Art Books

GARLAND REFERENCE LIBRARY OF THE HUMANITIES (VOL. 1264)

Art Books

*A Basic Bibliography
of Monographs on Artists,
Second Edition*

Editor
Wolfgang M. Freitag

GARLAND PUBLISHING, INC.
New York & London
1997

Library of Congress Cataloging-in-Publication Data

Freitag, Wolfgang M.
    Art Books : a basic bibliography of monographs on artists / editor,
Wolfgang M. Freitag. — 2nd ed.
        p.   cm. — (Garland reference library of the humanities ;
vol. 1264)
    Includes bibliographical references and index.
    ISBN 0-8240-3326-4 (acid-free paper)
    1. Art—Bio-bibliography. 2. Artists—Bibliography.   I. Title. II. Series.
Z5938.F73   1996
[N40]
016.9'092'2—dc20   96-28425
                                    CIP

Printed on acid-free, 250-year-life paper
Manufactured in the United States of America

Contents

"There is properly no history; only biography."

Ralph Waldo Emerson
Essays in History

Preface

For this second edition of *Art Books: A Basic Bibliography of Monographs on Artists,* the vast number of new books published since 1985 was surveyed and evaluated. This has resulted in the selection of 3,395 additional titles. These selections, reflective of the increase in the monographic literature on artists during the last ten years, are evidence of the activities of a larger number of art historians in more countries worldwide, of the increasingly diverse and ambitious exhibition programs of museums whose number has also increased dramatically, and also of a lively international art market and the attendant gallery activities. The selections of the first edition have been reviewed, errors have been corrected and important new editions and reprints have been noted.

The second edition contains 278 names of artists not represented in the first edition. These additional listings are by no means only of artists lifted out of obscurity. They include a surprising number of older masters, some of them well known through their oeuvre on view in major public collections, to whom, surprisingly, no monographs had been devoted before, and, as might be expected, many younger contemporary artists whose importance has only recently been acknowledged in monographs. A larger proportion of architects and designers is also included.

Like the first edition, the second includes works in all relevant genres of monographic writing: the analytical and critical, the biographical, and the enumerative. Formats range from books and catalogues raisonnés to exhibition and auction sale catalogues. In response to suggestions from users, the coverage of artists' writings is more thorough. Another departure from the strict principles of selection applied to in the first edition, where in order to be included a monograph had to deal with the whole oeuvre of an artist, is the more elastic definition of "monograph" which has allowed us to include treatises which, although purporting to deal with only a part of an artist's oeuvre, do actually illuminate the totality of an artist's life, works, and historical importance.

The Introduction to the first edition is still relevant to the purposes of the second which follows the same pattern of scope, style, and arrangement.

There are several new additions to the arsenal of the great encyclopedic and biographical art dictionaries of which two stand out and must be prominently mentioned, since both contain not only biographical but also substantial bibliographical material on individual artists. The first is the new version of *Thieme-Becker,* of which a new edition had been in preparation by the state-owned East German publishing firm, A.E. Seemann Verlag (VEB), Leipzig, at the time of the German reunification. By absorbing the three already published volumes of *T.-B.2,* a new start was made in 1992 by K.G. Saur who purchased the project and renamed it *Allgemeines Künstlerlexikon: Die bildenden Künstler aller Zeiten und Völker.* (Munich and Leipzig, K.G. Saur, 1992—). By the end of 1996 thirteen volumes had been published under the new title, of a total of 60 projected. The second new reference work in which fruitful bibliographical searches for monographic literature about artists might start is the *Dictionary of Art* (New York, Grove's Dictionaries, Inc., 1996), which is topical as well as biographical in scope and whose 34 volumes, published together, may, for its subject coverage, also be considered a legitimate successor to the still very useful *Encyclopedia of World Art* (New York, McGraw-Hill, 1959–68, 15 vols.)

These and several other important new reference works relevant to the objective of this book will be found listed in "A Selection of Biographical Dictionaries and Other Reference Works Containing Information on Artists" which has been expanded and updated for the second edition.

Attention is also called to the third and again improved edition of Lois Swan Jones' useful book *Art Information: Research Methods and Resources* (1990). Jones' Chapter 8: "Research on People" contains excellent advice for the student who looks for information on the lesser-known artists. In this same context it is necessary to mention a unique source for information on artists active in the United States that is all too often overlooked: The Archives of American Art. Founded in 1954, this Bureau of the Smithsonian Institution headquartered in Washington, D.C. with six regional branches in major U.S. cities, is dedicated to the collection, preservation, and study of the letters, diaries, and a great variety of other primary and largely unpublished records of artists and craftspeople active in the United States. Another bibliographical tool that the researcher overlooks at his or her own peril, because it contains abstracts of the most recent monographs and one-person exhibition catalogues, is the new international serial bibliography and abstracting journal *Bibliography of the History of Art (BHA)/Bibliographie d'Histoire de l'Art,* which is the successor to both *International Repertory of the Literature of Art, (RILA) 1975–1989* and *Répertoire d'Art et d'Archéologie (RAA), 1910–1989.*

To the list of the many friends who helped me with the compilation of the first edition I must add the name of the person who did for the second edition much of what Bob Sennett did for the first—albeit now with benefit of computer—Christi Nelson. Without her diligence, intuition, and savvy, the second edition would not have gotten off the ground as easily. I am also indebted to my son Tilman for making the author index to the second edition and greatly improving it. The index now includes not only the proper names of the principal personal and corporate authors, as did the index to the first edition, but also of co-authors, editors, co-editors and compilers as well as of contributors to works of multiple authorship, such as museum, collection and exhibition catalogues and conference proceedings. Last, but not least, very special thanks go to my friend James Hodgson who volunteered as proofreader.

W.M.F.
Spring, 1997

Introduction to the First Edition

The most basic kind of publication that art historians produce is probably the monograph on a particular artist. In it, all the artist's works will be sorted out and catalogued, with illustrations to match; and an interpretive essay will usually be provided to go along with this. There, the development of the artist's work will be dealt with from different points of view (style, subject matter, technique, and so on), and the discussion of how the artist developed and of his total achievement may well shade into criticism.[1]

As every librarian knows, artists' monographs form the core and account for the bulk of every art book collection, constituting well over fifty percent of the holdings; they have always been and remain—the importance which periodicals have attained notwithstanding—the principal vessels in which research results are packaged and transmitted, a fact which is corroborated by several empirical studies of the research habits of art historians.[2, 3, 4]

Lois Swan Jones notes in her study guide, *Art Research Methods and Resources*, that at present "there is no single reference work that lists all of the monographs, catalogues raisonnés, and *oeuvres* catalogues that have been compiled on various artists."[5] Indeed, the best and most useful bibliography of monographs deals with artists from only one field: printmaking.[6] The only work in which a general list has been attempted is E. Louise Lucas' *Art Books: A Basic Bibliography* (Greenwich, CT: New York Graphic Society, 1968), which contains a selected bibliography of monographs on about 550 artists from all fields. As this title is now out of print, a researcher wishing to locate additional books and catalogues on individual artists must turn to the bibliography sections appended to the entries in the great biographical dictionaries such as *Thieme-Becker* or *Bénézit*, to encyclopedias like the *Encyclopedia of World Art* or to the multi-volume handbooks of which the *Pelican History of Art* and the *Propyläen-Kunstgeschichte* are prominent examples. The titles found therein can be supplemented further by searching various national art bibliographies and published library catalogues and—if one wishes to bring one's search up to date—by recourse to national and trade bibliographies or serial abstracting and indexing services of which RILA, the *Répertoire d'Art et d'Archéologie*, and *Art Bibliographies Modern* are the most frequently used.

Many of the monographs listed contain substantial bibliographies that will lead to further study. If one intends to pursue research on an artist in depth, the user of this volume will disregard them at his or her peril. A select list of multi-artist biographical dictionaries and other reference works that contain useful data has been added in order to increase the usefulness of this volume.

Art Books: A Basic Bibliography of Monographs on Artists is designed primarily for the graduate student who needs a tool that is compact and affordable yet fairly comprehensive and that can take its place on the personal reference shelf alongside such standard works as Schlosser's *La Letteratura Artistica*, Chamberlin's *Art Reference Books*, Arntzen and Rainwater's *Guide to the*

Literature of Art History, and the bibliographies incorporated in a recent spate of study guides of which those by Jones, Kleinbauer and Muehsam are three outstanding examples.[7, 8, 9] In compiling this bibliography, I have also been mindful of the usefulness of such a volume to librarians who are charged with the task of collection building and naturally also to book dealers in acquiring stock and preparing catalogues.

Contained here are monographs and works of a monographic character on 1,870 artists from all historical periods and from all countries. The 10,543 titles represent the following media: painting and drawing (64%), sculpture (11%), architecture (11%), graphic arts (8%), photography (5%), and decorative and applied arts (1%).

Since it was my aim to do justice to artists from every historical epoch and from all parts of the world, my approach had to be severely selective if, in accordance with the publisher's plans, the one-volume format of the bibliography was to be preserved. To achieve this compactness I have thought it best to concentrate on artists who interest the American art student, the collector, and the ever-growing number of passionate art lovers among the general public. Many of the artists included are represented with their works in American or Canadian museums or have been shown in travelling exhibitions that have toured the continent; others are the subject of academic courses and lectures on the graduate and undergraduate level in North American colleges and universities.

The proportion of citations per national schools or geographical regions are as follows—Italy: 20%; Austria, Germany, and Switzerland: 18%; North America: 16%; France: 15%; Great Britain and Ireland: 9%; Belgium and the Netherlands: 7%; Russia: 4%; Scandinavia: 3%; Spain, Portugal, Latin America: 3%; Eastern Europe: 2%; the Middle East, India and Far East: 2%; and Modern Greece: 1%.

The term "monograph" has been defined broadly to include treatises (and published dissertations), biographies, *catalogues raisonnés* and other works catalogues, personal bibliographies, and artists' writings that are of an autobiographical or theoretical nature and illuminate the artist's creative process. I have selectively included the letters but have excluded the poetry, plays, and fiction produced by visual artists. Articles on single artists appearing in periodicals or collections (e.g., *Festschriften*, yearbooks, and general museum catalogues) are also not listed.

Every bibliography that selects from thousands of titles is in the final analysis always a matter of personal taste and reflects not only the selector's background but also what is in vogue at a given time. The present volume is no exception. No apology is offered for titles omitted that another compiler might have included, but I would certainly like to know why my readers would have selected differently and invite their suggestions, just as I shall be grateful for suggestions on how to improve the quality of the work overall.

I have made a serious effort to include books that reflect the current research interests of graduate students at a major university and have tried to anticipate trends. This is not easy in a field as protean as art history that now includes many subjects that were not considered germane to it when the first monograph bibliographies were compiled by Miss Lucas for her original *Harvard List of Books on Art* (Cambridge, Mass., Harvard University Press, 1938), its predecessors, and its successors.

In a day when it is possible to program a computer to spin off bibliographies on any subject by printing out relevant and appropriately coded titles from bibliographic data bases that are in themselves the machine-generated products of national and trade bibliographies, the present volume may seem like an anachronism. Before they were found worthy of being included, the books for the present compilation were personally examined in the stacks of a mature and well-stocked art library in order to identify publications that ought to be the backbone of the monographs collection of a much younger art library with a comprehensive scope and provide guidance for its acquisitions program.

The books were chosen for a variety of reasons. Some are acknowledged as definitive standard works, others, although perhaps unfamiliar, have been included because I considered them superior to the better-known standard works; some are the only works available on a given artist. The latter is especially true for artists who have not yet received monographic treatment but have received critical attention through substantial exhibitions and the catalogues accompanying them.

It is my hope that this volume, even if it does not immediately fill the gap that exists in the bibliographical literature on artists' monographs, will have a useful function until the field produces a better one.

I dedicate this book to the memory of Edna Louise Lucas, who as a librarian and a bibliographer has helped innumerable scholars and students of art history and who, by her example, taught me the joys of making personal bibliographies.

Wolfgang M. Freitag
Cambridge, Massachusetts
Spring 1985

Notes

1. Roskill, Mark. *What Is Art History?* New York: Harper & Row, 1976, p. 14.
2. Nelson, Diane. "Methods of Citation Analysis in the Fine Arts." *Special Libraries,* 68 (11), Nov. 1977, pp. 390–95.
3. Simonton, Wesley C. *Characteristics of the Research Literature of the Fine Arts during the Period 1948–1957.* Ph.D. diss., Univ. of Illinois (Urbana), 1960.
4. Stam, Deirdre C. *The Information-Seeking Practices of Art Historians in Museums and Colleges in the United States, 1982–83.* Ph.D. diss., Columbia Univ., School of Library Service, 1984.
5. Jones, Lois S. *Art Research Methods and Resources.* 2 ed., rev. and enlarged. Dubuque, Iowa: Kendall/Hunt, 1984, p. 53.
6. Riggs, Timothy A., compiler. *The Print Council Index to Oeuvre-Catalogues of Prints by European and American Artists.* Millwood, N.Y.: Kraus International, 1983.
7. Jones, Lois S. *op. cit.*
8. Kleinbauer, W. Eugene, and Slavens, Thomas P. *Research Guide to the History of Western Art.* Chicago: American Library Association, 1983.
9. Muehsam, Gerd. *Guide to Information Sources in the Visual Arts.* Santa Barbara, Cal./ Oxford, England: Jeffrey Norton, 1978; distrib. by ABC-Clio.

Acknowledgments

For help with the present work I am much indebted to Robert S. Sennett, who assisted me in selecting from the mass of the available literature the principal and most noteworthy titles, who was indefatigable in combing the stacks of the Harvard Fine Arts Library for copies to be inspected, who verified the entries, and who also had a major hand in organizing the material and preparing the manuscript for the press. I am also grateful to William S. Johnson, presently editor of the *International Photography Index*, formerly a lecturer in photography at Harvard and public services librarian in its Fine Arts Library, who is responsible for the selection of the photographers and the monographs devoted to them that are included.

Special thanks go to Martha Older and Caroline Ware Rusten, who typed most of the manuscript, and to Judy Morrison, my secretary, for sundry contributions to the work while it was in progress.

Grateful recognition must also be made to the staff of the Harvard Fine Arts Library for their forbearance—especially during the early stages of the project when our requests for recalls, shelflist and in-process information for books that were not immediately accessible were testing their patience daily.

The list of acknowledgments would be incomplete if it did not mention the assistance I have received from members of the faculty of the Fine Arts Department and from Harvard students who have contributed so much to this work, either indirectly by letting me observe them daily in their research and study habits or directly by their frank criticism of books they have used and by making suggestions for new purchases.

Finally, I would like to express my profound gratitude to the officers of the J. Paul Getty Trust, without whose most generous support I could neither have spared the time nor afforded the bibliographical and technical support necessary to bring the project of the bibliography to fruition.

W.M.F.

Notes on Style and Use

The material in this bibliography has been organized in a form convenient for the user. The arrangement is alphabetical by the artists' and authors' full last names. When an artist is known by several names, I have, in general, used the one by which he or she is best known. Cross-references are provided when the preferred form of the name is not clear, as in the case of Man Ray, or for artists who are known chiefly by their pseudonyms. Medieval and Renaissance artists, especially the early Italians whose real name is joined to that of their father, birthplace, or workshop are listed under their best-known names. Thus, for example, Desiderio da Settignano is found under Desiderio, and Andrea Del Sarto, whose family name was D'Agnolo, is found under Sarto. In the first case, a reference from Settignano leads the user to look under Desiderio; in the second, the cross-reference has been omitted because the artist's real name is practically never used. If the artist is known by several variations of his name, the entry is made under the most common form and as many references are made as needed.

Works whose subjects include more than one artist are found under the artist whose name comes first in the alphabet. Thus, a book on Turner, Cole, and Hunt will be listed under Cole, with cross-references to that entry under Turner and Hunt. The exception to this occurs when the identifying artist has not been the subject of a separate monograph. In such cases, the item is found under the artist whose name follows in the alphabet. For instance, Kensan and His Tradition: Kenzan, Koetsu, Korin, and Sotatsu will be found under Koetsu since there is no separate listing for Kenzan. Members of the same family are listed together and the monographs on them entered in one alphabet, so that all the books on the Della Robbias, for example, will be found together, without regard to the subject's first name.

Anonymous artists that are known to us only by their initials or marks (monograms) or by artificial catch-names beginning with Master or *Meister* are found in their appropriate place in the alphabet. The idiosyncrasies of certain archaic and foreign spellings such as "J" for "I" have been retained. The Dutch letter "IJ" is customarily transcribed as "Y" in English texts, and that is done here. Thus, Van Dijck remains Van Dyck.

Diacritical marks that alter the sound of a vowel or affect the position of a consonant (as in Slavic vernacular alphabets) have been ignored in the alphabetizing of foreign names. For instance, the German *umlaut* (ü) is considered "U," not "UE," and, consequently, entries for Müller follow those for Mueller. Transliterations of the names of artists that do not originally appear in the roman alphabet, i.e., Larianov, follow the standard form adopted by the Library of Congress. Foreign names that include prepositions such as Van, Von, De, or Della are entered under the part of the name which follows the prefix: Dyck, Anthony Van or Porta, Guglielmo Della.

These rules for alphabetization apply equally to the entries for artists and to the names of the authors. Institutions such as museums and galleries or associations and corporate bodies that appear as authors of catalogues and congress proceedings are found under the vernacular form of their official name, and if their location is not part of the name it has been added in parentheses in the accepted Engish version.

The bibliographical description for each entry follows exactly the information presented on the title page of the book in hand. In some cases, this has meant accepting variations of forms of a name for the same author. In such cases, the "literary units principle" adopted in many library catalogues to bring together all the works of an author under one form of the name, has *not* been upheld, and all the variant spellings found on the title pages appear in the text. An effort has been made, however, to bring such entries together in the author index, and thus an exact correlation between author entries in the index and author entries in the text does not necessarily exist. This applies to both individual authors and to corporate bodies as authors (e.g., museums).

When several forms of entry are possible preference is given to the personal author or authors, rather than to the sponsoring institution. An exception to this are exhibition catalogues, which are usually found under the name of the sponsoring institution. So-called "museum monographs," i.e., books which accompany an exhibition but are the work of one author, are treated as monographs and not as exhibition catalogues.

When two authors have written a work jointly or a publishing house imprint includes two cities, both are listed. However, if three or more authors are involved, only the first author is listed, and multiple authorship is indicated by et al., and when three or more cities are places of publication, only the first is given without mention of the others.

In the few rare instances when a book is a compilation of several short monographs without the aegis of an institution and without an editor, the work is listed under the name of the contributor whose piece appears first.

Entries are cited in the index by item number not by page.

The abbreviation CR is used throughout the text to stand for *catalogue raisonné*.

A Selection of Biographical Dictionaries and other Reference Works Containing Information on Artists

The most recent works are still in print, the others are readily found in large public and art libraries.

International

Allgemeines Künstlerlexikon: Die bildenden Künstler aller Zeiten und Völker. v.1– . München/Leipzig, Saur, 1992– .

Arntz, Wilhelm F. Verzeichnis der seit 1945 erschienenen Werkkataloge zur Kunst des 20. Jahrhunderts. Haag/Obb., Verlag Gertrud Arntz—Winter, 1975.

Bartsch, Adam von. Le peintre graveur. 21 v. Wien, Degen, 1803–1821. Reprints: Leipzig, Barth, 1854–1876; Hildesheim, Olms, 1970.

Blättel, Harry. International dictionary, miniature painters, porcelain painters, silhouettists. München, Arts & Antiques Edition Munich, 1992.

Browne, Turner and Parnow, Elaine. Macmillan biographical encyclopedia of photographic artists and innovators. N.Y., Macmillan, 1983.

Bryan, Michael. A biographical and critical dictionary of painters and engravers. 2 v. London, Carpenter, 1816.

Castagno, John. Artists as illustrators: an international directory with signatures and monograms, 1800–present. Metuchen, N.J., Scarecrow Press, 1989.

Chiarmonte, Paula L., ed. Women artists, a resource and research guide. [Tucson, Ariz., Art Libraries Society of North America, 1982].

Clement, Clara E. Women in the fine arts. Boston and N.Y., Houghton Mifflin, 1904.

Colnaghi & Co. (London). Photography: the first eighty years. [catalogue of an exhibition] 27 October to 1 December 1976. Text by Valerie Lloyd. London, P. & D. Colnaghi, 1967.

Columbia University Libraries. Avery Architectural Library. Avery obituary index of architects and artists. Boston, G.K. Hall, 1980. 2 ed.

Contemporary artists. Edited by Muriel Emanuel et al. London, Macmillan, 1983. 2 ed.

Darmstaedter, Robert. Reclam's Künstlerlexikon. Stuttgart, 1979.

Delteil, Loÿs. Le peintre-graveur illustré. 31 v. Paris, Delteil, 1906–30.

The Dictionary of art. Edited by Jane Turner; Hugh Brigstocke, consulting editor. 34 v. London and New York, Grove's Dictionaries Inc., 1996.

Dictionary of contemporary artists. Edited by V. Babington Smith. Oxford/Santa Barbara, Calif., ABC-Clio Press, 1981.

Drake, Wilfred J. A dictionary of glasspainters and "glasyers" of the tenth to eighteenth centuries. N.Y., Metropolitan Museum of Art, 1955.

Edouard-Joseph, René. Dictionnaire biographique des artistes contemporains 1910–1930. 3 v. Paris, Art et Edition, 1931–33. With 1st supplement, 1936.

Edwards, Gary. International guide to nineteenth-century photographers and their works: based on catalogues of auction houses and dealers. Boston, G.K. Hall, 1988.

Enciclopedia dell'arte antica, classica e orientale. Dir. di redazione Ranuccio Bianchi Bandinelli. 7 v., atlas and 1st supplement. Roma, Encyclopedia Italiana, 1959–73.

Fanelli, Giovanni and Godoli, Ezio. Dizionario degli illustratori simbolisti e Art Nouveau. 2 v. Firenze, Cantini, 1990.

Fleming, John and Honour, Hugh. *The Penguin dictionary of decorative arts*. London, Lane, 1977.

Forschungsunternehmen der Fritz Thyssen Stiftung. *Bibliographie zur Kunstgeschichte des 19. Jahrhunderts: Publikationen der Jahre 1940–1966*. Zusammengestellt von Hilda Lietzmann. München, Prestel, 1968 (Studien zur Kunst des neunzehnten Jahrhunderts, Bd. 4).

————. *Bibliographie zur Kunstgeschichte des 19. Jahrhunderts: Publikationen der Jahre 1967–1979, mit Nachträgen zu den Jahren 1940–1966*. Zusammengestellt von Marianne Prause. München, Prestel, 1984 (Studien zur Kunst des neunzehnten Jahrhunderts, Bd. 31).

Goldstein, Franz. *Monogramm-Lexikon; internationales Verzeichnis der Monogramme bildenden Künstler seit 1850*. Berlin, de Gruyter, 1964. (continues Nagler, G.K., *Die Monogrammisten*.)

Gould, John. *Biographical dictionary of painters, sculptors, engravers and architects*. 2 v. London, Wilson, 1835.

Gowing, Lawrence. *A biographical dictionary of artists*. London, Macmillan, 1983.

Graves, Algernon. *A dictionary of artists who have exhibited works in the principal London exhibitions from 1760–1893*. London, Henry Graves, 1901. 3 ed. Reprint: Bath, Kinsmead, 1969; N.Y., Burt Franklin, 1970.

Havlice, Patricia P. *Index to artistic biography*. Metuchen, N.J., Scarecrow Press, 1973. With 1st supplement, 1981.

Heller, Nancy. *Women artists: an illustrated history*. N.Y., Abbeville Press, 1987.

Jakovsky, Anatole. *Peintres naïfs: a dictionary of primitive painters*. N.Y., Universe, 1967. (2 ed.: Basel, Basilius, 1976)

Johnson, William S. *Nineteenth-century photography: an annotated bibliography, 1839–1879*. Boston, G.K. Hall; London, Mansell, 1990.

Kindler's Malereilexikon. Ed. by Germain Bazin et al. 6 v. Zürich, Kindler, 1964–71.

Macmillan Encyclopedia of architects. Edited by Adolf K. Placzek. 4 v. N.Y., The Free Press, 1982.

Marks, Claude, ed. *World artists 1980–1990: an H.W. Wilson biographical dictionary*. N.Y., H.W. Wilson, 1991.

Mathews, Oliver. *Early photographs and early photographers; a survey in dictionary form*. London, Reedminster, 1973.

Mayer, Leo A. *Bibliography of Jewish art*. Jerusalem, Magnes, 1967.

Nagler, Georg K. *Die Monogrammisten und diejenigen bekannten und unbekannten Künstler aller Schulen*. 5v. München, Franz, 1858–79. *General-Index. . . .*, München, Hirth, 1920. Reprint: Nieuwkoop, De Graaf, 1966, (including the *Index*).

————. *Neues allgemeines Künstler-Lexicon*. 22 v. München, 1835–1852. Reprint: Leipzig, Schwarzenberg & Schumann, 1924 (25 v.).

Naylor, Colin and P-Orrige, Genesis. *Contemporary artists*. N.Y., St. Martin's Press, 1977.

Newhall, Beaumont, and Newhall, Nancy. *Masters of photography*. N.Y. Braziller, 1958.

Osborne, Harold. *The Oxford companion to art*. Oxford, Clarendon Press, 1970.

————. *The Oxford companion to the decorative arts*. Oxford, Clarendon Press, 1975.

Osterwalder, Marcus. *Dictionnaire des illustrateurs, 1800–1914: (illustrateurs, caricaturistes et affichistes)*. Avec la collaboration de Gérard Pussey, Marie Leroy-Crèveoeur et Boris Moissard. Introduction de Bernard Noèl. Neuchâtel, Suisse, Ides et Calendes, 1989.

————. *Dictionnaire des illustrateurs, 1890–1945: XXe siècle, première génération, illustrateurs du monde entier nés avant 1885 (artistes du livres, dessinateurs de la presse et de la mode, caricaturistes, bédéistes et affichistes. Avec la collaboration de J.A. Agelink van Rentergem . . . [et al.]*. Neuchâtel, Suisse, Ides et Calendes, 1992.

Pavière, Sydney, H. *A dictionary of flower, fruit, and still life painters*. 4 v. Leigh-on-Sea, Lewis, 1962–4.

Petteys, Chris. *Dictionary of women artists: an international dictionary of women artists born before 1900*. With the assistance of Hazel Gustow, Ferris Olin, Verna Ritchie. Boston, G.K. Hall, 1985.

Pevsner, Niklolaus, Fleming, John, and Honour, Hugh. *A dictionary of architecture*. Rev. and enlarged. London, Lane, 1975.

Portoghesi, Paolo. *Dizionario enciclopedico di archittetura e ubanistica*. 6 v. Roma,

Istituto Editorale Romano, 1968–9.

Riggs, Timothy A. *The Print Council index to oeuvre-catalogues of prints by European and American artists.* Millwood, N.Y., Kraus, 1983.

Robertson, Jack. *Twentieth-century artists on art: an index to artists' writings, statements, and interviews.* Boston, G.K. Hall, 1985.

Rosenblum, Naomi. *A history of women photographers.* Paris/N.Y., Abbeville Press, 1994.

Schidlof, Leo. *The miniature in Europe in the 16th, 17th, 18th, and 19th centuries.* 4 v. Graz, Akademische Druck- und Verlagsanstalt, 1964.

Smith, Veronica B. *International directory of exhibiting artists.* v. 1– . 1983– . Oxford/Santa Barbara, Calif., ABC-Clio Press, 1983.

Spooner, S. *A biographical history of the fine arts.* N.Y., Putnam, 1852.

Thieme, Ulrich, and Becker, Felix. *Allgemeines Lexikon der bildenden Künstler von der Antike bis zur Gegenwart.* 37 v. Leipzig, Seemann, 1907–50.

Vollmer, Hans. *Allgemeines Lexikon der bildenden Künstler des XX. Jahrhunderts.* 6 v. Leipzig, Seemann, 1953–62.

Tufts, Eleanor. *Our hidden heritage, five centuries of women artists.* London/N.Y., Paddington, 1974.

Vinson, James, ed. *International dictionary of art and artists.* With a foreword by Cecil Gould. Chicago, St. James Press, 1990.

Wasmuths Lexikon der Baukunst. 5 v. Berlin, 1929–37.

Weilbach, Philip. *Weilbachs Kunstnerleksikon.* 3 v. København, Aschehoug, 1947–52. 3 ed.

Who's Who in architecture: from 1400 to the present day. Gen. ed. J.M. Richards; Adolf K. Placzek, American consultant. N.Y., Rinehart and Winston, 1977.

Australia and New Zealand

Germaine, Max. *Artists and galleries of Australia and New Zealand.* Sydney, etc. Landsdowne, 1979.

———. *A dictionary of women artists of Australia.* Foreword by Anne von Bertouch. Roseville East, NSW, Australia; N.Y., STBS Ltd. [distributor], 1991.

McCulloch, Alan. *Encyclopedia of Australian art.* London, Hutchinson, 1968.

Austria

Schmidt, Rudolf. *Österreichisches Künstlerlexikon von den Anfängen bis zur Gegenwart.* v. 1– . Wien, Tusch, 1974– .

Canada

Harper, J. Russell. *Early painters and engravers in Canada.* Toronto, Univ. of Toronto Press, 1970.

MacDonald, Colin S. *Dictionary of Canadian artists.* Ottawa, Canadian Paperbacks, 1967– .

Eastern Europe and Russia

Gorina, Tatiana G., and Vol'tsenburg, Oskar E. *Khudozhniki narodov SSSR.* Biobibliograficheskii slovar. Moskva, Iskusstvo, 1970.

Maurin-Bialostocka, Jolanta et al. *Słownik artystów polskich i obcych w Polsce dzai la jacych: malarze, rzezbiarze, graficy.* v. 1–Wroclaw, Zakładł. Narodowy im Ossolinskich, 1971– .

Mazalič, Doko. *Leksikon umjetnika: alikara, vajara, graditelja, zlatara, kaligrafa i drugih koji su radili u Bosni i Hercegovini.* Sarajevo, Veselin Maslěsa, 1967.

Neumann, Wilhelm. *Lexikon baltischer Künster.* Riga, Jonck & Doliewsky, 1908. Reprinted: Hannover-Döhren, Hirschheydt, 1972.

Prut, Constantin. *Dictionar de arta moderna.* Bucuresti, Albatross, 1982.

Rainov, Bogomil N. *Portreti.* Sofia, Bulgarski pisatel, 1975.

Toman, Prokop, and Toman, Prokop H. *Dodatky, Ke slovniku; československych výtvarných umělcu.* Praha, Nakladatelstvi Krásné literatury, hudby a umeni, 1955.

Zador, Anna, and Istvan, Genthon. *Müveszeti lexikon.* 4 v. Budapest, Akademiai Kiado, 1965–68.

France

Auvray, Louis. *Dictionnaire, général des artistes de l'école française.* 2 v. Paris,

Renouard, 1882–1885. (Supplement, 1887. Reprint: N.Y. Garland, 1979)

Baudicour, Prosper de. *Le graveur français continué, ou catalogue raisonné des estampes gravées par les peintres et les dessinateurs de l'école française nés dans le XVIIIe siècle.* 2 v. Paris, Bouchard Huzard, Rapilly [etc.], 1859–1861. Reprint: Paris, de Nobele, 1967.

Bénézit, Emmanuel. *Dictionnaire critique et documentaire des peintres, sculpteurs, dessinateurs et graveurs.* 10 v. Paris, Gründ, 1976. 3 ed.

Bonafons, Louis A., *Known as* Abbé de Fontenai. *Dictionnaire des artistes.* 2 v. Paris, Vincent, 1776. Reprint: Genève, Minkoff, 1972.

Germany

Andresen, Andreas. *Der deutsche Peintre-Graveur, oder Die deutschen Maler als Kupferstecher nach ihrem Leben und ihren Werken, von dem letzten Drittel des 16. Jahrhunderts bis zum Schluss des 18. Jahrhunderts, und in Anchluss an Bartsch's Peintre-graveur.* 5 v. Leipzig, Rudolph Weigel, Alexander Danz, 1864–78. Reprints: N.Y., Collectors Editions, 1969; Hildesheim, Olms, 1973.

———. *Die deutschen Maler-Radirer (Peintres-Graveurs) des neunzehnten Jahrhunderts nach ihren Leben und Werken.* 5 v. Leipzig, Alexander Danz, 1878. Reprints: Hildesheim, Olms, 1971; N.Y., Garland, 1978.

Hollstein, F.W.H. *German engravings, etchings and woodcuts, c. 1400–1700.* v.1– . Amsterdam, Hertzberger, 1954– .

Great Britain

Colvin Howard. *A biographical dictionary of British architects, 1600–1840.* London, Murray, 1978.

Garton, Robin. *British printmakers, 1855–1955: a century of printmaking from the Etching Revival to St Ives.* London, Garton & Co. in association with Scolar Press, 1992.

Harvey, John. *English medieval architects; a biographical dictionary down to 1550, incl. master masons, carpenters, carvers, building contractors and others respon-*sible for design . . . with contributions by Arthur Oswald. London, Batsford, 1954.

Johnson, J., and Greutzner, A. *The dictionary of British artists 1880–1940; an Antique Collectors' Club Research Project listing 41,000 artists.* Woodbridge, Suffolk, Antique Collectors' Club, 1976.

Redgrave, Samuel. *A dictionary of artists of the English school: painters, sculptors, architects, engravers and ornamentists; with notices of their lives and work.* London, Bell, 1878. 2 ed. Reprint: Amsterdam, Hissink, 1970.

Strickland, Walter G. *A dictionary of Irish artists.* 2 v. Dublin, Maunsel, 1913. Reprint: N.Y., Hacker, 1968.

Waters, Grant M. *Dictionary of British artists working 1900–1950.* Eastbourne, Eastbourne Fine Art, 1975.

Who's who in art. Havant, England, Art Trade Press, 1982.

Wood, Christopher. *The dictionary of Victorian painters.* Woodbridge, Suffolk, Christopher Wood Ltd., 1978. 2 ed.

Italy

Baldinucci, Filippo. *Notizie de' professori del disegno da Cimabue [etc.].* 21 v. Firenze, Stecchi e Pagani, 1767–74. *Index* published in Florence by Allegrini in 1813.

Bellori, Giovanni P. *Le vite de' pittori, scultori et architetti moderni.* A cura di Evelina Borea. Introd. by Giovanni Previtali. Torino, Einaudi, 1976.

Bessone-Aurelj, Antonietta M. *Dizionario degli scultori ed architetti italiani.* Genova, etc., Editrice Dante Alighieri, 1947.

Catalogo nazionale Bolaffi d'arte moderna. Torino, Bolaffi, 1962–.

Commanduci, Agostino M. *Dizionario illustrato dei pittori, disegnatori e incisori italiani moderi e contemporanei.* 4 ed. . . . a cura di una redazione diretta da Luigi Servolini. 5 v. Milano, Patuzzi, 1970–74.

Dizionario Bolaffi degli scultori italiani moderni. Torino, Bolaffi, 1972.

Dizionario enciclopedia Bolaffi dei pittori e degli incisori italiani, dall XI al XX secolo. 11 v. Torino, Bolaffi, 1972–76.

Dominici, Bernardo de'. *Vite dei pittori, scultori, ed architetti napoletani.* 3 v. Napoli, Ricciardi, 1742–44.

Lanzi, Luigi. A. *Storia pittorica della Italia dal risorgimento delle belle arti fin* presso al fine del XVIII secolo. 3 v. 3d rev. ed. Bassano, Remondini, 1809. Eng. trans. by Thomas Roscoe, 6 v.: London, Simpkin and Marshall, 1828.

Malvasia, Carol C. *Felsina pittrice vite dei pittori bolognesi.* 2 v. Bologna, Tipografia Guidi all' Ancora, 1841. Reprint: Bologna, Forni, 1967.

Pascoli, Lione. *Vite de' pittori, scultori ed architetti moderni.* 2 v. Roma, de Rossi, 1730–1736. Reprint: Roma, Calzone, 1933.

Temanza, Tommaso. *Vite dei piu celebri architetti e scultore veneziani.* Venezia, Palese, 1778. Reprint: Milan, Labor, 1966.

Vasari, Giorgio. *Le vite de' piu eccellenti pittori, scultori e architettori.* Di nuovo dal medesimo riviste et ampliate. 3 v. Fiorenza, Giunti, 1568. Eng. ed. by Blashfield & Hopkins, 4 v.: New York, Scribner, 1896. New Ital. ed.: A cura di Rosanna Bettarini. Commentato secolare a cura di Paola Barocchi, 7 v. Firenze, Sansoni, 1966–76.

Venturi, Adolfo. *Storia dell' arte italiana.* 11 v. Milano, Hoepli, 1901–40. Reprint: Nendeln, Liechtenstein, Kraus, 1967.

———. Index. Prepared by Jacqueline D. Sisson. Nendeln, Liechtenstein, Kraus, 1975 [Section 2 = *Artists Index*].

The Netherlands and Belgium

Bernt, Walther. *Die niederländischen Maler und Zeichner des 17. Jahrhunderts.* 5 v. München, Bruckmann, 1979–80. (CR).

Le dictionnaire des peintres belges du XIVe siècle á nos jours. Edited by Carine Dechaux, et al. 3 v. Louvain-la-Neuve, La Renaissance du Livre, 1994.

Friedländer, Max J. *Die altniederländische Malerei.* 14 v. Berlin, Cassirer, 1924–1937. Eng. ed.: *Early Netherlandish painting.* 14 v. Leyden, Sijthoff, 1967–1976.

Gemar-Koeltzsch, Erika. *Holländische Stillebenmaler im 17. Jahrhundert: dreibändiges Bild-Lexikon.* 3 v. Lingen, Luca Verlag, 1995.

Hofstede de Groot, Cornelis. *Beschreibendes und kritisches Verzeichnis der Werke des hervorragendsten holländischen Maler des XVII. Jahrhunderts; nach dem Muster von John Smith's Catalogue raisonné zusammengestellt von Dr. C. Hofstede de Groot.* 10 v. in 9. Esslingen, P. Neff, 1907–1928. (CR).

Hollstein, F.W.H. *Dutch and Flemish etchings, engravings and woodcuts, c. 1450–1700.* v. 1– . Amsterdam, Hertzberger, 1949– . (Editor, place, and publisher vary).

Hymans, Henri S. *Près de 700 biographies d'artistes belges, parues dans La Biographie nationale, dans L'Art flamand et hollandais, dans Le Dictionnaire des Drs. Thieme et Becker et dans diverses publications du pays et de l'etranger.* Bruxelles, Hayez, 1920.

Jacobs, P.M.J. *Beeldend Nederland: biografisch handboek.* 2 v. Tilburg, P.M.J. Jacobs, 1993. [Updates Sheen's Lexicon].

Maere, Jan de, and Wabbes, Maria. *The illustrated dictionary of 17th century Flemish painters.* 3 v. Louvain-la-Neuve, La Renaissance du Livre, 1993.

Mander, Carel van. *Het schilder-boek.* Haerlem, voor Pachier van Wesbusch, 1604. Eng. ed., trans. by Constant van de Wall: N.Y., MacFarlane, 1936. Reprint: N.Y., Arno, 1969.

Scheen, Pieter A. *Lexicon Nederlandse beeldende Kunstenaars 1750–1950.* 2 v. s' Gravenhage, Pieter A. Scheen, 1969–70. (Reprint: 1994).

Seyn, Eugène M.H. de. *Dessinateurs, graveurs et peintres des anciens Pays-Bas; écoles flamande et hollandaise.* Turnhout (Belgique), Brépols (1949?).

Smith, John. *A catalogue raisonné of the works of the most eminent Dutch, Flemish and French painters.* 9 v. London, Sands & Co., 1908. (CR).

Wilenski, Reginald Howard. *Flemish painters, 1430–1830.* 2 v. N.Y., Viking Press, [1960].

Wurzbach, Alfred von. *Niederländisches Künstler Lexicon, auf Grund archivalischer Forschungen.* 3 v. Wien, Halm, 1906–11. Reprint: Amsterdam, Israël, 1968.

Scandinavia

Gelsteds kunstner-leksikon 1900–1942. [Redigeret av Otto Gelsted]. København, Arthur Jensens Forlag, 1942.

Gran, Henning, and Anker, Peter. *Illustrert norsk kunstnerleksikon: stemmeberettigede, malere, grafikere/tegnere, billedhoggere.* Oslo, Broen, 1956. 2 ed.

Koroma, Kaarlo. *Suomen kuvataiteilijat.*

Suomen taiteilijaseuran julkaisema elämäkerrasto. Porvoo, Söderström, 1962.

Lilja, Gösta, et al. *Svenskt konstnärs lexikon; tiotusen svenska konstnärers liv och verk.* 5 v. Malmö, Allhems Förlag, 1952–67.

Munksgaards kunstnerleksikon. Redigeret av Svend P. Jørgenen. København, Munksgaard, [1962].

Norsk kunstnerleksikon: Bildende kunstnere—arkitekter—kunsthandverkere. Redigert av nasjonalgalleriet [Leif Østby, editor]. 2 v.- . Oslo, Universitetsforlaget, 1982–83.

Spain and Portugal

Ceán Bermudez, Juan A. *Diccionario histórico de los mas illustres profesores de las bellas artes en España.* 6 v. Madrid, Ibarra, 1800. Reprint: N.Y., Kraus, 1965.

Ossorio y Bernard, Manuel. *Galeria biográfica de artistas españoles del siglo XIX.* Continuacion del *Diccionario* de Ceán Bermudez hasta el año 1882. Madrid, Moreno y Rojas, 1883–84. Reprint: Madrid, Gaudi, 1975.

Pamplona, Fernando de. *Dicionário de pintores e escultores portugueses ou que trabalharam em Portugal.* 4 v. Lisboa, 1954–59.

Rafols, José F. *Diccionario de artistas de Cataluña, Valencia y Baleares.* 5 v. Barcelon/Bilbao, Edicions Catalanes y La Gran Enciclopedia Vasca, 1980–81.

Spanish artists from the fourth to the twentieth century; a critical dictionary. Edited by the Frick Art Reference Library. v. 1– . N.Y., G.K. Hall & Co., 1993– .

Tannock, Michael. *Portuguese twentieth century artists; a biographical dictionary.* Shopwyke Hall, Chichester, W. Sussex, England, Phillmore, 1978.

Switzerland

Brun, Carl. *Schwizerisches Künstlerlexikon.* 4 v. Frauenfeld, Huber, 1905–17. Reprint: Nendeln, Liechtenstein, Kraus, 1967.

Plüss, Eduard, and Tavel, Hans C. von. *Künstlerlexicon der Schweiz: XX. Jahrhundert.* 2 v. Frauenfeld, Huber, 1958–67.

United States

The Britannica encyclopedia of American art. Chicago, Encyclopedia Britannica; dist. N.Y., Simon & Schuster, 1973.

Cederholm, Theresa D. *Afro-American artists; a bio-bibliographical directory.* Boston, Trustees of the Boston Public Library, 1973.

Chiarmonte, Paula, ed. *Women artists in the United States: a selective bibliography and resource guide on the fine and decorative arts, 1750–1986.* Boston, G.K. Hall, 1990.

Collins, Jimmie L. *Women artists in America; eighteenth century to the present.* 2 v. Chattanooga, Univ. of Tennessee Press, 1973–75.

Cummings, Paul. *A dictionary of contemporary American artists.* N.Y., St. Martin's Press, 1977. 3 ed.

Davis, Lenwood G., and Sims, Janet L. *Black artists in the United States; an annotated bibliography of books, articles, and dissertations on black artists, 1779–1979.* Westport, Conn., Greenwood Press, 1980.

Fielding, Mantle. *American engravers upon copper and steel.* Biographical sketches and check lists of engravings; a supplement to David McNeely Stuffer's *American engravers.* Philadelphia, privately printed, 1917.

———. *Dictionary of American painters, sculptors, and engravers.* Philadelphia, Printed for the subscribers, 1926. Enlarged and revised edition by Genevieve C. Doran. Green Farms, Conn., 1974.

Groce, George C., and Wallace, David H. *The New-York Historical Society's dictionary of artists in America 1564–1860.* New Haven, Yale University Press, 1957.

Igoe, Lynn M., with James Igoe. *250 years of Afro-American art; an annotated bibliography.* N.Y./London, Bowker, 1981.

Karpel, Bernard. *Arts in America, a bibliography.* 4 v. Washington, D.C., Smithsonian Institution Press, 1979.

Rosenberg, Bernard. *Olana's guide to American artists; a contribution toward a bibliography.* 2 v. Riverdale, NY, Olana Gallery (printed for private distribution only), 1978.

Rubinstein, Charlotte Streifer. *American women artists: from early Indian times to the present.* N.Y., Avon; Boston, G.K. Hall, 1982.

———. *American women sculptors: a history of women working in three dimensions.* Boston, G.K. Hall, 1990.

Samuels, Peggy, and Samuels, Harold. *The illustrated biographical encyclopedia of artists of the American West.* Garden City, NY, Doubleday, 1976.

Stouffer, David McNeely. *American engravers upon copper and steel.* 2 v. N.Y., Grolier Club, 1907.

Who's Was Who in American Art. Edited by Peter H. Falk. Madison, CT.: Sound View Press, 1985.

Withey, Henry F., and Withey, Elsie. *Biographical dictionary of American architects.* Los Angeles, Hennessey & Ingalls, 1970.

Wodehouse, Lawrence. *American architects from the Civil War to the First World War.* Detroit, Gale, 1976.

————. *American architects from the first World War to the present.* Detroit, Gale, 1977.

Latin America

Findlay, James A. *Modern Latin American art: a bibliography.* Westport, Conn./London, Greenwood Press, 1983.

Handbook of Latin American art—Manual de arte latino americano. Gen. ed. Joyce W. Bailey. 2 v. Santa Barbara, Calif./Oxford, ABC-Clio Information Services, 1984.

Merlino, Adrian. *Diccionario de artistas plasticos de la Argentina, siglos XVIII-XIX-XX.* Buenos Aires, Instituciones de la Argentina Vinculadas a las Artes Plasticas, 1954.

Ortega Ricaurte, Carmen. *Diccionario de artistas en Colombia.* Bogota, Ediciones Tercer Mundo, 1965.

Pontul, Roberto. *Dicionario das artes plásticas no Brasil.* Rio de Janeiro, Editora Civilição Brasileira, 1969.

The Near East and Israel

Encyclopedia of Islam. New ed. by H.A.R. Gibb et al. Leiden, Brill/London, Luzac, 1954– .

Israel Museum (Jerusalem). *Here and now: Israeli art.* [catalogue of an exhibition] autums 1982. Jerusalem, Israel Museum, 1982.

The Jewish Museum (New York). *Artists of Israel, 1920–1980* [catalogue of an exhibition]. Exhibition curator Susan Tumarkin Goodman. Detroit, Wayne State Univ. Press, 1981.

Martin, Fredrik R. *The miniature painting and painters of Persia, India and Turkey, from the 8th to the 18th century.* London, Quaritch, 1912.

Meyer, Leo A. *Bibliography of Jewish art.* Edited by Otto Kurz. Jerusalem, Magnes Press, 1967.

————. *Islamic architects and their works.* Geneva, Kundig, 1950.

————. *Islamic metalworkers and their works.* Geneva, Kundig, 1959.

————. *Islamic woodcarvers and their works.* Geneva, Kundig, 1958.

The Far East and India

Blakemore, Frances. *Who's who in modern Japanese prints.* N.Y./Tokyo, Weatherhill, 1975.

Cahill, James. *An index of early Chinese painters and paintings.* Berkeley, Univ. of California Press, 1980.

Kim, Yong-Yun. *Hanguk sohwa immyong saso.* Seoul, Hangyang munhwasa, 1959.

Lalit Kala Akademi (New Delhi). *Artists directory, covering painters, sculptors, and engravers.* New Delhi, Lalit Kala Akademi, 1966 (?).

Roberts, Laurence P. *A dictionary of Japanese artists. Painting, sculpture, ceramics, prints, lacquer.* With a foreword by John M. Rosenfield. Tokyo/N.Y., Weatherhill, 1976.

Siren, Osvald. *Chinese painting: leading masters and principles.* 7 v. New York, Ronald, 1956–58.

The T.L. Yuan bibliography of Western writings on Chinese art and archaeology. Harrie A. Vanderstappen, editor. London, Mansell, 1975.

Waley, Arthur. *An index of Chinese artists represented in the Sub-department of Oriental Prints and Drawings.* London, British Museum, 1922.

South Africa

Berman, Esmé. *Art and artists of South Africa; an illustrated biographical dictionary and historical survey of painters, sculptors and graphic artists since 1875.* New updated and enlarged ed. of work first published 1970. Cape Town/Rotterdam, A.A. Balkema, 1983.

South Africa

Berman, Esmé. *Art and artists of South Africa; an illustrated biographical dictionary and historica survey of painters, sculptors and graphic artists since 1875.* New updated and enlarged ed. of work first published 1970. Cape Town/ Rotterdam, A.A. Balkema, 1983.

Art Books

A

Aalto, Alvar, 1898–1976

1. Aalto, Alvar. *Synopsis: painting, architecture, sculpture.* Basel, Birkhäuser, 1970. (Geschichte und Theorie der Architektur, 12)
2. Fleig, Karl. *Alvar Aalto, 1922–1962.* Scarsdale, N.Y., Wittenborn, 1963.
3. *Alvar Aalto, 1963–1970.* New York, Praeger, 1971. 2 ed., 1975.
4. ———. *Alvar Aalto.* Zürich, Artemis, 1974. [rev. ed. of *Alvar Aalto, 1922–1962* and *Alvar Aalto, 1963–1970*].
5. ———. *Alvar Aalto.* Barcelona, G. Gili, 1991. 2 ed.(Spanish/English)
6. ———. *Alvar Aalto: Gesamtwerk. Oeuvres complètes. Complete works.* 3v., Zürich Artemis, 1970–1978.
7. Gozaka A. *Arkhitektura i gumanizm; sbornik statei Alvar Aalto.* Moskva, Progress, 1979.
8. Gutheim, Frederick. *Alvar Aalto.* New York, Braziller, 1960.
9. Mikkola, Kirmo. *Aalto. Jyvaskylassa, Gummerus, 1985*
10. Miller, William Charles. *Alvar Aalto; a bibliography.* Monticello, Ill., Council of Planning Librarians, 1976.
11. Museum Folkwang (Essen). *Alvar Aalto; das architektonische Werk.* Ausstellung 18. März–22. April 1979. Katalog Redaktion, Zdenek Felix. Essen, Museum Folkwang, 1979.
12. Museum of Modern Art (New York). *Architecture and furniture: Aalto.* New York, Museum of Modern Art, 1938.
13. Neuenschwander, Eduard and Neuenschwander, Claudia. *Alvar Aalto and Finnish architecture.* London, Architectural Press; New York, Praeger, 1954.
14. Palazzo Strozzi (Florence). *L'opera di Alvar Aalto.* Cat. della mostra a cura di Leon Mosso, 14. nov. 1965–9 genn. 1966. Milano, Edizioni de Comunità, 1965.
15. Pearson, Paul David. *Alvar Aalto and the international style.* New York, Watson-Guptill, 1978.
16. Quantrill, Malcolm. *Alvar Aalto.* London, Secker & Warburg, 1982.
17. Schildt, Göran. *Alvar Aalto sketches.* Ed. by G. Schildt. Trans. from Swedish by Stuart Utrede. Cambridge, Mass., M.I.T. Press, 1978.
18. ———. *Alvar Aalto: the decisive years.* New York, Rizzoli, 1986
19. ———. *The sculptures of Alvar Aalto.* Helsinki, Otava, 1967.

Aaltonen, Vaino Waldemar, 1894–1966

20. Okkonen, Onni. *Wäinö Aaltonen.* Helsinki, Söderström, 1951. 2 ed.

Abbate, Niccolo dell', ca. 1512–1571

21. Beguin, Sylvie M. *Mostra di Nicolo dell'Abate.* Catalogo critico a cura di S. M. Beguin. Bologna, Palazzo dell' Archiginnasio, 1 sett.–20 ott. 1969. Bologna, Ediz. Alfa, 1969.
22. Bellochi, Ugo. *Il Mauriziano.* Gli affreschi di Nicolo dell'Abate nel nido di Ludovico Ariosto. Modena, Muratori, 1974. (Deputazione di storia patria per le antiche provincie Modenesi. Monumenti, 25).
23. Godi, Giovanni. *Nicolo dell'Abate e la presunta attivita del Parmigianino a Soragna.* Parma, Luigi Battei, 1976. (Collana di storia, arti figurative e architettura diretta da Gianni Capelli, 11).
24. Zanotti, Giovanni Pietro Cavazzoni. *Le pitture de Pellegrino Tibaldi e di Niccolo Abbati esistente nell'Instituto di Bologna, descrite et illustrate da Giampietro Zanotti.* Venezia, Pasquali, 1756.

Abbati, Giuseppe, 1836–1868

25. Dini, Piero. *Giuseppe Abbati; l'opera completa [ricerche d'archivio a cura di Alba Del*

Soldato; ricerche bibliografiche a cura di Francesca Dini]. Torino, Allemandi, 1987.

Abbey, Edwin Austin, 1852–1911

26. Lucas, Edward V. *Edwin Austin Abbey, royal academician; the record of his life and work.* 2 v. London, Methuen/New York, Scribner, 1921.
27. Yale University Art Gallery (New Haven). *Edwin Austin Abbey, 1852–1911.* [Catalog of] an exhibition, Dec. 6, 1973–Feb. 17, 1974. Introd. by Alan Shestak. Essays by Kathleen Foster and Michael Quick. New Haven, Yale University Art Gallery, 1973.

Abbott, Berenice, 1898–1991

28. Abbott, Berenice. *Berenice Abbott.* With an essay by Julia van Haften. New York, Aperture Books, 1988.
29. ———. *Berenice Abbott: photographs.* Foreword by Muriel Rukeyser. Introduction by David Vestal. Washington, D.C., Smithsonian Institution Press, 1990. (1st ed., New York, Horizon, 1970).
30. Marlborough Gallery (New York). *Berenice Abbott.* Exhibition, Jan. 4–Jan. 24, 1976. New York, Marlborough Gallery, 1976.
31. O'Neal, Hank. *Berenice Abbott, American photographer.* Introd. by John Canaday; commentary by Berenice Abbott. New York, McGraw-Hill, 1982.

Ackermann, Max, 1887–1975

32. Grohmann, Will. *Max Ackermann.* Stuttgart, Kohlhammer, 1955.
33. Hoffmann, Dieter. *Max Ackermann: Zeichnungen und Bilder.* Frankfurt a.M., Societäts-Verlag, 1965.
34. Langenfeld, Ludwig. *Max Ackermann: Aspekte seines Gesamtwerkes.* Stuttgart, Kohlhammer, 1972.
35. Leonhard, Kurt. *Max Ackermann: Zeichnungen und Bilder aus fünf Jahr-zehnten.* Frankfurt a.M., Societäts-Verlag, 1966.
36. Mittelrhein-Museum (Koblenz). *Max Ackermann: Gemälde 1908–1967.* Ausstellung, 2. Sept.–29. Okt. 1967. Katalog Bearbeitung Maria Velte. Koblenz, Mittel-rhein Museum, 1967.
37. Tittel, Lutz, Hrsg. *Max Ackermann, 1887–1975, zum 100. Geburtstag.* Stuttgart, Hatje, 1987.
38. Württembergischer Kunstverein (Stuttgart). *Max Ackermann: Aspekte des abstrakten Werkes 1919 bis 1973.* Ausstellung, 8. Aug.–30. Sept. 1973. Stuttgart, Württ. Kunstverein, 1973.

Adam, Henri Georges, 1904–1967

39. Waldemar-George [pseud.]. *Adam.* Par W.-George et Ionel Jianov. Paris, Arted, 1968.

Adam, James, 1758–1794
Robert, 1728–1792

40. Adam, Robert. *Ruins of the palace of the emperor Diocletian at Spalato in Dalmatia.* London, Printed for the Author, 1764.
41. ———. *The Works in architecture of Robert and James Adam.* Ed. with an introd. by Robert Oresko. London, Academy Editions/New York, St. Martin's, 1975. [Rev. and enl. version of 1902 ed. publ. in 3 v. by Thecard].
42. Beard, Geoffrey W. *The work of Robert Adam.* New York, Arco, 1978.
43. Bolton, Arthur T. *The architecture of Robert and James Adam (1758–1794).* 2 v. London, Country Life, 1922.
44. Fitzgerald, Percy. *Robert Adam, artist and architect; his works and his system.* London, Fisher Unwin, 1904.
45. Fleming, John. *Robert Adam and his circle in Edinburgh and Rome.* Cambridge, Mass., Harvard University Press/London, Murray, 1962.
46. Harris, Eileen. *The furniture of Robert Adam.* London, Tiranti, 1963.
47. Lees-Milne, James. *The age of Adam.* London, Batsford, 1947.
48. Musgrave, Clifford. *Adam and Hepplewhite and other neoclassical furniture.* London, Faber, 1966.
49. Spiers, Walter L. *Catalogue of the drawings and designs of Robert and James Adam in Sir John Soane's Museum.* Cambridge, Chadwyck-Healey/Teaneck, N.J., Somerset House, 1979.
50. Stillman, Damie. *The decorative work of Robert Adam.* London, Tiranti, 1966.
51. Swarbrick, John. *Robert Adam and his brothers; their lives, work and influence on English architecture, decoration and furniture.* London, Batsford, 1915.
52. Yarwood, Doreen. *Robert Adam.* New York, Scribner, 1970.

Adams, Ansel, 1902–1984

53. Adams, Ansel. *Ansel Adams: Letters and images, 1916–1984.* Ed. by Mary Street Alinder and Andrea Gray Stillman; foreword by Wallace Stegner. Boston, Little Brown, 1988. A New York Graphic Society Book.
54. ———. *The portfolios of Ansel Adams.* Boston, New York Graphic Society, 1977.
55. Newhall, Nancy W. *Ansel Adams, the eloquent light. His photographs and the classic biography.* Millerton, New York, distributed in U.S. by Harper & Row, New York, 1980.

Adriaenssen, Alexander, 1587–1661

56. Spiessens, Godelieve. *Leven en werk van de Antwerpse schilder Alexander Adriaenssen (1587–1661).* Brussels, AWLSK, 1990. (Verhandlingen van de Kgl. Academie voor Wet-

enschapen, Letteren en schone Kunsten van Belgie. Klasse der schone Kunsten, Jaarg. 52, no. 48).

Aertsen, Pieter, 1508–1575

57. Kloek, Wouter et al. *Pieter Aertsen.* The Hague, 1990. (Netherlands Yearbook for the History of Art,40).
58. Moxey, Keith P. F. *Pieter Aertsen, Joachim Beuckelaer and the rise of secular painting in the context of the Reformation.* New York, Garland, 1977.
59. Sievers, Johannes. *Pieter Aertsen; ein Beitrag zur Geschichte der niederländischen Kunst im XVI. Jahrhundert.* Leipzig, Hiersemann, 1908.

Agam, Yaacov, 1928–

60. Agam, Yaacov. *Yaacov Agam.* Texts by the artist. Ed. by Paul Kanelski. Trans. from the French by Haakon Chevalier. Neuchâtel, Editions du Griffon, 1962.
61. Metken, Günter. *Yaakov Agam.* Trans. by John Gabiel. London, Thames and Hudson, 1977.
62. Popper, Frank. *Agam.* New York, Abrams, 1990. 3d rev. ed.(1st ed., 1976).
63. Reichardt, Jasia. *Yaacov Agam.* London, Methuen, 1966.

Agasse, Jaques-Laurent, 1767–1849

64. Tate Gallery (London). *Jacques Laurent Agasse (1767–1849).* [Catalog of an exhibition organised by the Tate Gallery and the Musée'd Art et d'Histoire, Geneva]. London, Tate Gallery Publications, 1988.

Agostino di Duccio, 1418–1481

65. Bacci, Mina. *Agostino di Duccio.* Milano, Fabbri, 1966.
66. Pointer, Andy. *Die Werke des florentinischen Bildhauers Agostino d'Antonio di Duccio.* Strassburg, 1909. (Zur Kunstgeschichte des Auslandes, 68).

Aichl, Jan Santin *see* Santini-Aichl, Jan Blažej

Aigner, Lucien, 1901–

67. Aigner, John P., ed. *Lucien Aigner.* Introd. by Cornell Capa. New York, International Center for Photography, 1979. (ICP Library of photographers, 7).

Aivazovskii, Ivan Konstantinovich 1817–1900

68. Barsamov, Nikolai Stepanovich. *Ivan Konstantinovich Aivazovskii, 1817–1900.* Moskva, Isskustvo, 1962.

Albani, Francesco, 1578–1660

69. Bolognini Amorini, Antonio. *Vita del celebre pittore Francesco Albani.* Bologna, Tip. della Volpe al Sassi, 1837.

Albers, Josef, 1888–1976

70. Albers, Josef. *Homage to the square; ten works by J. Albers.* New Haven, Yale University Press, 1962.
71. ———. *Interaction of color.* 2 v. New Haven, Yale University Press, 1963.
72. ———. *Interaction of color.* Rev. pocket edition. New Haven, Yale University Press, 1975.
73. ———. *Search versus research; three lectures by J. Albers at Trinity College, April 1965.* Hartford, Conn., Trinity College Press, 1969.
74. Alviani, Getulio, Ed. *Josef Albers.* Introductory texts by: Getulio Alviani, Nicholas Fox Weber, Friedrich W. Heckmans. Milano, L'Arcaedizioni, 1988.
75. Gomringer, Eugen. *Josef Albers, his work as contribution to visual articulation in the twentieth century.* With articles by Clara Diament de Sujo [and others]. New York, Wittenborn, 1968.
76. Museum of Modern Art (New York). *Josef Albers: Homage to the square.* An exhibition organized by the Museum of Modern Art under the auspices of its International Council. New York, Museum of Modern Art, 1964. Distributed by Doubleday, Garden City, N.Y.
77. Solomon R. Guggenheim Museum (New York). *Josef Albers. A retrospective.* With contributions by Nicholas Fox-Weber, Mary Emma Harris, E. Rickart and Neal Benzara. New York, Abrams, 1988.
78. Spies, Werner. *Albers.* Trans. from German by Herman Plummer. New York, Abrams, 1970.
79. Wissmann, Jürgen. *Josef Albers.* Recklinghausen, Bongers, 1971. (Monographien zur rheinisch-westfälischen Kunst der Gegenwart, 27).
80. Yale University Art Gallery (New Haven). *Josef Albers: paintings, prints, projects.* A catalogue prepared by George Heard Hamilton for an exhibition arranged by Sewell Stillman, April 25–June 18, 1956. New York, Clarke and Way, 1956.

Alberti, Leon Battista, 1404–1472

81. Alberti, Leon Battista. *De pictura praestantissima, et nunquam satis laudata arte libri tres absolutissimo.* Basileae, 1540.
82. ———. *De re aedificatoria.* Florentiae, Laurentii, 1485.

83. ———. *De statua*. Introd. di O. Morisani. Catania, Università di Catania, Facolta di Lett. e Filosofia, 1961. (Pubblicazioni, 1).

84. ———. *L'architettura (De re aedificatoria)*. Testo latino e traduzione a cura di G. Orlandi. Introd. e note di P. Portoghesi. 2 v. Milano, Polifilo, 1966.

85. ———. *Leone Battista Alberti's kleinere kunsttheoretische Schriften*. I, Originaltext hrsg., übersetzt, erläutert, mit e. Einleitung und Excursen versehen von Dr. Hubert Janitschek. Wien, Braumüller, 1877. (Quellenschriften für Kunstgeschichte und Kunsttechnik, 11).

86. ———. *On painting*. Trans. by J. R. Spencer. New Haven, Yale University Press, 1966. [Trans. of *De Pictura*, first publ. Basel, 1540].

87. ———. *On painting and On sculpture*. The Latin texts of *De Pictura* and *De Statua*. Ed. with trans., introd. and notes by Cecil Grayson. London, Phaidon, 1972.

88. ———. *On the art of building in ten books*. Trans. by Joseph Rykwert, Neil Leach, and Robert Tavernor. Introd. by Joseph Rykwert. [Trans. of *De re aedificatoria*, first publ. Florence, 1485]. Cambridge, Mass., MIT Press, 1988.

89. ———. *Opera volgari;* a cura di Cecil Grayson. 3 v. Bari, Laterza, 1960–1973. (Scrittore d'Italia, 218, 234, 254).

90. Borsi, Franco. *Leon Battista Alberti*. Milano, Electa, 1975.

91. ———. *Leon Battista Alberti*. Trans. by R. G. Carpanini. New York, Harper, 1977.

92. Flemming, Willi. *Die Begründung der modernen Aesthetik und Kunstwissenschaft durch Leon Battista Alberti*. Leipzig, Teubner, 1916.

93. Gadol, Joan. *Leon Battista Alberti, universal man of the early Renaissance*. Chicago, Chicago University Press, 1969.

94. Jarzombek, Mark. *On Leon Battista Alberti: his literary and artistic theories*. Cambridge, Mass., MIT Press, 1990.

95. Luecke, Hans-Karl. *Alberti Index: Leon Battista Alberti, De re aedificatoria, Florence, 1485, Index verborum*. 4 v. München, Prestel, 1975–1979.

96. Mancini, Girolamo. *Vita di Leone Battista Alberti*. Firenze, Carnesecchi, 1911. 2 ed.

Albertinelli, Mariotto, 1474–1515

97. Borgo, Ludovico. *The works of Mariotto Albertinelli*. New York, Garland, 1976.

Alcamenes, 5th c. B.C.

98. Capuis, Loredana. *Alkamenes. Fonti storiche e archeologiche*. Firenze, Olschki, 1968. (Univ. di Padova. Pubblicaz. della Fac. di Lettere e Filosofia, 44).

99. Langlotz, Ernst. *Alkamenes-Probleme*. Berlin, de Gruyter, 1952. (Winckelmannsprogramm der Archaeologischen Gesellschaft zu Berlin, 108).

Aldegrever, Heinrich, 1502–1558

100. Fritz, Rolf. *Heinrich Aldegrever als Maler*. Dortmund, Ardey, 1959.

101. Geisberg, Max. *Heinrich Aldegrever*. Dortmund, Ruhfus, 1939. (Westfälische Kunsthefte, 9).

102. ———. *Die münsterischen Wiedertäufer und Aldegrever*. Strassburg, Heitz, 1907. (Schriften zur deutschen Kunstgeschichte, 76).

103. Luckhardt, Jochen. *Heinrich Aldegrever und die Bildnisse der Wiedertäufer*. [Ausstellung, Westfälisches Landesmuseum, 5. Mai–17 Juni, 1985]. Katal. und Ausstellung, J. Luckhardt unter Mitarbeit von Angelika Lorenz. Münster, Westf. Landesmuseum, 1985.

104. Zschelletzschky, Herbert. *Das graphische Werk Heinrich Aldegrevers*. Strassburg, Heitz, 1933. (Studien zur deutschen Kunstgeschichte, 292).

Alechinsky, Pierre, 1927–

105. Alechinsky, Pierre. *Pierre Alechinsky: margin and center*. [Catalog of an exhibition]. New York, Solomon R. Guggenheim Museum, 1987.

106. Alechinsky, Pierre. *Paintings and writings. Eugène Ionesco: three approaches*. Paris, Ives Rivière—Arts et Métiers Graphiques, 1977. [Catalogue of an exhibition, Carnegie Instit., Pittsburgh, Oct. 28, 1977–Jan. 8, 1978, and at the Art Gallery of Ontario, Toronto, March 10–April 20, 1978].

107. ———. *Pierre Alechinsky: 20 Jahre Impressionen*. Oeuvre-Katalog, Druckgraphik. Introd. by Yvon Taillandier. München: Galerie van de Loo, 1967.

108. Andre Emmerich Gallery (New York). *Pierre Alechinsky; new work*. [Catalog of an exhibition, May 3 to 25, 1990]. New York, Andre Emmerich Gallery, 1990.

Alessi, Galeazzo, 1512–1572

109. Alessi, Galeazzo. *Galeazzo Alessi: mostra di fotografie, rilievi, disegni*. Genova, Palazzo Bianco, 16 apr.–12 magg. 1974. Genova, Sagep, 1974.

110. ———. *Galeazzo Alessi e l'architettura del cinquecento; atti del convegno internazionale di studi*. Genova, 16–20 apr. 1974. Genova, Sagep, 1974.

111. Negri, Emmina de. *Galeazzo Alessi, architetto a Genova*. Genova, Univ. di Genova, 1957. (Quaderni dell' Ist. di Storia dell'arte dell'Univ. di Genova, 1).

Alexander, Francesca (Esther Frances), 1837–1917

112. Alexander, Constance Grosvenor. *Francesca Alexander: a hidden secret*. Cambridge, Mass., Harvard University Press, 1927.

Alfieri, Benedetto Innocente, 1700–1767

113. Bellini, Amedeo. *Benedetto Alfieri*. Milano, Electa, 1978.

Algardi, Alessandro, 1602–1654

114. Heimburger-Revalli, Minna. *Alessandro Algardi, scultore*. Città di Castello, Ist. di Studi Romani, 1973.
115. Montagu, Jennifer. *Allessandro Algardi*. 2 v. New Haven, Yale University Press, 1985.

Alkamenes *see* **Alcamenes**

Allan, David, 1744–1796

116. Gordon, Thomas Crouther. *David Allan of Alloa, the Scottish Hogarth*. Alva, Printed by Cunningham, 1951.

Allori, Cristofano, 1577–1621

117. Palazzo Pitti (Florence). *Cristofano Allori, 1577–1621*. catalogo a cura di Miles L. Chappell. Firenze, Centro Di, 1984.

Allston, Washington, 1779–1843

118. Allston, Washington. *Lectures on art, and poems*. Ed. by Richard H. Dana. New York, Baker and Scribner, 1850. Reprint: Gainesville, Scholars' Facsimiles, 1967.
119. Bjelajac, David. *Millenial desire and the apocalyptic vision of Washington Allston*. Washington, D.C., Smithsonian Institution Press, 1988.
120. Flagg, Jared. *The life and letters of Washington Allston*. New York, Scribner, 1892. Reprint: New York, Blom, 1969.
121. Gerdts, William Henry. *"A man of genius": the art of Washington Allston (1779–1843)* by W. H. Gerdts and Theodore E. Stebbins. Boston, Museum of Fine Arts, 1979.
122. Harding's Gallery (Boston). *Exhibition of pictures painted by Washington Allston*. Boston, Eastburn, 1839.
123. Richardson, Edgar P. *Washington Allston, a study of the romantic artist in America*. Chicago, Chicago University Press, 1948.
124. [Sweetser, Moses Foster]. *Allston*. Boston, Osgood, 1879.
125. Ware, William. *Lectures on the works and genius of Washington Allston*. Boston, Phillips, Sampson, 1852.

Alma-Tadema, Lawrence, 1836–1912

126. Ash, Russell. *Sir Lawrence Alma-Tadema*. New York, Abrams, 1990.
127. Borger, Rykle. *Drei Klassizisten: Alma-Tadema, Ebers, Vosmaer. Mit einer Bibliographie der Werke Alma-Tadema's*. Leiden, Ex Oriente Lux, 1978. (Mededelingen en verhandlingen van het voorziatisch-egyptisch genootschap "Ex Oriente Lux," 20).
128. City Art Galleries, Sheffield. *Sir Lawrence Alma-Tadema*. Exhibition at the Mappin Art Gallery, Weston Park, Sheffield, Jul. 3–Aug. 8, 1976. Cat. by Anne L. Goodchild. Sheffield, City Art Galleries, 1976.
129. Ebers, Georg. *Lorenz Alma Tadema; his life and works*. Trans.by Mary J. Safford. New York, Gottsberger, 1886. Trans. of artcle. orig. publ. in *Westermanns Monatshefte*, Bd.59, Oct./Nov. 1885).
130. Lippincott, Louise. *Lawrence Alma-Tadema: Spring*. Malibu, Calif., J. Paul Getty Museum, 1990.
131. Lovett, Jennifer Gordon and Johnston, William R. *Elysium revisited: the art of Sir Lawrence Alma-Tadema*. With contributions by Patricia R. Ivinski, Kathryn L. Calley, and Vern G. Swanson. Williamstown, Mass., Sterling and Francine Clark Art Institute, 1991.
132. Metropolitan Museum of Art (New York). *Victorians in togas: paintings by Sir Lawrence Alma-Tadema from the collection of Allen Funt*. Exhib. March–April, 1973. Cat. by Christopher Forbes. New York, Metropolitan Museum, 1973).
133. Royal Academy of Arts (London). *Exhibition of works by Sir Lawrence Alma-Tadema, R. A., O. M.* London, Cloves, 1913. (Winter exhibition, 44th Year).
134. Stephens, Frederic George. *Laurence Alma-Tadema, R. A. A sketch of His life and work*. London, 1895.
135. Standing, Percy Cross. *Sir Lawrence Alma-Tadema*. London, 1905.
136. Swanson, Vern G. *The biography and catalogue raisonné of Sir Lawrence Alma-Tadema, OM, RA*. London, Scolar Press, 1990.
137. ———. *Sir Lawrence Alma-Tadema, the painter of the Victorian vision of the Ancient World*. London, Ash and Grant, 1977.
138. Zimmern, Helen. *Sir Lawrence Alma-Tadema, R. A.* London, Bell, 1902.

Alt, Rudolf von, 1812–1905

139. Hevesi, Ludwig. *Rudolf von Alt: sein Leben und sein Werk*. Wien, Stülpnagel, 1905.
140. Koschatzky, Walter. *Rudolf von Alt, 1812–1905*. Salzburg, Residenz Verlag, 1975.
141. Rössler, Arthur. *Rudolf von Alt*. Wien, Graeser, 1921.

Altdorfer, Albrecht, c. 1480–1538

142. Altdorfer, Albrecht. *Altdorfer et le réalisme fantastique dans l'art allemand*. [Catalogue

d'une exposition présentée au Centre culturel du Marais, du 3 avril au 15 juillet 1984]. Rédigée par Jacqueline et Maurice Guillaud. Paris, Le Centre, 1984.

143. ———. *Altdorfer and fantastic realism in German art.* Edited by Jacqueline and Maurice Guillaud. New York, Rizzoli, 1985. (Trade edition of the English translation of above).

144. Baldass, Ludwig von. *Albrecht Altdorfer.* Wien, Gallus/Zürich, Scientia, 1941. 2 ed.

145. ———. *Albrecht Altdorfer. Studien über die Entwicklungsfaktoren im Werk des Künstlers.* Wien, Hölzel, 1923. (Kunstgeschichtliche Einzeldarstellungen, 2).

146. Bayerische Staatsgemäldesammlung (Munich). *Albrecht Altdorfer und sein Kreis.* Amtlicher Katalog der Gedächtnisausstellung zum 400. Todesjahr Altdorfers. München, Wolf, 1938.

147. Becker, Hanna L. *Die Handzeichnungen Albrecht Altdorfers.* München, Filser, 1938. (Münchener Beiträge zur Kunstgeschichte, 1).

148. Benesch, Otto. *Der Maler Albrecht Altdorfer.* Wien, Schroll, 1939.

149. Friedländer, Max J. *Albrecht Altdorfer.* Berlin, Cassirer, 1923.

150. Goldberg, Gisela. *Albrecht Altdorfer: Meister von Landschaft, Raum, Licht.* München, Schnell & Steiner, 1988.

151. Janzen, Reinhild. *Albrecht Altdorfer: four centuries of criticism.* Ann Arbor, UMI Research Press, 1980.

152. Oettinger, Karl. *Altdorfer-Studien.* Nürnberg, Carl, 1959. (Erlanger Beiträge zur Sprach- und Kunstwissenschaft, 3).

153. Ruhmer, Eberhard. *Albrecht Altdorfer.* München, Bruckmann, 1965.

154. Tietze, Hans. *Albrecht Altdorfer.* Leipzig, Insel, 1923.

155. Voss, Hermann G. A. *Albrecht Altdorfer und Wolf Huber.* Leipzig, Klinkhardt und Biermann, 1910.

156. Waldmann, Emil. *Albrecht Altdorfer.* London and Boston, Medici Society, 1923.

157. Winzinger, Franz. *Albrecht Altdorfer: die Gemälde, Tafelbilder, Miniaturen, Wandbilder, Bildhauerarbeiten; Werkstatt und Umkreis. Gesamtausgabe.* München, Hirmer, 1975.

158. ———. *Albrecht Altdorfer: Graphik, Holzschnitte, Kupferstiche, Radierungen.* München, Piper, 1963.

159. ———. *Albrecht Altdorfer: Zeichnungen. Gesamtausgabe.* München, Piper, 1952.

160. Wolf, Georg Jacob. *Altdorfer.* Bielefeld, Velhagen, 1925.

161. Wood, Christopher S. *Albrecht Altdorfer and the origins of landscape.* London, Reaktion Books, 1933.

Altechieri, Altechiero *see* Altechiero da Zevio

Altechiero da Zevio, 1320–1385

162. Bronstein, Leo. *Altechieri, l'artiste et son oeuvre.* Paris, Vrin, 1932.

163. Mellini, Gian Lorenzo. *Altechiero e Jacopo Avanzi.* Milano, Ediz. di Comunitá, 1967.

164. Pettenella, Plinia. *Altichiero e la pittura Veronese del Trecento.* Verona, Vita Veronese, 1961. (Collana monografie d'arte, 3).

165. Schubring, Paul. *Altichiero und seine Schule.* Leipzig, Hiersemann, 1898.

Altherr, Heinrich, 1878–1947

166. Überwasser, Walter and Braun, Wilhelm. *Der Maler Heinrich Altherr, sein Weg und Werk.* Zürich, Orell Füssli, 1938.

Altink, Jan, 1885–1971

167. Altink, Jan. *Jan Altink, 21 Oct. 1885–6 Dec. 1971.* Texts by D.H. Douvee and W.J. de Gruyter. 2 v. Heemskerk, Jan Altink Stichting, 1978.

Altomonte, Bartolomeo, 1702–1779 Martino (Martin Hohenberg), 1657–1745

168. Aurenhammer, Hans. *Martino Altomonte.* Mit einem Beitrag: Martino Altomonte als Zeichner und Graphiker, von Gertrude Aurenhammer. Wien, Herold, 1965.

169. Heinzl, Brigitte. *Bartolomeo Altomonte.* Wien, Herold, 1964.

Alunno, Niccolo di Liberatore *see* Niccolo da Foligno

Amadeo, Giovanni Antonio, 1447–1522

170. Malaguzzi-Valeri, Francesco. *Giovanni Antonio Amadeo, scultore e architetto lombardo (1447–1522).* Bergamo, Ist. Ital. d'Arti Grafiche, 1904.

Amalteo, Pomponio, 1505–1588

171. Mantoani, Jacopo. *Elogio di Pomponio Amalteo.* San-Vito, Pascatti, 1838.

172. Truant, Giuseppe. *Pomponio Amalteo e le sue opere.* Pordenone, Grafiche Editoriali Artistiche Pordenonesi, 1980.

Amasis Painter, 6th c. B.C.

173. Von Bothmer, Dietrich. *The Amasis Painter and his world: vase painting in sixth-century B.C., Athens.* With an introduction by Alan L. Boegehold. Malibu, Calif, J. Paul Getty Museum/ New York, Thames and Hudson, 1985.

174. ———. *Papers on the Amasis Painter and his world.* Based on a colloquium and symposium held at the J. Paul Getty Museum in

1986 in connection with the opening of the exhibition *The Amasis Painter and his world*. Malibu, Calif. The J. Paul Getty Museum, 1987.

Ames, Ezra, 1768–1836

175. Bolton, Theodore. *Ezra Ames of Albany, portrait painter, craftsman, Royal Arch mason, banker, 1768–1836*. Catalogue of his works by Irwin F. Cortelyou. New York, New York Historical Soc., 1955.

Amiet, Cuno, 1868–1961

176. Amiet, Cuno. *Über Kunst und Künstler*. Bern, Bernische Kunstgesellschaft, 1948.

177. Galeries Georges Petit (Paris). *Exposition Cuno Amiet, 1–18 mars 1932*. Paris, Galerie Georges Petit, 1932.

178. Jedlicka, Gotthard. *Cuno Amiet, 1868–1961*. Olten, Kunstverein, 1961.

179. Kunsthalle Bern. *Cuno Amiet. Ausstellung zum neunzigsten Geburtstag, 29. März–4. Mai 1958*. Text von Franz Meyer. Bern, Kunsthalle, 1958.

180. ———. *Jubiläumsausstellung Cuno Amiet, 1868–1961; Giovanni Giacometti, 1868–1933, Werke bis 1920. 8. März–28. April 1968*. Bern, Kunsthalle, 1968.

181. Kunsthaus Zürich. *Cuno Amiet und die Maler der Brücke*. [Ausstellung]. Kunsthaus Zürich, 18. Mai–5. Aug. 1979; Brücke Museum, Berlin, 31. Aug.–4 Nov. 1979. Zürich, Kunsthaus, 1979.

182. Müller, Josef. *Cuno Amiet*. Neuchâtel, Editions du Griffon, 1954.

183. Pennsylvania State University Museum of Art (University Park, Penn.). *Cuno Amiet, Giovanni Giacometti, Augusto Giacometti: Three Swiss painters*. An exhib. organized by the Museum of Art, the Pennsylvania State Univ. Selection and cat. by George Manner. 23 Sept.–4 Nov. 1973. Busch-Reisinger Museum, Harvard Univ., 16 Jan.–16 Feb. 1974. University Park, Penn. State Univ., 1973.

184. Sydow, Eckart von. *Cuno Amiet; eine Einführung in sein malerisches Werk*. Strassburg, Heitz, 1913. (Zur Kunstgeschichte des Auslandes, 106).

185. Tatarinoff-Eggenschwiler, Adele. *Cuno Amiet; ein Malerleben*. Solothurn, Vogt-Schild, 1958.

Amigoni, Jacopo, 1675–1752

186. Holler, Wolfgang. *Jacopo Amigonis Frühwerk in Süddeutschland*. Hilldesheim/New York, G. Olms, 1986.

187. Scarpa Sonino, Annalisa. *Jacopo Amigoni*. Soncino, Edizioni dei Soncino, 1994. (Mensili darte, 16). 1994.

Amman, Jost, 1539–1591

188. Amman, Jost. *Kunst- und Lehrbüchlein für die anfahenden Jungen daraus Reissen und Malen zu lernen*. Frankfurt a.M., Feyeraband, 1578.

189. Becker, Carl. *Jost Amann, Zeichner und Formschneider, Kupferätzer und Stecher*. Nebst Zusätzen von R. Weigel. Leipzig, Weigel, 1854. Reprint: Nieuwkoop, De Graaf, 1961.

Ammanati, Bartolomeo, 1511–1592

190. Fossi, Mazzino. *Bartolomeo Ammanati, architetto*. Napoli, Morano, 1966/68. (Univ. di Firenze, Fac. di Magistero, Pubblicazioni, 10).

191. Kinney, Peter. *The early sculpture of Bartolomeo Ammanati*. New York, Garland, 1976.

Anderson, Alexander, 1775–1870

192. Burr, Frederick M. *Life and works of Alexander Anderson, M. D., the first American wood engraver*. New York, Burr, 1893.

193. Duyckinck, Evert Augustus. *A brief catalogue of books illustrated with engravings by Dr. Alexander Anderson, with a biographical sketch of the artist*. New York, Thompson and Moreau, 1885.

Andre, Carl, 1935–

194. Andre, Carl. *Carl Andre*. Catalogue of an exhibition]. Den Haag: Haags Gemeentemuseum; Eindhoven; Stedelijk Van Abbemuseum, 1987.

195. ———. *Carl Andre, die Milchstrasse, der Frieden von Münster und andere Skulpturen*. [Katalog einer Ausstellung des Westfälischen Kunstvereins Münster 1984; Berliner Künstlerprogramm des DAAD (Galerie im Körnerpark) 1984; Kunstraum München 1985. Berlin, das Künstlerprogramm [des DAAD], 1985.

196. Lauter, Rolf. *Carl Andre: extraneous roots*. Frankfurt am Main. Museum für Moderne Kunst, 1991.

Andrea da Salerno *see* Sabatini, Andrea

Andriolli, Michael Elwir, 1836–1893

197. Piatkowski, Henryk. *Andriolli w sztuce i zyciu*. Spolecznym przez H. Piatkowskiego i H. Dobrzyckiego. Warzawa, Dobrzyckiego, 1904.

198. Wiercinska, Janina. *Andriolli, swadek swoich czasow: Listy i wspomnienia*. Wroclaw, Zakl. Narod. im Ossolinskich, 1976. [Polska Akad. Nauk, Inst. Sztuki].

199. Alce, Venturino. *"Omelie" del Beato Angelico*. Bologna. Edizione Studio Dominicano, 1988.

Angelico, Fra (Giovanni da Fiesole), 1387–1455

200. Angelico, Fra Giovanni da Fiesole. *L'opera completa dell' Angelico*. Presentazione di Elsa Morante. Apparati critici e filologici di Umberto Baldini. Milano, Rizzoli, 1970. (Classici dell'arte, 38).

201. Argan, Giulio C. *Fra Angelico, biographical and critical study*. Trans. by James Emmons. Geneva, Skira, 1955. (The taste of our time, 10).

202. Baldini, Umberto. *Beato Angelico*. Firenze, Edizioni d'arte il Fiorino, 1986.

203. Bazin, Germain. *Fra Angelico*. Trans. by Marc Loge; ed. by André Gloeckner. London, Hyperion, 1949.

204. *Beato Angelico: miscellanea di studi*. A cura della Postulazione generale dei Domenicani. Roma, Pontificia commissione centrale per l'arte sacra in italia, 1984. (Pubblicazioni della Pontificia commissione centrale per l'arte sacra in italia, 6).

205. Becherucci, Luisa. *Le celle di San Marco*. 2 v. Firenze, Alinari, 1955.

206. Bering, Kunibert. *Fra Angelico: mittelalterlicher Mystiker oder Maler der Renaissance?* Essen, Blaue Eule, 1984.

207. Berti, Luciano. *Beato Angelico*. Milano, Fabbri, 1964. (I maestri del colore, 19).

208. Boskovits, Miklos. *Un 'Adorazione dei Magi' e gli inizi dell'Angelico*. Bern, Abegg-Stiftung, 1976. (Monographien der Abegg-Stiftung, 2).

209. Cartier, Etienne. *Vie de Fra Angelico de Fiesole de l'ordre des Frères Precheurs*. Paris, Poussielgue-Rusand, 1857.

210. Didi-Huberman. Georges. *Fra Angelico: dissemblance et figuration*. Paris, Flammarion, 1990.

211. Douglas, Robert Langton. *Fra Angelico*. London, Bell, 1902, 2 ed.

212. Hausenstein, Wilhelm. *Fra Angelico*. Trans. by Agnes Blake. London, Methuen, 1928.

213. Muratov, Pavel Pavlovich. *Fra Angelico*. Trans. by E. Law-Gisiko; with 296 reproductions in collotype. London/New York, Warne, 1930.

214. Musei di San Marco (Florence). *Mostra delle opere del beato Angelico nel quinto centenario della morte, 1455–1955*. Magg.–sett. 1955. Firenze, Mus. di S. Marco, 1955.

215. Orlando, Stefano. *Beato Angelico; monografia storica della vita e delle opere, con un'appendice di nuovi documenti inediti*. Premessa di Mario Salmi. Firenze, Olschki, 1964.

216. Pope-Hennessy, John Wyndham. *Fra Angelico*. Firenze, Scala; New York, Riverside, 1981. repr. 1989. (The Library of Great Masters).

217. ———. *The paintings of Fra Angelico*. London/New York, Phaidon, 1952. 2 ed.: London, Phaidon/Ithaca, Cornell University Press, 1974.

218. Procacci, Ugo. *Beato Angelico al Museo di San Marco a Firenze*. (Parallel texts in Italian, French, English and German). Milano, Silvana, n.d.

219. Rothes, Walter. *Die Darstellungen des Fra Giovanni Angelico aus dem Leben Christi und Mariae. Ein Beitrag zur Ikonographie des Meisters*. Strassburg, Heitz, 1902. (Zur Kunstgeschichte des Auslandes, 12).

220. Salmi, Mario, ed.'[catalogo della] *Mostra del beato Angelico nel quinto centenario della morte (1455–1955)*. Firenze, maggio-settembre, 1955. 1956.(1st and 2 eds, 1955).

221. Schneider, Edouard. *Fra Angelico da Fiesole*. Paris, A. Michel, 1924.

222. Schottmüller, Frida. *Fra Angelico da Fiesole*. Stuttgart, Deutsche Verlagsanstalt, 1924. 2 ed. (Klassiker der Kunst, 18).

223. Valenziano, Crispino. *Via pulchritudinis: teologia sponsale del beato Angelico*. Roma, Pontificio Istituto Liturgico, 1988.

224. Vegas, Liana, Castelfranchi. *L'Angelico e l'Umanesimo*. Milano, Jaca Book, 1989.

225. Williamson, George C. *Fra Angelico*. London, Bell, 1901.

226. Wingenroth, Max. *Angelico da Fiesole*. Bielefeld/Leipzig, Velhagen und Klasing, 1906. (Künstler-Monographien, 85).

Angermair, Christoph, d. 1633

227. Grünewald, Michael D. *Christoph Angermair. Studien zu Leben und Werk des Elfenbeinschnitzers und Bildhauers*. München, Schnell und Steiner, 1971

Angers, Pierre Jean David de *see* David D'angers, Pierre Jean

Anguissola, Sofonisba, 1532–1625

228. Anguissola, Sofonisba. *Sofonisba Anguissola e le sue sorelle*.[Catalogue of an exhibition held at the Centro culturale "Citta di Cremona" Santa Maria della Pieta, Sept. 17–Dec. 11, 1994, the Vienna Kunsthistorisches Museum, Jan.–March, 1995 and the National Museum of Women in the Arts, Washington, D.C., April–June 1995. Roma, Leonardo Arte, 1994.

229. Caroli, Flavio. *Sofonisba Anguissola e le sue sorelle*. Milano, Mondadori, 1987.

230. Perlingieri, Ilya Sandra. *Sofonisba Anguissola*. New York, Rizzoli, 1992.

Anker, Albert, 1831–1910

231. Gantenbein, Leo. *Der Maler Albert Anker*. Zürich, Rigoletto, 1980.

232. Higgler, Max. *Albert Anker, 1831–1910, der Maler und sein Dorf.* Bern, Wyss, 1977.

233. Kuthy, Sandor. *Albert Anker.* Sandor Kuthy und Hans A. Lüthy: Zwei Autoren über einen Maler. Zürich, Orell-Füssli, 1980.

234. Kunstmuseum Bern. *Albert Anker.* Katalog der Gemälde und Ölstudien. Bern, Kunstmuseum, 1962.

235. Rytz, Daniel Albrecht. *Der Berner Maler Albert Anker: ein Lebensbild.* Bern, Stämpfli, 1911.

Annigoni, Pietro, 1910–

236. Cammell, Charles Richard. *Memoirs of Annigoni.* London, Wingate, 1956.

237. ———. *Pietro Annigoni.* With an introd. by C. R. Cammell, and a foreword by Lord Moran. London, Batsford, 1954.

238. Rasmo, Nicolo. *Pietro Annigoni.* Monograph presented by N. Rasmo. Firenze, Edam, 1961.

Antelami, Benedetto (Benedetto di Parma), fl. 1177–1233

239. Forster, Kurt W. *Benedetto Antelami, der grosse romanische Bildhauer Italiens.* Aufnahmen von Leonhard von Matt. München, Hirmer, 1961.

240. Francovich, Géza de. *Benedetto Antelami, architetto e scultore, e l'arte del suo tempo.* 2 v. Milano, Electa, 1952.

Antes, Horst, 1936–

241. Antes, Horst. *Horst Antes: Lithographien.* Werkverzeichnis von Bernd Lutze mit e. Einleitung von Klaus Gallwitz. Stuttgart, Belser, 1976. (CR).

242. ———. *Horst Antes: Metallplastik.* Werkverzeichnis. Engl. trans. Leslie Owen, Fr. trans. Leopold Jaumonet. München, Bruckmann, 1976.

243. ———. *Horst Antes: Neue Bilder 1987–1990.* Ed. by Jens Christian Jensen. [Catalog of an exhibition at the Kunsthalle Kiel, 10 June–29 July, 1990]. Düsseldorf, Kunsthalle, 1990.

244. ———. *Horst Antes: Werkverzeichnis der Radierungen* von Günther Gercken. München, Galerie Stangl, 1968.

245. Staatliche Kunsthalle Baden-Baden. *Antes: Bilder 1965–1971.* Ausstellung 30. Juli 1971–26. März 1972. Katalog Klaus Gallwitz. Baden-Baden, Staatl. Kunsthalle und Gesellschaft d. Freunde Junger Kunst, 1971.

Anthoons, Willy, 1911–

246. Seuphor, Michel [pseud., Berckelaers, Ferdinand Louis]. *Willy Anthoons.* Anvers, De Sikkel, 1954.

Antokolskii, Mark Matveevich, 1843–1902

247. Antokol'skii, Mark Matveevich. *Mark Matveevich Antokol'skii; ego zhizn, tvorenia pisma i stati.* Pod. red. V.V. Stasova. S.-Petersburg, Izd. T-va M.O. Volf, 1905.

248. Lebedev, Andrei Konstantinovich. *Tvorcheskoe sodruzhestvo: M. M. Anto-kolskii i V. V. Stasov.* [By] A. Lebedev [and] G. Burova. Leningrad, Khudoznik RSFSR, 1968.

Antolinez, José, 1639–1676

249. Angulo Iniguez, Diego. *José Antolinez.* Madrid, Instituto Diego Velazquez, 1957.

Antonello da Messina, 1430–1479

250. Antonello da Messina. *L'opera completa di Antonello da Messina.* Presentazione di Leonardo Sciascia. Apparati critici e filologici di Gabriele Mandel. Milano, Rizzoli, 1967. (Classici dell'arte, 10).

251. Bottari, Stefano. *Antonello da Messina, con 64 tavole fuori testo.* Messina/Milano, Principato, 1939. (Monumenti hist. ed artisti di Sicilia, 1).

252. ———. *Antonello da Messina.* Messina/Milano, Principato, 1953.

253. ———. *Antonello da Messina.* Greenwich, Conn., New York Graphic Society, 1956.

254. Lauts, Jan. *Antonello da Messina.* Wien, Schroll, 1940.

255. Museo Regionale, Messina. *Antonello da Messina.* [Mostra] ott. 1981–jan. 1982. Catalogo a cura di Alessandro Marabottini e Fiorella Stricchia Santoro. Roma, de Luca, 1981.

256. Palazzo Comunale, Messina. *Antonello da Messina e la pittura del '400 in Sicilia.* Catalogo della mostra, a cura di Giorgio Vigni e Giovanni Caradente. Con introduzione di Giuseppe Fioco. Venezia, Alfieri, 1953.

257. Sricchia Santoro, Fiorella. *Antonello e l' Europa.* Milano, Jaca Book 1986. (CR).

258. Vigni, Giorgio. *All the paintings of Antonello da Messina.* Trans. by Anthony F. O'Sullivan. New York, Hawthorn Books, 1963. (The complete library of world art, 14).

Anuszkiewicz, Richard, 1930–

259. Lunde, Karl. *Anuszkiewicz.* New York, Abrams, 1976.

Apelles, 4th c. B.C.

260. Housseye, Henry. *Histoire d'Apelles.* Paris, Didier, 1867. 2 ed. [3 ed. 1868].

261. Lepik-Kopaczynska, Wilhelmina. *Apelles, der berühmteste Maler der Antike.* Berlin, Akademie-Verlag, 1962. (Lebendiges Altertum, 7).

262. Wustmann, Gustav. *Apelles' Leben und Werke*. Leipzig, Engelmann, 1870.

Apollonio di Giovanni, 1415–1465

263. Callman, Ellen. *Apollonio di Giovanni*. Oxford, Clarendon Press, 1974.

Apollonio da Ripatransone *see* Apollonio di Giovanni

Appel, Karel, 1921–

264. Appel, Karel. *Karel Appel: works on paper*. Improvisation and essay by Jean-Clarence Lambert. Engl. version by Kenneth White. Foreword by Marshall McLuhan. New York, Abbeville, 1980.

265. Centraal Museum Utrecht. *Appel's oogappels*. [Tentoon-stelling] 4. Sept.–15. Nov. 1970. Utrecht, Centraal-museum, 1970.

266. Centre National d'Art Contemporain (Paris). *Karel Appel reliefs, 1966–1968*. Exposition. Paris, Ministère des Affaires Culturelles, 1968.

267. Claus, Hugo. *Karel Appel, painter*. Trans. by Cornelis de Dood. Amsterdam, Strengholt, 1962.

268. Kuspit, Donald B. *Karel Appel sculpture: a catalogue raisonné*. New York, H.N. Abrams, 1994. (CR).

269. Ragon, Michel. *Karel Appel. Peinture 1937–1957*. Paris, editions Galilée, 1988.

Arbus, Diane, 1923–1971

270. Arbus, Diane. *Diane Arbus*. Ed. and designed by D. Arbus and Marvin Israel. Millerton, N.Y., Aperture, 1972.

Arca, Niccolo dell' *see* Niccolo dell' Arca

Archipenko, Alexander, 1887–1964

271. Archipenko, Alexander. *Archipenko-Album*. Einführung von Theodor Däubler und Ivan Goll. Mit einer Dichtung von Blaise Cendrars. Potsdam, Kiepenheuer, 1921.

272. ———. *Alexander Archipenko*. Berlin, Der Sturm, [1920].

273. ———. *Alexander Archipenko, son oeuvre*. 66 reproductions avec un portrait de l'artiste et une introduction par Hans Hildebrandt. Berlin, Editions "Ukrainske slowo," 1923.

274. ———. *Archipenkpo; content and continuity, 1908–1963*. By Donald H. Karshan. Pref. by Marjorie B. Kovler. Chicago, Kovler Gallery, 1968.

275. ———. *Archipenko: fifty creative years, 1908–1958*, by A. Archipenko and fifty art historians. New York, Tekhne, 1960.

276. ———. *Archipenko, international visionary*. Ed. by Donald H. Karshan. Washington, D.C., Smithsonian Press for The National Collection of Fine Arts, 1969.

277. ———. *Archipenko; the American years, 1923–1963*. [Catalog] Exhibition July 23–Aug. 15, 1970, Bernard Danenberg Galleries, New York. New York, Danenberg Galleries, 1970.

278. ———. *Archipenko: the sculpture and graphic art, including a print catalogue raisonné by Donald Karshan*. Tübingen, Wasmuth, 1974. (CR).

279. Michaelsen, Katherine Janszky. *Archipenko; a study of the early works, 1908–1920*. New York, Garland, 1977.

Arcimboldi, Guiseppe, 1527–1593

280. Geiger, Benno. *I dipinti ghiribizzosi di Guiseppe Arcimboldi, pittore illusionista del Cinquecento (1527–1593)*. Con una nota su l'Arcimboldi musicista di Lionello Levi, ed un epilogo di Oskar Kokoschka. Firenze, Valecchi, 1954.

281. Legrand, Francine Claire and Sluys, Felix. *Arcimboldo et les arcimboldesques*. Aalter, Belg., de Rache, 1955.

282. Pieyre de Mandiargues, André. *Arcimboldo the marvelous* by A. Pieyre de Mandiargues. Concept. by Yasha David; editor Patricia Egan. Trans. I. Mark Paris. New York, Abrams, 1978.

Arikha, Avigdor, 1929–

283. Arikha, Avigdor. *Arikha*. Texts by Richard Channin . . . [et al.]; interviews, Barbara Rose, Joseph Shannon, Maurice Tuchman. Paris, Hermann, 1985.

284. Thomas, Duncan. *Arikha*. London, Phaidon, 1994.

Arman (Fernandez, Armand), 1928–

285. Andrew Crispi Gallery (New York). *Arman: concrete lyrics*. [Exhibition catalogue]. New York, Andrew Crispi Gallery, 1974.

286. Arman [Fernandez, Armand]. *Arman, or: Four and twenty blackbirds baked in a pie; or: Why settle for less when you can settle for more*. Text by Henry Martin. New York, Abrams, 1973.

287. ———. *Selected works, 1958–1974*. An exhibition organized by the La Jolla Museum of Contemporary Art, Sept. 15–Oct. 29, 1974. La Jolla, Calif., Museum of Contemp. Art, 1974.

288. Hahn, Otto. *Arman*. Paris, Hazan, 1972.

289. Kuspit, Donald. *Arman: Monochrome accumulations, 1986–1989*. New York, Abbeville Press, 1992.

290. Marck, Jan van der. *Arman*. New York. Abbeville, 1992.

291. Otmezguine, Jane and Moreau, Marc. *Arman estampes. Catalogue raisonné*. Avec la collaboration de Corice Arman. Paris. Marval 1990.

Armand, Fernandez *see* **Arman**

Armitage, Kenneth, 1916–

292. Penrose, Roland. *Kenneth Armitage.* Amriswil, Switz., Bodensee-Verlag, 1960. (Künstler unserer Zeit, 7).

Arnolfo di Cambio, 13th c.

293. Abbate, Francesco. *Arnolfo di Cambio.* Milano, Fabbri, 1966. (I maestri della scultura, 4).

294. Mariani, Valerio. *Arnolfo di Cambio.* Roma, Tumminelli, 1943.

295. ———. *Arnolfo e il gotico italiano.* Napoli, Libreria Scient. Edit., 1967.

296. Romanini, Angiola Maria. *Arnolfo di Cambio e lo "stil novo" del gotico italiano.* Milano, Ceschina, 1969. [2d ed.: Firenze, Sansoni, 1980].

Arosenius, Ivar, 1878–1909

297. Sandström, Sven. *Ivar Arosenius, hans konst och liv.* Stockholm, Bonnier, 1959.

Arp, Hans Jean, 1887–1966

298. Andreotti, Margherita. *The early sculpture of Jean Arp.* Ann Arbor, UMI Research Press, 1989.

299. Arp, Hans. *Arp on Arp: Poems, essays, memories.* Ed. by Marcel Jean. Trans. by Joachim Neugroschel. New York, Viking, 1971.

300. Bleikasten, Aimée et al. *Arp 1886–1966.* [Exhibition catalogue]. Stuttgart. Hatje, 1986.

301. Fauchereau, Serge. *Arp.* Trans. by Kenneth Lyons. New York, Rizzoli, 1988. (Transl. of *Hans Arp*, Madrid, Ediciones Poligrafa, 1988).

302. ———. *On my way; poetry and essays, 1912–1947.* New York, Wittenborn, 1948. (The Documents of Modern Art, 6).

303. ———. *Jours éffeuillés: Poèmes, essais, souvenirs, 1920–1965.* Préf. de Marcel Jean. Paris, Gallimard, 1966.

304. Arntz, Wilhelm F. *Hans (Jean) Arp: das graphische Werk—L'oeuvre gravé—The graphic work, 1912–1966.* Haag, Obb., Arntz-Winter, 1980.

305. Art of This Century Gallery (New York). *Arp.* [Cat. of an exhibition held in February 1944] with a note by Max Ernst. New York, Art of This Century, 1944.

306. Beyer, Victor, ed. *Hommage à Jean Arp.* Exposition à l'Ancienne Douane, Strasbourg, du 11 juin au 1er oct. 1967. Strasbourg, Soc. d'Edition de la Basse-Alsace, 1967.

307. Brzekowski, Jean. *Hans Arp.* Lodz, Collection "a.r.," 1936.

308. Cathelin, Jean. *Arp.* Paris, Fall, 1959.

309. Galerie Denise René (Paris). *Hommage à Jean Arp.* Paris, Gal. Denise René, 1974.

310. Galerie Surréaliste (Paris). *Arp.* [Exposition] 21. nov.–9 déc. 1927. Paris, Gal. Surréaliste, 1927.

311. Giedion-Welcker, Carola. *Hans Arp.* Dokumentation [von] Marguerite Hagenbach. Stuttgart, Hatje, 1957.

312. ———. *Jean Arp.* English trans. by Norbert Guterman. New York, Abrams, 1957.

313. Jianou, Ionel. *Jean Arp.* Paris, Arted, 1973.

314. Klipstein and Kornfeld (Bern). *Hans Arp Zeichnungen und Collagen—Papiers déchirés und Reliefs.* [Ausstellung] 11. Jan.–24. Feb. 1962. Bern, Klipstein und Kornfeld, 1962.

315. Marchiori, Guiseppe. *Arp.* Avec deux poèmes de Arp. Milano, Alfieri, 1964.

316. Metropolitan Museum of Art (New York). *Jean Arp; from the collection of Mme. Marguerite Arp and Arthur and Madeleine Lejwa.* Exhibition, May 24–Sept. 10. New York, Metropolitan Museum of Art, 1972.

317. Musée National d'Art Moderne (Paris). *Arp.* [Exposition] 21 fév.–21 avril 1962. Paris, Musée Natl. d'Art Moderne, 1962.

318. Öffentliche Kunstsammlung Basel. *Sammlung Marguerite Arp-Hagenbach.* Ausstellung vom 4. Nov. 1967–7 Jan. 1968. Katalog von Carlo Huber und Susanne Meyer. Basel, Kunstmuseum, 1968.

319. Poley, Stefanie. *Hans Arp: Die Formensprache im plastischen Werk. Mit einem Anhang unveröffentlicher Plastiken.* Stuttgart, Hatje, 1978.

320. Rau, Bernd. *Jean Arp: the reliefs. Catalogue of complete works.* Introd. by Michel Seuphor. New York, Rizzoli, 1981.

321. Read, Herbert. *The art of Jean Arp.* New York, Abrams, 1968.

322. Seuphor, Michel [pseud., Berckelaers, Ferdinand Louis]. *Arp; sculptures.* Paris, Hazan, 1964. (Petit encyclopédie de l'art, 61).

323. Soby, James Thrall. *Arp.* Ed. with an introd. by J. T. Soby. Texts by R. Huelsenbeck, R. Melville, C. Giedion-Welcker, with an original article by Arp. New York, Museum of Modern Art, 1958. Distributed by Doubleday, Garden City, N.Y.

324. Trier, Eduard. *Hans Arp Skulpturen, 1957–1966.* Einleitung von E. Trier. Bibliographie von Marguerite Arp-Hagenbach. Skulpturenkatalog von François Arp. Stuttgart, Hatje, 1968.

325. Weber, C. Sylvia. *Hans Arp.* Sigmaringen, Jan Thorbecke, 1994.

Arp, Sophie Henriette (Taeuber) *see* **Taeuber-Arp, Sophie Henriette**

Artschwager, Richard, 1924–

326. Albright-Knox Art Gallery (Buffalo, N.Y.).

Richard Artschwager's themes. Buffalo, The Gallery, 1979.

327. Armstrong, Richard. *Artschwager, Richard.* [Catalogue of an exhibition]. New York, Whitney Museum of American Art in association with W.W. Norton, 1988.

328. Artschwager, Richard. *Richard Artschwager.* [Exhbition catalogue: Kunsthalle Basel, 6.10.–10.11. 1985; Stedelijk Van Abbe-museum Eindhoven, 22.11. 1985–3.1. 1986; Musée d'art contemporain de Bordeaux, 22.2.–26.4.1986.] Redaktion, Jean-Christophe Amman und Margrit Suter. Basel, Die Kunsthalle, 1985.

329. ———. *Richard Artschwager: complete multiples.* [Catalogue of an exhibition]. New York, Brooke Alexander Editions, 1991.

330. ———. *Richard Artschwager, public (public).* [Catalogue of an exhibition], September 14–November 10, 1991. Organized by Russell Panczenko, with essays by Germano Celant, Herbert Muschamp, and Russell Panczenko. Madison, Wis., Elvehjem Museum of Art, University of Wisconsin. Madison, 1991.

Asam, Cosmas Damian, 1686–1739
Egid Quirin, 1692–1750
Hans Georg, 1649–1711

331. Halm, Philipp Maria. *Die Künstlerfamilie der Asam; ein Beitrag zur Kunstgeschichte Süddeutschlands im 17. und 18. Jahrhundert.* München, Lentner, 1896.

332. Hanfstaengl, Erika. *Die Brüder Cosmas Damian und Egid Quirin Asam.* Aufnahmen von Walter Hege. München, Deutscher Kunst-Verlag, 1955.

333. Rupprecht, Bernhard. *Die Brüder Asam. Sinn und Sinnlichkeit im bayerischen Barock.* Photographische Aufnahmen W.-C. von der Mülbe. Regensburg, Pustet, 1980.

Asselijn, Jan, 1610–1652

334. Steland-Stief, Anne Charlotte. *Jan Asselijn nach 1610 bis 1652.* Amsterdam, Van Gendt, 1971.

335. ———. *Die Zeichnungen des Jan Asselijn.* Offenbach, Graf Klenau, 1989.

Atget, Eugene, 1857–1927

336. Abbott, Berenice. *Eugène Atget.* [By] Berenice Abbottova. Praha, Statni nakladatelstvi kràsné literatury a umeni, 1963.

337. ———. *The world of Atget.* New York, Horizon, 1964.

338. Atget, Eugène. *Atget, photographe de Paris.* Préf. par Pierre Mac-Orlan. New York, Weyhe, 1930.

339. ———. *A vision of Paris. The photographs of Eugène Atget; the words of Marcel Proust.* Ed. with an introd. by Arthur D. Trotten-

berg. New York, Macmillan, 1963.

340. ———. *Atget: voyages en ville.* Présentation de Pierre Gassmann, texte de Romeo Martinez et Alain Pougetoux. Paris, Editions du Chêne/Hachette, 1979.

341. Leroy, Jean. *Atget magicien du vieux Paris en son époque.* Paris, Balbo, 1975.

342. Szarkowski, John, and Hambourg, Maria M. *The work of Atget.* 4 v. [Vol. 1: *Old France*; Vol. 2: *The art of old Paris*; Vol. 3: *The ancien régime*; Vol. 4: *Modern times*]. New York, Museum of Modern Art, 1981– .

Atlan, Jean, 1913–1960

343. Dorival, Bernard. *Atlan; essai de biographie artistique.* Paris, Tisné, 1962.

344. Musée National d'Art Moderne (Paris). *Atlan: oeuvres des collections publiques françaises.* Exposition organisée par la Bibliothèque Nationale et le Musée National d'Art Moderne, Centre Georges Pompidou, 23 jan.–17 mars 1980. Paris, Mus. Natl. d'Art Moderne, 1980.

345. Ragon, Michel. *Atlan.* Paris, Fall, 1962.

346. ———. *Jean Atlan.* Textes de M. Ragon et André Verdet, images de Roger Hauert. Genève, Kister, 1960.

347. Verdet, André. *Atlan.* Paris, Fall, 1956.

Auberjonois, René Victor, 1872–1957

348. Auberjonois, René Victor. *René Auberjonois: dessins, textes, photographies.* Précédé de L'atelier du peintre, par Fernand Auberjonois. Lausanne, Mermod, 1958.

349. Galerie Beyeler (Basel). *René Auberjonois.* Ausstellung Februar–März 1964. Basel, Gal. Beyeler, 1964.

350. Musée Cantonal des Beaux Arts (Lausanne). *Rétrospective René Auberjonois, 1872–1957.* Exposition, 6 Sept.–19 Oct. 1958. Préfaces de Gustave Roud et de Guido Fischer. Lausanne, Musée Cantonal des Beaux Arts, 1958.

351. Kunsthalle Bern. *René Auberjonois.* [Ausstellung] 4. März–9. April 1961. Bern, 1961.

352. Kunsthalle Bremen. *René Auberjonois, 1872–1957.* [Ausstellung] 3. Juli–21 Aug. 1977. Bremen, Kunsthalle, 1977.

353. Ramuz, Charles Ferdinand. *René Auberjonois.* Lausanne, Mermod, 1943.

354. Wagner, Hugo. *René Auberjonois: l'oeuvre peint—Das gemalte Werk: catalogue des huiles, pastels et peintures sous verre.* Zürich, Institut suisse pour l'étude d l'art. Denges-Lausanne, Editions du Verseau, 1987. (Oeuvrekataloge Schweizer Künstler, 13).

Audubon, John James, 1785–1851

355. Audubon, John James. *The art of Audubon: the complete birds and mammals, with an*

introd. by Roger Tory Peterson. New York Times Books, 1979.

356. ———. *Audubon and his journals.* Ed. by Maria R. Audubon. Freeport, New York, Books for Libraries Press, 1972.

357. ———. *The birds of America.* New York, Macmillan, 1937.

358. ———. *Letters of John James Audubon, 1826–1840.* Ed. by Howard Corning. Boston, Club of Odd Volumes, 1930. Reprint: New York, Kraus Reprint Co., 2 v., 1969.

359. ——— and Bachman, John. *The imperial collection of Audubon animals: the quadrupeds of North America.* Ed. by Victor H. Cahalane. New York, Bonanza, 1967.

360. Adams, Alexander B. *John James Audubon, a biography.* New York, Putnam, 1966.

361. Arthur, Stanley C. *Audubon; an intimate life of the American woodsman.* New Orleans, Harmanson, 1937.

362. Chancellor, John. *Audubon; a biography.* New York, Viking, 1978.

363. Fries, Waldemar H. *The double elephant folio: the story of Audubon's Birds of America.* Chicago, American Library Association, 1973.

364. Herrick, Francis H. *Audubon the naturalist; a history of his life and time.* 2 v. New York, Dover, 1968.

365. Lyman Allyn Museum (New London, Conn.). *John J. Audubon Centennial Exhibition, Oct. 9–Nov. 11, 1951.* New London, Conn., Lyman Allyn Museum, 1951.

366. Munson-Williams-Proctor Institute (Utica, N.Y.). *Audubon* watercolors and drawings. Catalog of an exhibition, 11 Apr.–30 May, 1965, by Edward H. Dwight. Also shown at the Pierpont Morgan Library, 15 June–30 July, 1965. Utica, M.-W.-P. Institute, 1965.

367. Peattie, Donald C., ed. *Audubon's America; the narratives and experiences of John James Audubon.* Boston, Houghton Mifflin, 1940.

368. Rourke, Constance. *Audubon.* New York, Harcourt Brace, 1936.

Avati, Mario, 1921–

369. Mario. *Avati, gravures, dessins, pastels, sculptures, de 1936 a 1984.* [Exposition]. Musée de l'Arsenal de Graveliones, 1er décembre 84–27 janvier, 1985. Collection minucipale du dessin et de l'estampe originale. Gravellines, editions du Musée de Gravelines, 1984.

370. Cailler, Pierre. *Mario Avati, 1921.* Documentation réunie par P. Cailler. Genève, Cailler, 1958. (Les cahiers d'art—Documents, 96).

371. Passeron, Roger. *Mario Avati: l'oeuvre gravé.* Préface de Thomas P. F. Hoving. Paris, Bibliothèque des Arts, 1973.

Avedon, Richard, 1923–

372. Avedon, Richard. *Observations.* Photographs by R. Avedon, comments by Truman Capote. New York, Simon and Schuster, 1959.

373. ———. *In the American West, 1979–1984.* New York, Abrams, 1985.

374. ———. *Photographs, 1947–1977.* Essay by Harold Brodkey. New York, Farrar, Straus & Giroux, 1978.

375. Lartigue, Jacques Henri. *Diary of a century.* Ed. Richard Avedon. Designed by Bea Feitter. New York, Viking, 1970.

376. Minneapolis Institute of Arts. *Avedon.* [Exhibition] July 2–Aug. 30, 1970. Minneapolis, Minn., Inst. of Arts, 1970.

Avercamp, Barent, 1612–1679
Hendrick, 1585–1635

377. Blankert, Albert, et al. *Hendrick Avercamp, 1585–1634; Barent Avercamp, 1612–1679: Frozen silence; Paintings from museums and private collections.* Amsterdam, K. & V. Waterman, 1882.

378. Welcker, Clara J. *Hendrick Avercamp, 1585–1634, bijgenaamd "de Stomme van Campen," en Barent Avercamp, 1612–1679, "schilders tot Campen." Bewerking Oeuvre catalogue D.J. Hensbroek van der Pool.* Doornspijk, DAVACO, 1979. First publ. Zwolle, Tijl, 1933.

Averlino, Antonio di Pietro *see* Filarete

Avery, Milton, 1893–1965

379. Avery, Milton. *Milton Avery.* Introd. by A.D. Breeskin. Catalog of the exhibition, Dec. 12, 1969–Jan. 25, 1970, at the National Collection of Fine Arts, Smithsonian Institution, Washington, D.C. Washington, D.C. Distributed by New York Graphic Society, Greenwich, Conn., 1969.

380. ———. *Milton Avery: prints and drawings, 1930–1964.* Text by Una E. Johnson. Commemorative essay by Mark Rothko. Brooklyn, N.Y., The Brooklyn Museum, 1966. (American graphic artists of the twentieth century, 4).

381. ———. *Milton Avery.* Text by Bonnie Lee Grad. Foreword by Sally Michel Avery. Royal Oak, Strathcona, 1981.

382. Breeskin, Adelyn. *Milton Avery.* Monograph and catalog of a retrospective exhibition. New York, American Federation of Arts, 1960.

383. Brutvan, Cheryl A. *Milton Avery: his works on paper.* Exhibition, Sterling and Francine Clark Art Institute, May 30–July 13, 1980. Catalogue by C. A. Brutvan. Williamstown, Mass., Clark Institute, 1980.

384. Grace Borgenicht Gallery (New York). *Milton Avery: Oil crayons.* [Exhibition] March 31–April 26, 1973. New York, Borgenicht, 1973.

385. Hobbs, Robert C. Milton Avery. *Milton Avery.* Introduction by Hilton Kramer. New York, Hudson Hills Press. Distrib. in the U.S. by Rizzoli International Publications, 1990.

386. Lunn, Harry H. *Milton Avery: Prints 1933–1955.* Comp. and ed. by H.H. Lunn, Jr. Washington, D.C., Graphics International, 1973.

387. University of California Art Gallery (Irvine). *Milton Avery: late paintings, 1958–1963.* [Exhibition] Feb. 16–March 14, 1971. Irvine, Univ. of Calif., 1971.

388. William Benton Museum of Art, University of Connecticut (Storrs). *Milton Avery and the landscape.* Selection and introd. essay by Stephanie Terenzio. [Exhibition] March 15–April 16, 1976. Storrs, William Benton Museum of Art, 1976.

Avetisian, Minas, 1928–1975

389. Avetisian, Minas. *Minas Avetisian.* [Catalogue of works] compiled and introduced by G. Igitian, designed by L. Yatsenko. Leningrad, Aurora, 1975.

390. Igitian, Genrikh. *Minas Avetisian.* Moskva, Sovietskii Khudozhnik, 1970.

B

Bachiacca, Il *see* Ubertini, Francesco

Baciccio, Giovanni Battista *see* Gaulli, Giovanni Battista

Backer, Jacob Adrianszoon, 1608–1651
391. Bauch, Kurt. *Jakob Adriaensz. Backer; ein Rembrandtschüler aus Friesland.* Berlin, Grote, 1926.

Backoffen, Hans, d. 1519
392. Kautzsch, Paul. *Die Werkstatt und Schule des Bildhauers Hans Backoffen in Mainz; ein Beitrag zur Geschichte der Mainzer Plastik von 1500 zu 1530.* Halle a.S., Erhardt Karras, 1909.

Baco, Jacomart, d. 1461
393. Tormo y Monzo, Elias. *Jacomart y el arte hispano-flamenco cuatrocentista.* Madrid, Centro de Estudios Historicos, 1913.

Bacon, Francis, 1909–
394. Alley, Ronald. *Francis Bacon.* Introd. by John Rothenstein, Catalogue raisonné and documentation by R. Alley. New York, Viking, 1964. (CR).
395. Alphen, Ernst van. *Francis Bacon and the loss of self.* Cambridge, Mass., Harvard Univ. Press, 1993.
396. Bacon, Francis. *Francis Bacon.* Paris, Maeght, 1966. (Derrière le miroir, 162).
397. ———. *Francis Bacon.* Trans. from the Spanish by John Weightman. London, Thames and Hudson, 1988. Publ. originally in Barcelona by Ediciones Poligrafa, 1987.
398. ———. *Francis Bacon in conversation with Michel Archimbaud.* London, Phaidon Press, 1993. (French ed., Paris, JC Lattes, 1992).
399. Marlborogh Gallery (New York). *Francis Bacon: paintings.* [Catalog of an exhibition,

May 23–June 1990]. New York, Marlborough Gallery, 1990.
400. Dückers, Alexander. *Francis Bacon; painting 1946.* Stuttgart, Reclam, 1971.
401. Galeries Nationales du Grand Palais (Paris). *Francis Bacon* [exposition]. Paris, Galeries Nationales du Grand Palais, 26 oct. 1971–10 Jan. 1972; Düsseldorf, Kunsthalle, 7 mars–7 mai 1972. Paris, Centre Natl. d'Art Contemporain, 1971.
402. Galleria Civica d'Arte Moderna (Torino). *Bacon* [mostra] 11 sett.–14 ott. 1962. Torino, Gall. d'Arte Moderna, 1962.
403. Leiris, Michel. *Francis Bacon; ou la vérité criante.* Montpellier, Fata Morgana, 1974. (Scholies, 8)
404. Marlborough-Gerson Gallery (New York). *Francis Bacon; recent paintings.* [Exhibition] Nov.–Dec. 1968. New York, Marlborough-Gerson Gallery, 1968.
405. Metropolitan Museum of Art (New York). *Francis Bacon; recent paintings 1968–1974.* [Exhibition] March 20–June 29, 1975. New York, Metropolitan Museum of Art, 1975.
406. Russell, John. *Francis Bacon.* London, Thames and Hudson, 1979. Revised ed. [1st ed., 1971]. (World of Art series).
407. ———. *Francis Bacon.* Greenwich, Conn., New York Graphic Society, 1977.
408. Sinclair, Andrew. *Francis Bacon: his life and violent times.* London, Sinclair-Stevenson; New York, Crown, 1993.
409. Solomon R. Guggenheim Museum (New York). *Francis Bacon* [exhibition] Oct. 1963–Jan. 1964. The Solomon R. Guggenheim Museum, New York in collaboration with The Art Institute of Chicago. Catalog by Lawrence Alloway. New York, Solomon R. Guggenheim Museum, 1963.
410. Sylvester, David. *Interviews with Francis Bacon.* London, Thames and Hudson, 1975.

411. Trucchi, Lorenza. *Francis Bacon.* Trans. by John Shepley. New York, Abrams, 1975.

412. Tate Gallery (London). *Francis Bacon.* [Exhibition] May 24–July 1, 1962. London, Tate Galley, 1962.

Bagnacavallo, Bartolomeo Ramenghi, 1484–1542

413. Bernardini, Carla. *Il Bagnacavallo senior: Bartolomeo Ramenghi pittore (1484?–1542?).* Catalogo generale. Collaborazione di Sara Vicini. Rimini, Luise, 1990

Baj, Enrico, 1921

414. Baj, Enrico. *Catalogo generale delle stampe originali.* Milano, Electa, 1986.(CR)

415. ———.*I Baj ceramisti.* A cura di Luciano Caprile e Gian Carlo Bojani. Firenze, Centro Di, 1991. (Strumenti di studio per la ceramica del XIX e XX secolo, 14).

416. Ballasi, Pietro . . . [et al.]. *Enrico Baj.* [Catalogue of an exhibition]. Locarno, Pinacoteca Comunale, Casa Rusca,1993–1994.2 v. Locarno, Pinacoteca Comunale, 1993.

417. Crispolti Enrico. *Catalogo generale Bolaffi dell' opera i Enrico Baj.* Torino, Giulio Bolaffi, 1973. (CR).

418. Petit, Jean, ed. *Baj: catalogue of the graphic work and multiples.* Vol 1 (1952–1970): Geneva, NP, 1972. (CR).

Bakst, Leon, 1866–1924

419. Borisovskaia, Natal'ia Anatol'evna. *Lev Bakst.* Moskva, "Isskustvo," 1979.

420. Buffalo Fine Arts Academy. *Catalogue of an exhibition of original works by L. Bakst.* With an introduction by Martin Birnbaum, Jan. 4–Feb. 1, 1914. New York, De Vinne Press, 1913.

421. Fine Art Society, London. *Bakst.* [Exhibition] 21 Aug.–11 Sept. 1976, Edinburgh; 16 Sept.–9 Oct. 1976, London. London, The Society, 1976.

422. Levinson, Andrei Iakovlevich. *Bakst; the story of Leon Bakst's Life.* New York, Brentano's, 1922.

423. Pruzhan, Irina Nikolaevna. *Lev Samoilovich Bakst.* Leningrad, "Isskustvo," 1975.

424. Réau, Louis, et al. *Inedited works of Bakst.* Essays on Bakst by Louis Réau, Denis Roche, V. Svietlov and A. Terrier, New York, Brentano's, 1927.

425. Schouvaloff, Alexander. *Leon Bakst: the theatre art.* London, Sotheby's Publications; New York, Distrib. by Rizzoli International, 1991.

426. Spencer, Charles. *Leon Bakst.* New York, St. Martin's Press, 1973.

Baldovinetti, Alesso, 1425–1499

427. Londi, Emilio. *Alesso Baldovinetti, pittore fiorentino.* Florence, Alfani, 1907.

428. Kennedy, Ruth W. *Alesso Baldovinetti, a critical and historical study.* New Haven, Yale University Press, 1938.

Baldung, Hans, 1480–1545

429. Baumgarten, Fritz. *Der Freiburger Hochaltar, kunstgeschichtlich gewürdigt.* Strassburg, Heitz, 1904. (Studien zur deutschen Kunstgeschichte, 49).

430. Bernhard, Marianne. *Hans Baldung Grien: Handzeichnungen, Druckgraphik.* Herausgeg. von M. Bernhard. München, Südwest Verlag, 1978.

431. Bussmann, Georg. *Manierismus im Spätwerk Hans Baldung Griens.* Heidelberg, Winter, 1966.

432. Curjel, Hans. *Hans Baldung Grien.* München, Recht, 1923.

433. Escherich, Mela. *Hans Baldung-Grien; Bibliographie 1509–1915.* Strassburg, Heitz, 1916. (Studien zur deutschen Kunstgeschichte, 189).

434. Fischer, Otto. *Hans Baldung Grien.* München, Bruckmann, 1939.

435. Graphische Sammlung Albertina (Wien). *Hans Baldung Grien.* Ausstellung im 450. Geburtsjahr des Meisters im Frühjahr 1935. Wien, Schroll, 1935.

436. Hartlaub, Gustav Friedrich. *Hans Baldung Griens Hexenbilder.* Stuttgart, Reclam, 1961. (Werkmonographien zur bildenden Kunst, 61).

437. Koch, Carl. *Die Zeichnungen Hans Baldung Griens.* Berlin, Deutscher Verlag für Kunstwissenschaft, 1941.

438. Kunstmuseum Basel. *Hans Baldung Grien im Kunstmuseum Basel.* Texte von Paul H. Boerlin, Tilman Falk, Richard W. Gassen, Dieter Keopplin. Basel, Kunstmuseum, 1978. (Schriften des Vereins der Freunde des Kunstmuseums Basel, 2).

439. Martin, Kurt. *Skizzenbuch des Hans Baldung Grien: "Karlsruher Skizzenbuch."* 2 v. Basel, Holbein, 1950. (Veröff. d. Holbein-Gesellschaft, 2). 2 ed. 1959.

440. Mende, Matthias. *Hans Baldung Grien: das graphische Werk.* Vollst. Bild-Katalog der Einzelholzschnitte, Buch-illustrationen u. Kupferstiche. Hrsg. von den Stadtgeschichtl. Museen Nürnberg u. d. Stadt Schwäbisch Gmünd. Unterschneidheim, Uhl, 1978. (CR).

441. Oldenbourg, Maria Consuelo. *Die Buchholzschnitte des Baldung Grien; ein bibliographisches Verzeichnis ihrer Verwendungen.* Baden-Baden, Heitz, 1962. (Studien zur deutschen Kunstgeschichte, 335).

442. Osten, Gert von der. *Hans Baldung Grien: Gemälde und Dokumente.* Berlin, Deutscher Verlag für Kunstwissenschaft, 1983. (CR). (Jahresgabe des Deutschen Vereins für

Kunstwissenschaft, 1981/1982.)

443. Schmitz, Hermann. *Hans Baldung, gen. Grien.* Bielefeld/Leipzig, Velhagen & Klasing, 1922. (Künstler-Monographien, 113).

444. Staatliche Kunsthalle Karlsruhe. *Hans Baldung Grien.* Ausstellung unter dem Protektorat des I.C.O.M., 4 Juli–27 Sept. 1959. Karlsruhe, Staatl. Kunsthalle, 1959.

445. Staatliche Museen (Berlin). *Hans Baldung Grien.* Gedächtnisausstellung zur 450. Wiederkehr seines Geburtsjahres. Berlin, Staatliche Museen, 1934.

446. Terez, Gabriel (Gabor) von. *Die Gemälde des Hans Baldung gen. Grien in Lichtdruck-Nachbildungen nach den Originalen.* 2 v. (of plates). Strassburg, Heitz, 1896–1900.

447. ———. *Die Handzeichnungen des Hans Baldung gen. Grien.* 3 v. Strassburg, Heitz, 1894–1896.

448. Weihrauch, Hans Robert. *Hans Baldung Grien.* Mainz, Kupferberg, 1948.

449. Winkler, Friedrich. *Hans Baldung Grien, ein unbekannter Meister deutscher Zeichnung.* Burg, Hopfer, 1941. 2 ed.

Balestra, Antonio, 1666–1740

450. Polazzo, Marco. *Antonio Balestra, pittore veronese, 1666–1740.* Verona, Libreria Cortina, 1978.

451. ———. *Antonio Balestra pittore veronese del Settecento.* Verone. Centro per la formazione professionale grafica "San Zeno", 1990. (Aspetti e figure dell'arte veronese, 7).

Balla, Giacomo, 1871–1958

452. Balla, Elica. *Con Balla.* 3 v. Milano, Multipla Edizioni, 1984–1986

453. Balla, Giacomo. *Balla, the futurist.* [Catalogue of an exhibition held at the Scottish National Gallery of Art, Edinburgh, June 6–July 19, 1987. Milano, Mazzotta, 1987.

454. De Machis, Giorgio. *Giacomo Balla: l'aura futurista.* Torino, Einaudi, 1971. (Einaudi letteratura, 51)

455. Dorazio, Virginia Dortch. *Giacoma Balla, an album of his life and work.* Introd. by Giuseppe Ungaretti. New York, Wittenborn, 1969.

456. Fagiolo dell'Arco, Maurizio. *Futur Balla.* Roma, Bulzoni, 1970.

457. Galleria Civica d'Arte Moderna (Torino). *Giacomo Balla.* Catalogo a cura di E. Crispolti. Torino, Museo Civico, 1963.

458. Galleria Fonte d'Abisso (Modena). *Giacomo Balla; opere dal 1912 al 1930.* Tipologie di astrazione. [Mostra] 15 marzo–15 maggio 1980. Catalogo a cura di Sergio Poggianella. Modena, Gall. Fonte d'Asisso, 1980.

459. Galleria Nazionale d'Arte Moderna (Roma). *Giacomo Balla 1871–1958.* [Mostra] 23 dic. 1971–27 febb. 1972. Roma, de Luca, 1971.

460. Lista, Giovanni. *Balla.* Modena, Ediz. Galleria Fonte d'Abisso, 1982.

461. Museo di Castelvecchio (Verona). *Giacomo Balla: studi, ricerchi, oggetti.* [Mostra] febbraio–marzo 1976. Schede e notazioni a cura di Luigi Marcucci. Verona, Grafiche AZ, 1976.

462. Robinson, Susan Barnes. *Giacomo Balla: Divisionism and Futurism 1871–1912.* Ann Arbor, UMI Research Press, 1977. (Studies in Fine Arts: The Avant-garde, 14)

Balthus (Count Balthasar Klossowski de Rola), 1908–

463. Balthus. *Balthus.* Testi Jean Leymarie, Federico Fellini. Milano, Ediz. La Biennale di Venezia, 1980.

464. ———. *Balthus: Zeichnungen.* Text by Antonin Artaud . . . et al].[Catalogue of an exhibition held at the Kunstmuseum Bern]. Bern, Kunstmuseum, 1994.

465. Galerie Claude Bernard, Paris. *Balthus; dessins et aquarelles.* Ouvrage édité à l'occasion de l'exposition en octobre 1971. Préf. de Jean Leymarie. Paris, Edits. Gal. Claude Bernard, 1971.

466. Klossowski de Rola, Stanislaus. *Balthus.* London, Thames and Hudson, 1983.

467. Leymarie, Jean. *Balthus.* New York, Skira/Rizzoli, 1979.

468. Pierre Matisse Gallery (New York). *Balthus: "La chambre turque, Les trois soeurs."* Drawings and water colours 1933–1966. March 28–April 22, 1967. New York, Pierre Matisse, 1967.

469. ———. *Balthus: paintings and drawings 1934 to 1977.* Nov. 15–Dec. 15, 1977. New York, Pierre Matisse, 1977.

470. Soby, James Thrall. *Balthus.* New York, Museum of Modern Art, 1956. (Bulletin 24, no. 3)

471. Tate Gallery (London). *Balthus.* A retrospective exhibition arr. by John Russell for the Arts Council of Great Britain, 4 Oct.–10 Nov. 1968. London, Tate Gallery, 1968.

472. Union Centrale des Arts Décoratifs (Paris). *Balthus* [exposition]. Musée des Arts Décoratifs, 12 mai–27 juin 1966. Préf. par Gaetan Picon. Paris, Musée des Arts, Déc., 1966.

Banco, Nanni di *see* Nanni di Banco

Bandinelli, Bartolommeo Bandini, 1493–1560

473. Ward, Roger. *Baccio Bandinelli, 1493–1560.* Drawings from British collections. selected and catalogued by R. Ward. Cambridge, Fitzwilliam Museum, 1988; London, Sotheby's, 1988.

Barbari, Jacopo de', 1440–1515

474. Hevesy, André de. *Jacopo de Barbari, le maître au caducée.* Paris, van Oest, 1925.
475. Sevolini, Luigi. *Jacopo de Barbari.* Padova, Tre Venezie, 1944.

Barbieri, Giovanni Francesco *called* Il Guercino, 1591–1666

476. Barbieri, Giovanni Francesco. *Guercino, disegni.* Scelta e introduzione di Stefano Bottari, note di Renato Roli e Anne Ottani Cavina. Firenze, La Nuova Italia, 1966.
477. Atti, Gaetano. *Intorno alla vita e alle opere di Gian-Francesco Barbieri detto Il Guercino da Cento; commentario.* Roma, Tip. delle Scienze Mat. E Fisiche, 1861.
478. Bagni, Prisco. *Guercino a Cento.* Bologna, Nuova Alfa, 1984.
479. ———. *Il Guercino e i suoi incisori.* Roma, Ugo Bozzi, 1988.
480. ———. *Il Guercino e il suo falsario.* 2 v. Bologna, la Nuova Alfa, 1985, 1990.
481. Calvi, Jacopo Alessandro. *Notizie della vita e delle opere del cavaliere Gio. Francesco Barbieri, detto Il Guercino da Cento.* Bologna, Guidi all'Ancora, 1842. 2 ed.
482. Grimaldi, Nefta. *Il Guercino, Gian Francesco Barbieri, 1591–1666.* Bologna, Tamari, 1957.
483. Guercino. *Giovanni Francesco Barbieri, il Guercino, 1591–1666.* Bologna, Museo civico archeologico; Cento, Pinacoteca civica, Chiesa del Rosario, 6 settembre–10 novembre 1991. A cura di Denis Mahon; con scritti di Prisco Bagni . . . [et al.]. Intro-doduzione di Andrea Emiliani. Bologna, Nuova Alfa, 1991.
484. ———. *Il Guercino, Giovanni Francesco Barbieri, 1591–1666: disegni.* Bologna, Museo civico archeologico, 5 settembre–10 novembre 1991. A cura di Denis Mahon. Bologna, Nuova Alfa, 1992.
485. Helston, Michael & Russell, Francis. *Guercino in Britain. Paintings from British collections.* Exhibition, National Gallery, London. London, National Gallery, 1991.
486. Mahon, Denis. *I disegni del Guercino della collezione Mahon.* Catalogo critico. Bologna, Alfa, 1967.
487. ———. *The drawings of Guercino in the Collection of Her Majesty the Queen at Windsor Castle.* [By] D. Mahon and Nicholas Turner. Cambridge, Cambridge University Press, 1989.
488. ———. *Guercino: Master painter of the Baroque.* [By] Sir Denis Mahon, with contributions by Andrea Emiliani, Diane De Grazia, Sybille Ebert-Schifferer. Washington, D.C., National Gallery of Art, 1992.
489. Marangoni, Matteo. *Guercino.* Milano, Martello, 1959.

490. Musée du Louvre (Paris). *Le Guercin en France.* Texts by Stéphane Loire, Introduction by Sir Denis Mahon. Paris, Editions de la Réunion des musées nationaux, 1990. (Les dossiers du Départment des peintures, 38).
491. Roli, Renato. *I fregi centesi del Guercino.* Introd. di Stefano Bottari. Préf. di Francesco Arcangeli. Bologna, Patron, 1968.
492. Russell, Archibald G. B. *Drawings by Guercino.* London, Arnold, 1923.
493. Salerno, Luigi. *I dipinti del Guercino.* Con la consulenza di Sir Denis Mahon. Roma, Ugo Bozzi, 1988.
494. VII Mostra Biennale d'Arte Antica, Bologna. *Il Guercino, Giovanni Francesco Barbieri, 1591–1666.* Catal. critico dei dipinti a cura di Denis Mahon. Exposizione, Palazzo dell'Archiginnasio, 1 sett.–18 nov. 1968. Bologna, Alfa, 1969. 2 ed. corretta.
495. Stone, David M. *Guercino: Master draftsman. Works from North American collections.* Bologna, Nuova Alfa, 1991. (Catalogue of the exhibition held at Harvard University Art Museums, February 16–March 31, 1991).
496. Tuyll van Serooskerken Carel van. *Guercino (1591–1666): drawings, from Dutch collections.* The Hague, Gary Schwartz/SDU, 1992.

Barendsz, Dirck, 1534–1592

497. Judson, Jay Richard. *Dirck Barendsz, 1534–1592.* Amsterdam, Vangendt, 1970.

Bari, Niccolo da see Niccolo Dell'arca

Barlach, Ernst, 1870–1938

498. Barlach, Ernst. *Ernst Barlach.* Mit einem Essay von Wilhelm Kurth. Stuttgart Kohlhammer, 1985.
499. ———. *Die Briefe, 1888–1938.* Hrsg. von Friedrich Dross, 2 v. München, Piper, 1968–1969.
500. ———. Ernst Barlach: *Plastiken, Entwurfszeichnungen.* Hrsg., Ausstellung und Katalog Jürgen Schilling. Ratzeburg, E. und H. Barlach, 1986.
501. ———. *Ein selbsterzähltes Leben.* München, Piper, 1948.
502. ———. *Ernst Barlach. Werk und Wirkung. Berichte, Gespräche, Erinnerungen.* Gesammelt und hrsg. von Elmar Jansen. Frankfurt a.M., Athenäum, 1972.
503. Barlach, Karl. *Mein Vetter Ernst Barlach.* Bremen, Heye, [1960].
504. Bevilacqua, Giuseppe. *Ernst Barlach; letteratura e critica.* Urbino, Argalla, 1963.
505. Carls, Carl Dietrich. *Ernst Barlach; das plastische, graphische und dichterische Werk.* Berlin, Rembrandt-Verlag, 1968. [First publ. 1931].

506. Ernst Barlach Haus, Hamburg-Klein Flott-bek. [Katalog der Sammlungen]. Hamburg, Stiftung Hermann F. Reemtsma, 1966. 2 ed.

507. Fechter, Paul. *Ernst Barlach.* Gütersloh, Bertelsmann, 1957.

508. Flemming, Willi. *Ernst Barlach, Wesen und Werk.* Bern, Francke, 1958. (Sammlung Dalp, 88)

509. Franck, Hans. *Ernst Barlach, Leben und Werk.* Stuttgart, Kreuz-Verlag, 1961.

510. Fuehmann, Franz. *Ernst Barlach, das schlimme Jahr; Grafik, Zeichnungen, Plastik, Dokumente.* Rostock, Hinstorff, 1963.

511. Gloede, Gunter. *Barlach, Gestalt und Gleichnis.* Hamburg, Furche, 1966.

512. Gross, Helmut. *Zur Seinserfahrung bei Ernst Barlach; eine ontologische Untersuchung von Barlachs dichterischem und bild-nerischem Werk.* Freiburg, Herder, 1967.

513. Hooper, Kent William. *Ernst Barlach's liter-ary and visual art: the issue of multiple tal-ent.* Ann Arbor, UMI Research Press, 1987.

514. Jansen, Elmar, Hrsg. *Barlach im Gespräch.* Friedrich Schult, mit ergänzenden Aufz-eichnungen des Verfassers. 2 Aufl., Leipzig, Insel Verlag, 1987. First publ. 1985.

515. Jansen, Elmar. *Ernst Barlach—Käthe Kollwitz. Berührungen, Grenzen, Geg-enbilder.* Berlin, Gebr. Mann Verlag, 1989.

516. Knobling, Harald. *Studien zum zeich-nerischen Werk Ernst Barlachs: 1892–1912.* Worms, Wernersche Verlagsgesell-schaft, 1989.

517. Kunsthalle Bremen. *Ernst Barlach: das druckgraphische Werk, Dore und Kurt Reutti-Stiftung.* Ausstellung Kunsthalle Bre-men, 28. Jan.–24. März, 1968. Bremen, Kunsthalle, 1968. (Sammlungskataloge der Kunsthalle Bremen, 4).

518. Schult, Friedrich. *Ernst Barlach: das plastische Werk.* Hamburg, Hauswedell, 1960. (*Ernst Barlach Werkverzeichnis,* Bd. I). (CR).

519. ———. *Ernst Barlach: das graphische Werk.* Hamburg, Hauswedell, 1958. (*Ernst Barlach Werkverzeichnis,* Bd. II). (CR).

520. ———. *Ernst Barlach: Werkkatalog der Zeichnungen.* Hamburg, Hauswedell, 1971. (*Ernst Barlach Werkverzeichnis,* Bd. III). (CR).

521. Schurek, Paul. *Begegnungen mit Barlach; ein Erlebnisbericht.* Gütersloh, Rufer-Verlag, 1954, 2 ed.

522. ———. *Barlach; eine Bildbiographie.* Mün-chen, Kindler, 1961.

523. Starczewski, Hanns Joachim. *Barlach; Inter-pretationen.* München, Starczewski-Verlag, 1964.

524. Stubbe, Wolf. *Ernst Barlach. Plastik.* Mün-chen, Piper, 1959.

525. ———. *Ernst Barlach; Zeichnungen.* Mün-chen, Piper, 1961.

526. Werner, Alfred. *Ernst Barlach, his life and work.* New York, McGraw-Hill, 1966.

Barnard, George, 1819–1902

527. Barnard, George N. *Photographic views of Sherman's campaign.* New York, Barnard, 1866. (Reprinted, with a new introduction by Beaumont Newhall: New York, Dover, 1977).

Barocci, Federigo, 1528–1612

528. Brigata Urbinate degli Amici dei Mon-umenti. *Studie notizie su Federigo Barocci.* Firenze, Ist. Micrografico Italiano, 1913.

529. Emiliani, Andrea. *Federico Barocci (Urbino 1535–1612).* 2v. Bologna, Nuova Alpha, 1985.

530. Krommes, Rudolf H. *Studien zu Federigo Barocci.* Leipzig, Seemann, 1912.

531. Olsen, Harald. *Federico Barocci.* Køben-havn, Munksgaard, 1962. 2 ed. (CR)

532. Pietro, Filippo di. *Disegni sconosciuti e disegni finora non identificati di Federigo Barocci negli Uffizi.* Firenze, Ist. Micro-grafico Italiano, 1913.

Barozzio *see* Vignola

Barraud, Maurice, 1889–1954

533. Barraud, Maurice. *Réflexions à perte de vue.* Vesenaz-Genève, Cailler, 1944.

534. Bovy, Adrien. *Barraud.* Lausanne, Librairie des beaux-arts F. Roth, 1940.

535. Cailler, Pierre and Darel, Henri. *Catalogue illustré de l'oeuvre gravé et lithographié de Maurice Barraud.* [Par] P. Cailler et H. Darel. Genève, Skira, 1944.

Barry, Charles, 1795–1860

536. Barry, Alfred. *The life and works of Sir Charles Barry.* London, Murray, 1867.

Barry, James, 1741–1806

537. Barry, James. *Lectures on painting by the royal academicians, Barry, Opie and Fuseli.* Ed. with an introduction and notes critical and illustrative, by Ralph N. Wornum. Lon-don, Bohn, 1848.

538. ———. *A letter to the Dilettanti Society, re-specting the obtention of certain matters es-sentially necessary for the improvement of public taste, and for accomplishing the origi-nal views of the Royal Academy of Great Britain.* London, J. Walker, 1799.

539. Pressly, William L. *The life and art of James Barry.* New Haven, Yale University Press, 1981.

B

Bartholdi, Frederic-Auguste, 1834–1904

540. Betz, Jacques. *Bartholdi*. Paris, Editions de Minuit, 1954.

541. Gschaedler, André. *True light on the Statue of Liberty and its creator*. Narberth, Pa., Livingston, 1966.

Bartning, Otto, 1883–1959

542. Bartning, Otto. *Kirchen: Handbuch für den Kirchenbau*. Mithrsg. Willy Weyres (Buch I), Otto Bartning (Buch II). München, Callwey, 1959.

543. Mayer, Hans K. F. *Der Baumeister Otto Bartning und die Wiederentdeckung des Raumes*. Heidelberg, Schneider, 1951.

Bartolini, Lorenzo, 1777–1850

544. Associazione Turistica Pratese. *L'opera di Lorenzo Bartolini, 1777–1850: sculture, disegni, cimeli*. [Mostra] Palazzo Banci Buonamici, Palazzo Pretorio. Cat. curato da Mario Bellandi e Gaetano Siciliano. Prato, Associazione Turistica Pratese, 1956.

545. Bonaini, Francesco. *Dell'arte secondo la mente di Lorenzo Bartolini; discorso*. Firenze, Le Monnier, 1852.

546. Tinti, Mario. *Lorenzo Bartolini, con prefazione di Romano Romanelli*. Roma, Reale Accademia d'Italia, 1936.

Bartoli di Fredi, 1330–1410

547. Freuler, Gaudenz. *Bartolo di Fredio Cini: ein Beitrag zur sienesischen Malerei des 14. Jahrhunderts*. [Disentis] Desertina Verlag, 1994.

548. Harpring, Patricia. *The Sienese Trecento painter Bartolo di Fredi*. Rutherford, Farleigh Dickinson University Press; London/Cranbury, NJ, Associated University Presses, 1993.

Bartolommeo, Fra, 1472–1517

549. Baxter, Lucy E. *Fra Bartolommeo* [and Mariotto Albertinelli, Andrea del Sarto]. By Leader Scott [pseud.]. London, Low, 1892.

550. Borgo, Ludovico. *The works of Mariotto Albertinelli [and Fra Bartolommeo]*. New York, Garland, 1976.

551. Fischer, Chris. *Fra Bartolommeo, master draughtsman of the high renaissance: a selection from the Rotterdam Album and landscape drawings from various collections*. Rotterdam, Museum Boymans-van Beuningen; Seattle, Distrib. in U.S.A., University of Washington Press, 1992.

552. Gabelentz, Hans von der. *Fra Bartolommeo und die Florentiner Renaissance*. 2 v. Leipzig, Hiersemann, 1922.

553. Knapp, Fritz. *Fra Bartolommeo della Porta und die Schule von San Marco*. Halle, Knapp, 1903.

554. Rouches, Gabriel. *Fra Bartolommeo, 1472–1517; quatorze dessins*. Paris, Musées Nationaux, 1942.

Bartolozzi, Francesco, 1727–1815

555. Baudi di Vesme, Alessandro. *Francesco Bartolozzi; catalogue des estampes et notice biographique d'après les manuscrits de A. de Vesmé, entièrement réformés et complétés d'une étude critique par A. Calibi*. Milan, G. Modiano, 1928.

556. Hind, Arthur Mayger. *Bartolozzi and other stipple engravers working in England at the end of the eighteenth century*. New York, Stokes, 1912.

557. Tuer, Andrew W. *Bartolozzi and his works*. 2 v. London, Field & Tuer, 1881.

Barye, Antoine Louis, 1796–1875

558. Alexandre, Arsène. *A. L. Barye*. Paris, Libr. de l'Art, 1889.

559. DeKay, Charles. *Barye. Life and works of Antoine Louis Barye . . . in memory of an exhibition of his bronzes, paintings and water-colors held in New York in aid of the fund for his monument at Paris*. New York, Barye Monument Association, 1889.

560. Lengyel, Alfonz. *Life and art of Antoine Louis Barye*. Dubuque, Iowa, Brown, 1963.

561. Pivar, Stuart. *The Barye Bronzes, a catalogue raisonné*. Woodbridge, Antique Collectors' Club, 1974. (CR).

562. Roger-Ballu. *L'oeuvre de Barye*. Précédé d'une introduction de M. Eugène Guillaume. Paris, Quantin, 1890.

563. Saunier, Charles. *Barye*. Paris, Rieder, 1925.

564. Walters, William Thompson. *Antoine-Louis Barye. From the French of various critics*. Baltimore, n.p. [Press of Isaac Friedenwald], 1885.

565. Zieseniss, Charles Otto. *Les aquarelles de Barye; étude critique et catalogue raisonné*. Paris, Massin, 1955. (CR).

Baschenis, Evaristo, 1617–1677

566. Angelini, Luigi. *I Baschenis*. Bergamo, Ediz. Orobiche, 1946. 2 ed. (Collana di monografie su artisti bergamaschi, 2).

567. Baschenis, Evaristo. *Evaristo Baschenis*. Testo di Angelo Geddo. Bergamo, Perolari, 1965.

568. Galleria Lorenzelli (Bergamo). *Evaristo Baschenis (1607–1677)*. [Mostra] sett.–ott. 1965. Bergamo, Galleria Lorenzelli, 1965.

569. Rosci, Marco. *Baschenis, Bettera & Co. Produzione e mercato della natura morta del seicento in Italia*. Milano, Görlich, 1971.

Baselitz, Georg, 1938–

570. Baselitz, Georg. *Baselitz: Paintings, 1960–1983*. Edited by Nicholas Serota and Mark Francis. London, Whitechapel Gallery, 1983.

571. Baselitz, Georg. *Georg Baselitz: Holzschnitt 1966–1989* Stuttgart, Edition Cantz, 1989.

572. ———. *Georg Baselitz: Pastelle, 1985–1990.* Mit Texten von Diane Waldman, Emil Maurer, Siegfried Gohr. Bern, Gachang & Springer, 1990.

573. ———. *Georg Baselitz: Zeichnungen und druckgraphische Werke* aus dem Kupferstichkabinett Basel. Text, Dieter Koepplin; Redaktion und Werkliste, Paul Tanner. Basel, Wiese, 1989.

574. ———. *Georg Baselitz: works of the seventies.* New York, Michael Werner, 1992.

575. Dahlem, Franz. *Georg Baselitz.* [Essays by Franz Dahlem and Georg Baselitz in English, German, French]. Köln, Benedikt Taschen, 1990.

576. Franzke, Andreas. *Georg Baselitz,* by A. Franzke; idea and concept Edward Quinn. Trans. from the German by David Britt. München, Prestel; New York, Distrib. in the U.S.A. and Canada by te Neues Pub. Co., 1989.

577. Gohr, Siegfried. *Georg Baselitz: Druckgraphik—print—estampes, 1963–1983.* München, Prestel, 1984.

578. ———. *Georg Baselitz. Retrospektive 1964–1991.* [Catalog of an exhibition, München, Kunsthalle der Hypo-Kulturstiftung, 1992.] München,

579. Güse, Ernst-Gerhard, ed. *Baselitz: Werke, 1981–1993.* [Catalogue of an exhibition held at the Saarland Museum, Saarbrücken]. Mit Beiträgen von Georg Baselitz, Heinrich Heil und Ernest W. Uthemann. Stuttgart, G. Hatje, 1994.

580. Jahn, Fred. *Baselitz: peintre-graveur;* F. Jahn in Zusammenarbeit mit Johannes Gachnang. Bern, Gachnang & Springer. Vol. 1– , 1983– .

581. Kunsthalle Bremen. *Georg Baselitz; das Motiv: Bilder und Zeichnungen, 1987–1988.*[Ausstellung, 18. IX.–30. X., 1988 in Zusammenarbeit mit dem Förderkreis für Gegenwartskunst im Kunstverein Bremen. [Ausstellung und Katalog, Annette Meyer zu Eissen, Detlev Gretenkort]. Bremen, Kunsthalle, 1988.

582. Museum Ludwig (Cologne). *Georg Baselitz: Pastorale, 4. Juli–16.August 1987.* [Ausstellung und Katalog: Siegfried Gohr, A.M. Fischer]. Köln, Museum Ludwig, 1987.

583. Nationalgalerie (Berlin). *Georg Baselitz; Bilder aus Berliner Privatbesitz.* [Catalog of an exhibition, Nationalgalerie, Altes Museum, 4. April–4. Juni 1990]. Katalog, Hartmut Ackermeier; Mitarbeit, Tina Aujesky, Brigitte Crockett, H.U. Davitt. Herausgeber Hartmut Ackermeier. Berlin, Nicolaische Verlagsbuchhandlung, 1990.

Baskin, Leonard, 1922–

584. Baskin, Leonard. *Baskin; the graphic work, 1950–1970.* Catalog of an exhibition held at the Far Gallery, New York, Feb. 10–Mar. 1, 1970. Text by Herman J. Wechsler and Dale Roylance. New York, Far Gallery, 1970.

585. ———. *Sculpture, drawings and prints.* New York, Braziller, 1970.

586. ———. *Catalog of the exhibition held June 12–July 26, 1970, at the National Collection of Fine Arts of the Smithsonian Institution.* Essay by Alan Fern, Washington, D.C., Smithsonian Press, 1970.

587. Bowdoin College Museum of Fine Arts (Brunswick, Maine). *Leonard Baskin.* [Catalog of an exhibition]. Brunswick, Maine, Bowdoin College, 1962.

Bassano, Jacopo, 1510–1592

588. Arslan, Walt. *I Bassano.* 2 v. Milano, Ceschina, 1960.

589. Bassano, Jacopo. *Jacopo Bassano.* Catalogo della mostra a cura di Pietro Zampetti. Venezia, Palazzo Ducale, 29 giugno–27 ottobre 1957. Venezia, Arte Veneta-Alfieri, 1957.

590. Bettini, Sergio. *L'arte di Jacopo Bassano.* Bologna, Apollo, 1933.

591. Brown, Beverly Louise and Marini, Paola, eds. *Jacopo Bassano, c1510–1592.* Bologna, Nuova Alpha, 1992.

592. Rearick, William R. *Iacobus a Ponte Bassanensis. Vol I: Disegni giovanili e della prima maturita, 1538–1548; Vol. II: Disegni della maturita, 1549–1567; Vol. III: I disegni della tarda maturita, 1568–1574.* Bassano nel Grappa, vols. I–II, G.B. Verci; vol. III, Comitato per la Storia del Bassano, 1986–1989.

593. Zampetti, Pietro. *Jacopo Bassano.* Rome, Ist. Poligrafico, 1958.

594. Zottmann, Ludwig. *Zur Kunst der Bassani.* Strassburg, Heitz, 1908. (Zur Kunstgeschichte des Auslandes, 57).

Bastien-Lepage, Jules, 1848–1884

595. Ady, Julia Cartwright. *Jules Bastien-Lepage,* by Julia Cartwright (Mrs. Henry Ady). London, Seely/New York, Macmillan, 1894.

596. Fourcaud, Louis de. *Bastien-Lepage, sa vie et ses oeuvres, 1848–1884.* Paris, Galerie des artistes modernes, 1885.

597. Theuriet, André, et al. *Jules Bastien-Lepage and his art. A Memoir,* by A. Theuriet with articles by G. Clausen, Walter Sickert. Includes a study of Marie Bashkirtseff by Mathilde Blind. London, Unwin, 1892.

Battoni, Pompeo, 1708–1787.

598. Batoni, Pompeo. *Mostra di Pompeo Batoni.*

[Catalogue of an exhibition. Promossa dall'Amministrazione provinciale di Lucca (luglio–settembre 1967). Catalogo a cura di Isa Belli Barsali. Lucca, M. Pacini Fazzi, 1985. 2 ed.

599. ———. *Pompeo Batoni and his British patrons.* [Exhibition]. The Iveagh Bequest, Kenwood. London, Greater London Council, 1982.

600. Clark, Anthony M. *Pompeo Battoni. A complete catalogue of his works with an introductory text.* Edited and prepared for publication by Edgar Peters Bowron. New York, New York University Press, 1985.

Battke, Heinz, 1900–1966

601. Cuppers, Joachim. *Heinz Battke; Werkkatalog von J. Cuppers mit einer Würdigung "Der Zeichner Heinz Battke" von Wieland Schmied.* Hamburg, Hauswedell, 1970. (CR).

602. Frankfurter Kunstkabinett Hanna Bekker vom Rath. *Heinz Battke zum Gedächtnis.* [Ausstellung] 12.1.–25.2. 1967. Frankfurt a.M., Frankfurter Kunstkabinett, 1967.

Baugin, Lubin, 1610/12–1663

603. Galerie Eric Coatalem (Paris). *Lubin Baugin.* Paris, Galerie Coatalem, 1994.

Baumeister, Willi, 1889–1955

604. Akademie der Künste, Berlin. *Willi Baumeister, 1889–1955.* Ausstellung in der Akademie der Künste vom 30. Mai bis 4. Juli 1965. Katalog: Herta Elisabeth Killy, Berlin, 1965.

605. Baumeister, Willi. *Zeichnungen, Gouachen, Collagen.* [Catalog of an exhibition at the Staatsgalerie Stuttgart]. Ausstellung und Katalog Ulrike Gauss. Stuttgart, Edition Cantz, 1989.

606. Grohmann, Will. *Willi Baumeister; Leben und Werk.* Köln, Dumont Schauberg, 1963.

607. ———. *Willi Baumeister; life and works.* Trans. by Robert Allen. New York, Abrams, 1966.

608. Nationalgalerie (Berlin). *Willi Baumeister.* [Catalog of an exhibition, 7.4.–28.5. 1989]. Ausstellung und Katalog: Angela Schneider unter Mitarbeit von Christine Hopfengart. Stuttgart, Edition Cantz, 1989.

609. Ponert, Dietmar J. *Willi Baumeister: Werkverzeichnis. der Zeichnungen, Gouachen und Collagen.* Köln, DuMont, 1988.

Bayard, Hippolyte, 1801–1887

610. Jammes, André. *Hippolyte Bayard, ein verkannter Erfinder und Meister der Photographie.* Luzern/Frankfurt a.M., Bucher, 1975. (Bibiliotek der Photographie, 8).

611. Lo Duca, Joseph-Marie. *Bayard.* Paris, Prisma, 1943. (Reprint: New York, Arno, 1979).

Bayer, Herbert, 1900–

612. Bayer, Herbert. *Bauhaus, 1919–1928.* Edited by Herbert Bayer, Walter Gropius, Ise Gropius. New York, Museum of Modern Art, 1938. 1st ed.; 3rd printing: Boston, Branford, 1959. 3. Aufl. Teufen, Switzerland, Niggli and Verkauf, 1955 (in German).

613. ———. *Herbert Bayer. Painter, designer, architect.* New York, Reinhold/London, Studio Vista, 1967.

614. Chanzit, Gwen Finkel. *Herbert Bayer and modernist design in America.* Ann Arbor/London, UMI Research Press, 1987.

615. Denver Art Museum. *Herbert Bayer; a total concept.* Exhibition, Nov. 11–Dec. 23, 1973. Denver, Colorado Art Museum, 1973.

616. Doner, Alexander. *The way beyond 'art'; the work of Herbert Bayer.* New York, Wittenborn, 1947. Reprint: New York, New York University, 1958.

617. Neue Galerie der Stadt Linz. *Herbert Bayer: Beispiele aus dem Gesamtwerk 1919–1974.* [Ausstellung] 12. Mai–12. Juni 1976. Linz, Neue Galerie Wolfgang-Gurlitt-Museum, 1976.

Bayeu y Subias, Francisco, 1734–1795

618. Sambricio, Valentin de. *Francisco Bayeu.* Madrid, Instituto Diego Velazquez, 1955.

619. Valenzuela la Rosa, José. *Los tiempos de Bayeu; discurso de ingreso en la Academia Aragonesa de Nobles y Bellas Artes . . . celebrada el dia 18 de Noviembre de 1934. . . .* Zaragoza, Heraldo de Aragon, 1934.

Bazille, Frederick, 1841–1870

620. Daulte, François. *Frédéric Bazille et les débuts de l'Impressionisme* Paris. (CR).

621. ———. *Frederick Bazille et son temps.* Genève, Cailler, 1952. (Peintres et sculpteurs d'hier et d'aujourd'hui, 24).

622. Poulain, Gaston. *Bazille et ses amis.* Paris, La Renaissance du Livre, 1932.

623. ———. *Frédéric Bazille, 1841–1870.* Paris, Assoc. des Etudiants Protestants, 1935.

624. Wildenstein, Daniel. *Bazille exposition,* organisée [par D. Wildenstein et Philippe Huisman] au profit du musée de Montpellier, juin–juillet 1950. Paris, Wildenstein, 1950.

Bazzi, Giovanni Antonio *see* Sodoma, II

Bazzani, Giuseppe, c. 1690–1769

625. Caroli, Flavio. *Giuseppe Bazzani e la linea d'ombra dell'arte lombarda.* Milano, Mondadori, 1988.

Bearden, Romare, 1914–1988

626. Schwartzman, Myron. *Romare Bearden: His life and art.* New York, Abrams, 1990.

627. State University of New York Art Gallery, Albany. *Romare Bearden: paintings and projections.* November 25 through December 22, 1968. Introduction by Ralph Ellison. Albany, SUNY Art Gallery, 1968.

628. Washington, M. Bunch. *The art of Romare Bearden: the prevalence of ritual.* Introduction by John A. Williams. New York, Abrams, 1972.

Beardsley, Aubrey, 1872–1898

629. Beardsley, Aubrey. *The best of Aubrey Beardsley.* Compiled and with text by Kenneth Clark, New York, Doubleday, 1978.

630. ———. *A book of fifty drawings by Aubrey Beardsley.* With iconography by Agnes Vallance. London, Smithers, 1897.

631. ———. *A second book of fifty drawings.* London, Smithers, 1899.

632. ———. *The early work of Aubrey Beardsley, with a note by H. C. Marillier.* London/New York, Lane, 1899.

633. ———. *The later work of Aubrey Beardsley.* London/New York, Lane, 1901.

634. ———. *The early and later work.* 2 v. New York, Da Capo, 1967.

635. ———. *Letters from Aubrey Beardsley to Leonard Smithers.* Edit. by R. A. Walker. London, First Edition Club, 1937.

636. ———. *The letters of Aubrey Beardsley.* Edited by Henry Maas, J. L. Duncan and W. G. Good. Rutherford, N.J., Fairleigh Dickinson University Press, 1970.

637. Benkovitz, Miriam J. *Aubrey Beardsley, an account of his life.* London, Hamish Hamilton, 1981.

638. Gallatin, Albert E. *Aubrey Beardsley; catalogue of drawings and bibliography.* New York, The Grolier Club, 1945. (CR).

639. Langenfeld, Robert, ed. *Reconsidering Aubrey Beardsley.* With an annotated secondary bibliography by Nicholas Salerno. Ann Arbor/London, UMI Research Press, 1989.

640. MacFall, Haldane. *Aubrey Beardsley, the man and his work.* London, Lane, 1928.

641. ———. *Aubrey Beardsley: The clown, the harlequin, the Pierrot of his age.* New York, Simon and Schuster, 1927.

642. Reade, Brian. *Aubrey Beardsley.* Introd. by John Rothenstein. New York, Viking, 1967.

643. Victoria and Albert Museum (London). *Aubrey Beardsley exhibition held 20th May–18th Sept., 1966.* Catalogue of the original drawings, letters, manuscripts, paintings, and books, posters, photographs, documents, etc. by B. Reade and Frank Dickinson. London, HMSO, 1966.

644. Weintraub, Stanley. *Beardsley, a biography.* New York, Braziller, 1967.

Beaton, Cecil Walter Hardy, 1904–1980

645. Danziger, James. *Beaton.* New York, Viking, 1980.

646. Beaton, Cecil. [*Diaries* (variously titled). 6 v.]. London, Weidenfeld and Nicolson, 1961–78.

647. ———. *Photobiography.* Garden City, N.Y., Doubleday, 1951.

Beaudin, André, 1895–

648. Beaudin, André. *André Beaudin, oeuvres 1921–1970.* Edité à l'occasion de l'ex-position realisée dans les Galeries Natl. d'exposition du Grand Palais, 21 oct.–30 nov. 1970. [Texte] Reynold Arnould. Paris, Centre Natl. d'Art Contemporain, 1970.

649. Galerie Louise Leiris (Paris). *A. Beaudin, peintures 1927–1957.* [Exposition] 31 mai–22 juin 1957. Paris, Gal. Louise Leiris, 1957.

650. ———. *Sculptures 1930–1963.* [Exposition] 14. nov.–14 déc. 1963. Paris, Gal. Louise Leiris, 1963.

651. International Galleries (Chicago). *Retrospective exhibition of André Beaudin, paintings, watercolors, drawings, graphic works, sculptures held March, 1967.* Chicago, Intl. Galleries, 1967.

652. Limbour, Georges. *André Beaudin.* Paris, Verve, 1961.

Beaux, Cecilia, 1863–1942

653. Beaux, Cecilia. *Background with figures; autobiography of Cecilia Beaux.* Boston/New York, Houghton Mifflin, 1930.

654. Oakley, Thornton. *Cecilia Beaux.* Philadelphia, Biddle, 1943.

655. Pennsylvania Academy of Fine Arts. *The paintings and drawings of Cecilia Beaux.* Philadelphia, 1955.

Beccafumi, Domenico, 1486–1551

656. Barocchi, Paola, Santoro, Fiorella Scricchia, et al. *Domenico Beccafumi.* [Catalog of an exhibition at the Pinacoteca Nazionale, Siena). Milano, Electa, 1990.

657. Gibellino Krasceninnicova, Maria. *Il Beccafumi.* Con prefazione di Adolfo Venturi. Siena, Ist. communale d'arte e di storia, 1933.

658. Judey-Barosin, Jacob. *Domenico Beccafumi.* Diss.: Freiburg i.Br. Berlin, [printed by] Michel, 1932.

659. Sanminiatelli, Donato. *Domenico Beccafumi.* Milano, Bramante, 1967.

Becker, Paula Modersohn *see* Modersohn-Becker Paula

Beckmann, Max, 1884–1950

660. Beckmann, Max. *Briefe im Kriege.* Berlin, Cassirer, 1916.

661. ———. *Max Beckmann: Aquarelle und Zeichnungen, 1903–1950.* [Ausstellung] i. d. Kunsthalle Bielefeld. Bielefeld, Kunsthalle, 1977.

662. ———. *Max Beckmann: Catalogue raisonné of his prints.* [Text: James Hofmaier]. 2v. Bern, Gallery Kornfeld, 1990. (CR).

663. ———. *Max Beckmann: die Druckgraphik.* Radierungen, Lithographien, Holzschnitte. [Ausstellung] Badischer Kunstverein Karlsruhe, 27. Aug.–18. Nov. 1962. Karlsruhe, Bad. Kunstverein, 1962. 2 ed.

664. ———. *Max Beckmann: Gemälde, 1905–1950.* [Ausstellung], Leipzig, Museum der Bildenden Künste, 21.7.–23.9., 1990. Klaus Gallwitz, et al. Stuttgart, Hatje, 1990.

665. ———. *Max Beckmann: das Portrait; Gemälde, Aquarelle, Zeichnungen.* [Ausstellung] Badischer Kunstverein Karlsruhe, 26. Aug.–17. Nov. 1963. Karlsruhe, Bad. Kunstverein, 1963.

666. ———. *Max Beckmann 1948.* Retrospective exhibition organized by the City Art Museum of St. Louis. St Louis, City Art Museum, 1948.

667. ———. *On my painting.* New York, Buchholz Gallery Curt Valentin, 1941.

668. ———. *Die Realität der Träume in den Bildern: Schriften und Gespräche.* Herausgegeben und mit einem Vorwort versehen von Rudolf Pillep. München, Piper, 1990.

669. ———. *Tagebücher, 1940–1950.* Zusammengestellt von Mathhilde A. Beckmann, hrsg. von Erhard Göpel. München, Langen-Müller, 1955. Erweiterte und neu durchgesehene Ausgabe, 1973. 2 ed.

670. Beckmann, Peter and Schaffer, Joachim, Hrsg. *Die Bibliothek Max Beckmanns—Unterstreichungen, Kommentare, Notizen und Skizzen in seinen Büchern.* Worms, Werner'sche Verlagsgesellschaft, 1992.

671. Beckmann, Peter. *Max Beckmann. Sichtbares und Unsichtbares.* Einf. von Peter Selz. Stuttgart, Belser, 1965.

672. Buchheim, Lothar G. *Max Beckmann.* Feldafing, Buchheim, 1959.

673. Busch, Günter. *Max Beckmann. Eine Einführung.* München, Piper, 1960.

674. Erffa, Hans Martin Frhr. von. *Blick auf Beckmann; Dokumente und Vorträge.* München, Piper, 1962. (Schriften der Max Beckmann Gesellschaft, 2).

675. Fischer, Friedhelm W. *Der Maler Max Beckmann.* Köln, DuMont Schauberg, 1972.

676. ———. *Max Beckmann, Symbol und Weltbild des Gesamtwerkes.* München, Fink, 1972.

677. Göpel, Erhard and Göpel, Barbara. *Max Beckmann: Katalog der Gemälde.* 2 v. Bern, Kornfeld, 1976. (Schriften der Max Beckmann Gesellschaft, 3). (CR).

678. Janasch, Adolf. *Max Beckmann als Illustrator.* Neu-Isenburg, Tiessen, 1969. (Monographien und Materialien zur Buchkunst, 1).

679. Kessler, Charles S. *Max Beckmann's triptychs.* Cambridge, Mass., Belknap Press of Harvard University Press, 1970.

680. Lackner, Stephan. *Ich erinnere mich gut an Max Beckmann.* Mainz, Kupferberg, 1967. (English ed.)

681. Reifenberg, Benno and Hausenstein, Wilhelm. *Max Beckmann.* München, Piper, 1949.

682. Selz, Peter. *Max Beckmann.* With contributions by Harold Joachim and Perry T. Rathbone. The Museum of Modern Art, New York, in collaboration with the Museum of Fine Arts, Boston, and the Art Institute of Chicago. New York, distributed by Doubleday, 1964.

683. Simon, Heinrich. *Max Beckmann.* Berlin/Leipzig, Klinkhardt und Biermann, 1930. (Junge Kunst, 56).

684. Wiese, Stephan von. *Max Beckmanns zeichnerisches Werk 1903–1925.* Düsseldorf, Droste, 1978.

Beham, Barthel, 1502–1540
Hans Sebald, 1500–1550

685. Burlington Fine Arts Club (London). *Exhibition of the works of Hans Sebald Beham, born 1500, died 1550, and Barthel Beham, born 1502, died 1540.* London, Burlington Fine Arts Club, 1877.

686. Koetschau, Karl. *Barthel Beham und der Meister von Messkirch; eine kunstgeschichtliche Studie.* Strassburg, Heitz, 1893.

687. Pauli, Gustav. *Barthel Beham; ein kritisches Verzeichnis seiner Kupferstiche, Radierungen, Holzschnitte.* Mit vollständiger Reproduktion in Faksimile. Baden-Baden, Heitz, 1958. First ed. 1911. (Studien zur deutschen Kunstgeschichte, 318). (CR).

688. Rosenberg, Adolf. *Sebald und Barthel Beham, zwei Maler der deutschen Renaissance.* Leipzig, Seemann, 1875.

689. Zschelletzschky, Herbert. *Die "Drei gottlosen Maler" von Nürnberg: Sebald Beham, Barthel Beham und Georg Pencz. Historische Grundlagen und chronologische Probleme ihrer Graphik zur Reformations–und Bauernkriegszeit.* Leipzig, Seemann, 1975.

Behrens, Peter, 1868–1940

690. Behrens, Peter. *Peter Behrens : Umbautes Licht.* Ed.by Bernhard Buderath. [Catalog of an exhibition, 12. März–12. Juni, 1990]. Frankfurt, Hoechst AG, 1990.

691. Buddensieg, Tilmann and Rogge, Henning. *Industriekultur. Peter Behrens und die AEG 1907–1914.* Berlin, Mann, 1979.

692. Hoeber, Fritz. *Peter Behrens.* München, Müller and Rentsch, 1913.

693. Kadatz, Hans-Joachim. *Peter Behrens, Architekt, Maler, Grafiker und Formgestalter, 1868–1940.* Leipzig, Seemann, 1977.

694. Windsor, Alan. *Peter Behrens, architect and designer.* London, Architectural Press, 1981.

Bella, Stefano della, 1610–1664

695. Massar, Phyllis Dearborn. *Presenting Stefano della Bella, seventeenth century printmaker.* New York, Metropolitan Museum of Art, 1971.

696. Cabinet des Dessins, Musée du Louvre (Paris). *Dessins de Stefano della Bella, 1610–1664.* Françoise Viatte, éditeur. Paris, Editions des Musées Nationaux, 1974. (Inventaire général des dessins italiens, 2).

Bellange, Hippolyte, 1800–1860

697. Adeline, Jules. *Hippolyte Bellange et son oeuvre.* Paris, Quantin, 1880.

698. Association des Artistes (Paris). *Exposition des oeuvres d'Hippolyte Bellange à l'Ecole des Beaux Arts.* Etude biographique par Francis Way. Paris, Assoc. des Artistes, 1867.

Bellano, Bartolomeo, c. 1434–1497

699. Krahn, Volker. *Bartolomeo Bellano: Studien zur Paduaner Plastik des Quattrocento.* Muenchen, Scraneg, 1988.

Belling, Rudolf, 1886–1972

700. Akademie der Künste (Berlin). *Rudolf Belling.* Ausstellung vom 6. Mai–17. Juni 1962. Katalog: Herta Elisabeth Killy, mit e. Einleitung von Werner Hofmann. Berlin, Akademie der Künste, 1962.

701. Nationalgalerie Berlin. *Rudolf Belling Skulpturen und Architekturen.* Berlin, National-Galerie, 1924.

702. Schmoll gen. Eisenwerth, Josef Adolf. *Rudolf Belling.* St. Gallen, Erker-Verlag, 1971. (Künstler unserer Zeit, 17).

Bellini, Gentile, 1429–1507
Giovanni, 1430–1516
Jacopo, 1400–1470

703. Bellini, Jacopo. *Venedig—Jacopo Bellini.* In Zusammenarbeit mit Joachim Eberhardt, unter Mitwirkung von Ulrike Bauer-Eberhardt, Dorothea Stichel und mit einem Beitrag von Ursula Lehmann-Brockhaus. 4 v. Berlin, Gebr. Mann, 1990. (Corpus der italienischen Zeichnungen, 1300–1450; 5–8).

704. Bottari, Stefano. *Tutta la pitture di Giovanni Bellini.* 2 v. Milano, Rizzoli, 1963.

705. Dussler, Luitpold. *Giovanni Bellini.* Wien, Schroll, 1949.

706. Eisler, Colin. *The genius of Jacopo Bellini: the complete paintings and drawings.* New York, Abrams, 1989.

707. Fry, Roger E. *Giovanni Bellini.* London, Unicorn, 1899.

708. Gamba, Carlo. *Giovanni Bellini.* Milano, Hoepli, 1937.

709. Goloubew, Victor. *Les dessins de Jacopo Bellini au Louvre et au British Museum.* 2 v. Bruxelles, van Oest, 1908–1912.

710. Gronau, Georg. *Giovanni Bellini.* Stuttgart, Deutsche Verlagsanstalt, 1930; also: New York, E. Weyhe, 1930. (Klassiker der Kunst, 36).

711. ———. *Die Künstlerfamilie Bellini.* Bielefeld, Velhagen & Klasing, 1909. (Künstler-Monographien, 96).

712. ———. *Die Spätwerke des Giovanni Bellini.* Strassburg, Heitz, 1928. (Zur Kunstgeschichte des Auslandes, 125).

713. Heinemann, Fritz. *Giovanni Bellini e i belliniani.* 2 v. Venezia, Neri Pozza, 1962. (Saggi e studi di storia dell'arte, 6).

714. Hendy, Philip and Goldscheider, Ludwig. *Giovanni Bellini.* New York, Phaidon, 1945.

715. Huse, Norbert. *Studien zu Giovanni Bellini.* Berlin/New York, de Gruyter, 1972. (Beiträge zur Kunstgeschichte, 7).

716. Moschini, Vittorio. *Disegni di Jacopo Bellini.* Bergamo, Ist. Ital. d'Arti Grafiche, 1943.

717. ———. *Giambellino.* Bergamo, Ist. Ital. d'Arti Grafiche, 1943.

718. Pallucchini, Rodolfo. *Giovanni Bellini.* Milano, Martello, 1959. English edition: New York, Humanities Press, 1962.

719. ———. *Catalogo illustrato [della] mostra di Giovanni Bellini.* Venezia, Pallazzo Ducale, 12 guigno–5 ott. 1949. Con la collaborazione di Giovanni Mariacher per la raccolta del materiale bibliografico. Venezia, Alfieri, 1949.

720. Pignatti, Terisio. *L'opera completa di Giovanni Bellini.* Presentazione di Renato Ghiotto. Milano, Rizzoli, 1969. (Classici dell'arte, 28).

721. Ricci, Corrado. *Jacopo Bellini e i suoi libre di disegni.* 2 v. Florence, Alinari, 1908.

722. Robertson, Giles. *Giovanni Bellini.* Oxford, Clarendon Press, 1968.

723. Röthlisberger, Marcel. *Studi su Jacopo Bellini.* Venezia, Pozza, 1960. (Estratto da saggi e memorie de storia dell'arte della Fondazione Giorgio Cini, 2).

724. Zuffi, Stefano. *Giovanni Bellini.* Milano,

Bellmer, Hans, 1902–1975

725. Bellmer, Hans. *L'anatomie de l'image.* Paris, Le Terrain Vague, 1957.

B

726. ———. *Die Puppe.* Carlsruhe, Oberschlesien, Privately publ., 1934.

727. ———. *La poupée.* Paris, Levis-Mano, 1936.

728. ———. *Les jeux de la poupée.* Paris, Editions Premières-Marcel Zerbib, 1949.

729. Centre National d'Art Contemporain (Paris). *Hans Bellmer.* Publié à l'occasion de l'exposition Bellmer, 30 nov. 1971–17 jan. 1972. Paris, C.N.A.C., 1971. (CNAC Archives, 1).

730. Jelenski, Constantin. *Les dessins de Hans Bellmer.* Paris, Denoël, 1966.

731. ———. *Hans Bellmer.* Ed. by Alex Grall, with an introduction by Constantin Jelenski. London, Academy Editions/ New York, St. Martin's Press, 1972–73. (English trans. of *Les dessins*).

732. Kestner Gesellschaft Hannover. *Hans Bellmer.* [Katalog der Ausstellung] 28. April–4. Juni 1967. Hannover, Kestner Gesellschaft, 1967.

733. Pieyre de Mandiargues, André. *Hans Bellmer, oeuvre gravé.* Paris, Denoël, 1969.

734. William and Noma Copley Foundation. *Hans Bellmer.* Biographical note by Alain Jouffroy. Chicago, Copley Foundation, 1959. (Printed in London by Lund Humphries).

Bellotto, Bernardo, 1720–1780

735. Camesasca, Ettore. *L'opera completa del Bellotto.* Introdotta e coordinata da E. Camesasca. Milano, Rizzoli, 1974. (Classici dell'arte, 78).

736. Fritzsche, Hellmuth A. *Bernardo Bellotto, genannt Canaletto.* Burg b.M., Hopfer, 1936. (Beiträge zur Kunstgeschichte, 3).

737. Gemäldegalerie Alte Meister (Dresden). *Bernardo Bellotto genannt Canaletto in Dresden und Warschau.* Ausstellung vom 8. Dez. 1963–31 Aug. 1964, im Albertinum, Dresden. Dresden, Staatl. Kunstsammlungen, 1963.

738. Kozakiewicz, Stefan. *Bernardo Bellotto genannt Canaletto.* 2 v. Bd. I: Leben und Werk, Bd. II: Katalog. Recklinghausen, Bongers, 1972. (CR).

739. Lippold, Gertraude. *Bernardo Bellotto, genannt Canaletto.* Leipzig, Seemann, 1963.

740. Lorentz, Stanislaw, and Kozakiewicz, Stefan. *Bellotto a Varsavia.* Milano, Alfieri, 1955.

741. Marinelli, Sergio., ed. *Bernardo Bellotto: Verona e le città europee.* A cura di S. Marinelli. Scritti di Gisela Barche [et. al.]. Milano, Electa, 1990.

742. Oesterreichische Kulturvereinigung (Vienna). *Bernard Bellotto genannt Canaletto.* Ausstellung [Oesterr. Galerie] Wien, Oberes Belvedere, 29. April–25 Juli 1965, unter der Leitung von: Staatl. Kunstsammlungen Dresden; National-Museum Warschau; Kunsthistorisches Museum Wien. Wien, Oesterr. Kulturvereinigung, 1965.

743. Pallucchini, Rodolfo. *Vedute del Bellotto.* Milano, Martello, 1961.

744. Rizzi Alberto. *Bernardo Bellotto. L'opera completa.* 3 v. Milano, Berenice, 1992.

745. Uzanne, Louis Octave. *Les deux Canaletto.* Biographie critique. Paris, Laurens, 1907.

746. ———. *Les Canaletto: L'oncle et le neveu, Antonio da Canal, 1697–1768, le maître et le disciple, Bernardo Bellotto, 1723–1780.* Paris, Nilsson, 1925.

747. Valcanover, Francesco. *Bernardo Bellotto.* Milano, Fabbri, 1966. (I maestri del colore, 190).

748. Villa Hügel, Essen. *Europäische Veduten des Bernardo Bellotto genannt Canaletto.* 29. April–31 Juli 1966. Essen-Bredeney, Gemeinnütziger Verein Villa Hügel, 1966.

749. Wallis, Mieczyslaw. *Canaletto the painter of Warsaw.* Warsaw, Panstwowy Instytut Wydawniczy, 1954.

Bellows, George Wesley, 1882–1925

750. Bellows, George W. *George Bellows: his lithographs.* Comp. by Emma Louise Bellows, with an introd., "George W. Bellows," by Thomas Beer. New York, Knopf, 1928.

751. ———. *The paintings of George Bellows.* Comp. by E. L. Bellows. New York, Knopf, 1929.

752. Boswell, Peyton. *George Bellows.* New York, Crown, 1942.

753. Braider, Donald. *George Bellows and the Ashcan School of painting.* Garden City, N.Y., Doubleday, 1971.

754. Columbus Museum of Art (Columbus, Ohio). *George Wesley Bellows: paintings, drawings, and prints.* [Catalog of the exhibition] April 1–May 8, 1979. Columbus, Ohio, 1979.

755. Doezema, Marianne. *George Bellows and urban America.* New Haven, Yale University Press, 1992.

756. Eggers, George W. *George Bellows.* New York, Macmillan, 1931.

757. Eisler, Colin. *The genius of Jacopo Bellini: the complete paintings and drawings.* New York, Abrams, 1989. (CR).

758. Goffen, Rona. *Giovanni Bellini.* New Haven and London, Yale University Press, 1989.

759. Mason, Lauris. *The lithographs of George Bellows; a catalogue raisonné.* L. Mason assisted by Joan Ludman. Foreword by Charles H. Morgan. Millwood, N.Y., KTO Press, 1977. (CR).

760. Metropolitan Museum of Art (New York). *Memorial exhibition of the work of George Bellows, Oct. 12–Nov. 22, 1925.* New York, Metropolitan Museum of Art, 1925.

761. Morgan, Charles H. *George Bellows, painter of America*. New York, Reynal, 1965.
762. ———. *The drawings of George Bellows*. Alhambra, Calif., Borden, 1973.
763. Myers, Jane and Ayres, Linda. *George Bellows: the artist and his lithographs, 1916–1924*. With an introduction by Jean Bellows Booth. Fort Worth, Texas, Amon Carter Museum, 1988.
764. Nugent, Frances F. *George Bellows, American painter*. Chicago, Rand McNally, 1963.
765. Quick, Michael, et al. *The paintings of George Bellows*. New York, Abrams, 1992.
766. Young, Mahonri S. *The paintings of George Bellows*. New York, Watson-Guptill, 1973.

Benbridge, Henry, 1743–1812
767. National Portrait Gallery, Smithsonian Institution (Washington, D.C.). *Henry Benbridge (1743–1812): American portrait painter*. April 2–May 16, 1971; catalogue by Robert G. Stewart. Washington, D.C., Smithsonian Institution Press, 1971.

Benedetto da Maiano, 1442–1497
768. Cendali, Lorenzo. *Guiliano e Benedetto da Majano, Fiesole*. Firenze, Societa Ed. Toscana, 1926.
769. Dussler, Luitpold. *Benedetto da Majano, ein florentiner Bildhauer des späten Quattrocento*. München, Schmidt, 1924.

Benedetto di Parma *see* **Antelami, Benedetto**

Benson, Ambrosius, d. 1550
770. Marlier, Georges. *Ambrosius Benson et la peinture à Bruges au temps du Charles-Quint*. Damme, Musée van Maulant, 1957.

Benton, Fletcher, 1931–
771. Lucie-Smith, Edward. *Fletcher Benton*. New York, Abrams, 1991

Benton, Thomas Hart, 1889–1975
772. Adams, Henry. *Thomas Hart Benton: an American original*. New York. Knopf, Distrib. by Random House, 1989.
773. ———. *Thomas Hart Benton: Drawing from life*. New York, Abbeville, 1992.
774. Baigell, Matthew. *Thomas Hart Benton*. New York, Abrams, 1974.
775. Benton, Thomas Hart. *An American in art; a professional and technical autobiography*. Lawrence, Univ. Press of Kansas, 1969.
776. ———. *An artist in America*. New York, McBride, 1937. New and rev. ed., Kansas City, Univ. of Kansas City Press, 1951. 3d rev. ed., Columbia, University of Missouri Press, 1968.
777. ———. *A Thomas Hart Benton miscellany; selections from his published opinions, 1916–1960*. Ed. by Matthew Baigell. Lawrence, Univ. Press of Kansas, 1971.
778. Braun, Emily. *Thomas Hart Benton: The America Today murals*. With essays by E. Braun and Thomas Branchick. Williamstown, Mass, Williams College Museum of Art, 1985.
779. Burroughs, Polly. *Thomas Hart Benton, a portrait*. Garden City, N.Y., Doubleday, 1981.
780. Chiappini, Rudy, ed. *Thomas Hart Benton*. [Catalogue of an exhibition held at the Museo d'Arte Moderna, Lugano]. Milano, Electa, 1992.
781. Doss, Erika Lee. *Benton, Pollock, and the politics of modernism: from regionalism to abstract expressionism*. Chicago, Chicago University Press, 1991.
782. Fath, Creekmore. *The lithographs of Thomas Hart Benton*. Compiled and edited by C. Fath. Austin, University of Texas Press, 1969. New ed. 1979.
783. Guedon, Mary Scholz. *Regionalist art: Thomas Hart Benton, John Stewart Curry and Grant Wood. A guide to the literature*. Metuchen, N.J., Scarecrow Press, 1982.
784. Marling, Karal Ann. *Tom Benton and his drawings: a biographical essay and a collection of his sketches, studies and mural cartoons*. Columbia, MO. University of Missouri Press, 1985.

Benziger, August, 1867–1955
785. Benziger, Marieli. *August Benziger, portrait painter*. Glendale, Calif., Clark, 1958.
786. Braungart, Richard. *August Benziger; sein Leben und sein Werk*. München, Bruckmann, 1922.

Berain, Jean, 1639–1711
787. Weigert, Roger Armand. *Jean I. Bérain, dessinateur de la chambre et du cabinet du roi (1640–1711)*. 2 v. Paris, Editions d'Art et d'Histoire, 1936.

Berettini, Pietro *see* **Pietro da Cortona**

Berg, Magnus, 1666–1739
788. Pausen, Ashlid. *Magnus Berg: En kunstner ved kongens hoff*. Oslo, Dreyer, 1990.(CR).

Bergh, Sven Richard, 1858–1919
789. Bergh, Richard. *Efterlamnade skrifter om konst och annatomi*. Stockholm, Bonnier, 1921.
790. Osterman, Gunhold. *Richard Bergh och Nationalmuseum; nagra dokument*. Lund, Berlingska Bokts., 1958

791. Rapp, Birgitta. *Richard Bergh; konstnär och kultur-politiker 1890–1915*. Stockholm, Raben and Sjögren, 1978.

Berghe, Frits van den, 1883–1939
792. Hecke, Paul Gustave van. *Frits van den Berghe*. Anvers, De Sikkel, 1950. (Monographies de l'art belge, 2. ser., 9).
793. Langui, Emile. *Frits van den Berghe. De mens en zijn werk: 1883–1939*. Antwerpen, Mercatorfonds, 1968.
794. ———. *Frits van den Berghe, 1883–1939*. Catalogue raisonné de son oeuvre peint. Bruxelles, Laconti, 1966. (Maîtres de la peinture contemporaine en Belgique, 2). (CR).
795. Palais des Beaux-Arts (Brussels). *Frits van den Berghe*. [Exposition] Mai 1962. Bruxelles, Palais des Beaux-Arts, 1962.

Berlage, Hendrick Petrus, 1856–1934
796. Singelenberg, Pieter. *H. P. Berlage; idea and style. The quest for modern architecture*. Utrecht, Haentjens Dekker en Gumbert, 1972.
797. Berlage, Hendrick Petrus. *H. P. Berlage, 1856–1934, een bouwmeester en zijn tijd*. Red. C.H.A. Broos, P. Singelenberg, E.R.M. Taverne. Bussum, Fibula van Dishoeck, 1975.

Berlin Painter, fl. 500–460 B.C.
798. Kurtz, Donna C. *The Berlin painter*. Drawings by Sir John Beazley. Oxford, Clarendon Press, 1983.

Bermejo, Bartolome, 1430–1498
799. Tormo y Monzo, Elias. *Bartolome Bermejo, el mas recio de los primitivos espanoles*. Madrid, p.p. 1926.
800. Young, Eric. *Bartolomé Bermejo, the great Hispano-Flemish master*. London, Elek, 1975.

Bernard, Emile, 1868–1941
801. Bernard, Emile. *Souvenirs sur Paul Cézanne, une conversation avec Cézanne*. Paris, Michel, 1926.
802. Hautecoeur, Louis. *Eloge d'Emile Bernard*. Avec des lithographies en couleurs et des gravures sur bois. Paris, Bruker, 1962.
803. Luthi, Jean-Jacques. *Catalogue raisonné de l'oeuvre d'Emile Bernard*. Paris, 1962. (CR).
804. ———. *Emile Bernard, chef de l'école de Pont-Aven*. Par J. J. Luthi; préf. d'Ambrose Vollard. Paris, Nouvelles Editions Latines, 197?.
805. Mornard, Pierre. *Emile Bernard et ses amis: Van Gogh, Gauguin, Toulouse-Lautrec, Cézanne, Odilon Redon*. Genève, Cailler, 1957.
806. Sainte-Marie, Jean Pierre, ed. *Hommage de la Bourgogne à Emile Bernard (1868–1941) à l'occasion de centenaire de sa naissance*. [Exposition] Musées d'Auxerre, Cellier de l'Abbaye Saint-Germain, 7 juillet–8 septembre, 1968. Auxerre, L'Yonne Republicaine, 1968.
807. Stevens, Mary Anne, Boyle-Turner, Caroline, et. al. *Emile Bernard, 1868–1941. A pioneer of modern art/Ein Wegbereiter der Moderne*. Catalogue of the exhibition at the Städtische Kunsthalle, Mannheim and the Van Gogh Museum, Amsterdam. Zwolle, Waanders Publishers, 1990.

Bernard, Joseph, 1866–1931
808. Cantinelli, Richard. *Joseph Bernard; catalogue de l'oeuvre sculpté*. Paris, van Oest, 1928.
809. Musée Rodin (Paris). *Joseph Bernard*. [Exposition] au Musée Rodin, Paris, 1973. Paris, Musée Rodin, 1973.

Bernath, Aurel, 1895–
810. Bernath, Aurel. *So lebten wir in Pannonien*. Übers. aus dem Ungarischen von Heinrich Weissling. Berlin, Union, 1964. [Trans. of Igy eltünk Pannoniaban].
811. Genthon, Istvan. *Bernath Aurel*. Budapest, Kepzomüveszeti Alap Kiadovallata, 1964. (A Müveszet Kiskönyvtara, 58).

Bernini, Giovanni Lorenzo, 1598–1680
812. Baldinucci, Filippo. *The life of Bernini*. Trans. by Catherine Engass. Foreword by Robert Engass. University Park/London, Penn. State University Press, 1966. [Trans. of Vita del cavaliere Lorenzo Bernino, scultore, architetto, epittore. Scritta da F. B. Fiorentino, Florence, 1682].
813. ———. *Vita di Gian Lorenzo Bernini*. Con l'inedita vita del Baldinucci, scritta dal Figlio Francesco Saverio. Studio e note de Sergio Saniek Ludovici, Milano, Edizioni del Milione, 1948.
814. ———. *Vita des Giovanni Lorenzo Bernini*. Mit Übersetzung und Kommentar von Alois Riegl; aus seinem Nachlass herausgegeben von Arthur Burdin und Oskar Pollak. Wien, Schroll, 1912.
815. Bauer, George C., ed. *Bernini in perspective*. Englewood Cliffs, N.J., Prentice-Hall, 1976.
816. Benkard, Ernst. *Giovanni Lorenzo Bernini*. Frankfurt a.M., Iris-Verlag, 1926. (Meister der Plastik, 3).
817. Bernini, Domenico. *Vita del cav. Gio. Lorenzo Bernini, descritta da Domenico Bernini suo figlio*. Roma, a spese di Rocco Bernabo, 1713.
818. Bernini, Giovanni Lorenzo. *Selected drawings of Gian Lorenzo Bernini*. Ed. by Ann Sutherland Harris. New York, Dover, 1977.

819. ——. *Die Zeichnungen des Gianlorenzo Bernini*. Hrsg. von Heinrich Brauer und Rudolf Wittkower. Berlin, Keller, 1931. (Römische Forschungen, 9–10).

820. Birindello, Massimo. *La machina heroica*. Il disegno di Gian Lorenzo Bernini per Piazza San Pietro. Roma, Universitá. Ist. di Fondamenta dell'Architettura, 1980. (Saggi di storie dell'architettura, 4).

821. Boehn, Max von. *Lorenzo Bernini; seine Zeit, sein Leben, sein Werk*. Bielefeld/Leipzig, Velhagen & Klasing, 1912.

822. Borsi, Franco. *Bernini architetto*. Milano, Electa, 1980.

823. Chantelou, Paul Friart de. *Journal du voyage in France du cavalier Bernini*. Ed. by G. Charensol. Paris, Ateliers, 1930.

824. ——. *Journal du voyage du cavalier Bernini en France*. Manuscrit inédit publié et annoté par Ludovic Lalanne. Paris, Gazette des Beaux-Arts, 1885.

825. Comitato Vaticano per l'Anno Berniniano. *Bernini in Vaticano*. [Mostra] Braccio di Carlo Magno, maggio–luglio 1981. Roma, de Luca, 1981.

826. Fagiolo dell'Arco, Maurizio. *Bernini, una introduzione al gran teatro del barocco* [di] Maurizio e Marcello F. dell'Arco. Roma, Bulzoni, 1967.

827. Fraschetti, Stanislao. *Il Bernini la sua vita, la sua opera, il suo tempo*. Con prefazione di Adolfo Venturi. Milano, Hoepli, 1900.

828. Gould, Cecil Hilton M. *Bernini in France; an episode in seventeenth century history*. London, Weidenfeld and Nicolson, 1981. (American edition: Princeton, N.J., Princeton University Press, 1982).

829. Grassi, Luigi. *Disegni del Bernini*. Bergamo, Ist. Ital. d'Arti Grafiche, 1944.

830. ——. *Gianlorenzo Bernini*. Roma, Ateneo, 1962.

831. Hibbard, Benjamin H. *Bernini*. London, Penguin, 1966.

832. Kauffmann, Hans. *Giovanni Lorenzo Bernini: die figürlichen Kompositionen*. Berlin, Mann, 1970.

833. Kitao, Timothy K. *Circle and oval in the square of Saint Peter's. Bernini's art of planning*. New York, New York University Press, 1968. (Monographs on archaeology and the fine arts, 29).

834. Lavin, Irving. *Bernini and the crossing of Saint Peter's*. New York, New York University Press, 1968. (Monographs on archaeology and the fine arts, 17).

835. ——. *Bernini and the unity of the visual arts*. 2 v. New York/London, Pierpont Morgan Library and Oxford University Press, 1980.

836. ——. *Drawings by Gianlorenzo Bernini from the Museum der Bildenden Künste, Leipzig, German Democratic Republic*. Exhibition and catalogue prepared in a graduate seminar, Department of Art and Archaeology, Princeton University. Princeton, N.J., Princeton University Art Museum, 1981.

837. Mariani, Valerio. *Gian Lorenzo Bernini*. Napoli, Soc. Editrice Vapoletana, 1974.

838. Martinelli, Valentino. *Bernini: disegni* Firense, La Nuova Italia.1981

839. ——. *I ritratti di pontefici di G. L. Bernini*. Roma, Ist. di studi romani, 1956. (Quaderni di storia del'arte, 3).

840. Pane, Roberto. *Bernini architetto*. Venezia, Pozza, 1953.

841. Perlove, Shelley Karen. *Bernini and the idealization of death: the "Blesssed Ludovica Albertoni" and the Altieri Chapel*. University Park, Pennsylvania State University Press, 1990.

842. Scribner, Charles. *Gianlorenzo Bernini*. New York, Abrams,1991.

843. Wittkower, Rudolf. *Gian Lorenzo Bernini, the sculptor of the Roman Baroque*. London, Phaidon, 1955. 2 ed. 1966.

844. ——. *Gian Lorenzo Bernini, the sculptor of the Roman Baroque*. Rev. by Howard Hibbard, Thomas Martin and Margot Wittkower, Oxford, Phaidon, 1981. 3 ed.

Berrocal, Miguel, 1933–

845. Berrocal, Miguel. *Miguel Berrocal: Skulpturen*. Offenbach am Main, Die Galerie, 1987.

Berruguete, Alonso Gonzalez, 1480?–1561
Pedro, 1483?–1503

846. Angulo Iniguez, Diego. *Pedro Berruguete en paredes de nava, estudio critico*. Barcelona, Juventud, 1946. (Obras maestras del arte espanol, 6).

847. Azcarate, Jose Maria de. *Alonso Berruguete. Quatro ensayos*. Valladolid, Publ. por la Direccion General de Bellas Artes, 1963.

848. Castro, Luis de. *El enigma de Berruguete: la danza y la escultara*. Valladolid, El Ateneo de Valladolid, 1953.

849. Gaya Nuno, Juan Antonio. *Alonso Berruguete en Toledo*. Barcelona, Juventud, 1944. (Obras maestras del arte espanol, 4).

850. Gomez-Moreno, Manuel. *Las aguilas del renacimiento espanol: Bartolomé Ordonez, Diego Silóee, Pedro Machuca, Alonso Berruguete*. Madrid, Graficas Uguina, 1941.

851. Lainez Alcala, Rafael. *Pedro Berruguete, pintor de Castilla; ensayo critico biografico*. Madrid, Espasa-Calpe, 1935.

852. Orueta, Ricardo de. *Berruguete y su obra*. Madrid, Callega, 1917.

Bertholle, Jean, 1909–

853. Ferrier, Jean-Louis. *Bertholle*. Paris, 1959.

Bertoia, Harry, 1915–

854. Nelson, Junek. *Harry Bertoia, sculptor.* Detroit, Wayne State University Press, 1970.

Bertoia, Jacopo,

855. De Grazia, Diane. *Bertoia, Mirola and the Farnese Court.* Bologna, Nuova Alfa Editoriale, 1991.

Bertoldo, Giovanni di, 1410–1491

856. Bode, Wilhelm von. *Bertoldo und Lorenzo di Medici: die Kunstpolitik des Lorenzo il Magnifico im Spiegel der Werke seines Lieblingsschülers.* Freiburg i.Br., Pontos, 1925.
857. Draper, James David. *Bertoldo di Giovanni, sculptor of the Medici household. Critical reappraisal and catalogue raisonn*é. Columbia, Missouri, 1992.

Bertram, Meister von Minden, 1345?–1415

858. Dorner, Alexander. *Meister Bertram von Minden.* Berlin, Rembrandt-Verlag, 1937.
859. Martens, Friedrich A. *Meister Bertram; Herkunft, Werk und Wirken.* Berlin, Deutscher Verein fur Kunstwissenschaft, 1936.
860. Portmas, Paul Ferdinand. *Meister Bertram.* Zürich, Rabe, 1963.

Bertrand, Gaston, 1910–

861. Selevoy, Robert L. *Gaston Bertrand.* Anvers, De Sikkel, 1954.

Besnard, Albert, 1849–1934

862. Besnard, Albert. *Zeichnungen von Albert Besnard.* Mit einer Einleitung von Hans W. Singer. Leipzig, Schumann, 1913.
863. Coppier, André Charles. *Les eaux-fortes de Besnard.* Paris, Berger-Levrault, 1920.
864. Mauclair, Camille. *Albert Besnard, l'homme et l'oeuvre.* Paris, Delagrave, 1914.
865. Mourey, Gabriel, et al. *Albert Besnard . . . accompagné de quelques écrits d'Albert Besnard et des opinions de quelques écrivains et artistes sur son oeuvre. . . .* Paris, Davoust, 1906.

Betti, Bernardino *see* Pinturicchio

Beuckelaer, Joachim, 1533–1573

866. Museum voor schone Kunsten (Gent). *Het markt- en keukenstuk in de Nederlanden, 1550–1650.* Gent, The Museum, 1987.

Beuys, Joseph, 1921–

867. Adriani, Götz, et al. *Joseph Beuys,* [von] Götz Adriani, Winfried Konnertz, Karin Thomas. Köln, DuMont Schauberg, 1973.
868. Bastian, Heiner, Hrsg. *Joseph Beuys: Zeich-*

nungen. [Catalog of an exhibition at the Sara Hildénin Taidmuseo, Tampere and the Städtisches Museum Abteiberg, M. Gladbach]. Tampere, Finland /Mönchen Gladbach, 1985.

869. Beuys, Joseph. *Beuys vor Beuys: frühe Arbeiten aus der Sammlung van der Grinten: Zeichnungen, Aquarelle, Ölstudien, Collagen.* Mit Textbeiträgen von Klaus Gallwitz. Köln, DuMont, 1987.
870. ———.*Der erweiterte Kunstbegriff.* Darmstadt. Georg Büchner Buchhandlung, 1989.
871. ———. *Joseph Beuys.* [Catalogue of an exhibition held at the Kunsthaus Zürich, Nov. 26, 1993–Feb. 20, 1994, the Museo Nacional, Centro de Arte Reina Sofia, Madrid, Mar. 15–June 6, 1994, and the Centre national d'art et de culture Georges Pompidou, Paris, June 30–Oct.3, 1994]. Catalogue conception, Fabrice Hergott avec la collaboration de Marion Hohlfeldt. Paris, Musée d'art moderne, 1994.
872. ———. *Joseph Beuys: Handzeichnungen.* Ausstellung des Kupferstichkabinetts, 11. Dezember 1970 bis 31 Januar 1971. Braunschweig, Herzog Anton Ulrich Museum, 1971.
873. ———. *Joseph Beuys: Block Beuys.* Mit Farbaufnahmen von Claudio Abate im Hessischen Landesmuseum in Darmstadt. München, Schirmer/Mosel, 1990.
874. ———. *Joseph Beuys: Eine innere Mongolei: Dschingis Khan, Schamanen, Aktricen: Ölfarben, Wasserfarben, und Bleistiftzeichnungen aus der Sammlung van der Grinten.* Hrsg. von Carl Haenlein; [Redaktion, Carsten Ahrens und Carl Haenlein]. Hannover, Kestner-Gesellschaft, 1990.
875. ———. *Joseph Beuys in America: energy plan for the Western man.* Writings by and interview with the artist, compiled by Carin Kuoni. New York, Four Walls Eight Windows, 1990.
876. ———. *Joseph Beuys: multiples.* Catalogue raisonné, multiples and prints 1965–80. Ed. by Jörg Schellmann and Bernd Klüser, trans. by C. Tisdall. New York, New York University Press, 1980. 5 ed.
877. ———. *Joseph Beuys: multiples.* Werkverzeichnis der Auflagenobjekte und Druckgraphik, 1965–1986. Ed. by Jörg Schellmann. München, Schellmann, 1992. 7 ed.
878. ———. *Joseph Beuys: Natur, Materie, Form.* Kunstsammlung Nordrhein-Westfalen, 3. November, 1991–9 Februar 1992. [Konzeption der Ausstellung und des Katalogs, Armin Zweite].
879. Bojescul, Wilhelm. *Zum Kunstbegriff des Joseph Beuys.* Essen, 1985.
880. ———. *Joseph Beuys: Plakate.* [Catalog of

an exhibition, Bayerische Staatsbibliothek, 8.4.–8.5., 1991]. München, Schneider-Henn, 1991. (Ausstellungskataloge der Bayr. Staatsbibliothek; 55).

881. Borstel, Stephan von, Hrsg. *Die unsichtbare Skulptur: zum erweiterten Kunstbegriff von Joseph Beuys.* Herausgegeben von der FIU-Kassel. Stuttgart, Urachhaus, 1989.

882. Burckhardt, Jacqueline, Hrsg. *Joseph Beuys, Enzo Cucchi, Anselm Kiefer, Jannis Kounellis. Ein Gespräch/ Una discussione.* Zürich. Verlag Parkett, 1986.

883. Burgbacher-Krupka, Ingrid. *Prophete rechts, Prophete links: Joseph Beuys.* Stuttgart, Belser, 1977.

884. Celant, Germano. *Beuys tracce in Italia.* Naples, Amelio, 1978.

885. Grinten, Franz Joseph and Grinten, Hans van der. *Joseph Beuys: Bleistiftzeichnungen aus den Jahren 1946–1964.* Berlin, Propyläen: Edition Heiner Bastian, 1973.

886. Haenlein, Carl, Hrsg. *Joseph Beuys: Eine innere Mongolei: Dschingis Khan, Schamanen, Aktricen.* Ölfarben, Wasserfarben und Bleistiftzeichnungen aus der Sammlung van der Grinten. Hannover, Kestner-Gesellschaft, 1990.

887. Harlan, Volker. *Sozial Plastik.* Materialien zu Joseph Beuys/Harlan, Rappmann, Schata. Achberg, Achberger Verlagsanstalt, 1976.

888. Joachimides, Christos M. *Joseph Beuys Richtkräfte.* Berlin, Nationalgalerie, 1977.

889. Romain, Lothar and Wedewer, Rolf. *Über Beuys.* Düsseldorf, Droste, 1972.

890. Stachelhaus, Heiner. *Joseph Beuys.* Düsseldorf, Claassen, 1987. (English Trans. by David Britt. New York, Abbeville Press, 1991)

891. Temkin, Ann and Rose, Bernice. *Thinking is form: the drawings of Joseph Beuys.* New York, Thames and Hudson, 1993.

892. Tisdall, Caroline. *Joseph Beuys.* Preface by Thomas M. Messer. Introduction by Joseph Beuys. [An exhibition book]. New York, The Solomon R. Guggenheim Museum, 1979.

893. ———. *Joseph Beuys Coyote.* München, Schirmer Mosel, 1976.

894. Vischer, Theodora. *Joseph Beuys, die Einheit des Werkes: Zeichnungen, Aktionen, plastische Arbeiten, soziale Skulptur.* Köln, Verlag der Buchhandlung W. König, 1991.

895. Weber, Christa. *Vom "Erweiterten Kunstbegriff" zum "Erweiterten Pädagogikbegriff": Versuch einer Standortbestimmung von Joseph Beuys.* Frankfurt a.M., Verlag für Interkulturelle Kommunikation, 1991.

Bewick, John, 1760–1795
Thomas, 1753–1828

896. Bain, Ian. *The watercolours and drawings of Thomas Bewick and his workshop apprentices.* 2 v. London, Gordon Fraser, 1981.

897. Bewick, Thomas. *Memoir of Thomas Bewick written by himself, 1822–1828.* With an introduction by Selwyn Image. London, Lane, 1924.

898. ———. [Another edition]. With an introduction by Edmund Blunden. London, Centaur, 1961.

899. ———. *Memorial edition of Thomas Bewick's works.* 5 v. London, Quariet, 1885–1887.

900. Dobson, Austin, i.e., Henry Austin. *Thomas Bewick and his pupils.* Boston, Osgood, 1884.

901. Hugo, Thomas. *The Bewick collector. A descriptive catalogue of the works of Thomas and John Bewick . . . with an appendix of portraits, autographs, works of pupils, etc., etc. The whole described from the originals contained in the largest and most perfect collection ever formed. . . .* London, Reeve, 1866.

902. ———. *The Bewick collector. A supplement.* London, Reeve, 1868.

903. Roscoe, S. *Thomas Bewick, a bibliography raisonné of editions of the General history of quadrupeds, the History of British birds and the Fables of Aesop, issued in his lifetime.* London, Oxford University Press, 1953.

904. Ruzicka, Rudolph. *Thomas Bewick, engraver.* New York, The Typophiles, 1943. (Typophile Chap Book, 8).

905. Thomson, David Croal. *The life and works of Thomas Bewick; being an account of his career and achievements in art, with a notice of the works of John Bewick.* London, The Art Journal Office, 1882.

906. ———. *The water-colour drawings of Thomas Bewick.* London, Barbizon House, 1930.

907. Weekley, Montague. *Thomas Bewick.* London, Oxford University Press, 1953.

Bianchi, Mosé, 1845–1904

908. Marangoni, Guido. *Mosé Bianchi.* Bergamo, Istit. Italiano d'Arti Grafiche, n.d.

909. Nebbia, Ugo. *Mosé Bianchi.* Busto Arsizio, Bramante Editrice, 1960.

Bibiena, Galli da *see* Galli da Bibiena

Biddle, George, 1885–1974

910. Biddle, George. *An American artist's story.* Boston, Little Brown, 1939.

911. ———. *Artist at war.* New York, Viking, 1944.

912. ———. *Tahitian journal.* Minneapolis, University of Minnesota Press, 1968.

913. ———. *The yes and no of contemporary art;*

an artist's evaluation. Cambridge, Mass., Harvard University Press, 1957.

Biederman, Charles Joseph, 1906–

914. Biederman, Charles Joseph. *Art as the evolution of visual knowledge*. Red Wing, Minn., Biederman, 1948.

915. ———. *Charles Biederman; a retrospective exhibition with especial emphasis on structurist works of 1936–69*. London, Arts Council of Great Britain, 1969.

916. ———. *Letters on the new art*. Red Wing, Minn., Biederman, 1957.

Bierstadt, Albert, 1830–1902

917. Baigell, Matthew. *Albert Bierstadt*. New York, Watson Guptill, 1981.

918. Ferber, Linda S. and Anderson, Nancy K. *Albert Bierstadt: Art and enterprise*. With a contribution by Helena E. Wright. New York, Hudson Hills, 1991. (Published in conjunction with an exhibition at the Brooklyn Museum).

919. Hendricks, Gordon. *Albert Bierstadt, 1830–1902*. [Exhibition] Sept. 15–Oct. 10, 1972. M. Knoedler & Co., New York, Knoedler, 1972.

920. ———. *Albert Bierstadt: painter of the American West*. New York, Abrams, 1973.

921. ———. *Bierstadt. An essay and catalogue to accompany a restrospective exhibition of the work of Albert Bierstadt*. Fort Worth. Amon Carter Museum, 1972.

Bill, Max, 1908–

922. Centre National d'Art Contemporaine (Paris). *Max Bill; oeuvres 1928–1969*. [Catalogue de] l'exposition, 30 oct.–10 déc. 1969. Paris, Centre National d'Art Contemporaine, 1969.

923. Galerie im Erker, St. Gallen. *Max Bill*. [Ausstellung] 8. April–27. Mai 1967. St. Gallen, Gallerie im Erker, 1967.

924. Gomringer, Eugen, ed. *Max Bill* [von] Max Bense et al. Zum 50. Geburtstag am 22. Dezember 1958. Teufen, Niggli, 1958.

925. Kestner-Gesellschaft, Hannover. *Max Bill*. [Ausstellung] 14. Juni–14. Juli, 1968. Hannover, Kestner-Gesellschaft, 1968.

926. Kunsthaus Zürich. *Max Bill*. [Ausstellung] 23. Nov. 1968–5. Jan. 1969. Zürich, Kunsthaus, 1968.

Bindesbøll, Gottlieb, 1800–1856

927. Millech, Knud. *Bindesbøll Museum*. København, Thorvaldsens Museum, 1960.

928. Wanscher, Vilhelm. *Arkitekten G. Bindesbøll*. København, Køster, 1903.

Bingham, George Caleb, 1811–1879

929. Blad, E. Maurice. *The drawings of George Caleb Bingham with a catalogue raisonné*. Columbia, Mo., University of Missouri Press, 1975. (CR).

930. McDermott, John F. *George Caleb Bingham, river portraitist*. Norman, University of Oklahoma Press, 1959.

931. Rash, Nancy. *The painting and politics of George Caleb Bingham*. London, Yale University Press, 1991.

Bischof, Werner, 1916–1954

932. Bischof, Marco and Burri, René, eds. *Werner Bischof, 1916–1954*. Introduction by Hugo Loetscher. Text by Marco Bischof and Guido Magnaguagno. Boston, Little Brown, 1990.

933. Burri, Rosellina Bischof and Bischof, René, eds. *Werner Bischof*. Introd. by Bhupendra Karia and Manuel Gasser. New York, Grossman, 1974. (ICP Library of Photography, 2).

934. Flüeler, Niklaus. *Werner Bischof*. Luzern/ Frankfurt a.M., Bucher, 1973. (Bibliothek der Photographie, 6).

935. Smithsonian Institution (Washington, D.C.). *The world of Werner Bischof, a photographer's Odyssey*. [Sponsored by the Foundation Pro Helvetia]. Zürich, Die Arche, 1961.

Bishop, Isabel, 1902–

936. Lunde, Karl. *Isabel Bishop*. New York, Abrams, 1975.

937. University of Arizona Museum of Art (Tucson, Ariz.). *Isabel Bishop*. Tucson, Ariz., University of Arizona Museum of Art, 1974.

938. Teller, Susan Pirpiris. *Isabel Bishop: Etchings and aquatints; a catalogue raisonné*. New York, Associated American Artists, 1985. (CR).

939. Yglesias, Helen. *Isabel Bishop*. Foreword by John Russell. New York, Rizzoli, 1989.

Bissen, Herman Vilhelm, 1789–1868

940. Rostrup, Haavard. *Billedhuggeren H. W. Bissen, 1798–1868*. 2 v. København, Kunstforeningen, 1945.

Bissier, Julius, 1893–1965

941. Bissier, Julius. *Julius Bissier, 1893–1965: a retrospective exhibition*. Essay by Thomas Messer. San Francisco, San Francisco Museum of Art, 1968.

942. ———. *Julius Bissier, 1893–1965: an exhibition from the Kunstsammlung Nordrhein-Westfalen, the National Gallery of Ireland, City Museum and Art Gallery, Birmingham, Graves Art Gallery, Sheffield*. London, Arts Council, 1977.

943. Kunstverein Braunschweig. *Julius Bissier, 1893–1965*. [Ausstellung] 21. Dez. 1980–15. Feb. 1981. Katalog [von] Jürgen Schilling. Braunschweig, Kunstverein, 1980.

944. Schmalenbach, Werner. *Julius Bissier.* Köln, DuMont Schauberg, 1974.

945. ———. *Julius Bissier: Tuschen und Aquarelle—Brush Paintings and Watercolors—Encres de Chine et aquarelles.* Frankfurt a.M., Propyläen, 1978.

Bissiere, Roger, 1888-1964

946. Fouchet, Max Pol. *Bissière.* Paris, Fall, 1955.

947. Musée des Beaux-Arts (Bordeaux). *Bissière, Bordeaux, 1965.* [Catalogue of the exhibition]. Bordeaux, Musée des Beaux-Arts, 1965.

948. Musée National d'Art Moderne (Paris). *Bissière* [Exposition] 9 avril–10 mai 1959. Paris, Editions des Musées Nationaux, 1959.

Blake, William *1757-1827*

949. Bentley, Gerald E. and Nurmi, Martin K. *A Blake bibliography.* Minneapolis, University of Minnesota Press, 1964.

950. Blake, William. *The complete writings of William Blake.* Ed. by Geoffrey Keynes. London, etc., Nonesuch, 1957. 1st ed

951. ———. *Letters.* Ed. by Geoffrey Keynes. London, Hart-Davis, 1956.

952. ———. *Jerusalem: the emanation of the giant Albion.* Edited with an introduction and notes by Morton D. Paley. Princeton, N.J., William Blake Trust/Princeton University Press, 1991. (Blake's illuminated books; v.1).

953. ———. *Songs of innocence and experience.* Eedited with an introduction and notes by Andrew Lincoln. Princeton, N.J.,William Blake Trust/ Princeton University Press, 1991. (Blake's illuminated books, v.2).

954. Bindman, David. *Blake as an artist.* Oxford, Phaidon/New York, Dutton, 1977.

955. ———. *The complete graphic works of William Blake.* D. Bindman, asssisted by Deirdre Toomey. New York, Putnam, 1978.

956. Binyon, Laurence. *The drawings and engravings of William Blake,* by L. Binyon. Ed. by Geoffrey Holme. London, Studio, 1922.

957. Blunt, Anthony. *The art of William Blake.* New York, Columbia University Press, 1969. (Bampton Lectures, 12).

958. Bronowski, Jacob. *William Blake, 1757–1827; a man without a mask.* London, Secker & Warburg, 1944.

959. Butlin, Martin. *The paintings and drawings of William Blake.* 2 v. New Haven, Yale University Press, 1981.

960. ———. *William Blake* [exhibition, 9 March–21 May, 1978]. Catalog by Martin Butlin. London, Tate Gallery, 1978.

961. ———. *William Blake, 1757–1827.* London, Tate Gallery, 1990. (Tate Gallery collections; v.5).

962. Cary, Elisabeth Luther. *The art of William*

Blake: his sketch-book, his water-colours, his painted books. New York, Moffat, 1907.

963. Chester, Gilbert Keith. *William Blake.* London, Duckworth/New York, Dutton, 1910.

964. Damon, Samuel Foster. *William Blake, his philosophy and symbols.* Boston/New York, Houghton Mifflin, 1924.

965. DeSelincourt, Basil. *William Blake.* London, Duckworth, 1909.

966. Ellis, Edwin John. *The real Blake; a portrait biography.* London, Chatto & Windus, 1907.

967. Erdman, David V. *The illuminated Blake.* All of William Blake's illuminated works with a plate-by-plate commentary. Garden City, N.Y., Doubleday, 1974. (CR).

968. Essick, Robert N., ed. *The visionary hand; essays for the study of William Blake's art and aesthetics.* Edited and with an introd. by Robert N. Essick. Los Angeles, Hennessey & Ingalls, 1973.

969. ———. *William Blake, printmaker.* Princeton, New Jersey, Princeton University Press, 1980.

970. Figgis, Darrell. *The paintings of William Blake.* London, Benn, 1925.

971. Fitzwilliam Museum (Cambridge). *William Blake.* Catalogue of the collection in the Fitzwilliam Museum, Cambridge. Ed. by David Bindman. Cambridge, Heffer, 1970.

972. Gilchrist, Alexander. *Life of William Blake.* "*Pictor ignotus.*" With selections from his poems and other writings . . . Illus. in facsimile by W. J. Linton . . . with a few of Blake's own plates. 2 v. London/Cambridge, Macmillan, 1863. 1st ed.

973. Hamburger Kunsthalle. *William Blake, 1757–1827.* [Ausstellung] 6. März–27. April 1975 in der Hamburger Kunsthalle. München, Prestel, 1975.

974. Henry E. Huntington Library and Art Gallery, San Marino, Calif. *Catalogue of William Blake's drawings and paintings in the Huntington Library.* By C. H. Collins Baker. San Marino, 1938.

975. ———. *William Blake at the Huntington: an introduction to the William Blake Collection in the Henry E. Huntington Library and Art Gallery, San Marino, California.* [By] Robert N. Essick. New York, H.N. Abrams, 1944.

976. Keynes, Geoffrey Langdon. *A bibliography of William Blake.* New York, Grolier Club, 1921.

977. ———. *Blake studies: notes on his life and works in seventeen chapters.* London, Hart-Davis, 1949.

978. ———. *William Blake's illuminated books; a census.* Compiled by G. Keynes and Edwin Wolf. New York, Grolier Club, 1953.

B

979. Langridge, Irene. *William Blake; a study of his life and art work.* London, Bell, 1904.

980. Lindsay, Jack. *William Blake; his life and work.* New York, Braziller, 1979.

981. Lister, Raymond. *Infernal methods; a study of William Blake's art techniques.* London, Bell, 1975.

982. ———. *The paintings of William Blake.* New York, Cambridge University Press, 1986.

983. Mitchell, W. J. Thomas. *Blake's composite art; a study of the illuminated poetry.* Princeton, N. J., Princeton University Press, 1978.

984. Philadelphia Museum of Art. *William Blake, 1757–1827; a descriptive catalogue of an exhibition of the works of William Blake selected from collections in the United States.* Catalog [by] Agnes Mongan. Philadelphia, The Philadelphia Museum of Art, 1939.

985. Raine, Kathleen Jessie. *Blake and tradition.* 2 v. Princeton, Princeton Unviersity Press, 1968. (The A. W. Mellon lectures in the Fine Arts, 11. Bollingen series, 35).

986. ———. *William Blake.* New York, Praeger, 1971.

987. Swinburne, Algernon Charles. *William Blake. A critical essay.* London, Hotten, 1868.

988. Symons, Arthur. *William Blake.* London, Constable, 1907.

989. Wilson, Mona. *The life of William Blake.* London, Nonesuch, 1927.

990. Tate Gallery (London). *William Blake (1757–1827); a catalogue of the works of William Blake.* Introd. by A. Blunt, with a foreword by John Rothenstein. London, Tate Gallery, 1957.

Blanchet, Thomas, 1614–1689

991. Galactéros-de Boissier, Lucie. *Thomas Blanchet, 1614–1689.* Preface de Jacques Thuillier. Paris, Athena, 1991.

Blanquart-Evrard, Louis-Désiré, 1802–1872

992. Blanquart-Evrard, [Louis-Désiré]. *On the intervention of art in photography.* Trans. by Alfred Harrad. London, Sampson Low, 1864. (Reprinted in *The Collodion Process and the Ferrotype.* New York, Arno, 1973.

993. ———. *Photographie; ses origines, ses progrès, ses transformations.* Lille, Daniel, 1870. (Reprint: New York, Arno, 1979).

994. ———. *Traité de photographie sur papier.* Paris, Librairie encyclopédique de Roret, 1851.

995. Jammes, Isabelle. *Blanquart-Evrard et les origines de l'édition photographique française.* Catalogue raisonné des albums photographiques édités 1851–1855. Genève, Librairie Droz, 1981. (CR).

Blavot, Marie Elisabeth Boulanger *see* **Cavé, Marie Elisabeth (Blavot) Boulanger**

Blechen, Carl, 1798–1840

996. Blechen, Carl. *Karl Blechen, 1798–1840; Ölskizzen, Aquarelle, Sepiablätter, Zeichnungen, Entwürfe.* Ausstellung Berlin 1973. Berlin, Staatl. Museen-Nationalgalerie, 1973.

997. Heider, Gertrud. *Carl Blechen.* Leipzig, Seemann, 1970.

998. National Galerie (Berlin). *Karl Blechen: Leben, Würdigungen, Werk.* Introd. Paul Ortwin Rave. Berlin, Dt. Verein für Kunstwissenschaft, 1940. (CR).

999. Paul-Pescatore, Anni. *Karl Blechen. Sechzig Bilder.* Hrsg. von A. Paul-Pescatore. Königsberg, Kanter-Verlag, 1944.

1000. Schuster, Peter-Klaus, Hrsg. *Carl Blechen: Zwischen Romantik und Realismus.* München, Prestel, 1990. (Dieses Buch erschien anlässlich der Ausstellung in der Nationalgalerie Berlin, 31. August–4. November, 1990).

Bloemaert, Abraham, 1564–1651

1001. Delbanco, Gustav. *Der Maler Abraham Bloemaert 1564–1651.* Strassburg, Heitz, 1928. (Studien zur deutschen Kunstgeschichte, 253).

1002. Roethlisberger, Marcel. *Abraham Bloemart and his sons: paintings and prints.* Marcel G. Roethlisberger; biographies and prints, Marten Jan Bok. 2 v. Doornspijk, Davaco, 1993. (Aetas aurea, 11).

Blondeel, Lancelot, 1496–1561

1003. Bautier, Pierre. *Lancelot Blondeel.* Bruxelles, van Oest, 1910.

Blondel, Jacques Francois, 1705–1774

1004. Blondel, Jacques F. *De la distribution des maisons de plaisance, et de la décoration des édifices en général.* 2 v. Paris, Jombert, 1737/1738. Reprint: Farnsborough, England, Gregg, 1967.

1005. ——— et Patte, Pierre. *Cours d'architecture.* 9 v. Paris, Desaint, 1771–1777.

1006. Prost, Auguste. *Jean François Blondel et son oeuvre.* Metz, Rousseau-Pallez, 1860.

Blossfeldt, Karl, 1865–1932

1007. Blossfeldt, Karl. *Art forms in nature.* Second series. London, Zwemmer, 1932.

1008. ———. *Karl Blossfeldt, 1865–1932: das fotografische Werk.* [Text by Gert Mattenklott]. München, Schirmer/Mosel, 1981.

1009. ———. *Urformen der Kunst.* Berlin, Wasmuth, [1928].

1010. Rheinisches Landesmuseum (Bonn). *Karl*

Blossfeldt, Fotographien 1900–1932. [May 19–June 20, 1976; text by Klaus Honnef]. Bonn, Rheinisches Landesmuseum, 1976. (Kunst und Altertum am Rhein: Führer des Rheinischen Landesmuseum in Bonn, 65).

Bluemmer, Oscar, 1867–1938

1011. Hayes, Jeffrey Russell. *Oscar Bluemmer: Landscapes of sorrow and joy.*[Catalog of the exhibition at the Corcoran Gallery of Art, Washington, D.C., December 10, 1988–February 19, 1989]. Washington, D.C., The Corcoran Gallery of Art, 1988.

1012. ———. *Oscar Bluemmer.* Cambridge [England]; New York, Cambridge University Press, 1991.

Boccaccino, Boccaccio, 1467–1524

1013. Puerari, Alfredo. *Boccaccino.* Milano, Ceschina, 1957.

Boccioni, Umberto, 1882–1916

1014. Argan, Giulio Carlo. *Umberto Boccioni.* Scelta degli scritti regesti, bibliografia e catalogo della opera a cura di Maurizio Calvesi. Roma, de Luca, 1953.

1015. Ballo, Guido. *Umberto Boccioni. La vita e l'opere.* Milano, Saggiatore, 1964.

1016. Bellini, Paolo. *Catalogo completo dell'opera grafica di Boccioni.* Milano: Salamon e Agustoni, 1972.

1017. Boccioni, Umberto. *Gli scritti editi e inediti.* A cura di Zeno Birolli; Prefazione di Mario de Micheli. Milano, Feltrinelli, 1971.

1018. ———. *L'opera completa di Boccioni.* Presentazione di Aldo Palazzeschi. Apparati critici e filologici di Gianfranco Bruno. Milano, Rizzoli, 1969. (Classici dell'arte, 34).

1019. Calvesi, Maurizio and Coen, Ester. *Boccioni. Catalogo generale.* Milano, Electa, 1983.

1020. Grada, Raffaele de. *Boccioni, il mito del moderno.* Milano, Club del Libro, 1962.

1021. Marinetti, F. *Umberto Boccioni, con uno scritto di Umberto Boccioni sul dinamismo plastico.* Milano, Bottega di Poesia, 1924.

1022. Taylor, Joshua Charles. *The graphic work of Umberto Boccioni.* New York, Museum of Modern Art, 1961.

Boeckl, Herbert, 1894–1966

1023. Boeckl, Herbert. *Boeckl: 17 Zeichnungen, 51 Bilder.* Interpretationen von Otto Benesch et al. Wien, Metten, 1947.

1024. ———. *Zeichnungen und Aquarelle.* Ausgewählt und eingeleitet von Werner Hofmann. Wien, Rosenbaum, 1968.

1025. Museum des 20. Jahrhunderts (Wien). *Herbert Boeckl.* [Sonderausstellung] 18 Dez. 1964–14. Febr. 1965. Wien, Museum des 20. Jahrhunderts, 1964.

1026. Pack, Claus. *Der Maler Herbert Boeckl.* Wien, Schroll, 1964.

Boecklin, Arnold, 1827–1901

1027. Andree, Rolf. *Arnold Böcklin, die Gemälde.* Basel, Reinhardt/München, Prestel, 1977. (Schweizer. Inst. für Kunstwissenschaft. Oeuvrekataloge Schweizer Künstler, 6).

1028. Barth, Wilhelm. *Arnold Böcklin.* Frauenfeld, Huber, 1928. (Die Schweiz im deutschen Geistesleben, 11).

1029. Berger, Ernst. *Böcklins Technik.* München, Callwey, 1906. (Sammlung maltechnischer Schriften, 1).

1030. Boecklin, Angela. *Böcklin Memoiren: Tagebuchblätter von Böcklin's Gattin Angela.* Mit dem gesamten brieflichen Nachlass hrsg. von Ferdinand Runkel. Berlin, Internat. Verlagsanstalt für Kunst und Literatur, 1910.

1031. Boecklin, Arnold. *A. Böcklin 1827–1901.* Ausstellung zum 150. Geburtstag veranstaltet vom Magistrat der Stadt Darmstadt. Mathildenhöhe, 23. Oktober–11. December 1977. 2 v. Darmstadt, 1977.

1032. ———. *Neben meiner Kunst: Flugstudien, Briefe und Persönliches.* Hrsg. von Ferd. Runkel und Carlo Böcklin. Berlin, Vita, 1909.

1033. Floerke, Gustav. *Zehn Jahre mit Böcklin.* Aufzeichnungen und Entwürfe von Gustav Floerke. München, Bruckmann, 1902. 2 ed. (A 3rd edition ed. by Hanns Floerke has title: *Arnold Böcklin und seine Kunst.* München, Bruckmann, 1921.)

1034. Graborsky, Adolf. *Der Kampf um Böcklin.* Berlin, Cronbach, 1906.

1035. Hayward Gallery, London. *Arnold Böcklin, 1827–1901.* 20 May–27 June, 1971. An exhibition organized by the Arts Council of Great Britain and the Pro Helvetia Foundation of Switzerland. London, Arts Council of Great Britain, 1971.

1036. Kunstmuseum Basel. *Arnold Böcklin, 1827–1901. Gemälde, Zeichnungen, Plastiken.* Ausstellung zum 150. Geburtstag, veranstaltet vom Kunstmuseum Basel und vom Kunstverein, 11. Juni–11. September 1977. Basel/Stuttgart, Schwabe, 1977.

1037. Meier-Graefe, Julius. *Der Fall Böcklin und die Lehre von den Einheiten.* Stuttgart, Hoffmann, 1905.

1038. Ostini, Fritz von. *Böcklin.* Bielefeld/Leipzig, Velhagen & Klasing, 1904. (Künstler-Monographien, 70).

1039. Ritter, William. *L'art en Suisse: Arnold Böcklin.* Gand, Typ. Siffer, 1895.

1040. Schick, Rudolf. *Tagebuch-Aufzeichnungen aus den Jahren 1866, 1868, 1869 über Arnold Böcklin . . .* Hrsg. Hugo von Tschudi; gesichtet von Cäsar Flaischlen. Berlin, Fleischel, 1903.

1041. Schmid, Heinrich Alfred. *Arnold Böcklin.* München, Bruckmann, 1919.
1042. ———. *Böcklin: Verzeichnis der Werke.* München, Bruckmann, 1903.
1043. Schneider, Max Ferdinand. *Arnold Böcklin, ein Maler aus dem Geiste der Musik.* Basel, Holbein-Verlag, 1943.
1044. Thode, Henry. *Arnold Böcklin.* Heidelberg, Winter, 1905.

Boekhorst, Johannes, 1605–1668
1045. Boekhorst, Johannes. *Jan Boeckhorst, 1604–1668: Maler der Rubenszeit.* [Catalogue of an exhibition] Rubenshaus, Antwerpen, 7.7.–2.9. 1990, Westfälisches Landesmuseum für Kunst und Kulturgeschichte Münster, 16.9.–11.11. 1990. [Konzeption von Ausstellung und Katalog, Jochen Luckhardt in Abstimmung mit Hans Vlieghe; Übersetzung, C.P. Baudisch]. Freren, Luca, 1990.

Boilly, Louis Leopold, 1761–1845
1046. Harrisse, Henry. *L. L. Boilly, peintre, dessinateur et lithographe; sa vie et son oeuvre.* Paris, Societé des Livres d'Art, 1888.
1047. Marmottan, Paul. *Le peintre Louis Boilly.* Paris, Gateau, 1913.

Bol, Ferdinand, 1616–1680
1048. Blankert, Albert. *Kunst als regeringzaak in Amsterdam in de 17e eeuw: rondom schilderingen van Ferdinand Bol.* Lochem: De Tijdstroom, 1975.
1049. ———. *Ferdinand Bol (1616–1680), Rembrandt's pupil.* Trans. from Dutch by Ina Rikel. Doornspijk, Neth., Davaco, 1982. (Aetas aurea: Monographs on Dutch & Flemish painting, 2).

Bologna, Giovanni da *see* Giovanni sa Bologna

Bomberg, David, 1890–1957
1050. Cork, Richard. *David Bomberg.* New Haven, Yale University Press, 1987.

Bon, Bartolomeo *see* Buon, Bartolomeo

Bon, Giovanni *see* Buon, Giovanni

Bondone, Giotto di *see* Giotto di Bondone

Bonheur, Rosa, 1822–1899
1051. Ashton, Dore. *Rosa Bonheur, a life and a legend.* Text by D. Ashton; illus. and captions by Denise Brown Hare. London, Secker and Warburg/New York, Viking, 1981.
1052. Digne, Danielle. *Rosa Bonheur, ou l'insolence: l'histoire d'une vie, 1822–1899.* Paris, Denoël Gonthier, 1980.
1053. Galerie Georges Petit (Paris). *Atelier Rosa Bonheur.* Préface et catalogue analytique par L. Roger-Milès. 2 v. Paris, Petit, 1900 (CR).
1054. Klumpke, Anna. *Rosa Bonheur: sa vie, son oeuvre.* Paris, Flammarion, 1909.
1055. Lepelle de Bois-Gallais, F. *Memoir of Mademoiselle Rosa Bonheur.* Trans. by James Parry. New York, Williams, 1857.
1056. Roger-Milès, Léon. *Rosa Bonheur: sa vie, son oeuvre.* Paris, Societé d'édition artistique, 1900.
1057. Shriver, Rosalia. *Rosa Bonheur. With a checklist of works in American collections.* Philadelphia, Art Alliance/London, Assoc. University Presses, 1982.
1058. Stanton, Theodore. *Reminiscences of Rosa Bonheur.* London, Melrose, 1910.

Bonifazio di'pitati *see* Bonifazio Veronese

Bonifazio Veronese, 1487–1531
1059. Westphal, Dorothee. *Bonifazio Veronese (Bonifazio dei Pitati).* München, Bruckmann, 1931.

Bonington, Richard Parkes, 1801–1828
1060. Cormack, Malcolm. *Bonington.* Oxford, Phaidon, 1989.
1061. Curtis, Atherton. *Catalogue de l'oeuvre lithographié et gravé de R.P. Bonington.* Paris, Prouté, 1939.
1062. Dubuisson, A. *Richard Parkes Bonington: his life and work.* By A. Dubuisson; trans. with annotations by C. E. Hughes. London, Lane, 1924.
1063. Noon, Patrick. *Richard Parkes Bonington, 'On the pleasure of painting.'* New Haven, Yale University Press, 1991. (The book served as the exhibition catalogue for Bonington's paintings, watercolors, and prints shown at the Yale Center for British Art).
1064. Shirley, Andrew. *Bonington.* London, Kegan, 1940.

Bonnard, Pierre, 1867–1947
1065. Beer, François Joachim. *Pierre Bonnard.* Par F.-J. Beer suivi d'un texte de Louis Gillet. Préface par Raymond Cogniat. Marseille, Editions Françaises d'Art, 1947.
1066. Bonnard, Pierre. *Bonnard dans sa lumière.* Préfaces de Marcel Arland et Jean Leymarie. [Paris], Maeght Editeur, 1978.
1067. Bouvet, François. *Bonnard, the complete graphic work.* Introduction by Antoine Terrasse. Trans. from the French by Jane Brenton. New York, Rizzoli, 1981. (CR).
1068. Courthion, Pierre. *Bonnard, peintre du merveilleux.* Lausanne, Marguerat, 1945.
1069. Dauberville, Jean and Dauberville, Henry. *Bonnard; catalogue raisonné de l'oeuvre peint.* 4 v. Paris, Bernheim, 1966–1974. (CR).

1070. Fondation Maeght (Saint-Paul). *Bonnard dans son lumière*. [Exposition] du 12 juillet–28 septembre 1975. Paris, Adrien Maeght, 1975.

1071. Galerie Beyeler Bâle. *Bonnard*. Exposition septembre–15 novembre 1966. Basel, Galerie Beyeler, 1966.

1072. Haus der Kunst München. *Pierre Bonnard*. [Ausstellung]. Haus der Kunst München, 8 Okt. 1966–1 Jan. 1967; Musée du Louvre, Paris, 13. Jan.–15. April 1967. Katalog: M. Antoine Terrasse. München, Haus der Kunst, 1966.

1073. Heilbrun, Françoise and Négu. *Pierre Bonnard: photographs and paintings*. New York, Aperture Foundation, 1988. (Originally publishe in France in conjunction with the exhibition *Bonnard Photographe* at the Musée d'Orsay and produced for the Réunion des Musées Nationaux by Editions Sers, Paris, 1987).

1074. Ives, Colta, Giambruni, Helen, and Sasha M. Newman. *Pierre Bonnard: the graphic art*. New York, Metropolitan Museum of Art; distributed by Abrams, 1989.

1075. Museum of Modern Art (New York). *Bonnard and his environment*. Texts by James Thrall Soby, James Elliott, and Monroe Wheeler, New York; Museum of Modern Art; distributed by Doubleday, Garden City, N.Y., 1964.

1076. Natanson, Thadée. *Le Bonnard que je propose, 1867–1947*. Genève, Cailler, 1951.

1077. Rewald, John. *Pierre Bonnard*. New York, Museum of Modern Art, 1948.

1078. Royal Academy of Arts (London). *Pierre Bonnard 1867–1947*. Winter exhibition 1966; text by Denys Sutton. London, Royal Academy of Arts, 1966.

1079. Terrasse, Antoine. *Bonnard*. Paris, Gallimard, 1988.

1080. ———. *Bonnard; biographical and critical study*. Trans. by S. Gilbert. Cleveland, World (Skira), 1964. (Originally published in French by Floury, Paris, 1927).

1081. Vaillant, Annette. *Pierre Bonnard, ou le bonheur de voir*. Neuchâtel, Ides, 1966.

1082. Villa Medici (Rome). *Bonnard 1867–1947*. Mostra all'Accademia di Francia, Villa Medici, Roma, 18 nov. 1971–23 genn. 1972. Roma, de Luca, 1971.

1083. Watkins, Nicholas. *Bonnard*. London Phaidon Press, 1994.

1084. Werth, Léon. Bonnard. *"Cahiers d'Aujourd'hui."* Paris, Crès, 1923. Nouv. éd.

Bonnet, Louis Marin, 1736–1793

1085. Herold, Jacques. *Louis-Marin Bonnet, 1736–1793. Catalogue de l'oeuvre gravé*. Paris, Rousseau, 1935. (CR).

Bonvicino, Alessandro *see* **Moretto, Il**

Bonvin, Francois, 1817–1887
Léon, 1834–1866

1086. Hôtel Drouot (Paris). *Catalogue de tableaux, aquarelles et dessins par Bonvin*. Déc. 14, 1893 [auction cat.]. Paris, Drouot, 1893.

1087. Moreau-Nélaton, Etienne. *Bonvin raconté par lui-même*. Paris, Laurens, 1927.

1088. Weisberg, Gabriel P. *The drawings and watercolors of Léon Bonvin*. Introductory essay by William R. Johnson. Cleveland, Ohio, Cleveland Museum of Art; distributed by Indiana University Press, Bloomington, Ind., 1980.

Bordone, Paris, ca. 1500–1571

1089. Bordone, Paris. *Paris Bordon e il suo tempo*. Atti del convegno internazionale di studi, Treviso, 28–30 ottobre, 1985. Treviso, Canova, 1987. (Essays by Rodolfo Palucchini et al.).

1090. Canova, Giordana. *Paris Bordone*. Con prefazioni di Rudolfo Pallucchini. Venezia, Alfieri, 1964. (Profili e saggi di Arte Veneta, 2).

1091. Schefer, Jean Louis. *Scénographie d'un tableau*. Paris, Editions du Seuil, 1969.

Borduas, Paul-Emile, 1905–1960

1092. Borduas, Paul Emile. *Refus Global: projections libérantes*. Nouv. éd. augm. d'une introduction de François-Marc Gagnon et suivie de Notes biographiques de Borduas et l'automatisme par Marcel Fournier et Robert Laplante et de Dimensions de Borduas par Claude Gauvreau. Montréal, Parti Pris, 1977. (Collection Projections Libérantes, 1).

1093. Ethie-Blais, J. *Autour de Borduas* Essai d'histoire intellectuelle. Montréal, Les Presses de l'Université de Montréal, 1979.

1094. Gagnon, François-Marc. *Paul-Emile Borduas*. [Catalogue of an exhibition at the Montreal Museum of Fine Arts, from May 6 to August 7, 1988, and at the Art Gallery of Ontario from September 3 to November 13, 1988. Montreal, Montreal Museum of Fine Arts, 1988.

1095. ———. *Paul-Emile Borduas, 1905–1960. Biographie critique et analyse de l'oeuvre*. Montréal, Fides, 1978.

1096. Musée d'Art Contemporain Montréal. *La collection Borduas du Musée d'Art Contemporain*. Montréal, Musée d'Art Contemporain, 1976.

1097. Robert, Guy. *Borduas*. Montréal, Presses de l'Université du Québec, 1972.

1098. ———. *Borduas: ou le dilemme culturel québécois*. Montréal, Stanke, 1977.

Borglum, John Gutzon de la Mothe, 1867–1941

1099. Casey, Robert Joseph. *Give the man room: the story of Gutzon Borglum.* By R. J. Casey and Mary Borglum. Indianapolis, Bobbs-Merrill, 1952.

1100. Price, Willadene. *Gutzon Borglum, artist and patriot.* Chicago, Rand McNally, 1961.

Borromini, Francesco, 1599–1667

1101. Argan, Giulio C. *Borromini.* Milano, Mondadori, 1952. (Biblioteca moderna Mondadori, 300).

1102. Blunt, Anthony. *Borromini.* Cambridge, Mass., Harvard University Press, 1979.

1103. Bruschi, Arnaldo. *Borromini, manierismo spaziale oltre il Barocco.* Bari, Dedalo libri, 1978. (Universale di architettura, 8).

1104. Convegno di studi Borromino. *Atti del convegno promosso dall'Accademia Nazionale di San Luca.* 2 v. Roma, 1967–1972. (Vol. 2 pub. by de Luca).

1105. Del Piazzo, Marcello. *Ragguagli borrominiani; mostra documentaria.* Catalogo a cura di Marcello Del Piazzo. Roma, 1968.

1106. Hempel, Eberhard. *Francesco Borromini.* Wien, Schroll, 1924.

1107. Modiano, Ignacio. *La ciudad en la obra de Borromini; y otros ensayos.* Santiago de Chile, Ediciones del Pirato, 1988.

1108. Munoz, Antonio. *Francesco Borromini.* Roma, Società Ed. d'Arte Illus., 1921.

1109. Perrotti, Maria Venturi. *Borromini.* Milano/Firenze, Electa, 1951.

1110. Portoghesi, Paolo. *Borromini nella cultura europea.* Roma, Officini Ediz., 1964.

1111. ———. *Disegni di Francesco Borromini.* Catalogo a cura di Paolo Portoghesi, Roma, de Luca, 1967.

1112. ———. *The Rome of Borromini. Architecture as language.* Trans. by Barbara L. LaPenta. New York, Braziller, 1968.

1113. Sedlmayr, Hans. *Die Architektur Borrominis.* Berlin, Frankfurter Verlags-Anstalt, 1930.

1114. Thelen, Heinrich. *Francesco Borromini; die Handzeichnungen.* Graz, Akad. Druck und Verlagsanstalt, 1967. (Veröffentlichungen der Albertina, 2).

Bos, Cornelis, 1506–1556

1115. Schele, Sune. *Cornelis Bos; a study of the origins of the Netherlands grotesque.* Stockholm, Almquist, 1965. (Stockholm Studies in the History of Art, 10).

Bosch, Hieronymus van Aken, 1450–1516

1116. Baldass, Ludwig von. *Hieronymus Bosch.* New York, Abrams, 1960.

1117. Bax, Dirk. *Hieronymus Bosch: his picture-writing deciphererd.* Tranlated by M.A. Bax-

Botha. Rotterdam, A.A. Balkema, 1979.

1118. Bosch, Hieronymus van Aken. *Hieronimus Bosch.* Bijdragen bij gelegenheid van de herdenkings-tentoonstelling to s'Hertogenbosch. s'Hertogenbosch, Hieronymus Bosch Exhibition Foundation, 1967.

1119. Combe, Jacques. *Jérôme Bosch.* Paris, Tisné, 1957.

1120. Daniel, Howard. *Hieronymus Bosch.* New York, Hyperion, 1947.

1121. Fraenger, Wilhelm. *Hieronymus Bosch.* Von W. Fraenger mit einem Beitrag von Patrik Reuterswärd. Dresden, Verlag der Kunst, 1975.

1122. ———. *Hieronymus Bosch: das tausendjährige Reich.* Grundzüge einer Auslegung. Amsterdam, Castrum Peregrini, 1969. 2 ed. 1st ed.: Coburg, Winkler, 1947 as his Hieronymus Bosch, 1. (Castrum Peregrini, 86/88).

1123. ———. *The millennium of Hieronymus Bosch.* Trans. by E. Wilkins and E. Kaiser. Chicago, Chicago University Press, 1951.

1124. Gauffreteau-Sévy, Marcelle. *Jérôme Bosch.* Paris, Editions du Temps, 1965.

1125. Gerlach, Pater, O.F.M. Cap. *Jheronimus Bosch: opstellen over leven en werk.* Samenstelling en redactie P.M. le blanc. s'-Hertogenbosch, Vereeniging "Gerlach-Publikaties"; 's-Gravenhage, SDU Uitg., 1988.

1126. Gibson, Walter S. *Hieronymus Bosch; an annotated bibliography.* Boston, G.K. Hall, 1983.

1127. ———. *Hieronymus Bosch.* New York, Praeger, 1973.

1128. Lafond, Paul. *Hieronymus Bosch: the complete prints.* Catalogue raisonné. First English language edition. Revised and supplemented. San Francisco, Alan Wofsy, 1993. (CR).

1129. ———. *Hieronymus Bosch—son art, son influence, ses disciples.* Paris, van Oest, 1914.

1130. Leymarie, Jean. *Jérôme Bosch.* Paris, Somogy, 1949.

1131. Linfert, Carl. *Hieronymus Bosch: the paintings. Complete edition.* Trans. from the German by Joan Spencer. London, Phaidon, 1959.

1132. ———. *Hieronymus Bosch.* Köln, Du Mont Schauberg, 1970.

1133. ———. *Hieronymus Bosch.* Translated by Robert Erich Wolf. New York, Abrams; London, Thames and Hudson, 1972.

1134. ———. *Hieronymus Bosch.* New York, Abrams 1989.

1135. Marijnissen, Roger H., et al. *Jérôme Bosch.* Bruxelles, Arcade, 1972.

1136. ———., and Ruyffelaere, P. *Bosch.* Amsterdam, Mercatorfonds, 1987.

1137. Pfister, Kurt, ed. *Hieronymus Bosch: das Werk*. Potsdam, Kiepenheuer, 1922.

1138. Puyvelde, Leo van. *Le peinture flamande au siècle de Bosch et Breughel*. Paris, Elsevier, 1962.

1139. Reuterswärd, Patrik. *Hieronymus Bosch*. Stockholm, Almquist & Wiksell, 1970. (Uppsala Studies in the History of Art, N.S. 7).

1140. Schuder, Rosemarie. *Hieronymus Bosch*. Wien, Tusch, 1975.

1141. Schurmeyer, Walter. *Hieronymus Bosch*. München, Piper, 1923.

1142. Tolnay, Charles de. *Hieronymus Bosch*. Trans. by M. Bullock and H. Minns. New York, Reynal, 1966.

1143. Unverfehrt, Gerd. *Hieronymus Bosch. Die Rezeption seiner Kunst im frühen 16. Jahrhundert*. Berlin, Mann, 1980.

1144. Vandenbroeck, Paul. *Jheronimus Bosch: tussen volksleven en stadscultuur*. Berchem, EPO, 1987.

1145. Wertheim-Aymes, Clement A. *Hieronymus Bosch; eine Einführung in seine geheime Symbolik, dargestellt am "Garten der himmlischen Freuden," am Heuwagen-Triptychon, am Lissaboner Altar und an Motiven aus anderen Werken*. Amsterdam, van Ditmar, 1957.

Boschini, Marco, 1613–1678

1146. Boschini, Marco. *I gioielli pittoreschi: virtuoso ornamento della citta di Vicenza*. Sala Bolognese, A. Forni, [1976]. (Reprint of the 1677 edition, published in Venice by F. Nicolini).

1147. Sohm, Philip L. *Pittoresco: Marco Boschini, his critics, and their critiques of painterly brushwork in seventeenth- and eighteenth-century Italy*. Cambridge; New York, Cambridge University Press, 1991.

Bosschaert, Ambrosius, 1573–1621

1148. Bol, Laurens Johannes. *The Bosschaert dynasty, painters of flowers and fruit*. Trans. by A. M. de Bruin-Cousins. Leigh-on-Sea, Lewis, 1960.

Bosse, Abraham, 1602–1676

1149. Blum, André. *L'oeuvre gravé d'Abraham Bosse*. Paris, Morance, 1924.

1150. Bosse, Abraham. *Le peintre converty aux précises et universelles règles de son art. Sentiments sur la distinction des diverses manières de peinture, dessin et gravure*. Introduction par Roger-Armand Weigert. Paris, Hermann, 1964. [First published 1649].

1151. ———. *Le XVII siècle vu par Abraham Bosse, graveur du roy*. Texte de presentation par Nicole Villa. Paris, Editions Dacosta, 1967.

1152. ———. *Traité des manières de dessiner les ordres de l'architecture antique en toutes leurs parties*. Paris, l'auteur, 1664.

1153. Duplessis, Georges. *Catalogue de l'oeuvre de Abraham Bosse*. Paris, Revue Universelle des Arts, 1859. (CR).

1154. Servolini, Luigi. *Abraham Bosse e il suo trattato della calcografia*. Bologna, Ratta, 1937.

1155. Smith College Museum of Art (Northampton, Mass.). *Abraham Bosse, 1602–1676*. [Exhibition] Feb.–March, 1956. Northampton, Smith College, 1956.

1156. Valabrègue, Antony. *Abraham Bosse*. Paris, Librairie de l'Art, 1892.

Botero, Fernando, 1932–

1157. Arciniegas, German. *Fernando Botero*. Trans. by Gabriela Arciniegas. New York, Abrams, 1977.

1158. Botero, Fernando. *Fernando Botero: Bilder, Zeichnungen, Skulpturen*. Herausgegeben von Werner Spies; mit Beiträgen von Alberto Moravia [et al.]; einer Biographie von Dörte de Chaisemartin; sowie sechs Kurzgeschichten von Fernando Botero. München, Prestel-Verlag, 1986.

1159. ———. *Fernando Botero*. Catalog of an exhibition, comp. by Cynthia Jaffee McCabe. Hirshhorn Museum and Sculpture Garden, Washington, D.C., 20 Dec. 1979–10 Feb. 1980 and Art Museum of South Texas, Corpus Christi, 27 March–10 May, 1980. Washington, U.S. Govt. Print. Office, 1979.

1160. ———. *Fernando Botero*. Museum Boymans-Van Beuningen, Rotterdam, 27 maart–19 mei 1975. Rotterdam, Museum Boymans-Van Beuningen, 1975.

1161. ———. *Fernando Botero: esculturas*. Bogota, Litografia Arco, 1979.

1162. Ratcliff, Carter. *Botero*. New York, Abbeville Press, 1980.

1163. Sgarbi, Vittorio. *Botero: dipinti, sculture, disegni*. Milano, Mondadori Arte, 1991.

1164. Soavi, Giorgio. *Fernando Botero*. Milano, Fabbri Editori, 1988.

1165. Spiess, Werner. *Fernando Botero*. München, Prestel; distrib. te Neues Pub. Co., New York, 1992.

1166. Sullivan, Edward J. *Botero, sculpture*. New York, Abbeville Press, 1986.

Both, Jan, 1618–1652

1167. Burke, James. *Jan Both: paintings, drawings, prints*. New York, Garland, 1976.

Botticelli, Sandro, 1447–1510

1168. Argan, Giulio Carlo. *Botticelli: biographical*

and critical study. Trans. from the Italian by James Emmons. New York, Skira, 1957. (The Taste of Our Time, 19).

1169. ———. *Botticelli*. Roma, Newton Compton-Skira, 1989. (Grandi Tascabili Economici, Collezione d'Arte Skira/Newton Compton; 5).

1170. Baldini, Umberto. *Botticelli*. Firenze, Edizioni d'arte Il Fiorino, 1988.

1171. Bargellini, Piero. *Botticelli: la vita e l'opere*. Edizione aggiornata a cura di Simone Bargellini. Firenze, Nardini, 1990.

1172. Bertini, Aldo. *Botticelli*. Testo di Aldo Bertini. Milano, Marbello, 1953.

1173. Bettini, Sergio. *Botticelli*. Bergamo, Instituto Italiano d'Arti Grafiche, 1947.

1174. Binyon, Laurence. *The art of Botticelli; an essay in pictorial criticism*. London, Macmillan, 1913.

1175. Bode, Wilhelm von. *Botticelli; des Meisters Werke*. Stuttgart, Deutsche Verlagsanstalt, 1926. 2 ed.

1176. Botticelli, Sandro. *L'opera completa del Botticelli*. Presentazione di Carlo Bo. Apparati critici e filologici di Gabriele Mandel. Milano, Rizzoli, 1967. (Classici dell'arte, 5).

1177. Caneva, Caterina. *Botticelli: catalogo completo dei dipinti*. Firenze, Cantini, 1990. (CR).

1178. Chastel, André. *Botticelli*. Greenwich, Conn., New York Graphic Society, 1958.

1179. Clark, Kenneth. *The drawings by Sandro Botticelli for Dante's Divine Comedy*. After the originals in the Berlin museums and the Vatican. New York, Harper & Row, 1976.

1180. Ettlinger, Leopold David. *Botticelli*. By L.D. and Helen S. Ettlinger. London, Thames and Hudson, 1976.

1181. Gamba, Carlo. *Botticelli*. Trans. by Jean Chuzeville. Paris, Gallimard, 1937.

1182. Hartt, Frederick. *Sandro Botticelli*. New York, Abrams, 1953.

1183. Horne, Herbert P. *Alessandro Filipepi, commonly called Sandro Botticelli, painter of Florence*. London, Bell, 1908. (Reprint, 3v., Firenze, Studio per edizioni scelte, 1986–1987).

1184. Lightbown, Michael. *Botticelli*. 2 v. I: *Life and work*. II: *Complete catalogue*. Berkeley, Univ. of California Press/London, Paul Elek, 1978. (CR).

1185. ———. *Sandro Botticelli; life and work*. New York, Abbeville Press, 1989.

1186. Mandel, Gabriele. *The complete paintings of Botticelli*. Introduction by Michael Levey. New York, Abrams, 1967.(Italian edition, *L'opera completa del Botticelli*. Milano, Rizzoli, 1978)

1187. Mesnil, Jacques. *Botticelli*. Paris, Albin Michel, 1938. (Les maîtres du Moyen Age et de la Renaissance, 9).

1188. Pons, Nicoletta. *Botticelli; catalogo completo*. Milano, Rizzoli, 1989. (CR).

1189. Pucci, Eugenio. *Botticelli nelle opere e nella vita del suo tempo*. Milano, Ceschina, 1955.

1190. Salvini, Roberto. *All the paintings of Sandro Botticelli*. Trans. by John Grillenzoni. 4 v. New York, Hawthorn, 1965. (The Complete Library of World Art, vols. 25–28).

1191. ———. *Tutta la pittura del Botticelli*. 2 v. Milano, Rizzoli, 1958. (Biblioteca d'arte Rizzoli, 32–35).

1192. Steinmann, Ernst. *Botticelli*. Bielefeld/Leipzig, Velhagen & Klasing, 1925. 4 ed. 1st ed. 1897. (Künstler-Monographien, 24).

1193. ———. *Botticelli*. Trans. by Campbell Dodgson. New York, Lemcke & Buechner, 1904. (Monographs on Artists, 6).

1194. Ulmann, Hermann. *Sandro Botticelli*. München, Verlagsanstalt für Kunst und Wissenschaft F. Bruckmann, 1893.

1195. Venturi, Adolfo. *Botticelli*. London, Zwemmer, 1927.

1196. Venturi, Lionello. *Botticelli*. New York, Phaidon, 1961.

1197. Yashiro, Yukio. *Sandro Botticelli and the Florentine renaissance*. London, Medici Society, 1929. 2 ed.

Bouchardon, Edmé, 1698–1762

1198. Bouchardon, Edmé. *Edmé Bouchardon, sculpteur du roi, 1698–1762*. Exposition du bi-centenaire. Catalogue rédigé par Odile Colin. Chaumont, Musée de Chaumont, 1962.

1199. Roserot, Alphonse. *Edmé Bouchardon*. Paris, Librairie Centrale des Beaux-Arts, E. Lévy, 1910.

Boucher, François, 1703–1770

1200. Ananoff, Alexandre. *François Boucher*. Par A. Ananoff avec la collaboration de Daniel Wildenstein. 2 v. Lausanne, Bibliothèque des Arts, 1976.

1201. ———. *L'oeuvre dessiné de François Boucher (1703–1770), catalogue raisonné*. V. I– . Paris, de Nobele, 1966– . (CR).

1202. Boucher, François. *Boucher et les femmes*. [comportant un texte inédit de Georges Brunel]. Paris, Arts et metiers graphiques; Editions du Centre Pompidou, Flammarion, Skira; distributor: Flammarion, 1986.

1203. Boucher, François. *François Boucher in North American Collections: 100 Drawings*. Text by Regina Shoolman Slatkin. Washington, D.C., National Gallery of Art, 1973.

1204. Fenaille, Maurice. *François Boucher*. Par M. Fenaille avec une préface de Gustave Geffroy. Paris, Nilsson, 1925.

1205. Hind, Arthur Mayger. *Watteau, Boucher, and the French engravers and etchers of the earlier eighteenth century.* New York, Stokes, 1911.

1206. Kahn, Gustave. *Boucher; biographie critique.* Paris, Laurens, 1904.

1207. Levallée, Pierre. *François Boucher, 1703–1770; quatorze dessins.* Paris, Musées Nationaux, 1942.

1208. Macfall, Haldane. *Boucher; the man, his times, his art, and his significance, 1703–1770.* London, The Connoisseur, 1908.

1209. Mantz, Paul. *François Boucher, Lemoyne et Natoire.* Paris, Quantin, 1880.

1210. McInnes, Ian. *Painter, King & Pompadour: François Boucher at the court of Louis XV.* London, Muller, 1965.

1211. Musée du Louvre (Paris). *François Boucher: gravures et dessins provenant du Cabinet des dessins et de la Collection Edmond de Rothschild.* Exposition organisée à l'occasion au bicentenaire de la mort de l'artiste. Musée du Louvre 12 Mai–Sept. 1971. Catalogue par Pierette Jean-Richard. Paris, Réunion des Musées Nationaux, 1971.

1212. ———. *L'oeuvre gravé de François Boucher dans la collection Edmond de Rothschild.* Par Pierette Jean-Richard. Paris, Editions des Musées Nationaux, 1978. (Its inventaire général des gravures: Ecole française, 1).

1213. Nolhac, Pierre de. *François Boucher, premier peintre du roi, 1703–1770.* Paris, Goupil, 1907.

Boudin, Eugène, 1824–1898

1214. Benjamin, Ruth L. *Eugène Boudin.* New York, Raymond and Raymond, 1937.

1215. Boudin, Eugene. *Eugene Boudin raconté par lui-même: sa vie, son atelier, son oeuvre.* [Edited by] Gilbert de Knyff. Paris, Mayer, 1976.

1216. Cahen, Gustave. *Eugène Boudin, sa vie et son oeuvre.* Paris, Floury, 1900.

1217. Cario, Louis. *Eugène Boudin.* Paris, Rieder, 1928.

1218. Jean-Aubry, Georges. *Eugène Boudin.* By G. Jean-Aubry with Robert Schmit. Trans. by Caroline Tisdall. Greenwich, Conn., New York Graphic Society, 1968.

1219. ———. *La vie et l'oeuvre d'après les lettres et les documents inédits d'Eugène Boudin.* Par G. Jean-Aubry. Avec la cooperation de Robert Schmit. Neuchatel, Editions Ides et Calendes, 1968. 1st ed. 1922: Paris, Bernheim-Jeune.

1220. Musée Eugene Boudin (Honfleur). *Eugène Boudin, 1824–1898.* [Catalogue of an exhibition]. Honfleur, Societé des amis du Musée Eug ene Boudin, 1992.

1221. Musée National du Louvre (Paris). *Boudin: aquarelles et pastels.* Catalogue établi par Lise Duclaux et Geneviève Monnier. Paris, Réunion des Musées Nationaux, 1965.

1222. Schmit, Robert. *Eugène Boudin, 1824–1898.* 3 v. Paris, Imp. Union, 1973.

1223. Sutton, Peter C. *Boudin: impressionist marine paintings.* With an historical essay by Daniel Finamore. Salem, Mass., Peabody Museum of Salem, 1991.

Bouguereau, William Adolphe, 1825–1905

1224. Baschet, Ludovic. *Catalogue illustré des oeuvres de W. Bouguereau.* Paris, Librairie d'Art, 1885.

1225. Bouguereau, William Adolphe. *William Bouguereau, 1825–1905.* [Catalogue of an exhibition]. Musée du Petit Palais, Paris 9 Feb.–6 May, 1984; the Montreal Museum of Fine Arts, 22 June–23 September, 1984; the Wadsworth Atheneum, Hartford, Conn., 27 October 1984–13 January, 1985. Montreal, Mmontreal Museum of Fine Arts, 1984.

1226. Vachon, Marius. *W. Bouguereau.* Paris, A. Lahure, 1900.

Boulanger, Louis, 1806–1867

1227. Marie, Aristide. *Le peintre poète Louis Boulanger.* Paris, Floury, 1925.

Boulanger, Marie Elisabeth (Blavot) *see* Cavé, Marie Elisabeth (Blavot) Boulanger

Boullee, Etienne-Louis, 1728–1799

1228. Perouse de Montclos, Jean Marie. *Etienne-Louis Boullée, 1728–1799, de l'architecture classique à l'architecture révolutionnaire.* Paris, Arts et Métiers Graphiques, 1969.

Boumeester, Christine, 1904–1971

1229. Goetz, Henri. *Christine Boumeester.* Introduction de Vercors. [Paris]. Maeght, 1968.

1230. Sireuil, Jean. *Christine Boumeester.* Preface de Henri Goetz. Paris, Editions Cercle d'art, 1988.

Bourdelle, Emile-Antoine, 1861–1929

1231. Auricoste, Emmanuel. *Emile-Antoine Bourdelle, 1861–1929.* Paris, Braun, 1955.

1232. Cannon-Brookes, P. *Emile Antoine Bourdelle: an illustrated commentary.* London, Trefoil Books; National Museum of Wales, 1983.

1233. Jianou, Ionel. *Bourdelle.* Par Ionel Jianou et Michel Dufet. Paris, Arted, 1965.

1234. Lavrillier, Carol-Marc. *Bourdelle et la critique de son temps.* Rev. ed. by C.-M. Lavrillier [and] Michel Dufet. Paris, Editions Paris-Musées, 1992.

1235. Lorenz, Paul. *Bourdelle, sculptures et dessins.* Paris, Rombaldi, 1947.

1236. Starodubova, Veronika Vasi'evna. *Emil'-Antuan Burdel.* Moskva, Iskusstvo, 1970.
1237. Varenne, Gaston. *Bourdelle par lui-même; sa pensée et son art.* Paris, Fasquelle, 1937.

Bourdon, Sebastien, 1616–1671
1238. Ponsonailhe, Charles. *Sébastien Bourdon: sa vie et son oeuvre d'après des documents inédits tirés des archives de Montpellier.* Paris, Rouam, 1886.

Bouts, Dierck, 1420–1475
1239. Denis, Valentin. *Thierry Bouts.* Bruxelles, Elsevier, 1957. (Connaissance des primitifs flamands, 2).
1240. Palais des Beaux-Arts (Brussels). *Dieric Bouts, Tentoonstelling, Paleis voor Schone Kunsten Brussel, Prinsenhof Delft, 1957–1958.* Catalogus door Frans Baudouin on K.G. Boon. Brussel, Editions de la Connaissance, 1957.
1241. Schöne, Wolfgang. *Dieric Bouts und seine Schule.* Berlin, Verlag für Kunstwissenschaft, 1938.
1242. Wauters, Alphonse. *Thierri Bouts ou de Harlem et ses fils.* Bruxelles, Devroye Impr., 1863.

Bracht, Eugen, 1842–1921
1243. Bracht, Eugen. *Eugen Bracht 1842–1921.* [Ausstellung]. Kunsthalle Darmstadt, 14. Sept.–15 Nov. 1970. Katalogbearbeitung Hans-Günther Sperlich. Darmstadt, Kunstverein, 1970.
1244. Osborn, Max. *Eugen Bracht.* Bielefeld/Leipzig, Velhagen & Klasing, 1909. (Künstler-Monographien, 97).

Brady, Mathew B., 1823–1896
1245. Horan, James D. *Mathew Brady, historian with a camera.* New York, Crown, 1955.
1246. Kunhardt, Dorothy M. and Kunhardt, Philip B., Jr. *Mathew Brady and his world.* Alexandria, Va., Time-Life, 1977.
1247. Meredith, Roy. *Mr. Lincoln's camera man: Mathew B. Brady.* New York, Dover, 1974. Rev. ed.
1248. ———. *The World of Mathew Brady; portraits of the Civil war period.* Los Angeles, Brooke House, 1976.

Braekeleer, Henri de, 1840–1888
1249. Conrady, Charles. *Henri di Braekeleer.* Bruxelles, Elsevier, 1957.
1250. Gilliams, Maurice. *Inleiding tot de idee Henri de Braekeleer.* Antwerpen, Nederlandsche Boekhandel, 1945.
1251. Vanzype, Gustave. *Henri de Braekeleer.* Bruxelles, van Oest, 1923.

Bramante, Donato, 1444–1514
1252. Baroni, Costantino. *Bramante.* Bergamo, Ist. Ital. d'Arti Grafiche, 1944.
1253. Bramante, Donato. *L'opera completa di Bramantino e Bramante pittore.* Presentazione di Gian Alberto dell'Acqua; apparati critici e filologici di Germano Mulazzini. Milano, Rizzoli, 1978. (Classici dell'arte 45).
1254. Bruschi, Arnaldo. *Bramante.* Foreword by Peter Murray. London, Thames and Hudson, 1977.
1255. ———. *Bramante architetto.* Bari, Laterza, 1969.
1256. Comitato Nazionale per le Celebrazzioni Bramantesche. *Bramante fra umanesimo e manierismo.* Mostra storico-critica, sett. 1970. Palazzo reale Milano. Roma, Istit. Grafico Tiberino, 1970.
1257. Congresso Internazionale di Studi Bramanteschi. *Studi bramanteschi.* Atti del Congresso internazionale. Milano, Urbino, Roma, 1970. Roma, de Luca, 1974.
1258. Forster, Otto Helmut. *Bramante.* Wien, Schroll, 1956.
1259. Raymond, Marcel. *Bramante et l'architecture italienne au XVIe siècle.* Paris, Laurens, 1914.
1260. Suida, William Emil. *Bramante pittore e il bramantino.* Milano, Ceschina, 1953.
1261. Wolff-Metternich, Franz. *Bramante und St. Peter.* München, Fink, 1975. (Collectanea artis historiae, 2).

Bramer, Leonard, 1596?–1674
1262. Barnes, Donna R. *Street scenes: Leonard Braamer's drawings of 17th-century Dutch daily life.* [Catalogue of an exhibition held at the Hoftra Museum] April 9–May 17, 1991. Catalog essays by Donna R. Barnes and Jane ten Brink Goldsmith. Hempstead, N.Y., Hoftra Museum, Hofstra Univertsity, 1991.
1263. Hofrichter, Ferima Fox. *Leonaert Bramer 1596–1674: a painter of the night.* [Catalogue of an exhibition] by Frima Fox Hofrichter; with essays by Walter Liedtke, Leonard J. Slatkes, Arthur Wheelock, Jr. Milwaukee, Patrick and Beatrice Haggerty Museum of Art, Marquette University, 1992.
1264. Kersten, Michiel. *Leonaert Bramer, 1596–1674.* [Catalogue of an exhibition]. Delft, Delft Gemeente Musea, 1994.

Brancusi, Constantin 1876–1957
1265. Brancusi, Constantin. *Brancusi, photographer.* Pref. by Pontus Hulten. Photos selected by Marielle Tabart and Isabelle Monod-Fontaine. Trans. by Kim Sichel. New York, Agrinde, 1979.

1266. Brezianu, Barbu. *Brancusi in Romania.* Bucuresti, Edit. Acad. Rep. Socialiste România, 1976. (1st ed. 1974 has title *Opera lui Constantin Brancusi in Romania*).

1267. Chave, Anna. *Constantin Brancusi: shifting the bases of art.* New Haven, Yale University Press, 1993.

1268. Geist, Sidney. *Brancusi. A study of the Sculpture; an oeuvre catalogue.* New York, Grossmann, 1983. 2 ed. 1st ed. 1968. (CR).

1269. ———. *Brancusi; the sculpture and drawings.* New York, Abrams, 1975.

1270. Giedion-Welcker, Carola. *Constantin Brancusi.* Basel, Schwabe, 1958.

1271. Hulten, (Karl Gunnar) Pontus. *[By] Pontus Hulten, with Natalia Dumitresco, Alexander Istrati.* Milano, Mondadori, 1986. *(English language edition, New York, Abrams, 1987).*

1272. Jianou, Ionel. *Brancusi.* Paris, Arted, 1963.

1273. Klein, Ina. *Constatin Brancusi: Natur, Struktur, Skulptur, Architektur.* 2 v. Köln, W.. König, 1994.

1274. Pandrea, Petre. *Brancusi, amintiri si exegeze.* Bucuresti, Meridiane, 1976. (Biblioteca de arta, 177).

1275. Pogorilovschi, Ion. *Comentarea Capodoperei: ansamblul sculptural Brancusi de la Tirgu-Jiu.* Iasi, Janimea, 1976.

1276. Shanes, Eric. *Constantin Brancusi.* New York, Abbeville, 1989. (Modern masters series, 12).

1277. Solomon R. Guggenheim Museum (New York). *Constantin Brancusi, 1876–1957: a retrospective exhibition.* Catalog by Sidney Geist. New York, Solomon R. Guggenheim Foundation, 1969.

1278. Varia, Radu. *Brancusi.* New York, Rizzoli, 1986.

1279. Zervos, Christian. *Constantin Brancusi: sculptures, peintures, fresques, dessins.* Paris, Editions "Cahiers d'art," 1957.

Brandt, Bill, 1904–1984

1280. Brandt, Bill. *Camera in London.* London/New York, Focal Press, 1948.

1281. ———. *Portraits.* Introd. by Alan Ross. London, Fraser, 1982.

1282. ———. *Shadow of light.* New York, Da Capo, 1977.

Brangwyn, Frank, 1867–1956

1283. Boyd, James D. *The drawings of Sir Frank Brangwyn, 1867–1956.* By J. D. Boyd. Leigh-on-Sea, Lewis, 1967.

1284. Brangwyn, Frank. *Frank Brangwyn, R. A.* Introd. by G. S. Sandilands. London, The Studio, 1928. (Famous water-colour painters, 1).

1285. Brangwyn, Rodney. *Brangwyn.* London, Kimber, 1978.

1286. Bunt, Cyril G. E. *Sir Frank Brangwyn.* Leigh-on-Sea, Lewis, 1949.

1287. ———. *The water-colours of Sir Frank Brangwyn, 1867–1956.* Leigh-on-Sea, Lewis, 1958.

1288. Furst, Herbert E. A. *The decorative art of Frank Brangwyn.* London, Lane/New York, Dodd Mead, 1924.

1289. Galloway, Vincent. *The oils and murals of Sir Frank Brangwyn 1867–1956.* Leigh-on-Sea, Lewis, 1962.

1290. Gaunt, William. *The etchings of Frank Brangwyn; a catalogue raisonné* by W. Gaunt. London, The Studio, 1926.

1291. Marechal, Dominique. *Collectie Frank Brangwyn.* Bruxelles, Stedelijke Musea and Generale Bank, 1987.

1292. Sparrow, Walter Shaw. *Frank Brangwyn and his work.* London, Kegan Paul, etc., 1910.

1293. ———. *Prints and drawings by Frank Brangwyn, with some other phases of his art.* London, Lane, 1919.

Braque, Georges, 1881–1963

1294. Braque, Georges. *Georges Braque* [Exposition]. Orangerie des Tuileries, 10 oct. 1973–14 jan. 1974. Catalogue rédigé par Michèle Richet et Nadine Pouillon. Paris, Editions des Musées Nationaux, 1973.

1295. Brunet, Christian. *Braque et l'espace.* Paris, Klincksieck, 1971.

1296. Cogniat, Raymond. *Georges Braque.* Trans. by I. M. Paris. New York, Abrams, 1980.

1297. Cooper, Douglas. *Braque: the great years.* Catalogue of an exhibition held at the Art Institute of Chicago, Oct. 7–Dec. 3, 1972. Chicago, Art Institute, 1972.

1298. Einstein, Carl. *Georges Braque.* New York, Weyhe, 1934.

1299. Engelberts, Edwin. *Georges Braque.* Oeuvre graphique original. Hommage de René Char. Genève, Cabinet des Estampes du Musée d'Art ed d'Histoire and Galerie Nicolas Rauch, 1958.

1300. Fondation Maeght (Saint-Paul). *Georges Braque: 5 juillet–30 septembre 1980.* Exposition réalisée par Jean-Louis Prat. St. Paul, La Fondation, 1980.

1301. Fumet, Stanislas. *Sculptures de Braque.* Paris, Damase, 1951.

1302. Gallatin, Albert Eugène. *Georges Braque: essay and bibliography.* New York, Wittenborn, 1943.

1303. Gieure, Maurice. *Braque: Dessins.* Paris, Editions Deux Mondes, 1955.

1304. ———. *Georges Braque.* Paris, Tisné, 1956.

1305. Hofmann, Werner. *Georges Braque: das graphische Werk,* Einleitung W. Hofmann. Stuttgart, Hatje, 1961.

1306. ———. *Georges Braque: His graphic work.*

Introd. by W. Hofmann. New York, Abrams, 1961.

1307. Hope, Henry R. *Georges Braque*. The Museum of Modern Art, New York, in collaboration with the Cleveland Museum of Art. New York, Museum of Modern Art; distributed by Simon and Schuster, 1949.

1308. Leymarie, Jean. *Braque*. Trans. by James Emmons. New York, Skira, 1961. (The Taste of Our Time, 35).

1309. Leymarie, Jean. *Georges Braque*. Herausgegeben von J. Leymarie; mit Beiträgen von J. Leymarie, Magdalena M. Moeller und Carla Schulz-Hoffmann. München Prestel-Verlag, 1988.

1310. Mangin, Nicole S. *Catalogue de l'oeuvre de Georges Braque: Peintures 1916–23, 1924–27, 1928–35, 1936–41, 1942–47, 1948–57*. 6 v. Paris, Maeght Editeur, 1959–1973.

1311. Monod-Fontaine, Isabelle. *Braque, the papiers collés*. By I. Monod-Fontaine with E. A. Carmeau and contrib. by T. Clark et al. Washington, D.C., National Galley of Art, 1982.

1312. Paulhan, Jean. *Braque le patron*. Genève/Paris, Editions des Trois Collines, 1946.

1313. Prat, Jean-Louis. *Georges Braque*. [Catalogue of an exhibition, 13 juin au 8 novembre, 1992]. Martigny, Suisse, Fondation Pierre Gianadda, 1992.

1314. Ponge, Francis, et al. *G. Braque de Draeger*. [Par] F. Ponge, P. Descargues, A. Malraux. Paris, Draeger, 1971.

1315. ———. *Georges Braque lithographe*. Préface de F. Ponge. Notices et catalogue établis par Fernand Mourlot. Monte Carlo, Sawret, 1963.

1316. Richardson, John. *Braque*. New York, New York Graphic Society, 1961. 1st pub. by Penguin Books, Harmondsworth, Eng., 1959. (Penguin Modern Painters, 20).

1317. Russell, John. *G. Braque*. London, Phaidon, 1959.

1318. Vallier, Dora. *Braque: the complete graphics*. New York, Alpine, 1984. (CR).

1319. Worms de Romilly, Nicole and Laude, Jean. *Braque: le cubisme fin 1907–1914*. Paris, Maeght, 1982.

1320. Zurcher, Bernard. *Georges Braque, life and work*. Trans. by Simon Nye. New York, Rizzoli, 1988.

Brassaï (Gyula Halasz), 1899–

1321. Brassaï. *Brassaï*. Introduction by Roger Grenier. New York, Pantheon books, ; Paris, Centre national de la photographie, 1988.

1322. ———.Brassaï. *The artists of my life*. Trans. by Richard Muller. New York, Viking, 1982.

1323. ———. *Brassaï présente images du camera*. Paris, Hachette, 1964.

1324. ———. *The secret Paris of the 30's*. Trans. by Richard Muller. New York, Pantheon, 1976.

1325. Durrell, Lawrence. *Brassaï*. New York, Museum of Modern Art, 1968; distributed by New York Graphic Society, Greenwich, Conn.

Breenbergh, Bartholomeus, 1599–1659

1326. Roethlisberger, Marcel. *Bartholomeus Breenbergh: Handzeichnungen*. Berlin/New York, de Gruyter, 1969.

1327. ———. *Bartholomeus Breenbergh: The paintings*. Berlin/New York, de Gruyter, 1981.

Breker, Arno, 1900–1991

1328. Breker, Arno. *Schriften*. Vorwort von Franz Joseph Hall; hrsg. von Volker G. Probst. Bonn/Paris/New York, Marco, 1983.

1329. Despiau, Charles. *Arno Breker*. Paris, Flammarion, 1942.

1330. Grothe, Heinz. *Arno Breker: sechzig Bilder*. Königsberg, [1943].

1331. Noel, Bernard. *Arno Breker et l'art officiel*. Paris, J. Damase, 1981.

1332. Probst, Volker G. *Der Bildhauer Arno Bre-ker; eine Untersuchung*. Bonn/Paris, Marco, 1978.

1333. ———. *Das Bildnis des Menschen im Werk von Arno Breker*. Herausgegeben von Volker G. Probst. Berlin, Studio d l'art; Yeadon, Pa. Distribution Morenas-Art, 1981.

1334. ———. *Das Pieta-Motiv bei Arno Breker: eine Untersuchung*. Bonn/Paris, Marco, 1978.

Breker, Walter, 1904–1980

1335. Breker, Walter. *Marken und "Marken": Walter Breker und die Gebrauchgrafik, 1904–1980*. Hrsg. von Hanspeter Wilberg; mit einem Beitrag von Klaus Popitz. Berlin, Gebr. Mann, 1984.

Bremer, Uwe, 1940–

1336. Rosenbach, Detlev. *Bremer: Werkverzeichnis der Radierungen, 1964–1973*. Hannover, Edition Rosenbach, 1974. (CR).

Bresdin, Rodolphe, 1825–1885

1337. Bresdin, Rodolphe. *Rodolphe Bresdin 1822–1885*, [tentoonstelling] *Haags Gemeentemuseum 27 oktober 1978–14 januari 1979*. Catalogus Dirk van Gelder and John Sillevis. s'Gravenhage, Staatsuitgeverij, 1978.

1338. Gelder, Dirk van. *Rodolphe Bresdin*. Monographie et catalogue raisonné de l'oeuvre. 2 v. The Hague, Nijhoff, 1976. (CR).

1339. Museum of Modern Art (New York). *Odilon Redon, Gustave Moreau [and] Rodolphe Bresdin*. The Museum of Modern Art, New York, in collaboration with the Art Institute of Chicago. Garden City, N.Y.; distributed by Doubleday, 1961.

Breuer, Marcel, 1902–

1340. Blake, Peter. *Marcel Breuer, architect and designer*. New York, Architectural Record in collaboration with the Museum of Modern Art, 1949.

1341. Breuer, Marcel. *Sun and shadow; the philosophy of an architect.* New York, Dodd Mead, 1956.

Breuer, Peter, 1472–1541

1342. Hentschel, Walter. *Peter Breuer.* Eine spätgotische Bildschnitzer-Werkstatt. Berlin, Union, 1952. 2 ed. (Forschungen zur sächsischen Kunstgeschichte, 1).

Brigman, Anne W., 1869–1950

1343. Brigman, Anne. *Songs of a pagan.* Caldwell, Id., Caxton Printers, 1949.

1344. Oakland Museum, Oakes Gallery (Oakland, Calif.). *Anne Brigman; pictorial photographer/pagan/member of the photosecession.* September 17 through November 17, 1974. [Text by Therese Thau Heyman]. Oakland, Calif., The Oakland Museum Art Department, 1974.

Brill, Matthäus, 1550–1584
Paul, 1554–1626

1345. Baer, Rudolf. *Paul Brill; Studien zur Entwicklungsgeschichte der Landschaftsmalerei um 1500.* München, Grassi, 1930.

1346. Mayer, Anton. *Das Leben und die Werke der Brüder Matthäus und Paul Brill.* Leipzig, Hiersemann, 1910.

Briosco, Andrea *see* Riccio, Andrea

Bronzino, Agnolo, 1503–1572

1347. Bronzino, Agnolo. *L'opera completa del Bronzino.* Introdotta da scritti del pittore e coordinata da Edi Baccheschi. MIlano, Rizzoli 1973. (Classici dell'arte, 70).

1348. Emiliani, Andrea. *Il Bronzino.* Milano, Bramante, 1960.

1349. Goldschmidt, F. *Pontorino, Rosso und Bronzino; ein Versuch zur Geschichte der Raumdarstellung mit einem Index ihrer Figurenkomposition.* Leipzig, Klinkhardt und Biermann, 1911.

1350. McComb, Arthur K. *Agnolo Bronzino; his life and works.* Cambridge, Mass., Harvard University Press, 1928.

1351. McCorguodale, Charles. *Bronzino.* New York, Harper & Row, 1981.

1352. Schulze, Hanns. *Die Werke Angelo Bronzinos.* Von Hanns Schulze. Strassburg, Heitz, 1911. (Zur Kunstgeschichte des Auslandes, 81).

1353. Smyth, Craig H. *Bronzino as draughtsman.* An introduction. With notes on his portraiture and tapestries. Locust Valley, N.Y., Augustin, 1977.

1354. Tinti, Mario. *Bronzino.* Firenze, Alinari, 1927. (Piccola collezione d'arte, 10).

Brooks, Romaine, 1874–1970

1355. Breeskins, Adelyn D. *Romaine Brooks, thief of souls.* [Published in conjunction with an exhibition at the National Collection of Fine Arts, Smithsonian Institution, Washington, D.C., 24 Feb.–4 April, 1971]. Washington, D.C., Smithsonian Institution Press, 1971.

1356. Gramont, Elizabeth de. *Romaine Brooks: portraits, tableaux, dessins.* Paris, Braun, 1952.

1357. Morand, Paul et al. *Romaine Brooks.* Paris, Pauvert, 1968.

1358. Secrest, Meryle. *Between me and life; a biography of Romaine Brooks.* Garden City, N.Y., Doubleday, 1974.

Brosse, Salomon de, 1571–1626

1359. Coope, Rosalys. *Salomon de Brosse and the development of the classical style in French architecture from 1565 to 1630.* London, Zwemmer, 1972. (Studies in architecture, 11).

1360. Pannier, Jacques. *Un architecte français au commencement du XVIIᵉ siècle: Salomon de Brosse.* Paris, Libr. Centrale d'Art et d'Archit., 1911.

Brouwer, Adriaen, 1606–1638

1361. Bode, Wilhelm von. *Adriaen Brouwer, sein Leben und seine Werke.* Berlin, Euphorion, 1924.

1362. Böhmer, Günter. *Der Landschafter Adriaen Brouwer.* München, Neuer Filser-Verlag, 1940.

1363. Höhne, Erich. *Adriaen Brouwer.* Leipzig, Seemann, 1960.

1364. Knuttel, Gerhardus. *Adriaen Brouwer; the master and his work.* Trans. by J. G. Talma-Schilthuis and R. Wheaton. The Hague, Boucher, 1962.

1365. Schmidt-Degener, Frederik. *Adriaen Brouwer et son évolution artistique.* Brussels, van Oest, 1908.

Brown, Ford Madox, 1821–1893

1366. Art Gallery, Manchester, England. *Loan exhibition of works by Ford Madox Brown and the Pre-Raphaelites.* Manchester, Autumn, 1911. Manchester, Art Gallery, 1911.

1367. Brown, Ford Madox. *The diary of Ford Madox Brown.* Edited by Virginia Surtees. New Haven, publ. for the Paul Mellon Centre for Studies in British Art by Yale University Press, 1981.

1368. ———. *Ford Madox Brown; a record of his life and work.* London, Longmans, 1896.

1369. Rabin, Lucy Feiden. *Ford Madox Brown and the Pre-Raphaelite history picture.* New York, Garland, 1978.

1370. Walker Art Gallery (Liverpool). *Ford Madox Brown, 1821–1893.* Exhibition organized by the Walker Art Gallery, Liverpool. Liverpool, 1964.

Brown, Lancelot "Capability," 1716–1783

1371. Hyams, Edward. *Capability Brown and Humphry Repton*. New York, Scribner, 1971.
1372. Stroud, Dorothy. *Capability Brown*. With an introduction by Christopher Hussey. London, Faber, 1975. 2 ed.

Brown, Mather, 1761–1831

1373. Evans, Dorinda. *Mather Brown: early American artist in England*. New York, Harper & Row, 1983.

Brueghel, Jan, (the elder) 1568–1625
Jan (the younger) 1601–1678
Pieter (the elder), 1525–1569
Pieter (the younger), 1564–1638

1374. Barker, Virgil. *Pieter Brueghel the elder: a study of his paintings*. New York, Arts Publ. Corp., 1926.
1375. Barnouw, Adriaan Jacob. *The fantasy of Pieter Brueghel*. New York, Lear, 1947.
1376. Bastelaer, Rene van. *Peter Bruegel l'ancien, son oeuvre et son temps*. 2 v. Bruxelles, van Oest, 1908.
1377. Baumgart, Fritz Erwin. *Blumen-Brueghel (Jan Brueghel d. Ä.). Leben und Werk*. Köln, DuMont, 1978. (DuMont Kunst-Taschenbücher, 67).
1378. Bianconi, Piero. *Bruegel*. Bologna, Capitol, 1979. (Collana d'arte Paola Malipiero, 2).
1379. Bruegel, Pieter, the elder. *Bruegel, the painter and his world*. Catalogue realised on the occasion of the exhibit. "Bruegel and his world"; commemorating the 400th anniversary of Bruegel's death, at the Royal Museums of Fine Arts of Belgium, Brussels, 20 Aug.–16 Nov. 1969. Brussels, Lacconti, 1969.
1380. ———. *The complete paintings of Bruegel*. Introd. by Robert Hughes; notes and catalogue by Piero Bianconi. New York, Abrams, 1970.
1381. ———. *Opera completa*. Presentazione di Giovanni Arpino. Apparati critici e filologici di Piero Bianconi. Milano, Rizzoli, 1967. (Classici dell'arte, 7).
1382. Bruhns, Leo. *Das Bruegel Buch*. Wien, Schroll, 1941.
1383. Denuce, Jean. *Brieven en documenten betreffend Jan Brueg el I en II*. Antwerp, De Sikkel, 1934.
1384. Dvorak, Max. *Pierre Brueghel l'ancien*. Wien, Oester. Staatsdruckerei, 1930.
1385. Ertz, Klaus. *Jan Brueghel der Ältere (1568–1625): die Gemälde: mit kritischem Oeuvrekatalog*. Köln, DuMont, 1979. (CR). (Based on the author's thesis, Universität des Saarlandes, 1974; abridged version 1981 in DuMonts Bibliothek grosser Maler).

1386. ———. *Jan Brueghel der Jüngere (1601–1678): die Gemälde mit kritischem Oeuvrekatalog*. Freren, Luca, 1984. (CR). (Flämische Maler im Umkreis der grossen Meister, 1). German and English.
1387. ———. *Jan Brueghel the elder: [catalog of] a loan exhibition of paintings, 21 June–20 July at the Brod Gallery, London*. Introduction by Klaus Ertz. London. Brod Gallery, 1979.
1388. Fierens, Paul. *Pieter Bruegel; sa vie, son oeuvre, son temps*. Paris, Richard-Masse, 1949.
1389. Fraenger, Wilhelm. *Der Bauern-Bruegel und das deutsche Sprichwort*. Erlenbach-Zürich, Rentsch, 1923.
1390. Friedländer, Max J. *Pieter Bruegel*. Berlin, Propyläen, 1921.
1391. Gibson, Walter S. *Bruegel*. London, Thames and Hudson, 1977.
1392. Glück, Gustav. *Das grosse Bruegel-Werk*. Wien, Schroll, 1951. (Based on the author's *Bruegels Gemälde* and *Bilder aus Bruegels Bildern*).
1393. ———. *Pieter Brueghel, the elder*. Trans. by E. B. Shaw. London, Commodore, 1936. 1st German ed.: Wien, Schroll, 1932.
1394. Grauls, Jan. *Volkstaal en volksleven in het werk van Pieter Bruegel*. Antwerpen, Standaard-Boekhandel, 1957.
1395. Grossman, Fritz. *Pieter Bruegel: complete edition of the paintings*. New York, Phaidon [distributed by Praeger], 1973. 3 ed. First 2 eds. published under title: *Bruegel, the paintings*. 1955, 1966.
1396. Hausenstein, Wilhelm. *Der Bauern-Bruegel*. Mit einem Vorwort zur neuen Ausgabe über Bruegel den Belgier. München, Piper. (Klassische Illustratoren, 6).
1397. Jedlicka, Gotthard. *Pieter Bruegel der Maler in seiner Zeit*. Erlenbach-Zürich, Rentsch, 1938.
1398. Klein, H. Arthur. *Graphic worlds of Peter Bruegel the elder, reproducing 64 engravings and a woodcut after designs by Peter Bruegel the elder*. Selected, edited and with commentary by H. A. Klein, New York, Dover, 1963.
1399. Kunsthandel P. de Boer Amsterdam. *De helsche en de fluweelen Brueghel en hun invloed op de kunst in de Nederlanden naar aanleiding van de tentoonstelling, 10 febr.–26 maart, 1934*. Amsterdam, DeBoer, 1934.
1400. Lavalleye, Jacques. *Lucas van Leyden, Peter Bruegel l'ancien; gravures. Oeuvre complet*. Paris, Arts et Métiers Graphiques, 1966.
1401. Lebeer, Louis. *Catalogue raisonné des estampes de Bruegel l'ancien*. Publ. in conjunction with the 400th anniversary exhibition at the Bibliothèque Royale Albert Ier, Sept.–Nov. 1969. Bruxelles, 1969.
1402. ———. *Les estampes de Pierre Bruegel l'ancien*. Avant-propos de Herman Libaers. Antwerpen, Fond Mercator, 1976.

1403. Marijnissen, Roger H. *Bruegel.* Text, catalogue and notes by R. H. Marijnissen. Photographs by Max Seidel, 1971.

1404. Marlier, Georges. *Pierre Brueghel le jeune;* édition posthume mise au point et annotée par Jacqueline Fobie. Bruxelles, Vinck, 1969.

1405. Michel, Emile. *Les Brueghel.* Paris, Allison, 1892.

1406. Münz, Ludwig. *Bruegel; the drawings. Complete edition.* London, Phaidon, 1961.

1407. Palais des Beaux-Arts, Bruxelles. *Bruegel, une dynastie de peintres.* [Exposition] 18 Sept.–18 Nov. 1980. Bruxelles, Europalia, 1980.

1408. Stechow, Wolfgang. *Pieter Bruegel, the elder.* New York, Abrams, 1972. (First published, 1969; in French as *Peter Bruegel l'ancien,* Paris, Editions Cercle d"Art , 1987).

1409. Stridbeck, Carl Gustaf. *Bruegel Studien. Untersuchungen zu den ikonologischen Problemen bei Pieter Bruegel d. Ä. sowie dessen Beziehungen zum niederländischen Romanismus.* Stockholm, Almquist & Wiksell, 1956. (Stockholm Studies in the History of Art, 2). (Reprint: Doornspijk, Davaco, 1976).

1410. Tolnay, Charles de. *Pierre Bruegel l'ancien.* 2 v. Bruxelles, Nouv. S oc. d'Edit., 1935.

1411. Visser, M.J. C. *Pieter Brueghel; en nieuwe interpretatie.* Zutphen, De Walburg Pers, 1984.

1412. Winkelmann-Rhein, Gertraude. *The paintings and drawings of Jan 'Flower' Bruegel.* New York, Abrams, 1969.

Bruguiere, Francis, 1879–1945

1413. Enyeart, James. *Bruguiere, his photographs and his life.* New York, Knopf, 1977.

Brühlmann, Hans, 1878–1911

1414. Frauenfelder, Rudolf. *Hans Brühlmann.* Zeichnungen, hrsg. und eingeleitet von R. Frauenfelder mit dem Katalog der späten Zeichnungen von Rudolf Hanhart. Zürich, Artemis, 1961.

1415. Kempter, Lothar. *Der Maler Hans Brühlmann 1878–1911.* St. Gallen, Tschudy, 1954. (Der Bogen, 42).

1416. Roessler, Arthur. *Hans Brühlmann, ein Beitrag zur Geschichte der modernen Kunst.* Wien, Lanyi, 1918.

Brunelleschi, Filippo, 1377–1446

1417. Argan, Giulio C. *Brunelleschi.* Milano, Mondadori, 1955. (Biblioteca moderna Mondadori, 415).

1418. Baldinucci, Filippo. *Vita di Filippo di Ser Brunellesco, architetto fiorentino . . . ora per la prima volta pubblicata . . . .* Firenze, N. Carli, 1812.

1419. Battisti, Eugenio. *Filippo Brunelleschi.* Milano, Electa, 1976.

1420. ———. *Filippo Brunelleschi, the complete work.* Trans. from Italian by R. E. Wolf. New York, Rizzoli, 1981.

1421. Benigni, Paola. *Filippo Brunelleschi, l'uomo e l'artista: ricerche brunelleschiane.* Mostra documentaria. Catalogo a cura di P. Benigni. Firenze, Archivio di Stato di Firenze, 1977. (Pubblicazione degli Archivi di Stato, 94).

1422. Bozzoni, Corrado. *Filippo Brunelleschi: saggio di bibliografia.* Di C. Bozzoni, Giovanni Carbonara. 2 v. Roma, Istituto di Fondamenti dell'architettura dell'Universitá, 1977–1978.

1423. Brunelleschi, Filippo. *Filippo Brunelleschi, la sua opere e il suo tempo.* 2 v. Papers presented at an international conference held in Florence, Oct. 16–22, 1977, organized by Guglielmo DeAngelis d'Ossat, Franco Borsi, and others. Firenze, Centro Di, 1980.

1424. Carli, Enzo. *Brunelleschi.* Firenze, Electa, 1949.

1425. Fabriczy, Cornelius von. *Filippo Brunelleschi. La vita e le opere.* A cura di Anna Maria Poma. Prefazione di Franco Borse. 2 v. Firenze, Uniedit, 1979. 1st ed.: Stuttgart, Cotta, 1892.

1426. Fanelli, Giovanni. *Brunelleschi.* Firenze, Becocci, 1977.

1427. Folnesics, Hans. *Brunelleschi; ein Beitrag zur Entwicklungsgeschichte der Frührenaissance-Architektur.* Wien, Schroll, 1915.

1428. Hyman, Isabelle. *Brunelleschi in perspective.* Englewood Cliffs, N.J., Prentice-Hall, 1974.

1429. Klotz, Heinrich. *Die Frühwerke Brunelleschis und die mittelalterliche Tradition.* Berlin, Mann, 1970.

1430. Luporini, Eugenio. *Brunelleschi; forma e ragione.* Milano, Ediz. di Comunita, 1964. (Studi e documenti di storia dell'arte, 6).

1431. Manetti, Antonio di Tuccio. *The life of Brunelleschi.* Introduction and critical text edition by Howard Saalman. Engl. trans. of the Italian text by Catherine Engass. University Park, Penn./London, Pennsylvania State University Press, 1970.

1432. Museo Nazionale del Bargello, (Florence). *Brunelleschi scultore.* Mostra celebrativa nel sesto centenario della nascita. Magg.–ott. 1977. Catalogo a cura di Emma Micheletti e Antonio Paolucci. Firenze, Museo Nazionale del Bargello, 1977.

1433. Ragghianti, Carlo Ludovico. *Filippo Brunelleschi, un uomo, un universo.* Firenze, Vallecchi, 1977.

1434. Sanpaolesi, Piero. *Brunelleschi.* Milano, Club del Libro, 1962.

Bruyn, Barthel, 1493–1555

1435. Firmenich-Richartz, Eduard. *Bartholomaeus Bruyn und seine Schule.* Leipzig, Seemann,

1891. (Beiträge zur Kunstgeschichte, N.F. 14).

1436. Wallraf-Richartz-Museum (Cologne). *Barthel Bruyn, 1493–1555.* Gesamtverzeichnis seiner Bildnisse und Altarwerke. Gedächtnisausstellung aus Anlass seines vierhundertsten Todesjahres. Köln, Wallraf-Richartz-Museum, 1955. (CR).

1437. Westhoff-Krummacher, Hildegard. *Barthel Bruyn der Aeltere als Bildnismaler.* München, Deutscher Kunstverlag, 1965. (Kunstwissenschaftliche Studien, 35).

Bryen, Camille, 1907–

1438. Bryen, Camille. *Bryen, abhomme.* Textes réunis et intro-duits par Daniel Abadie. Bruxelles, La Connaissance, 1973.

1439. Musée National d'Art Moderne (Paris). *Bryen.* [Cat. d'une exposition] 14. fév.–30 avril 1973. Paris, Editions des Musées Nationaux, 1973.

Brzeska, Henri Gaudier *see* Gaudier-Brzeska, Henri

Buchser, Frank, 1828–1890

1440. Buchser, Frank. *Mein Leben und Streben in Amerika; Begegnungen und Bekenntnisse eines schweizer Malers, 1866–1871.* Eingel. und hrsg. von G. Wälchli. Zürich/Leipzig, Orell Füssli, 1942.

1441. Lüdeke, Henry. *Frank Buchsers amerikanische Sendung 1866–1871, die Chronik seiner Reisen.* Basel, Holbein-Verlag, 1941.

1442. Wälchli, Gottfried. *Frank Buchser, 1828–1890; Leben und Werk.* Zürich/Leipzig, Orell Füssli, 1941. (Monographien zur schweizer Kunst, 9).

Buerkel, Heinrich, 1802–1869

1443. Buerkel, Ludwig von. *Heinrich Buerkel, 1803–1869, ein Malerleben der Biedermeierzeit.* Erzählt und mit einem Register der Werke ergänzt von seinem Enkel. München, Bruckmann, 1940.

Buffet, Bernard, 1928–

1444. Berge, Pierre. *Bernard Buffet.* Genève, Cailler, 1958. 1st. ed.; 2nd ed., rev. et augm., 1964. (Peintres et sculpteurs d'hier et d'aujourd'hui, 45).

1445. Buffet, Bernard. *Oeuvre gravé.* Préf. par Georges Simenon. Catalogue établi par Fernand Mourlot. Lithographies, 1952–1966. Paris, Mazo, 1967.

1446. Descargues, Pierre. *Bernard Buffet.* Suivi de *Bernard Buffet, peintre ou témoin* par P. de Boisdeffre. Paris, Editions universitaires, 1959. (Témoins du XXᵉ siècle, 15).

1447. Le Pichon, Yann. *Bernard Buffet, 1943–1981.* 2 v. Paris, Garnier, 1986.

1448. Rheims. Maurice. *Bernard Buffet, graveur. 1948–1980.* [Trad. japonaise: préface, Mitsue Himoriu-Lejan, texte Paris-Dayori; trad. anglaise, Bernard Cotnoir]. Nice, Editions d'Aart de Francony; Paris Editions M. Garnier, 1983.

1449. Sorlier, Charles. *Bernard Buffet lithographe.* Paris, Draeger/Trinckvel, 1980.

Buhot, Félix Hilaire, 1847–1898

1450. Bourchard, Gustave. *Félix Buhot.* Catalogue descriptif de son oeuvre gravé. New York, Gordon, 1979. Reprint of 1899 ed., Paris, Floury.

1451. Uzanne, Octave. *Félix Buhot, dessinateur et aquafortiste.* Paris, Quantin, 1888.

Bulfinch, Charles, 1763–1844

1452. Bulfinch, Charles. *The life and letters of Charles Bulfinch, architect, with other family papers.* Ed. by Ellen S. Bulfinch. Boston, Houghton, 1896.

1453. Kirker, Harold. *Bulfinch's Boston, 1787–1817.* [By] H. and James Kirker. New York, Oxford University Press, 1964.

1454. Place, Charles A. *Charles Bulfinch, architect and citizen.* Boston, Houghton, 1925.

Bullock, Wynn, 1902–1975

1455. Bullock, Barbara. *Wynn Bullock.* San Francisco, Scrimshaw Press, 1971.

1456. ———. *Wynn Bullock; photography: a way of life.* Edited by Liliane DeCock. Dobbs Ferry, N.Y., Morgan & Morgan, 1973.

1457. Fuess, David. *Wynn Bullock.* Millerton, N.Y., Aperture, 1976. (The Aperture history of photography, 4).

Buon, Bartolomeo, d. 1464
Giovanni, fl. 1382–1443

1458. Schulz, Anne. *The sculpture of Giovanni and Bartolomeo Buon and their workshop.* Philadelphia, American Philosophical Society, 1978. (Transactions of the American Philosophical Society, 68, pt. 3).

Buonarroti *see* Michelangelo

Buoninsegna, Duccio *see* Duccio di Buoninsegna

Buontalenti, Bernardo, 1531–1608

1459. Fara, Amelio. *Bernardo Buontalenti: l'architettura, la guerra e l'elemento geo-metrico.* Genova, Sagep, 1988.

1460. Galleria degli Uffizi (Florence). *Mostra di disegni di Bernardo Buontalenti, 1531–1608.* Firenze, Olschki, 1968.

Burchfield, Charles, 1893–1967

1461. Baigell, Matthew. *Charles Burchfield.* New

York, Watson Guptil, 1976.

1462. Baur, John I. H. *Charles Burchfield*. New York, Macmillan, 1956.

1463. ———. *The islander: life and work of Charles Burchfield, 1893–1967.* Newark, University of Delaware Press/New York, Cornwall Books, 1982.

1464. Burchfield Center at State University College, Buffalo, N.Y. *Works by Charles E. Burchfield: a tribute from Tom Sisti.* Catalogue of an exhibition 21 Oct.–9 Dec. 1979, held at the Burchfield Center. Buffalo, State University College, 1979.

1465. Burchfield, Charles. *Charles Burchfield.* Catalogue of paintings in public and private collections. Utica, N.Y., Munson-Williams-Proctor Institute, 1970.

1466. ———. *Charles Burchfield's journals: the poetry of place.* Edited by J. Benjamin Townsend. Albany, State University of New York Press, 1992.

Burges, William, 1827–1881

1467. Crook, J. Mordaunt. *William Burges and the High Victorian dream.* London, Murray, 1981.

1468. Pullan, R. P. *The architectural designs of William Burges.* London, Batsford, 1887.

Burgkmair, Hans, 1475–1531

1469. Burkhard, Arthur. *Hans Burgkmair d. Ae.* Leipzig, Insel, 1934.

1470. Falk, Tilman. *Hans Burgkmair. Studien zu Leben und Werk des Augsburger Malers.* München, Bruckmann, 1968.

1471. Feuchtmayr, Karl. *Das Malerwerk Hans Burgkmairs von Augsburg.* Kritisches Verzeichnis anlässlich der im Sommer 1931 von der Direktion der Bayerischen Staatsgemäldesammlungen in Augsburg und München veranstalteten Burgkmair-Ausstellung, Augsburg, Filser, 1931.

Burne-Jones, Edward, 1833–1898

1472. Bell, Malcolm. *Sir Edward Burne-Jones; a record and review.* London, Bell, 1903. 4 ed.

1473. Benedetti, Maria Teresa, and Piantoni, Gianna. *Burne-Jones, dal preraffaellismo al simbolisdmo.* Milano, Mazzotta, 1986.

1474. Burne-Jones, Georgina M. *Memorials of Edward Burne-Jones. With a new introduction John Christian.* 2 v. London/New York, Macmillan, 1993. (First published: London, Macmillan, 1904; 2 ed., 1909).

1475. Cecil, David. *Visionary and dreamer; two poetic painters: Samuel Palmer and Edward Burne-Jones.* Princeton, N.J., Princeton University Press, 1969. (Bollingen series, 35).

1476. Grossman, Fritz. *Burne-Jones; paintings.* London, Phaidon, 1956.

1477. Harrison, Martin. *Burne-Jones.* [By] Martin Harrison and Bill Waters. New York, Putnam, 1973.

1478. Hayward Gallery, London. *Burne-Jones: the paintings, graphic and decorative work of Sir Edward Burne-Jones, 1833–1898.* Exhibition, 5 Nov. 1975–4 Jan. 1976. Catalogue ed. by Penelope Marcus. London, Arts Council of Great Britain, 1975.

1479. Wood, T. Martin. *Drawings of Sir Edward Burne-Jones.* New York, Scribner, 1907.

Burnham, Daniel Hudson, 1846–1912

1480. Hines, Thomas S. *Burnham of Chicago, architect and planner.* New York, Oxford University Press, 1974.

1481. Moore, Charles H. *Daniel H. Burnham, architect and planner of cities.* 2 v. Boston, Houghton, 1921.

Bury, Pol, 1922–

1482. Ashton, Dore. *Pol Bury.* Paris, Maeght, 1970. (Collection monographies, 31).

1483. Bury, Pol. *Pol Bury.* [Catalog of an exhibition held by the Kestner Gesellschaft Hannover, Nov. 20, 1971–Feb. 20, 1972]. Katalogredaktion André Balthazar and Wieland Schmied. Hannover, Kestner Gesellschaft, 1971.

Busch, Wilhelm, 1832–1908

1484. Busch, Wilhelm. *Wilhelm Busch, Lebenszeugnisse. Aus der Sammlung des Wilhelm-Busch-Museums Hannover.* Herausgegeben von Herwig Guratzsch. Stuttgart, G. Hatje, 1987.

1485. Bohne, Friedrich. *Wilhelm Busch: Leben, Werk, Schicksal.* Zürich, Fretz & Wasmuth, 1958.

1486. Gmelin, Hans Georg. *Wilhelm Busch als Maler.* Mit einem vollständigen Werkverzeichnis nach Vorarbeiten von Reinhold Behrens. Berlin, Mann, 1980. (CR).

1487. Niedersächsisches Landesmuseum (Hannover). *Wilhelm Busch 1832–1908.* 3 v. Berlin, Mann, 1982.

1488. Nöldeke, Hermann. *Wilhelm Busch,* von Hermann, Adolf und Otto Noldeke. München, Lothar Joachim-Verlag, 1909.

1489. Novotny, Fritz. *Wilhelm Busch als Zeichner und Maler.* Wien, Schroll, 1949.

Busch, Wilhelm Martin, 1908–1987

1490. Küster, Bernd. *Wilhelm M. Busch; Kunst und Illustration.* Marburg, Hitzeroth, 1990.

Buson, Yosa, 1716–1784

1491. The University of Michigan Museum of Art (Ann Arbor, Mich.). *The poet-painters: Buson and his followers.* January 9–Febru-

B

ary 17, 1974. Ann Arbor, Mich., University
of Michigan Museum of Art, 1974.

Buytewech, Willem Pieterszoon, 1591/92–1624

1492. Havercamp-Begemann, Egbert. *Willem Buytewech*. Amsterdam, Hertzberger, 1959.
1493. Kunstreich, Jan S. *Der geistreiche Willem; Studien zu Willem Buytewech 1591–1624*. Kiel, Kunsthist. Institut der Universität Kiel, 1959.
1494. Museum Boymans-van Beuningen (Rotterdam). *Willem Buytewech 1591–1624*. Text and catalogue by Egbert Havercamp-Begemann. Rotterdam, Museum Boymans-van Beuningen, 1975.

C

Cades, Giuseppe, 1750–1799

1495. Carracciolo, Maria Teresa. *Giuseppe Cades (1750–1799) et la Rome de son temps.* Préface de Giuliano Briganti. Paris, Arthena, 1992.

Caffi, Ippolito, 1809–1866

1496. Avon Caffi, Guiseppe. *Ippolito Caffi, 1809–1866.* Padova, Amicucci, 1967.

1497. Pittaluga, Mary. *Il pittore Ippolito Caffi.* Vincenza, Pozza, 1971.

Caillebotte, Gustave, 1848–1894

1498. Berhaut, Marie. *Caillebotte: sa vie et son oeuvre: catalogue raisonné des peintures et pastels.* Paris, Bibliothèque des Arts, 1978. (CR). New ed. rev. et augm., 1994.

1499. Distel, Anne . . . [et al.]. *Gustave Caillebotte, urban impressionist.* [Catalogue of an exhibition held at the Musée d'Orsay, Paris and at the Art Institute of Chicago]. Paris, Réunion des musées nationaux in association with Abbeville Press. New York Abbeville Press, 1995.

1500. Galerie Brame et Lorenceau, Paris. *Gustave Caillebotte, 1848–1894: Dessins, études, peintures.* [Catalogue of an exhibition]. 28 février – 24 mars, 1989. Paris, Galerie Brame et Lorenceau, 1989.

1501. Caillebotte, Gustave. *Gustave Caillebotte: a retrospective exhibition, 1976–1977.* Museum of Fine Arts, Houston, Oct. 22, 1976–Jan. 2, 1977, The Brooklyn Museum, Feb. 12–Apr. 24. Catalogue by Kirk T. Varnedoe and Thomas P. Lee. Houston, Museum of Fine Arts, 1976.

1502. Varnedoe, Kirk. *Gustave Caillebotte.* New Haven, Yale University Press, 1987.

1503. Wildenstein and Co. Ltd., London. *Gustave Caillebotte, 1848–1894.* A loan exhibition in aid of the Hertford British Hospital in Paris, 15 June–16 July, 1966. London, 1966.

1504. Wittmer, Pierre. *Caillebotte and his garden at Yerres.* Preface by Bernard Lorenceau. New York, Abrams, 1991.

Calamis, fl. 460 B.C.

1505. Studniczka, Franz. *Kalamis, ein Beitrag zur griechischen Kunstgeschichte.* Leipzig, Teubner, 1907. (Abhandlungen der philologisch-historischen Klasse der königl. sächsischen Gesellschaft der Wissenschaften, 4).

Caldecott, Randolph, 1846–1886

1506. Blackburn, Henry. *Randolph Caldecott: a personal memoir of his early art career.* New York, Routledge, 1886 (issued in large and small paper).

1507. Caldecott, Randolph. *Catalogue of drawings by Randolph Caldecott, the property of C. K. Seaman . . . and from other sources.* London, Christie's [sale], June 15, 1936.

Calder, Alexander, 1898–1976
Alexander Milne, 1848–1923
Alexander Stirling, 1870–1945

1508. Arnason, H. Harvard. *Calder.* Photographs by Pedro E. Guerrero. Princeton, N.J., Van Nostrand, 1966.

1509. Bourdon, David. *Calder: mobilist, ringmaster, innovator.* New York, Macmillan, 1980.

1510. Calder, Alexander. *Calder.* Photos and design by Ugo Mulas. Introd. by H. Harvard Arnason, with comments by Alexander Calder. New York, Viking, 1971.

1511. ———. *Calder.* Text by Maurice Bruzeau. Photos by Jacques Masson. Trans. by I. M. Paris. New York, Abrams, 1979.

1512. ———. *Calder: an autobiography with pictures.* New York, Pantheon, 1966.

1513. ———. *Calder, l'artiste et l'oeuvre.* Paris, Maeght, 1971. (Archives Maeght, 1).

1514. Fondation Maeght (Saint-Paul de Vence). *Calder.* Exposition du 2 avril au mai 1969.

St.-Paul, Fondation Maeght, 1969.

1515. Hayes, Margaret Calder. *Three Alexander Calders: a family memoir.* Introd. by Malcolm Cowley. Middlebury, Vt., Eriksson, 1977.

1516. Lipman, Jean. *Calder's universe.* By Jean Lipman and Ruth Wolfe, editorial director. New York, Viking, 1976. (A traveling exhibition based on this book began at the Whitney Museum of American Art in New York, Oct. 14, 1976–Feb. 6, 1977).

1517. Marchesseau, Daniel. *The intimate world of Alexander Calder.* Trans. by Eleanor Levieux and Barbara Shuey. Paris, Solange Thierry. Distrib. by Harry N. Abrams, New York, 1989.

1518. Marter, Joan. *Alexander Calder.* New York, Abbeville, Press, 1984.

1519. ———. *Alexander Calder.* New York, Cambridge University Press, 1992.

1520. Sims, Patterson. *Alexander Calder, a concentration of works from the permanent collection of the Whitney Museum of American Art: a 50th anniversary exhibition, Feb. 17–May 3, 1981.* New York, Whitney Museum of American Art, 1981.

1521. Solomon R. Guggenheim Museum (New York). *Alexander Calder: a retrospective exhibition by the Solomon R. Guggenheim Museum and Musée National d'Art Moderne, Paris.* New York, 1964.

1522. Sweeney, James J. *Alexander Calder.* New York, Museum of Modern Art, 1951.

Calderara, Antonio, 1903–

1523. Mendes, Murillo. *Antonio Calderara, pitture dal 1925 al 1965.* Milano, All'Insegna del Pesce d'Oro, 1965. (Arte moderna italiana, 52).

1524. Saba Sardi, Francesco. *Calderara.* Milano, All'Insegna del Pesce d'Oro, 1965. (Antologia di punto, 2).

Callahan, Harry, 1912–

1525. Bunnell, Peter C. *Harry Callahan.* New York, American Federation of the Arts, 1978.

1526. Callahan, Harry. *Photographs.* Santa Barbara, Calif., El Mochuelo Gallery, 1964. (Monograph series, 1).

1527. Paul, Sherman. *The photography of Harry Callahan.* New York, Museum of Modern Art, 1967.

1528. Szarkowski, John, ed. *Callahan.* [Published in conjunction with an exhibition at the Museum of Modern Art, New York, December 2, 1976–February 8, 1977]. Millerton, N.Y., Aperture, 1976.

1529. Tow, Robert and Winsor, Ricker, eds. *Harry Callahan: color, 1941–1980.* Foreword by Jonathan Williams; afterword by A. D. Coleman. Providence, R.I., Matrix Publications, 1980.

Callot, Jacques, 1592–1635

1530. Albertina (Vienna). *Jacques Callot und sein Kreis. Werke aus dem Besitz der Albertina und Leihgaben aus den Uffizien.* Wien, Albertina, 1969. (Die Kunst der Graphik, 5).

1531. Bechtel, Edwin de T. *Jacques Callot.* New York, Braziller, 1955.

1532. Bibliothèque Nationale (Paris). *Jacques Callot, étude de son oeuvre gravé.* [Par] J. Cain, R.-A. Weigert [et] P. A. Lemoigne. Paris, Editions des Bibliothèques Nationales, 1935.

1533. Bonchot, Henri. *Jacques Callot, sa vie, son oeuvre et ses continuateurs.* Paris, Hachette, 1889.

1534. Bouchot-Saupique, Jacqueline. *Jacques Callot, 1592–1635; quatorze dessins.* Paris, Musées Nationaux, 1942.

1535. Bruwaert, Edmond. *Jacques Callot, biographie critique.* Paris, Laurens, 1913.

1536. ———. *Vie de Jacques Callot, graveur lorrain, 1592–1635.* Paris, Imprimerie Nationale, 1912.

1537. Callot, Jacques. *Jacques Callot, 1592–1635.* By the Department of Art, Brown University at the Museum of Art, Rhode Island School of Design, March 5–April 11, 1970. Providence, Museum of Art, Rhode Island School of Design, 1970.

1538. Daniel, Howard. *The world of Jacques Callot.* New York, Lear, 1948.

1539. Lieure, J. *Jacques Callot.* 2 pts. in 5 v. Editions de la Gazette des Beaux-Arts, 1924–1929. (CR). (Reprint: San Francisco, Alan Wofsy, 1989; 2 v.).

1540. Meaume, Edouard. *Recherches sur la vie et les ouvrages de Jacques Callot, suite au Peintre-graveur français de Robert-Dumesnil.* 2 v. Paris, Renouard, 1860.

1541. Nasse, Hermann. *Jacques Callot.* Leipzig, Klinkhardt & Biermann, 1919. 2 ed. (Meister der Graphik, 1).

1542. National Gallery of Art (Washington, D.C.). *Jacques Callot: prints and related drawings.* H. Diane Russell, Jeffrey Blanchard, theater section. John Krill, technical appendix. Washington, D.C., National Gallery of Art, 1975.

1543. Plan, Pierre Paul. *Jacques Callot maître graveur (1593–1635), suivi d'un catalogue raisonné et accompagné de la réproduction de 282 estampes et de deux portraits.* Bruxelles, van Oest, 1911. (CR).

1544. Sadoul, Georges. *Jacques Callot, miroir de son temps.* Paris, Gallimard, 1969.

1545. Schroeder, Thomas. *Jacques Callot. Das gesamte Werk.* 2 v. München, Rogner & Bernhard, 1971.

1546. Ternois, Daniel. *L'art de Jacques Callot.* Paris, de Nobele, 1962.

1547. ———. *Jacques Callot; catalogue complet de son oeuvre dessiné.* Paris, de Nobele, 1962. (CR).

1548. Zahn, Leopold. *Die Handzeichnungen des Jacques Callot, unter besonderer Berücksichtigung der Petersburger Sammlung.* München, Recht, 1923.

Camaino, Tino da *see* **Tino da Camaino**

Cambiaso, Luca, 1527–1585

1549. Cambiaso, Luca. *The Genoese Renaissance, grace and geometry: paintings and drawings by Luca Cambiaso from the Suida-Manning Collection.* By Bertina Suida Manning and Robert L. Manning. Houston, Museum of Fine Arts, 1974.

1550. Ente manifestazioni genovesi. *Luca Cambiaso e la sua fortuna.* [Mostra] Genova, Palazzo dell'Accademia, guigno–ottobre 1956. Genova, Ente manifestazioni genovesi, 1956.

1551. Suida Manning, Bertina. *Luca Cambiaso, la vita e le opere.* A cura di Bertina Suida Manning e William Suida. Milano, Ceschina, 1957.

Cameron, Charles, 1740–1812

1552. Arts Council of Great Britain. *Charles Cameron, ca. 1740–1812; architectural drawings and photographs from the Hermitage collection, Leningrad and Architectural Museum, Moscow.* [Exhibition] English Speaking Union Gallery, Edinburgh, August 19–Sept. 9, 1967. London, Arts Council of Great Britain, 1967.

1553. Cameron, Charles. *The baths of the Romans explained and illustrated: with the restorations of Palladio corrected and improved.* To which is prefixed an introductory preface, pointing out the nature of the work; and a dissertation upon the state of the arts during the different periods of the Roman empire. London, Leacroft, 1775.

1554. Lukomskii, Georgii Kreskentévich. *Charles Cameron (1740–1812). An illustrated monograph on his life and work in Russia. . . .* Adapted into English and edited by Nicholas de Gren, with a foreword by the Princess Romanovsky-Pavlovsky, an introduction by D. Talbot Rice . . . and historical notes and bibliography. London, Nicholson & Watson, 1943.

1555. Rae, Isobel. *Charles Cameron, architect to the court of Russia.* London, Elek, 1971.

Cameron, David Young, 1865–1945

1556. Cameron, David Young. *Sir D. Y. Cameron, R. A.* Introduction by Malcolm C. Salaman. 2 v. London, The Studio, 1925–1932. (Modern Masters of Etching, 7, 33).

1557. Rinder, Frank. *D. Y. Cameron; an illustrated catalogue of his etched work, with introductory essay and descriptive notes on each plate.* Glasgow, Maclehose, 1912.

Cameron, Julia Margaret, 1815–1879

1558. Gernsheim, Helmut. *Julia Margaret Cameron, her life and photographic work.* Millerton, N.Y., Aperture Press, 1975.

1559. Hill, Brian. *Julia Margaret Cameron; a Victorian family portrait.* London, Owen, 1973.

1560. Ovenden, Graham, ed. *A Victorian album: Julia Margaret Cameron and her circle.* Introductory essay by Lord David Cecil. New York, Da Capo, 1975.

Campagna, Girolamo, ca. 1550–1626

1561. Rossi, Paola. *Girolamo Campagna.* Presentazione di Rodolfo Palluchini. Verona, Vita Veronese, 1968. (Monografie d'arte, 8).

1562. Tomofiewitsch, Wladimir. *Girolamo Campagna: Studien zur venezianischen Plastik um das Jahr 1600.* München, Fink, 1972.

Campalans, Jusep Torres *see* **Torres Campalans, Jusep**

Campbell, Colen, 1676–1729

1563. Campbell, Colen. *Vitruvius Britannicus, or the British architect.* 3 v. London, 1715–1725. (Reprint: New York, Blom, 1967).

1564. Stuchbury, Howard E. *The architecture of Colen Campbell.* Cambridge, Mass., Harvard University Press, 1967.

Campen, Jacob van, 1595–1657

1565. Swillens, P. T. A. *Jacob van Campen, schilder en bouwmeester, 1595–1657.* Assen, Van Gorcum, 1961. (Van Gorcum's historische bibliotheek, 63).

Campendonk, Heinrich, 1889–1957

1566. Engles, Mathias Toni. *Campendonk. Holzschnitte. Werkverzeichnis.* Stuttgart, Kohlhammer, 1959. (CR).

1567. ———. *Heinrich Campendonk.* Köln, Seemann, 1957. (Monografien zur rheinisch-westfälischen Kunst der Gegenwart, 8).

1568. Firmenich, Andrea. *Heinrich Campendonk (1889–1957); Leben und expressionistisches Werk.* Mit Werkkatalog des malerischen Oeuvres. Recklinghausen, Bongers, 1989. CR).

1569. Wember, Paul. *Heinrich Campendonk; Krefeld 1889–1957.* Amsterdam. Krefeld, Scherpe, 1960.

Camphuysen, Rafael Govertsz, 1597–1657

1570. Bachmann, Fredo. *Der Landschaftsmaler Rafael Govertsz*. Camphuysen, München, Delp, 1980.

Campigli, Massimo, 1895–1971

1571. Appolonio, Umbro. *Campigli*. Venezia, Cavallino, 1958.

1572. Campigli, Massimo. *Scrupoli*. Venezia, Cavallino, 1955.

1573. Cardazzo, Carlo. *Campigli*. Venezia, Cavallino, 1958.

1574. Cassou, Jean. *Campigli*. Présenté par J. Cassou avec un texte de l'artiste. Paris, Ed. "L'Oeuvre gravée," 1957.

1575. Ente manifestazioni milanesi. *Mostra di Massimo Campigli*. Scritti di M. Campigli et al. Catalogo a cura di Giuseppe L. Mele. Giugno 1967, Milano, Palazzo reale. Milano, Moneta, 1967.

1576. Galerie de France (Paris). *Campigli*. Album édité à l'occasion de l'exposition des oeuvres récentes de Campigli, 1 juin–17 juillet 1965. Paris, Galerie de France, 1965.

1577. ———. *Les idoles de Campigli.* . . . Editée à l'occasion de l'exposition des oeuvres de Campigli, mai 1961. Paris, Galerie de France, 1961.

Campin, Robert *see* Master of Flémalle

Canale, Antonio, 1697–1768

1578. Baetjer, Katharine and J.G. Links. *Canaletto*. [Catalogue of an exhibition at the Metropolitan Museum of Art, New York, Oct. 30, 1989–Jan 21, 1990]. New York, Metropolitan Museum of Art, 1989; distributed by Harry N. Abrams.

1579. Barcham, William L. *The imaginary view scenes of Antonio Canaletto*. New York/London, Garland, 1977.

1580. Berto Giuseppe. *L'opera completa del Canaletto*. Milano, Rizzoli, 1981. (Classici dell'arte Rizzoli, 18).

1581. Brandi, Cesare. *Canaletto*. Milano, Mondadori, 1960. (Biblioteca moderna Mondadori, 596).

1582. Bromberg, Ruth. *Canaletto's etchings; a catalogue and study illustrating and describing the known states, including those hitherto unrecorded*. London/New York, Sotheby Parke Bernet, 1974.

1583. Constable, William G. *Canaletto*. Catalogue of an exhibition held at the Art Gallery of Toronto, Oct. 17–Nov. 15, 1964, and subsequently at the National Gallery of Canada, Ottawa, and the Museum of Fine Arts, Montreal. (n. p.), 1964.

1584. ———. *Canaletto, Giovanni Antonio Canal, 1697–1768*. 2 v. New York, Clarendon Press, 1962; 2 ed., revised by J. G. Links, 1976.

1585. Corboz, Andre. *Canaletto: una Venezia immaginaria*. 2 v. Milano, Alfieri-Electa, 1985.

1586. Ferrari, Giulio. *Les deux Canaletto, Antonio Canal, Bernardo Bellotto, peintres*. Torino, Celanza, 1914.

1587. Hadeln, Detlev von. *The drawings of Antonio Canal, called Canaletto*. Trans. by C. Dodgson. London, Duckworth, 1929.

1588. Kainen, Jacob. *The etchings of Canaletto*. Washington, Smithsonian Press, 1967.

1589. Levey, Michael. *Canaletto paintings in the collection of her Majesty the Queen*. London, Phaidon, 1964.

1590. Links, J. G. *Canaletto*. Ithaca, N.Y., Cornell University Press, 19

1591. ———. *Canaletto and his patrons*. New York, New York University Press, 1977.

1592. ———. *Views of Venice by Canaletto*. Engraved by A. Visentini. New York, Dover, 1971.

1593. Martin, Gregory. *Canaletto: Paintings, drawings and etchings*. London, Folio Society, 1967.

1594. Meyer, Rudolph. *Die beiden Canaletto, Antonio Canale und Bernardo Belotto; Versuch einer Monographie der radierten Werke beider Meister*. Dresden, Verlag des Verfassers, 1878.

1595. Moschini, Vittorio. *Canaletto*. Milano, Giunti-Martello, 1978. 3d ed. 1s (1st ed. 1954, 2d. ed. 1963).

1596. Moureau, Adrien. *Antonio Canal, dit le Canaletto*. Paris, Librairie de l'Art, 1894.

1597. Pallucchini, Rodolfo. *Le acqueforti del Canaletto*. Venezia, Guarnati, 1945. (Serie Brunetto Fanelli, 1).

1598. Parker, Karl T. *The drawings of Antonio Canaletto in the collection of His Majesty the King at Windsor Castle*. London, Phaidon, 1948. (2 ed. with an appendix to the catalogue by Charlotte Crawley. Bologna, Nuova Alfa Editoriale, 1990).

1599. Pignatti, Terisio. *Antonio Canal detto Il Canaletto*. Milano, Martello-Giunti, 1976.

1600. ———. *Canaletto disegni*. Scelti e annotati da T. Pignatti. Firenze, Nuova Italia, 1969.

1601. ———. *Canaletto; selected drawings*. Trans. by Stella Rudolph. University Park, Penn., Pennsylvania State University Press, 1970.

1602. ———. *Il quaderno di disegni del Canaletto alle gallerie di Venezia*. Milano, Guarnati, 1958.

1603. ———. *Das venezianische Skizzenbuch von Canaletto*. Trans. Erich Steingräber. 2 v. München, Callwey, n.d.

1604. Potterton, Homan. *Pageant and panorama; the elegant world of Canaletto*. Oxford, Phaidon, 1978.

1605. Puppi, Lionello, and Berto, Giuseppe. *The complete paintings of Canaletto.* Introd. by David Bindman, notes and catalogue by L. Puppi. New York, Abrams, 1968.

1606. ———. *L'opera completa del Canaletto.* Milano, Rizzoli, 1968. (Classici dell'arte, 18).

1607. Salamon, Harry. *Catalogo completo delle incisioni di Giovanni Antonio Canal detto Il Canaletto.* Milano, Salamon e Agustoni, 1971.

1608. Uzanne, L. G. *Les Canaletto: l'oncle et le neveu, le maître et le disciple.* Antonio da Canal, 1697–1768; Bernardo Bellotto, 1723–1780. Paris, Nilsson, 1925.

1609. ———. *Les deux Canaletto: biographie critique.* Paris, Laurens, 1907.

1610. Watson, Francis J. B. *Canaletto.* London, Elek, 1954. 2 ed.

Canaletto *see* Canale, Antonio; *see also* Bellotto, Bernardo

Canina, Luigi, 1795–1856

1611. Canina, Luigi. *L'architettura antica descritta e dimonstrata coi monumenti.* 6 v. Roma, Canina, [1830]–1844.

1612. ———. *Gli edifizi di Roma antica.* 6 v. Roma, Canina, 1848–1856.

1613. ———. *Richerche sull'architettura piu propria dei tempi cristiani.* Roma, Canina, 1843.

1614. Raggi, Oreste. *Della vita e delle opere di Luigi Canina, architetto e archeologo di Casal Monferrato.* Casal Monferrato, Nanni, 1857.

Cano, Alonso, 1601–1667

1615. Bernales Ballestros, Jorge. *Alonso Cano en Sevilla.* Sevilla, Diputacion Provincial, 1976.

1616. Cano, Alonso. *[Tercer] centenario de la muerte de Alonso Cano en Granada.* 2 v. (1) Estudios, (2) Catalogo de la exposición, Hospital real, jun. 28–jul. 31 1968. Granada, Ministerio de Educación y Ciencia, 1968.

1617. Diaz-Jiménez y Molleda, Eloy. *El escultor Alonso Cano, 1601–1667.* Madrid, Suarez, 1943. (Monografias de critica artistica, 1).

1618. Martinez Chumillas, Manuel. *Alonso Cano estudio monografico de la obra del insegne racionero que fue de la Catedral de Granada.* Madrid, Jaime, 1948.

1619. Wethey, Harold E. *Alonso Cano: painter, sculptor, architect.* Princeton, N.J., Princeton University Press, 1955.

Canova, Antonio, 1757–1822

1620. Albrizzi, Isabella. *Opere di scultura e di plastica di Antonio Canova descritte da Isabella Albrizzi nata Teotochi.* 4 v. Pisa, Capurro, 1826.

1621. ———. *The works of Antonio Canova, in sculpture and modelling.* Engraved in outline by Henry Moses. With description from the Italian of the Countess Albrizzi and a biographical memoir by Count Cicognara. 3 v. London, Bohn, 1849. (2 ed.: London, Rowett, 1824; repr. 1887. 3 ed.: Boston, Osgood, 1876–1878. 2 v.).

1622. Argan, Giulio C. *Antonio Canova.* A cura di Elisa Debenedetti. Roma, Bulzoni, 1969. (Univ. di Roma. Fac. di Lettere e Filosofia, Anno academico 1968–69).

1623. Barbieri, Franco. *Canova scultore, pittore, architetto a Possagno.* Padua, Biblos Edizioni, 1990.

1624. Bassi, Elena. *Canova.* Bergamo, Ist. Ital. d'Arti Grafiche, 1943.

1625. Canova, Antonio. *Pensieri su le belli arti.* Milano, Bettoni, 1824.

1626. ———. *Antonio Canova.* [Catalogue of an exhibition held at the Museo Correr, Venice and the Gipsoteca, Possagno, March 22–September 30, 1992]. Catalogo a cura di Giuseppe Pavenello e Giandomenico Romanelli. Venezia, Marsilio, 1992.

1627. ———. *I quaderni di viaggio, 1779–1780.* Ed. e commento a cura di E. Bassi. Venezia, Ist. per la collab. culturale, 1959. (Fonti e documenti per la storia dell'arte veneta, 2).

1628. Cicognara, Leopoldo. *Biografia di Antonio Canova.* Venezia, Missiaglia, 1823.

1629. ———. *Lettere ad Antonio Canova.* A cura di Gianni Venturi. Urbino, Argalia, 1973.

1630. Foratti, Aldo. *Antonio Canova, 1757–1822.* Milano, Caddeo, 1922.

1631. Licht, Fred. *Canova.* Photographs by David Finn. New York, Abbeville Press, 1983.

1632. Malamani, Vittorio. *Canova.* Milano, Hoepli, 1911.

1633. Memes, John Smythe. *Memoirs of Antonio Canova, with a critical analysis of his works, and an historical view of modern sculpture.* Edinburgh, Constable, 1825.

1634. Meyer, Alfred G. *Canova.* Bielefeld/Leipzig, Velhagen & Klasing, 1898. (Künstler-Monographien, 36).

1635. Missirini, Melchiorre. *Della vita di Antonio Canova libri quattro.* 2 v. Milano, Bettoni, 1824–1825.

1636. Museo Correr (Venice). *Antonio Canova.* [Catalogue of an exhibition]. Venezia, Museo Correr, 1992.

1637. Munoz, Antonio. *Antonio Canova: le opere.* Roma, Palombi, 1957.

1638. Pantaleoni, Massimo. *Disegni anatomici di Antonio Canova.* Roma, Istituto Superiore di Sanita—Fondazione Emanuele Paterno, 1949.

1639. Paravia, Pier Alessandro. *Notizie intorno alla vita di Antonio Canova.* Giuntovi il catalogo cronologico di tutte le sue opere. Venezia, Orlandelli, 1822.

1640. Praz, Mario. *L'opera completa del Canova*. Presentazione di Mario Praz. Apparati critici e filologici di Giuseppe Pavanello. Milano, Rizzoli, 1976. (Classici dell'arte, 85).

1641. Quatremère de Quincy. *A. C. Canova, et ses ouvrages, ou Mémoires historiques sur la vie et les travaux de ce célèbre artiste*. Paris, LeClerc, 1836. 2 ed.

1642. Stefani, Ottorino. *Canova pittore*. Milano, Electa, 1992.

1643. ———. *I rilievi del Canova*. Milano, Elacta, 1990.

Canuti, Domenico Maria, 1620–1684

1644. Stagni, Simonetta. *Domenico Canuti pittore (1626–1684)*. Con traduzione in Inglese di Lionella Casadio. Rimini, Luise Editore, 1988.

Capa, Robert, 1913–1954

1645. Capa, Robert. *Children of war, children of peace*. [a fall 1991 ICP exhibition]. Ed. by Cornell Capa and Richard Whelan. Boston, Little Brown, Bulfinch Press, 1991.

1646. Capa, Robert. *Robert Capa*. A cura di Romeo Martinez. Milano, Mondadori, 1979.

1647. ——— *Robert Capa, 1913–1954*. Edited by Cornell Capa and Bhupendra Karia. New York, Grossmann, 1974. (ICP library of photographers, 1).

1648. ———. *Slightly out of focus*. New York, Holt, 1947.

Capek, Josef, 1887–1945

1649. Pecirka, Jaromir. *Josef Capek*. Praze, Melantrich, 1937. (Prameny, sbirka dobreho umeni, 16).

1650. Thiele, Vladimir. *Josef Capek a kniha; soupis kniszni grafiky*. Vladimir Thiele, Jiri Ketalik. Praha, Nakl. Československých vytvarnych umělců, 1958. (Ceska Kniha, 2).

Capelle, Jan Van de, 1624/6–1679

1651. Russel, Margarita. *Jan van de Cappelle, 1624/6–1679*. Leigh-on-Sea, Lewis, 1975.

Capogrossi, Guiseppe, 1900–

1652. Argan, Giulio Carlo. *Capogrossi*. Roma, Editalia, 1967.

1653. Tapié, Michel. *Capogrossi*. Testo di Michel Tapié. Note biografiche a cura di Carlo Cardazzo. Venezia, Edizioni di Cavallino, 1962.

Caponigro, Paul, 1932–

1654. Caponigro, Paul. *Paul Caponigro, an Aperture monograph*. [Chronology and bibliography compiled by Peter C. Bunnell]. Mil-

lerton, N.Y., Aperture, 1972. 2 ed.

1655. Photography Gallery (Philadelphia). *Paul Caponigro; photography: 25 years*. [October 16–November 22, 1981]. Philadelphia, The Photography Gallery, 1981.

Caracciuolo, Battistello (i.e. Giovanni Battista), 1570–1637.

1656. Bologna, Ferdinando, ed. *Battistello Caracciolo 3 il primo naturalismo a Napoli*. [Catalogue of an exhibition held at Castel Sant Elmo, Naples, 991–1992]. Napoli, Electa, 1991.

Capuccino, Il *see* Strozzi, Bernardo

Caravaggio, Michelangelo Merisi sa, 1565–1610

Caravaggio, Polidoro Caldara, detto Il *see* Polidoro, sa Caravaggio

1657. Accademia Nazionale dei Lincei. *Colloquio sul tema Caravaggio e i caravaggeschi, Roma, 12–14 febbraio, 1973*. Roma, Accademia Nazionale dei Lincei, 1974. (Accademia Nazionale dei Lincei, Anno CCCLI–1974, Quaderno 205).

1658. Bardon, Françoise. *Caravage ou l'experience de la matière*. Paris, Presses Universitaires de France, 1978. (Publications. Univ. de Poitiers. Lettres et sciences humaines, 19).

1659. Baroni, Costantino. *All the paintings of Caravaggio*. Trans. by Anthony F. O'Sullivan. New York, Hawthorn, 1962.

1660. ———. *Tutta la pittura di Caravaggio*. Milano, Rizzoli, 1956, 4 ed. (Biblioteca d'arte Rizzoli, 2).

1661. Baumgart, Fritz Erwin. *Caravaggio. Kunst und Wirklichkeit*. Berlin, Mann, 1955.

1662. Benkard, Ernst. *Caravaggio-Studien*. Berlin, Keller, 1928.

1663. Berenson, Bernard. *Caravaggio, his incongruity and his fame*. London, Chapman, 1953.

1664. Brehm, Margrit Franziska. *Der Fall Caravaggio*. Eine Rezeptionsgeschichte. Frankfurt/Bern, Peter Lang.1992.

1665. Calvesi, Maurizio. *Le realta dal Caravaggio*. Torino, Einaudi, 1990.

1666. ———. *L'ultimo Caravaggio e la cultura artistica a Napoli, in Sicilia e Malta*. Siracusa, Ediprint, 1987. (Barocco in Sicilia, 2).

1667. Cinotti, Mia. *Caravaggio*. Bergamo, Edizioni Bolis, 1991.

1668. ———. *Michelangelo Merisi detto Il Caravaggio; tutte le opere*. Saggio critico di Gian Alberto dell'Acqua. Bergamo, Bolis, 1983. (Estrattto da 'I Pittori Bergamschi' Il Seicento, I).

1669. DeLogu, Giuseppe. *Caravaggio*. New York, Abrams, n.d.

1670. Friedländer, Walter F. *Caravaggio studies.* Princeton, N.J., Princeton University Press, 1955.

1671. Hibbard, Howard. *Caravaggio.* London, Thames & Hudson, 1983.

1672. Hinks, Roger P. *Michelangelo Merisi da Caravaggio, his life, his legend.* London, Faber, 1953.

1673. Joffroy, Berne. *Le dossier Caravage.* Paris, Editions de Minuit, 1959.

1674. Kirsta, Georg and Zahn, Leopold. *Caravaggio.* 44 Lichtdrucktafeln und 12 Abb. im Text, mit einem Kapitel über "*Caravaggio und die Kunst der Gegenwart.*" Berlin, Albertus-Verlag, 1928.

1675. Kitson, Michael. *The complete paintings of Caravaggio.* New York, Abrams, 1967.

1676. Longhi, Roberto. *Il Caravaggio.* Milano, Martello, 1952.

1677. ———. *Caravaggio, Michelangelo Merisi, 1573–1610.* Milano, Martello, 1956.

1678. Marangoni, Matteo. *Il Caravaggio.* Firenze, Battistelli, 1922.

1679. Marini, Maurizio. *Caravaggio: Michelangelo Merisi da Caravaggio "pictor praestantissimus."* Roma, Newton Compton, 1989. (Quest'Italia, 117).

1680. ———. *Io Michelangelo da Caravaggio.* Roma, Bestetti, 1974. 2 ed.

1681. Metropolitan Museum of Art (New York). *The age of Caravaggio.* [Exhibition catalogue]. Texts by Luigi Salerno, Richard Spear, Mina Gregori. New York, Electa International, 1985.

1682. Moir, Alfred. *Caravaggio.* New York, Abrams, 1982.

1683. ———. *Caravaggio and his copyists.* New York, New York University Press, 1976. (Monographs on archaeology and the fine arts, 31).

1684. ———. *The Italian followers of Caravaggio.* 2 v. Cambridge, Harvard University Press, 1967.

1685. Nicholson, Benedict. *The international Caravaggesque movement; lists of pictures by Caravaggio and his followers throughout Europe from 1590 to 1650.* Oxford, Phaidon, 1979.

1686. Ottino della Chiesa, Angela. *Caravaggio.* Bergamo, Istituto Italiano d'Arti Grafiche, 1962.

1687. Palazzo Pitti (Florence). *Caravaggio e caravaggeschi nelle gallerie di Firenze.* Catalogo della mostra a cura di Evelina Borea. Paris, Editions de Minuit, 1959.

1688. Palazzo Reale (Milan). *Mostra del Caravaggio e dei Caravaggeschi.* Aprile–giugno, 1951. [Catalogo a cura di Achille Marazza e Roberto Longhi]. Milano, Palazzo Reale, 1951.

1689. Petrucci, Alfredo. *Il Caravaggio, acqua-fortista e il mondo calcografico romano.* L'Indovina, Leoni, Borgianni, Maggi, Villamena, Onofri, Mercati, amici del Caravaggio. Roma, Palombi, 1956.

1690. Prater, Andreas. *Licht und Farbe bei Caravaggio.* Studien zur Ästhetik und Ikonologie des Helldunkels. Stuttgart, Franz Steiner Verlag, 1992.

1691. Regione Lombardia. *Immagine del Caravaggio.* Mostra didattica itinerante. . . . Catalogo a cura di Mia Cinotti. Milano, Pizzi, 1973.

1692. Röttgen, Herwarth. *Il Caravaggio.* Ricerche e interpretazionei. Roma, Bulzoni, 1974. (Biblioteca di storia dell'arte, 9).

1693. Samek Ludovici, Sergio. *Vita del Caravaggio dalle testimonazione del suo tempo.* Milano, Edizioni del Milione, 1956. (Vite, lettere, testimonianze di artisti italiani, 2).

1694. Schneider, Arthur von. *Caravaggio und die Niederländer.* Amsterdam, Israel, 1967.

1695. Schudt, Ludwig. *Caravaggio.* Wien, Schroll, 1942.

1696. Spear, Richard E. *Caravaggio and his followers.* Cleveland, Cleveland Museum of Art, 1971.

1697. Venturi, Lionello. *Il Caravaggio.* Con prefazione di Benedetto Croce. Sotto gli auspici del Comitato della Città di Caravaggio. Novara, Ist. Geografico De Agostini, 1963. 2 ed.

1698. Witting, Felix. *Michelangelo da Caravaggio; eine kunsthistorische Studie.* Strassburg, Heitz, 1916. (Zur Kunstgeschichte des Auslandes, 113).

Cardi, Lodovico *see* **Cigoli, Lodovico Cardi da**

Cariani, Giovanni de' Busi, 1485–1547

1699. Gallina, Luciano. *Giovanni Cariani; materiale per uno studio.* Bergamo, Ediz. "Documenti Lombardi," 1954.

Carlevarijs, Luca, 1663–1730

1700. Mauroner, Fabio. *Luca Carlevarijs.* Padova, Le Tre Venezie, 1945.

1701. Rizzi, Aldo. *Disegni, incisioni, e bozzetti del Carlevarijs.* Catalogo della mostra a cura di Aldo Rizzi. Udine, Loggia del Lionello, 29 dic. 1963–2 febbr. 1964.

1702. ———. *Luca Carlevarijs.* Con una prefazione di Rodolfo Pallucchini. Venezia, Alfieri, 1967. (Profili e saggi di arte veneta, 5).

Carnovali, Giovanni, 1806–1873

1703. Caversazzi, Ciro. *Giovanni Carnovali, il picchio.* Bergamo, Ist. Ital. d'Arti Grafiche, 1946.

1704. Palazzo della ragione (Bergamo). *Il Picchio*

e artisti bergamaschi del suo tempo. 14 settembre–10 novembre, 1974. Bergamo, Palazzo della ragione, 1974.

Caro, Anthony, 1924–

1705. Kunstverein Braunschweig. *Anthony Caro, table and related sculptures, 1966–1978*. 18. Mai 1979 bis 1. Juli 1979. [Text in English and German]. Braunschweig, Kunstverein Braunschweig, 1979.

1706. Moorhouse, Paul. *Anthony Caro; sculpture towards architecture*. [Catalogue of an exhibition held at the Tate Gallery, London, Oct. 16, 1991–Jan 26, 1992]. London, Tate Gallery 1991.

1707. Rubin, William Stanley. *Anthony Caro*. New York, Museum of Modern Art/Boston, New York Graphic Society, 1975.

1708. Waldman, Diane. *Anthony Caro*. New York, Abbeville Press, 1982.

1709. Whelan, Richard. *Anthony Caro* [by] Richard Whelan. With additional texts by Clement Greenberg. Harmondsworth/Baltimore, Penguin Books, 1974.

Caron, Antoine, 1521–1599

1710. Ehrmann, Jean. *Antoine Caron, peintre à la cour des Valois, 1521–1599*. Introd. P.-A. Lemoigne. Genève/Lille, Droz/Giard, 1955. (Travaux d'humanisme et renaissance, 18).

Carpaccio, Vittore, 1455–1525

1711. Fiocco, Giuseppe. *Carpaccio*. Trans. by Jean Chuzeville. Paris, Crès, 1931.

1712. ———. *Carpaccio*. Novara, Ist. Geografico De Agostini, 1958.

1713. Hausenstein, Wilhelm. *Das Werk des Vittore Carpaccio*. Stuttgart, Deutsche Verlagsanstalt, 1925.

1714. Humfrey, Peter. *Carpaccio. Catalogo completo dei dipinti*. Firenze, Cantini, 1991.

1715. Lauts, Jan. *Carpaccio; paintings and drawings*. New York, Phaidon, 1962.

1716. Ludwig, Gustave and Molmenti, Pompeo G. *Vittore Carpaccio. La vita e le opere*. Milano, Hoepli, 1906.

1717. Molmenti, Pompeo G. *The life and works of Vittore Carpaccio*. Trans. by R. H. H. Cust. London, Murray, 1907.

1718. Murray, Michelangelo. *Carpaccio*. Firenze, Il Fiorino, 1966. (Il più eccelenti. Collano di monografie di artisti, 2).

1719. Palazzo Ducale (Venice). *Vittore Carpaccio*. Guignio–ottobre 1963. [Catalogo a cura di Pietro Zampetti]. Venezia, Palazzo Ducale, 1963.

1720. Pallucchini, Anna. *Carpaccio*. Milano, Martello, 1963.

1721. Perocco, Guido. *L'opera completa del Carpaccio*. Presentazione di Manlio Can-

cogni. Milano, Rizzoli, 1967. (Classici dell'arte, 13).

1722. Valcanover, Francesco. *Carpaccio*. Trans. by Lisa Pelletti. New York, Riverside Books, 1989. (The library of great masters).

1723. Zampetti, Pietro. *Vittore Carpaccio*. Venezia, Alfieri, 1966.

Carpeaux, Jean Baptiste, 1827–1875

1724. Clément-Carpeaux, Louise. *La vérité sur l'oeuvre et la vie de J.-B. Carpeaux (1827–1875)*. 2 v. Paris, Dousset, 1934–1935.

1725. Laran, Jean and LeBas, Georges. *Carpeaux*. Paris, Libr. Centrale des Beaux-Arts, 1912.

1726. Lecomte, Georges C. *La vie héroïque et glorieuse de Carpeaux*. Paris, Plon, 1928.

1727. Musée des Beaux-Arts, Valenciennes. *Catalogue des peintres et sculptures de Jean-Baptiste Carpeaux*. Catalogue [par] André Hardy and Anny Braunwald. Valenciennes, Musée des Beaux-Arts, 1978.

1728. Sarradin, Edouard. *Carpeaux*. Paris, Rieder, 1927.

1729. Wagner, Anne Middleton. *Jean-Baptiste Carpeaux*. New Haven, Yale University Press, 1986.

Carpi, Girolamo da, 1501–1556

1730. Mezzetti, Amalia. *Girolamo da Ferrara detto da Carpi: l'opera pittorica*. Milano, Silvana, 1977.

Carpioni, Giulio, 1613–1679

1731. Pilo, Giuseppe Maria. *Giulio Carponi. Tutta la pittura*. Venezia, Alfieri, 1961.

Carr, Emily, 1871–1945

1732. Blanchard, Paula. *Life of Emily Carr*. Seattle, University of Washington Press, 1987.

1733. Carr, Emily. *Growing pains; the autobiography of Emily Carr*. With a foreword by Ira Dilworth. Toronto, Oxford University Press, 1946.

1734. ———. *Hundreds and thousands; the journals of Emily Carr*. Toronto, Clarke-Irwin, 1966.

1735. Shadbolt, Doris. *The art of Emily Carr*. Seattle, University of Washington Press, 1990. 2 ed. [First published, 1979; paperback ed., 1988].

1736. Tippett, Maria. *Emily Carr, a biography*. Toronto/New York, Oxford University Press, 1979.

Carrà, Carlo, 1881–1966

1737. Carrà, Carlo. *La mia vita*. Presentazione di Vittorio Fagone. Milano, Feltrinelli, 1981.

1738. Carrà, Massimo. *L'opera completa di Carrà, dal futurismo alla metafisica e al realismo mitico, 1910–1930*. Presentazione di Piero

Bigongiari. Apparati critici e filologici di Massimo Carrà. Milano, Rizzoli, 1970. (Classici dell'arte, 44).

1739. ———. *Carlo Carrà; opera grafica (1922–1964).* A cura di M. Carrà, con un saggio di Marco Valsecchi. Vicenza, Pozza, 1976. (Grafica, 2).

1740. ———. *Carrà; tutta l'opera pittorica.* 3 v. Milano, Ediz. dell'Annunciata, 1967–68.

1741. ———. *Carra: tutti gli scritti.* Milano, Feltrinelli, 1978.

1742. Galleria civica d'arte moderna (Ferrara). *Carlo Carrà con il patrocinio della regione Emilia-Romagna.* 2 luglio–9 ottobre 1977. [Ferrara, Galleria civica d'arte moderna, 1977].

1743. Palazzo Reale, Milano. *Carra: mostra antologica,* 8 aprile–28 giugno, 1987. Milano, Mazzotta, 1987.

1744. Pacchioni, Guglielmo. *Carlo Carrà pittore.* Milano, Milione, 1959. 2 ed.

Carracci, Agostino, 1557–1602
Annibale, 1560–1609
Ludovico, 1555–1619

1745. Bellori, Giovanni Pietro. *The lives of Annibale and Agostino Carracci.* Trans. from the Italian by Catherine Enggass. Foreword by Robert Enggass. University Park, Penn., Pennsylvania State University Press, 1968.

1746. Biennali d'Arte Antica, Bologna. *Mostra dei Carracci, sett.–ott. 1956.* Catalogo critico a cura di Gian Carlo Cavalli, Francesco Arcangeli, Andrea Emiliani, Maurizio Calvesi. Con una nota di Denis Mahon. Saggio introduttivo di Cesare Gnudi. Bologna, Alfa, 1956. 2 ed.

1747. ———. *Mostra dei Carracci, sett.–ott. 1956.* Catalogo critico dei disegni, a cura di Denis Mahon. Trad. di Maurizio Calvesi. Bologna, Alfa, 1963. 2 ed. corr. e augmenta.

1748. Bodmer, Heinrich. *Lodovico Carracci.* Burg, Hopfer, 1939. (Beiträge zur Kunstgeschichte, 6).

1749. Bohlin, Diane DeGrazia. *Prints and related drawings by the Carracci family.* A catalogue raisonné. Published in conjunction with the exhibition at the National Gallery, March–May, 1979. Bloomington, Indiana University Press/Washington, D.C., National Gallery of Art. (CR).

1750. Emiliani, Andrea, ed. *Dall'avanguardia dei Carracci al secolo barocco: Bologna 1580–1600.* A cura di A. Emiliani; con scritti di Grazia Agostini . . . [et al.]. Bologna, Nuova Alfa, 1988.

1751. Foratti, Aldo. *I Carracci nella teoria e nella practica.* Castello, Lapi, 1913.

1752. Goldstein, Carl. *Visual facts over verbal fiction. A study of the Carracci and the criticism, theory, and practice of art in renaissance and baroque Italy.* Cambridge, Cambridge University Press, 1988.

1753. Perini, Giovanna, ed. *Gli scritti dei Caracci: Ludovico, Annibale, Agostino, Antonio, Giovanni Antonio.* Bologna, Nuova Alfa, 1990.

1754. Posner, Donald. *Annibale Carracci. A study in the reform of Italian painting around 1590.* London, Phaidon, 1971.

1755. Rouchès, Gabriel. *La peinture bolonaise à la fin du XVI siècle (1575–1619): les Carrache.* Paris, Alcan, 1913.

1756. Wittkower, Rudolf. *The drawings of the Carracci in the collection of Her Majesty the Queen at Windsor Castle.* London, Phaidon, 1952.

Carriera, Rosalba, 1675–1757

1757. Carriera, Rosalba. *Journal de Rosalba Carriera pendant son séjour à Paris en 1720 et 1721.* Trad., annoté et augmenté d'une biographie et de documents inédits sur les artistes et les amateurs du temps par Alfred Sensier. Paris, Techener, 1865.

1758. Malamani, Vittorio. *Rosalba Carreira.* Bergamo, Ist. Ital. d'Arti Grafiche, 1910. (Collezione di monografie illustrate; pittori, scultori, architetti, 8).

Carrière, Eugène, 1849–1906

1759. Bantens, Robert James. *Eugène Carrière: his work and his influence.* Ann Arbor, Mich., UMI Research Press, 1982.

1760. Dubray, Jean Paul. *Eugène Carrière; essai critique.* Paris, Seheur, 1931.

1761. Faure, Elie. *Eugène Carrière, peintre et lithographe.* Paris, Floury, 1908.

1762. Morice, Charles. *Eugène Carrière; l'homme et sa pensée, l'artiste et son oeuvre, essai de nomenclature des oeuvres principales.* Paris, Mercure de France, 1906.

1763. Musée de l'Orangerie (Paris). *Eugène Carrière et le symbolisme.* Exposition en l'honneur du centenaire de la naissance d'Eugène Carrière, déc. 1949–jan. 1950. Introd. et cat. par Michel Florisoone, notices par Jean Leymarie. Paris, Editions des Musées Nationaux, 1950.

1764. Séailles, Gabriel. *Eugène Carrière; essai de biographie psychologique.* Paris, Colin, 1917. 2 ed.

Carruci, Jacopo *see* Pontormo, Jacopo

Carstens, Asmus Jakob, 1754–1798

1765. Fernow, Carl Ludwig. *Carstens Leben und Werke.* Hrsg. und ergänzt von Herman Riegel. Hannover, Rumpler, 1867.

1766. Heine, Albrecht-Friedrich. *Asmus Jakob Carstens und die Entwicklung des Figuren-*

bildes. Strassburg, Heitz, 1928. (Studien zur deutschen Kunstgeschichte, 264).

1767. Kamphausen, Alfred. *Asmus Jakob Carstens.* Neumünster, Wachholtz, 1941. (Studien zur schleswig-holsteinischen Kunstgeschichte, 5).

1768. Sach, August. *Asmus Jakob Carstens' Jugend- und Lehrjahre nach urkundlichen Quellen.* Halle, Verlag der Buchhandlung des Waisenhauses, 1881.

Cartier-Bresson, Henri, 1908–

1769. Cartier-Bresson, Henri. *Henri Cartier-Bresson: photographer.* Text translated from the French by Frances Frenage. Boston, New York Graphic Society, 1979.

1770. ———. *The photographs of Henri Cartier-Bresson.* Texts by Lincoln Kirstein and Beaumont Newhall. New York, Museum of Modern Art, 1947.

1771. Scottish Arts Council (Edinburgh). *Henri Cartier-Bresson: his archive of 390 photographs from the Victoria and Albert Museum.* A Scottish Arts Council exhibition arranged in association with the V. and A. Museum. [First shown at] Fruit Market Gallery, Edinburgh, 19 Aug.–10 Sept. 1978. Catalogue with an essay by Ernst Gombrich. Edinburgh, Scottish Arts Council, 1978.

Carus, Karl Gustav, 1789–1869

1772. Carus, Karl Gustav. *Briefe über Landschaftsmalerei. Zuvor ein Brief von Goethe als Einleitung.* Nach der 2., vermehrten Ausg. von 1835 mit einem Nachwort hrsg. von Dorothea Kuhn. Heidelberg, Schneider, 1972.

1773. ———. *Die Proportionslehre der menschlichen Gestalt.* Zum ersten Male morphologisch und physiologisch begründet von C. G. Carus. Leipzig, Brockhaus, 1854.

1774. ———. *Symbolik der menschlichen Gestalt.* Neu bearbeitet und erweitert von Theodor Lessing. Celle, Kampmann, 1925. 3 ed.

1775. Kaiser, Konrad. *Carl Gustav Carus und die zeitgenössische Dresdner Landschaftsmalerei.* Gemälde aus der Sammlung Georg Schäfer, Schweinfurt. Ausstellung im Alten Rathaus Schweinfurt vom 14. bis 25. Oktober 1970. Schweinfurt, 1970.

1776. Prause, Marianne. *Carl Gustav Carus: Leben und Werk.* Berlin, Deutscher Verlag für Kunstwissenschaft, 1968.

Carzou, Jean Marie, 1907–

1777. Cailler, Pierre. *Catalogue raisonné de l'oeuvre gravé et lithographié de Carzon.* Avec une préface de Jean Bouret. Genève, Cailler, 1962. (Catalogues d'oeuvres gravés et lithographiés, 4). (CR).

1778. Carzou, Jean-Marie. *Carzou: les années 30–40.* Paris, De Francony Editeur, 1988.

1779. Fels, Florent. *Carzou.* Avec une biographie, une bibliographie et une documentation complète sur le peintre et son oeuvre. Genève, Cailler, 1955. (Peintres et sculpteurs d'hier et d'aujourdhui, 34).

1780. Furhange, Maguy. *Carzou, graveur et lithographe.* Catalogue raisonné et commenté de l'oeuvre gravé et lithographié. Préface de Roger Caillois. Nice, Editions d'art de Francony, 1971–1975. (Text in French and English).

1781. Lambertin, Pierre. *Carzou.* Paris, Julliard, 1961.

1782. Verdet, André. *Carzou: Provence.* Introd. de Pierre Cabanne. Monte Carlo, Sauret, 1966.

Cassatt, Mary, 1844–1926

1783. Breeskin, Adelyn D. *The graphic art of Mary Cassatt.* Introd. by A. D. Breeskin. Foreword by Donald H. Karshan. New York, Museum of Graphic Art, 1967.

1784. ———. *Mary Cassatt: a catalogue raisonné of the graphic work.* 2 ed., rev. Washington, Smithsonian Institution Press, 1979. (CR).

1785. ———. *Mary Cassatt: a catalogue raisonné of the oils, pastels, watercolors, and drawings.* Washington, Smithsonian Institution Press, 1970. (CR).

1786. Breuning, Mary. *Mary Cassatt.* New York, publ. by Hyperion Press, distributed by Duell, Sloan and Pearce, 1944.

1787. Bullard, E. John. *Mary Cassatt, oils and pastels.* New York, Watson-Guptill, 1972.

1788. Carson, Julia M. *Mary Cassatt.* New York, McKay, 1966.

1789. Cassatt, Mary. *Mary Cassatt.* Edited by Edith Valerio. Paris, Editions G. Cres, 193).

1790. Getlein, Frank. *Mary Cassatt: paintings and prints.* New York, Abbeville, 1980.

1791. Hale, Nancy. *Mary Cassatt.* New York, Doubleday, 1975.

1792. Love, Richard H. *Cassatt, the independent.* Chicago, Love, 1980.

1793. Mathews, Nancy Mowll. *Cassat and her circle; selected letters.* New York, Abbeville Press, 1984.

1794. ———. *Mary Cassatt: the color prints.* Nancy M. Mathews and Barbara Stern Shapiro. [Catalogue of an exhibition held at the National Gallery of Art, Washington, D.C., June 18–Aug.27, 1989, at the Museum of Fine Arts, Boston, Mass., Sept. 9–Nov.5, 1989, and the Williams College Museum of Art, Williamstown, Mass., Nov. 23–Jan 21, 1990. New York, Harry N. Abrams, in association with Williams College Museum of Art, 1989.

1795. Segard, Achille. *Mary Cassatt. Un peintre des enfants et des mères.* Paris, Ollendorff, 1913. 2 ed.

1796. Sweet, Frederick A. *Miss Mary Cassatt, impressionist from Pennsylvania*. Norman, University of Oklahoma Press, 1966.

1797. Watson, Forbes. *Mary Cassatt*. New York, Macmillan, 1932.

Castagno, Andrea del, 1423–1457

1798. Berti, Luciano. *Andrea del Castagno*. Firenze, Sadea/Sansoni, 1966.

1799. Fortuna, Alberto M. *Andrea del Castagno*. Firenze, Olschki, 1957. (Pocket library of "studies" in art, 9).

1800. Horster, Marita. *Andrea del Castagno*. Complete edition with a critical catalogue. Oxford, Phaidon, 1980.

1801. Richter, George M. *Andrea del Castagno*. Chicago, University of Chicago Press, 1943.

1802. Salmi, Mario. *Andrea del Castagno*. Novara, Agostini, 1961.

1803. Spencer, John R. *Andrea Castagno and his patrons*. Durham, N.C., Duke University Press, 1991.

1804. Zanoli, Anna. *Andrea del Castagno*. Milano, Fabbri, 1965. (I maestri del colore, 48).

Castellani, Enrico, 1930–

1805. Agnetti, Vincenzo. *Enrico Castellani pittore*. Milano, Mauri, 1969.

1806. Castellani, Enrico. *Enrico Castellani*. Saggi di Achille Bonito Oliva, Arturo Carlo Quintavalle; inoltre testi di Vincenzo Agnetti. Parma, Univ. di Parma, 1976. (Quaderni, 32).

Castiglione, Giovanni Benedetto, *called* Il Grechetto, 1610?–1670?

1807. Blunt, Anthony. *The drawings of G. B. Castiglione and Stefano della Bella in the collection of Her Majesty the Queen at Windsor Castle*. London, Phaidon, 1954.

1808. Delogu, Giuseppe. *G. B. Castiglione detto Il Grechetto*. Bologna, Apollo, 1928.

1809. Percy, Ann. *Giovanni Benedetto Castiglione, master draughtsman of the Italian Baroque*. [Catalogue of an exhibition held at the Philadelphia Museum of Art, Sept. 17–Nov. 28, 1971]. Foreword by A. Blunt. Philadelphia Museum of Art, 1971.

Castiglione, Giuseppe, 1688–1766

1810. Beurdeley, Cécile. *Giuseppe Castiglione, a Jesuit painter at the court of the Chinese emperors*. By Cécile and Michel Beurdeley. Trans. by Michael Bullock. Rutland, Vt., Tuttle, 1971.

Castillo, Jorge, 1933–

1811. Haftmann, Werner. *Jorge Castillo: Gemälde, Aquarelle, Zeichnungen*. Text von Werner Haftmann; Bildbeschreibung, Jean-Luc Daval. Frankfurt a.M., Propyläen, 1975.

Castleden, George Frederick, 1861–1945

1812. Castleden, Louise Decatur. *George Frederick Castleden, etcher-painter; a brief biography*. With a foreword by Elihu Root, Jr. New York, Exposition Press, 1954.

Catena, Vincenzo, ca. 1470–ca. 1531

1813. Robertson, Giles. *Vincenzo Catena*. Edinburgh, Edinburgh University Press, 1954.

Catesby, Mark, ca. 1679–1749

1814. Frick, George F. and Stearns, Raymond P. *Mark Catesby, the colonial Audubon*. Urbana, Ill., University of Illinois Press, 1961.

Catlin, George, 1796–1872

1815. Catlin, George. *Catlin's North American Indian Portfolio*. New York, Abbeville Press, 1992. [A Library of Congress/ Abbeville Presfacsimile].

1816. Catlin, George. *Letters and notes on the North American Indian*. Ed. and introd. by Michael M. Mooney. New York, Potter, 1975 (Reprint of 1841 ed.).

1817. ———. *The letters of George Catlin and his family*. Ed. by Marjorie Catlin Roehm. Berkeley/Los Angeles, University of California Press, 1966.

1818. Dippie, Brian W. *George Catlin and his contemporaries: the politics of patronage*. Lincoln, Neb. University of Nebraska Press, 1990.

1819. Haberly, Lloyd. *Pursuit of the horizon. A life of George Catlin, painter recorder of the American Indian*. New York, Macmillan, 1948.

1820. McCracken, Harold. *George Catlin and the Old Frontier*. New York, Crown, 1959.

1821. Plate, Robert. *Palette and tomahawk: the story of George Catlin*. New York, McKay, 1962.

1822. Truettner, William H. *The natural man observed: a study of George Catlin's Indian Gallery*. Washington, D.C., Smithsonian Institution Press, 1979.

Cavalli, Vitale *see* Vitale sa Bologna, fl. 1320–1359

Cavallini, Pietro, ca. 1250–ca. 1330

1823. Matthaie, Guglielmo. *Pietro Cavallini*. Milano, Ist. Italiane Editoriale, 1972.

1824. Lavagnino, Emilio. *Pietro Cavallini*. Roma, Palombi, 1953.

1825. Sindona, Enio. *Pietro Cavallini*. Milano, Istituto Editorial Italiano, 1958. (Arte e pensiero, 2).

1826. Toesca, Pietro. *Pietro Cavallini*. Trans. by Elizabeth Andrews. New York, McGraw-Hill, 1960. (Collezione silvana, 19).

Cavé, Marie Elisabeth (Blavot) Boulanger, b. 1810

1827. Angrand, Pierre. *Marie-Elisabeth Cavé, disciple de Delacroix.* [Lausanne/Paris], La Bibliotheque des arts, 1966.

Cellini, Benvenuto, 1500–1571

1828. Calamandrei, Piero. *Scritti e inediti celliniarni.* A cura di Carlo Cordie. Firenze, La Nuova Italia, 1971. (Documenti di storia italiana, ser. 3, pt. 3, v. 4).

1829. Cellini, Benvenuto. *Autobiography.* Ed. by John Pope-Hennessy. New York, Phaidon, 1960.

1830. ———. *The autobiography of Benvenuto Cellini.* Trans. by George Bull. London, Folio Society, 1966.

1831. ———. *Due trattati di Benvenuto Cellini, . . . uno dell'oreficeria, l'altro della scultura.* Firenze, Tartini e Franchi, 1731. 2 ed.

1832. ———. *The life of Benvenuto Cellini, a Florentine artist. Written by himself.* Trans by Thomas Nugent. 2 v. London, Davies, 1771.

1833. ———. *L'opera completa del Cellini.* Presentazione di Charles Avery. Apparati critici e filologici di Susanna Barbaglia. Milano, Rizzoli, 1981. (Classici dell'arte, 104).

1834. ———. *Tutta l'opera del Cellini.* A cura di Ettore Camesasca. Milano, Rizzoli, 1955. (Biblioteca d'arte Rizzoli, 21).

1835. ———. *La vita scritta da lui medesimo.* [A cura] di A. Cocci. Napoli, 1728.

1836. ———. *La Vita.* A cura di Bruno Maier. Novara, Ist. Geografico de Agostini, 1962. (I classici di tutti i tempi, 2. Serie memorialisti e viaggiatori, 1).

1837. Cervigni, Dino S. *The Vita of Benvenuto Cellini: literary tradition and genre.* Ravenna, Longo, 1979. (L'intreprete, 13).

1838. Cust, Robert H. H. *Life of Benvenuto Cellini.* 2 v. London, Methuen, 1910.

1839. Goethe, Johann Wolfgang von. *Benvenuto Cellini.* Mit Steinzeichnungen von Max Slevogt. Berlin, Cassirer, 1913.

1840. Plon, Eugène. *Benvenuto Cellini, orfevre, médailleur, sculpteur; recherches sur sa vie, sur son oeuvre et sur les pièces qui lui sont attribuées.* 2 v. Paris, Plon, 1883–1884.

1841. Supino, Igino B. *L'art di Benvenuto Cellini, con nuovi documenti sull'oreficeria fiorentina del secolo XVI.* Firenze, Alinari, 1901.

Cerdá, Ildefonso, 1815–1876

1842. Cerdá, Ildefonso. *Teoría general de la urbanización.* 2 v. Madrid, Imprenta Espanola, 1867. (Reprint: 3 v. Madrid, Instituto de Estudios Fiscales, 1968).

Cermák, Jaroslav, 1830–1878

1843. Cerny, Vratislav. *Zivot, a dílo Jaroslava Cermáka.* Sepsali Vratislav Cerny, F.V. Mokry, V. Naprstek. Praha, Vytvarny odbor Umeleké besedý, 1930.

1844. Siblik, Emmanuel. *Le peintre Jaroslav Cermák, 1830–1878.* Prague, Umelecká beseda, 1930.

Ceruti, Giacomo, fl. ca. 1720–1750

1845. Gregori, Mina. *Giacomo Ceruti.* Bergamo, Credito Bergamsco, 1982.

1846. Passamini, Bruno, ed. *Giacomo Ceruti, il pittocchetto.* Milano, Mazzotta, 1987.

Cézanne, Paul, 1839–1906

1847. Adriani, Götz. *Paul Cézanne: Zeichnungen.* [Katalog] der Ausstellung in der Kunsthalle Tübingen, 21 Okt.–31 Dezember 1978. Köln, DuMont, 1978.

1848. Anderson, Wayne. *Cézanne's portrait drawings.* Cambridge, M.I.T. Press, 1970.

1849. Badt, Kurt. *The art of Cézanne.* Trans. by S. A. Ogilvie. Berkeley, University of California Press, 1965.

1850. Barnes, Albert C. and De Mazia, Violette. *The art of Cézanne.* New York, Harcourt, Brace & Co., 1939.

1851. Bernard, Emile. *Souvenirs sur Paul Cézanne, une conversation avec Cézanne, la méthode de Cézanne.* Paris, Michel, 1926. 3 ed.

1852. Berthold, Gertrude. *Cézanne und die alten Meister. Die Bedeutung der Zeichnungen Cézannes nach Werken anderer Künstler.* Stuttgart, Kohlhammer, 1958.

1853. Biederman, Charles. *The new Cézanne.* Red Wing, Minnesota, Art History, 1958.

1854. Boisdeffre, Pierre de, et al. *Cézanne.* Paris, Hachette et Société d'Etudes et de Publications Economiques, 1966. (Génies et réalités, 26).

1855. Brion-Guerry, Liliane. *Cézanne et l'expression de l'espace.* Paris, Michel, 1966.

1856. Cézanne, Paul. *Album de Paul Cézanne.* [Par] Adrien Chappuis. Préface de Roseline Bacori. 2 v. Paris, Berggruen & Cie., 1966.

1857. ———. *Cézanne by himself: drawings, paintings, writings.* Edited by Richard Kendall. London. Macdonald Orbis, 1988.

1858. ———. *Paul Cézanne, correspondance.* Recueillie, annotée et préfacée par John Rewald. Nouv. éd. rev. et augm. Paris, Grasset, 1978. 2 ed.

1859. ———. *Paul Cézanne, letters.* Edited by John Rewald. Trans. by Seymour Hacker. Rev. and augmented edition. New York, Hacker Art Books, 1981.

1860. ———. *Paul Cézanne sketchbook, 1875–1885.* Introd. by John Rewald; trans. by Olivier Bernier. New York, Johnson Reprint Corp., 1982.

1861. Chappuis, Adrien. *Les dessins de Paul Cézanne au Cabinet des Estampes du Musée des Beaux-Arts, Bâle.* 2 v. Oeten/Lausanne, Graf, 1962.

1862. ———. *The drawings of Paul Cézanne: a catalogue raisonné.* 2 v. Greenwich, Conn., New York Graphic Society, 1973. (CR).

1863. Cherpin, Jean. *L'oeuvre gravé de Cézanne.* Préf. par Paul Gachet. Lettres de Paul Gachet à propos de Cézanne. Marseilles, Arts et Livres de Provence, 1972.

1864. Dorival, Bernard. *Cézanne.* Paris, Tisné, 1948.

1865. Faure, Elie. *Cézanne.* Trans. by Walter Pach. New York, Assoc. of American Painters and Sculptors, 1913.

1866. ———. *Les constructeurs.* Paris, Editions Crès, 1921.

1867. Fry, Roger E. *Cézanne, a study of his development. With an introduction by Richard Shiff.* Chicago, University ofChicago Press, 1989. [First publ.: London, L. & V. Woolf, 1927, 3 ed., New York, Farrar, 1958.]

1868. Gasquet, Joachim. *Cézanne.* Paris, Bernheim-Jeune, 1921.

1869. ———. *Joachim Gasquet's Cézanne; a memoir with conversations.*Trans. by Christopher pemberton. Preface by John Rewald. Introduction by Richard Shiff. New York, Thames and Hudson, 1991.

1870. Gatto, Alfonso. *L'opera completa di Cézanne.* Presentazione di A. Gatto; apparati critici e filologici di Sandra Orienti. Milano, Rizzoli, 1970. (Classici dell'arte, 39).

1871. Geist, Sidney. *Interpreting Cézanne.* Cambridge, Mass., Harvard University Press, 1988.

1872. Glaser, Curt. *Paul Cézanne.* Leipzig, Seemann, 1922. (Bibliothek der Kunstgeschichte, 50).

1873. Gowing, Lawrence. *Cézanne, the early years, 1859–1872.* Catalogue by Lawrence Gowing; with contributions by Götz Adriani . . . [et al.]. Edited by Mary Ann Stevens. London, Royal Academy of Arts; in association with Weidenfeld and Nicolson, 1988.

1874. Guerry, Liliane. *Cézanne et l'expression de l'espace.* Paris, Michel, 1966. 2 ed.

1875. Guillaud, Jacqueline. *Cézanne in Provence.* By Jacqueline and Maurice Guillaud, with the collaboration of Jean-Louis Ferrier. New York, Potter; Paris/New York, Guillaud Editions, 1989.

1876. Huyghe, René. *Cézanne.* Paris, Somogy, 1961.

1877. Levêcque, Jean-Jacques. *La vie et l'oeuvre de Paul Cézanne.* Paris, ACR Edition, 1988.

1878. Lewis, Mary Tompkins. *Cézanne's early imagery.* Berkeley, Calif./ Los Angeles/ London, University of California Press, 1989.

1879. Lindsay, Jack. *Cézanne; his life and art.* Greenwich, Conn., New York Graphic Society, 1969.

1880. Loran, Erle. *Cézanne's composition; analysis of his form with diagrams and photographs of his motifs.* Berkeley, University of California Press, 1963. 3 ed.

1881. Mack, Gerstle. *Paul Cézanne.* Trans. by J. Holroyd-Reece. New York, Knopf, 1942. 2 ed.

1882. McLeave, Hugh. *A man and his mountain: the life of Paul Cézanne.* New York, Macmillan, 1977.

1883. Meier-Graefe, Julius. *Cézanne.* Trans. by J. Holroyd-Reece. London, Benn, 1927.

1884. ———. *Paul Cézanne.* München, Piper, 1923. 5 ed. First publ. 1910.

1885. Murphy, Richard W. *The world of Cézanne, 1839–1906.* New York, Time-Life Books, 1968.

1886. Museum of Modern Art (New York). *Cézanne: the late work.* Essays by Theodore Reff et al. Edited by William Rubin. Published on the occasion of the exhibition "Cezanne: The Late Work." New York, Museum of Modern Art, 1977; distributed by New York Graphic Society, Boston.

1887. Neumeyer, Alfred. *Cézanne drawings.* New York, Yoseloff, 1958.

1888. Novotny, Fritz. *Cézanne.* New York, Phaidon, 1961.

1889. ———. *Cézanne und das Ende der wissenschaftlichen Perspektive.* Wien/München, Schroll, 1970. (Reprint of 1938 ed.).

1890. Orangerie des Tuileries (Paris). *Cézanne dans les musées nationaux.* 19 juillet–14 octobre 1974. Paris, Editions des Musées Nationaux, 1974.

1891. Perruchot, Henri. *La vie de Cézanne.* Paris, Hachette, 1956.

1892. Phillips Collection (Washington, D.C.). *Cézanne; an exhibition in honor of the fiftieth anniversary of the Phillips Collection.* Feb. 27–March 28, 1971. Introd. by John Rewald; catalogue entries by Anne d'Harnoncourt. Washington, D.C., The Phillips Collection, 1971.

1893. Ponente, Nello. *Cézanne.* Bologna, Capitol, 1980. (Collana d'arte Paola Malipiero, 9).

1894. Reynal, Maurice. *Cézanne; biographical and critical studies.* Trans. by James Emmons. Geneva, Skira, 1954. (The Taste of Our Time, 8).

1895. Rewald, John. *Cézanne and America: dealers, collectors, artists and critics, 1891–1921.* By John Rewald; with the rersearch asssistance of Frances Weitzenhoffer. Princeton, Prince-ton University Press, 1989.

1896. ———. *Cézanne et Zola.* Paris, Sed-rowski, 1936.

1897. ———. *Paul Cézanne, a biography.* New

C

York, Abrams, 1986. [First ed., New York, Schocken, 1968].

1898. ———. *Paul Cézanne, carnet des dessins.* Préface et catalogue raisonné. 2 v. Paris, Quatre Chemins-Editart, 1957. (CR).

1899. ———. *Paul Cézanne: the watercolors.* A catalogue raisonnée by John Rewald. Boston, New York Graphic Society, 1983.(CR).

1900. Rubin, William. *Cézanne, the late work.* London, Thames and Hudson, 1978.

1901. Schapiro, Meyer. *Paul Cézanne.* New York, Abrams, 1965. 3 ed.

1902. Twitchell, Beverly Hamilton. *Cézanne and formalism in Bloomsbury.* Ann Arbor, Mich., UMI Research Press, 1987. (Studies in the fine arts. Criticism, 20).

1903. Venturi, Lionello. *Cézanne; son art, son oeuvre.* 2 v. Paris, Rosenberg, 1936. (Reprint: San Francisco, Alan Wofsy, 1989).

1904. Verdi, Richard. *Cézanne.* London, Thames and Hudson, 1992.

1905. Vollard, Ambroise. *Paul Cézanne; his life and art.* Trans. by H. L. Van Doren. New York, Brown, 1923.

1906. Wechsler, Judith. *Cézanne in perspective.* Englewood Cliffs, Prentice-Hall, 1975.

1907. ———. *The interpretation of Cézanne.* Ann Arbor, Mich., UMI Research Press, 1981. (Studies in the fine arts. Art Theory, 8).

Chadwick, Lynn, 1914–

1908. Musée National d'Art Moderne (Paris). *Lynn Chadwick.* Exposition organisée par le British Council et des musées de France, 7 fev.–10 mars 1957. Paris, Editions des Musées Nationaux, 1957.

1909. Read, Herbert. *Lynn Chadwick.* Amriswil, Switzerland, Bodensee-Verlag, 1958.

Chadwick, William, 1879–1962

1910. Love, Richard H. *William Chadwick, 1879–1962: an American impressionist.* Chicago, R. H. Love Galleries, 1978.

Chagall, Marc, 1887–1985

1911. Aronson, Boris. *Mark Shagal.* Petropolis [i.e. Berlin], Petropolis-Verlag, 1923.

1912. Bibliothèque Nationale (Paris). *Chagall, l'oeuvre gravé.* [Catalogue de l'exposition] par Françoise Voimant, 1970.

1913. Bidermanis, Izis. *The world of Marc Chagall.* Photographed by I. Bidermanis. Text by Roy McMullen. Garden City, N.Y., Doubleday, 1968.

1914. Cain, Julien. *Chagall lithographe.* Avant-propos de Marc Chagall. Notices de Fernand Mourlot. 6 v. Monte-Carlo, Sauret, 1960–1986. (CR).

1915. Cassou, Jean. *Chagall.* Trans. by Alice Jaffa. New York, Praeger, 1965.

1916. Chagall, Marc. *Chagall by Chagall.* Ed. by Charles Sorlier, trans. by John Shepley. New York, Abrams, 1979.

1917. ———. *Marc Chagall.* Berlin, Verlag Der Sturm, 1920. (Sturm Bilderbücher, 1).

1918. ———. *My life.* Trans. by E. Abbott. New York, Grossman, 1960.

1919. Compton, Susan. *Marc Chagall, 'My life, my dream': Berlin and Paris, 1922–1940.* München, Prestel; New York, distributed by the Neues Pub. Co., 1990.

1920. Crespelle, Jean-Paul. *Chagall, l'amour, le rêve et la vie.* Paris, Presses de la Cité, 1969.

1921. Däubler, Theodor. *Marc Chagall.* Roma, Edit. de Valori Plastici, 1922.

1922. Debenedetti, Elisa. *I miti di Chagall.* Milano, Longanesi, 1962.

1923. Efros, Abram M. *Die Kunst Marc Chagalls.* Von A. Efros und J. Tugenhold. Autorisierte Übersetzung aus dem Russischen von F. Ichak-Rubiner. Potsdam, Kiepenheuer, 1921.

1924. Erben, Walter. *Marc Chagall.* Trans. by Michael Bullock. Rev. ed., New York, Praeger, 1966.

1925. Forestier, Sylvie. *Les Chagall de Chagall.* Paris, Albin Michel, 1988.

1926. Haftmann, Werner. *Marc Chagall.* Köln, DuMont, 1972.

1927. Kamensky, Aleksandr. *Chagall: The Russian years, 1907–1922.* Translated from the French by Catherine Phillips. Picture research, Isabelle d'Hauteville. London, Thames and Hudson, 1989.

1928. Kornfeld, Eberhard. *Marc Chagall: das graphische Werk.* Bern, Kornfeld und Klipstein, 1970.

1929. Lassaigne, Jacques. *Chagall.* Paris, Maeght, 1957.

1930. ———. *Chagall: unpublished drawings.* Genève, Skira, 1968.

1931. Leymarie, Jean. *Marc Chagall: monotypes.* Catalogue établie par Gerald Cramer. 2 v. Genève, Cramer, 1966–1977.

1932. Mathey, François. *Chagall.* 2 v. Paris, Hazan, 1959. (Petite encyclopédie de l'art, 27–28).

1933. Meyer, Franz. *Marc Chagall; his graphic work.* Documentation: Hans Bolliger. New York, Abrams, 1957.

1934. ———. *Marc Chagall; life and work.* Trans. by Robert Allen. New York, Abrams, 1964.

1935. Musée des Arts Décoratifs (Paris). *Marc Chagall.* Juin–octobre 1959, Palais du Louvre, Pavillon de Marsan. Catalogue par François Mathey. Paris, 1959.

1936. Salmon, André. *Chagall.* Paris, Editions des Chroniques du Jour, 1928.

1937. Sidney, Alexander. *Marc Chagall; a biography.* New York, Putnam, 1978.

1938. Sorlier, Charles. *Les affiches de Marc Chagall.* Préf. de Léopold Senghor; introd. de Jean Adhémar. Paris, Draeger-Vilo, 1975. (CR).

1939. ——. *Les céramiques et sculptures de Chagall*. Catalogue raisonné. Préf. de André Malraux. Monaco, Editions Sauret, 1972. (CR).

1940. ——. *Chagall, le patron*. Paris, Librairie Seguier, 1989.

1941. ——. *Chagall lithographs, 1974–1979*. Preface by Robert Marteau. Notes and catalogue by C. Sorlier. New York, 1984.

1942. ——. *Chagall lithographs, 1980–1985*. Foreword by Roger Passeron, New York, 1986.

1943. ——. *Marc Chagall et Ambrose Vollard*. Catalogue complet des gravures exécutés par Marc Chagall à la demande de Ambrose Vollard. Textes de Marc Chagall, André Malraux, Robert Marteneau. Paris, Editions Galerie Matignon, 1981. (CR).

1944. ——. *Marc Chagall: le livre des livres/ the illustrated books*. Paris. Sauret and Trickvel, 1990. (Text in French and English).

1945. Sweeney, James Johnson. *Marc Chagall*. The Museum of Modern Art in New York in collaboration with the Art Institute of Chicago. New York, Museum of Modern Art, 1946.

1946. Venturi, Lionello. *Chagall; a biographical and critical study*. Trans. by S. J. C. Harrison and James Emmons. New York, Skira, 1956. (The Taste of Our Time, 18).

1947. Vitali, Christoph, Hrsg. *Marc Chagall: die russischen Jahre, 1906–1922*. [Katalog zur Ausstellung].Framkfurt am Main, Schirn Kunsthalle, 1991.

1948. With, Karl. *Marc Chagall*. Leipzig, Klinkhardt & Biermann, 1923. (Junge Kunst, 35).

Chambers, William, 1723–1796

1949. Chambers, William. *A treatise on civil architecture in which the principles of that art are laid down, and illustrated by a great number of plates, accurately designed, and elegantly engraved by the best hands*. London, Printed for the author by J. Haberkorn, 1759.

1950. ——. *A treatise on the decorative part of civil architecture*. Illustrated by fifty original, and three additional plates, engraved by old Rooker, old Foudrinier, Charles Grignion, and other eminent hands. London, Smeeton, 1791. 3 ed.

1951. Harris, John. *Sir William Chambers, Knight of the Polar Star*. With contributions by J. Mordaunt Crook and Eileen Harris. London, Zwemmer, 1970. (Studies in Architecture, 9).

Champaigne, Jean Baptiste de,1631–1681 Philippe de, 1602–1674

1952. Dorival, Bernard. *Jean-Baptiste de Champaigne (1631–1681), la vie l'homme*. Paris. Léonce Laget, 1992.

1953. Dorival, Bernard. *Philippe de Champaigne, 1602–1674: la vie, l'oeuvre,et le catalogue raisonné de l'oeuvre*. 2. v. Paris, Léonce Laget, 1976. (CR).

1954. ——. *Supplement au catalogue raisonné de l'oeuvre de Philippe de Champaigne*. Paris, Chez l'auteur; Distributeur, L. Laget, 1992. (CR).

1955. Gazier, A. L. *Philippe et Jean Baptiste de Champaigne*. Paris, Librairie de l'Art, 1923.

1956. Orangerie des Tuileries (Paris). *Philippe de Champaigne*. Exposition [fév.–mars 1952] en l'honneur du trois cent cinquantième anniversaire de sa naissance. Avant-propos de Mauricheau-Beaupré. Catalogue par Bernard Dorival. Paris, Editions des Musées Nationaux, 1952.

Chang, Ta-Chien, 1899–

1957. Fu, Shen. *Challenging the past: the paintings of Chang Dai-chien*. By Shen C.Y. Fu. With major contributions and translated by Jan Stuart. Selected poems and inscriptions translated by Stephen D. Allee. Washington, D.C., Arthur M. Sackler Gallery; Smithsonian Institution, in association with University of Washington Press, Seattle, 1991.

Chardin, Jean-Baptiste Siméon, 1699–1779

1958. Consibee, Philip. *Chardin*. Oxford, Oxford University Press, 1983.

1959. Dayot, Armand P. M. *J.-B. Siméon Chardin, avec un catalogue complet de l'oeuvre du maître par Jean Guiffrey*. Paris, Piazza, 1907.

1960. De La Mare, Walter. *Chardin (1699–1779)*. London, Faber and Faber, 1948.

1961. Denvir, Bernard. *Chardin*. New York, Harper, 1950.

1962. Florisoone, Michel. *Chardin*. Paris, Skira, 1938. (Les trésors de la peinture française; XVIIIᵉ siècle, 2).

1963. Fourcaud, Louis de. *J. B. Siméon Chardin*. Paris, Ollendorff, 1900.

1964. Furst, Herbert E. A. *Chardin*. London, Methuen, 1911.

1965. Konody, Paul George. *Chardin*. London, Jack/New York, Stokes, 1909.

1966. Lazarev, Viktor N. *Jean-Baptiste Siméon Chardin*. Dresden, Verlag der Kunst, 1966.

1967. Leclère, Tristan. *Chardin*. Paris, Nilsson, 1924.

1968. Mittelstädt, Kuno. *Jean-Baptiste Siméon Chardin*. Berlin, Henschel, 1963.

1969. Normand, Charles. *J.-B. Siméon Chardin*. Paris, Librairie de l'Art/E. Moreau, 1901.

1970. Ridder, André de. *J.-B. S. Chardin*. Paris, Floury, 1932.

1971. Roland Michel, Marianne. *Chardin*. Paris, Hazan, 1994.

1972. Rosenberg, Pierre. *Chardin, biographical*

and critical study. Trans. by Helga Harrison. Lausanne, Skira, 1963. (The Taste of Our Time, 40).

1973. ———. *Chardin, 1699–1779.* A special exhibition organized by the Réunion des Musées Nationaux, Paris, the Cleveland Museum of Art, and Museum of Fine Arts, Boston. Cleveland, Cleveland Museum of Art in cooperation with Indiana University Press, 1979.

1974. Rothschild, Henri de. *Documents sur la vie et l'oeuvre de Chardin.* Réunies et annotés par André Pascal [pseud.] et Roger Gaucheron. Paris, Editions de la Galerie Pigalle, 1931.

1975. Schéfer, Gaston. *Chardin, biographie critique.* Paris, Laurens, 1907.

1976. Wildenstein, Georges. *Chardin.* Zurich, Manesse, 1963. Rev. and enl. ed. by Daniel Wildenstein. Trans. by Stuart Gilbert. Oxford, Cassirer, 1969. (CR).

1977. ———. *Chardin: biographie et catalogue critique.* Paris, Les Beaux-arts, 1933. (CR).

1978. Zolotov, Iurii K. *Jean-Baptiste Siméon Chardin.* Moscow, Iskusstvo, 1956.

Charlet, Nicolas-Toussaint, 1792–1845

1979. Dayot, Armand P. M. *Charlet et son oeuvre. . . . 118 compositions, lithographiques, peintures à l'huile, aquarelles, sépias et dessins inédits.* Paris, Librairies-Imprimeries Réunies, 1892.

1980. ———. *Les peintres militaires: Charlet et Raffet.* Paris, Librairies-Imprimeries Réunies, n.d.

1981. LaCombe, Joseph F. L. de. *Charlet, sa vie, ses lettres, suivie d'une description raisonné de son oeuvre lithographique.* Paris, Paulin et Le Chevalier, 1856.

1982. Lhomme, François. *Charlet.* Paris, Librairie de l'Art, 1892.

Chasseriau, Theodore, 1819–1856

1983. Bénédite, Léonce. *Théodore Chasseriau, sa vie et son oeuvre;* manuscrit inédit publié par André Dezarrois. 2 v. Paris, Braun, 1932.

1984. Chevillard, Valbert. *Un peintre romantique: Théodore Chasseriau.* Avec une eau-forte de Bracquemond. Paris, Lemerre, 1893.

1985. Fogg Art Museum, Harvard University (Cambridge, Mass.). *Between the empires; Géricault, Delacroix, Chasseriau, painters of the Romantic movement, April 30–June 1, 1946.* Cambridge, Mass. Fogg Art Museum, Harvard University, 1946.

1986. Laran, Jean. *Chasseriau . . . Par J. Laran . . .* précédée d'une introduction biographique et critique par Henry Marcel. Paris, La Renaissance du Livre, J. Gulleguin, 1911. (L'art de notre temps, 1).

1987. Musée de l'Orangerie (Paris). *Exposition Chasseriau, 1819–1856.* Préf. de Jean-Louis Vaudoyer. Paris, Musée de l'Orangerie, 1933.

1988. Sandoz, Marc. *Théodore Chasseriau, 1819–1856.* Catalogue raisonné des peintures et estampes. Paris, Arts et Métiers Graphiques, 1974. (CR).

Chéret, Jules, 1836–1932

1989. Maindron, Ernest. *Les affiches illustrées; ouvrage orné de 20 chromalithographies par Jules Chéret et de nombreuses reproductions en noir et en couleur d'après les documents originaux.* Paris, Launette, 1886.

1990. Mauclair, Camille. *Jules Chéret.* Paris, Le Garrec, 1930.

Chillida, Eduardo, 1924–

1991. Chillida, Eduardo. *Chillida.* Hayward Gallery, London. 6 September–4 November, 1990. London, South Bank Centre, 1990.

1992. ———. *Chillida: Escala humana.* Gijon, Caja de Ahorros de Asturias, 1991.

1993. ———. *Eduardo Chillida: XLIV Esposizione internazionale d'arte.* La Biennale di Venezia. Venezia. Edizioni Biennale, 1990.

1994. ———. *Eduardo Chillida: Zeichnung als Skulptur, 1948–1989.* [Ausstellung] Städtisches Kunstmuseum Bonn, 20. Juni bis 6. August, 1989; Westfälisches Landesmuseum Münster, 24 September bis 26 November, 1989. Redaktion: Katharina Schmidt, Mario-Andreas von Lüttichau. Bonn, Städtisches Kunstmuseum, 1989.

Chimenti da Empoli, Jacopo

1995. Marabottini, Alessandro. *Jacopo di Chimenti da Empoli.* Roma, De lucaEdizioni d'Arte, 1988. (CR)

1996. Vries, Simonetta de. *Jacopo Chimenti da Empoli.* Firenze, Olschki, 1933.

Chini, Galileo, 1873–1956

1997. Chini, Galileo. *Galileo Chini: dipinti, decorazioni, ceramiche. Opere, 1895–1952.* A cura di Fabio Benzi, Gilda Cefariello Grosso. Milano, Electa, 1988.

1998. ———. *Galileo Chini: Liberty ed oltre.* Firenze, Arnaud Becocci, 1989.

Chippendale, Thomas, 1718–1779

1999. Brackett, Oliver. *Thomas Chippendale; a study of his life, work and influence.* Boston, Houghton Mifflin, 1925.

2000. Chippendale, Thomas. *The gentleman & cabinet-maker's director, being a large collection of the most elegant and useful designs of household furniture in the most fashionable taste.* London, Chippendale, 1762. 3 ed. (Reprint: New York, Dover, 1966).

2001. Gilbert, Christopher. *The life and work of*

Thomas Chippendale. 2 v. London, Studio Vista/Christie's, 1978.

2002. Hayden, Arthur. *The furniture designs of Thomas Chippendale.* London, Gibbings, 1910.

2003. Layton, Edwin J. *Thomas Chippendale; a review of his life and origin.* London, Murray, 1928.

2004. Lowe, John. *Möbel von Thomas Chippendale.* Darmstadt, Schneekluth, n.d. (Wohnkunst und Hausrat einst und jetzt, 15).

Chirico, Giorgio de, 1888–1978

2005. Arco, Maurizio Fagiolo dell'. *Giorgio de Chirico all epoca del Surrealismo.* Milano, Electa, 1991.

2006. Chirico, Giorgio de. *Giorgio di Chirico: catalogo dell'opere grafica 1969–1977.* A cura di Edoardo Brandani; schede critiche di Giorgio Di Genova; schede tecniche di Patrizia Bonfiglioli. Bologna, Bora, 1990.

2007. Chirico, Giorgio de. *Catalogo generale Giorgio de Chirico.* Coordin. Claudio Bruni con collab. di Giorgio de Chirico e Isabella Far, e con la consulenza speciale di Giuliana Briganti. 7 v. Milano, Electa, [1971–1983]. (CR).

2008. ———. *The memoirs of Giorgio de Chirico.* Trans. from Italian and with introd. by Margaret Crosland. London, Owen, 1971.

2009. ———. *Memorie della vita mia.* Milano, Rizzoli, 1962. 2 ed.

2010. ———. *De Chirico nel centenario della nascita.* In collaborazione con la Galleria Nazionale d'Arte Mpderna, Roma e la Fondazione Giorgio e Isa de Chirico. Milano, Mondadori; Roma, De Luca, 1988.

2011. Guzzi, Domenico. *Giorgio De Chirico: arma virumque cano: il mito classico dell'eroe guerriero.* Pref. di Giulio Andreotti. Roma, Leonardo Arte, 1989.

2012. Ciranna, Alfonso. *Giorgio de Chirico.* Catalogo delle opere grafiche: incisioni e litografie, 1921–1969. A cura di Alfonso Ciranna con introd. critica di Cesare Vivaldi. Milano, Ciranna, 1969.

2013. Costantini, Constanzo. *Il pittore glorioso.* Milano, Sugar Co., 1978.

2014. Far, Isabella. *De Chirico.* Trans. from French by Joseph M. Bernstein. New York, Abrams, 1968.

2015. Ragghianti, Carlo Ludovico. *Il caso de Chirico: saggi e studi 1934–1978.* Firenze, Critica d'Arte, 1979.

2016. Soby, James Thrall. *The early Chirico.* New York, Dodd, Mead, 1941; rev. ed.: *Giorgio de Chirico,* New York, Museum of Modern Art, 1955.

2017. Spaguoli, Luisa. *Lunga vita di Giorgio de Chirico.* Milano, Longanesi, 1971.

2018. Waldemar-George [pseud.]. *Chirico.* Avec des fragments littéraires de l'artiste. Paris, Editions des Chroniques du Jour, 1928. (Les maîtres nouveaux, 15).

Chodowiecki, Daniel Nikolaus, 1726–1801

2019. Bauer, J. *Daniel Nikolaus Chodowiecki, 1726–1801. Das druckgraphische Werk.* Hannover, Galerie Bauer, 1982.

2020. Bredt, E. W. *Chodowiecki. Zwischen Rokoko und Romantik.* München, Hugo Schmidt, n.d.

2021. Brinitzer, Carl. *Die Geschichte des Daniel Chodowicki; ein Sittenbild des 18. Jahrhunderts.* Stuttgart, Deutsche Verlagsanstalt, 1973.

2022. Chodowiecki, Daniel. *Briefe an Anton Graff.* Hrsg. von Charlotte Steinbrucker. Berlin/Leipzig, de Gruyter, 1921.

2023. ———. *Briefe an die Gräfin von Solms-Laubach.* Hrsg. von Charlotte Steinbrucker. Strassburg, Heitz, 1928. (Studien zur deutschen Kunstgeschichte, 250).

2024. ———. *Briefwechsel zwischen Daniel Chodowicki und seinen Zeitgenossen.* Hrsg. von Charlotte Steinbrucker. Berlin, Duncker, 1919.

2025. ———. *Journal gehalten auf einer Lustreise von Berlin nach Dresden im Jahre 1789.* Mit einer Einleitung von Adam Wiecek. Berlin, Akademie-Verlag, 1961. (Schriften zur Kunstgeschichte, 6).

2026. ———. *Unveröffentlichte Handzeichnungen zu dem Elementarwerk von Johann Bernhard Basedow.* Mit einem Vorworte von Max von Boehn. Frankfurt, Voigtländer-Tetzner, 1922. (Veröffentlichung der Prestel-Gesellschaft, 10).

2027. ———. *Unveröffentlichte Handzeichnungen zu dem moralischen Elementarbuche von Christian Gotthelf Salzman.* Mit einem Vorworte von Max von Boehn. Frankfurt, Voigtländer-Tetzner, 1922. (Veröffentlichung der Prestel-Gesellschaft, 11).

2028. ———. *Von Berlin nach Danzig. Eine Künstlerfahrt im Jahre 1773 von Daniel Chodowiecki.* 108 Lichtdrucke nach Originalen in der Königl. Akademie der Künste in Berlin. Mit erläuterndem Text und einer Einführung von Wolfgang von Oet-tingen. Leipzig, Insel, 1923.

2029. Denkert, Paul. *Daniel Chodowiecki.* Berlin, Rembrandt-Verlag, 1977.

2030. Engelmann, Wilhelm. *Daniel Chodowiecki's sämmtliche Kupferstiche.* Beschrieben, mit historischen, literarischen und bibliographischen Nachweisungen, der Lebensbeschreibung des Künstlers und Registern versehen von Wilhelm Engelmann. Mit drei Kupfertafeln Copien der seltensten Blätter des Meisters enthaltend. Leipzig, Engelmann, 1857. (Reprint: Hildesheim, Olms, 1969).

2031. ———. *Nachträge und Berichtigungen.* Leipzig, Engelmann, 1860. (Reprint: see above).

2032. Jahn, Johannes. *Daniel Chodowiecki und die künstlerische Entdeckung des Berliner bürgerlichen Alltags.* Berlin, Henschelverlag, 1954. (Berlin in der Kunst. Veröff. der Deutschen Akademie der Künste, 1).

2033. Kaemmerer, Ludwig J. K. *Chodowiecki.* Bielefeld/Leipzig, Velhagen & Klasing, 1897. (Künstler-Monographien, 21).

2034. Laundau, Paul. *Chodowieckis Illustrationen zu den deutschen Klassikern.* Berlin, Bard, 1920.

2035. Meyer, Ferdinand. *Daniel Chodowiecki der peintre-graveur. Im Lichte seiner und unsere Zeit dargestellt.* Berlin, Mückenberger, 1888.

2036. Oettingen, Wolfgang von. *Daniel Chodowiecki; ein Berliner Künstlerleben im achtzehnten Jahrhundert.* Berlin, Grote, 1895.

2037. Redslob, Edwin. *Daniel Chodowiecki.* Berlin, Berlin-Museum, 1965. (Veröffentlichungen des Berlin-Museums, 2).

2038. Rümann, Arthur. *Daniel Chodowiecki (Bibliographie).* Berlin. (Das Werk, Sammlung praktischer Bibliographien, 1: Das graphische Werk).

2039. Städelsches Kunstinstitut (Frankfurt a.M.). *Bürgerliches Leben im 18. Jahrhundert: Daniel Chodowiecki, 1726–1801. Zeichnungen und Druckgraphik.* Katalog der Ausstellung vom 8. Juni–20 August, 1978. Katalogbearbeitung Peter Märker. Frankfurt a.M., Städel, 1978.

2040. Turnau, Irena. *Kultura materialna oswiecenia w rycinach Daniela Chod-owieckiego.* Wrocław, etc. Zaktad Narodowy Imienia Ossolinskich Wydawnictwo Polskiej Akademii Nauk, 1968.

Christo (Christo Javacheff), 1935–

2041. Christo. *Christo.* Text by David Bourdon. New York, Abrams, 1972.

2042. ———. *The Pont Neuf, wrapped, Paris, 1975–1985.* Photographs [by] Wolfgang Volz,; picture commentary, David Bourdon; the Pont-Neuf and Paris [by] Bernard de Montgolfier. New York, Harry N. Abrams, 1990.

2043. ———. *Running Fence, Sonoma and Marin Counties, California, 1972–76.* Photos by Gianfranco Gorgoni; chronicle by Calvin Tomkins; text by David Bourdon. New York, Abrams, 1978.

2044. ———. *Valley Curtain, Rifle, Colorado, 1970–72.* Photos: Harry Shunk. New York, Abrams, 1973.

2045. Houdenakk, Pei and Schellmann, Jorg. *Christo: The complete editions, 1964–1982.*

New York University Press, 1982.

2046. Institute of Contemporary Art (Boston). *Urban projects; a survey [by Christo].* May 9–July 1, 1979. Boston, Institute of Contemporary Art, 1979.

2047. Laporte, Dominique G. *Christo.* Trans. by Abby Pollak. New York, Pantheon Books, 1986.

2048. Princeton University Art Museum. *Christo: Oceanfront.* Text by Sally Yard; photos by Gianfranco Gorgoni. Princeton, N.J., University Art Museum; distributed by Princeton University Press, 1975.

2049. Schellmann, Jörg and Benecke, Josèphine, eds. *Christo: prints and objects, 1963–1987; a catalogue raisonné.* Introduction by Werner Spies. München, Edition Schellmann; New York, Edition Schellmann and Abbeville Press, 1988. (CR).

Christus, Petrus *see* Cristus, Petrus

Chu Ta, c. 1630–c. 1705

2050. Chang, Wan-li and Hu Jen-mou. *The selected paintings and calligraphy of Pa-Ta-Shan-Jeh [Chu Ta].* 2 v. Hong Kong, Cafa, 1969.

2051. Vassar College Art Gallery. *Chu Ta, selected paintings and calligraphy.* December 2, 1972–January 28, 1973. New York, New York Cultural Center, 1973.

Church, Frederic Edwin, 1826–1900

2052. Carr, Gerald L. *Frederic Edwin Church: catalogue rasionné of works of art of Olana State Historic Site.* Cambridge[England]/New York, Cambridge University Press, 1994. (CR).

2053. Huntington, David C. *The landscape of Frederic Edwin Church; vision of an American era.* New York, Braziller, 1966.

2054. Kelly, Franklin. *Frederic Edwin Church.* [Catalogue of an exhibition held at the National Gallery of Art, Washington, D.C., October 8, 1989–March 18, 1990].

2055. ———. *Frederic Edwin Church.* F. Kelly, with Stephen Jay Gould, James Anthony Ryan, and Debora Rindge. Washington, D.C., National Gallery of Art; Smithsonian Institution Press, 1989.

2056. Metropolitan Museum of Art (New York). *Paintings by Frederic E. Church; special exhibition, May 28 to Oct. 15, 1900.* New York, Metropolitan Museum of Art, 1900.

2057. National Collection of Fine Arts (Washington, D.C.). *Frederic Edwin Church; an exhibition, Feb. 12–Mar. 13, 1966.* Preface by Richard Wunder. Washington, D.C., Smithsonian Institution-N.C.F.A., 1966.

Cignani, Carlo, 1628–1719

2058. Fabbri, Beatrice Buscaroli. *Carlo Cignani:*

alfreschi, dipinti, disegni. Bologna, Nuova Alfa Editrice, 1991.

2059. Vitelli Buscaroli, Syra. *Carlo Cignani, 1628–1719.* Bologna, Arti Grafiche, 1953.

Cigoli, Lodovico Cardi da, 1559–1613

2060. Battelli, Guido. *Lodovico Cardi, detto il Cigoli.* Firenze, Alinari, 1922. (Piccola collezione d'arte, 38).

Cima da Conegliano, Giovanni Battista, 1460–1517

2061. Botteon, Vincenzo. *Ricerche intorno alla vita e alle opere di Giambattista Cima.* Conegliano, Cagnani, 1893.

2062. Burckhardt, Rudolf F. *Cima da Conegliano; ein venezianischer Maler des Übergangs vom Quattrocento zum Cinquecento.* Leipzig, Hiersemann, 1905. (Kunstgeschicht-liche Monographien, 2).

2063. Coletti, Luigi. *Cima da Conegliano.* Venezia, Pozza, 1959.

2064. Humfrey, Peter. *Cima.* Cambridge, Cambridge University Press, 1983.

2065. Menegazzi, Luigi. *Cima da Conegliano.* Treviso, Canova, 1981.

2066. Palazzo de Trecento (Venice). *Cima da Conegliano.* 26 agosto–11 novembre 1962. Venezia, Pozza, 1962.

Cimabue, Giovanni, 1240–1302

2067. Battisti, Eugenio. *Cimabue.* Milano, Istituto Editoriale Italiano, 1963. (Arte e pensiero, 5). English ed.: University Park, Penn., Pennsylvania State University Press, 1966.

2068. Nicholson, Alfred. *Cimabue; a critical study.* Princeton, N.J., Princeton University Press, 1932. (Princeton Monographs in Art and Archaeology, 16).

2069. Salvini, Roberto. *Cimabue.* Roma, Tuminelli, 1946.

Cingria, Alexandre, 1879–1945

2070. Bouvier, Jean Bernard. *Alexandre Cingria, peintre, mosaïste et verrier.* Genève-Annemasse, Editions du Mont Blanc, 1944.

2071. Fosca, François. *Portrait d'Alexandre Cingria.* Lausanne, Payot, 1930. (Les Cahiers romands, 11).

2072. Musée Rath (Geneva). *Alexandre Cingria (1879–1945).* 14 mai–27 juin 1965. Genève, 1965.

Civitali, Matteo, 1436–1501

2073. Meli, Filippo. *L'arte di Matteo Civitali.* Lucca, Baroni, 1934.

2074. Yriarte, Charles E. *Sculpture italienne, XV. siècle; Matteo Civitali, sa vie et son oeuvre.* Paris, Rothschild, 1886.

Clark, Robert *see* Indiana, Robert

Claude Lorrain (Claude Gellée), 1600–1682

2075. Blum, André. *Les eaux-fortes de Claude Gellée.* Paris, Documents d'Art, 1923.

2076. Bouyer, Raymond. *Claude Lorrain.* Paris, Laurens, 1905.

2077. Christoffel, Ulrich. *Poussin und Claude Lorrain.* Einleitung von U. Christoffel. Die Auswahl der Bilder besorgte Bernhard Dörries. München, Bruckmann, 1942.

2078. Claude Lorrain. *Liber veritatis; or, a collection of prints, after the original designs of Claude Lorrain, in the collection of His Grace, the Duke of Devonshire.* 3 v. London, Boydell, 1777–1819.

2079. Cotté, Sabine. *Claude Lorrain.* Trans. by Helen Sebba. New York, Braziller, 1971.

2080. Courthion, Pierre. *Claude Gellée dit Le Lorrain.* Paris, Floury, 1932.

2081. Demonts, Louis. *Les dessins de Claude Gellée dit Le Lorrain.* Paris, Morancé, 1923.

2082. Dulles, Owen J. *Claude Gellée Le Lorrain.* London, Sampson Low, 1887.

2083. Friedländer, Walter. *Claude Lorrain.* Berlin, Cassirer, 1921.

2084. Grahame, George. *Claude Lorrain, painter and etcher.* London, Seeley/New York, Macmillan, 1895. (Portfolio Artistic Monographs, 15).

2085. Graphische Sammlung Albertina (Vienna). *Claude Lorrain und die Meister der römischen Landschaft im XVII. Jahrhundert.* 16. Nov.–15. Feb. 1965. Wien, Albertina, 1964.

2086. Hetzer, Theodor. *Claude Lorrain.* Frankfurt a.M., Klostermann, 1947.

2087. Hind, Arthur M. *Catalogue of the drawings of Claude Lorrain in the Print Dept. of the British Museum.* London, British Museum, 1926.

2088. ———. *The drawings of Claude Lorrain.* London, Halton/New York, Minton, 1925.

2089. Langdon, Helen. *Claude Lorrain.* Oxford, Phaidon, 1989.

2090. Manocci, Lino. *The etchings of Claude Lorrain.* New Haven/ London, Yale University Press, 1988.

2091. Kitson, Michael. *Claude Lorrain, Liber veritatis.* London, British Museum Publications, 1978.

2092. Langdon, Helen. *Claude Lorrain.* Oxford, Phaidon, 1989.

2093. Manwaring, Elizabeth W. *Italian landscape in eighteenth century England; a study chiefly of the influence of Claude Lorrain and Salvator Rosa on English taste, 1700–1800.* New York, Oxford University Press, 1925.

2094. Marotte, Léon. *Claude Gellée dit Le Lorrain.* Cinquante-deux reproductions de L. Marotte avec un catalogue et une vie du peintre par J. de Sandrart, nouvellement traduit de l'allemand par Charles Martine. Paris, Helleu, 1922. (Dessins de maîtres français, 2).

2095. Pattison, Emily F. *Claude Lorrain, sa vie et ses oeuvres, d'après des documents inédits.* Par Mme. Mark Pattison. Suivi d'un catalogue des oeuvres de Claude Lorrain, conservées dans les musées et dans les collections particulières de l'Europe. Paris, Rouam, 1884.

2096. Röthlisberger, Marcel. *Claude Lorrain: the drawings.* 2 v. Berkeley, University of California Press, 1968. (California Studies in the History of Art, 8).

2097. ———. *Claude Lorrain: The Paintings.* New Haven, Yale University Press, 1961. 2 v.(Yale Publications in the History of Art, 13). Reprint: New York, Hacker, 1979.

2098. ———. *L'opera completa di Claude Lorrain.* Presentazione di M. Röthlisberger, apparati critici e filologici a cura di Doretta Cecchi. Milano, Rizzoli, 1975. (Classici dell'arte, 83).

2099. Russell, H. Diane. *Claude Lorrain, 1600–1682.* Washington, D.C., National Gallery of Art, 1982.

2100. Sweetser, Moses F. *Claude Lorrain.* Boston, Houghton Mifflin, 1878. (Artist-biographies, 6).

2101. Wine, Humphrey. *Claude, the poetic landscape.* London, National Gallery, 1994.

Claudel, Camille, 1864–1943.

2102. Paris, Reine-Marie. *Camille; the life of Camille Claudel, Rodin's muse and mistress.* Trans. by Liliane Emery Tuck. New York, Seaver Books, 1988.

2103. Paris, Reine-Marie and Arnaud de la Chapelle. *L'oeuvre de Camille Claudel;* catalogue raisonné. Nouvelle édition, revisée et completée Paris, Editions d'art et d'histoire Arhis, 1991. (CR).

Clerici, Fabrizio, 1913–

2104. Brion, Marcel. *Fabrizio Clerici.* Milano, Electa, 1955.

2105. Carrieri, Raffaele. *Fabrizio Clerici.* Milano, Electa, 1955.

2106. Museo Civico (Bologna). *Fabrizio Clerici: I disegni per L'Orlando Furioso.* 28 marzo–3 maggio 1981. Bologna, Grafis industrie, 1981.

Cleve, Joos van, ca. 1485–ca. 1540

2107. Baldass, Ludwig von. *Joos van Cleve der Meister des Todes Mariä.* Wien, Krystall-Verlag, 1925.

Clodion, Claude Michel, 1738–1814

2108. Poulet, Anne L. and Scherf, Guilhelm. *Clo-dion, 1738–1814.* [Catalogue of an exhibition held at the] Musée du Louvre, 17 mars–29 juin, 1992. Paris. Réunion des Musées nationaux, 1992.

2109. Thirion, Henri. *Les Adam et Clodion.* Paris, A.Quantin, 1885.

Close, Chuck, 1940–

2110. Lyons, Lisa, and Robert Storr. *Chuck Close.* New York, Rizzoli, 1987

Clouet, François, 1505–1572
Jean, 1475–1541

2111. Bibliothèque Nationale, Paris. *Les Clouet et la cour des rois de France.* [Exposition] catalogue: Jean Adhémar. Paris, Bibliothèque Nationale, 1970.

2112. Clouet, François. *Three hundred French portraits representing personages of the courts of Francis I, Henry II, and Francis II.* Autolithographed from the originals at Castle Howard, Yorkshire, by Lord Ronald Gower. London, Low/Paris, Hachette, 1875.

2113. Fourreau, Armand. *Les Clouet.* Paris, Rieder, 1929.

2114. Germain, Alphonse. *Les Clouet; biographie critique.* Paris, Laurens, 1907.

2115. Jolly, Alphonse. *Les crayons de Jean Clouet.* Paris, Marceau, 1952.

2116. Malo, Henri. *Les Clouet de Chantilly.* Paris, Laurens, 1932.

2117. Mellen, Peter. *Jean Clouet: complete edition of drawings, miniatures and paintings.* London, Phaidon, 1971.

2118. Moreau-Nélaton, Etienne. *Les Clouet et leurs émules.* 3 v. Paris, Laurens, 1924.

2119. ———. *Les Clouet, peintres officiels des rois de France.* Paris, Levy, 1908.

Clovio, Giulio (Macedo), 1498–1578

2120. Bradley, John W. *The life and works of Giorgio Giulio Clovio, miniaturist, with notices of his contemporaries and of the art of book decoration in the sixteenth century.* London, Quaritch, 1891.

2121. Gamulin, Grego and Cionini-Visani, Maria. *Giulio Clovio. A catalogue raisonné.* New York, Alpine, 1980. (CR).

Coburn, Alvin Langdon, 1882–1966

2122. Coburn, Alvin Langdon. *Alvin Langdon Coburn, photographer; an autobiography.* Ed. by Helmut and A. Gernsheim. New York, Praeger, 1966.

2123. George Eastman House (Rochester, New York). *Alvin Langdon Coburn: an exhibition of photographs from the International Museum of Photography.* Rochester, New York, George Eastman House/London, Arts Council of Great Britain, 1978.

Coducci, Mauro, c. 1440-1504

2124. Angelini, Luigi. *Le opere in Venezia di Mauro Codussi.* Milano, Bestetti, 1945.

2125. Puppi, Lionello [and] Loredana O. *Mauro Codussi.* Fotografie di Paolo Monti. Milano, Electa, 1977.

Coecke, Pieter, 1502-1550

2126. Corbet, August. *Pieter Coecke van Aelst.* Antwerpen, De Sikkel, 1950. (Maerlant-bibliotheek, 21).

2127. Friedländer, Max J. *Jan van Scorel and Pieter Coeck van Aelst.* Comments and notes by H. Pauwels and G. Lemmen. Assisted by Monique Gierts and Anne-Marie Hess. Trans. by Heinz Norden. Leyden, Sijthoff/ Brussels, La Connaissance, 1975. (Early Netherlandish Painting, 12).

2128. Marlier, Georges. *Pierre Coeck d'Alost, 1502-1550; la renaissance flamande.* Bruxelles, Finck, 1966.

Coello, Alonso Sanchez *see* Sanchez Coello, Alonso

Coldstream, William, 1908-1987.

2129. Gowing, Lawrence. *The Paintings of William Coldstream, 1908-1987.* London, Tate Gallery Publications, 1990.

Cole, Thomas, 1801-1848

2130. Baigell, Matthew. *Thomas Cole.* New York, Watson-Guptill, 1981.

2131. Baltimore Museum of Art. *Studies on Thomas Cole, an American romanticist.* Essays by Howard S. Merritt and William H. Gerdts, Jr. Baltimore Museum of Art, 1967.

2132. Noble, Louis L. *The Course of Empire, Voyage of Life, and other pictures of Thomas Cole, N.A., with selections from his letters and miscellaneous writings.* New York, Cornish, Lamport, 1853. (New ed.: *The life and works of Thomas Cole.* Edited by Eliot S. Vesell. Cambridge, Mass., Harvard University Press, 1964).

2133. Parry Ellwood C. *The art of Thomas Cole; ambition and imagination.* Newark, University of Delaware Press; London and Toronto, Associated University Presses, 1988.

2134. Powell, Earl A. *Thomas Cole.* New York, Harry N. Abrams, 1990.

2135. Wadsworth Atheneum (Hartford). *Thomas Cole, 1801-1848; one hundred years later, a loan exhibition, Nov. 12, 1948-Jan. 2, 1949.* Hartford, Wadsworth Atheneum, 1948.

Colombe, Michel, 1430-1512

2136. Fillon, Benjamin. *Documents relatifs aux oeuvres de Michel Colombe, exécutées pour le Poitou, l'Aunis et le Pays Natais.* Fontenay-le-Comte, Robuchon, 1865.

2137. Pradel, Pierre. *Michel Colombe, le dernier imagier gothique.* Paris, Plon, 1953.

2138. Vitra, Paul. *Michel Colombe et la sculpture française de son temps.* Paris, Librairie Centrale des Beaux-Arts, 1901.

Conegliano, Giovanni Battista Cima da *see* Cima da Conegliano, Giovanni Battista

Constable, John, 1776-1837

2139. Bunt, Cyril G. E. *John Constable, the father of modern landscape.* Leigh-on-Sea, Lewis, 1948. (The Lewis "Introduction to painters" series, 1).

2140. Constable, John. *Correspondence, edited by R. B. Bechet with an introduction and notes.* 6 v. London, HMSO, 1962-1968.

2141. ———. *John Constable, R.A. (1776-1837).* An exhibition [of] paintings, drwawings, watercolors, mezzotints. By Graham Reynolds, Charles Rhyne, with essays from 'Modern art: the struggle for painting'(vol. 1, 1906), by Julius Meier-Graefe. New York, Salander-O'Reilly Galleries, 1988.

2142. ———. *Sketch-books of 1813 and 1814.* Reproduced in facsimile. Introdcution by Graham Reynolds. 3 v. London, H.M. Stationery Office, 1973. (Reprint: London, Victoria and Albert Museum, 1991).

2143. Cormack, Malcolm. *Constable.* Oxford, Phaidon, 1986.

2144. Darracott, Joseph. *England's Constable: the life and letters of John Constable.* London, Folio Society, 1985.

2145. Fleming-Williams, Ian. *Constable and his drawings.* London, Philip Wilson, 1990.

2146. Fraser, John Lloyd. *John Constable, 1776-1837: the man and his mistress.* London, Hutchinson, 1976.

2147. Gadney, Reg. *Constable and his world.* London, Thames and Hudson, 1976.

2148. Holmes, Charles J. *Constable and his influence on landscape painting.* Westminster, Constable, 1902.

2149. Ivy, Judy Crosby. *Constable and the critics, 1802-1837.* Woodbridge, Suffolk; Rochester, NY, USA, Boydell in association with the Suffolk Records Society, 1991.

2150. Leslie, Charles R. *Memoirs of the life of John Constable, Esq., R. A.; composed chiefly of his letters.* With an introduction by Benedict Nicolson. London, Phaidon, 1951. 2 ed. (The Chiltern library, 29).

2151. Parris, Leslie. *Constable.* [Catalogue of an exhibition] by L. Parris and Ian Fleming-Williams. London, Tate Gallery, 1991.

2152. ———. *Constable: pictures from the exhibition.* London, Tate Gallery, 1991.

2153. Peacock, Carlos. *John Constable, the man and his work.* Greenwich, Conn., New York Graphic Society, 1956.

2154. Reynolds, Graham. *Constable, the natural painter.* New York, McGraw-Hill, 1965.

2155. ———, ed. *Constable with his friends in 1806; sketchbooks in facsimile.* 5 v. London, Trianon Press/Genesis, 1983.

2156. ———. *The later paintings and drawings of John Constable.* 2 v. Haven and London, Yale University Press, 1984

2157. Rhyne, Charles S. *John Constable; toward a complete chronology.* Portland, Oregon, Published by the editor, 1990.

2158. Rosenthal, Michael. *Constable; the painter and his landscape.* New Haven, Yale University Press, 1982.

2159. Shirley, Andrew. *John Constable.* London, Medici Society, 1948.

2160. Smart, Alastair. *Constable and his country.* By A. Smart and Attfield Brooks. London, Elek, 1976.

2161. Tate Gallery (London). *Constable: paintings, watercolours and drawings.* 18 Feb.–25 Apr. 1976. [Catalogue by Leslie Parris et al.]. London, Tate Gallery, 1976. 2 rev. ed.

2162. Taylor, Basil. *Constable; paintings, drawings and watercolours.* London, Phaidon, 1975. 2 ed.

2163. Victoria and Albert Museum (London). *Catalogue of the Constable collection.* By Graham Reynolds. London, HMSO, 1960.

2164. Walker, John. *John Constable.* New York, Abrams, 1978.

2165. Windsor, J. *John Constable.* London, Walker Scott/New York, Scribner, 1903.

Cooper, Samuel, 1609–1672

2166. Foskett, Daphne. *Samuel Cooper, 1609–1672.* London, Faber, 1974.

2167. Foster, Joshua J. *Samuel Cooper and the English miniature painters of the XVII century.* London, Dickinsons, 1914–16.

2168. National Portrait Gallery (London). *Samuel Cooper and his contemporaries.* [Text by Daphne Foskett et al.]. London, HMSO, 1974.

Copley, John Singleton, 1738–1815

2169. Bayley, Frank W. *The life and works of John Singleton Copley,* founded on the work of Augustus Thorndike Perkins. Boston, Taylor, 1915.

2170. Copley, John Singleton. *Letters and papers of John Singleton Copley and Henry Pelham, 1739–1776.* New York, Kennedy Graphics, 1970. (Republication of 1st ed., 1914, which appeared as vol. 71 of the "Collections of the Massachusetts Historical Society").

2171. Flexner, James T. *The double adventure of John Singleton Copley, first major painter of the new world.* Boston, Little Brown, 1969.

2172. ———. *John Singleton Copley.* Boston, Houghton-Mifflin, 1948.

2173. Frankenstein, Alfred Victor. *The world of Copley, 1738–1815.* New York, Time-Life Books, 1970.

2174. Morgan, John H. *John Singleton Copley, 1737/8–1815.* Windham, Conn., The Walpole Society, 1939.

2175. National Gallery of Art (Washington, D.C.). *John Singleton Copley, 1738–1815.* Catalog of an exhibition at the National Gallery of Art, Washington; the Metropolitan Museum of Art, New York, and the Museum of Fine Arts, Boston. Text by Jules D. Brown. New York, October House, 1965.

2176. Parker, Barbara N. and Wheeler, Anne B. *John Singleton Copley; American portraits in oil, pastel, and miniature.* Boston, Museum of Fine Arts, 1938.

2177. Perkins, Augustus T. *A sketch of the life and a list of some of the works of John Singleton Copley.* Boston, Osgood, 1873.

2178. Prown, Jules D. *John Singleton Copley.* 2 v. Publ. for the National Gallery of Art. Cambridge, Mass., Harvard University Press, 1966.

Corinth, Lovis, 1858–1925

2179. Badischer Kunstverein, Karlsruhe. *Lovis Corinth: das Portrait, Gemälde, Aquarelle, Zeichnungen.* 4. Juni–3. Sept. 1967. Katalogredaktion: Klaus Gallwitz. Karlsruhe, Badischer Kunstverein, 1967.

2180. Biermann, Georg. *Lovis Corinth.* Bielefeld/Leipzig, Velhagen & Klasing, 1913. (Künstler-Monographien, 107).

2181. ———. *Der Zeichner Lovis Corinth.* Dresden, Arnold, 1924.

2182. Corinth, Charlotte Berend. *Die Gemälde von Lovis Corinth: Werkkatalog.* Mit einer Einführung von H. K. Röthel. München, Bruckmann, 1958.

2183. ———. *Lovis.* München, Langen, 1958.

2184. ———. *Mein Leben mit Lovis Corinth.* München, List, 1947.

2185. Corinth, Lovis. *Das Erlernen der Malerei.* Berlin, Cassirer, 1920. 3 ed. (Reprint: Hildesheim, Gerstenberg, 1979).

2186. ———. *Gesammelte Schriften.* Berlin, Gurlitt, 1920. (Maler-Bücher, 1).

2187. ———. *Lovis Corinth; eine Dokumentation.* Zusammengestellt und erläutert von Thomas Corinth. Tübingen, Wasmuth, 1979.

2188. ———. *Selbstbiographie.* Leipzig, Hirzel, 1926.

2189. Klein, Rudolf. *Lovis Corinth.* Paris, Librairie Artistique et Littéraire, 1909.

2190. Kuhn, Alfred. *Lovis Corinth.* Berlin, Propyläen-Verlag, 1925.

2191. Kunsthalle Köln. *Lovis Corinth: Gemälde,*

Aquarelle, Zeichnungen und druckgraph-ische Zyklen. Ausstellung des Wallraf-Richartz-Museums in der Kunsthalle, 10. Januar–21. März 1976. Vorwort von Horst Keller, Katalogbearbeitung Siegfried Gohr. Köln, Museum der Stadt Köln, 1976.

2192. Müller, Heinrich. *Die späte Graphik von Lovis Corinth.* Hamburg, Lichtwarkstiftung; distributed by W. Gurlitt, München, 1960.

2193. Nationalgalerie (Berlin). *Lovis Corinth.* Ausstellung von Gemälden und Aquarellen zu seinem Gedächtnis. Einführung von Ludwig Justi. Berlin, Nationalgalerie, 1926. 4 ed.

2194. Osten, Gert von der. *Lovis Corinth.* München, Bruckmann, 1955. 2 ed.

2195. Rhode, Alfred. *Der Junge Corinth.* Berlin, Rembrandt-Verlag, 1941.

2196. Röthel, Hans K. *Lovis Corinth.* Zur Feier seines hun-dertsten Geburtstages. Aus-stellung, 7. Juli–17. August 1958. Gemälde: Städtische Galerie; Aquarelle, Zeichnung, Druckgraphik: Staatl. Graphische Samm-lung. 50 graph. Selbstbildnisse: Galerie Gurlitt. München, 1958.

2197. Schwarz, Karl. *Das graphische Werk von Lovis Corinth.* San Francisco, Alan Wofsy, 1985. 3 ed., rev. and enlarged, with all the works illustrated, and with an English trans-lation of the technical terms.

2198. Singer, Hans W. *Zeichnungen von Lovis Corinth.* Leipzig, A. Schumann's Verlag, 1921. (Meister der Zeichnung, 8).

2199. Städtische Galerie im Lenbachhaus München. *Lovis Corinth 1858–1925.* Gemälde und Druckgraphik. München, Prestel, 1975.

2200. Uhr, Horst. *Lovis Corinth.* Berkeley, Univer-sity of California Press, 1990.

Cornelisz, Cornelis, van Haarlem, 1562–1638

2201. McGee, Julie L. *Cornelis Corneliszoon van Haarlem, 1562–1638: patrons, friends and Dutch humanists.* Nieuwkoop, the Nether-lands, De Graaf, 1991. (Bibliotheca Human-istica and Reformatorica, 48).

Cornelisz, Jakob, van Oostsanen, ca. 1470–1533

2202. Steinbart, Kurt. *Das Holzschnittwerk de Jakob Cornelisz von Amsterdam.* Burg, Hop-fer, 1937.

2203. ———. *Die Tafelgemälde de Jakob Cornelisz von Amsterdam.* Strassburg, Heitz, 1922. (Studien zur deutschen Kunstgesch-ichte, 221).

Cornelius, Peter, 1783–1867

2204. Eckert, Christian L. M. *Peter Cornelius.* Bielefeld/Leipzig, Velhagen & Klasing, 1906.

(Künstler-Monographien, 82).

2205. Kuhn, Alfred. *Peter Cornelius und die geistigen Strömungen seiner Zeit.* Mit den Briefen des Meisters an Ludwig I von Bayern und an Goethe. Berlin, Reimer, 1921.

2206. Riegel, Herman. *Cornelius der Meister der deutschen Malerei.* Hannover, Rümpler, 1870. 2 ed.

2207. ———. *Peter Cornelius.* Festschrift zu des grossen Künstlers hundertstem Geburtstage. Berlin, Decker, 1883.

2208. Simon, Karl. *Die Frühzeit des Peter Cor-nelius.* Düsseldorf, Schwann, 1925. (Pem-pelfort; Sammlung kleiner Düsseldorfer Kunstschriften, 4).

Cornell, Joseph, 1903–1972

2209. Cornell, Joseph. *Joseph Cornell's theater of the mind: selected diaries, letters, and files of a great American artist.* Edited, with an in-troduction by Mary Ann Caws. Preface by John Ashbery. New York, Thames and Hudson, 1992.

2210. Jaguer, Edouard. *Joseph Cornell.* [Exposi-tion] du 13 mars au 8 avril 1989. Galerie 1900–2000, Paris. Paris, La Galerie, 1989.

2211. McShine, Kynaston, ed. *Joseph Cornell.* With essays by Dawn Ades, Carter Ratcliff, et al. New York, Museum of Modern Art, 1980. (Reprint: New York, Museum of Modern Art/ Prestel, 1990).

2212. Simic, Charles. *Dime-store alchemy; the art of Joseph Cornell.* Hopewell, N.J., Ecco Press, 1992.

Corot, Jean-Baptiste Camille, 1796–1875

2213. Art Institute of Chicago. *Corot 1796–1875.* An exhibition of his paintings and graphic works, Oct. 6–Nov. 13, 1960. Introduction by S. Lane Faison. Notes by James Merrill. Chicago, 1960.

2214. Baud-Bovy, Daniel. *Corot.* Genève, Jullien, 1957.

2215. Bazin, Germain, *Corot.* Paris, Tisné, 1942.

2216. Bibliothèque Nationale (Paris). *Estampes et Dessins de Corot.* Exposition organisée avec le concours de Musée du Louvre. Paris, Edi-tions des Bibliothèques Nationales, 1931.

2217. Clarke, Michael. *Corot and the art of land-scape.* London, British Museum Press, 1991.

2218. Coquis, André. *Corot et la critique contem-poraine.* Paris, Dervy, 1959.

2219. Cornu, Paul. *Corot.* Paris, Michaud, 1889.

2220. Corot, Jean-Baptiste C. *Corot, raconté par lui-même et par ses amis.* Ed. by Etienne Moreau-Nélaton. 2 v. Genève, Cailler, 1946.

2221. Faure, Elie. *Corot.* Paris, Crès, 1931.

2222. Gaillot, Edouard. *La vie secrète de Jean-Baptiste-Camille Corot, peintre, graveur et sculpteur; d'après des documents nouveaux et quelques anciens nouvellement élucidés.* Paris, Guitard, 1934.

2223. Galassi, Peter. *Corot in Italy: open-air painting and the classical landscape tradition.* New Haven, Yale University Press, 1991.

2224. Gensel, Walther. *Corot und Troyon.* Bielefeld/Leipzig, Velhagen & Klasing, 1906. (Künstler-Monographien, 83).

2225. Leymarie, Jean. *Corot.* Trans. by S. Gilbert. A biographical and critical study. Lausanne, Skira/Cleveland, World, 1966. (The Taste of Our Time, 44).

2226. Mauclair, Camille. *Corot, peintre-poète de la France.* Paris, Michel, 1962.

2227. Meier-Graefe, Julius. *Corot.* Berlin, Cassirer/ Klinkhardt und Biermann, 1930.

2228. ———. *Corot und Courbet.* München, Piper, 1912. 2 ed.

2229. Meynell, Everard. *Corot and his friends.* London, Methuen, 1908.

2230. Michel, Emile. *Corot.* Paris, Librairie de l'Art, 1905.

2231. Musée de l'Orangerie (Paris). *Hommage à Corot: peintures et dessins des collections françaises, 6 juin–29 sept. 1975.* Catalogue par Hélène Toussaint, Geneviève Monnier et Martine Servot. Paris, Editions des Musées Nationaux, 1975.

2232. Musée Nationale du Louvre (Paris). *Dessins de Corot, 1796–1875.* Catalogue établi par Martine Servot. Paris, 1962. (Cabinet des Dessins du Louvre).

2233. ———. *Figures de Corot.* Juin–septembre 1962. Paris, Ministère d'Etat pour Affaires Culturelles, 1962.

2234. Palais Galliera (Paris). *Exposition organisée au profit du monument du centenaire de Corot.* Catalogue des chefs-d'oeuvre prêtés par les musées de l'état et les grandes collections de France et de l'étranger. Paris, Georges Petit, 1895.

2235. Philadelphia Museum of Art. *Corot 1796–1875.* [Catalog of the exhibition]. Foreword by Henri Marceau. Introduction by Lionello Venturi. Philadelphia, 1946.

2236. Robaut, Alfred and Moreau-Nélaton, Etienne. *L'oeuvre de Corot.* 5 v. Paris, Floury, 1905. (Reprint: Paris, Laget, 1965, 1966). (CR).

2237. Schoeller, André and Dieterle, Jean. *Corot.* Premier supplément à *L'oeuvre de Corot* par A. Robaut et Moreau-Nélaton. Paris, Arts et Métiers Graphiques, 1948. (CR).

2238. ———. *Corot.* Deuxième supplément à *L'oeuvre de Corot* par A. Robaut et Moreau-Nélaton. Paris, Quatre Chemins-Editart, 1974. (CR).

2239. ———. *Corot.* Troisième supplément à *L'oeuvre de Corot* par A. Robaut et Moreau-

Nélaton. Paris, Quatre Chemins-Editart, 1974. (CR).

2240. Selz, Jean. *La vie et l'oeuvre de Camille Corot.* Courbevoie, Paris, ACR, 1988.

2241. Sérullaz, Maurice. *Corot.* Paris, Hazan, 1951.

2242. Traz, Georges de. *Corot, sa vie et son oeuvre.* Par François Fosca [pseud.]. Bruxelles, Elsevier, 1958. (Les grands maîtres de l'art français, 2).

Correggio, Antonio Allegri, 1489–1534

2243. Acqua, Marzio dall',ed. *Correggio e il suo tempo.* Parma, Ministero per i Beni Culturali e Ambientali; Archivo di Stato di Parma, 1984

2244. Bigi, Quirino. *Della vita e delle opere certe ed incerte di Antonio Allegri detto il Correggio; opere posthuma.* Modena, Vicenzi, 1880.

2245. Bodmer, Heinrich. *Correggio und die Malerei der Emilia.* Wien, Denticke, 1942.

2246. Bottari, Stefano. *Correggio.* Milano Edizioni per Il Club del Libro, 1961. (Collana d'arte del Club del Libro, 1).

2247. Correggio, Antonio Allegri. *L'opera completa del Correggio.* Presentazione di Alberto Bevilacqua. Apparati critici e filologici di A. C. Quintavalle. Milano, Rizzoli, 1970. (Classici dell'arte, 41).

2248. Ercoli, Giuliano. *Arte e fortuna del Correggio.* Modena, Artioli, 1982.

2249. De Vito Battaglia, Silvia. *Correggio bibliografia.* Con prefazione di Corrado Ricci. Roma, Palombi, 1934. (R. Istituto di Archeologia e Storia dell'Arte. Bibliografie e cataloghi, 3).

2250. Ghidiglia Quintavalle, Augusta. *Gli affreschi del Correggio in San Giovanni Evangelista a Parma.* Presentazione di Roberto Longhi. Milano, Silvana, 1962.

2251. Giampalo, Mario di and Muzzi, Andrea. *Correggio: i disegni.* Presentazione di Federico Zeri. Torino, Allemandi, 1989.

2252. Gould, Cecil H. P. *The paintings of Correggio.* London, Faber/Ithaca, N.Y., Cornell University Press, 1976.

2253. ———. *The School of Love and Correggio's mythologies.* London, National Gallery, 1970.

2254. Gronau, Georg. *Correggio; des Meisters Gemälde.* Stuttgart, Deutsche Verlagsanstalt, 1907.

2255. ———. *The work of Correggio.* Abridged from G. Gronau. New York, Brentano's, 1908. (Classics in art series, 8).

2256. Hagen, Oskar F. L. *Correggio Apokryphen; eine kritische Studie über die sogenannten Jugendwerke des Correggio.* Berlin, Hyperion, 1915.

2257. Longhi, Roberto. *Il Correggio e la Camera di San Paolo a Parma*. A cura di A. Ghidiglia, Quintavalle. Milano, Silvana, 1973.

2258. Martini, Pietro. *Il Correggio*. Studi. Parma, Grazioli, 1871.

2259. Mecklenburg, Carl Gregor, Herzog zu. *Correggio in der deutschen Kunstanschauung in der Zeit von 1750 bis 1850; mit besonderer Berücksichtigung der Frühromantik*. Baden-Baden, Heitz, 1970. (Studien zur deutschen Kunstgeschichte, 347).

2260. Meyer, Julius. *Antonio Allegri da Correggio*. Trans. with an introduction by Mrs. Charles Heaton. London, Macmillan, 1876.

2261. ———. *Correggio*. Leipzig, Engelmann, 1871.

2262. Moore, Thomas S. *Correggio*. London, Duckworth/New York, Scribner, 1911.

2263. Mottini, Guido E. *Il Correggio*. Bergamo, Ist. italiano d'arte grafiche, 1935.

2264. Musée du Louvre (Paris). *Dessins de l'école de Parme: Corrège, Parmesan, XXXIIIe exposition du Cabinet des Dessins*. Paris, 1964.

2265. Musée de l'Orangerie (Paris). *Hommage à Corrège*. Catalogue des dessins du maître et de ses élèves et des artistes qui ont subi son influence, exposés à l'occasion du quatrième centenaire de sa mort (1534); catalogue rédigé par Jean Vernet-Ruiz. Paris, 1934.

2266. National Gallery of Art (Washington, D.C.). *The age of Correggio and the Carracci: Emilian painting of the sixteenth and seventeenth centuries*. [Translations by Robert Erich Wolf . . . et al.]. Washington, D.C., National Gallery of Art, 1986.

2267. Panofsky, Erwin. *The iconography of Correggio's Camera di San Paolo*. London, Warburg Institute of the University of London, 1961. (Warburg Institute Studies, 26).

2268. Piva, Paolo. *Correggio giovane e l'affresco ritrovato di san Benedetto in Polirone*. Prefazione di Cecil Gould. Torino, Allemandi, 1988.

2269. Popham, Arthur E. *Correggio's drawings*. New York, Oxford University Press, 1957.

2270. Pungileoni, Luigi. *Memorie istoriche di Antonio Allegri, detto il Correggio*. 3 v. Parma, Stamperia ducale, 1817–21.

2271. Ricci, Corrado. *Antonio Allegri de Coregio, his life, his friends, and his time*. Trans. by Florence Simmonds. London, Heinemann, 1896.

2272. ———. *Correggio*. London/New York, Warne, 1930.

2273. Roi, Pia. *Il Correggio*. Firenze, Alinari, 1921.

2274. Thode, Henry. *Correggio*. Bielefeld/Leipzig, Velhagen & Klasing, 1898. (Künstler-Monographien, 30).

2275. Toscano, Giuseppe M. *Nuovi studi sul Correggio*. Parma, Libreria Aurea, 1974.

2276. Venturi, Adolfo. *Correggio*. Roma, Stock, 1926.

2277. Venturi, Adolfo, et al. *Manifestazioni parmensi nel IV. centenario della morte del Correggio*. 21 Aprile–28 ottobre XIII (1936). A cura della Federazione dei Fasci di Combattimento di Parma. Parma, Federazione dei Fasci di Combattimento di Parma, 1936.

2278. ———. *Mostra nazionale del Correggio, organizzata per gli auspici della R. Accademia d'Italia dalla Federazione dei Fasci di Combattimento di Parma*. . . . maggio–ottobre 1935. Parma, Crispoli, 1935.

Cortona, Pietro da, 1596–1669

2279. Briganti, Giuliano. *Pietro da Cortona o della pittura barocca*. Firenze, Sansoni, 1962.

2280. Campbell, Malcolm. *Pietro da Cortona at the Pitti Palace, a study of the planetary rooms and related projects*. Princeton, N.J., Princeton University Press, 1977. (Princeton Monographs in Art and Archaeology, 41).

2281. Noehles, Karl. *La chiesa dei SS. Luca e Martina nell'opera di Pietro da Cortona, con contributi di G. Incisa della Rocchetta e Carlo Pietrangelli, presentazione di Mino Maccari*. Roma, Bozzi, 1970. (Saggi e studi di storia dell'arte, 3).

Cortona, Urbano da *see* Urbano da Cortona

Cosindas, Marie, 1925–

2282. Cosindas, Marie. *Marie Cosindas, color photographs*. With an essay by Tom Wolfe. Boston, New York Graphic Society, 1978.

2283. Museum of Modern Art (New York). *Marie Cosindas, Polaroid color photographs*. [April 12–July 4, 1966]. New York, [Museum of Modern Art], 1966.

Cossa, Francesco del, 1435–1477

2284. Ortolani, Sergio. *Cosmè Tura, Francesco del Cossa, Ercole de'Roberti*. Milano, Hoepli, [1941].

2285. Ruhmer, Eberhard. *Francesco del Cossa*. Mit vollständigem Werkverzeichnis. München, Bruckmann, 1959. (CR).

2286. Scassellati-Riccardi, Vincenza. *Francesco del Cossa*. Milano, Fabbri, 1957. (I maestri del colore, 110).

Cosway, Richard, 1742–1821

2287. Daniell, Frederick B. *A catalogue raisonné of th engraved works by Richard Cosway, R. A., with a memoir of Cosway by Sir Philip Currie*. London, Daniell, 1890. (CR).

2288. Williamson, George C. *Richard Cosway, R. A., and his wife and pupils*. London, Bell, 1897.

C

Cotes, Francis, 1726–1770

2289. Johnson, Edward M. *Francis Cotes: complete edition with a critical essay and a catalogue.* Oxford, Phaidon, 1976.

Cotman, John Joseph, 1814–1878
John Sell, 1782–1842
Miles Edmund, 1811–1858

2290. Binyon, Laurence. *John Crome and John Sell Cotman.* London, Seely/New York, Macmillan, 1897. (The Portfolio Artistic Monographs, 32).

2291. Holcomb, Adele M. *John Sell Cotman.* London, British Museum Publications, 1978.

2292. Kitson, Sydney D. *The life of John Sell Cotman.* London, Faber & Faber, 1937.

2293. Rajnai, Miklos. *John Sell Cotman: drawings of Normandy in Norwich Castle Museum,* by M. Rajnai Assisted by Marjorie Allthorpe-Guyton. Norwich, Norfolk Museums Service, 1975.

2294. ———. *John Sell Cotman, 1782–1842: early drawings (1798–1812) in Norwich Castle Museum.* By M. Rajnai assisted by Marjorie Allthorpe-Guyton. Norwich, Norfolk Museums Service, 1979.

2295. Rienaecker, Victor G. R. *John Sell Cotman, 1782–1842.* Leigh-on-Sea, Lewis, 1953.

2296. Tate Gallery (London). *Exhibition of works by John Sell Cotman, and some related painters of the Norwich School: Miles Edmund Cotman, John Joseph Cotman, John Thirtle.* April 7–July 3, 1922. London, National Gallery, 1922.

2297. Turner, Dawson. *Architectural antiquities of Normandy, by John Sell Cotman; accompanied by historical and descriptive notices by Dawson Turner.* 2 v. London, Arel, 1822.

Courbet, Gustave, 1819–1877

2298. Aragon, Louis. *L'exemple de Courbet.* Paris, Editions Cercle d'art, 1952.

2299. Bénédite, Léonce. *Gustave Courbet, with notes by J. Laran and Ph. Baston-Dreyfus.* Philadelphia, Lippincott, 1913.

2300. Boas, George. *Courbet and the naturalistic movement.* New York, Russell, 1938.

2301. Bonniot, Roger. *Gustave Courbet en Saintonge, 1862–1863.* Préf. de Yves Brayer. Paris, Klincksieck, 1973.

2302. Borel, Pierre. *Le roman de Gustave Courbet d'après une correspondance originale du grand peintre.* Préf. de C. Mauclair. Paris, Chiberre, 1922.

2303. Boudaille, Georges. *Gustave Courbet, painter in protest.* Trans. by Michael Bullock. Greenwich, Conn., New York Graphic Society, 1969.

2304. Bowness, Alan. *Courbet's L'Atelier du Peintre.* Newcastle upon Tyne, University of Newcastle, 1972. (Charlton Lectures on Art, 50).

2305. Castagnary, Jules A. *Gustave Courbet et la colonne Vendome; plaidoyer pour un ami mort.* Paris, Dentu, 1883.

2306. Clark, Timothy J. *Image of the people; Gustave Courbet and the second French Republic, 1848–1851.* Greenwich, Conn., New York Graphic Society, 1973.

2307. Courbet, Gustave. *Courbet in perspective.* Edited by Petra ten-Doesschate-Chu. Englewood Cliffs, N.J., Prentice-Hall, 1977.

2308. ———. *Letters of Gustave Courbet.* Edited and translated by Petra ten-Doesschate Chu. Chicago, University of Chicago Press, 1992.

2309. ———. *Courbet, raconté par lui-même et par ses amis; sa vie et ses oeuvres.* Genève, Cailler, 1948. (Collection les grands artistes vus par eux-mêmes et par leurs amis, 7).

2310. ———. *Lettres de Gustave Courbet à Alfred Bruyas.* Publiées par P. Borel. Genève, Cailler, 1951. (Collection Ecrits et documents de peintres, 8).

2311. Courthion, Pierre. *Courbet.* Paris, Floury, 1931.

2312. Duret, Théodore. *Courbet.* Paris, Bernheim, 1918.

2313. Estignard, Alexandre. *Courbet: sa vie, ses oeuvres.* Besançon, Delagrange-Louys, 1896.

2314. Faunce, Sarah and Nochlin, Linda. *Courbet reconsidered.* New Haven, distributed for the Brooklyn Museum by Yale University Press, 1988.

2315. Fermigier, André. *Courbet; étude biographique et critique.* Genève, Skira, 1971.

2316. Fernier, Robert. *Gustave Courbet, peintre de l'art vivant.* Préface de René Huyghe. Paris, Bibliothèque des arts, 1969.

2317. ———. *La vie et l'oeuvre de Gustave Courbet: catalogue raisonné.* 2 v. Lausanne, Bibliothèque des Arts, 1977–1978. (CR).

2318. Foucart, Bruno. *G. Courbet.* Trans. by Alice Sachs. New York, Crown, 1977.

2319. Fried, Michael. *Courbet's realism.* Chicago, University of Chicago Press, 1990.

2320. Galerie Claude Aubry (Paris). *Courbet dans les collections privées françaises.* Exposition organisée au profit du Musée Courbet, 5 mai–25 juin 1966. Paris, Galerie C. Aubry, 1966.

2321. Grand Palais (Paris). *Gustave Courbet: 1819–1877.* 30 sept. 1977–6 jan. 1978. Catalogue par Hélène Toussaint. Paris, Ministère de la culture et de l'environment, Editions des Musées Nationaux, 1977.

2322. Hamburger Kunsthalle. *Courbet und Deutschland.* 19. Oktober–17 Dezember 1978. [Edited by Werner Hoffman and Klaus Herding]. Köln, DuMont, 1978.

2323. Herding, Klaus. *Courbet: to venture inde-*

pendence. Trans. John William Gabriel. New Haven, Yale University Press, 1991.

2324. Léger, Charles. *Courbet*. Paris, Crès, 1929.

2325. ———. *Courbet et son temps; lettres et documents inédits*. Paris, Editions universelles, 1948.

2326. Lindsay, Jack. *Gustave Courbet; his life and art*. Bath, Adams and Dart. Distributed by Jupiter Books, London, 1973.

2327. Mack, Gerstle. *Gustave Courbet*. New York, Knopf, 1951.

2328. Meier-Graefe, Julius. *Corot und Courbet*. München, Piper, 1912.

2329. ———. *Courbet*. München, Piper, 1921.

2330. Musée Gustave Courbet (Ornans). *Hommage à Courbet: catalogue de l'exposition organisée à l'occasion du centenaire de la mort du maître-peintre*. 2 juillet–16 octobre 1977. Paris, Les amis de Gustave Courbet, 1977.

2331. Nochlin, Linda. *Gustave Courbet: a study of style and society*. New York, Garland, 1976.

2332. Philadelphia Museum of Art. *Gustave Courbet, 1819–1877*. Philadelphia Museum of Art, Dec. 17, 1959–Feb. 14, 1960; Museum of Fine Arts, Boston, Feb. 26–Apr. 14, 1960. Boston, Museum of Fine Arts, 1960.

2333. Riat, Georges. *Gustave Courbet, peintre*. Paris, Floury, 1906.

2334. Zahar, Marcel. *Courbet*. Genève, Cailler, 1952. (Collection Les problèmes de l'art, 2).

Cousin, Jean (the elder), ca. 1490–1560/61
Jean (the younger), ca. 1522–ca. 1594

2335. Cousin, Jean (the elder). *Livre de perspective de Iehan Cousin senonois, maistre painctre à Paris*. Paris, Le Royer, 1560.

2336. Cousin, Jean (the younger). *The book of fortune; two hundred unpublished drawings*. With introduction and notes by Ludovic Lalanne. Trans. by H. Mainwaring Dunstan. Paris, Librairie de l'art, 1883.

2337. Didot, Ambroise F. *Recueil des oeuvres choisies de Jean Cousin reproduites en facsimile*. Paris, Didot, 1873.

2338. Lobet, Jean. *Quelques preuves sur Jean Cousin, peintre, sculpteur, géomètre et graveur*. Paris, Renouard, 1881.

Cousins, Samuel, 1801–1887

2339. Whitman, Alfred. *Samuel Cousins*. London, Bell, 1904.

Coypel, Antoine, 1661–1722
Charles, 1664–1752

2340. Garnier, Nicole. *Antoine Coypel, 1661–1722*. Paris, Arthena, Association pour la diffusion de l'histoire de l'art, 1989.

2341. ———. *Antoine Coypel, 1661–1722*. Paris,

Galerie de Bayser, 1989. (Cahiers du dessin français, 6).

2342. Jamieson, I. *Charles-Antoine Coypel, premier peintre de Louis XV. . . . (1694–1752)*. Paris, Hachette, 1930.

2343. Lefrançois, Thierry. *Charles Coypel, peintre du roi (1694–1752)*. Préf. par Pierre Rosenberg. Paris, Arthena, 1994. (CR).

Coysevox, Antoine, 1640–1720

2344. Jouin, Henry. *Antoine Coyzevox, sa vie, son oeuvre et ses contemporains*. Paris, Didier, 1883.

2345. Keller-Dorian, Georges. *Antoine Coysevox (1640–1720); catalogue raisonné de son oeuvre*. Précédé d'une introd. par Paul Vitry. 2 v. Paris, Keller-Dorian, 1920. (CR).

Cozens, Alexander, 1717–1786
John Robert, 1752–1797

2346. Bell, C. F. and Girtin, Thomas. *The drawings and sketches of John Robert Cozens; a catalogue with an historical introduction*. Oxford, Johnson, 1935. (Walpole Society, London annual volume, 23 [1934–35]).

2347. Burlington Fine Arts Club. *Exhibition of the Herbert Horne collection of drawings, with special reference to the works of Alexander Cozens, with some decorative furniture and other objects of art*. London, Burlington Fine Arts Club, 1916.

2348. Sloan, Kim. *Alexander and Robert Cozens: the poetry of landscape*. New Haven and London, Yale University Press. Published in association with the Art Gallery of Ontario (Toronto), 1986.

2349. Oppé, Adolf P. *Alexander and John Robert Cozens*. With a reprint of Alexander Cozen's *A new method of assisting the invention in drawing original compositions of landscape*. London, Black, 1952.

Craig, Edward Gordon, 1872–1966

2350. Craig, Edward. *Gordon Craig: the story of his life*. New York, Limelight Editions, 1985. [c. 1986].

2351. Craig, Edward Gordon. *Woodcuts, and some words, by E. G. Craig*; with an introduction by Campbell Dodgson. London/Toronto, Dent, 1924.

2352. Innes, Christopher D. *Edward Gordon Craig*. Cambridge/New York, Cambridge University Press, 1983.

2353. Nash, George. *Edward Gordon Craig, 1872–1966*. London, HMSO, 1967. (Victoria and Albert Museum. Large picture book, 35).

Cram, Ralph Adams, 1863–1942

2354. Muccigrosso, Robert. *American Gothic: the mind and art of Ralph Adams Cram*. Washington, D.C., University Press of America, 1980.

2355. Tucci, Douglas S. *Ralph Adams Cram, American medievalist*. Catalogue of an exhibition. Boston, Boston Public Library, 1975.

Cranach, Lucas (the elder), 1472–1553
Lucas (the younger), 1515–1586

2356. Coburger Landesstiftung. *Lucas Cranach d. Ae. 1472–1553*. Aus dem Kupferstichkabinett der Kunstsammlungen der Veste Coburg. [Ausstellung] anlässlich der 500. Wiederkehr des Geburtstages von Lucas Cranach d. Ae. 16. Juli–30 Sept. 1972. Coburg, Kunstsammlungen der Veste Coburg, 1972.

2357. Friedländer, Max J. and Rosenberg, Jakob. *The paintings of Lucas Cranach*. Catalogue trans. by Heinz Norden; introd. trans. by Ronald Taylor. Ithaca, N.Y., Cornell University Press, 1978. Rev. and enlarged ed. (Original publ.: Berlin, Deutscher Verein für Kunstwissenschaft, 1932).

2358. Glaser, Curt. *Lukas Cranach*. Leipzig, Insel, 1923.

2359. Grote, Ludwig. *Lucas Cranach, der Maler der Reformation; eine biographische Skizze*. Dresden, Naumann, 1883.

2360. Heyck, Eduard. *Lukas Cranach*. Bielefeld/Leipzig, Velhagen & Klasing, 1927. 2 ed. (Künstler-Monographien, 95).

2361. Jahn, Johannes. *Lucas Cranach als Graphiker*. Leipzig, Seemann, 1955.

2362. Koepplin, Dieter and Falk, Tilman. *Lukas Cranach*. Ausstellung in Kunstmuseum, Basel, 15. Juni–8 September 1974. 2 v. Basel, Birkhäuser, 1974–1976.

2363. Kunsthistorisches Museum (Wien). *Lucas Cranach der Ältere und seine Werkstatt*. Jubiläumsausstellung museumseigener Werke, 1472–1972. Wien, Kunsthistorisches Museum, 1972.

2364. Lilienfein, Heinrich. *Lukas Cranach und seine Zeit*. Bielefeld/Leipzig, Velhagen & Klasing, 1942.

2365. Lüdecke, Heinz. *Lucas Cranach der Ältere; der Künstler und seine Zeit*. Berlin, Henschel, 1953.

2366. ———. *Lucas Cranach der Ältere im Spiegel seiner Zeit, aus Urkunden, Chroniken, Briefen, Reden und Gedichten*. Berlin, Rütten & Loening, 1953.

2367. Ohly, Friedrich. *Gesetz und Evangelium: zur Typologie bei Luther und Lucas Cranach*. Münster, Aschendorff, 1985. (Schriftenreihe der Westfälischen Wilhelms-Universität; n.F.,1).

2368. Posse, Hans. *Lucas Cranach*. Wien, Schroll, 1942.

2369. Schade, Werner. *Cranach, a family of painters*. Trans. by Helen Sebba. New York, Putnam, 1980.

2370. Schlossmuseum Weimar. *Lucas Cranach, 1472–1553; ein grosser Maler in bewegter Zeit*. Ausstellung zu seinem 500. Geburtstag, 22. Juni–15. Oktober 1972. Redaktion: Gerhard Pommeranz-Liedke. Weimar, Kunstsammlungen, 1972.

2371. Schuchardt, Christian. *Lucas Cranach des Aelteren: Leben und Werke*. 3 v. Leipzig, Brockhaus, 1851–71.

2372. Schwarz, Herbert. *Lucas Cranach der Ältere: Führer durch Leben und Werk*. Kronach, Link, 1972.

2373. Thöne, Friedrich. *Lukas Cranach des Älteren Meister-zeichnungen*. Burg, Hopfer, 1939.

2374. Thulin, Oskar. *Cranach-Altäre der Reformation*. Berlin, Evangelische Verlagsanstalt, 1955.

Crane, Walter, 1845–1915

2375. Konody, Paul G. *The art of Walter Crane*. London, Bell, 1902.

2376. Massé, Gertrude C. E. *A bibliography of first editions of books illustrated by Walter Crane*. With a preface by Heyward Sumner. London, Chelsea Publ. Co., 1923.

2377. Schleinitz, Otto J. W. von. *Walter Crane*. Bielefeld/Leipzig, Velhagen & Klasing, 1902. (Künstler-Monographien, 62).

2378. Spencer, Isobel. *Walter Crane*. New York, Macmillan, 1975.

Crayer, Gaspar de, 1584–1669

2379. Vlieghe, Hans. *Gaspar de Crayer, sa vie et ses oeuvres*. 2 v. Bruxelles, Arcade, 1972.

Credi, Lorenzo di *see* Lorenzo di Credi

Crespi, Giuseppe Maria, 1665–1747

2380. Crespi, Giuseppe Maria. *Giuseppe Maria Crespi, 1665–1747*. [Catalogue of an exhibition]. Bologna, Palazzo Popoli Campograndi (Pinacoteca nazionale di Bologna), 7 settembre–1 novembre,1990. A cura di Andrea Emiliani e August B. Rave; con scritti di Anton A.W. Boschloo . . . [et al.]. Bologna, Nuova Alfa, 1990. (Also at Staatsgalerie, Stuttgart; Pushkin Museum, Moscow).

2381. Merriman, Mira Pajes. *Giuseppe Maria Crespi*. English trans. by Elena Gozzer and Gemma Verchi. Milano Rizzoli, 1980.

2382. Spike, John T. *Giuseppe Maria Crespi and the emergence of genre painting in Italy*. With essays by Mira Pajes Merriman ansd Giovanna Perini. Fort Worth, Kimbell Art Museum, ; Firenze, Centro Di, 1986.

Crippa, Roberto, 1921–1972

2383. Crippa, Roberto. *Crippa*. Prefazione di Giampièro Giani. Venezia, Edizioni del Cavallino, 1954.

2384. Giani, Giampièro. *Crippa*. Venezia, Edizioni del Cavallino, 1956.

2385. Jouffroy, Alain. *Crippa*. Milano, Schwarz Galleria d'Arte, 1962.

2386. Palazzo Reale (Milan). *Roberto Crippa*. Novembre–dicembre 1971. Milano, Arti Grafiche Fiorin, 1971.

Cristus (Christus), Petrus, 1420–1472/73

2387. Ainsworth, Maryan Wynn. *Petrus Christus: Renaissance master of Bruges*. [By] Maryan W. Ainsworth, with contributions by Maximiliaan P.J. Martens. New York, Metropolitan Museum of Art, distributed by H.N. Abrams, 1994.

2388. Panhans-Bühler, Ursula. *Eklektizismus und Originalität im Werk des Petrus Christus*. Wien, Holzhausens Nfg., 1978.

2389. Schabracker, Peter H. *Petrus Christus*. Utrecht, Dekker & Gumbert, 1974.

2390. Upton, Joel Morgan. *Petrus Christus: his place in fifteenth-century Flemish painting*. University Park, Pennsylvania State University Press, 1990.

Crivelli, Carlo, 1430–1493
Taddeo, fl. 1452–1476
Vittore, 1440–1502

2391. Bertoni, Giulio. *Il maggior miniatore della bibbia di Borso d'Este, Taddeo Crivelli*. Modena, Oriandini, 1925.

2392. Crivelli, Carlo. *L'opera completa del Crivelli*, introdotta e coordinata de Anna Bovero. Milano, Rizzoli, 1975. (Classici dell'arte, 80).

2393. ———. *Tutta la pittura del Crivelli*. A cura d'Anna Bovero. Milano, Rizzoli, 1961. (Biblioteca d'arte Rizzoli, 44–45).

2394. Davies, Martin. *Carlo Crivelli*. London, National Gallery, 1972. (Themes and painters in the National Gallery, 4).

2395. Di Provvido, Sandra. *La pittura di Vittore Crivelli*. L'Aquila, Japadre, 1972.

2396. Drey, Franz. *Carlo Crivelli und seine Schule*. München, Bruckmann, 1927.

2397. Palazzo Ducale (Venice). *Carlo Crivelli e i Crivelleschi*. Catalogo della mostra a cura di Pietro Zampetti, 10 giugno–10 ottobre 1961. Venezia, Alfieri, 1961.

2398. Rushforth, Gordon M. *Carlo Crivelli*. London, Bell, 1900.

2399. Zampetti, Pietro. *Carlo Crivelli*. Milano, Martello, 1961.

2400. ———. *Carlo Crivelli*. Firenze, Nardini, 1986. (CR).

Crome, John, 1768–1821

2401. Baker, Charles H. *Crome*. With an introduction by C. J. Holmes. London, Methuen, 1921.

2402. Binyon, Laurence. *John Crome and John Sell Cotman*. London, Seeley/New York, Macmillan, 1897. (The Portfolio Artistic Monographs, 32).

2403. Clifford, Derek P., and Clifford, Timothy. *John Crome*. London, Faber, 1968.

2404. Mallalieu, Huon. *The Norwich school: Crome, Cotman and Their Followers*. London, Academy Eds./New York, St. Martin's, 1974.

2405. Mottram, Ralph H. *John Crome of Norwich*. London, Lane, 1931.

2406. Norwich Castle Museum. *John Crome, 1768–1821; an exhibition of paintings and drawings organized by the Arts Council to mark the bicentenary of the artist's birth*. 3 August–29 September, 1968. London, Arts Council, 1968.

2407. Smith, Solomon C. K. *Crome, with a note on the Norwich school*. With an introduction by C. H. Collins Baker. London, Allan, 1923.

Cross, Henri Edmond, 1856–1910

2408. Compin, Isabelle. *H. E. Cross*. Préf. de Bernard Dorival. Paris, Quatre Chemins-Editart, 1964.

2409. Rewald, John. *Henri-Edmond Cross; carnet de dessins*. 2 v. Paris, Berggruen, 1959.

Cruikshank, George, 1792–1878

2410. Buchanan-Brown, John. *The book illustrations of George Cruikshank*. North Pomfret, Vt., David & Charles, 1980.

2411. Chesson, Wilfrid H. *George Cruikshank*. London, Duckworth/New York, Dutton, 1908.

2412. Cohn, Albert Mayer. *A biographical catalogue of the printed works illustrated by George Cruikshank*. London/New York, Longmans, Green, 1914.

2413. Evans, Hilary and Evans, Mary. *The life and art of George Cruikshank, 1792–1878; the man who drew the Drunkard's Daughter*. Chatham, N.Y., Phillips, 1978.

2414. Gough, John B. *The works of George Cruikshank in oil, watercolors, original drawings, etchings, woodcuts, lithographs, and glypographs, collected by J. Gough*. Boston, The Club of Odd Volumes, 1890.

2415. Hamilton, Walter. *A memoir of George Cruikshank, artist and humorist*. London, Stock, 1878.

2416. Jerrold, Blanchard. *The life of George Cruikshank in two epochs*. London, Chatto and Windus, 1898. 2 ed.

2417. McLean, Ruari. *George Cruikshank, his life and work as a book illustrator*. New York, Pellegrini & Cudahy, 1948.

2418. Patten, George, ed. *George Cruikshank: a revaluation*. Princeton, N.J., Princeton University Press, 1992.

2419. ———. *George Cruikshank's life, times and*

art. Volume I: 1792–1835. Cambridge, Lutterworth, 1992.

2420. Rosenbach, A. S. W. *A catalogue of the works illustrated by George Cruikshank and Isaac and Robert Cruikshank in the Library of Harry Elkins Widener.* Philadelphia, Rosenbach, 1918.

2421. Speed Art Museum (Louisville, Ky.). *The inimitable George Cruikshank: an exhibition of illustrated books, prints, drawings and manuscripts from the collection of David Borowitz.* Oct. 12–Nov. 15, 1968. Louisville, Ky., Univ. of Louisville Libraries, 1968.

2422. Stephens, Frederick G. *A memoir of George Cruikshank by F. G. Stephens; and an essay on the genius of George Cruikshank by William Makepeace Thackeray.* London, Sampson Low, 1891.

2423. Wardroper, John. *The caricatures of George Cruikshank.* London, Gordon Fraser Gallery, 1977.

2424. Wynn Jones, Michael. *George Cruikshank: his life and London.* London, Macmillan, 1978.

Cucchi, Enzo, 1950–

2425. Cucchi, Enzo. *Enzo Cucchi.* Catalogo [di] Amnon Barzel con la collaborazione die Marina Berio. [Mostra, 22 marzo–15 giugno, 1989]. Prato, Museo d'Arte Contemporanea Luigi Pecci, 1989.

2426. ———. *Enzo Cucchi: Skulptur für Basel.* Text by Jean Christophe Amman. München, Bernd Klüser Gallery, 1985.

2427. Perucchi-Petri, Ursula. *Enzo Cucchi, "La Disegna": Zeichnungen 1975 bis 1988.* Mit einem Beitrag von Theodora Vischer. München, Prestel, 1988.

2428. Waldman, Diane. *Enzo Cucchi.* New York. Solomon R. Guggenheim Museum, 1986.

Cunningham, Imogen, 1883–1976

2429. Cunningham, Imogen. *After Ninety.* Introd. by Margaretta Mitchell. Seattle/London, University of Washington Press, 1977.

2430. ———. *Imogen Cunningham: selected texts and bibliography* Edited by Amy Rule. Essay by Richard Lorenz. Oxford, Clio Press, 1992. (World Photographers Reference Series, 2).

2431. ———. *Photographs.* Introd. by Margery Mann. Seattle, University of Washington Press, 1971.

2432. Dater, Judy. *Imogen Cunningham, a portrait.* Boston, New York Graphic Society, 1979.

2433. Henry Art Gallery (Seattle). *Imogen! Imogen Cunningham; photographs, 1910–1973.* Introd. by Margery Mann. [March 23–April 21, 1974]. Seattle, Henry Art Gallery, 1974.

Curry, John Steuart, 1897–1946

2434. Cole, Sylvan. *The lithographs of John Steuart Curry: a catalogue raisonné.* Compiled and edited by S. Cole; introd. by Laurence Schmeckebier. New York, Associated American Artists, 1976. (CR).

2435. Curry, John Steuart. *John Steuart Curry.* New York, American Artists Group, 1945. (American Artists Group Monograph, 14).

2436. ———. *John Steuart Curry, 1897–1946: rural America.* Exhibition, May 1990. Chicago, Mongerson Wunderlich, 199o.

2437. ———. *Prairie vision and circus wonders: the complete lithographic suite by John Steuart Curry (1897–1946).* Davenport, Iowa, Davenport Art Gallery, March 9–April 27, 1980. Ed. by Ann C. Madonia, Curator of Collections. Davenport, Iowa, the Gallery, 1980.

2438. Czestochowski, Joseph H. *John Steuart Curry and Grant Wood: a portrait of rural America.* Columbia, Mo./London, University of Missouri Press, 1981.

2439. Guedon, Mary Scholz. *Regionalist art: Thomas Hart Benton, John Steuart Curry, and Grant Wood. A guide to the literature.* Metuchen, N.J., Scarecrow Press, 1982

2440. Kendall, M. Sue. *Rethinking regionalism: John Steuart Curry and the Kansas mural controversy.* Washington, D.C., Smithsonian Institution Press, 1986.

2441. Schmeckebier, Laurence E. *John Steuart Curry's pageant of America.* New York, American Artists Group, 1943.

Cuvillies, Francois, 1695–1768

2442. Braunfels, Wolfgang. *François Cuvilliés, der Baumeister der galanten Architektur des Rokoko.* München, Süddeutscher Verlag, 1986.

2443. Wolf, Friedrich. *François de Cuvilliés (1695–1768), der Architekt und Dekorschöpfer.* München, Histor. Verein von Oberbayern, 1967. (Oberbayerisches Archiv, 89).

Cuyp, Aelbert, 1620–1691

2444. Dordrechts Museum (Dordrecht, Netherlands). *Aelbert Cuyp en zijn familie.* 12 Nov. 1977–8 Jan. 1978. Dordrecht, Dordrechts Museum, 1977.

2445. Reiss, Stephen. *Aelbert Cuyp.* Boston, New York Graphic Society, 1975.

2446. ———. *Albert Cuyp in British Collections.* Catalog of an exhibition held at the National Gallery, London, 3 Jan.–11 Feb. 1973. Colchester, Benham, 1972.

D

Dadd, Richard, 1817–1886

2447. Allderidge, Patricia. *The late Richard Dadd, 1817–1886.* London, Tate Gallery, 1974. .

Daddi, Bernardo, 1280–1350

2448. Bacci, Pèleo. *Dipinti inediti e sconosciuti di Pietro Lorenzetti, Bernardo Daddi, etc., in Siena e nel contado.* Con documenti, commenti critici e 70 illustrazioni. Siena, Accademia per le arti e per le lettere, 1939.

2449. Vitzthum von Eckstädt, Georg. *Bernardo Daddi.* Leipzig, Hiersemann, 1903.

Dagoty, Pierre Edouard, 1775–1871

2450. Du Pasquier, Jacqueline. *Pierre-Edouard Dagoty, 1775–1871 et la miniature bordelaise au XIXᵉ siècle; biographie critique et catalogue raisonné de l'oeuvre.* Préf. de F. G. Pariset. Chartres, Laget, 1974. (CR).

Daguerre, Louis Jacques Mande, 1787–1851

2451. Daguerre, [Louis J. M.]. *Histoire et description des procédés du daguerreotype et du diorama.* Paris, Giroux, 1839. (Reprinted, with an introduction by Beaumont Newhall and with a facsimile of the first English edition published in London by McLean & Nutt in 1839, by Winter House, New York, 1971).

2452. Gernsheim, Helmut and Gernsheim, Alison. *L. J. M. Daguerre, the world's first photographer.* Cleveland, World, 1956.

2453. Hôtel de Malestroit à Bry-sur-Marne. *Hommage à Daguerre, magicien de l'image.* 23 octobre–7 novembre 1976. Bry-sur-Marne, Office culturel de Bry-sur-Marne, 1976.

2454. Mentienne, Adrien. *La découverte de la photographie en 1839.* Paris, Dupont, 1892. (Reprint: New York, Arno, 1979).

Dahl, Johan Christian Clausen, 1788–1857

2455. Bang, Marie L'drup. *Johan Christian Dahl, 1788–1857: life and works.* 3 v. Oslo, Norwegian University Press; Oxford, Oxford University Press [distributor], 1987. (CR).

2456. Nasjonal galleriet (Oslo). *Dahl's Dresden: utstilling.* [11 October–7 December 1980]. Kat. Pontus Grate redaksjon Magne Malmanger. Oslo, Nasjonalgalleriet, 1980.

2457. ———. *Johan Christian Dahl, 1788–1857: Jubileumsutstillning 1988,* Nasjonalgalleriet 27 feb.–1 mai 1988; Bergen Billedgalleri 19. mai–3. juli 1988. Oslo, Nasjonalgalleriet, 1988.

2458. ———. *Johan Christian Dahl, tegninger og akvareller.* Innledning av Leif Østby. Oslo, Nasjonalgalleriet og Bergens billedgalleri, 1957.

2459. Neue Pinakothek München. *Johan Christian Dahl, 1788–1857: ein Malerfreund Caspar David Friedrichs.* 11. November 1988 bis 15. Januar 1989. [Katalogredaktion, Christoph Heilmann]. München, Lipp, 1988.

2460. Venturi, Lionello. *Johan Christian Dahl.* Oslo, Gyldendal, 1957.

Dali, Salvador, 1904–1989

2461. Ades, Dawn. *Dali.* London, Thames and Hudson, 1983.

2462. Bosquet, Alain. *Entretiens avec Salvador Dali.* Paris, Belfond, 1966.

2463. Centre Georges Pompidou (Paris). *Salvador Dali: rétrospective 1920–1980, 18 décembre 1979–14 avril 1980.* Centre Georges Pompidou, Musée national d'art moderne. Catalogue conçu et réalisé par Daniel Abadie. Paris, Centre Georges Pompidou, 1979.

2464. ———. *La vie publique de Salvador Dali.* [Catalogue d'une exposition] publié à l'occasion de la rétrospective Salvador Dali. Catalogue par Daniel Abadie. Documentation par Evelyne Pomey. Paris, Centre Georges Pompidou, 1979.

2465. Dali, Ana Maria. *Salvador Dali vue par sa soeur.* Introd., traduction et notes de Jean Martin. Paris, Arthaud, 1960.

2466. Dali, Salvador. *Diary of a genius.* Trans. by Richard Howard. New York, Doubleday, 1965.

2467. ———. *On modern art; the cuckolds of antiquated modern art.* Trans. by Haakon M. Chevalier. New York, Dial, 1957.

2468. ———. *400 Obres de 1914 a 1983: Salvador Dali.* [Catalogacio de les obres, Paloma Esteban, Maria José Salazar]. 2 v. [Madrid]: Generalat de Catalunya, Ministerio de Cultura, Obra Cultural de la Caixa de Pensions, 1983.

2469. ———. *Oui; méthode paranoïaque-critique, et autres textes.* Paris, Denoël-Gonthier, 1971. (Bibliotheque médiations, 88).

2470. ———. *Salvador Dali, 1904–1989.* Einführung und Katalog, Karin v. Maur. Stuttgart, Hatje; Heiden, A. Niggli, 1989.

2471. ———. *Salvador Dali: catalogue raisonné of etchings and mixed media prints, 1924–1980.* Edited by Ralf Michler and Lutz W. Lopsinger; incorporating entries from Charles Sahli's *Salvador Dali—257 éditions originales, 1964–1985,* published by J.P. Schneider; and including a foreword by Robert Descharmes. Munich, Prestel, 1994. (CR).

2472. ———. *Salvador Dali: the early years.* Ian Gibson . . . [et al.]. Ed. by Michael Raeburn. London, South Bank Centre, 1994.

2473. ———. *The unspeakable confessions of Salvador Dali.* Trans. by Harold J. Salemson. New York, Morrow, 1976.

2474. Descharnes, Robert. *Salvador Dali.* Trans. by Eleanor R. Morse. New York, Abrams, 1976.

2475. ———. *The world of Salvador Dali.* Trans. by Albert Field. New York, Harper & Row, 1962.

2476. Etherington-Smith, Meredith. *Dali: a biography.* London, Sinclair-Stevens, 1992.

2477. Fornes, Eduard. *Les contradiccions del cas Dali.* Barcelona, Prensa Catalana, 1989.

2478. ———. *Dali y los libros.* [Catalogo, Eduard Fornes; con la colaboracion de Felip Casañas y Jordy Oliveras]. Barcelona, Mediterrania, 1985. (French edition, *Dali et les livres.* Nîmes, 1984).

2479. Gaya Nuno, Juan Antonio. *Salvador Dali.* Barcelona, Omega, 1950.

2480. Gomez de la Serna, Ramón. *Dali.* Paris, Flammarion, 1979.

2481. Lake, Carlton. *In quest of Dali.* New York, Putnam, 1969.

2482. Maddox, Conroy. *Dali.* New York, Crown, 1979.

2483. Montreal Museum of Fine Arts. *Salvador Dali.* [Catalog of the exhibition presented . . . from April 27 to July 29, 1990, . . . organized by Pierre Théberge]. Montreal, Montreal Museum of Fine Arts, 1990.

2484. Morse, Albert Reynolds. *Dali: a study of his life and work.* Text by A. Reynolds Morse and a special appreciation by Michel Tapié. Greenwich, Conn., New York Graphic Society, 1958.

2485. ———. *Salvador Dali; a panorama of his art: ninety-three oils 1917–1970.* Written and edited by A. Reynolds Morse. Cleveland, Ohio, Salvador Dali Museum, 1974.

2486. Museum Boymans-Van Beuningen (Rotterdam). *Dali, 21 november 1970–10 januari 1971.* Exposition Dali, avec la collection de Edward F. W. James. [Samengesteld] door R. Hammacher-Van der Brande en L. Brandt Corstius. Rotterdam, Museum Boymans-Van Beuningen, 1970.

2487. Rey, Henri François. *Dali dans son labyrinthe.* Paris, Grasset, 1974.

2488. Rom, Luis. *Psicodalico Dali.* Barcelona, Mediterrania, 1991.

2489. Salvador Dali Museum (Cleveland). *Salvador Dali: catalog of a collection; ninety-three oils, 1917–1970.* Cleveland, Ohio, 1972.

2490. ———. *Salvador Dali, Spanish (1904–).* A guide to his works in public museums. Cleveland, The Dali Museum, published for the Reynolds Morse Foundation, 1973.

2491. Secrest, Meryle. *Salvador Dali.* New York, Dutton, 1986.

2492. Soby, James Thrall. *Salvador Dali.* New York Museum of Modern Art, 1946. Reprinted by Arno Press, New York, 1969.

2493. Staatliche Kunsthalle Baden-Baden. *Dali: Gemälde, Zeichnungen, Objekte, Schmuck.* Ausstellung Salvador Dali unter Einschluss der Sammlung Edward F. W. James, 29. Jan.– 18. April 1971. Baden-Baden, Staatl. Kunsthalle, 1971.

2494. Tuchel, Hans Gerd. *Salvador Dali: Literarische Zyklen.* Katalog [der] Ausstellung, Schloss Drachenburg 1982, Königswinter. Bearbeitet von Hermann Wünsche; Texte von Hand G. Tuchel. Heidelberg, Galerie Apokalypse, 1982.

Dalou, Aimé Jules, 1838–1902

2495. Caillaux, Henriette. *Aimé-Jules Dalou (1838–1902).* Paris, Delagrave, 1935.

2496. Delestre, François. *Jules Dalou, 1838–1902.* Exposition, 9 nov.–18 déc. 1976, Galerie Delestre, Paris. Catalogue rédigé par F. Delestre et Robert Stoppenbach. Paris, Delestre, 1976.

2497. Dreyfous, Maurice. *Dalou, sa vie et son oeuvre.* Paris, Laurens, 1903.

Danby, Francis, 1793–1861

2498. Adams, Eric. *Francis Danby: varieties of poetic landscape.* New Haven, Yale University Press, 1973.

2499. City Art Gallery (Bristol). *The Bristol school of artists; Francis Danby and painting in Bristol, 1810–1840.* Exhibition, 4 Sept.–10 Nov. 1973. Catalogue by Francis Greenacre. Bristol, City Art Gallery, 1973.

2500. Malins, Edward G. *James Smetham and Francis Danby: two 19th century Romantic painters.* By E. G. Malins and Morchard Bishop. London, Stevens, 1974.

Daniell, Samuel, 1775–1811
Thomas, 1749–1840
William, 1769–1837

2501. Shellim, Maurice. *Oil paintings of India and the East by Thomas Daniell, 1749–1840, and William Daniell, 1769–1837.* Foreword by Mildred Archer. London, Inchcape, 1979.

2502. Sutton, Thomas. *The Daniells; artists and travellers.* London, Bodley Head, 1954.

2503. Victoria Memorial (Calcutta). *A descriptive catalogue of Daniells work in the Victoria Memorial (Museum).* Calcutta, Victoria Memorial, 1976.

Dannecker, Johann Heinrich Von, 1758–1841

2504. Dannecker, Johann Heinrich von. *Johann Heinrich Dannecker.* [Catalogue of an exhibition held at the Staatsgalerie Stuttgart. Feb 14 –May 31, 1987]. 2 v.: (1) *Der Bildhauer* [by] Christian von Holst; (2) *Der Zeichner* [by] Ulrike Gauss. Stuttgart, Staatsgalerie Stuttgart; Stutgart-Bad Cannstatt, Edition Cantz, 1987.

2505. Spemann, Adolf. *Dannecker.* Berlin/Stuttgart, Spemann, 1909.

2506. ———. *Johann Heinrich Dannecker: das Leben, das Werk, der Mensch.* München, Bruckmann, 1958.

Dantan, Jean Pierre, 1800–1869

2507. Hale, Richard W. *Dantan, jeune, 1800–1869, and his satirical and other sculpture, especially his Portraits chargés.* With Christmas greetings from Richard Walden Hale. Meriden, Conn., Meriden Gravure Co., 1940.

2508. Seligman, Janet. *Figures of fun; the caricature-statuettes of Jean-Pierre Dantan.* London/New York, Oxford University Press, 1957.

Darley, Felix Octavius Carr, 1822–1888

2509. Bolton, Theodore. *The book illustrations of Felix Octavius Carr Darley.* Worcester, Mass., American Antiquarian Society, 1952.

2510. Delaware Art Museum (Wilmington). *". . . . illustrated by Darley," an exhibition of original drawings by the American book illustrator Felix Octavius Carr Darley (1822–1888).* May 4–June 18, 1978. Wilmington, Delaware Art Museum, 1978.

2511. King, Ethel M. *Darley, the most popular illustrator of his time.* Brooklyn, Gaus, 1964.

Da Silva, Marie Helena Vieira *see* Vieira da Silva, Marie Helena

Daubigny, Charles François, 1817–1878
Karl Charles Pierre, 1846–1856

2512. Fidell-Beaufort, Madeleine. *Daubigny.* [By] M. Fidell-Beaufort [and] Janine Bailly-Herzberg. Textes anglais de Judith Schub. Paris, Geoffroy-Dechaume, 1975.

2513. Hellebranth, Robert. *Charles-François Daubigny, 1817–1878.* Morges, Matute, 1976.

2514. Henriet, Frédéric. *C. Daubigny et son oeuvre gravé, eaux fortes et bois inédits par C. Daubigny, Karl Daubigny, Léon Lhermitte.* Paris, Lévy, 1875.

2515. Moreau-Nélaton, Etienne. *Daubigny, raconté par lui-même.* Paris, Laurens, 1925.

Daumier, Honoré Victorin, 1788–1856

2516. Adhémar, Jean. *Honoré Daumier.* London, Zwemmer, 1954.

2517. Alexandre, Arsène. *Honoré Daumier, l'homme et l'oeuvre.* Paris, Laurens, 1888.

2518. Balzer, Wolfgang. *Der junge Daumier und seine Kampfgefährten; politische Karikatur in Frankreich, 1830–1835.* Dresden, Verlag der Kunst, 1965.

2519. Baudelaire, Charles. *Les dessins de Daumier.* Paris, Crès, n.d. (Ars graphica, 2).

2520. Bertels, Kurt. *Honoré Daumier als Lithograph.* München/Leipzig, Piper, 1908. (Klassische Illustratoren, 4).

2521. Bibliothèque Nationale (Paris). *Daumier: lithographies, gravures sur bois, sculptures.* Paris, Editions des Bibliothèques Nationales de France, 1934.

2522. ———. *Daumier: le peintre graveur.* Préface par Julien Cain. Texte par George Duhamel, Claude Roger-Marx et Jean Vallery-Radot. Paris, 1958.

2523. Bouvy, Eugène. *Daumier, l'oeuvre gravé du maitre.* 2 v. Paris, Le Garrec, 1933. (Reprint: San Francisco, Alan Wofsy, 1993).

2524. Cary, Elisabeth. *Honoré Daumier.* New York, Putnam, 1907.

2525. Cassou, Jean. *Daumier.* Lausanne, Marguerat, 1950.

2526. Champfleury, Jules F. *Honoré Daumier.* Catalogue de l'oeuvre lithographié et gravé. Paris, Librairie Parisienne, 1878.

2527. Château de Blois (Blois, France). *Hommage à Honoré Daumier*. Exhibition presented by La Ville de Blois and organized by Roger Passeron. Paris, Presses de A. Lahure, 1968.

2528. Courthion, Pierre. *Daumier, raconté par lui-même et par ses amis*. Genève, Cailler, 1945.

2529. Daumier, Honoré Victorin. *La chasse et la pêche*. Préface de Paul Vialac; catalogue et notices de Jacqueline Armingeat. Paris, Editions Vilo, 1968.

2530. ———. *Commerces et commerçants*. Préface de Jean Fernicot; notices de Jacqueline Perrot. Paris, Editions Vilo, 1979.

2531. ———. *Les gens d'affaires (Robert Macaire) par Daumier*. Préface, catalogue et notices de Jean Adhémar. Paris, Editions Vilo, 1968.

2532. ———. *Les gens de médecine dans l'oeuvre de Daumier*. [Texte de Henri] Mondor; catalogue raisonné de Jean Adhémar. Paris, Impr. nationale, A. Sauret, 1960.

2533. ———. *Intellectuelles (bas bleus) et femmes socialistes*. Préface de Françoise Parturier. Catalogue et notices de Jacqueline Armingeat. Paris, Editions Vilo, 1974.

2534. ———. *Locataires et propriétaires*. Préface de Paul Guth; catalogue et notices de Jacqueline Armingeat. Paris, Vilo, 1977.

2535. ———. *Moeurs conjugales*. Préface, catalogue et notices de Philippe Roberts-Jones. Paris, Editions Vilo/Monte Carlo, Sauret, 1967.

2536. ———. *Les tracas de Paris*. Préface de Pierre Mazars, catalogue et notices de Jacqueline Armingeat. Paris, Editions Vilo, 1978.

2537. ———. *Les transports en commun*. Préface de Max Gallo. Catalogue et notices de Jacqueline Armingeat. Paris, Editions Vilo, 1976.

2538. Escholier, Raymond. *Daumier et son monde*. Nancy, Berger-Levrault, 1965.

2539. Delteil, Loys. *Daumier: l'oeuvre lithographié, 1830–37*. Paris, Delteil. 1925. (Reprint with new illustrations and an English language translation of the introduction: San Francisco, Alan Wofsy, 1993).

2540. ———. *Daumier, peintre et lithographe*. Paris, Floury, 1923.

2541. Fontainas, André. *La peinture de Daumier*. Paris, Crès, n.d. (Ars graphica, 1).

2542. Fuchs, Eduard. *Honoré Daumier; Holzschnitte, 1833–1870*. München, Langen, 1918.

2543. ———. *Honoré Daumier; Lithographien*. 3 v. München, Langen, 1920–1922.

2544. ———. *Der Maler Daumier; Nachtrag*. München, Langen, 1930.

2545. Galeries Durand-Ruel (Paris). *Exposition des peintures et dessins de Honoré Daumier*. Paris, 1878.

2546. Gobin, Maurice. *Daumier sculpteur, 1808–1879, avec un catalogue raisonné et illustré de l'oeuvre sculpté*. Genève, Cailler, 1952. (CR). (Peintures et sculpteurs d'hier et d'aujourd'hui, 27).

2547. Hausenstein, Wilhelm. *Daumier; Zeichnungen*. München, Piper, 1918.

2548. Hazard, Nicolas A. *Catalogue raisonné de l'oeuvre lithographie de Honoré Daumier*. Par N. A. Hazard et Loys Delteil. Orrouy (Oise), Hazard, 1904. (CR).

2549. Kalitina, Nina N. *Onore Dom'e*. Moskva, Iskusstvo, 1955.

2550. Klossowski, Erich. *Honoré Daumier*. München, Piper, 1923. 2 ed.

2551. Larkin, Oliver W. *Daumier, man of his time*. New York, McGraw-Hill, 1966.

2552. Lejeune, Robert. *Honoré Daumier*. Köln, Kiepenheuer & Witsch, 1953.

2553. Los Angeles County Museum of Art. *Daumier in retrospect, 1808–1879*. March 20–June 3, 1979. [Text by Elizabeth Mongan]. Los Angeles, Armand Hammer Foundation, 1979.

2554. Maison, Karl E. *Honoré Daumier; catalogue raisonné of the paintings, watercolours and drawings*. 2 v. Greenwich, Conn., New York Graphic Society, 1968. (CR).(Reprint: San Francisco, Alan Wofsy, 1993).

2555. Mandel, Gabriele. *L'opera pittorica completa di Daumier*. Presentazione di Luigi Barzini, apparati critici e filo-logici di G. Mandel. Milano, Rizzoli, 1971. (Classici dell'arte, 47).

2556. Mondor, Henri. *Doctors and medicine in the works of Daumier*. Notes and catalogue by Jean Adhémar. Pref. by Arthur W. Heintzelman. Trans. by C. de Chabanne. Boston, Boston Book and Art Shop, 1960.

2557. Musée de l'Orangerie (Paris). *Daumier: peintures, aquarelles, dessins*. Préface de Anatole de Monzie, introduction de Claude Roger-Marx. Paris, Musée de l'Orangerie, 1934.

2558. Neue Gesellschaft für Bildende Kunst, Berlin. *Honoré Daumier und die ungelösten Probleme der bürgerlichen Gesellschaft*. Hrsg. zur Ausstellung im Schloss Charlottenburg, Mai–Juni 1974. Berlin, NGBK, 1974.

2559. Passeron, Roger. *Daumier, témoin de son temps*. Paris, Bibliothèque des Arts, 1979.

2560. Rey, Robert. *Honoré Daumier*. Trans. by Norbert Guterman. New York, Abrams, 1966.

2561. Roger-Marx, Claude. *Daumier*. Paris, Plon, 1938.

2562. Rossel, André. *H. Daumier; oeuvres politiques et sociales: lithographies, bois, peintures, sculptures*. Paris, Editions de la Courtille, 1971.

2563. Roy, Claude. *Daumier; étude biographique et critique.* Genève, Skira, 1971. (Le goût de notre temps, 50).

2564. Rümann, Arthur. *Honoré Daumier, sein Holzschnittwerk.* München, Delphin, 1914.

2565. Saint-Guilhelm, F. et Schrenk, Klaus. *Honoré Daumier: l'oeuvre lithographique.* Présentation de F. Saint-Guilhelm et Klaus Schrenk; suivi d'un texte contemporain de l'artiste par Charles Baudelaire. Paris, Hubschmid, 1978.

2566. Vincent, Howard P. *Daumier and his world.* Evanston, Ill., Northwestern University Press, 1968.

2567. Wassermann, Jeanne L. *Daumier sculpture; a critical and comparative study.* By Jeanne L. Wasserman, assisted by Joan M. Lukach and Arthur Beale. Catalog of an exhibition Fogg Art Museum, Harvard University, May 1–June 23, 1969. Greenwich, Conn., distributed by New York Graphic Society, 1969.

Dauzats, Adrien, 1808–1868

2568. Guinard, Paul. *Dauzats et Blanchard, peintres de L'Espagne romantique.* Paris, Presses Universitaires de France, 1967.

David, Gerard, 1460–1523

2569. Bodenhauser-Degener, Eberhard von. *Gerard David und seine Schule.* München, Bruckmann, 1905.

2570. Boon, Karel G. *Gerard David.* Amsterdam, Becht, 1948. (Palet serie, 20).

2571. Migroet, H. van. *Gerard David.* Antwerpen, Mercatorfonds, 1989.

2572. Musée Communal des Beaux Arts (Bruges). *Gerard David.* 18 June–21 August 1949. Bruxelles, Editions de la Connaissance, 1949.

2573. Weale, William H. J. *Gerard David, painter and illuminator.* London, Seeley/New York, Macmillan, 1895. (The Portfolio Artistic Monographs, 24).

David, Jacques-Louis, 1748–1825

2574. Cantinelli, Richard. *Jacques-Louis David, 1748–1825.* Paris, van Oest, 1930.

2575. David, Jacques Louis Jules. *Le peintre Louis David.* 2 v. Paris, Havard, 1880–82.

2576. Delécluze, Etienne J. *Louis David, son école et son temps.* Souvenirs par M. E. J. Delécluze. Paris, Didier, 1855. (Nouv. ed. annotée par Jean-Pierre Mouilleseaux: Paris, Macula, 1983).

2577. Dowd, David. *Pageant master of the republic: J. L. David and the French revolution.* Lincoln, University of Nebraska Press, 1948. Reprint: Freeport, N.Y., Books for Libraries, 1969.

2578. Herbert, Robert L. *David, Voltaire, Brutus and the French Revolution; an essay in art and politics.* New York, Viking, 1973.

2579. Kuznetsova, Irina A. *Lui David; monograficheskii ocherk.* Moskva, Iskus-stvo, 1965.

2580. Maret, Jacques. *David.* Monaco, Documents d'Art, 1943.

2581. Maurois, André. *J.-L. David.* Paris, Dimanche, 1948.

2582. Miette de Villars. *Memoires de David, peintre et député à la Convention.* Paris, Chez tous les libraires, 1850.

2583. Musée de l'Orangerie (Paris). *David, exposition en l'honneur du deuxième centenaire de sa naissance.* Exposition, juin–septembre 1948. Préface de René Huyghe. . . . catalogue par Michel Florisoone. Paris, Editions des Musées Nationaux, 1948.

2584. Serullaz, Maurice. *J.-L. David, 1748–1825; quatorze dessins.* Paris, Musées Nationaux, 1939.

2585. Schnapper, Antoine. *David.* New York, Alpine Fine Arts Ltd., 1983.

2586. Thome, Antoine. *Vie de David.* Paris, Marchands de nouveautés, 1826.

2587. Valentiner, Wilhelm R. *Jacques Louis David and the French revolution.* New York, Sherman, 1929.

2588. Verbraeken, René. *Jacques-Louis David jugé par ses contemporains et par la posterité.* Suivi de la liste des tableaux dont l'authenticité est garantie. Avec une bibliographie chronologique. Préface par Louis Hautecoeur. Paris, Laget, 1973. (CR).

2589. Wildenstein, Daniel. *Documents complémentaires au catalogue de l'oeuvre de Louis David par Daniel et Guy Wildenstein.* Paris, Wildenstein, 1973. (CR).

David d'angers, Pierre-Jean, 1788–1856

2590. David d'Angers, Pierre-Jean. *Les carnets de David d'Angers.* Publiés pour la première fois intégralement, avec une introduction par André Bruel. 2 v. Paris, Plon, 1958.

2591. ———. *David d'Angers et ses relations littéraires.* Correspondance du maître avec Victor Hugo, Lamartine, Chateaubriand [etc.]. Publiée par Henry Jouin. Paris, Plon, 1890.

2592. ———. *Oeuvres complètes de P. J. David d'Angers, statuaire, membre de l'Institut de France, lithographiées par Eugène Marc.* 3 v. Paris, 1856.

2593. David d'Angers, Robert. *David d'Angers, un grand statuaire, sa vie, ses oeuvres, par son fils.* Paris, Charavay, Mantons, Martin, 1891.

2594. De Caso, Jacques. *David d'Angers: l'avenir de la mémoire. Etude sur l'art signalétique à l'époque romantique.* Paris, Flammarion, 1988.

2595. ———. *David d'Angers: sculptural communication in the age of romanticism.* Trans. Dorothy Johnson and Jacques de Caso.

Princeton: Princeton University Press, 1992. (English language edition of David d'Angers: l'avenir de la mémoire).

2596. Jouin, Henri A. *David d'Angers, sa vie, son oeuvre, ses écrits et ses contemporains.* 2 v. Paris, Plon, 1878.

2597. Schazmann, Paul E. *David d'Angers, profils de l'Europe.* Genève, Editions de Bonvent, 1973.

2598. Valotaire, Marcel. *David d'Angers; étude critique.* Paris, Laurens, 1932.

Davies, Arthur Bowen, 1862–1928

2599. Ackerman, Martin S. and Ackerman, Diane L., eds. *Arthur B. Davies: essays on his art, with illustrations.* Essays by Dwight Williams and others. New York, Arco, 1974. (Arco collectors' series, 2).

2600. Cortissoz, Royal. *Arthur B. Davies.* New York, Whitney Museum of American Art, 1931.

2601. Czestochowski, Joseph S. *Arthur B. Davies, a catalogue raisonné of the prints.* Newark, Del. University of Delaware Press; London, Associated University Presses, 1987. (CR).

2602. Metropolitan Museum of Art (New York). *Catalogue of a memorial exhibition of the works of Arthur B. Davies, Feb. 17–March 30, 1930.* New York, Metropolitan Museum of Art, 1930.

2603. Pennsylvania State University, Museum of Art (University Park, Penn.). *Works by Arthur B. Davies from the collection of Mr. and Mrs. Herbert Brill.* Exhibition June 24–Sept. 9, 1979. Catalogue compiled and annotated by John P. Driscoll. University Park, Penn., Pennsylvania State University Museum of Art, 1979.

2604. Phillips Memorial Art Gallery (Washington, D.C.). *Arthur B. Davies; essays on the man and his art.* A symposium. Cambridge, Mass., The Riverside Press, 1924. (The Phillips Publications, 3).

2605. Price, Frederic N. *The etchings and lithographs of Arthur B. Davies.* New York, Kennerley, 1929.

2606. Sims, Lowery Stokes. *Stuart Davis: American painter.* With contributions by William c. Agee et al. New York, Metropolitan Museum of Art; distrib. by Harry N. Abrams, 1991.

Davis, Alexander Jackson, 1803–1892

2607. Davis, Alexander J., et al. *Rural residences.* New York, New York University, 1837. (Reprint, with an introduction by Jane B. Davies: New York, Da Capo, 1980).

2608. Newton, Roger H. *Town & Davis, architects: pioneers in American revivalist architecture, 1812–1870.* New York, Columbia University Press, 1942.

Davis, Stuart, 1894–1964

2609. Blesh, Rudi. *Stuart Davis.* New York, Grove Press, 1960. (Evergreen gallery book, 11).

2610. Goossen, E. C. *Stuart Davis.* New York, Braziller, 1959.

2611. Kelder, Diane. *Stuart Davis.* New York, Praeger, 1971.

2612. Lane, John R. *Stuart Davis: art and art theory.* Brooklyn, N.Y., Brooklyn Museum, 1978.

2613. National Collection of Fine Arts (Washington, D.C.). *Stuart Davis memorial exhibition, 1894–1964.* Washington, D.C. Smithsonian Institution Press, 1965. (Smithsonian Publication, 4614).

2614. Sweeney, James J. *Stuart Davis.* New York, Metropolitan Museum of Art, 1945.

Day, Frederick Holland, 1864–1933

2615. Jussim, Estelle. *Slave to beauty: the eccentric life and controversial career of F. Holland Day, photographer, publisher, aesthete.* Boston, Godine, 1981.

2616. Wellesley College Museum (Wellesley, Mass.). *The photographic work of F. Holland Day.* February 21–March 24, 1975. [Introduction and catalogue by Ellen Fritz Clattenberg]. Wellesley, Mass., Wellesley College Museum, 1975.

Dayez, Georges, 1907–

2617. Duchateau, Jacques. *Dayez.* Paris, Musée de Poche, 1967. (Eng. ed. by George Schwab).

Decamps, Alexandre Gabriel, 1803–1860

2618. Chaumelin, Marius. *Decamps, sa vie, son oeuvre, ses imitateurs.* Marseille, Camoin, 1861.

2619. Clément, Charles. *Decamps.* Paris, Librairie de l'Art, 1887.

2620. Du Colombier, Pierre. *Decamps.* Paris, Rieder, 1928.

2621. Moreau, Adolphe. *Decamps et son oeuvre, avec des gravures en facsimile, des planches originales les plus rares.* Paris, Jouaust, 1869.

2622. Mosby, Dewey F. *Alexandre-Gabriel Decamps, 1803–1860.* 2 v. New York, Garland, 1977.

De Feure, Georges, 1868–1943

2623. Millman, Ian. *Georges de Feure: maître du symbolisme et de l'art nouveau.* Courbevoie (Paris), ACR, 1992.

Defregger, Franz von, 1835–1921

2624. Defregger, Hans P. *Defregger.* Rosenheim, Rosenheimer Verlagshaus, 1983.

2625. Kunstverein München. *Franz von Defregger 1835–1921.* Ehrenausstellung anlässlich seines 100. Geburtstages. München, Kunstverein, 1935.

2626. Rosenberg, Adolf. *Defregger*. Bielefeld/Leipzig, Velhagen & Klasing, 1897. (Künstler-Monographien, 18).

Degas, Hilaire Germain Edgar, 1834–1917

2627. Adhémar, Jean [and] Cachin, Françoise. *Degas, gravures et monotypes*. Paris, Arts et Métiers Graphiques, 1973.

2628. Armstrong, Carol M. *Odd man out: readings of the work and reputation of Edgar Degas*. Chicago, University of Chicago Press, 1991.

2629. Boggs, Jean S. *Drawings by Degas*. New York, Abrams, 1967.

2630. ———. *Portraits by Degas*. Berkeley, University of California Press, 1962.

2631. Browse, Lillian. *Degas dancers*. New York, Studio Publications, n.d.

2632. Churchill, Karen L. *Degas and photography*. An annotated bibliography and list of published images. Tempe, Arizona, Arizona State University, 1990.

2633. City Art Museum of St. Louis. *Drawings by Degas*. Essay and catalogue of the exhibition, Jan. 20–Feb. 26, 1967, by Jean S. Boggs. St. Louis, City Art Museum, 1967.

2634. Coquiot, Gustave. *Degas*. Paris, Ollendorff, 1924. 2 ed.

2635. Degas, Edgar. *Degas by himself: drawings, prints, paintings, writings*. Edited by Richard Kendall. Boston, Little Brown, 1987.

2636. ———. *Letters*. Ed. by Marcel Guérin. Oxford, Cassirer, 1947.

2637. Dunlop, Ian. *Degas*. New York, Harper & Row, 1979.

2638. Galerie Georges Petit, Paris. *Ventes atelier Degas*. Catalogue des tableaux, pastels et dessins par Edgar Degas et provenant de son atelier. Ventes I–IV. 4 v. Paris, Petit, 1918–1919.

2639. Grand Palais (Paris).*Dégas*. [Exposition] Galeries Nationales du Grand Palais, Paris, 9 février–16 mai 1988: Musée des Beaux-Arts du Canada, Ottawa, 16 juin–28 aout 1988: The Metropolitan Museum of Art, New York, 27 septembre 1988–8 janvier, 1989. Paris, Ministère de la Culture et de la Communication. Editions de la Reunion des Musées Nationaux, 1988.

2640. Guillaud, Maurice, ed. *Degas: form and space* [designed and edited by M. Guillaud]. Paris, Centre Culturel du Marais, 1984.

2641. Hertz, Henri. *Degas; art et esthétique*. Paris, Alcan, 1920.

2642. Jamot, Paul. *Degas*. Paris. Gazette de Beaux-arts, 1939.

2643. Janis, Eugenia P. *Degas Monotypes*. Essay, catalogue and checklist [of the exhibition held at the] Fogg Arts museum, Harvard University, April 25–June 14, 1968. Cambridge, Mass., Fogg Art Museum, 1968. (CR).

2644. Kendall, Richard and Pollock, Griselda, editors. *Dealing with Degas: representations of women and the politics of vision*. London, Pandora, 1992.

2645. Lafond, Paul. *Degas*. 2 v. *Paris, Floury, 1918–1919*.

2646. Lefevre Gallery (London). *The complete sculptures of Degas*. With an introduction by John Rewald. 18 Nov.–21. Dec., 1976. London, Lefevre, 1976.

2647. Lemoisne, Paul A. *Degas et son oeuvre*. 4v. Paris, Brame, 1947.

2648. Lévêque, Jean-J. *Edgar Degas*. Paris, Editions Siloé, 1978.

2649. Leymarie, Jean. *Les Degas du Louvre*. Paris, Librairie des Arts Décoratifs, 1947.

2650. Liebermann, Max. *Degas*. Berlin, Cassirer, 1902.

2651. Lipton, Eunice. *Looking into Degas*. Uneasy images of women and modern life. Berkeley, University of California Press, 1986.

2652. Los Angeles County Museum of Art. *An exhibition of works by Edgar Hilaire Degas, 1834–1917*. March, 1958. Los Angeles. Los angeles County Museum of Art, 1958.

2653. Loyrette, Henri. *Degas*. Paris, Fayard, 1991.

2654. Maheux, Anne F. *Degas pastels*. Ottawa, National Gallery of Canada, 1988.

2655. Mauclair, Camille. *Degas*. Paris, Hyperion Press, 1937.

2656. Meier-Graefe, Julius. *Degas; ein Beitrag zur Geschichte der modernen Malerei*. München, Piper, 1920.

2657. ———. *Degas*. Trans. by J. Holroyd-Reece. London, Benn, 1923.

2658. Millard, Charles W. *The sculpture of Edgar Degas*. Princeton, Princeton University Press, 1976.

2659. O'Brian, John. *Degas to Matisse: the Maurice Wertheim Collection*. Pref. by Barbara Wertheim Tuchman and Anne Wertheim Werner. New York, Harry N. Abrams; and the Fogg Art Museum. Harvard University Art Museums, 1988.

2660. Pečirka, Jaromir. *Edgar Degas: drawings*. London, Nevill, 1963.

2661. Reff, Theodore F. *Degas: the artist's mind*. New York, Metropolitan Museum of Art, 1976. (Reprint: Cambridge, Mass., Belknap Press of Harvard University Press, 1987).

2662. ———. *The notebooks of Edgar Degas.: a catalogue of the thirty-eight notebooks in the Bibliotheque Nationale and other collections*. 2 v. Oxford, Clarendon Press, 1976.

2663. Rewald, John. *Degas: sculpture, the complete works*. Photographed by Leonard von Matt. Trans. from the French by John Coleman and Noel Moneton. London, Thames and Hudson, 1957. (CR).

2664. ———. *Degas' complete sculpture.* Catalogue raisonné. New edition. San Francisco, Alan Wofsy, 1990. (CR).

2665. Rich, Daniel C. *Degas.* New York, Abrams, 1951.

2666. Rivière, Henri. *Les dessins de Degas.* 2 v. Ser. I–II. Paris. Demotte, 1922–1923.

2667. Rouart, Denis. *Degas a la recherche de sa technique.* Paris, Floury, 1945.

2668. ———. *Degas: Collection palettes.* Paris, Braun, 1949

2669. ———. *Degas dessins.* Paris, Braun, 1949.

2670. Russoli, Franco, e Minervino, Fiorella. *L'opera completa di Degas.* Presentazione di Franco Russoli. Apparati critici e filologici di Fiorella Minervino. Milano, Rizzoli, 1970. (Classici dell'arte, 45). (CR).

2671. Thomson, Richard. *Degas: the nudes.* London, Thames and Hudson, 1988.

2672. Traz, Georges de. *Degas.* Trans. by James Emmons. Geneva, Skira, 1954. (The Taste of Our Time, 5).

2673. Valéry, Paul. Degas. *Danse dessin.* Paris, Gallimard, 1928.

2674. Vollard, Ambroise. *Degas, an intimate portrait.* Trans. by R. T. Weaver. New York, Greenberg, 1927.

De Kooning, Willem, 1904–

2675. Gaugh, Harry F. *Willem de Kooning.* New York, Abbeville Press, 1983.

2676. Hess, Th.B. *Willem de Kooning.* New York, Braziller, 1959.

2677. ———. Willem de Kooning. New York, Museum of Modern Art; distributed by New York Graphic Society, Greenwich, Conn., 1968.

2678. ———. *Willem de Kooning: drawings.* London, Secker and Warburg, 1972.

2679. Rosenberg, Harold. *De Kooning.* New York, Abrams, 1974.

2680. Stedelijk Museum (Amsterdam). *Willem de Kooning.* 19. Sept.–17. Nov. 1968. Amsterdam, Dienst der Gemeentemusea, 1968.

2681. Walker Art Center (Minneapolis). *De Kooning: drawings, sculptures.* An exhibition organized by the Walker Art Center, March 10–April 21, 1974. Text by Philip Larson and Peter Schjeldahl. New York, Dutton, 1974.

Delacroix, Eugène, 1798–1863

2682. Athanassoglou-Kallmyer, Nina M. *Eugène Delacroix: prints, politics, and satire, 1814–1822.* New Haven, Yale University Press, 1991.

2683. Badt, Kurt. *Eugène Delacroix drawings.* Oxford, Cassirer, 1946.

2684. Baudelaire, Charles. *Eugène Delacroix, his life and work.* Trans. by J.M. Bernstein. New York, Lear, 1947.

2685. Cassou, Jean. *Delacroix.* Paris, Dimanche, 1947.

2686. Courthion, Pierre. *La vie de Delacroix.* Paris, Gallimard, 1927. 6 ed.

2687. Delacroix, Eugène. *Album de croquis.* Préface et catalogue raisonné par Maurice Sérullaz. 2 v. Paris, Quatre Chemins-Editart, 1961.(CR).

2688. ———. *Correspondance générale d'Eugène Delacroix.* Publiée par André Joubin. 5 v. Paris, Plon, 1936–1938.

2689. ———. *Delacroix in Morocco*: exhibition organized by the Institut du monde arabe, 27 September 1994–15 January 1995. [Conception of the catalogue, Brahim Alaoui. Trans. by Tamara Blondel]. Paris/New York, Flammarion; Paris, The Institute, 1994.

2690. ———. *Journal de Eugène Delacroix.* Avec notes par André Joubin. 3 v. Paris. Plon, 1932. (English ed., trans. by Lucy Norton: London, Phaidon, 1952).

2691. ———. *Oeuvres littéraires.* 2 pt. in 1 v. Paris, Crès, 1923.

2692. Escholier, Raymond. *Delacroix, peintre, graveur, écrivain.* 3 v. Paris, Floury, 1926–1929.

2693. Huyghe, René. *Delacroix.* Trans. by Jonathan Griffin. New York, Abrams, 1963.

2694. Johnson, Lee. *Delacroix.* New York, Norton, 1963.

2695. ———. *Eugène Delacroix: Further correspondence, 1817–1863.* New York, Oxford University Press, 1991.

2696. ———. *The Paintings of Eugène Delacroix, 1816–1831: a critical catalogue.* Oxford, Clarendon Press; New York, Oxford University Press, 1981–1989. (CR).

2697. Kunstmuseum Bern. *Eugène Delacroix. 16 Nov. 1963–19 Jan. 1964.* Katalog bearbeitet von Felix Baumann und Hugo Wagner. Bern, Kunstmuseum, 1963.

2698. Lavallée, Pierre. *Eugène Delacroix, quatorze dessins.* Paris, Musées Nationaux, 1938.

2699. Moreau-Nélaton, Etienne. *Delacroix, raconté par lui-même; étude biographique d'après ses lettres, son journal.* 2 v. Paris, Laurens, 1916.

2700. Moss, Armand. *Baudelaire et Delacroix.* Paris, Nizet, 1973.

2701. Mras, George P. *Eugène Delacroix's theory of art.* Princeton, N.J., Princeton University Press, 1966.

2702. Musée du Louvre (Paris). *Centenaire d'Eugène Delacroix, 1798–1863.* Exposition, mai–septembre 1963. Paris. Ministère d'Etat Affaires Culturelles, 1963.

2703. Planet, Louis de. *Souvenirs de travaux de*

peinture avec M. *Eugène Delacroix.* Pub. avec une introd. et des notes par André Joubin. Paris, Colin, 1929.

2704. Robaut, Alfred. *L'oeuvre complet de Eugène Delacroix: peintures, dessins, gravurers, lithographies.* Paris, Charavay, 1885.

2705. Rossi Bortolatto, Luigina. *L'opera pittorica completa di Delacroix.* Milano, Rizzoli, 1972. (Classici dell' arte, 57).

2706. Rudrauf, Lucien. *Eugène Delacroix et le problème du romantisme artistique.* Paris, Laurens, 1942.

2707. Sérullaz, Maurice. *Eugène Delacroix.* New York, Abrams, 1971.

2708. ———. *Les peintures murales de Delacroix.* Paris, Les Editions du Temps, 1963.

2709. Signac, Paul. *D'Eugène Delacroix au néo-impressionisme.* Paris, Floury, 1939. 4 ed.

2710. Tourneux, Maurice. *Eugène Delacroix; biographie critique.* Paris, Renouard, 1904.

2711. ———. *Eugène Delacroix devant ses contemporains, ses écrits, ses biographies, ses critiques.* Paris, Librairie de l'Art /Jules Rouam, 1886.

2712. Trapp, Frank A. *The attainment of Delacroix.* Baltimore, Johns Hopkins Press, 1970.

Delacroix, Henri-Edmond *see* Cross, Henri-Edmond

Delaunay, Robert, 1885–1941
Sonia, 1885–1979

2713. Albright-Knox Art Gallery (Buffalo, New York). *Sonia Delaunay; a retrospective, Feb. 2–March 16, 1980.* Foreword by Robert T. Buck, essays by Sherry A. Buckberrough; chronology by Susan Krane. Buffalo, New York. Albright-Knox Art Gallery, 1980.

2714. Cohen, Arthur A. *Sonia Delaunay.* New York, Abrams, 1975.

2715. Delaunay, Robert and Delaunay, Sonia. *The new art of color. The writings of Robert and Sonia Delaunay.* Ed. with introd. by Arthur A. Cohen. Trans. by David Shapiro and A. A. Cohen. New York, Viking, 1978.

2716. Delaunay, Sonia. *Nous irons jusqu'au soleil.* Avec la collaboration de Jacques Damase et de Patrick Raynaud. Paris, Laffont, 1978.

2717. Dorival, Bernard. *Robert Delaunay 1885–1941.* Paris/Bruxelles, Jacques Damase Gallery, 1975.

2718. ———. *Sonia Delaunay, sa vie, son oeuvre 1885–1979. Notes biographiques.* Paris, Jacques Damase Editeur, 1980.

2719. Gilles de la Tourette, F. *Robert Delaunay.* Préf. par Yvon Bizardel. Paris, Massin, 1950.

2720. Hoog, Michel. *Robert Delaunay.* Paris, Flammarion, 1976.

2721. ———. *Robert et Sonia Delaunay: Paris, Musée National d'Art Moderne.* Paris, Edi-

tions des Musées Nationaux, 1967. (Inventaire des collections publiques fran-çaises, 15).

2722. Orangerie des Tuileries (Paris). *Robert Delaunay (1885–1941).* 25 mai–30 août 1976. Préf. de Jean Cassou; introduction de Michel Hoog. Paris, Editions des Musées Nationaux, 1976.

Delorme, Philibert, 1512–1570

2723. Blunt, Anthony. *Philibert de l'Orme.* London, Zwemmer, 1958. (Studies in architecture, 1).

2724. Clouzot, Henri. *Philibert de l'Orme.* Paris, Plon-Nourrit, 1910.

2725. Delorme, Philibert. *L'oeuvre de Philibert Delorme, comprenant le premier tome de l'architecture et les nouvelles inventions pour bien bastir et a petitt frais.* Paris, Morel, 1567. (Reprint: Paris, Librairies imprimeries réunies, 1894).

2726. Prévost, Jean. *Philibert Delorme.* Paris, Gallimard, 1948.

2727. Vachon, Marius. *Philibert de l'Orme.* Paris, Librairie de l'Art, 1887.

Delvaux, Laurent, 1698–1778

2728. Devigne, Marguerite. *Laurent Delvaux et ses élèves.* Bruxelles/Paris, van Oest, 1928.

2729. Musées Royaux des Beaux-Arts de Belgique (Brussels). *Laurent Delvaux—Jacob de Wit.* Dec. 5, 1968–Jan. 1, 1969. Préf. Ph. Roberts-Jones, introd. H. Pauwels; textes F. Popelier et F. De Wilde. Bruxelles, Musées Royaux des Beaux-Arts de Belgique, 1968.

2730. Willame, Georges. *Laurent Delvaux, 1696–1778.* Bruxelles et Paris, van Oest, 1914.

Delvaux, Paul, 1897–

2731. Bock, Paul A. de. *Paul Delvaux: l'homme, le peintre, psychologie d'un art.* Paris, Pauvert/ Bruxelles, Laconti, 1967.

2732. Butor, Michel, et al. *Delvaux.* [By] M. Butor, Jean Clair, Suzanne Houbart-Wilkin. Bruxelles, Cosmos, 1975.

2733. Jacob, Mira. *Paul Delvaux: l'oeuvre gravé.* Monaco, André Sauret, 1976. (English ed., trans. by Howard Brasyn. New York, Rizzoli, 1976). (CR).

2734. Musées Royaux des Beaux-Arts de Belgique (Brussels). *Hommage à Paul Delvaux.* 13 juillet–25 septembre 1977. Bruxelles, Musées Royaux des Beaux Arts, 1977.

2735. Museum Boymans-van Beuningen (Rotterdam). *Paul Delvaux.* 13 apr.–17 juni 1973. Rotterdam, Mus. Boymans-van Beuningen, 1973.

2736. Nadeau, Maurice. *Les dessins de Paul Delvaux.* Paris, Denoël, 1967.

2737. Scott, David. *Surrealizing the Nude.* London,

Reaktion Books; Seattle, Wash., distributed in USA and Canada by the University of Washington Press, 1992.

2738. Spaak, Claude. *Paul Delvaux*. Antwerp, De Sikkel, 1948.

2739. Terrasse, Antoine. *Paul Delvaux: la septième face du dé*. Paris, Filipaichi, 1972.

Demachy, Robert, 1859–1936

2740. Demachy, Robert [and] Puyo, C. *Les procédés d'art en photographie*. Paris, Photo-Club de Paris, 1906. (Reprint: New York, Arno, 1979).

2741. Jay, Bill. *Robert Demachy, 1859–1936; photographs and essays*. London, Academy Editions/New York, St. Martin's, 1974.

Demarne, Jean-Louis, 1752–1829

2742. Watelin, Jacques. *Le peintre J.-L. de Marne, 1752–1829*. Paris, Bibliothèque des arts, 1962). (La Bibliothèque des arts, 10).

Demuth, Charles Henry, 1883–1935

2743. Eiseman, Alvord L. *Charles Demuth*. New York, Watson-Guptill, 1982.

2744. Farnham, Emily. *Charles Demuth: behind a laughing mask*. Norman, University of Oklahoma Press, 1971.

2745. Gallatin, Albert E. *Charles Demuth*. New York, Rudge, 1927.

2746. Murrell, William. *Charles Demuth*. New York, Macmillan, 1931.

2747. Norton, Thomas E., ed. *Homage to Charles Demuth, still life painter of Lancaster*. Ed. and with an introd. by Thomas E. Norton. Essays by Alvord L. Eiseman, Sherman E. Lee, and Gerald S. Lestz. Valedictory by Marsden Hartley. Ephrata, Penn., Science Press, 1978.

2748. Ritchie, Andrew C. *Charles Demuth*. New York, Metropolitan Museum of Modern Art, 1950.

Denis, Maurice, 1870–1943

2749. Denis, Maurice. *Journal*. 3 v. Paris, La Colombe, 1957–1959.

2750. ———. *Théories, 1890–1910. Du symbolisme et de Gauguin; vers un nouvel ordre classique*. Paris, Rouart et Watelin, 1920.

2751. ———. *Nouvelles théories; sur l'art moderne, sur l'art sacré, 1914–1921*. Paris, Rouart et Watelin, 1922.

2752. Fosca, François [pseud., Georges de Traz]. *Maurice Denis*. Paris, Nouvelle Revue Français, 1924. (Les peintres français nouveaux, 17).

2753. Jamot, Paul. *Maurice Denis*. Paris, Plon, 1945.

Derain, André, 1880–1954

2754. Arts Council of Great Britain. *Derain, an exhibition of paintings, drawings, sculpture, and theatre designs* [at The Royal Academy, London]. 30 Sept.–5 Nov., 1967. London, Arts Council, 1967.

2755. Basler, Adolphe. *André Derain*. Paris, Librairie de France, 1929. (Albums d'art Druet, 21).

2756. ———. *Derain*. Paris, Crès, 1931.

2757. Cailler, Pierre. *Catalogue raisonné de l'oeuvre sculpté de André Derain; première partie: l'oeuvre édité*. Aigle, Imprimerie de la Plaine du Rhone, 1965. (CR).

2758. Carra, Carlo. *André Derain*. Roma, Valori Plastici, 1924.

2759. Derain, André. *Lettres à Vlaminck*. Paris, Flammarion, 1955.

2760. Diel, Gaston. *Derain*. Paris, Flammarion, 1964.

2761. Dunoyer de Segonzac, André. *Album André Derain*. Paris, Editions d'Art du Lion, 1961.

2762. Faure, Elie. *A. Derain*. Paris, Crès, 1926.

2763. Grand Palais (Paris). *André Derain*. 15 février–11 avril 1977. Paris, Editions des Musées Nationaux, 1977.

2764. Henry, Daniel [pseud., Daniel H. Kahnweiler]. *André Derain*. Leipzig, Klinkhardt und Biermann, 1920. (Junge Kunst, 15).

2765. Hilaire, Georges. *Derain*. Genève, Cailler, 1959.

2766. Kalitina, Nina N. *André Derain*. Leningrad, Aurora, 1976.

2767. Kellermann, Michel. *Paintings by André Derain*. Volume I: 1895–1915. Paris, Galerie Schmit, 1992.

2768. Leymarie, Jean. *André Derain ou le retour à l'ontologie*. Genève, Skira, 1948.

2769. Lee, Jane. *Derain*. *Oxford*. Oxford University Press, 1990.

2770. Papazoff, George. *Derain, mon copain*. Paris, SNEV, 1960.

2771. Parke-Taylor. *André Derain in North American collections*. Organized by the Norman Mackenzie Art Gallery, University of Regina, 29 October–5 December, 1982. Regina, Sask., Norman Mackenzie Art Gallery, 1982.

2772. Salmon, André. *André Derain*. Paris, Editions des Chroniques du Jour, 1928.

2773. Sutton, Denys. *André Derain*. London, Phaidon, 1959.

2774. Vaughan, Malcolm. *Derain*. New York, Hyperion Press/Harper, 1941.

Deruet, Claude, 1588–1660

2775. Fessenden, De Witt H. *The life and works of Claude Deruet, court painter, 1588–1660*. Brooklyn, N.Y., Fessenden, 1952.

Desiderio da Settignano, 1428–1464

2776. Cardellini, Ida. *Desiderio da Settignano*. Milano, Edizioni di Communità, 1962. (Studi e documenti di storia dell'arte, 3).

2777. Planiscig, Leo. *Desiderio da Settignano.* Wien, Schroll, 1943.

Desmarees, George *see* Marees, George des

Desnoyer, Francois, 1894–1972
2778. Bouret, Jean. *Desnoyer: dessins.* Paris, Galerie Guiot, 1944.
2779. Dorival, Bernard. *Desnoyer.* Paris, Braun, 1943.
2780. Galerie Marcel Guiot (Paris). *Desnoyer: Venise.* Oct. 1963. Paris, Guiot, 1963.
2781. Gay, Paul. *Desnoyer.* Saint Jeoire en Faucigny (Hte. Savoie), La Peinture pour Tous, 1951.
2782. Musée Ingres (Montauban). *F. Desnoyer, cinquante ans de peinture.* 26 juin–15 sept. 1968. Catalogue par Duchein et Mathieu Méras. Montauban, Musée Ingres, 1968.

Despiau, Charles, 1874–1946
2783. Basler, Adolphe. *Despiau.* Paris, Druet, 1927. (Les albums d'art Druet, 9).
2784. Deshairs, Léon. *C. Despiau.* Paris, Crès, 1930.
2785. George, Waldemar. *Despiau.* Amsterdam, De Lange, 1954.
2786. ———. *Despiau vivant, l'homme et l'oeuvre.* London, Dupont, 1947.
2787. Musée Rodin (Paris). *Charles Despiau, sculptures et dessins.* [Catalogue by Claude Roger-Marx]. Paris, Musée Rodin, 1974.
2788. Roger-Marx, Claude. *Charles Despiau.* Paris, Gallimard, 1922. (Les sculpteurs français nouveaux, 1).

Detaille, Edouard, 1848–1912
2789. Chanlaine, Pierre. *Edouard Detaille.* Paris, Bonne, 1962.
2790. Detaille, Edouard. *Types et uniformes: L'amée française, par Edouard Detaille; texte par Jules Richard.* 2 v. Paris, Boussod, Valadon, 1885–1889.
2791. Humbert, Jean. *Edouard Detaille; l'heroïsme d'un siècle.* Paris, Editions Copernic, 1979.
2792. Vachon, Marius. *Detaille.* Paris, Lahure, 1898.

Deutsch, Niklaus Manuel *see* Manuel-Deutsch, Niklaus

Deveria, Achille, 1800–1857
Eugène, 1805–1865
2793. Gauthier, Maximilien. *Achille et Eugène Devéria.* Paris, Floury, 1925.
2794. Musée des Beaux-Arts, Pau (France). *Eugène Devéria (Paris 1805–Pau 1865).* 29 oct.–31 déc. 1965. Pau, Musée des Beaux-Arts, 1965.

Diaz, Daniel Vazquez *see* Vazquez-Diaz, Daniel

Dientzenhofer, Christoph, 1655–1722
Kilian Ignaz, 1689–1751
Wolfgang, 1648–1706
2795. Franz, Heinrich G. *Die Kirchenbauten des Christoph Dientzenhofer.* Brünn, Rohrer, 1942. (Beiträge zur Geschichte der Kunst im Sudeten- und Karpathenraum, 5).
2796. Gürth, Alcuin H. *Über Wolfgang Dientzenhofer; Materialen zur Geschichte der oberpfälzischen Barockarchitektur.* Kallmünz, Lassleben, 1959.
2797. Norberg-Schulz, Christian. *Kilian Ignaz Dientzenhofer e il barocco boemo.* Roma, Officina, 1968.
2798. Weigmann, Otto A. *Eine Bamberger Baumeister-Familie um die Wende des 17. Jahrhunderts.* Ein Beitrag zur Geschichte der Dientzenhofer. Strassburg, Heitz, 1902. (Studien zur deutschen Kunstgeschichte, 34).

Dietterlin, Wendel, 1550–1599
2799. Dietterlin, Wendel. *Architectura von Austheilungs Symetria und Proportion der fünff Seulen, und aller daraufs volgender Kunst Arbeit, von Fenstern, Caminen, Thurgerichten, Portalen, Bronnen, und Epi-taphien.* Nürnberg, Caymox, 1598. (Repr.: Darmstadt, Wissenschaftliche Buchgesellschaft, 1954; Einführung von Hans Gerhard Evers; also: New York, Dover, 1968; introd. by Adolf K. Placzek).
2800. Ohnesorge, Karl. *Wendel Dietterlin, Maler von Strassburg; ein Beitrag zur Geschichte der deutschen Kunst in der zweiten Hälfte des sechzehnten Jahrhunderts.* Leipzig, Seemann, 1893. (Beiträge zur Kunstgeschichte, N.F. 21).

Dillis, Cantius, 1779–1856
Johann Georg, 1759–1841
2801. Bayerische Staatsgemäldesammlungen (Munich). *Johann Georg von Dillis, 26. Dezember 1759–28. September 1841: Ausstellung, 15 Dez. 1959–14. Feb. 1960.* München, Prestel, 1959.
2802. Galerie Arnoldi-Livie (Munich). *Johann Georg von Dillis, 1759–1841; Cantius Dillis, 1779–1856.* 40 Aquarelle und Zeichnungen aus e. Privatsammlung. Herbst 1979. München, Galerie Arnoldi-Livie, 1979.
2803. Lessing, Waldemar. *Johann Georg von Dillis als Künstler und Museumsmann, 1759–1841.* München, Bruckmann, 1951.
2804. Messerer, Richard. *Georg von Dillis; Leben und Werk.* München, 1961. (Oberbayerisches Archiv, 84).

Dine, Jim, 1935–

2805. Beal, Graham W., et al. *Jim Dine: five themes.* New York, Abbeville Press, 1984.

2806. Dine, Jim. *Jim Dine.* A cura di Attilio Codognato. Milano, Mazotta, 1988.

2807. Dine, Jim. *Jim Dine designs for A Midsummer Night's Dream.* Selected from the drawings and prints collection of the Museum of Modern Art. Introd. by Virginia Allen. General editor S. Lieberman. New York, Museum of Modern Art, 1968.

2808. D'Oench, Ellen and Feinberg, Jean E. *Jim Dine prints, 1977–1985.* New York, Harper & Row, 1986.

2809. Shapiro, David. *Jim Dine. Painting what one is.* New York, Abrams, 1981.

2810. Whitney Museum of American Art (New York). *Jim Dine.* Feb. 27–April 19, 1970. [Text by John Gordon]. New York, Whitney Museum of American Art, 1970.

Dinglinger, Johann Melchior, 1664–1731

2811. Watzdorf, Erna von. *Johann Melchior Dinglinger der Goldschmied des deutschen Barock.* 2 v. Berlin, Mann, 1962.

Dix, Otto, 1891–1969

2812. Akademie der Künste Berlin. *Otto Dix; Gemälde und Graphik von 1912–1957.* 12. April–31. Mai 1957. Redaktion und Gestaltung [von] Gerhard Pommeranz-Liedke. Berlin, Akademie der Künste, 1957.

2813. Barton, Brigid S. *Otto Dix und die Neue Sachlichkeit, 1918–1925.* Ann Arbor, UMI Research Press, 1981. (Studies in the fine arts. The avant-garde, 11).

2814. Dix, Otto. *Otto Dix, 1891–1969.* [Catalog of an exhibition held at the Tate Gallery, March 11–May 17, 1992]. London, Tate Gallery, 1992.

2815. ———. *Otto Dix im Selbstbildnis.* Mit 126 Abbildungen, 43 Farbreproduktionen und einer Sammlung von Schriften, Briefen und Gesprächen von Dieter Schmidt. Berlin, Henschel, 1978.

2816. Fischer, Lothar. *Otto Dix; ein Malerleben in Deutschland.* Berlin, Nicolai, 1981.

2817. Galerie der Stadt Stuttgart. *Otto Dix, Menschenbilder.* Gemälde, Aquarelle, Gouachen und Zeichnungen. 3 Dez. 1981–31 Jan. 1982. Katalog Eugen Keuerleber; wiss. Mitarbeit Brigitte Reinhardt. Stuttgart, Die Galerie, 1981.

2818. ———. *Otto Dix zum 80. Geburtstag: Gemälde, Aquarelle, Gouachen, Zeichnungen und Radierfolge Der Krieg.* 2. Okt.–28. Nov. 1971. Stuttgart, Die Galerie, 1971.

2819. Hartley, Keith. *Otto Dix, 1891–1969.* London, Tate Gallery; Seattle, University of Washington Press, 1992.

2820. Karcher, Eva. *Dix.* München, Südwest Verlag, 1986. (English trans: New York, Crown, 1987).

2821. ———. *Eros und Tod im Werk von Otto Dix. Studien zur Geschichte des Körpers in den zwanziger Jahren.* Münster, Lit, 1984.

2822. ———. *Otto Dix, 1891–1969: Leben und Werk.* Hrsg. von Ingo F. Walter. Köln, Benedikt Taschen Verlag, 199.

2823. Karsch, Florian. *Otto Dix: das graphische Werk.* Eingeleitet von Hans Kinkel. Hannover, Fackelträger Verlag, Schmidt Küster, 1970. (CR).

2824. Kunsthalle zu Kiel. *Otto Dix: Zeichnungen aus dem Nachlass 1911–1942.* 30. März–21. Mai 1980. Katalog von Jens Christian Jensen. Kiel, Kunsthalle und Schleswig-Holsteinischer Kunstverein, 1980.

2825. Löffler, Fritz. *Otto Dix: Bilder zur Bibel und zu Legenden, zu Vergänglichkeit und Tod.* Stuttgart/Zürich, Belser Verlag, 1987.

2826. ———. *Otto Dix: Leben und Werk.* Dresden, Verlag der Kunst, 1977. 4 ed.

2827. ———. *Otto Dix, 1891–1969: Oeuvre der Gemälde.* Recklinghausen, Bongers, 1981.

2828. McGreevy, Linda F. *The life and works of Otto Dix, a German critical realist.* Ann Arbor, UMI Research Press, 1981. (Studies in the fine arts. The avant-garde, 12).

2829. Schmidt, Johann Karl [and] Reinhart, Brigitte . . . [et al.]. *Otto Dix: Bestandskatalog: Gemälde, Aquarelle, Pastelle, Zeichnungen, Holzschnitte, Radierungen, Lithographien.* Hrsg von J.K. Schmidt. Bearbeitung von Katalog und Bibliographie, Dieter Scholz. Engl. trans. Joy Fischer. Stuttgart, Galerie der Stadt Stuttgart; Edition Cantz, 1989.

2830. Schubert, Dietrich. *Otto Dix in Selbstzeugnissen und Bilddokumenten.* Reinbeck, Rowohlt, 1980. (Rowohlts Monographien, 287).

Dobson, Frank, 1886–1963

2831. Arts Council of Great Britain. *Frank Dobson, 1886–1963; memorial exhibition [of] sculpture, drawings and designs.* Arts Council Gallery, 22 June–23 July 1966. London, Arts Council, 1966.

2832. Earp, Thomas W. *Frank Dobson, sculptor.* London, Tiranti, 1945.

Doesburg, Theo van, 1883–1931

2833. Baljeu, Joost. *Theo van Doesburg.* New York, Macmillan, 1974.

2834. Doesburg, Theo van. *Grundbegriffe der neuen gestaltenden Kunst.* München, Langen, 1925. (Bauhausbücher, 6).

2835. ———. *Principles of neo-plastic art.* With an introd. by Hans M. Wingler and a postscript by H. L. C. Jaffé. Trans. by Janet Seligman. Greenwich, Conn., New York Graphic Society, 1968.

2836. ———. *Klassiek—barok—modern; lezing.* Antwerpen, De Sikkel, 1920.

2837. ———. *De nieuwe beweging in de schilderkunst.* Delft, Waltman, 1917.

2838. ———. *Scritti di arte e di architettura.* A cura di Sergio Polano. Roma, Officina Edizioni, 1979. (Collana di architettura, 19).

2839. Hedrick, Hannah L. *Theo van Doesburg, propagandist and practitioner of the avant-garde, 1909–1923.* Ann Arbor, UMI Research Press, 1980. (Studies in the fine arts. The avant-garde, 5).

2840. Mansbach, Steven A. *Visions of totality: Laszlo Moholy-Nagy, Theo van Doesburg, and El Lissitzky.* Ann Arbor, UMI Research Press, 1980. (Studies in the fine arts. The avant-garde, 6).

2841. Musée National d'Art Moderne (Paris). *Théo van Doesburg: projets pour l'Aubette.* Centre national d'art et de culture Georges Pompidou, 12 oct.–12 déc. 1979. Paris, Centre Georges Pompidou, 1977.

2842. Stedelijk van Abbemuseum Eindhoven. *Theo van Doesburg 1883–1931.* Eindhoven, van Abbemuseum, 1968.

2843. Weyergraf, Clara. *Piet Mondrian und Theo van Doesburg: Deutung von Werk und Theorie.* München, Fink, 1979.

Domela, César, 1900–

2844. Clairet, Alain. *Domela: un catalogue raisonné de l'oeuvre de César Domela-Nieuwenhuis; peintures, reliefs, sculptures.* Traduction anglaise de Madeleine Hage. Paris, Carmen Martinez, 1978. (CR).

2845. Kunsthalle Düsseldorf. *César Domela, Werke 1922–1972.* 12. Okt.–3 Dez. 1972. Bearb. und Gestaltung: Karl-Heinz Hering. Düsseldorf, Kunstverein für die Rheinlande und Westfalen, 1972.

Domenichino (Domenico Zampieri), 1581–1641

2846. Borea, Evelina. *Dominichino.* Milano, Club del libro, 1965. (Collana d'arte del Club del libro, 12).

2847. Pope-Hennessy, John. *The drawings of Domenichino in the collection of His Majesty the King at Windsor Castle.* London, Phaidon, 1948.

2848. Serra, Luigi. *Domenico Zampieri, detto il Domenichino.* Rome, Calzone, 1909.

2849. Spear, Richard E. *Domenichino.* 2 v. New Haven, Yale University Press, 1982.

Donatello (Donato di Niccolo di Betto Bardi), 1386–1466

2850. Bennett, Bonnie A. *Donatello.* By Bonnie A. Bennet and David G. Wilkins. Oxford, Phaidon Press, 1984.

2851. Bertela, Giovanna Gaeta. *Donatello.* [Trans. Nancy Pearson and Anthony Brierley]. Florence, Scala, 1991.

2852. Cecci, Emilio. *Donatello.* Rome, Tumminelli, 1942.

2853. Colasanti, Arduino. *Donatello.* Roma, Valori Plastici, n.d.

2854. ———. *Donatello.* Trans. de Jean Chuzeville. Paris, Crès, 1931.

2855. Convegno Internazionale di Studi sul Rinascimento VIII. *Donatello e il suo tempo.* Atti del convegno 25 sett.–1 ott. 1966, Firenze-Padova. Firenze, Istituto Nazionale di Studi sul Rinascimento, 1968.

2856. Crawford, David A. E. L. (Lord Balcarres). *Donatello.* New York, Scribner, 1903.

2857. Donatello. *Donatello e il suo tempo.* Atti dell' VIII Convegno Internazionale di Studi sul Rinascimento, Firenze-Padova, 25 settembre–1 ottobre, 1966. Firenze, Istituto Nazionale di Studi sul Rinascimento, 1968.

2858. ———. *Donatello e i suoi: scultura fiorentina del primo Rinascimento.* A cura di Alan Phipps Darr e Giorgio Bonsanti. Milano, Mondadori, 1986.

2859. ———. *Donatello-Studien.* Redaktion Monika Cammerer. München, Bruckmann, 1989. (Italienische Forschungen; 3. Folge, Bd. 16).

2860. Fechheimer, Samuel S. *Donatello und die Reliefkunst; eine kunstwisenschaftliche Studie.* Strassburg, Heitz, 1904. (Zur Kunstgeschichte des Auslandes, 17).

2861. Goldscheider, Ludwig. *Donatello.* London, Phaidon, 1944.

2862. Grassi, Luigi. *All the sculpture of Donatello.* Trans. by Paul Colacicchi. New York, Hawthorn Books, 1964. (The Complete Library of World Art, 23–24).

2863. Hartt, Frederick. *Donatello, prophet of modern vision.* Photographs by David Finn. New York, Abrams, 1973.

2864. Istituto Statale d'Arte, Firenze. *Donatello e il primo Rinascimento del nei calchi della Gipsoteca.* Firenze, S.P.E.S., 1985

2865. Janson, Horst W. *The sculpture of Donatello.* 2 v. Princeton, N.J., Princeton University Press, 1957. (Rev. ed., incorporating the notes of Jenö Lányi, 1963).

2866. Kauffmann, Hans. *Donatello. Eine Einführung in sein Bilden und Denken.* Berlin, Grote, 1935.

2867. Lightbown, Ronald W. *Donatello and Michelozzo: an artistic partnership and its patrons in the early Renaissance.* 2 v. London, Miller, 1980.

2868. Meyer, Alfred G. *Donatello.* Trans. by P. G. Konody. Bielefeld/Leipzig, Velhagen & Klasing, 1904. (Monographs on artists, 8). (Rev., 3 ed., in German, 1926).

2869. Milanesi, Gaetano. *Catalogo delle opere di Donatello e bibliografia degli autori che ne hanno scritto.* Firenze, Tipi dell'arte della stampa, 1887.

2870. Morisani, Ottavio. *Studi su Donatello.* Venezia, Pozza, 1952.

2871. Parronchi, Alessandro. *Donatello e il potere.* Bologna, Cappelli/Firenze, Il Portolano, 1980.

2872. Planiscig, Leo. *Donatello.* Wien, Schroll, 1939. 3 ed.

2873. Poeschke, Joachim. *Donatello, Figur und Quadro.* München, Fink, 1980.

2874. ———. *Die Skulptur der Renaissance in Italien. Band 1.: Donatello und seine Zeit.* München, Hirmer, 1990.

2875. Pope-Hennessy, John Wyndham. *Donatello,* [by] John Pope-Hennessy; fotografie di Liberto Perugi; apparati critici di Giovanna Ragionieri. Firenze, Cantini, 1985. (Reprint of the author's 1968 text).

2876. Rosenauer, Artur. *Donatello.* Milano, Electa, 1993. (CR).

2877. ———. *Studien zum frühen Donatello; Skulptur im projektiven Raum der Neuzeit.* Wien, Holzhausen, 1975. (Wiener kunstgeschichtliche Forschungen, 3).

2878. Schottmüller, F. *Donatello. Ein Beiträg zum Verständnis seiner künstlerischen Tat.* München, Bruckmann, 1904.

2879. Schubring, Paul. *Donatello; des Meisters Werke.* Stuttgart, Deutsche Verlagsanstalt, 1922. 2 ed.

2880. Semper, Hans. *Donatello. Seine Zeit und Schule; eine Reihenfolge von Abhandlungen. Im Anhange: Das Leben des Donatello von Vasari. Der Tractat des Francesco Bocchi über den S. Georg des Donatello.* Wien, Braumüller, 1875.

2881. ———. *Donatellos Leben und Werke.* Eine Festschrift zum fünfhundertjährigen Jubiläum seiner Geburt in Florenz. Innsbruck, Wagner, 1887.

2882. Wundram, Manfred. *Donatello und Nanni di Banco.* Berlin, de Gruyter, 1969. (Beiträge zur Kunstgeschichte, 3).

Donato di Niccolo di Betto Bardi *see* Donatello

Dongen, Kees van, 1877–1968

2883. Adrichem, Jan van, Kuspit, Donald, and Michel Hoog, editors. *Kees van Dongen.* [Catalog of an exhibition held at the Museum Boymans-van Beuningen, Rotterdam, 17/12/89–11/02/90]. Rotterdam. Het Museum, 1989.

2884. Chaumeil, Louis. *Van Dongen, l'homme et l'artiste: la vie et l'oeuvre.* Genève, Cailler, 1967.

2885. Courières, Eduard des. *Van Dongen.* Paris, Floury, 1925.

2886. Dongen, Kees van. *La Hollande, les femmes et l'art.* Paris, Flammarion, 1927.

2887. Fierens, Paul. *Van Dongen, l'homme et l'oeuvre.* Paris, Les Ecrivains Réunis, 1929.

2888. Museum Boymans-van Beuningen (Rotterdam). *Tentoonstelling Kees van Dongen, Werken van 1894 tot 1949.* 28 mei–10 juli 1949. Rotterdam, Museum Boymansvan Beuningen, 1949.

2889. ———. *Van Dongen.* 8 dec. 1967–28 jan. 1968. Museum Boymans-van Beuningen, Rotterdam. Rotterdam, Museum Boymans-van Beuningen, 1967.

2890. Musée Cantini (Marseille). *Hommage à van Dongen.* Juin–septembre 1969. Catalogue par Daniele Giraudy, avec le concours de Frédérique Cuchet. Marseille, Presses Municipales, 1969.

2891. Musée de Lyon. *Van Dongen.* Introduction par René Déroudille. Lyon, Musée de Lyon, 1967.

2892. Page, Suzanne, Marquet, Françoise, Gilbert Lascault et al. *Kees van Dongen le peintre, 1877–1968.* [Catalogue of an exhibition held at the Musée d'Art Moderne de la Ville de Paris, 22 mars–17 juin, 1990]. Paris, Amis du Musée d'Art Moderne, 1990.

2893. Stedelijk Museum (Amsterdam). *Kees van Dongen tentoonstelling 9 april–8 mei 1927.* Georganiseerd door weekblad Het Leven. Amsterdam, Stedelijk Museum, 1927.

2894. ———. *Van Dongen 1877–1937.* Dec. 1937–jan. 1938. Amsterdam, Stedelijk Museum, 1937.

Donner, Georg Raphael, 1693–1741

2895. Blauensteiner, Kurt. *Georg Raphael Donner.* Mit 96 Bildern nach Aufnahmen von Helga Glassner. Wien, Schroll, 1944.

2896. Pigler, Andor. *Georg Raphael Donner.* Leipzig, Epstein, 1929.

2897. Schlager, J. E. *Georg Rafael Donner; ein Beitrag zur österreichischen Kunstgeschichte.* Wien, Kaulfuss-Prandel, 1853.

2898. Schwarz, Michael. *Georg Raphael Donner: Kategorien der Plastik.* München, Fink, 1968.

Doré, Gustave, 1832–1883

2899. Cercle de la Librairie (Paris). *Catalogue de l'exposition de Gustave Doré: catalogue des dessins, aquarelles et estampes exposés dans les salons du Cercle de la Librairie (mars 1885), avec une notice biographique par M. G. Duplessis.* Paris, Cercle de la Librairie, 1885. (Reprint: New York, Garland, 1981.)

2900. Delormé, René. *Gustave Doré; peintre,*

sculpteur, dessinateur et graveur. Paris, Librairie d'Art Baschet, 1879.

2901. Doré Gallery (London). *Descriptive catalogue of pictures by Gustave Doré.* London, 1869.

2902. Farner, Konrad. *Gustave Doré, der industrialisierte Romantiker.* 2 v. Dresden, Verlag der Kunst, 1963.

2903. Forberg, Gabriele. *Gustave Doré; das graphische Werk.* Ausgewählt von G. Forberg; Nachwort von Günter Metken. 2 v. München, Rogner & Bernhard, 1975.

2904. Gosling, Nigel. *Gustave Doré.* New York, Praeger, 1974.

2905. Hartlaub, Gustav F. *Gustave Doré.* Leipzig, Klinkhardt & Biermann, 1923. (Meister der Graphik, 12).

2906. Jerrold, Blanchard. *Life of Gustave Doré.* London, Allen, 1891. (Reprint: Detroit, Singing Tree Press, 1969).

2907. ———. *London; a pilgrimage.* By Gustave Doré and B. Jerrold. London, Allen, 1872. (Reprint: New York, Blom, 1968).

2908. Leblanc, Henri. *Catalogue de l'oeuvre complet de Gustave Doré; illustrations, peintures, dessins, sculptures, eaux fortes, lithographies.* Paris, Bosse, 1931.

2909. Lehmann-Haupt, Hellmut. *The terrible Gustave Doré.* New York, Marchbanks Press, 1943. (Reprint: Westport, Conn., Greenwood, 1976).

2910. Richardson, Joanna. *Gustave Doré: a biography.* London, Cassell, 1980.

2911. Roosevelt, Blanche [pseud.]. *Life and reminiscences of Gustave Doré; compiled from material supplied by Doré's relations and friends and from personal recollection.* New York, Cassell, 1885.

2912. Rose, Millicent. *Gustave Doré.* London, Pleiades Books, 1946.

2913. Valmy-Baysse, Jean. *Gustave Doré.* Bibliographie et catalogue complet de l'oeuvre par Louis Dézé. Paris, Seheur, 1930.

Dossi, Battista (Battista de Lutero), d. 1548

Dosso (Giovanni de Lutero), 1479–1542

2914. Gibbons, Felton L. *Dosso and Battista Dossi, court painters at Ferrara.* Princeton, N.J., Princeton University Press, 1968. (Princeton Monographs in Art and Archaeology, 39).

2915. Mendelsohn, Henriette. *Das Werk der Dossi.* München, Müller & Rentsch, 1914.

2916. Mezzetti, Amalia. *Il Dosso e Battista, Ferranesi.* Milano, Silvana, 1965.

2917. Zwanziger, Walter C. *Dosso Dossi, mit besonderer Berücksichtigung seines künstlerischen Verhältnisses zu seinem Bruder Battista.* Leipzig, Klinkhardt und Biermann, 1911.

Dou, Gerard, 1613–1675

2918. Martin, Wilhelm. *Gerard Dou; des Meisters Gemälde in 247 Abbildungen.* Stuttgart/Berlin, Deutsche Verlagsanstalt, 1913. (Klassiker der Kunst in Gesamtausgaben, 24).

2919. ———. *Gerard Dou.* Trans. by Clara Bell. London, Bell, 1902.

2920. ———. *Het leven en de werken van Gerrit Dou, beschouwd in Verband met het schildersleven van zijn tijd.* Leiden, van Doesburgh, 1901.

Dove, Arthur Garfield, 1880–1946

2921. Newman, Sasha M. *Arthur Dove and Duncan Phillips, artist and patron.* Foreword by Laughlin Phillips; exhibition history and reviews [by] Jan Lancaster. Washington, D.C., Phillips Collection/New York, Braziller, 1981.

2922. Wight, Frederick S. *Arthur G. Dove.* Berkeley, University of California Press, 1958.

2923. Worcester Art Museum (Worcester, Mass.). *Paintings and water colors by Arthur G. Dove lent by the William H. Lane Foundation.* 17 July–17 Sept. 1961. Text by Daniel C. Rich. Worcester, Mass., Worcester Art Museum, 1961.

Dubbels, Hendrik Jacobszoon, 1621–1707

2924. Middendorf, Ulrike. *Hendrik Jacobsz. Dubbels (1621–1707). Gemälde und Zeichnungen mit kritischem Oeuvrekatalog.* Freren, Luca Verlag, 1989.

Dubuffet, Jean, 1901–

2925. Akademie der Künste (Berlin). *Dubuffet Retrospektive.* 7. Sept.–26. Okt. 1980. Berlin, Akademie der Kunst, 1980. (Akademie-Katalog, 130).

2926. Barilli, Renato. *Dubuffet, le cycle de l'Hourloupe.* Paris, Editions du Chêne, 1976.

2927. Cordier, Daniel. *The drawings of Jean Dubuffet.* Trans. by Cecily Mackworth. New York, Braziller, 1980.

2928. Dubuffet, Jean. *Jean Dubuffet, 1943–1963: Paintings, sculptures, assemblages.* With contributions by James T. Demetrion, Susan J. Cooke, Jean Planque and Peter Schjeldahl. Washington, D.C. published with the Hirshhorn Museum and Sculpture Garden [by] Smithsonian Institution Press, 1993.

2929. Fitzsimmons, James. *Jean Dubuffet, brève introduction à son oeuvre.* Bruxelles, Editions de la Connaissance, 1958.

2930. Franzke, Andreas. *Dubuffet.* Trans. by Robert E. Wolf. New York, Abrams, 1981.

2931. ———. *Dubuffet Zeichnungen.* München, Rogner und Bernhard, 1980.

2932. Gagnon, François. *Jean Dubuffet: aux sources de la figuration humaine.* Montréal, Les Presses de l'Université de Montreal, 1972.

2933. Loreau, Max. *Dubuffet et le voyage au centre de la perception.* Paris, La Jeune Parque, 1966.

2934. ———. *Dubuffet. Catalogue des travaux.* V. 1–(33). Paris, Pauvert, 1964– . (CR).

2935. ———. *Jean Dubuffet; délits, déportements, lieux de haut jeu.* Paris, Weber, 1971.

2936. ———. *Jean Dubuffet: stratégie de la création.* Paris, Gallimard, 1973.

2937. Musée des Arts Décoratifs (Paris). *Jean Dubuffet, 1942–1960.* [16 déc. 1960–25 fév. 1961]. Palais du Louvre, Pavillon de Marsan. Catalogue rédigé par François Mathey. Paris, Musée des Arts Décoratifs, 1960.

2938. Picon, Gaétan. *Le travail de Jean Buffet.* Genève, Skira, 1973.

2939. Selz, Peter. *The work of Jean Dubuffet.* New York, Museum of Modern Art, 1962; distributed by Doubleday, New York.

2940. Trucchi, Lorenza. *Jean Dubuffet.* Roma, de Luca, 1965.

2941. Webel, Sophie. *L'Oeuvre gravé et les livres illustrés par Jean Dubuffet: catalogue raisonné.* Préface de Daniel Abadie. Paris, Lebon, 1991. (CR).

Duccio, Agostino di *see* **Agostino di Duccio**

Du Cerceau, Jacques Androuet, c. 1515–1585

2942. Chevalley, Denis A. *Der grosse Tuilerienentwurf in der Überlieferung du Cerceaus.* Bern, Lang, 1973. (Kieler kunsthistorische Studien, 3).

2943. Du Cerceau, Jacques A. *Les plus excellents bastiments de France.* Paris, Du Cerceau, 1576–79. (New ed., revised: Paris, Levy, 1868–70. 2 v.).

2944. Geymüller, Henry de. *Les du Cerceau; leur vie et leur oeuvre.* Paris, Rouam/London, Wood, 1887.

2945. Ward, W. H. *French chateaux and gardens in the XVIth century; a series of reproductions of contemporary drawings hitherto unpublished by Jacques Androuet du Cerceau, selected and described with an account of the artist and his works.* London, Batsford, 1909.

Duccio di Buoninsegna, ca. 1255–1319

2946. Baccheschi, Edi. *L'opera completa di Duccio.* Presentazione di Giulio Cataneo. Milano, Rizzoli, 1972.

2947. Brandi, Cesare. *Duccio.* Firenze, Vallecchi, 1951.

2948. Carli, Enzo. *Duccio di Buoninsegna.* Milano, Electa, 1959.

2949. Jannella, Cecilia. *Duccio di Buoninsegna.* [Trans. Laura Molinaro Bailache]. Florence, Scala, 1991].

2950. Stubblebine, James H. *Duccio di Buoninsegna and his school.* Princeton, N.J., Princeton University Press, 1979.

2951. Weigelt, Curt H. *Duccio di Buoninsegna; Studien zur Geschichte der frühsienesischen Tafelmalerei.* Leipzig, Hiersemann, 1911. (Kunstgeschichtliche Monographien, 15).

2952. White, John. *Duccio: Tuscan art and the medieval workshop.* London, Thames and Hudson, 1979.

Duchamp, Gaston *see* **Villon, Jacques**

Duchamp, Marcel, 1887–1968
Suzanne, 1889–1963
Duchamp-Villon, Raymond, 1876–1918

2953. Adcock, Craig E. *Marcel Duchamp's notes from the 'Large Glass'.* An N-Dimensional analysis. Ann Arbor. UMI Research Press, 1983.

2954. Agee, William C. *Raymond Duchamp-Villon, 1876–1918.* Introd. by George Heard Hamilton. New York, Walker, 1967.

2955. Bonk, Ecke. *Marcel Duchamp, the 'Portable Museum'.* London, Thames and Hudson, 1989.

2956. Cabanne, Pierre. *The brothers Duchamp: Jacques Villon, Raymond Duchamp-Villon, Marcel Duchamp.* Boston, New York Graphic Society, 1976.

2957. ———. *Dialogues with Marcel Duchamp.* Trans. by Ron Padgett. New York, Viking, 1971.

2958. ———. *Ingénieur du temps perdu: entretiens avec Pierre Cabanne.* Paris, Belfond, 1977.

2959. Clair, Jean. *Duchamp et la photographie: essai d'analyse d'un primat technique sur le développement d'une oeuvre.* Paris, Chêne, 1977.

2960. ———. *Marcel Duchamp: abécédaire; approches critiques.* Réalisé sous la direction de Jean Clair avec la collaboration de Ulf Linde. Paris, Musée National d'Art Moderne, Centre National d'Art et de Culture Georges Pompidou, 1977. (Série des catalogues, No. 8, t. 3).

2961. ———. *Marcel Duchamp: catalogue raisonné.* Paris, Centre National d'Art et de Culture Georges Pompidou, Musée d'Art Moderne, 1977. (Série des catalogues, No. 8, t. 2). (CR).

2962. ———. *Marcel Duchamp ou le grand fictif.* Essai de mythanalyse du grand verre. Paris, Editions Galilée, 1975.

2963. Clearwater, Bonnie, ed. *West Coast Duchamp.* Miami Beach, Florida, Grassfield Press; published in association with the Shoshana Wayne Gallery, Santa Monica, Calif., 1991.

2964. Duchamp, Marcel. *The bride stripped bare*

by her bachelors, even; a typographic version by Richard Hamilton of Marcel Duchamp's Green Box. Trans. by George Heard Hamilton. New York, Wittenborn, 1960. (The Documents of Modern Art, 14).

2965. ———. *From the Green Box.* Trans. and with a pref. by George Heard Hamilton. New Haven, Readymade Press, 1957.

2966. ———. *Notes and projects for the Large Glass.* Selected, ordered and with an introduction by Arturo Schwarz. New York, Abrams, 1969.

2967. ———. *Salt seller; the writings of Marcel Duchamp.* Ed. by Michel Sanouillet and Elmer Peterson. New York, Oxford University Press, 1973.

2968. Duchamp-Villon, Raymond. *Raymond Duchamp-Villon: sculpteur (1876–1918).* Paris, Povolozky, 1924.

2969. Duve, Thierry de., ed. *The Definitively unfinished Marcel Duchamp.* Halifax, Nova Scotia College of Art and Design; Cambridge, Mass., MIT Press, 1991.

2970. Galerie Louis Carré, Paris. *Duchamp-Villon: le cheval majeur.* [Exposition] sous la direction de Marcel Duchamp, réalisée avec l'aide de Gilioli. Paris, Galerie Louis Carré, 1966.

2971. ———. *Sculptures de Duchamp-Villon.* 17 juin–30 juillet 1963. Paris, Galerie Louis Carré, 1963.

2972. Golding, John. *Marcel Duchamp: The bride stripped bare by her bachelors, even.* New York, Viking Press, 1973.

2973. Gough-Cooper, Jennifer [and] Caumont, Jacques. *Plan pour écrire une vie de Marcel Duchamp.* Paris, Centre National d'Art et de Culture Georges Pompidou, Musée d'Art Moderne, 1977. (Série des catalogues, No. 8, pt. 1).

2974. Harnoncourt, Anne d' and McShine, Kynaston, eds. *Marcel Duchamp.* Published on occasion of the exhibition organized by the Philadelphia Museum of Art and the Museum of Modern Art. Greenwich, Conn., New York Graphic Society, 1973.

2975. Hulten, Pontus, ed. and intro. *Marcel Duchamp: work and life.* Texts by Jennifer Gough-Cooper and Jacques Caumont. Cambridge, Mass., MIT Press, 1993.

2976. Kuenzli, Rudolf E. and Naumann, Francis M., eds. *Marcel Duchamp, artist of the century.* Cambridge, Mass., M.I.T. Press, 1989.

2977. Lebel, Robert. *Marcel Duchamp.* With chapters by Marcel Duchamp, André Breton and H. P. Roché. Trans. by George Heard Hamilton. New York, Grove, 1959.

2978. Lyotard, Jean F. *Les transformateurs Duchamp.* Paris, Editions Galilée, 1977.

2979. ———. *Duchamp's TRANS/formers.* Venice, Ca Lapis, 1990.

2980. Mashek, Joseph. *Marcel Duchamp in perspective.* Englewood Cliffs, N.J., Prentice-Hall, 1975.

2981. Musée des Beaux-Arts (Rouen). *Les Duchamps: Jacques Villon, Raymond Duchamp-Villon, Marcel Duchamp, Suzanne Duchamp.* 15 avril–1 juin 1967. Rouen, Musée des Beaux-Arts, 1967.

2982. Musée National d'Art Moderne (Paris). *Raymond Duchamp-Villon, 1876–1918, Marcel Duchamp, 1887– .* 7 juin–2 juillet 1967. Paris, Musée National d'Art Moderne, 1967.

2983. Museum Ludwig (Cologne). *Duchamp.* [Katalog einer] Ausstellung im Museum Ludwig, Köln. Köln, Museen der Stadt, 1984.

2984. Paz, Octavio. *Marcel Duchamp, appearance stripped bare.* Trans. by Rachel Phillips and Donald Gardner. New York, Viking Press, 1978.

2985. Schwarz, Arturo. *The complete works of Marcel Duchamp.* New York, Abrams, 1969.

2986. ———. *Marcel Duchamp: 66 creative years.* From the first painting to the last drawing, over 260 items. [Cat. of an exhibition, 12 Dec. 1972–28 Feb. 1973]. Milano, Gallery Schwarz, 1972.

2987. Tomkins, Calvin. *The bride and the bachelors; the heretical courtship in modern art.* New York, Viking, 1965.

2988. ———. *The world of Marcel Duchamp.* New York, Time-Life, 1966.

Dufresne, Charles, 1876–1938

2989. Fosca, François. *Charles Dufresne.* Paris, La Bibliothèque des Arts, 1958.

2990. Hirschl and Adler Galleries (New York). *Charles Dufresne, 1876–1936.* A retrospective exhibition April 27–May 21, 1971. New York, Hirschl and Adler Galleries, 1971.

Dufy, Raoul, 1877–1953

2991. Berr de Turique, Marcelle. *Raoul Dufy.* Paris, Floury, 1930.

2992. Brion, Marcel. *Raoul Dufy; paintings and watercolours selected by René ben Sussan with an introduction by M. Brion.* Trans. by Lucy Norton. London, Phaidon, 1959.

2993. Cassou, Jean. *Raoul Dufy, poète et artisan.* Genève, Skira, 1946.

2994. Cogniat, Raymond. *Dufy, décorateur.* Genève, Cailler, 1957. (Les maîtres de l'art décoratif contemporain, 3).

2995. ———. *Raoul Dufy.* Paris, Flammarion, 1962.

2996. Courthion, Pierre. *Raoul Dufy.* Paris, Editions des Chroniques du Jour, 1929.

2997. ———. *Raoul Dufy.* Genève, Cailler, 1951.

(Peintres et sculpteurs d'hier et d'aujourd'hui, 19. Les Grandes monographies, 1).

2998. Galerie Louis Carré (Paris). *Tapisseries de Raoul Dufy.* Paris, Galerie Louis Carré, 1963.

2999. Gieure, Maurice. *Dufy, dessins.* Paris, Editions de Deux Mondes, 1952. (Dessins des grands peintres, 4).

3000. Guillon-Laffaille, H. *Dufy, catalogue raisonné des aquarelles, gouaches et pastels.* 2 v. Paris, Carré, 1981. (CR).

3001. Haus der Kunst, München. *Raoul Dufy, 1877–1953.* 30. Juni–30 Sept. 1973. Katalog-Redaktion: Maurice Lafaille und Fanny Guillon. München, Haus der Kunst, 1973.

3002. Hayward Gallery (London). *Raoul Dufy: paintings, drawings, illustrated books, mural decorations, Aubusson tapestries, fabric designs and fabrics for Bianbchini-Férier, Paul Poiret dresses, ceramics, posters.* [Catalogue of an exhibition held at the Hayward Gallery, London, 9 November 1983–5 February 1984]. London, Arts Council of Great Britain, 1983.

3003. Hunter, Sam. *Raoul Dufy.* New York, Abrams, 1954.

3004. Kunsthalle Bern. *Raoul Dufy.* 12. Juni–11. Juli 1954. Bern, Kunsthalle, 1954.

3005. Lafaille, Maurice. *Raoul Dufy; catalogue raisonné de l'oeuvre peint.* Avant-propos de Maurice Lafaille. Préf. de Marcelle Berr de Turique. Biographie de Bernard Dorival. 4 v. Genève, Motte, 1972–1977. (CR).

3006. ———. *Raoul Dufy; catalogue raisonné de l'oeuvre peint. Supplement.* Paris, Louis Carré, 1985. (CR).

3007. Lassaigne, Jacques. *Dufy: biographical and critical studies.* Trans. by James Emmons. Genève, Skira, 1954. (The Taste of Our Time, 9).

3008. Musée Jules Chéret (Nice). *Raoul Dufy à Nice: collection du Musée des beaux-arts Jules Chéret.* Nice, Direction des Musées de Nice, 1977.

3009. Musée National d'Art Moderne (Paris). *Raoul Dufy, 1877–1953.* Catalogue par Bernard Dorival. Paris, Editions des Musées Nationaux, 1953.

3010. Museum Folkwang (Essen). *Raoul Dufy: Gemälde, Aquarelle, Gouachen, Zeichnungen.* 18. Feb.–14. April 1968. Hrsg. vom Kunstverein in Hamburg. Hamburg, Kunstverein, 1968.

3011. Perez-Tibi, Dora. *Dufy.* Paris, Flammarionm, 1989.

3012. San Francisco Museum of Art. *Raoul Dufy, 1877–1953.* May 12–July 4, 1954. San Francisco, San Francisco Museum of Art, 1954.

3013. Tate Gallery (London). *Raoul Dufy; an exhibition of paintings and drawings organized by the Arts Council of Great Britain and the Assoc. Française d'Action Artistique.* 9 Jan.–7 Feb., 1954. London, Tate Gallery, 1954.

3014. Werner, Alfred. *Raoul Dufy (1877–1953).* New York, Abrams (in assoc. with Pocket Books), 1953. (The Pocket Library of Great Art, A5). Reprint: 1987.

3015. Zervos, Christian. *Raoul Dufy.* Paris, Editions Cahiers d'Art, 1928.

Dughhet, Gaspard, 1615–1675

3016. Boisclair, Marie Nicole. *Gaspard Dughet, sa vie et son oeuvre (1615–1675).* Préface de Jacques Thuillier. Paris, Arthena, 1986. (CR).

Dunlap, William, 1766–1839

3017. Coad, Oral S. *William Dunlap: a study of his life and works and of his place in contemporary culture.* New York, Dunlap Society, 1917.

3018. Dunlap, William. *The diary of William Dunlap (1766–1839).* 3 v. New York, New York Historical Society, 1930.

3019. ———. *History of the rise and progress of the arts of design in the United States.* 2 v. New York, Scott, 1834. (New ed., illustrated, edited, and with additions by Frank W. Bayley and Charles E. Goodspeed, in 3 v.: Boston, Goodspeed, 1918).

Dunoyer de Segonzac, Andre *see* Segonzac, Andre Dunoyer de

Dupré, Giovanni, 1817–1882

3020. Dupré, Giovanni. *Giovanni Dupré scultore.* Torino, 1919. 2 ed. (I maestri dell'arte; monografie d'artisti italiani moderni, 2).

3021. ———. *Pensieri sull'arte e ricordi autobiografici.* Firenze, Le Monnier, 1880.

3022. ———. *Scritti minori e lettere.* Con un'appendice ai suoi *Ricordi autobiografici* per Luigi Venturi. Firenze, Le Monnier, 1882.

3023. ———. *Thoughts on art and autobiographical memories.* Trans. by E. M. Peruzzi. Edinburgh, Blackwood, 1884.

3024. ———. *Vocazione d'artista, da Pensieri sull'arte e Ricordi autobiografici.* A cura di Enzo Petrini. Firenze, Marzocco, 1958.

3025. Frieze, Henry Simmons. *Giovanni Dupré.* With two dialogues on art from the Italian of Augusto Conti. London, Low, Marston, Searle & Rivington, 1888.

Dupré, Jules, 1811–1889

3026. Aubrun, Marie M. *Jules Dupré, 1811–1889: catalogue raisonné et l'oeuvre peint, dessiné et gravé.* Préf. de M. Jacques Thuillier. Paris, Laget, 1974. Supplement: Nantes, Chiffoleau, 1982. (CR).

3027. Dixon Gallery and Gardens (Memphis, Tenn.). *Jules Dupré, 1811–1889; a loan exhibition. Sept. 9–Oct. 21, 1979. [Text by Michael Milkovich]. Memphis, Tenn., Dixon Gallery, 1979.

3028. Galerie du Fleuve (Paris). *Jules Dupré, 1811–1889.* 21 novembre au 22 décembre 1973. Paris, Galerie du Fleuve, 1973.

Durand, Asher Brown, 1796–1886

3029. Durand, John. *The life and times of A. B. Durand.* New York, Scribner's, 1894. Reprint: New York, Kennedy Graphics and DaCapo Press, 1970.

3030. Lawall, David B. *Asher B. Durand: a documentary catalogue of the narrative and landscape paintings.* New York, Garland, 1978. (Garland Reference Library of the Humanities, 74). (CR).

3031. ———. *Asher Brown Durand, his art and art theory in relation to his times.* New York, Garland, 1977.

3032. Montclair Art Museum (Montclair, New Jersey). *A. B. Durand, 1796–1886.* Oct. 24–Nov. 28, 1971. Essay by David Lawall. Montclair, New Jersey, Montclair Art Museum, 1971.

Dürer, Albrecht, 1471–1528

3033. Albertina (Vienna). *Die Dürerzeichnungen der Albertina, von Walter Koschatzky und Alice Strobl.* Salzburg, Residenz-Verlag, 1971.

3034. ———. *Albrecht Dürer: kritischer Katalog der Zeichnungen,* bearbeitet von F. Anzelewsky und Hans Mielke. Berlin, Staatliche Museen Preussischer Kulturbesitz, Kupferstichkabinett, 1984. (CR).

3035. Anzelewsky, Fedja. *Albrecht Dürer: das malerische Werk.* Berlin, Deutscher Verlag für Kunstwissenschaft, 1971. (Neuausgabe in 2 v., 1991).

3036. ———. *Dürer: Werk und Wirkung.* Stuttgart, Electa/Klett-Cotta, 1980.

3037. Arend, Henrich C. *Das Gedechtniss der Ehren. . . . Albrecht Dürers.* Goslar, König, 1728.

3038. Bohatta, Hanns. *Versuch einer Bibliographie der kunsttheoretischen Werke Albrecht Dürers.* Wien, Gilhofer & Ranschburg, 1928.

3039. Brion, Marcel. *Dürer, his life and work.* Trans. by James Cleugh. New York, Tudor, 1960.

3040. Conway, William Martin. *Literary remains of Albrecht Dürer.* With transcripts from the British Museum manuscripts, and notes upon them by Lina Eckenstein. Cambridge, Cambridge University Press, 1889. (New ed.: *The writings of Albrecht Dürer.* New York, Philosophical Library, 1958).

3041. Dodgson, Campbell. *Albrecht Dürer.* London/Boston, Medici Society, 1926.

3042. Dürer, Albrecht. *Reliquien von Albrecht Dürer, seinen Verehrern geweiht.* Nürnberg, Campe, 1828.

3043. ———. *Schriftlicher Nachlass.* Hrsg. von Hans Rupprich. 3 v. Berlin, Deutscher Verein für Kunstwissenschaft, 1956–1969.

3044. ———. *Writings.* Trans. by W. M. Conway. Ed. by Alfred Werner. New York, Philosophical Library, 1958.

3045. Eye, August von. *Leben und Wirken Albrecht Dürers.* Nördlingen, Beck, 1860.

3046. Flechsig, Eduard. *Albrecht Dürer; sein Leben und seine künstlerische Entwicklung.* 2 v. Berlin, Grote, 1928–1931.

3047. Friedländer, Max J. *Albrecht Dürer.* Leipzig, Insel Verlag, 1921.

3048. Germanisches Nationalmuseum (Nuremberg). *Albrecht Dürer Ausstellung im Germanischen Museum.* Nürnberg, Germanisches Museum, 1928.

3049. ———. *Albrecht Dürer, 1471–1971.* 21. Mai–1. Aug. 1971. München, Prestel-Verlag, 1971.

3050. ———. *Vorbild Dürer: Kupferstiche und Holzschnitte Albrecht Dürers im Spiegel der europäischen Druckgraphik des 16. Jahrhunderts.* Katalog der Ausstellung 8. Juli–10. Sept. 1978. München, Prestel, 1978.

3051. Grote, Ludwig. *Dürer; biographical and critical study.* Trans. by Helga Harrison. Geneva, Skira; distributed by World Pub. Co., Cleveland, 1965. (The Taste of Our Time, 43).

3052. Haendcke, Berthold. *Die Chronologie der Landschaften Albrecht Dürers.* Strassburg, Heitz, 1899. (Studien zur deutschen Kunstgeschichte, 19).

3053. Hamel, Maurice. *Albert Durer.* Paris, Librairie de l'art ancien et moderne, 1904.

3054. Heidrich, Ernst. *Dürer und die Reformation.* Leipzig, Klinkhardt & Biermann, 1909.

3055. ———. *Geschichte des Dürer'schen Marienbildes.* Leipzig, Hiersemann, 1906. (Kunstgeschichtliche Monographien, 3).

3056. Hind, Arthur M. *Albrecht Dürer, his engravings and woodcuts.* New York, Stokes, 1911.

3057. Hofmann, Walter J. *Über Dürers Farbe.* Nürnberg, Carl, 1971. (Erlanger Beiträge zur Sprach- und Kunstwissenschaft, 42).

3058. Hollstein, Friedrich W. H. *German engravings, etchings and woodcuts, ca. 1400–1700: Albrecht and Hans Dürer.* Ed. by K. G. Boon and R. W. Scheller. Amsterdam, Hertzberger, 1962. (German engravings, etchings and woodcuts, 7).

3059. Hutchison, Jane Campbell. *Albrecht Dürer: a biography.* Princeton, N.J., Princeton University Press, 1990.

3060. Hütt, Wolfgang. *Albrecht Dürer, 1471 bis 1528; das gesamte graphische Werk.* 2 v.

München, Rogner & Bernard, 1971.

3061. Jahn, Johannes. *Entwicklungsstufen der Dürerforschung.* Berlin, Akademie-Verlag, 1971. (Sitzungsberichte der Sächs. Akademie der Wissenschaften zu Leipzig. Philol. Hist. Klasse, Bd. 115, Heft 1).

3062. Kauffmann, Hans. *Albrecht Dürers rhythmische Kunst.* Leipzig, Seemann, 1924.

3063. Kehrer, Hugo. *Dürers Selbstbildnisse und die Dürer-Bildnisse.* Berlin, Mann, 1934.

3064. Knappe, Karl Adolf. *Dürer; complete engravings, etchings and woodcuts.* New York, Abrams, 1965. (Trans. of *Albrecht Dürer: Das graphische Werk.* Wien, Schroll, 1964).

3065. Knorr, Georg W. *Historische Künstler-Belustigung oder Gespräche in dem Reiche der Todten, zwischen denen beeden weltbekannten Künstlern Albrecht Dürer und Raphael de Urbino.* Nürnberg, Knorr, 1738.

3066. Koehler, Sylvester R. *A chronological catalogue of the engravings, drypoints and etchings of Albert Dürer.* New York, Grolier Club, 1897. (CR).

3067. Koschatzky, Walter. *Albrecht Dürer: die Landschaftsaquarelle.* Wien/München, Jugend und Volk, 1971.

3068. Kurth, Willi. *The complete woodcuts of Albrecht Dürer.* Trans. by S. M. Welsh. New York, Crown, 1946. (Reprint: Magnolia, Mass., Peter Smith, 1963).

3069. Levey, Michael. *Dürer.* New York, Norton, 1964.

3070. Lippmann, Friedrich. *Drawings by Albrecht Dürer.* 7 v. Berlin, Grote, 1883–1929. (CR).

3071. Lorenz, Ludwig. *Die Marien-Darstellungen Albrecht Dürers.* Strassburg, Heitz, 1904. (Studien zur deutschen Kunstgeschichte, 55).

3072. Lüdecke, Heinz and Heiland, Susanne. *Dürer und die Nachwelt.* Urkunden, Briefe, Dichtungen und wissenschaftliche Betrachtungen aus vier Jahrhunderten, gesammelt und erläutert von Heinz Lüdecke und Susanne Heiland. Berlin, Rütten & Leoning, 1955.

3073. Meder, Joseph. *Dürer Katalog: ein Handbuch über Albrecht Dürers Stiche, Radierungen, Holzschnitte, deren Zustände, Ausgaben und Wasserzeichen.* Wien, Gilhofer & Ranschburg, 1932.

3074. Mende, Matthias. *Dürer Bibliographie.* Wiesbaden, Harrassowitz, 1971.

3075. Müller, Franz L. *Die Ästhetik Albrecht Dürers.* Strassburg, Heitz, 1910. (Studien zur deutschen Kunstgeschichte, 123).

3076. Museum of Fine Arts (Boston). *Albrecht Dürer: master printmaker.* Nov. 17, 1970–Jan. 16, 1971. Boston, Museum of Fine Arts, 1971.

3077. Musper, Theodor. *Albrecht Dürer.* Trans. by Robert E. Wolf. New York, Abrams, 1966.

3078. ———. *Albrecht Dürer.* Köln, DuMont Schauberg, 1971.

3079. ———. *Albrecht Dürer; der gegenwärtige Stand der Forschung.* Stuttgart, Kohlhammer, 1952.

3080. ———. *Dürers Kaiserbildnisse.* Köln, DuMont Schauberg, 1969.

3081. National Gallery of Art (Washington, D.C.). *Dürer in America, his graphic work.* Charles W. Talbot, ed. Notes by Gaillard F. Ravenel and Jay A. Levenson. April 25–June 6, 1971. Washington, D.C., National Gallery of Art, 1971.

3082. Panofsky, Erwin. *Albrecht Dürer.* 2 v. Princeton, N.J., Princeton University, 1943. (This is the original edition with the catalogue. A 2d rev. ed. in 2 vols. was published in 1945 and reprinted as a 3d ed. The 4th ed. of 1955 is in 1 vol. and lacks the critical catalogue.)

3083. ———. *Dürers Kunsttheorie.* Berlin, Reimer, 1915.

3084. ———. *Dürers Stellung zur Antike.* Wien, Hölzel, 1922.

3085. Retberg, Ralf Leopold von. *Dürers Kupferstiche und Holzschnitte. Ein kritisches Verzeichnis.* München, Ackermann, 1871.

3086. Rupprich, Hans, ed. *Albrecht Dürer, schriftlicher Nachlass.* Berlin, Deutscher Verein für Kunstwissenschaft, 1956.

3087. Scherer, Valentin. *Dürer; des Meisters Gemälde, Kupferstiche und Holzschnitte.* Stuttgart, Deutsche Verlaganstalt, 1928. 4 ed. (Klassiker der Kunst in Gesamtausgaben, 4).

3088. ———. *Die Ornamentik bei Albercht Dürer.* Strassburg, Heitz, 1902. (Studien zur deutschen Kunstgeschichte, 38).

3089. Schöber, David G. *Albrecht Dürers . . . Leben, Schriften und Kunstwerke.* Leipzig/Schleiz, Mauke, 1769.

3090. Singer, Hans W. *Versuch einer Dürer Bibliographie.* Strassburg, Heitz, 1928. 2 ed.

3091. Stechow, Wolfgang. *Dürer and America.* Washington, D.C., National Gallery of Art, 1971.

3092. Strauss, Walter L., ed. *Albrecht Dürer: woodcuts and wood blocks.* New York, Abaris, 1975.

3093. ———. *All of Dürer's engravings, etchings, and drypoints.* New York, Abaris, 1981. 3 ed.

3094. ———. *The complete drawings of Albrecht Dürer.* 6 v. New York, Abaris, 1974. Supplements: New York, Abaris, 1977– . (CR).

3095. ———. *The intaglio prints of Albrecht Dürer: engravings, etchings & drypoints.* Expanded ed. New York, Kennedy Galleries, 1977.

3096. Strieder, Peter. *Albrecht Dürer: paintings, prints, drawings.* Trans. by Nancy M. Gordon and Walter L. Strauss. New York, Abaris, 1982.

3097. ———. *The hidden Dürer*. Trans. by Vivienne Menkes. Oxford, Phaidon, 1978.

3098. Suida, Wilhelm. *Die Genredarstellung Albrecht Dürers*. Strassburg, Heitz, 1900. (Studien zur deutschen Kunstgeschichte, 27).

3099. Thausing, Moritz. *Dürer; Geschichte seines Lebens und seiner Kunst*. 2 v. Leipzig, Seemann, 1884. 2 ed.

3100. Tietze, Hans and Tietze-Conrat, Erika. *Kritische Verzeichnis der Werke Albrecht Dürers*. 2 v. (in 3). Augsburg, Filser, 1928–1938. (CR).

3101. Waetzoldt, Wilhelm. *Dürer and his times*. Trans. by R. H. Boothroyd. London, Phaidon, 1950.

3102. Waldmann, Emil. *Albrecht Dürer*. Leipzig, Insel-Verlag, 1923.

3103. ———. *Albrecht Dürers Handzeichnungen*. Leipzig, Insel-Verlag, 1920.

3104. ———. *Albrecht Dürers Stiche und Holzschnitte*. Leipzig, Insel, 1920.

3105. Weise, Adam. *Albrecht Dürer und sein Zeitalter; ein Versuch*. Leipzig, Gleditsch, 1819.

3106. Weise, Georg. *Dürer und die Ideale der Humanisten*. Tübingen, Kunsthist. Institut der Universität, 1953. (Tübinger Forschungen zur Kunstgeschichte, 6).

3107. White, Christopher. *Dürer: the artist and his drawings*. London, Phaidon, 1971.

3108. Winkler, Friedrich. *Albrecht Dürer, Leben und Werk*. Berlin, Mann, 1957.

3109. ———. *Die Zeichnungen Albrecht Dürers*. 4 v. Berlin, Deutscher Verein für Kunstwissenschaft, 1936–1939.

3110. Winzinger, Franz. *Albrecht Dürer in Selbstzeugnissen und Bilddokumenten*. Reinbeck bei Hamburg, Rowohlt, 1971. (Rowohlts Monografien, 177).

3111. Wölfflin, Heinrich. *The art of Albrecht Dürer*. Trans. by Alastair and Heide Grieve. London, Phaidon, 1971.

3112. ———. *Die Kunst Albrecht Dürers*. München, Bruckmann, 1905.

3113. Zahn, Albert von. *Dürers Kunstlehre und sein Verhältnis zur Renaissance*. Leipzig, Weigel, 1866.

Duris, fl. 500 B.C.

3114. Pottier, Edmond. *Douris and the painters of Greek vases*. Trans. by Bettina Kahlweiler, with a preface by Jane Ellen Harrison. London, Murray, 1909.

Du Ry, Charles Louis, 1692–1757
Paul, 1640–1714
Simon Louis, 1726–1799

3115. Boehlke, Hans-Kurt. *Simon Louis Du Ry, ein Wegbereiter klassizistischer Architektur in Deutschland*. Kassel, Stauda, 1980.

3116. Gerland, Otto. *Paul, Charles, und Simon Louis du Ry; eine Künstlerfamilie der Barockzeit*. Stuttgart, Neff, 1895.

Dyce, William, 1806–1864

3117. Art Gallery and Industrial Museum (Aberdeen, Scotland). *Centenary exhibition of the work of William Dyce, R. A. (1806–1864), Aug. 7–Sept. 13, 1964*. Aberdeen, Art Gallery, 1964.

3118. Pointon, Marcia R. *William Dyce, 1806–1864: a critical biography*. Foreword by Quentin Bell. Oxford, Clarendon Press, 1979.

Dyck, Anthony van, 1599–1641

3119. Carpenter, William H. *Pictorial notices consisting of a memoir of Sir Anthonis van Dyck, with a descriptive catalogue of the etchings*. London, J. Carpenter, 1844.

3120. Cust, Lionel H. *Anthony van Dyck, an historical study of his life and works*. London, Bell, 1900.

3121. ———. *Anthony van Dyck*. A further study by L. Cust, with twenty-five illustrations in colour executed under the supervision of the Medici Society. New York/London, Hodder and Stoughton, 1911.

3122. Delacre, Maurice. *Le dessin dans l'oeuvre de van Dyck*. Brussels, Hayez, 1934.

3123. Didière, Pierre. *Antoine van Dyck*. Suivi d'un portrait d'Antoine Van Dyck par Eugène Fromentin. Bruxelles, Meddens, 1969.

3124. Dyck, Anthony van. *Antwerp sketchbook*. Ed. by Michael Jaffé. 2 v. London, Macdonald, 1966.

3125. ———. *Italienisches Skizzenbuch*. Hrsg. von Gert Adriani. Wien, Schroll, 1940.

3126. Fierens-Gevaert, Hippolyte. *Van Dyck; biographie critique*. Paris, Laurens, 1903.

3127. Glück, Gustav. *Van Dyck; des Meisters Gemälde in 571 Abbildungen*. Stuttgart, Deutsche Verlagsanstalt, 1931; distributed by F. Kleinberger, New York. 2 ed. of the work edited by E. Schaeffer. (Klassiker der Kunst in Gesamtausgaben, 13). (See also 3148).

3128. Guiffrey, Jules M. J. *Antoine van Dyck, sa vie et son oeuvre*. Paris, Quantin, 1882.

3129. Head, Percy R. *Van Dyck*. New York, Scribner and Welford, 1879.

3130. Hind, Arthur M. *Van Dyck and portrait engraving and etching in the seventeenth century*. New York, Stokes, 1911.

3131. ———. *Van Dyck, his original etchings and his iconography*. New York, Houghton Mifflin, 1915.

3132. Knackfuss, Hermann. *A. van Dyck*. Bielefeld/Leipzig, Velhagen & Klasing, 1896. (Künstler-Monographien, 13).

3133. ———. *Van Dyck*. Trans. by Campbell Dodgson. Bielefeld/Leipzig, Velhagen &

Klasing/New York, Lemcke & Buechner, 1899. (Monographs on Artists, 4).

3134. Knoedler & Company, New York. *The portrait etchings of Anthony van Dyck*. Catalogue of an exhibition. New York, Knoedler, 1934.

3135. Koninklijk Muzeum voor Schoone Kunsten (Antwerp). *Album der Van Dycktentoonstelling, uitgegeven onder de Bescherming der Commissie van de tentoonstelling*. Bruxelles, Editions Lyon-Claesen, 1899.

3136. ———. *Van Dyck tentoonstelling juli–august 1949*. Antwerpen, Nederlandsche Boekhandel, 1949.

3137. ———. *Van Dijk tentoonstelling ter gelegenheid der 300e verjaring der geboorte van den meester, 12 aug.–15 oct., 1899*. Antwerpen, 1899.

3138. Larsen, Erik. *L'opera completa di Van Dyck, 1626–1641*. Milano, Rizzoli, 1980. (Classici dell'arte, 103).

3139. ———. *The paintings of Anthony van Dyck*. 2 v. Freren, Luca Verlag, 1988.

3140. Maugouy-Hendrickx, Marie. *L'iconographie d'Antoine van Dyck*. Catalogue raisonné. 2 v. Bruxelles, Académie Royale de Belgique, 1956. (CR).

3141. Mayer, August L. *Anthonis van Dyck*. München, Recht, 1923.

3142. Michiels, Alfred. *Van Dyck et ses élèves*. Paris, Renouard, 1882. 2 ed.

3143. National Gallery of Canada (Ottawa). *The young van Dyck/le jeune van Dyck*. Sept. 19–Nov. 9, 1980. [Text by Alan McNairn]. Ottawa, National Museums of Canada, 1980.

3144. Newbolt, Francis G. *Etchings of Van Dyck*. London, Newnes/New York, Scribner, 1906.

3145. Palazzo dell'Accademia (Genoa). *Cento opere di Van Dyck*. Catalogo della mostra, guigno–agosto 1955. Genova, 1955.

3146. Royal Academy of Arts (London). *Exhibition of works by Van Dyck, 1599–1641*. London, Clowes, 1900.

3147. Rubenshuis (Antwerp). *Antoon Van Dyck: tekeningen en olieverfschetsen*. 1 juli–31 aug. 1960. [Text by Roger-A. d'Hulst and Horst Vey]. Antwerpen, Rubenshuis, 1960.

3148. Schaeffer, Emil. *Van Dyck; des Meisters Gemälde in 537 Abbildungen*. Stuttgart/Leipzig, Deutsche Verlagsanstalt, 1909. (Klassiker der Kunst in Gesamtausgaben, 13). (See also 3127).

3149. Sweetser, Moses F. *Van Dyck*. Boston, Houghton, Osgood, 1878. (Artist-biographies, 10).

3150. Szwykowski, Ignaz von. *Anton van Dyck's Bildnisse bekannter Personen. . . .* Leipzig, Weigel, 1859.

3151. Vey, Horst. *Die Zeichnung Anton van Dycks*. 2 v. Brüssel, Arcade, 1962. (Natl. Centrum voor de Plastiche Kunsten van de XVIde en XVIIde eeuw. Monographien, 1).

3152. Wheelock, Arthur K. Anthony van Dyck. A.K. Wheelock, Susan J. Barnes, Julius Held [principal authors]. . . . et al. *Anthony van Dyck*. [Published in connection with an exhibition held at the National Gallery of Art, Washington, D.C.]. New York, Abrams, 1990.

3153. Wibiral, Franz. *L'Iconographie d'Antoine van Dyck d'après les recherches de H. Weber*. Leipzig, Danz, 1877.

3154. Wijngaert, Frank van den. *Antoon van Dyck*. Antwerpen, Nederlandsche Boekhandel, 1943.

E

Eakins, Thomas, 1844–1916

3155. Carnegie Institute (Pittsburgh). *Thomas Eakins centennial exhibition, 1844–1944.* Pittsburgh, Carnegie Institute, Dept. of Fine Arts, 1945.

3156. Coe Kerr Gallery (New York). *A family album, photographs by Thomas Eakins, 1880–1890.* New York, Coe Kerr Gallery, 1976.

3157. Corcoran Gallery of Art (Washington, D.C.). *The sculpture of Thomas Eakins.* Washington, D.C., Corcoran Gallery of Art, 1960.

3158. Danly, Susan and Leibold, Cheryl. *Eakins and the photograph.* By S. Danly and Cheryl Leibold with Elizabeth Johns, Anne McCauley, and Mary Panzer. [Catalogue of an exhibition]. Washington, D.C., Smithsonian Institution, 1994.

3159. Foster, Kathleen A. *Writing about Eakins: the manuscripts in Charles Bregler's Thomas Eakins collection.* Kathleen A. Foster with Cheryl Leibold. Philadelphia, published for the Pennsylvania Academy of Fine Arts by the University of Pennsylvania Press, 1989.

3160. Fried, Michael. *Realism, writing, disfiguration: on Thomas Eakins and Stephen Crane.* Chicago, University of Chicago Press, 1987.

3161. Goodrich, Lloyd. *Thomas Eakins, his life and work.* New York, Macmillan, 1933.

3162. ———. *Thomas Eakins.* 2 v. Cambridge, Harvard University Press, 1982 (revision of earlier work). (CR). New York, Grossman, 1974.

3163. Hendricks, Gordon. The life and work of Thomas Eakins. New York, Grossman, 1974.

3164. ———. *The photographs of Thomas Eakins.* New York, Grossman, 1972.

3165. Homer, William Innes. *Thomas Eakins: his life and art.* New York, Abbeville Press, 1992.

3166. Hoopes, Donelson F. *Eakins watercolours.*

New York, Watson-Guptill, 1971.

3167. Johns, Elizabeth. *Thomas Eakins: the heroism of modern life.* Princeton, Princeton University Press, 1983.

3168. Lubin, David M. *Act of portrayal: Eakins, Sargent, James.* New Haven, Yale University Press, 1985

3169. McKinney, Roland J. *Thomas Eakins.* New York, Crown, 1942.

3170. Metropolitan Museum of Art (New York). *Loan exhibition of the works of Thomas Eakins.* [Nov. 5, 1917–Dec. 3, 1917]. New York, Metropolitan Museum of Art, 1917.

3171. National Gallery of Art (Washington, D.C.). *Thomas Eakins, a retrospective exhibition.* [Oct. 8, 1961–Nov. 12, 1961]. Washington, D.C., National Gallery of Art, 1961.

3172. Pennsylvania Academy of the Fine Arts (Philadelphia). *Memorial exhibition of the works of the late Thomas Eakins.* [Dec. 23, 1917–Jan. 13, 1918]. Philadelphia, Penn., Academy of Fine Arts, 1918.

3173. ———. *Thomas Eakins, his photographic works.* Philadelphia, Penn., Academy of Fine Arts, 1969.

3174. Porter, Fairfield. *Thomas Eakins.* New York, Braziller, 1959.

3175. Rosenzweig, Phyllis D. *The Thomas Eakins Collection of the Hirshhorn Museum and Sculpture Garden.* Washington, D.C., Smithsonian Institution, 1977.

3176. Schendler, Sylvan. *Eakins.* Boston, Little, Brown, 1967.

3177. Sewell, Darrel. *Thomas Eakins, artist of Philadelphia.* [Catalog of an exhibition, Philadelphia Museum of Art, May 19, 1982–Aug. 1, 1982]. Philadelphia, Penn., Philadelphia Museum of Art, 1982.

3178. Siegl, Theodor. *The Thomas Eakins Collection.* [Philadelphia Museum of Art]. Philadelphia, Philadelphia Museum of Art, 1978. (Handbooks in American Art, No. 1).

3179. Soyer, Raphael. *Hommage to Thomas Eakins, etc.* South Brunswick, N.J., Thomas Yoseloff, 1966.

3180. Whitney Museum of American Art (New York). *Thomas Eakins, a retrospective exhibition.* By Lloyd Goodrich. [Sept. 22, 1970–Nov. 21, 1970]. New York, Whitney Museum, 1970.

3181. Wilmerding, John,. ed. *Thomas Eakins (1844–1916) and the art of American life.* London, National Portrait Gallery, 1993.

Earl, Ralph, 1751–1801

3182. Gallery of Fine Arts, Yale University (New Haven). *Connecticut portraits by Ralph Earl, 1751–1801.* [Published in conjunction with Connecticut Tercentenary, 1635–1935]. New Haven, Gallery of Fine Arts, 1935.

3183. Goodrich, Laurence B. *Ralph Earl, recorder for an era.* Albany, State Univ. of New York, 1967.

3184. Kornhauser, Elizabeth Mankin. *Ralph Earl: the age of the young republic.* E. M. Kornhauser with Richard L. Bushman, Stephen H. Kornhauser, Aileen Ribeiro. New Haven, Yale University Press, 1991.

3185. Sawitzky, William. *Ralph Earl, 1751–1801.* [Catalog of an exhibition, Oct. 16, 1945–Nov. 21, 1945]. New York, Whitney Museum of American Art, 1946.

3186. William Benton Museum of Art (Storrs, Conn.). *The American Earls: Ralph Earl, James Earl, R. E. W. Earl.* [Pub. in conjunction with an exhibition, Oct. 14–Nov. 12, 1972]. Storrs, University of Connecticut, 1972.

Eastlake, Charles Lock, 1793–1865

3187. Eastlake, Sir Charles Lock. *Contributions to the literature of the fine arts.* London, John Murray, 1848.

3188. ———. *Materials for a history of oil painting.* 2 v. London, Longman Brown, 1847–1869. (Reprint: New York, Dover, 1960).

3189. Robertson, David. *Sir Charles Eastlake and the Victorian art world.* Princeton, N.J., Princeton University Press, 1978.

Eckersberg, Christoffer Wilhelm, 1783–1853

3190. Christensen, Laura J. *Graenselandets Maler, Christoffer Wilhelm Eckersberg.* Sonderborg, Clausens, 1962.

3191. Hannover, Emil. *Maleren C. W. Eckersberg, en studie i dansk kunsthistorie.* København, Thiele, 1898.

3192. Johansen, Peter. *Den danske Malerkunsts Fader, Christoffer Wilhelm Eckersberg, 1783–1853.* København, Slesvigsk, 1925.

3193. Weilback, Philip. *Eckersbergs leved og värker.* København, Lind, 1872.

3194. Zahle, Eric. *C. W. Eckersberg.* Odense, Flensteds, 1945.

Eckmann, Otto, 1865–1902

3195. Eckmann, Otto. *Neue Formen, dekorative Entwürfe für die Praxis.* Berlin, Max Spielmeyer, 1897.

3196. Kaiser-Wilhelm-Museum (Krefeld, Germany). *Otto Eckmann (1865–1902), ein Hauptmeister des Jugendstils.* (Nov. 6, 1977–Jan. 8, 1978). Krefeld, Kaiser Wilhelm Museum, 1978.

Edelfelt, Albert Gustaf Aristides, 1854–1905

3197. Hintze, Bertel. *Albert Edelfelt.* 3 v. Helsingfors, Söderström, 1942–44.

Edelinck, Gerard, 1640–1707

3198. Delaborde, Henri. *Gerard Edelinck.* Paris, Librairie de l'art, 1886. (Les artistes célèbres).

Edgerton, Harold E., 1903–

3199. Edgerton, Harold E. and Killian, James R., Jr. *Flash! Seeing the unseen by ultra high-speed photography.* Boston, Branford, 1954. 2 ed.

3200. ———. *Moments of vision; the stroboscopic revolution in photography.* Cambridge, Mass., MIT Press, 1979.

3201. ———. *Stopping time: the photographs of Harold Edgerton.* Foreword by H. E. Edgerton; Text by Estelle Jussim; edited by Gus Kayafas. New York, H.N. Abrams, 1987

Egell, Paul, 1691–1752

3202. Lankheit, Klaus. *Der kurpfälzische Hofbildhauer Paul Egell, 1691–1752.* 2 v. München, Hirmer, 1988.

Egger-Lienz, Albin, 1868–1926

3203. Hammer, Heinrich. *Albin Egger-Lienz, ein Buch für das deutsche Volk.* Innsbruck, Deutscher Alpenverlag, 1938.

3204. ——— and Kollreider, Franz. *Albin Egger-Lienz, ein Bildwerk.* Innsbruck, Tyrolia, 1963.

3205. Soyka, Josef. *A. Egger-Lienz, Leben und Werke.* Wien, Carl Konegen, 1925.

3206. Tiroler Landesmuseum Ferdinandeum (Innsbruck). *Albin Egger-Lienz, 1868–1926.* [May 25, 1976–July 15, 1976]. Innsbruck, Tiroler Landesmuseum Ferdinandeum, 1976.

3207. Weigelt, Curt H. *Albin Egger-Lienz, eine Studie.* Berlin, Weise, 1914.

Eichenberg, Fritz, 1902–

3208. Eichenberg, Fritz. *The art of the print; mas-*

terpieces, history, techniques. New York, Abrams, 1976.

3209. ———. *Fritz Eichenberg: a retrospective of prints, 1922 to 1986.* [Catalog of an exhibition] January 6 through 31, 1987. New York, Associated American Artists, 1987.

3210. ———. *Fritz Eichenberg: Werkkatalog der illustrierten Bücher, 1922–1987.* Hrsg. von Curt Visel; Bibliographie von David Maslyn und Hildegard Nägele. Memmingen, Edition Curt Visel, 1988. (CR).

3211. ———. *Vier Meister des Holzschnitts: Fritz Eichenberg, Johannes Lebek, Hans Alexander Müller, Hellmuth Weissenborn.* Memmingen, Edition Curt Visel, 1988.

3212. ———. *The wood and the graver; the work of Fritz Eichenberg.* New York, Clarkson Potter, 1976.

3213. New York Public Library (New York). *Fritz Eichenberg, illustrator and printmaker.* [Exhibition, Feb.–Mar. 1949]. New York, AIGA, 1949.

Eiffel, Alexandre Gustave, 1832–1923

3214. Besset, Maurice. *Gustave Eiffel, 1832–1923.* Milano, Electa Editrice, 1957. (Astra-Arengarum collana di monografie d'arte, Serie architetti).

3215. Eiffel, Gustave. *La tour de trois cents mètres.* 2 v. Paris, Société des Imprimeries Lemercier, 1900.

3216. Keim, Jean A. *La tour Eiffel.* [Text in French and English]. Paris, Editions Tel, 1950.

3217. Marrey, Bernard. *Gustave Eiffel, une enterprise exemplaire.* Ed. nouv., Paris, Institute, 1988.

3218. ———. *La vie et l'oeuvre extraordinaire de Monsieur Gustave Eiffel . . .* Paris, Graphite, 1984

3219. Prévost, Jean. *Eiffel.* Paris, Rieder, 1929. (Maîtres de l'art moderne).

Eisenstaedt, Alfred, 1898–

3220. Eisenstaedt, Alfred. *Eisenstaedt on Eisenstaedt: a self-portrait.* Photos and text by A. Eisenstaedt; Introduction by Peter Adam. New York, Abbeville Press, 1985.

3221. ———. *Eisenstaedt: remembrances.* Edited by Doris C. O'Neil; introduction by Bryan Holmer. Boston, Little Brown, 1990.

3222. ———. *The eye of Eisenstaedt,* as told to Arthur Goldsmith. New York, Viking, 1969.

3223. ———. *People.* New York, Viking, 1973.

3224. ———. *Witness to our time.* Foreword by Henry R. Luce. Harmondsworth, England, Penguin, 1980. 2 ed.

Eishi, Hosoda, 1756–1829

3225. Brandt, Klaus J. *Hosoda Eishi, 1756–1829; der japanische Maler und Holzschnittmeister und seine Schüler.* Stuttgart, Brandt, 1977.

3226. Hosoda, Eishi. *The thirty-six immortal women poets:* a poetry album with illustrations by Chobunsai Eishi. Introduction, commentaries, and translations by Andrew J. Pekarik. New York, G. Braziller in association with New York Public Library, 1991.

Elsheimer, Adam, 1578–1610

3227. Andrews, Keith. *Adam Elsheimer; paintings, drawings, prints.* New York, Rizzoli, 1977.

3228. Bode, Wilhelm von. *Adam Elsheimer, der römische Maler deutscher Nation.* München, Schmidt, 1920.

3229. Drost, Willi. *Adam Elsheimer als Zeichner.* Stuttgart, Kohlhammer, 1957.

3230. ———. *Adam Elsheimer und sein Kreis.* Potsdam, Athenaion, 1933. (Die Grossen Deutschen Maler).

3231. Lenz, Christian. *Adam Elsheimer: die Gemälde im Städel.* Hrsg. Klaus Gallwitz. Frankfurt am Main, Städelsches Kunstinstitut und Städtische Galerie, 1989.

3232. Möhle, Hans. *Die Zeichnungen Adam Elsheimers.* Berlin, Deutscher Verlag für Kunstwissenschaft, 1966.

3233. Sello, Gottfried. *Adam Elsheimer, 1578–1610.* München, C.H. Beck, 1988.

3234. Städelsches Kunstinstitut (Frankfurt a.M.). *Adam Elsheimer; Werk, künstlerische Herkunft und Nachfolge.* [Katalog der Ausstellung, Dec. 2, 1966–Jan. 31, 1967.] Frankfurt, Städelsches Kunstinstitut, 1967.

3235. Weizsäcker, Heinrich. *Adam Elsheimer, der Maler von Frankfurt.* 2 v. [V. 2: *Des Künstlers Leben und Werke,* ed. H. Möhle]. Berlin, Deutscher Verein f. Kunstwissenschaft, 1936–1952.

3236. ———. *Die Zeichnungen Adam Elsheimers.* Frankfurt a.M., Baer, 1923.

Emerson, Peter Henry, 1856–1936

3237. Emerson, Peter H. *Naturalistic photography for students of the art.* New York, Scovil & Adams, 1899. 3 ed. (Reprint: New York, Arno, 1973).

3238. Newhall, Nancy W. *P. H. Emerson: the fight for photography as a fine art.* Millerton, N.Y., Aperture, 1975. (Aperture, 19: 2–3).

3239. Turner, Peter and Wood, Richard. *P. H. Emerson, photographer of Norfolk.* London, Fraser, 1974.

Ende, Edgar, 1901–1965

3240. Ende, Edgar. *Edgar Ende, 1901–1965: Gemälde, Gouachen und Zeichnungen: Katalog für die Ausstellungen in der Städtischen Galerie im Lenbachhaus München, in der Hamburger Kunsthalle, in der Städtischen Kunsthalle Mannheim und im Von der Heydt-Museum der Stadt Wuppertal. Hrs. von Jörg Krichbaum; mit Beiträgen von

Harald Behm [et al.]. Stuttgart, Edition Weitbrecht, 1987.

3241. Ende, Michael. *Die Archäologie der Dunkelheit:* Gespräche über Kunst und das Werk des Malers Edgar Ende. M. Ende [und] Jörg Krichbaum. Stuttgart, Edition Weitbrecht, 1985.

Engel, Johann Carl Ludwig, 1778–1840

3242. Hein, Birgit. *Carl Ludwig Engel, Baukunst in Helsinki.* Köln, Universität Köln, 1966.

3243. Meissner, Carl. *Carl Ludwig Engel, deutscher Baumeister in Finnland.* Berlin, Deutscher Verein für Kunstwissenschaft, 1937. (Forschungen zur deutschen Kunstgeschichte, v. 20).

Ensor, James, 1860–1949

3244. Arts Council of Great Britain. *The works of James Ensor.* [Catalogue of an exhibition]. London, Arts Council of Great Britain, 1946.

3245. Colin, Paul. *James Ensor.* Berlin, Klinkhardt & Biermann, 1931. (Junge Kunst, 59).

3246. Cuypers, Firmin. *Aspects & propos de James Ensor.* Bruges, A. G. Stainforth, 1946.

3247. Damase, Jacques. *L'oeuvre gravé de James Ensor.* Genève, Editions Motte, 1967.

3248. [Electa]. *Ensor; dipinti, disegni, incisioni.* Milano, Electa Editrice, 1981.

3249. Elsevier (publishers). *James Ensor; portraitiste, peintre de squelettes et de sujets grotesques, peintre de masques, peintre "réaliste" et "fantaisiste."* 4 v. Bruxelles, Elsevier, 1959. (CR).

3250. Ensor, James. *Ecrits.* [Ed. by H. Vandeputte]. Bruxelles, Lumière, 1944.

3251. ———. *Ensor.* [Catalogue of an exhibition at the Museé du dessin et de l'estampe originale en l'Arsenal de Gravelines, du 8 juin au 7 septembre 1986 et Musée d'art moderne de Troyes, du 1er octobre au 15 décembre 1986. Réalisation et conception du catalogue, Dominique Tonneau-Ryckelnyck]. Gravelines, Musée de Gravelines, 1986.

3252. Fierens, Paul. *James Ensor.* Paris, Editions Hypérion, 1946.

3253. Haesaerts, Paul. *James Ensor.* New York, Abrams, 1959.

3254. Janssens, Jacques. *Ensor.* New York, Crown, 1978.

3255. Legrand, Francine-Claire. *Ensor cet inconnu.* Bruxelles, Collection Renaissance Art, 1971.

3256. LeRoy, Grégoire. *James Ensor.* Bruxelles, van Oest, 1922. (Librairie Nationale d'Art et d'Histoire).

3257. Marlborough Fine Art, Ltd. (London). *James Ensor, 1860–1949; a retrospective centenary exhibition.* London, Marlborough Fine Art, Ltd., 1960.

3258. Musée du Petit Palais (Paris). *James Ensor, 27 avril–22 juillet 1990.* Paris, Paris-Musées, 1990.

3259. Museum voor Schone Kunsten (Ghent). *Ik James Ensor: tekeningen en prenten.* [Tentoonstelling] Museum voor Schone Kunsten, Gent, 8 mei–28 juni 1987; Rijksprentenkabinet, Rijksmuseum, Amsterdam, 11 juli–27 september 1987. Voor de texten: Robert Hoozee, Sabine Bown-Taevernier, J. F. Heijbroek. Brussel, Ludion, in samenwerking met het Museum vor Schone Kunsten, Gent en het Rijksprenten-Kabinet, Rijksmuseum van Amsterdam, 1987.

3260. Ollinger-Zinque, Gisèle. *Ensor by himself.* Bruxelles, Laconti, 1976.

3261. Ridder, André de. *James Ensor.* Paris, Rieder, 1930. (Maîtres de l'ar t moderne).

3262. Rousseau, Blanche, et al. *James Ensor, peintre & graveur.* Paris, Librairie de la Société Anonyme "La Plume," 1899.

3263. Taevernier, Aug. *James Ensor; illustrated catalogue of his engravings, their critical description, and inventory of the plates.* Ghent, Ledeberg, 1973.

3264. ———. *Le drame Ensorien, les auréoles du Christ ou les sensibilités de la lumière.* Ghent, Ledeberg, 1976.

3265. Tannenbaum, Libby. *James Ensor.* New York, Museum of Modern Art, 1951; distributed by Simon & Schuster, New York.

3266. Tricot, Xavier. *Ensor: catalogue raisonné of the paintings.* 2v. Antwerp, Pandora, 1992. (CR).

3267. Verhaeren, Emile. *James Ensor.* Bruxelles, van Oest, 1908.

Epstein, Jacob, 1880–1959

3268. Arts Council of Great Britain. *Epstein* [memorial exhibition]. London, Arts Council of Great Britain, 1961.

3269. Black, Robert. *The art of Jacob Epstein.* Cleveland, World, 1942.

3270. Buckle, Richard. *Jacob Epstein, sculptor.* Cleveland, World, 1963.

3271. Dieran, Bernard van. *Epstein.* London, Lane, 1920.

3272. Epstein, Jacob. *Jaob Epstein: sculpture and drawings.* [Text by Evelyn Silber . . . et al.]. Leeds, W.S. Maney and Son, in association with the Henry Moore Centre for the Study of Sculpture, 1989.

3273. ———. *An autobiography.* [Revised ed. of earlier work]. New York, Dutton, 1955.

3274. ———. *Let there be sculpture, an autobiography.* London, Joseph, 1940.

3275. ———. *The sculptor speaks, a series of conversations on art.* [Edited by Arnold L. Haskell]. London, Heinemann, 1931.

3276. Epstein, Kathleen. *Epstein drawings.* With

notes by Lady Epstein. London, Faber, 1962.

3277. Powell, L. B. *Jacob Epstein.* London, Chapman & Hall, 1932.

3278. Schinman, Edward P. and Schinman, Barbara Ann. *Jacob Epstein, a catalogue of the collection of Edward P. Schinman.* Rutherford, N.J., Fairleigh Dickinson University Press, 1970.

3279. Silber, Evelyn. *The sculpture of Epstein; with a complete catalogue.* Lewisburg, Pa., Bucknell University Press, 1986. (CR).

3280. Wellington, Hubert. *Jacob Epstein.* London, Benn, 1925. (Contemporary British Artists).

Erfurth, Hugo, 1874–1948

3281. Lohse, Bernd, ed. *Hugo Erfurth, 1874–1948; der Fotograf der goldenen zwanziger Jahre.* Seebruck a. Chiemsee, Heering, 1977.

Erni, Hans, 1909–

3282. Burckhardt, Carl J. *Hans Erni.* Zürich, Scheidegger, 1964.

3283. Cailler, Pierre. *Catalogue raisonné de l'oeuvre lithographié et gravé de Hans Erni.* 2 v. Genève, Cailler, 1969–1971. (CR).

3284. Erni, Hans. *Skizzenbuch.* Zürich, Scheidegger, 1963.

3285. ———. *Skizzen 1982/83.* Frauenfeld, Edition Scheidegger im Verlag Huber, 1984.

3286. ———. *Skizzenbuch 2: Afrika.* Vorwort von Leopold Sédar Senghor. Zürich, Scheidegger, 1966.

3287. ———. *Wo steht der Maler in der Gegenwart?* Zürich, Büchergilde Gutenberg, 1947.

3288. Farner, Konrad. *Weg und Zielsetzung des Künstlers.* Zürich, Amstutz Herdeg, 1943.

3289. ———. *Hans Erni, ein Maler unserer Zeit.* Zürich, Kultur und Volk, 1945.

3290. Gabus, Jean. *Les fresques de Hans Enri, ou la part du peintre en ethnographie.* Neuchâtel, La Baconnière, 1955.

3291. Gafner, Raymond. *Hans Erni: OlympArt.* Texte, Raymond Gafner, Alfred A. Häsler, Silvio Blatter. Vorworte, Adolf Ogi, Juan Antonio Samaranch. Zürich, ABC Verlag, 1990.

3292. Roy, Claude. *Hans Erni.* Genève, Cailler, 1955.

3293. Rüegg, Walter. *Hans Erni, das malerische Werk.* Bern, Erpf, 1980.

Ernst, Max, 1891–1976

3294. Bibliothèque Nationale (Paris). *Max Ernst, estampes et livres illustrés.* [Catalogue de l'exposition]. Paris, Bibliothèque Nationale, 1975.

3295. Bosquet, Joe and Tapié, Michel. *Max Ernst.* Paris, Drouin, 1950.

3296. Cahiers d'Art. *Max Ernst, oeuvres de 1919 à 1936.* Paris, Cahiers d'Art, 1937.

3297. Camfield, William A. *Max Ernst: Dada and the dawn of surrealism.* Munich, Prestel, 1993.

3298. Diehl, Gaston. *Max Ernst.* New York, Crown, 1973.

3299. Ernst, Max. *Beyond Painting and other writings by the artist and his friends.* New York, Wittenborn, 1948. (The Documents of Modern Art).

3300. ———. *Ecritures.* Paris, Gallimard, 1970.

3301. ———. *Max Ernst, beyond surrealism: a retrospective of the artist's books and prints.* Edited by Robert Rainwater; with essays by Anne Hyde Greet, Evan M. Maurer, and Robert Rainwater and a foreword by Vartan Gregorian. New York, New York Public Library; Oxford University Press, 1986.

3302. ———. *Max Ernst, das Rendezvous der Freunde.* [Catalog of an exhibition held at the Museum Ludwig, Köln, 22. Juni bis 8. September 1991]. Ausstellung und Katalog, Ludger Derenthal. Köln, das Museum, 1991.

3303. ———. *Le néant et son double.* Paris, etc., Alexandre Jolas, 1988.

3304. Gatt, Giuseppe. *Max Ernst.* London, Hamlyn, 1970. (Twentieth-Century Masters).

3305. Herzogenrath, Wulf. *Max Ernst in Köln, die rheinische Kunstszene bis 1922.* Köln, Rheinland, 1980.

3306. Konnertz, Winfried. *Max Ernst.* Köln, DuMont, 1980.

3307. Kunstmuseum Hannover. *Max Ernst: Gemälde, Skulpturen, Collagen, Frottagen, Zeichnungen, Druckgraphik und Bücher.* [Verzeichnis der Bestände]. Hannover, Kunstmuseum, 1981. (CR).

3308. Lake, Johannes auf der. *Skulpturen von Max Ernst: aesthetische Theorie und Praxis.* Frankfurt am Main/ New York, P. Lang, 1986.

3309. Le Point Cardinal (Paris). *Max Ernst; oeuvre sculpté, 1913–1961.* [15 novembre–fin décembre 1961]. Paris, Le Point Cardinal, 1962.

3310. Leffin, Gudrun. *Bildtitel und Bildlegenden bei Max Ernst:* ein interdisziplinärer Beitrag zur Kunst des zwanzigsten Jahrhunderts. Frankfurt am Main/New York, P. Lang, 1988. (Europäische Hochschulschriften, Reihe XXVII; Kunstgeschichte, Bd. 80).

3311. Legge, Elizabeth M. *Max Ernst: the psychoanalytic sources.* Ann Arbor, Michigan/ London, UMI Research Press, 1991.

3312. Museum of Modern Art (New York). *Max Ernst.* [March 1, 1961–May 7, 1961]. New York, Museum of Modern Art, 1961.

3313. Musée d'Art et d'Histoire (Geneva). *Max Ernst, oeuvre gravé.* [Cabinet des estampes, 30 mai–9 août, 1970]. Genève, Musée d'Art et d'Histoire, 1970.

E

3314. Oehlers, Helmut. *Figur und Raum in den Werken von Max Ernst, René Magritte, Salvador Dali und Paul Delvaux, zwischen 1925 und 1938.* Frankfurt am Main/ New York, P. Lang, 1986. (Europäische Hochschulschriften, Reihe XXVII; Kunstgeschichte, Bd. 54).

3315. O'Hara, J. Philip. *Max Ernst.* Chicago, O'Hara, 1972.

3316. Patyk, Urs. *Max Ernst und Paul Delvaux: Bildstruktur und Erzählmodi in den Bildern zwischen 1938 und 1960.* Frankfurt am Main/New York, P. Lang, 1988. (Europäische Hochschulschriften, Reihe XXVIII; Kunstgeschichte, Bd. 89).

3317. Quinn, Edward. *Max Ernst.* Zürich, Atlantis, 1977.

3318. Russell, John. *Max Ernst, life and work.* New York, Abrams, 1967.

3319. Sala, Carlo. *Max Ernst et la démarche onirique.* Paris, Klincksieck, 1970.

3320. Schneede, Uwe M. *Max Ernst.* New York, Praeger, 1973.

3321. Solomon R. Guggenheim Museum (New York). *Max Ernst, a retrospective.* [Catalogue of an exhibition]. New York, Guggenheim Museum, 1975.

3322. Spies, Werner. *Max Ernst, Collagen; Inventar und Widerspruch.* Köln, DuMont, 1974.

3323. ———. *Max Ernst collages: the invention of the surrealist universe.* Trans. from the German by John William Gabriel. New York, H.N. Abrams, 1991.

3324. ———. *Max Ernst: Druckgraphische Werke und illustrierte Bücher.* Compl. by A.M. Fischer; Gabriele Lohberg. Köln, Wienand, 1990.

3325. ———. *Max Ernst, Frottages.* London, Thames and Hudson, 1969.

3326. ———. *Max Ernst, Loplop: the artist's other self.* London, Thames and Hudson, 1983.

3327. ———. *Max Ernst, Oeuvre-Katalog.* 5 v. Köln, DuMont, 1974–76. (Menil Foundation). (CR).

3328. ———. *The return of la belle jardinière; Max Ernst, 1950–1970.* New York, Abrams, 1971.

3329. Tate Gallery (London). *Max Ernst: a retrospective.* [Catalogue of an exhibition held at the Tate Gallery, London, Feb. 1–April 21, 1991, at the Staatsgalerie, Stuttgart, May 18–Aug. 4, 1991, and at the Kunstsammlung Nordrhein-Westfalen, Düsseldorf, Aug. 24–Nov. 3, 1991]. Edited and with an introduction by Werner Spies; essays by Karin von Maur . . . [et al.]; translations from the German by John William Gabriel.Munich, Prestel; New York, distributed on behalf of Prestel-Verlag by te Neues Pub. Co, 1991.

3330. Trier, Eduard. *Max Ernst.* Recklinghausen, Bongers, 1959. (Monographien zur rheinisch-westfälischen Kunst der Gegenwart).

3331. Waldberg, Patrick. *Max Ernst.* Paris, Pauvert, 1958.

3332. ———. *Ernst: peintures.* Paris, Hazan, 1969.

Escher, Maurits Cornelis, 1898–1971

3333. Ernst, Bruno. *The magic mirror of M. C. Escher.* New York, Random House, 1976.

3334. Escher, Maurits, Cornelis. *Escher.* With a complete catalogue of the graphic works, [compiled by] F.H. Bool, J.L. Locher, F. Wierda]; including essays by M.C. Escher. General editor, J.L. Locher; translated from the Dutch by Tony Langham and Plym Peters. London, Thames and Hudson, 1982. (CR).

3335. Escher, M. C. *The world of M. C. Escher.* New York, Abrams, 1971.

3336. ———. *Escher on Escher: exploring the infinite.* M.C. Escher with a contribution by J.W. Vermeulen; translated from the Dutch by Karin Ford. New York, H.N. Abrams, 1989.

3337. ———. *Grafiek in tekeningen.* Zwolle, Tijl, 1962.

3338. ———. *The graphic work of M.C. Escher; Introduced and explained by the artist.* New York, Ballantine Books, 1973. New and rev. ed., [1 ed. 1967].

3339. ———. *Le monde de M.C. Escher:* l'oeuvre de M.C. Escher, commenté par J.L. Locher . . . [et al.]; sous la direction de J.L. Locher; [traduction en français des textes hollandais par Jeanne A. Renault. Paris, Chêne, 1986. 12 ed. [1 ed. 1972].

3340. International Congress on M.C. Escher (Rome, Italy, March 26–28, 1985). *M.C. Escher, art and science.* Edited by H.S.M. Coxeter, M. Emmer, R. Penrose, M.L. Teuber. Amsterdam; New York, North Holland. Distrib. in the U.S.A. and Canada, Elsevier Science Pub. Co., 1986. [2 ed. 1987].

3341. Macgillavry, Caroline H. *Fantasy & symmetry, the periodic drawings of M. C. Escher.* New York, Abrams, 1976. (Reprint of the original edition published for the International Union of Crystallography by A. Osthoek's Uitgeversmaatschappij, Utrecht, under the title: Symmetry aspects of M.C. Escher's periodic drawings).

3342. Schattschneider, Doris. *Visions of Symmetry: notebooks, periodic drawings, and related work of M.C. Escher.* New York, W.H. Freeman, 1990. Published for the International Union of Crystallography by A. Oosthoek's Uitgeversmaatschappij NV, Utrecht) under title: *Symmetry aspects of M.C. Escher's periodic drawings.*

3371. Museum of Modern Art (New York). *Walker Evans.* Introd. by John Szarkowski. New York, Museum of Modern Art, 1980; distributed by New York Graphic Society, Boston, Mass. 2 ed.

3372. Southall, Thomas. *Of time and place: Walker Evans* and William Christenberry. [By] T. Southall; with excerpts by James Agee and stories by William Christenberry. San Francisco, Friends of Photography; Fort Worth, Amon Carter Museum in association with the University of New Mexico Press, Albuquerque, 1990.

3373. Ward, Joseph Anthony. American silences: the realism of James Agee, *Walker Evans,* and Edward Hopper. Baton Rouge, Louisiana State University Press, 1985.

Evenepoel, Henry Jacques Edouard, 1872–1899

3374. Derrey-Capon, Danielle. *Henri Evenepoel, 1872–1899.* Brussels, Musées Royaux des Baux-arts de Belgique, 1994. (CR).

3375. Evenepoel, Henri. *Henri Evenepoel à Paris; lettres choisies 1892–1899.* Editées avec une introduction et des notes par Francis E. Hyslop. Bruxelles, La Renaissance du Livre, 1972.

3376. ———. *Lettres à mon père.* Edited by Danielle Derrey-Capon. 2 v. Bruxelles, Editions des Musées Royaux des Beaux-arts de Belgique, 1994.

3377. Hellens, Franz. *Henri Evenepoel.* Anvers, De Sikkel, 1947. (Monographies de l'art belge).

3378. Hyslop, Francis E. *Henri Evenepoel, Belgian painter in Paris, 1892–1899.* University Park, Penn. State University Press, 1975.

3379. Lambotte, Paul. *Henri Evenepoel.* Bruxelles, van Oest, 1908. (Collection des artistes belges contemporains).

3380. Musée Royaux des Beaux-Arts de Belgique, Bruxelles. *Hommage à Henri Evenepoel, 1872–1899; oeuvres des collections publiques de Belgique.* 2 ed. Bruxelles, Musée Royaux des Beaux-Arts de Belgique, 1973.

3381. Wilde, Eliane De. *Henri Evenepoel, 1872–1899.* [By] Eliane De Wilde . . . et al. Brussels, Crédit Communal, 1994.

Exekias, 6th c. b.c.

3382. Technau, Werner. *Exekias.* Leipzig, Keller, 1936. (Bilder griechischer Vasen, 9).

Eyck, Hubert van, 1366–1426
Jan van, 1390–1440

3383. Baldass, Ludwig. *Jan van Eyck.* New York, Phaidon, 1952.

3384. Beenken, Hermann. *Hubert und Jan van Eyck.* München, Bruckmann, 1943. 2 ed.

3385. Brignetti, Raffaello. *L'opera completa dei van Eyck.* Milano, Rizzoli, 1968. (Classici dell'arte, 17).

3386. Brockwell, Maurice W. *The van Eyck Problem.* London, Chatto & Windus, 1954.

3387. Bruyn, Josua. *Van Eyck problemen.* Utrecht, Kunsthistorisches Institut, 1957.

3388. Conway, Martin. *The van Eycks and their followers.* London, Murray, 1921.

3389. Coremans, Paul. *L'agneau mystique au laboratoire, examen et traitement.* Anvers, De Sikkel, 1953. (Les Primitifs Flamands, III: Contributions à l'étude des Primitifs Flamands, 2).

3390. ——— and Bisthoven, A. Jannssens de. *Van Eyck, the adoration of the mystic lamb.* Antwerp, Nederlandsche Boekhandel, 1948.

3391. Cornette, A. H. *De protretten van Jan van Eyck.* Antwerpen, De Sikkel, 1947. (Maerlantbibliotheek, 20).

3392. Devigne, Marguerite. *Van Eyck.* Bruxelles, Kryn, 1926.

3393. Dhanens, Elisabeth. *Van Eyck, the Ghent altarpiece.* New York, Viking, 1973.

3394. Durand-Greville, E. *Hubert et Jean van Eyck.* Bruxelles, van Oest, 1910.

3395. Dvorak, Max. *Das Rätsel der Kunst der Brüder van Eyck.* München, Piper, 1925.

3396. Faggin, Giorgio T. *The complete paintings of the van Eycks.* New York, Abrams, 1968.

3397. Friedländer, Max J. *Die van Eyck, Petrus Christus.* Berlin, Cassirer, 1924. (Die Altniederländische Malerei, 1).

3398. Harbison, Craig. *Jan van Eyck: the play of realism.* London, Reaktion Books; Seattle, distributed in USA and Canada by the University of Washington Press, 1991.

3399. Hotho, H. G. *Die Malerschule Huberts van Eyck, nebst deutschen Vorgängern und Zeitgenossen.* 2 v. Berlin, Veit, 1858.

3400. Hymans, Henri. *Les van Eyck.* Paris, H. Laurens, 1908.

3401. Jansen, Dieter. *Similitudo: Untersuchungen zu den Bildnissen Jan van Eycks.* Köln, Böhlau, 1988.

3402. Kaemmerer, Ludwig. *Hubert und Jan van Eyck.* Leipzig, Velhagen & Klasing, 1898. (Künstler-Monographien, 35).

3403. Kerbert, Ottmar. *Hubert van Eyck, die Verwandlung der mittelalterlichen in die neuzeitliche Gestaltung.* Frankfurt a.M., Klostermann, 1937.

3404. Knuttel, G. *Hubert en Jan van Eyck.* Amsterdam, Becht, 1949. (Palet serie, 1).

3405. Konody, P. G. *The brothers van Eyck.* London, Bell, 1907.

3406. Lejeune, Jean. *Les van Eyck, peintres de Liège et de sa cathédrale.* Liège, Thone, 1956.

3407. Pächt, Otto. *Altniederländische Malerei: von Rogier van der Weyden bis Gerard David.*

Hrsg. von Monika Rosenauer. München, Prestel, 1994.

3408. ———. *Van Eyck: die Begründung der altniederländischen Malerei.* Hrsg. von Maria Schmidt-Dengler. München, Prestel, 1989.

3409. ———. *Van Eyck and the founders of early Netherlandish painting.* Edited by Maria Schmidt-Dengler and translated from the German by David Britt. London, Harvey Miller, 1994

3410. Pfister, Kurt. *Van Eyck.* München, Delphin, 1922.

3411. Philip, Lotte Brand. *The Ghent altarpiece and the art of Jan van Eyck.* Princeton, N.J., Princeton University Press, 1971.

3412. Philippe, Joseph. *Van Eyck et la genèse mosane de la peinture des anciens pays-bas.* Liège, Bénard et Centrale, 1960.

3413. Puyvelde, Leo van. *Van Eyck, the holy lamb.* Paris, Marion Press, 1947.

3414. Renders, Emile. *Hubert van Eyck, personnage de légende.* Paris, van Oest, 1933.

3415. ———. *Jean van Eyck et le polyptyque, deux problèmes résolus.* Bruxelles, Librairie Générale, 1950.

3416. ———. *Jean van Eyck, son oeuvre, son style, son évolution et la légende d'un frère peintre.* Bruges, Beyaert, 1935.

3417. Scheewe, L. *Hubert und Jan van Eyck, ihre literarische Würdigung bis ins 18. Jahrhundert.* Haag, Nijhoff, 1933.

3418. Schmarsow, August. *Hubert und Jan van Eyck.* Leipzig, Hiersemann, 1924. (Kunstgeschichtliche Monographien, 19).

3419. Schopenhauer, Johanna. *Johann van Eyck und seine Nachfolger.* Frankfurt a.M., Wilmans, 1822.

3420. Waagen, Gustav Friedrich. *Ueber Hubert und Johann van Eyck.* Breslau, Max, 1822.

3421. Weale, W. H. James. *Hubert and John van Eyck, their life and work.* London, Lane, 1908.

3422. ——— and Brockwell, Maurice W. *The van Eycks and their art.* London, Lane, 1912.

3423. Ziloty, Alexandre. *La découverte de Jean van Eyck et l'évolution du procédé de la peinture à l'huile du moyen age à nos jours.* Paris, Librairie Floury, 1941.

E

F

Fabriano, Gentile da *see* **Gentile da Fabriano**

Fabritius, Barent, 1624–1673
3424. Miomandre, Francis de. *Trois chefs-d'oeuvre de Barent Fabritius.* Paris, Brunner, 1914.
3425. Point, Daniël. *Barent Fabritius, 1624–1673.* Utrecht, Drukkerij Trio, 1958.

Fabritius, Carel, 1622?–1654
3426. Brown, Christopher. *Carel Fabritius, complete edition with a catalogue raisonné.* Oxford, Phaidon, 1981. (CR).
3427. Hofstede de Groot, Cornelis. *Jan Vermeer of Delft and Carel Fabritius; photogravures of all their known paintings.* With biographical and descriptive text by C. Hofstede de Groot. Amsterdam, Scheltema, 1909.
3428. Schuurman, K. E. *Carel Fabritius.* Amsterdam, Becht, 1947.
3429. Tietze-Conrat, E. *Die Delfter Malerschule; Carel Fabritius, Pieter de Hooch, Jan Vermeer.* Leipzig, Seemann, 1922.

Fadrusz, János, 1858–1903
3430. Béla, Lázár. *Fadrusz János élete és müveszete.* Budapest, Athenaeum, 1923.
3431. Soos, Gyula. *Fadrusz Janos.* Budapest, Kepzomuveszeti Alap Kiadovallalata, 1961.

Faed, Thomas, 1826–1900
3432. [James R. Osgood and Company]. *The Faed gallery; a series of the most renowned works of Thomas Faed, reproduced in heliotype.* Boston, Osgood, 1878.

Faichtmayer, Joseph Anton *see* **Faichtmayr, Joseph Anton**

Faichtmayr, Joseph Anton, 1696–1770
3433. Boeck, Wilhelm. *Feuchtmayer Meisterwerke.* Tübingen, Wasmuth, 1963.

3434. ———. *Joseph Anton Feuchtmayer.* Tübingen, Wasmuth, 1948.
3435. Sauer, Horst. *Herkunft und Anfänge des Bildhauers Joseph Anton Faichtmeyer.* Leipzig, Gerhardt, 1932.

Falconet, Etienne Maurice, 1716–1791
3436. Diderot, Denis. *Le pour et le contre: correspondence polémique sur le respect de la posterité. Pline et les anciens auteurs qui ont parlé de peinture et de sculpture. Diderot et Falconet;* introduction et notes de Yves Benot. Paris, Editeurs Français Réunis, 1958.
3437. [Falconet, Etienne]. *Oeuvres d'Etienne Falconet, statuaire; contenant plusieurs écrits relatifs aux beaux arts.* 6 v. Lausanne, Société Typographique, 1781. (CR).
3438. ———. *Oeuvres diverses concernant les arts.* 3 v. Paris, Didot, 1787. Nouvelle édition.
3439. Hildebrandt, Edmund. *Leben, Werke und Schriften des Bildhauers E.-M. Falconet, 1716–1791.* Strassburg, Heitz, 1908. (Zur Kunstgeschichte des Auslandes, 63).
3440. Levitine, George. *The Sculpture of Falconet.* Greenwich, Conn., New York Graphic Society, 1972.
3441. Réau, Louis. *Etienne-Maurice Falconet.* 2 v. Paris, Demotte, 1922.
3442. Vallon, Fernand. *Falconet; Falconet et Diderot, Falconet et Catherine II.* Senlis, Imprimeries réunies, 1927.
3443. Weinshenker, Anne B. *Falconet, his writings and his friend Diderot.* Genève, Droz, 1966.

Fansaga, Cosimo *see* **Fanzago, Cosimo**

Fanzago, Cosimo, 1593–1678
3444. Fogaccia, Piero. *Cosimo Fanzago.* Bergamo, Istituto italiano d'arti grafiche, 1945.
3445. Winther, Annemarie. *Cosimo Fanzago und die Neapler Ornamentik des 17. und 18. Jahrhunderts.* Bremen, Hauschild, 1973.

Fantin-Latour, Ignace Henri Jean Theodore, 1836–1904

3446. Bénédite, Léonce. *Catalogue des lithographies originales de Henri Fantin-Latour.* Paris, Motteroz, 1899.

3447. ———. *Fantin-Latour.* Paris, Librairie de L'Art Ancien et Moderne, 1903. (Les artists de tous les temps; Série D—le XXᵉ siècle).

3448. ———. *Fantin-Latour.* Exhibition organized by the Réunion des musées nationaux and the National Gallery of Canada, in conjunction with the Fine Arts Museum of San Francisco; Douglas Druick, Michel Hoog. Ottawa, National Gallery of Canada; National Museums of Canada, 1983.

3449. ———. *L'oeuvre de Fantin-Latour, recueil de cinquante reproductions.* Paris, Librairie Centrale des Beaux-Arts, 1906.

3450. [Fantin-Latour]. *L'oeuvre lithographique de Fantin-Latour; collection complète de ses lithographies reproduites et réduites en facsimilé par le procédé héliographique boyet.* Paris, Delteil, 1907.

3451. Fantin-Latour, Victoria D. *Catalogue de l'oeuvre complet (1849–1904) de Fantin-Latour.* Paris, Floury, 1911. Reprint: New York, Da Capo, 1969. (CR).

3452. Gibson, Frank W. *The art of Henri Fantin-Latour.* London, Drane, 1924.

3453. Hédiard, Germain. *Fantin-Latour, catalogue de l'oeuvre lithographique du maître.* Paris, Librairie de L'Art Ancien et Moderne, 1906. (Les maîtres de la lithographie). (CR).

3454. ———. *Fantin-Latour: toute la lithographie.* Genève, Musée d'art et d'histoire, 1980. [Catalogue of an exhibition wich contains a reprint of Hédiard's catalogue raisonné of 1906 with illustrations added together with a supplement of previously uncatalogued prints]. (CR).

3455. Jullien, Adolphe. *Fantin-Latour, sa vie et ses amitiés; lettres inédites et souvenirs personnels.* Paris, Laveur, 1909.

3456. Kahn, Gustave. *Fantin-Latour.* New York, Dodd, Mead, 1927.

3457. Lucie-Smith, Edward. *Henri Fantin-Latour.* New York, Rizzoli, 1977.

3458. Musée d'Art et d'Histoire (Geneva). *Fantin-Latour lithographies.* [19 décembre–11 février 1981]. Genève, Editions du Tricorne, 1981.

3459. Palais de L'Ecole National des Beaux-Arts (Paris). *Exposition de l'oeuvre de Fantin-Latour, mai–juin 1906.* 2 ed. Paris, Librairie Centrale des Beaux-Arts, 1906.

3460. Smith College Museum of Art (Northampton, Mass.). *Henri Fantin-Latour.* [April 28–June 6, 1966]. Northampton, Mass., Smith College Museum of Art, 1966.

Fanzago, Cosimo, 1591–1678

3461. Cantone, Gaetana. *Napoli barocca e Cosimo Fanzago.* Napoli, Banco di Napoli, 1984.

Farinati, Paolo, 1524–1606

3462. Farinati, Paolo. *Giornale (1573–1606).* A cura di Lionello Puppi. Firenze, Olschki, 1968. (Civiltà Veneziana fonti e testi, VIII; Serie prima, 5).

3463. Forno, Federico dal. *Paolo Farinati, 1524–1606.* Verona, Vita Veronese, 1965. (Collana monografie d'arte, 6).

Fattori, Giovanni, 1825–1908

3464. Baboni, Andrea. *Le incisioni di Giovanni Fattori nella collezione Franconi, e catalogo generale dell'opera incisa Fattoriana.* Prefazione di Federico Zeri. [Traduzioni dei testi di Luigi Franconi . . . et al.]. Firenze, Edizioni Panatini, 1987. (CR).

3465. Bianciardi, Luciano. *L'opera completa di Fattori.* Milano, Rizzoli, 1970. (Classici dell'arte, 42).

3466. Centro d'Arte Dolomiti (Cortina d'Ampezzo). *Omaggio a Giovanni Fattori.* Cortina d'Ampezzo, Centro d'Arte Dolomiti, 1972.

3467. Cisternino del Pocciani (Livorno). *La giovinezza di Fattori, catalogo della mostra, ottobre–dicembre 1980.* Roma, de Luca, 1980. (Archivio dei Macchiaioli, 2).

3468. Di Micheli, Mario. *Giovanni Fattori.* Busto Arsizio, Bramante, 1961. (I grandi pittori italiani dell'ottocento, 4).

3469. Durbe, Dario. *Fattori e la scuola di Castiglioncello.* 2 v. Roma, De Luca, 1982–1983.

3470. Franchi, Anna. *Giovanni Fattori, studio biografico.* Firenze, Alinari, 1910.

3471. ———. *Giovanni Fattori, Silvestro Lega, Telemaco Signorini; conferenze e saggi.* Milano, Ceschina, 1953.

3472. Francini Ciaranfi, Anna M. *Incisioni del Fattori.* Bergamo, Istituto italiano d'arti grafiche, 1944.

3473. Galleria Nazionale d'Arte Moderna (Roma). *Disegni di Giovanni Fattori del Museo Civico di Livorno.* 19 dicembre 1970–31 gennaio 1971. Rome, de Luca, 1970.

3474. Ghiglia, Oscar. *L'opera di Giovanni Fattori.* Firenze, Edizioni Self, 1913.

3475. Malesci, Giovanni. *Catalogazione illustra della pittura ad olio di Giovanni Fattori.* Novara, de Agostini, 1961.

3476. La Meridiana di Palazzo Pitti (Florence). *Le acqueforti di Fattori della collezione Rosselli.* 12 giugno–31 dicembre 1976. Firenze, La Meridiano di Palazzo Pitti, 1976. (Galleria d'arte moderna di Palazzo Pitti, Firenze, 1).

3477. Paolieri, Ferdinando. *Giovanni Fattori, il maestro Toscano del secolo XIX*. Firenze, Benaglia, 1925.

3478. Pepi, Carlo. *Giovanni fattori in una raccolta privata*. v.1—Valpiana, (Grosseto), Il Parnasso, 1991– .

Fauconnier, Henri Victor Gabriel *see* **Le Fauconnier, Henri Victor Gabriel**

Fautrier, Jean, 1898–1964

3479. Argan, Gian-Carlo. *Fautrier, matière et mémoire; testo: italiano, francese, inglese, tedesco*. Milano, Apollonaire, 1960.

3480. Bucarelli, Palma. *Jean Fautrier, pittura e materia*. Milano, Il Saggiatore, 1960. (La Cultura, Vol. XX).

3481. Fautrier, Jean. *Fautrier, 1898–1964*. [Exposition] 25 mai–24 septembre 1989. Musée d'art moderne de la Ville de Paris. Paris, Paris—Musées; amis du musée d'art moderne de la Ville de Paris, 1989.

3482. ———. *Jean Fautrier: Gemälde, Skulpturen und Handzeichnungen*. [Ausstellung], Josef-Haubrich-Kunsthalle, Köln, 23. Februar bis 7. April, 1980. Köln, Die Kunsthalle, 1980.

3483. Galerie Engleberts (Geneva). *Jean Fautrier; oeuvre gravé, oeuvre sculpté; essai d'un catalogue raisonné*. Genève, Galerie Engleberts, 1969. (CR).

3484. Josef-Haubrich-Kunsthalle (Cologne). *Jean Fautrier; Gemälde, Skulpturen und Handzeichnungen*. 23. Februar bis 7. April 1980. Köln, Josef-Haubrich-Kunsthalle, 1980.

3485. Kunstverein Hamburg. *Jean Fautrier*. 19. Mai–17. Juni 1973. Hamburg, Kunstverein, 1973.

3486. Mason, Rainer Michael. *Jean Fautrier: les estampes; nouvel essai de catalogue raisonné*. R.M. Mason; avec deux notes de Castor Seibel, Marcel-André Stalter. Genève, Cabinet des estampes, 1986. (CR).

3487. Musée d'Art Moderne de la Ville de Paris. *Jean Fautrier, rétrospective, avril–mai 1964*. Paris, Les Presses Artistiques, 1964.

3488. Paulhan, Jean. *Fautrier l'enragé*. Paris, Gallimard, 1962.

3489. ———. *Fautrier, oeuvres (1915–1943)*. Paris, Drouin, 1943.

3490. Peyré, Yves. *Fautrier, ou, Les outrages de l'impossible*. Iconographie réunie par Isabelle d'hauteville et l'auteur. Paris, rtegard, 1990. (CR).

3491. Ragon, Michel. *Fautrier*. Paris, Fall, 1957. (Le Museé de Poche).

Feichtmayr, Joseph Anton *see* **Faichtmayr, Joseph Anton**

Feininger, Lyonel, 1871–1956

3492. Dorfles, Gillo. *Lyonel Feininger*. Milano,
Scheiwiller, 1958. (All'Insegna de Pesce d'Oro, Serie illustrata, 62).

3493. Feininger, Lyonel. *Feininger and Tobey: years of friendship, 1944–1956; the complete correspondence*. Edited and annotated by Stephan E. Hauser. New York, Achim Moeller Fine Art, 1991.

3494. ———. *Lyonel Feininger: Gemälde, Aquarelle und Zeichnungen, Druckgraphik*. [Ausstellung] 19. Juni bis 29. August 1982. Kunsthalle zu Kiel der Christian-Albrechts-Universität in Kiel in Zusammenarbeit mit dem Schleswig-Holsteinischen Kunstverein und im Auftrag der Landeshauptstadt Kiel. Herausgeber, Konzeption, Katalogbearbeitung, Kataloggestaltung: Jens Christian Jensen. Kiel, Die Kunsthalle, 1982.

3495. ———. *Lyonel Feininger: die Halle-Bilder*. Hrsg. und mit Beiträgen von Wolfgang Buche, Andreas Huneke und Peter Romanus. München, Prestel-verlag, 1991.

3496. ———. *Lyonel Feininger: Städte und Küsten; Aquarelle, Zeichnungen, Druckgrafik*. Ausstellung zum 200. Jubiläum der Albrecht Dürer Gesellschaft (1793–1992). Marburg, Hitzeroth, 1992.

3497. ———. *Lyonel Feininger: la variante tematica e tecnica nello sviluppo del processo creativo*. [Curatori della mostra, Manuela Kahn-Rossi, Marco Franciolli]. Lugano, Fidia, 1991.

3498. Feininger, T. Lux. *Lyonel Feininger, city at the edge of the world*. New York, Praeger, 1965.

3499. Haus der Kunst (Munich). *Lyonel Feininger, 1871–1956*. 24. März bis 13. Mai 1973. München, Haus der Kunst, 1973.

3500. Hess, Hans. *Lyonel Feininger*. New York, Abrams, 1961.

3501. Luckhardt, Ulrich. *Lyonel Feininger, die Karikaturen und das zeichnerische Frühwerk: der Weg der Selbstfindung zum unabhängigen Künstler. Mit einem Exkurs zu den Karikaturen von Emil Nolde und George Grosz*. München, Scaneg, 1987.

3502. ———. *Lyonel Feininger*. Munich, Prestel; New York, distributed in the USA and Canada by te Neues, 1989.

3503. Museum für Kunst und Gewerbe (Hamburg). *Lyonel Feininger; Karikaturen, Comic strips, Illustrationen, 1888–1915*. [9. Januar–22. Februar 1981]. Hamburg, Museum für Kunst und Gewerbe, 1981.

3504. Museum of Modern Art (New York). *Lyonel Feininger; Marsden Hartley*. New York, Museum of Modern Art, 1944.

3505. Ness, June L., ed. *Lyonel Feininger [letters]*. New York, Praeger, 1974. (Documentary Monographs in Modern Art).

3506. Prasse, Leona E. *Lyonel Feininger; a descriptive catalogue of his graphic work: etchings, lithographs, woodcuts.* Cleveland, Cleveland Museum of Art, 1972.

3507. Ruhmer, Eberhard. *Lyonel Feininger; Zeichnungen, Aquarelle, Graphik.* München, Bruckmann, 1961.

3508. Sabarsky, Serge. *Lyonel Feininger: Zeichnungen und Aquarelle.* München, Oktagon, 1991.

3509. Scheyer, Ernst. *Lyonel Feininger, caricature & fantasy.* Detroit, Wayne State University Press, 1964.

3510. Wolfradt, Willi. *Lyonel Feininger.* Leipzig, Klinkhardt & Biermann, 1924. (Junge Kunst, 47).

Feke, Robert, 1705?–1750

3511. Bayley, Frank W. *Five colonial artists of New England: Joseph Badger, Joseph Blackburn, John Singleton Copley, Robert Feke, John Smibert.* Boston, [Privately printed], 1929.

3512. Foote, Henry W. *Robert Feke, colonial portrait painter.* Cambridge, Harvard University Press, 1930.

3513. Poland, William C. *Robert Feke, the early Newport portrait painter and the beginnings of colonial painting.* Providence, Rhode Island Historical Society, 1907.

3514. Smith, Albert D. *Robert Feke, native colonial painter.* [Exhibition, Nov. 2–Nov. 10, 1946]. Huntington, N.Y., Heckscher Art Museum, 1946.

3515. Whitney Museum of American Art (New York). *Robert Feke.* October 8–30, 1946. [Text by Lloyd Goodrich]. New York, Whitney Museum, 1946.

Felixmüller, Conrad, 1897–1977

3516. Felixmüller, Conrad. *Conrad Felixmueller: Das druckgraphische Werk 1912–1976 im Kunstmuseum Düsseldorf: Schenkung Titus Felixmüller und Luca Felix Müller.* Bearbeitet von Friedrich W. Heckmanns. [Redaktion, Friedrich W. Heckmanns, Gerhard Leistner]. Düsseldorf, Das Kunstmuseum, 1986.

3517. Germanisches Nationalmuseum (Nuremberg). *Conrad Felixmüller, Werke und Documente.* [Dec. 3, 1981–Jan. 31, 1982]. Nürnberg, Germanisches Nationalmuseum, 1982.

3518. Gleisberg, Dieter. *Conrad Felixmüller, Leben und Werk.* Dresden, Verlag der Kunst, 1982.

3519. Heinz, Hellmuth. *Conrad Felixmüller, gezeichnetes Menschenbild.* Dresden, Verlag der Kunst, 1958.

3520. Rathke, Christian. *Conrad Felixmüller: Gemälde, Aquarelle, Zeichnungen, Druckgraphik, Skulpturen* [Katalog der Ausstellung] Schleswig, Schleswig-Holsteinisches Landesmuseum, 1.4.–17.6. 1990. Schleswig,

Schleswig-Holsteinische Landesmuseum, 1990.

3521. Söhn, Gerhart. *Conrad Felixmüller, das graphische Werk, 1912–1974.* Düsseldorf, Graphik-Salon, 1975.

3522. ———. *Conrad Felixmüller, von ihm—über ihn.* Düsseldorf, Graphik-Salon, 1977.

3523. Verein Berliner Künstler. *Conrad Felixmüller: Ausstellungen seiner Malereien von 1913 bis 1973.* Gemälde, 12. Okt.–11. Nov. 1973 in den Räumen der ehemaligen Nationalgalerie; Aquarelle, 13. Okt.–11. Nov. 1973 in der Galerie des Vereins. Berlin, Verein Berliner Künstler, 1973.

3524. Wächter, Bernhard. *Das kleine Holzschnittbuch von Conrad Felixmüller.* Rudolstadt, Greifenverlag, 1958.

Fenton, Roger, 1819–1869

3525. Fenton, Roger. *Roger Fenton;* with an essay by Richard Pare. New York, Aperture, 1987. (Aperture masters of photography, 4).

3526. Fenton, Roger. *Roger Fenton, photographer of the 1850s.* Hayward Gallery, London, 4 February to 17 April 1988. [London], South Bank Board, 1988.

3527. Gernsheim, Helmut and Gernsheim, Alison. *Roger Fenton, photographer of the Crimean War; his photographs and his letters from the Crimea.* London, Secker & Warburg, 1954. Reprint: New York, Arno, 1973.

3528. Hannavy, John. *Roger Fenton of Crimble Hall.* London, Fraser, 1975. (The Gordon Fraser photographic monographs, 3).

Ferenczy, Károly, 1862–1917

3529. Genthon, István. *Ferenczy Károly.* Budapest, Képzömüvészeti Alap Kiadóvállata, 1963.

3530. Magyar Nemzeti Gelerija (Budapest). *Die Familie Ferenczy.* Budapest, Magyar Nemzeti Galeria, 1968.

3531. Petrovics, Elek. *Ferenczy.* Budapest, Athenaeum, 1943.

Fernandez, Arman D. *see* Arman

Ferrari, Gaudenzio, 1480–1546

3532. Bordiga, Gaudenzio. *Notizie intorno alle opere di Gaudenzio Ferrari, pittore e plasticatore.* Milano, Pirotta, 1821.

3533. ———, et al. *Le opere del pittori e plasticatore Gaudenzio Ferrari.* Milano, Molina, 1835–1846.

3534. Colombo, Giuseppe. *Vita ed opera di Gaudenzio Ferrari pittore con documenti inediti.* Torino, Bocca, 1881.

3535. Ferrari, Gaudenzio. *Gaudenzio Ferrari e la sua scuola: i cartoni cinquecenteschi dell' Accademia Albertina.* [Mostra], marzo–maggio 1982, Torino, Accademia Albertina di belli arti; a cura di Giovanni Romano. Torino, Ages Arti Grafiche, 1982.

3536. Halsey, Ethel. *Gaudenzio Ferrari*. London, Bell, 1904.

3537. Mallé, Luigi. *Incontri con Gaudenzio, raccolta di studi e note su problemi gaudenziani*. Torino, Tipografia Impronta, 1969.

3538. Museo Borgogna (Vercelli). *Mostra da Gaudenzio Ferrari*. Aprile–guigno 1956. Milano, Molina, 1956.

3539. Perpenti, A. *Elogio di Gaudenzio Ferrari, pittore e plastificatore*. Milano, Molina, 1843.

3540. Regaldi, Giuseppe. *Nella solenne inaugurazione del monumento a Gaudenzio Ferrari in Varallo-Sesai, 6 settembre 1874*. Firenze, Cellini, 1875.

3541. Testori, Giovanni. *Il gran teatro montano, saggi su Gaudenzio Ferrari*. Milano, Feltrinelli, 1965.

3542. Viale, Vittorio. *Gaudenzio Ferrari*. Torino, Edizioni RAI, 1969.

3543. Weber, Siegfried. *Gaudenzio Ferrari und seine Schule*. Strassburg, Heitz, 1927.

Ferrer Bassa, 1290–1348

3544. Trens, Manuel. *Ferrer Bassa i les pintures de pedrables*. Barcelona, Institut d'Estudis Catalans, 1936. (Memòries de la Seccio Històrico-Arqueològica, 6).

Fetti, Domenico, c. 1589–1624

3545. Fetti, Domenico. *Domenici Feti: venticinque riproduzioni, con test e catalogo a cura di R[udolf] Oldenbourg*. Roma, Societa editrice della Biblioteca d'arte illustrata, 1921.

3546. Safarik, Eduard A. *Fetti*. Milano, Electa, 1990. (CR).

Feuchtmayr, Joseph Anton see Faichtmayr, Joseph Anton

Feuerbach, Anselm, 1829–1880

3547. Allgeyer, Julius. *Anselm Feuerbach*. 2 v. Berlin, Spemann, 1904.

3548. ———. *Anselm Feuerbach, sein Leben und seine Kunst*. Bamberg, Buchner, 1894.

3549. Christoffel, Ulrich. *Anselm Feuerbach*. München, Bruckmann, 1944.

3550. Ecker, Jürgen. *Anselm Feuerbach, Leben und Werk: kritischer Katalog der Gemälde, Ölskizzen und Ölstudien*. München, Hirmer, 1991. (CR).

3551. Feuerbach, Anselm. *Briefe an seine Mutter*. Berlin, Meyer & Jessen, 1911.

3552. ———. *Ein Vermächtnis*. Wien, Gerald'ssohn, 1890. 3 ed.

3553. Gerstenberg, Kurt. *Anselm Feuerbach, aus unbekannten Skizzenbüchern der Jugend*. München, Piper, 1925.

3554. Heyck, Eduard. *Anselm Feuerbach*. Bielefeld/Leipzig, Velhagen & Klasing, 1905. (Künstler-Monographien, 76).

3555. Kupper, Daniel, Hrsg. *Anselm Feuerbachs Vermächtnis: Die originalen Aufzeichnungen*. München, Deutscher Verlag für Kunstwissenschaft, 1992. (Quellen zur deutschen Kunstgeschichte vom Klassizismus bis zur Gegenwart, 2).

3556. Oechelhaeuser, Adolf von. *Aus Anselm Feuerbachs Jugendjahren*. Leipzig, Seemann, 1905.

3557. Staatliche Kunsthalle Karlsruhe. *Anselm Feuerbach, 1829–1880, Gemälde und Zeichnungen*. 5. Juni–15. August, 1976. Karlsruhe, Staatliche Kunsthalle, 1976.

3558. Uhde-Bernays, Hermann. *Feuerbach; des Meisters Gemälde*. Stuttgart, Deutsche Verlags-Anstalt, 1913. (Klassiker der Kunst, 23).

3559. ———. *Feuerbach; beschreibender Katalog seiner sämtlichen Gemälde*. München, Bruckmann, 1929. (CR).

3560. Waldmann, Emil. *Anselm Feuerbach*. Berlin, Rembrandt, 1942. (Die Kunstbücher des Volkes, 41).

Feure, Georges de see De Feure, Georges

Field, Robert, ca. 1769–1819

3561. Art Gallery of Nova Scotia (Halifax). *Robert Field, 1769–1819*. Oct. 5 to Nov. 27, 1978. [Text in English and French]. Halifax, Art Gallery of Nova Scotia, 1978.

3562. Piers, Harry. *Robert Field, portrait painter in oils, miniatures, and water-colours, and engraver*. New York, Sherman, 1927.

Fiesole, Mino da see Mino da Fiesole

Filarete, 1400–1469

3563. Filarete. *Treatise on architecture, being the treatise by Antonio di Piero Averlino, known as Filarete*. 2 v. New Haven, Yale University Press, 1965. (Yale publications in the history of art, 16).

3564. Lazzaroni, Michele and Munoz, Antonio. *Filarete, scultore e architetto del secolo XV*. Roma, Modes, 1908.

3565. Moos, Stanislaus von. *Die Kastelltyp-Variationen des Filarete*. Zürich, Atlantis, 1971.

3566. Oettingen, Wolfgang von. *Über das Leben und die Werke des Antonio Averlino gennant Filarete, eine Studie*. Leipzig, Seemann, 1888. (Beiträge zur Kunstgeschichte, N.F., 6).

3567. Tigler, Peter. *Die Architekturtheorie des Filarete*. Berlin, de Gruyter, 1963. (Neue Münchner Beiträge zur Kunstgeschichte, 5).

Filonov, Pavel Nikolaevich, 1883–1941

3568. Filonov, Pavel Nikolaevich. *Filonov*. [Catalogue conception et réalisation, Evgueni

Kovtoune, Stanislas Zadora, Nicole Ouvrard]. Paris, Centre Georges Pompidou, 1990.

3569. ———. *Pavel Filonow und seine Schule.* [Ausstellung] Städtische Kunsthalle Düsseldorf, in Zusammenarbeit mit dem Staatlichen Russischen Museum, Leningrad. Hrsg. Jürgen Harten und Jewgenija Petrowa. Köln, Dumont, 1990.

Fini, Tommaso di Cristofero *see* **Masolino da Panicale**

Finiguerra, Tommaso, 1426–1464

3570. Colvin, Sidney. *A Florentine picture-chronicle, being a series of ninety-nine drawings representing scenes and personages of ancient history sacred and profane, by Masso Finiguerra.* [With] a critical and descriptive text by Sidney Colvin. London, Quaritch, 1898. Reprint: New York, Bloom, 1970.

Fiorenzo di Lorenzo, 1445–1525

3571. Graham, Jean C. *The problem of Fiorenzo di Lorenzo of Perugia, a critical and historical study.* Perugia, Domenico Terese, 1903.

3572. Weber, Siegfried. *Fiorenzo di Lorenzo, eine kunsthistorische Studie.* Strassburg, Heitz, 1904. (Zur Kunstgeschichte des Auslandes, 27).

Fiori, Ernesto da, 1884–1945

3573. Bardi, Pietro Maria. *Ernesto de Fiori.* Milano, Hoepli, 1950.

3574. Szittya. Emilio. *Ernesto de Fiori.* Milano, Ulrico Hoepli, 1927.

3575. Vierneisel, Beatrice. Ernesto de Fiori: *Das plastische Werk 1911–1936:* Katalogbuch zur Ausstellung im Georg-Kolbe-Museum Berlin, 14. März bis 17. Mai 1992. Mit Beiträgen von Ursel Berger, Mayra Laudanna und Ursula Merkel. Berlin, Dietrich Reimer, 1992.

Firenze, Agostino da *see* **Agostino di Duccio**

Fischer, Johann Michael, 1692–1766

3576. Hagen-Dempf, Felicitas. *Der Zentralbaugedanke bei Johann Michael Fischer.* München, Schnell & Steiner, 1954.

3577. Heilbronner, Paul. *Studien über Johann Michael Fischer.* München, Heller, 1933.

3578. Lieb, Norbert. *Johann Michael Fischer: Baumeister und Raumschöpfer im späten Barock Süddeutschlands.* Regensburg, Pustet, 1982.

Fischer von Erlach, Johann Bernhard, 1656–1723
Joseph Emanuel, 1693–1742

3579. Aurenhammer, Hans. *J. B. Fischer von Erlach.* Cambridge, Mass., Harvard University Press, 1973.

3580. ———. *Johann Bernhard Fischer von Erlach, 1656–1723.* Katalog der Ausstellung: Graz, Wien, Salzburg, 1956–57. Wien/München, Schroll, 1956.

3581. ———. *Johann Bernhard Fischer von Erlach.* Wien, Bergland, 1957. (Österreich-Reihe, 35/37).

3582. Fischer von Erlach, Johann Bernhard. *Entwurff einer historischen Architectur.* Leipzig, 1725. (Reprint: Boston, Gregg, 1964; English trans.: 1737).

3583. Frey, Dagobert. *Johann Bernhard Fischer von Erlach, eine Studie über seine Stellung in der Entwicklung der Wiener Palastfassade.* Wien, Hölzel, 1923. (Kunstgeschichtliche Einzeldarstellungen, 6).

3584. Ilg, Albert. *Die Fischer von Erlach.* Wien, Konegen, 1895.

3585. Kreul, Andreas. *Die Barockbaumeister Fischer von Erlach:* Bibliographie zu Leben und Werk. Wiesbaden, Otto Harrassowitz, 1988.

3586. Kunoth, George. *Die historische Architektur Fischers von Erlach.* Düsseldorf, Schwann, 1956. (Bonner Beiträge zur Kunstwissenschaft, 5).

3587. Lorenz, Hellmut. *Johann Bernhard Fischer von Erlach.* Zürich, Verlag für Architektur, 1992.

3588. Lanchester, Henry V. *Fischer von Erlach.* London, Benn, 1924.

3589. Schmidt, Justus. *Fischer von Erlach der Jüngere.* Wien, Verein für Geschichte der Stadt Wien, 1933.

3590. Sedlmayr, Hans. *Johann Bernhard Fischer von Erlach.* Wien, Herold, 1976. 2 ed.

3591. Zacharias, Thomas. *Joseph Emanuel Fischer von Erlach.* Wien/München, Herold, 1960.

Flaxman, John, 1755–1826

3592. Bentley, G. A., Jr. *The early engravings of Flaxman's classical designs, a bibliographical study.* New York, New York Public Library, 1964.

3593. Colvin, Sidney. *The drawings of Flaxman in the gallery of University College, London.* London, University College, 1876.

3594. Constable, William G. *John Flaxman, 1755–1826.* London, University of London, 1927.

3595. Essick, Robert and LaBelle, Jenijoy. *Flaxman's illustrations to Homer; drawn by John Flaxman, engraved by William Blake and others.* Edited with an introduction and commentary. New York, Dover, 1977.

3596. Flaxman, John. *Anatomical studies of the bones and muscles for the use of artists.* London, Nattali, 1833.

3597. ———. *Lectures on sculpture.* London, Murray, 1829.

3598. Hamburger Kunsthalle. *John Flaxman, Mythologie und Industrie.* 20. April bis 3. Juni 1979. Hamburg, Hamburger Kunsthalle, 1979.

3599. Irwin, David. *John Flaxman, 1755–1826; sculptor, illustrator, designer.* New York, Rizzoli, 1979.

3600. Sparkes, John C. L. *Flaxman's classical outlines; notes on their leading characteristics, with a brief memoir of the artist.* London, Seeley, Jackson and Halliday, 1879.

3601. Symmons, Sarah. *Flaxman and Europe: the outline illustrations and their influence.* New York, Garland, 1984.

3602. Wark, Robert R. *Drawings by John Flaxman in the Huntington Collection.* San Marino, Calif., Huntington Library, 1970.

3603. Whinney, Margaret and Gunnis, Rupert. *The collection of models by John Flaxman, R. A., at University College, London; a catalogue and introduction.* London, Athlone Press, 1967.

Flegel, Georg, 1563–1638

3604. Müller, Wolfgang J. *Der Maler Georg Flegel und die Anfänge des Stillebens.* Frankfurt a.M., Kramer, 1956. (Schriften des Historischen Museums, 8).

3605. Winkler, Friedrich. *Georg Flegel, sechs Aquarelle.* Berlin, Deutscher Verein fur Kunstwissenschaft, 1954.

Fleischmann, Adolf, 1892–1968

3606. Galerie der Stadt Esslingen, Villa Merkel. *Adolf Fleischmann.* 18. April bis 1. Juni 1975. Esslingen, Kulturamt der Stadt Esslingen, 1975.

3607. Wedewer, Rolf. *Adolf Fleischmann.* Stuttgart, Hatje, 1977.

Flettner, Peter, ca. 1485–1546

3608. Bange, E. F. *Peter Flötner.* Leipzig, Klinkhardt & Biermann, 1926. (Meister der Graphik, 14).

3609. Germanisches Nationalmuseum (Nuremberg). *Peter Flötner und die Renaissance in Deutschland.* 14. Dezember 1946–28. Februar 1947. Nürnberg, Die Egge, 1947.

3610. Haupt, Albrecht. *Peter Flettner, der erste Meister des Ott-Heinrichsbaus zu Heidelberg.* Leipzig, Hiersemann, 1904. (Kunstgeschichtliche Monographien, 1).

3611. Lange, Konrad. *Peter Flötner, ein Bahnbrecher der deutschen Renaissance.* Berlin, Grote, 1897.

3612. Leitschuh, Franz F. *Flötner-Studien, 1: das Plakettenwerk Peter Flötners in dem Verzeichnis des Nürnberger Patriziers Paulus Behaim.* Strassburg, Beust, 1904.

3613. Reimers, J. *Peter Flötner nach seinen Hand-* *zeichnungen und Holzschnitten.* München/Leipzig, Hirth, 1890.

3614. Röttinger, Heinrich. *Peter Flettners Holzschnitte.* Strassburg, Heitz, 1916. (Studien zur deutschen Kunstgeschichte, 186).

Flötner, Peter *see* Flettner, Peter

Floris, Cornelis, 1514–1575
Frans, 1517–1570

3615. Corbet, August. *Cornelis Floris en de bouw van het stadhuis van Antwerpen.* Antwerpen, De Sikkel, 1937.

3616. Hedicke, Robert. *Cornelis Floris und die Florisdekoration.* 2 v. Berlin, Bard, 1913.

3617. Velde, Carl van de. *Frans Floris (1519/20–1570), leven en werken.* 2 v. Brussel, Academie voor Wetenschapen, 1975.

3618. Zuntz, Dora. *Frans Floris, ein Beitrag zur Geschichte der niederländischen Kunst im XVI. Jahrhundert.* Strassburg, Heitz, 1929. (Zur Kunstgeschichte des Auslands, 130).

Fohr, Carl Philipp, 1795–1818

3619. Dieffenbach, Philipp. *Das Leben des Malers Karl Fohr.* Erstmalig gedruckt 1823. Frankfurt a.M., Voigtländer-Tetzner, 1918.

3620. Hardenberg, Kuno F. Graf von [and] Schilling, Edmund. *Karl Philipp Fohr, Leben und Werk eines deutschen Malers der Romantik.* Freiburg i.Br., Urban Verlag, 1925.

3621. Jensen, Jens. *Carl Philipp Fohr in Heidelberg und im Neckartal, Landschaften und Bildnisse.* Karlsruhe, Braun, 1968.

3622. Poensgen, Georg. *Carl Philipp Fohr und das Café Greco. Die Künstlerbildnisse des Heidelberger Romantikers im geschichtlichen Rahmen der berühmten Gaststätte an der Via Condotti zu Rom.* Heidelberg, Kerle, 1957.

3623. Schneider, Arthur von. *Carl Philipp Fohr, Skizzenbuch. Bildniszeichnungen deutscher Künstler in Rom.* Berlin, Mann, 1952.

3624. Städelsches Kunstinstitut (Frankfurt a.M.). *Karl Philipp Fohr, 1795–1818.* 21. Juni–11. August 1968. Frankfurt a.M., Städelsches Kunstinstitut, 1968.

Folgore da San Gimignano, fl. 1309–1317

3625. Caravaggi, Giovanni. *Folgore da S. Gimignano.* Milano, Ceschina, 1960. (Pubblicazioni della Facoltà di Filosofia e Lettere dell'Università di Pavia, 10).

Fontana, Carlo, 1634–1714

3626. Braham, Allan and Hager, Hellmut. *Carlo Fontana, the drawings at Windsor Castle.* London, Zwemmer, 1977. (Studies in architecture, 18).

3627. Coudenhove-Erthal, Eduard. *Carlo Fontana*

*und die Architektur des römischen Spät-
barocks.* Wien, Schroll, 1930.

3628. Fontana, Carolo. *Templum Vaticanum et
ipsius origo, cum aedificiis maxime con-
spicuis antiquitus & recens ibidem con-
stitutis.* Romae, Jo. Francisci Buagni, 1694.

Fontana, Domenico, 1543–1607

3629. Fontana, Domenico. *Della trasportatione
dell'obelisco Vaticano et delle fabriche di
Nostro Signore Papa Sisto V.* Roma,
Domenico Basa, 1590. Reprint: Milano,
Edizioni il Profilo, 1978.

3630. Munoz, Antonio. *Dominico Fontana,
architetto, 1543–1607.* Roma, Cremonese,
1944. (Quaderni Italo-Svizzeri, 3).

Fontana, Lavinia, 1552–1614

3631. Cantaro, Maria Teresa. *Lavinia Fontana
bolognese "pittora singulare,"* 1552–1614.
Milano, Jandi Sapi Editore, 1989.

3632. Galli, Romeo. *Lavinia Fontana, pittrice,
1552–1614.* Imola, Galeati, 1940.

Fontana, Lucio, 1899–1968

3633. Ballo, Guido. *Lucio Fontana.* New York,
Praeger, 1971.

3634. Castello Sforzesco (Milan). *Fontana, disegni;
opere donate alle collezioni civiche de Milano.* 19 maggio–31 luglio, 1977. Milano,
Electa, 1977.

3635. Crispolti, Enrico. *Carriera "barocca" di
Fontana, un saggio e alcune note.* Milano,
all'Insegna del Pesce d'Oro, 1963. (Fascicoli
del verri, 10).

3636. ———. *Fontana. Catalogo generale.* 2v.
Milano, Electa, 1986. (CR).

3637. ———. *Lucio Fontana: la scultura in
ceramica.* Milano, Electa, 1991.

3638. ———. *Lucio Fontana.* Saggio critico di
Enrico Crispolti. Lugano, Fidia, 1991.

3639. Fontana, Lucio. *Fontana e lo spazialismo*
[mostra]: 19 settembre–29 novembre 1987.
Villa Malpensata, Riva Caccia 5, Lugano.
Dicastero Musei e Cultura, Citta di Lugano.
Lugano, Edizioni Citta di Lugano, 1987.

3640. ———. *Lucio Fontana, 1899–1968.* [Cata-
logue]: Paris, Musée National d'Art
Moderne, Centre Georges Pompidou, 13
octobre 1987–11 Janvier, 1988. [Documen-
tation et iconographie Catherine Grenier,
Giovanni Joppolo, Giorgio Verzotti]. Paris,
Eitions du Centre Georges Pompidou, 1987.
(Also: Barcelona, Fundacio Caixa de Pensions, 8 de febrer–27 de març de 1988, with
a separate catalogue published by Fundacio
Caixa de Pensions, Barcelona, 1988, as well
as at Amsterdam, Stedelijk Museum, and
London, Whitechapel Art Gallery).

3641. Istituto Italo-Latino Americano (Rome). *L.*

Fontana. 1972, 2 marzo–15 aprile. Roma,
Istituto Italo-Latino Americano, 1972.

3642. Joppolo, Giovanni. *Lucio Fontana: "qui sait
comment est Dieu?":* biographie 1899–
1968. Marseille, Images en Manoeuvres,
1992.

3643. Marck, Jan van der, and Crispolti, Enrico.
Lucio Fontana. 2 v. Bruxelles, La Connaissance, 1974. (CR).

3644. Palazzo Pitti (Florence). *Fontana.* Aprile-
giugno 1980. Firenze, Vallecchi, 1980.

3645. Schulz-Hoffmann, Carla. *Lucio Fontana.*
Mit einem Beitrag von Cornelia Syre. München, Prestel-Verlag, 1983.

3646. Palazzo Reale (Milan). *La donazione Lucio
Fontana.* Proposta per una sistemazione
museografica. 28 novembre 1978–31 gennaio 1979. Milano, Multhipla Edizioni,
1978.

3647. Persico, Eduardo. *Lucio Fontana.* Milano,
Campo Grafico, 1936.

3648. Pica, Agnoldomenico. *Fontana.* Venezia,
Cavallino, 1953.

3649. Solomon R. Guggenheim Museum (New
York). *Lucio Fontana, 1899–1968; a retrospective.* New York, Guggenheim Foundation, 1977.

3650. Tapié, Michel. *Devenir de Fontana.* Torino,
Pozzo, 1961.

3651. Zocchi, Juan. *Lucio Fontana.* Buenos Aires,
Poseidon, 1946.

Fontanesi, Antonio, 1818–1882

3652. Bernardi, Marziano. *Antonio Fontanesi.*
Milano, Mondadori, 1933.

3653. ———. *Fontanesi.* Torino, RAI, 1968.

3654. Calderini, Marco. *Antonio Fontanesi,
pittore-paesista, 1818–1882.* Torino, Paravia, 1901.

3655. Carrà, Carlo. *Antonio Fontanesi.* Rome,
Valori Plastici, 1924.

3656. Carrà, Massimo. *Antonio Fontanesi.* Milano, Fabbri, 1966.

3657. Museo Nazionale d'Arte Moderna, Tokyo.
*Fontanesi, ragusa e l'arte giapponese nel
primo periodo Meiji.* 7 ott.–27 nov. 1977.
Tokyo, Museo Nazionale d'Arte Moderna,
1977.

Foppa, Vincenzo, 1428–1516

3658. Cipriani, Renata, et al. *La Cappella Portinari
in Sant'eustorgio a Milano.* Milano, Electa,
1963.

3659. Ffoulkes, Constance J. *Vincenzo Foppa of
Brescia, founder of the Lombard school; his
life and work.* London, Lane, 1909.

3660. Matalon, Stella. *Vincenzo Foppa.* Milano,
Fabbri, 1965. (I maestri del colore, 58).

3661. Rotondi, Pasquale. *Vincenzo Foppa in S.
Maria di Castello a Savona.* Genova [pri-

vately printed], 1958. (Quaderni della soprintendenza alle gallerie et opere d'arte della Liguria, 8).

3662. Wittgens, Fernanda. *Vincenzo Foppa.* Milano, Pizzi, [1948].

Forain, Jean Louis, 1852–1931

3663. Bibliothèque Nationale (Paris). *J.-L. Forain, peintre, dessinateur et graveur; exposition organisée pour le centenaire de sa naissance.* Juin–septembre 1952. Paris, Bibliothèque Nationale, 1952.

3664. Bory, Jean-François. *Forain [les dessin satiriques].* Paris, Veyrier, 1979.

3665. Browse, Lillian. *Forain, the painter; 1852–1931.* London, Elek, 1978.

3666. D. Caz-Delbo Galleries (New York). *Exhibition Forain; paintings, drawings, prints.* [Nov. 25–Dec. 25, 1931]. New York, Caz-Delbo Galleries, 1931.

3667. Danforth Museum (Framingham, Mass.). *Jean-Louis Forain, 1852–1931; works from New England Collections.* 14 Oct.–31 Nov., 1979. Framingham, Danforth Museum, 1979.

3668. Daudet, Alphonse. *Album de Forain.* Paris, Empis, 1893.

3669. Dodgson, Campbell. *Forain; draughtsman, lithographer, etcher.* New York, Knoedler, 1936.

3670. Faxon, Alicia Craig. *Jean-Louis Forain, a catalogue raisonné of the prints.* New York, Garland, 1982. (CR).

3671. Guérin, Marcel. *J.-L. Forain, aquafortiste; catalogue raisonné de l'oeuvre gravé de l'artiste.* 2 v. Paris, Floury, 1912. (CR). (Reprint: San Francisco, Alan Wofsy, 1980).

3672. ———. *J.-L. Forain, lithographe; catalogue raisonné de l'oeuvre lithographié de l'artiste.* Paris, Floury, 1910. (CR). (Reprint: San Francisco, Alan Wofsy, 1980).

3673. Museum of Fine Arts (Springfield, Mass.). *Jean-Louis Forain, 1852–1931.* April 15–May 20, 1956. Springfield, Museum of Fine Arts, 1956.

3674. Salaman, Malcolm C. *J. L. Forain.* London, The Studio, 1925. (Modern Masters of Etching, 4).

Forli, Melozzo da *see* Melozzo da Forli

Fortuny y Marsal, Mariano *see* Fortuny y Carbo, Mariano Jose Maria Bernardo

Fortuny y Carbo, Mariano José Maria Bernardo, 1838–1874

3675. Ciervo, Joaquin. *El arte y el vivir de Fortuny.* Barcelona, Bayes, n.d.

3676. Davillier, Jean C. *Fortuny, sa vie, son oeuvre, sa correspondance.* Paris, Aubry, 1875. (CR).

3677. Gil Fillol, Luis. *Mariano Fortuny: su vida, su obra, su arte.* Barcelona, Iberia, 1952.

3678. Gonzalez, Carlos (Gonzalez Lopez). *Mariano Fortuny Marsal.* Por Carlos Gonzalez Lopez y Montserrat, Marti Ayxela; prologo de Joan Ainaud de Lasarte. 2v. Barlelona, Diccionari Rafols, 1989. (CR).

3679. Pompey Salgueiro, Francisco. *Fortuny.* Madrid, Publicaciones Españolas, 1958. (Temas espanoles, 72).

3680. Yriarte, Charles E. *Fortuny.* Librairie d'Art, 1886. (Les artistes célèbres).

3681. Yxart y Morgas, José. *Fortuny; noticia biografica critica.* Barcelona, Arte y Letras, 1881.

Foujita, Tsugoharu, 1886–1974

3682. Bauer, Gerard. *Foujita, l'homme et le peintre.* Paris, Les Presses Artistiques, 1958.

3683. Buisson, Sylvie et Buisson, Dominique. *La vie et l'oeuvre de Leonard-Tsuguharu Foujita.* Paris, ACR Editions, 1987. (CR).

3684. George Walter Vincent Smith Art Gallery (Springfield, Mass.). *Modern French paintings and prints, also drawings and prints by M. Foujita Tsugoharu.* Springfield, Mass., George Walter Vincent Smith Art Gallery, 1931.

3685. Morand, Paul. *Foujita, avec des souvenirs d'enfance de l'artiste et un commentaire par Charles-Albert Cingria.* Paris, Chroniques du Jour, 1928.

3686. Tanaka, Jo. *Hyoden Fujita Tsuguharu.* Tokyo, Geijutsu Shinbunsha, 1988.

3687. Vaucaire, Michel-Gabriel. *Foujita.* Paris, Crès, 1924.

Fouquet, Jean, 1415–1480

3688. Bazin, Germain. *Fouquet.* Genève, Skira, 1942. (Les trésors de la peinture française, Tome I, 4).

3689. Castelnuovo, E. *Jean Fouquet.* Milano, Fabbri, 1966. (I maestri del colore, 168).

3690. Cox, Trenchard. *Jehan Foucquet, native of Tours.* London, Faber, 1931.

3691. Deutsch, Guy N. *Iconographie de l'Illustration de Flavius Josephe au temps de Jean Fouquet.* Leiden, Brill, 1986.

3692. Durrieu, Paul. *Les antiquités judaïques et le peintre Jean Fouquet.* Paris, Plon, 1908.

3693. ———. *Livre d'heures peint par Jean Fouquet pour maître Etienne Chevalier.* Paris, La Société Française, 1923.

3694. Fouquet, Jehan. *Jean Fouquet: die Bilder der Grandes Chroniques de France:* mit der originalen Wiedergabe aller 51 Miniaturen von Manuscrit français 6465 der Bibliothèque Nationale in Paris. Beiträge von Françoise Avril, Marie-Therèse Gousset, Bernard Guenée. Graz, Austria, Akademische Druck- und Verlagsanstalt, 1987.

3695. Fouquet, Jehan. *Oeuvre*. 2 v. Paris, Curmer, 1866–1867.

3696. Gruyer, François Anatole. *Chantilly, les quarante Fouquet*. Paris, Plon, 1897.

3697. Heywood, Florence. *The Life of Christ and his Mother according to Jean Fouquet*. London, Methuen, 1927.

3698. Lafenestre, Georges. *Jehan Fouquet*. Paris, Baranger, 1905.

3699. Melet-Sanson, J. *Fouquet*. Paris, Scrépel, 1977.

3700. Perls, Klaus G. *Jean Fouquet*. London/Paris/New York, Hyperion, 1940.

3701. Sterling, Charles and Schaefer, Claude. *The hours of Etienne Chevalier [by] Jean Fouquet*. New York, Braziller, 1971.

3702. Thompson, Henry Y. *Facsimiles of two "Histoires" by Jean Foucquet from Vols. I and II of the Anciennetés des Juifs . . . to which is added a notice with two photographs and four three-colour photographs*. [Notes by Henry Yates Thompson]. London, Chiswick Press, 1903.

3703. Wescher, Paul. *Jean Fouquet and his time*. Trans. E. Winkworth. [London], Pleiades, 1947.

Fra Angelico *see* **Angelico, Fra**

Fragonard, Jean Honoré, 1732–1806

3704. Ananoff, Alexandre. *L'oeuvre dessiné de Jean-Honoré Fragonard (1732–1806)*. 4 v. Paris, de Nobele, 1961–70. (CR).

3705. Ashton, Dore. *Fragonard in the universe of painting*. Washington, Smithsonian Institution Press, 1988.

3706. Cabanne, Pierre. *Fragonard*. Paris, Somogy, 1987.

3707. Cuzin, Jean Pierre. *Jean-Honoré Fragonard, vie et oeuvre: catalogue complet des peintures*. Fribourg, Office du Livre, 1987. (CR). (English ed.: New York: Abrams, 1988).

3708. Feuillet, Maurice. *Les dessins d'Honoré Fragonard et de Hubert Robert des Bibliothèque et Musée de Besançon*. Paris, Delteil, 1926. (Les plus beaux dessins des musées de France, 1).

3709. Fragonard, Jean-Honoré. *J.H. Fragonard e H. Robert a Roma:* [mostra] Villa Medici, 6 dicembre 1990– 24 febbraio 1991. Roma Palombi: Edizioni Caerte Segrete, 1990.

3710. Galeries Nationales du Petit Palais (Paris). *Fragonard et le dessin français au XVIIIe siècle dans les collections du Petit Palais*. [Catalogue of the exhibition held at the Petit Palais, October 1992–February, 1993]. Paris, Editions Paris-Musées, 1992

3711. Grappe, Georges. *H. Fragonard, peintre de l'amour au XVIIIe siècle*. 2 v. Paris, Piazza, 1913.

3712. ———. *La vie et l'oeuvre de J.-H. Frago-nard*. Paris, Les Editions Pittoresques, 1929.

3713. Guimbaud, Louis. *Fragonard*. Paris, Plon, 1947.

3714. ———. *Saint-Non et Fragonard, d'après des documents inédits*. Paris, Goupy, 1928.

3715. Josz, Virgile. *Fragonard*. Paris, Société du Mercure de France, 1901.

3716. Kahn, Gustave. *Jean Honoré Fragonard*. Paris, Librairie Internationale, 1907.

3717. Leveque, Jean Jacques. *La vie et l'oeuvre de Jean-Honoré Fragonard*. Paris, ACR, 1987.

3718. Mandel, Gabriele. *L'opera completa di Fragonard*. Milano, Rizzoli, 1972. (Classici dell'arte, 62).

3719. Massengale, Jean Montague. *Jean-Honoré Fragonard*. New York, H.N. Abrams, 1993.

3720. Mauclair, Camille. *Fragonard, biographie critique*. Paris, Laurens, 1904.

3721. Mongan, Elizabeth, et al. *Fragonard, drawings for Ariosto*. Published for the National Gallery of Art, Washington, D.C. [and] the Harvard College Library, Cambridge, Mass., New York, Pantheon, 1945.

3722. Musée des Arts Décoratifs (Paris). *Exposition d'oeuvres de J.-H. Fragonard*. 7 juin–10 juillet 1921. Paris, Musée des Arts Décoratifs, 1921.

3723. Naquet, Félix. *Fragonard*. Paris, Librairie de l'Art, 1890.

3724. National Museum of Western Art (Tokyo). *Fragonard*. 18 March–11 May 1980. Tokyo, National Museum of Western Art, 1980.

3725. Noldac, Pierre de. *J.-H. Fragonard, 1732–1806*. Paris, Goupil, 1906.

3726. Portalis, Roger. *Honoré Fragonard, sa vie et son oeuvre*. 2 v. Paris, Rothschild, 1889.

3727. Réau, Louis. *Fragonard*. Paris, Skira, 1938. (Les trésors de la peinture française).

3728. ———. *Fragonard, sa vie et son oeuvre*. Bruxelles, Elsevier, 1956.

3729. Rosenberg, Pierre. *Fragonard*. [Published in conjunction with the exhibition "Fragonard," held at the Galeries Nationales du Grand Palais, Paris, September 24, 1987–January 4, 1988, and at the Metropolitan Museum of Art, New York, February 2–May 8, 1988]. New York, The Metropolitan Museum of Art, 1988.

3730. Sheriff, Mary D. *Fragonard: art and eroticism*. Chicago, University of Chicago Press, 1990.

3731. Sollers, Philippe. *Les surprises de Fragonard*. Paris, Gallimard, 1987.

3732. Thuillier, Jacques. *Fragonard*. Geneva, Skira, 1967; dist. by Cleveland, World. (The Taste of Our Time, 46). (Reprint: New York, Rizzoli, 1987).

3733. Traz, Georges de. *Les dessins de Fragonard*. Paris, Perret, 1954.

3734. Wakefield, David. *Fragonard*. London, Oresko, 1976.

3735. Wildenstein, Georges. *The paintings of Fragonard, complete edition*. London, Phaidon, 1960.

3736. Williams, Eunice. *Drawings by Fragonard in North American collections*. [National Gallery of Art, Washington; Nov. 19, 1978–Jan. 21, 1979]. Washington, D.C., National Gallery of Art, 1978.

Francesca, Piero della, 1416–1492

3737. Alazard, Jean. *Piero della Francesca*. Paris, Plon, 1948.

3738. Battisti, Eugenio. *Piero della Francesca*. 2 v. Milano, Istituto Editoriale Italiano, 1971.

3739. Bertelli, Carlo. *Piero della Francesca: la forza divina della pittura*. [Cinisello Balsamo], Silvana, 1991.

3740. Berenson, Bernard. *Piero della Francesca or the ineloquent in art*. London, Chapman & Hall, 1954.

3741. Bianconi, Piero. *All the paintings of Piero della Francesca*. New York, Hawthorne, 1962. (Complete Library of World Art, 5).

3742. Borra, Pompeo. *Piero della Francesca*. Milano, Istituto Editoriale Italiano, 1950.

3743. Brilli, Attilio. *In search of Piero: a guide to the Tuscany of Piero della Francesca*. [Translation, Deborah Hodges]. Milano, Electa, 1990. (Italian ed.: Milano, Electa, 1991).

3744. Buono, O. del and Vecchi, P. de. *L'opera completa di Piero della Francesca*. Milano, Rizzoli, 1967. (Classici dell'arte, 9).

3745. Chiasserini, Vera. *La pittura a Sansepolcro e nell'alta valle Tiberina, primo di Piero della Francesca*. Firenze, Olschki, 1951. (Collana di monografie storiche e artistiche Altotiberine, 1).

3746. Clark, Kenneth. *Piero della Francesca, complete edition*. London/New York, Phaidon, 1969.

3747. Cole, Bruce. *Piero della Francesca: tradition and innovation in Renaissance art*. New York, Icon Editions, 1991.

3748. Cook, Albert Spaulding. *Temporalizing space: the triumphant strategies of Piero della Francesca*. New York, P. Lang, 1992.

3749. Davis, Margaret D. *Piero della Francesca's mathematical treatises, the Trattato d'abaco and Libellus de quinque corporibus regularibus*. Ravenna, Longo, 1977.

3750. Focillon, Henri. *Piero della Francesca*. Paris, Colin, 1952.

3751. Formaggio, Dino. *Piero della Francesca*. Milano, Mondadori, 1957. (Biblioteca moderna Mondadori, 492).

3752. Francesca, Piero della. *Piero della Francesca e il Novecento: prospettiva, spazio, luce, geometria, pittura murale, tonalismo, 1920–1983*. A cura di Maria Mimita Lamberti e Maurizio Fagiolo dell'Arco. Venezia, Marsilio, 1991.

3753. ———. *Piero teoretico dell'arte*. A cura di Omar Calabrese; scritti di H. Damisch . . . [et al.]. Roma, Gangemi, 1985. (Semiosis; collana di studi semiotici, 1).

3754. ———. *De prospectiva pingendi*. A cura di Nico Fasola. 2 v. Firenze, Sansoni, 1942. (Raccolta di fonti per la storia dell'arte, 5).

3755. ———. *Trattato d'abaco*. Pisa, Domus Galilaeana, 1970. (Testimonianze di storia della cienza, 6).

3756. Gilbert, Creighton. *Change in Piero della Francesca*. Locust Valley, N.Y., Augustin, 1968.

3757. Ginzburg, Carlo. *The enigma of Piero: Piero della Francesca: The baptism, The Arezzo cycle, The flagellation*. C. Ginzburg; with an introduction by Peter Burke; translated by Martin Ryle and Kate Soper. London, Verso, 1985.

3758. Graber, Hans. *Piero della Francesca, achtundsechzig Tafeln mit einführendem Text*. Basel, Schwabe, 1922.

3759. Guillaud, Jacqueline. *Piero della Francesca, poet of form: the frescoes of San Francesco di Arezzo; by J. and Maurice Guillaud*. New York, C.N. Potter; Paris/New York, Guillaud, 1988.

3760. Hendy, Philip. *Piero della Francesca and the early Renaissance*. New York, Macmillan, 1968.

3761. Jahnsen, Angeli. *Perspektivregeln und Bildgestaltung bei Piero della Francesca*. München, W. Fink, 1990.

3762. Lightbown, Ronald W. *Piero della Francesca*. New York, Abbeville Press, 1992.

3763. Longhi, Roberto. *Piero della Francesca, 1927, con aggiunte fino al 1962*. Firenze, Sansoni, 1963. (English ed.: New York/London, Warne, 1930).

3764. Paolucci, Antonio. *Piero della Francesca: catalogo completo*. Firenze, Cantini, 1989. (CR).

3765. ———. *Piero della Francesca. Notizie sulla conservazione*. di Margherita Moriondo Lenzini. Firenze, Cantini, 1989.

3766. Pichi, Giovanni F. *La vita e le opere di Piero della Francesca*. Sansepolcro, Becamorti, 1892.

3767. Pope-Hennessy, John. *The Piero della Francesca trail*. London, Thames and Hudson, 1992. (23rd of the Walter Neurath memorial lectures).

3768. Previtali, Giovanni. *Piero della Francesca*. Milano, Fabbri, 1965. (I maestri del colore, 89).

3769. Ricci, Corrado. *Piero della Francesca*. Roma, Anderson, 1910. (L'opera dei grande artisti italiani, 1).

3770. Salmi, Mario. *La pittura di Piero della Francesca*. Novara, Istituto Geografico de Agostini, 1979.

F

3771. Venturi, Adolfo. *Piero della Francesca.* Firenze, Alinari, 1922.
3772. Venturi, Lionello. *Piero della Francesca.* Geneva, Skira, 1954. (The Taste of Our Time, 6).
3773. Vita, Alessandro del. *Piero della Francesca.* Firenze, Alinari, 1921. (Piccola collezione d'arte, 20).
3774. Waters, William George. *Piero della Francesca.* London, Bell, 1901.
3775. Witting, Felix. *Piero dei Franceschi, eine kunsthistorische Studie.* Strassburg, Heitz, 1898.

Franceschi, Piero dei *see* **Francesca, Piero della**

Francesco di Giorgio Martini, 1439–1502
3776. Brinton, Selwyn. *Francesco di Giorgio Martini of Siena, painter, sculptor, engineer, civil and military architect (1439–1502).* London, Besant, 1934.
3777. Ericsson, Christoffer H. *Roman architecture expressed in sketches by Francesco di Giorgio Martini.* Helsinki, Societas Scientiarum Fennica, 1980. (Commentationes Humanorum Litterarum, 66).
3778. Fiore, F. Paolo. *Città e macchine del '400 nei disegni di Francesco di Giorgio Martini.* Firenze, Olschki, 1978.
3779. Francesco di Giorgio Martini. *La praticha di gieometria dal Codice Ashburnham 361 della Biblioteca Medicea Laurenziana di Firenze.* Firenze, Giunti, 1970. (Istituto italiano per la storia della tecnica, Sez. 1, Vol. 1).
3780. ———. *Trattati di architettura ingegneria e arte militare.* 2 v. Milano, Il Polifilo, 1967.
3781. ———. *Il Trattato di Francesco di Giorgio Martini e Leonardo: il Codice Estense restituito.* Massimo Mussini. Parma, Universita di Parma. Istituto di storia dell'arte, 1991.
3782. ———. Das Skizzenbuch des Francesco di Giorgio Martini.[facsim. of Vat.Urb.Cod. lat. 1757]. Einführung von Luigi Michelini Tocci; [aus dem Italienischen von Katherina Dobai]. 2 v. Zürich, Belser, 1989 (Codices Vaticanis selecti; vol. 80).
3783. Pantanelli, Antonio. *Di Francesco di Giorgio Martini, pittore, scultore e architetto Senese del secolo XV e dell'arte de' suoi tempi in Siena.* Siena, Gati, 1870.
3784. Papini, Roberto. *Francesco di Giorgio, architetto.* 3 v. Firenze, Electa, 1946.
3785. Promis, Carlo. *Vita di Francesco di Giorgio Martini.* Torino, Chirio e Mina, 1841.
3786. Salmi, Mario. *Disegni di Francesco di Giorgio nella collezione Chigi Saracini.* Siena, Ticci, 1947. (Quaderni dell'accademia Chigiana, 11).
3787. Toledano, Ralph. *Francesco di Giorgio Martini, pittore e scultore.* Milano, Electa, 1987.
3788. Weller, Allen S. *Francesco di Giorgio, 1439–1501.* Chicago, University of Chicago Press, 1943.

Francesco di Stefano *see* **Pesellino**

Francia, 1450–1518
3789. Calvi, Jacopo A. *Memorie della vita, e delle opere di Francesco Raibolini detto Il Francia, pittore Bolognese.* Bologna, Lucchesini, 1812.
3790. Cartwright, Julia. *Mantegna and Francia.* New York, Scribner and Welford, 1881.
3791. Lipparini, Giuseppe. *Francesco Francia.* Bergamo, Istituto italiano d'arti grafiche, 1913. (Collezione di monografie illustrate, Serie: Pittori, scultori, architetti, 9).
3792. Malaguzzi-Valeri, Francesco. *Il Francia.* Firenze, Alinari, 1921. (Piccola collezione d'arte, 23).
3793. Williamson, George C. *Francesco Raibolino, called Francia.* London, Bell, 1901.

Francis, Sam, 1923–
3794. Albright-Knox Art Gallery (Buffalo, N.Y.). *Sam Francis, paintings, 1947–1972.* Buffalo, Buffalo Fine Arts Academy, 1972.
3795. Francis, Sam. *Sam Francis, etchings, 1973–1985.* Bern, Galerie Kornfeld, 1985.
3796. Klipstein & Kornfeld (Berne). *Sam Francis Ausstellung. 25. September bis 5. November 1957.* Bern, Klipstein & Kornfeld, 1957.
3797. Lembark, Connie W. *The prints of Sam Francis: a catalogue raisonné, 1960–1990.* Introd. by Ruth E. Fine. New York, Hudson Hills Press; distributed in the U.S. by Rizzoli International Publications, 1992. (CR).
3798. Los Angeles County Museum of Art. *Sam Francis.* March 13–May 11, 1980. Los Angeles, Los Angeles County Museum of Art, 1980.
3799. Selz, Peter. *Sam Francis.* New York, Abrams, 1975; rev. ed., 1982.
3800. Waldberg, Michel. *Sam Francis: metaphysics of the void.* Paris, Moos Book Publishing, 1987.

Francke, Meister, 15th c.
3801. Kunsthalle Hamburg. *Meister Francke und die Kunst um 1400. 30. Aug.–19. Okt. 1969.* Hamburg, Kunsthalle, 1969.
3802. Lichtwark, Alfred. *Meister Francke, 1424.* Hamburg, Kunsthalle zu Hamburg, 1899.
3803. Martens, Bella. *Meister Francke.* 2 v. Hamburg, Friederichsen, 1929.

Francken, Frans (the elder), 1542–1616
Francken, Frans (the younger), 1581–1642
3804. Härting, Ursula. Hans Francken der Jüngere

(1581–1642) die Gemälde mit kritischem Oeuvrekatalog. Freren, Luca Verlag, 1989. (CR). (Flämische Maler im Umkreis der grossen Meister, 2).

Frank, Robert, 1924–

3805. Frank, Robert. *The Americans.* Introd. by Jack Kerouac. New York, Grossman, 1969. 2 ed.

3806. ———. *The lines of my hand.* Los Angeles, Lustrum, 1972.

3807. ———. *Robert Frank.* Millerton, N.Y., Aperture, 1976. (History of photography, 2).

Frankenthaler, Helen, 1928–

3808. Carmean, E.A. *Helen Frankenthaler, a paintings retrospective.* New York, Abrams; in association with the Modern Art Museum of Fort Worth, 1989.

3809. Corcoran Gallery of Art (Washington, D.C.). *Helen Frankenthaler: paintings, 1969–1974.* April 20–June 1, 1975. Washington, D.C., Corcoran Gallery of Art, 1975.

3810. Elderfield, John. *Frankenthaler.* New York, Abrams, 1989.

3811. Krens, Thomas. *Helen Frankenthaler, prints, 1961–1979.* [Catalogue of an exhibition, Sterling and Francine Clark Art Institute, Williamstown, Mass., April 11–May 11, 1980]. New York, Harper & Row, 1980. (CR).

3812. Rose, Barbara. *Frankenthaler.* New York, Abrams, 1972.

3813. Rose Art Museum, Brandeis University (Waltham, Mass.). *Frankenthaler: the 1950's.* May 10–June 28, 1981. Waltham, Mass., Rose Art Museum, 1981.

3814. Whitney Museum of American Art (New York). *Helen Frankenthaler.* February 20–April 6, 1969. New York, Whitney Museum of American Art, 1969. ·

3815. Wilkin, Karen. *Frankenthaler: works on paper, 1949–1984.* New York, G. Braziller; International Exhibitions Foundation, 1984.

Fredi Bartolo di *see* Bartolo di Fredi

French, Daniel Chester, 1850–1931

3816. Adams, Adeline. *Daniel Chester French, sculptor.* Boston, Houghton Mifflin, 1932.

3817. Cresson, Margaret French. *Daniel Chester French.* New York, Norton, 1947. (American Sculptor Series, 4).

3818. ———. *Journey into fame, the life of Daniel Chester French.* Cambridge, Mass., Harvard University Press, 1947.

3819. French, Mrs. Daniel Chester. *Memories of a sculptor's wife.* Boston, Houghton Mifflin, 1928.

3820. Richman, Michael. *Daniel Chester French, an American sculptor.* [Catalogue of an exhibition, Nov. 4, 1976–Jan. 10, 1977]. New York, Metropolitan Museum of Art, 1976.

Freud, Lucian, 1921–

3821. Freud, Lucian. *Lucian Freud: dipinti e opere su carta 1940–1991.* [Exhibition]. Rome, Plazzo Ruspoli, 1991.

3822. ———. *Lucian Freud: works of art on paper.* London, Thames and Hudson. 1988.

3823. Gowing, Lawrence. *Lucian Freud.* New York, Thames and Hudson, 1982.

3824. Hughes, Robert. *Lucian Freud: paintings.* New York, Thames and Hudson, 1987.

3825. Lampert, Catherine. *Lucian Freud, recent work.* New York, Rizzoli, 1993.

Friedlander, Lee, 1934–

3826. Friedlander, Lee. *The American monument.* New York, Eakins, 1976.

3827. ———. *Lee Friedlander.* Introduction by Loic Malle. New York, Pantheon Books; Paris, Centre National de la Photographie, 1988.

3828. ———. *Photographs.* New City, N.Y., Haywire, 1978.

3829. ———. *Portraits.* Foreword by R.B. Kitaj. Boston, Little Brown, 1985.

3830. ———. *Self-portrait.* New City, N.Y., Haywire, 1970.

Friedrich, Caspar David, 1774–1840

3831. Aubert, Andreas. *Caspar David Friedrich: Gott, Freiheit, Vaterland.* Berlin, Cassirer, 1915.

3832. Bauer, Franz. *Caspar David Friedrich, ein Maler der Romantik.* Stuttgart, Schuler, 1961.

3833. Börsch-Supan, Helmut. *Caspar David Friedrich.* 1st ed.: München, Prestel, 1973. (1st English ed.: New York, Braziller, 1974; 2nd.English ed. based on the 4th ed. and rev. German edition: München, Prestel; New York, Distributed in the US and Canada by te Neues Publications, 1990).

3834. ———. *Caspar David Friedrich; Gemälde, Druckgraphik und bildmässige Zeichnungen.* München, Prestel, 1973.

3835. ———. *L'opera completa di Friedrich.* Milano, Rizzoli, 1976. (Classici dell'arte, 84).

3836. Eimer, Gerhard. *Caspar David Friedrich und die Gotik.* Hamburg, von der Ropp, 1963.

3837. Einem, Herbert von. *Caspar David Friedrich.* Berlin, Rembrandt, 1938.

3838. Emmrich, Irma. *Caspar David Friedrich.* Weimar, Böhlau, 1964.

3839. Fiege, Gertrud. *Caspar David Friedrich in Selbstzeugnissen und Bilddokumenten.* Hamburg, Rowohlt, 1977. (Rowohlts Monographien, 252).

3840. Friedrich, Caspar David. *Caspar David Friedrich: line and transparency.* [Exhibition]. Paris, Centre Culturel du Marais, 1984.

3841. ———.*The romantic vision of Caspar David Friedrich*: paintings and drawings from the U.S.S.R.. Essays by Robert Rosenblum and Boris I. Asvarishch; edited by Sabine Rewald. New York, Metropolitan Museum of Art/ Art Institute of Chicago. New York, Distributed by H.N. Abrams, 1990.

3842. Gärtner, Hannelore, ed. *Caspar David Friedrich; Leben, Werk, Diskussion.* Berlin, Union, 1977.

3843. Geismeier, Willi. *Caspar David Friedrich.* Wien/München, Schroll, 1975.

3844. Grote, Ludwig. *Caspar David Friedrich, Skizzenbuch aus den Jahren 1806 und 1818.* Berlin, Mann, 1942.

3845. Guillaud, Maurice. *Caspar David Friedrich: Paysage au temps de l'oubli/Landscape from the time of forgetting.* With an essay by William Vaughan. Paris/New York, Guillaud Editions, 1991.

3846. Hamburger Kunsthalle. *Caspar David Friedrich, 1774–1840.* 14. September bis 3. November 1974. München, Prestel, 1974.

3847. Hinz, Berthold, et al. *Bürgerliche Revolution und Romantik; Natur und Gesellschaft bei Caspar David Friedrich.* Giessen, Anabas, 1976. (Kunstwissenschaftliche Untersuchungen des Ulmer Vereins, Verband für Kunst und Kulturwissenschaften, 6).

3848. Hofmann, Werner, ed. *Caspar David Friedrich und die deutsche Nachwelt.* Frankfurt a.M., Suhrkamp, 1974.

3849. Hofstätter, Hans H. *Caspar David Friedrich, das gesamte graphische Werk.* Herrsching, Pawlak, 1982. 2 ed. (CR).

3850. Koerner, Joseph Leo. *Caspar David Friedrich and the subject of landscape.* London, Reaktion Books, 1990.

3851. Leighton, John. *Caspar David Friedrich: Winter landscape.* [Exhibition]. The National Gallery, London, 28 March–28 May, 1990.[Catalogue by] John Leighton and Colin J. Bailey. London, National Gallery Publications, 1990.

3852. Leonhardi, Klaus. *Die romantische Landschaftsmalerei: Caspar David Friedrich.* Würzburg, Mayr, 1936.

3853. Monrad, Kasper. *Caspar David Friedrich og Danmark/ Caspar David Friedrich und Dänemark.* [Exhibition]. Statens Museum for Kunst, 12 Oktober–8 December 1991; aft Kasper Monrad og Colin J. Bailey. København, Statensmuseum for Kunst, 1991.

3854. National Museum for Modern Art (Tokyo). *Caspar David Friedrich and his circle.* February 11–April 2, 1978. Tokyo, National Museum for Modern Art, 1978.

3855. Nemitz, Fritz. *Caspar David Friedrich. Die unendliche Landschaft.* München, Bruckmann, 1938.

3856. Prybram-Gladona, Charlotte Margarethe de. *Caspar David Friedrich.* Paris, Les Editions d'Art et d'Histoire, 1942.

3857. Rautmann, Peter. *Caspar David Friedrich, Landschaft als Sinnbild entfalteter bürgerlicher Wirklichkeitsaneignung.* Frankfurt a.M./Bern/Las Vegas, Lang, 1979. (Kunstwissenschaftliche Studien, 7).

3858. Richter, Gottfried. *Caspar David Friedrich, der Maler der Erdenfrömmigkeit.* Stuttgart, Urachhaus, 1953.

3859. Sala, Charles. *Caspar David Friedrich et la peinture romantique.* Paris, Terrail, 1993.

3860. Schmied, Wieland. *Caspar David Friedrich.* Köln, DuMont Schauberg, 1975.

3861. Sigismund, Ernst. *Caspar David Friedrich: eine Umrisszeichnung.* Dresden, Jess, 1943.

3862. Städtische Kunsthalle Mannheim. *Caspar David Friedrich in seiner Zeit: Zeichnungen der Romantik und des Biedermeier;* bearbeitet von Hans Dickel. Weinheim, VCH, Acta Humaniora, 1991. (Die Zeichnungen und Aquarelle des 19. Jahrhunderts der Kunsthalle Mannheim, Bd.3).

3863. Sumowski, Werner. *Caspar David Friedrich-Studien.* Weisbaden, Steiner, 1970.

3864. Tassi, Roberto. *Caspar David Friedrich.* Milano, Fabbri, 1966. (I maestri del colore, 195).

3865. Tate Gallery (London). *Caspar David Friedrich, 1774–1840. Romantic landscape painting in Dresden.* [6 September–16 October, 1972]. London, Tate Gallery, 1972.

3866. Wolfradt, Willi. *Caspar David Friedrich und die Landschaft der Romantik.* Berlin, Mauritius, 1924.

Fries, Hans, 1465–1523?

3867. Kelterborn-Haemmerli, Anna. *Die Kunst des Hans Fries.* Strassburg, Heitz, 1927. (Studien zur deutschen Kunstgeschichte, 245).

Frith, William Powell, 1819–1903

3868. Frith, William P. *My autobiography and reminiscences.* 2 v. New York, Harper, 1888.

3869. Noakes, Aubrey. *William Frith, extraordinary Victorian painter; a biography & critical essay.* London, Jupiter, 1978.

Friesz, Othon, 1879–1949

3870. Fleuret, Fernand, et al. *Friesz, oeuvres (1901–1927).* Paris, Editions des Chroniques du Jour, 1928. (Les maîtres nouveaux, 1).

3871. Galerie Charpentier (Paris). *Rétrospective Othon Friesz.* Paris, Galerie Charpentier, 1950.

3872. Gauthier, Maximilien. *Othon Friesz.* Genève, Cailler, 1957.

3873. Salmon, André and Aubert, Georges. *Emile-*

Othon Friesz. Paris, La Nouvelle Revue Française, 1920. (Les peintres français nouveaux, 5).

Froment, Nicolas, ca. 1435–ca. 1484

3874. Chamson, Lucie. *Nicolas Froment et l'école Avignonaise au XVe siècle.* Paris, Rieder, 1931. (Maîtres de l'art ancien, 18).

3875. Marignane, M. *Nicolas Froment.* Paris, Morancé, 1955.

Fromentin, Eugène, 1820–1876

3876. Association des Artistes, Peintres, Sculpteurs, Architectes, Graveurs et Dessinateurs. *Exposition des oeuvres de Eugène Fromentin à l'Ecole National des Beaux Arts.* Paris, Claye, 1877.

3877. Beaume, Georges. *Fromentin.* Paris, Louis-Michaud, 1911.

3878. Bibliothèque Municipale (La Rochelle). *Fromentin, le peintre et l'écrivain, 1820–1876.* La Rochelle, Bibliothèque Municipale, 1970.

3879. Christin, Anne-Marie. *Fromentin, conteur d'espace: essai sur l'oeuvre algerienne.* Paris, Sycomore, 1982

3880. Dorbec, Prosper. *Eugène Fromentin, biographie critique.* Paris, Laurens, 1926.

3881. Fromentin, Eugène. *Correspondance et fragments inédits.* Paris, Plon, 1912.

3882. ———. *Dominique/Eugene Fromentin* [Correspondence]; texte presenté et commenté par Anne-Marie Christin; illustrations d'Etienne Lodeho. Paris, Imprimerie nationale, 1988.

3883. ———. *Lettres de jeunesse.* Paris, Plon, 1909.

3884. ———. *The masters of past time; Dutch & Flemish painting from van Eyck to Rembrandt.* London, Phaidon, 1960.

3885. Gonse, M. Louis. *Eugène Fromentin, painter and writer.* Boston, Osgood, 1883.

3886. Lafouge, Jean-pierre. *Etude sur l'orientalisme d'Eugène Fromentin dans ses "récits algériens".* New York, P. Lang, 1988.

3887. Lagrange, Andrée. *L'art de Fromentin.* Paris, Dervy, 1952.

3888. Marcos, Fouad. *Fromentin et l'Afrique.* Sherbrooke, Québec, Editions Cosmos, 1973.

Fuchs, Ernst, 1930–

3889. Fuchs, Ernst. *Architectura Caelestis, die Bilder des verschollenen Stils.* Salzburg, Residenz, 1966.

3890. ——— and Brion, Marcel. *Ernst Fuchs.* New York, Abrams, 1979.

3891. ——— and Hartmann, Richard P. *Ernst Fuchs, das graphische Werk, 1967–1980.* München/Zürich, Piper, 1980. (Klassiker der Neuzeit, 4). (CR).

3892. ——— and Hartmann, Richard P. *Der Feuerfuchs.* Frankfurt am Main, Umschau Verlag, 1988.

3893. Weis, Helmut. *Ernst Fuchs, das graphische Werk.* Wien/München, Verlag für Jugend und Volk, 1967. (CR).

Fuessli, Johann Heinrich see Fuseli, Henry

Fuga, Ferdinando, 1699–1781

3894. Bianchi, Lidia. *Disegni di Ferdinando Fuga e di altri architetti del settecento.* Roma, Gabinetto Nazionale delle Stampe, 1955.

3895. Matthiae, Guglielmo. *Ferdinando Fuga e la sua opera Romana.* Roma, Palombi, 1952.

3896. Pane, Roberto. *Ferdinando Fuga.* Napoli, Scientifiche Italiane, 1956.

Fuller, Richard Buckminster, 1895–1983

3897. Edmondson, Amy C. *A Fuller explanation: the synergetic geometry of R. Buckminster Fuller.* Boston, Birkhäuser, 1987.

3898. Fuller, R. Buckminster. *The artifacts of R. Buckminster Fuller: a comprehensive collection of hsi designs and drawings; edited with descriptions by james wrd.* New York, Garland, 1985.

3899. ———. *Ideas & integrities, a spontaneous autobiographical disclosure.* Englewood Cliffs, N.J., Prentice-Hall, 1963.

3900. Grimaldi, Roberto. *R. Buckminster Fuller, 1895–1983.* Roma, Officina Edizioni, 1990.

3901. Hatch, Alden. *Buckminster Fuller at home in the universe.* New York, Crown, 1974.

3902. Kenner, Hugh. *Bucky, a guided tour of Buckminster Fuller.* New York, Morrow, 1973.

3903. Marks, Robert W. *The Dymaxion world of Buckminster Fuller.* New York, Reinhold, 1960.

3904. McHale, John. *R. Buckminster Fuller.* New York, Braziller, 1962.

3905. Robertson, Donald W. *Mind's eye of Richard Buckminster Fuller.* New York, Vantage, 1974.

3906. Rose Art Museum, Brandeis University (Waltham, Mass.). *Two urbanists; the engineering-architecture of R. Buckminster Fuller and Paolo Soleri.* December 21, 1964–January 17, 1965. Waltham, Mass., Rose Art Museum, 1964.

3907. Sieden, Lloyd Steven. *Buckminster Fuller's universe.: an appreciation.* Foreword by Norman Cousins. New York, Plenum Press, 1989.

Fungai, Bernardino, 1460–1516

3908. Bacci, Pèleo. *Bernardino Fungai, pittore Senese (1460–1516).* Siena, Lazzeri, 1947.

Furini, Francesco, 1604–1646

3909. Cantelli, Giuseppe. *Disegni di Francesco*

Furini e del suo ambiente. Firenze, Olschki, 1972. (Gabinetto disegni e stampe degli Uffizi, 36).

3910. Toesca, Elena. *Francesco Furini.* Roma, Tumminelli, 1950. (Quaderni d'arte, 11).

Fuseli, Henry (Heinrich Füssli), 1741–1825
see also Barry, James

3911. Antal, Frederick. *Fuseli studies.* London, Routledge & Kegan Paul, 1956.

3912. Federmann, Arnold. *Johann Heinrich Füssli, Dichter und Maler, 1741–1825.* Zürich/Leipzig, Orell Füssli, 1927.

3913. Füssli, Heinrich. *Aphorismen über die Kunst.* Klosterberg/Basel, Schwabe, 1944.

3914. ———. *Briefe.* Klosterberg/Basel, Schwabe, 1942.

3915. ———. *The collected English letters of Henry Fuseli,* edited by David H. Weiun-glass. Millwood, N.Y., Kraus International, 1982.

3916. ———. *Füssli e Dante.* [catalogo]. A cura di Corrado Gizzi. Milano, Mazzotta, 1985.

3917. ———. *Johann Heinrich Füssli: Zeichnunen.* Zürich, Kunsthaus Zürich, 1986. (Kunsthaus Zürich Sammlungsheft, 12).

3918. ———. *Lectures on painting delivered at the Royal Academy.* London, Colburn and Bentley, 1830.

3919. Ganz, Paul. *Die Zeichungen Hans Heinrich Füsslis (Henry Fuseli).* Bern, Urs, 1947. (English ed.: London, Parrish, 1949).

3920. Hamburger Kunsthalle. *Johann Heinrich Füssli, 1741–1825.* 4. Dez. 1974 bis 19. Jan. 1975. München, Prestel, 1974.

3921. Jaloux, Edmond. *Johann-Heinrich Füssli.* Genève, Cailler, 1942.

3922. Knowles, John. *The life and writings of Henry Fuseli.* 3 v. London, Colburn and Bentley, 1831.

3923. Kunsthaus Zürich. *Johann Heinrich Füssli, 1741–1825; Gemälde und Zeichnungen.* 17. Mai bis 6 Juli 1969. Zürich, Kunsthaus Zürich, 1969

3924. Mason, Eudo C. *The mind of Henry Fuseli; selections from his writings with an introductory study.* London, Routledge & Kegan Paul, 1951.

3925. Powell, Nicolas. *Fuseli—The Nightmare.* New York, Viking, 1973.

3926. Pressly, Nancy L. *The Fuseli circle in Rome; early romantic art of the 1770's.* New Haven, Yale Center for British Art, 1979.

3927. Schiff, Gert. *Johann Heinrich Füssli, 1741–1825.* 2 v. Zürich, Berichthaus; München, Prestel, 1973. (CR). (Oeuvrekataloge schweizer Künstler, 1).

3928. ——— and Viotto, Paola. *L'opera completa di Füssli.* Milano, Rizzoli, 1977. (Classici dell'arte, 94).

3929. Schnyder-Seidel, Barbara. *J.H. Füssli und seine schönen Zürcherinnen:* Verwirrungen um Bildnisse im Umkreis von Goethe, Füssli, und Tischbein. Zürich, W. Classen, 1986.

3930. Tate Gallery (London). *Henry Fuseli, 1741–1825.* [19 February–31 March, 1975]. London, Tate Gallery, 1975.

3931. Tomory, Peter. *The life and art of Henry Fuseli.* New York/Washington, Praeger, 1972.

3932. Weinglass, David H. *Engraved illustrations by and after Henry Fuseli: a cataqlogue raisonné.* Aldershot, Hampshire; Brookfield, VT, 1993. (CR).

G

Gabo, Naum, 1890–1977

3933. Gabo, Naum. *Gabo: constructions, sculpture, paintings, drawings, engravings.* Introd. by Herbert Read and Leslie Martin. Cambridge, Mass., Harvard University Press, 1957.

3934. ———. *Of divers arts.* New York, Pantheon, 1962. (Bollingen series, 35. The A. W. Mellon lectures in the fine arts, 8).

3935. ———. *Sixty years of constructivism, including catalogue raisonné of the constructions and sculptures.* Edited by Steven A. Nash and Jørn Merkert. Munich, Prestel, 1985. (CR).

3936. Galerie Percier (Paris). *Constructivistes russes: Gabo et Pevsner: peintures, constructions.* Exposition du 19 juin au 5 juillet 1924. Paris, Galerie Percier, 1924.

3937. Musée de Peinture et de Sculpture (Grenoble). *Naum Gabo.* Exposition, Grenoble sept.–oct. 1971; Paris, Musée National d'Art Moderne nov.–déc. 1971. Catalogue rédigé par Marie-Claude Beaud. Paris, Réunion des musées nationaux, 1971.

3938. Museum of Modern Art (New York). *Naum Gabo [and] Antoine Pevsner.* Introd. by Herbert Read; text by Ruth Olson and Abraham Chanin. New York, Museum of Modern Art, 1948.

3939. Pevsner, Alexei. *A biographical sketch of my brothers Naum Gabo and Antoine Pevsner.* Amsterdam, Augustin & Schoonman, 1964.

Gabriel, Jacques Ange, 1698–1782

3940. Bottineau, Yves. *L'art d'Ange-Jacques Gabriel à Fontainebleau, 1735–1774.* Paris, De Boccard, 1962.

3941. Despierres, Gérasième (Bonnaire). *Les Gabriel; recherches sur les origines provinciales de ces architects.* Paris, Plon, 1895.

3942. Fels, Edmond, Comte de. *Ange-Jacques Gabriel premier architecte du roi, d'après des documents inédits.* Paris, Laurens, 1924. 2 ed. 1 ed.: Paris, Emile-Paul, 1912.

3943. Tadgell, Christopher. *Ange-Jacques Gabriel.* London, Zwemmer, 1978. (Studies in architecture, 19).

Gaddi, Agnolo, 1350–1396
Gaddo, D. 1312
Taddeo, 1300–1366

3944. Cole, Bruce. *Agnolo Gaddi.* Oxford/New York, Clarendon Press, 1977. (Oxford Studies in the History of Art and Architecture).

3945. Donati, Pier P. *Taddeo Gaddi.* Firenze, Sadea/Sansoni, 1966.

3946. Ladis, Andrew. *Taddeo Gaddi: a critical reappraisal and catalogue raisonné.* Columbia, University of Missouri Press, 1982. (CR).

3947. Mather, Frank J. *The Isaac Master; a reconstruction of the work of Gaddo Gaddi.* Princeton, N.J., Princeton University Press/ London, Oxford University Press, 1932. (Princeton Monographs in Art and Archaeology, 17).

3948. Salvini, Roberto. *L'arte di Agnolo Gaddi.* Firenze, Sansoni, 1936. (Monographie e studi. Istituto di storia dell'arte della Università di Firenze, 1).

Gaertner, Eduard, 1801–1877

3949. Berlin Museum. *Eduard Gaertner.* Architekturmaler in Berlin. Ausstellung, 6. Sept.–4 Okt. 1968. Katalog: Irmgard Wirth. Berlin, Berlin Museum, 1968.

3950. Wirth, Irmgard. *Eduard Gaertner, der Berliner Architekturmaler.* Frankfurt a.M., Propyläen, 1979.

Gärtner, Friedrich von, 1792–1847

3951. Eggert, Klaus. *Friedrich von Gärtner, der Baumeister König Ludwigs I.* München, Stadtarchiv München, 1963. (Neue Schriftenreihe d. Stadtarchivs München, 15).

3952. Gärtner, Friedrich von. *Friedrich von Gärtner: ein Architektenleben, 1791–1847.* Mit den Briefen an Johann Martin von Wagner. [Hrsg.] Winfried Nerdinger. München, Klinkhardt & Biermann, 1992.

3953. Hederer, Oswald. *Friedrich von Gärtner, 1792–1847: Leben, Werk, Schüler.* München, Prestel, 1976. (Studien zur Kunst des neunzehnten Jahrhunderts, 30).

Gainsborough, Thomas, 1727–1788

3954. Armstrong, Walter. *Gainsborough and his place in English art.* London, Heinemann, 1898. New ed.: New York, Dutton, 1906.

3955. ———. *Thomas Gainsborough.* London, Seeley/New York, Macmillan, 1894. (The Portfolio Artistic Monographs, 9).

3956. Boulton, William B. *Thomas Gainsborough, his life, work, friends and sitters.* London, Methuen, 1905.

3957. Brock-Arnold, George M. *Gainsborough.* London, Low, Marston, 1901. (Illustrated Biographies of the Great Artists).

3958. Chamberlain, Arthur B. *Thomas Gainsborough.* London, Duckworth/New York, Dutton, n.d.

3959. Cormack, Malcolm. *The paintings of Thomas Gainsborough.* Cambridge; New York, Cambridge University Press, 1991.

3960. Dibdin, Edward R. *Thomas Gainsborough, 1727–1788.* New York, Funk & Wagnalls, 1923.

3961. Fulcher, George W. *Life of Thomas Gainsborough.* London, Longman, 1856.

3962. Gainsborough, Thomas. *Letters.* Ed. by Mary Woodall. Greenwich, Conn., New York Graphic Society, 1963.

3963. Galeries Nationales du Grand Palais (Paris). *Gainsborough, 1727–1788:* [exposition], Grand Palais, 6 février–27 avril 1981. Organisée par le British Council et la Réunion des musées nationaux, avec la collaboration de la Tate Gallery. Paris, Ministère de la Culture et de la Communication, Editions de la Réunion des musées nationaux, 1981.

3964. Gower, Ronald S. *Thomas Gainsborough.* London, Bell, 1903. (The British Artists series).

3965. Hayes, John T. *Thomas Gainsborough.* Catalog of an exhibition held at the Tate Gallery, Oct. 8, 1980–Jan. 4, 1981. London, Tate Gallery, 1980.

3966. ———. *Gainsborough: paintings and drawings.* London, Phaidon, 1975.

3967. ———. *Gainsborough as printmaker.* London, Zwemmer, 1971.

3968. ———. *The drawings of Thomas Gainsborough.* 2 v. New Haven, Yale University Press, for the Paul Mellon Centre for Studies in British Art, 1971.

3969. ———. *The landscape paintings of Thomas Gainsborough:* a critical text and catalogue raisonné. 2 v. Ithaca, N.Y., Cornell University Press, 1982.

3970. Leonard, Jonathan N. *The world of Gainsborough.* New York, Time-Life, 1969.

3971. Lindsay, Jack. *Thomas Gainsborough, his life and art.* New York, Universe, 1981.

3972. Millar, Oliver. *Thomas Gainsborough.* New York, Harper, 1949.

3973. Mourey, Gabriel. *Gainsborough, biographie critique.* Paris, Librairie Renouard, Henri Laurens, 1905. (Les grands artistes).

3974. Pauli, Gustav. *Gainsborough.* Bielefeld/Leipzig, Velhagen & Klasing, 1904.

3975. Tate Gallery (London). *Thomas Gainsborough, 1727–1788: an exhibition of paintings arranged by the Arts Council of Great Britain and the Tate Gallery.* London, Tate Gallery, 1953.

3976. Waterhouse, Ellis K. *Gainsbourough.* London, Hulton, 1958.

3977. Whitley, William T. *Thomas Gainsborough.* London, Murray, 1915.

3978. Williamson, Geoffrey. *The ingenious Mr. Gainsborough; Thomas Gainsborough, a biographical study.* New York, St. Martin's, 1972.

3979. Woodall, Mary. *Gainsborough's landscape drawings.* London, Faber, 1939.

3980. ———. *Thomas Gainsborough, his life and work.* London, Phoenix, 1949.

Gallé, Emile, 1846–1904

3981. Charpentier, Françoise-Thérèse. *Emile Gallé.* Nancy, Université de Nancy II, 1978.

3982. Gallé, Emile. *Ecrits pour l'art; floriculture, art décoratif, notices d'exposition (1884–1889).* Paris, Renouard, 1908. (Repr.: Marseille, Laffitte, 1980).

3983. ———. *Gallé.*[Exhibition]. Paris, Musée du Luxembourg, 29 novembre, 1985–2 février, 1986. Paris Mnistère de la Culture, Editions de la Réunion des musées nationaux, 1985.

3984. ———. *Keramik von Émile Gallé.* [Ausstellung]. Hetjens-Museum, Deutsches Keramik-Museum, Düsseldorf, 27.9.1981–10.1.1982: Keramik Museum Mettlach, Mettlach/Saar, 6.3. 1982–6.6.1982. Bearbeitet von Bernd Hakenjos. Düsseldorf, Hetjens-Museum, 1981.

3985. Garner, Philippe. *Emile Gallé.* New York, Rizzoli, 1976. (2 ed., with new col. illus., London, Academy Editions 1990).

3986. Münchner Stadtmuseum. *Nancy 1900; Jugendstil in Lothringen, zwischen Historismus und Art Déco.* 28. August bis 23. November 1980. Mainz/Murnau, von Zabern, 1980.

3987. Museum Bellerive (Zurich). *Emile Gallé: Keramik, Glas und Möbel des Art Nouveau.*

28. Mai–17. August 1980. Zürich, Museum Bellerive, 1980. (Wegleitung des Kunstgewerbemuseums Zürich, 329).

3988. Warmus, William. *Emile Gallé: dreams into glass*. Corning, N.Y., Corning Museum of Glass, 1984.

Gallego, Fernando, ca. 1440–ca. 1507

3989. Gaya Nuño, Juan A. *Fernando Gallego*. Madrid, Istituto Diego Velazquez, 1958.

3990. Quinn, R. M. *Fernando Gallego and the retablo of Ciudad Rodrigo*. Tucson, University of Arizona, 1961.

Gallen-Kallela, Akseli, 1865–1931

3991. Gallen-Kallena, Kirsti. *Isäni, Akseli Gallen-Kallena*. 2 v. Helsinki, Söderström, 1964–5.

3992. Knuuttila, Seppo. *Akseli Gallen-Kallelan Väinämöiset*. Helsinki, Suomalaisen Kirjallisuuden Seura, 1978.

3993. Okkonen, Onni. *A. Gallen-Kallela, elämä ja taide*. Helsinki, Söderström, 1949. (Suomen tiedettä, 6).

Galli da Bibiena, Ferdinando, 1657–1743
Giuseppe, 1696–1756

3994. Beaumont, Maria Alice Mourisca. *Eighteenth-Century scenic and architectural design: drawings by the Galli Bibiena family from collections in Portugal*. Alexandria, Va., Art Services International, 1990.

3995. Casa del Mantegan (Mantua). *I Bibiena: disegni e incisioni nelle collezioni del Museo teatrale alla Scala*. 7 sett.–4 nov. 1975. Catalogo a cura di Mario Monteverdi; con un contributo di Ercolano Marani. Milano, Electa, 1975.

3996. Galli da Bibiena, Fernando. *Direzioni a' giovani studenti nel disegno dell'architettura civile, nell'Accademia Clementina dell'Istituto delle Scienze unite da F. G. Bibiena*. 2 v. Venezia, 1796.

3997. Galli da Bibiena, Giuseppe. *Architectural and perspective designs dedicated to His Majesty Charles VI, Holy Roman Emperor*. Introd. by A. Hyatt Mayor. New York, Dover, 1964. (Repr. of 1740 edition).

3998. Hadamowsky, Franz. *Die Familie Galli-Bibiena in Wien; Leben und Werk für das Theater*. Wien, Prachner, 1962. (Museion; Reihe 1, Bd. 2).

3999. Mayor, Alpheus Hyatt. *The Bibiena family*. New York, Bittner, 1945.

4000. Muraro, Maria T. and Povoledo, Elena. *Disegni teatrali dei Bibiena*. Catalogo della mostra a cura di M. T. Muraro e Elena Povoledo. Presentazione di Gianfranco Folena. Venezia, Pozza, 1970. (Fondazione Giorgio Cini. Cataloghi di mostre, 31).

4001. Ricci, Corrado. *I Bibiena, architetti teatrali . . . opere esposte alla mostra scenografica nel*

Museo teatrale alla Scala in Milano, primavera, 1915. Milano, Alfieri, 1915.

Gandolfi, Francesco, 1824–1873

4002. Bagni, Prisco. *I Gandolfi: affreschi, dipinti, bozzetti, disegni*. Bologna, Nuova Alfa, 1992.

4003. Cazort, Mimi. *Bella pittura: the art of the Gandolfi*. [By] Mimi Cazort; with an essay by Giovanna Perini. Ottawa, National Gallery of Canada, 1993.

4004. Pozzo, Matteo. *Il pittore Francesco Gandolfi nato in Chiavari nel 1824 morto in Genova nel 1873*. Genova, Tip. della Gioventu, 1910.

Gardella, Ignazio, 1905–

4005. Argan, Giulio Carlo. *Ignazio Gardella*. Milano, Comunità, 1959.

4006. Gardella, Ignazio. *L'Architettura di Ignazio Gardella*. A cura di Marco Porta; presentazione di Giulio Carlo Argan; saggio introduttivo di Roberto Gabetti; testimonianze di Franco Purini . . . et al.]. Milano, Etas libri, 1985.

4007. ———. *Ignazio Gardella: progetti e architetture, 1933–1990*. A cura di Franco Buzzi Ceriani; contributi di Guido Canella . . . [et al.]. Venezia, Marsilio, 1992.

4008. Samonà, Alberto. *Ignazio Gardella e il professionismo italiano*. Roma, Officia, 1981.

4009. Zermani, Paolo. *Ignazio Gardella*. Roma-Bari, Laterza, 1991.

Gaudi, Antonio, 1852–1926

4010. Bassegoda Nonell, Juan. *El gran Gaudi*. Sabadell, Barcelona, AUSA, 1989.

4011. ———. *Obras completas de Gaudi*. 2 v. Tokyo, Rikuyosha, 1979.

4012. Bergós, Joan. *Gaudí, l'home i l'obra*. Barcelona, Ariel, 1954.

4013. Casanelles, Enric. *Nueva vision de Gaudí*. Barcelona, Poligrafa, 1965. (English ed.: Greenwich, Conn., New York Graphic Society, 1965).

4014. Cirlot, Juan-Eduardo. *Introduccion a la arquitectura de Gaudí*. Barcelona, Editorial RM, 1966.

4015. Collins, George R. *Antonio Gaudí*. New York, Braziller, 1960.

4016. ——— and Bassegoda Nonell, Juan. *The designs and drawings of Antonio Gaudi*. Princeton, N.J., Princeton University Press, 1981.

4017. Dalisi, Riccardo. *Gaudi furniture*. London, Academy Editions, 1980.

4018. Flores, Carlos. *Gaudí, Jujol y el Modernismo Catalan*. 2 v. Madrid, Aguilar, 1982.

4019. Güell, Xavier. *Gaudi guide*. Barcelona, G. Gili, 1992.

4020. Hitchcock, Henry-Russell. *Gaudí.* New York, Museum of Modern Art, 1957.

4021. Lahuerta, Juan José. *Antoni Gaudi, 1852–1926: architettura, ideologia e politica.* Milano, Electa, 1992.

4022. Martinell, Cèsar. *Antonio Gaudí.* Milano, Electa, 1955. (Astra-Arengarium collana di monografie d'arte, serie architetti, 39).

4023. Martinell i Brunet, Cèsar. *Gaudí; su vida, su teoria, su obra.* Barcelona, Colegio de Arquitectos de Cataluna y Baleares, Comision de Cultura, 1967. (English ed.: Cambridge, Mass., MIT Press, 1975).

4024. O'Neal, William B., ed. *Antonio Gaudí and the Catalan Movement, 1870–1930.* Charlottesville, Virginia, University Press of Virginia, 1973. (American Association of Architectural Bibliographers, Papers v. 10).

4025. Palazzo Vecchio (Florence). *Antoni Gaudí.* Luglio–settembre, 1979. Firenze, Vallecchi, 1979.

4026. Pane, Roberto. *Antoni Gaudí.* Milano, Edizioni di Comunità, 1964. (Studi e documenti di storia dell' arte, 5).

4027. Perucho, Juan. *Gaudí, una arquitectura de anticipacion.* Barcelona, Poligrafa, 1967.

4028. Prévost, Clovis and Descharnes, Robert. *La vision artistica y religiosa de Gaudí.* Barcelona, Aymá, 1971.

4029. Pujols, Francesc. *La visio' artística; religiosa d'En Gaudí.* Barcelona, Llibereria Catalònia, 1927.

4030. Ràfols, Josep F. *Antoni Gaudí.* Barcelona, Canosa, 1928.

4031. ———. *Gaudí, 1852–1926.* Barcelona, Aedos, 1952.

4032. Sugranes, Jose M.ª Guix. *Defensa de Gaudi.* Reus, Monterols, 1960.

4033. Sweeney, James Johnson and Sert, Josep Lluís. *Antoni Gaudí.* New York, Praeger, 1960.

4034. Willaume, Alain. *Imagenes y mitos: Gaudi.* Fotografia Alain Willaume; texto, Jordi Castellanos, Juan José Lahuerta. Barcelona, Lunwerg, 1991.

4035. Zerbst, Rainer. *Gaudi, 1852–1926: Antoni Gaudi i Cornet—a life devoted to architecture.* Köln, Taschen, 1991.

Gaudier-Brzeska, Henri, 1891–1915

4036. Brodzky, Harold. *Henri Gaudier-Brzeska.* London, Faber, 1933.

4037. Cole, Roger. *Burning to speak, the life and art of Henri Gaudier Brzeska.* Oxford, Phaidon, 1978.

4038. Ede, H. S. *A life of Gaudier-Brzeska.* London, Heinemann, 1930.

4039. ———. *Savage Messiah.* New York, Knopf, 1931.

4040. Gaudier-Brzeska, Henri. *Henri Gaudier-Brzeska, 1891–1915, vu et raconté par les*

élèves du Lycée Professionel de Saint-Jean-de-Braye. Saint-Jean-de-Braye, Le Lycée, 1986.

4041. Kunsthalle der Stadt Bielefeld. *Henri Gaudier-Brzeska, 1891–1915, Skulpturen, Zeichnungen, Briefe, programmatische Schriften.* Bielefeld, Kunsthalle der Stadt, 1969.

4042. Levy, Mervyn. *Gaudier-Brzeska, drawings and sculpture.* New York, October House, 1965.

4043. Pound, Ezra. *Gaudier-Brzeska, a memoir.* New York, New Directions, 1970.

4044. Secrétain, Roger. *Un sculpteur 'maudit'; Gaudier-Brzeska, 1891–1915.* Paris, Le Temps, 1979.

Gauermann, Friedrich, 1807–1862

4045. Feuchtmüller, Rupert. *Friedrich Gauermann, 1897–1862; der Tier- und Landschaftsmaler des österreichischen Biedermeier.* Wien, Österreichische Staatsdruckerei, 1962.

4046. ———. *Friedrich Gauermann, 1807–1862.* Rosenheim, Rosenheimer Verlagshaus, 1987. (CR).

4047. Jenni, Ulrike. *Friedrich Gauermann, 1807–1862: Ölskizzen und Zeichnungen im Kupferstichkabinett; zur Arbeitsmethode des Malers. Mit einem Beitrag von Robert Wagner.* Wien, Kupferstichkabinett der Akademie der Bildenden Künste, 1987. (Kataloge des Kupferstichkabinetts der Akademie der Bildenden Künste. Neue Reihe, 2).

4048. Niederösterreichischer Ausstellungsverein (Vienna). *Biedermeier Ausstellung; Friedrich Gauermann und seine Zeit.* 19. Mai bis 18. Oktober 1962. Wien, Niederösterreichisches Landesmuseum, 1962.

Gauguin, Paul, 1848–1903

4049. Alexandre, Arsène. *Paul Gauguin, sa vie et le sens de son oeuvre.* Paris, Bernheim-Jeune, 1930.

4050. Amishai-Maisels, Ziva. *Gauguin's religious themes.* New York, Garland, 1985. [Based on ther author's thesis (Ph.D.)—Hebrew University, 1969].

4051. Andersen, Wayne. *Gauguin's paradise lost.* New York, Viking, 1971.

4052. Art Institute of Chicago. *Gaugin; paintings, drawings, prints, sculpture.* [February 12–March 19, 1959]. Chicago, Art Institute of Chicago, 1959.

4053. Becker, Beril. *Paul Gaugin, the calm madman.* New York, Boni, 1931.

4054. Bodelsen, Merete. *Gauguin's ceramics, a study in the development of his art.* London, Faber, 1964.

4055. Boudaille, Georges. *Gauguin.* Paris, Somogy, 1963.

4056. Boyle-Turner, Caroline. *Gauguin and the*

School of Pont-Aven: prints and paintings. Catalogue of an exhibition held at the Royal Academy of Arts, London, Sept. 9–Nov. 19, 1989, and at the National Gallery of Scotland, Edinburgh, Dec. 4, 1989–Feb.4, 1990. [By] C. Boyle-Turner with Samuel Josefowitz; foreword by Douglas Druick. London, Royal Academy of Arts in association with Weidenfeld and Nicolson, 1986.

4057. Burnett, Robert. *The life of Paul Gauguin.* London, Cobden-Sanderson, 1936; New York, Oxford University Press, 1937.

4058. Cachin, Françoise. *Gauguin. Translated by Bambi Ballard.* Paris, Flammarion, 1990. New York, Abbeville Press, 1992.

4059. ———. *Gauguin: "ce malgré moi de sauvage".* Paris, Gallimard; Réunion des musées nationaux, 1989. (Découvertes Gallimard 49: Peinture).

4060. Chassé, Charles. *Gauguin et le groupe de Pont-Aven, documents inédits.* Paris, Floury, 1921.

4061. ———. *Gauguin et son temps.* Paris, La Bibliothèque des Arts, 1955.

4062. Cogniat, Raymond. *Gauguin.* Paris, Tisné, 1947.

4063. ———. *Paul Gauguin, a sketchbook.* 3 v. New York, Hammer Galleries, 1962.

4064. Danielsson, Bengt. *Gauguin in the South Seas.* Trans. by Reginald Spink. London, Allen and Unwin, 1965.

4065. ——— and O'Reilly, Patrick. *Gauguin, journaliste à Tahiti & ses articles des Guêpes.* Paris, Société des Océanistes, 1966.

4066. Daix, Pierre. *Paul Gauguin.* Paris, J.-C. Lattès, 1989.

4067. Estienne, Charles. *Gauguin.* Geneva, Skira, 1953. (The Taste of Our Time, 1).

4068. Fletcher, John E. *Paul Gauguin, his life and art.* New York, Brown, 1921.

4069. Gauguin, Paul. *Le chemin de Gauguin: genèse et rayonnement.* [Catalogue of an exhibition held Oct. 7, 1985 to March 2,1986 at the Musée du Prieuré. Yvelines, France; written by Marie-Amélie Anquetil and others. Saint-Germain-en Laye, Yvelines [France], Musée départmental du Prieuré, 1985.

4070. ———. *Gauguin: actes du colloque Gauguin,* Musée d'Orsay, 11–13 janvier, 1989. Paris, Documentation française, 1991.

4071. ———. *Gauguin, a retrospective.* Edited by Marla Prather and Charles F. Stuckey. New York, Hugh Lauter Levin Associates; distributed by Macmillan Pub. Co., 1987.

4072. ———. *Gauguin: letters from Brittany and the South Seas: the search for paradise.* Selected and introduced by Bernard Denvir. 1st American ed. New York, Clarkson Potter Publishers, 1992.

4073. ———. *The letters of Paul Gauguin to Georges Daniel de Monfried.* Trans. by Ruth Pielkovo. London, Heinemann, 1923.

4074. ———. *Letters to his wife and friends.* Ed. by M. Malingue. Cleveland, World, 1949.

4075. ———. *Noa-Noa, première édition du texte authentique de Gauguin, établi sur le manuscript initial retrouvé.* Paris, Ballard, 1966.

4076. ———. *Noa-Noa.* Réalisé et presenté par Gilles Artur, Jean-Pierre Fourcade, Jean-Pierre Zingg. Tahiti, Association des Amis du Musée Gauguin; New York, Gauguin and Oceania Foundation, 1987.

4077. ———. *Paul Gauguin et Vincent van Gogh 1887–1888: lettres retrouvées, sources ingnorées.* Taravao, Tahiti, Avant et après, 1989.

4078. ———. *Paul Gauguin's intimate journals.* Trans. by Van Wyck Brooks. New York, Crown, 1936.

4079. Gauguin, Pola. *My father, Paul Gauguin.* New York, Knopf, 1937.

4080. Goldwater, Robert. *Gauguin.* New York, Abrams, 1957.

4081. Graber, Hans. *Paul Gauguin, nach eigenen und fremden Zeugnissen.* Basel, Schwabe, 1946.

4082. Gray, Christopher. *Sculpture and ceramics of Paul Gauguin.* Baltimore, Johns Hopkins, 1963.

4083. Guérin, Daniel. *The writings of a savage, Paul Gauguin.* Trans. by Eleanor Levieux. New York, Viking, 1978.

4084. Guérin, Marcel. *L'oeuvre gravé de Gauguin.* 2 v. Paris, Floury, 1927.

4085. Hanson, Lawrence and Hanson, Elisabeth. *The noble savage; a life of Paul Gauguin.* London, Chatto & Windus, 1954.

4086. Huyge, René. *Les carnets de Paul Gauguin.* 2 v. Paris, Quatre Chemins-Editart, 1952.

4087. ———. *Gauguin.* New York, Crown, 1959.

4088. ———, et al. *Gauguin.* Paris, Hachette, 1960. (Collection génies et réalités).

4089. Jaworska, Wladyslawa. *Paul Gauguin et l'école de Pont-Aven.* Neuchâtel, Editions Ides et Calandes, 1971.

4090. Kunstler, Charles. *Gauguin.* Paris, Floury, 1934.

4091. Le Pinchon, Yann. *Gauguin: life, art, inspiration.* Translated from the French by I. Mark Paris. New York, Abrams, 1987.,

4092. ———. *Sur les traces de Gauguin.* Paris. R. Laffont, 1986.

4093. Leprohon, Pierre. *Paul Gauguin.* Paris, Gründ, 1975.

4094. Leymarie, Jean. *Paul Gauguin; watercolours, pastels and drawings in colour.* London, Faber, 1961.

4095. Malingue, Maurice. *Gauguin, le peintre et son oeuvre.* Avant-propos de Pola Gauguin. Paris, Presses de la Cité, 1948.

G

4096. Mongan, Elizabeth. *Paul Gauguin, catalogue raisonné of his prints.* Manuscript written by Elizabeth Mongan, Eberhard W. Kornfeld, Harold Joachim; produced with the assistance of Christine E. Stauffer. Bern, Galerie Kornfeld, 1988. (CR).

4097. Morice, Charles. *Paul Gauguin.* Paris, Floury, 1919.

4098. Museum of Modern Art (New York). *First loan exhibition, New York, November 1929: Cézanne, Gauguin, Seurat, van Gogh.* New York, Museum of Modern Art, 1929.

4099. National Gallery of Art (Washington, D.C.). *The art of Paul Gauguin.* Catalog by Richard Brettell of an exhibition held at the National Gallery of Art, Washington, 1 May–31 July, 1988; the Art Institute of Chicago, 17 September–11 December 1988; and the Grand Palais, Paris, France, 10 January-20 April 1989. Washington, D.C., National Gallery of Art, 1988.

4100. O'Reilly, Patrick. *Catalogue du Musée Gauguin, Papeari, Tahiti.* Paris, Foundation Singer-Polignac, 1965.

4101. Perruchot, Henri. *Gauguin.* Trans. by Humphrey Hare. Cleveland/New York, World, 1963.

4102. Pickvance, Ronald. *The drawings of Gauguin.* London, Hamlyn, 1970.

4103. Read, Herbert. *Gauguin (1848–1903).* London, Faber, 1954.

4104. Rewald, John. *Gauguin.* Paris, Hyperion, 1938.

4105. ———. *Gaugin drawings.* New York/London, Yoseloff, 1958.

4106. ———. *Paul Gauguin.* New York, Abrams, 1952.

4107. Rey, Robert. *Gauguin.* Trans. by F. C. de Sumichrast. New York, Dodd, Mead, 1924.

4108. Rotonchamp, Jean de. *Paul Gauguin, 1848–1903.* Paris, Drouet, 1906.

4109. Schneeberger, Pierre-Francis. *Gauguin à Tahiti.* Lausanne, International Art Book, 1961.

4110. Sugana, G. M. *L'opera completa di Gauguin.* Milano, Rizzoli, 1972. (Classici dell'arte, 61).

4111. Sýkorová, Libuše. *Gauguin woodcuts.* London, Hamlyn, 1963.

4112. Tate Gallery (London). *Gauguin and the Pont-Aven group.* 7 January–13 February [1966]. London, Arts Council, 1966.

4113. Thomson, Belinda. *Gauguin.* New York, Thames and Hudson, 1987.

4114. Wildenstein, Georges. *Gauguin.* Paris, Les Beaux Arts, 1964. (CR).

Gaul, August, 1869–1921

4115. Rosenhagen, Hans. *Bildwerke von August Gaul.* Berlin, Cassirer, 1905.

4116. Waldmann, Emil. *August Gaul.* Berlin, Cassirer, 1919.

4117. Walther, Angelo. *August Gaul.* Leipzig, Seemann, 1973.

Gaulli, Giovanni Battista (Baciccio), 1639–1709

4118. Allen Memorial Art Museum (Oberlin, Ohio). *An exhibition of paintings, bozzetti, and drawings made by Baciccio, January 16 to February 13, 1967.* (Allen Memorial Art Museum Bulletin, v. 24, 2).

4119. Brugnoli, Maria Vittoria. *Il Baciccio.* Milano, Fabbri, 1966. (I maestri del colore, 214).

4120. Enggass, Robert. *The paintings of Baciccio, Giovanni Battista Gaulli, 1639–1709.* University Park, Penn., Pennsylvania State University Press, 1964. (CR).

4121. Kunstmuseum Düsseldorf. *Die Handzeichnungen von Guglielmo Cortese und Giovanni Battista Gaulli.* Düsseldorf, Kunstmuseum Düsseldorf, 1976. (Kataloge des Kunstmuseums Düsseldorf III, 2/1).

Gebhardt, Eduard von, 1838–1925

4122. Burckhardt, Rudolf F. *Zum Schauen bestellt: Eduard von Gebhardt, der Düsseldorfer Meister der biblischen Historie.* Stuttgart, Quell-Verlag, 1928. (Aus klaren Quellen, 19).

4123. Rosenberg, Adolf. *E. von Gebhardt.* Bielefeld/Leipzig, Velhagen & Klasing, 1899. (Künstler-Monographien, 38).

4124. Thomson, Erik. *Eduard von Gebhardt: Leben und Werk.* Aus dem Nachlass bearbeitet und mit einem Nachwort versehen von Günter Krüger. Lüneburg, Verlag Norddeutsches Kulturwerk, 1991.

Geertgen tot Sint Jans, 1465–1495

4125. Balet, Leo. *Der Frühholländer Geertgen tot Sint Jans.* Haag, Nijhoff, 1910.

4126. Friedländer, Max J. *Geertgen tot Sint Jans and Jerome Bosch.* Leyden, Sijthoff/Brussels, La Connaissance, 1969. (Early Netherlandish Painting, 5).

4127. Kessler, Johann H. H. *Geertgen tot Sint Jans, zijn herkomst en invloed in Holland.* Utrecht, Oosthoek, 1930.

4128. Vogelsang, W. *Geertgen tot Sint Jans.* Amsterdam, Becht, [n.d.]. (Palet serie, 21).

Geiler, Hans, fl. 1513–1534

4129. Strub, Marcel. *Deux maîtres de la sculpture Suisse du XVIᵉ siècle: Hans Geiler et Hans Gieng.* Fribourg, Editions Universitaires, 1962.

Gelder, Arent de, 1645–1727

4130. Lilienfeld, Karl. *Arent de Gelder, sein Leben und seine Kunst.* Haag, Nijhoff, 1914.

(Quellenstudien zur holländischen Kunstgeschichte, 4).

4131. Moltke, J.W. von. *Aert de Gelder (1645–1727)*. By J.W. von Moltke. Ed. by Kristin Belkin. With chapters by Alan Choing; Christian Tümpel. Documents by Gabriel Pastoor. Doornspijk, Davaco, 1994. (Aetas aurea, 5).

Gellée, Claude *see* Claude Lorrain

Genelli, Bonaventura, 1798–1868

4132. Christoffel, Ulrich. *Buonaventura Genelli, aus dem Leben eines Künstlers*. Berlin, Propyläen, 1922.

4133. Ebert, Hans. *Buonaventura Genelli, Leben und Werk*. Weimar, Hermann Böhlaus Nachfolger, 1971.

4134. Marshall, Hans. *Buonaventura Genelli*. Leipzig, Xenien-Verlag, 1912.

Generalić, Ivan, 1914–

4135. Bašičević, Dimitrije. *Ivan Generalić*. Zagreb, Društvo Historicara Umjetnostri NRH, 1962.

4136. Tomasević, Nebojša. *Magični svet Ivana Generalića*. Beograd, Jugoslovenska Revija, 1976. (English ed.: New York, Rizzoli, 1976).

4137. Zdunić, Drago, et al. *Ivan Generalić*. Zagreb, Spektar, 1973.

Gennai, Hiraga, 1729–1780

4138. Hirano, Imao. *Hiraga Gennai no shogai: yomigaeru Redo no Reonarudo da Binchi*. Tokyo, Chikuma Shobo, 1989.

4139. Mäes, Hubert. *Hiraga Gennai et son temps*. Paris, Ecole Fr. d'Extrème-Orient, 1970.

Gensler, Günther, 1803–1884
Jakob, 1808–1845
Martin, 1811–1881

4140. Bürger, Fritz. *Die Gensler, drei Hamburger Malerbrüder des 19. Jahrhunderts*. Strassburg, Heitz, 1916. (Studien zur deutschen Kunstgeschichte, 190).

Gentile da Fabriano, 1370–1427

4141. Bellosi, Luciano. *Gentile da Fabriano*. Milano, Fabbri, 1966. (I maestri del colore, 159).

4142. Christiansen, Keith. *Gentile da Fabriano*. Ithaca, N.Y., Cornell University Press, 1982.

4143. Colasanti, Arduino. *Gentile da Fabriano*. Bergamo, Ist. Ital. d'Arti Grafiche, 1909.

4144. Grassi, Luigi. *Tutta la pittura di Gentile da Fabriano*. Milano, Rizzoli, 1953.

4145. Micheletti, Emma. *L'opera completa di Gentile da Fabriano*. Milano, Rizzoli, 1976. (Classici dell'arte, 86). (CR).

4146. Molajoli, Bruno. *Gentile da Fabriano*. Fabrino, Edizioni Gentile, 1927. (2 ed., 1934).

Gentileschi, Artemisia, ca.1597–ca.1651
Gentileschi, Orazio, 1563–1640?

4147. Bissell, Raymond Ward. *The baroque painter Orazio Gentileschi; his career in Italy*. 2 v. Ann Arbor, Mich., University Microfilms, 1975.

4148. ———. *Orazio Gentileschi and the poetic tradition in Caravaggesque painting*. University Park, Penn., Pennsylvania State University Press, 1982.

4149. Garrard, Mary D. *Artemisia Gentileschi: the image of the female hero in Italian Baroque art*. Princeton, N.J., Princeton University Press, 1989

4150. Gentileschi, Artemisia. *Artemisia*. [Catalogue of an exhibition held at the Casa Buanarotti, Florence, June 18–Nov. 4, 1991]. A cura di Roberto Contini e Gianni Papi, con un saggio di Luciano Berti. Roma, Leonardo/De Luca, 1991.

4151. Rosci, Marco. *Orazio Gentileschi*. Milano, Fabbri, 1965. (I maestri del colore, 83).

Gerard, François, 1770–1837

4152. Gérard, Henri. *Lettres adressées au Baron François Gérard, peintre d'histoire, par les artistes et les personnages célèbres de son temps*. 2 v. Paris, Quantin, 1888. 3 ed.

4153. ———. *Oeuvres du Baron François Gérard, 1789–1836*. 3 v. Paris, Vignières, 1852–57.

4154. Lenormant, Charles. *François Gérard, peintre d'histoire*. Paris, René, 1847.

Gerard, Jean Ignace Isidore *see* Grandville

Gerhaert, Nicolaus van Leyden, 1420/30–1473

4155. Fischel, L. *Nicolaus Gerhaert und die Bildhauer der deutschen Spätgotik*. München, Bruckmann, 1944.

4156. Maier, August R. *Niclaus Gerhaert von Leiden, ein niederländer Plastiker des 15. Jahrhunderts*. Strassburg, Heitz, 1910. (Studien zur deutschen Kunstgeschichte, 131).

4157. Recht, Roland. *Nicolas de Leyde et la sculpture à Strasbourg, 1460–1525*. Strasbourg, Presses universitaires de Strasbourg, 1987.

4158. Wertheimer, Otto. *Nicolaus Gerhaert, seine Kunst und seine Wirkung*. Berlin, Deutscher Verein für Kunstwissenschaft, 1929.

Gericault, Théodore, 1791–1824

4159. Aimé-Azam, Denise. *La passion de Géricault*. Paris, Fayard, 1970.

4160. ———. *Mazeppa; Géricault et son temps*. Paris, Plon, 1956.

4161. Bazin, Germain. *Théodore Géricault.; étude critique, documents et catalogue raisonné.* 5 v. Paris, La Bibliothèque des arts, 1987–1992. (CR).

4162. Berger, Klaus. *Géricault: drawings & watercolors.* New York, Bittner, 1946.

4163. ———. *Géricault und sein Werk.* Wien, Schroll, 1952. (English ed., Lawrence, Kansas, University of Kansas, 1955).

4164. Clement, Charles. *Géricault, étude biographique et critique.* Paris, Didier, 1879. 3 ed., illustrée. Reprint: Paris, Laget, 1973; English ed.: New York, Da Capo, 1974. (CR).

4165. Courthier, Pierre, ed. *Géricault, raconté par lui-même et par ses amis.* Vésenaz-Genève, Cailler, 1947.

4166. Eitner, Lorenz. *Géricault, an album of drawings in the Art Institute of Chicago.* Chicago, University of Chicago Press, 1960.

4167. ———. *Géricault, his life and work.* Ithaca, New York, Cornell University Press, 1982.

4168. ———. *Géricault, 1791–1824.* [Exhibition]. Lorenz E.A. Eitner, Steven A. Nash. San Francisco, Fine Arts Museums of San Francisco, 1989.

4169. Gauthier, Maximilien. *Géricault.* Paris, Braun, 1935.

4170. Géricault, Théodore. *Géricault.*[Exposition]. Galeries nationales du Grand Palais, Paris, 10 octobre 1991–6 janvier 1992. Paris, Réunion des musées nationaux, 1991.

4171. ———. *Théodore Géricault (1791–1824); an exhibition: paintings, drawings, watercolors, prints and sculpture.* Essays by Lorenz Eitner, Hans Lüthy. New York, Salander-O'Reilly Galleries, 1987.

4172. Guercio, Antonio del. *Géricault.* Milano, Club del Libro, 1963. (Collana d'arte del Club del Libro, 4).

4173. ———. *Théodore Géricault.* Milano, Fabbri, 1965. (I maestri del colore, 46).

4174. Hôtel Jean Charpentier (Paris). *Exposition de l'oeuvres de Géricault.* 24 avril au 16 mai 1924. Paris, La Sauvegarde de l'Art Français, 1924. (CR).

4175. Musée des Beaux-Arts de Rouen. *Géricault; tout l'oeuvre gravé et pièces en rapport.* 28 novembre 1981–28 février 1982. Rouen, Musée des Beaux-Arts, 1981.

4176. Oprescu, Georges. *Géricault.* Paris, La Renaissance du Livre, 1927.

4177. Régamey, Raymond. *Géricault.* Paris, Rieder, 1926.

4178. Rosenthal, Léon. *Géricault.* Paris, Librairie de l'Art Ancien et Moderne, 1905.

4179. Thuillier, Jacques. *L'opera completa di Géricault.* Milano, Rizzoli, 1978. (Classici dell'arte, 92).

4180. Villa Medici (Rome). *Géricault.* Novembre 1979–gennaio 1980. Roma, Edizioni dell'Elefante, 1979.

Gérôme, Jean Léon, 1824–1904

4181. Ackermann, Gerald M. *The life and work of Jean-Léon Gérôme. With a catalogue raisonné.* London, P. Wilson for Sotheby's Publications; New York, Harper and Row, 1986. (CR).

4182. Dayton Art Institute (Dayton, Ohio). *Jean-Léon Gérôme (1824–1904).* November 10–December 30, 1972. Dayton, Dayton Art Institute, 1972.

4183. Hering, Fanny F. *Gérôme; the life and works of Jean Léon Gérôme.* New York, Cassell, 1892.

4184. Moreau-Vauthier, Charles. *Gérôme, peintre et sculpteur, l'homme et l'artiste.* Paris, Hachette, 1906.

4185. Musée de Vesoul. *Gérôme: Jean-Léon Gérôme, 1824–1904; peintre, sculpteur et graveur.* Vesoul, Ville de Vesoul, 1981.

Ghiberti, Lorenzo, 1378–1455

4186. Ghiberti, Lorenzo. *Der dritte Kommentar Lorenzo Ghibertis: Naturwissenschaften und Medizin in der Kunsttheorie der Frührennaissance.* Eingeleitet, kommentiert und übersetzt von Klaus Bergdolt. Weinheim, VCH, Acta Humaniora, 1988.

4187. Goldscheider, Ludwig. *Ghiberti.* London, Phaidon, 1949.

4188. Gollob, Hedwig. *Lorenzo Ghibertis künstlerischer Werdegang.* Strassburg, Heitz, 1929. (Zur Kunstgeschichte des Auslandes, 126).

4189. Gonelli, Guiseppe. *Elogio di Lorenzo Ghiberti.* Firenze, Piatti, 1822.

4190. Krautheimer, Richard. *Lorenzo Ghiberti.* Princeton, N.J., Princeton University Press, 1956. (Rev. ed.: 2 v., 1970).

4191. ———, et al. *Lorenzo Ghiberti nel suo tempo, atti del convegno internazionale di studi (Firenze, 18–21 ottobre 1978).* 2 v. Firenze, Olschki, 1980.

4192. Marchini, Giuseppe. *Ghiberti architetto.* Firenze, La Nuova Italia, 1978.

4193. Museo dell'Accademia e Museo di San Marco (Florence). *Lorenzo Ghiberti, materia e ragionamenti.* 18 ottobre 1978/31 gennaio 1979. Firenze, Centro Di, 1978. (CR).

4194. Perkins, Charles. *Ghiberti et son école.* Paris, Librairie de l'Art, 1886.

4195. Planiscig, Leo. *Lorenzo Ghiberti.* Wien, Schroll, 1940.

4196. Rosito, Massimiliano, ed. *Ghiberti e la sua arte nella Firenze del '3–'400.* Firenze, Città di Vita, 1979.

4197. Schlosser, Julius. *Leben und Meinungen des florentinischen Bildners Lorenzo Ghiberti.* Basel, Holbein, 1941.

4198. ———. *Lorenzo Ghibertis Denkwürdigkeiten (I commentarii).* 2 v. Berlin, Bard, 1912.

Ghirlandaio, Domenico, 1449–1494

4199. Bargellini, Piero. *Il Ghirlandaio del bel mondo fiorentino.* Firenze, Arnaud, 1946.

4200. Biagi, Luigi. *Domenico Ghirlandaio.* Firenze, Alinari, 1928. (Piccola collezione d'arte, 42).

4201. Chiarini, Marco. *Domenico Ghirlandaio.* Milano, Fabbri, 1966. (I maestri del colore, 156).

4202. Davies, Gerald S. *Ghirlandaio.* London, Methuen, 1908.

4203. Hauvette, Henri. *Ghirlandaio.* Paris, Plon, 1908.

4204. Küppers, Paul E. *Die Tafelbilder des Domenico Ghirlandajo.* Strassburg, Heitz, 1916. (Zur Kunstgeschichte des Auslandes, 111).

4205. Lauts, Jan. *Domenico Ghirlandajo.* Wien, Schroll, 1943.

4206. Micheletti, Emma. *Domenico Ghirlandaio.* Firenze, Scala, 1990.

4207. Sabatini, Attilio. *Domenico Ghirlandaio.* Firenze, Illustrazione Toscana, 1944.

4208. Steinmann, Ernst. *Ghirlandajo.* Bielefeld/Leipzig, Velhagen & Klasing, 1897. (Künstler-Monographien, 25).

4209. Weiser von Inffeld, Josepha. *Das Buch um Ghirlandaio, eine Florentiner Chronik.* Zürich/Stuttgart, Rascher, 1957.

Giacometti, Alberto, 1901–1966
Augusto, 1877–1947
Diego, 1902–1985
Giovanni, 1868–1933

4210. Bonnefoy, Yves. *Alberto Giacometti: a biography of his work.* Translated by Jean Stewart. Paris, Flammariuon, 1991.

4211. Bucarelli, Palma. *Giacometti.* Roma, Editalia, 1962.

4212. Carluccio, Luigi. *Giacometti, a sketchbook of interpretive drawings.* Trans. by Barbara Luigia La Penta. New York, Abrams, 1968.

4213. du Bouchet, André. *Alberto Giacometti: dessin.* Paris, Maeght, 1991.

4214. ———. *Alberto Giacometti, dessins, 1914–1965.* Paris, Maeght, 1969.

4215. du Carrois, Norbert R. *Giovanni Giacometti; Katalog des graphischen Werkes, 1888–1933.* Zürich, P & P Galerie, 1977.

4216. Dupin, Jacques. *Alberto Giacometti.* Paris, Maeght, 1963.

4217. Fletcher, Valerie. J. *Alberto Giacometti, 1901–1966.* V.J. FLetcher; with essays by Silvio Berthoud and Reinhold Hohl. Washington, D.C., Published for the Hirshhorn Museum and Sculpture Garden by the Smithsonian Institution Press, 1988.

4218. Fondation Maeght (Paris). *Alberto Giacometti.* 8 juillet–30 septembre 1978. Paris, Fondation Maeght, 1978. (CR).

4219. Genêt, Jean. *L'atelier d'Alberto Giacometti.* Décines (Isère), Barbezat, 1963.

4220. Giacometti, Alberto. *Alberto Giacometti: [Ausstellung] Nationalgalerie, Berlin,* Staatliche Museen Preussischer Kulturbesitz, 9.10. 1987–3.1. 1988. Staatsgalerie Stuttgart, 29.1.–20.3. 1988. Katalog, Angela Schneider; Mitarbeit Octavia Heidemann . . . et al. Berlin, Die Museen, 1987.

4221. ———. *Alberto Giacometti.* Basel, Galerie Beyeler, 1989.

4222. ———. *Alberto Giacometti:* exposicion y catalogo [by] Kosme Maria de Baranano. Madrid, Museo Nacional Centro de Arte Reina Sofia, Ministerio de Cultura: Lunwerg, 1990.

4223. ———. *Alberto Giacometti, sculptures, peintures, dessins:* [exposition] 30 novembre 1991–15 mars 1992; réalisée sur la direction de Suzanne Pageé. Paris, Musée d'art moderne de la ville de Paris; Diffusion, Paris-Musées, 1991.

4224. ———. *Die Sammlung der Alberto Giacometti-Stiftung.* [Catalogue]. Zürich, Zürcher Kunstgesellschaft, 1990.

4225. ———. *Alberto Giacometti: Skulpturen, Gemälde, Zeichnungen, Graphik.* Hrsg. von Peter Beye und Dieter Honisch; mit Beiträgen von Alexander Dückers . . . [et al.]. München, Prestel, 1987.

4226. Giacometti, Augusto. *Augusto Giacometti 1877–1947: Gemälde, Aquarelle, Pastelle, Entwürfe.* [Ausstellung]: Clemens-Sels-Museum, Neuss 1. Februar bis 22. März 1987. Katalogredaktion Hans van der Grinten in Zusammenarbeit mit Gisela Götte und Beat Stutzer. Nijmegen, Netherlands, Nijmeegs Museum "Commanderie Van Sint-Jan", 1986.

4227. ———. *Von Florenz bis Zürich, Blätter der Erinnerung.* Zürich, Rascher, 1948.

4228. ———. *Von Stampa bis Florenz, Blätter der Erinnerung.* Zürich, Rascher, 1943.

4229. Giacometti, Diego. *Diego Giacometti: catalogue de l'oeuvre.* Réalisé par Françoise Francisci; photos Daniel Frasnay; portraits Ralph Crane. Textes [by] Françoise Francisci, Robert Wernick, Claude Delay. v. 1– . Paris, EOLIA, 1986– .

4230. Marchesseau, Daniel. *Diego Giacometti.* Préface de Jean Leymarier. Paris, Hermann, 1986.

4231. Hartmann, Hans. *Augusto Giacometti, ein Leben für die Farbe: Pionier der abstrakten Malerei.* Chur, Bündner Kunstverein; Bündner Kunstmuseum Chur, 1981. (Schriftenreihe des Bündner Kunstmuseums, Chur, 211).

4232. Hohl, Reinhold. *Alberto Giacometti.* Trans. by Gerd Hatje. New York, Abrams, 1972.

4233. Huber, Carla. *Alberto Giacometti.* Zürich, Ex Libris, 1970.

4234. Hugelshofer, Walter. *Giovanni Giacometti, 1868–1933.* Zürich/Leipzig, Füssli, 1936.

4235. Köhler, Elisabeth E. *Giovanni Giacometti, 1868–1933; Leben und Werk.* Zürich, Fischer, 1969.

4236. Lord, James. *Alberto Giacometti, drawings.* Greenwich, Conn., New York Graphic Society, 1971.

4237. ———. *A Giacometti portrait.* New York, Farrar, Straus & Giroux, 1980.

4238. Lust, Herbert C. and Taylor, John L. *Giacometti, the complete graphics and fifteen drawings.* New York, Tudor, 1970.

4239. Martini, Alberto. *Giacometti.* Milano, Fabbri, 1967. (I maestri del colore, 79).

4240. Matter, Herbert. *Alberto Giacometti.* Photographed by Herbert Matter; text by Mercedes Matter; foreword by Louis Finkelstein; with an introduction by Andrew Forge. New York, Abrams, 1987.

4241. Meyer, Franz. *Alberto Giacometti; eine Kunst existentieller Wirklichkeit.* Frauenfeld/Stuttgart, Huber, 1968.

4242. Moulin, Raoul-Jean. *Giacometti, sculptures.* Trans. by Bettina Wadia. New York, Tudor, 1964.

4243. Museum of Modern Art (New York). *Alberto Giacometti.* New York, Museum of Modern Art; distributed by Doubleday, Garden City, N.Y., 1965.

4244. Negri, Mario. *Giacometti.* Milano, Fabbri, 1969. (I maestri della scultura, 57).

4245. Pierre Matisse Gallery (New York). *Exhibition of sculptures, paintings, drawings [by Alberto Giacometti].* Introduction by Jean-Paul Sartre and a letter from Alberto Giacometti. January 19 to February 14, 1948. New York, Pierre Matisse Gallery, 1948.

4246. Poeschel, Erwin. *Augusto Giacometti.* Zürich/Leipzig, Füssli, 1928. (Monographien zur Schweizer Kunst, 3).

4247. Soavi, Giorgio. *Giacometti: la ressemblance impossible = Resemblance defeated = Unerreichbare Ähnlichkeit.* [By] G. Soavi [and] Peter Knapp. [France], A. Sauret; M. Trinckvel, 1991.

4248. Solomon R. Guggenheim Museum (New York). *Alberto Giacometti, a retrospective exhibition.* New York, Guggenheim Foundation, 1974.

4249. Stutzer, Beat. *Augusto Giacometti: Leben und Werk.* B. Stutzer [and] Lutz Windhöfel. Chur, Verlag Bündner Monatsblatt, 1991.

4250. Zendralli, A. M. *Augusto Giacometti.* Zurigo/Lipsia, Füssli, 1936.

Gibbons, Grinling, 1648–1721

4251. Bullock, Albert E., ed. *Grinling Gibbons and his compeers.* London, Tiranti, 1914.

4252. Green, David. *Grinling Gibbons, his work as carver of statuary.* London, Country Life, 1964.

4253. Tipping, H. Avray. *Grinling Gibbons and the woodwork of his age (1648–1720).* London, Country Life, 1914.

4254. Whinney, Margaret D. *Grinling Gibbons in Cambridge.* Cambridge, Cambridge University Press, 1948.

Gibbs, James, 1682–1754

4255. Gibbs, James. *Designs of buildings and ornaments; a collection of the best plates from this work.* Washington, D.C., The Reprint Co., 1909.

4256. ———. *The rules for drawing the several parts of architecture.* The first edition reduced. London, Hodder and Stoughton, 1924.

4257. Little, Bryan. *The life and work of James Gibbs, 1682–1754.* London, Batsford, 1955.

Gibson, John, 1790–1866

4258. Eastlake, Elizabeth R. *Life of John Gibson, R. A., sculptor.* London, Longmans, Green, 1870.

4259. Matthews, T. *The biography of John Gibson, R. A., sculptor, Rome.* London, Heinemann, 1911.

Gilbert, Alfred, 1854–1934

4260. Bury, Adrian. *Shadow of Eros, a biographical and critical study of the life and works of Sir Alfred Gilbert, R. A., M.V.O., D.C.L.* London, The Dropmore Press, 1952.

4261. Cox, E. M. *Commemorative catalogue of an exhibition of models and designs by the late Sir Alfred Gilbert, R. A., held at the Victoria and Albert Museum, autumn 1936.* Oxford, Oxford University Press, 1936.

4262. Gilbert, Alfred. *The studio diary of Alfred Gilbert for 1889: the identities of the saints on the Duke of Clarence Memorial.* Cecil Gilbert. Newcastle upon Tyne, C. Gilbert, 1987.

4263. Hatton, Joseph. *The life and work of Alfred Gilbert.* London, The Art Journal, 1903.

4264. McAllister, I. G. *Alfred Gilbert.* London, Black, 1929.

4265. Minneapolis Institute of Arts. *Victorian High Renaissance: George Frederick Watts, 1817–1904; Frederic Leighton, 1830–1939; Albert Moore, 1841–93; Alfred Gilbert, 1854–1939.* 19 November–7 January, 1979. Minneapolis, Minneapolis Institute of Arts, 1978.

Gill, Eric, 1882–1940

4266. Brady, Elizabeth A. *Eric Gill, twentieth-century book designer.* Metuchen, New Jersey, Scarecrow Press, 1974.

4267. Brewer, Roy. *Eric Gill, the man who loved letters.* London, Muller, 1973.

4268. Collins, Judy. *Eric Gill Sculpture.* [Accompanies the] Exhibition, London, Barbican. London, Lund Humphries, 1992.

4269. Gill, Eric. *Art.* London, Bodley Head, 1934.

4270. ———. *Autobiography.* London, Cape, 1940.

4271. ———. *Autobiography.* With a new introduction by Fiona MacCarthy. London, Lund-Humphries, 1992

4272. ———. *Beauty looks after herself.* London/New York, Sheed & Ward, 1933. (Reprint: Freeport, New York, Books for Libraries, 1956).

4273. ———. *The engravings of Eric Gill.* Wellingborough, Eng., Skelton's Press, 1983. (Reprint: London, The Herbert Press, 1990).

4274. ———. *It all goes together; selected essays.* New York, Devin, 1944.

4275. ———. *Letters.* Ed. by Walter Shewring. New York, Devin, 1948.

4276. Gill, Evan R. *Bibliography of Eric Gill.* London, Cassell, 1953. (Revised ed. with title: *Eric Gill: a bibliography*; revised by D. Steven Corey and Julia MacKenzie. Winchester, St. Paul's Bibliographies; Detroit, Omnigraphics, 1991.

4277. ———. *The inscriptional work of Eric Gill, an inventory.* London, Cassell, 1964. (CR).

4278. Physick, J. F. *The engraved work of Eric Gill.* London, Her Majesty's Stationery Office, 1963. (CR).

4279. ———. *The engraved work of Eric Gill.* [A photographic supplement of works in the Victoria and Albert Museum]. London, Her Majesty's Stationery Office, 1963.

4280. Speaight, Robert. *The life of Eric Gill.* London, Methuen, 1966.

4281. Thorp, Joseph and Marriott, Charles. *Eric Gill.* London, Cape, 1929.

4282. Yorke, Malcolm. *Eric Gill, man of flesh and spirit.* New York, Universe, 1982.

Gilles, Werner, 1894–1961

4283. Akademie der Künste (Berlin). *Werner Gilles, 1894–1961.* Berlin, Akademie der Künste, [1962?]. (Kunst und Altertum am Rhein, 43).

4284. Hentzen, Alfred. *Werner Gilles.* Köln, DuMont Schauberg, 1960.

4285. Rheinisches Landesmuseum (Bonn). *Werner Gilles, 1894–1961; ein Rückblick.* [January 17–February 25, 1973]. Köln, Rheinisches Landesmuseum, 1973.

4286. Schwenger, Marlis. *Werner Gilles, 1894–1961: stilistische und ikonographische Studien zu seinem Werk. Mit einem Verzeichnis der Druckgraphik.* Köln, DME-Verlag, 1985. (CR).

Gillray, James, 1757–1815

4287. Arts Council of Great Britain. *James Gillray, 1756–1815; drawings and caricatures.* [Arts Council Gallery, January 6–February 4, 1967]. London, The Arts Council, 1967.

4288. Gillray, James. *Fashionable contrasts; caricatures.* Introduced and annotated by Draper Hill. London, Phaidon, 1966.

4289. ———. *The works of James Gillray, from the original plates, with the addition of many subjects not before collected.* 2 v. London, Bohn, 1851.

4290. Hill, Draper. *Mr. Gillray, the caricaturist; a biography.* London, Phaidon, 1965. (U.S. distributors: Greenwich, Conn., New York Graphic Society).

4291. Wright, Thomas and Evans, R. H. *Historical and descriptive account of the caricatures of James Gillray, comprising a political and humorous history of the latter part of the reign of George the third.* [As an accompaniment to his collected works published . . . by H. G. Bohn]. London, Bohn, 1851. (CR).

Gilly, Friedrich, 1772–1800

4292. Gilly, Friedrich. *Friedrich Gilly, 1772–1800, und die Privatgesellschaft junger Architekten.* [Ausstellung] Berlin Museum, 21. September bis 4. November, 1984. Berlin, Verlag W. Arenhövel, 1984.

4293. Oncken, Alste. *Friedrich Gilly, 1772–1800.* Berlin, Deutscher Verein für Kunstwissenschaft, 1935. (CR). (Forschungen zur deutschen Kunstgeschichte, 5).

4294. Rietdorf, Alfred. *Gilly, Wiedergeburt der Architektur.* Berlin, Hugo, 1940.

Gilpin, William, 1724–1804

4295. Barbier, Carl P. *William Gilpin; his drawings, teachings, and theory of the picturesque.* Oxford, Oxford University Press, 1963.

4296. Templeman, William D. *The life and work of William Gilpin.* Urbana, Ill., University of Illinois Press, 1939.

Gimmi, Wilhelm, 1886–1965

4297. Cailler, Pierre. *Catalogue raisonné de l'oeuvre lithographié de Wilhelm Gimmi.* Genève, Cailler, 1956. (CR). (Catalogue d'oeuvres gravés et lithographiés, 1).

4298. Jacometti, Nesto. *Wilhelm Gimmi.* Genève, Skira, 1943. (Peintres d'hier et d'aujourd'hui, 1).

4299. Jedlicka, Gotthard. *Begegnung mit Wilhelm Gimmi.* Zürich, Füssli, 1961.

4300. Peillex, Georges. *Wilhelm Gimmi, catalogue raisonné des peintures.* Zürich, Füssli, 1978. (CR).

4301. ——— [and] Scheidegger, Alfred. *Wilhelm Gimmi.* Zürich, Füssli, 1972.

G

Giocondo, Fra Giovanni, 1435–1515

4302. Brenzoni, Raffaello. *Fra Giovanni Giocondo Veronese, Verona 1435–Roma 1515.* Firenze, Olschki, 1960.

4303. Fontana, Vincenzo. *Fra' Giovanni Giocondo, architetto 1433 c. 1515.* Vicenza, Neri Pozza, 1988.

4304. Geymüller, Heinrich. *Cento disegni di architettura d'ornato e di figure di Frà Giovanni Giocondo.* Firenze, Bocca, 1882.

Giordano, Luca, 1635–1705

4305. Benesch, Otto. *Luca Giordano.* Wien, Hölzel, 1923.

4306. Brooks Memorial Art Gallery (Memphis, Tenn.). *Luca Giordano in America; a loan exhibition, April 1964.* [Catalogue by Michael Milkovich]. Memphis, Tenn., Brooks Memorial Art Gallery, 1964.

4307. Ferrari, Oreste [and] Scavizzi, Giuseppe. *Luca Giordano.* 3 v. Napoli, Edizioni Scientifiche Italiane, 1966.

4308. ———. *Luca Giordano; l'opera completa.* 2 v. O. Ferrari [and] Giuseppe Scavizzi. Napoli. Electa Napoli, 1992. (CR).

4309. *Saggi e documenti per la storia dell'arte dedicato a luca Giordano.* Milano, L & T, 1991.

4310. Petraccone, Enzo. *Luca Giordano, opera postuma.* Napoli, Ricciardi, 1919.

4311. Rinaldis, Aldo de. *Luca Giordano.* Firenze, Alinari, 1922. (Piccola collezione d'arte, 40).

Giorgio, Francesco di *see* Francesco di Giorgio Martini

Giorgione da Castelfranco, 1477–1510

4312. Baldass, Ludwig von. *Giorgione.* Trans. by J. M. Brownjohn. New York, Abrams, 1965.

4313. Calvesi, Maurizio, ed. *Giorgione e la cultura veneta tra '400 e '500; mito, allegoria, analisi iconologica.* Roma, de Luca, 1981.

4314. Castelfranco Veneto (Venice). *Giorgione, guida alla mostra: i tempi di Giorgione.* Firenze, Alinari, 1978.

4315. Coletti, Luigi. *All the paintings of Giorgione.* New York, Hawthorn, 1961. (Complete Library of World Art, 3).

4316. Conti, Angelo. *Giorgione, studio.* Firenze, Alinari, 1984.

4317. Conway, William M. *Giorgione, a new study of his art as a landscape painter.* London, Benn, 1929.

4318. *Convegno internazionale di studi per il V centenario della nascita di Giorgone 1978.* Castelfranco Veneto, and Asolo, Italy. Atti del convegno, 29–31 maggio 1978; comune di Castelfranco Veneto, Comitato per le celebrazioni giorgionesche. [S.l.], Banca popolare di Asolo e Montebelluna, 1979.

4319. Cook, Herbert F. *Giorgione.* London, Bell, 1904. 2 ed.

4320. Dreyfous, Georges. *Giorgione.* Paris, Alcan, 1914.

4321. Ferriguto, Arnaldo. *Attraverso i 'misteri' di Giorgione.* Castelfranco Veneto, Arti Grafiche Trevisan, 1933.

4322. Fiocco, Giuseppe. *Giorgione.* Bergamo, Ist. Ital. d'Arti Grafiche, 1948. 2 ed.

4323. Fossi, Piero. *Di Giorgione e della critica d'arte.* Firenze, Olschki, 1957. (Pocket Library of Studies in Art, 7).

4324. Giorgione. *Giorgione e l'umanesimo veneziano.* A cura di Rodolfo Palucchini, 2 v. Firenze, L.S. Olschki, 1981.

4325. ———. *Giorgione, tutta la pittura.* [Testi di Davide Banzato . . . et. al.]. Firenze, Nardini, 1988.

4326. Hartlaub, G. F. *Giorgiones Geheimnis; ein kunstgeschichtlicher Beitrag zur Mystik der Renaissance.* München, Allgemeine Verlagsanstalt, 1925.

4327. Hermanin, Federico. *Il mito di Giorgione.* Spoleto, Argentieri, 1933.

4328. Hourticq, Louis. *Le problème de Giorgione; sa légende, son oeuvre, ses élèves.* Paris, Hachette, 1930.

4329. Justi, Ludwig. *Giorgione.* 2 v. Berlin, Reimer, 1936. 3 ed.

4330. Laudau, Paul. *Giorgione.* Berlin, Bard, 1903. (Die Kunst, 20).

4331. Magugliani, Lodovico. *Introduzione a Giorgione ed alla pittura veneziana del Rinascimento.* Milano, Ceschina, 1970.

4332. Morassi, Antonio. *Giorgione.* Milano, Hoepli, 1942.

4333. Palazzo Ducale (Venice). *Giorgione e i Giorgioneschi, catalogo della mostra.* 11 giugno–23 ottobre 1955. Venezia, Casa Editrice Arte Veneta, 1955.

4334. Pallucchini, Rodolfo, ed. *Giorgione e l'umanesimo veneziano.* 2 v. Firenze, Olschki, 1981. (Civiltà veneziana saggi, 27).

4335. Pergola, Paolo della. *Giorgione.* Milano, Martello, 1955.

4336. Phillips, Duncan. *The leadership of Giorgione.* Washington, D.C., The American Federation of the Arts, 1937.

4337. Pignatti, Terisio. *Giorgione, complete edition.* Trans. by Clovis Whitfield. London, Phaidon, 1971. (Rev. ed.: Milano, Alfieri, 1978).

4338. Richter, George M. *Giorgio da Castelfranco, called Giorgione.* Chicago, University of Chicago Press, 1937.

4339. Schaukal, Richard von. *Giorgione; oder, Gespräche über die Kunst.* München, Müller, 1907.

4340. Trevisan, Luca L. *Giorgione.* Venezia, Emiliana, 1951.

4341. Tschmelitsch, Günther. *Zorzo, genannt Giorgione; der Genius und sein Bannkreis.* Wien, Braumüller, 1975.

4342. Venturi, Lionello. *Giorgione e il Giorgionismo.* Milano, Hoepli, 1913.

4343. Villard, Ugo Monneret de. *Giorgione da Castelfranco; studio critico.* Bergamo, Istituto Italiano d'Arti Grafiche, 1904.

4344. Zampetti, Pietro. *L'opera completa de Giorgione.* Milano, Rizzoli, 1968. (I classici dell'arte, 16). (CR). (English ed.: New York, Abrams, 1968).

Giotto di Bondone, 1266–1337

4345. Alazard, Jean. *Giotto, biographie critique.* Paris, Librairie Renouard, 1918.

4346. Baccheschi, Edi. *The complete paintings of Giotto.* New York, Abrams, 1966. (CR).

4347. Bandera Bistoletti, Sandrina. *Giotto: catalogo completo dei dipinti.* Firenze, Cantini, 1989. (CR).

4348. Barasch, Moshe. *Giotto and the language of gesture.* Cambridge, [Cambridgeshire]/ New York, Cambridge University Press, 1987.

4349. Battisti, Eugenio. *Giotto, biographical and critical study.* Trans. by James Emmons. Lausanne, Skira, 1960; U.S. distribution: World, Cleveland.

4350. Baxandall, Michael. *Giotto and the orators; humanist observers of painting in Italy and the discovery of pictorial composition, 1350–1450.* Oxford, Oxford University Press, 1971.

4351. Bayet, Charles. *Giotto.* Paris, Librairie de l'art ancien et moderne, 1907.

4352. Bellinati, Claudio. *La cappella di Giotto all'Arena (1300–1306).* Padova, Tipografia del Seminario di Padova, 1967.

4353. Bellosi, Luciano. *Giotto: complete works.* Firenze, Scala; New York, Riverside, 1990. (1st printing: 1981). (The library of great masters).

4354. Bologna, Ferdinando. *Novità su Giotto; Giotto al tempo della cappella Peruzzi.* Torino, Einaudi, 1969.

4355. Carli, Enzo. *Giotto.* Firenze, Electa, 1951. (Astra-Arengarium collana di monografie d'arte, pittori, 19).

4356. Carrà, Carlo. *Giotto.* London, Zwemmer, 1925.

4357. Cecci, Emilio. *Giotto.* Milano, Hoepli, 1937.

4358. ———. *Giotto.* Trans. by Elizabeth Andrews. New York, McGraw-Hill, 1961. (Not the same title as above).

4359. Cole, Bruce. *Giotto and Florentine painting, 1280–1375.* New York, Harper & Row, 1976.

4360. de Selincourt, Basil. *Giotto.* London, Duckworth, 1905. (U.S. ed.: New York, Scribner, 1911).

4361. Edgerton, Samuel Y. *The heritage of Giotto's geometry: art and science on the eve of the scientific revolution.* Ithaca, Cornell University Press, 1991.

4362. Gabrielli, Margherita. *Giotto e l'origine del realismo.* Roma, Bardi. 1981.

4363. Gioseffi, Decio. *Giotto architetto.* Milano, Edizioni di Comunità, 1963.

4364. Gnudi, Cesare. *Giotto.* Milano, Martelli, 1959.

4365. Gosebruch, Martin. *Giotto und die Entwicklung des neuzeitlichen Kunstbewusstseins.* Köln, DuMont Schauberg, 1962.

4366. ———, et al. *Giotto di Bondone.* Konstanz, Leonhardt, 1970. (Persönlichkeit und Werk, 3).

4367. Hausenstein, Wilhelm. *Giotto.* Berlin, Propyläen, 1923.

4368. Hetzer, Theodor. *Giotto, Grundlegung der neuzeitlichen Kunst.* Mittenwald/Mäander/ Stuttgart, Urachhaus, 1981. (Schriften Theodor Hetzers, 1).

4369. Mariani, Valerio. *Giotto.* Napoli, Libreria Scientifica, 1966.

4370. ———. *Giotto, 1337–1937.* Roma, Palombi, 1937.

4371. Luzzatto, Guido L. *L'arte di Giotto.* Bologna, Zanichelli, 1927.

4372. Marle, Raimond van. *Recherches sur l'iconographie de Giotto et de Duccio.* Strassburg, Heitz, 1920.

4373. Perkins, F. Mason. *Giotto.* London, Bell, 1902.

4374. Previtali, Giovanni. *Giotto.* 2 v. Milano, Fabbri, 1964. (I maestri del colore, 26–27).

4375. ———. *Giotto e la suo bottega.* Milano, Fabbri, 1974.

4376. Quilter, Harry. *Giotto.* London, Sampson Low, 1880.

4377. Rintelin, Friedrich. *Giotto und die Giotto-Apokryphen.* München/Leipzig, Müller, 1912. (Rev. ed.: Basel, Schwabe, 1923).

4378. Rosenthal, Erwin. *Giotto in der mittelalterlichen Geistesentwicklung.* Augsburg, Filser, 1924.

4379. Ruskin, John. *Giotto and his works in Padua, being an explanatory notice of the series of woodcuts executed for the Arundel Society after the frescoes in the Arena Chapel.* [London], Arundel Society, 1854. (Reprint: London, Allen, 1905).

4380. Salvini, Roberto. *All the paintings of Giotto.* Trans. by Paul Colacicchi. 2 v. New York, Hawthorn, 1964. (Complete Library of World Art, 18–19).

4381. ——— and Benedictis, Cristina de. *Giotto bibliografia.* 2 v. Roma, Palombi, 1938/ Roma, Istituto Nazionale d'Archeologia e Storia dell'Arte, 1973. (Istituto nazionale d'archeologia e storia dell'arte, bibliografie e cataloghi, 4).

4382. Schneider, Laurie, ed. *Giotto in perspective.*

Englewood Cliffs, N.J., Prentice-Hall, 1974.

4383. Sirén, Osvald. *Giotto and some of his followers.* Trans. by Frederick Schenck. 2 v. Cambridge, Mass., Harvard University Press, 1917. (Reprint: New York, Hacker, 1975).

4384. Smart, Alastair. *The Assisi problem and the art of Giotto.* Oxford, Oxford University Press, 1971.

4385. Supino, Igino B. *Giotto.* 2 v. Firenze, Ist. di Ediz. Artistiche, 1920.

4386. Thode, Henry. *Giotto.* Bielefeld/Leipzig, Velhagen & Klasing, 1899. (Künstler-Monographien, 43).

4387. Vigorelli, Giancarlo. *L'opera completa di Giotto.* Milano, Rizzoli, 1966. (CR). (Classici dell'arte, 3).

4388. Weigelt, Curt H. *Giotto: des Meisters Gemälde.* Stuttgart, Deutsche Verlagsanstalt, 1925. (Klassiker der Kunst in Gesamtausgaben, 19).

Giovanni da Bologna (called Giambologna), 1529–1608

4389. Avery, Charles. *Giambologna: the complete sculpture.* C. Avery; principal photographs by David Finn. Mt. Kisco, N.Y., Moyer Bell, 1987.

4390. Desjardins, Abel. *La vie et l'oeuvre de Jean Bologne.* Paris, Quantin, 1883.

4391. Dhanens, Elisabeth. *Jean Boulogne, Giovanni Bologna Fiammingo; Douai 1529–Florence 1608.* Brussels, Paleis der Academiën, 1956. (Vlaamsche Academie voor Wetenschappen, Lettern en Schoone Kunsten van Belgie, Brussels; Klasse der Schoone Kunsten; Verhandelingen, 11).

Giovanni da Milano, 1300–1370

4392. Boscovits, Miklos. *Giovanni da Milano.* Firenze, Sadea/Sansoni, 1966. (I diamanti dell'arte, 13).

4393. Castelfranchi-Vegas, Liana. *Giovanni da Milano.* Milano, Fabbri, 1965. (I maestri del colore, 111).

4394. Cavadini, Luigi. *Giovanni da Milano.* Valmorea, Comune di Valmorea, 1980.

4395. Marabottini, Alessandro. *Giovanni da Milano.* Firenze, Sansoni, 1950. (Monografie e studi a cura dell'Istituto di Storia dell'Arte dell'Università di Firenze, 5).

Giovanni da Fiesole *see* Angelico, Fra

Giovanni da Udine, 1487–1561

4396. Bartolini, Elio. *Giovanni da Udine: la vita.* Udine, Casamassima, 1987.

4397. Dacos, Nicole and Furlan, Caterina. *Giovanni da Udine, 1487–1561.* Udine, Casamassima, 1987.

4398. Giovanni da Udine. *Giovanni da Udine.* 3 v. [Udine], Casamassima, 1987.

4399. ———. *I Libri dei conti.* A cura di Liliana Cargnelutti. Udine, Casamassima, 1987.

Giovanni da Verona, 1457–1525

4400. Lugano, Placido. *Di Fra Giovanni da Verona, maestro d'intaglio e di tarsia e della sua scuola.* Siena, Lazzeri, 1905.

Giovanni di Paolo, 1403–1482

4401. Brandi, Cesare. *Giovanni di Paolo.* Firenze, Le Monnier, 1947.

4402. Pope-Hennessy, John. *Giovanni di Paolo, 1403–1483.* London, Chatto, 1937.

Giovanni di Pietro *see* Spagna, Lo

Girardon, Francois, 1628–1715

4403. Corrard de Breban. *Notice sur la vie et les oeuvres de François Girardon de Troyes.* Troyes, Fèvre, 1850. 2 ed.

4404. Francastel, Pierre. *Girardon; biographie et catalogue critiques; l'oeuvre complète de l'artiste.* Paris, Beaux-Arts, 1928. (CR).

4405. Musée des Beaux-Arts (Troyes). *Mignard et Girardon.* 25 juin au 2 octobre 1955. Troyes, Musée des Beaux-Arts, 1955.

Girodet-Trioson, Anne Louis, 1767–1824

4406. Bernier, Georges. *Anne-Louis Girodet, 1764–1824, prix de Rome 1789.* Paris, Damase, 1975.

4407. Coupin, P. A. *Oeuvres posthumes de Girodet-Trioson, peintre d'histoire.* 2 v. Paris, Renouard, 1829.

4408. Grasset, August. *Girodet-Trioson, tableau inédit de ce célèbre peintre.* Paris, Loones, 1872.

4409. Leroy, Paul Auguste. *Girodet-Trioson, peintre d'histoire.* Orléans, Herluison, 1892.

4410. Musée de Montargis. *Girodet, 1767–1824; exposition du deuxième centenaire.* Montargis, Musée de Montargis, 1967.

4411. Souesme, Etienne. *Girodet.* Paris, Delauney, 1825.

Girtin, Thomas, 1775–1802

4412. Binyon, Laurence. *Thomas Girtin, his life and works; an essay.* London, Seeley, 1900.

4413. Burlington Fine Arts Club (London). *Exhibition on the works of Thomas Girtin, born 1773, died 1802.* London, Spottiswoode, 1875.

4414. Davies, Randall. *Thomas Girtin's watercolours.* London, Studio, 1924.

4415. Girtin, Thomas and Loshak, David. *The art of Thomas Girtin.* London, Black, 1954. (CR).

4416. Mayne, Jonathan. *Thomas Girtin.* Leigh-on-Sea, Lewis, 1949.

4417. Whitworth Art Gallery, University of Manchester (Manchester, England)/Victoria and

Albert Museum (London). *Watercolours by Thomas Girtin.* January–February, 1975/ March–April, 1975. London, Victoria and Albert Museum, 1975.

Gislebertus, fl. 1125–1150

4418. Grivot, Denis and Zarnecki, George. *Gislebertus, sculptor of Autun.* New York, Orion, 1961.

Giulio Romano, 1499–1546

4419. Carpeggiani, Paolo. *Giulio Romano a Mantova: "—una nuova e strava ganta maniera."* P. Carpeggiani, Chiara Tellini Perinia. Mantova, Sintesi, 1987.

4420. Carpeggiani, Paolo, et al. *Studi su Giulio Romano; omaggio all'artista nel 450 della venuta a Mantova (1524–1974).* San Benedetto Po, Accademia Polironiana, 1975. (Biblioteca Polironiana di Fonti e Studi, 2).

4421. Carpi, Piera. *Giulio Romano ai servigi di Federico II Gonzaga.* Mantova, Mondovi, 1920.

4422. *Convegni internazionale di studi su "Giulio Romano e l'espansione europea del Rinascimento,"* Mantua, 1989. Mantova, Palazzo ducale, Teatro scientifico del Bibiena, 1–5 ottobre, 1989. Relatori, Oriana Baracchi ... [et al.]. Mantova. Accademia nazionale virgiliana, 1989.

4423. D'Arco, Carlo. *Istoria della vita e delle opere di Giulio Pippi Romano.* Mantua, Negretti, 1842. 2 ed.

4424. Grand Palais (Paris). *Jules Romain: l'Histoire de Scipion; tapisseries et dessins.* 26 mai–2 octobre 1978. Paris, Editions de la réunion des musées nationaux, 1978.

4425. Hartt, Frederick. *Drawings by Giulio Romano in the National Museum in Stockholm.* [Stockholm], Nationalmusei Arsbok, 1939.

4426. ———. *Giulio Romano.* 2 v. New Haven, Yale University Press, 1958.

4427. Romano, Giulio. *Giulio Romano.* Saggi di Ernst H. Gombrich ... [et al.]. Milano, Electa, 1989.

Glackens, William James, 1870–1938

4428. Allyn, Nancy E. *William Glackens a catalogue of book and magazine illustrations.* N.E. Allyn and Elizabeth Hawkes. Wilmington, Del. Delaware Art Museum, 1987.

4429. DuBois, Guy P. *William J. Glackens.* New York, Whitney Museum of American Art, 1931.

4430. Glackens, Ira. *William Glackens and the Ashcan Group; the emergence of the realism in American art.* New York, Crown, 1957.

4431. Watson, Forbes. *William Glackens.* New York, Duffield, 1923.

4432. Whitney Museum of American Art (New York). *William Glackens, memorial exhibition.* December 14, 1938, to January 15, 1939. New York, Whitney Museum of American Art, 1938.

Gleizes, Albert, 1881–1953

4433. Alibert, Pierre. *Albert Gleizes: naissance et avenir du cubisme.* Paris, Aaubin-Visconti, 1982.

4434. Cassou, Jean, ed. *Albert Gleizes [hommage].* [Lyon], Atelier de la Rose, 1954.

4435. Chevalier, Jean, ed. *Albert Gleizes et le Cubisme.* [Text in French, German, and English]. Basel, Basilius Presse, 1962.

4436. Gleizes, Albert and Metzinger, Jean. *Du Cubisme.* Paris, Figuière, 1912. (English ed.: London, Unwin, 1913).

4437. ———. *L'art sacré d'Albert Gleizes.* [Exposition], 22 mai–31 aout, 1985. Caen, Musée des Beaux-arts de Caen, 1985.

4438. Solomon R. Guggenheim Museum (New York). *Albert Gleizes, 1881–1953; a retrospective exhibition.* New York, Guggenheim Foundation, 1964. (CR).

Gleyre, Marc Charles Gabriel, 1806–1874

4439. Clément, Charles. *Gleyre; étude biographique et critique, avec le catalogue raisonné de l'oeuvre du maitre.* Paris, Didier, 1878. (CR).

4440. Grey Art Gallery and Study Center, New York University (New York). *Charles Gleyre, 1806–1874.* February 6–March 22, 1980. New York, Grey Art Gallery and Study Center, 1980.

4441. Kunstmuseum (Winterthur, Switzerland). *Charles Gleyre ou les illusions perdues.* [Includes reprint of Clément's catalogue raisonné]. Zürich, Schweizerisches Institut für Kunstwissenschaft, 1974. (CR).

4442. Lugeon, Raphael. *Charles Gleyre, le peintre et l'homme.* Lausanne, Imprimérie centrale, 1939.

4443. Thévoz, Michel. *L'académisme et ses fantasmes: le réalisme imaginaire de Charles Gleyre.* Paris, Editions de minuit, 1980.

Gloeden, Wilhelm von, 1856–1931

4444. Barthes, Roland. *Wilhelm von Gloeden; interventi di Joseph Beuys, Michelangelo Pistoletta, Andy Warhol.* Napoli Amelio, 1978.

4445. Falzone del Barbaró, Michele, et al. *Le fotografie di von Gloeden.* Milano, Longanesi, 1980.

4446. Gloeden, Wilhelm von. *Photographs of the classic male nude.* Preface by Jean-Claude Lemagny. New York, Camera/Graphic, 1977.

4447. Kunsthalle Basel. *Wilhelm von Gloeden*

(1856–1931). 15. Juli bis 9. September 1979. [Text by Ekkehard Hieronimus]. Basel, Kunsthalle, 1979.

4448. Pohlmann. Ulrich. *Wilhelm von Gloeden: Sehnsucht nach Arkadien.* Berlin, Nishen, 1987.

Goes, Hugo van der, 1435?–1482

4449. Denis, Valentin. *Hugo van der Goes.* Bruxelles, Elsevier, 1956. (Connaissance des primitifs Flamands, 1).

4450. Destrée, Joseph. *Hugo van der Goes.* Bruxelles/Paris, Librairie d'art et d'histoire/van Oest, 1914.

4451. Friedländer, Max J. *Hugo van der Goes.* Trans. by Heinz Norden. Leyden, Sijthoff/Brussels, La Connaissance, 1969. (Early Netherlandish Painting, 4).

4452. Knipping, John B. *Hugo van der Goes.* Amsterdam, Becht, 1940. (Palet serie, 3).

4453. Pfister, Kurt. *Hugo van der Goes.* Basel, Schwabe, 1923.

4454. Rey, Robert. *Hugo van der Goes.* Bruxelles, Cercle d'Art, 1945.

4455. Sander, Jochen. Hugo van der Goes: Stilentwicklung und Chronologie. Mainz, P. von Zabern, 1992. (Nerliner Schriften zur Kunst, 2).

4456. Wauters, Alphonse. *Hugues van der Goes, sa vie et ses oeuvres.* Bruxelles, Hayez, 1872.

4457. Winkler, Friedrich. *Das Werk des Hugo van der Goes.* Berlin, de Gruyter, 1964.

Gogh, Vincent van, 1853–1890

4458. Andriesse, Emmy. *De Wereld van van Gogh.* [Photographs; text in Dutch/English/French]. Haag, Daamen, 1953.

4459. Artaud, Antonin. *Van Gogh, le suicidé de la société.* Paris, K éditeur, 1947.

4460. Arts Council of Great Britain. *Vincent van Gogh, 1853–1890; an exhibition of paintings and drawings.* London, Arts Council of Great Britain, 1947.

4461. Badt, Kurt. *Die Farbenlehre van Goghs.* New ed. Köln, DuMont Schauberg, 1981.

4462. Bailey, Martin. *Young Vincent: the story of Van Gogh's years in England.* London, W.H. Allen, 1990.

4463. Bauer, Walter. *Die Sonne von Arles; das Leben von Vincent van Gogh.* Hattingen (Ruhr), Hundt, 1956. 2 ed.

4464. Beucken, Jean de. *Un portrait de Vincent van Gogh.* Liège, Editions du Balancier, 1938.

4465. Bonafoux, Pascal. *Van Gogh.* Translated from the French by Alexandra Campbell. New York, H. Holt, 1990. 1st American ed.

4466. ———. *Van Gogh par Vincent.* Paris, Denoël, 1986 (2nd printing, 1988).

4467. ———. *Van Gogh, the passionate eye.* New York, H.N. Abrams, 1992.

4468. Bourniquel, Camille, et al. *Van Gogh.* [Pa-

ris], Hachette, 1968.

4469. Braunfels, Wolfgang, ed. *Vincent van Gogh: ein Leben in Einsamkeit und Leidenschaft.* Berlin, Safari, 1962.

4470. Bremmer, Henricus P. *Vincent van Gogh, inleidende beschouwingen.* Amsterdam, Versluys, 1911.

4471. Bronkhorst, Hans. *Vincent van Gogh.* New York, Portland House, [1990?].

4472. Brooks, Charles M. *Vincent van Gogh; a bibliography comprising a catalogue of the literature published from 1890 through 1940.* New York, Museum of Modern Art, 1942.

4473. Buchmann, Mark. *Die Farbe bei Vincent van Gogh.* Zürich, Bibliander, 1948.

4474. Cabanne, Pierre. *Van Gogh.* Paris, Somogy, 1961.

4475. Callow, Philip. *Vincent Van Gogh: a life.* Chicago, I.R. Dee, 1990.

4476. Chetham, Charles S. *The role of Vincent van Gogh's copies in the development of his art.* New York, Garland, 1976.

4477. Cogniat, Raymond. *Van Gogh.* Paris, Somogy, 1958. (U.S. ed.: New York, Abrams, 1959).

4478. Colin, Paul E. *Van Gogh.* Trans. by Beatrice Moggridge. New York, Dodd, Mead, 1926.

4479. Cooper, Douglas [and] Hofmannsthal, Hugo von. *Drawings and watercolors by Vincent van Gogh.* New York, Macmillan, 1955.

4480. Courthion, Pierre, ed. *Van Gogh, raconté par lui-même et par ses amis.* Vésenaz-Genève, Cailler, 1947.

4481. Dantzig, Maurits M. van. *Vincent? A new method of identifying the artist and his work and of unmasking the forger and his products.* Amsterdam, Keesing, 1953.

4482. Doiteau, Victor et Leroy, Edgard. *La folie de Vincent van Gogh.* Paris, Editions Aesculape, 1928.

4483. Duret, Théodore. *Van Gogh, édition définitive.* Paris, Bernheim-Jeune, 1919.

4484. Elgar, Frank. *Van Gogh.* Trans. by James Cleugh. New York, Praeger, 1966.

4485. Erpel, Fritz. *Van Gogh, self-portraits.* Oxford, Cassirer, 1964.

4486. Estienne, Charles. *Van Gogh.* Trans. by S. J. C. Harrison. Genève, Skira, 1953.

4487. Faille, Jacob B. de la. *L'époque française de van Gogh.* Paris, Bernheim-Jeune, 1927.

4488. ———. *Les faux van Gogh.* Paris et Bruxelles, van Oest, 1930.

4489. ———. *L'oeuvre de Vincent van Gogh; catalogue raisonné.* 4 v. Paris/Bruxelles, van Oest, 1928. (Rev., English ed.: Amsterdam, Meulenhoff International, 1970. New ed. in 2 v.: San Francisco, Alan Wofsy, 1992). (CR).

4490. ———. *Vincent van Gogh.* Paris, Hyperion, 1939.

4491. Feilchenfeldt, Walter. *Vincent van Gogh &*

Paul Cassirer, Berlin: the reception of van Gogh in Germany from 1901 to 1914. W. Feilchenfeldt; catalogue of the drawings compiled by Han Veenenbos. Zwolle, Waanders. 1988.

4492. Fels, Florent. *Vincent van Gogh*. Paris, Floury, 1928.

4493. Fierens, Paul. *Van Gogh*. Paris, Braun, 1949.

4494. Florisoone, Michel. *Van Gogh*. Paris, Plon, 1937.

4495. Formaggio, Dino. *Van Gogh*. Milano, Mondadori, 1952. (Biblioteca moderna Mondadori, 275).

4496. Forrester, Viviane. *Van Gogh, ou l'enterrement dans les blés*. Paris, Seuil, 1983.

4497. Galerie H. O. Miethke (Vienna). *Vincent van Gogh, Kollektiv Ausstellung*. Jänner 1906. Wien, Ohwala, [1906].

4498. Gemeentemuseum (The Hague). *Vincent van Gogh, herdenkingstentoonstelling*. 30 Maart–17 Mei 1953. 's Gravenhage, [Gemeentemuseum], 1953.

4499. Gogh, Elizabeth du Quesne van. *Personal recollections of Vincent van Gogh*. Trans. by Katherine S. Dreier. Boston/New York, Houghton Mifflin, 1913.

4500. Gogh, Vincent van. *The complete letters*. Trans. by Mrs. J. van Gogh-Bonger and C. de Dood. 3 v. Greenwich, Conn., New York Graphic Society, 1959. 2 ed.

4501. ———. *Letters, 1886–1890; a facsimile edition*. 2 v. London, The Scolar Press, 1977.

4502. ———. *Letters from Provençe*. Selected and introduced by Martin Bailey. London, Collins & Brown, 1990.

4503. ———. *The Mythology of Vincent Van Gogh*. Kodera Tsukasa, editor; Yvette Rosenberg, English editor. Amsterdam/Philadelphia, PA, John Benjamins Pub., 1993.

4504. ———. *Vincent van Gogh and the modern movemenmt, 1890–1914*. Exhibition and catalogue concept, Roland Dorn, Fred Leeman. Translation from the German, Eileen Martin. Freren [Germany], Luca Verlag, 1990.

4505. ———. *Vincent van Gogh: die Rohrfederzeichnungen*. Hrsg. und eingeleitet von Fritz Erpel. München, Schirmer/ Mosel, 1990.

4506. Goldscheider, Ludwig. *Vincent van Gogh*. London, Phaidon, 1947.

4507. Graetz, H. R. *The symbolic language of Vincent van Gogh*. New York, McGraw-Hill, 1963.

4508. Grappe, Georges. *Van Gogh*. Genève, Skira, 1943. (Les trésors de la peinture française, 18).

4509. Hammacher, Abraham M. *Genius and disaster; the ten creative years of Vincent van Gogh*. New York, Abrams, 1968.

4510. ———. *Van Gogh, a documentary biography*. New York, Macmillan, 1982.

4511. Hanson, Lawrence and Hanson, Elisabeth. *Portrait of Vincent, a Van Gogh biography*. London, Chatto & Windus, 1955.

4512. Hautecoeur, Louis. *Van Gogh*. Monaco, Documents d'Art, 1946.

4513. Heinich, Nathalie. *La gloire de Van Gogh: essai d'anthropologie de l'admiration*. Paris, Minuit, 1991. English ed.: Princeton, 1996).

4514. Huisman, Philippe. *Van Gogh, portraits*. Lausanne, International Art Book, 1960. (Rhythmes et couleurs, 5).

4515. Hulsker, Jan. *The complete Van Gogh: paintings, drawings, sketches*. New York, Abrams, 1980.

4516. ———. *Van Gogh in close-up*. Amsterdam, Meulenhoff, 1993. (Meulenhoff editie, 1370).

4517. ———. *Vincent and Theo van Gogh: a dual biography*. James M. Miller, editor. Ann Arbor, Fuller Publications, 1990.

4518. Keulen, Jan van. *Met Van Gogh in de Provençe: verblijf, brieven, werk*. s'-Gravenhage, Staatsuitgeverij, 1987.

4519. Huyge, René. *Van Gogh*. New York, Crown, 1958.

4520. Keller, Horst. *Vincent van Gogh; die Jahre der Vollendung*. Köln, DuMont Schauberg, 1969. (U.S. ed.: New York, Abrams, 1970).

4521. Knapp, Fritz. *Vincent van Gogh*. Bielefeld/ Leipzig, Velhagen & Klasing, 1930. (Künstler-Monographien, 118).

4522. Krauss, André. *Vincent van Gogh: studies in the social aspects of his work*. Göteborg, Acta Universitatis Göthoburgensis, 1983. (Gothenburg Studies in Art and Architecture, 2).

4523. Kuhn-Foelix, August. *Vincent van Gogh, eine Psychographie*. Bergen, Müller & Kiepenheuer, 1958.

4524. Lecaldano, Paolo. *L'opera pittorica completa di Van Gogh e i suoi nessi grafici*. 2 v. Milano, Rizzoli, 1971. (CR). (Classici dell'arte, 51–52).

4525. Leprohon, Pierre. *Vincent van Gogh*. Paris, Bonne, 1972.

4526. Leymarie, Jean. *Van Gogh*. [Paris], Tisné, [1951].

4527. ———. *Who was Van Gogh?* Trans. by James Emmons. Genève, Skira, 1968; U.S. distributors: World, Cleveland.

4528. Leeuw, Ronald de. *The Van Gogh Museum: paintings and pastels*. Trans. by Andrew McCormick. Zwolle, Waanders, 1994.

4529. Lubin, Albert J. *Stranger on earth, a psychological biography of Vincent van Gogh*. New York, Holt, Rinehart, 1972.

4530. McQuillan, Melissa A. *Van Gogh*. New York, Thames and Hudson, 1989.

4531. Mauron, Charles. *Van Gogh, études psycho-critiques*. Paris, Librairie José Corti, 1976.

4532. Meier-Graefe, Julius. *Vincent van Gogh, a*

G

biographical study. Trans. by John Holroyd Reece. 2 v. London/Boston, The Medici Society, 1926. 2 ed.

4533. ———. *Vincent van Gogh, der Zeichner.* Berlin, Wacker, 1928.

4534. Metropolitan Museum of Art (New York). *Van Gogh, paintings and drawings; a special loan exhibition.* New York, Metropolitan Museum of Art, 1949.

4535. Musée d'Orsay (Paris). *Van Gogh à Paris.* [Exposition] Musée d'Orsay, 2 février–15 mai 1988. [Traduit de l'anglais par J.C. Garcias . . . et al.] Paris, Ministère de la Culture et de la Communication, Editions de la Réunion des musées nationaux, 1988.

4536. Museum of Modern Art (New York). *First loan exhibition, November 1929: Cézanne, Gaugin, Seurat, Van Gogh.* New York, Museum of Modern Art, 1929.

4537. ———. *Vincent van Gogh.* [Nov. 4, 1935–Jan. 5, 1936]. New York, Museum of Modern Art, 1935. (Reprint: New York, Arno, 1966).

4538. Nagera, Humberto. *Vincent Van Gogh.* Foreword by Anna Freud. Madison, Conn., International Universities Press. 1990. (1st ed. has title: *Vincent van Gogh, a psychological study.* New York, International Universities Press, 1967).

4539. Nordenfalk, Carl. *The life and work of Van Gogh.* New York, Philosophical Library, 1953.

4540. Orangerie des Tuileries (Paris). *Vincent van Gogh; collection du Musée National Vincent van Gogh à Amsterdam.* 21 décembre 1971–10 avril 1972. Paris, Réunion des Musées Nationaux, 1971.

4541. Pach, Walter. *Vincent van Gogh, 1853–1890; a study of the artist and his work in relation to his times.* New York, Artbook Museum, 1936.

4542. Perruchot, Henri. *La vie de van Gogh.* Paris, Hachette, 1955.

4543. Pfister, Kurt. *Vincent van Gogh.* Berlin, Kiepenheuer, 1929.

4544. Pickvance, Ronald. *Van Gogh in Saint-Rémy and Auvers.* New York, Metropolitan Museum of Art; H.N. Abrams, 1986.

4545. Piérard, Louis. *The tragic life of Vincent van Gogh.* Trans. by Herbert Garland. Boston/New York, Houghton Mifflin, 1925.

4546. Pollock, Griselda and Orton, Fred. *Vincent van Gogh, artist of his time.* Oxford, Phaidon, 1978.

4547. Robin, Michel. *Van Gogh, ou la remontée vers la lumière.* Paris, Plon, 1964.

4548. Schapiro, Meyer. *Vincent van Gogh.* New York, Abrams, 1950.

4549. Scherjon, W. and Gruyter, Jos. de. *Vincent van Gogh's great period; Arles, St. Rémy and Auvers-sur-Oise.* 2 v. Amsterdam, de Spieghel, 1937. (CR)

4550. Stedelijk Museum (Amsterdam). *Vincent van Gogh; paintings, watercolours and drawings.* Amsterdam, Stedelijk Museum, 1966.

4551. Stone, Irving, ed. *Dear Theo: the autobiography of Vincent van Gogh.* Boston, Houghton Mifflin, 1937.

4552. Sweetman, David. *The love of many things: a life of Vincent van Gogh.* London, Hodder & Stoughton, 1990. (1st American ed.: *Van Gogh, his life and his art.* New York, Crown Publishers, 1990).

4553. Terrasse, Charles. *Van Gogh.* Paris, Floury, 1935.

4554. Tralbaut, Marc Edo. *Vincent van Gogh.* New York, Viking, 1969.

4555. ———. *Vincent van Gogh.* New York, Alpine Fine Arts, 1981.

4556. ———. *Van Gogh, eine Bildbiographie.* München, Kindler, 1958.

4557. Uhde, Wilhelm. *Vincent van Gogh in full colour.* [London], Phaidon, 1951.

4558. Uitert, Evert van. *Van Gogh drawings.* Trans. by Elizabeth Willems-Treeman. Woodstock, New York, Overlook Press, 1978.

4559. ———. *Vincent van Gogh, Leben und Werk.* Köln, DuMont Schauberg, 1976.

4560. Valsecchi, Marco. *Van Gogh.* Milano, Electa, 1952. (Astra-Arengarium collana di monografie d'arte, pittori, 35).

4561. Vanbeselaere, Walther. *De Hollandsche periode (1880–1885) in het werk van Vincent Van Gogh (1863–1890).* Antwerpen, De Sikkel, 1937. (CR)

4562. Varenne, Daniel. *Van Gogh: Zundert-Anvers.* Périgueux, P. Fanlac, 1989.

4563. Wadley, Nicholas. *The drawings of van Gogh.* London, Hamlyn, 1969.

4564. Weisbach, Werner. *Vincent van Gogh, Kunst und Schicksal.* 2 v. Basel, Amerbach, 1949.

4565. Wheldon, Keith. *Van Gogh.* London, Brompton Books, 1989.

4566. Wilkie, Kenneth. *The Van Gogh file: a journey of discovery.* London: Souvenir Press, 1990. Rewritten and enl. ed.

4567. Wolk, Johannes van der. *The seven sketchbooks of Vincent van Gogh.* Translated from the Dutch by Claudia Swan. London, Thames and Hudson, 1987. Facsimile ed.

4568. Zemel, Carol M. *The formation of a legend: Van Gogh criticism, 1890–1920.* Ann Arbor, Mich., UMI Research Press, 1980.

4569. Zurcher, Bernard. *Vincent Van Gogh: art, life and letters.* Translated from the French by Helga Harrison. New York, Rizzoli, 1985.

Goltzius, Hendrik, 1558–1617

4570. Bialler, Nancy. *Chiaroscuro Woddcuts: Hen-*

drick Goltzius and his time (1558–1617). Seattle, University of Washington Press, 1993.

4571. Hirschmann, Otto. *Hendrick Goltzius.* Haag, Nijhoff, 1916.

4572. ———. *Verzeichnis des graphischen Werks von Hendrick Goltzius, 1558–1617.* Leipzig, Klinkhardt & Biermann, 1921. (Reprint: Braunschweig, Klinkhardt & Biermann, 1976).

4573. Museum Boymans (Rotterdam). *H. Goltzius als Tekenaar.* Van 23 mei tot 13 juli 1958. Rotterdam, Museum Boymans, 1958.

4574. Museum of Art, University of Connecticut (Storrs, Conn.). *Hendrik Goltzius & the printmakers of Haarlem.* April 22–May 21, 1972. Storrs, Conn., University of Connecticut, 1972.

4575. Nichols, Lawrence W. *The "pen" works of Hendrick Goltzius.* [By] Lawrence W. Nichols, assistant curator, John G. Johnson Collection. Philadelphia, PA, Philadelphia Museum of Art, 1991.

4576. Reznicek, Emil K. J. *Die Zeichnungen von Henrik Goltzius, mit einem beschreibenden Katalog.* 2 v. Utrecht, Haentjens Dekker & Gumbert, 1961. (Utrechtse kunsthistorische Studien, 6). (CR).

4577. Strauss, Walter L., ed. *Hendrick Goltzius, 1558–1617; the complete engravings and woodcuts.* 2 v. New York, Abaris, 1977. (CR).

Golub, Leon, 1922–

4578. Golub, Leon. *Leon Golub.* [Ausstellungs- und Katalogkonzeption, Martin Kunz und Karl-Egon Vester]. Luzern, Kunstmuseum Luzern, 1987.

4579. ———. *Leon Golub: paintings, 1987–92.* [Catalog of an exhibition] curated by Patrick T. Murphy; with an essay by Carrie Rickey. Philadelphia, Institute of Contemporary Art, University of Pennsylvania, 1992.

4580. Gumpert, Lynn. *Golub/Lynn Gumpert/Ned Rifkin.* New York, New Museum of Modern Art, 1984.

4581. Kuspit, Donald. *Leon Golub, existential/activist painter.* New Brunswick, N.J., Rutgers University Press, 1985.

4582. Marzorati, Gerald. *A painter of darkness: Leon Golub and our times.* New York, Viking, 1990.

Gonçalves, Nuño, fl. 1450–1471

4583. Figueiredo, José de. *O pintor Nuño Conçalves.* Lisboa, Typ. do Annuario Commercial, 1910. (Arte portugueza primitiva, 1).

4584. Francis, Anne F. *Voyage of re-discovery; the veneration of Saint Vincent.* Hicksville, New York, Exposition Press, 1979.

4585. Gusmao, Adriano de. *Nuño Gonçalves.* Lis-

boa, Europa-America, 1957.

4586. ———. *Nuño Gonçalves.* [Lisbon], Artis, 1958. (Nova colecçao de arte Portuguesa, 11).

4587. Lapa, Albino. *Historia dos painéis de Nuño Gonçalves.* Lisboa, [Beleza], 1935.

4588. Santos, Reynaldo dos. *Nuño Gonçalves, the great Portuguese painter of the fifteenth century and his altar-piece for the Convent of St. Vincent.* Trans. by Lucy Norton. London, Phaidon, 1955.

Goncharova, Nathalia, 1881–1962 see Larianov, Mikhail

Gonzalès, Eva, 1849–1883

4589. Gonzalès, Eva. *Catalogue des peintures et pastels de Eva Gonzalès.* Préface de Philippe Burty; camée de Théodore de Banville, eau forte de Guérard. Paris, Imprimé par Ch. Delevoye, 1885. (Reprint: New York, Garland Pub., 1981).

4590. Sainsaulieu, Marie-Caroline and Mons, Jacques de. *Eva Gonzalès, 1849–1883.* Etude critique et cataloguer raisonné. Paris, Bibliothèque des arts, 1991.(CR).

Gonzales, Joan, 1868–1908
Julio, 1876–1942
Roberta, 1909–

4591. Cerni, Vicente Aguilera. *Julio Gonzalez.* Roma, Edizioni dell'Ateneo, 1962. (Contributi alla storia dell'arte, 1).

4592. ———. *Julio, Joan, Roberta Gonzalez, itinerario de una dinastia.* [Text in Spanish/English/French/German]. Barcelona, Polígrafa, 1973. (CR).

4593. Galerie Chalette (New York). *Julio Gonzalez.* October–November 1961. [Text by Hilton Kramer]. New York, Galerie Chalette, 1961.

4594. Galerie de France (Paris). *Joan Gonzalez, 1868–1908; Julio Gonzalez, 1876–1942; Roberta Gonzalez; peintures et dessins inédits.* 9 avril–30 mai 1965. Paris, Galerie de France, 1965.

4595. Gilbert, Josette. *Julio Gonzalez, dessins.* 9 v. Paris, Martinez, 1975. (CR).

4596. Museum of Modern Art (New York). *Julio Gonzalez.* New York, Museum of Modern Art, 1956.

4597. Pradel de Grandry, Marie. *Julio Gonzalez.* Milano, Fabbri, 1966. (I maestri della sculture, 25).

4598. Withers, Josephine. *Julio Gonzales, les materiaux de son expression.* 2 v. [Text in French/English/Spanish/German]. Paris, Galerie de France, 1970.

4599. Whitechapel Art Gallery (London). *Julio Gonzalez: Sculptures and drawings.* [Catalogue of] an exhibition organised by the

South Bank Centre and the Whitechapel Gallery. London, The Southbank Centre, Whitechapel, 1990.

Gorky, Arshile, 1905–1948

4600. Gorky, Arshile. *Arshile Gorky, 1904–1948: 17 October–23 December 1989, Sala de Exposiciones de la Fundacion Caja de Pensiones, Madrid; 19 January–25 March 1990, Whitechapel Art Gallery, London.* London, Trustees of the Whitechapel Art Gallery, 1990.

4601. Gorky, Arshile. *Arshile Gorky: oeuvres sur papier 1929–1947 = Arbeiten auf Papier 1929–1947.* Textes par Erika Billeter . . . [et al.]; et les reimpressions des textes de André Breton, Frank O'Hara. Bern, Benteli Verlag; Lausanne, Musée cantonal des beaux arts, 1990.

4602. Jordan, Jim M. and Goldwater, Robert. *The paintings of Arshile Gorky, a critical catalogue.* New York/London, New York University Press, 1982. (CR).

4603. Lader, Melvin P. *Arshile Gorky.* New York, Abbeville Press, 1985.

4604. ———. *Arshile Gorky: three decades of drawings.* New York, G. Peters Gallery in assocoation with John Van Doren, 1990.

4605. Levy, Julien. *Arshile Gorky.* New York, Abrams, 1966.

4606. Mooradian, Karlen. *Arshile Gorky Adoian.* Chicago, Gilgamesh, 1978. (Rev. ed.: *The many worlds of Arshile Gorky,* 1980).

4607. Rand, Harry. *Arshile Gorky; the implications of symbols.* Montclair, N.J./London, Allanheld & Schram/Prior, 1980. (Reprint: Berkeley, University of California Press, 1991).

4608. Rosenberg, Harold. *Arshile Gorky; the man, the time, the idea.* New York, Horizon, 1962.

4609. Schwabacher, Ethel. *Arshile Gorky.* New York, Macmillan, 1957.

4610. Seitz, William C. *Arshile Gorky; paintings, drawings; studies.* [Exhibition catalogue, Museum of Modern Art, New York]. New York, Museum of Modern Art, 1962; distributed by Doubleday, Garden City, N.Y.

4611. Waldman, Diane. *Arshile Gorky, 1904–1948; a retrospective.* [at the Solomon R. Guggenheim Museum, New York, April 24–July 19, 1981]. New York, Abrams, 1981. (CR).

4612. Whitney Museum of American Art (New York). *Arshile Gorky, memorial exhibition.* January 5–February 18, 1951. New York [Whitney Museum], 1951.

Gossaert, Jan, 1478–1532

4613. Gossart, Maurice. *Un des peintres peu connus de l'école flamande de transition: Jean Gossart de Maubeuge, sa vie & son oeuvre.* Lille, Editions du Beffroi, [1902].

4614. Museum Boymans-van Beuningen (Rotterdam). *Jan Gossaert genaamd Mabuse. 15 mei–27 juni 1965.* [Rotterdam, Museum Boymans-van Beuningen, 1965]. (CR).

4615. Segard, Achille. *Jean Gossaert, dit Mabuse.* Bruxelles et Paris, van Oest, 1923.

4616. Weisz, Ernst. *Jan Gossart gennant Mabuse, sein Leben und seine Werke.* Parchim i.M., Freises, 1913.

Goujon, Jean, 1510–1565

4617. Du Colombier, Pierre. *Jean Goujon.* Paris, Michel, 1949. (Les maîtres du Moyen Age et de la Renaissance, 11).

4618. Gailhabaud, Jules. *Quelques notes sur Jean Goujon.* Paris, Pillet, 1863.

4619. Jarrin, Charles. *Alexandre Goujon.* Bourg, Imprimérie du Courrier de l'Ain, 1886.

4620. Jouin, Henry. *Jean Goujon.* Paris, Librairie de l'Art [1906].

4621. Lister, Reginald. *Jean Goujon, his life and work.* London, Duckworth, 1903.

4622. Vitry, Paul. *Jean Goujon, biographie critique.* Paris, Laurens, 1908.

Gouthière, Pierre, 1732–1813

4623. Robiquet, Jacques. *Gouthière; sa vie, son oeuvre.* Paris, Laurens, 1912.

Goya y Lucientes, Francisco José de, 1746–1828

4624. Adhémar, Jean. *Goya.* Trans. by Denys Sutton and David Weston. Paris, Tisné, 1948; distributed by Continental Book Center, New York.

4625. Alcala Flecha, Roberto. *Literatura e ideologia en el arte de Goya.* Zaragoza, Diputacion General de Aragon, 1988.

4626. Almoisna, José. *La pósthuma peripecia de Goya.* [Mexico City], Imprenta Universitaria, 1949.

4627. Arnaiz, Jose Manuel. *Francisco de Goya: cartones y tapices.* Madrid, Espasa Calpe, 1987.

4628. Art Institute of Chicago. *The art of Goya; paintings, drawings, and prints.* January 30 to March 2, 1941. Chicago, Art Institute of Chicago, 1941.

4629. Bareau, Juliet Wilson. *Goya: truth and fantasy: the small paintings.* Exhibition curated by Juliet Wilson-Bareau, Manuela B. Mena Marqués. Madrid, Museo del Prado; London, Royal Academy of Arts; Chicago, Art Institute of Chicago, 1994.

4630. Baticle, Jeannine. *Goya.* Paris, Fayard, 1992.

4631. Beruete y Moret, Aureliano de. *Goya as portrait painter.* Trans. by Selwyn Brinton. Boston and New York, Houghton Mifflin, 1922.

4632. Brunet, Gustave. *Etude sur Francisco Goya; sa vie et ses travaux; notice biographique et artistique.* Paris, Aubry, 1865.

4633. Calvert, Albert F. *Goya, an account of his life and works.* London, Lane, 1908.

4634. Camon Aznar, José. *Francisco de Goya.* [3 v., ongoing]. [Zaragoza], Caja de Ahorros de Zaragoza, Aragón y Rioja, [1980–]. (CR).

4635. Chabrun, Jean-François. *Goya.* Trans. by J. Maxwell Brownjohn. London, Thames and Hudson, 1965.

4636. Chastenet, Jacques, et al. *Goya, collection génies et réalités.* [Paris], Hachette, 1964.

4637. Cruzada Villaamil, D. G. *Los tapices de Goya.* Madrid, Rivadeneyra, 1870. (Biblioteca de el arte en España, 8).

4638. De Angelis, Rita. *L'opera pittorica completa di Goya.* Milano, Rizzoli, 1974. (Classici dell'arte, 74).

4639. Delteil, Loys. *Francisco Goya.* 2 v. Paris, [Delteil], 1922. (Le peintre graveur illustré, 14–15).

4640. Desparmet Fitz-gerald, Xavière. *L'oeuvre peint de Goya, catalogue raisonné.* 4 v. Paris, de Nobele, 1928–1950. (CR).

4641. Encina, Juan de la [pseud., Gutierrez Abascal, Ricardo]. *El mundo historico y poetico de Goya.* México, D.F., La Casa de Espana, 1939.

4642. ———. *Goya en zig-zag; bosquejo de interpretacion biográfica.* Madrid, Espasa-Calpe, [1928].

4643. Estarico, Leonard. *Francisco de Goya, el hombre y el artista.* Buenos Aires, El Ateneo, [1942].

4644. Esteve Botey, Francisco. *Francisco de Goya y Lucientes, intérprete genial de su época.* Barcelona, Amaltea, 1944.

4645. Estrada, Genaro. *Bibliografia de Goya.* [Mexico City], La Casa de Espana, 1940.

4646. Ezquerra del Bayo, Joaquin. *La duquesa de Alba y Goya, estudio biografico y artistico.* Madrid, Hermanos, 1928.

4647. Formaggio, Dino, ed. *Goya.* [Milano], Mondadori, 1951. (Biblioteca moderna Mondadori, 166).

4648. Gantner, Joseph. *Goya, der Künstler und seine Welt.* Berlin, Mann, 1974.

4649. Gassier, Pierre. *The drawings of Goya: the sketches, studies, and individual drawings.* New York, Harper & Row, 1975.

4650. ———. *Goya, biographical and critical study.* Trans. by James Emmons. New York, Skira, 1955. (The Taste of Our Time, 13).

4651. Gassier, Pierre and Wilson, Juliet. *Goya, his life and work, with a catalogue raisonné of the paintings, drawings and engravings.* London, Thames and Hudson, 1971. (CR).

4652. Glendinning, Nigel. *Goya and his critics.* New Haven/London, Yale University Press, 1977.

4653. Goya, Francisco. *El cuaderno Italiano, 1771–1786. Los origins del arte de Goya.* 2 v. Madrid, Museo del Prado, 1994.

4654. ———. *Goya and the spirit of enlightenment.* [Catalogue of an exhibition]. Alfonso E. Perez Sanchez and Eleanor A. Sayre, codirectors of the exhibition; with contributions by Gonzalo Aners . . . [et al.]. Boston, Museum of Fine Arts, 1989.

4655. ———. *Goya, 1746–1828.* [Catalogue of an exhibition held at the Galleria internazionale d'arte moderna di Ca' Pesaro, Venice, May 7–July 30, 1989].

4656. ———. *The sleep of reason: reality and fantasy in the print series of Goya:* works by Francisco de Goya from the Algur H. Meadows Collection, Meadows Museum, Southern Methodist University, Dallas, Texas, and the gift of Norton Simon, Pomona College, Claremont, California. Washington, D.C., The Trust for Museum Exhibitions, 1992.

4657. Gudiol, José. *Goya.* New York, Hyperion Press, 1941.

4658. ———. *Goya, 1746–1828; biography, analytical study and catalogue of his paintings.* Trans. by Kenneth Lyons. 4 v. New York, Tudor, 1971. (CR).

4659. Guerlin, Henri. *Goya, biographie critique.* Paris, Laurens, 1923.

4660. Guillaud, Jacqueline and Guillaud, Maurice. *Goya: the phantasmal vision.* Paris/New York, Guillaud Editions; New York, C. Potter; distributed by Crown Publishers, 1987.

4661. Harris, Tomás. *Goya, engravings and lithographs.* 2 v. Oxford, Cassirer, 1964. (CR). (Reprint: San Francisco, Alan Wofsy, 1983).

4662. Hamburger Kunsthalle. *Goya; das Zeitalter der Revolutionen, 1789–1830.* 17. Oktober bis 4. Januar 1981. Hamburg, Hamburger Kunsthalle/Prestel, 1980.

4663. Held, Jutta. *Farbe und Licht in Goyas Malerei.* Berlin, de Gruyter, 1964.

4664. Helman, Edith. *Trasmundo de Goya.* Madrid, Revista de Occidente, 1963.

4665. Hofmann, Julius. *Francisco de Goya, Katalog seines graphischen Werkes.* Wien, Gesellschaft für Vervielfältigende Kunst, 1907. (CR).

4666. Hofmann, Werner, Hrsg. *Goya: Das Zeitalter der Revolutionen, 1789–1830.* Herausgeber, Werner Hofmann; Katalogredaktion, Werner Hofmann . . . et al.]. München, Prestel, 1980.

4667. Holscher, Thomas. *Bild und Exzess: Näherungen zu Goya.* München, Matthes & Seitz, 1988.

4668. Hull, Anthony H. *Goya: man among kings.* New York, Hamilton Press, 1987.

4669. Huxley, Aldous L. *The complete etchings of Goya.* New York, Crown, 1943.

4670. Lafond, Paul. *Goya.* Paris, Baranger, [1901].

G

4671. Lafuente Ferrari, Enrique. *Antecedentes, coincidencias e influencias del arte de Goya.* Catalogo ilustrado de la exposicion celebrada en 1932. Ahora publicado con un estudio preliminar sobre la situacion y la estela del arte de Goya. Madrid, Sociedad Española de Amigos del Arte, 1947. (Reprint: Madrid, Amigos del Museu del Prado, 1987).

4672. Lefort, Paul. *Francisco Goya, étude biographique et critique, suivie de l'essai d'un catalogue raisonné de son oeuvre gravé et lithographié.* Paris, Renouard, 1877. (CR).

4673. Lewis, D. B. Wyndham. *The world of Goya.* New York, Clarkson Potter, 1968.

4674. Licht, Fred, ed. *Goya in perspective.* Englewood, Cliffs, N.J., Prentice-Hall, 1973.

4675. ———. *Goya, the origins of the modern temper in art.* New York, Universe Books, 1979.

4676. Lopez-Rey, José. *A cycle of Goya's drawings; the expression of Truth and Liberty.* New York, Macmillan, 1956.

4677. ———. *Goya y el mundo a su alrededor.* Buenos Aires, Editorial Sudamericana, 1947.

4678. Malraux, André. *Dessins de Goya au Musée du Prado.* [Genève], Skira, 1947.

4679. ———. *Saturn, an essay on Goya.* Trans. by C. W. Chilton. London, Phaidon, 1957; distributed by Garden City Books, N.Y. (New ed.: Saturne; le destin, l'art et Goya, Paris, Gallimard, 1978).

4680. Matheron, Laurent. *Goya.* Paris, Schulz et Thuillie, 1858.

4681. Mayer, August L. *Francisco de Goya.* Trans. by Robert West. London, Dent, 1924.

4682. Museo del Prado (Madrid). *Catálogo ilustrado de la exposition de pinturas de Goya, celebrada para commemorar el primer centenario de la muerte del artista.* Abril–mayo 1928. Madrid, [Museo del Prado], 1928.

4683. Muther, Richard. *Francisco de Goya.* New York, Scribner, 1905.

4684. Nordström, Folke. *Goya, Saturn and Melancholy; studies in the art of Goya.* Stockholm, Almquist & Wicksell, 1962. (Uppsala Studies in the History of Art, New Series, 3).

4685. Oertel, Richard. *Goya.* Bielefeld/Leipzig, Velhagen & Klasing, 1929. 2 ed. (Künstler-Monographien, 89).

4686. Onieva, Antonio J. *Goya, estudio biografico y critico.* Madrid, Offo, 1962.

4687. Ortega y Gasset, José. *Goya.* Madrid, Revista de Occidente, 1958.

4688. Paris, Pierre. *Goya.* Paris, Plon, 1928.

4689. Perez Sanchez, Alfonso. *Goya.* Translated by Alexandra Campbell. London, Barrie & Jenkins, 1990.

4690. Pompey, Francisco. *Goya, su vida y sus obras.* Madrid, Aguado, 1945.

4691. Poore, Charles. *Goya.* New York/London, Scribner, 1938.

4692. Rothe, Hans. *Francisco Goya; Handzeichnungen.* München, Piper, 1943.

4693. Rothenstein, William. *Goya.* New York, Longmans/London, Unicorn Press, 1901.

4694. Roy, Claude. *Goya.* Paris, Cercle d'Art, 1952.

4695. Ruiz Cabraida, Agustin. *Aportación a una bibliografía de Goya.* Madrid, Junta Téchnica de Archivos, 1946.

4696. Saint-Paulien [pseud., Sicard, Maurice I.]. *Goya; son temps, ses personnages.* Paris, Plon, 1965.

4697. Salas, Xavier de. *Goya.* Trans. by G. T. Culverwell. London, Cassell, 1979.

4698. Sambricio, Valentin de. *Tapices de Goya.* Madrid, Patrimonio Nacional, 1946. (CR).

4699. Sanchez-Canton, Francisco J. *Como vivia Goya; I. El inventario de sus bienes; II. Leyanda e historia de la Quinta del Sordo.* Madrid, Instituto Diego Velazquez, 1946.

4700. ———. *Goya.* Trans. by Georges Pillement. New York, Reynal, 1964.

4701. ———. *Los dibujos de Goya.* 2 v. Madrid, Museo del Prado, 1954. (CR).

4702. ———. *Vida y obras de Goya.* Madrid, Editorial Peninsular, 1951.

4703. Sayre, Eleanore A. *The changing image; prints by Francisco Goya.* [Catalogue of an exhibition at the Museum of Fine Arts, Boston, October 24–December 29, 1974]. Boston, Museum of Fine Arts, 1974; distributed by New York Graphic Society, Boston.

4704. Schlosser, Julius. *Francisco Goya.* Leipzig, Seemann, 1922. (Bibliothek der Kunstgeschichte, 26).

4705. Sociedad Espanola de Amigos del Arte. *Antecedentes, coincidencias e influencias del arte de Goya.* Catalogo ilustrado de la exposicion celebrada en 1932, ahora publicado con un estudio preliminar sobre la situacion y la estela del arte de Goya por Enrique Lafuente Ferrari. Madrid, Sociedad Espanola de Amigos del Arte, 1947.

4706. Städtische Galerie im Städtischen Kunstinstitut, Frankfurt am Main. *Goya, Zeichnungen und Druckgraphik.* 13. Februar bis 5. April 1981. Frankfurt a.M., Städtische Galerie, 1981.

4707. Starkweather, William E. B. *Paintings and drawings by Francisco Goya in the collection of the Hispanic Society of America.* New York, Hispanic Society of America, 1916.

4708. Stokes, Hugh. *Francisco Goya, a study of the work and personality of the eighteenth century Spanish painter and satirist.* London, Jenkins, 1914.

4709. Symmons, Sarah. *Goya, in pursuit of patronage.* London, G. Fraser, 1987.

4710. Terrasse, Charles. *Goya y Lucientes, 1746–*

1828. Paris, Floury, 1931.

4711. Tomlinson, Janis Angela. *Francisco Goya: the tapestry cartoons and early career at the court of Madrid.* Cambridge [England]/New York, Cambridge University Press, 1989.

4712. ———. *Francisco Goya y Lucientes, 1746– 1828.* London, Phaidon, 1994.

4713. ———. *Goya in the twilight of the Enlightenment.* New Haven, Yale University Press, 1992.

4714. ———. *Graphic evolutions: the print series of Francisco Goya.* With an introduction by David Rosand. New York, Columbia University Press, 1989.

4715. Vallentin, Antonina. *This I saw; the life and times of Goya.* Trans. by Katherine Woods. New York, Random House, 1949.

4716. Vinaza, Cipriano Munoz y Manzano. *Goya; su tiempo, su vida, sus obras.* Madrid, Hernández, 1887.

4717. Williams, Gwyn A. *Goya and the impossible revolution.* New York, Pantheon, 1976.

4718. Yriarte, Charles. *Goya; sa biographie, les fresques, les toiles, les tapisseries, les eaux-fortes et le catalogue de l'oeuvre.* Paris, Plon, 1867. (CR).

Goyen, Jan van, 1596–1656

4719. Beck, Hans-Ulrich. *Jan van Goyen, 1596– 1656; ein Oeuvreverzeichnis in zwei Bänden.* 2 v. Amsterdam, van Gendt, 1972. (CR).

4720. ———. *Künstler um Jan van Goyen: Maler und Zeichner.* Doornspijk, Davaco, 1991.

4721. Dobrzycka, Anna. *Jan van Goyen, 1596– 1959.* [Text in French]. Poznán, Pánstwowe Wydawn, 1966.

4722. Goyen, Jan van. *The sketchbook of Jan van Goyen from the Bredius-Kroning Collection.* [Edited] by Edwin Buijsen. 2v. The Hague, Bredius Genootschaap, 1993.

4723. Volhard, Hans. *Die Grundtypen der Landschaftsbilder Jan van Goyens und ihre Entwicklung.* Frankfurt, Hemp, 1927.

4724. Waal, Henri van de. *Jan van Goyen.* Amsterdam, Becht, [1954]. (Palet serie, 12).

4725. Waterman Gallery (Amsterdam). *Jan van Goyen, 1596–1656: Conquest of space; paintings from museums and private collections.* Amsterdam, Waterman Gallery, 1981.

Gozzoli, Benozzo, 1420–1497

4726. Bargellini, Piero. *La fiaba pittorica de Benozzo Gozzoli.* Firenze, Arnaud, 1946.

4727. Contaldi, Elena. *Benozzo Gozzoli, la vita, le opere.* Milano, Hoepli, 1928.

4728. Hoogewerff, Goffredo J. *Benozzo Gozzoli.* Paris, Alcan, 1930.

4729. Lagaisse, Marcelle. *Benozzo Gozzoli, les traditions trecentistes et les tendances nouvelles chez un peintre florentin du quattorcento.* Paris, Laurens, 1934.

4730. Mengin, Urbain. *Benozzo Gozzoli.* Paris, Plon, 1909.

4731. Padoa Rizzo, Anna. *Benozzo Gozzoli: catalogo completo dei dipinti.* Firenze, Cantini, 1992. (CR).

4732. ———. *Benozzo Gozzoli, pittore fiorentino.* Firenze, Edam, 1972.

4733. Scarpellini, Pietro. *Benozzo Gozzoli.* Milano, Fabbri, [1966]. (I maestri del colore, 188).

4734. Wingenroth, Max. *Die Jugendwerke des Benozzo Gozzoli; eine kunstgeschichtliche Studie.* Heidelberg, Winter, 1897.

Graf, Urs, ca. 1485–ca. 1528

4735. Amiet, Jacob. *Urs Graf, ein Künstlerleben aus alter Zeit.* Basel/Genf, Georg, 1873.

4736. Koegler, Hans. *Beschreibendes Verzeichnis der Basler Handzeichnungen des Urs Graf.* Nebst einem Katalog der Basler Urs Graf-Ausstellung, 1 Juli. bis 15 September 1926. [Oeffentliche Kunstsammlung]. Basel, Schwabe, 1926.

4737. Lüthi, Walter. *Urs Graf und die Kunst der alten Schweizer.* Zürich unde Leipzig, Füssli, 1928. (Monographien zur schweizer Kunst, 4).

4738. Major, Emil. *Urs Graf; ein Beitrag zur Geschichte der Goldschmiedekunst im 16. Jahrhundert.* Strassburg, Heitz, 1907.

4739. ——— and Gradmann, Erwin. *Urs Graf.* London, Home & van Thal, 1947.

Graff, Anton, 1736–1813

4740. Berckenhagen, Eckhart. *Anton Graff, Leben und Werk.* Berlin, Deutscher Verlag für Kunstwissenschaft, 1967.

4741. Börsch-Supan, Helmut. Die deutsche Malerei von *Anton Graff* bis Hans von Marées, 1760–1870. München, C.H. Beck: Deutscher Kunstverlag, 1988.

4742. Muther, Richard. *Anton Graff, sein Leben und seine Werke.* Leipzig, Seemann, 1881. (Beiträge zur Kunstgeschichte, 4).

4743. Staatliche Museen zu Berlin, Nationalgalerie. *Anton Graff, 1736–1813.* Berlin, Staatliche Museen zu Berlin, 1963.

4744. Vogel, Julius. *Anton Graff, Bildnisse von Zeitgenossen des Meisters in Nachbildungen der Originale.* Leipzig, Breitkopf & Härtel, 1898. (K. Sächsische Kommission für Geschichte. Schriften, 1).

4745. Waser, Otto. *Anton Graff, 1736–1813.* Frauenfeld und Leipzig, Huber, 1926.

Gran, Daniel, 1695–1757

4746. Albertina (Vienna). *Daniel Gran, 1694– 1757.* Gedächtnisausstellung, Sommer 1957. Wien, Albertina, 1957.

4747. Knab, Eckhart. *Daniel Gran.* Wien/München, Herold, 1977. (CR).

G

Grandville (Jean Ignace Isidore Gérard), 1803–1847

4748. Applebaum, Stanley. *Bizarreries and fantasies of Grandville; 266 illustrations from Un Autre Monde and Les Animaux.* New York, Dover, 1974.

4749. Blanc, Charles. *Grandville.* Paris, Audois, 1855. (Reprint: Paris, Garnier, 1979; introd. by Roland Topor).

4750. Garcin, Laure. *J. J. Grandville, revolutionnaire et précurseur de l'art du mouvement.* Paris, Losfeld, 1970.

4751. Nollet, Jules. *Eloge historique de J. J. Grandville.* Anvers, Kornicker, 1853.

4752. Renonciat, Annie. *La vie et l'oeuvre de J.J. Grandville.* Préface de René Huyghe; catalogue de l'oeuvre par Claude Rebeyrat. Paris, ACR: Vilo, 1985. (CR).

4753. Sello, Gottfried. *Grandville; das gesamte Werk.* 2 v. München, Rogner & Bernhard, 1969. (CR).

Granet, François-Marius, 1775–1849

4754. Daguerre, Isabelle Neto. *Granet, peintre de Rome.* Isabelle Neto Dragon, Denis Coutagne. Aix-en-Provençe, Association des Amis du Musée Granet, 1992.

4755. Munhall, Edgar. *François-Marius Granet: Watercolors from the Musée Granet at Aix-en-Provence.* With the memoirs of the Painter Granet translated and annotated by Joseph Focarino. New York, The Frick Collection, 1988.

4756. Musée Granet (Aix-en-Provençe). *Granet: paysages de l'Ile de Françe; aquarelles et dessins; collections du Musée Granet, Aix-en-Provençe.* Aix-en-Provençe, Le Musée, 1984.

4757. Toussaint, *Gabriel. Granet: paintre provençal et franciscain, 1775–1849.* Aix-en-Provençe, Librairie A. Dragon : Librairie Makaire, 1927.

Grant, Duncan, 1885–1978.

4758. Grant, Duncan. *Private: the erotic art of Duncan Grant, 1885–1978.* Introd. by Douglas Blair Turnbaugh. London, Gay Mens Press, 1989.

4759. Whatney, Simon. *The Art of Duncan Grant.* London, Murray, 1990.

Grasser, Erasmus, 1450–1518

4760. Halm, Philipp M. *Erasmus Grasser.* Augsburg, Filser, 1928. (Jahresgabe des deutschen Vereins für Kunstwissenschaft, 1927.

4761. Otto, Kornelius. *Erasmus Grasser und der Meister des Blutenburger Apostelzyklus:* Studien zur Münchner Plastik des späten 15. Jahrhunderts. München, Komissionsverlag UNI-Druck, 1988. (Neue Schriftenreihe des Stadtarchivs München: Miscellanea Bavarica Monacensia, 150).

Greco, El, 1541–1614

4762. Ballo, Guido. *El Greco.* [Milano], Mondadori, 1952. (Biblioteca moderna Mondadori, 297).

4763. Barres, Maurice et Lafond, Paul. *Le Greco.* Paris, Floury, [1911].

4764. Béritens, Germán. *Aberraciones del Greco, científicamente consideradas.* Madrid, Fé, 1913.

4765. Bronstein, Leo. *El Greco (Domenicos Theotocopoulos).* New York, Abrams, [1950].

4766. Brown, Jonathan, et al. *El Greco of Toledo.* Boston, New York Graphic Society, 1982.

4767. Calvert, Albert F. and Hartley, C. Gasquoine. *El Greco, an account of his life and works.* London, Lane, 1909.

4768. Calvo Serraller, Francisco. *El Greco: Entierro del conde de Orgaz.* Milano, Electa, 1994.

4769. Camón Aznar, José. *Dominico Greco.* 2 v. Madrid, Espasa-Calpe, 1970. 2 ed. (CR).

4770. Cassou, Jean. *Le Greco.* Paris, Rieder, 1931.

4771. Cocteau, Jean. *Le Greco.* [Paris], Au Divan, [1943].

4772. Cossio, Manuel B. *El Greco.* 2 v. Madrid, Suarez, 1908. (Edicion definitiva al cuidado de Natalia Cossio de Jiminez. Barcelona, Editorial R.M., 1972). (CR).

4773. Crastre, Victor. *Le mythe Greco.* Genève, Cailler, 1961. (Les problèmes de l'art, 9).

4774. *Domenikos Theotokopoulos Kres: ekthese me aphorme ta 450 chronia apo te gennese tou = El Greco of Crete: exhibition on the occasion of the 450th anniversary of his birth.* Epimeleia, Nikou Chatsenikolaou. Herakleiou, Demos Herakleiou, 1990.

4775. Emmrich, Irma. *El Greco.* Leipzig, Koehler & Amelang, 1987.

4776. Escholier, Raymond. *Greco.* Paris, Floury, 1937.

4777. Esclasans, Agustín. *El Greco y su tiempo.* Barcelona, Juventud, 1953.

4778. Encina, Juan de la. *Domenico Greco.* [Mexico City], Leyenda, 1944.

4779. Gallart y Folch, José. *El espíritu y l técnica de "El Greco."* Barcelona, Porter, 1946.

4780. Goldscheider, Ludwig. *El Greco; paintings, drawings and sculptures.* New York. Phaidon, 1954. 3 ed.; distributed by Garden City Books, N.Y.

4781. Gomez de la Serna, Ramón. *El Greco, el visionario de la pintura.* Santiago de Chile, Ercilla, 1941.

4782. Gudiol y Ricart, Josep. *Domenikos Theotokopoulos; El Greco, 1541–1614.* Trans. by Kenneth Lyons. New York, Viking, 1973.

4783. Guinard, Paul. *El Greco, biographical and*

critical study. Trans. by James Emmons. [Lausanne], Skira, 1956. (The Taste of Our Time, 15).

4784. Hadjinikolaou, Nicos, ed. *El Greco: Byzantium and Italy.* [Rethymno], Crete University Press, 1990.

4785. ———. *El Greco: Documents on his life and work.* [Rethymno], Crete University Press, 1990.

4786. ———. *El Greco: Works in Spain.* Rethymno, Crete University Press, 1990.

4787. Ipser, Karl. *El Greco, der Maler des christlichen Weltbildes.* Berlin/Braunschweig, Klinkhardt & Biermann, 1960.

4788. Jorge, Ricardo. *El Greco; nova contríbuiçao biográfica, crítica e médica ao estudo do pintor Doménico Theotocópuli.* Coimbra, Imprensa da Universidade, 1913.

4789. Kehrer Hugo. *Die Kunst des Greco.* München, Schmidt, 1914. 3 ed.

4790. ———. *Greco als Gestalt des Manierismus.* München, Filser, 1939.

4791. ———. *Greco in Toledo; Höhe und Vollendung, 1577–1614.* Stuttgart, Kohlhammer, 1960.

4792. Keleman, Pál. *El Greco revisited: Candia, Venice, Toledo.* New York, Macmillan, 1961.

4793. Lafond, Paul. *Le Greco; essai sur sa vie et sur son oeuvre, suivi d'un catalogue et d'une bibliographie illustré de nombreuses reproductions.* Paris, Sansot, [1913].

4794. Lafuente Ferrari, Enrique. *El Greco, the expressionism of his final years.* Trans. by Robert Erich Wolf. New York, Abrams, 1969.

4795. Lassaigne, Jacques. *El Greco.* Trans. by Jane Brenton. London, Thames & Hudson, 1974.

4796. Legendre, Maurice. *El Greco (Domenico Theotocopuli).* New York, Hyperion Press/ Duel, Sloan and Pearce, 1947.

4797. ——— and Hartmann, A. *Domenikos Thetokopoulos, called El Greco.* London, Commodore, Press, 1937.

4798. Mann, Richard G. *El Greco and his patrons: three major projects.* Cambridge [England]/ New York, Cambridge University Press, 1986.

4799. Manzini, Gianna. *L'opera completa del Greco.* Milano, Rizzoli, 1969. (Classici dell'arte, 35). (CR).

4800. Maranón, Gregorio. *El Greco y Toledo.* Madrid, Espasa-Calpe, 1958. 2 ed.

4801. Marias, Fernando [and] Bustamante Garcia, Agustín. *Las ideas artisticas de El Greco; comentarios a un texto inédito.* Madrid, Ediciones Cátedra, 1981.

4802. Martini, Pietro. *Del pittore Domenico Theotocopulo e di suo dipinto.* Torino, Botta, 1862.

4803. Mayer, August L. *Dominico Theotocopuli,*

El Greco; kritisches und illustriertes Verzeichnis des Gesamtwerkes. München, Hanfstaengl, 1926. (CR).

4804. ———. *El Greco.* Berlin, Klinkhardt & Biermann, 1931.

4805. ———. *El Greco; eine Einführung in das Leben und Wirken des Dominico Theotocopuli gennant El Greco.* München, Delphin, 1916.

4806. Merediz, José A. *La transformación espanola de El Greco.* Madrid, Plutarco, 1930.

4807. Pallucchini, Anna. *El Greco.* Milano, Fabbri, 1964. (I maestri del colore, 42).

4808. Pita Andrade, José Manuel. *El Greco.* [Con la collaborazione di José Alvarez Lopera]. Milano, Mondadori, 1986.

4809. Pye, Patrick. *The time gatherer; a study of El Greco's treatment of the sacred theme.* Dublin, Four Courts Press, 1991.

4810. Reimann, Georg J. *El Greco.* Wien/München, Schroll, 1966.

4811. Rutter, Frank. *El Greco (1541–1614).* N.Y., Weyhe, [1930].

4812. Salas, Xavier de. *El Greco arte de su tiempo: las notas de El Greco a Vasari.* Textos de Xavier de Salas, Fernando Marías. Spain, Iberdrola; Madrid, Real Fundación de Toledo, Junta de Comunidades de Castilla-La Mancha, 1992.

4813. San Román y Fernández, Francisco de Borja de. *El Greco en Toledo; nuevas investigaciones acerca de la vida y obra de Dominico Theotocópuli.* Madrid, Suárez, 1910.

4814. Sanchez de Palacios, Mariano. *El Greco, estudio biografico y critico.* Madrid, Offo, 1961.

4815. Trapier, Elizabeth du Gué. *El Greco.* New York, Hispanic Society of America, 1925.

4816. ———. *El Greco; early years at Toledo, 1576–1586.* New York, Hispanic Society of America, 1958.

4817. Vallentin, Antonina. *El Greco.* Trans. by Andrew Révai and Robin Chancellor. Garden City, N.Y., Doubleday, 1955.

4818. Vázquez Campo, Antonio. *El divino Greco, puntualizaciones en torno a su vida y obra.* Madrid, Prensa Española, 1974.

4819. Villegas López, Manuel, ed. *El Greco, antologia de textos en torno a su vida y obra.* Madrid, Taurus, 1960. (Ser y tiempo, temas de España, 10).

4820. Wethey, Harold E. *El Greco and his school.* 2 v. Princeton, N.J., Princeton University Press, 1962.

4821. Willumsen, Jens F. *La jeunesse du peintre El Greco; essai sur la transformation de l'artiste byzantin en peintre européen.* 2 v. Paris, Crès, 1927.

4822. Zervos, Christian. *Les oeuvres du Greco en Espagne.* Paris, Cahiers d'Art, 1939.

G

Greenaway, Kate, 1846–1901

4823. Greenaway, Kate. *The complete Kate Greenaway, featuring The Language of Flowers and listing all her illustrated books with value guide.* Watkins Glen, N.Y., Century House, 1967.

4824. Schuster, Thomas E. *Printed Kate Greenaway: a catalogue raisonné.* Thomas E. Schuster and Rodney Engen. London, T.E. Schuster, 1986. (CR).

4825. Spielmann, M. H. and Layard, G. S. *Kate Greenaway.* London, Black, 1905.

4826. Taylor, Ina. *The art of Kate Greenaway: a nostalgic portrait of childhood.* Gretna, La. Pelican Pub. Co., 1991.

Greenough, Horatio, 1805–1852

4827. Greenough, Horatio. *Form and function; remarks on art, design, and architecture.* Ed. by Harold A. Small. Berkeley, University of California Press, 1969.

4828. ———. *Letters of Horatio Greenough, American sculptor.* Ed. by Nathalia Wright. Madison, Wis., University of Wisconsin Press, 1972.

4829. ———. *Letters of Horatio Greenough to his brother, Henry Greenough.* Ed. by Frances Boott Greenough. Boston, Ticknor, 1887.

4830. ———. *The travels, observations, and experience of a Yankee stonecutter.* By Horace Bender [pseud.]. New York, Putnam, 1852. (Reprint: Scholars' Facsimiles & Reprints, Gainesville, Fla., 1958. Introd. by Nathalia Wright).

4831. Tuckerman, Henry T. *A memorial of Horatio Greenough, consisting of a memoir, selections from his writings, and tributes to his genius.* New York, Putnam, 1853.

4832. Wright, Nathalia. *Horatio Greenough, the first American sculptor.* Philadelphia, University of Pennsylvania Press, 1963.

Greuze, Jean Baptiste, 1725–1805

4833. Brookner, Anita. *Greuze, the rise and fall of an eighteenth century phenomenon.* Greenwich, Conn., New York Graphic Society, [1972].

4834. *Diderot et Greuze: actes du colloque de Clermont-Ferrand, 16 novembre 1984;* réunis par Antoinette et Jean Ehrard. Clermont-Ferrand, Adosa, 1986.

4835. *Greuze et Diderot: vie familiale et education dans la seconde moitié du XVIIIème siècle.*(Clermont-Ferrand]: Conservation des musées d'art de la ville de Clermont-Ferrand, 1984.

4836. Greuze, Jean-Baptiste. *Jean-Baptiste Greuze.* [Compiled and introduced by Irina Novoselskaya; translated from the Russian by Ruslan Smirnov]. Leningrad, Aurora Art, 1987.

4837. Hautecoeur, Louis. *Greuze.* Paris, Alcan, 1913.

4838. Houssaye, Arsène, et al. *Greuze, sa vie et son oeuvre; sa statue, le Musée Greuze.* Paris, Plon, [1868]. (L'artiste, revue du XIXe siècle, 37).

4839. Martin, Jean. *Catalogue raisonné de l'oeuvre peint et dessiné de Jean-Baptiste Greuze, suivi de la liste des gravures executées d'après ses ouvrages.* Paris, Kadar, [1908]. (CR).

4840. Mauclair, Camille. *Greuze et son temps.* Paris, Michel, 1926.

4841. ———. *Jean-Baptiste Greuze.* Paris, Piazza, [1905]. (CR).

4842. Normand, Charles. *J. B. Greuze.* Paris, Allison, [1892].

4843. Pilon, Edmund. *J.-B. Greuze, peintre de la femme et la jeune fille du XVIII. siècle.* Paris, Piazza, [1912].

4844. Rivers, John. *Greuze and his models.* London, Hutchinson, 1912.

4845. Wadsworth Atheneum (Hartford, Conn.). *Jean-Baptiste Greuze/1725–1805.* 1 December 1976–23 January 1977. Hartford, Conn., Wadsworth Atheneum, 1976.

Grien, Hans Baldung *see* Baldung, Hans

Grieshaber, Hap (i.e., Helmut Andreas Paul), 1909–1981

4846. Boeck, Wilhelm. *Hap Grieshaber, Holzschnitte.* Pfullingen, Neske, 1959.

4847. Eingangshalle des Rathauses, Stadt Reutlingen. *Grieshaber in Reutlingen.* 25. März 1979 bis 6. Mai 1979. Reutlingen, Stadt Reutlingen, 1979.

4848. Fuerst, Margot. *Grieshaber: Die Druckgrafik.* Werkverzeichnis Band 2. 1966–1981. Stuttgart, Hatje, 1984. (CR).

4849. ———. *Grieshaber: ein Lebenswerk.* Stuttgart, Hatje, 1984.

4850. ———. *Grieshaber: Malbriefe.* Stuttgart, Hatje, 1967.

4851. Gobel, Johannes [and] Glockner, Wolfgang. *Grieshaber, der Holzschneider als Maler: Gouachen, Malbriefe, Aquarelle, Holzschnitte, Zeichnungen.* Bonn, Bouvier, 1989.

4852. Grieshaber, Helmut A.P. *Liebe Nanni, liebe Ricca . . .: Malbriefe und Holzschnitte von der Achalm;* mit einem Bericht von der Familie und Fotos von Ricca Achalm; herausgegeben von Hans Marquardt. Frankfurt a.M., Röderberg Verlag, 1986.

4853. Hannsmann, Margarete. *Pfauenschrei: die Jahre mit HAP Grieshaber.* München, H. Knaus, 1986.

4854. Museum für Kunst und Gewerbe (Hamburg). *Grieshaber, der Drucker und Holzschneider.* [September 8–October 6, 1965]. Stuttgart, Hatje, 1965.

4855. Pfäfflin, Friedrich [and] Fuerst, Margot.

Grieshaber; die Plakate, 1934–1979. Stuttgart, Hatje, 1979.

4856. Sandberg, Willem and Fuerst, Margot. *Grieshaber. Der betroffene Zeitgenosse*. Stuttgart, Hatje, 1978.

4857. Studentenstudio für Moderne Kunst (Tübingen). *H. A. P. Grieshaber; eine Ausstellung des graphischen Werkes*. Stuttgart, Verlag KG, 1949.

4858. Universitätsbibliothek (Tübingen). *Grieshaber und das Buch*. 25. Mai bis 14. Juli 1979. Tübingen, Universitätsbibliothek, 1979.

Grimm, Ludwig Emil, 1790–1863

4859. Grimm, Ludwig Emil. *Ludwig Emil Grimm: Briefe*. Herausgegben und kommentiert von Egbert Koolman. 2v. Marburg, N.G. Elwert, 1985. (Bd.I: Textband; Bd.II: Kommentarband).

4860. ———. *Ludwig Emil Grimm: 1790–1863. Maler, Zeichner, Radierer*. Ausstellung, Kassel, Museum Fridericianum, 1.6.–15.9. 1985; Hanau, Schloss Steinheim, 16.11.– 15.12. 1985. Kassel, Weber & Weidemeyer, 1985.

4861. Koszinowski, Ingrid. *Ludwig Emil Grimm: Zeichnungen und Gemälde*. Werkverzeichnis, Ingrid Kosziniwski, Vera Leuschner. 2v. Marburg, Hitzeroth, 1990. (CR).

Gris, Juan, 1887–1927

4862. Cooper, Douglas. *Juan Gris, catalogue raisonné de l'oeuvre peint établi avec le collaboration de Margaret Potter*. 2 v. Paris, Berggruen, 1977. (CR).

4863. ———. *Juan Gris, ou le goût du solennel*. Paris, Skira, [1949]. (Les trésors de la peinture française, 11).

4864. Gaya-Nuño, Juan Antonio. *Juan Gris*. Trans. by Kenneth Lyons. Boston, New York Graphic Society, 1975.

4865. Green, Christopher. *Juan Gris*. [By] Christopher Green with contributions by Christian Derouet and Karin von Maur. London, Whitechapel Art Gallery; New Haven, Yale University Press, 1992.

4866. Gris, Juan. *Juan Gris: correspondence, dessins 1915–1921*. IVAM Centre Julio Gonzalez du 23 octobre 1990 au 13 janvier 1991, Centre Georges Pompidou, Musée national d'art moderne du 29 janvier 1991 au 1er avril 1991. Texte établi et annoté par Christian Derouet. Valencia, IVAM Centre Juio Gonzalez; Paris, Centre Georges Pompidou, 1990.

4867. ———. *Letters of Juan Gris [1913–1927]*. Collected by Daniel-Henry Kahnweiler; translated and edited by Douglas Cooper. London, [Douglas Cooper], 1956.

4868. ———. *Posibilidades de la pintura y otros escritas*. Córdoba, Argentina, Assandri, 1957.

4869. Kahnweiler, Daniel H. *Juan Gris*. Milano, Fabbri, [1967]. (I maestri del colore, 177).

4870. ———. *Juan Gris, his life and work*. Trans. by Douglas Cooper. New York, Valentin, 1947; rev. ed.: Abrams, New York, 1969.

4871. ———. *Juan Gris von Daniel Henry* [pseud.]. Leipzig/Berlin, Klinkhardt & Biermann, 1929. (Junge Kunst, 55).

4872. Kunsthalle Baden-Baden. *Juan Gris*. [July 20–September 29, 1974]. Baden-Baden, Staatliche Kunsthalle, 1974.

4873. Museum of Modern Art (New York). *Juan Gris*. April 9–June 1, 1958. [Text by James Thrall Soby]. New York, Museum of Modern Art, 1958.

4874. Raynal, Maurice. *Juan Gris, vingt tableaux*. Paris, Editions de l'effort Moderne, 1920.

4875. Rosenthal, Mark. *Juan Gris*. New York, Abbeville, 1983.

Gromaire, Marcel, 1892–1971

4876. Gromaire, Marcel. *Marcel Gromaire, 1892–1971: works on paper*. With an introductory essay by R. Stanley Johnson. Chicago, Johnson Fine Art, 1987.

4877. ———. *Marcel Gromaire, 1892/1971:* [exposition] 12 juin/28 septembre 1980. Musée d'art moderne de la ville de Paris. Rédaction du catalogue, Marie-Odile Briot. Paris, Le Musée, 1980.

4878. ———. *Marcel Gromaire: Peinture 1921–1939*. Avant-propos de M.O. Briot et de François Gromaire. Paris, Denoël-Gonthier, 1980.

Gropius, Walter, 1883–1969

4879. Busch-Reisinger Museum. *The Walter Gropius Archive: an illustrated catalogue of the drawings, prints, and photographs in the Walter Gropius Archive at the Busch-Reisinger Museum, Harvard University*. Ed. by Winfried Nerdinger. 4 v. New York, Garland Pub. and Harvard University Art Museums, 1990–1991. (CR).

4880. Cook, Ruth V. *A bibliography: Walter Gropius, 1919 to 1950*. Chicago, American Institute of Architects, 1951.

4881. Fitch, James M. *Walter Gropius*. New York, Braziller, 1960.

4882. ——— [and] Gropius, Ise. *Walter Gropius; buildings, plans, projects, 1906–1969*. Lincoln, Mass., International Exhibitions Foundation, 1972.

4883. Franciscono, Marcel. *Walter Gropius and the creation of the Bauhaus in Weimar: the ideals and artistic theories of its founding years*. Urbana, Ill., University of Illinois Press, 1971.

4884. Giedion, Sigfried. *Walter Gropius*. Paris, Crès, 1931.

4885. ———. *Walter Gropius, l'homme et l'oeuvre*. Paris, Morancé, 1954. (U.S. ed.: *Walter Gropius, work and teamwork*. New York, Reinhold, 1954.)

4886. Gropius, Walter. *Bauhausbauten Dessau*. München, Langen, 1930. (Bauhausbücher, 12). (Reprint: Mainz, Kupferberg, 1974).

4887. ———. *Idee und Aufbau des staatlichen Bauhauses*. Weimar/München, Bauhaus-verlag, 1923.

4888. ———. *Internationale Architektur*. München, Langen, 1925. (Bauhausbücher, 1). (Reprint: Mainz, Kupferberg, 1981).

4889. ———. *The new architecture and the Bauhaus*. Trans. by P. Morton Shand. New York, Museum of Modern Art/London, Faber, [1937].

4890. ———. *Scope of total architecture*. New York, Harper, 1955. (World Perspectives, 3).

4891. Isaacs, Reginald R. *Gropius; an illustrated biography of the creator of the Bauhaus*. Boston, Little Brown, 1991.

4892. Museum of Modern Art (New York). *Bauhaus, 1919–1928*. Edited by Herbert Bayer, Walter Gropius, Ise Gropius. New York, Museum of Modern Art, 1938.

4893. Rudolph, Paul and Gropius, Walter. *Walter Gropius et son école* [being the entire contents of the February, 1950, issue of *L'Architecture d'aujourd'hui*]. Paris, L'Architecture d'aujourd'hui, 1950.

4894. Wingler, Hans M. *The Bauhaus: Weimar, Dessau, Berlin, Chicago*. Cambridge, Mass., MIT Press, 1969.

Gros, Antoine Jean, 1771–1835

4895. Dargenty, G. [pseud., Arthur Auguste Mallebay du Cluseau d'Echérac]. *Le Baron Gros*. Paris, Librairie de l'Art, [1887]. (Les artistes célèbres, 18).

4896. Delestre, Jean-Baptiste. *Gros et ses ouvrages, ou mémoires historiques sur la vie et les travaux de ce célèbre artiste*. Paris, Labitte, [1845]; 2 ed.: Paris, Renouard, 1867.

4897. Escholier, Raymond. *Gros, ses amis et ses élèves*. Paris, Floury, 1936.

4898. Lemonnier, Henry. *Gros; biographie critique*. Paris, Laurens, 1905.

4899. Petit Palais (Paris). *Gros; ses amis, ses élèves*. [Mai–juillet, 1936]. [Paris, Petit Palais, 1936]. (CR).

4900. Tripier le Franc, J. *Histoire de la vie et de la mort du Baron Gros, le grand peintre*. Paris, Martin et Baur, 1880.

Grossmann, Rudolf, 1882–1941

4901. Grossmann, Rudolf. *Homenaje a Rodolfo Grossmann: Festschrift zu seinem 85. Geb-urtstag*. [Von] Sabine Horl, José M. Navarro de Adriaensens, Hans-Karl Schneider, [unter Mitarbeit von Erika Lorenz]. Frankfurt am Main/ Bern/ Las Vegas, Lang, 1977.

4902. Hausenstein, Wilhelm. *Rudolf Grossmann*. Leipzig, Klinkhardt & Biermann, 1919. (Junge Kunst, 7).

4903. Kunstgalerie Esslingen. *Rudolf Grossmann, 1882–1941*. Juni/Juli 1974. Esslingen, Kunstgalerie Esslingen, 1974.

4904. Staatsgalerie Stuttgart. *Rudolf Grossmann, Zeichnungen und Druckgraphik*. September bis Oktober 1963. Karlsruhe, Staatliche Kunsthalle, 1963.

Grosz, George, 1893–1959

4905. Ballo, Ferdinando, ed. *Grosz*. Milano, Rosa e Ballo, 1946. (Documenti d'arte contemporanea, 3).

4906. Baur, John I. H. *George Grosz*. Exhibition and catalogue by the Whitney Museum of Modern Art. January 14–March 7, 1954. New York, Whitney Museum of American Art, 1954.

4907. Bazalgette, Léon. *George Grosz, l'homme & l'oeuvre*. Paris, Escrivains Réunis, 1926.

4908. Becher, Ulrich. *Flaschenpost: Geschichte einer Freundschaft Ulrich Becher, George Grosz*. Herausgegeben von Uwe Naumann und Michael Toteberg. Basel, Lenos, 1989.

4909. Dückers, Alexander. *George Grosz, das druckgraphische Werk*. Frankfurt a.M., Propyläen, 1979. (CR).

4910. Flavell, Mary Kay. *George Grosz, a biography*. New Haven, Yale University Press, 1988.

4911. Grosz, George. *Briefe, 1913–1959*. Herausgegeben von Herbert Knust. Reinbek bei Hamburg, Rowohlt, 1979.

4912. ———. *Drawings, with an introduction by the artist*. New York, Bittner, 1944.

4913. ———. *A little yes and a big no; the autobiography of George Grosz*. New York, Dial, 1946.

4914. Hess, Hans. *George Grosz*. New York, Macmillan, 1974. (Reprint: New Haven, Yale University Press, 1985).

4915. Lewis, Beth I. *George Grosz; art and politics in the Weimar Republic*. Madison, Wis., University of Wisconsin Press, 1971. (Revised edition: Princeton, Princeton University Press, 1991).

4916. Mynona [pseud., Salomon Friedländer]. *George Grosz*. Dresden, Kaemmerer, 1922. (Künstler der Gegenwart, 3).

4917. Ray, Marcel. *George Grosz*. Paris, Crès, 1927.

4918. Sabarsky, Serge. *George Grosz: the Berlin years*. [With] contributions by Marty Grosz . . . [et al.]. New York, Rizzoli, 1985.

4919. Schneede, Uwe M. *George Grosz, his life and work*. Trans. by Susanne Flatauer. London, Fraser, 1979.

Grottger, Artur, 1837–1867

4920. Antoniewicz, Jan B. *Grottger*. Lwów, Altenberga, 1910.

4921. Kanteckiego, Klemensa. *Artur Grottger, szkic biograficzny*. Lwów, Przewodnika naukowego i literackiego, 1879.

4922. Potocki, Antoni. *Grottger*. Lwów, Altenberga, 1907.

4923. Ratajczak, Jozef. *Romantyczni kochankowie: Zygmunt Krasisnski, Fryderyk Chopin, Artur Grottger*. Poznan, Wydawnictwo Poznanskie, 1989.

4924. Rogosz, Józef. *Artur Grottger, Jan Matejko: studja o sztuce w Polsce*. Lwów, Redakcji Tygodnia, 1876.

4925. Táborský, Frantisek. *Arthur Grottger, jeho láska a dílo*. Praze, Orbis, 1933. (Práce Slovanského Ùstavu v Praza, 10).

4926. Wolska, Maryla i Pawlikowski, Michal. *Arthur i Wanda; dzieje milósci Arthura Grottgera i Wandy Monné*. 2 v. Medyka/Lwów, Biblioteki Medyckiej, 1928.

Groux, Henry de, 1867–1930

4927. Baumann, Emile. *La vie terrible d'Henry de Groux*. Paris, Grasset, 1936.

4928. Souguenet, Léon, et al. *L'oeuvre de Henry Groux*. Paris, La Plume, 1899.

Grundig, Hans, 1901–1958
Lea Langer, 1906–1977

4929. Feist, Günther. *Hans Grundig*. Dresden, Verlag der Kunst, 1979.

4930. Frommhold, Erhard. *Hans und Lea Grundig, Einführung*. Dresden, Verlag der Kunst, 1958.

4931. Grundig, Hans. *Künstlerbriefe aus den Jahren 1926 bis 1957*. Mit einem Vorwort herausgegeben von Bernhard Wächter. Rudolstadt, Greifenverlag, 1966.

4932. ———. *Zwischen Karneval und Aschermittwoch, Erinnerungen eines Malers*. Berlin, Dietz, 1957.

4933. Grundig, Lea. *Gesichte und Geschichte*. Berlin, Dietz, 1958.

4934. Hütt, Wolfgang. *Lea Grundig*. Dresden, Verlag der Kunst, 1969.

4935. Ladengalerie (West Berlin). *Lea Grundig, Werkverzeichnis der Radierungen*. Westberlin, Ladengalerie, 1973.

4936. Staatliche Museen zu Berlin, National-Galerie. *Hans Grundig; Malerei, Zeichnungen; Druckgraphik*. Juli bis August 1962. Berlin, Staatliche Museen, 1962.

Grünewald, Matthias, 1470–1528

4937. Behling, Lottlisa. *Die Handzeichnungen des Mathis Gothart Nithart genannt Grünewald*. Weimar, Böhlaus, 1955.

4938. Bianconi, Piero. *L'opera completa di Grünewald*. Milano, Rizzoli, 1972. (Classici dell'arte, 58). (CR).

4939. Bock, Franz. *Die Werke des Mathias Grünewald*. Strassburg, Heitz, 1904. (Studien zur deutschen Kunstgeschichte, 54).

4940. Brion, Marcel. *Grünewald*. Paris, Plon, 1939.

4941. Burkhard, Arthur. *Matthias Grünewald, personality and accomplishment*. Cambridge, Mass., Harvard University Press, 1936. (Reprint: New York, Hacker, 1976).

4942. Dittmann, Lorenz. *Die Farbe bei Grünewald*. München, Wolf & Sohn, 1955.

4943. Escherich, Mela. *Grünewald-Bibliographie (1489–Juni 1914)*. Strassburg, Heitz, 1914. (Studien zur deutschen Kunstgeschichte, 177).

4944. Feurstein, Heinrich. *Matthias Grünewald*. Bonn am Rhein, Verlag der Buchgemeinde, 1930. (Buchgemeinde Bonn, Religiöse Schriftenreihe, 6).

4945. Fraenger, Wilhelm. *Matthias Grünewald in seinen Werken, ein physiognomischer Versuch*. Berlin, Rembrandt, 1936.

4946. Gasser, Helmi. *Das Gewand in der Formensprache Grünewalds*. Bern, Francke, 1962. (Basler Studien zur Kunstgeschichte, N.F., 3).

4947. Hagen, Oskar F. L. *Matthias Grünewald*. München, Piper, 1923. 4 ed.

4948. Hausenberg, Margarethe. *Matthias Grünewald im Wandel der deutschen Kunstanschauung*. Leipzig, Weber, 1927.

4949. Hotz, Walter. *Meister Mathis der Bildschnitzer; die Plastik Grünewalds und seines Kreises*. Aschaffenburg, Pattloch, 1961. (Veröffentlichungen des Geschichts- und Kunstvereins Aschaffenburg e.V., 5).

4950. Hürlimann, Martin. *Grünewald, das Werk des Meisters Mathis Gothardt Neithardt*. Berlin, Atlantis, 1939.

4951. Huysmans, Joris-Karl. *Les Grunewald du Musée de Colmar: des primitifs au retable d'Issenheim*. Edition critique par Pierre Brunel, André Guyaux et Christian Heck. Paris, Hermann, 1988.

4952. Huysmans, Joris K. *Mathias Grünewald*. München, Recht, 1923.

4953. Josten, Hanns H. *Matthias Grünewald*. Bielefeld/Leipzig, Velhagen & Klasing, 1921. (Künstler-Monographien, 108).

4954. Kehl, Anton. *Grünewald-Forschungen*. Neustadt a.d. Aisch, Schmidt, 1964.

4955. Kromer, Joachim. *Matthias Grünewald; die Schlüsselkompositionen seiner Tafeln*. Baden-Baden, Koerner, 1978. (Studien zur deutschen Kunstgeschichte, 356).

4956. Lanckorońska, Maria. *Matthäus Gotthart Neithart, Sinngehalt und historischer Unter-*

grund der Gemälde. Darmstadt, Roether, 1963.

4957. ———. *Matthäus Neithart Sculptor, der Meister des Blaubeurer Altars und seine Werke.* München, Frühmorgen, 1965.

4958. ———. *Neithart in Italien, ein Versuch.* München, Frühmorgen, 1967.

4959. Mayer, August L. *Matthias Grünewald.* München, Delphin, 1920.

4960. Monick, Eugene. *Evil, sexualityy , and disease in Grunewald's body of Christ.* With a foreword by David L. Miller. Dallas, TX, Spring Publications, 1993.

4961. Naumann, Hans H. *Das Grünewald—Problem und das neuentdeckte Selbstbildnis des 20jährigen Mathis Nithart aus dem Jahre 1475.* Jena, Diederichs, 1930.

4962. Pevsner, Nikolaus and Meier, Michael. *Grünewald.* New York, Abrams, 1958.

4963. Réau, Louis. *Mathias Grünewald et le Retable de Colmar.* Nancy, Berger-Levrault, 1920.

4964. Reichenauer, Berta. *Grünewald.* Thaur, Kulturverlag, 1992.

4965. Rolfs, Wilhelm. *Die Grünewald—Legende, kritische Beiträge zur Grünewald-Forschung.* Leipzig, Hiersemann, 1923.

4966. Ruhmer, Eberhard. *Grünewald drawings, complete edition.* Trans. by Anna R. Cooper. London, Phaidon, 1970.

4967. Saran, Bernhard. *Matthias Grünewald, Mensch und Weltbild.* München, Goldmann, 1972.

4968. Schmidt, Heinrich A. *Die Gemälde und Zeichnungen von Matthias Grünewald.* 2 v. Strassburg, Heinrich, 1907/1911. (CR).

4969. Schoenberger, Guido. *The drawings of Mathis Gothart Nithart, called Grünewald.* New York, Bittner, 1948.

4970. Schulze, Ingrid. *Die Erschütterung der Moderne: Grünewald im 20. Jahrhundert; eine Studie.* Leipzig, E.A. Seemann, 1991.

4971. Société pour la conservation des monuments historiques d'Alsace/Société Schongauer. *Grünewald et son oeuvre.* Acts de la Table Ronde organisée par le Centre National de la Recherche Scientifique à Strasbourg et Colmar du 18 au 21 octobre 1974. Strasbourg, Imprimerie des Dernières Nouvelles, [1974].

4972. Vogt, Adolf M. *Grünewald: Mathis Gothart Nithart, Meister gegenklassischer Malerei.* Zürich/Stuttgart, Artemis, 1957.

4973. Weixlgärtner, Arpad. *Grünewald.* Wien/München, Schroll, 1962. (Neue Sammlung Schroll, 3).

4974. Zülch, Walter K. *Der historische Grünewald, Mathis Gothardt-Neithardt.* München, Bruckmann, 1938.

Grupello, Gabriel, 1644–1730

4975. Berghe, Gustaaf van den. *Gabriel Grupello; Opperbeltsnyder van Syne Majesteit.* Geraardsbergen, G. van den Berghe-Steenhoudt, 1958.

4976. Kultermann, Udo. *Gabriel Grupello.* Berlin, Deutscher Verlag für Kunstwissenschaft, 1968.

4977. Kunstmuseum Düsseldorf. *Europäische Barockplastik am Niederrhein; Grupello und seine Zeit.* 4. April bis 20. Juni 1971. Düsseldorf, Kunstmuseum Düsseldorf, 1971.

Grzimek, Waldemar, 1918–1984

4978. Grzimek, Waldemar. *Berliner Kunst von 1770–1930: Studiensammlung Waldemar Grzimek:* 2 Oktober bis 7. November 1982. Redaktion und Organisation, Gertrud Weber; wissenschaftliche Mitarbeit, Willmuth Arenhövel . . . [et al.]. Ausstellungskonzept, Waldemar Grzimek. Berlin, Berlin Museum, 1882.

4979. ———. *Waldemar Grzimek 1918–1984: Plastik, Zeichnungen,* Grafik. [Ausstellung]. Magdeburg, Kloster unserer Lieben Frauen, 12.2.–14.5. 1989. Magdeburg, Kloster unserer Lieben Frauen, 1988.

4980. ———. *Waldemar Grzimek: Plastiken, Zeichnungen, Graphik, 1932–1979.* Berlin, Neuer Berliner Kunstverein, 1979.

4981. Hoffmann, Raimund. *Waldemar Grzimek.* Berlin, Henschelverlag, 1989.

4982. Roters, Eberhard. *Der Bildhauer Waldemar Grzimek.* Mit einem vollständigen Werkverzeichnis. Berlin, Propyläen, 1979. (CR).

Guardi, Francesco, 1712–1793
Giacomo, 1764–1835
Giovanni Antonio, 1699–1760

4983. Binion, Alice. *Antonio and Francesco Guardi; their life and milieu, with a catalogue of their figure drawings.* New York/London, Garland, 1976. (CR).

4984. Bortolatto, Luigina R. *L'opera completa di Francesco Guardi.* Milano, Rizzoli, 1974. (Classici dell'arte, 71).

4985. Damerini, Gino. *L'arte di Francesco Guardi.* Venezia, Istituto Veneto di Arti Grafiche, 1912.

4986. Fiocco, Giuseppe. *Francesco Guardi.* Firenze, Battistelli, 1923.

4987. Goering, Max. *Francesco Guardi.* Wien, Schroll, 1944.

4988. *Guardi: metamorfosi dell'imagine.* [mostra] Castello di Gorizia, giugno–settembre 1987. Scritti di Paolo Casadio . . . [et al.]. [Gorizio], Il Comune, Assessorato alla cultura; Venezia, Stamperia di Venezia, 1987.

4989. Maffei, Fernanda de. *Gian Antonio Guardi,*

pittore di figura. Verona, Libreria Dante, 1948.

4990. Morassi, Antonio. *Guardi: Antonio e Francesco Guardi.* 2 v. Venezia, Alfieri, [1973]. (CR). (Profili e saggi di arte veneta, 11).

4991. ———. *Guardi: i dipinti* [together with] *Guardi: i disegni.* 3 v. Milano, Electa, 1984. [Vol. I: I dipinti, Vol. II: I dipinti; Vol. III: I disegni].

4992. ———. *Guardi: tutti i disegni di Antonio, Francesco e Giacomo Guardi.* Venezia, Alfieri, 1975. (Profile e saggi di arte veneta, 13).

4993. Moschini, Vittorio. *Francesco Guardi.* Milano, Martello, 1952.

4994. Pallucchini, Rodolfo. *Francesco Guardi.* Milano, Fabbri, 1965. (I maestri del colore, 104).

4995. ———. *I disegni del Guardi al Museo Correr di Venezia.* Venezia, Guarnati, 1943.

4996. Pedrocco, Filippo and Montecuccoli degli Erri, Federico. *Antonio Guardi.* Milano, 1992.

4997. Pignatti, Terisio. *Disegni dei Guardi.* Firenze, La Nuova Italia, 1967.

4998. Shaw, J. Byam. *The drawings of Francesco Guardi.* London, Faber, 1951.

4999. Simonson, George A. *Francesco Guardi, 1712–1793.* London, Methuen, 1904.

5000. Zampetti, Pietro. *Mostra dei Guardi.* Palazzo Grassi, Venezia, 5 giugno–10 ottobre 1965. Venezia, Alfieri, 1965.

Guarienti, Carlo, 1923–

5001. Briganti, Giuliano. *Guarienti, disegni e acquerelli.* A cura di Pier Luigi Gerosa; traduzione in francese di Marina Jeronimidis. Oggiono, Edizioni della Seggiola, 1984.

5002. Cortenova, Giorgio. *Carlo Guarienti.* Testi di Giorgio Cortenova, Giuseppe Mazzariol, Andrée Chedid. Milano, Mondadori; Roma, De Luca, 1988.

5003. Sgarbi, Vittorio. *Carlo Guarienti.* Introduzione di Alberto Moravia. Milano, Fabbri, 1985.

Guarini, Guarino, 1624–1683

5004. Accademia delle Scienze di Torino. *Guarino Guarini e l'internazionalità del Barocco; atti del convegno internazionale.* 2 v. 30 settembre–5 ottobre 1968. Torino, Accademia delle Scienze, 1970.

5005. Anderegg-Tille, Maria. *Die Schule Guarinis.* Winterthur, Keller, 1962.

5006. Bernardi Ferrero, Daria de. *I Disegni d'architettura civile et ecclesiastica di Guarino Guarini e l'arte del maestro.* Torino, Albra, 1966.

5007. Guarini, Guarino. *Architettura civile.* Torino, Mairesse, 1737. (Reprint: London, Gregg, 1964. 2 v.).

5008. ———. *Architettura civile.* Introduzione di Nino Carboneri; note e appendice a cura di Bianci Tavassi La Greca. Milano, Polifilo, 1968. (Trattati di architettura, 8).

5009. Meek, Harold Alan. *Guarino Guarini and his architecture.* New Haven/London, Yale University Press, 1988.

5010. Passanti, Mario. *Nel mondo magico di Guarino Guarini.* Torino, Toso, 1963.

5011. Portoghesi, Paolo. *Guarino Guarini, 1624–1683.* Milano, Electa, 1956. (Astra-Arengarium collana di monografie d'arte, serie architetti, 40).

5012. Ruotolo, Renato [et al.]. *I dipinti dei Guarino e le arti decorative nella Collegiata di Solofra.* Napoli, Edizioni Scientifiche Italiane, 1987.

Günther, Ignaz, 1725–1775

5013. Feulner, Adolf. *Ignaz Günther, der grosse Bildhauer des bayerischen Rokoko.* München, Münchner Verlag, 1947.

5014. ———. *Ignaz Günther, kurfürstlich bayrischer Hofbildhauer.* Wien, Österreichische Staatsdruckerei, 1920. (Jahresgabe des deutschen Vereins für Kunstwissenschaft, 1921).

5015. Heikamp, Detlef. *Ignaz Günther.* Milano, Fabbri, 1966. (I maestri della scultura, 18).

5016. Schoenberger, Arno. *Ignaz Günther.* München, Hirmer, 1954.

5017. Städtische Kunstsammlungen Augsburg. *Matthäus Günther, 1705–1788: Festliches Rokoko für Kirchen, Klöster, Residenzen.* [Katalog der Ausstellung, 25.6.–11.9. 1988]. Mit Beiträgen von Rolf Biedermann, Tilman Falk, Bärbel Hamacher, [et al.]. München, Klinkhardt & Biermann, 1988.

5018. Volk, Peter. *Ignaz Günther: Vollendung des Rokoko.* Fotografische Aufnahmen , Wolf-Christian von der Mülbe. Regensburg, Friedrich Pustet, 1991.

5019. Woeckel, Gerhard P. *Franz Ignaz Günther, der grosse Bildhauer des bayerischen Rokoko.* Regensburg, Pustet, 1977.

5020. ———. *Ignaz Günther, die Handzeichnungen des kurfürstlich bayerischen Hofbildhauers Franz Ignaz Günther (1725–1775).* Weissenhorn, Konrad, 1975.

Guercino, Il *see* Barbieri, Giovanni Francesco *called* Il Guercino

Gütersloh, Albert Paris [pseud.], 1887–1973

5021. Doderer, Heimito. *Der Fall Gütersloh, ein Schicksal und seine Deutung.* Wien, Haybach, 1930.

5022. ———, et al., eds. *Albert Paris Gütersloh, Autor und Werk.* München, Piper, 1962.

5023. Gütersloh, Albert Paris [pseud.]. *Bekennt-*

nisse eines modernen Malers. Wien/Leipzig, Zahn und Diamond, 1926.

5024. ———. *Zur Situation der modernen Kunst; Aufsätze und Reden*. Wien, Forum, 1963.

5025. Hutter, Heribert, ed. *A. P. Gütersloh, Beispiele; Schriften zur Kunst, Bilder, Werkverzeichnis*. Wien/München, Jugend und Volk, 1977. (CR).

Guidi, Tommaso *see* Masaccio

Guido da Siena, 13th cent.

5026. Stubblebine, James H. *Guido da Siena*. Princeton, N.J., Princeton University Press, 1964. (CR).

Guillaumin, Jean Baptiste Armand, 1841– 1927

5027. Courières, Edouard des. *Armand Guillaumin*. Paris, Floury, 1924.

5028. Gray, Christopher. *Armand Guillaumin*. Chester, Conn., Pequot Press, 1972. 2 ed., 1991.

5029. Guillaumin, *Jean Baptiste Armand. Armand Guillaumin, 1841–1927: les années impressionistes*. [Exposition]. Pontoise, Musée Pissaro, 5 octobre–17 novembre 1991, Aulnay-sous-Bois, Galerie de l'Hotel de ville, 23 novembre–17 decembre 1991. [Commissaires de l'exposition, Christophe Duvivier, Gérard Boute]. Pontoise, Le Musée; Aulnay-sous-Bois, La Galérie, 1991.

5030. Lecomte, Georges. *Guillaumin*. Paris, Bernheim, 1926.

5031. Serret, Georges [and] Fabiani, Dominique. *Armand Guillaumin, 1841–1921; catalogue raisonné de l'oeuvre peint*. Paris, Mayer, 1971. (CR).

Guimard, Hector, 1867–1942

5032. Rheims, Maurice. *Hector Guimard*. Photographs by Félipe Ferré; explanatory captions and chronology by Georges Vigne. New York, Harry N. Abrams, 1988.

Guston, Philip, 1913–1980

5033. Ashton, Dore. *A critical study of Philip Guston*. Berkeley, University of California Press, 1990. (Revised edition of Yes, but . . .).

5034. ———. *Yes, but . . .: a critical study of Philip Guston*. New York, Viking Press, 1976

5035. Dabrowski, Magdalena. *The drawings of Philip Guston*. New York, Museum of Modern Art, 1988.

5036. Guston, Philip. *Philip Guston: paintings, 1969–1980*. [Edited by Nicholas Serota]. London, Whitechapel Art Gallery, 1982.

5037. Mayer, Musa. *Night studio: a memoir of Philip Guston*. By his daughter, Musa Mayer. New York, Knopf, 1988.

5038. Storr, Robert. *Philip Guston*. New York, Abbeville Press, 1986.

Guttuso, Renato, 1912–

5039. Assemblea Regionale Siciliana. *Catalogo della mostra ontologica dell'opera di Renato Guttuso*. Palermo, Palazzo dei Normanni, 13 febbraio–14 marzo 1971. Palermo, Banco di Sicilia, 1971.

5040. Brandi, Cesare. *Guttuso: antologia critica*. C. Brandi; a cura di Viottorio Rubiu. Milano, Gruppo Editoriale Fabbri, 1983.

5041. Crispolti, Enrico. *Leggere Guttuso*. Milano, A. Mondadori, 1987.

5042. ———. *Guttuso: disegni, 1932–1986*. Poggibonsi, Lalli, 1987.

5043. De Micheli, Mario. *Guttuso*. Milano, [Edizioni il Torchietto], 1966.

5044. Grasso, Franco. *Renato Guttuso, "pittore di Bagheria"*. Catania, Tringale, 1982.

5045. Guttuso, Renato. *Mestiere di pittore; scritti sull'arte e la società*. Bari, de Donato, 1972.

5046. Guttuso, Renato, et al. *Renato Guttuso, negli scritti*. Milano, Fabbri, 1976.

5047. Marchiori, Giuseppe. *Renato Guttuso*. Milano, Edizione d'Arte Moneta, 1952. (Collezione monografie artisti contem-poranei, 1).

5048. Moravia, Alberto [pseud.]. *Renato Guttuso*. [Including] *La vita e l'opera di Guttuso* [by] Franco Grasso. Palermo, Edizioni Il Punto, 1962.

5049. Morosini, Duilio. *Renato Guttuso*. Roma, Cusmano, [1960].

5050. Rubiu, Vittorio. *Guttuso: opere dal 1938– 1985*. Milano, Mazzotta, 1986.

5051. Vittorini, Elio. *Storia de Renato Guttuso e nota congiunta sulla pittura contemporanea*. Milano, Edizioni del Milione, 1960. (Pittori italiani contemporanei, seconda serie, 1).

Guys, Constantin, 1805–1892

5052. Baudelaire, Charles. *Le peintre de la vie moderne, Constantin Guys*. Paris, Kieffer, 1923.

5053. Dubray, Jean-Paul. *Constantin Guys*. Paris, Rieder, 1930.

5054. Duflo, Pierre. *Constantin Guys: fou de dessin, grand reporter, 1802–1892*. Paris, A. Seydoux, 1988.

5055. Galeries Barbazanges (Paris). *Exposition des oeuvres de Constantin Guys*. Préface par Armand Dayot. 18 mai au 1 juin [1904]. Paris, Galeries Barbazanges, 1904.

5056. Geffroy, Gustave. *Constantin Guys, l'historien du Second Empire*. Paris, Galli-mard, 1904.

5057. Grappe, Georges. *Constantin Guys*. Paris, Librairie Artistique et Littéraire, [1910]. (L'art et le beau, quatrième année, 1).

5058. Guys, Constantin. *Constantin Guys, il pit-*

tore della vita moderna. [Mostra] Roma, Palazzo Braschi, 10 settembre–5 ottobre 1980. [Con un saggio di Charles Baudelaire; a cura di Gilda Piersanti. [Milano], Savelli, 1980.

5059. Konody, P. G. *The painter of Victorian life, a study of Constantin Guys with an introduction and a translation of Baudelaire's "Peintre de la vie moderne."* Edited by C. Geoffrey Holme. New York, Rudge; London, Studio, 1930.

5060. Ober, William B. *Great men of Guy's,* with an introduction by William Ober, with a foreword by Lord Brock. Metuchen, N.J. Scarecrow Reprint Corp., 1973.

5061. Palazzo Braschi (Rome). *Constantin Guys; il pittore della vita moderna.* 10 settembre–5 ottobre 1980. Milano, Savelli, 1980.

G

H

Hackert, Jacob Philipp, 1737–1807

5062. Goethe, J. W. *Philipp Hackert. Biographische Skizze, meist nach dessen eigenen Aufsätzen entworfen.* Tübingen, Cotta, 1811.

5063. Lohse, Bruno. *Jakob Philipp Hackert, Leben und Anfänge seiner Kunst.* Emsdetten, Lechte, 1936.

5064. Nordhoff, Claudia. *Jakob Philipp Hackert 1737–1801: Verzeichnis seiner Werke.* [By] Claudia Nordhoff and Hans Reimer. 2 v. Berlin, Akademie Verlag, 1994. (CR).

Hagenau, Niklaus von (called Niclas Hagnower), 1445–1538

5065. Vöge, Wilhelm. *Niclas Hagnower, der Meister des Isenheimer Hochaltars und seine Frühwerke.* Freiburg im Breisgau, Urban-Verlag, 1931.

Hagnower, Niclas *see* Hagenau, Niklaus von

Halász, Gyula *see* Brassaï.

Hals, Frans, 1584–1666

5066. Baard, Henricus Petrus. *Frans Hals.* Trans. by George Stuck. New York, Abrams, 1981.

5067. Bode, Wilhelm von. *Frans Hals und seine Schule.* Leipzig, Seemann, 1871.

5068. ———, ed. *Frans Hals, his life and work.* With an essay by M. J. Binder. Trans. by Maurice W. Brockwell. 2 v. Berlin, Photographische Gesellschaft, 1914; London agents: The Berlin Photographic Company.

5069. Dantzig, Maurits Michel van. *Frans Hals, echt of onecht.* Amsterdam, Paris, 1937.

5070. Davies, Gerald S. *Frans Hals.* London, Bell, 1902.

5071. Descargues, Pierre. *Hals, biographical and critical study.* Lausanne, Skira, 1968. (The Taste of Our Time, 48).

5072. Dülberg, Franz. *Frans Hals, ein Leben und ein Werk.* Stuttgart, Neff, 1930.

5073. Fontainas, André. *Frans Hals.* Paris, Laurens, 1908.

5074. Gratama, Gerrit David. *Frans Hals.* Haag, Oceanus, 1943.

5075. Grimm, Claus. *Frans Hals: the complete work.* Translated from the German by Jürgen Riehle. New York, Abrams, 1990.

5076. ———. *Frans Hals; Entwicklung, Werkanalyse, Gesamtkatalog.* Berlin, Mann, 1972. (CR).

5077. ———. *L'opera completa di Frans Hals.* Milano, Rizzoli, 1974. (I classici dell'arte, 76).

5078. Knackfuss, Hermann. *Franz Hals.* Biele-feld/Leipzig, Velhagen & Klasing, 1897. 3 ed. (Künstler-Monographien, 12).

5079. Luns, Theo M. *Frans Hals.* Amsterdam, Becht, [1948]. (Palet serie, [27]).

5080. Martin, Wilhelm. *Frans Hals in zijn tijd.* Amsterdam, Meulenhoff, 1935. (De Hollandsche Schilderkunst in de zeventiende Eeuw, 1).

5081. Moes, Ernst W. *Frans Hals, sa vie et son oeuvre.* Trans. by Jean de Bosschère. Brussels, van Oest, 1909.

5082. Peladan, Joséphin. *Frans Hals, 1580(?)–1666.* Paris, Goupil, 1912.

5083. Slive, Seymour. *Frans Hals.* 3 v. London, Phaidon, 1970. (National Gallery of Art, Kress Foundation Studies in the History of European Art, 4). (CR).

5084. ———. *Frans Hals.* With contributions by Peter Biesboer, Martin Bijl, Karin Groen and Ella Hendriks . . . [et al.]. Edited by Seymour Slive. First published on the occasion of the exhibition 'Frans Hals,' National Gallery of Art, Washington, D.C, 1 October–31 December 1989; Royal Academy of Arts, London, 13 January–8 April, 1990; Frans Hals Museum, Haarlem, 11 May–22 July 1990. Munich, Prestel-Verlag in association with Mercatorfonds, Antwerp, 1989.

5085. Trivas, Numa S. *The paintings of Frans Hals, complete edition.* London, Phaidon, 1949. 2 ed.; distributed by Oxford University Press, New York.

5086. Valentiner, Wilhelm R. *Frans Hals, des Meisters Gemälde.* Stuttgart, Deutsche Verlags-Anstalt, 1923. 2 ed. (Klassiker der Kunst in Gesamtausgaben, 28).

Halsman, Philippe, 1906–1979

5087. Halsman, Philippe. *The jump book.* New York, Simon & Schuster, 1959.

5088. ———. *Portraits.* Selected and edited by Yvonne Halsman. New York, McGraw-Hill, 1983.

5089. ———. *Sight and insight.* Garden City, N.Y., Doubleday, 1972.

5090. International Center for Photography (New York). *Halsman '79.* June 9–July 22, 1979. New York, International Center for Photography, 1979.

Hamilton, Richard, 1922–

5091. Hamilton, Richard. *Richard Hamilton: collected words, 1953–1982.* London/ New York, Thames and Hudson, 1982.

5092. Hamilton, Richard. *Richard Hamilton.* Edited by Richard Morphet. London, Tate Gallery; Seattle, distributed in North America by University of Washington Press, 1993.

Hammershøj, Vilhelm, 1864–1916

5093. Hammershøi, Wilhelm. *60 Autotypier i Sorttryk efter Fotografier af Originalerne.* [København], Gad, 1916. (Smaa kunstbøger, 13).

5094. Michaëlis, Sophus [and] Bramsen, Alfred. *Vilhelm Hammershøi, Kunstneren og hans Vaerk.* København, Gyldendal, 1918.

5095. Vad, Poul. *Vilhelm Hammershø.* [København], Gyldendal, 1957.

5096. ———. *Vilhelm Hammershoi and Danish art at the turn of the century.* Translated by Kenneth Tindall. New Haven Yale University press, 1992.

Hans von Tübingen, ca. 1400–1462

5097. Oettinger, Karl. *Hans von Tübingen und seine Schule.* Berlin, Deutscher Verein für Kunstwissenschaft, 1938.

Hansen, Christian Frederik, 1756–1845

5098. Altonaer Museum in Hamburg. *Architekt Christian Frederik Hansen, 1756–1845. 26. Juni bis 1. September 1968.* Hamburg, [Altonaer Museum, 1968].

5099. Jakstein, Werner. *Landesbaumeister Christian Friedrich Hansen, der nordische Klassizist.* Neumünster in Holstein, Wachholtz, 1937. (Studien zur schleswig-holsteinischen Kunstgeschichte, 2).

5100. Rubow, Jorn. *C. F. Hansens Arkitektur.* København, Gad, 1936.

5101. Smidt, Carl Martin. *Arkitekten C. F. Hansen og hans Bygninger.* København, Gad, 1911.

5102. Wietek, Gerhard, ed. *C. F. Hansen, 1756–1845, und seine Bauten in Schleswig-Holstein.* Neumünster, Wachholtz, 1982. (Kunst in Schleswig-Holstein, 23).

Hanson, Duane, 1925–

5103. Bush, Martin H. *Sculptures by Duane Hanson.* Wichita, Kan., Edwin A. Ulrich Museum of Art, Wichita State University, 1985.

5104. Hobbs, Robert. *Duane Hanson: the new objectivity.* Talahassee, Fla., Florida State University Art Gallery and Museum; Seattle, distributed by University of Washington Press, 1991.

5105. Livingstone, Marco. *Duane Hanson.* [Catalogue of an exhibition]. Montreal, Montreal Museum of Fine Arts, 1994.

5106. Varnedoe, Kirk. *Duane Hanson.* New York, Abrams, 1985.

Haring, Keith, 1958–

5107. Bindeman, Barry. *Keith Haring: Future primeval.* [Exhibition catalogue]. New York, Abbeville Press for the Galleries of Illinois State University, Normal, 1990.

5108. Gruen, John. *Keith Haring: the authorized biography.* New York, Prentice Hall Press, 1991.

Harnett, William Michael, 1848–1892

5109. Frankenstein, Alfred. *After the hunt; William Harnett and other American still life painters, 1870–1900.* Berkeley/Los Angeles, University of California, 1953. (Rev. ed., University of California, Berkeley/Los Angeles, 1969; California Studies in the History of Art, 12). (CR).

Harrison, Peter, 1716–1775

5110. Bridenbaugh, Carl. *Peter Harrison, first American architect.* Chapel Hill, University of North Carolina Press, 1949.

Hartley, Marsden, 1877–1943 *see also* Lyonel Feininger

5111. Hartley, Marsden. *Adventures in the arts; informal chapters on painters, vaudeville, and poets.* New York, Boni and Liveright, 1921.

5112. Ludington, Townsend. *Marsden Hartley; the biography of an American Artist.* Boston, Little Brown, 1992.

5113. McCausland, Elizabeth. *Marsden Hartley.* Minneapolis, University of Minnesota Press, 1952.

5114. Scott, Gayl R. *Marsden Hartley.* New York, Abbeville, 1988.

5115. Whitney Museum of American Art (New York). *Marsden Hartley.* March 4–May 25, 1980. New York, Whitney Museum of Modern Art/New York University Press, 1980.

Hartung, Hans, 1904–

5116. Apollonio, Umbro. *Hans Hartung.* Trans. by John Shepley. New York, Abrams, [1972].

5117. Aubier, Dominique. *Hartung.* Paris, Le Musée de Poche, 1961.

5118. Daix, Pierre. *Hans Hartung.* Paris/ Bordas, Daniel Gervis, 1991.

5119. Descargues, Pierre. *Hartung.* Paris, Cercle d'Art, 1977.

5120. Gindertael, Roger van. *Hans Hartung.* [Paris], Tisné, 1960.

5121. Hartung, Hans. *Autoportrait.* Paris, Grasset, 1976.

5122. ———. *Hans Hartung, Malerei, Zeichnung, Photographie.* [Ausstellung]. Kunsthalle Düsseldorf. [Redaktion des Katalogs, Ulrich Krempel]. Berlin, Kunstbuch Berlin, 1981.

5123. ———. *Hartung: oeuvres de 1922 à 1939.* [Exposition]. Musée d'art moderne de la ville de Paris, 31 mars–21 septembre 1980. Paris, Musée d'art moderne de la ville de Paris, 1980.

5124. Rousseau, Madeleine. *Hans Hartung.* [Text in English, French, German]. Stuttgart, Domnick, [1949].

5125. Schmücking, Rolf. *Hans Hartung, Werkverzeichnis der Graphik, 1921–1965.* Braunschweig, Galerie Schmücking, 1965. (CR).

5126. Städtische Kunsthalle Düsseldorf. *Hans Hartung; Malerei, Zeichnung, Photographie.* 12. September bis 11. Oktober 1981. Berlin, Kunstbuch Berlin, 1981.

Harunobu, Suzuki, 1725–1770

5127. Hájek, Lubor. *Harunobu.* Trans. by Hedda Veselá Stránská. London, Spring, [1958].

5128. Kondō, Ichitarō. *Suzuki Harunobu.* Trans. and adapted by Kaoru Ogimi. Tokyo/Rutland, Vermont, Tuttle, [1956]. (Kodansha Library of Japanese Art, 7).

5129. Kurth, Julius. *Suzuki Harunobu.* München/Leipzig, Piper, 1923. 2 ed.

5130. Noguchi, Yone. *Harunobu.* London, Kegan Paul/Yokohama, Yoshikawa, 1940. (CR).

5131. Philadelphia Museum of Art. *Suzuki Harunobu, an exhibition of his colour-prints and illustrated books on the occasion of the bicentenary of his death in 1770.* 18 September to 22 November 1970. Philadelphia, Philadelphia Museum of Art, 1970.

5132. Smidt, Hermann. *Harunobu, Technik und Fälschungen seiner Holzschnitte.* Wien, Gesellschaft für Vervielfältigende Kunst, 1911.

5133. Takahashi, Seiichirō. *Harunobu.* English adaptation by John Bester. Tokyo/Palo Alto, Calif., Kodansha, 1968. (Masterworks of Ukiyo-e, 6).

5134. Waterhouse, David B. *Harunobu and his age; the development of colour printing in Japan.* London, Trustees of the British Museum, 1964.

Haseltine, William Stanley, 1835–1900

5135. Simpson, Marc. *Expressions of place: the art of William Stanley Haseltine.* By Marc Simpson, Andrea Henderson, and Sally Mills. San Francisco, Fine Arts Museum of San Francisco; New York, distributed by Hudson Hills Press, 1992.

Hasenclever, Johann Peter, 1810–1853

5136. Bestvater-Hasenclever, Hanna. *J. P. Hasenclever, ein wacher Zeitgenosse des Biedermeier.* Recklinghausen, Bongers, 1979.

5137. Hasenclever, Hermann, ed. *Das Geschlecht Hasenclever im ehemaligen Herzogtum Berg in der Provinz Westfalen und zeitweise in Schlesien.* 2 v. Leipzig, Gohlis, 1922/4.

Hassam, Childe, 1859–1935

5138. Adams, Adeline. *Childe Hassam.* New York, American Academy of Arts and Letters, 1938.

5139. Cortissoz, Royal. *Catalogue of the etchings and dry-points of Childe Hassam.* New York/London, Scribner, 1925.

5140. Curry, David Park. *Childe Hassam; an island garden revisited.* Denver, Colo., Denver Art Museum; New York, distributed by W.W. Norton, 1990. (Revised edition: San Francisco, A. Wofsy, 1989).

5141. Eliasoph, Paula. *Handbook of the complete set of etchings and drypoints . . . of Child Hassam . . . from 1883 till October 1933.* New York, The Leonard Clayton Gallery, 1933. (CR).

5142. Griffith, Fuller. *The lithographs of Childe Hassam, a catalog.* Washington, D.C., Smithsonian Institution, 1962. (Smithsonian Institution Bulletin, 232). (CR).

5143. Hoopes, Donelson F. *Childe Hassam.* New York, Watson-Guptill, 1979.

5144. University of Arizona Museum of Art (Tucson). *Childe Hassam, 1859–1935.* February 5 to March 5, 1972. Tucson, Arizona, University of Arizona Museum of Art, [1972].

5145. Weir, J. Alden and Zigrosser, Carl. *Childe Hassam.* New York, Keppel, 1916.

Hausmann, Raoul, 1886–1971

5146. Benson, Timothy O. *Raoul Hausmann and Berlin Dada.* Ann Arbor, UMI Research Press, 1987

5147. Giroud, Michel, ed. *Raoul Hausmann: je ne suis pas un photographe.* Paris, Chêne, 1975.

5148. Haus, Andreas. *Raoul Hausmann, Kamera-*

fotografien 1927–1957. München, Schirmer/ Mosel, 1979.

5149. Hausmann, Raoul. *Courrier Dad*. Suivi d'une bio-bibliographie de l'auteur par Poupard-Lieussou. Paris, Le Terrain Vague, 1958.

5150. ———. *Gegen den kalten Blick der Welt: Raoul Hausmann, Fotografien 1927–1933*. Ausstellungskatalog. Österreichisches Fotoarchiv im Museum Moderner Kunst, Wien. Hrsg. von Hildegund Amanshauser und Monika Faber. Wien, Das Archiv, 1986.

5151. Kestner-Gesellschaft Hannover. *Raoul Hausmann, Retrospektive*. 12. Juni bis 9. August 1981. Hannover, Kestner-Gesellschaft, 1981. (Katalog 4/1981).

Haussmann, Georges-Eugène, 1809–1891

5152. Cars, Jean des. *Haussmann: la gloire du Second Empire*. Paris, Perrin, 1978.

5153. Chapman, Joan M. and Chapman, Brian. *The life and times of Baron Haussmann: Paris in the Second Empire*. London, Weidenfeld, 1957.

5154. Des Cars, Jean. *Haussmann, la gloire du Second Empire*. Paris, Librairie académique Perrin, 1978.

5155. Gaillard, Jeanne. *Paris, la ville, 1852–1870: l'urbanisme parisien à l'heure d'Haussmann*. Paris, Champion, 1977.

5156. Haussmann, Georges-Eugène. *Mémoires*. 3 v. Paris, Havard, 1890–1893. (Reprint: Paris, Durier, 1979).

5157. Laronze, Georges. *Le Baron Haussmann*. Paris, Alcan, 1932.

5158. Londei, Enrico F. *La Parigi di Haussmann: la transformazione urbanistica di Parigi durante il seconda impero*. Roma, Kappa, 1982.

5159. Saalman, Howard. *Haussmann: Paris transformed*. New York, Braziller, 1971.

5160. Touttain, Pierre-André. *Haussmann: artisan du Second Empire, créateur du Paris moderne*. Paris, Grund, 1971.

Hawes, Josiah J. *see* Southworth, Alfred S.

Hawksmoor, Nicholas, 1661–1736

5161. Downes, Kerry. *Hawksmoor*. London, Zwemmer, 1979. 2 ed.

5162. Goodhart-Rendel, H. S. *Nicholas Hawksmoor*. New York, Scribner, 1924.

Haydon, Benjamin Robert, 1786–1846

5163. George, Eric. *The life and death of Benjamin Robert Haydon, 1786–1846*. London, Oxford University Press, 1948.

5164. Haydon, Benjamin Robert. *Correspondence and table-talk*. With a memoir by his son Frederic Wordsworth Haydon. 2 v. London, Chatto and Windus, 1876.

5165. ———. *The diary of Benjamin Robert Haydon*. 5 v. Ed. by Willard Bissell Pope. Cambridge, Mass., Harvard University Press, 1960–63.

5166. ———. *Lectures on painting and design*. 2 v. London, Longman, Brown, Green, 1844–46.

5167. Haydon, Benjamin Robert. *Neglected genius: the diaries of Benjamin Robert Haydon, 1808–1846*. Eedited by John Joliffe. London, Hutchinson, 1990.

5168. Olney, Clarke. *Benjamin Robert Haydon, historical painter*. Athens, Ga., University of Georgia Press, 1952.

5169. Paston, George [pseud., Emily Morse Symonds]. *B. R. Haydon and his friends*. London, Nisbet, 1905.

5170. Saumarez Smith, Charles. *The building of Castle Howard*. London/Boston, Faber, 1990.

5171. Taylor, Tom, ed. *Life of Benjamin Robert Haydon, historical painter, from his autobiography and journals*. 3 v. London, Longman, Brown, Green, 1853. (New ed. with an introduction by Aldous Huxley, 2 v. New York, Harcourt, Brace, [1926]).

Hayez, Francesco, 1791–1882

5172. Castellaneta, Carlo. *L'opera completa di Hayez*. Milano, Rizzoli, 1971. (Classici dell'arte, 54).

5173. Hayez, Francesco. *Hayez*. A cura di Maria Cristina Gozzoli e Fernando Mazzocca. Milano, Electa, 1983.

5174. ———. *Le mie memorie*. Milano, Reale Accademia de Belle Arti in Milano, 1890.

5175. Nicodemi, Giorgio. *Francesco Hayez*. 2 v. Milano, Ceschina, 1962. (CR).

Hayman, Francis, 1708–1776

5176. Allen, Brian. *Francis Hayman*. New Haven, Yale University Press, 1987.

Hayter, Stanley William, 1901–1988

5177. Black, Peter and Moorhead, Desirée. *The prints of Stanley Hayter: a complete catalogue*. London, Phaidon, 1992. (CR).

Hebert, Ernest, 1817–1908

5178. Patrie d'Uckermann, René. *Ernest Hébert, 1817–1908*. Paris Ministère de la culture, Editions de la Réunion des musées nationaux, 1982.

5179. Peladan, Joséphin. *Ernest Hébert, son oeuvre et son temps*. Paris, Delagrave, 1910.

Heckel, Erich, 1883–1970

5180. Dube, Annemarie und Dube, Wolf-Dieter. *Erich Heckel, das graphische Werk*. 3 v. New York, Rathenau, 1974; distributed by Hauswedell, Hamburg. (CR).

5181. Henze, Anton. *Erich Heckel, Leben und Werk.* Stuttgart, Belser, 1983.

5182. Köhn, Heinz. *Erich Heckel, Aquarelle und Zeichnungen.* München, Bruckmann, 1959.

5183. Lucke, Mechthild. *Erich Heckel, Lebensstufen: Die Wandbilder im Angermuseum zu Erfurt.* Dresden, Verlag der Kunst, 1992.

5184. Moeller, Magdalena M. *Erich Heckel: Aquarelle, Zeichnungen, Druckgraphik aus dem Brücke-Museum Berlin.* München, Hirmer, 1991.

5185. Schleswig-Holsteinisches Landesmuseum (Schleswig, W. Germany). *Erich Heckel.* [Ausstellung]. 2. November 1980–4. Januar 1981. Schleswig, Schleswig-Holsteinisches Landesmuseum, 1980.

5186. Thormaehlen, Ludwig. *Erich Heckel.* Berlin, Klinkhardt & Biermann, 1931. (Junge Kunst, 58).

5187. Vogt, Paul. *Erich Heckel.* Recklinghausen, Bongers, 1965. (CR).

Heemskerk, Martin van, 1498–1574

5188. Filippi, Elena. *Maarten van Heemskerck, inventio urbis.* Milano, Berenice, 1990.

5189. Garff, Jan. *Tegninger af Maerten van Heemskerck, illustreret katalog.* København, Statens Museum vor Kunst, 1971. (CR).

5190. Grosshans, Rainald. *Maerten van Heemskerck: die Gemälde.* Berlin, H. Boettcher, 1980.

5191. Harrison, Jefferson Cabel. *The paintings of Maerten van Heemskerck. Catalogue raisonné.* (Volumes I and II = text only). Ann Arbor, UMI Dissertation Abstracts, Diss. PhD. University of Virginia, 1987.(CR).

5192. Huelsen, Christian and Egger, Hermann. *Die römischen Skizzenbücher von Marten van Heemskerk im königlichen Kupferstichkabinett zu Berlin.* 2 v. Berlin, Bard, 1913–1916.

5193. Kerrich, Thomas. *A catalogue of the prints which have been engraved after Martin Heemskerck; or rather, an essay towards such a catalogue.* London, Rodwell, 1829.

5194. Preibisz, Leon. *Martin van Heemskerck, ein Beitrag zur Geschichte des Romanismus in der niederländischen Malerei des XVI. Jahrhunderts.* Leipzig, Klinkhardt & Biermann, 1911.

5195. Veldman, Ilja M. *Maarten van Heemskerck and Dutch humanism in the sixteenth century.* Trans. by Michael Hoyle. Maarssen, Schwartz, 1977.

5196. ———. *Maarten van Heemskerck.* 2 v. Comp. by I.M. Veldman; edited by Ger Luijten. Roosendaal, Kon. van Poll; Publ. in cooperation with the Rijksprentenkabinet, Rijksmuseum, Amsterdam, 1993–1994. (CR). (New Hollstein Dutch and Flemish Etchings, Engravings and Woodcuts, 1450–1700, 1).

Hegenbarth, Josef, 1884–1962

5197. Hegenbarth, Josef. *Aufzeichnungen über seine Illustrationsarbeit.* Hamburg, Christians, 1964.

5198. ———. *Der Illustrator Josef Hegenbarth, 1884–1962: Zeichnungen, farbige Blätter, Grafiken und illustrierte Bücher.* [Ausstellung]. Klingspor-Museum Offenbach, 13. Juni–16. August 1987, Galerie Christian Zwang, Hamburg, 28. September–13. November 1987. Konzeption der Ausstellung und Katalog, Ulrich Zesch. Stuttgart, U. Zesch, 1987.

5199. Löffler, Fritz. *Josef Hegenbarth.* Dresden, Verlag der Kunst, 1980. 2 ed.

5200. Reichelt, Johannes. *Josef Hegenbarth.* Essen, Baedeker, 1925. (Charakterbilder der neuen Kunst, 5).

Hegi, Franz, 1774–1850

5201. Appenzeller, Heinrich. *Der Kupferstecher Franz Hegi von Zürich, 1774–1850; sein Leben und seine Werke, beschreibendes Verzeichnis seiner sämtlichen Kupferstiche.* Zürich, Appenzeller, 1906. (CR).

5202. Dönz-Breimaier, Maria Gertrud. *Franz Hegi und sein Kreis.* Chur, Ebner, 1944.

Heiliger, Bernhard, 1915–

5203. Flemming, Hanns Theodor. *Bernhard Heiliger.* Berlin, Rembrandt, 1962.

5204. Hammacher, Abraham M. *Bernhard Heiliger.* Trans. by Guy Atkins. St. Gallen, Erker-Verlag, 1978. (Künstler unserer Zeit, 20).

5205. Heiliger, Bernhard. *Bernhard Heiliger, Retrospektive.* Wilhelm-Lehmbruck-Museum der Stadt Duisburg, 1. September bis 13. Oktober 1985: Städtische Museen Heilbronn, 7. Februar bis 6. April 1986. Ausstellung und Katalog, Christian Brockhaus und Barbara Lepper in Zusammenarbeit mit Bernhard Heiliger. Duisburg, Wilhelm-Lehmbruck-Museum der Stadt Duisburg, 1985.

5206. Neuer Berliner Kunstverein und Akademie der Künste. *Bernhard Heiliger, Skulpturen und Zeichnungen, 1960–1975.* 13. April bis 25. Mai 1975. Berlin, Neuer Berliner Kunstverein und Akademie der Künste, 1975.

5207. Salzmann, Siegfried. *Bernhard Heiliger.* S. Salzmann [und] Lothar Romain. Berlin, Propyläen Verlag, 1989.

Heintz, Joseph, der Ältere, 1564–1609

5208. Zimmer, Jürgen. *Joseph Heintz der Ältere: Zeichnungen und Dokumente.* München, Deutscher Kunstverlag, 1988.

Heldt, Werner, 1904–1954

5209. Heldt, Werner. *Werner Heldt.* Herausgegeben von Lucius Grisebach; mit Beiträgen von Annie Bardon, Thomas Fohl, Lucius Grisebach, Dieter Schmidt. Berlin, Nicolaische Verlagsbuchhandlung, 1989.

5210. Heldt, Werner. *Werner Heldt, 'Berlin am Meer': Bilder und Graphik von 1927–1954.* Zur Ausstellung mit Bildern und Graphik von Werner Heldt vom 5. September bis 31. Oktober 1927. Galerie Brusberg, Berlin. Erstellt von Christiane Grathwohl und Stephanie Tasch; herausgegeben von Dieter Brusberg. Texte von Alfred Hentzen; . . . [et al.] Berlin, Edition Brusberg, 1987.

5211. Kestner-Gesellschaft (Hannover). *Werner Heldt.* 8. März bis 7. April 1968. Hannover, Kestner-Gesellschaft, 1968.

5212. Schmied, Wieland. *Werner Heldt.* Mit einem Werkkatalog von Eberhard Seel. Köln, DuMont, 1976. (CR).

Helleu, Paul Cesar, 1859–1927

5213. Adhémar, Jean. *Helleu.* Paris, Bibliothèque Nationale, 1957.

5214. Helleu, Paul Cesar. *Paul Helleu, 1859–1927: drypoints and drawings.* [Exhibition] 14 June–July 22, 1983. London, Lumley Cazalat, 1983.

5215. Montesquiou-Fezensac, Robert. *Paul Helleu, peintre et graveur.* Paris, Floury, 1913.

Helst, Bartolomeus van der, 1613–1670

5216. Gelder, Jan J. *Bartholomeus van der Helst.* Rotterdam, Brusse, 1921. (CR).

Hennequin, Philippe Auguste, 1762–1833

5217. Benoit, Jérémie. *Philippe-Auguste Hennequin, 1762–1833.* Paris, Arthena, 1994. (CR).

Henner, Jean Jacques, 1829–1905

5218. Crastre, François. *Henner.* Trans. by Frederic Taber-Cooper. New York, Stokes, 1913.

5219. Henner, Jean-Jacques. *J.J. Henner.* Mulhouse, Musée des beaux-arts de Mulhouse. v.1– . Steinbrunn-le-Haut, Editions du Rhin, 1988– .

5220. Muenier, Pierre-Alexis. *La vie et l'art de Jean-Jacques Henner, peintures et dessins.* [Paris], Flammarion, 1927.

5221. Soubies, Albert. *J.-J. Henner (1829–1905); notes biographiques.* Paris, Flammarion, 1905.

Henri, Robert, 1865–1929

5222. Henri, Robert. *The art spirit.* Compiled by Margery Ryerson. Philadelphia, Lippincott, 1960. 4 ed.

5223. Homer, William Innes and Organ, Violet. *Robert Henri and his circle.* Ithaca, N.Y., Cornell University Press, 1969. (Revised edition: New York, Hacker Art Books, 1988).

5224. Metropolitan Museum of Art (New York). *Catalogue of a memorial exhibition of the work of Robert Henri.* [March 9–April 19, 1931]. New York, Metropolitan Museum of Art, 1931.

5225. Read, Helen A. *Robert Henri.* New York, Whitney Museum of American Art, 1931.

5226. Yarrow, William and Bouche, Louis. *Robert Henri, his life and works.* New York, Boni & Liveright, 1921.

Hepplewhite, George, D. 1786 *see also* Adam, Robert

5227. Hepplewhite, A[lice], and Co. *The cabinetmaker and upholsterer's guide.* London, Taylor, 1788.

5228. Hinckley, F. Lewis. *Hepplewhite, Sheraton & Regency furniture.* New York, Washingston Mews Book, 1987

Hepworth, Barbara, 1903–1975

5229. Bowness, Alan. *The sculpture of Barbara Hepworth, 1960–1969.* New York/Washington [D.C.], Praeger, 1971.

5230. Curtis, Penelope and Wilkinson, Alan G. *Barbara Hepworth.* [Catalogue of a travelling exhibition organized by the Tate Gallery]. Liverpool/London, Tate Gallery, 1894.

5231. Gibson, William. *Barbara Hepworth, sculptress.* London, Faber, 1946.

5232. Hammacher, Abraham M. *Barbara Hepworth.* Trans. by James Brockway. London, Thames and Hudson, 1968. (Revised edition, 1987).

5233. Hepworth, Barbara. *Carvings and drawings.* Introduction by Herbert Read. London, Humphries, 1952.

5234. ———. *A pictorial autobiography, new and extended edition.* Bradford-on-Avon, Moonraker Press, 1978.

5235. Hodin, Josef Paul. *Barbara Hepworth.* Catalogue by Alan Bowness. New York, McKay, 1961.

5236. Shepherd, Michael. *Barbara Hepworth.* London, Methuen, 1963.

Herkomer, Hubert von, 1849–1914

5237. Baldry, Alfred Lys. *Hubert von Herkomer, R. A., a study and a biography.* London, Bell, 1901.

5238. Courtney, William Leonard. *Professor Hubert Herkomer, his life and work.* London, Art Journal, 1892. (Art Annual, 9).

5239. Herkomer, Sir Hubert von. *Etching and mezzotint engraving; lectures delivered at Oxford.* London/New York, Macmillan, 1892.

5240. ———. *The Herkomers.* 2 v. London, Macmillan, 1910.

5241. ———. *My school and my gospel*. London, Constable, 1908.

5242. Pietsch, Ludwig. *Herkomer*. Bielefeld/Leipzig, Velhagen & Klasing, 1901. (Künstler-Mongraphien, 54).

Herrera, Juan de, c.1530–1597

5243. Zerner, Catherine Wilkinson. *Juan de Herrera: Architect to Philip II of Spain*. New Haven, Yale University Press, 1993.

Hesse, Eva, 1936–1970

5244. Barrette, Bill. *Eva Hesse sculpture: catalogue raisonné*. New York, Timken; distrib. Rizzoli, 1992.

5245. Cooper, Helen A. *Eva Hesse, a retrospective*. [Catalogue of an exhibition at the Yale University Art Gallery]. New Haven, Yale Art Gallery, 1992.

Heyden, Jan van der, 1637–1712

5246. Fuchs, Rudi. *J.C.J. van der Heyden*. [Catalogue of an exhibition]. Rotterdam, Museum Boymans van Beuningen, 1990.

5247. Heyden, Jan van der. *Jan van der Heyden 1637–1712: kunstenaar en iutvinder*. [Exhibition catalogue]. By Lyckle de Vries, Piet Sleperda and Albert Boeijink. Groningen, Kunsthistorisch Instituut, nd.

5248. Wagner, Helga. *Jan van der Heyden, 1637–1712*. Amsterdam/Haarlem, Scheltema & Holkema, 1971. (CR).

Higgins, Victor, 1884–1949

5249. Porter, Dean A. *Victor Higgins, an American master*. Salt Lake City, Pregrine Smith Books, 1991.

Hildebrand, Adolf von, 1847–1921

5250. Esche-Braunfels, Sigrid. *Adolf von Hildebrand*. Berlin, Deutscher Verlag für Kunstwissenschaft, 1994.

5251. Hass, Angela. *Adolf von Hildebrand: das plastische Portrait*. München, Prestel, 1984.

5252. Hausenstein, Wilhelm. *Adolf von Hildebrand*. München, Filser, 1947. (Meisterwerke der Kunst, 5).

5253. Heilmeyer, Alexander. *Adolf Hildebrand*. Bielefeld/Leipzig, Velhagen & Klasing, 1902. (Künstler-Monographien, 60).

5254. ———. *Adolf von Hildebrand*. München, Langen, 1922. (CR).

5255. Hildebrand, Adolf von. *Gesammelte Schriften zur Kunst*. Bearbeitet von Henning Bok. Köln/Opladen, Westdeutscher Verlag, 1969. (Wissenschaftliche Abhandlungen der Arbeitsgemeinschaft für Forschung des Landes Nordrhein-Westfalen, 39).

5256. ———. *The problem of form in painting and sculpture*. Trans. by Max Meyer and Robert Morris Ogden. New York, Stechert, 1932. 2 ed. (Reprint: New York/London, Garland, 1978; Connoisseurship, Criticism and Art History in the Nineteenth Century, 11).

5257. Sattler, Bernhard, ed. *Adolf von Hildebrand und seine Welt; Briefe und Erinnerungen*. München, Callwey, 1962.

Hildebrandt, Johann Lukas von, 1668–1745

5258. Grimschitz, Bruno. *Johann Lucas von Hildebrandt*. Wien/München, Herold, 1959.

5259. ———. *Johann Lucas von Hildebrandt. Künstlerische Entwicklung bis zum Jahre 1725*. Wien, Hölzel, 1922 (Kunstgeschichtliche Einzeldarstellungen, 1).

Hilder, Rowland, 1905–

5260. Hilder, Rowland. *Rowland Hilder's England; a personal record by the artist introduced by Denis Thomas*. London, Herbert Press, 1986.

5261. Lewis, John. *Rowland Hilder, painter and illustrator*. London, Barrie & Jenkins, 1978.

5262. ———. *Rowland Hilder, painter of the English landscape*. Woodbridge, Antique Collectors' Club, 1987. 2 ed.

Hiler, Hilaire, 1898–

5263. George, Waldemar. *Hilaire Hiler and structuralism, new conception of form-color*. New York, Wittenborn, [1958].

5264. Hiler, Hilaire. *Notes on the technique of painting*. London, Faber, 1934.

5265. ———. *The painter's pocket-book of methods and materials*. New York, Harcourt, Brace, 1938.

5266. ———. *Why abstract?* [With a note on Hilaire Hiler by William Saroyan and a letter from Henry Miller]. New York, New Directions, 1945.

Hill, Carl Frederik, 1849–1911

5267. Anderberg, Adolf. *Carl Hill, hans liv och hans konst*. Malmö, Allhems, 1951.

5268. Blomberg, Erik. *Carl Fredrik Hill, hans friska och sjuka konst*. Stockholm, Natur och Kultur, 1949.

5269. Ekelöf, Gunnar. *C. F. Hill*. Göteborg, Förlagsaktiebolaget Bokkonst, 1946.

5270. Lindhagen, Nils. *C. F. Hill, sjukdomsarens konst*. Malmö, Bernce, 1976.

5271. Polfeldt, Ingegerd. *Möte med Carl Fredrik Hill*. Stockholm, Liber, 1979.

Hill, David Octavius, 1802–1870

5272. Bruce, David. *Sun pictures; the Hill-Adamson calotypes*. Greenwich, Conn., New York Graphic Society, 1973.

5273. Elliot, Andrew. *Calotypes by D. O. Hill and*

R. Adamson, illustrating an early stage in the development of photography. Edinburgh, [privately printed], 1928.

5274. Ford, Colin and Strong, Roy. *An early Victorian album; the Hill/Adamson collection.* London, Cape, 1974.

5275. Nickel, Heinrich. *David Octavius Hill, Wurzeln und Wirkungen seiner Lichtbildkunst.* Saale, Fotokinoverlag, 1960.

5276. Schwarz, Heinrich. *David Octavius Hill, Master of photography.* Trans. by Helene E. Fraenkel. New York, Viking, 1931.

5277. Scottish Arts Council Gallery (Edinburgh). *A centenary exhibition of the work of David Octavius Hill, 1802–1848.* May 2–31, 1970. Edinburgh, Scottish Arts Council, 1970.

5278. Stevenson, Sara. *David Octavius Hill and Robert Adamson, catalogue of their calotypes taken between 1843 and 1847 in the collection of the Scottish National Portrait Gallery.* Edinburgh, National Galleries of Scotland, 1981. (CR).

5279. Ward, John. *Printed light: the scientific art of William Henry Fox Talbot and David Octavius Hill* with Robert Adamson, John Ward, Sara Stevenson. Edinburgh, Scottisch National Portrait Gallery, H.M.S.O., 1986.

Hilliard, Nicholas, ca. 1537–1619

5280. Auerbach, Erna. *Nicholas Hilliard.* London, Routledge & Kegan Paul, 1961. (CR).

5281. Edmond, Mary. *Hilliard and Oliver: the lives and works of two great miniaturtists.* London, Hale, 1983.

5282. Pope-Hennessy, John. *A lecture on Nicholas Hilliard.* London, Home and Van Thal, 1949.

5283. Reynolds, Graham. *Nicholas Hilliard & Isaac Oliver.* London, HMSO, 1971. 2 ed.

5284. Strong, Roy. *Nicholas Hilliard.* London, Joseph, 1975.

Hine, Lewis Wickes, 1874–1940

5285. Gutman, Judith Mara. *Lewis W. Hine, 1874–1940; two perspectives.* New York, Grossman, 1974.

5286. ———. *Lewis W. Hine and the American social conscience.* New York, Walker, 1967.

5287. Hine, Lewis W. *Men at work; photographic studies of modern men and machines.* New York, Macmillan, 1932. (Reprinted, with a supplement: New York, Dover, 1977).

5288. ———. *Photo story: selected letters and photographs of Lewis W. Hine,* edited by Daile Kaplan. Washington, D.C., Smithsonian Institution Press, 1992.

5289. Trachtenberg, Alan, et al. *America & Lewis Hine, photographs 1904–1940.* Millerton, N.Y., Aperture, 1977.

Hiroshige, 1797–1858

5290. Addiss, Stephen, ed. *Tōkaidō, adventures on the road in old Japan.* Lawrence, Kansas, The Helen Foresman Spencer Museum of Art, 1980.

5291. Amsden, Dora [and] Happer, John Stewart. *The heritage of Hiroshige; a glimpse at Japanese landscape art.* San Francisco, Elder, 1912.

5292. Ando Hiroshige. *Hiroshige: birds and flowers.* Introduction by Cynthia Bogel; commentaries on the plates by Israel Goldman; poetry translated from the Japanese by Alfred Marks. New York, G. Braziller in association with Rhode Island School of Design, 1988.

5293. Exner, Walter. *Hiroshige.* Trans. by Marguerite Kay. New York, Crown, 1960.

5294. Fenollosa, Mary McNeil. *Hiroshige, the artist of mist, snow, and rain.* San Francisco, Vickery, Atkins & Torrey, 1901.

5295. Narazaki, Muneshige. *Hiroshige, famous views.* English adaptation by Richard L. Gage. Tokyo/Palo Alto, Calif., Kodansha, 1968. (Masterpieces of Ukiyo-e, 5).

5296. Noguchi, Yone. *Hiroshige.* New York, Orientalia, 1921.

5297. ———. *Hiroshige.* London, Kegan Paul, 1934.

5298. Oka, Isaburō. *Hiroshige.* Trans. by Stanleigh H. Jones. Tokyo, Kodansha, 1982.

5299. ———. *Hiroshige: Japan's great landscape artist.* Translated by Stanleigh H. Jones. Tokyo/ New York, Kodansha International. Distributed in the U.S. by Kodansha America, 1992.

5300. Strange, Edward F. *The colour-prints of Hiroshige.* London, Cassell, 1925.

5301. Takahashi, Sei-ichiro. *Andō Hiroshige (1797–1858).* English adaptation by Charles E. Perry. Rutland, Vermont/Tokyo, Tuttle, 1956. (Kodansha Library of Japanese Art, 3).

Hirschvogel, Augustin, 1503–1553

5302. Friedrich, Carl. *Augustin Hirschvogel als Töpfer, seine Gefässentwürfe, Öfen und Glasgemälde.* Nürnberg, Schrag, 1885.

5303. Schwarz, Karl. *Augustin Hirschvogel, ein deutscher Meister der Renaissance.* Berlin, Bard, 1917.

Hitchens, Sydney Ivon, 1893–1979

5304. Bowness, Alan [and] Rosenthal, T. G. *Ivon Hitchens.* London, Humphries, 1973.

5305. Tate Gallery (London). *Ivon Hitchens, a retrospective exhibition.* 11 July–18 August, 1963. London, Arts Council of Great Britain, 1963.

Hobbema, Meindert, 1638–1709

5306. Broulhiet, Georges. *Meindert Hobbema (1638–1709)*. Paris, Firmin-Didot, 1938.

5307. Héris, Henri Joseph. *Notice raisonnée sur la vie et les ouvrages de Mindert Hobbema*. Paris, Febvre, 1854.

5308. Michel, Emile. *Hobbema et les paysagistes de son temps en Hollande*. Paris, Librairie de l'Art, 1890.

Höch, Hannah, 1889–

5309. Höch, Hannah. *Hannah Höch: eine Lebenscollage*. Herausgegeben von der Berlinischen Galerie; Bearbeitet von Cornelia Thater-Schulz. Bd. I– . Berlin, Argon, 1989– .

Hockney, David, 1937–

5310. Hockney, David. *David Hockney*. [Editor, Andreas C. Papadakis]. London, Academy Editions; New York, St. Martin's Press, 1988.

5311. ———. *David Hockney, a retrospective*. Organized by Maurice Tuchman and Stephanie Barron. Los Angeles, Los Angeles County Museum of Art; New York, Abrams, 1988.

5312. ———. *Hockney on photography*. Conversations with Paul Joyce.[Transcribed and edited by Wendy Brown]. London, Jonathan Cape, 1988.

5313. ———. *That's the way I see it*. London, Thames and Hudson, 1993.

5314. Livingstone, Marco. *David Hockney: etchings and lithographs*. London, Thames and Hudson, 1988.

5315. Melia, Paul and Luckhardt, Ulrich. *David Hockney paintings*. München, Prestel Verlag, 1994.

5316. Stangos, Niklos, ed. *David Hockney by David Hockney: My early Years*. New York, Abrams, 1988.

Hodler, Ferdinand, 1853–1918

5317. Bender, Ewald. *Das Leben Ferdinand Hodlers*. Zürich, Rascher, 1922.

5318. ——— and Müller, Werner Y. *Die Kunst Ferdinand Hodlers*. 2 v. Zürich, Rascher, 1923/1941.

5319. Brüschweiler, Jura. *Eine unbekannte Hodler-Sammlung aus Sarajewo*. Bern, Benteli, 1978. (Hodler-Publikation, 1).

5320. ———. *Ferdinand Hodler, Selbstbildnisse als Selbstbiographie*. Bern, Benteli, 1979. (Hodler-Publikation, 2).

5321. Dietschi, Peter. *Der Parallelismus Ferdinand Hodlers; ein Beitrag zur Stilpsychologie der neueren Kunst*. Basel, Birkhäuser, 1957. (Basler Studien zur Kunstgeschichte, 16).

5322. Frey, Adolf. *Ferdinand Hodler*. Leipzig, Haessel, 1922.

5323. Guerzoni, Stéphanie. *Ferdinand Hodler; sa vie, son oeuvre, son enseignement, souvenirs personnels*. Genève, Cailler, 1957. (Les grands artistes racontés par eux-mêmes et par leurs amis, 13).

5324. Hirsh, Sharon L. *Ferdinand Hodler*. New York, Braziller, 1982.

5325. Hodler, Ferdinand. *Ferdinand Hodler*. [Ausstellung] Kunsthaus Zürich. Bildredaktion, Jura Bruschweiler, Guido Magnaguagno. Zürich, Kunsthaus Zürich, 1983.

5326. ———. *Ferdinand Hodler landscapes*. Introductory essays by Stephen F. Eisenman and Oskar Batschmann; catalogue by Lukas Gloor; translations from the German by Danielle Nathanson; edited by the Swiss Institute for Art Research, Zurich. Zurich, The Institute, 1987.

5327. ———. *Ferdinand Hodler und das schweizer Künstlerplakat, 1890–1920*. [Ausstellung] Kunstgewerbemuseum der Stadt Zürich, Museum für Gestaltung, 10. November 1883–22. Januar 1984, Vereinigung Bildender Künstler Wiener Sezession, 7. Februar–7. März 1984, Musée des arts decoratifs de la Ville de Lausanne, 29. März–27. Mai 1984. Konzept und Leitung, Oskar Bätschmann; Redaktionsassistenz, Susanne Jossen. Zürich, Kunstgewerbemuseum der Stadt Zürich, 1983. (Wegleitungen des Kunstgewerbemuseums der Stadt Zürich, 346).

5328. ———. *Ferdinand Hodler: Vom Frühwerk bis zur Jahrhundertwende: Zeichnungen aus der Gaphischen Sammlung des Kunsthauses Zürich*. Katalog und Ausstellung, Bernhard von Waldkirch; mit Beiträgen von Rudolf Schindler und Christian Steinhoff. Zürich, Das Kunsthaus, 1990.

5329. ———. *Die Mission des Künstlers/ la mission de l'artiste*. Texte, Ivonne Lenherr, Margrit Hahnloser-Ingold, Hans A.Lüthy; Redaktion, Yvonne Lenherr; traduction des textes allemands, Ivan Andrey. Bern, Benteli, 1981.

5330. Hugelshofer, Walter. *Ferdinand Hodler, eine Monographie*. Zürich, Rascher, 1952.

5331. Kesser, Herman. *Zeichnungen Ferdinand Hodlers*. Basel, Rhein-Verlag, 1921.

5332. Klein, Rudolf. *Ferdinand Hodler & the Swiss*. Washington, D.C., Brentano, 1910.

5333. Loosli, Carl A. *Ferdinand Hodler; Leben, Werk und Nachlass*. 4 v. Bern, Sluter, 1921–1924. (CR).

5334. Maeder, Alphonse. *F. Hodler, eine Skizze seiner seelischen Entwicklung und Bedeutung für die schweizerisch-nationale Kultur*. Zürich, Rascher, 1916.

5335. Mühlestein, Hans. *Ferdinand Hodler, ein Deutungsversuch*. Weimar, Kiepenheuer, 1914.

5336. —— und Schmidt, Georg. *Ferdinand Hodler, 1853–1918; sein Leben und sein Werk.* Erlenbach/Zürlich, Rentsch, 1942.

5337. Museum für Kunst und Geschichte (Freiburg i.Ue.). *Hodler, die Mission des Künstlers.* 11. Juni–20. September 1981. [Text in German and French]. Bern, Benteli, 1981. (Hodler-Publikation, 4).

5338. Roffler, Thomas. *Ferdinand Hodler.* Frauenfeld/Leipzig, Huber, [1926].

5339. Schweizerisches Institut für Kunstwissenschaft (Zurich). *Der frühe Hodler, das Werk 1870–1890.* 11. April bis 14. Juni 1981. Bern, Benteli, 1981. (Hodler-Publikation, 3).

5340. Selz, Peter. *Ferdinand Hodler.* [Published in conjunction with an exhibition, University Art Museum, Berkeley, Calif., November 22, 1972–January 7, 1973; with contributions by Jura Brüschweiler, Phyllis Hattis, and Eva Wyler]. Berkeley, Calif., University Art Museum, 1972.

5341. Steinberg, Solomon David. *Ferdinand Hodler, ein Platoniker der Kunst.* Zürich, Rascher, 1947.

5342. Ueberwasser, Walter and Spreng, Robert. *Hodler, Köpfe und Gestalten.* Zürich, Rascher, 1947.

5343. Weese, Artur. *Ferdinand Hodler.* Bern, Francke, 1910.

Hofer, Karl, 1878–1955

5344. Akademie der Künste (Berlin). *Karl Hofer, 1878–1955.* 7. November 1965–2. Januar 1966. Berlin, Akademie der Künste, [1965].

5345. Feist, Ursula. *Karl Hofer.* Berlin, Henschel, 1977.

5346. Hofer, Karl. *Aus Leben und Kunst.* Berlin, Rembrandt, 1952.

5347. ——. *Erinnerungen eines Malers.* Berlin/Grunewald, Herbig, 1953.

5348. ——. *Karl Hofer, Bilder im Schlossmuseum Ettlingen.* [Hrsg. von der Stadt Ettlingen und vom Karl Hofer Archiv Berlin. Berlin, Frölich & Kaufmann, 1983.

5349. ——. *Karl Hofer, Theodor Reinhart: Maler und Mäzen, ein Briefwechsel in Auswahl.* Herausgegeben von Ursula und Gunter Feist. Berlin, Edition Hentrich, 1989

5350. ——. *Malerei hat eine Zukunft: Briefe, Aufsätze, Reden.* Herausgegeben von Andreas Huneke. Leipzig, Kiepenheuer, 1991.

5351. ——. *Über das Gesetzliche in der bildenden Kunst.* Berlin, Akademie der Künste, 1956. (Monographien und Biographien, 1).

5352. Reifenberg, Benno. *Karl Hofer.* Leipzig, Klinkhardt & Biermann, 1924. (Junge Kunst, 48).

5353. Staatliche Kunsthalle (Berlin). *Karl Hofer, 1878–1955.* 16. April bis 14. Juni 1978. Berlin, Staatliche Kunsthalle, 1978. (CR).

Hoffman, Malvina Cornell, 1887–1966

5354. Alexandre, Arsène. *Malvina Hoffman.* Paris, Pouterman, 1930.

5355. Hoffman, Malvina. *Heads and tales.* New York, Scribner, 1936.

5356. ——. *Sculpture inside and out.* New York, Norton, 1939.

5357. ——. *Yesterday is tomorrow, a personal history.* New York, Crown, 1965.

Hoffmann, Josef (Franz, Maria), 1870–1956

5358. Baroni, Daniele e D'Aruia, Antonio. *Josef Hoffman e la Wiener Werkstätte.* Milano, Electa, 1981.

5359. Fagiolo, Maurizio. *Hoffmann, i mobili semplici; Vienna 1900–1910.* [Rome], Galleria dell'Emporio Floreale, [1977].

5360. Hoffmann, Josef, F.M. *Josef Hoffmann, 1870–1956: Ornament zwischen Hoffnung und Verbrechen.* Die Sammlungen des Österreichischen Museums für angewandte Kunst, der Hochschule für angewandte Kunst, Wien, mit Objekten aus dem Historischen Museum der Stadt Wien. Hrsg. von Peter Noeven und Oswald Oberhuber. Wien, Peter Noeven und Oswald Oberhuber, 1987.

5361. ——. *Josef Hoffmann, Wien: Jugendstil und Zwanziger Jahre.* [Ausstellung]. Museum Bellerive, Zürich, 25. Mai–14. August 1983. Zürich, Kunstgewerbemuseum und Museum Bellerive, 1983. (Wegleitung des Kunstgewerbemuseums und des Museums Bellerive, 344).

5362. Kleiner, Leopold. *Josef Hoffmann.* Berlin, Hübsch, 1927.

5363. Langseth-Christensen, Lillian. *A design for living.* New York, Viking, 1987.

5364. Sekler, Eduard. *Josef Hoffmann, the architectural work. Monograph and catalogue of works.* Trans. by the author. Catalogue of works trans. by John Maass. Princeton, N.J., Princeton University Press, 1985.(CR). (Translation of *Josef Hoffmann: das architektonische Werk. Monographie und Werkverzeichnis.* Salzburg, Residenz Verlag, 1982. 2 ed., 1986).

5365. Veronesi, Giulia. *Josef Hoffmann.* Milano, Il Balcone, 1956. (Architetti del movimento moderno, 17).

5366. Weiser, Armand. *Josef Hoffmann.* Genf, Meister der Baukunst, 1930.

Hofmann, Hans, 1880–1966

5367. Goodman, Cynthia. *Hans Hofmann.* New York, Abbeville Press, 1986.

5368. ——. ed. *Hans Hofmann.* With essays by Cynthia Goodman, Irving Sandler, Clement Greenberg. Munich, Prestel-Verlag; New York, Whitney Museum of Art. Distributed in the USA and Canada by the Neues Publishing Company, 1990.

5369. Greenberg, Clement. *Hofmann*. Paris, Fall, 1961. (Musée de poche, 1).

5370. Hofmann, Hans. *Search for the real and other essays*. Andover, Mass., Addison Gallery of American Art, 1948.

5371. Hoyland, John. *Hans Hofmann, late paintings*. London, Tate Gallery, 1988.

5372. Hunter, Sam. *Hans Hofmann*. New York, Abrams, 1963.

5373. Museum of Modern Art (New York). *Hans Hofmann*. September 11–November 28, 1963. Text by William C. Seitz. New York, Museum of Modern Art, 1963; distributed by Doubleday, Garden City, N.Y. (Reprint: New York, Arno, 1972).

5374. Wight, Frederick S. *Hans Hofmann*. Los Angeles, University of California Press, 1957.

Hogarth, William, 1697–1764

5375. Antal, Frederick. *Hogarth and his place in European art*. New York, Basic Books, 1962.

5376. Beckett, Ronald B. *Hogarth*. London, Routledge, 1949.

5377. Benoit, François. *Hogarth*. Paris, Laurens, [1904].

5378. Berry, Erick [pseud., Allena Best]. *The four Londons of William Hogarth*. New York, McKay, 1964.

5379. Bindman, David. *Hogarth*. London, Thames and Hudson, 1981.

5380. Blum, André. *Hogarth*. Paris, Alcan, 1922.

5381. Bowen, Marjorie. *William Hogarth, the Cockney's mirror*. New York/London, Appleton-Century, 1936.

5382. Brown, Gerard B. *William Hogarth*. New York, Scribner, 1905.

5383. Burke, Joseph and Caldwell, Colin. *Hogarth, the complete engravings*. London, Thames and Hudson, 1968.

5384. Cook, Thomas. *Hogarth restored; the whole works of the celebrated William Hogarth as originally published, now re-engraved, accompanied by anecdotes of Mr. Hogarth*. 2 v. London, [Cook] and Robinson, 1802.

5385. Dobson, Austin. *William Hogarth*. London, Heinemann/New York, McClure, Phillips, 1902.

5386. Garnett, Edward. *Hogarth*. London, Duckworth/New York, Dutton, [1911].

5387. Gaunt, William. *The world of William Hogarth*. London, Cape, 1978.

5388. Gowing, Lawrence. *Hogarth*. [Catalogue of an exhibition, The Tate Gallery, 2 December 1971–6 February 1972]. London, The Tate Gallery, 1971.

5389. Hogarth, William. *The analysis of beauty, written with a view of fixing the fluctuating ideas of taste*. London, Reeves, 1753. (New edition: Oxford, Clarendon Press, 1955).

5390. ———. *The works of William Hogarth . . . with a sketch of Hogarth's life and career by William Makepeace Thackeray and an essay on the genius and character of Hogarth by Charles Lamb*. Boston, Osgood, 1876.

5391. Ireland, John. *Hogarth illustrated*. 3 v. London, Boydell, 1793. 2 ed.

5392. Lichtenberg, Georg Christoph. *W. Hogarth's Zeichnungen, nach den Originalen in Stahl gestochen*. 2 v. Stuttgart, Literatur-Comptoir, 1840.

5393. ———. *Witzige und launige Sittengemälde nach Hogarth*. Wien, Commission der Gassler'schen Buchhandlung, 1811.

5394. ———. *The world of Hogarth, Lichtenberg's commentaries on Hogarth's engravings*. Trans. by Innes and Gustav Herdan. Boston, Houghton Mifflin, 1966.

5395. Lindsay, Jack. *Hogarth; his art and his world*. New York, Taplinger, 1979.

5396. Mandel, Gabriele. *L'opera completa di Hogarth pittore*. Milano, Rizzoli, 1967. (Classici dell'arte, 15).

5397. Meier-Graefe, Julius. *William Hogarth*. München/Leipzig, Piper, 1907.

5398. Moore, Robert E. *Hogarth's literary relationships*. Minneapolis, University of Minnesota Press, 1948.

5399. [Nichols, John, ed.]. *Anecdotes of William Hogarth written by himself, with essays on his life and genius, and criticisms on his works selected from Walpole, Gilpin, J. Ireland, Lamb, Phillips, and others*. London, Nichols, 1833. (Reprint: London, Cornmarket Press, 1970).

5400. Nichols, John and Steevens, George. *The geniune work of William Hogarth, illustrated with biographical anecdotes, a chronological catalogue and commentary*. 2 v. London, Longman, Hurst, Rees, and Orme, 1808/1810 [with a supplementary volume containing *Clavis Hogarthiana* purported to be by Edmund Ferres and other illustrative essays, with fifty additional plates, London, Nichols, Son, and Bentley, 1817].

5401. Oppé, Adolf P. *The drawings of William Hogarth*. New York, Phaidon, 1948.

5402. Quennell, Peter. *Hogarth's progress*. London, Collins, 1955.

5403. Paulson, Ronald. *The art of Hogarth*. London, Phaidon; New York, distrib. by Praeger Publishers, 1975.

5404. ———. *Hogarth*. 3 v. New Brunswick, N.J., Rutgers University Press, 1991–1993. (Fully revised and updated edition of the work first published in 2 vols., *Hogarth, his life, art and times*, New Haven, Yale University Press, 1971).

5405. ———. *Hogarth, his life, art and times.* 2 v. New Haven/London, Yale University Press, 1971.

5406. ———. *Hogarth, his life art times.* 1 v. Abridged by Anne Wilde. New Haven, Yale University Press, 1974.

5407. ———. *Hogarth's graphic work.* 2 v. London, The Print Room, 1989. 3 d. revised edition. (2 rev. ed.: New Haven, Yale University Press, 1970).

5408. Sala, George Augustus. *William Hogarth, painter, engraver and philosopher; essays on the man, the work and the time.* London, Smith, Elder, 1866.

5409. Trusler, John. *Hogarth moralized, being a complete edition of Hogarth's works . . . with an explanation . . . and a comment on their moral tendency.* London, Hooper [and] Jane Hogarth, 1768.

5410. Webster, Mary. *Hogarth.* London, Studio Vista, 1979.

5411. Weitenkampf, Frank. *A bibliography of William Hogarth.* Cambridge, Mass., The Library of Harvard University, 1890. (Library of Harvard University, Bibliographic Contributions, 37).

5412. Wheatley, Henry B. *Hogarth's London; pictures of the manners of the eighteenth century.* New York, Dutton, 1909.

Hohenberg, Martin *see* Altomonte, Martino, 1657–1745

Hokusai (Katsushika Hokusai), 1760–1849

5413. Bowie, Theodore. *The drawings of Hokusai.* Bloomington, Ind., Indiana University Press, 1964.

5414. Dickins, Frederick V. *Fugaku Hiyaku-kei, or a hundred views of Fuji.* London, Batsford, 1880.

5415. [Fenellosa, Ernest F.]. *Catalogue of the exhibition of paintings of Hokusai held at the Japan Fine Art Association, Uyeno Park, Tokio, from 13th to 30th January, 1900.* Tokio, Bunshichi Kobayashi, 1901.

5416. Focillon, Henri. *Hokousaï.* Paris, Alcan, 1914.

5417. Forrer, Matthi. *Hokusai, a guide to the serial graphics.* Philadelphia/London, Heron Press, 1974.

5418. ———. *Hokusai.* With texts by Edmond de Goncourt. New York, Rizzoli, 1988.

5419. ———. *Hokusai: prints and drawings.* Munich, Prestel; New York, distributed in the USA and Canada by te Neues Pub. Co., 1991.

5420. Goncourt, Edmond de. *Hokousaï.* Paris, Bibliothèque Charpentier, 1896.

5421. Hillier, Jack R. *The art of Hokusai in book illustration.* London, Sotheby Parke Bernet/

Berkeley and Los Angeles, University of California, 1980.

5422. ———. *Hokusai; paintings, drawings, and woodcuts.* New York, Phaidon, 1955; distributed by Garden City Books, Garden City, N.Y.

5423. Holmes, Charles J. *Hokusai.* London, At the Sign of the Unicorn, 1900. (Artist's library, 1).

5424. Honolulu Academy of Arts. *Prints by Utagawa Hiroshige in the James A. Michener Collection.* Essay by Kobayashi Tadashi; catalogue by Howard A. Link. 2 v. Honolulu, Honolulu Academy of Arts, 1991.

5425. Katsushika Hokusai. *Hokusai: one hundred views of Mt. Fuji.* Introduction and commentaries on the plates by Henry D. Smith II. New York, George Braziller, 1988.

5426. Lane, Richard. *Hokusai: life and work.* London. Barrie & Jenkins, 1989.

5427. Michener, James A. *The Hokusai sketchbooks; selections from the Manga.* Rutland, Vermont/Tokyo, Tuttle, 1958.

5428. Nagassé, Takeshiro. *Le paysage dans l'art de Hokouçai.* Paris, Les Editions d'Art et d'Histoire, 1937.

5429. Narazaki, Muneshige. *Hokusai, sketches and paintings.* English adaptation by John Bester. Tokyo/Palo Alto, Calif., Kodansha, 1969.

5430. ———. *Hokusai, the thirty-six views of Mt. Fuji.* English adaptation by John Bester. Tokyo/Palo Alto, Calif., Kodansha, 1968.

5431. Noguchi, Yone. *Hokusai.* London, Elkin Mathews, 1925.

5432. Perzynski, Friedrich. *Hokusai.* Bielefeld/Leipzig, Velhagen & Klasing, 1904. (Künstler-Monographien, 68).

5433. Revon, Michel. *Etude sur Hoksaï.* Paris, Lecène, Oudin, 1896.

5434. Strange, Edward F. *Hokusai, the old man mad with painting.* London, Siegle, Hill, 1906. (Langham series of art Monographs, 17).

Holbein, Hans (the elder), 1460–1524
Hans (the younger), 1497–1543

5435. Benoit, François. *Holbein.* Paris, Librairie de l'Art Ancien et Moderne, [1905].

5436. Beutler, Christian and Thiem, Günther. *Hans Holbein d. Ä., die spätgotische Altar- und Glasmalerei.* Augsburg, Rösler, 1960. (Abhandlungen zur Geschichte der Stadt Augsburg, Schriftenreihe des Stadtarchivs Augsburg, 13).

5437. Bushart, Bruno. *Hans Holbein der Ältere.* Hrsg. vom Ausburger Holbein-Kuratorium. Ausburg, Verlag Hofmann-Druck, 1987. 2 ed.

5438. Chamberlain, Arthur B. *Hans Holbein the*

younger. 2 v. London, Allen, 1913.

5439. Chamberlaine, John. *Imitations of original drawings by Hans Holbein in the collection of His Majesty for the portraits of illustrious persons of the Court of Henry VIII, with biographical tracts* [by Edmund Lodge]. London, Bulmer, 1792.

5440. Christoffel, Ulrich. *Hans Holbein d. J.* Berlin, Verlag des Druckhauses Tempelhof, 1950.

5441. Cohn, Werner. *Der Wandel der Architekturgestaltung in den Werken Hans Holbein d. J., ein Beitrag zur Holbein-Chronologie.* Strassburg, Heitz, 1930. (Studien zur deutschen Kunstgeschichte, 278).

5442. Davies, Gerald S. *Hans Holbein the younger.* London, Bell, 1903.

5443. Fougerat, Emmanuel. *Holbein.* Paris, Alcan, 1914.

Ford, Ford M. *see* Hueffer, Ford Madox

5444. Frölicher, Elsa. *Die Porträtkunst Hans Holbein des Jüngeren und ihr Einfluss auf die schweizerische Bildnismalerei im XVII. Jahrhundert.* Strassburg, Heitz, 1909. (Studien zur deutschen Kunstgeschichte, 117).

5445. Ganz, Paul. *Les dessins de Hans Holbein le jeune.* 9 v. Genève, Boissonas, [1911–1939]. (CR).

5446. ———. *Die Handzeichnungen Hans Holbein d.J., kritischer Katalog.* Berlin, Bard, 1937. (CR).

5447. ———. *Hans Holbein d.J., des Meisters Gemälde.* Stuttgart/Leipzig, Deutsche Verlags-Anstalt, 1912. (Klassiker der Kunst, 20).

5448. ———. *The paintings of Hans Holbein, first complete edition.* Trans. by R. H. Boothroyd and Marguerite Kay. London, Phaidon, 1950.

5449. Gauthiez, Pierre. *Holbein, biographie critique.* Paris, Laurens, [1907].

5450. Glaser, Curt. *Hans Holbein d. J., Zeichnungen.* New York, Weyhe, [1924].

5451. ———. *Hans Holbein der Ältere.* Leipzig, Hiersemann, 1908. (Kunstgeschichtliche Monographien, 11).

5452. Hegner, Ulrich. *Hans Holbein der Jüngere.* Berlin, Reimer, 1827.

5453. Holbein, Hans. *Todtentanz.* Lyon, Trechfelz fratres, 1538. (Reprint: München, Hirth, 1884).

5454. ———. *The dance of death.* With an introduction and notes by James M. Clark. London, Phaidon, 1947.

5455. ———. *Icones historiarvm Veteris Testamenti.* Lvdgvni [Lyons], Apud I. Frellonium, 1547. (Reprint: Manchester [England], Holbein Society, 1869).

5456. Hueffer, Ford Madox. *Hans Holbein, the younger; a critical monograph.* London, Duckworth/New York, Dutton, 1905.

5457. Knackfuss, Hermann. *Holbein.* Trans. by Campbell Dodgson. Bielefeld/Leipzig, Velhagen & Klasing/London, Grevel, 1899. (Monographs on Artists, 2).

5458. Koegler, Hans. *Hans Holbein d. J.; die Bilder zum Gebetbuch Hortulus animae.* 2 v. Basel, Schwabe, 1943.

5459. Kunstmuseum Basel zur Fünfhundertjahrfeier der Universität Basel. *Die Malerfamilie Holbein in Basel. 4. Juni–25. September 1960.* Basel, Kunstmuseum Basel, 1960.

5460. Landolt, Hanspeter. *Das Skizzenbuch Hans Holbein des Älteren im Kupferstichkabinett Basel.* 2 v. Olten, Urs Graf-Verlag, 1960.

5461. Leroy, Alfred. *Hans Holbein et son temps.* Paris, Michel, 1943.

5462. Lieb, Norbert and Strange, Alfred. *Hans Holbein der Ältere.* [München], Deutscher Kunstverlag, [1960].

5463. Mantz, Paul. *Hans Holbein.* Paris, Quantin, 1879.

5464. Michael, Erika. *The drawings by Hans Holbein the Younger for Erasmus' "Praise of Folly."* New York, Garland, 1986. (Outstanding dissertaions in the fine arts).

5465. Müller, Christin. *Hans Holbein d.J.: Zeichnungen. aus dem Kupferstichkabinett der Öffentlichen Kunstsammlung Basel.* Basel, Kunstmuseum Basel, 1988.

5466. Parker, Karl T. *The drawings of Hans Holbein in the collection of His Majesty the King at Windsor Castle.* London, Phaidon, 1945.

5467. Pinder, Wilhelm. *Holbein der Jüngere und das Ende der altdeutschen Kunst.* Köln, Seemann, 1951.

5468. Richter, Julius Wilhelm. *Hans Holbein der Jüngere; eine altdeutsche Künstlergeschichte.* Berlin, Schall, 1901.

5469. Rousseau, Jean. *Hans Holbein.* Paris, Rouam, 1885.

5470. Rumohr, Karl Friedrich von. *Hans Holbein der Jüngere in seinem Verhältniss zum deutschen Formschnittwesen.* Leipzig, Weigel, 1836.

5471. Schmid, Heinrich A. *Hans Holbein der Jüngere, sein Aufstieg zur Meisterschaft und sein englischer Stil.* 3 v. Basel, Holbein-Verlag, 1948/1955.

5472. Stein, Wilhelm. *Holbein.* Berlin, Bard, 1929.

5473. Strong, Roy. *Holbein and Henry VIII.* London, Routledge & Kegan Paul, 1967.

5474. Waetzoldt, Wilhelm. *Hans Holbein der Jüngere; Werk und Welt.* Berlin, Grote, 1938.

5475. Wornum, Ralph N. *Some account of the life and works of Hans Holbein, painter of Augsburg.* London, Chapman and Hall, 1867.

5476. Woltmann, Alfred. *Holbein and his time.* Trans. by F. E. Bunnètt. London, Bentley, 1872.

5477. ———. *Holbein und seine Zeit.* 2 v. Leipzig, Seemann, 1874/1876. 2 ed.

H

5478. Zoege von Manteuffel, Kurt. *Hans Holbein der Maler.* München, Schmidt, 1920.

5479. ———. *Hans Holbein der Zeichner für Holzschnitt und Kunstgewerbe.* München, Schmidt, 1920.

Holl, Elias, 1573–1646

5480. Baum, Julius. *Die Bauwerke des Elias Holl.* Strassburg, Heitz, 1908. (Studien zur deutschen Kunstgeschichte, 93).

5481. Dirr, Pius. *Handschriften und Zeichnungen Elias Holls.* Augsburg, [Schlosser], 1907.

5482. Hieber, Hermann. *Elias Holl, der Meister der deutschen Renaissance.* München, Piper, 1923.

5483. Holl, Elias. *Elias Holl und das Augsburger Rathaus.* [Ausstellung]. Hrsg. von Wolfram Baer, Hanno-Walter Kruft, Bernd Roeck. Regensburg, F. Pustet, 1985.

5484. Roeck, Bernd. *Elias Holl; Architekt einer europäischen Stadt.* Regensburg, F. Pustet, 1985.

5485. Vogt, Wilhelm. *Elias Holl, der Reichsstadt Augsburg bestellter Werkmeister.* Bamberg, Buchnersche Verlagsbuchhandlung, 1890. (Bayerische Bibliothek, 7).

5486. Wagenseil, Christian Jakob. *Elias Holl, Baumeister zu Augsburg, biographische Skizze.* Ausgburg, Braun, 1818.

Hollar, Wenceslaus, 1607–1677

5487. Borovský, František. *Wenzel Hollar. Ergänzungen zu G. Parthey's beschreibendem Verzeichniss seiner Kupferstiche.* Prag, [Rivnác], 1898. (CR).

5488. Denkstein, Valdimír. *Václav Hollar, Kresby.* [Praha], Odeon, 1977.

5489. Dolenský, Antonin. *Václav Hollar, cesky rytec.* Praha, Veraikon, 1919.

5490. Dostál, Eugène. *Venceslas Hollar.* Prague, Stenc, 1924.

5491. Eerde, Katherine S. van. *Wenceslaus Hollar, delineator of his time.* Charlottesville, Va., Folger Shakespeare Library/University Press of Virginia, 1970.

5492. Griffiths, Antony. *Wenceslaus Hollar: prints and drawings from the collections of the National Gallery, Prague, and the British Museum,* London. A. Griffiths and Gabriela Kesnerova. London, British Museum Publications, 1983.

5493. Hind, Arthur M. *Wenceslaus Hollar and his views of London and Windsor in the seventeenth century.* London, Lane, 1922.

5494. Hollar, Wenceslaus. *Wenzel Hollar, die Kölner Jahre: Zeichnungen und Radierungen 1632–1636.* Die Bestände des Kölnischen Stadtmuseums ergänzt durch Leihgaben aus Bonn, Chatsworth, Düsseldorf, Köln, Odenthal, Prag und Windsor. Hrsg. von Werner

Schafke. Köln, Kölnisches Stadtmuseum, 1992.

5495. Hollar, Wenceslaus. *Wenzel Hollar, 1607–1677: Reisebilder vom Rhein:* Städte und Burgen am Mittelrhein in Zeichnungen und Radierungen. [Ausstellung]. Landesmuseum Mainz, 16. November 1986 bis 6. Januar 1987. Hrsg. Berthold Roland. Katalogtexte und Redaktion, Ralph Melville, Horst Reber, Norbert Suhr. Mainz, Das Landesmuseum, 1986.

5496. Institut Néerlandais (Paris). *Wenzel Hollar, 1607–1677; dessins, gravures, cuivres.* 11 janvier–25 février 1979. Paris, Institut Néerlandais, 1979.

5497. Mielke, Hans. *Wenzel Hollar; Radierungen und Zeichnungen aus dem Berliner Kupferstichkabinett.* Berlin, Staatliche Museen Preussischer Kulturbesitz, 1984.

5498. Parry, Graham. *Hollar's England, a mid-seventeenth century view.* Salisbury, Russell, 1980.

5499. Parthey, Gustav. *Wenzel Hollar, beschreibendes Verzeichniss seiner Kupferstiche.* Berlin, Verlag der Nicolaischen Buchhandlung, 1853. (CR).

5500. ———. *Nachträge und Verbesserungen zum Verzeichnisse der Hollar'schen Kupferstiche.* Berlin, Verlag der Nicolaischen Buchhandlung, 1858. (CR).

5501. Richter, Stanislav. *Václav Hollar, umelec a jeho doba 1607–1677.* Praha, Vysehrad, 1977.

5502. Sprinzels, Franz. *Hollar, Handzeichnungen.* Wien, Passer, 1938.

5503. Urzidil, Johannes. *Hollar, a Czech emigré in England.* London, The Czechoslovak, 1942.

5504. ———. *Wenceslaus Hollar, der Kupferstecher des Barock.* Leipzig, Passer, 1936.

5505. Vertue, George. *A description of the works of the ingenious delineator and engraver Wencelas Hollar.* London, William Bathoe, 1759. 2 ed.

Holst, Theodor von, 1840–1844

5506. Browne, Max. *The romantic art of Theodor von Holst, 1840–44.* London, Lund Humphries, 1994.

Homer, Winslow, 1836–1910

5507. Beam, Philip C. *Winslow Homer at Prout's Neck.* Boston/Toronto, Little, Brown, 1966.

5508. ———. *Winslow Homer in the 1890s, Prout's Neck observed.* [Catalogue of an exhibition]. Philip Beam, Lois Homer Graham et al. New York, Hudson Hills Press, in association with the Memorial Art Gallery of the University of Rochester. New York, Hudson Hills Press, 1991.

5509. ———. *Winslow Homer's magazine engrav-*

ings. New York, Harper & Row, 1979.

5510. Cikovsky, Nicolai. *Winslow Homer.* New York, Harry N. Abrams, 1990.

5511. ———. *Winslow Homer: Watercolors.* Southport, Conn.: Levin, 1991; distrib. Macmillan.

5512. Cooper, Helen A. *Winslow Homer watercolours.* [Catalogue of an exhibition held at the National Gallery of Art, Washington, D.C., March 2–May 11, 1986]. New Haven, Yale University Press, 1986.

5513. Cox, Kenyon. *Winslow Homer.* New York, [Frederick Fairchild Sherman], 1914.

5514. Davis, Melinda D. *Winslow Homer, an annotated bibliography of periodical literature.* Metuchen, N.J., Scarecrow Press, 1975.

5515. Downes, William Howe. *The life and works of Winslow Homer.* Boston/New York, Houghton Mifflin, 1911.

5516. Flexner, James Thomas. *The world of Winslow Homer, 1836–1910.* New York, Time, Inc., 1966.

5517. Foster, Allen E. *A check list of illustrations by Winslow Homer in Harper's Weekly and other periodicials.* New York, New York Public Library, 1936.

5518. Gardner, Albert Ten Eyck. *Winslow Homer, American artist; his world and his work.* New York, Clarkson Potter, 1961.

5519. Gelman, Barbara. *The wood engravings of Winslow Homer.* New York, Bounty, 1970.

5520. Goodrich, Lloyd. *American watercolor and Winslow Homer.* Minneapolis, Walker Art Center, 1945.

5521. ———. *The graphic art of Winslow Homer.* [Washington, D.C.], Smithsonian Institution Press, 1968. (CR).

5522. ———. *Winslow Homer.* New York, Whitney Museum of American Art/Macmillan, 1944.

5523. ———. *Winslow Homer.* New York, Braziller, 1959.

5524. ———. *Winslow Homer's America.* New York, Tudor, 1969.

5525. Gould, Jean. *Winslow Homer, a portrait.* New York, Dodd, Mead, 1962.

5526. Grossman, Julian. *Echo of a distant drum; Winslow Homer and the Civil War.* New York, Abrams, 1974.

5527. Hannaway, Patti. *Winslow Homer in the tropics.* Richmond, Virginia, Westover, 1973.

5528. Hendricks, Gordon. *The life and work of Winslow Homer.* New York, Abrams, 1979. (CR).

5529. Hoopes, Donelson F. *Winslow Homer, watercolors.* New York, Watson-Guptill, 1969.

5530. Hyman, Linda. *Winslow Homer, America's old master.* New York, Doubleday, 1973.

5531. Judge, Mary A. *Winslow Homer.* New York, Crown Publishers, 1986.

5532. Metropolitan Museum of Art (New York). *Winslow Homer, memorial exhibition.* February 6–March 19, [1911]. New York, Metropolitan Museum of Art, 1911.

5533. National Gallery of Art (Washington, D.C.). *Winslow Homer, a retrospective exhibiton.* November 23, 1958–January 4, 1959. [Text by Albert Ten Eyck Gardner]. Washington, D.C., National Gallery of Art, 1958.

5534. Ripley, Elizabeth. *Winslow Homer, a biography.* Philadelphia, Lippincott, 1963.

5535. Robertson, Bruce. *Reckoning with Winslow Homer: his late paintings and their influence.* [Exhibition catatalogue]. Cleveland, The Cleveland Museum of Art in cooperation with Indiana University Press, 1990.

5536. Tatham, David. *Winslow Homer and the illustrated book.* Syracuse, Syracuse University Press, 1992.

5537. Watson, Forbes. *Winslow Homer.* New York, Crown, 1942.

5538. Whitney Museum of American Art (New York). *Winslow Homer, centenary exhibition.* December 15, 1936 to January 15, 1937. [Text by Lloyd Goodrich]. New York, Whitney Museum of American Art, 1936.

5539. Wilmerding, John. *Winslow Homer.* New York, Praeger, 1972.

Honnecourt, Villard de See Villard de Honnecourt

Honthorst, Gerrit van, 1590-1656

5540. Hoogewerff, Godefritus J. *Gerrit van Honthorst.* The Hague, Naeff, 1924.

5541. Judson, J. Richard. *Gerrit van Honthorst, a discussion of his position in Dutch art.* The Hague, Nijhoff, 1959. (CR). (Utrechtse Bijdragen tot de Kunstgeschiedenis, 6).

Hooch, Pieter de, 1629-1684 *see also* Fabritius, Carel

5542. Rudder, Arthur de. *Pieter de Hooch et son oeuvre.* Bruxelles, van Oest, 1914.

5543. Scala, André. *Pieter de Hooch.* Paris, Editions Séguier, 1991.

5544. Sutton, Peter C. *Pieter de Hooch, complete edition.* Oxford, Phaidon, 1980. (CR).

5545. Thienen, Frithjof Willem Sophi van. *Pieter de Hooch.* Amsterdam, Becht, [1945].

5546. Valentiner, Wilhelm R. *Pieter de Hooch, the master's paintings.* New York, Weyhe, [1930].

Hopper, Edward, 1882-1967

5547. Beck, Hubert. *Der melancholische Blick: die Großstadt im Werk des amerikanischen Malers Edward Hopper.* Frankfurt am Main/New York, P. Lang, 1988. (European university studies. Series XXVIII, History of art, 86).

5548. DuBois, Guy P. *Edward Hopper.* New York, Whitney Museum of American Art, 1931.

5549. Goodrich, Lloyd. *Edward Hopper.* New York, Abrams, [1971].

5550. ———. *Edward Hopper: das Frühwerk.* [Ausstellung]. Westfälisches Landesmuseum für Kunst und Kulturgeschichte, 16.4.–31.5.1981. Redaktion des Kataloges, Ernst Gerhard Güse und Nicola Borger-Keweloh. Münster Landschaftsverband Westfalen-Lippe, 1981.

5551. ———. *Edward Hopper, light years.* [Exhibition], October 1 to November 12, 1988. Essay by Peter Schjeldahl. New York, Hirschl & Adler Galleries, 1988.

5552. ———. *Edward Hopper und die Fotografie: die Wahrheit des Sichtbaren.* Hrsg. von Georg-W. Koltzsch und Heinz Liesbrock; mit Beiträgen von Gerd Blum . . . [et al.]. Essen, Museum Folkwang, 1992.

5553. Hopper, Edward. *Hopper drawings: 44 works.* New York, Dover Publications, 1989.

5554. Levin, Gail. *Edward Hopper as illustrator.* New York, Norton/Whitney Museum of American Art, 1979. (CR).

5555. ———. *Edward Hopper, the art and the artist.* New York, Norton/Whitney Museum of American Art, 1980.

5556. ———. *Edward Hopper, the complete prints.* New York, Norton/Whitney Museum of American Art, 1979. (CR).

5557. Museum of Modern Art (New York). *Edward Hopper, retrospective exhibition.* November 1–December 7, 1933. [Text by Alfred H. Barr, Jr., Charles Burchfield, and Edward Hopper]. New York, Museum of Modern Art, 1933.

5558. Whitney Museum of American Art (New York). *Edward Hopper, retrospective exhibition.* February 11–March 26, 1950. [Text by Lloyd Goodrich]. New York, Whitney Museum of American Art, 1950.

Hoppner, John, 1758–1810

5559. McKay, William and Roberts, William. *John Hoppner, R. A.* London, Colnaghi/Bell, 1909. (CR).

Horta, Victor, 1861–1947

5560. Borsi, Franco [and] Portoghesi, Paolo. *Victor Horta.* Roma, Laterza, 1982.

5561. ———. *Victor Horta.* [By] F. Borsi, P. Portoghesi; foreword by Jean Delhaye. Translated from the Italian by Marie-Helene Agueros. New York, Rizzoli, 1991.

5562. Delhaye, Jean. *La maison du peuple de Victor Horta.* Textes presentés et commentés par Françoise Dierkens-Aubry. Bruxelles, Atélier Vokaer, 1987.

5563. Dierkens-Aubry, Françoise. The Horta Museum, Brussels, Saint-Gilles. Brussels, Crédit Communal, 1990

5564. Horta, Victor. *Mémoires.* Texte établi, annoté et introduit par Cecile Duliere. [Bruxelles], Ministère de la Communauté français de Belgique, Administration du Patrimoine culturel, 1985.

5565. Delevoy, Robert L. *Victor Horta.* Bruxelles, Elsevier, 1958.

5566. Oostens-Wittamer, Yolande. *Horta en Amérique, décembre 1915–janvier 1919.* Bruxelles, Editions Lebeer Hossman, 1986.

5567. ———. *Victor Horta; l'Hôtel Solvay/the Solvay House.* Trans. by John A. Gray, Jr. 2 v. [Text in French and English]. Louvain-la-neuve, Institut supérieur d'archéologie et d'histoire de l'art, 1980. (Publications d'histoire de l'art et d'archéologie de l'Université Catholique de Louvain, 20).

Houdon, Jean Antoine, 1741–1828

5568. Arnason, H. H. *The sculptures of Houdon.* London, Phaidon, 1975.

5569. Chinard, Gilbert, ed. *Houdon in America, a collection of documents in the Jefferson papers in the Library of Congress.* Baltimore, Johns Hopkins/London, Oxford University Press, 1930. (Historical Documents, Institut Français de Washington, 4).

5570. Dierks, Hermann. *Houdons Leben und Werke; eine kunsthistorische Studie.* Gotha, Thienemanns, 1887.

5571. Délerot, Emile et Legrelle, Arsène. *Notice sur J. A. Houdon de l'Institut (1741–1828).* Versailles, Montalant-Bongleux, 1856.

5572. Gandouin, Ernest. *Quelques notes sur J.-A. Houdon, statuaire, 1741–1828.* Paris, Nouvelle Imprimerie, [1900].

5573. Giacometti, Georges. *La vie et l'oeuvre de Houdon.* 2 v. Paris, Camoin, [1921]. (CR).

5574. Hart, Charles Henry and Biddle, Edward. *Memoirs of the life and works of Jean Antoine Houdon, the sculptor of Voltaire and of Washington.* Philadelphia, printed for the authors, 1911.

5575. Maillard, Elisa. *Houdon.* Paris, Rieder, 1931.

5576. Réau, Louis. *Houdon, biographie critique.* Paris, Laurens, 1930.

5577. ———. *Houdon, sa vie et son oeuvre; ouvrage posthume suivi d'un catalogue systématique.* 2 v. Paris, de Nobele, 1964. (CR).

Houel, Jean-Pierre-Laurent, 1735–1813.

5578. Bloberg, Maurice. *Jean Houel, peintre et graveur.* Paris, Naert, 1930.

5579. Houël, Jean-Pierre-Laurent. *Houël, voyage en Sicile, 1776–1779.* [Catalogue, Musée du

Louvre. Cabinet des Dessins] Madeleine Pionault, avec la participation de Kate de Kersauson et André Le Prat]. Paris, Herscher; Ministère de la culture, de la communication, des grands travaux et du Bicentenaire/ Réunion des musées nationaux, 1990.

Hrdlicka, Alfred, 1928–

5580. Buderath, Bernhard. *Alfred Hrdlicka: Anatomien des Leids.* Stuttgart, Klett-Cotta, 1984.

5581. Hrdlicka, Alfred. *Alfred Hrdlicka, von Robespierre zu Hitler: Die Pervertierung der Revolution seit 1789.* Hrsg. von Walter Schurian. Hamburg, Rasch und Röhring Verlag, 1988.

5582. ———. *Alfred Hrdlicka.* [Katalog der Ausstellung]. Kestner-Gesellschaft, Hanover, 15. März bis 5. Mai 1974. Hannover, Kest-ner-Gesellschaft, 1974. (Katalog 2/1974).

5583. ———. *Die Ästhetik des automatischen Faschismus:* Essays und neue Schriften. Hrs. von Michael Lewin, Wien, Europaverlag, 1989.

5584. ———. *Drei Zyklen: Winckelmann, Haarmann, Roll over Mondrian.* Essays und Bildtexte, Johann Muschik. Wien/München, Verlag für Jugend und Volk, 1986.

5585. ———. *Das Frauenbild: Alfred Hrdlicka.* Mit Beiträgen von Eva Blimlinger . . . [et al]; hrsg. von Ernst Hilger. Wien, Galerie Hilger; Vertrieb, Europaverlag, 1989?.

5586. ———. *Alfred Hrdlicka: Texte und Bilder zum sechzigsten Geburtstag des Bildhauers A H.* Hrsg. von Ulrike Jenni und Theodor Scheufele. Gräfelfing vor München, Moos & Partner, 1988.

5587. Lewin, Michael. *Alfred Hrdlicka: Druckgraphik.* [Katalog]. Berlin, Staatliche Kunsthalle, 1989.

5588. ———. *Alfred Hrdlicka, das Gesamtwerk.* Wien, Europaverlag in Zusammenarbeit mit der Galerie Hilger. 1987– . (CR). [v. 1, 3–4 published to-date].

5589. Menekes, Friedhelm. *Kein schlechtes Opium: Das Religiöse im Werk von Alfred Hrdlicka.* Stuttgart, Katholisches Bibelwerk, 1987.

5590. Sotriffer, Christian. *Alfred Hrdlicka: Randolectil.* Mit einem Werkkatalog sämtlicher Radierungen 1947–1968. Wien/München, Edition Tusch im Verlag Anton Schroll & Co. 1969. (CR). (Österreichische Druckgraphiker der Gegenwart,1).

Hsü-Kuo, 1823–1896

5591. Tsao, Jung Ying. *The paintings of Xugu and Qi Baishi.* By Jung Yin Tsa; edited by Carol Ann Bardoff. San Francisco, Far East Fine Arts; Seattle, University of Washington Press, 1993.

Huang Kung-Wang, 1269–1354

5592. Hay, John. *Huang Kung-Wang's Dwelling in the Fu-ch'un Mountains: the dimensions of landscape.* Ann Arbor, Michigan, University Microfilms, 1978.

Huang, Pin-Hung, 1865–1965

5593. Kuo Chi-sheng. *Innovation within tradition: the painting of Huang Pin-hung.* By Jason C. Kuo, with an introduction by Richard Edwards and a contribution by Tao Ho. Hong Kong, Hanart Gallery in association with Williams College Museum of Art, Williamstown, Massachusetts. Williamstown. Mass., 1989.

Huber, Wolf, 1485–1553

5594. Heinzle, Erwin. *Wolf Huber, um 1485–1553.* Innsbruck, Wagner, [1953].

5595. Riggenbach, Rudolf. *Der Maler und Zeichner Wolfgang Huber (ca. 1490–nach 1542).* Basel, Gasser, 1907.

5596. Weinberger, Martin. *Wolfgang Huber.* Leipzig, Insel-Verlag, 1930.

5597. Winzinger, Franz. *Wolf Huber, das Gesamtwerk.* 2 v. München, Hirmer/München [und] Zürich, Piper, 1979. (CR).

Huet, Paul, 1803–1869

5598. Burty, Philippe. *Paul Huet, notice biographique et critique, suivie du catalogue de ses oeuvres exposées en partie dans les salons de l'Union artistique.* Paris, Claye, 1869.

5599. Huet, René Paul. *Paul Huet (1803–1869) d'après ses notes, sa correspondance, ses contemporains, documents recueillis et précédés d'une notice biographique par son fils.* Paris, Renouard, 1911.

5600. Miquel, Pierre. *Paul Huet de l'aube romantique à l'aube impressionniste.* Sceaux, Editions de la Martinelle, 1962.

5601. Musée des Beaux-Arts (Rouen). *Paul Huet (1803–1869).* 28 mai–15 septembre 1965. Rouen, Musée des Beaux-Arts, 1965.

Huguet, Jaume, 1448–1487

5602. Gudiol Ricart, José [and] Ainaud de Lasarte, Juan. *Huguet.* Barcelona, Instituto Amateller de Arte Hispánico, 1948.

5603. Huguet, Jaume. *Jaume Huguet, 500 Anys; ponencies i communicacions presentadas a les jornades d'estudi.* Desembre 1992, Valls, (Tarragona). Barcelona, Generalitat Catalunya, 1993.

5604. Rowland, Benjamin, Jr. *Jaume Huguet, a study of late Gothic painting in Catalonia.* Cambridge, Mass., Harvard University Press, 1932.

Hundertwasser, Friedensreich, 1928–

5605. Bockelmann, Manfred. *Hundertwasser: Regentag, Rainy Day, Jour de pluie: Idee,*

Fotografie und Gestaltung. [By] Manfred Bockelmann. [Text in German, English, and French]. München, Bruckmann, [1972].

5606. Chipp, Herschel B. and Richardson, Brenda. *Hundertwasser.* [Catalogue of an exhibition, October 8–November 10, 1968]. Berkeley, Calif., University Art Museum, University of California, 1968. Distributed by New York Graphic Society, Greenwich, Conn.

5607. Haus der Kunst (Munich). *Hundertwasser, Friedensreich: Regentag.* München, Gruener Janura, 1975.

5608. Hundertwasser, Friedensreich. *Das Haus Hundertwasser.* Texte von Hundertwasser . . . [et al.]. Wien, Oesterreichischer Bundesverlag; Compress Verlag, 1985.

5609. ———. *Hundertwasser: Tapisserien.* [Ausstellung]. Museum für Angewante Kunst, Wien, Dezember 1978–Feber 1979. Wien, Das Museum, 1978.

5610. Kestner-Gesellschaft Hannover. *Hundertwasser.* 25. März bis 3. Mai 1964. Hannover, Kestner-Gesellschaft, 1964. (Katalog 5, Ausstellungsjahr 1963/64).

5611. Koschatzky, Walter. *Friedensreich Hundertwasser,* the complete graphic work, 1951–1986. W. Koschatzky with Janine Kertesz; translated by Charles Kessler, New York, Rizzoli, 1986. (CR).

5612. Rand, Harry. *Hundertwasser, der Maler.* München, Bruckmann, 1986.

Hunt, William Henry, 1790–1864

5613. Witt, John. *William Henry Hunt (1790–1864); life and work, with a catalogue.* London, Barrie & Jenkins, 1982. (CR).

Hunt, William Holman, 1827–1910

5614. Amor, Anne Clark. *William Holman Hunt, the true Pre-Raphaelite.* London, Constable, 1989.

5615. Farrar, Frederick William and Meynell, Mrs. [Alice]. *William Holman Hunt, his life and work.* London, Art Journal, 1893.

5616. Gissing, Alfred C. *William Holman Hunt, a biography.* London, Duckworth, 1936.

5617. Holman-Hunt, Diana. *My grandfather, his wives and loves.* London, Hamish Hamilton, 1969.

5618. Hunt, William H. *Pre-Raphaelitism and the pre-Raphaelite brotherhood.* 2 v. New York, Dutton, 1914. 2 ed.

5619. Landow, George P. *William Holman Hunt and typological symbolism.* New Haven/ London, Yale University Press, 1979.

5620. Maas, Jeremy. *Holman Hunt and the Light of the world.* London/Berkeley, Calif., Scolar Press, 1984.

5621. Schleinitz, Otto von. *William Holman Hunt.* Bielefeld/Leipzig, Velhagen & Klasing, 1907. (Künstler-Monographien, 88).

5622. [Stephens, Frederic George]. *William Holman Hunt and his works; a memoir of the artist's life with description of his pictures.* London, Nisbet, 1860.

5623. Walker Art Gallery (Liverpool). *William Holman Hunt.* March–April 1969. Liverpool, Walker Art Gallery, 1969. (CR).

5624. Williamson, George C. *Holman Hunt.* London, Bell, 1902.

Hunt, William Morris, 1824–1879

5625. Angell, Henry C. *Records of William M. Hunt.* Boston, Osgood, 1881.

5626. Hunt, William Morris. *Talks on art.* [Extracts edited by Helen M. Knowlton]. Boston, Houghton, Mifflin, 1875.

5627. Knowlton, Helen M. *Art-life of William Morris Hunt.* Boston, Little, Brown, 1899.

5628. Museum of Fine Arts (Boston). *William Morris Hunt, a memorial exhibition.* [June 27–August 19, 1979; text by Martha J. Hoppin and Henry Adams]. Boston, Museum of Fine Arts, 1979.

5629. Shannon, Martha A. S. *Boston days of William Morris Hunt.* Boston, Marshall Jones, 1923.

5630. Webster, Sally. *William Morris Hunt.* Cambridge [England]/New York, Cambridge University Press, 1991.

I

Ibbetson, Julius Caesar, 1759–1817 *see also* **Morland, George**
5631. Clay, Rotha M. *Julius Caesar Ibbetson, 1759–1817.* London, Country Life, 1948.

Indiana, Robert, 1928–
5632. Indiana, Robert. *Robert Indiana: Druckgraphik und Plakate, 1961–1971/The prints and posters.* Einführung, William Katz; Kommentar, Robert Indiana. [Übersetzung, Klaus Reichert. Farbfotos, Dieter Schwille]. Stuttgart/New York, Domberger, 1971.
5633. McCoubrey, John W. *Robert Indiana, an introduction, with statements by the artist.* [Catalogue of an exhibition, Institute of Contemporary Art of the University of Pennsylvania, April 17 to May 17, 1968]. [University Park, Penn.], Institute of Contemporary Art, 1968.
5634. Mecklenburg, Virginia M. *Wood works: constructions by Robert Indiana.* Washington, D.C. Published for the National Museum of American Art by the Smithsonian Institution Press, 1984.
5635. Sheehan, Susan. *Robert Indiana prints, a catalogue raisonné, 1951–1991.* By S. Sheehan, with the assistance of Poppy Gandler Orchier and Catherine Mennenga; introduction and interview by Poppy Gandler Orchier. New York, Susan Sheehan Gallery, 1991. (CR).
5636. University Art Museum (Austin, Texas). *Robert Indiana.* September 25–November 6, 1977. Austin, Texas, University of Texas Press, 1977.
5637. Weinhardt, Carl J. *Robert Indiana.* New York, Abrams, 1990.

Ingres, Jean-Auguste Dominique 1780–1867
5638. Alazard, Jean. *Ingres et l'ingrisme.* Paris, Michel, 1950.
5639. Amaury-Duval, Eugène E. *L'Atelier d'Ingres.* Paris, Charpentier, 1878.

5640. ———. *L'Atelier d'Ingres.* Edition critique de l'ouvrage publié a Paris en 1878. Introduction, notes, postface et documents par Daniel., Ternois. Paris, Arthena, 1993.
5641. Angrand, Pierre. *Monsieur Ingres et son époque.* Lausanne/Paris, La Bibliothèque des Arts, 1967.
5642. Blanc, Charles. *Ingres, sa vie et ses ouvrages.* Paris, Renouard, 1870.
5643. Cassou, Jean. *Ingres.* Bruxelles, Editions de la Connaissance, 1947.
5644. Courthion, Pierre, ed. *Ingres raconté par lui-même et par ses amis.* 2 v. Vésenaz-Genève, Cailler, 1947/1948. (Les grands artistes racontés par eux-mêmes et par leur amis, 5).
5645. D'Agen, Boyer. *Ingres d'après une correspondance inédite.* Paris, Daragon, 1909.
5646. Delaborde, Henri. *Ingres; sa vie, ses travaux, sa doctrine.* Paris, Plon, 1870. (CR).
5647. L'Ecole Impériale des Beaux-Arts (Paris). *Catalogue des tableaux, études peintes, dessins, et croquis de J.-A.-D. Ingres. . . exposés dans les galeries du palais de l'école.* Paris, Lainé et Havard, 1867.
5648. Fogg Art Museum, Harvard University (Cambridge, Mass.). *Works by J.-A.-D. Ingres in the collection of the Fogg Art Museum.* [By] Marjorie B. Cohn and Susan L. Siegfried. Cambridge, Mass. Fogg Art Museum, Harvard University, 1980.
5649. Fouquet, Jacques. *La vie d'Ingres.* Paris, Gallimard, 1930. 3 ed. (Vie des hommes illustres, 62).
5650. Fröhlich-Blum, Lili. *Ingres, his life & art.* Trans. by Maude V. White. London, Heinemann, 1926.
5651. Gatti, Lelio. *Ingres, l'idealista della forma.* Milano, Bietti, 1946.
5652. Ingres, Jean-Auguste Dominique. *Ecrits sur l'art; textes recueillis dans les carnets et dans la correspondance de Ingres.* Paris, La Jeune Parque, 1947.
5653. Ingres, Jean-Auguste Dominique. *Ingres und*

Delacroix: Aquarelle und Zeichnungen. Hrsg. von Ernst Goldschmidt und Götz Adriani; mit Beiträgen von Helene Lassalle . . . [et al.]. Übersetzung aus dem Englischen, Elisabeth Brockmann, aus dem Französischen, Clemens-Carl Harle und Karin Hirschmann. Köln, DuMont, 1986.

5654. Lapauze, Henry. *Les dessins de J.-A.-D. Ingres du Musée de Montauban.* Paris, Bulloz, 1901.

5655. ———. *Ingres, sa vie et son oeuvre (1780–1867) d'après des documents inédits.* Paris, Petit, 1911.

5656. Merson, Olivier. *Ingres, sa vie et ses oeuvres.* Paris, Hetzel, [1867].

5657. Mirecourt, Eugène de. *Ingres.* Paris, Havard, 1855.

5658. Momméja, Jules. *Ingres, biographie critique.* Paris, Laurens, [1903].

5659. Mongan, Agnes and Naef, Hans. *Ingres; centennial exhibition, 1867–1867.* Fogg Art Museum, Harvard University (Cambridge, Mass.). Feburary 12–April 9, 1967. Cambridge, Mass., Harvard College, 1967.

5660. Montrond, Maxime de. *Ingres, étude biographique et historique.* Lille, Lefort, [1868].

5661. Musée de Montauban. *Dessins d'Ingres du Musée de Montauban,* Pavillion des arts, 7 juin–3 septembre 1989. Catalogue redigé par Marie-Christine Boucher. Paris, Paris-Musées, 1989.

5662. ———. *Ingres et son temps: exposition organisée pour le centenaire de la mort d'Ingres (Montauban 1780–Paris 1867).* Montauban, Musée Ingres, 24 juin–15 septembre 1967. [Commissaire, Daniel Ternois, assisté de Jean Lacambre]. Montauban, Ministère des affaires culturelles; Réunion des musées nationaux, 1967.

5663. Naef, Hans. *Die Bildniszeichnungen von J.-A.-D. Ingres.* 5 v. Bern, Benteli, 1977–1980. (CR).

5664. Pach, Walter. *Ingres.* New York, Harper, 1939.

5665. Picon, Gaëtan. *Jean-Auguste-Dominique Ingres.* Trans. by Stuart Gilbert. New York, Rizzoli, 1980.(Pbk. ed.: Geneva, Skira; New York, Rizzoli, 1991).

5666. Radius, Emilio [and] Camesasca, Ettore. *L'opera completa di Ingres.* Milano, Rizzoli, 1968. (CR). (Classici dell'arte, 19).

5667. Rosenblum, Robert. *Jean-Auguste-Dominique Ingres.* New York, Abrams, 1967.(Reprint: 1985).

5668. Schlenoff, Norman. *Ingres, ses sources littéraires.* Paris, Presses Universitaires de France, 1956.

5669. Ternois, Daniel. *Ingres.* [Paris?], Nathan, 1980; distributed by Mondadori, Milano.

5670. Toussaint, Hélène. *Les portraits d'Ingres: peintures de musées nationaux.* Paris, Ministère de la Culture, Editions de la Reunion des musées nationaux, 1985.

5671. Wildenstein, Georges. *Ingres.* London, Phaidon, 1954; distributed by Garden City Books, Garden City, N.Y.

Inness, George, 1825–1894

5672. Cikovsky, Nicolai, Jr. *George Inness.* New York, Praeger, 1971.

5673. ———. *George Inness.* [Catalogue of an exhibition]. By N. Cikovsky, Jr., Michael Quirk. Los Angeles, Los Angeles County Museum of Art, 1985.

5674. ———. *The life and work of George Inness.* New York, Garland, 1977.

5675. Daingerfield, Elliott. *George Inness, the man and his art.* New York, [Frederic Fairchild Sherman], 1911.

5676. Innes George. *George Inness.* Washington, D.C., National Gallery of Art, 1987.

5677. Innes, George, Jr. *Life, art and letters of George Inness.* New York, Century, 1917.

5678. Ireland, Le Roy. *The works of George Inness, an illustrated catalogue raisonné.* Austin, Texas/London, University of Texas, 1965. (CR).

5679. McCausland, Elizabeth. *George Inness, an American landscape painter, 1825–1894.* [Catalogue of an exhibition, George Walter Vincent Smith Art Museum, February 25 to March 24, 1946]. Springfield, Mass., Smith Art Museum, 1946.

5680. Trumble, Alfred. *George Inness, N. A.; a memorial of the student, the artist, and the man.* New York, The Collector, 1895.

5681. Werner, Alfred. *Inness landscapes.* New York, Watson-Guptill, 1973.

Isabey, Eugène, 1803–1886
Jean-Baptiste, 1767–1855

5682. Basily-Callimaki, Mme. E. de. *J.-B. Isabey; sa vie, son temps, 1767–1855, suivi du catalogue de l'oeuvre gravée par et d'après Isabey.* 2 v. Paris, Frazier-Soye, 1909. (CR).

5683. Curtis, Atherton. *Catalogue de l'oeuvre lithographié de Eugène Isabey.* Paris, Proute, [1939].

5684. Hediard, Germain. *Eugène Isabey, étude suivie du catalogue de son oeuvre.* Paris, Delteil, 1906. (CR).

5685. ———. *J.-B. Isabey.* Chateaudun, Société Typographique, 1896.

5686. Miquel, Pierre. *Eugène Isabey, 1803–1886; la marine au XIXe siècle.* 2 v. Maurs-la-Jolie, Editions de la Martinelle, 1980. (CR).

5687. Osmond, Marion W. *Jean-Baptiste Isabey, the fortunate painter, 1767–1855.* London, Nicholson & Watson, 1947.

5688. Taigny, Edmond. *J.-B. Isabey, sa vie et ses oeuvres*. Paris, Panckoucke, 1859.

Israëls, Jozef, 1824–1911

5689. Dake, Carel L. *Jozef Israëls*. Berlin, Internationale Verlagsanstalt für Kunst und Literatur, [1909].

5690. Dekkers, Dieuwertje. *Jozef Israëls, Een succesvol schilder van het vissersgenre*. Leiden, Primavera Pers, 1994.

5691. Eisler, Max. *Josef Israëls*. London, The Studio, 1924.

5692. Gelder, Hendrik E. van. *Jozef Israëls*. Amsterdam, Becht, 1947. (Palet serie, [32]).

5693. Liebermann, Max. *Jozef Israëls, kritische Studie*. Berlin, Cassirer, 1902. 2 ed.

5694. Netscher, Frans et Zilcken, Philippe. *Jozef Israëls, l'homme et l'artiste*. Amsterdam, Schalekamp, 1890.

5695. Phythian, J. Ernest. *Jozef Israëls*. London, Allen, 1912.

5696. Veth, Jan P. *Jozef Israëls en zijn kunst*. Arnhem en Nijmegen, Cohen, 1904.

Itten, Johannes, 1882–1967

5697. Itten, Johannes. *The art of color*. Trans. by Ernst van Haagen. New York, Reinhold, 1961.

5698. ———. *Design and form, revised edition; the basic course at the Bauhaus and later*. New York, Van Nostrand Reinhold, 1975.

5699. ———. *Tagebücher: Stuttgart 1913–1916; Wien, 1916–1919*. Abbildung und Transkription. Hrsg. von Eva Badura-Triska. 2v. Wien, Löcker, 1989.

5700. Rotzler, Willy. *Johannes Itten, Werke und Schriften*. Werkverzeichnis von Anneliese Itten. Zürich, Füssli, 1972. (CR).

5701. Tavel, Hans Christoph von and Helfenstein, Josef, Hrsg. *Johannes Itten: Künstler und Lehrer*. Bern, Kunstmuseum, 1984.

5702. Westfälisches Landesmuseum für Kunst und Kulturgeschichte, Münster. *Johannes Itten; Gemälde, Gouachen, Aquarelle, Tuschen, Zeichnungen*. 24. August bis 5. Oktober 1980. Münster, Landschaftsverband Westfalen-Lippe/Landesmuseum, 1980.

Ivanov, Aleksandr Andreevich, 1806–1858

5703. Alpatov, Mikhail V. *Aleksandr Ivanov*. Moskva, Molodaia gvardiia, 1959.

5704. Botkin, Izdal M. *Aleksandr Andreevich Ivanov; ego zhizn' i perepiska, 1806–1858*. Sanktpeterburg, Stasiulevicha, 1880. (German ed.: *Alexander Andejewitsch Iwanoff, 1806–1858; biographische Skizze*. Berlin, Asher, 1880).

5705. Gosudarstvennaia Tret'iakovskaia galleria (Moscow). *Aleksandr Andreevich Ivanov; 150 let so dnia rozhdenia, 1806–1956*. Moskva, Iskusstvo, 1956. (CR).

J

Jackson, William Henry, 1843–1942

5706. Forsee, Aylesa. *William Henry Jackson, pioneer photographer of the West.* Illustrated with drawings by Douglas Gorsline and with photographs by William Henry Jackson. New York, Viking, 1964.

5707. Jackson, Clarence S. *Picture maker of the old West: William H. Jackson.* New York, Scribner, 1971. 2 ed.

5708. Jackson, William H. *Time exposure: the autobiography of William Henry Jackson.* New York, Cooper Square, 1940.

5709. ———. *William Henry Jackson's Colorado.* Compiled by William C. Jones and Elizabeth B. Jones. Foreword by Marshall Sprague. Boulder, Col., Pruett, 1975.

5710. ——— and Driggs, Howard R. *The pioneer photographer; Rocky Mountain adventures with a camera.* Yonkers-on-Hudson, N.Y., World, 1929.

5711. Newhall, Beaumont and Edkins, Diane E. *William H. Jackson.* With a critical essay by William L. Broecker. Dobbs Ferry, N.Y., Morgan & Morgan/Fort Worth, Texas, Amon Carter Museum of Western Art, 1974.

Jacob, Georges, 1739–1814
Jacob-Desmalter, François-Honoré-Georges, 1770–1841

5712. Dumanthier, Ernest. *Les sièges de Georges Jacob.* Paris, Morancé, 1922.

5713. Lefuel, Hector. *François-Honoré Jacob-Desmalter, ébéniste de Napoléon Ier et de Louis XVIII.* Paris, Morancé, 1925.

5714. ———. *Georges Jacob, ébéniste du XVIIIe siècle.* Paris, Morancé, 1923.

Jacobi, Lotte, 1896–

5715. Wise, Kelley, ed. *Lotte Jacobi.* Dunbury, N.H., Addison House, 1978.

Jacomart, Jaime Bacó *see* Bacó, Jacomart

Jacque, Charles Emile, 1813–1894

5716. Guiffrey, Jules. *L'oeuvre de Ch. Jacque; catalogue de ses eaux-fortes et pointes sèches.* Paris, Lemaire, 1866. (CR).

5717. Wickenden, Robert J. *Charles Jacque.* [Boston], Museum of Fine Arts/Houghton Mifflin, 1914.

Jamnitzer, Wenzel, 1508–1585

5718. Frankenburger, Max. *Beiträge zur Geschichte Wenzel Jamnitzers und seiner Familie.* Strassburg, Heitz, 1901. (Studien zur deutschen Künstgeschichte, 30).

5719. Rosenberg, Marc. *Jamnitzer; alle erhaltenen Goldschmiede-Arbeiten, verlorene Werke, Handzeichnungen.* Frankfurt a.M., Baer, 1920.

Janssen, Horst, 1929–

5720. Albertina (Vienna). *Horst Janssen, Zeichnungen.* 1. April bis 2. Mai 1982. [Text by Walter Koschatzky and Wolfgang Hildesheimer]. München, Prestel, 1982.

5721. Kestner-Gesellschaft Hannover. *Horst Janssen.* 23. März bis 6. Mai 1973. Hannover, Kestner-Gesellschaft, 1973. (Katalog 3/1973).

5722. Janssen, Horst. *Landschaften, 1942–1989. . . .* Zusammengetragen und herausgegeben von Dierck Lemcke. Hamburg, Verlag St. Gertrude, 1989.

5723. Schack, Gerhard. *Horst Janssen, die Kopie.* Hamburg, Christians, 1977.

Javacheff, Christo *see* Christo

Jawlensky, Alexej, 1864–1941

5724. Galerie im Ganserhaus (Wasserburg). *Alexej Jawlensky.* 15. September bis 28. Oktober 1979. Wasserburg, Künstlergemeinschaft Wasserburg, 1979.

5725. Jawlensky, Maria, Lucia, and Angelica.

Alexej Jawlensky: Catalogue of the oil paintings 1890–1914. London, Philip Wilson, 1991. (CR).

5726. Pasadena Art Museum. *Alexei Jawlensky, a centennial exhibition.* April 14–May 19, 1964. [Text by James T. Demetrion]. Pasadena, Pasadena Art Museum, 1964.

5727. Rathke, Ewald. *Alexej Jawlensky.* Hanau, Peters, 1968.

5728. Schultze, Jürgen. *Alexej Jawlensky.* Köln, DuMont Schauberg, 1970.

5729. Weiler, Clemens. *Alexej Jawlensky.* Köln, DuMont Schauberg, 1959. (CR).

Jeanneret-Gris, Charles Edouard *see* Le Corbusier

Jefferson, Thomas, 1745–1826

5730. Adams, William Howard, ed. *Jefferson and the arts: an extended view.* Washington, D.C., National Gallery of Art, 1976.

5731. Frary, Ihna T. *Thomas Jefferson, architect and builder.* Richmond, Va., Garret & Massie, 1931.

5732. Guinness, Desmond and Sadler, Julius T., Jr. *Mr. Jefferson, architect.* New York, Viking, 1973.

5733. Kimball, Fiske. *Thomas Jefferson, architect.* Boston, Riverside Press, 1916. (Reprint, with a new introduction by Frederick Doveton Nichols: New York, DaCapo, 1968. Da Capo Press Series in Architecture and Decorative Art, 5).

5734. Lambeth, William A. and Manning, Warren H. *Thomas Jefferson as an architect and a designer of landscapes.* Boston/New York, Houghton Mifflin, 1913.

5735. McLaughlin, Jack. *Jefferson and Monticello: the biography of a builder.* New York, Henry Holt, 1988.

5736. Nichols, Frederick D. *Thomas Jefferson's architectural drawings compiled and with commentary and a check list.* Boston, Massachusetts Historical Society/Charlottesville, Va., Jefferson Memorial Foundation and University of Virginia Press, 1961. 2 ed., revised and enlarged.

5737. ———— and Griswold, Ralph E. *Thomas Jefferson, landscape architect.* Charlottesville, Va., University Press of Virginia, 1978.

5738. O'Neal, William B. *A checklist of writings on Thomas Jefferson as an architect.* [Charlottesville, Va., American Association of Architectural Bibliographers], 1959. (American Association of Architectural Bibliographers, 15).

5739. Stein, Susan. *The worlds of Thomas Jefferson at Montecello.* New York, H.N. Abrams in association with the Thomas Jefferson Memorial Foundation, Inc., 1993.

John, Augustus, 1878–1961

5740. Dodgson, Campbell. *A catalogue of etchings by Augustus John, 1901–1914.* London, Chenil, 1920.

5741. Earp, Thomas W. *Augustus John.* London/Edinburgh, Nelson/Jack, [1904].

5742. Easton, Malcolm and Holroyd, Michael. *The art of Augustus John.* London, Secker & Warburg, 1974.

5743. Evans, Mark L. *Portraits by Augustus John: Family, friends, and the famous.* Cardiff, National Museum of Wales, 1988.

5744. Holroyd, Michael. *Augustus John, a biography.* New York, Holt, Rinehart and Winston, 1975.

5745. John, Augustus. *Chiaroscuro; fragments of autobiography.* London, Cape, 1952.

5746. ————. *Finishing touches.* London, Cape, 1964.

5747. Rothenstein, John. *Augustus John.* Oxford/London, Phaidon, 1945. 2 ed.

Johns, Jasper, 1930–

5748. Bernstein, Roberta. *Jasper Johns' paintings and sculptures, 1954–1974.:"the changing focus of the eye".* Ann Arbor, Mich., UMI Research Press, 1985.

5749. Boudaille, Georges. *Jasper Johns.* New York, Rizzoli, 1989.

5750. Castleman, Riva. *Jasper Johns, a print retrospective.* [Catalog of an exhibition]. Museum of Modern Art. New York; Boston, distributed by New York Graphic Society/Little Brown Books, 1986.

5751. Crichton, Michael. *Jasper Johns.* [Catalogue of an exhibition at the Whitney Museum of American Art, New York, Oct. 17, 1977–Jan. 22, 1978]. New York, Abrams, 1977.

5752. Field, Richard S. *Jasper Johns: prints 1960–1970.* Philadelphia, Philadelphia Museum of Art, 1970. (CR).

5753. Kozloff, Max. *Jasper Johns.* New York, Abrams, [1968].

5754. Rosenthal, Nan. *The drawings of Jasper Johns.* [By] Nan Rosenthal, Ruth E. Fine with Marla Panther and Amy Mizrahi Zorn. [Catalogue of an exhibition]. Washington, National Gallery of Art, 1990.

5755. Shapiro, David. *Jasper Johns drawings, 1954–1984.* Text by D. Shapiro; project director, David Whitney; editor, Christopher Sweet. New York, Abrams, 1984.

5756. Steinberg, Leo. *Jasper Johns.* New York, Wittenborn, 1963.

Johnson, Joshua, fl. 1796–1824

5757. Weekley, Carolyn J. *Joshua Johnson: freeman and early American portrait painter.* [By] C.J. Weekley, Stiles Tuttle Colwill; with Leroy Graham, Mary Ellen Hayward. Willamsburg, Va. Abby Aldrich Rockefeller Folk Art Center, The Colonial Williamsburg Foundation; Baltimore, Md., Maryland Historical Society, 1987.

Johnson, Philip Cortelyou, 1906–

5758. Hitchcock, Henry R. *Philip Johnson; architecture, 1949–1965.* New York, Holt, Rinehart and Winston, 1966.

5759. Jacobus, John M., Jr. *Philip Johnson.* New York, Braziller, 1962.

5760. Johnson, Philip. *Philip Johnson.* Introduction and notes by Charles Noble; with photographs by Yukio Futagawa. London, Thames and Hudson, 1972.

5761. ———. *Philip Johnson/John Burgee: architecture 1979–1985.* Introduction by Carleton Knight III. New York, Rizzoli, 1985.

5762. ———. *Writings.* New York, Oxford University Press, 1979.

5763. Noble, Charles. *Philip Johnson.* New York, Simon & Schuster, 1972.

Johnston, Frances Benjamin, 1864–1952

5764. Art Museum and Galleries and the Center for Southern California Studies in the Visual Arts, California State University, Long Beach. *Frances Benjamin Johnston: women of class and station.* February 12–March 11, 1979. [Text by Constance W. Glenn and Leland Rice]. Long Beach, Calif., Art Museum and Galleries, California State University, 1979.

5765. Daniel, Pete and Smock, Raymond. *A talent for detail; the photographs of Miss Frances Benjamin Johnston, 1889–1910.* New York, Harmony, 1974.

5766. Johnston, Frances B. *The early architecture of North Carolina; a pictorial survey.* With an architectural history by Thomas Tileston Waterman. Chapel Hill, North Carolina, University of North Carolina Press, 1941.

Johnston, Joshua, 1765–1830

5767. Pleasants, J. Hall. *Joshua Johnston: an early Baltimore Negro portrait painter.* [Windham, Conn.], The Walpole Society, 1940.

Jones, Inigo, 1573–1652

5768. Cerutti Fusco, Annarosa. *Inigo Jones, Vitruvius Britannicus: Jones e Palladio nella cultura architettonica inglese, 1600–1740.* Prefazione di Claudio Tiberi. Rimini, Maggioli, 1985.

5769. Cunningham, Peter. *Inigo Jones, a life of the architect [with] remarks on some of his sketches for masques and dramas by J. R. Planché, Esq., and five court masques edited from the original mss. . . . by J. Payne Collier, Esq.* London, Shakespeare Society, 1848.

(Shakespeare Society Publications, 39).

5770. Gotch, John A. *Inigo Jones.* London, Methuen, 1928.

5771. Harris, John. *Inigo Jones: complete architectural drawings.* [Compiled by] J. Harris and Gordon Higgott. London, P. Wilson for A. Zwemmer; New York, The Drawing Center. Distrib. in the USA by Harper and Row, 1989.

5772. [Jones, Inigo]. *The designs of Inigo Jones, consisting of plans and elevations for publick and private buildings, published by William Kent with some additional designs.* London, [Kent], 1727. (Reprint: [Ridgewood, N.J.], Gregg, 1967).

5773. [———]. *Inigo Jones on Palladio, being the notes by Inigo Jones in the copy of I Quattro Libri dell'Architettura di Andrea Palladio, 1601 in the Library of Worcester College, Oxford.* 2 v. Edited by Bruce Allsopp. Oxford, Oriel Press, 1970.

5774. Lees-Milne, James. *The age of Inigo Jones.* London, Batsford, 1953.

5775. Orgel, Stephen and Strong, Roy. *Inigo Jones; the theatre of the Stuart court, including the complete designs for productions at court.* 2 v. London, Sotheby Parke Bernet/Berkeley and Los Angeles, University of California Press, 1973. (CR).

5776. Ramsey, Stanley C. *Inigo Jones.* London, Benn, 1924.

5777. Simpson, Percy and Bell, Charles F. *Designs by Inigo Jones for masques & plays at court, a descriptive catalogue of drawings for scenery and costumes.* Oxford, Walpole Society, 1924. (The Walpole Society, 12).

5778. Summerson, John. *Inigo Jones.* Harmondsworth, Eng., Penguin, 1966.

Jones, Lois Mailou, 1905–

5779. Museum of Fine Arts (Boston). *Reflective moments; Lois Mailou Jones; retrospective, 1930–1972.* March 11–April 15, 1973. Boston, Museum of Fine Arts, 1973.

5780. Porter, James A. *Lois Mailou Jones; peintures, 1935–1951.* Tourcoing (France), Frère, 1952.

Jongkind, Johan Barthold, 1819–1891

5781. Colin, Paul. *J. B. Jongkind.* Paris, Rieder, 1931.

5782. Hefting, Victorine. *Jongkind d'après sa correspondance.* Utrecht, Haentjens Dekker & Gumbert, 1969.

5783. ———. *J.B. Jongkind: voorloper van het impressionisme.* Amsterdam, B. Bakker, 1992.

5784. ———. *Jongkind; sa vie, son oeuvre, son époque.* Paris, Arts et Métiers Graphiques, 1975. (CR).

5785. Moreau-Nélaton, Etienne, ed. *Jongkind raconté par lui-même.* Paris, Laurens, 1918.

5786. Roger-Marx, Claude. *Jongkind.* Paris, Crès, 1932.

5787. Signac, Paul. *Jongkind.* Paris, Crès, 1927.

Jordaens, Jakob, 1593–1678

5788. Buschmann, Paul, Jr. *Jacob Jordaens, eene studie.* Amsterdam, Veen, 1905.

5789. Coopman, Henrik. *Jordaens.* Bruxelles, Kryn, 1926.

5790. Fierens-Gevaert, Hippolyte. *Jordaens; biographie critique.* Paris, Laurens, 1905.

5791. Hulst, Rogier Adolf d'. *Jacob Jordaens.* Trans. by P. S. Falla. Ithaca, N.Y., Cornell University Press, 1982.

5792. ———. *Jacob Jordaens, 1593–1678.* By Rogier A. d'Hulst; Nora d Poorter; M. van den Ven; C. Tümpel. 2 v. Bruxelles, Crédit Communal, 1993. [Catalogue of an exhibition held in the Royal Museum of Fine Arts, Antwerp from 27 March–27 June, 1993]. (Published in English and Dutch editions).

5793. ———. *Jordaens drawings.* 4 v. Brussels, Arcade, 1974. (CR). (Monographs of the National Centrum voor de Plastiche Kunsten van de XVIde en XVIIde Eeuw, 5).

5794. ———. *De Tekeningen van Jakob Jordaens.* Brussel, Paleis der Academiën, 1956. (Verhandelingen van de Koninklijke Vlaamse Academie voor Wetenschappen, Letteren en Schone Künsten van België, Klasse der Schone Künsten, 10).

5795. National Gallery of Canada (Ottawa). *Jacob Jordaens, 1593–1678.* [29 November 1968– 5 January 1969; selection and catalogue by Michael Jaffe]. Ottawa, National Gallery of Canada, 1968.

5796. Puyvelde, Leo van. *Jordaens.* Paris/Bruxelles, Elsevier, 1953.

5797. Rooses, Max. *Jacob Jordaens, his life and work.* Trans. by Elisabeth C. Broers. London, Dent/New York, Dutton, 1908.

Jorn, Asger, 1914–1973

5798. Atkins, Guy. *Asger Jorn, the crucial years: 1954–1964.* London, Humphries, 1977. (CR).

5799. ———. *Asger Jorn, the final years: 1965– 1973.* London, Humphries, 1980. (CR).

5800. ———. *Asger Jorn, supplement to the oeuvre catalogue of his paintings from 1930 to 1973.* [By] G. Atkins with the help of Troels Andersen. London, Asger Jorn Foundation in association with Lund Humphries, 1986. (CR).

5801. ———. *A bibliography of Asger Jorn's writings to 1963 (Bibliografi over Asger Jorns skrifter til 1963).* With Erik Schmidt. København, Permild & Rosengreen, 1964.

5802. ———. *Jorn in Scandinavia, 1930–1953.* London, Humphries, 1968. (CR).

5803. Birtwistle, Graham M. *Living art: Asger Jorns comprehensive theory of art between Helhesten and Cobra, 1946–1949.* Utrecht, Reflex, 1986.

5804. Jansen, Per Hofman. *Bibliografi over Asger Jorns skrifter* udarbejdet af Per Hofman Hansen = *A bibliography of Asger Jorn's writings* compiled by Per Hofman Hansen. Silkeborg, Denmark, Silkeborg Kunstmuseum, 1988.

5805. Jorn, Asger. *Asger Jorn 1914–1973: Gemälde, Zeichnungen, Aquarelle, Gouachen, Skulpturen.* [Katalog der Ausstellung im Lenbachhaus, 21. Januar–29. März 1987] Hrsg. von Armin Zweite. [Übersetzungen: Gunhild Baier Nilsen, Johannes Feil Sohlman, Inge Leipold]. München, Städtische Galerie im Lenbachhaus, 1987.

5806. Kestner-Gesellschaft Hannover. *Asger Jorn.* 16. Februar–18. März 1973. Hannover, Kestner-Gesellschaft, 1973. (Kestner-Gesellschaft Katalog 2/1973).

5807. Schade, Virtus. *Asger Jorn.* København, Venderkaers, 1968. 2 ed.

5808. Schmied, Wieland, ed. *Jorn.* St. Gallen, Erker-Verlag, 1973.

Josephson, Ernst Abraham, 1851–1906

5809. Blomberg, Erik. *Ernst Josephson, hans liv.* Stockholm, Wahlstrom & Widstrand, 1951.

5810. ———. *Ernst Josephsons konst; från näcken till gåslisa.* Stockholm, Norstedt, 1959.

5811. ———. *Ernst Josephsons konst: historie-, porträtt- och genremåleren.* Stockholm, Norstedt, 1956.

5812. Millner, Simon L. *Ernst Josephson.* New York, Machmadim Art Editions, 1948.

5813. Pauli, Georg. *Ernst Josephson.* Stockholm, Norstedt, 1914. 2 ed.

5814. Schneede, Marina [and] Schneede, Uwe M. *Vor der Zeit:* Carl Fredrik Hill, *Ernst Josephson,* zwei Künstler des späten 19. Jahrhunderts. [Katalog einer Ausstellung]: Kunstverein in Hamburg, 13. Oktober bis 25. November 1984; Städtische Galerie im Lenbachhaus, München, 19. Dezember 1984 bis 10. Februar 1985, Württemberg. Kunstverein Stuttgart, 6. März bis 14. April 1985. Berlin, Frölich & Kaufmann, 1984[?].

5815. Städtisches Kunstmuseum (Bonn). *Ernst Josephson, 1851–1906; Bilder und Zeichnungen.* 22. März bis 6. Mai 1979. Bonn, Städtisches Kunstmuseum, [1979].

5816. Wåhlin, Karl. *Ernst Josephson, 1851–1906; en minnesteckning.* 2 v. Stockholm, Svenges Allmänna Konstforenings, 1911/1912. (Svenges allmänna konstforenings publikations, 19/20).

5817. Zennström, Per-Olav. *Ernst Josephson, en studie.* Stockholm, Norstedt, 1946.

Jourdain, Frantz, 1847–1935
Francis, 1876–1958
Frantz-Philippe, 1906–

5818. Barre-Despond, Arlette. *Jourdain: Frantz— 1847–1935, Francis—1876–1958, Frantz-Philippe—1906–1990. "Francis Jourdain"* by Suzanne Tise. Photography by Jean Baptiste Rouault. Archival material courtesy of Stephen Jourdain. New York, Rizzoli, 1991.

Jouvenet, Jean, 1644–1717

5819. Leroy, François N. *Histoire de Jouvenet.* Paris, Didron, 1860.

5820. Schnapper, Antoine. *Jean Jouvenet, 1644– 1717, et la peinture d'histoire à Paris.* Paris, Laget, 1974. (CR).

Jujoli i Gibert, Josep Maria, 1879–1949

5821. Bassegoda i Nonell, Juan. *Jujol.* Barcelona, Ediciones de Nuevo Arte Thor, 1990. (Gent nostra, 77).

5822. Duran i Albareda, Montserrat. *Josep Ma. Jujol a Sant Joan Despi: projectes i obra, 1913–1949.* Fotografies, Xavier Miserachs. Barcelona, Corporació Metropolitana de Barcelona, Assessoria de Comunicació i Relacions, Servei de Publicacions, [1987].

5823. Flores, Carlos. *Gaudí, Jujol y el modernismo catalán.* 2 v. Prologo de George R. Collins. Madrid, Aquilar, 1982.

5824. Jujol i Gibert, Josep Maria. *Joseph Maria Jujol architecte, 1879–1949*: 19 décembre 1990–25 février 1991, Centre de Crèation Industrielle Centre Georges Pompidou. Paris, Editions du Centre Pompidou, 1990.

5825. Solá-Morales Rubió, Ignasi. *Jujol.* Photographs, Melba Levick. New York, Rizzoli, 1991.

Jungstedt, Kurt, 1894–

5826. Strömberg, Martin. *Kurt Jungstedt.* Stockholm, Bonniers, 1945.

Juni, Juan de, ca. 1507–1577

5827. García Chico, Esteban. *Juan de Juni.* Valladolid [Spain], Escuela de Artes y Oficios Artisticos de Valladolid, 1949.

5828. Griseri, Andreina. *Juan de Juni.* Milano, Fabbri, 1966. (I maestri della scultura, 72).

5829. Martín Gonzales, Juan José. *Juan de Juni, vida y obra.* Madrid, Dirección General de Bellas Artes, Ministerio de Educación y Ciencia, 1974.

5830. Museo National de Escultura (Valladolid, Spain). *Juan de Juni y su epoca; exposicion commorative del IV centenario de la muerte de Juan de Juni.* Abril–Mayo 1977. Valladolid, Museo Nacional de Escultura, 1977.

Juvarra, Filippo, 1678–1736

5831. Boscarino, Salvatore. *Juvarra architetto.* Roma, Officina Edizioni, 1973.

5832. Gritella, Gianfranco. *Juvarra: l'architettura.* 2 v. Modena, Panini, 1992.

5833. Millon, Henry A. *Filippo Juvarra: drawings from the Roman period, 1704–1714.* v. 1– . Roma, Edizioni dell'Elefante, 1984– .

5834. Pommer, Richard. *Eighteenth-century architecture in Piedmont;* the open structures of Juvarra, Alfieri & Vittone. New York, New York University Press, 1967.

5835. Rovere, Lorenzo, et al. [Comitato per le onoranze a Filippo Juvarra]. *Filippo Juvarra.* Milano, Oberdan Zucci, 1937.

5836. Telluccini, Augusto. *L'arte dell'architetto Filippo Juvara in Piemonte.* Torino, Crudo, 1926.

K

Kaendler, Johann Joachim, 1706–1775

5837. Gröger, Helmuth. *Johann Joachim Kaendler, der Meister des Porzellans.* Dresden, Jess, 1956. (Dresdener Beiträge zur Kunstgeschichte, 2).

5838. Handt, Ingelore. *Johann Joachim Kändler und die Meissner Porzellanplastik des 18. Jahrhunderts.* Dresden, Verlag der Kunst, 1954. (Das kleine Kunstheft, 7).

5839. Sponsel, Jean Louis. *Kabinettstücke der Meissner Porzellan-Manufaktur von Johann Joachim Kändler.* Leipzig, Seemann, 1900.

Kahlo, Frida, 1907–1954

5840. Drucker, Malka. *Frida Kahlo: torment and triumph in her life and art.* Introduction by Laurie Anderson. New York, Bantam Books, 1991.

5841. Herrera, Hayden. *Frida Kahlo: the paintings.* New York, Harper Collins, 1991.

5842. Jamis, Randa. *Frida Kahlo: un portrait d'une femme.* Paris, Presses del la Renaissance, 1988.

5843. Kahlo, Frida. *Frida Kahlo: das Gesamtwerk.* Hrsg. von Helga Prignitz Poda. [Die Übertragung aus dem Amerikanischen besorgte Bodo Schulze]. Frankfurt am Main, Verlag Neue Kritik, 1988.

5844. Kettenmann, Andrea. *Frida Kahlo 1907–1954; pain and passion.* Cologne, Benedikt Taschen Verlag, 1992.

5845. Lowe, Sarah M. *Frida Kahlo.* New York, Universe Books. 1991.

5846. Olmedo, Lola. *The Frida Kahlo Museum.* Mexico City, M. Galas,1970.

5847. Tibol, Raquel. *Frida Kahlo, an open life.* Trans. by Elinor Randall, Albuquerque, University of New Mexico Press, 1993.

5848. Zamora, Martha. *Frida Kahlo: the brush of anguish.* San Francisco, Chronicle Books, 1990.

Kahn Louis I., 1901–1974

5849. [American Association of Architectural Bibliographers]. *Louis Kahn and Paul Zucker, two bibliographies.* [Kahn bibliography compiled by Jack Perry Brown]. New York/ London, Garland, 1978. (Papers of the American Association of Architectural Bibliographers, 12).

5850. Büttiker, Urs. *Louis I. Kahn: light and space.* Trans. by David Bean. Basel/Boston, Birkhäuser Verlag, 1993.

5851. Giurgola, Romaldo and Mehta, Jaimini. *Louis I. Kahn.* Boulder, Colo., Westview Press, 1975.

5852. Kahn Louis I. *Louis I. Kahn.* Tokyo, A&U Publishing Co.1975.

5853. ———. *Personal drawings from the Kahn Collection on permanent loan to the University of Pennsylvania.* Introduced by Vincent Scully. 7 v. New York, Garland , 1988.

5854. Komendant, August E. *18 years with architect Louis I. Kahn.* Englewood, N.J., Aloray, 1975.

5855. Lobell, John. *Between silence and light; spirit in the architecture of Louis I. Kahn.* Boulder, Colo., Shambhala, 1979; distributed by Random House, New York.

5856. Norberg-Schultz, Christian. *Louis I. Kahn, idea e immagine.* Roma, Officina Edizioni, 1980.

5857. Ronner, Heinz, et al. *Louis I. Kahn; complete works, 1935–74.* Boulder, Colo., Westview Press/Zürich, Institute for the History and Theory of Architecture, 1977. (CR).

5858. Scully, Vincent, Jr. *Louis I. Kahn.* New York, Braziller, 1962.

5859. Wurman, Richard S. and Feldman, Eugene. *The notebooks and drawings of Louis I. Kahn.* Cambridge, Mass./London, MIT Press, 1973. 2 ed.

Kandinsky, Wassily, 1866–1944

5860. Barnett, Vivian E. *Kandinsky at the Guggenheim.* New York, Abbeville Press, 1983.

5861. ———. *Kandinsky watercolours: catalogue raisonné.* 2 v. Ithaca, N.Y., Cornell University Press, 1992–1993.(CR).

5862. Bill, Max. *Wassily Kandinsky.* Boston, Institute of Contemporary Art/Paris, Maeght, 1951.

5863. Brion, Marcel. *Kandinsky.* Paris, Somogy, 1961.

5864. Eichner, Johannes. *Kandinsky und Gabriele Münter; von den Ursprüngen moderner Kunst.* München, Bruckmann, 1957.

5865. Geddo, Angelo. *Commento a Kandinsky.* Bergamo, San Marco, 1960.

5866. Grohmann, Will. *Wassily Kandinsky.* Leipzig, Klinkhardt & Biermann, 1924. (Junge Kunst, 42).

5867. ———. *Wassily Kandinsky, life and work.* Trans. by Norbert Guterman. New York, Abrams, 1958.

5868. Hahl-Koch, Jelena. *Kandinsky.* New York, Rizzoli, 1993.

5869. Hanfstaengl, Erika. *Wassily Kandinsky, Zeichnungen und Aquarelle; Katalog der Sammlung in der Städtischen Galerie im Lenbachhaus München.* München, Prestel, 1974. (Materialien zur Künst des 19. Jahrhunderts, 13).

5870. Haus der Künst München. *Wassily Kandinsky, 1866–1944. 13. November 1976–30. Januar 1977.* München, Haus der Künst, 1976.

5871. Kandinsky, Nina. *Kandinsky und ich.* München, Kindler, 1976.

5872. Kandinsky, Wassily. *Concerning the spiritual in art.* Trans. by Michael Sadleir [et al.]. New York, Wittenborn, 1972. 3 ed.

5873. ———. *Complete writings on art.* Edited by Kenneth C. Lindsay and Peter Vergo. 2 v. Boston, G.K. Hall, 1982.

5874. ———. *Der frühe Kandinsky, 1900–1910.* Herausgegeben von Magdalena M. Moeller. Mit Beiträgen von Vivian Endicott Barnett . . . [et al.]. München, Hirmer, 1994.

5875. ———. *Ecrits complets.* 3 v. Paris, Denoël Gonthier, 1970–1975.

5876. ———. *Kandinsky in Munich. 1896–1914.* New York, Solomon R. Guggenheim Foundation, 1982.

5877. ———. *Kandinsky: Russian and Bauhaus years, 1915–1933.* New York, Solomon R. Guggenheim Museum, 1983.

5878. ———. *Kandinsky: Russische Zeit und Bauhausjahre, 1915–1933.* [Herausgeber, Peter Hahn; Redaktion, Christian Wolsdorff; Übersetzungen, Bernhard Schulz, Magdalena Droste]. Berlin, Bauhaus-Archiv, 1984. (Contains additional material not shown at the Guggenheim in 1982 and Kunsthaus Zürich, 1984).

5879. ———. *Point and line to plane.* Trans. by Howard Dearstyne and Hilla Rebay. New York, Solomon Guggenheim Foundation, 1947. Reprint: New York, Dover, 1979).

5880. ———. *Watercolors by Kandinsky at the Guggenheim Museum: a selection from the Solomon R. Guggenheim Museum and the Hilla von Rebay Foundation.* Introductory essay by Susan B. Hirschfeld. New York, Guggenheim Museum; distributed by Rizzoli, 1991.

5881. ———. *Kandinsky: watercolors and drawings.* Edited and with contributions by Vivian Endicott Barnett and Armin Zweite. Munich, Prestel; New York; distributed in the USA and Canada by te Neues Pub. Co., 1992.

5882. ——— and Marc, Franz. *The Blaue Reiter Almanac.* New documentary edition. New York, Viking, 1974.

5883. [and] Marc, Franz]. *Wassily Kandinsky, Franz Marc: Briefwechsel; mit Briefen von und an Gabriele Münter und Maria Marc.* Herausgegeben und eingeleitet und kommentiert von Klaus Lankheit. München, R. Piper, 1983.

5884. [and] Schönberg, Arnold. *Arnold Schönberg, Wassily Kandinsky; Briefe, Bilder und Dokumente einer ausser-gewöhnlichen Begegnung.* Herausgegeben von Jelena Hahl-Koch. Salzburg und Wien, Residenz, 1980.

5885. Kleine, Gisela. *Gabriele Münter und Wassily Kandinsky: Biographie eines Paares.* Frankfurt am Main, Insel Verlag, 1990.

5886. Korn, Rudolf. *Kandinsky und die Theorie der abstrakten Malerei.* Berlin, Henschel, 1960.

5887. Lassaigne, Jacques. *Kandinsky, biographical and critical study.* Trans. by H. S. B. Harrison. Genève, Skira, 1969; distributed by World, Cleveland.

5888. Levin, Gail. *Theme and improvisation: Kandinsky and the American avant-garde, 1912–1950.* [By] G. Levin and Marianne Lorenz. Boston, Little Brown, 1992.

5889. Long, Rose-Carol. *Kandinsky, the development of an abstract style.* Oxford, Clarendon Press, 1980.

5890. Overy, Paul. *Kandinsky, the language of the eye.* New York, Praeger, 1969.

5891. Ringbom, Sixten. *The sounding cosmos; a study in the spiritualism of Kandinsky and the genesis of abstract painting.* Åbo [Finland], Åbo Akademi, 1970.

5892. Roethel, Hans K. und Benjamin, Jean K. *Kandinsky: Werkverzeichnis der Ölgemälde.* 2 v. München, Beck, 1982/1984. (CR). (English edition: Ithaca, N.Y., Cornell University

Press, 1982–1984).

5893. Roskill, Mark W. *Klee, Kandinsky, and the thought of their time: a critical perspective.* Urbana, University of Illinois Press, 1992.

5894. Société Internationale d'Art XXᵉ Siècle. *Hommage à Wassily Kandinsky.* [Numéro spécial de XXᵉ Siècle]. Paris, XXᵉ Siècle, 1974.

5895. Solomon R. Guggenheim Museum (New York). *Vasily Kandinsky, 1866–1944; a retrospective exhibition.* [January–April 1963]. New York, Guggenheim Foundation, 1962.

5896. Thürlemann, Felix. *Kandinsky über Kandinsky: der Künstler als Interpret eigener Werke.* Herausgegeben von der Stiftung von Schnyder von Wartensee. Bern, Benteli, 1986.

5897. Zehder, Hugo. *Wassily Kandinsky.* Dresden, Kaemmerer, 1920. (Künstler der Gegenwart, 1).

Kanō, Eitoku, 1543–1590

5898. Takeda, Tsuneo. *Kanō Eitoku.* Trans. and adapted by H. Mack Horton and Catherine Kaputa. Tokyo, Kodansha, 1977.

Kanoldt, Alexander, 1881–1939

5899. Ammann, Edith, ed. *Das graphische Werk von Alexander Kanoldt.* Karlsruhe, Staatliche Kunsthalle, 1963. (Schriften der Staatlichen Kunsthalle Karlsruhe, 7).

5900. Kanoldt, Alexander. *Alexander Kanoldt, 1881–1939: Gemälde, Zeichnungen, Lithographien.* [Katalog der Ausstellung; Redaktion, Jochen Ludwig und Detlef Zinkel]. Freiburg i.Br., Museum für Neue Kunst, 1987.

Kaprow, Allan Joseph, 1927–

5901. Kaprow, Allan. *Assemblage, environments & happenings.* New York, Abrams, [1966].

5902. ———. *Blindsight/ Allan Kaprow.* [Exhibition catalogue]. Wichita, Kan., Wichita State University, Dept of Art Education, 1979.

5903. Pasadena Art Museum (Pasadena, Calif.). *Allan Kaprow.* September 15 through October 22, 1967. Pasadena, Calif., Pasadena Art Museum, 1967.

Kars, Georges, 1880–1945

5904. Fels, Florent. *Georges Kars.* Paris, Le Triangle, [1933].

5905. Jolinon, Joseph. *La vie et l'oeuvre de Georges Kars.* Lyon, Imprimerie Générale du Sud-Est, 1958.

Karsh, Yousuf, 1908–

5906. Karsh, Yousuf. *Faces of destiny.* Chicago/ New York, Ziff-Davis/London, Harrap, 1946.

5907. ———. *In search of greatness; reflections of Yousuf Karsh.* New York, Knopf, 1962.

5908. ———. *Karsh Canadians.* Toronto, University of Toronto Press, 1978.

5909. ———. *Karsh portraits.* Toronto, University of Toronto Press, 1976.

Käsebier, Gertrude, 1852–1934

5910. Delaware Art Museum (Wilmington, Del.). *A pictorial heritage: the photographs of Gertrude Käsebier.* March 2–April 22, 1979. [Text by William Innes Homer et al.]. Wilmington, Del., Delaware Art Museum, 1979.

5911. Michaels, Barbara. *Gertrude Käsebier: the photographer and her photographs.* New York, H.N. Abrams, 1992.

Kasiian, Vasyl' Illich, 1896–

5912. Kostiuk, S. P. *Vasyl' Kasiian, bibliohrafichnyi pokazhchyk.* L'viv, Akademiia Nauk Ukrains'koi RSR, 1976.

5913. Vladych, Leonid V. *Vasyl' Kasiian, p'iat' etiudiv pro khudozhynka.* Kyiv, Mystetsvko, 1978.

Kaspar, Adolf, 1877–1934

5914. Beneš Buchlovan, Bedřich. *Knizní ilustrace Adolfa Kašpara.* Praha, Šmidt, 1942.

5915. Scheybal, Josef V. *Adolf Kašpar, život a dílo.* Praha, Hudby a Umení, 1957.

5916. Táborský, Frantissěk. *A. Kašpar, ilustrátor, malíř, grafik.* Olomouc, Promberger, 1935.

Katz, Alex, 1927–

5917. Kuspit, Donald. *Alex Katz: the night paintings.* New York, H.N. Abrams, 1991.

5918. Maravell, Nicholas P. *Alex Katz: the complete prints.* [By] N.P. Maravell; interview with Carter Ratcliff. New York, Alpine Fine Arts Collection, 1983. (CR).

5919. Sandler, Irving. *Alex Katz.* New York, Abrams, 1979.

5920. ———, and Berkson, William, eds. *Alex Katz.* New York, Praeger, 1971.

5921. Walker, Barry. *Alex Katz, a print retrospective.* [Exhibition catalogue]. New York, Brooklyn Museum in association with Burton Skira Inc., 1987.

Kauffmann, Angelica, 1741–1807

5922. Baumgärtel, Bettina. *Angelica Kauffmann (1741–1807): Bedingungen weiblicher Kreativität in der Malerei des 18. Jahrhunderts.* Weinheim, Beltz, 1990. (Ergebnisse der Frauenforschung, 20).

5923. C. G. Boerner (Düsseldorf). *Angelika Kauffmann und ihre Zeit; Graphik und Zeichnungen von 1760–1810.* [Einladung zur Herbst-Ausstellung, 1.–22. September 1979]. Düsseldorf, Boerner, 1979. (Neue Lagerliste, 70).

5924. De Rossi, Giovanni Gherardo. *Vita di An-*

gelica Kauffmann, pittrice. Firenze, A spese di Molini, 1810.

5925. Gerard, Frances A. *Angelica Kauffman, a biography; new edition.* New York, Macmillan, 1893.

5926. Hartcup, Adeline. *Angelica, the portrait of an eighteenth-century artist.* Melbourne, Heinemann, 1954.

5927. Helbok, Claudia. *Miss Angel; Angelika Kauffmann, eine Biographie.* Wien, Rosenbaum, 1968.

5928. Kauffmann, Angelica. *Angelica Kauffmann: a continental artist in Georgian England.* [Exhibition catalogue]. Edited by Wendy Wassyng Roworth; with essays by David Alexander . . . [et al.]. London, Reaktion Books; published in association with the Royal Pavillion Art Gallery and Museums, Brighton; Seattle, WA, distributed in USA and Canada by the University of Washington Press, 1992.

5929. Manners, Victoria and Williamson, George C. *Angelica Kauffmann, R.A.; her life and her works.* London, Lane, 1924.

5930. Mayer, Dorothy M. *Angelica Kauffman, R.A., 1741–1807.* Gerrards Cross, Buckinghamshire, Smythe, 1972.

5931. Sandner, Oscar. *Hommage an Angelika Kauffmann.* [Exhibition catalogue]: Liechtensteinische Staatliche Kunstsammlung Vaduz, Juni–September 1992; Palazzo della permanente, Mailand, Dezember 1992–Jänner 1993. Milano, Nuova Mazzotta, 1992.

5932. Schram, Wilhelm. *Die Malerin Angelica Kauffmann.* Brunn, Rohrer, 1890.

5933. Thurnher, Eugen, ed. *Angelika Kauffmann und die deutsche Dichtung.* Bregenz, Russ, [1966]. (Vorarlberger Schrifttum, 10).

5934. Vorarlberger Landesmuseum (Bregenz). *Angelika Kauffmann und ihre Zeitgenossen.* 23. Juli bis 13. Oktober 1968. Bregenz, Vorarlberger Landesmuseum, 1968.

Kaulbach, Wilhelm von, 1805–1874
Friedrich August von, 1850–1920
Hermann, 1846–1909

5935. Dürck-Kaulbach, Josefa. *Erinnerungen an Wilhelm von Kaulbach und sein Haus.* München, Delphin, 1917. 3 ed.

5936. Kaulbach, Isidore. *Friedrich Kaulbach; Erinnerungen an mein Vaterhaus.* Berlin, Mittler, 1931.

5937. Lehmann, Evelyn [and] Riemer, Elke. *Die Kaulbachs, eine Künstlerfamilie aus Arolsen.* Arolsen, Waldeckischer Geschichtsverein, 1978.

5938. Müller, Hans. *Wilhelm Kaulbach.* Berlin, Fontane, 1893.

5939. [Ostini, Fritz von]. *Fritz August von Kaul-*
bach, Gesamtwerk. München, Hanfstaengl, [1911].

5940. ———. *Wilhelm von Kaulbach.* Bielefeld/Leipzig, Velhagen & Klasing, 1906. (Künstler-Monographien, 84).

5941. Rosenberg, Adolf. *Friedrich August von Kaulbach.* Bielefeld/Leipzig, Velhagen & Klasing, 1910. 2 ed. (Künstler-Monographien, 48).

5942. Schasler, Max. *Die Wandgemälde Wilhelm von Kaulbachs im Treppenhause des Neuen Museums zu Berlin.* Berlin, Wolff, 1854.

5943. Zimmermans, Klaus. *Friedrich August von Kaulbach, 1850–1920; Monographie und Werkverzeichnis.* München, Prestel, 1980. (CR). (Materialien zur Kunst des 19. Jahrunderts, 26).

Kaván, František, 1866–1941

5944. Kovárna, František. *František Kaván.* Praha, Jednotaŭmelcŭ výtvarných, 1942.

5945. Vancl, Karel. *František Kaván.* Liberci, Severoćeské Krajské, 1962.

Kawai, Gyokudō, 1873–1957

5946. Takahaski, Seiichiro. *Gyokudō Kawai.* [Text in Japanese and English]. Tokyo, Bijutsu Shippansha, 1958.

Kazan, Watanabe *see* Watanabe, Kazan

Kazakov, Matveĭ Fedorovich, 1738–1813

5947. [Beletskoi, E. A.]. *Arkhitekturnye al'bomy M. F. Kazakova.* Moskva, Gosizdat litry po stroitel'stvu i arkhitekture, 1956.

5948. Bondarenko, Ilia Evgrafovich. *Arkhitekor Matvyeĭ Fedorovich Kazakov.* Moskva, Institut Moskovskogo arkhitekturnogo obshchestva, 1912.

Keene, Charles Samuel, 1823–1891

5949. Hudson, Derek. *Charles Keene.* London, Pleiades, 1947.

5950. Layard, George S. *The life and letters of Charles Samuel Keene.* London, Sampson Low, 1892.

5951. Pennell, Joseph. *The work of Charles Keene.* London, Unwin, 1897.

Keith, William, 1838–1911

5952. Art Institute of Chicago. *Exhibition of paintings by the late William Keith.* April 22 to May 6, 1913. Chicago, Art Institute of Chicago, 1913.

5953. Cornelius, Fidelis. *Keith, old master of California.* [Vol. 1] New York, Putnam's, 1942. [Vol. 2] Fresno, California, Academy Library Guild, 1956.

5954. Hay, Emily. *William Keith as prophet painter.* San Francisco, Elder, 1916. (Reprint:

San Francisco, Kenneth Starosciak, [1981]).

5955. Oakland Art Museum (Oakland, Calif.). *An introduction to the art of William Keith.* [Text by Paul Mills; published upon the opening of the William Keith Memorial Gallery]. Oakland, Calif., Oakland Art Museum, 1956.

Keller, Ferdinand, 1842–1922

5956. Gaertner, Friedrich W. *Ferdinand Keller.* Karlsruhe, Müller, 1912.

5957. Koch, Michael. *Ferdinand Keller (1842–1922), Leben und Werk.* Karlsruhe, Müller, 1978. (CR).

Kelly, Ellsworth, 1923–

5958. Axsom, Richard H. *The prints of Ellsworth Kelly, a catalogue raisonné, 1949–1985.* [By] R.H. Axsom with the assistance of Phyllis Floyd. New York, Hudson Hills Press, in association with the American Federation of Arts, 1987.(CR).

5959. Bois, Yve Alain. *Ellsworth Kelly.* [Exhibition catalogue by] Yve-Alain Bois, Jack Cowart, Alfred Pacquement. Washington, National Gallery of Art; Munich, Prestel Verlag, 1992.

5960. Coplans, John. *Ellsworth Kelly.* New York, Abrams, 1973. (CR).

5961. Goossen, Eugene C. *Ellsworth Kelly.* [Catalogue of an exhibition, Museum of Modern Art, Sept. 12–Nov. 4, 1973]. New York, Museum of Modern Art, 1973; distributed by New York Graphic Society, Greenwich, Conn.

5962. Kelly, Ellsworth. *Ellsworth Kelly, curves, rectangles.* Essay by Barbara Rose. New York, Blum Helman, 1989.

5963. Metropolitan Museum of Art (New York). *Ellsworth Kelly, recent paintings and sculptures.* April 26–June 24, 1979. New York, Metropolitan Museum of Art, 1979.

5964. Sims, Patterson. *Ellsworth Kelly, sculpture.* [Catalogue of an exhibition, Whitney Museum of American Art; Dec. 17, 1982–Feb. 21, 1983]. New York, Whitney Museum of American Art, 1982.

5965. Upright, Diane. *Ellsworth Kelly: works on paper.* [Catalog of an exhibition by] Diane Upright; introduction by Henry Geldzahler. New York, H.N. Abrams, in association with the Fort Worth Art Museum, 1987.

5966. Waldman, Diane. *Ellsworth Kelly; drawings, collages, prints.* Greenwich, Conn., New York Graphic Society, 1971.

Kemeny, Zoltan, 1907–1965

5967. Fondation Maeght (Paris). *Kemeny.* 23 mars–31 mai 1974. [Text by Michel Ragon]. Paris, Fondation Maeght, 1974.

5968. Giedion-Welcker, Carola. *Zoltan Kemeny.* [Text in German, French and English]. St. Gallen, Erker, 1968. (Artists of Our Time, 15).

5969. Kunstmuseum Bern. *Zoltan Kemeny.* [March 9–May 9, 1982]. [Text in German and French]. Bern, Kunstmuseum Bern, 1982.

5970. Ragon, Michel. *Zoltan Kemeny.* [Text in French, English, and German]. Neuchâtel, Editions du Griffon, 1960.

Kemp-Welch, Lucy Elizabeth, 1869–1958

5971. Messum, David. *The life and work of Lucy Kemp-Welch.* [N.p.], Antique Collectors' Club, 1976.

Kent, Rockwell, 1882–1971

5972. Armitage, Merle. *Rockwell Kent.* New York, Knopf, 1932.

5973. Chegodaev, Andrei. *Rokwell Kent, zhivopis', grafika.* Moskva, Akad. khudozhestv SSSR, 1962.

5974. Kent, Rockwell. *It's me, O Lord; the autobiography of Rockwell Kent.* New York, Dodd, Mead, 1955.

5975. ———. *Later bookplates & marks of Rockwell Kent.* With a preface by the artist. New York, Pynson Printers, 1937.

5976. [——— and Zigrosser, Carl]. *Rockwellkentiana; few words and many pictures by R. K. and, by Carl Zigrosser, a bibliography and a list of prints.* New York, Harcourt, Brace, 1933.

5977. Johnson, Fridolf. *The illustrations of Rockwell Kent; 231 examples from books, magazines and advertising art.* New York, Dover, 1976.

5978. ———. *Rockwell Kent, an anthology of his works.* New York, Knopf, 1982.

5979. Jones, Dan B. *The prints of Rockwell Kent, a catalogue raisonné.* Chicago/London, University of Chicago Press, 1975. (CR).

5980. Traxel, David. *An American saga; the life and times of Rockwell Kent.* New York, Harper & Row, 1980.

5981. West, Richard V. *"An enkindled eye": the paintings of Rockwell Kent, a retrospective exhibition.* [Catalogue by] R. West with contributions by Fridolf Johnson and Dan Burne Jones. Santa Barbara, CA, Santa Barbara Museum of Art, 1985.

Kent, William, 1685–1748

5982. Hunt, John Dixon. *William Kent, landscape garden designer; an assessment and catalogue of his designs.* London, A. Zwemmer, 1987.

5983. Jourdain, Margaret. *The work of William Kent; artist, painter, designer, and landscape gardener.* Introduction by Christopher Hussey. London, Country Life, 1948.

5984. Wilson, Michael I. *William Kent: architect, designer, painter, gardener, 1685–1748.* London, Routledge & Kegan Paul, 1984.

Kenzan, ca. 1662–1743 *see* Koetsu

Kerkovius, Ida, 1879–1970
5985. Galerie der Stadt Stuttgart. *Ida Kerkovius, 1879–1970; Gesichter.* 19. Juli bis 16. September 1979. Stuttgart, Galerie der Stadt, 1979.
5986. Kerkovius, Ida. *Ida Kerkovius, 1879–1970: Reisebilder und Übungszeichnungen: 30 unveröffentlichte Arbeiten.* [Ausstellung] Galerie Adriana, Stuttgart, vom 4. Dezember 1987 bis 20. Januar 1988. [Katalog und Konzeption der Ausstellung Adriana Schmidt]. Stuttgart, Galerie Adriana, 1987.
5987. Leonhard, Kurt. *Ida Kerkovius, Leben und Werk.* Köln, DuMont Schauberg, 1967.
5988. ———. *Die Malerin Ida Kerkovius.* Stuttgart, Kohlhammer, 1954.
5989. Roditi, Eduard. *Ida Kerkovius.* Konstanz, Simon und Koch, 1961.

Kersting, Georg Friedrich, 1785–1847
5990. Schnell, Werner. *Georg Friedrich Kersting, 1785–1847.* Berlin, Deutscher Verlag für Kunstwissenschaft, 1994. (CR).

Kertesz, André, 1894–
5991. Gaillard, Agathe. *André Kertész.* Paris, Belfond, 1980.
5992. Kertesz, André. *André Kertesz: diary of light 1912–1985.* Foreword by Cornell Capa; essay by Hal Hinson; edited by Susan Harder with Hiroji Kubota. New York, Aperture in association with the International Center of Photography, 1987
5993. Kertész, André. *Hungarian memories.* Introduction by Hilton Kramer. Boston, New York Graphic Society, 1982.
5994. ———. *J'aime Paris; photographs since the twenties.* Ed. by Nicolas Ducrot. New York, Grossman, 1974.
5995. ———. *A lifetime of perception.* Introduction by Ben Lifson. Ed. by Jane Corkin. New York, Abrams, 1982.
5996. ———. *Kertesz on Kertesz: a self-portrait;* photos and text by André Kertész; introduction by Peter Adam, New York, Abbeville Press, 1985.
5997. ———. *Sixty years of photography, 1912–1972.* Ed. by Nicolas Ducrot. New York, Grossman, 1972.
5998. Museum of Modern Art (New York). *A. Kertész, photographer.* Introductory essay by John Szarkowski. New York, Museum of Modern Art, 1964.
5999. Phillips, Sandra S. *André Kertesz of Paris and*

New York. [Exhibition catalogue by] Sandra S. Phillips, David Travis, Weston J. Naef. Chicago, Art Institute of Chicago; New York, Metropolitan Museum of Art; London, Thames and Hudson, 1985.

Keyser, Hendrick Cornelis de, 1565–1621
6000. [Bray, Salomon de]. *Architectura moderna of te Bouwinge van onsen tyt.* Introd.: E. Tavern. Soest, Davaco, 1971.
6001. Nuerdenburg, Elisabeth. *Hendrick de Keyser, beeldhouwer en bouwmeester van Amsterdam.* Amsterdam, Scheltema & Holkema, 1930.

Khnopff, Fernand, 1858–1921
6002. Delevoy, Robert L. *Fernand Khnopff.* [Catalogue de l'oeuvre et bibliographie: Catherine De Croës et Giselle Ollinger-Zinque]. Bruxelles, Cosmos Monographies [Editions Lebeer-Hossmann], 1979. (CR). (2 ed. rev. et aug.: Paris, Bibliotheque des arts, 1987).
6003. Dumont-Wilden, Louis. *Fernand Khnopff.* Bruxelles, van Oest, 1907.
6004. Howe, Jeffery W. *The symbolist art of Fernand Khnopff.* [Ann Arbor, Mich.], University of Michigan Press, 1982. (Studies in Fine Arts: the Avant-Garde, 28).
6005. Khnopff, Fernand. *Fernand Khnopff et ses rapports avec la Secession viennoise.* [Exposition]. Bruxelles, Musées royaux des Beaux-Arts de Belgique, 2 octobre–6 décembre, 1987.
6006. Musée des Arts Décoratifs (Paris). *Fernand Khnopff, 1858–1921.* 10 octobre–31 décembre, 1979. [Brussels], Ministère de la Communauté française de Belgique, 1979.
6007. Verhaeren, Emile. *Quelques notes sur l'oeuvre de Fernand Khnopff, 1881–1887.* Bruxelles, Veuve Monnom, 1887.

Kiefer, Anselm, 1945–
6008. Beeren, Wim. *Anselm Kiefer: Bilder 1980–1986.* [Exhibition catalogue]. Amsterdam, Stedelijk Museum, 1986.
6009. Gilmour, John. *Fire on earth: Anselm Kiefer and the postmodern world.* Philadelphia, Temple University Press, 1990.
6010. Hutchinson, John. *Anselm Kiefer.* [Catalogue of an exhibition]. Dublin, Douglas Hyde Gallery, 1990.
6011. Kiefer, Anselm. *The books of Anselm Kiefer, 1969–1990.* Trans. by Bruni Mayor. Edited by Götz Adriani, New York, G. Braziller 1991.
6012. ———. *The high priestess;* with an essay by Arnim Zweite. New York, H.N. Abrams in association with Anthony d'Offay Gallery. London, 1989.
6013. ———. *Über Räume und Völker.* Nachwort

von Klaus Gallwitz. Frankfurt am Main, Suhrkamp, 1990.

6014. Marian Goodman Gallery (New York). *Anselm Kiefer: Bruch und Einung.* [Catalogue of an exhibition]. New York, Marian Goodman Gallery, 1987.

6015. ———. *Anselm Kiefer: Lilith.*[Catalogue of an exhibition]. New York, Marian Goodman Gallery,1991.

6016. Meier, Cordula. *Anselm Kiefer: Die Rückkehr des Mythos in der Kunst.* Essen, Verlag Die Blaue Eule, 1992.

6017. Rosenthal, Mark. *Anselm Kiefer.* [Catalogue of an exhibition] organized by A. James Speyer, Mark Rosenthal. Chicago, Art Institute of Chicago; Philadelphia, Philadelphia Museum of Art. New York; distributed in the U.S. and Canada by te Neues Pub. Co., 1987.

Kienholz, Edward, 1927–1994
Nancy Reddin, 1943–

6018. Baur, Karl Friedrich. *Edward Kienholz, Nancy Reddin Kienholz: Medien, Macht, Manipulation.* [Ausstellung und Katalog, K.F. Baur, Thomas Buchsteiner, Hans Gercke]. Stuttgart, Hatje, 1987.

6019. Kienholz, Edward. *Edward Kienholz.* Paris, Maeght éditeur, 1979. (Derrière le miroir, 236).

6020. Pincus, Robert L. *On a scale that competes with the world: the art of Edward and Nancy Kienholz.* Berkeley, University of California Press, 1990.

6021. Schmidt, Hans-Werner. *'The portable war memorial': moralischer Appell und politische Kritik.* Frankfurt am Main, Fischer Taschenbuch Verlag, 1988.

Kirchner, Ernst Ludwig, 1880–1938

6022. Crispolti, Enrico. *Ernst Kirchner.* Milano, Fabbri, 1966. (I maestri del colore, 137).

6023. Dube, Annemarie and Dube, Wolf-Dieter. *E. L. Kirchner, das graphische Werk.* 2 v. München, Prestel, 1980. 2 ed. (CR).

6024. Dube-Heynig, Annemarie. *Kirchner; his graphic art.* Greenwich, Conn., New York Graphic Society, 1961.

6025. Froning, Hubertus. *E.L. Kirchner und die Wandmalerei; Entwürfe zur Wandmalerei im Museum Folkwang.* Recklinghausen, A. Bbongers, 1991.

6026. Gordon, Donald E. *Ernst Ludwig Kirchner.* Cambridge, Mass., Harvard University Press, 1968. (CR).

6027. Grisebach, Lothar. *E. L. Kirchners Davoser Tagebuch; eine Darstellung des Malers und eine Sammlung seiner Schriften.* Köln, DuMont Schauberg, 1968.

6028. Grohmann, Will. *Das Werk Ernst Ludwig Kirchners.* München, Wolff, 1926.

6029. ———. *E. L. Kirchner.* New York, Arts, 1961.

6030. ———. *Zeichnungen von Ernst Ludwig Kirchner.* Dresden, Arnold, 1925.

6031. Ketterer, Roman N., et al. *Ernst Ludwig Kirchner; Zeichnungen und Pastelle.* Stuttgart/Zürich, Belser, 1979. (English ed.: New York, Alpine, 1982).

6032. Kirchner, Ernst Ludwig. *Briefe an Nele und Henry van de Velde.* München, Piper, 1961.

6033. ———. *Briefwechsel 1910–1935/1938: mit Briefen von und an Luise Schiefler und Erna Kirchner sowie weiteren Dokumenten aus Schieflers Korrespondenz-Ablage.* Bearbeitet von Wolfgang Henze in Verbindung mit Annemarie Dube-Heynig und Magdalena Kraemer-Noble. Stuttgart, Belser, 1990.

6034. ———. *Ernst Ludwig Kirchner: Briefwechsel mit einem jungen Ehepaar, 1227–1937: Elfriede Dumler und Hansgeorg Knoblauch.* Bern, Verlag Kornfeld, 1989.

6035. ———. *Ernst Ludwig Kirchner in der Graphischen Sammlung der Staatsgalerie: Bestandskatalog der Zeichnungen, Aquarelle, Pastelle, Holzschnitte, Radierungen, Lithograohien und illustrierten Bücher.* Für die Ausstellung bereichert durch Leihgaben aus württembergischen Sammlungen. Graphische Sammlung Staatsgalerie Stuttgart, 14. Juni bis 31. August 1980. Katalog: Karin Becker und Gunther Thiem. Stuttgart, Die Galerie, 1980.

6036. ———. *Ernst Ludwig Kirchner: Postkarten und Briefe an Erich Heckel im Altonaer Museum in Hamburg.* [By] Annemarie Dube-Heynig; herausgegeben von Roman Norbert Ketterer unter Mitwirkung von Wolfgang Henze. Köln, DuMont, 1984.

6037. ———. *Ernst Ludwig Kirchner: Werke 1917–1923.* Ausstellung, 17. Dezember 1988–2. April 1989, Ernst Ludwig Kirchner Museum, Davos Platz. [Katalogtexte und Gestaltung, E.W. Kornfeld]. Davos-Platz, Das Museum, 1989.

6038. Kornfeld, Eberhard W. *Ernst Ludwig Kirchner, Nachzeichnung seines Lebens.* Katalog der Sammlung von Werken von Ernst Ludwig Kirchner im Kirchner-Haus Davos. Bern, Kornfeld und Ketterer, 1979.

6039. Museum der Stadt Aschaffenburg. *E. L. Kirchner; Zeichnungen, Pastelle, Aquarelle. Dokumente: Fotos, Schriften, Briefe.* 2 v. [Text and compilation by Karlheinz Gabler]. 19. April bis 26. Mai 1980. Aschaffenburg, Museum der Stadt, 1980.

6040. Museum of Fine Arts (Boston). *Ernst Ludwig Kirchner, a retrospective exhibition.* [Text by Donald E. Gordon]. March 20–April 27, 1969, Boston, Museum of Fine Arts, 1968.

6041. Schiefler, Gustav. *Die Graphik Ernst Ludwig*

Kirchners. 2 v. Berlin, Euphorion, 1924/
1931.

Kisling, Moïse, 1891–1953

6042. Charensol, Georges. *Moïse Kisling.* Paris, Editions de Clermont, 1948. (Art-Present, 2).

6043. Einstein, Carl. *M. Kisling.* Leipzig, Klinkhardt & Biermann, 1922. (Junge, 31).

6044. Kesel, Joseph. *Kisling.* New York, Abrams, 1971. (CR).

6045. Troyat, Henri and Kisling, Jean. *Moïse Kisling: catalogue raisonné de l'oeuvre peint.* Paris, Kisling, 1982. 2 ed. (CR).

Kitagawa, Utamaro *see* Utamaro Kitagawa

Kitaj, Ronald B., 1937–

6046. Kinsman, Jane. *The prints of R.B. Kitaj.* [By] Jane Kinsman; afterwords by R.B. Kitaj. Aldershot, Hants., Scolar Press; Brookfield, Vt., Ashgate Pub., 1994.

6047. Kitaj, R.B. *First Diasporist manifesto.* London, Thames and Hudson, 1989.

6048. ———. *Kitaj: paintings, drawings, pastels.* [Exhibition catalog] by John Ashbery . . . [et al.]. New York, Thames and Hudson, 1983.

6049. ———. *R.B. Kitaj.* [Catalogue of an] Exhibition organized by John Shannon. Washington, D.C., Smithsonian Institution Press, 1981.

6050. ———. *R.B. Kitaj:* Nov.–Dec. 1985, Marlborough Fine Art (London) Ltd.: March 1986, Marlborough Gallery Inc., New York. London, Marlborough Fine Art, 1985.

6051. ———. *R.B. Kitaj: a retrospective.* Ed. by Richard Morphet. London, Tate Gallery Publications, 1994.

6052. Livingstone, Marco. *R.B. Kitaj.* New York, Rizzoli, 1985. [2 ed., rev., exp. pbk. New York/London, Thames and Hudson, 1992].

Kiyonaga, Torii *see* Torii, Kiyonaga

Klapheck, Konrad, 1935–

6053. Klapheck, Konrad. *Konrad Klapheck: Werkverzeichnis der Druckgraphik, 1977–1980.* Düsseldorf, Wolfgang Wittrock Kunsthandel. 1980.

6054. ———. *Konrad Klapheck, Retrospektive 1955–1985.* [Exhibition catalogue]. Hrsg. von Werner Hofmann; mit zwei Essays von Konrad Klapheck, sowie Beiträgen von Werner Hofmann und Peter-Klaus Schuster. München, Prestel-Verlag, 1985.

6055. Museum Boymans-van Beuningen (Rotterdam). *Konrad Klapheck.* [September 14–November 3, 1974]. Rotterdam, Museum Boymans-van Beuningen, 1974.

6056. Pierre, José. *Konrad Klapheck.* Köln, DuMont Schauberg, 1970.

Klee, Paul, 1879–1940

6057. [Armitage, Merle, ed.]. *5 essays on Klee.* New York, [designed by Merle Armitage and distributed by] Duell, Sloan & Pearce, 1950.

6058. Bischoff, Ulrich. *Paul Klee.* München, Bruckmann, 1992.

6059. Cherchi, Placido. *Paul Klee teorico.* Bari, De Donato, 1978.

6060. Compte, Philippe. *Paul Klee.* Trans. by Carol Marshall. Woodstock, N.Y., Overlook Press, 1991.

6061. Crone, Rainer. *Paul Klee: legends of the sign.* [By] R. Crone and Joseph Leo Koerner. New York, Columbia University Press, 1991.

6062. Di San Lazzaro, Gualtieri. *Klee Study of his life and work.* Trans. from the Italian by Stuart Hood. New York, Praeger, 1957.

6063. Franciscono, Marcel. *Paul Klee: his work and thought.* Chicago, University of Chicago Press, 1991.

6064. Geist, Hans Friedrich. *Paul Klee.* Hamburg, Ernst Hauswedell, 1948.

6065. Giedion-Welcker, Carola. *Paul Klee.* Trans. by Alexander Gode. New York, Viking, 1952. (2 ed.: Stuttgart, Hatje, 1954).

6066. ———. *Paul Klee in Selbstzeugnissen und Bilddokumenten.* [Reinbeck bei Hamburg], Rowohlt, 1961. (Rowohlt Monographien, 52).

6067. Glaesemer, Jürgen. *Paul Klee; die farbigen Werke im Kunstmuseum Bern.* Bern, Kornfeld, 1976. (Sammlungskataloge des Berner Kunstmuseums: Paul Klee, 1).

6068. ———. *Paul Klee; Handzeichnungen.* 3 v. Bern, Kunstmuseum Bern, 1973–1979. (CR). (Sammlungskataloge des Berner Kunstmuseums: Paul Klee, 2–4).

6069. Grohmann, Will. *Paul Klee.* Paris, Cahiers d'art, 1929.

6070. ———. *Paul Klee.* New York, Abrams, [1954].

6071. ———. *Paul Klee: Handzeichnungen.* Köln, DuMont Schauberg, 1959.

6072. Grote, Ludwig. *Erinnerungen an Paul Klee.* München, Prestel, 1959.

6073. Haftmann, Werner. *The mind and work of Paul Klee.* New York, Praeger, 1954.

6074. Haxthausen, Charles W. *Paul Klee, the formative years.* New York, Garland, 1981.

6075. Helfenstein, Josef. *Paul Klee: Das Schaffen im Todesjahr.* [Catalogue of an exhibition]. By, J. Helfenstein [und] Stefan Frey. Bern, Kunstmuseum, 1990.

6076. Huggler, Max. *Paul Klee, die Malerei als Blick in den Kosmos.* Frauenfeld/Stuttgart, Huber, 1969. (Wirkung und Gestalt, 7).

6077. Jardi, Enric. *Paul Klee.* Trans. by Jennifer Jackson and Kerstin Engström. New York, Rizzoli, 1991.

6078. Kagan, Andrew. *Paul Klee, art & music.* Ithaca/London, Cornell University Press, 1983.

6079. Kahnweiler, Daniel-Henry. *Klee*. [Text in French, English, and German]. Paris, Braun/ New York, Herrmann, 1950.

6080. Klee, Felix. *Paul Klee, his life and works in documents*. New York, Braziller, 1962.

6081. Klee, Paul. *Beiträge zur bildnerischen Formlehre*. Faksimilierte Ausgabe des Originalmanuskripts. Herausgegeben von Jürgen Glaesemer. Bael/Stuttgart, Schwabe, 1979.

6082. ———. *Briefe an die Familie, 1893–1940*. [Edited by Felix Klee]. Köln, DuMont Schauberg, 1979.

6083. ———. *The diaries of Paul Klee, 1898–1918*. Edited, with an introduction, by Felix Klee. Berkeley and Los Angeles, University of California Press, 1964.

6084. ———. *Journal*. Trans. by Pierre Klossowski. Paris, Grasset, 1959.

6085. ———. *The nature of nature. The notebooks of Paul Klee [vol. 2]*. Edited by Jürgen Spiller; trans. by Heinz Norden. New York, Wittenborn, 1973. (Documents of Modern Art, 17).

6086. ———. *On modern art*. Trans. by Paul Findlay. London, Faber, 1948.

6087. ———. *Paul Klee*. [Published on the occasion of the Paul Klee exhibition at the Museum of Modern Art, New York]. Edited by Carolyn Lanchner. Boston. Distributed by New York Graphic Society Books/Little Brown, 1987.

6088. ———. *Paul Klee notebooks [Transl. of Form- und Gestaltungslehre]*. Edited by Jörg Spiller. 2 v. London, Lund Humphries; Woodstock, N.Y., Overlook Press, 1992.

6089. ———. *Paul Klee. Oeuvreverzeichnis*, Band 1: *Die Werke des Jahres 1940*. Hrsg von der Paul-Klee-Stiftung. Stuttgart, Hatje Verlag, Winter 1990/91– .

6090. ———. *Paul Klee: opere dal 1885 al 1933*. [Scelte delle opere, Felix Klee, Michele Reiner; testi, Felix Klee . . . et al; traduzioni, Vera Segre-Rutz, Michele Reiner]. [Mendrisio], Municipio di Mendrisio, 1987.

6091. ———. *Paul Klee, opere 1900–1940: dalla collezione Felix Klee*. [Catalogo] a cura di Carmine Benincasa. Firenze, Electa, 1981.

6092. ———. *Pedagogical sketchbook*. Trans. by Sibyl Moholy-Nagy. New York, Praeger, 1953.

6093. ———. *Schriften; Rezensionen und Aufsätze*. [Edited by Christian Geelhaar]. Köln, DuMont Schauberg, 1976.

6094. ———. *Tagebücher, 1898–1918*. Hrsg. von der Paul- Klee-Stiftung, Kunstmuseum Bern; bearbeitet von Wolfgang Kersten. Stuttgart, G. Hatje; Teufen, A. Niggli, 1988. Textkritische Neued.

6095. ———. *The thinking eye; the notebooks of Paul Klee [vol. 1]*. Edited by Jürgen Spiller; trans. by Ralph Manheim. New York, Wittenborn, 1961. (Documents of Modern Art, 15).

6096. ———, et al. *The inward vision; watercolors, drawings, writings*. Trans. by Norbert Guterman. [Text by Paul Klee with Werner Haftmann, Carola Giedion-Welcker, et al.]. New York, Abrams, 1959.

6097. Hopfengart, Christine. *Klee, vom Sonderfall zum Publikumsliebling*: Stationen seiner öffentlichen Resonanz in Deutschland 1905–1960. Mainz, P. von Zabern, 1989.

6098. Miller, Margaret. *Paul Klee*. New York, Museum of Modern Art, 1945.

6099. Mösser, Andeheinz. *Das Problem der Bewegung bei Paul Klee*. Heidelberg, Winter, 1976. (Heidelberger Kunstgeschichtliche Abhandlungen, Neue Folge, 12).

6100. National Gallery of Canada (Ottawa). *A tribute to Paul Klee, 1879–1940*. 2 March–15 April 1979. [Text by David Burnett]. Ottawa, National Gallery of Canada, 1979.

6101. Naubert-Riser, Constance. *La création chez Paul Klee; étude de la relation théoriepraxis de 1900 à 1924*. Paris, Klincksieck/Ottawa, Editions de l'Université d'Ottawa, 1978.

6102. Osterwold, Tilman. *Paul Klee, ein Kind träumt sich*. Stuttgart, Hatje, [1979].

6103. Partsch, Susanna. *Paul Klee 1879–1940*. Köln, DuMont, 1990.

6104. Pfeiffer-Belli, Erich. *Klee, eine Bildbiographie*. München, Kindler, 1964.

6105. Plant, Margaret. *Paul Klee, figures and faces*. London, Thames and Hudson, 1978.

6106. Ponente, Nello. *Klee, biographical and critical study*. Trans. by James Emmons. Lausanne, Skira, 1960; distributed by World, Cleveland.

6107. Roskill, Mark W. *Klee, Kandinsky, and the thought of their time: a critical perspective*. Urbana, University of Illinois Press, 1992.

6108. San Lazzaro, Gualtieri di. *Klee, a study of his life and work*. Trans. by Stuart Hood. New York, Praeger, 1957.

6109. Soby, James T. *The prints of Paul Klee*. New York, Valentin, 1945. 2 ed.

6110. Solomon R. Guggenheim Museum (New York). *Paul Klee, 1879–1940*. New York, Guggenheim Foundation, 1977.

6111. Tower, Beeke Sell. *Klee and Kandinsky in Munich and at the Bauhaus*. Ann Arbor, Mich., UMI Research Press, 1981. (Studies in the fine arts. The Avant-garde, 16).

6112. Verdi, Richard. *Klee and nature*. New York, Rizzoli, 1985.

6113. Wedderkop, Hermann von. *Paul Klee*. Leipzig, Klinkhardt & Biermann, 1920. (Junge Kunst, 13).

6114. Werckmeister, Otto Karl. *The making of Paul Klee's career, 1914–1920*. Chicago, University of Chicago Press, 1989.

6115. ———. *Versuch über Paul Klee.* Frankfurt a.M., Syndikat, 1981.

6116. Zahn, Leopold. *Paul Klee; Leben/Werk/Geist.* Potsdam, Kiepenheuer, 1920.

Klein, César, 1876–1954

6117. Däubler, Theodor. *César Klein.* Leipzig, Klinkhardt & Biermann, 1923. 2 ed.

6118. Pfefferkorn, Rudolph. *César Klein.* Berlin, Rembrandt, 1962. (Die Kunst unserer Zeit, 14).

Klein, Johann Adam, 1792–1875

6119. Jahn, Carl. *Das Werk von Johann Adam Klein.* München, Montmorillon'sche Kunsthandlung, 1863.

6120. Schwemmer, Wilhelm. *Johann Adam Klein, ein Nürnberger Meister des 19. Jahrhunderts.* Nürnberg, Carl, 1966.

6121. Stadtgeschichtliche Museen (Nuremberg). *Johann Adam Klein, 1792–1875; Zeichnungen und Aquarelle.* Nürnberg, Stadtgeschichtliche Museen, 1975. (Bestandskatalog, 1).

Klein, Yves, 1928–1962

6122. [Klein, Yves]. *Yves Klein, 1928–1962; selected writings.* Trans. by Barbara Wright. [Edited by Jacques Caumont and Jennifer Gough-Cooper]. London, Tate Gallery, 1974.

6123. Künsthalle Bern. *Yves Klein.* 4.–29. August 1971. [Hannover, Kunstverein Hannover, 1971].

6124. Martano, Giuliano. *Yves Klein, il mistero ostentato.* Torino, Martano, 1970. (Nadar, ricerche sull'arte contemporanea, 6).

6125. McEveilley, Thomas, et al. *Yves Klein, 1928–1962; a retrospective.* Houston, Tex., Institute for the Arts, Rice University, 1983.

6126. Restany, Pierre. *Yves Klein.* Trans. by John Shepley. New York, Abrams, 1982.

6127. Wember, Paul. *Yves Klein.* Köln, DuMont Schauberg, 1969. (CR).

Klenze, Leo von, 1784–1864

6128. Hederer, Oswald. *Leo von Klenze, Persönlichkeit und Werk.* München, Callwey, 1964.

6129. Klenze, Leo von. *Sammlung architektonischer Entwürfe für die Ausführung bestimmt oder wirklich ausgeführt.* 5 v. München, Cotta, 1847–50. 2 ed.

6130. Lieb, Norbert [and] Hufnagl, Florian. *Leo von Klenze, Gemälde und Zeichnungen.* München, Callwey, 1979.

6131. Wiegmann, Rudolf. *Der Ritter Leo von Klenze und unsere Kunst.* Leipzig, Fleischer, 1839.

Kleophrades Painter, fl. 430–410 b.c.

6132. Beazley, John D. *The Kleophrades painter.*

Mainz, von Zabern, 1974. 4 ed. (Bilder griechischer Vasen, 6).

Klimt, Gustav, 1861–1918

6133. Breicha, Otto. *Gustav Klimt, die goldene Pforte; Werk-Wesen-Wirkung; Bilder und Schriften zu Leben und Werk.* Salzburg, Galerie Welz, 1978.

6134. Comini, Alessandra. *Gustav Klimt.* New York, Braziller, 1975.

6135. Dobai, Johannes. *L'opera completa di Klimt.* Milano, Rizzoli, 1978. (CR). (Classici dell'arte,).

6136. Eisler, Max, ed. *Gustav Klimt, eine Nachlese.* Wien, Oesterreichische Staatsdruckerei, 1920. (English ed.: *Gustav Klimt, an aftermath.* Vienna, 1931).

6137. Frodl, Gerbert. *Klimt.* Translated by Alexandra Campbell. London, Barrie & Jenkins, 1992.

6138. Hofmann, Werner. *Gustav Klimt.* Trans. by Inge Goodwin. Boston, New York Graphic Society, 1971.

6139. Hofstätter, Hans H. *Gustav Klimt, erotische Zeichnungen.* Köln, DuMont, 1979.

6140. Klimt, Gustav. *Gustav Klimt: Landscaspes.* With an essay by Johannes Dobai and a biography of Gustav Klimt. Translated from the German by Ewald Osers. London, Weidenfeld and Nicolson, 1988.

6141. ———. *Gustav Klimt masterpieces.* [By] Gabriella Belli, [edited by Fernando Orlando]. Boston, Little Brown, 1990.

6142. ———. *Gustav Klimt, Women.* With an essay by Angelica Baumer and a biography of Gustav Klimt. Translated from the German by Ewald Osers. London, Weidenfeld and Nicolson, 1986.

6143. Nebehay, Christian Michael, ed. *Gustav Klimt: Das Skizzenbuch aus dem Besitz von Sonja Knips.* Wien, Edition Tusch, 1987.

6144. ———. Christian Michael. ed. *Gustav Klimt, Dokumentation.* Wien, Galerie Christian M. Nebehay, 1969.

6145. ———. *Gustav Klimt, Egon Schiele und die Familie Lederer.* C.M. Nebehay mit einem Vorwort von Ottokar von Jacobs. Bern, Verlag Galerie Kornfeld, 1987.

6146. ———. *Gustav Klimt, von der Zeichnung zum Bild.* Wien, C. Brandstätter, 1992.

6147. Novotny, Fritz and Dobai, Johannes. *Gustav Klimt.* Salzburg, Galerie Welz, 1967. (CR).

6148. Pirchan, Emil. *Gustav Klimt.* Wien, Bergland, 1956.

6149. Sabarsky, Serge. *Gustav Klimt.* [By] Serge Sabarsky; testi, Peter Baum . . . [et al.]; apparato critico e schede, Laura Lombardi. Firenze, Artificio, 1991.

6150. Salten, Felix. *Gustav Klimt, gelegentliche Anmerkungen.* Wien, Wiener Verlag, 1903.

6151. Strobl, Alice. *Gustav Klimt; die Zeich-*

nungen. Mit einem Geleitwort von Walter Koschatzky]. 3 v. Salzburg, Galerie Welz, 1980–89. (CR). (Veröffentlichungen der Albertina, 15).

6152. Whitford, Frank. *Klimt.* London, Thames and Hudson, 1990.

Kline, Franz Josef, 1910–1962

6153. Dawson, Fielding. *An emotional memoir of Franz Kline.* New York, Pantheon, 1967.

6154. Gaugh, Harry F. *The vital gesture: Franz Kline.* [Catalogue of an exhibition held at the Cincinnati Art Museum]. New York, Abbeville Press, 1985.

6155. Whitney Museum of American Art (New York). *Franz Kline, 1910–1962.* October 1–November 24, 1968. [Text by John Gordon]. New York, Whitney Museum of American Art, 1968.

Klinger, Max, 1857–1920

6156. Avenarius, Ferdinand. *Max Klinger als Poet.* München, Callwey, [1919]. 3 ed.

6157. Brieger-Wasservogel, Lothar. *Max Klinger.* Leipzig, Seemann, 1902. (Männer der Zeit, 12).

6158. Dückers, Alexander. *Max Klinger.* Berlin, Rembrandt, 1976.

6159. Heyne, Hildegard. *Max Klinger, im Rahmen der modernen Weltanschauung und Kunst.* Leipzig, Wigand, 1907.

6160. Klinger, Max. *Briefe . . . aus den Jahren 1874 bis 1919.* Herausgegeben von Hans Wolfgang Singer. Leipzig, Seemann, 1924.

6161. ———. *Max Klinger, Carl Schirren: Briefwechsel 1910–1920.* Mit einem essay von H.G. Pfeiffer; hrsg. von Carl Schirren. Hamburg, R. Kramer, 1988.

6162. ———. *Max Klinger: Wege zum Gesamtkunstwerk.* Mit Beiträgen von Manfred Boetzkes . . . [et al.] und einer umfassenden Klinger-Dokumentation. Mainz am Rhein, P. von Zabern; Hildesheim, Roemer- und Pelizaeus-Museum, 1984.

6163. ———. *Gedanken und Bilder aus der Werkstatt des werdenden Meisters.* Herausgegeben von Dr. [Hildegard] Heyne. Leipzig, Koehler & Amelang, 1925.

6164. ———. *Malerei und Zeichnungen.* Leipzig, Insel, 1885. (Insel-Bücherei, 263).

6165. Kuhn, Paul. *Max Klinger.* Leipzig, Breitkopf, 1907.

6166. Künsthalle Bielefeld. *Max Klinger.* [October 10–November 11, 1976]. Bielefeld, Kunsthalle Bielefeld, 1976.

6167. Mathieu, Stella W., ed. *Max Klinger, Leben und Werk in Daten und Bildern.* Frankfurt a.M., Insel, 1976. (Insel Taschenbuch, 204).

6168. Meissner, Franz H. *Max Klinger.* Berlin/Leipzig, Schuster & Loeffler, 1899. (Das Künstlerbuch, 2).

6169. ———. *Max Klinger: Radierungen, Zeichnungen, Bilder und Sculpturen des Künstlers.* München, Hanfstaengl, 1896.

6170. Michalski, Martin. *Max Klinger: künstlerische Entwicklung und Wandel weltanschaulicher Gehalte in den Jahren 1878–1910.* Augsburg, AV-Verlag, 1986.

6171. Museum Boymans-van Beuningen (Rotterdam). *Max Klinger, 1857–1920; Beeldhouwwerken, Schilderijen, Tekeningen, Grafiek.* 30 September–12 November 1978. Rotterdam, Museum Boymans-van Beuningen, 1978.

6172. National Gallery of Victoria (Melbourne). *Max Klinger; love, death, and the beyond.* 26 February–12 April 1981. Melbourne, National Gallery of Victoria, 1981.

6173. Pastor, Willy. *Max Klinger.* Berlin, Amsler, 1919. 2 ed.

6174. Pfeifer, Hans-Georg. *Max Klingers (1857–1920) Graphikzyklen: Subjektivität und Kompensation im künstlerischen Symbolismus als Parallelentwicklung zu den Anfängen der Psychoanalyse.* Giessen , W. Schmitz, 1980. (Giessener Beiträge zur Kunstgeschichte, 5).

6175. Schmid, Max. *Klinger.* Bielefeld/Leipzig, Velhagen & Klasing, 1901. 2 ed. (Künstler-Monographien, 41).

6176. Servaes, Franz. *Max Klinger.* [Berlin], Bard, [1904].

6177. Singer, Hans W. *Max Klingers Radierungen, Stiche und Steindrucke; wissenschaftliches Verzeichnis.* Berlin, Amsler und Ruthardt, 1909. (CR). (Reprint: San Francisco, Wofsy, 1991).

6178. ———. *Zeichnungen von Max Klinger.* Leipzig, Schumann, 1912. (Meister der Zeichnung, 1).

6179. Tauber, Henry. *Max Klingers Exlibriswerk.* Wiesbaden. C. Wittal, 1989.

6180. Treu, Georg. *Max Klinger als Bildhauer.* Leipzig/Berlin, Seemann, 1900.

6181. Varnedoe, J. Kirk T. and Streicher, Elizabeth. *The graphic work of Max Klinger.* New York, Dover, 1977.

6182. Vogel, Julius. *Max Klinger und seine Vaterstadt Leipzig.* Leipzig, Scholl, 1923.

6183. ———. *Max Klingers Leipziger Skulpturen.* Leipzig, Seemann, 1902. 2 ed.

Kneller, Godfrey, 1646–1723

6184. Ackermann, Wilhelm A. *Der Portraitmaler Sir Godfrey Kneller.* Leipzig, Weigel, 1845.

6185. Killanin, Michael M. *Sir Godfrey Kneller and his times, 1646–1723, being a review of English portraiture of the period.* London, Batsford, 1948.

6186. Stewart, J. Douglas. *Sir Godfrey Kneller.* London, Bell, 1971. (New ed.: Oxford, Clarendon Press, 1983).

Knight, Laura, 1877–1970

6187. Bolling, G. Fredric and Whithington, Valerie, editors. *The graphic work of Laura Knight, including a catalogue raisonné of her prints.* Introduction by Irving Grose. Aldershot; Brookfield, Vermont, Scolar Press, 1993. (CR.)

6188. Fox, Caroline. *Dame Laura Knight.* Oxford, Phaidon, 1988.

Knobelsdorff, Georg Wenceslaus von, 1699–1753

6189. Eggeling, Tilo. *Studien zum friderizianischen Rokoko; Georg Wenceslaus von Knobelsdorff als Entwerfer von Innendekorationen.* Berlin, Mann, 1980.

6190. Kadatz, Hans-Joachim. *Georg Wenzeslaus von Knobelsdorff: Baumeister Friedrichs II.* Text, Hans-Joachim Kadatz; Fotos, Gerhard Murza. München, C.H. Beck, 1983.

6191. Streichhan, Annelise. *Knobelsdorff und das friderizianische Rokoko.* Burg, Hopfer, 1932.

6192. Westarp, Franz G. von. *Knobelsdorffs Rheinsberger Werk.* Würzburg, Verlagsdruckerei Würzburg, 1929.

Kobell, Ferdinand, 1740–1799
Wilhelm Alexander Wolfgang von, 1766–1855

6193. Beringer, Joseph A. *Ferdinand Kobell, eine Studie über sein Leben und Schaffen.* Mannheim, Nemnich, 1909.

6194. Biedermann, Margret. *Ferdinand Kobell, 1740–1799; das malerische und zeichnerische Werk.* München, Galerie Margret Biedermann, 1973.

6195. Gassen, Richard W. *Kobell: Handzeichnungen und Druckgraphik der Künstlerfamilie Kobell* aus städtischem Kunstbesitz. [Katalog, Richard W. Gassen]. Ludwigshafen am Rhein, Stadtmuseum, 1987.

6196. Goedl-Roth, Monika. *Wilhelm von Kobell, Druckgraphik; Studien zur Radierung und Aquatinta mit kritischem Verzeichnis.* München, Bruckmann, 1974. (CR).

6197. Kugler, Franz. *Radirungen von Ferdinand Kobell.* Stuttgart, Goepel, [1842].

6198. Lessing, Waldemar. *Wilhelm von Kobell.* München, Bruckmann, 1923. (2 ed., rev. by Ludwig Grote, 1966).

6199. Stengel, Etienne. *Catalogue raisonné des estampes de Ferdinand Kobell.* Nürnberg, Riegel et Wiesner, 1822. (CR).

6200. Wichmann, Siegfried. *Wilhelm von Kobell, Monographie und kritisches Verzeichnis der Werke.* München, Prestel, 1970. (CR).

Koch, Joseph Anton, 1768–1839

6201. Gizzi, Corrado. *Koch e Dante.* Milano, Mazzotta, 1988. [Catalogo d'una esposizone alla "Casa di Dante in Abruzzo, Castello Gizzi, Torre de' Passeri, sett.–ott., 1988].

6202. Holst, Christian von. *Joseph Anton Koch, 1768–1839, Ansichten der Natur.* [Katalog der Ausstellung]. Staatsgalerie Stuttgart, 26 August bis 29. Oktober 1989. Stuttgart, Edition Cantz, 1989.

6203. Jaffé, Ernst. *Joseph Anton Koch, sein Leben und sein Schaffen.* Innsbruck, Wagner, 1905.

6204. Lutterotti, Otto R. von. *Joseph Anton Koch, 1768–1839.* Berlin, Deutscher Verein für Künstwissenschaft, 1940.

6205. Mark, Hans. *Der Maler Joseph Anton Koch und seine Tiroler Heimat.* Innsbruck, Wagner, 1939.

Koch, Rudolf, 1876–1934

6206. Haupt, Georg. *Rudolf Koch der Schreiber.* Leipzig, Insel, 1936.

6207. Koch, Rudolph. *The book of signs, which contains all manner of symbols used from the earliest times to the middle ages by primitive peoples and early Christians.* Trans. by Vyvyan Holland. New York, Dover, [1957].

Koenig, Fritz, 1924–

6208. Koenig, Fritz. *Fritz Koenig: Skulptur und Zeichnung.* Hrsg. von Peter-Klaus Schuster. Mit Beiträgen von Dietrich Clarenbach, Eugen Gomringer, et al. . . . [Katalog der Ausstellung in der Neuen Pinakothek, München, vom 6. Mai bis 10. Juli, 1988 und in der Akademie der Künste, Berlin vom 5. März bis 30. April 1989]. München. Prestel-Verlag, 1988.

Koenig, Leo von, 1871–1944

6209. Kroll, Bruno. *Leo von König.* Berlin, Rembrandt, 1941.

6210. Nemitz, Fritz. *Leo von König.* Berlin-Frohnau, Ottens, 1930.

6211. Schneider, Reinhold. *Gestalt und Seele, das Werk des Malers Leo von König.* Leipzig, Insel, 1936.

Koetsu, Homani, 1558–1637

6212. Leach, Bernard H. *Kenzan and his tradition; the lives and times of Koetsu, Sotatsu, Korin, and Kenzan.* London, Faber, 1966.

6213. Ushikubo, D. *J. R. Life of Kôyetsu.* [Text in English]. Kyoto, Igyoku-do, 1926.

Kokei, Kobayashi, 1883–1957

6214. Kawakita, Michiaki. *Kobayashi Kokei (1883–1957).* English adaptation by Ray Andrew Miller. Rutland, Vt./Tokyo, Tuttle, 1957. (Kodansha Library of Japanese Art, 11).

Kokoschka, Oskar, 1886–1980

6215. Biermann, Georg. *Oskar Kokoschka.* Leipzig/Berlin, Klinkhardt & Biermann, 1929. (Junge Kunst, 52).

6216. Braham, Helen. Kokoschka: *Prints, illustrated books, drawings in the Princes Gate Collection. With notes on the paintings.* [Catalogue of an exhibition held at the Courtauld Institute Galleries, from 9 September to 28 October 1992]. London, The Galleries, 1992.

6217. Bultmann, Bernhard. *Oskar Kokoschka.* Salzburg, Galerie Welz, 1959.

6218. Calvocoressi, Richard. *Kokoschka.* Recklinghausen, Bongers, 1992.

6219. Gatt, Giuseppe. *Oskar Kokoschka.* Firenze, Sansoni, 1970. (I maestri del novecento, 15).

6220. Goldscheider, Ludwig. *Kokoschka.* London, Phaidon, 1963; distributed by New York Graphic Society, Greenwich, Conn., 1966.

6221. Hodin, Josef P. *Kokoschka, the artist and his time.* Greenwich, Conn., New York Graphic Society, 1966.

6222. ———. *Oskar Kokoschka, eine Psychographie.* Wien, Europa, 1971.

6223. ———, ed. *Bekenntnis zu Kokoschka, Erinnerungen und Deutungen.* Berlin/Mainz, Kupferberg, 1963.

6224. Hoffmann, Edith. *Kokoschka, his life and work.* London, Faber, 1947.

6225. Kokoschka, Oskar. *Briefe.* 4 v. Herausgegeben von Olda Kokoschka und Heinz Spielmann. Düsseldorf, Claassen Verlag, 1984–1988.

6226. ———. *My life.* Trans. by David Britt. New York, Macmillan, 1974.

6227. ———. *Oskar Kokoschka: Letters 1905–1976.* Edited by Olda Kokoschka and Alfred Marnau. Foreword by E.H. Gombrich. Trans. Mary Whitall. New York, Thames and Hudson, 1992.

6228. ———. *Oskar Kokoschka, 1886–1980: Welt-Theater, Bühnenbilder und Illustrationen 1907–1975.* Ein Werkverzeichnis bearbeitet von Heinz Spielmann, mit Beriträgen von Otto Breicha, Martin Hürlimann und H. Spielmann. [Katalog der Ausstellungen: Museum für Kunst und Gewerbe Hamburg, 1. März–27. April 1986; Salzburger Landessammlungen Rupertinum, Juni/Juli 1986]. Hamburg, Museum für Kunst und Gewerbe, 1986.

6229. ———. *Das schriftliche Werk.* Ed. by Heinz Spielmann. 4 v. Hamburg, Christians, 1973–76.

6230. Institute of Contemporary Art (Boston). *Oskar Kokoschka, a retrospective exhibition, with an introduction by James S. Plaut.* New York, Chanticleer Press, 1948.

6231. Rathenau, Ernst, ed. *Oskar Kokoschka, Handzeichnungen.* 5 v. New York, Rathenau/Berlin, Euphorion, 1936–1977. (CR).

6232. Sabarsky, Serge. *Oscar Kokoschka, die frühen Jahre, 1906–1926: Aquarelle und Zeichnungen.* S. Sabarsky; mit Beiträgen von Werner Hofmann und Willi Hahn. München, R. Jentsch, 1986.

6233. Salzburger Residenzgalerie (Salzburg). *Oskar Kokoschka vom Erlebnis im Leben.* März/April 1976. Salzburg, Galerie Welz, 1976.

6234. Schröder, Klaus Albrecht and Winkler, Johann, eds. *Oskar Kokoschka.* München, Prestel Verlag, 1991.

6235. Schvey, Henry I. *Oskar Kokoschka, the painter as playwright.* Detroit, Wayne State University Press, 1982.

6236. Solomon R. Guggenheim Museum (New York). *Oskar Kokoscha, 1886–1980.* [Catalogue of an exhibition]. Texts by Richard Calvocoressi and Katharina Schulz. New York, Guggenheim Foundation, 1986.

6237. Tate Gallery (London). *Oskar Kokoschka, 1886–1980.* [Exhibition catalogue]. London, Tate Gallery, 1986.

6238. Werner, Norbert. *Kokoschka: Leben und Werk in Daten und Bildern.* Herausgegeben von N. Werner. Frankfurt am Main. Inselverlag, 1991.

6239. Westheim, Paul. *Oskar Kokoschka.* Berlin, Cassirer, 1925. 2 ed.

6240. Whitford, Frank. *Oskar Kokoschka, a life.* New York, Atheneum, 1986.

6241. Wingler, Hans M. *Oskar Kokoschka, the work of the artist.* Salzburg, Galerie Welz, 1956.

6242. ———, ed. *Oskar Kokoschka, ein Lebensbild in zeitgenössischen Dokumenten.* München, Langen/Müller, 1956. (Langen-Müller's kleine Geschenkbücher, 56).

6243. ——— [and] Welz, Friedrich. *Oskar Kokoschka, das druckgraphische Werk.* Salzburg, Galerie Welz, 1975. (CR).

Kolbe, Georg, 1877–1947

6244. Berger, Ursel. *Georg Kolbe, Leben und Werk.* Mit dem Katalog der Kolbe-Plastiken im Georg-Kolbe-Museum Berlin. Berlin, Gebr. Mann Verlag, 1990.(CR).

6245. Binding, Rudolf G. *Vom Leben der Plastik; Inhalt und Schönheit des Werkes von Georg Kolbe.* Berlin, Rembrandt, 1933.

6246. Justi, Ludwig. *Georg Kolbe.* Berlin, Klinkhardt & Biermann, 1931. (Junge Kunst, 60).

6247. Kolbe, Georg. *Auf Wegen der Kunst; Schriften, Skizzen, Plastiken.* Berlin-Zehlendorf, Lemmer, 1949.

6248. ———. *Briefe und Aufzeichnungen.* [Ed. by] Maria Freifrau von Tiesenhausen. Tübingen, Wasmuth, 1987.

6249. Pinder, Wilhelm. *Georg Kolbe, Zeichnungen.* Berlin, Rembrandt, 1942.

6250. Scheibe, Richard. *Georg Kolbe, 100 Licht-drucktafeln.* Marburg/Lahn, Verlag des Künstgeschichtlichen Seminars, 1931.

6251. Valentiner, Wilhelm R. *Georg Kolbe, Plastik und Zeichnungen.* München, Wolff, 1922.

Kollwitz, Käthe Schmidt, 1867–1945

6252. Akademie der Künste (Berlin). *Käthe Kollwitz, 1867–1945.* 10. Dezember 1967 bis zum 7. Januar 1968. Berlin, Akademie der Künste, 1967.

6253. Art Museum and Galleries, California State University (Long Beach, Calif.). *Käthe Kollwitz/Jake Zeitlin Bookshop and Gallery: 1937.* November 26–December 19, 1979. Long Beach, Calif., Art Museum and Galleries, 1979.

6254. Bauer, Arnold. *Käthe Kollwitz.* Berlin, Colloquium, 1967. (Köpfe des XX. Jahrhunderts, 19).

6255. Bittner, Herbert. *Käthe Kollwitz drawings.* New York, Yoseloff, 1959.

6256. Bonus, Arthur. *Das Kaethe Kollwitz-Werk.* Dresden, Reissner, 1914.

6257. Bonus-Jeep, Beate. *Sechzig Jahre Freundschaft mit Käthe Kollwitz.* Boppard, Rauch, 1948. (Reprint: Bremen, Schünemann, 1963).

6258. Diel, Louise. *Käthe Kollwitz, ein Ruf ertönt: eine Einführung in das Lebenswerk der Künstlerin.* Berlin, Furche, 1927.

6259. Fanning, Robert J. *Kaethe Kollwitz.* Karlsruhe, Müller, 1956; distributed by Wittenborn, New York.

6260. Heilborn, Adolf. *Käthe Kollwitz.* Berlin, Lemmer, 1949. 2 ed.

6261. Hinz, Renate. *Käthe Kollwitz: Druckgrafik, Plakate, Zeichnungen.* Berlin, Elefanten Press, 1981. 2 ed.

6262. Kaemmerer, Ludwig. *Kaethe Kollwitz, Griffelkunst und Weltanschauung.* Dresden, Richter, 1923.

6263. Kearns, Martha. *Käthe Kollwitz: woman and artist.* Old Westbury, N.Y., Feminist Press, 1976.

6264. Klein, Mina C. [and] Klein, H. Arthur. *Käthe Kollwitz; life in art.* New York, Holt, Rinehart, 1972.

6265. Klipstein, August. *Käthe Kollwitz; Verzeichnis des graphischen Werkes.* Bern, Klipstein, 1955. (CR).

6266. Koerber, Lenka von. *Erlebtes mit Käthe Kollwitz.* Berlin, Rütten & Loening, 1957.

6267. Kollwitz, Hans, ed. *Käthe Kollwitz, das plastische Werk.* Hamburg, Wegner, 1967.

6268. Kollwitz, Käthe. *Aus meinem Leben.* München, List, 1957. (List-Bücher, 92).

6269. ———. *Briefe an den Sohn 1904–1945.* Hrsg. von Jutta Bohnke-Kollwitz. Berlin, Siedler, 1992.

6270. ———. *The diary and letters of Käthe Kollwitz.* Ed. by Hans Kollwitz. Trans. by Richard and Clara Winston. Chicago, Regnery, 1955. (2 ed.: Evanston, Ill., Northwestern University Press, 1988).

6271. ———. *Ich sah die Welt mit liebevollen Blicken; ein Leben in Selbstzeugnissen.* Ed. by Hans Kollwitz. Hannover, Fackelträger, 1968.

6272. ———. *Ich will wirken in dieser Zeit.* Berlin, Mann, 1952.

6273. ———. *Käthe Kollwitz: Druckgraphik, Handzeichnungen, Plastik.* Hrsg. von Herwig Guratzsch. Stuttgart, G. Hatje, 1990.

6274. ———. *Käthe Kollwitz: works in color.* Edited and with an introduction by Tom Fecht. Trans. by A.S. Wensinger and R.H. Wood. New York, Schocken Books, 1988.

6275. ———. *Die Kollwitz-Sammlung des Dresdner Kupferstich-Kabinettes: Graphik und Zeichnungen, 1890–1912.* Hrsg. von Werner Schmidt. Köln, Käthe Kollwitz Museum: DuMont, 1988.

6276. ———. *Tagebuchblätter und Briefe.* Ed. by Hans Kollwitz. Berlin, Mann, 1948.

6277. ———. *Die Tagebücher.* Hrsg. von Jutta Bohnke-Kollwitz; [Redaktion der Anmerkungen, Volker Frankl. Berlin, Siedler, 1989.

6278. Nagel, Otto. *The drawings of Käthe Kollwitz.* New York, Crown, 1972. (CR).

6279. ———. *Käthe Kollwitz.* Trans. by Stella Humphries. Greenwich, Conn., New York Graphic Society, 1971.

6280. Prelinger, Elizabeth. *Käthe Kollwitz.* [Catalogue of an exhibition] by] E. Prelinger with essays by Alessandra Comini and Hildegard Bachert. Foreword by J. Carter Brown. New Haven, Yale University Press in association with the National Gallery of Art, 1992.

6281. Schneede, Uwe M. *Käthe Kollwitz, das zeichnerische Werk.* München, Schirmer-Mosel, 1981.

6282. Sievers, Johannes. *Die Radierungen und Steindrucke von Käthe Kollwitz innerhalt der Jahre 1890 bis 1912; ein beschreibendes Verzeichnis.* Dresden, Holst, 1913. (CR).

6283. Singer, Hans W. *Käthe Kollwitz.* Esslingen, Neff, 1908. (Führer zur Kunst, 15).

6284. Strauss, Gerhard. *Käthe Kollwitz.* Dresden, Sachsenverlag, 1950.

6285. Wagner, A. *Die Radierungen, Holzschnitte, und Lithographien von Käthe Kollwitz; eine Zusammenstellung der seit 1912 entstandenen graphischen Arbeiten in chronologischer Folge.* Dresden, Richter, 1927. (CR).

6286. Zigrosser, Carl. *Kaethe Kollwitz.* New York, Bittner, 1946.

Koninck, Philips, 1619–1688

6287. Gerson, Horst. *Philips Koninck, ein Beitrag zur Erforschung der holländischen Malerei des XVII. Jahrhunderts.* Berlin, Mann, 1980. 2 ed. (CR).

Konrad von Soest *see* Soest, Conrad von

Kooning, Willem de *see* De Kooning, Willem

Koons, Jeff, 1955–

6288. Koons, Jeff. *Jeff Koons.* [Organisatie tentoonstelling, Wim Beeren]. Amsterdam, Stedelijke Museum, 1992.

6289. ———. *Jeff Koons.*[Exhibition catalogue]. San Francisco Museum of Modern Art. San Francisco, San Francisco Museum of Modern Art, 1992.

6290. ———. *The Jeff Koons handbook.* Introduction by Robert Rosenblum. New York, Rizzoli, 1992.

Korin, Ogata, 1658–1716 *see also* Koetsu, Honami

6291. Mizuo, Hiroshi. *Edo painting: Sotatsu and Korin.* Trans. by John M. Shields. New York, Weatherhill, 1972. (Heibonsha survey of Japanese art, 18).

6292. Noguchi, Yone. *Korin.* London, Matthews, 1922.

6293. Perzyński, Friedrich. *Korin und seine Zeit.* Berlin, Marquart, [1907].

Krafft, Adam, ca. 1455–ca. 1509

6294. Daun, Berthold. *Adam Krafft und die Künstler seiner Zeit.* Berlin, Hertz, 1897.

6295. Schwemmer, Wilhelm. *Adam Kraft.* Nürnberg, Carl, 1958.

6296. Stern, Dorothea. *Der Nürnberger Bildhauer Adam Kraft, Stilentwicklung und Chronologie seiner Werke.* Strassburg, Heitz, 1916. (Studien zur deutschen Kunstgeschichte, 191).

6297. Wanderer, Friedrich. *Adam Krafft und seine Schule, 1490–1507.* [Text in German, French and English]. Nürnberg, Schrag, 1868.

Kraft, Adam *see* Krafft, Adam

Kramskoi, Ivan Nikolaevich, 1837–1887

6298. Davydova, Alla S. *Kramskoi.* Moskva, Iskusstvo, 1962.

6299. Goldshtein, Sofia N. *Ivan Nikolaevich Kramskoi, zhizn' i tvorchestvo.* Moskva, Iskusstvo, 1965.

6300. Kramskoi, Ivan N. *Pis'ma.* 2 v. [Moskva], Gosudarstvennoe izdatel'stvo izobrazitel'nykh iskusstvo, 1937.

6301. ———. *Kramskoi ob iskusstve.* [Sostavitel', avtor vstupitel'noi stat'i i primechanii T.M.

Kovalenskaia]. Moskva, "Izobrazitel'noe iskusstvo", 1988.

6302. Kurochkina, Tatiana I. *Ivan Nikolaevich Kramskoi.* Moskva, Izobrazitel'noe iskusstvo, 1980. (2 ed.: Leningrad, Khudozhnik RSFSR, 1989).

6303. Lapunova, Nina F. *Ivan Nikolaevich Kramskoi, monograficheskii ocherk.* Moskva, Iskusstvo, 1964.

6304. Stasiv, V., ed. *Ivan Nikolaevich Kramskoi; ego zhizn', perepiska, i khudozhestvennoe kriticheskie stat'i, 1837–1887.* S. Petersburg, Suvorin, 1888.

Krasner, Lee, 1908–

6305. Hobbs, Robert Carleton. *Lee Krasner.* New York, Abbeville Press, 1993.

6306. Krasner, Lee. *Lee Krasner; collages.* [Exhibition catalogue]. Essay by Bryan Robertson; introduction by Robert Hughes. New York, Robert Miller Gallery, 1986.

6307. ———. *Lee Krasner: Paintings from the late fifties.* [Exhibition catalogue]. Robert Miller Gallery, Otober 26–November 20, 1982. New York, the Gallery, 1982.

6308. ———. *Lee Krasner: umber paintings, 1959-1962.* [Exhibition catalogue]. Interview by Richard Howard; organized by John Cheim. New York, Robert Miller Gallery, 1993.

6309. Rose, Barbara. *Lee Krasner, a retrospective.* [Exhibition catalogue]. Houston, Houston Museum of Fine Arts; New York, Museum of Modern Art. 1983.

Kricke, Norbert, 1922–

6310. Morschel, Jürgen. *Norbert Kricke.* Stuttgart, Hatje, 1976.

6311. Museum of Modern Art (New York). *Norbert Kricke.* [March 2–April 2, 1961]. New York, Museum of Modern Art, 1961.

6312. Thwaites, John A. *Kricke.* New York, Abrams, 1964.

6313. Trier, Eduard. *Norbert Kricke.* Recklinghausen, Bongers, 1963. (Monographien zur rheinisch-westfälischen Kunst der Gegenwart, 28).

6314. Wilhelm-Lehmbruck-Museum der Stadt Duisburg/Städtische Kunsthalle Düsseldorf. *Norbert Kricke.* [June 28–August 31, 1975]. Duisburg/Düsseldorf, Museum/Kunsthalle, 1975.

Ku K'ai-Chih, c. 345–405

6315. Chen, Shih-Hsiang. *Biography of Ku K'ai-chih.* Trans. and annotated by Chen Shih-Hsiang. Berkeley and Los Angeles, University of California Press, 1953. (University of California Institute of East Asiatic Studies, Chinese Dynastic Histories Translations, 2).

Kubin, Alfred, 1877–1959

6316. Bayerische Akademie der Schönen Künste (Munich). *Alfred Kubin, 1877–1959.* 26. Juni bis 9. Oktober 1964. München, Bayerische Akademie der Schönen Künste, 1964.

6317. Bisanz, Hans. *Alfred Kubin; Zeichner, Schriftsteller und Philosoph.* München, Spangenberg, 1977.

6318. Bredt, Ernst W. *Alfred Kubin.* München, Schmidt, 1922.

6319. Breicha, Otto, ed. *Alfred Kubin Weltgeflecht, ein Kubin-Kompendium; Schriften und Bilder zu Leben und Werk.* München, Spangenberg, 1978.

6320. Esswein, Hermann. *Alfred Kubin, der Künstler und sein Werk.* München, Müller, [1911].

6321. Horodisch, Abraham. *Alfred Kubin Taschenbibliographie.* Amsterdam, Erasmus, 1962.

6322. ———, ed. *Alfred Kubin, book illustrator.* New York, Aldus, 1950.

6323. Kubin, Alfred. *Aus meinem Leben.* Ed. by Ulrich Riemerschmidt. München, Spangenberg, 1974.

6324. ———. *Aus meiner Werkstatt.* Ed. by Ulrich Riemerschmidt. München, Nymphenburger, 1973.

6325. ———. *Die wilde Rast; Alfred Kubin in Waldhäuser.* Briefe an Reinhold und Hanne Koeppel. Ed. by Walter Boll. München, Nymphenburger, 1972.

6326. Künstgeschichtliches Institut der Johannes Gutenberg-Universität Mainz. *Handzeichnungen, Aquarelle und Druckgraphik von Alfred Kubin, 1877–1959.* [Text by Friedrich Gerke]. 2. Dezember 1964–10. Januar 1965. Mainz, Kunstgeschichtliches Institut, 1964. (Kleine Schriften der Gesellschaft für Bildende Kunst in Mainz, 24).

6327. Kunstsammlung der Universität Göttingen. *Alfred Kubin; Mappenwerke, Bücher, Einzelblätter aus der Sammlung Hedwig und Helmut Goedeckemeyer.* [January 20–March 30, 1980]. Göttingen, Kunstgeschichtliches Seminar der Universität Göttingen, 1980.

6328. Marks, Alfred. *Der Illustrator Alfred Kubin, Gesamtkatalog seiner Illustrationen und buchkünstlerischen Arbeiten.* München, Spangenberg, 1977. (CR).

6329. Mitsch, Erwin. *Alfred Kubin, Zeichnungen.* Salzburg, Galerie Welz, 1967.

6330. Müller-Thalheim, Wolfgang K. *Erotik und Dämonie im Werk Alfred Kubins, eine psychopathologische Studie.* München, Nymphenburger, 1970.

6331. Raabe, Paul, ed. *Alfred Kubin; Leben, Werk, Wirkung.* Hamburg, Rowohlt, 1957.

6332. Rhein, Philip H. *The verbal and visual arts of Alfred Kubin.* Riverside, Calif., Ariadne Press, 1989.

6333. Rosenberger, Ludwig. *Wanderungen zu Alfred Kubin, aus dem Briefwechsel.* München, Heimeran, 1969.

6334. Schmidt, Paul F. *Alfred Kubin.* Leipzig, Klinkhardt & Biermann, 1924. (Junge Künst, 44).

6335. Schmied, Wieland. *Der Zeichner Alfred Kubin.* Salzburg, Residenz, 1967.

6336. Schneditz, Wolfgang. *Alfred Kubin.* Wien, Rosenbaum, 1956.

6337. Seipel, Wilfried. *Alfred Kubin, der Zeichner 1877–1959.* Wien, C. Brandstätter, 1988.

6338. Staatliche Kunsthalle Baden-Baden. *Alfred Kubin, das zeichnerische Frühwerk bis 1904.* 1. April bis 30. Mai 1977. Baden-Baden, Staatliche Kunsthalle, 1977.

6339. Van Zon, Gabriele. *Word and picture, a study of the double talent in Alfred Kubin and Fritz von Hermanovsky-Orlando.* New York, P. Lang, 1991.

Kuepper, Christian E. M. *see* Doesburg, Theo van

Kuhn, Walt, 1877–1949

6340. Adams, Philip R. *Walt Kuhn, painter; his life and work.* Columbus, Ohio, Ohio State University Press, 1978. (CR).

6341. Bird, Paul. *Fifty paintings by Walt Kuhn.* New York, Studio, 1940.

6342. Kuhn, Walt. *The story of the Armory show.* New York, Kuhn, 1938.

6343. University of Arizona Art Gallery (Tucson, Ariz.). *Painter of vision, a retrospective exhibition of oils, watercolors, and drawings by Walt Kuhn, 1877–1949.* Feb. 6– March 31, [1966]. Tucson, Ariz., Board of Regents of the Universities and State College of Arizona, 1966.

Kulmbach, Hans Suess von, 1480–1522

6344. Koelitz, Karl. *Hans Suess von Kulmbach und seine Werke.* Leipzig, Seemann, 1891. (Beiträge zur Kunstgeschichte, neue Folge, 12).

6345. Stadler, Franz. *Hans von Kulmbach.* Wien, Schroll, 1936.

6346. Winkler, Friedrich. *Hans von Kulmbach, Leben und Werk eines fränkischen Künstlers der Dürerzeit.* [Kulmbach], Staatsarchiv Kulmbach, 1959. (Die Plassenburg, Schriften für Heimatforschung und Kulturpflege in Ostfranken, 14).

6347. ———. *Die Zeichnungen Hans Süss von Kulmbachs und Hans Leonhard Schäufeleins.* Berlin, Deutscher Verein für Kunstwissenschaft, 1942.

Kuniyoshi, Utagawa, 1798–1861

6348. Forrer, Matthi. *Drawings by Utagawa Kuniyoshi from the collection of the National Museum of Ethnology, Leiden.* The Hague, SDU Publishers, 1988.

6349. Robinson, Basil W. *Kuniyoshi*. London, HMSO, 1961.

6350. ———. *Kuniyoshi, the warrior prints.* Ithaca, N.Y., Cornell University Press/London, Phaidon, 1983.

6351. Speiser, Werner. *Kuniyoshi*. Bad Wildungen, Siebenberg, 1969.

6352. Springfield Museum of Fine Arts (Springfield, Mass.). *Utagawa Kuniyoshi*. Springfield, Mass., Springfield Library and Museums Association, 1980.

Kuniyoshi, Yasuo, 1893–1953

6353. Davis, Richard A. *Yasuo Kuniyoshi:the complete graphic work.* San Francisco, Alan Wofsy Fine Arts, 1991.(CR).

6354. Goodrich, Lloyd. *Yasuo Kuniyoshi*. New York, Whitney Museum of American Art/Macmillan, 1948.

Kupecký, Jan, 1667–1740

6355. Dvořák, František. *Kupecký, the great baroque portrait painter.* Trans. by. Hedda Stránská. Prague, Artia, [1956].

6356. Nyári, Alexander. *Der Porträtmaler Johann Kupetzky, sein Leben und seine Werke.* Wien, Hartleben, 1889.

6357. Šafařik, Eduard. *Joannes Kupezky, 1667–1740.* Prague, Orbis, 1928.

Kupelwieser, Leopold, 1796–1862

6358. Feuchtmüller, Rupert. *Leopold Kupelwieser und die Kunst der österreichischen Spätromantik.* Wien, Österreichischer Bundesverlag für Unterricht, Wissenschaft und Kunst, 1970.

Kupezky, Johann *see* Kupecky, Jan

Kupka, Frank *see* Kupka, František

Kupka, František, 1871–1957

6359. Arnold-Grémilly, Louis. *Frank Kupka*. Paris, Povolozky, 1922.

6360. Cassou, Jean et Fédit, Denise. *Kupka*. Paris, Tisné, 1964.

6361. Fauchereau, Serge. *Kupka*. Paris, Editions Albin Michel, 1988.

6362. Galerie Gmurzynska (Cologne). *Frank Kupka*. Februar–April 1981. [Text in German and English]. Köln, Galerie Gmurzynska, 1981.

6363. Kupka, František. *František Kupka, 1871–1957, ou, L'invention d'une abstraction.* Musée d'art moderne de la ville de Paris, 22 novembre 1989–25 février 1990. Paris, Paris-Musées, 1989.

6364. Solomon R. Guggenheim Museum (New York). *Frantisek Kupka, 1871–1957; a retrospective.* [May 1975]. New York, Guggenheim Foundation, 1975.

6365. Vachtová, Ludmila. *Frank Kupka, pioneer of modern art.* Trans. by Zdenek Lederer. New York, McGraw-Hill, 1968. (CR).

Kuznetsov, Pavel Varfoloneevich, 1878–1968

6366. Stupples, Peter. *Pavel Kuznetsov: his life and art.* Cambridge, Cambridge, etc. Cambridge University Press, 1989.

L

Labille-Guiard, Adélaï de, 1749–1803

6367. Passez, Anne M. *Adélaïde Labille-Guiard, 1749–1803; biographie et catalogue raisonné de son oeuvre.* Paris, Arts et Métiers Graphiques, 1973. (CR).

6368. Portalis, Roger. *Adélaïde Labille-Guiard.* Paris, Petit, 1902.

Laboureur Jean Émile, 1877–1943

6369. Godefroy, Louis. *L'oeuvre gravé de Jean Laboureur.* v.1– . Paris, Godefroy, 1929– . (All published). CR).

6370. Laboureur, Jean-Émile. *Jean-Émile Laboureur.* [Exhibition catalogue]. Musée du Dessin et de l'Estampe originale en l'Arsenal de Gravelines, 1987.

6371. ———. *Jean-Émile Laboureur, 1877–1843: prints, drawings, and books.* New York, French Institute/ Alliance française, 1977.

6372. Laboureur, Sylvain. *Catalogue complet de l'oeuvre de Jean-Emile Laboureur.* 4 v. Neuchatel, Ides et Calendes, 1989–1991. (CR)

6373. Loyer, Jacqueline. *Laboureur: l'oeuvre gravé et lithographié.* Paris, Imprimerie Tournon, 1962.

Lachaise, Gaston, 1882–1935

6374. Carr, Carolyn Kinder. *Gaston Lachaise: portrait, sculpture.* By C. Kinder Carr and Margaret C.S. Christman. Washington, D.C., National Portrait Gallery, Smithsonian Institution, in association with the Smithsonian Institution Press, 1985.

6375. Gallatin, Albert E. *Gaston Lachaise.* New York, Dutton, 1924.

6376. Kramer, Hilton, et al. *The sculpture of Gaston Lachaise.* New York, Eakins Press, 1967.

6377. Lachaise, Gaston. *Gaston Lachaise: sculpture.* Essay by Barbara Rose. [Exhibition catalogue]. New York, Salander-O'Reilly Galleries; Houston, Texas, Meredith Long & Co., 1991.

6378. Museum of Modern Art (New York). *Gaston Lachaise, retrospective exhibition.* January 30–March 7, 1935. [Text by Lincoln Kirstein]. New York, Museum of Modern Art, 1935.

6379. Nordland, Gerald. *Gaston Lachaise, the man and his work.* New York, Braziller, 1974.

6380. Wassermann, Jeanne L. *Three American Sculptors and the female nude: Lachaise, Nadelman, Archipenko.* By Jeanne L. Wasserman, with contributions by James B. Cuno. Cambridge, Mass., Fogg Art Museum, 1980.

6381. Whitney Museum of American Art (New York). *Gaston Lachaise, a concentration of works from the permanent collection.* March 5–April 27, 1980. New York, Whitney Museum of American Art, 1980.

La Farge, John, 1835–1910

6382. Adams, Henry, et al. *John La Farge.* New York, Abbeville, 1987.

6383. Cortissoz, Royal. *John La Farge, a memoir and a study.* Boston/New York, Houghton Mifflin, 1911. (Reprint: New York, Da Capo, 1971).

6384. La Farge, John. *An American artist in the South Seas. [Reminiscences of the South Seas].* London; New York, KPI; New York, distributed by Methuen, 1987.

6385. La Farge, John. *An artist's letter from Japan.* New York, Century, 1897.

6386. ———. *Considerations on painting; lectures given in the year 1893 at the Metropolitan Museum of New York.* New York, Macmillan, 1895.

6387. Metropolitan Museum of Art (New York). *An exhibition of the work of John La Farge.* March 23 to April 26, 1936. New York, Metropolitan Museum of Art, 1936.

6388. Waern, Cecilia. *John La Farge, artist and writer.* London, Seeley/New York, Macmillan, 1896. (Portfolio Monographs, 26).

6389. Yarnall, James L. *John La Farge, watercolors and drawings.* [Exhibition catalogue]. With an introduction by Barbara Bloemink. Yonkers, N.Y., Hudson River Museum of Westchester, 1990.

Lafrensen, Nicolas, 1737–1807

6390. Bibliothèque Nationale (Paris). *Lavreince; Nicolas Lafrensen, peintre suédois, 1737–1807.* Mai–juin, 1949. Paris, Bibliothèque Nationale, 1949.

6391. Bocher, Emmanuel. *Nicholas Lavreince, catalogue raisonné des estampes.* Paris, Librairie des Bibliophiles, 1874. (Les gravures francaises du XVIIIe siècle, 2). (CR).

6392. Levertin, Oscar I. *Nicolas Lafrensen d. y. och forbindelserna mellan svensk och fransk mâlarkonst pâ 1700—talet, konsthistorisk studie.* Stockholm, Bonnier, 1910. 2 ed.

6393. Wennberg, Bo G. *Niclas Lafrensen, den yngre.* Malmö, Allhem, 1947.

La Fresnaye, Roger de, 1885–1925

6394. Allard, Roger. *R. de La Fresnaye.* Paris, Editions de la Nouvelle Revue Française, 1922.

6395. Cogniat, Raymond [and] George, Waldemar. *Oeuvre complète de Roger de la Fresnaye.* Paris, Rivarol, 1950.

6396. Gaffé, René. *Roger de La Fresnaye.* Bruxelles, Editions des Artistes, 1956.

6397. Nebelthau, Eberhard. *Roger de La Fresnaye.* Paris, Montaignac, 1935.

6398. Seligman, Germain. *Roger de La Fresnaye.* Greenwich, Conn., New York Graphic Society, 1969. (CR).

Lairesse, Gérard de, 1640–1711

6399. Roy, Alain. *Gérard de Lairesse, 1640–1711.* Préface de Jacques Thuillier, Paris, Arthena, 1992.

Lalique, René, 1860–1945

6400. Barten, Sigrid. *René Lalique; Schmuck und Objets d'art, 1890–1910.* Monographie und Werkkatalog. München, Prestel, 1977. (CR). (Materialen zur Künst des 19. Jahrhunderts, 22).

6401. Bayer, Patricia. *The Art of René Lalique.* By P. Bayer and Mark Waller. London, Bloomsbury Publishing, 1988.

6402. Lalique, Marie-Claud. *Lalique.* Genève, EDIPOP, 1988.

6403. Lalique, René. *René Lalique: jewelry glass.* [Exhibition director, Yvonne Brunhammer; translation. Deke Dusinberre . . . et al.]. Paris, Musée des arts décoratifs, Réunion des musées nationaux, 1991.

6404. Geffroy, Gustave. *Renee Lalique.* Paris, Mary, 1922.

6405. Marcilhac, Félix. *René Lalique, 1860–1945,*

maître verrier. Analyse de l'oeuvre et catalogue raisonné. Paris, Editions de l'amateur, 1989. (CR).

6406. McClinton, Katharine M. *Lalique for collectors.* New York, Scribner, 1975.

6407. Percy, Christopher V. *The glass of Lalique, a collector's guide.* London, Studio Vista, 1977.

Lam, Wifredo, 1902–1982

6408. Lam, Wifredo. *Wifredo Lam.* [Exhibition]. Museo Nacional Centro de Arte Reina Sofia, Madrid/Fundacion Joan Miro, Barcelona. Madrid, Museu Nacional, 1992.

6409. ———. *Wifredo Lam.* Mit Beiträgen von Pierre Gaudibert . . . [et al.] und einem Geleitwort von Graham Greene. [Ausstellung und Katalog] von Ulrich Krempell. Düsseldorf, Kunstsammlungen Nordrhein-Westfalen, 1988.

6410. ———. *Exposicion "Homenaje Wifredo Lam" 1902–1982:* Museo Nacional de Arte Contemporaneo, Musée d'art modene de la ville de Paris, Musee d'Ixelles, Bruxelles. Catalogo, José Ayllon. Madrid, Ministerio de Cultura de España, Direccion General de Bellas Artes, Archivos y Bibliotecas, 1982.

Lamberti, Niccolò, d. 1451 Piero, fl. 1393–1437

6411. Goldner, George R. *Niccolò and Piero Lamberti.* New York and London, Garland, 1978.

6412. Salmi, Mario. *La vita di Niccolò di Piero, scultore e architetto aretino.* Arezzo, Presso gli Amici dei Monumenti, 1910.

Lami, Eugène Louis, 1800–1890

6413. Lemoisne, Paul-André. *Eugène Lami, 1800–1890.* Paris, Goupil, 1912.

6414. ———. *L'oeuvre d'Eugène Lami (1800–1890); lithographiés, dessins, aquarelles, peintures.* Essai d'un catalogue raisonné. Paris, Champion, 1914. (CR).

Lancret, Nicolas, 1690–1743

6415. Ballot de Sovot. *Eloge de Lancret, peintre du roi [1743].* Accompagné de diverses notes sur Lancret, de pièces inédites et du catalogue de ses tableaux et de ses estampes. Réunis et publiés par J. J. Guiffrey. Paris, Baur, [1874]. (Collection de travaux sur l'art français, 5).

6416. Bocher, Emmanuel. *Nicolas Lancret.* Paris, Librairie des Bibliophiles, 1877. (CR). (Les gravures françaises du XVIIIe siècle, 4).

6417. Holmes, Mary Tavener. *Nicolas Lancret, 1690–1743.* Edited by Joseph Focarino. New york, H.N. Abrams in association with the Frick Collection, 1991.

6418. Wildenstein, Georges. *Lancret, biographie et catalogue critique.* Paris, Servant, 1924. (CR).

Landseer, Edwin Henry, 1802–1873

6419. Dafforne, James. *Pictures by Sir Edwin Landseer, Royal Academician; with descriptions and a biographical sketch of the painter.* London, Virtue, [1874].

6420. Hurll, Estelle M. *Landseer, a collection of pictures with introduction and interpretation.* Boston, Houghton Mifflin, 1901. (Riverside Art Series, 9).

6421. Lennie, Campbell. *Landseer, the Victorian paragon.* London, Hamilton, 1976.

6422. Manson, James A. *Sir Edwin Landseer, R. A.* London, Scott/New York, Scribner, 1902.

6423. Monkhouse, William C. *The works of Sir Edwin Landseer, R. A., with a history of his art-life.* London, Virtue, 1879.

6424. Ormond, Richard. *Sir Edwin Landseer.* With contributions by Joseph Rishel and Robin Hamlyn. Philadelphia, Philadelphia Museum of Art; London, Tate Gallery, 1981.

6425. Philadelphia Museum of Art. *Sir Edwin Landseer.* October 25, 1981–January 3, 1982. [Text by Richard Ormond and Joseph Rishel]. Philadelphia, Philadelphia Museum of Art, 1981.

6426. Scott, McDougall. *Sir Edwin Landseer, R. A.* London, Bell, 1903.

6427. Stephens, Frederick. *Sir Edwin Landseer.* London, Sampson Low, 1881. 3 ed.

6428. [Sweetser, Moses F.]. *Landseer.* Boston, Houghton, Osgood, 1879.

Lane, Fitz Hugh, 1804–1865

6429. Cape Ann Historical Association (Gloucester, Mass.). *Paintings and drawings by Fitz Hugh Lane.* Gloucester, Mass., Cape Ann Historical Association, 1974.

6430. Wilmerding, John. *Fitz Hugh Lane.* New York, Praeger, 1971.

6431. Wilmerding, John. *Paintings by Fitz Hugh Lane.* [By] John Wilmerding; with contributions by Elizabeth Garrity Ellis . . . [et al.]. Washington, National Gallery of Art; New York, Abrams, 1988.

Lanfranco, Giovanni, 1582–1647

6432. Bernini, Giovanni Pietro. *Giovanni Lanfranco, 1582–1647.* [Calestano?], Centro studi della Val Baganza; Terenzo, Associazione "Comunità di Terenzo", 1985.

6433. Schleier, Erich. *Disegni di Giovanni Lanfranco (1582–1647).* Catalogo della mostra a cura di Erich Schleier. Firenze, L.S. Olschki, 1983.

Lange, Dorothea, 1895–1965

6434. Heyman, Therese T., et al. *Celebrating a collection: the work of Dorothea Lange.* Oakland, Calif., The Oakland Museum, 1978.

6435. Lange, Dorothea. *Dorothea Lange.* With an essay by Christopher Cox. New York, N.Y., Aperture, 1987.

6436. ———. *Dorothea Lange, eloquent witness: an exhibition of vintage photographs.* [Chicago, Ill.], Edwynn Houk Gallery, 1989.

6437. Lange, Dorothea. *Dorothea Lange looks at the American country woman; a photographic essay with a commentary by Beaumont Newhall.* Fort Worth, Tex., Amon Carter Museum of Western Art, 1967.

6438. ———. *Dorothea Lange; photographs of a lifetime.* With an essay by Robert Coles. Millerton, N.Y., Aperture, 1982.

6439. ——— [and] Mitchell, Margaretta, K. *To a cabin.* New York, Grossman, 1973.

6440. ——— and Taylor, Paul S. *An American exodus; a record of human erosion.* New York, Reynal & Hitchcock, 1939. (Reprint: New York, Arno Press, 1975).

6441. Levin, Howard M. and Northrup, Katherine, eds. *Dorothea Lange: Farm Security Administration photographs [from the Library of Congress], 1935–1939.* With writings by Paul S. Taylor. 2 v. Glencoe, Ill., Text-Fiche Press, 1980.

6442. Meltzer, Milton. *Dorothea Lange, a photographer's life.* New York, Farrar, Straus & Giroux, 1978.

6443. Museum of Modern Art (New York). *Dorothea Lange.* [Text by George P. Elliott]. New York, Museum of Modern Art, 1966; distributed by Doubleday, Garden City, N.Y.

6444. Ohrn, Karin B. *Dorothea Lange and the documentary tradition.* Baton Rouge, La., Louisiana State University Press, 1980.

Langhans, Carl Gotthard, 1732–1808

6445. Hinrichs, Walther T. *Carl Gotthard Langhans, ein schlesischer Baumeister, 1733–1808.* Strassburg, Heitz, 1909. (Studien zur deutschen Kunstgeschichte, 116).

Lansere, Evgenii Evgenevich, 1875–1946

6446. Borovskii, Aleksandr Davydovich. *Evgenii Evgen'evich Lansere.* Leningrad, Khudozhnik RSFSR, 1975.

6447. Podobedova, O. I. *Evgenii Evgen'evich Lansere, 1875–1946.* Moskva, Sovetskii Khudozhnik, 1961.

Lapicque, Charles René, 1898–

6448. Balanci, Bernard [and] Auger, Elmina. *Charles Lapicque, catalogue raisonné de l'oeuvre peint et de la sculpture.* Paris, Mayer, 1972. (CR).

6449. et Blache, Gérard. *Catalogue raisonné de l'oeuvre gravé de Charles Lapicque.* Paris, Amateur, 1982. (CR).

6450. Centre National d'Art et de Culture Georges

L

Pompidou, Musée National d'Art Moderne (Paris). *Les dessins de Lapicque au Musée National d'Art Moderne.* l mars–23 avril 1978. [Paris], Centre National d'Art et de Culture Georges Pompidou, 1978.

6451. Lapicque, Charles. *Dessins de Lapicque.* 3 v. [Vol. 1:

6452. ———. *Essais sur l'espace, l'art et la destinée.* Paris, Grasset, 1958.

6453. ———. *Lapicque.* Catalogue text by Sarah Wilson; with a foreword by Peter Nathan. London, ASB Gallery, 1987.

6454. Lescure, Jean. *Lapicque.* Paris, Galanis, 1956.

6455. Perregaux, Aloys. *Espace et présence dans la peinture de Lapique.* Neuchâtel, Paul Attinger, 1981.

6456. ———. *Lapicque.* Neuchâtel, Editions Ides et Calendes, 1983.

Lardera, Berto, 1911–

6457. Jianou, Ionel. *Lardera.* Paris, Arted, 1968. (CR).

6458. Kunstverein Hannover. *Berto Lardera.* 24. April bis 6. Juni 1971. Hannover, Kunstverein Hannover, 1971.

6459. Seuphor, Michel. *Berto Lardera.* [Text in French, English and German]. Neuchâtel, Editions du Griffon, 1960.

6460. Wilhelm-Lehmbruck-Museum der Städt Duisburg. *Berto Lardera; Plastiken, Collagen, Graphiken.* 9. Mai bis 20. Juni 1976. Duisburg, Wilhelm-Lehmbruck Museum, 1976.

Largillierre, Nicolas de, 1656–1746

6461. Pascal, Georges. *Largillierre.* Paris, Les Beaux-Arts, 1928.

6462. Rosenfeld, Myra N. *Largillierre and the eighteenth-century portrait.* [Catalogue of an exhibition, Montreal Museum of Fine Arts, September 19 to November 15, 1981]. Montreal, Montreal Museum of Fine Arts, 1982.

Larionov, Mikhail, 1881–1964

6463. Arts Council of Great Britain. *A retrospective exhibition of paintings and designs for the theatre; Larionov and Goncharova.* [Leeds, City Art Gallery, 9–30 September, 1961, et al.]. London, Arts Council, 1961.

6464. Chamot, Mary. *Goncharova.* Paris, Bibliothèque des Arts, 1972.

6465. Eganbiuri, Eli. *Natalia Goncharova, Mikhail Larionov.* Moskva, Münster, 1913.

6466. Larionov, Mikhail Fedorovich. *Mikhail Larionov: la voie vers l'abstraction: oeuvres sur papier 1908–1915.* [Conception] Andrei Boris Nakov. = *Der Weg in die Abstraktion: Werke auf Papier 1908–1915 /* [Konzeption

Andrei Boris Nakov]. Stuttgart, Edition Cantz, 1987.

6467. Marion Kogler McNay Art Museum (San Antonio). *Goncharova/Larionov.* [Exhibition catalogue]. the Tobin Wing, ntonio, Marion Kogler McNay Art Museum, San Antonio, Texas, 1987.

6468. George, Waldemar. *Larionov.* Paris, Bibliothèque des Arts, 1966.

6469. Musée d'Ixelles (Bruxelles). *Retrospective Larionov, Gontcharova.* 29 avril au 6 juin 1976. [Bruxelles, Musée d'Ixelles, 1976].

6470. Musée Toulouse-Lautrec (Albi). *Michel Larionov et son temps.* Juin–septembre 1973. [Albi, Musée Toulouse-Lautrec, 1973].

6471. Parnakh, Valentin. *Gontcharova Larionov; l'art décoratif théâtral moderne.* Paris, Edition La Cible, 1919.

6472. Parton, Anthony. *Mikhail Larionov and the Russian avant-garde.* Princeton, N.J., Princeton University Press, 1993.

Larsen, Johannes, 1867–1961

6473. Heltoft, Kjeld. *En bryllupsgave: fem ungdomsbilleder af maleren Johannes Larsen.* 27. december 1967. Odense, Andelsbogtrykkeriet i Odense, 1967.

6474. Jensen, Johannes V. *Johannes Larsen og hans billeder; med et kapitel af hans erindringer.* København, Gyldendal, 1947. 2 ed.

6475. La Cour, Tage. *Johannes Larsen, tegninger og grafik.* [København], Selskabet Bogvennerne, [1963].

6476. ——— and Madsen, Herman. *Johannes Larsen tegninger.* København, Gyldendal, 1938.

6477. ——— and Marcus, Aage, eds. *En hilsen til Johannes Larsen å 80 årsdagen.* København, Glydendal, 1947.

6478. Madsen, Herman. *Johannes Larsen.* København, Jensen, 1937.

6479. Marcus, Aage. *Maleren Johannes Larsen, en mindebog.* København, Gyldendal, 1962.

6480. Mentze, Ernst. *Johannes Larsen, kunstnerens erindringer; med biografiske oplysninger, noter og kommentarer.* København, Berlingske Forlag, 1955.

6481. Rasmussen, Holger M. *Johannes Larsens grafiske arbejder, en illustreret fortegnelse.* København, Fischer, 1938.

6482. Vinding, Ole. *Med Johannes Larsen i naturen; illustreret af kunstneren.* [København], Munksgaard, [1957].

Larsson, Carl Olaf, 1853–1919

6483. Alfons, Harriet, [and] Alfons, Sven, eds. *Carl Larsson skildrad av honom själv i text och bilder.* Stockholm, Bonniers, 1952.

6484. Frieberg, Axel. *Karin, en bok om Carl Lar-*

ssons hustru. Stockholm, Bonniers, 1967.

6485. Kruse, John. *Carl Larsson.* Wien, Gesellschaft für Vervielfältigende Kunst, 1905.

6486. Larson, Carl O. *Das Haus in der Sonne.* Königstein im Taunus, Langewiesche, 1909. (Die Blauen Bücher).

6487. ———. *Jag.* Stockholm, Bonniers, 1953.

6488. Lindwall, Bo. *Carl Larsson och Nationalmuseum.* Stockholm, Rabén & Sjögren, 1969. (Årsbok för Svenska statens konstsamlingar, 16).

6489. Nordensvan, Georg. *Carl Larsson.* 2 v. Stockholm, Norstedt, 1920–1. (Sveriges allmanna konstförenings publikation, 29–30).

6490. Zweigbergk, Eva von. *Hemma hos Carl Larssons.* Stockholm, Bonniers, 1968.

Lastman, Pieter, 1583–1633

6491. Freise, Kurt. *Pieter Lastman, sein Leben und sein Künst.* Leipzig, Klinkhardt & Biermann, 1911. (Kunstwissenschaftliche Studien, 5).

6492. Tümpel, Astrid. *Pieter Lastman: leermeister van Rembrandt.* [By] A. Tümpel & Peter Schatborn; met bijdragen van Christian Tümpel, Ed de Heer, Marikke Holtrop. Zwolle, Waandsers; Amsterdam, Het Rembradthuis, 1991.

La Tour, Georges Dumesnil de, 1593–1652

6493. Arland, Marcel [and] Marsan, Anna. *Georges de La Tour.* Paris, Editions du Dimanche, 1953.

6494. Bajou, Thierry. *De La Tour.* [By] Thierry Bajou; introduction de Pierre Rosenberg. Paris, Hazan, 1985.

6495. Bloch, Vitale. *Georges de La Tour, een beschouwing over zijn werk voorafgegaan door een catalogus van zijn oeuvre.* Amsterdam, de Bussy, 1950.

6496. Bourgier, Annette M. *La mystique de Georges de La Tour.* Bruges, Desclee de Brouwer, 1963.

6497. Furness, S. M. *Georges de La Tour of Lorraine, 1593–1652.* London, Routledge and Kegan Paul.

6498. Jamot, Paul. *Georges de La Tour.* Paris, Floury, 1942.

6499. Musee de l'Orangerie (Paris). *Georges de la Tour.* 10 mai–25 septembre 1972. Paris, Editions des Musees Nationaux, 1972.

6500. Nicholson, Benedict and Wright, Christopher. *Georges de La Tour.* London, Phaidon, 1974. (CR).

6501. Ottani Cavina, Anna. *La Tour.* Milano, Fabbri, 1966. (I maestri del colore, 140).

6502. Pariset, François-Georges. *Georges de La Tour.* Paris, Laurens, 1948.

6503. Reinbold, Anne. *Georges de la Tour.* Paris, Fayard, 1991.

6504. Rosenberg, Pierre. *Georges de la Tour: catalogo completo dei dipinti.* [By] P. Rosenberg, Marina Mojana. Firenze, Cantini, 1992.

6505. ——— [and] Macé de l'Epinay, François. *Georges de La Tour, vie et oeuvre.* Fribourg, Office du Livre, 1973. (CR).

6506. Solesmes, François. *Georges de La Tour.* Lausanne, Clairefontaine, 1973.

6507. Thuillier, Jacques. *Georges de la Tour.* Paris, Flammarion, 1992. (CR).

6508. ———. *L'opera completa di Georges de La Tour.* Milano, Rizzoli, 1973. Classici dell'arte, 65).

6509. Zolotov, Iurii K. *Zhorzh de La Tur.* Moskva, Iskusstvo, 1979.

Latour, Ignace Henri Jean Theodore, Fantin *see* Fantin-Latour, Ignace Henri Jean Theodore

La Tour, Maurice-Quentin de, 1704–1788

6510. Besnard, Albert. *La Tour, la vie et l'oeuvre de l'artiste.* [With a] catalogue critique par Georges Wildenstein. Paris, Les Beaux-Arts, 1928. (CR).

6511. Bury, Adrian. *Maurice-Quentin de La Tour, the greatest pastel portraitist.* London, Skilton, 1971.

6512. Champfleury [pseud., Jules Fleury]. *De La Tour.* Paris, Didron/Dumoulin, 1855.

6513. Debrie, Christine. *Maurice-Quentin de la Tour: peintre de portraits au pastel. 1704–1788; au Musée Antoine Lécuyer de Saint-Quentin.* [By] C. Debrie; préface de Pierre Rosenberg. Thonon-les-Bains, Haute Savoie; L'Albaron-Societé: Présence du livre, 1991.

6514. Desmaze, Charles. *Maurice-Quentin de La Tour, peintre du roi Louis XV.* Paris, Levy, 1854.

6515. ———. *Le reliquaire de La Tour; sa correspondance et son oeuvre.* Paris, Leroux, 1874.

6516. Dreolle de Nodon, Ernest. *Eloge biographique de M. Q. de La Tour.* Paris, Amyot, 1856.

6517. Duplaquet, Charles-Vincent. *Eloge historique de M. Q. de La Tour, peintre du roi.* Saint-Quentin et Paris, Hautoy, 1788.

6518. Erhard, Hermann. *La Tour, der Pastellmaler Ludwigs XV.* München, Piper, 1917. (Französische Kunst, 1).

6519. Goncourt, Edmond et Goncourt, Jules de. *La Tour, étude.* Paris, Dentu, 1867.

6520. Lapauze, Henry. *La Tour et son oeuvre au Musée de Saint-Quentin.* 2 v. Paris, Goupil, 1905.

6521. Leroy, Alfred. *Maurice-Quentin de La Tour et la société française du XVIII siècle.* Paris, Michel, 1953.

6522. Nolhac, Pierre de. *La vie et oeuvre de Maurice-Quentin de La Tour.* Paris, Piazza, 1930.

6523. Patoux, Abel. *Les dernières années de M.-Q. de La Tour.* Saint-Quentin, Poëtte, 1880.

6524. Tourneux, Maurice. *La Tour, biographie critique.* Paris, Laurens, 1904.

Latrobe, Benjamin, 1764–1820

6525. Carter, Edward C., II, ed. *The Virginia journals of Benjamin Henry Latrobe, 1795–1798.* 2 v. New Haven, Yale University Press, 1977.

6526. ———, et al., eds. *The journals of Benjamin Henry Latrobe, 1799–1820: from Philadelphia to New Orleans.* New Haven, Yale University Press, 1980.

6527. Hamlin, Talbot F. *Benjamin Henry Latrobe.* New York, Oxford, 1955.

6528. Latrobe, Benjamin H. *Impressions respecting New Orleans; diary and sketches, 1818–1820.* Edited, with an introduction and notes, by Samuel Wilson, Jr. New York, Columbia University Press, 1951.

6529. ———. *Latrobe's view of America, 1795–1820.* Selections from the watercolors and sketches. Edited by Edward G. Carter, John C. van Horne, and Charles E. Brownell. New Haven, Yale University Press, 1985.

6530. Norton, Paul F. *Latrobe, Jefferson and the National Capital.* New York/London, Garland, 1977.

6531. Stapleton, Darwin H., ed. *The engineering drawings of Benjamin Henry Latrobe.* New Haven, Yale University Press, 1980.

Laurana, Francesco, 1430–1502

6532. Burger, Fritz. *Francesco Laurana, eine Studie zur italienischen Quattrocentoskulptur.* Strassburg, Heitz, 1907. (Kunstgeschichte des Auslandes, 50).

6533. Chiarini, Marco. *Francesco Laurana.* Milano, Fabbri, 1966. (I maestri della scultura, 47).

6534. Patera, Benedetto. *Francesco Laurana in Sicilia.* Palermo, Novecento, 1992.

6535. Rolfs, Wilhelm. *Franz Laurana.* 2 v. Berlin, Bong, 1907.

Laurencin, Marie, 1885–1956

6536. Allard, Roger. *Marie Laurencin.* Paris, Editions de la Nouvelle Revue Française, 1921. (Les peintres français nouveaux, 10).

6537. Day, George [pseud.]. *Marie Laurencin.* Paris, Editions du Dauphin, 1947.

6538. Gere, Charlotte. *Marie Laurencin.* New York, Rizzoli, 1977.

6539. Groult, Flora. *Marie Laurencin.* Paris, Mercure de France, 1987.

6540. Hyland, Douglas. *Marie Laurencin, artist and muse.* [By] Douglas K.S. Hyland [and] Heather McPherson. [Exhibition catalogue].

Birmingham Museum of Art; Seattle, distrib. by University of Washington Press, 1989.

6541. Laurencin, Marie. *Le carnet des nuits.* Genève, Cailler, 1956. (Ecrits et documents de peintres, 12).

6542. Marchesseau, Daniel. *Marie Laurencin, 1883–1956: catalogue raisonné de l'oeuvre peint.* Chino, Japan, Editions du Musée Marie Laurencin, 1986.(CR).

6543. Wedderkop, H. von. *Marie Laurencin.* Leipzig, Klinkhardt & Biermann, 1921. (Junge Kunst, 22).

Laurens, Henri, 1885–1954

6544. Arts Council of Great Britain. *Henri Laurens, 1895,* [i.e., 1885]–1954.

6545. Falcidia, Giorgio. *Henri Laurens.* Milano, Fabbri, 1966. (I maestri della scultura, 41).

6546. Grand Palais (Paris). *Henri Laurens.* Exposition de la donation aux Musées Nationaux. Mai–août 1967. Paris, Réunion des Musées Nationaux, 1967.

6547. Hofmann, Werner. *The sculpture of Henri Laurens.* With recollections of Henri Laurens by Daniel-Henry Kahnweiler.

6548. Kuthy, Sandor. *Henri Laurens, 1885–1954.* [By] S. Kuthy, mit Texten [von] Claude Laurens, Marthe Laurens, Magdalena M. Moeller, Isabelle Monod-Fontaine. Bern, Kunstmuseum Bern; München, Museum Villa Stuck, 1985.

6549. Laurens, Henri. *Henri Laurens: le cubisme, constructions et papiers collées, 1915–1919.* [Exposition]. Centre Georges Pompidou, Musée national d'art moderne, Salle d'art graphique, 18 décembre 1985–16 février 1986. [Catalogue par] Isabelle Monod-Fontaine, avec la collaboration de Brigitte Léal]. Paris, Le Centre, 1989.

6550. ———. *Henri Laurens: opere su carta.* [Catalogue of an exhibition held at the Galleria Pieter Coray, Lugano, 1991]. Introduction, Jean Leymarie. Milano, Electa, 1991.

6551. ———. *Henri Laurens, rétrospective.* [Catalogue d'une exposition]: Musée d'art moderne Villeneuve d'Asq, Communauté de Lille, 1992. Paris, Réunion des musées nationaux, 1992.

6552. ———. *Henri Laurens (1885–1954): Skulpturen, Collagen, Zeichnungen, Aquarelle, Druckgraphik:* Bestandskatalog und Ausstellungskatalog; Oeuvreverzeichnis der Druckgraphik: 3. März bis 28. April 1985. [Ausstellung und Katalog, Norbert Nobis]. Hannover, Sprengel Museum Hannover, 1985. (CR).

6553. Laurens, Marthe, ed. *Henri Laurens, sculpteur, 1885–1954.* [Années 1915 à 1924]. Paris, [Bérès], 1955.

6554. Waldberg, Patrick. *Henri Laurens ou la femme placée en amîbe.* Paris, Le Sphinx-Veyrier, 1980.

Lavery, Sir John, 1856–1941

6555. Lavery, John. *The life of a painter.* Boston, Little, Brown, 1940.
6556. Shaw-Sparrow, Walter. *John Lavery and his work.* London, Kegan Paul, [1911].

Lavreince, Nicolas *see* Lafrensen, Nicolas

Lawrence, Jacob Armstead, 1917–

6557. Brown, Milton W. *Jacob Lawrence.* New York, Dodd, Mead, 1974.
6558. Detroit Institute of Arts. *Jacob Lawrence: John Brown series.* October 14–November 26, 1978. Detroit, Detroit Institute of Arts, 1978.

Lawrence, Sir Thomas, 1769–1830

6559. Armstrong, Walter. *Lawrence.* New York, Scribner, 1913.
6560. Garlick, Kenneth. *A catalogue of the paintings, drawings, and pastels of Sir Thomas Lawrence.* London, Walpole Society, 1964. (Walpole Society, 39).
6561. ———. *Sir Thomas Lawrence.* London, Routledge & Kegan Paul, 1954.
6562. ———. *Sir Thomas Lawrence: a complete catalogue of the oil paintings,* by Kenneth Garlick. Oxford, Phaidon, 1989. (CR).
6563. ———. *Sir Thomas Lawrence: portraits of an age, 1790–1830.* Alexandria, Va., Art Services International, 1993.
6564. Goldring, Douglas. *Regency portrait painter; the life of Sir Thomas Lawrence, P. R.A.* London, Macdonald, 1951.
6565. Gower, Ronald S. *Sir Thomas Lawrence.* London, Goupil, 1900.
6566. Knapp, Oswald G. *An artist's love story, told in the letters of Sir Thomas Lawrence, Mrs. Siddons, and her daughter.* London, Allen, 1905.
6567. Layard, George S., ed. *Sir Thomas Lawrence's letter-bag, with recollections of the artist by Miss Elizabeth Croft.* London, Allen, 1906.
6568. Williams, D. E. *The life and correspondence of Sir Thomas Lawrence.* 2 v. London, Colburn & Bentley, 1831.

Lawson, Ernest, 1873–1939

6569. Berry-Hill, Henry and Berry-Hill, Sidney. *Ernest Lawson, American impressionist; 1873–1939.* With a foreword by Ira Glackens. Leigh-on-Sea, Lewis, 1968.
6570. Du Bois, Guy Pène. *Ernest Lawson.* New York, Whitney Museum of American Art, 1932.
6571. Price, Frederic N. *Ernest Lawson, Canadian-American.* New York, Ferargil, 1930.
6572. University of Arizona Museum of Art (Tucson, Ariz.). *Ernest Lawson, 1873–1939.* February 11–March 8, 1979. [Tucson, Ariz.], Arizona Board of Regents, 1979.

Leal, Juan de Valdes *see* Valdes Leal, Juan de

Lear, Edward, 1812–1888

6573. Arts Council of Great Britain. *Edward Lear, 1812–1888. An exhibition of oil paintings, water-colours and drawings, books and prints, manuscripts, photographs and records.* [Arts Council Gallery, London, 5 July–26 July, 1958]. London, Arts Council, 1958.
6574. Chitty, Susan. *That singular person called Lear: a biography of Edward Lear, artist, traveler, and prince of nonsense. New York, Atheneum, 1989.* (First publ.: London, Weidenfeld and Nicolson, 1988).
6575. Davidson, Angus. *Edward Lear, landscape painter and nonsense poet (1812–1888).* London, Murray, 1938. (Reprint: Port Washington, N.Y., Kennikat Press, 1968).
6576. Dehejia, Vidya. *Impossible picturesqueness: Edward Lear's Indian Watercolors.* With an essay by Allen Staley. New York, Columbia University Press, 1989.
6577. Field, William B. *Edward Lear on my shelves. [A bibliography and catalogue].* München, privately printed [for William B. Field] by the Bremer Presse, 1933.
6578. Hark, Ina Rae. *Edward Lear.* Boston, Twayne Publishers, 1982.
6579. Hofer, Philip. *Edward Lear.* New York, Oxford University Press, 1962.
6580. ———. *Edward Lear as a landscape draughtsman.* Cambridge, Mass., Belknap Press, 1967.
6581. Hyman, Susan. *Edward Lear's birds.* Introduction by Philip Hofer. New York, Morrow, 1980.
6582. Lear, Edward. *The Corfu years: a chronicle presented through his letters and journals.* Edited and introduced by Philip Sherrard. Athens, D. Harvey, 1988.
6583. ———. *Journals of a landscape painter in Corsica.* London, Bush, 1870. (Reprint: London, Kimber, 1966).
6584. ———. *Journals of a landscape painter in Greece and Albania.* London, Bentley, 1851. (Reprint: London, Kimber, 1965).
6585. ———. *Journals of a landscape painter in Greece and Albania.* With an introduction by Steven Runciman. London, Century, 1988.
6586. ———. *Journals of a landscape painter in Southern Calabria, &c.* London, Bentley, 1852. (Reprint: London, Kimber, 1964).

6587. ———. *Edward Lear in the Levant: travels in Albania, Greece, and Turkey in Europe, 1848–1849.* Compiled and edited by Susan Hyman. London, J. Murray, 1988.

6588. Lehmann, John. *Edward Lear and his world.* [London], Thames and Hudson, 1977.

6589. Noakes, Vivien. *Edward Lear, 1812–1888.* [By] V. Noakes; with an introduction by Sir Steven Runciman and an essay by Jeremy Maas. London, Royal Academy of Arts; published in association with Weidenfed and Nicolson, 1985.

6590. ———. *Edward Lear: the life of a wanderer.* London, Collins, 1968.

6591. ———. *The painter Edward Lear.* [By] V. Noakes; with a foreword by HRH the Prince of Wales, Newton Abbott, David & Charles, 1991.

6592. Strachey, Constance, ed. *Later letters of Edward Lear.* London, Unwin, 1911.

6593. ———. *Letters of Edward Lear.* London, Unwin, 1907.

Lebek, Johannes, 1901–1985

6594. Lebek, Johannes. *Der Holzschneider Johannes Lebek: Leben und Werk.* München, R. Schneider, 1988.

6595. Wegner, Hubert. *Werkverzeichnis Johannes Lebek, der Jahre 1922–1950.* Bearbeitet und herausgegeben von Hubert Wegner. *[Langenhagen],* H. Wegner, 1980. *(CR).*

Le Brun, Charles, 1619–1690

6596. Château de Versailles. *Charles Le Brun, 1619–1690; peintre et dessinatuer.* Juillet-octobre 1963. Paris, Ministère d'Etat Chargé des Affaires Culturelles, 1963.

6597. Fontaine, André. *Quid senserit Carolus Le Brun, de arte sua; thesim proponebat.* [Paris], Apud Fontemoing Bibliopolam, [1903].

6598. Genevay, Antoine. *Le style Louis XIV: Charles Le Brun, décorateur; ses oeuvres, son influence, ses collaborateurs et son temps.* Paris, Rouam, 1886.

6599. Jouin, Henri A. *Charles Le Brun et les arts sous Louis XIV, le premier peintre, sa vie, son oeuvre, ses ecrits, ses contemporains, son influence, d'après le manuscrit de Nivelon et de nombreuses pièces inédits.* Paris, Imp. Nat., 1889.

6600. Le Brun, Charles. *Conférence . . . sur l'expression générale et particulière.* Paris, Picard, 1698. (English ed.: London, Smith, 1701).

6601. ———. *A series of lithographic drawings illustrative of the relation between the human physiognomy and that of the brute creation, with remarks on the system.* London, Carpenter, 1827.

6602. Marcel, Pierre. *Charles Le Brun.* Paris, Plon-Nourrit, [1909].

6603. Mignard, Paul. *Ode à M. Le Brun, premier peintre du roy.* Paris, Le Petit, 1683.

Le Brun, Marie Louise Elisabeth Vigee *see* **Vigee-Le Brun, Elisabeth Louise**

Lechter, Melchior, 1865–1937

6604. Hoffmann, Marguerite. *Mein Weg mit Melchior Lechter.* Amsterdam, Castrum Peregrini Presse, [1966]. (Castrum Peregrini, 72–74).

6605. Lechter, Melchior. *Briefe: Melchior Lechter und Stefan George.* Kritische Ausgabe herausgegeben von Günter Heintz. Stuttgart, Dr. Ernst Hauswedell & Co. Verlag, 1991.

6606. ———. *Melchior Lechter, der Meister des Buches, 1865–1937: eine Kunst für und wider Stefan George.* Amsterdam, Castrum Peregrini, 1987.

6607. Rapsilber, Maximilian. *Melchior Lechter.* Berlin, Wasmuth, 1904. (Berliner Kunst, 3).

6608. Raub, Wolfhard. *Melchior Lechter als Buchkünstler; Darstellung, Werkverzeichnis, Bibliographie.* Köln, Greven, 1969. (CR).

6609. Wissman, Jürgen. *Melchior Lechter.* Recklinghausen, Bongers, 1966. (Monographien zur rheinisch-westfälischen Kunst der Gegenwart, 19).

6610. Wolters, Friedrich. *Melchior Lechter.* München, Hanfstaengl, 1911.

Le Clerc, Sebastien, 1637–1714

6611. Jombert, Charles-Antoine. *Catalogue raisonné de l'oeuvre de Sébastian Le Clerc, chevalier romain, dessinateur & graveurdu cabinet du Roi.* 2 v. Paris, [Jombert], 1774. (CR).

6612. LeClerc, Sébastien. *Pratique de la géométrie sur le papier et sur le terrain, avec un nouvel ordre et une méthode particulière.* Paris, [Quay des Augustins, à l'image Nostre-Dame], 1682. 2 ed.

6613. ———. *Traité d'architecture avec des remarques et des observations très-utiles pour les jeunes gens qui veulent s'appliquer à ce bel art.* Paris, Giffart, 1714. (English ed., trans. by Mr. Chambers: London, Bateman and Taylor, 1724).

6614. ———. *Traité de géométrie.* Paris, Gaubert, 1690.

6615. ———. *Traité de géometrie théorique et pratique à l'usage des artistes.* Nouv. éd. Paris, C.A. Jombert, 1774.

6616. Meaume, Edouard. *Sébastien Le Clerc et son oeuvre.* Paris, Baur/Rapilly, 1877.

6617. Musée de Metz. *Sébastien Le Clerc (1637–1714); guide et catalogue de l'exposition organisée à l'occasion du III centenaire de sa naissance.* Nancy, Edition du Pays Lorrain, 1937.

Le Corbusier, 1887–1965

6618. Alazard, Jean. *Le Corbusier.* New York, Universe, 1960.

6619. Baker, Geoffrey Howard. *Le Corbusier: an analysis of form.* London, van Nostrand Reinhold, 1988. 2 ed.

6620. Besset, Maurice. *Who was Le Corbusier?* Trans. by Robin Kemball. Genève, Skira, 1968; distributed by World, Cleveland. (First paperback edition: New York, Rizzoli, 1987).

6621. Blake, Peter. *Le Corbusier, architecture and form.* Baltimore, Penguin, 1960.

6622. Boesiger, Willy. *Le Corbusier.* [English and Spanish]. Traduccion, Lucy Nussbaum, Graham Thomson]. Barcelona, Gustavo Gili, 1991. (Originally published: Zürich, Verlag für Architektur Artemis, 1972. (First paperback edition: Barcelona, G. Gilli, 1982).

6623. Brady, Darlene A. *Le Corbusier: an annotated bibliography.* New York, Garland Publishing, 1985.

6624. Brooks, H. Allen, ed. *The Le Corbusier archives.* 32 v. [Titled variously]. New York/London, Garland [and] Paris, Fondation Le Corbusier, 1982–83.

6625. Choay, Françoise. *Le Corbusier.* New York, Braziller, 1960.

6626. Cohen, Jean-Louis. *Le Corbusier and the mystique of the USSR: theories and projects for Moscow, 1928–1936.* Trans. from the French by Kenneth Hylton. Princeton, Princeton University Press, 1992.

6627. Cresti, Carlo. *Le Corbusier.* London, Hamlyn, 1970.

6628. Curtis, William J.R. *Le Corbusier: ideas and forms.* New York, Rizzoli, 1986.

6629. Daria, Sophie. *Le Corbusier, sociologue de l'urbanisme.* Paris, Seghers, 1964.

6630. Denti, Giovanni [et al.]. *Le Corbusier in Italia.* A cura di G. Denti, Andrea Savio, Gianni Calzá. Interventi di Lodovico Belgioiso . . . [et al.]. Milano, CLUP, 1988.

6631. Ducret, André [et.al.]. *Le Corbusier, le peintre derrière l'architecte.* [By] A. Ducret . . . et al.]. Grenoble, Presses Universitaires, 1988.

6632. [L'Esprit Nouveau]. *L'Esprit Nouveau,* Nos. 1–28. 8 v. New York, Da Capo, 1968–69.

6633. Evenson, Norma. *Le Corbusier: the machine and the grand design.* New York: Braziller, 1969.

6634. Fusco, Renato De. *Le Corbusier, designer: furniture, 1929.* Woodbury, N.Y., Barron's, 1977.

6635. Gabetti, Roberto e Olmo, Carlo. *Le Corbusier e L'Esprit Nouveau.* Torino, Einaudi, 1975.

6636. Gardiner, Stephen. *Le Corbusier.* New York, Viking, 1974.

6637. Gauthier, Maximilien. *Le Corbusier ou l'architecture au service de l'homme.* Paris, Denoël, 1944.

6638. Gerosa, Pier G. *Le Corbusier—urbanisme et mobilité.* Basel/Stuttgart, Birkhäuser, 1978. (Studien aus dem Institut für Geschichte und Theorie der Architektur, 3).

6639. Girsberger, Hans. *Im Umgang mit Le Corbusier—mes contacts avec Le Corbusier.* [Text in German and French]. Zürich, Editions d'Architecture Artemis, 1981.

6640. Gresleri, Giuliano, et al. *L'esprit nouveau: Parigi-Bologna; costruzione e ricostruzione di un prototipo dell'architettura moderna.* Milano, Electa, 1979.

6641. Guiton, Jacques, ed. *The ideas of Le Corbusier on architecture and urban planning.* Trans. by Margaret Guiton. New York, Braziller, 1981.

6642. Hayward Gallery (London). *Le Corbusier, architect of the century.* Hayward Gallery, London, 5 March–7 June 1987: a centenary exhibition organized by the Arts Council of Great Britain in collaboration with the Fondation Le Corbusier, Paris. London, The Arts Council of Great Britain, 1987.

6643. Hervé, Lucien. *Le Corbusier, as artist, as writer.* Introduction by Marcel Joray. Trans. by Haakon Chevalier. Neuchâtel, Editions du Griffon, 1970.

6644. ———. *Etude sur le mouvement d'art decoratif en Allemagne.* La Chaux-de-Fonds, Haefel, 1912.

6645. Hilpert, Thilo. *Die funktionelle Stadt: Le Corbusiers Stadtvision: Bedingungen, Motive, Hintergründe.* Braunschweig, Vieweg, 1978.

6646. Jencks, Charles. *Le Corbusier and the tragic view of architecture.* Cambridge, Mass., Harvard University Press, 1973.

6647. Jordan, Robert F. *Le Corbusier.* London, Dent, 1972.

6648. Kaufmann, Emil. *Von Ledoux bis Le Corbusier: Ursprung und Entwicklung der Autonomen Architektur.* Stuttgart, G. Hatje, 1985. (First published: Wien, Passer, 1933).

6649. Kunsthaus Zürich. *Le Corbusier: Architektur, Malerei, Plastik, Wandteppiche.* 5. Juni–31. August 1957. Zürich, Kunsthaus, 1957.

6650. Le Corbusier [i.e. Jeanneret-Gris, Charles, Edouard]. *Almanach d'architecture moderne.* Paris, Cres, [1925].

6651. ———. *Le Corbusier et la Mediterranée:* ouvrage réalisé à l'occasion de l'exposition . . . Marseille, Centre de la Vieille Charité, 27 juin–27 septembre, 1987.

6652. ———. *Le Corbusier: Buildings and projects, 1933–1937.* New York, Garland Publishing; Paris, Fondation le Corbusier, 1983.

6653. ———. *Le Corbusier: Early buildings and projects, 1912–1923.* New York, Garland

Publishing; Paris, Fondation Le Corbusier, 1982.

6654. ———. *Le Corbusier: Early works by Charles-Edouard Jeanneret-Gris,* with contributions by Geoffrey Baker and Jacques Gubler. London, Academy; New York, St. Martin's Press, 1987.

6655. ———. *L'art décoratif d'aujord'hui.* Paris, Crès, [1925].

6656. ———. *Croisade ou le créspuscule des académies.* Paris, Crès, 1932.

6657. ———. *The ideas of Le Corbusier on architecture and urban planning.* Texts edited and presented by Jacques Guiton; translation by Margaret Guiton. New York, G. Baziller, 1981.

6658. ———. *Journey to the East. [Voyage d'Orient].* [By] Le Corbusier (Charles-Edouard Jeanneret). Edited and annotated by Ivan Zaknic; trans. Ivan Zaknic in collaboration with Nicole Pertuiset. Cambridge, Mass., M.I.T. Press, 1987.

6659. ———. *Un maison-un palais.* Paris, Crès, 1928.

6660. ———. *Last works.* Ed. by Willy Boesiger. Trans. by Henry A. Frey. [Text in French, English, and German]. New York/Washington, D.C., Praeger, 1970.

6661. ———. *Le Corbusier et la nature:* rencontres des 14–15 juin 1991. Paris, Fondation Le Corbusier, 1991.

6662. ———. *Le Corbusier, oeuvre tissé.* Préface de François Mathey; introduction d'Annick Davy et Martine Mathias; texte et catalogue raisonné par Martine Mathias. Paris, P. Sers, 1987. (CR)

6663. ———. *Le Corbusier: textes et planches.* Préface de Maurice Jardot. Paris, Vincent, Fréal, 1960.

6664. ———. *Le Corbusier the artist:* works from the Heidi Weber Collection. Zürich, H. Weber, 1988.

6665. ———. *Manière de penser l'urbanisme.* Paris, Denoël/Gonthier, [1977]. 2 ed. (English trans. of 1st ed. by Eleanor Levieux: New York, Grossman, 1971).

6666. ———. *The modulor: a harmonious measure to the human scale universally applicable to architecture and mechanics.* Trans. by Peter de Francia and Anna Bostock. Cambridge, Mass., Harvard University Press, 1954. 2 ed.

6667. ———. *Modulor 2: 1955 (Let the user speak next).* Continuation of *The modulor,* 1948. Trans. by Peter de Francia and Anna Bostock. Cambridge, Mass., Harvard University Press, 1956.

6668. ———. *My work.* Trans. by James Palmes. London, Architectural Press, 1960.

6669. ———. *The new world of space.* New York, Reynal & Hitchcock/Boston, Institute of Contemporary Art, 1948.

6670. ———. *Oeuvre complète.* 7 v. Ed. by Willy Boesiger et al. Zürich, Les Editions d'Architecture, 1930–71. (CR).

6671. ———. *Le poème électronique.* [Paris], Edition de Minuit, 1958.

6672. ———. *Précisions sur un état présent de l'architecture et de l'urbanisme.* Paris, Crès, 1930.

6673. ———. *Propose d'urbanisme.* Paris, Bourrelier, 1946. (English ed.: London, Architectural Press, 1947).

6674. ———. *Selected drawings.* Introduction by Michael Graves. London, Academy, 1981.

6675. ———. *Sketchbooks [1914–1964].* 4 v. Preface by André Wogenscky. Introduction by Maurice Besset. Notes by Franoise Franclieu. New York, Architectural History Foundation/Cambridge, Mass., MIT Press in collaboration with the Fondation Le Corbusier, Paris, 1981–82.

6676. ———. *Urbanisme.* Paris, Crès, [1925]. (Reprint: Paris, Arthaud, 1980; English ed. trans. by Frederick Etchells: *The city of tomorrow and its planning.* London, Rodka, 1929; new ed.: Cambridge, Mass., MIT Press, 1971).

6677. ———. *Vers une architecture.* Paris, Crès, 1923. (English ed., trans. by Frederick Etchells: London, Architectural Press, 1927; new ed.: New York, Praeger, 1946).

6678. ———. *When the cathedrals were white; a journey to the country of timid people.* Trans. by Francis E. Hyslop, Jr. New York, Reynal & Hitchcock, 1947.

6679. [———]. *Le Corbusier et P. Jeanneret.* 7 v. Paris, Morance, [1927–1936].

6680. Lucan, Jacques, ed. *Le Corbusier, une encyclopédie.* [Also catalogue of an exhibition]. Direction de l'ouvrage, Jacques Lucan. Paris, Centre Georges Pompidou, 1987.

6681. Messina, Bruno Salvatore. *Le Corbusier: eros e logos.* B. S. Messina; prefazione di Francesco Venezia. Napoli, CLEAN, 1987.

6682. Moos, Stanislaus von. *Le Corbusier; elements of a synthesis.* Cambridge, Mass., MIT Press, 1979.

6683. ———. *L'Esprit nouveau: Le Corbusier et l'industrie 1920–1925.* [Catalogue of an exhibition held at the Museum für Gestaltung, Zürich, 28 March–10 May 1987, and at three other locations, 23 May–31 October 1987]. Berlin, W. Ernst, 1987. (Tranlation of: L'Esprit nouveau: Le Corbusier und die Industrie, 1920–1925).

6684. ———. *Le Corbusier: l'architecte et son mythe.* [s.l.], Horizons de France, 1971.

6685. Musee National d'Art Moderne (Paris). *Le Corbusier.* Novembre 1962–janvier 1963.

Paris, Ministère d'Etat Chargé d'Affaires Culturelles, 1962.

6686. Museo Correr (Milan). *Le Corbusier, pittore e scultore.* Comitato ordinatore della mostra, Giuseppe Mazzariol . . . [et al.]. Milano, Arnoldo Mondadori, 1986.

6687. Papadaki, Stamo. *Le Corbusier, architect, painter, writer.* New York, Macmillan, 1948.

6688. Pawley, Martin. *Le Corbusier.* New York, Simon and Schuster, 1970.

6689. Perruchot, Henri. *Le Corbusier.* Paris, Editions Universitaires, 1958. (Témoins du XXᵉ siècle, 10).

6690. Petit, Jean. *Le Corbusier lui-même.* Genève, Rousseau, 1970.

6691. Ragot, Gilles. *Le Corbusier en France: réalisations et projets.* [By] Gilles Ragot, Mathilde Dion. Paris, Electa Moniteur, 1987.

6692. Riehl, Martin. *'Vers une architecture': Das moderne Bauprogramm des Le Corbusier.* München, Scaneg, 1992. (Beiträge zur Kunstwissenschaft, 44).

6693. Rodrigues dos Santos, Cecilia [et al.]. *Le corbusier e o Brasil.* Sao Paulo, Tessela: Projeto. 1987.

6694. Sekler, Mary P. *The early drawings of Charles-Edouard Jeanneret (Le Corbusier), 1902–1908.* New York/London, Garland, 1977.

6695. Serenyi, Peter, ed. *Le Corbusier in perspective.* Englewood Cliffs, N.J., Prentice-Hall, 1975.

6696. Turner, Paul Venable. *The education of Le Corbusier.* New York/ London, Garland, 1977. (French edition: *La formation de Le Corbusier: idéalisme et mouvement moderne.* Traduction par Pauline Choay. Paris, Macula, 1987).

6697. Walden, Russell, ed. *The open hand: essays on Le Corbusier.* Cambridge, Mass./London, MIT Press, 1977.

Ledoux, Claude Nicolas, 1736–1806

6698. Christ, Yvan. *Projets et divagations de Claude-Nicolas Ledoux, architecte du Roi.* Paris, Editions du Minotaure, 1961.

6699. Gallet, Michel. *Claude-Nicolas Ledoux, 1736–1806.* Paris, Picard, 1980.

6700. Kaufmann, Emil. *Die Stadt des Architekten Ledoux: Zur Erkenntnis der Autonomen Architektur.* Frankfurt am Main, Frankfurter Verlagsanstalt, [1933?]. (Reprint: Stuttgart, G. Hatje, 1985).

6701. Ledoux, Claude-Nicolas. *L'architecture considérée sous le rapport de l'art, des moeurs et de la législation.* Paris, [Ledoux], 1804. (Plates published in Paris by Daniel Ramée, 1847; both vols. reprinted by Fernand de Nobele, Paris, 1962).

6702. ———. *Architecture de C.N. Ledoux.* Princeton, N.J., Princeton Architectutal Press

in association with the Avery Architectural and Fine Arts Library of Columbia University. New York, Columbia University, 1983.

6703. ———. *Architecture de Ledoux: inédits pour un tome III, précédés d'un texte de Michel Gallet.* Paris, Editions du Demi Cercle,1991.

6704. ———. *Claude-Nicolas Ledoux, unpublished projects.* With an essay by Michel Gallet. English translation, Michael Robinson. Berlin [Germany], Ernst & Sohn, 1992.

6705. ———. *Ledoux et Paris.* [Catalogue of an exhibition]. Paris, Rotonde de la Villette, 1979. (Cahiers de la Rotonde, 3).

6706. ———. *Origines de l'architecture moderne: de Ledoux à Le Corbusier.* Paris, Edition Fondation C.N. Leroux, 1987.

6707. Levallée-Haug, Géneviève. *Claude-Nicolas Ledoux.* Paris/Strasbourg, Istra, 1934.

6708. Raval, Marcel H. *Claude-Nicolas Ledoux, 1736–1806.* Paris, Arts et Métiers Graphiques, 1946.

6709. Stoloff, Bernard. *L'affaire Claude-Nicolas Ledoux; autopsie d'un mythe.* Bruxelles/ Liège, Mardaga, 1977. (Architecture + recherches, 7).

6710. Vidler, Anthony. *Claude-Nicholas Ledoux: architecture and social reform at the end of the Ancien Règime.* Cambridge, Mass., MIT Press, 1990.

Lee, Russell, 1903–

6711. Hurley, F. Jack. *Russell Lee, photographer.* Introduction by Robert Coles. Dobbs Ferry, N.Y., Morgan & Morgan, 1978.

6712. Lee, Russel. *Threads of culture: photography in New Mexico 1939–1943.* Photographs by Russel Lee, John Collier, Jr., and Jack Delano. Santa Fee, Museum of Fine Arts, 1993.

Leech, John, 1817–1864

6713. Brown, John. *John Leech and other papers.* Edinburgh, Douglas, 1882.

6714. Chambers, Charles E. S. *A list of works containing illustrations by John Leech; a bibliography.* Edinburgh, Brown, 1892.

6715. Field, William B. *John Leech on my shelves.* München, privately printed [for William B. Field], 1930. (CR).

6716. Frith, William P. *John Leech, his life and work.* 2 v. London, Bentley, 1891.

6717. Grolier Club (New York). *Catalogue of an exhibition of the works of John Leech (1817–1864) held at the Grolier Club from January 22 until March 8, 1914.* New York, The Grolier Club, 1914.

6718. Kitton, Fred G. *John Leech, artist and humorist; a biographical sketch.* New edition, revised. London, Redway, 1884.

6719. Leech, John. *Pictures of life & character from the collection of Mr. Punch.* 5 v. London, Bradbury and Evans, 1854–1869.

6720. Tidy, Gordon. *A little about Leech*. London, Constable, 1931.

Le Fauconnier, Henri Victor Gabriel, 1881–1946

6721. Ridder, André de. *Le Fauconnier*. Bruxelles, Editions de l'Art Libre, 1919.

6722. Romains, Jules. *Le Fauconnier*. Paris, Seheur, 1927. (L'art et la vie, 3).

Léger, Fernand, 1881–1955

6723. Bauquier, Georges. *Fernand Léger, catalogue raisonné: le catalogue raisonné de l'oeuvre paint, établi par Georges Bauquier; assisté de Nelly Maillard*. v.1– , Paris, A. Maeght, 1990– . (CR).

6724. Cassou, Jean et Leymarie, Jean. *Fernand Léger; dessins et gouaches*. Paris, Chêne, 1972.

6725. Cooper, Douglas. *Fernand Léger et le nouvel espace*. London, Lund Humphries/Genève-Paris, Editions des Trois Collines, 1949.

6726. Couturie, Marie A., et al. *Fernand Léger; la forme humaine dans l'espace*. Montréal, Les Editions de l'Arbre, 1945.

6727. de Francia, Peter. *Fernand Léger*. New Haven, Yale University Press, 1983.

6728. Delevoy, Robert L. *Léger, biographical and critical study*. Trans. by Stuart Gilbert. Genève, Skira, 1962; distributed by World, Cleveland. (The Taste of Our Time, 38).

6729. Descargues, Pierre. *Fernand Léger*. Paris, Cercle d'Art, 1955.

6730. Diehl, Gaston. *F. Léger*. New York, Crown Publishers, 1985.

6731. Garaudy, Roger. *Pour un réalisme du XXᵉ siècle; dialogue posthume avec Fernand Léger*. Paris, Grasset, 1968.

6732. George, Waldemar. *Fernand Léger*. Paris, Gallimard, 1929.

6733. Green, Christopher. *Léger and the avant-garde*. New Haven/ London, Yale University Press, 1976.

6734. Jardot, Maurice. *Léger*. Paris, Hazan, 1956.

6735. Kuh, Katharine. *Léger*. Urbana, Ill., University of Illinois, 1953.

6736. Kunsthalle Köln. *Fernand Léger, das fig-ürliche Werk*. 12. April bis 4. Juni 1978. Köln, Museen der Stadt Köln, 1978.

6737. Laugier, Claude et Richet, Michèle. *Léger; oeuvres de Fernand Léger (1881–1955)*. Paris, Centre Georges Pompidou, Musée National d'Art Moderne, 1981. (CR).

6738. Léger, Fernand. *Functions of painting*. Trans. by Alexandra Anderson. Ed. and introd. by Edward F. Fry. New York, Viking, 1973.

6739. ———, et al. *Entretien de Fernand Léger avec Blaise Cendrars et Louis Carré sur le paysage dans l'oeuvre de Léger*. Paris, Carré, 1956.

6740. ———. *Lettres à Simone*. Préface de Mau-

rice Jardot; correspondence établie et annotée par Christian Derouet. Genève, Skira; Paris, Musée national d'art moderne, Centre Georges Pompidou, 1987.

6741. Le Noci, Guido. *Fernand Léger: sa vie, son oeuvre, son rêve*. Milano, Apollinaire, 1971. (Inchiostri dell'Apollinaire, 5).

6742. Musée des Arts Décoratifs, Palais du Louvre, Pavillon de Marsan (Paris). *Fernand Léger, 1881–1955*. Juin–octobre 1956. Paris, Museé des Arts Décoratifs, 1956.

6743. Raynal, Maurice. *Fernand Léger, vingt tableaux*. Paris, L'Effort Moderne, 1920.

6744. Saphire, Lawrence. *Fernand Léger, the complete graphic work*. New York, Blue Moon Press, 1978. (CR)

6745. Staatliche Kunsthalle Berlin. *Fernand Léger, 1881–1965*. 24. Oktober 1980 bis 7. Januar 1981. Berlin, Staatliche Kunsthalle, 1980.

6746. Tate Gallery (London). *Léger and purist Paris*. 18 November 1970–24 January 1971. London, Tate Gallery, 1970.

6747. Tériade, E. *Fernand Léger*. Paris, Cahiers d'Art, 1928.

6748. Verdet, André. *Fernand Léger. Images de Robert Doisneau et Gilles Ehrmann*. Genève, Kister, 1956.

6749. ———. *Fernand Léger; le dynamisme pictural*. Genève, Cailler, 1955.

Legros, Alphonse, 1837–1911

6750. Bénédite, Léonce. *Alphonse Legros*. Paris, Ollendorff, 1900.

6751. [Bliss, Frank E.]. *A catalogue of the etchings, drypoints and lithographs by Professor Alphonse Legros (1837–1911) in the collection of Frank E. Bliss*. With a preface by Campbell Dodgson. London, [printed for private circulation], 1923.

6752. Poulet-Malassis, Auguste [and] Thibaudeau, A. *Catalogue raisonné de l'oeuvre gravé et lithographié de M. Alphonse Legros, 1855–1877*. Paris, Baur, 1877. (CR).

6753. Wilcox, Timothy. *Alphonse Legros, 1837–1911: catalogue de l'exposition présentée au Musée des beaux-arts de Dijon du 12 décembre 1987 au 15 février 1988*. Catalogue par Timothy Wilcox; notices des médailles par Philip Attwood; traduit de l'anglais par Marguerite Guillaume, avec le concours de Claudie Barral et Christaine Van Wersch-Cot. Dijon, Le Musée, 1988.

Lehmbruck, Wilhelm, 1881–1919

6754. Händler, Gerhard. *Wilhelm Lehmbruck, die Zeichnungen der Reifezeit*. Mit einem Nachwort von Siegfried Salzmann. Stuttgart, G. Hatje, 1985.

6755. Hoff, August. *Wilhelm Lehmbruck*. Berlin, Klinkhardt & Biermann, 1933. (Junge Kunst 61/62).

6756. ———. *Wilhelm Lehmbruck, Leben und Werk*. Berlin, Rembrandt, 1961 (Die Kunst unserer Zeit, 13). (CR).

6757. National Gallery of Art (Washington, D.C.). *The art of Wilhelm Lehmbruck*. May 20–August 13, 1972. [Text by Reinhold Heller]. Washington, D.C., National Gallery of Art, 1972.

6758. Petermann, Erwin. *Die Druckgraphik von Wilhelm Lehmbruck, Verzeichnis*. Stuttgart, Hatje, 1964. (CR).

6759. Schubert, Dietrich. *Die Kunst Lehmbrucks*. Worms, Wernersche Verlagsgesellchaft, 1981. (2 ed., i.e., zweite überarbeitete und erweiterte Auflage). Worms, Wernersche Verlagsgesellschaft; Dresden, Verlag der Kunst, 1993).

6760. Westheim, Paul. *Wilhelm Lehmbruck*. Berlin, Kiepenheuer, 1922. 2 ed.

6761. Wilhelm-Lehmbruck-Museum der Stadt Duisburg. *Hommage à Lehmbruck/Lehmbruck in seiner Zeit*. 25. Oktober–3. Januar 1982. Duisburg, Wilhelm-Lehmbruck-Museum, 1981.

Leibl, Wilhelm, 1844–1900

6762. Gronau, Georg. *Leibl*. Bielefeld/Leipzig, Velhagen & Klasing, 1901. (Künstler-Monographien, 50).

6763. Langer, Alfred. *Wilhelm Leibl*. Leipzig, Rosenheimer Verlagshaus, 1961. 2 ed.

6764. Mayr, Julius. *Wilhelm Leibl, sein Leben und sein Schaffen*. Berlin, Cassirer, 1919. 3 ed.

6765. Nasse, Hermann. *Wilhelm Leibl*. München, Schmidt, 1923.

6766. Rompler, Karl. *Wilhelm Leibl*. Dresden, Verlag der Künst, 1955.

6767. Ruhmer, Eberhard. *Der Leibl-Kreis und die Reine Malerei*. Rosenheim, Rosenheimer Verlagshaus, 1984.

6768. Städtische Galerie im Lenbachhaus München. *Wilhelm Leibl und sein Kreis*. 25. Juli bis 29. September 1974. [Text ed. by Michael Petzet]. München, Prestel, 1974.

6769. Waldmann, Emil. *Wilhelm Leibl als Zeichner*. München, Prestel, 1943.

6770. ———. *Wilhelm Leibl: eine Darstellung seiner Künst; Gesamtverzeichnis seiner Gemälde*. Berlin, Cassirer, 1914. (CR).

6771. Wallraf-Richartz-Museum (Köln). *Wilhelm Leibl; Gemälde, Zeichnungen, Radierungen*. 10.–31. März 1929. Berlin, Cassirer, 1929.

6772. Wolf, Georg J. *Leibl und sein Kreis*. München, Bruckmann, 1923.

Leighton, Frederick (Lord Stretton), 1830–1896

6773. Baldry, A. Lys. *Leighton*. London, Jack/New York, Stokes, [1908].

6774. Barrington, Mrs. Russell. *The life, letters and work of Frederic Leighton*. 2 v. New York, Macmillan, 1906.

6775. Gaunt, William. *Victorian Olympus*. London, Cape, 1975. Rev. ed.

6776. Lang, Leonora B. *Sir F. Leighton, president of the Royal Academy his life and work*. London, Virtue/New York, International News Company, 1884. (The Art Annual, 1884)

6777. Newall, Christopher. *The art of Lord Leighton*. Oxford, Phaidon; New York, Phaidon Universe, 1990.

6778. Ormond, Leonée and Ormond, Richard. *Lord Leighton*. New Haven/London, Yale University Press, 1975.

6779. Rhys, Ernest. *Frederic Lord Leighton, an illustrated record of his life and work*. London, Bell, 1900.

6780. Staley, Edgcumbe. *Lord Leighton of Stretton*. London, Scott/New York, Scribner's, 1906.

Leinberger, Hans, fl. 1511–1522

6781. Behle, Claudia. *Hans Leinberger: Leben und Eigenart des Künstlers, stilistische Entwicklung, Rekonstruktion der Gruppen und Altäre*. München, Kommissionsverlag UNI-Druck, 1984. (Miscellanea Bavarica Monacensia, 124).

6782. Liedke, Volker. *Hans Leinberger; Marginalien zur künstlerischen und genealogischen Herkunft des grossen Landshuter Bildschnitzers*. München, Weber, 1979.

6783. Lill, Georg. *Hans Leinberger der Bildschnitzer von Landshut*. München, Bruckmann, 1942.

6784. Lossnitzer, Max. *Hans Leinberger: Nachbildungen seiner Kupferstiche und Holzschnitte*. Berlin, Cassirer, 1913. (Graphische Gesellschaft, 18).

6785. Thoma, Hans. *Hans Leinberger: seine Stadt, seine Zeit, sein Werk*. Regensburg, Pustet, 1979.

Le Lorrain, Robert, 1666–1743

6786. Beaulieu, Michèle. *Robert Le Lorrain (1666–1743)*. Neuilly-sur-Seine, Arthena, 1982.

Lely, Peter, 1618–1680

6787. Baker, Charles H. *Lely and the Stuart portrait painters; a study of English portraiture before and after Van Dyck*. 2 v. London, Warner, 1912.

6788. Beckett, Ronald B. *Lely*. London, Routledge, 1951.

6789. Carlton House Terrace (London). *Sir Peter Lely, 1618–80*. 17 November 1978–18 March 1979. [Text by Sir Oliver Millar]. London, National Portrait Gallery, 1978.

Lemmen, Georges, 1865–1916

6790. Cardon, Roger. *Georges Lemmen (1865–1916).* Monographie générale suivie du catalogue raisonné de l'oeuvre gravé. Anwerpen, Pandora, 1990 (CR).

Lemmers, Georges, 1871–1944

6791. Berko, Patrick and Berko, Viviane. *Georges Lemmers, 1871–1944.* Knokke-Zoute, Berko, 1987. [New ed. by Patrick and Viviane Berko and Philippe Cruymans; Knokke-Zoute, Berko, 1993].

Le Moyne, François, 1688–1737

6792. Bordeaux, Jean-Luc. *François Le Moyne and his generation, 1688–1737.* Neuilly-sur-Seine, Arthena, 1984.

Le Moyne, Jacques *see* Le Moyne de Morgues, Jacques

Lemoyne, Jean-Baptiste, 1704–1778 *see also* Boucher, François

6793. Le Breton, Gaston. *Le sculpteur Jean-Baptiste Lemoyne et L'Académie de Rouen.* Paris, Plon, 1882.
6794. Réau, Louis. *Les Lemoyne; une dynastie de sculpteurs au XVIIIᵉ siècle.* Paris, Les Beaux-Arts, 1927.

Le Moyne De Morgues, Jacques, d. 1588

6795. Hulton, Paul. *The work of Jacques Le Moyne de Morgues, a Huguenot artist in France, Florida and England.* 2 v. London, The Trustees of the British Museum, 1977.
6796. Le Moyne de Morgues, Jacques. *Narrative of Le Moyne, an artist who accompanied the French expedition to Florida under Laudonnière, 1564.* Trans. from the Latin of De Bry by Frederick B. Perkins. Boston, Mass., 1875.
6797. Lorant, Stefan, ed. *The New World; the first pictures of America, made by John White and Jacques Le Moyne and engraved by Theodore De Bry.* New York, Duell, Sloan & Pearce, 1946.

Le Nain, Antoine, 1588–1648
Louis, 1593–1648
Mathieu, 1607–1677

6798. Champfleury [pseud., Jules Fleury]. *Les frères Le Nain.* Paris, Renouard, 1862.
6799. Fierens, Paul. *Les Le Nain.* Paris, Floury, 1933.
6800. Grand Palais (Paris). *Les frères Le Nain.* 3 octobre 1978–8 janvier 1979. [Text by Jacques Thuillier]. Paris, Editions de la Réunion des Musées Nationaux, 1978.
6801. Jamot, Paul. *Les Le Nain; biographie critique.* Paris, Laurens, 1929.

6802. Valabrègue, Antony. *Les frères Le Nain.* Paris, Baranger, 1904.

Lenbach, Franz von, 1836–1904

6803. Baranow, Sonja von. *Franz von Lenbach: Leben und Werk.* Köln, DuMont, 1986.
6804. Lenbach, Franz von. *Franz von Lenbach, 1836–1904:* [Katalog der] Ausstellung, 14. Dezember 1986–3. Mai 1987, Lenbachhaus, München. Vorbereitung und Bearbeitung von Ausstellung und Katalog, Rosel Gollek und Winfried Ranke. München, Prestel-Verlag, 1987.
6805. ———. *Franz von Lenbach: Unbekanntes und Unveröffentlichtes.* Hrsg. von Dieter Distl und Klaus Englert; mit einem Beitrag von Reinhard Horn und einer Einführung von Franz. J. Mayer. Pfaffenhofen, W. Ludwig, 1986.
6806. Mehl, Sonia. *Franz von Lenbach in der Städtischen Galerie im Lenbachhaus München.* München, Prestel, 1980. (CR). (Materialien zur Kunst des neunzehnten Jahrhunderts, 25).
6807. Reischl, Georg A. *Lenbach und seine Heimat.* Schrobenhausen [Oberbayern], [Reischl], 1954.
6808. Rosenberg, Adolf. *Lenbach.* Bielefeld/Leipzig, Velhagen & Klasing, 1898. (Künstler-Monographien, 34).
6809. Wichmann, Siegfried. *Franz von Lenbach und seine Zeit.* Köln, DuMont Schauberg, 1973.
6810. Wyl, Wilhelm [pseud., Wilhelm Ritter von Wymetal]. *Franz von Lenbach, Gespräche und Erinnerungen.* Stuttgart/Leipzig, Deutsche Verlags-Anstalt, 1904.

L'Enfant, Pierre Charles, 1754–1825

6811. Caemmerer, H. Paul. *The life of Pierre Charles L'Enfant.* Washington, D.C., National Republic Publishing Co., 1950. (Reprint: New York, Da Capo, 1970).
6812. Kite, Elizabeth S. *L'Enfant and Washington.* Baltimore, Johns Hopkins Press, 1929.
6813. Stephenson, Richard W. *A plan whol[l]y new: Pierre Charles L'Enfant's plan of the City of Washington.* Washington, Library of Congress, 1993.

Le Nôtre, André, 1613–1700

6814. Baubion-Mackler, Jeannie. *French royal gardens: the designs of André Le Nôtre.* Photographs by Jennie Baubion-Mackler; text by Vincent Scully. foreword by Simone Hoog; epilogue by Claude Roy. New York, Rizzoli, 1992.
6815. Fox, Helen M. *André Le Nôtre, garden architect to kings.* London, Batsford, 1963.
6816. Ganay, Ernest de. *André Le Nostre, 1613–*

1700. Paris, Vincent, Fréal, 1962.

6817. Guiffrey, Jules. *André LeNostre*. Paris, Laurens, 1912.

6818. Hazlehurst, F. Hamilton. *Gardens of illusion; the genius of André Le Nostre*. Nashville, Tenn., Vanderbilt University Press, 1980.

Leonardo da Vinci, 1452–1519

6819. Amoretti, Carlo. *Memorie storiche su la vita gli studi e le opere di Lionardo da Vinci*. Milano, Giusti, Ferrario, 1804.

6820. Argan, Giulio C., et al. *Leonardo: la pittura*. Firenze, Martello-Giunti, 1977.

6821. [Arte Lombarda, eds.]. *Leonardo; il Cenacolo*. Milano, Arte Lombarda, 1982. (Arte Lombarda, nuova serie, 62).

6822. Baratta, Mario. *Curiosità Vinciane*. Torino, Bocca, 1905. (Piccola biblioteca di scienze-moderne, 103).

6823. ———. *Leonardo da Vinci ed i problemi della terra*. Torino, Bocca, 1903.

6824. Beck, James. *Leonardo's rules of painting; an unconventional approach to modern art*. New York, Viking, 1979.

6825. Belt, Elmer. *Manuscripts of Leonardo da Vinci; their history, with a description of the manuscript editions in facsimile*. Catalogue by Kate T. Steinitz with the assistance of Margot Archer. Los Angeles, Elmer Belt Library of Vinciana, 1948.

6826. Beltrami, Luca. *Documenti e memorie riguardanti la vita e le opere di Leonardo da Vinci in ordine cronologico*. Milano, Treves, 1919.

6827. Bérence, Fred. *Léonard de Vinci*. Paris, Somogy, 1965. (Lesplusgrands, 10).

6828. Bode, Wilhelm von. *Studien über Leonardo da Vinci*. Berlin, Grote, 1921.

6829. Bossi, Giuseppe. *Del Cenacolo di Leonardo da Vinci*. Milano, Stamperia Reale, 1810.

6830. Boussel, Patrice. *Leonardo da Vinci*. Secaucus, N.J., Chartwell Books, 1986.

6831. Bovi, Arturo. *Leonardo; filosofo, artista, uomo*. Milano, Hoepli, 1952.

6832. Bramly, Serge. *Leonardo: discovering the life of Leonardo da Vinci*. Translated [from the French] by Siéan Reynolds. New York, Edward Burlingame Books, 1991.

6833. Brasil, Jaime. *Leonardo da Vinci e o seu tempo*. Lisboa, Portugália, 1959.

6834. Braunfels-Esche, Sigrid. *Leonardo da Vinci, das anatomische Werk*. Stuttgart, Schattauer, 1961. 2 ed.

6835. Brion, Marcel. *Léonard de Vinci, génie et destinée*. Paris, Michel, 1952.

6836. Brown, John W. *The life of Leonardo da Vinci with a critical account of his works*. London, Pickering, 1828.

6837. Calder, Ritchie. *Leonardo and the age of the eye*. New York, Simon & Schuster, 1970.

6838. Caroli, Flavio. *Leonardo: studi di fisiognomica*. Milano, Leonardo, 1991.

6839. Calvi, Gerolamo. *I manoscritti di Leonardo da Vinci dal punto di vista cronologico storico e biografico*. Bologna, Zanichelli, 1925. (Studi e testi vinciani, 6).

6840. Calvi, Ignazio. *L'architettura militare di Leonardo da Vinci*. Milano, Libreria Lombarda, 1943.

6841. Campana, Adelemo. *Leonardo; la vita, il pensiero, i testi esemplari*. Milano, Edizioni Accademia, 1973.

6842. Carotti, Giulio. *Leonardo da Vinci; pittore, scultore, architetto*. Studio biografico-critico. Torino, Celanza, 1921.

6843. Carpiceci, Alberto C. *L'architettura di Leonardo: indagine e ipotesi su tutta l'opera di Leonardo architetto*. Firenze, Bonechi, 1978.

6844. Castelfranco, Giorgio. *Studi vinciana*. Roma, de Luca, 1966.

6845. Ceccarelli, Anna. *L'idea pedagogica di Leonardo da Vinci*. Roma, Loescher, 1914.

6846. Chastel, André, ed. *Léonard de Vinci par lui-même*. Textes choisis, traduits et présentes par André Chastel, précédés de la vie de Léonard par Vasari. Paris, Nagel, 1952. (English ed.: *The genius of Leonardo da Vinci*. Trans. by Ellen Callmann. New York, Orion Press, 1961).

6847. Clark, Kenneth. *The drawings of Leonardo da Vinci in the collection of Her Majesty the Queen at Windsor Castle, revised with the assistance of Carlo Pedretti*. 3 v. London, Phaidon, 1968. 2 ed. (CR).

6848. ———. *Leonardo da Vinci, an account of his development as an artist*. Cambridge, Cambridge University Press, 1939.

6849. ———. *Leonardo da Vinci*. [rev. ed. of the preceeding title]. Introduction, Martin Kemp. London, Viking, 1988. (A rev. ed. was first published by Penguin Books, 1959. Now it is published with revisions and an introduction by Viking in 1988).

6850. Coleman, Marguerite. *Amboise et Léonard de Vinci à Amboise*. Préf. de Pierre Nolhac. Tours, Arrault, 1932.

6851. Colombo, Alfredo. *Ecco Leonardo*. Novara, Istituto Geografico de Agostini, 1952.

6852. [Comitato Nazionale per le Onoranze a Leonardo da Vinci nel Quinto Centenario della Nascita (1452–1952)]. *Leonardo, saggi e ricerche*. Roma, Istituto Poligrafico dello Stato, 1954.

6853. [Convegno di Studi Vinciani]. *Atti del convegno di studi vinciani, indetto dalla Unione Regionale delle province Toscane e dalle Università di Firenze, Pisa e Siena*. [Firenze/Pisa/Siena, 15–18 gennaio 1953]. Firenze, Olschki, 1953.

6854. Cook, Theodore A. *Leonardo da Vinci,*

sculptor. London, Humphreys, 1923.

6855. D'adda, Gerolamo. *Leonardo da Vinci e la sua libreria; note di un bibliofilo.* Milano, Bernardini, 1873.

6856. Duhem, Pierre. *Etudes sur Léonard de Vinci.* [3 v., published separately]. Paris, Hermann, 1906–1913. (Reprint: Paris, de Nobele, 1955).

6857. Einem, Herbert von. *Das Abendmahl des Leonardo da Vinci.* Köln, Westdeutscher Verlag, 1961.

6858. Eissler, Kurt R. *Leonardo da Vinci, psychoanalytic notes on the enigma.* London, Hogarth Press, 1962. (The International Psychoanalytical Library, 58).

6859. Farago, Claire J. *Leonardo da Vinci's Paragone: a critical interpretation with a new edition of the text in the Codex Urbinas.* Leiden, the Netherlands/New York, E.J. Brill, 1992.

6860. Feddersen, Hans. *Leonardo da Vincis Abendmahl.* Stuttgart, Urachhaus, 1975.

6861. Feldhaus, Franz M. *Leonardo der Techniker und Erfinder.* Jena, Diederichs, 1922.

6862. Firpo, Luigi. *Leonardo, architetto e urbanista.* Torino, Unione Tipografico-Editrice Torinese, 1963.

6863. Flora, Francesco. *Leonardo.* Milano, Mondadori, 1952. (Biblioteca moderna Mondadori, 279).

6864. Franzini, Elio. *Il mito di Leonardo: sulla fenomenologia della creazione artistica.* Milano, UNICOPLI, 1987. (Estetica contemporanea, 6).

6865. [Fratelli Treves, editori]. *Leonardo da Vinci, conferenze fiorentine.* [Text by Edmondo Solmi, Luca Beltrami, Benedetto Croce, et al.] Milano, Treves, 1910.

6866. Freud, Sigmund. *Leonardo da Vinci; a psychosexual study of an infantile reminiscence.* Trans. by A. Brill. New York, Moffat, Yard, 1916.

6867. Friedenthal, Richard. *Leonardo, eine Bildbiographie.* München, Kindler, 1959.

6868. Fumagalli, Giuseppina. *Eros di Leonardo.* Milano, Garzanti, 1952.

6869. ———. *Leonardo iere e oggi.* Pisa, Nistri-Lischi, 1959. (Saggi di varia umanità, 28).

6870. Galbiati, Giovanni. *Dizionario Leonardesco; repertorio generale delle voci e cose contenute nel Codice Atlantico.* Milano, Hoepli, 1939.

6871. Gallenberg, Hugo G. von. *Leonardo da Vinci.* Leipzig, Fleischer, 1834.

6872. Gantner, Joseph. *Leonardos Visionen von der Sintflut und vom Untergang der Welt; Geschichte einer kunstlerischen Idee.* Bern, Francke, 1958.

6873. Gault de Saint-Germain, Pierre M. *Vie de Leonard de Vinci, suivie du catalogue de ses*

ouvrages dans les beaux-arts. Paris, Perlet, 1803.

6874. Giacomelli, Raffaele. *Gli scritti di Leonardo da Vinci sul volo.* Roma, Bardi, 1936.

6875. Giglioli, Odoardo H. *Leonardo; iniziazione alla conoscenza de lui e delle questioni vinciane.* Firenze, Arnaud, 1944.

6876. Gilles de la Tourette, Franois. *Léonard de Vinci.* Paris, Michel, 1932. (Les maîtres du Moyen Age et de la Renaissance, 8).

6877. Goldscheider, Ludwig, ed. *Leonardo da Vinci.* London, Phaidon/New York, Oxford University Press, 1964. 7 ed.

6878. Gould, Cecil H. *Leonardo: the artist and the non-artist.* Boston, New York Graphic Society, 1975.

6879. Gronau, Georg. *Leonardo da Vinci.* Trans. by Frederic Pledge. London, Duckworth/New York, Dutton, [1903].

6880. Grothe, Hermann. *Leonardo da Vinci als Ingenieur und Philosoph; ein Beitrag zur Geschichte der Technik und der induktiven Wissenschaften.* Berlin, Nicolaische Verlags-Buchhandlung, 1874.

6881. Guerrini, Mauro. *Bibliotheca leonardiana, 1493–1989.* 3 v. Presentazione: Augusto Marinoni, Carlo Pedretti. Milano, Editrice Bibliografica, 1990. (Grandi opere, 3).

6882. Guillerm, Jean-Pierre. *Tombeau de Léonard de Vinci; le peintre et ses tableaux dans l'écriture symboliste et décadente.* Lille, Presses Universitaires de Lille, 1981.

6883. Guillion, Aimé. *Le Cénacle de Léonard de Vinci, rendu aux amis des beaux-arts, dans le tableau qu'on voit aujourd'hui chez un citoyen de Milan, et qui étoit ci-devant dans le réfectoire de l'insigne chartreuse de Pavie.* Essai historique et psychologique. Milano, Dumolard, Artaria/Lyon, Maire, 1811.

6884. ———. *Sur l'ancien copie de la Cène de Léonard de Vinci qu'on voit maintenant au Musée Royal; comparée à la plus célèbre de toutes, celle des Chartreux de Pavie; et à la copie récente d'après laquelle s'exécute à Milan, une mosaïque égale en dimentions à l'original.* Paris, Normant, 1817.

6885. Heaton, Mrs. Charles W. [and] Black, Charles C. *Leonardo da Vinci and his works, consisting of a life of Leonardo da Vinci, [by Mrs. Heaton], an essay on his scientific and literary works [by Mr. Black] and an account of his most important paintings.* London/New York, Macmillan, 1874.

6886. Heesvelde, Franois van. *Les signatures de Léonard de Vinci dans ses oeuvres.* Anvers, Blondé, 1962.

6887. Herzfeld, Marie. *Leonardo da Vinci; der Denker, Forscher und Poet.* Leipzig, Diederichs, 1904.

6888. Hevesy, André de. *Pèlerinage avec Léonard*

de Vinci. Paris, Fermin-Didot, 1939.

6889. Heydenreich, Ludwig H. *Leonardo da Vinci.* 2 v. New York, Macmillan/Basel, Holbein, 1954.

6890. ———. *Leonardo: the Last Supper.* New York, Viking, 1974.

6891. ———. *Die Sakralbau-Studien Leonardo da Vincis.* München, Fink, 1971. 2 ed.

6892. Hildebrandt, Edmund. *Leonardo da Vinci, der Künstler und sein Werk.* Berlin, Grote, 1927.

6893. Hoerth, Otto. *Das Abendmahl des Leonardo da Vinci, ein Beitrag zur Frage seiner künstlerischen Rekonstruktion.* Leipzig, Hiersemann, 1907. (Kunstgeschichtliche Monographien, 8).

6894. Houssaye, Arsène. *Histoire de Léonard de Vinci.* Paris, Didier, 1876. 2 ed.

6895. Istituto di Studi Vinciani di Roma. *Per il IV° centenario della morte di Leonardo da Vinci, [2] maggio [1919].* [Edited by Mario Cermenati]. Bergamo, Istituto Italiano d'Arti Grafiche, 1919.

6896. Janowitz, Günther J. *Leonardo da Vinci, Brunelleschi, Dürer: ihre Auseinandersetzung mit der Problematik der Zentralperspektive.* Einhausen, Hübner, 1986.

6897. Jordan, Max. *Das Malerbuch des Lionardo da Vinci; Untersuchung der Ausgaben und Handschriften.* Leipzig, Seemann, 1873.

6898. Kemp, Martin. *Leonardo da Vinci; the marvelous works of nature and man.* Cambridge, Mass., Harvard University Press, 1981.

6899. Klaiber, Hans. *Leonardostudien.* Strassburg, Heitz, 1907. (Zur Kunstgeschichte des Auslandes, 56).

6900. Knapp, Fritz. *Leonardo da Vinci.* Bielefeld/Leipzig, Velhagen & Klasing, 1938. (Künstler-Monographien, 33).

6901. Koenig, Frédéric [pseud., Just J. E. Roy]. *Léonard de Vinci.* Tours, Mame, 1869. 2 ed.

6902. *Léonard de Vinci.* [Feuillets inédits, variously titled]. 23 v. Paris, Rouveyre, 1901.

6903. ———. *Les manuscrits de Léonard de Vinci.* Avec transcription littérale, traduction française, préface et table méthodique par Charles Ravaisson-Mollien. 6 v. Paris, Quantin, 1881–91.

6904. ———. *Problèmes de géométrie et d'hydraulique.* Manuscrits inédits, reproduits d'après les originaux con-servés à la Forster Library, South Kensington Museum, London. 3 v. Paris, Rouveyre, 1901.

6905. ———. *Sciences physico-mathématiques.* Manuscrits inédits, reproduits d'après les originaux conservés au British Museum, London. 4 v. Paris, Rouveyre, 1901.

6906. ———. *Traité de la peinture [Trattato della pitttura].* Traduit et présenté par André Chastel. Paris, Berger-Levrault, 1987.

6907. Leonardo da Vinci. *Il Codice Atlantico della Biblioteca Ambrosiana di Milano. Transcrizione diplomatica e critica di Augusto Marinoni.* 12 v. Firenze, Giunti/Barbèra, 1975–1980.

6908. ———. *Il codice di Leonardo da Vinci della biblioteca del principe Trivulzio in Milano.* Transcritto ed anno-tato di Luca Beltrami. Milano, Hoepli, 1891.

6909. ———. *The complete paintings of Leonardo da Vinci.* Introduction by L. Ettlinger; notes and catalogue by Angela Ottino della Chiesa. Harmondsworth, Middlesex, Penguin Books; New York, Viking Penguin, 1985. (First publ. in Italian by Rizzoli, 1967. English transl. first publ. in Great Britain by Weidenfeld & Nicolson, 1969).

6910. ———. *I disegni d'architettura militare di Leonardo da Vinci (Ms. Saluzzo 312).* [Compiled by Giuseppe François and Luigi Ferrario]. 2 v. Firenze, Giunti, 1990.

6911. ———. *I disegni di Leonardo da Vinci e della sua cerchia nel Gabinetto disegni e stampe della Galleria degli Uffizi a Frenze.* Ordinati e presentati da Carlo Pedretti; catalogo di Gigetta Dalli Regoli. Firenze, Giunti Barbera, 1985.

6912. ———. *I disegni di Leonardo da Vinci e della sua cerchia nella Biblioteca reale di Torino.* Ordinati e presentati da Carlo Pedretti. Con la riproduzione integrale dell'opera inedita Disegni d'architettura militare di Leonardo da Vinci (Ms. Saluzzo 312). 2 v. Firenze, Giunti, 1990.

6913. ———. *The drawings of Leonado da Vinci and his circle in America.* Arranged and introduced by Carlo Pedretti; catalogue by Patricia Trutty-Coohill. Florence, Giunti, 1993.

6914. ———. *Leonardo da Vinci on the human body; the anatomical, physiological, and embryological drawings.* With transcription, emendations, and a biographical introduction by Charles D. O'Malley and J. B. Saunders. New York, Schuman, 1952.

6915. ———. *Leonardo on painting: an anthology of writings by Leonardo da Vinci with a selection of documents relating to his career as an artist.* Edited by Martin Kemp; selected and translated by Martin Kemp and Margaret Walker. New Haven, Yale University Press, 1989.

6916. ———. *I libri di meccanica, nella ricostruzione ordinata di Arturo Uccelli, preceduti da un'introduzione critica e da un esame della fonti.* Milano, Hoepli, 1940.

6917. ———. *The literary works of Leonardo da Vinci, compiled and edited from the original manuscripts by Jean Paul Richter.* Commentary by Carlo Pedretti. 2 v. Berkeley, Calif., University of California Press, 1977.

6918. ———. *The Madrid codices.* [Tratato de

L

estatica y mechanica en italiano; transcription and translation by Ladislao Reti]. New York, McGraw-Hill, 1974.

6919. ———. *I manoscritti e i disegni di Leonardo da Vinci pubblicati dalla Reale Commissione Vinciana*. A cura di Adolfo Venturi. 7 v. Roma, Danesi/La Libreria dello Stato, 1928–1952.

6920. ———. *The notebooks of Leonardo da Vinci*. Arranged, rendered into English, and introduced by Edward MacCurdy. Garden City, N.Y., Garden City Publishing Co., 1941–42.

6921. ———. *I pensieri*. A cura di Bruno Nardini. Firenze, Giunit, 1977.

6922. ———. *Quaderni d'anatomia; tredici fogli della Royal Library di Windsor*. Pubblicati da Ove C. L. Vangensten, A. Fonahn, [and] H. Hopstock. 6 v. [Text in English and Norwegian]. Christiania [Oslo], Dybwad, 1911–1916.

6923. ———. *Scritti scelti*. [Ed. by Anna Maria Brizio]. Torino, Unione Tipografico-Editrice Torinese, 1952. (Classici italiani, 40).

6924. ———. *Thoughts on art and life*. Trans. by Maurice Baring. Boston, Merrymount Press, 1906. (The Humanist's Library, 1).

6925. ———. *Treatise on painting (Codex Urbinas Latinus 1270)*. Translated and annotated by A. Philip McMahon, with an introduction by Ludwig H. Heydenreich. 2 v. (Vol. II: *Facsimile of the Codex*). Princeton, N.J., Princeton University Press, 1956.

6926. ———. *A treatise on painting*. [First English edition]. *Translated from the original Italian* [by John Senex] *and adorn'd with a great number of cuts*. London, Senex/Taylor, 1721.

6927. Lionardo da Vinci. *Trattato della pittura; nuovamente data in luce, colla vita dell'istesso autore scritta da Rafaelle du Fresne*. Paris, Langois, 1651.

6928. Lüdecke, Heinz. *Leonardo da Vinci im Spiegel seiner Zeit*. Berlin, Rutten und Loening, 1953. 2 ed.

6929. Luporini, Cesare. *La mente di Leonardo*. Firenze, Sansoni, 1953. (Biblioteca storica del Rinascimento, nuova serie, 2).

6930. McCurdy, Edward. *The mind of Leonardo da Vinci*. London, Cape, 1952.

6931. Malaguzzi Valeri, Francesco. *Leonardo da Vinci e la scultura*. Bologna, Zanichelli, 1922. (Studietesti vinciani, 5).

6932. Marani, Pietro C. *Leonardo e i leonardeschi nei musei della Lombardia*. Milano, Electa, 1990.

6933. Marcolongo, Roberto. *Leonardo da Vinci; artista, scienzato*. Milano, Hoepli, 1939.

6934. Marcus, Aage. *Leonardo da Vinci*. Stockholm, Bonniers, 1944.

6935. Marinoni, Augusto, et al. *Leonardo da Vinci, letto e commentato*. [Letture vinciane, 1–12].

Firenze, Barbara, 1974.

6936. ———. *I rebus di Leonardo da Vinci, raccolti e interpretati*. Firenze, Olschki, 1954.

6937. Mazenta, Giovanni A. *Le memorie su Leonardo da Vinci*. Ripubblicate e illustrate a cura di Luigi Gramatica. Milano, Alfieri e Lacroix, 1919.

6938. Mazzucconi, Ridolfo. *Leonardo da Vinci*. Firenze, Vallecchi, 1943. (Biblioteca Vallecchi, 38).

6939. McMullen, Roy. *Mona Lisa; the picture and the myth*. Boston, Houghton Mifflin, 1975.

6940. Moeller, Emil. *Das Abendmahl des Lionardo da Vinci*. Baden-Baden, Verlag für Kunst und Wissenschaft, 1952.

6941. Mourgue, Géraqrd. *Léonard de Vinci*. Paris, France-Empire, 1986.

6942. Müller-Walde, Paul. *Leonardo da Vinci; Lebensskizze und Forschungen über sein Verhältniss zur florentiner Kunst und zu Rafael*. München, Hirth, 1889–1890.

6943. Müntz, Eugène. *Leonardo da Vinci; artist, thinker, man of science*. 2 v. London, Heinemann/New York, Scribner's, 1898.

6944. Oberdorfer, Aldo. *Leonardo da Vinci*. Torino, Paravia, 1928.

6945. Ost, Hans. *Leonardo-Studien*. Berlin/New York, de Gruyter, 1975. (Beiträge zur Kunstgeschichte, 11).

6946. Ottino della Chiesa, Angela. *The complete paintings of Leonardo da Vinci*. Trans. by Madeline Jay. New York, Abrams, 1967.

6947. Panofsky, Erwin. *The Codex Huygens and Leonardo da Vinci's art theory*. London, Warburg Institute, 1940. (Studies of the Warburg Institute, 13). (Reprint: New York, Kraus, 1968).

6948. Payne, Robert. *Leonardo*. Garden City, N.Y., Doubleday, 1978.

6949. Pedretti, Carlo. *A chronology of Leonardo da Vinci's architectural studies after 1500*. Genève, Droz, 1962. (Travaux d'Humanisme et Renaissance, 54).

6950. ———. *Documenti e memorie rigvardanti Leonardo da Vinci a Bologna e in Emilia*. Bologna, Fiammenghi, 1953.

6951. ———. *Leonardo architect*. Translated by Sue Brill. New York, Rizzoli, 1985. (Translation of *Leonardo Architetto*. Milano, Electa, 1978).

6952. ———. *Leonardo da Vinci on painting; a lost book (Libro A), reassembled from the Codex Vaticanus Urbinas 1270 and from the Codex Leicester*. Foreword by Sir Kenneth Clark. Berkeley/Los Angeles, University of California Press, 1964. (California Studies in the History of Art, 3).

6953. ———. *Leonardo da Vinci: the Royal Palace at Romorantin*. Cambridge, Mass., Belknap Press, 1972.

6954. ———. *Leonardo, a study in chronology*

and style. Berkeley/Los Angeles, University of California Press, 1973.

6955. ———. *Studi vinciani; documenti, analisi e inediti leonardeschi.* Genève, Droz, 1957. (Travaux d'Humanisme et Renaissance, 27).

6956. Péladan, Joséphin. *La philosophie de Léonard de Vinci d'après ses manuscrits.* Paris, Alcan, 1910.

6957. Philipson, Morris, ed. *Leonardo da Vinci; aspects of the renaissance genius.* New York, Braziller, 1966.

6958. Piantanida, Sandro [and] Baroni, Constantino. *Leonardo da Vinci.* [Published in conjunction with the exhibition at the Palazzo dell'Arte, Milan, May 9–September 30, 1939]. Novaro, Istituto Geografico de Agostini, 1939. (English ed.: 1956).

6959. Pierantoni, Amalia C. *Studi sul libro della pittura di Leonardo da Vinci.* Roma, Scotti, 1921.

6960. Pino, Domenico. *Storia genuina del Cenacolo insigne dipinto da Leonardo da Vinci nel refettorio de' Padri Domenicani de Santa Maria delle Grazie de Milano.* Milano, Malatesta, 1796.

6961. Polifolo [pseud., Luca Beltrami]. *Leonardo e i disfattisti suoi,* [with] *Leonardo architetto di Luca Beltrami.* Milano, Treves, 1919.

6962. Pomilio, Mario. *L'opera completa di Leonardo pittore.* Milano, Rizzoli, 1967. (Classici dell'arte, 12).

6963. Popham, Arthur E. *The drawings of Leonardo da Vinci.* New York, Reynal, 1945.

6964. Reti, Ladislao, ed. *The unknown Leonardo.* New York, McGraw-Hill, 1974.

6965. Richter, Jean Paul. *Leonardo.* Trans. by Percy E. Pinkerton. London, Sampson Low, 1880.

6966. Rigollot, Marcel J. *Catalogue de l'oeuvre de Leonard de Vinci.* Paris, Dumoulin, 1849.

6967. Rinaldis, Aldo de. *Storia dell'opera pittorica de Leonardo da Vinci.* Bologna, Zanichelli, 1926. (Studi e testi vinciani, 7).

6968. Rio, Alexis F. *Léonard de Vinci et son école.* Paris, Bray, 1855.

6969. Roger-Milès, Léon. *Léonard de Vinci et les jocondes.* Paris, Floury, 1923.

6970. Rosci, Marco. *The hidden Leonardo.* Trans. by John Gilbert. Milano, Mondadori, 1977.

6971. Rosenberg, Adolf. *Leonardo da Vinci.* Bielefeld/Leipzig, Velhagen & Klasing, 1898. (Künstler-Monographien, 33).

6972. Santi, Bruno. *Leonardo da Vinci.* (Antella) Firenze, Scala; New York, Riverside, 1990.

6973. Sartoris, Alberto. *Léonard, architecte.* Paris, La Maison de Mansart, 1952.

6974. Turner, Richard. *Inventing Leonardo.* New York, Knopf; distrib. by Random House, 1993.

6975. Schiaparelli, Attilio. *Leonardo ritrattista.* Milano, Treves, 1921.

6976. Schumacher, Joachim. *Leonardo da Vinci, Maler und Forscher in anarchischer Gesellschaft.* Berlin, Wagenbach, 1974.

6977. Seailles, Gabriel. *Léonard de Vinci, l'artist & le savant; essai de biographie psychologique.* Paris, Perrin, 1892.

6978. Seidlitz, Woldemar von. *Leonardo da Vinci, der Wendepunkt der Renaissance.* Wien, Phaidon, 1935. 2 ed.

6979. Siren, Osvald. *Leonardo da Vinci.* 3 v. Paris, van Oest, 1928. 2 ed.

6980. Solmi, Edmondo. *Scritti vinciani.* Raccolta a cura di Arrigo Solmi. Firenze, La Voce, 1924.

6981. Steinitz, Kate T. *Leonardo da Vinci's Trattato della Pittura; a bibliography of the printed editions, 1651–1956, based on the complete collection in the Elmer Belt Library of Vinciana, preceded by a study of its sources and illustrations.* København, Munksgaard, 1958. (Library Research Monographs, 5).

6982. ———. *Pierre-Jean Mariette & le Comte de Caylus and their concept of Leonardo da Vinci in the eighteenth century.* Los Angeles, Zeitlin & Ver Brugge, 1974.

6983. Stites, Raymond S. *The sublimations of Leonardo da Vinci, with a translation of the Codex Trivulzianus.* Washington, D.C., Smithsonian Institution, 1970.

6984. Suida, Wilhelm. *Leonardo und sein Kreis.* München, Bruckmann, 1929.

6985. Sweetser, Moses F. *Leonardo da Vinci.* Boston, Houghton, Osgood, 1879.

6986. Thiis, Jens. *Leonardo da Vinci: the Florentine years of Leonardo & Verrocchio.* Trans. by Jessie Muir. Boston, Small, Maynard, [1913].

6987. Toni, Giambattista de. *Le piante e gli animali in Leonardo da Vinci.* Bologna, Zanichelli, 1922. (Studi e testi vinciani, 4).

6988. Ullmann, Ernst. *Leonardo da Vinci.* Leipzig, Seemann, 1980.

6989. Uzielli, Gustavo. *Ricerche intorno a Leonardo da Vinci, serie prima.* Torino, Loescher, 1896. 2 ed.

6990. ———. *Ricerche intorno a Leonardo da Vinci, serie seconda.* Roma, Salviucci, 1884.

6991. Valéry, Paul. *Les divers essais sur Léonard de Vinci de Paul Valéry, commentés et annotés par lui-même.* Paris, Editions du Sagittaire, 1931.

6992. Venturi, Adolfo. *Leonardo da Vinci, pittore.* Bologna, Zanichelli, 1920. (Studi e testi vinciani, 2)

6993. Venturi, Lionello. *La critica e l'arte de Leonardo da Vinci.* Bologna, Zanichelli, 1919. (Stu=di e testi vinciani, 1).

6994. Verga, Ettore. *Bibliografica Vinciana, 1493–1930.* 2 v. Bologna, Zanichelli, 1931. (Reprint: New York, Franklin, 1970.)

6995. ———. *Gli studi intorno a Leonardo da Vinci nell'ultimo cinquantennio (1872–1922).* Roma, Casa Libreria Editrice Italiana, 1923.

L

6996. Vuilliaud, Paul. *La pensée ésotérique de Léonard de Vinci*. Paris, Lieutier, 1945. 2 ed.

6997. Wasserman, Jack. *Leonardo da Vinci*. New York, Abrams, 1975.

6998. Wilhelm-Lehmbruck-Museum der Städt Duisburg. *Mona Lisa im 20. Jahrhundert.* [September 24–December 3, 1978]. Duisburg, Wilhelm-Lehmbruck-Museum, 1978.

6999. Zubov, Vasilii P. *Leonardo da Vinci*. Trans. by David H. Kraus. Cambridge, Mass., Harvard University Press, 1968.

Lepautre, Antoine, 1621–1691

7000. Berger, Robert W. *Antoine Lepautre, a French architect of the era of Louis XIV.* New York, Published for the College Art Association of America by New York University Press, 1969.

7001. [D'Aviler, Augustin C.]. *Les oeuvres d'architecture d'Anthoine Le Pautre, architecte ordinaire du Roy.* Paris, Jombert, 1652. (Reprint: Farnsborough, Eng., Gregg, 1966).

7002. [Lepautre, Jean]. *Collection des plus belles compositions de [Jean] Lepautre, gravée par Decloux, architecte, & Doury, peintre.* Paris, Caudrilier et Morel, [1854].

7003. ———. *Oeuvres d'architecture de Jean Le Pautre, architecte, dessinateur et graveur du Roi.* 3 v. Paris, Jombert, 1751.

Le Prince, Jean-Baptiste, 1734–1781

7004. Hedou, Jules P. *Jean Le Prince et son oeuvre.* Paris, Baur, 1879.

7005. [Le Prince, Jean-Baptiste]. *Oeuvres de Jean-Baptiste le Prince.* Paris, Basan & Poignant, 1782.

Lescaze, William, 1896–1969

7006. Lescaze, William H. *On being an architect.* New York, Putnam, 1942.

Le Sidaner, Henri-Eugene, 1862–1939

7007. Farinaux-Le Sidaner, Yann. *Le Sidaner: l'oeuvre peint et gravé.* Préface de Remy Le Sidaner. Monte Carlo, André Sauret, 1989.

7008. Mauclair, Camille. *Henri Le Sidaner.* Paris, Georges Petit, 19278.

Le Sueur, Eustache, 1617–1655

7009. Dussieux, Louis E., ed. *Nouvelles recherches sur la vie et les ouvrages d'Eustache LeSueur.* Paris, Dumoulin, 1852.

7010. Landon, Charles P. *Vie et oeuvre d'Eustache LeSueur.* Paris, Treuttel et Wurtz, 1811. (Vie et oeuvres des peintres les plus célèbres, 8).

7011. Merot, Alain. *Eustache Le Sueur:1616–1655.* Paris, Arthena, 1987.

7012. Rouchès, Gabriel. *Eustache Le Sueur.* Paris, Alcan, 1923.

7013. Vitet, Ludovic. *Eustache Le Sueur, sa vie et ses oeuvres.* Paris, Challamel, 1849.

Levine, Jack, 1915–

7014. Levine, Jack. *Jack Levine.* Commentary by Jack Levine. Introduction by Milton W. Brown. Compiled and edited by Stephen Robert Frankel. New York, Rizzoli, 1989. (CR).

7015. Prescott, Kenneth Wade. *The complete graphic work of Jack Levine.* K.W. Precott and Emma-Stine Prescott, New York, Dover, 1984.

Levitan, Isaak Il'ich, 1860–1900

7016. Fedora-Davydova, Aleksei A., ed. *Isaak Il'ich Levitan; dokumenty, materialy, bibliografiia.* Moskva, Iskusstvo, 1966.

7017. ———. *Isaak Il'ich Levitan i zhizn' i tvorchestvo, 1860–1900.* Moskva, Iskusstvo, 1976.

7018. Levitan, Isaak Il'ich. *Levitan.* Introduction by Alexai Fiodorov-Davydov; chronology by Tamara Yurova; compiled by Tamara Yurova.

7019. Prytkov, Vladimir A. *Levitan.* Moskva, Akademii Khudozhestv SSR, 1960.

7020. Razdobreyeva, Irina V. *Levitan.* [Text in Russian, French, German, and English]. Leningrad, Aurora Art Publishers, 1971.

7021. Turkov, Andrei M. *Isaak Il'ich Levitan.* Moskva, Iskusstvo, 1974.

Levitskii, Dmitrii Grigor'evich, 1735–1822

7022. Gershenzon-Chegodaeva, Natalia M. *Dmitrii Grigor'evich Levitskii.* Moskva, Iskusstvo, 1964.

7023. Levitskii, Dmitrii Grigor'evich. *Dmitrii Grigorevich Leviskii, 1735–1822: katalog,* G.N. Goldovskii, B.A. Kosolapov, S.V. Rimskaia-Korsakova; sostaviteli kataloga, G.B. Andreeva . . . et al. leningrad "Iskusstvo," Leningradskoe otd-nie, 1987.

7024. Maleva, Nina M. *Dmitrii Grigor'evich Levitskii.* Moskva, Iskusstvo, 1980.

7025. Roche, Denis. *D.M. Lévitski, un portraitiste petit-russien.* Paris, Gazette des Beaux-Arts, 1904.

Lewis, Wyndham, 1882–1957

7026. Ayers, David. *Wyndham Lewis and Western man.* Basingstoke, Macmillan Academic and Professional, 1991.

7027. Cork, Richard . . . [et al.]. *Wyndham Lewis et le vorticisme.* Paris, Centre Georges Poimpidou; Aix-en-Provence, Pandora Editions, 1982.

7028. Edwards, Paul. *Wyndham Lewis: art and war.* [By] P. Edwards; chronology and catalogue of plates by Catherine Wallace; foreword by Angela Weight. London, Wyndhaom Lewis Memorial Trust in association with Lund Humphries, 1992.

7029. Foshay, Toby. *Wyndham Lewis and the av-*

ant-garde: the politics of the intellect. Montreal; Buffalo, McGill-Queen's University Press, 1992.

7030. Grigson, Geoffrey. A master of our time; a study of Wyndham Lewis. London, Methuen, 1951.

7031. Handley-Read, Charles, ed. The art of Wyndham Lewis. With a critical evaluation by Eric Newton. London, Faber, 1951.

7032. Kush, Thomas. Wyndham Lewis's pictorial integer. Ann Arbor, UMI Research Press, 1981.

7033. Lewis, Wyndham. Blasting and bombardiering. London, Calder & Boyars, 1967. 2 ed.

7034. ———. The letters of Wyndham Lewis. Ed. by W. K. Rose. London, Methuen, 1963.

7035. ———. Wyndham Lewis: letteratura—pittura. A cura di Giovanni Cianci. Palermo, Sellerio, 1982.

7036. ———. Wyndham Lewis on art; collected writings, 1913–1956. Introduction and notes by Walter Michel and C. J. Fox. New York, Funk & Wagnalls, 1969.

7037. ———. Wyndham Lewis, the twenties. London, Anthony d'Offay, 1984.

7038. Manchester City Art Gallery (England). Wyndham Lewis. 1 October to 15 November 1980. Manchester, England, City of Manchester Cultural Services, 1980.

7039. Marrow, Bradford and Lafourcade, Bernard. A bibliography of the writings of Wyndham Lewis. Santa Barbara, Calif., Black Sparrow Press, 1978.

7040. Meyers, Jeffrey. The enemy: a biography of Wyndham Lewis. London/Henley, Routledge & Kegan Paul, 1980.

7041. Michel, Walter. Wyndham Lewis, paintings and drawings. Introductory essay by Hugh Kenner. Berkeley and Los Angeles, University of California Press, 1971. (CR).

7042. Normand, Tom. Wyndham Lewis the artist holding the mirror up to politics. Cambridge [England]; New York, Cambridge University Press, 1992.

7043. Porteus, Hugh G. Wyndham Lewis, a discursive exposition. London, Harmsworth, 1932.

7044. Wagner, Geoffrey. Wyndham Lewis: a portrait of the artist as the enemy. London, Routledge & Kegan Paul, 1957.

Lewitt, Sol, 1928–

7045. Kunsthalle Basel. Sol Lewitt, Graphik 1970–1975. Bern, Kornfeld/Basel, Kunsthalle, [1976].

7046. Lewitt, Sol. Sol Lewitt, prints, 1970–86. [Exhibition catalogue]. London, Tate Gallery, 1986.

7047. ———. Sol Lewitt, walldrawings. Hrsg. von Carl Haenlein. [Katalog der Ausstellung, Kestner-Gesellschaft, Hannover]. Hannover, Kestner-Gesellschaft, 1988. [Katalog der Kestner-Gesellschaft, 5/1988).

7048. ———. Sol Lewitt, walldrawings, 1984–1992. Editor, Susanna Singer; translation, Margaret Joss. [Katalog der Ausstellung in der Kunsthalle, Bern, Sala Rekalde, Addison Gallery of American Art]. Bern, Kunsthalle, 1989. (3rd rev. and expanded ed., 1992).

7049. Museum of Modern Art (New York). Sol Lewitt. [Text and catalogue edited and introduced by Alicia Legg]. New York, Museum of Modern Art, 1978.

Leyden, Gerhaert Nicolaus van *see* **Gerhaert, Nicolaus van Leyden**

Leyden, Lucas van *see* **Lucas van Leyden**

Leyster, Judith, 1609–1660

7050. Harms, Juliane. Judith Leyster, ihr Leben und ihr Werk. Amsterdam, Oud-Holland, 1929. (Oud-Holland, 44).

7051. Hofrichter, Frima Fox. Judith Leyster: a woman painter in Holland's Golden Age. Doornspijk, Davaco, 1989.

7052. Leyster, Judith. Judith Leyster: a Dutch master and her world. Project directors, James A. Welu, Pieter Biesboer; contributors, Pieter Biesboer . . . [et al.]. New Haven, Yale University Press, 1993.

Lhote, André, 1885–1962

7053. Artcurial (Centre d'Art Plastique Contemporain, Paris). André Lhote; retrospective 1907–1962: peintures, aquarelles, dessins. Octobre–novembre 1981. Paris, Artcurial, 1981.

7054. Brielle, Roger. André Lhote. Paris, Librairie de France, 1931.

7055. Courthion, Pierre. André Lhote. Paris, Gallimard, 1926. (Les peintres français nouveaux, 26).

7056. Jakovsky, Anatole. André Lhote, étude. Paris, Floury, 1947.

7057. Lhote, André. Figure painting. Trans. by W. J. Strachan. London, Zwemmer, 1953.

7058. ———. La peinture: le coeur et l'esprit. Correspondence inédite, 1907–1924: André Lhote, Alain-Fournier, Jacques Rivière. Texte établi et présenté par Alain Rivière, Jean Georges Morgenthaler et François Garcia. Bordeaux, France, V. Blake; Musée des beaux-arts de Bordeaux, 1986.

7059. ———. La peinture: le coeur et l'esprit, suivi de Parlons peinture; essais. Paris, Denoël, 1950. 2 ed.

7060. Mercereau, Alexandre. André Lhote. Paris, Povolzky, 1921.

Li Lung-Mien, fl. 1070–1106

7061. Meyer, A. E. *Chinese painting as reflected in the thought and art of Li Lung-mien, 1070–1106.* New York, Duffield, 1923. 2 ed.

Liberale da Verona, ca. 1445–1529

7062. Brenzoni, Raffaello. *Liberale da Verona (1445–1526).* Milano, Lucini, 1930.

7063. Carli, Enzo. *Miniature di Liberale da Verona dai Corali per il Duomo di Siena.* Milano, Martello, 1953. (Il fiore della miniatura italiana, 1).

7064. Del Bravo, Carlo. *Liberale da Verona.* Firenze, Edizioni d'Arte il Fiorino, 1967. (I più eccelenti, collana di monografie di artisti, 3).

7065. Eberhardt, Hans-Joachim. *Die Miniaturen von Liberale da Verona, Girolamo da Cremona und Venturino da Milano in den Chorbüchern des Doms von Siena:* Dokumentation—Attribution—Chronologie. München, H.J. Eberhardt in Kommission bei Wasmuth, 1983.

7066. Museo di Castelvecchio (Verona). *Liberale ritrovato nell'Esopo Veronese del 1479.* [Inaugurata il 22 dicembre 1973; testo di Giovanni Mardersteig con una nota introduttiva di Licisco Magagnato]. Verona, Museo di Castelvecchio, 1973.

Liberatore, Niccolo di *see* Niccolo da Foligno

Liberman, Alexander, 1912–

7067. Kazanjian, Dodie. *Alex; the life of Alexander Liberman.* [By] Dodie Kazanjian and Calvin Tomkins. New York, A.A. Knopf; distributed by Random House, 1993.

7068. Liberman, Alexander. *Alexander Liberman, new paintings: January 7 to 30.* [Catalog of an exhibition] New York, André Emmerich Gallery, 1988.

7069. Rose, Barbara. *Alexander Liberman.* New York, Abbeville, 1981.

Lichtenstein, Roy, 1923–

7070. Alloway, Lawrence. *Roy Lichtenstein.* New York, Abbeville Press, 1983.

7071. Busche, Ernst A. *Roy Lichtenstein, das Frühwerk, 1942–1960.* Berlin, Gebr. Mann, 1988.

7072. Coplans, John. *Roy Lichtenstein.* New York, Praeger, 1972.

7073. Corlett, Mary Lee. *The prints of Roy Lichtenstein: a catalogue raisonné, 1948–1993.* By M.L. Corlett; introduction by Ruth E. Fine. [Published in conjunction with an exhibition organized by the National Gallery of Art]. New York, Hudson Hills Press in association with the National Gallery of Art, Washington, D.C., 1994. (CR).

7074. Lichtenstein, Roy. *Lichtenstein: la grafica.* Di

Nina Sundell. Milano, Electa, 1990.

7075. Lichtenstein, Roy. *Roy Lichtenstein, bronze sculpture 1976–1989:.* [Catalog of an exhibition] May 19–July 1, 1989. Essay by Frederic Tuten. New York, N.Y. 65 Thompson Street, 1989.

7076. ———. *Roy Lichtenstein: landscape sketches 1984–1985.* With an introduction by Constance Glenn. New York, H.N. Abrams. 1986.

7077. ———. *Roy Lichtenstein: mural with blue brushstroke.* Essay by Calvin Tomkins. Photographs and interviews by Bob Adelman. New York, H.N. Abrams, 1987.

7078. ———. *Roy Lichtenstein, pop masterpieces, 1961–1964.* [Catalog of an exhibition] 5 May–6 June, 1987. New York, Blum-Helman Gallery, 1987.

7079. Pincus-Witten. Robert. *Roy Lichtenstein, a drawing retrospective: April 10 to May 12, 1984;* on the occasion of the twenty-fifth anniversary of the gallery. Text by R. Pincus-Witten; photographs, Nathan Rabin and Archival color, New York, James Goodman Gallery, 1984.

7080. Saint Louis Art Museum. *Roy Lichtenstein, 1970–1980.* May 8–June 28, 1981. [Text by Jack Cowart]. St. Louis, Saint Louis Art Museum, 1981.

7081. Waldman, Diane. *Roy Lichtenstein.* New York, Abrams, 1971.

7082. ———. *Roy Lichtenstein, drawings and prints.* New York, Chelsea House, 1969.

Liebermann, Max, 1847–1935

7083. Brauner, Lothar. *Max Liebermann.* Berlin Henschelverlag Kunst und Gesellschaft, 1986.

7084. Bunge, Matthias. *Max Liebermann als Künstler der Farbe: eine Untersuchung zum Wesen seiner Kunst.* Berlin, Gebr. Mann, 1990.

7085. Busch, Günter. *Max Liebermann: Maler, Graphiker, Zeichner.*Frankfurt am Main, s. Fischer, 1986.

7086. Elias, Julius. *Max Liebermann, eine Bibliographie.* Berlin, Cassirer, 1917.

7087. Friedländer, Max J., ed. *Max Liebermanns graphische Künst.* Dresden, Arnold, 1922. 2 ed. (Arnolds graphische Bücher, erste Folge, 1).

7088. Hancke, Erich. *Max Liebermann, sein Leben und sein Werk.* Berlin, Cassirer, 1914.

7089. Klein, Rudolf. *Max Liebermann.* Berlin, Bard, Marquardt, 1906. (Die Kunst, 55/56).

7090. Küster, Bernd., Max Liebermann, ein Maler-Leben. Hamburg, Ellert & Richter, 1988.

7091. Lichtwark, Alfred. *Briefe an Max Liebermann.* Im Auftrage der Lichtwark-Stiftung herausgegeben von Carl Schellenberg. Hamburg, Trautmann, 1947.

7092. Liebermann, Max. *Für Max Liebermann 1847–1935: eine Schwarzweiss-Ausstellung der Akademie dere Künste der DDR und des Kupferstichkabinetts der Staatlichen Museen zu Berlin Hauptstadt der DDR: Juli–August 1985*, Nationalgalerie Obergeschoss. Berlin, Staatliche Museen, 1985.

7093. Liebermann, Max. *Die Phantasie in der Malerei; Schriften und Reden.* Herausgegeben und eingeleitet von Günter Busch. Frankfurt a.M., Fischer, 1978.

7094. ———. *Siebzig Briefe.* Herausgegeben von Franz Landsberger. Berlin, Schocken, 1937.

7095. Meissner, Günter. *Max Liebermann.* Wien/ München, Schroll, 1974.

7096. Nationalgalerie Berlin. *Max Liebermann in seiner Zeit.* 6. September bis 4. November 1979. Berlin, Nationalgalerie Berlin, 1979. (CR).

7097. Pauli, Gustav. *Max Liebermann.* Stuttgart, Deutsche Verlags-Anstalt, 1911.

7098. Rosenhagen, Hans. *Liebermann.* Bielefeld/ Leipzig, Velhagen & Klasing, 1900. (Künstler-Monographien, 45).

7099. Scheffler, Karl. *Max Liebermann.* München, Piper, 1906. (New ed.: Wiesbaden, Insel, 1953).

7100. Schiefler, Gustav. *Das graphische Werk von Max Liebermann.* Berlin, Cassirer, 1906. (Fourth, revised ed.: San Francisco, Alan Wofsy, 1991).(CR).

7101. Stuttmann, Ferdinand. *Max Liebermann.* Hannover, Fackelträger, 1961.

7102. Wolff, Hans. *Zeichnungen von Max Liebermann.* Dresden, Arnold, 1922. (Arnolds graphische Bücher, zweite Folge, 4).

Lienz, Albin Egger *see* **Egger-Lienz, Albin**

Lievens, Jan, 1607–1674

7103. Herzog Anton Ulrich-Museum (Braunschweig). *Jan Lievens, ein Maler im Schatten Rembrandts.* 6. September bis 11. November 1979. Braunschweig, Herzog Anton Ulrich-Museum, 1979.

7104. Schatborn, Peter. *Jan Lievens, 1607–1674: prenten & tekeningen = prints and drawings.* [Catalogue of an exhibition] 5 november 1988–8 januari 1989. Museum het Rembrandthuis, Amsterdam. [Catalogue by] Peter Schatborn met bijdragen van Eva Ornstein-van Slooten. Amsterdam, Het Museum, 1988.

7105. Schneider, Hans. *Jan Lievens, sein Leben und sein Werk.* Haarlem, Bohn, 1932. (Reprinted, with a supplement by R. E. O. Ekkart: Amsterdam, Israel, 1973).

Lilien, Ephraim Mose, 1874–1925

7106. Brieger, Lothar. *E. M. Lilien, eine künstlerische Entwicklung um die Jahrhundert-* *wende.* Berlin/Wien, Harz, 1922.

7107. Levussove, Moses S. *The new art of an ancient people; the work of Ephraim Mose Lilien.* New York, Huebsch, 1906.

7108. Lilien, Ephraim M. *Briefe an seine Frau, 1905–1925.* Hrsg. von Otto Lilien und Eva Strauss; mit einer Einleitung von Ekkehard Hieronimus. Königstein/Ts., Jüdischer Verlag Athenäum, 1985.

7109. ———. *Jerusalem.* Introd. by Joseph Gutman. New York, Ktav, 1976.

7110. Regener, Edgar. *E. M. Lilien, ein Beitrag zur Geschichte der zeichnenden Künste.* Berlin/ Leipzig, Lattmann, 1905.

7111. Stadt Museum Braunschweig. *Der Grafiker E.M. Lilien (1874–1925).* 21. Mai–16. Juni 1974. [Catalogue by Ekkehard Hieronimus]. Braunschweig' Stadt Museum, 1974.

7112. Zweig, Stefan. *E. M. Lilien, sein Werk.* Berlin, Schuster & Loeffler, 1903.

Lindner, Richard, 1901–1978

7113. Ashton, Dore. *Richard Lindner.* New York, Abrams, 1969.

7114. Dienst, Rolf-Gunter. *Lindner.* Trans. by Christopher Cortis. New York, Abrams, 1970.

7115. Fondation Maeght (Paris). *Richard Lindner.* 12 mai–30 juin 1979. [Text by Werner Spies; trans. by Eliane Kaufholz]. [Paris], Fondation Maeght, 1979.

7116. Kramer, Hilton. *Richard Lindner,.* London, Thames and Hudson, 1975.

7117. Lindner, Richard. *Richard Lindner: Sammlung internationaler zeitgenössischer Kunst in der Kunsthalle Nürnberg.* [Katalog der Ausstellung] Kunsthalle Nürnberg in der Norrishalle, 12.2.1986–1.3.1987. Nürnberg, Die Kunsthalle, 1986.

7118. Tillim, Sidney. *Lindner,.* Chicago, William and Noma Copley Foundation, 1960.

Lindsay, Norman, 1879–1969

7119. Bloomfield, Lin, ed. *The world of Norman Lindsay.* South Melbourne, Macmillan, 1979.

7120. Chaplin, Harry F. *Norman Lindsay; his books, manuscripts and autograph letters in the library of and annotated by the author.* Sydney, Wentworth Press, 1969. (2 ed.: Sydney, Wentworth Books, 1978

7121. Hetherington, John. *Norman Lindsay, the embattled Olympian.* Melbourne, Oxford University Press, 1973.

7122. Lindsay, Norman. *Letters of Norman Lindsay.* Edited by R. G. Howarth and A. W. Barker. Sydney, Angus & Robertson, 1979.

7123. ———. *My mask, for what little I know of the man behind it: an autobiography.* Sydney, Angus & Richardson, 1970.

7124. ———. *Norman Lindsay watercolours.*

With an appreciation of the medium by Norman Lindsay and a survey of the artist's life and work by Geofrey Blunden. Sydney/London, Smith, 1969.

7125. Lindsay, Rose. *Model wife; my life with Norman Lindsay.* Sydney, Smith, 1967.

7126. Stewart, Douglas A. *Norman Lindsay, a personal memoir.* Melbourne, Nelson, 1975.

Linnell, John, 1792–1882

7127. Colnaghi & Co., Ltd. (London). *A loan exhibition of drawings, watercolours, and paintings by John Linnell and his circle.* 10 January to 2 February 1973. London, Colnaghi, 1973.

7128. Fitzwilliam Museum (Cambridge, Eng.). *John Linnell, a centennial exhibition.* Oct. 5–Dec. 12, 1981. [Selected and catalogued by Katherine Crouan]. Cambridge, Fitzwilliam Museum, 1982.

7129. Story, Alfred T. *The life of John Linnell.* 2 v. London, Bentley, 1892.

Lint, Peter Van, 1609–1690

7130. Busiri Vici, Andrea. *Peter, Hendrik e Giacomo van Lint: tre pittori di Anversa del '600 e '700 lavorano a Roma.* Roma, Ugo Bozzi, 1987.

Liotard, Jean Etienne, 1702–1789

7131. Fosca, François [pseud., Georges de Traz]. *La vie, les voyages et les oeuvres de Jean-Etienne Liotard, citoyen de Genève, dit le peintre turc.* Lausanne/Paris, Bibliothèque des Arts, 1956.

7132. Grijzenhout, Frans. *Liotard in Nederland.* Utrecht, Kwadraat, 1985.

7133. Herdt, Anne de. *Dessins de Liotard, suivie du catalogue de l'oeuvre dessiné.* Paris, Réunion des musées nationaux; Genève, Musée d'art et d'histoire, 1992. (CR).

7134. Humbert, Edouard, et al. *La vie et les oeuvres de Jean Etienne Liotard (1702–1789); étude biographique et iconographique.* Amsterdam, van Gogh, 1897.

7135. Liotard, Jean-Etienne. *Traité des principes et des règles de la peinture.* Pref. de Pierre Courthion. Vésenaz/ Genève, Cailler, 1945.

7136. Loche, Renée e Roethlisberger, Marcel. *L'opera completa di Liotard.* Milano, Rizzoli, 1978. (CR). (Classici dell'arte).

7137. Previtali, Giovanni. *Jean-Etienne Liotard.* Milano, Fabbri, 1966. (I maestri del colore, 240).

Lipchitz, Jacques, 1891–1973

7138. Arnason, H. Harvard. *Jacques Lipchitz: sketches in bronze.* New York, Praeger, 1969.

7139. Hammacher, Abraham M. *Jacques Lipchitz,*

his sculpture. New York, Abrams, 1975. 2 ed.

7140. Jenkins, David Fraser. *The Lipchitz gift: models for sculpture.* [By] D.F. Jenkins & Derek Pullen. London, Tate Gallery Publications, 1986.

7141. Lipchitz, Jacques. *Jacques Lipchitz, the cubist period (1913–1930).* [Catalogue of an exhibition]. October 15–November 14, 1987, Marlborough Gallery, New York. New York, The Gallery, 1987.

7142. ———. *My life in sculpture.* With H. H. Arnason. New York, Viking, 1972.

7143. Musee National d'Art Moderne, Centre Georges Pompidou (Paris). *Oeuvres de Jacques Lipchitz (1891–1973).* Catalogue établi par Nicole Barbier. Paris, Musée National d'Art Moderne, 1978.

7144. Museum of Modern Art (New York). *The sculpture of Jacques Lipchitz.* [May 18–August 1, 1954; text by Henry R. Hope]. New York, Museum of Modern Art, 1954.

7145. Patai, Irene. *Encounters; the life of Jacques Lipchitz.* New York, Funk & Wagnalls, 1961.

7146. Raynal, Maurice. *Lipchitz.* Paris, Action, 1920. (L'art d'aujourd'hui, 1).

7147. Van Bork, Bert. *Jacques Lipchitz; the artist at work.* With a critical evaluation by Dr. Alfred Werner. New York, Crown, 1966.

7148. Vitrac, Roger. *Jacques Lipchitz, une étude critique.* Paris, Gallimard, 1929. (Les sculpteurs français nouveaux, 7).

Lippi, Filippino, 1457–1504
Filippo, ca. 1406–1469
see also Masaccio

7149. Associazione Turistica Pratese, ed. *Saggi su Filippino Lippi, di Cesare Brandi, Roberto Salvini, Valerio Mariani [and] Giuseppe Fiocco.* Firenze, Arnaud, 1957.

7150. [Baldanzi, Ferdinando]. *Delle pitture di Fra Filippo Lippi nel coro della cattedrale di Prato e de' loro restauri.* Prato, Giachetti, 1835.

7151. Baldini, Umberto. *Filippo Lippi.* Milano, Fabbri, 1965. (I maestri del colore, 61).

7152. Berti, Luciano [and] Baldini, Umberto. *Filippino Lippi.* Firenze, Arnaud, 1957. (2 ed.: Firenze, Edizioni d'Arte Il Fiorino, 1991).

7153. Fossi, Gloria. *Filippo Lippi.* (Antella) Florence, SCALA; New York, Riverside, 1989.

7154. Gamba, Fiammetta. *Filippino Lippi nella storia della critica.* Firenze, Arnaud, 1958.

7155. Marchini, Giuseppe. *Filippo Lippi.* Milano, Electa, 1975.

7156. Mendelsohn, Henriette. *Fra Filippo Lippi.* Berlin, Bard, 1909.

7157. Mengin, Urbain. *Les deux Lippi.* Paris, Plon, 1932.

7158. Neilson, Katherine B. *Filippino Lippi; a critical study*. Cambridge, Mass., Harvard University Press, 1938.

7159. Oertel, Robert. *Fra Filippo Lippi*. Wien, Schroll, 1942.

7160. Peters-Schildgen, Susanne. *Die Bedeutung Filippino Lippis für den Manierismus; unter besonderer Berücksichtigung der Strozzi-Fresken in Santa Maria Novella zu Florenz.* Essen, Blaue Eule, 1989. (Kunstwissenschaft in der Blauen Eule, 3).

7161. Pittaluga, Mary. *Filippo Lippi*. Firenze, Del Turco, 1949.

7162. Ruda, Jeffrey. *Fra Filippo Lippi: life and work with a complete catalogue*. London, Phaidon; New York; distrib. in North America by H.N. Abrams. 1993. (CR).

7163. Sacher, Helen. *Die Ausdruckskraft der Farbe bei Filippino Lippi*. Strassburg, Heitz, 1929. (Zur Kunstgeschichte des Auslandes, 128).

7164. Scharf, Alfred. *Filippino Lippi*. Wien, Schroll, 1950.

7165. Strutt, Edward C. *Fra Filippo Lippi*. London, Bell, 1901.

7166. Supino, Igino B. *Les deux Lippi*. Trans. by J. de Crozals. Firenze, Alinari, 1904.

7167. ———. *Fra Filippo Lippi*. Firenze, Alinari, 1902.

Lippi, Lorenzo, 1606–1664

7168. Alterocca, Arnaldo. *La vita e l'opera poetica e pittorica di Lorenzo Lippi*. Catania, Battiato, 1914.

Lipton, Seymour, 1903–

7169. Elsen, Albert. *Seymour Lipton*. New York, Abrams, 1971.

7170. Rand, Harry. *Seymour Lipton: aspects of sculpture*. (Published in conjunction with an exhibition at the National Collection of Fine Arts, Smithsonian Institution, March 16–May 6, 1979). Washington, D.C., National Collection of Fine Arts, 1979.

Lisboa, Antonio Francisco, *called* O Aleijadinho, 1730–1814

7171. Alves Guimarães, Renato. *Antonio Francisco Lisboa (O Aleijadinho); monumentos e tradiçoes de Minas Geraes*. Sïo Paulo, Ferraz, 1931.

7172. Arias, Abelardo. *Inconfidencia: el Aleijadinho*. Buenos Aires, Editorial Sudamericana, 1979. (Fiction).

7173. Barbosa, Waldemar de Almeida. *O Aleijadinho de Villa Rica*. Belo Horizonte, Editorial Itatiaia; Sao Paulo, Editora da Universidade de Sao Paulo, 1985.

7174. Bazin, Germain. *Aleijadinho et la sculpture baroque au Brésil*. Paris, Le Temps, 1963.

7175. Feu de Carvalho, Theophilo. *O Aleijadinho (Antonio Francisco Lisboa)*. Bello Horizonte, Ediçoes Históricas, 1934.

7176. Jorge, Fernando. *O Aleijadinho; sua vida, suo obra, seu gênio*. Rio de Janeiro, Buccini/Sïo Paulo, Leia, 1961. 2 ed.

7177. Lima, Augusto de, Jr. *O Aleijadinho e a arte colonial*. Rio de Janeiro, [Lima], 1942.

7178. Marianno Filho, José. *Antonio Francisco Lisboa*. Rio de Janeiro, [Mendes], 1945.

7179. Pires, Heliodoro. *Mestre Aleijadinho; vida e obra de Antônio Francisco Lisboa, gigante da arte no Brasil*. Rio de Janeiro, Livraria Sïo José, 1961. 2 ed.

Liss, Johann, 1576–1629

7180. Cleveland Museum of Art. *Johann Liss*. December 17, 1975–March 7, 1976. Cleveland, Cleveland Museum of Art, 1975. (CR).

7181. Steinbart, Kurt. *Johann Liss, der Maler aus Holstein*. Berlin, Deutscher Verein für Kunstwissenschaft, 1940.

Lissitzky, El, 1890–1941

7182. Birnholz, Alan C. *El Lissitsky*. 2 v. Ann Arbor, Mich., University Microfilms, 1974.

7183. Galerie Gmurzynska (Cologne). *El Lissitzky*. (9. April bis Ende Juni 1976). [Text in German and English]. Köln, Galerie Gmurzynska, 1976.

7184. Hemken, Kai-Uwe. *El Lissitzky: Revolution und Avantgarde*. Köln, DuMont, 1990.

7185. Lissitzky, El. *El Lissitzky, 1890–1941: architect, painter, photographer, typographer.* [Catalogue of an exhibition]. Eindhoven, Municipal Van Abbemuseum; New York, distrib. by Thames and Hudson, 1990.

7186. ———. *El Lissitzky: experiments in photography*. [Exhibition]. April 17 to June 1, 1991. New York, Houk Friedman Gallery, 1991.

7187. ———. *El Lissitzky: Konstrukteur, Denker, Pfeifenraucher, Kommunist*. [Exhibition catalogue] hrsg. von Victor Malsy. Mainz, Hermann Schmidt, 1990.

7188. ———. *Russland, die Rekonstruktion der Architektur in der Sowjetunion*. Wien, Schroll, 1930. (English ed.: *Russia, an architecture for world revolution*. Trans. by Eric Dluhosch. Cambridge, Mass., MIT Press, 1970).(New ed.: Wiesbaden, Vieweg & Sohn, 1989).

7189. ———. *El Lissitzky, 1890–1941, Retrospektive*: Staatliche Galerie Moritzburg, Halle vom 7. Mai bis 3. Juli 1988. Katalog, Norbert Nobis . . . et al.]. Halle, Staatliche Galerie Moritzburg, 1988.

7190. ——— and Arp, Hans. *Die Kunstismen.* [Text in German, French, and English]. Zürich, Rentsch, 1925.

7191. Lissitzky-Kuppers, Sophie. *El Lissitsky; life, letters, texts.* Introd. by Herbert Read. Trans.

L

by Helene Aldwinckle and Mary Whittall. London, Thames and Hudson, 1968.

7192. Nisbet, Peter. *El Lissitzky, 1890–1941*. Catalogue for an exhibition of selected works from North American collections, the Sprengel Museum Hannover and the Staatliche Galerie Moritzburg, Halle. Exhibition and catalogue prepared by Peter Nisbet; Harvard University Art Museums: Busch-Reisinger Museum. Cambridge, Mass., The Museums, 1987.

7193. Richter, Horst. *El Lissitzky: Sieg über die Sonne; zur Kunst des Konstruktivismus.* Köln, Galerie Christop Czwiklitzer, 1958.

7194. Sprengel Museum (Hannover). *El Lissitzky, 1890–1941: Retrospektive, 24. Januar–10. April, 1988.* Katalog, Norbert Nobis; Mitarbeit, Kai-Uwe Hemken; [mit Beiträgen von Christian Grohn . . . et al.]. Hannover, Sprengel Museum; Frankfurt am Main, Ullstein, 1988.

7195. Stedelijk van Abbemuseum, Eindhoven (Holland). *El Lissitzky.* 3. Dezember 1965 bis 16. Januar 1966. Eindhoven, Stedelijk van Abbemuseum/Hannover, Kestner-Gesell-schaft, 1965. (Kestner-Gesellschaft Hannover, Katalog 4, Ausstellungsjahr 1965/66).

Lochner, Stefan, 1410–1451

7196. Forster, Otto H. *Stefan Lochner, ein Maler zu Köln.* Bonn, Auer, 1952. 3 ed.

7197. Kerber, Bernard. *Stephan Lochner.* Milano, Fabbri, 1965. (I maestri del colore, 99).

7198. May, Helmut. *Stefan Lochner und sein Jahrhundert.* Köln, Seemann, 1955.

7199. Schrade, Hubert. *Stephan Lochner.* München, Verlag der Wissenschaften, 1923. (Kompendien zur deutschen Kunst, 2).

Lohse, Richard Paul, 1902–

7200. Lohse, Richard Paul. *Fragen an Lohse.* Redaktion, Martin Kunzl. Luzern, Kunstmuseum Luzern, 1985.

7201. Lohse, Richard Paul. *Richard Paul Lohse: Bilder und Zeichnungen, 1945–1980.* [Ausstellung] 13. September bis 4. november 1982, Galerie Teufel, Köln. Köln, Die Galerie, 1982.

7202. ———. *Richard Paul Lohse, modulare und serielle Ordnungen.* [Ausstellung] Wiener Sezession, 20. März–27. April, 1986. Wien, Die Sezession, 1986.

7203. Riese, Hans-Peter. *Richard Paul Lohse, drawings, 1935–1985.* H.-P. Riese, Friedrich W. Heckmanns; foreword by Dieter Bachmann. New York, Rizzoli, 1986.

Lombard, Lambert, ca. 1505–1566

7204. Denhaene, Godelieve. *Lambert Lombard (1505/1566): Renaissance et humanisme à Liège.* Anvers, Fonds Mercator, 1990.

7205. Helbig, Jules. *Lambert Lombard, peintre et architecte.* Bruxelles, Baertsoen, 1893.

7206. Lampsonius, Dominicus. *Lamberti Lombardi apud Eburones pictoris celeberrimi vita, pictoribus, sculptoribus architectis, aliisque id artificibus utilis et necessaria.* Brugis, Goltzii, 1565.

7207. Musée de l'Art Wallon (Liège). *Dessins de Lambert Lombard ex-collection d'Arenberg.* 26 janvier–24 mars 1963. Liège, Musée de l'Art Wallon, 1963.

7208. ———. *Lambert Lombard et son temps.* 30 septembre–31 octobre 1966. Liege, Musee de l'Art Wallon, 1963.

Lombardo, Antonio, ca. 1458–1516
Pietro, ca. 1435–1515
Tullio, ca. 1455–1532

7209. Jestaz Bertrand. *La Chapelle Zen à Saint-Marc de Venise: d'Antonio à Tullio Lombardo.* Stuttgart, F. Steiner Verlag Wiesbaden, 1986.

7210. Wilk, Sarah. *The sculpture of Tullio Lombardo; studies in sources and meaning.* New York/London, Garland, 1978.

7211. Zandomeneghi, Luigi. *Elogio di Tullio ed Antonio fratelli Lombardo.* Venezia, Picotti, 1828.

7212. Zava Boccazzi, Franca. *I Lombardo.* Milano, Fabbri, 1968. (I maestri della scultura, 73).

Lomi, Aurelio, 1566–1622

7213. Ciardi, Roberto Paolo, Maria Clelia Galassi, Pierluigi Carofano. *Aurelio Lomi: maniera e innovazione.* Pisa, Pacini, 1989.

Longhena, Baldassare, 1596?–1682

7214. Cristinelli, Giuseppe. *Baldassare Longhena, architetto del '600 a Venezia.* Fotografie di Francesco Possani. Padua, Marsilio, 1978. 2 ed. (Le grande opere dell' architettura, 4).

7215. Semenzato, Camillo. *L'architettura di Baldassare Longhena.* Padova, CEDAM, 1954. (Università di Padova, pubblicazioni della Facoltà di Lettere e Filosofia, 29).

Longhi, Pietro, 1702–1795

7216. Longhi, Pietro. *Pietro Longhi: 24 dipinti da collezioni private* [mostra]; 7–21 maggio 1993. Introduzione di Terisio Pignatti; catalogo a cura di Andrea Daninos. Milano, Galleria Carlo Orsi, 1993.

7217. Moschini, Vittorio. *Pietro Longhi.* Milano, Martelli, 1956.

7218. Pignatti, Terisio. *Disegni di Pietro Longhi.* Milano, Berenice, 1990.

7219. ———. *L'opera completa di Pietro Longhi.* Milano, Rizzoli, 1974. (Classici dell'arte, 75).

7220. ———. *Pietro Longhi dal disegno alla pit-*

tura. Venezia, Alfieri, 1975.

7221. ———. *Pietro Longhi, paintings and drawings; complete edition.* Trans. by Pamela Wiley. London, Phaidon, 1969. (CR).

7222. Ravà, Aldo. *Pietro Longhi.* Firenzi, Alinari, 1923. 2 ed. (Collezione d'arte, 3).

7223. Valcanover, Francesco. *Pietro Longhi.* Milano, Fabbri, 1964. (I maestri del colore, 21).

Longhi, Roberto, 1890–1970

7224. Contini, Gianfranco. *Roberto Longhi: discorso ommemorativo* pronunciato dal linceo Gianfranco Contini nella seduta ordinaria del 13 gennaio 1973. Roma, Accademia nazionale dei Lincei, 1973.

7225. Testori, Giovanni. *Disegni di Roberto Longhi.* Milano, Compagnia del disegno, 1980. (Prima collana del Lanzone, 4).

Longo, Robert, 1953–

7226. Fox, Howard N. *Robert Longo.* With essays by Hal Foster, Katherine Dieckmann, Brian Wallis. [Published in conjunction with the exhibition Robert Longo, held at the Los Angeles County Museum of Art, October 1–December 31, 1989]. Los Angeles, Los Angeles County Museum of Art; New York, Rizzoli International, 1989.

7227. Gibson, William. *Robert Longo.* Kyoto, Japan., Kyoto Shoin International, 1991.

7228. Longo, Robert. *Men in the cities.1979–1982.* With an introduction and interview by Richard Price. New York, Abrams, 1986.

7229. Ratcliff, Carter. *Robert Longo.* New York, Rizzoli, 1985.

Loos, Adolf, 1870–1933

7230. Altenberg, Peter, et al. *Adolf Loos zum 60. Geburtstag am 10. Dezember 1930.* Wien, Lanyi, 1930.

7231. Glück, Franz. *Adolf Loos.* Paris, Cres, 1931.

7232. Gravagnuolo, Benedetto. *Adolf Loos, theory and works.* New York, Rizzoli, 1982.

7233. Kubinsky, Mihály. *Adolf Loos.* Berlin, Henschel, 1970.

7234. Loos, Adolf. *"Alle Architekten sind Verbrecher": Adolf Loos und die Folgen;* hrsg. von Adolf Opel und Marino Valdez. Wien, Edition Atelier, 1990.

7235. Loos, Adolf. *Sämtliche Schriften in zwei Bänden.* Herausgegeben von Franz Glück. 2 v. Wien/München, Herold, 1962.

7236. ———. *Spoken into the void: collected essays 1897–1900.* Introd. by Aldo Rossi. Trans. by Jane O. Newman and John H. Smith. Cambridge, Mass., MIT Press, 1982.

7237. ———. *Das Werk des Architekten.* Herausgegeben von Heinrich Kulka. Wien, Schroll, 1931. (Reprint: Wien, Locker, 1979).

7238. Marilaun, Karl. *Adolf Loos.* Wien/Leipzig, Wiener Literarische Anstalt, 1922. (Die Wiedergabe, 1. Reihe, 5. Band).

7239. Münz, Ludwig and Künstler, Gustav. *Adolf Loos; pioneer of modern architecture.* With an introduction by Nikolaus Pevsner and an appreciation by Oskar Kokoschka. London, Thames and Hudson, 1966.

7240. Posener, Julius. *Adolf Loos, 1870–1933; ein Vortrag.* Redaktion, Manfred Schlösser. Berlin, Akademie der Künste, 1984.

7241. Roth, Alfred. *Begegnungen mit Pionieren* Le Corbusier, Piet Mondrian, *Adolf Loos,* Josef Hoffmann, Auguste Perret, Henry van der Velde. Basel, Birkhäuser, 1973.

7242. Rukschcio, Burkhardt [and] Schachel, Roland. *Adolf Loos, Leben und Werk.* Salzburg und Wien, Residenz, 1982. (CR). (Veröffentlichungen der Albertina, 17).

7243. Volkman, Barbara [and] Raddatz, Rose-France. *Adolf Loos, 1870–1933: Raumplan-Wohnungsbau: Ausstellung der Akademie der Künste, 4 Dezember 1983 bis 15 Januar 1984.* Berlin, Akademie der Künste, 1983.

Lopez Mezquita, José María, 1883–1954

7244. Francés, José. *José María Lopez Mezquita.* [Madrid], Estrella, 1919.

7245. Lopez Mezquita, Jose Maria. *Lopez Mezquita.* Exposicion organizada por la Caja General de Ahorros y Monte de Piedad de Granada. [Museo Municipal, Madrid, 1985, enero–febrero]. Granada, Caja General de Ahorros y Monte de Piedad de granada, 1984.

7246. Nogales y Marquez de Prado, Antonio. *Lopez Mezquita, su personalidad en la pintura española.* Madrid, Aguirre Torre, 1954.

Lorenzetti, Ambrogio, ca. 1324–1345
Pietro, 1305–1348

7247. Boorsook, Eve. *Ambrogio Lorenzetti.* Firenze, Sadea, 1966. (I diamanti dell'arte, 6).

7248. Carli, Enzo. *Pietro e Ambrogio Lorenzetti.* Milano, Silvana, 1971.

7249. Cecci, Emilio. *Pietro Lorenzetti.* Milano, Treves, 1930.

7250. Dewald, Ernest T. *Pietro Lorenzetti.* Cambridge, Mass., Harvard University Press, 1930.

7251. Meyenburg, Ernst von. *Ambrogio Lorenzetti.* Ein Beitrag zur Geschichte der sienesischen Malerei im vierzehnten Jahrhundert. Zürich, Frey, 1903.

7252. Rowley, George. *Ambrogio Lorenzetti.* 2 v. Princeton, N.J., Princeton University Press, 1958. (Princeton Monographs in Art and Archeology, 32).

7253. Sinibaldi, Giulia. *I Lorenzetti.* Siena, Istituto Comunale d'Arte e di Storia, 1933.

7254. Skinner, Quentin. *Ambrogio Lorenzetti: the*

artist as political philosopher. London, British Academy, 1986. (Raleigh lecture on history, [1986]).

7255. Volpe, Carlo. *Pietro Lorenzetti.* A cura di Mauro Lucco. Milano, Electa, 1989.

Lorenzo da Bologna, 15th c.
7256. Lorenzoni, Giovanni. *Lorenzo da Bologna.* Venezia, Pozza, 1963. (Profili, 3).

Lorenzo di Credi, 1456–1557
7257. Brewer, Robert. *A study of Lorenzo di Credi.* Firenze, Giuntina, 1970.

7258. Dalli Regoli, Gigetta. *Lorenzo di Credi.* Milano, Edizioni di Comunità, 1966. (Raccolta Pisana di saggi e studi, 19).

Lorenzo, Fiorenzo di *see* Fiorenzo di Lorenzo

Lorenzo, Monaco, 1370–1425
7259. Bellosi, Luciano. *Lorenzo Monaco.* Milano, Fabbri, 1965. (I maestri del colore, 73).

7260. Golzio, Vincenzo. *Lorenzo Monaco; l'unification della tradizione senese con la fiorentina e il gotico.* Roma, Biblioteca d'Arte Editrice, 1931.

7261. Sirén, Osvald. *Don Lorenzo Monaco.* Strassburg, Heitz, 1905. (Zur Kunstgeschichte des Auslandes, 33).

Lorrain, Claude *see* Claude Lorrain

Lory, Gabriel, 1763–1840
7262. Mandach, Conrad de. *Deux peintres suisses: Gabriel Lory le père (1763–1840) et Gabriel Lory le fils (1784–1846).* Lausanne, Haeschel, 1920. (Reprint, Genève, Slatkine, 1978).

7263. Weitz, Hans-Joachim. *Ein Schweizer Maler bei Goethe.* Vortrag gehalten im Kunsthaus Zürich am 11. November 1976; im Kunstmuseum Bern am 28. Februar 1977. Zürich, Kunsthaus Zürich; Bern, Kunstmuseum Bern, 1978.

Losenko, Anton Pavlovich, 1737–1773
7264. Gavrilova, Evgeniia I. *Anton Pavlovich Losenko.* Leningrad, Khudozhnik RSFSR, 1977.

7265. Kaganovich, A. L. *Anton Losenko i russkoe iskusstvo serediny XVIII stoletiia.* Moskva, Izd-vo Akademiia Khudozhestv SSR, 1963.

Lotto, Lorenzo, 1480–1556
7266. Accademia Carrara (Bergamo). *Bergamo per Lorenzo Lotto.* [Dec. 15, 1980–March 31, 1981]. Bergamo, Bolis, 1980.

7267. Angelini, Luigi. *Gli affreschi di Lorenzo Lotto in Bergamo.* Bergamo, Istituto Italiano d'Arti Grafiche, 1953.

7268. Banti, Anna and Boschetto, Antonio. *Lorenzo Lotto.* Firenze, Sansoni, 1953.

7269. Berenson, Bernhard. *Lorenzo Lotto, an essay in constructive art criticism.* New York/London, Putnam, 1895. (Rev. ed.: *Lorenzo Lotto, complete edition.* London, Phaidon, 1956; distributed by Garden City Books, Garden City, N.Y.).

7270. Biagi, Luigi. *Lorenzo Lotto.* Roma, Tumminelli, 1942.

7271. Bianconi, Piero. *Lorenzo Lotto.* Trans. by Paul Colacicchi. 2 v. New York, Hawthorn, 1963. (Complete Library of World Art, 16–17).

7272. Caroli, Flavio. *Lorenzo Lotto.* Firenze, Edizioni d'Arte il Fiorino, 1975. (I più eccellenti; collana di monografie di artisti, 6; new ed.: *Lorenzo Lotto e la nascita della psicologia moderna.* Milano, Fabbri, 1980).

7273. Chiesa del Gesù, et al. (Ancona, Italy). *Lorenzo Lotto nelle Marche; il suo tempo, il suo influsso.* 4 luglio–11 ottobre 1981. Catalogo a cura di Paolo Dal Poggetto e Pietro Zampetti. Firenze, Centro Di, 1981.

7274. Chiodi, Luigi, ed. *Lettere inedite di Lorenzo Lotto su le tarsie di S. Maria Maggiore in Bergamo.* Bergamo, Edizioni Monumenta Bergomensia, 1962. (Monumenta bergomensia, 8).

7275. Cortesi Bosco, Francesca. *Il coro intarsiato di Lotto e Capoferri per Santa Maria Maggiore in Bergamo.* 2 v. Bergamo, Credito Bergamasco; Milano, Pizzi, 1987.

7276. ———. *Gli affreschi dell'Oratorio Suardi: Lorenzo Lotto nella crisi della Riforma.* Bergamo, Bolis, 1980.

7277. Dillon, Gianvittorio, ed. *Lorenzo Lotto a Treviso, ricerche e restauri.* Treviso, Canova, 1980.

7278. Galis, Diana W. *Lorenzo Lotto: a study of his career and character with particular emphasis on his emblematic and hieroglyphic works.* Ann Arbor, Mich., University Microfilms, 1980.

7279. Gentili, Augusto. *I giardini di contemplazione: Lorenzo Lotto.* Roma, Bulzoni, 1985

7280. Lotto, Lorenzo. *Il libro di spese diverse.* A cura di Pietro Zampetti. Venezia/Roma, Istituto per la Collaborazione Culturale, 1969.

7281. Mascherpa, Giorgio. *Invito a Lorenzo Lotto.* Milano, Rusconi, 1980.

7282. ———. *Lorenzo Lotto a Bergamo.* Milano, Cassa di Risparmio della Provincie Lombarde, 1971.

7283. Matthew, Louisa Chevalier. *Lorenzo Lotto and the patronage and production of Venetian altarpieces in the early sixteenth century.* 2 v. Ann Arbor, Mich., University Microfilms International, 1990. (Photoprint of a 1988 dissertation).

7284. Palazzo Ducale (Venice). *Mostra di Lorenzo Lotto*. 14 giugno–18 ottobre 1953. Catalogo ufficiale a cura di Pietro Zampetti. Venezia, Casa Editrice Arte Veneta, 1953.

7285. Pallucchini, Rodolfo [and] Mariani Canova, Giordana. *L'opera completa di Lotto*. Milano, Rizzoli, 1975. (CR). (Classici dell'arte, 79).

7286. Siedenberg, Margot. *Die Bildnisse des Lorenzo Lotto*. Lorrach, Schahl, 1964.

7287. Zampetti, Pietro. *Lorenzo Lotto*. Milano, Fabbri, 1965. (I maestri del colore, 115).

7288. ———. *Lorenzo Lotto nelle Marche*. Urbino, Istituto Statale d'Arte, 1953. (Collana di studi archeologici ed artistici marchigiani, 3).

7289. ———, ed. *Lorenzo Lotto nel suo e nel nostro tempo*. Urbino, Argalia, 1980. (Notizie da Palazzo Albani, anno IX, 1–2).

Loudon, John Claudius, 1783–1843

7290. Gloag, John. *Mr. Loudon's England: the life and work of John Claudius Loudon and his influence on architecture and furniture design*. Newcastle-upon-Tyne, Oriel, 1970.

7291. Loudon, John C. *An encyclopaedia of cottage, farm, and villa architecture*. London, Longman, 1833. (New ed., edited by Jane Loudon: London, Warne, 1844).

7292. ———. *An encyclopaedia of gardening*. 2 v. London, Longman, 1822. (New ed., edited by Jane Loudon: London, Longman, 1850; reprint of 1835 ed.: New York, Garland, 1982).

7293. ———. *Observations on the formation and management of useful and ornamental plantations, on the theory and practice of landscape gardening, and on gaining and embanking land from rivers or the sea*. Edinburgh, Constable/London, Longman, 1804.

7294. ———. *The suburban gardener and villa companion*. London, Printed for the author, 1838. (Reprint: New York, Garland, 1982).

7295. MacDougall, Elisabeth B., ed. *John Claudius Loudon and the early nineteenth century in Great Britain: papers*. Washington, D.C., Dumbarton Oaks Trustees for Harvard University, 1980. (Dumbarton Oaks Colloquium on the History of Landscape Architecture, 6).

7296. Simo, Melanie Louise. *Loudon and the landscape: from country seat to metropolis, 1783–1843*. New Haven, Yale University Press, 1988. (Yale publications in the history of art, 38).

Louis, Morris, 1912–1962

7297. Ashton, Dore. *Morris Louis*. [Catalogue of an exhibition]. Milano, Fabbri, 1990.

7298. Elderfield, John. *Morris Louis*. [Catalogue of an exhibition]. New York, Museum of Modern Art, 1986.

7299. Louis, Morris. *Morris Louis drawings, 1948-1953*. [Catalogue of an exhibition held at the André Emmerich Gallery, New York], April 4– 27, 1985. 1985. New York, The Gallery, 1985.

7300. ———. *Morris Louis, a commemorative exhibition* [held at the André Emmerich Gallery, New York], September 9–October 2, 1992. New York, The Gallery, 1992.

7301. Upright, Diane. *Morris Louis: the complete paintings; a catalogue raisonné*. New York, Abrams, 1985. (CR).

Loutherbourg, Philip James de, 1740–1812

7302. Baugh, Christopher. *Garrick and Loutherbourg*. Cambridge, [England]; Alexandria, Va., Chadwyck-Healy in association with the Consortium for Drama and Media in Higher Education, 1990.

7303. Joppien, Rüdiger. *Philippe Jacques de Loutherbourg, R.A., 1740–1812*. [Catalogue of an exhibition held at the Iveagh Bequest, Kenwood, Hampstead, England]. London, Greater London Council, 1973.

Lucas van Leyden, 1494–1533

7304. Baldass, Ludwig von. *Die Gemälde des Lucas van Leyden*. Wien, Hölzel, 1923.

7305. Bartsch, Adam von. *Catalogue raisonné de toutes les estampes qui forment l'oeuvre de Lucas de Leyde*. Wien, Degen, 1798. (CR).

7306. Beets, Nicholas. *Lucas de Leyde*. Bruxelles, van Oest, 1913.

7307. Dittrich, Christian. *Lucas van Leyden: das graphische Werk im Kupferstich-Kabinett zu Dresden*. Dresden, Staatliche Kunstsammlungen, 1983.

7308. Evrard, W. *Lucas de Leyde et Albert Dürer: la vie et l'oeuvre de Lucas de Leyde; son école, ses gravures, ses peintures, ses dessins; catalogue et prix de cinq cents de ses ouvrages*. Bruxelles, van Trigt, 1884.

7309. Friedländer, Max J. *Lucas van Leyden*. Berlin, de Gruyter, 1963.

7310. Hollstein, F. W. *The graphic art of Lucas van Leyden (1494–1533)*. Amsterdam, Hertzberger, [1968]. (CR).

7311. Jacobowitz, Ellen. *The prints of Lucas van Leyden and his contemporaries*. Washington, D.C., National Gallery of Art, 1983.

7312. Kahn, Rosy. *Die frühen Stiche des Lucas van Leyden*. Strassburg, Heitz, 1917. (Zur Kunstgeschichte des Auslandes, 118).

7313. Smith, Elise, Lawton. *The paintings of Lucas van Leyden, a new appraisal*. Columbia, Mo., University of Missouri Press, 1992. (CR).

7314. Volbehr, Theodor. *Lucas van Leyden; Ver-*

zeichniss seiner Kupferstiche, Radierungen und Holzschnitte. Hamburg, Haendcke & Lehmkuhl, 1888.

7315. Vos, Rik. *Lucas van Leyden.* Bentveld, Landshoff/Maarssen, Schwartz, 1978. (CR).

Lucchesi, Bruno, 1926–

7316. Merriam, Dana. *Bruno Lucchesi, scupltor of the human spirit.* Photographs by David Finn. New York, Hudson Hills Press, 1989.

Luchetto da Genova *see* Cambiaso, Luca

Luini, Bernardino, 1475–1533

7317. Beltrami, Luca. *Luini, 1512–1532; materiale di studio raccolto.* Milano, Allegretti, 1911.

7318. Civico Istituto di Cultura Popolare (Luino). *Sacro e profano nella pittura di Bernardino Luini.* [August 9– October 8, 1975]. Luino, Civico Istituto di Cultura Popolare, 1975.

7319. Della Chiesa, Angela O. *Bernardino Luini.* Novara, Istituto Geografico de Agostini, 1956.

7320. Gauthiez, Pierre. *Luini, biographie critique.* Paris, Laurens, [1905].

7321. Mason, James. *Bernardino Luini.* London, Jack/New York, Stokes, [1908].

7322. Reggiori, Giovanni B. *Bernardino Luini, cenni biografici preceduti da una introduzione sui magistri comacini.* Milano, Mohr, [1911].

7323. Williamson, George C. *Bernardino Luini.* London, Bell, 1907.

Lurçat, Jean, 1892–1966

7324. Faux, Claude. *Lurçat a haute voix: culs-de-lampe de Jean Lurçat.* Photographies de Pic. Paris, R. Julliard, 1962.

7325. Lurçat, Jean. *Designing tapestry.* Trans. by Barbara Crocker. London, Rockliff, 1950.

7326. ———. *Jean Lurçat et la renaissance de la tapisserie Aubusson.* Aubusson, Musée departemental de la tapisserie, 1992. (Colloque, 92).

7327. Musee Lurçat (Angers). *L'homme et ses lumieres: retrospective de l'oeuvre paint, tapisseries cosmiques et religieuses* [11 avril– 27 septembre, 1992]. Angers, Le Musé, 1992.

7328. Roy, Claude. *Jean Lurçat.* Genève, Cailler, 1956. 2 ed. (CR).

7329. Vercors [pseud., Jean Bruller]. *Tapisseries de Jean Lurçat, 1939–1957.* Belvès (Dordogne, France), Vorms, 1958.

Lutero, Giovanni de *see* Dossi, Dosso

Lutyens, Edwin Landseer, 1869–1944

7330. Butler, Arthur S. *The architecture of Sir Edwin Lutyens.* 3 v. London, Country Life, 1950. (CR).

7331. Gradidge, Roderick. *Edwin Lutyens, architect laureate.* London, Allen & Unwin, 1981.

7332. Hayward Gallery (London). *Lutyens: the work of the English architect Sir Edwin Lutyens (1869–1944).* 18 November 1981–31 January 1982. London, Arts Council of Great Britain, 1981.

7333. Hussey, Christopher. *The life of Sir Edwin Lutyens.* London, Country Life, 1950.

7334. Irving, Robert G. *Indian summer: Lutyens, Baker, and imperial Delhi.* New Haven/London, Yale University Press, 1981.

7335. Inskip, Peter. *Edwin Lutyens.* New York, Rizzoli, 1979. (Architectural Monographs, 6).

7336. Lutyens, Mary. *Edwin Lutyens.* London, Murray, 1980.

7337. O'Neill, Daniel. *Sir Edwin Lutyens, country houses.* With a preface by Sir Hugh Casson. London, Lund Humphries, 1980.

7338. Weaver, Lawrence. *Houses and gardens by E. L. Lutyens, described and criticized.* London, Country Life, 1913. (Reprint: London, Antique Collectors' Club, 1981).

Lys, Jan, *called* Pan *see* Liss, Johann

Lysippus, sculptor, 4th c. B.C.

7339. Collignon, Maxime. *Lysippe, étude critique.* Paris, Librairie Renouard, [1904].

7340. Johnson, Franklin P. *Lysippos.* Durham, N.C., Duke University Press, 1927.

7341. Lange, Konrad. *Das Motiv des aufgestützten Fusses in der antiken Kunst und dessen statuarische Verwendung durch Lysippos.* Leipzig, Seemann, 1879. (Beiträge zur Kunstgeschichte, 3).

7342. Löwy, Emanuel. *Lysipp und seine Stellung in der griechischen Plastik.* Hamburg, Richter, 1891.

7343. Maviglia, Ada. *L'attività artistica di Lisippo ricostruita su nuova base.* Roma, Loescher, 1914.

7344. Moreno, Paolo, ed. *Testimonianze per la teoria artistica di Lisippo.* Treviso, Canova, 1973.

7345. ———. *Vita e arte di Lisippo.* Milano, Il Saggiatore, 1987.

M

Mabuse *see* **Gossaert, Jan**

Macedo *see* **Clovio, Giulio**

Macke, August, 1887–1914

7346. Bartmann, Domenik. *August Macke, Kunsthandwerk: Glasbilder, Stickerien, Keramiken, Holzarbeiten und Entwürfe.* Berlin, Mann, 1979.

7347. Cohen, Walter. *August Macke.* Leipzig, Klinkhardt & Biermann, 1922. (Junge Künst, 32).

7348. Erdmann-Macke, Elisabeth. *Erinnerung an August Macke.* Stuttgart, Kohlhammer, 1962.

7349. Friesen, Astrid von. *August Macke, ein Maler-Leben.* Hamburg, Ellert & Richter Verlag, 1989.

7350. Heiderich, Ursula. *August Macke, Zeichnungen: Werkverzeichnis.* Stuttgart, Hatje, 1993. (CR).

7351. ———. *August Macke: Die Skizzenbücher.* 2 v. Stuttgart, Hatje, 1987.

7352. Macke, August. *Briefe an Elisabeth und die Freunde.* Hrsg. von Werner Frese und Ernst-Gerhard Güse. München, Bruckmann, 1987.

7353. [———]. *Die Rheinischen Expressionisten: Macke und seine Malerfreunde.* Recklinghausen, Bongers, 1980.

7354. ———, et al. *Tunisian watercolors and drawings.* Trans. by Norbert Guterman. New York, Abrams, 1969.

7355. [Macke, Wolfgang, ed.]. *August Macke; Franz Marc: Briefwechsel.* Köln, DuMont Schauberg, 1964.

7356. Moeller, Magdalena M. *August Macke.* Köln, DuMont, 1988.

7357. Städtisches Kunstmuseum (Bonn). *Die rheinischen Expressionisten: August Macke und seine Malerfreunde.* 30. Mai–29. Juli 1979. Recklinghausen, Bongers, 1979.

7358. Vriesen, Gustav. *August Macke.* Stuttgart, Kohlhammer, 1957. 2 ed. (CR).

7359. Westfälischer Kunstverein (Münster, Westfalen). *August Macke, Gedenkausstellung zum 70. Geburtstag.* 27. Januar–24. März 1957. Münster, Westfälischer Kunstverein, 1957.

7360. Weyandt, Barbara. *Farbe und Naturauffassung im Werk von August Macke.* Hildesheim, Olms, 1994. (Studien zur Kunstgeschichte, 86).

Mackintosh, Charles Rennie, 1868–1928

7361. Alison, Filippo. *Charles Rennie Mackintosh as a designer of chairs.* Trans. by Bruno and Christina del Piore. Milan/London, Warehouse, 1974.

7362. [Barnes, H. Jefferson, introd.]. *Some examples of furniture by Charles Rennie Mackintosh in the Glasgow School of Art Collection.* Glasgow, Glasgow School of Art, [1968].

7363. ———. *Some examples of iron work and metalwork by Charles Rennie Mackintosh at Glasgow School of Art.* Glasgow, Glasgow School of Art, [1968].

7364. Billcliffe, Roger. *Charles Rennie Macintosh; the complete furniture, furniture drawings, and interior designs.* London, J. Murray, 1986. 3 ed. (First publ.: New York, Taplinger, 1979. (CR).

7365. ———. *Mackintosh furniture.* Cambridge, Eng., Lutterworth Press, 1984.

7366. ———. *Mackintosh textile designs.* London, J. Murray, 1982.

7367. Bliss, Douglas Percy. *Charles Rennie Mackintosh and the Glasgow School of Art.* 3 v. Edited and annotated by H. Jefferson Barnes; text by Douglas Percy Bliss; photography by Ralph Burnett. Glasgow, G.S.A. Enterprises, 1988. 3 ed. (First published, 1961).

7368. ———. *Mackintosh, textile designs.* London, J. Murray, 1982.

7369. ——— *Mackintosh watercolours.* London, J. Murray, 1978. (CR).

7370. Brett, David. *C.R. Mackintosh: the poetics of workmanship.* London, Reaktion Books, 1992.

7371. Buchanan, William, ed. *Mackintosh's masterwork: the Glasgow School of Art.* Glasgow, R. Drew, 1989.

7372. Garcias, Jean-Claude. *Mackintosh.* Paris, Hazan, 1989.

7373. Grigg, Jocelyn. *Charles Rennie Mackintosh.* Glasgow, Drew Publishing, 1987.

7374. Howarth, Thomas. *Charles Rennie Mackintosh and the modern movement.* London, Routledge & Kegan Paul, 1977. 2 ed.

7375. Jones, Anthony. *Charles Rennie Mackintosh.* London, Studion Editions, 1990.

7376. Mackintosh, Charles R. *Architectural sketches & flower drawings.* Ed. by Roger Billcliffe. London, Academy, 1977.

7377. ———. *Charles Rennie Mackintosh, 1868–1928.* [Mostra] a cura di Guido Lagan; contributi di Andrew MacMillan . . . [et al.]. Milano, Electa, 1988.

7378. ———. *Mackintosh watercolours.* London, J. Murray, 1979. (Paperback ed.: 1992).

7379. Macleod, Robert. *Charles Rennie Mackintosh: architect and artist.* London, Collins, 1983. (Rev. ed. of his *Charles Rennie Mackintosh.* Feltham, Eng.,Country Life, 1968).

7380. Nuttgens, Patrick, ed. *Mackintosh and his contemporaries in Europe and America.* [P. Nuttgens, general editor]. London, J. Murray, 1988.

7381. Pevsner, Nikolaus. *Charles R. Mackintosh.* Milano, Il Balcone, 1950. (Reprinted in translation in: Pevsner, Nikolaus. *Studies in art, architecture and design.* 2 v. London, Thames and Hudson, 1968).

7382. Victoria and Albert Museum (London). *Charles Rennie Mackintosh (1868–1928), a centenary exhibition. Architecture, design and painting.* [30 October–29 December 1968; introduction, notes, and catalogue by Andrew McLaren Young]. Edinburgh, Scottish Arts Council, 1968.

McIntire, Samuel, 1757–1811

7383. Cousins, Frank and Riley, Phil M. *The woodcarver of Salem; Samuel McIntire, his life and work.* Boston, Little Brown, 1916. (Reprint: New York, AMS, 1970).

7384. Hipkiss, Edwin J. *Three McIntire rooms from Peabody, Massachusetts.* Boston, Museum of Fine Arts, 1931.

7385. Labaree, Benjamin W., ed. *Samuel McIntire; a bicentennial symposium, 1757–1957.* Salem, Mass. Essex Institute, 1957.

7386. Kimball, Fiske. *Mr. Samuel McIntire, carver; the architect of Salem.* Portland, Me., Southworth-Anthoensen Press, 1940. (Reprint: Gloucester, Mass., Peter Smith, 1966).

McKim, Charles Follen, 1847–1911

7387. Granger, Alfred H. *Charles Follen McKim, a study of his life and work.* Boston/New York, Houghton Mifflin, 1913. (Reprint: New York, Arno, 1972).

7388. Hill, Frederick P. *Charles F. McKim, the man.* Francestown, N.H., Jones, 1950.

7389. [McKim, Charles F., et al.]. *A monograph of the work of McKim, Mead & White, 1879–1915.* 4 v. New York, Architectural Book Publishing Co., 1915–1920. (New ed., with an essay and notes on the plates by Leland M. Roth; New York, Blom, 1973; student's edition, with an introduction by Alan Greenberg and notes by Michael George: New York, Architectural Book Publishing Co., 1981). (CR).

7390. Moore, Charles. *The life and times of Charles Follen McKim.* Boston/New York, Houghton Mifflin, 1929. (Reprint: New York, Da Capo, 1969).

7391. Reilly, C. H. *McKim, Mead & White.* London, Benn, 1924. (Reprint: New York, Blom, 1973).

7392. Roth, Leland M. *The architecture of McKim, Mead & White, 1870–1920: a building list.* New York, Garland, 1978. (Garland Reference Library of the Humanities, 114).

McLean, Bruce, 1944–

7393. Gooding, Mel. *Bruce McLean.* Oxford. Phaidon; New York, Phaidon Universe, 1990.

Maderno, Carlo, 1556–1629

7394. Caflisch, Nina. *Carlo Maderno, ein Beitrag zur Geschichte der römischen Barockarchitektur.* München, Bruckmann, 1934.

7395. Donati, Ugo. *Carlo Maderno, architetto ticinese a Roma.* Lugano, A cura del Banco di Roma per la Svizzera, 1957.

7396. Egger, Hermann. *Carlo Madernos Projekt für den Vorplatz von San Pietro in Vaticano.* Leipzig, Poeschel & Trepte, 1928 (Römische Forschungen der Bibliotheca Hertziana, 6).

7397. Hibbard, Howard. *Carlo Maderno and Roman architecture, 1580–1630.* London, Zwemmer, 1971. (Studies in Architecture, 10).

7398. Muñoz, Antonio. *Carlo Maderno.* Roma, Societá editrice della biblioteca d'arte illustrata, 1921.

Maderno, Stefano, 1576–1636

7399. Muñoz, Antonio. *Stefano Maderno: contributo allo studio della scultura barocca primi del Bernini.* Roma, Tipografia Editrice Romana, 1915.

7400. Nava Cellini, Antonia. *Stefano Maderno.* Milano, Fabbri, 1966. (I maestri della scultura, 60).

Madrazo, Federico de, 1815–1894
José, 1781–1859

7401. [Ceán Bermúdez and Musso y Valiente]. *Coleccion lithographica de cuadros del Rey de España, el señor, don Fernando VII*. Obra lithographica por hábiles artistas bajo le direccion de Jose de Madrazo. Madrid, Real Establecimienta Lithographico, 1826–32.

7402. Madrazo, Mariano de. *Federico de Madrazo*. 2 v. Madrid, Estrella, 1921.

Maes, Nicolaes, 1632–1693

7403. Valentiner, Wilhelm R. *Nicolaes Maes*. Stuttgart, Deutsche Verlags-Anstalt, 1924.

Maffei, Francesco, 1600/20(?)–1660

7404. *Basilica Palladiana di Vicenza. Mostra di Francesco Maffei*. Giugno–ottobre 1956. [Catalogue by Nicola Ivanoff]. Venezia, Pozza, 1956.

7405. Ivanoff, Nicola. *Francesco Maffei*. Padova, Le Tre Venezie, 1947. (Collection d'art, deuxième série, 6). (CR).

7406. Rossi, Paola. *Francesco Maffei: Catalogue raisonné*. Milano, Berenice, 1991. (CR).

Magini, Carlo, 1720–1806

7407. Zampetti, Pietro. *Carlo Magini*. A cura di Pietro Zampetti; testi di Rodolfo Bettistini, Bonita Cleri, Giuseppe Cucco. Milano, F. Motta, 1990. (CR)

Magnasco, Alessandro, 1667–1749

7408. Beltrami, Giuseppe. *Alessandro Magnasco, detto il Lissandrino*. Milano, Allegretti, 1913.

7409. Bonzi, Mario. *Saggi sul Magnasco*. Genova, Liguria, 1971. 3 ed.

7410. Dürst, Hans. *Alessandro Magnasco*. Teufen, Niggli, 1966.

7411. Franchini Guelfi, Fausta. *Alessandro Magnasco*. Genova, Pagano, 1977. (2 ed.: Soncino, Edizioni dei Soncino, 1991).

7412. Geiger, Benno. *Magnasco*. Bergamo, Istituto Italiano d'Arte Grafiche, 1949.

7413. ———. *Magnasco, i disegni*. Padova, Le Tre Venezie, 1945.

7414. Magnasco, Alessandro. *Il "Trattenimento in un girardino d'Albaro" di Alessandro Magnasco: un rerstauro a Palazzo Bianco*. A cura dei Clario Di Fabio; contributi di Paolo Bensi . . . [et al.]. Genova, Assessorato alle istituzioni e attivita culturali, 1990.

7415. Magnoni, Valentina. *Alessandro Magnasco*. Roma, Edizioni Mediterranee, [1965].

7416. Pospisil, Maria. *Magnasco*. Firenze, Alinari, 1944.

7417. Syamken, Georg G. *Die Bildinhalte des Alessandro Magnasco, 1667–1749*. Hamburg, Hintze & Sachse, 1963.

Magnelli, Alberto, 1888–1971

7418. Degand, Léon. *Magnelli*. Venezia, Edizioni del Cavallino, [1952].

7419. Lochard, Anne. *Magnelli, opere 1907–1939*. Roma, Il Collezionista, 1972.

7420. Maisonnier, Anne. *Alberto Magnelli, l'oeuvre peint: catalogue raisonné*. Paris, Société Internationale d'Art XXᵉ siècle, 1975. (CR).

7421. ———. *Magnelli: collages*. Catalogue raisonné, Anne Maisonnier-Lochard; préface de Maurice Besset. Paris, A. Biro, 1990. (CR).

7422. Mendes, Murillo, ed. *Alberto Magnelli*. [Texts in Italian, French and English]. Roma, Ateneo, 1964. (Contributi alla storia dell'arte, 2).

7423. Magnelli, Alberto. *Alberto Magnelli, a Florentine painter, 1888–1971*. [Catalogue of an exhibition]: October 18 to December 14,198 Leonard Hutton Galleries, New York, NY. New York, The Galleries, 1985.

7424. ———. *Alberto Magnelli: realismo imaginario. Disegni editi e inediti, 1920–1929*. [Mostra] Forte dei Marmi, 11 luglio–23 agosto 1987. A cura di Mario de Micheli. Milano, Fabbri, 1987.

7425. ———. *Magnelli*. [Catalogue of an exhibition]. Musée national d'art moderne avec le concours de l'Association "Pour Magnelli"; [conceptiom et direction del'ouvrage, Daniel Abadie]. Paris, Editions du Centre Pompidou, 1989.

7426. ———. *Magnelli, les années 20*. [Catalogue of an exhibition]. Préface de Achille Bonito Oliva. Paris, Galerie Maeght Lelong, 1986.

Magritte, René, 1898–1967

7427. Foucault, Michel. *This is not a pipe*. With illustrations and letters by René Magritte. Trans. and ed. by James Harkness. Berkeley, Calif., University of California Press, 1983.

7428. Gablik, Suzi. *Magritte*. Greenwich, Conn., New York Graphic Society, 1970.

7429. Gimferrer, Pere. *Magritte*. Trans. Kenneth Lyons. New York, Rizzoli, 1987.

7430. Hammacher, Abraham M. *René Magritte*. Trans. by James Brockway. New York, Abrams, 1973.

7431. Konersmann, Ralf. *René Magritte, die verbotene Reproduktion: über die Sichtbarkeit des Denkens*. Frankfurt am Main, Fischer Taschenbuch Verlag, 1991.

7432. Kunstverein und Kunsthaus Hamburg. *René Magritte und der Surrealismus in Belgien*. 23. Januar bis 28. März 1982. Brüssel, Lebeer Hossmann, 1982.

7433. Lebel, Robert. *Magritte, peintures*. Paris, Hazan, 1969.

7434. Magritte, René. *La destination: lettres à Marcel Mariën, 1937–1962*. Bruxelles, Lèvres, 1977.

7435. ———. *Ecrits complets.* Ed. par André Blavier. Paris, Flammarion, 1979.

7436. ———. *Lettres à André Bosmans, 1958–1967.* Edition établie et annotée par Francine Perceval. Paris, Seghers; Isy Brachot, 1990.

7437. ———. *Quatre vingt deux lettres de René Magritte à Mirabelle Dors et Maurice Rapin avec des lettres de Noël Arnaud et Georgette Magritte* [in facsimile]. Paris, [Georgette Magritte et al.], 1976.

7438. ———. *René Magritte: Catalogue raisonné.* Edited by David Sylvester . . . [et al.]. 5 v. Antwerpen, Mercator Fonds; distributed in the U.S.A. and Canada by Rizzoli, in association with the Menil Foundation, 1992–1993. (CR).

7439. ———. *René Magritte.* [Exposition] du 21 mai au 10 juillet 1988, le Musée national d'art moderne, Tokyo. Rédaction, Yoshikazu Iwasaki . . . [et al.]. Tokyo, Le Musée ; Le Tokyo Shimbun, 1988.

7440. ———. *René Magritte.* [Mostra] Gallerie civiche d'arte moderna, Palazzo dei diamanti, 30 giugno–12 ottobre 1986. Roma, SIAE, 1986.

7441. ———. *René Magritte, peintures et gouaches.* Ed. by Isy Brachot. Antwerp, Rony Van de Velde, 1994.

7442. Meuris, Jacques. *René Magritte.* Trans. from the French by J.A. Underwood. Wood-stock, N.Y., Overlook Press, 1990.

7443. Museum Boymans-von Beuningen (Rotterdam). *René Magritte: het mysterie van de werkelijkheid.* 4 augustus–24 september 1967. [Text in Dutch and French]. Rotterdam, Museum Boymans-van Beuningen, 1967.

7444. Museum of Modern Art (New York). *René Magritte.* [Dec. 15, 1965–Feb. 27, 1966; text by James T. Soby]. New York, Museum of Modern Art, 1965; distributed by Doubleday, Garden City, N.Y.

7445. Noël, Bernard. *Magritte.* Paris, Flammarion, 1976.

7446. Nougé, Paul. *René Magritte ou les images défendues.* Bruxelles, Les Augeurs Associés, 1943.

7447. Oehlers, Helmut. *Figur und Raum in den Werken von Max Ernst, René Magritte, Salvador Dali und Paul Delvaux, zwischen 1925 und 1938.* Frankfurt am Main/ New York, P. Lang, 1986. (European university studies. Series XXVIII, History of art, 54).

7448. Palais des Beaux-Arts (Brussels). *Rétrospective Magritte.* 27 ottobre–31 décembre 1978. Bruxelles, Département de la Culture Française de Belgique/Paris, Musée d'Art Modern, Centre Georges Pompidou, 1978.

7449. Passeron, René and Saucet, Jean. *René Magritte.* Trans. by Elisabeth Abbott. Chicago, O'Hara, 1972.

7450. Roberts-Jones, Philippe. *Magritte, poète visible.* Bruxelles, Laconti, 1972.

7451. Schliebler, Ralf. *Die Kunsttheorie René Magrittes.* München/Wien, Hanser, 1981.

7452. Schneede, Uwe M. *René Magritte: Leben und Werk.* Köln, DuMont Schauberg, 1973.

7453. Scutenaire, Louis. *Avec Magritte.* Bruxelles, Lebeer Hossmann, 1977.

7454. Sylvester, David. *Magritte.* New York, Praeger, 1969.

7455. ———. *Magritte.* London, Thames and Hudson in association with the Menil Foundation, 1992.

7456. Torczyner, Harry. *L'ami Magritte: correspondence et souvenirs.* Antwerp, Bibliothèque des Amis du Fonds Mercator, 1992.

7457. ———. *Magritte: ideas and images.* Trans. by Richard Miller. New York, Abrams, 1977.

7458. ———. *Magritte: the true art of painting.* With the collaboration of Bella Bessard. Trans. by Richard Miller. New York, Abrams, 1979.

7459. Waldberg, Patrick. *René Magritte.* Trans. by Austryn Wainhouse. Bruxelles, de Roche, 1965.

7460. Whitfield, Sarah. *Magritte.* [Catalogue of an exhibition]. London, South Bank Centre, 1992.

Maillol, Aristide Joseph Bonaventure, 1861–1944

7461. Albright Art Gallery (Buffalo, N.Y.). *Aristide Maillol* [commemorative exhibition]. Buffalo, N.Y., Buffalo Fine Arts Academy, 1945.

7462. Bouvier, Marguette. *Aristide Maillol.* Lausanne, Editions Margeurat, 1945.

7463. Chevalier, Denys. *Maillol.* Trans. by Eileen B. Hennessy. New York, Crown, 1970.

7464. Cladel, Judith. *Maillol; sa vie, son oeuvres, ses idées.* Paris, Grasset, 1937.

7465. Denis, Maurice. *A. Maillol.* Paris, Crès, 1925.

7466. ——— et Colombier, Pierre du. *Maillol, dessins et pastels.* Paris, Carré, 1942.

7467. Frère, Henri. *Conversations de Maillol.* Genève, Cailler, 1956. (Les grands artistes racontés par eux-mêmes et par leurs amis, 12).

7468. George, Waldemar. *Aristide Maillol et l'âme de la sculpture.* Paris, La Bibliothèque des Arts/Neuchâtel, Editions Ides et Calendes, 1977.

7469. Guérin, Marcel. *Catalogue raisonné de l'oeuvre gravé et lithographié de Aristide Maillol.* 2 v. Genève, Cailler, 1965–1967. (CR).

7470. Kuhn, Alfred. *Aristide Maillol: Landschaft, Werke, Gespräche.* Leipzig, Seemann, 1925.

7471. Linnenkamp, Rolf. *Aristide Maillol, die grossen Plastiken.* München, Bruckmann, 1960.

7472. Lorquin, Bertrand. *Maillol aux Tuileries.* Paris, A Biro, 1991.

7473. Maillol, Aristide. *Maillol.* [Exposition] mars–mai 1987, Galerie Dina Vierny. Paris, Galerie Vierny, 1987.

7474. Mirbeau, Octave. *Aristide Maillol.* Paris, Crès, 1921.

7475. Rewald, John. *Maillol.* London, Hyperion, 1939.

7476. ———. *The woodcuts of Aristide Maillol, a complete catalogue.* New York, Pantheon, 1951. 2 ed. (CR).

7477. Sentenac, Paul. *Aristide Maillol.* Paris, Peyre, [1936].

7478. Solomon R. Guggenheim Museum (New York). *Aristide Maillol, 1861–1944.* [Text by John Rewald]. New York, Guggenheim Foundation, 1965.

7479. Staatliche Kunsthalle Baden-Baden. *Maillol.* 17. Juni bis 3. September 1978. Herausgegeben von Hans Albert Peters. Baden-Baden, Staatliche Kunsthalle, 1978.

7480. Vierny, Dina. *Maillol, la Méditerranée* [Exposition]. Catalogue établi et redigée par Dina Vierny et Bernard Lorquin et Antoinette Le Normand-Romain. Paris, Ministère de la culture et de la communication, Editions de la réunion des musées nationaux, 1986. (Dossiers du Musée d'Orsay,4).

Makart, Hans, 1840–1884

7481. Bachelin, Léopold. *Hans Makart et les cinq sens.* Paris, Sandoz & Thullier, 1883.

7482. Frodel, Gerbert. *Hans Makart; Monographie und Werkverzeichnis.* Salzburg, Residenz, 1974. (CR).

7483. Makart, Hans. *Makart-Album.* Wien F. Bondy, 1882 (1883?).

7484. Pirchan, Emil. *Hans Makart.* Wien, Bergland, 1954. 2 ed.

7485. Staatliche Kunsthalle Baden-Baden. *Makart.* 23. Juni bis 17. September 1972. Baden-Baden, Staatliche Kunsthalle, 1972. 2 ed.

Malbone, Edward Greene, 1777–1807

7486. Tolman, Ruel P. *The life and works of Edward Greene Malbone.* Foreword by John Davis, Jr. Introd. by Theodore Bolton. New York, New York Historical Society, 1958. (CR).

Malevich, Kazimir Severinovich, 1878–1935

7487. Andersen, Troels. *Malevich: catalogue raisonné of the Berlin exhibition, 1927, including the collection of the Stedelijk Museum, Amsterdam.* Amsterdam, Stedelijk Museum, 1970. (CR).

7488. Crone, Rainer. *Kazimir Malevich: the climax of discourse.* [By] R. Crone, David Moos. Chicago, University of Chicago Press, 1991.

7489. Douglas, Charlotte. *Swans of other worlds; Kazimir Malevich and the origins of abstrac-

tion in Russia.* Ann Arbor, Mich., UMI Research Press, 1976. (Studies in the Fine Arts: the Avant-garde, 2).

7490. ———. *Malevich.* [By] C. Douglas, Galina Demosfenova . . . et al. Paris, Flammarion; distr. in the U.S.A. and Canada, New York, Abbeville Press, 1991.

7491. Fauchereau, Serge. *Kazimir Malévitch.* Paris, Editions Cercle d'art, 1991.

7492. Galerie Gmurzynska (Cologne). *Kasimir Malewitsch zum 100. Geburtstag.* June–July 1978. [Text in English and German]. Köln, Galerie Gmurzynska, 1978.

7493. Karshan, Donald. *Malevich: the graphic work, 1913–1930.* A print catalogue raisonné. [Published in conjunction with an exhibition, November 1975–January 1976]. Jerusalem, Israel Museum, 1975. (CR).

7494. [Malevich, Kazimir Severinovich]. *Écrits.* Traduits par Jean-Claude et Valentine Marcadé et al. 4 v. Lausanne, L'Age d'Homme, 1974–1981.

7495. ———. *[Essays on art].* Edited by Troels Andersen. Trans. by Xenia Glowacki-Prus [Hoffman], et al. 4 v. Copenhagen, Borgen, 1968–1978.

7496. ———. *Kazimir Malevich, 1878–1935:* [Catalogue of an exhibition]. National Gallery of Art, Washington, D.C., 16 September–4 November 1990, the Armand Hammer Museum of Art and Cultural Center, Los Angeles, 28 November 1990–13 January 1991, the Metropolitan Museum of Art, New York, 7 February–24 March 1991. Editor, Jeanne 'DAndrea]. Los Angeles, Armand Hammer Museum of Art and Cultural Center in association with the University of Washington Press, 1990.

7497. ———. *Kazimir Malevich, 1887–1935: werken in Staats Russisch Museum, Leningrad . . . = works from the State Russian Museum, Leningrad . . .* [Catalogue of an exhbition held at the Stedelijk Museum, Amsterdam]. Redactie, W.A.L. Beeren, J.M. Joosten; met medewerking van L. Veneman-Boersma. [Moscow], Ministerie van Cultuur USSR; Amsterdam, Nederland, Stedelijk Museum, 1988.

7498. Marcadé, Jean-Claude. *Malévitch, 1878–1978; actes du colloque international tenu au Centre Pompidou, Musée National d'Art Moderne, les 4 et 5 mai 1978.* Lausanne, L'Age d'Homme, 1979.

7499. ———. *Malévitch.* Paris, Casterman: Nouvelles Editions françaises, 1990.

7500. Martineau, Emmanuel. *Malévitch et la philosophie: la question de la peinture abstraite.* Lausanne, L'Age d'Homme, 1976.

7501. Musée National d'Art Moderne (Paris). *Malévitch: oeuvres de Casimir Severinovitch Malévitch (1878–1935).* Catalogue établi par Jean-Hubert Martin. Paris, Musée National d'Art Modern/Centre Georges Pompidou, 1980.

7502. Papadakis, Andreas C., ed. *Malevich*. London, Academy Editions; New York, St. Martins Press, 1989. (Art and design profile, 15).

7503. Petrova, Evgeniya . . . [et al]. *Malevich: artist and theoretician*. Paris, Flammarion, 1991.

7504. Sarab'ianov, Dmitri Vladimirovich. *Kazimir Malevich: zhivopis'; teoriia: al'bom monografiia*. [By] D. Sarab'ianov [and] A. Shatskii. Moskva, Isskustvo, 1993.

7505. Stachelhaus, Rainer. *Kasimir Malewitsch, ein tragischer Konflikt*. Düsseldorf, Claassen, 1989.

7506. Zhadova, Larisa. *Malevich: Suprematism and revolution in Russian art, 1910–1930*. Trans. by Alexander Lieven. New York, Thames & Hudson, 1982.

Man, Felix H., 1893–

7507. Man, Felix H. *60 Jahre Fotografie*. Bielefeld, Kunsthalle Bielefeld, 1978.

Man Ray *see* Ray, Man

Mander, Karel van, 1548–1606

7508. Greve, H. E. *De Bronnen van Carel van Mander*. Haag, Nijhoff, 1903. (Quellenstudien zur holländischen Kunstgeschichte, 2).

7509. Hoecker, Rudolf, ed. *Das Lehrgedicht des Karl van Mander; Text, Uebersetzung, und Kommentar*. Haag, Nijhoff, 1916. (Quellenstudien zur holländischen Kunstgeschichte, 8).

7510. Jacobsen, R. *Carel van Mander (1548–1606), dichter en prozaschrijver*. Rotterdam, Brusse, 1906.

7511. Mander, Karel van. *Karel van Mander: lives*. Ed. by Hessel Miedema. 6 v. Doornspijk, Davaco Spring, 1994.

7512. ———. *Het Schilder-boek*. Haarlem, Paschier von Wesbusch, 1604. (Reprint: Utrecht, Davaco, 1969; English trans. by Constant van de Wall: New York, McFarlane, 1936. 2v. Reprint: New York, Arno, 1969).

7513. Melion, Walter S. *Shaping the Netherlandisch canon: Karel van Mander's Schilderboek*. Chicago, University of Chicago Press, 1992.

7514. Miedema, Hessel. *Karel van Mander: Den grondt der edel vry schilder-const*. [Edited by] H. Miedema. Utrecht, Haentjens, 1973. 2 v. (Dutch text with English summary).

7515. Müller, Jürgen. *Concordia Pragensis: Karel van Manders Kunsttheorie im Schilderboeck: ein Beitrag zur Rhetorisierung von Kunst und Leben am Beispiel der Rudol-*

inischen Hofkünstler. München, Oldenbourg, 1993. (Veröffentlichungen des Collegium Carolinum, 77).

7516. Noë, Helen. *Carel van Mander in Italie*. Den Haag, Nijhoff, 1954.

7517. Plettinck, Leopold. *Studien over het leven en de werken van Karel van Mander, dichter, schilder en kunstgeschiedschrijver, 1598–1606*. 2. Ghent, Siffer, 1896.

7518. Valentiner, Elisabeth. *Karel van Mander als Maler*. Straßburg, Heitz, 1930. (Zur Kunstgeschichte des Auslandes, 123).

Manés, Josef, 1820–1871

7519. Chytil, Karel. *Josef Mánes a jeho rod*. Praha, Nákladem Kruhu pro pěstování dějin umení, 1934. (Knihova Kruhu pro pěstování dějin umeni, 2).

7520. Hlavaček, Luboš. *Josef Mánes a umelecka rodina Mánescu*. Praha, Melantrich, 1988.

7521. Kühndel, Jan, ed. *Dopisy Josefa Mánesa*. Praha, Odeon, 1968.

7522. Lamač, Miroslav. *Josef Mánes*. Praha, Nakldatelstvi československých výtvarných umelcu, 1956. 2 ed. (Umění lidů svazek, 2).

7523. Loriš, Jan. *Mánesovy podobizny*. Praha, Státí nakladatelství krásné literatury, hudby a umení, 1954.

7524. Máal, Karel B. *Josef Mánes, jeho život a díla*. Praze, Topié, 1905.

7525. Macková, Olga. *Josef Mánes*. Praha, Odeon, 1970.

7526. Matějček, Antonin. *Dílo Josefa Mánesa*. 4 v. Praha, Štenc, 1923–1940. (CR).

7527. Paur, Jaroslav. *Josef Mánes; výbor obrazů a kreseb z jehodíla*. Praha, Dědictví Komenského, 1949. 2 ed.

7528. Pěcírka, Jaromír. *Josef Mánes, živy pramen národní tradice*. Praze, Melantrich, 1941.

7529. Štencuv graficky kabinet (Prague). *Josefa Mánesa*. Praze, Štenc, 1920.

7530. Volavková, Hana. *Josef Mánes, malíř vzorků a ornamentu*. Praha, Odeon, 1981.

Manessier, Alfred, 1911–

7531. Cayrol, Jean. *Manessier*. Paris, Fall, 1966. 2 ed.

7532. Hodin, Josef Paul. *Manessier*. Bath (Eng.), Adams & Dart, 1972.

Manet, Edouard, 1832–1883

7533. Adler, Kathleen. *Manet*. Oxford, Phaidon, 1986.

7534. Bareau, Juliet Wilson. *The hidden face of Manet: an investigation of the artist's working processes*. [Catalogue of an exhibition held at the Courtauld Institute Galleries, Apr. 23–June 15, 1986]. With an introductory essay by John House. London, Burlington Magazine, 1986.

7535. Bataille, Georges. *Manet, biographical and*

critical study. Trans. by Austryn Wainhouse and James Emmons. New York, Skira, 1955. (The Taste of Our Time, 14; new ed.: Paris, Flammarion, 1980).

7536. Bazire, Edmond. *Manet: illustrations d'après les originaux et gravures de Guérard.* Paris, Quantin, 1884.

7537. Biez, Jacques de, ed. *Edouard Manet, conférence faite à la Salle des Capucines, le mardi 22 janvier, 1884.* Paris, Baschet, 1884.

7538. Blanche, Jacques-Emile. *Manet.* Paris, Rieder, 1924.

7539. Cachin, Françcoise. *Manet.* Trans. From the French by Emily Read. New York, Henry Holt, 1991. (First published: London, Barrie & Jenkins, 1991).

7540. Carr-Gomm, Sarah. *Manet.* London, Studio Editions, 1992.

7541. Clark, Timothy J. *The painting of modern life: Paris in the art of Manet and his followers.* New York, Knopf; distributed by Random House, 1985.

7542. Colin, Paul. *Edouard Manet.* Paris, Floury, 1932.

7543. Courthion, Pierre. *Edouard Manet.* New York, Abrams, 1962.

7544. ———— and Cailler, Pierre, eds. *Portrait of Manet by himself and his contemporaries.* Trans. by Michael Ross. New York, Roy, 1960.

7545. Darragon, Eric. *Manet.* Paris, Editions Citadelles, 1991.

7546. Duret, Théodore. *Histoire d'Edouard Manet et de son oeuvre.* Paris, Floury, 1902; new ed.: Paris, Bernheim-Jeune, 1926. (English ed., trans. by J. E. Crawford Flitch: New York, Crown, 1927).

7547. ————. *Manet and the French Impressionists.* Trans. by J. E. Crawford Flitch. London, Richards/Philadelphia, Lippincott, 1910.

7548. Ecole Nationale des Beaux-Arts. *Exposition des oeuvres d'Edouard Manet.* Préface de Emile Zola. [June 5–28, 1884]. Paris, Quantin, 1884.

7549. Farwell, Beatrice. *Manet and the nude: a study in iconography in the Second Empire.* New York/London, Garland, 1981.

7550. Fisher, Jay McKean. *The Prints of Edouard Manet.* [Catalogue of an exhibition held at the Detroit Institute of Arts, Detroit, Michigan and 4 other U.S. Museums]. Organized and circulated by the International Exhibitions Foundation, Washington, D.C., 1985–1986. Washington, D.C., The foundation, 1985.

7551. Florence, Penny. *Mallarmé, Manet, and Redon: visual and aural signs and the generation of meaning.* Camridge, England/New York, Cambridge University Press, 1986.

7552. Florisoone, Michel. *Manet.* Monaco, Documents d'Art, 1947.

7553. Galeries nationales du Grand Palais (Paris). *Manet, 1832–1883.* [Exposition] 22 avril–1er août 1983. Paris, Editions de la Réunion des Musées Nationaux, 1983.

7554. Graber, Hans. *Edouard Manet nach eigenen und fremden Zeugnissen.* Basel, Schwabe, 1941.

7555. Gramantieri, Tullo. *Il caso Manet.* Roma, Palombi, 1944.

7556. Guérin, Marcel. *L'oeuvre gravé de Manet.* Paris, Floury, 1944.

7557. Hamilton, George H. *Manet and his critics.* New Haven, Yale University Press, 1954. (Yale Historical Publications: History of art, 7; reprints: New York, Norton, 1969; New Haven, Yale University Press, 1986).

7558. Hanson, Anne C. *Manet and the modern tradition.* New Haven/London, Yale University Press, 1977.

7559. Harris, Jean C. *Edouard Manet, graphic work. A definitive catalogue raisonné.* New York, Collectors Editions, 1970. (Rev. ed. edited by Joel M. Smith: San Francisco, A. Wofsy Fine Arts, 1990). (CR).

7560. Hopp, Gisela. *Edouard Manet, Farbe und Bildgestalt.* Berlin, de Gruyter, 1968. (Beiträge zur Kunstgeschichte, 1).

7561. Jamot, Paul et Wildenstein, Georges. *Manet.* 2 v. Paris, Les Beaux-Arts, 1932. (CR).

7562. Jedlicka, Gotthard. *Edouard Manet.* Erlenbach/Zürich, Rentsch, 1941.

7563. Leiris, Alain de. *The drawings of Edouard Manet.* Berkeley/Los Angeles, University of California Press, 1969. (California Studies in the History of Art, 10).

7564. Leveque, Jacques. *Manet.* Paris, Quatre Chemins, 1983.

7565. Manet, Edouard. *The complete paintings of Manet.* Introduction by Phoebe Pool; notes and catalogue by Sandra Orienti. Harmondsworth, Middlesex, England, Penguin Books; New York, Viking Penguin, 1985. (Originally published in Italian by Rizzoli in 1967. This English translation first published in London by Weidenfeld & Nicolson, 1970). (CR).

7566. ————. *Lettres de jeunesse, 1848–1849: voyage à Rio.* Paris, Rouart, 1928.

7567. ————. *Lettres illustrées.* Introduction de Jean Guiffrey. Paris, Legarrec, 1929.

7568. ————. *Manet, 1832–1883.* [Exposition] Galeries nationales du Grand Palais, Paris, 22 avril–1er août 1983, Metropolitan Musem of Art, New York, 10 septembre–27 novembre 1983. Paris, Ministère de la Culture, Editions de la Réunion des musées nationaux, 1983.

7569. ————. *Manet by himself: correspondence and conversation, paintings, pastels, prints and drawings.* Edited by Juliet Wilson-Bareau. Boston, Little Brown, 1991. (First published: London, Macdonald & Co. Publishers, 1991).

7570. ———. *Manet, a retrospective*. Edited by Theresa A. Gronberg. New York, Hugh Lauter Levin Associates; distrib. by Macmillan Publishing Company, 1988.

7571. Mathey, Jacques. *Graphisme de Manet*. 3 v. Paris, de Nobele, 1961–66. (CR).

7572. Mauner, George. *Manet, peintre-philosophe: a study of the painter's themes*. University Park, Penn./London, Pennsylvania State University Press, 1975.

7573. Meier-Graefe, Julius. *Manet und sein Kreis*. Berlin, Bard, Marquardt, [1904]. 2 ed. (Die Kunst, 7).

7574. Moreau-Nélaton, Etienne. *Manet, raconté par lui-même*. 2 v. Paris, Laurens, 1926.

7575. Musée de l'Orangerie (Paris). *Exposition Manet, 1832–1883*. [June 16–October 9, 1932]. Préface de Paul Valéry; introd. de Paul Jamot. Ed. by Charles Sterling. Paris, [Musée de l'Orangerie], 1932.

7576. National Gallery of Art (Washington, D.C.). *Manet and modern Paris*. [Exhibition: Dec. 5, 1982–March 6, 1983; text by Theodore Reff]. Washington, D.C., National Gallery of Art, 1982.

7577. Perruchot, Henri. *La vie de Manet*. Paris, Hachette, 1959.

7578. Perutz Vivien. *Edouard Manet*. Lewisburg, Pa., Bucknell University Press; London, Associated University Presses, 1991.

7579. Philadelphia Museum of Art. *Edouard Manet, 1832–1883*. Exhibition: Nov. 3–Dec. 11, 1966. [Catalogue by Anne C. Hanson]. Philadelphia, Philadelphia Museum of Art, 1966.

7580. Piérard, Louis. *Manet l'incompris*. Paris, Sagittaire, 1945.

7581. Proust, Antonin. *Edouard Manet: souvenirs*. Paris, Laurens, 1913. (Reprint: Caen, L'Echoppe, 1988).

7582. Reff, Theodore. *Manet and modern Paris: one hundred paintings, drawings, prints, and photographs by Manet and his contemporaries*. Washington, D.C., National Gallery of Art, 1982. (Published in conjunction with the exhibition *Manet and modern Paris* held at the National Gallery of Art, 5 December 1982–6 March 1983).

7583. ———. *Manet: Olympia*. New York, Viking, 1976.

7584. Rewald, John. *Edouard Manet pastels*. Oxford, Cassirer, 1947.

7585. Rosenthal, Léon. *Manet, aquafortiste et lithographe*. Paris, Le Goupy, 1925.

7586. Rouart, Denis et Wildenstein, Daniel. *Edouard Manet, catalogue raisonné*. 2 v. Lausanne/Paris, La Bibliothèque des Arts, 1975. (CR).

7587. Rubin, James Henry. *Manet's silence and the poetics of bouquets*. Cambridge, Mass., Har-

vard University Press, 1994.

7588. Sandblad, Nils G. *Manet: three studies in artistic conception*. Trans. by Walter Nash. Lund (Sweden), Gleerup, 1954. (Publications of the New Society of Letters at Lund, 46).

7589. Tabarant, Adolphe. *Manet et ses oeuvres*. Paris, Gallimard, 1947.

7590. ———. *Manet: histoire catalographique*. Paris, Editions Montaigne, 1931.

7591. Tschudi, Hugo V. *Edouard Manet*. Berlin, Cassirer, 1909. 2 ed.

7592. Venturi, Marcello [and] Orienti, Sandra. *L'opera pittorica di Edouard Manet*. Milano, Rizzoli, 1967. (Classici dell'arte, 14).

7593. Waldmann, Emil. *Edouard Manet*. Berlin, Cassirer, 1923.

7594. Zola, Emile. *Edouard Manet, étude biographique et critique*. Paris, Dentu, 1867.

Manguin, Henri, 1874–1949

7595. Cabanne, Pierre. *Henri Manguin: hommages de André Dunoyer de Segonzac et Charles Terrasse; souvenirs de Madame Albert Marquet et Hans R. Hahnloser*. Neûchatel, Editions Ides et Calendes, 1964.

7596. Gassier, Pierre. *Manguin et les Fauves*. [Catalogue of an exhibition]. Martigny, Switzerland, Fondation Pierre Giannadda, 1983.

7597. Manguin, Henri Charles. *Henri Manguin: plus de cent cinquante oeuvres*. [Exposition] Février, mars, avril, 1969. Nice, Palais de la Méditerranée, 1969. Nice, Le Palais, 1969.

7598. ———. *Manguin in America; Henri Manguin, 1874–1949*. [Catalogue of an exhibition held at the University of Arizona Art Museum, Tucson. Introduction by W.E. Steadman; essay by D. Sutton. Tucson, Ariz., University of Arizona Museum of Art, 1974.

7599. Manguin, Lucile. *Henri Manguin. Catalogue raisonné de l'oeuvre peint*. [By] L. and Claude Manguin. Paris, Bibliothèque des arts, 1980.(CR).

7600. Sainsaulieu, Marie-Caroline. *Henri Manguin: catalogue raisonné de l'oeuvre peint*. Sous la direction de Lucile et Claude Manguin; avant-propos: Jacques Lassaigne; l'homme: Pierre Cabanne; l'oeuvre: Alain Mousseigne; catalogue raisonné: Marie-Caroline Sainsaulieu; notes biographiques: Jean-Pierre Manguin, Neuchâtel, Ides et Calendes, 1980. (CR).

7601. Städtische Kunsthalle Düsseldorf. *Henri Manguin: erste deutsche Retrospektive* [Ausstellung]. Städtische Kunsthalle Düsseldorf, 24. Oktober bis 7. Dezember 1969. Düsseldorf, Städtische Kunsthalle, 1969.

Manolo *see* Martinez Hugue, Manuel

Mansart, François, 1598–1666

7602. Blunt, Anthony. *François Mansart and the*

origins of French classical architecture. London, Warburg Inst., 1941. (Studies of the Warburg Institute, 14).

7603. Braham, Allan and Smith, Peter. *François Mansart.* 2 v. London, Zwemmer, 1973. (CR). (Studies in Architecture, 13).

7604. Marie, Alfred et Marie, Jeanne. *Mansart à Versailles.* 2 v. Paris, Fréal, 1972. (Versailles, son histoire, 2).

7605. ———. *Mansart et Robert de Cotte.* Paris, Imprimerie nationale, 1976. (Versailles, son histoire, 3).

Mansart, Jules Hardouin, 1646–1708

7606. Bibliothèque National (Paris). *Hardouin-Mansart et son école, exposition organisée à l'occasion du troisième centenaire de sa naissance.* 16 octobre–6 novembre 1946. Paris, Bibliothèque nationale, 1946.

7607. Bourget, Pierre et Cattaui, Georges. *Jules Hardouin Mansart.* Paris, Vincent, Fréal, 1956.

Manship, Paul, 1885–1966

7608. Gallatin, Albert E. *Paul Manship, a critical essay on his sculpture and an iconography.* New York, Lane, 1917.

7609. Manship, John. *Paul Manship.* New York, Abbeville Press, 1989.

7610. Manship, Paul. *Paul Manship: changing taste in America.* [Catalogue of an exhibition] 19 May to 18 August 1985. Minnesota Museum of Art, Landmark Center, Saint Paul, The Museum, 1985.

7611. Minnesota Museum of Art (St. Paul) [and] Bush Memorial Library, Hamline University (St. Paul, Minn.). *Paul Howard Manship, an intimate view.* [Museum exhibit: Dec.7, 1972– March 31, 1972; Library exhibit: Dec. 7, 1972–Jan. 31, 1973; text by Frederick D. Leach]. St. Paul, Minnesota Museum of Art, 1972.

7612. Rand, Harry. *Paul Manship.*[Catalogue of an exhibition] Washington, D.C., Published for the National Museum of American Art by the Smithsonian Institution Press, 1989.

7613. Murtha, Edwin. *Paul Manship.* New York, Macmillan, 1957.

7614. Smith, Carol Hynning. *Drawings by Paul Manship: the Minnesota Museum of Art collection.* Introduction by Paul Manship. St. Paul, Minn., The Museum, 1987.

7615. Vitry, Paul. *Paul Manship, sculpteur américain.* Paris, Editions de la Gazette de Beaux-Arts, 1927.

Mantegna, Andrea, 1431–1506 *see also* Francia

7616. Bell, Mrs. Arthur [Nancy]. *Mantegna.* London, Jack/New York, Stokes, [1911].

7617. Bellonci, Maria and Garavaglia, Niny. *L'opera completa del Mantegna.* Milano, Rizzoli, 1967. (Classici dell'arte, 8).

7618. Beyen, Hendrik G. *Andrea Mantegna en de verovering der ruinote on der schilderkunst.* Haag, Nijhoff, 1931.

7619. Blum, André. *Mantegna; biographie critique.* Paris, Laurens, 1912.

7620. Blum, Ilse. *Andrea Mantegna und die Antike.* Strassburg, Heitz, 1936. (Sammlung Heitz, III. Reihe, 8).

7621. Camesasca, Ettore. *Mantegna.* Milano, Club del Libro, 1964. (Collana d'arte del Club del Libro, 8).

7622. ———. *Mantegna.* Translated by Susan Madocks Lister. Florence, Scala, 1992.

7623. Cipriani, Renata. *All the paintings of Mantegna.* Trans. by Paul Colacicchi. 2 v. New York, Hawthorn, 1963. (Complete Library of World Art, 20/21).

7624. Cruttwell, Maud. *Andrea Mantegna.* London, Bell, 1901.

7625. Fiocco, Giuseppe. *L'arte di Andrea Mantegna.* Venezia, Pozza, 1959. 2 ed.

7626. ———. *Mantegna.* Milano, Hoepli, 1937.

7627. ———. *Mantegna, la Cappella Ovetori nella Chiesa degli Eremitani.* Milano, Pizzi, 1947. (New ed., in English, with an introduction by Teresio Pignatti: London, Phaidon, 1978.)

7628. Greenstein, Jack M. *Mantegna and painting as historical narrative.* Chicago, University of Chicago Press, 1992.

7629. Knapp, Fritz. *Andrea Mantegna; des Meisters Gemälde und Kupferstiche.* Stuttgart/Leipzig, Deutsche Verlags-Anstalt, 1910. (Klassiker der Kunst, 16).

7630. Kristeller, Paul. *Andrea Mantegna.* Trans. by S. Arthur Strong. London, Longmans, 1901.

7631. Lightbown, Ronald. *Mantegna. With a complete catalogue of the paintings, drawings and prints.* Oxford, Phaidon/Christie's, 1986.(CR).

7632. Martindale, Andrew. *The Triumphs of Caesar by Andrea Mantegna in the collection of Her Majesty the Queen at Hampton Court.* London, Miller, 1979.

7633. Martineau, Jane, ed. *Andrea Mantegna.* [By] Susanne Boorsch, Keith Christiansen, David Ekserdjian, Charles Hope, David Landau, and others. [Catalogue of an exhibition held at the Royal Academy of Arts, London and the Metropolitan Museum of Art, New York, 1992. New York, distrib. by Harry N. Abrams,1992. (Also distrib., London, Thames and Hudson; Milano, Electa).

7634. Meiss, Millard. *Andrea Mantegna as illuminator; an episode in Renaissance art, humanism, and diplomacy.* New York, Columbia University Press, 1957.

7635. Palazzo Ducale (Venice). *Andrea Mantegna.*

Settembre–ottobre 1961. Catalogo della mostra a cura di Giovanni Paccagnini. Venezia, Pozza, 1961.

7636. Thode, Henry. *Mantegna*. Bielefeld/Leipzig, Velhagen & Klasing, 1897. (Künstler-Monographien, 27).

7637. Tietze-Conrat, Erica. *Mantegna*. London, Phaidon, 1955; distributed by Garden City Books, N.Y.

7638. Yriarte, Charles. *Mantegna; sa vie, sa maison, son tombeau, ses oeuvres dans les musées et les collections.* Paris, Rothschild, 1901.

Manzoni, Piero, 1933–1963

7639. Agnetti, Vincenzo. *Piero Manzoni.* Testi di V. Agnetti, Franco Angeli, Nanni Balestrini, Piero Manzoni, Elio Pogliarani. Milano, Edizioni Vanni Scheiwiller, 1967.

7640. Celant, Germano. *Piero Manzoni.* [Catalogue of an exhibition held in Milan, Castello di Rivoli—Museo d'Arte Contempoanea]. Milano, Mondadori, 1992.

7641. ———. *Piero Manzoni: catalogo generale delle opere.* Milano, Prearo, 1975.

7642. Manzoni, Piero. *Piero Manzoni, 1933–1963.* [Ausstellung] Kunstverein Hannover, 26.1.–28.2. 1970. Hannover, Kunstverein, 1970.

7643. ———. *Piero Manzoni: paintings, reliefs and objects.* [Catalogue of an exhibition held at the Tate Gallery, 20 March–15 May 1974. Writings by Piero Manzoni translated from the Italian by Caroline Tisdale and Angelo Bozzola]. London, Tate Gallery Publications, 1974.

7644. ———. *Piero Manzoni.* Presentazione di Palma Bucarelli. Catalogo di Germano Celant. [Catalogue of an exhibition held at the Galleria Nazionale d'Arte Moderna, Rome]. Roma, De Lucca, 1971.

7645. Vergine, Lea. *Azimuth:* mostra documentaria, novembre–dicembre 1974, Primo Piano Galleria d'Arte, Roma. [Catalogo] a cura di L. Vergine. Roma, Primo Piano Galleria d'Arte, 1974.

Manuel-Deutsch, Niklaus, 1484–1530

7646. Beerli, Conrad A. *Le peintre poète Nicolas Manuel et l'évolution sociale de son temps.* Genève, Droz, 1953. (Travaux d'Humanisme et Renaissance, 4).

7647. Ganz, Paul. *Zwei Schreibbüchlein des Niklaus Manuel Deutsch von Bern.* Berlin, Bard; Im Auftrag des Deutschen Vereins für Kunstwissenschaft, 1909.

7648. Grüneisen, Karl van. *Niclaus Manuel, Leben und Werke eines Malers und Dichters, Kriegers, Staatsmannes und Reformators im sechzehnten Jahrhundert.* Stuttgart/Tübingen, Cotta, 1837.

7649. Haendcke, Berthold. *Nikolaus Manuel Deutsch als Künstler.* Frauenfeld, Huber, 1889.

7650. Koegler, Hans. *Beschreibendes Verzeichnis der Basler Handzeichnungen des Niklaus Manuel Deutsch.* Basel, Schwabe, 1930.

7651. Kunstmuseum Bern. *Niklaus Manuel Deutsch: Maler, Dichter, Staatsmann.* 22. September bis 2. Dezember 1979. Bern, Kunstmuseum Bern, 1979. (CR).

7652. Mandach, Conrad de. *Niklaus Manuel Deutsch.* Basel, Urs Graf, [1956]. 2 ed. (Basler Kunstbücher, 2).

7653. Stumm, Lucie. *Niklaus Manuel Deutsch von Bern als bildender Künstler.* Bern, Stämpfli, 1925.

7654. Tavel, Hans C. von. *Niklaus Manuel. Zur Kunst eines Eidgenossen der Dürerzeit.* Bern, Wyss Erben, 1979.

7655. Zinsli, Paul. *Der Berner Totentanz des Niklaus Manuel.* Bern, Haupt, 1953. (Berner Heimatbücher, 54/55).

Manzù, Giacomo, 1908–

7656. Accademia delle Arti del Disegno. *Giacomo Manzù: esposizione per le celebrazioni del suo settantesimo anno.* [Text by Cesare Brandi et al.]. Firenze, Barbèra, 1979.

7657. Ciranna, Alfonso. *Giacomo Manzù, catalogo delle opere grafiche, 1929–1968.* Milano, Ciranna, 1968. (CR).

7658. Micheli, Mario de. *Giacomo Manzù.* New York, Abrams, 1974.

7659. Pacchioni, Anna. *Giacomo Manzù.* Prefazione di Lionello Venturi. Milano, Edizioni del Milione, 1948. (New ed., text by Carlo L. Ragghianti: 1957).

7660. Rewald, John. *Giacomo Manzù.* Greenwich, Conn., New York Graphic Society, 1967.

7661. Ciranna, Alfonso. *Manzu: catalogo delle opere grafiche: incisioni e litografie 1929–1968.* Milano, Alfonso Ciranna, 1968. (CR).

7662. De Micheli, Mario. *Giacomo Manzu.* Milano, Fabbri, 1988. (Nuova ed. ampliata).

7663. Manzu, Giacomo. *Manzu: sacred and profane.* [Catalogue of an exhbition held at the Tasende Gallery, La Jolla, Calif.], September 30–December 2, 1989. La Jolla, Calif., The Gallery, 1989.

7664. ———. *Manzu.* [Catalogo] a cura di Rossana Bossaglia]. Milano, Electa, 1988.

7665. ———. *Giacomo Manzu, temas y variaciones: esculturas, dibujos y grabados, 1929–1985.* [Catalogue of an exhibition] a cura di Livia Velani. Milano, Electa, 1991.

7666. Manzu, Inge Schabel, ed. *Manzu pittore.* A cura di Inge Schabel Manzu con saggi di Giulio Carlo Argan . . . [et al.]. Introduzione ai temi di Silvana Milesi. Bergamo, Silvana Corponove, 1988.

7667. Velani, Livia, ed. *Manzu*. Edited by Livia Velani. [English translation Rosa Maria Letts, Ann Wisel]. Milan, Electa, 1987.

Mapplethorpe, Robert, 1946–1989
7668. Celant, Germano. *Mapplethorpe*. Milano, Electa, 1992.
7669. ———. *Mapplethorpe versus Rodin*. Milano, Electa, 1992.
7670. ———. *Robert Mapplethorpe: the perfect moment*. [Catalogue of an exhibition. Institute of Contemporary Art. University of Pennsylvania; with essays by David Joselit and Kay Larson, and [a] dedication by Patti Smith. Philadelphia, The Institute, 1988.
7671. Mapplethorpe, Robert. *Mapplethorpe*. Essay by Arthur C., Danto. New York, Random House, 1992.
7672. ———. *Robert Mapplethorpe: certain people, a book of portraits*. Pasadena, Calif., Twelvetrees Press, 1985.
7673. ———. *Robert Mapplethorpe, early works, 1970–1974*. [Exhibition] May 1991. Robert Miller, New York. [Edited and designed by John Chaim]. New York, Robert Miller, 1991.
7674. Marshall, Richard. *Robert Mapplethorpe*. With essays by Richard Howard, Ingrid Sischy. London, Secker & Warburg, 1986.

Marc, Franz, 1880–1916 *see also* Macke, August and Kandinsky, Wassily
7675. Bünemann, Hermann, ed. *Franz Marc: Zeichnungen, Aquarelle*. München, Bruckmann, 1952.
7676. Lankheit, Klaus. *Franz Marc im Urteil seiner Zeit*. Köln, DuMont Schauberg, 1960.
7677. ———. *Franz Marc, sein Leben und seine Kunst*. Köln, DuMont, 1976. (CR).
7678. ———. *Franz Marc: watercolors, drawings, writings*. Trans. by Norbert Guterman. New York, Abrams, 1960.
7679. Levine, Frederick S. *The apocalyptic vision: the art of Franz Marc as German expressionism*. New York, Harper & Row, 1979.
7680. Marc, Franz. *Der Blaue Reiter präsentiert Eurer Hoheit sein blaues Pferd. Karten und Briefe: Franz Marck—Else Lasker-Schüler*. [Catalogue of an exhibition] herausgegeben und kommentiert von Peter-Klaus Schuster. München, Prestel, 1987.
7681. ———. *Briefe aus dem Felde, 1914–1916*. Berlin, Rembrandt, 1959. 5 ed.
7682. ———. *Briefe, Aufzeichnungen und Aphorismen*. 2 v. Berlin, Cassirer, 1920.
7683. ———. *Schriften*. Herausgegeben von Klaus Lankheit. Köln, DuMont, 1978.
7684. März, Roland. *Franz Marc*. With eighteen plates in colour and fifty-four monochrome illustrations. Berlin, Henschelverlag, 1987.
7685. Pese, Claus. *Franz Marc, Leben und Werk*. Stuttgart, Belser, 1989.
7686. Rosenthal, Mark Lawrence. *Franz Marc*. München, Prestel; New York, distrib. in the USA and Canada by te Neues Publishing, 1989.
7687. Schardt, Alois J. *Franz Marc*. Berlin, Rembrandt, 1936.
7688. Schuster, Peter-Klaus. *Franz Marc: postcards to Prince Jussuf*. München, Prestel; New York, distrib. in the USA by te Neues Publishing, 1988.
7689. Städtische Galerie im Lenbachhaus (Munich). *Franz Marc, 1880–1916*. [Aug. 27–Oct. 26, 1980]. München, Prestel, 1980.
7690. University Art Museum, Berkeley. *Franz Marc; pioneer of spiritual abstraction*. Dec. 5, 1979–Feb. 3, 1980. [Text by Marc Rosenthal et al.]. Berkeley, Calif., University Art Museum, 1979.

Marcantonio *see* Raimondi, Marcantonio

Marcoussis *see* Markus, Louis

Marcks, Gerhard, 1889–1981
7691. Georg-Kolbe-Museum (Berlin). *Gerhard Marcks*. [April 11, 1979–June 1, 1980]. Berlin, Georg-Kolbe-Museum, 1979.
7692. Marcks, Gerhard. *Gerhard Marcks 1889–1981: Briefe und Werke*. Ausgewählt, bearbeitet und eingeleitet von Ursula Frenzel. Herausgeber: Archiv für Bildende Kunst im Germanischen Nationalmuseum Nürnberg. München, Prestel-Verlag, 1988.
7693. ———. *Gerhard Marcks, dem grossen Bildhauer zum Gedächtnis: Skulpturen, Ölkreiden, Zeichnungen, Graphiken*. Ausstellung, 16.2.–31.5.1983, Galerie Nierendorf, Berlin. Berlin Die Galerie, 1983.
7694. ———. *Gerhard Marcks, 1889–1981: Retrospektive*. Herausgegeben von Martina Rudloff im Auftrag der Gerhard Marcks-Stiftung Bremen. München, Hirmer, 1989.
7695. ———. *The letters of Gerhard Marcks and Marguerite Wildenhain, 1970–1981: a mingling of souls*. [Edited by] Ruth R. Kath in collaboration with Lawrence J. Thornton. Bibliography by Jane Kemp. Ames, Iowa. Iowa State University Press; Decorah, Iowa, Luther College Press, 1991.
7696. Rieth, Adolf. *Gerhard Marcks*. Recklinghausen, Bongers, 1959. (Monographien zur Rheinisch-Westfälischen Kunst der Gegenwart, 16).
7697. U.C.L.A. Art Gallery (Los Angeles). *Gerhard Marcks*. [Text by Werner Haftmann et al.]. Los Angeles, Regents of the University of California, 1969.

Marden, Brice, 1938–
7698. Kertesz, Klaus. *Brice Marden: paintings and*

drawings. Text by K. Kertesz. Project director, David Whitney. New York, H.N. Abrams, 1992.

7699. Lewison, Jeremy. *Brice Marden: prints 1961–1991: a catalogue raisonné*. London, Tate Gallery, 1992. (CR).

7700. Richardson, Brenda. *Brice Marden—Cold Mountain*. Houston, Tex., Houston Fine art Press, 1992.

Marees, Georges des, 1697–1776

7701. Heenmarck, Carl. *Georg Desmarées; Studien über die Rokoko-Malerei in Schweden und Deutschland*. Uppsala, Almquist & Wiksells, 1933.

Marees, Hans von, 1837–1887

7702. Degenhart, Bernhard. *Marées Zeichnungen*. Berlin, Mann, 1963. 2 ed.

7703. Domm, Anne-S. *Der "klassische" Hans von Marees und die Existenzmalerei Anfang des 20. Jahrhunderts*. München, Kommissionsverlag UNI-Druck, 1989 (Miscellanea Bavarica Monacensia, 146).

7704. Fiedler, Conrad. *Bilder und Zeichnungen von Hans von Marées, seinem Andenken gewidmet*. München, [Bruckmann], 1889. (New ed.: Frankfurt a.M., Heiderhoff, 1969).

7705. Gebäude der Secession (Berlin). *Ausstellung Hans von Marées. 28. Februar bis Anfang April 1909*. Berlin, Cassirer, [1909].

7706. Gerlach-Laxner, Uta. *Hans von Marées, Katalog seiner Gemälde*. München, Prestel, 1980. (CR).

7707. Kutter, Erich. *Hans von Marées; die Tragödie des deutschen Idealismus*. Dresden, Verlag der Kunst, 1958. 2 ed.

7708. Liebmann, Kurt. *Hans von Marées*. Dresden, Verlag der Kunst, 1972.

7709. Marées, Hans von. *Briefe*. München, Piper, 1920.

7710. ———. *Briefe*. Herausgegeben mit einem Nachwort versehen von Anne-S. Domm. München, Piper, 1987.

7711. ———. *Hans von Marées*. Herausgegeben von Christian Lenz, mit Beiträgen von Gottfried Boehm . . . [et al]. München, Prestel Verlag, 1987.

7712. ———. *Hans von Marées und die Moderne in Deutschland*. [Catalogue of an exhibition] bearbeitet von Erich Franz, mit Beiträgen von Anne S. Domm . . . [et al.]. Bielefeld. Kunsthalle Bielefeld, 1987.

7713. Meier-Graefe, Julius. *Hans von Marées, sein Leben und sein Werk*. 3 v. München/Leipzig, Piper, 1910.

7714. ———. *Der Zeichner Hans von Marées*. München, Piper, 1925.

Marees, Horst de, 1896–1988

7715. Marées, Horst de. *Horst de Marées, 1896–1988: Malerei und Zeichnungen*. [Catalogue of an exhibition] Höxter, Museum Höxter-Corvey, 1992.

Marin, John, 1870–1953

7716. Balken, Debra Bricker. *John Marin's Berkshire landscapes*. [Exhibition] June 9 through August 4, 1985. The Berkshire Museum. Pittsfield, Mass. Pittsfield, The Museum, 1985.

7717. Benson, Emanuel M. *John Marin, the man and his work*. Washington, D.C., American Federation of Arts, 1935.

7718. Fine, Ruth E. *John Marin*. Washington, National Gallery of Art; New York, Abbeville Press, 1990.

7719. Gray, Cleve, ed. *John Marin by John Marin*. New York, Holt, Rinehart & Winston, [1970].

7720. Helm, Mackinley. *John Marin*. New York, Pellegrini & Cuhady/Boston, Institute of Contemporary Art, 1948. (Reprint: New York, Kennedy Graphics/Da Capo, 1970).

7721. Institute of Contemporary Art (Boston). *John Marin, a restrospective exhibition, 1947*. The Institute of Modern Art, Boston. the Phillips Memorial Gallery, Washington, the Walker Art Center, Minneapolis. Boston, Institute of Contemporary art, 1947.

7722. Marin John. *John Marin and the sea*. [Exhibition] October 19–November 1982. Kennedy Galleries, New York. New York, The Galleries, 1982.

7723. ———. *John Marin's autumn*. [Exhibition] October 8–29, 1988 at Kennedy Galleries, New York. New York, Kennedy Galleries, Inc., 1988.

7724. ———. *John Marin's mountains*. [Exhibition] October 4–29, 1983. Kennedy Galleries, New York. New York, The Galleries, 1983.

7725. Marin, John. *Letters*. Edited, with an introduction by Herbert J. Seligmann. New York, [An American Place], 1931.

7726. ———. *The selected writings of John Marin*. Edited, with an introduction by Dorothy Norman. New York, Pellegrini & Cuhady, 1949.

7727. Museum of Modern Art (New York). *John Marin; watercolors, oil paintings, etchings*. New York, Museum of Modern Art, 1936.

7728. Philadelphia Museum of Art. *John Marin: etchings and related works*. 2 v. January 17–March 17, 1969. [Vol. I: *The complete etchings of John Marin; a catalogue raisonné* by Carl Zigrosser; Vol. II: *Oils, watercolors, and drawings which relate to his etchings* by

Sheldon Reich]. Philadelphia, Philadelphia Museum of Art, 1969. (CR).

7729. Reich, Sheldon. *John Marin, a stylistic analysis and catalogue raisonné.* 2 v. Tucson, Ariz., University of Arizona Press, 1970. (CR).

Marini, Marino, 1901–1980

7730. De Micheli, Mario. *Marino pittore.* A cura di Mario De Micheli, Carlo Pirovano. Milano, Electa, 1988.

7731. Drot, Jean-Marie. *Marino Marini: antologica, 1919–1978.* Testi di Jean-Marie Drot, Maurizio Calvesi, Erich Steingräber. Roma, Edizioni carte segrete, 1991.

7732. Guastalla, Giorgio. *Marino Marini: catalogo ragionato dell'opera grafica (incisioni e litografie), 1919–1980.* [By] Giorgio e Guido Guastalla, Saggio critico Mario De Micheli. Livorno, Graphis arte, 1990.(CR).

7733. Hunter, Sam. *Marino Marini: the sculpture.* Text by Sam Hunter; photographs by David Finn; introduction by Marina Marini. New York, Abrams, 1993.

7734. Marini, Marina. *Con Marino.* Milano, Bompiani, 1991.

7735. Marini, Marino. *Marino Marini, pittore.* Prefazione di Erich Steingräber; testo di Lorenzo Papi. [Traduzione inglese di John Iliffel]. Torino, Priuli & Verlucca, 1987.

7736. ———. *Marino Marini: sculture, pitture, disegni dal 1914 al 1977.* Catalogo a cura di Mario De Micheli. Firenze, Sansoni Editore, 1983

7737. ———. *Marino Marini.*[Catalogue of an exhibition]. Museo San Pancrazio, Firenze. Contributi di Gianfranco Contini . . . [et al.]. A cura di Carlo Pirovano. Milano, Electa, 1988.

7738. ———. *Marino Marini.* Milano, Electa, 1989.

7739. Read, Herbert, Waldberg, Patrick and G. Di SanLazzaro. *Marini Marini; complete works.* New York, Tudor Publishing Co., 1970. (CR).

7740. Schulz-Hoffmann, Carla, ed. *Marino Marini: Druckgraphik.* Werkkatalog. München, Bruckmann, 1976. (CR).

7741. Steingräber, Erich. *Marino Marini: Malerei/Peinture.* Bad Homburg, Scheffel, 1987. (CR).

Maris, Jacob, 1837–1899
Matthijs, 1835–1917
Willem, 1844–1910

7742. Arondéus, Willem. *Matthijs Maris, de tragick van den droom.* Amsterdam, Querido, 1939.

7743. Bock, Theophile E. A. *Jacob Maris.* Amsterdam, Scheltema & Holkema, 1902–3. (English ed.: London, Moring, 1904).

7744. Boer, H. de. *Willem Maris.* Haag, Zürcher, [n.d.].

7745. Fridlander, Ernest D. *Matthew Maris.* London/Boston, Warner, 1921.

7746. Gemeentemuseum (The Hague). *Maris tentoonstelling.* 22 December 1935 tot 2 Februari 1936. [Haag], Gemeentemuseum, [1935].

7747. Thomson, D. Croal. *The brothers Maris (James—Matthew—William).* Edited by Charles Holme. London/Paris, The Studio, 1907.

Marne, Jean-Louis de *see* Demarne, Jean-Louis

Marsh, Reginald, 1898–1954

7748. Laning, Edward. *The sketchbooks of Reginald Marsh.* [Compiled by] Edward Laning. Greenwich, Conn., New York Graphic Society, 1973.

7749. Marsh, Reginald. *Reginald Marsh.* Reginald Marsh, 1898–1954, paintings and works on paper: the Greenberg Gallery, St. Louis, Mo., January 18–March 1, 1986, Hirschl & Adler Galleries, New York, March 13–April 19, 1986. New York, Hirschl & Adler Galleries, 1985.

7750. Sasowsky, Norman. *The prints of Reginald Marsh.* New York, Clarkson N. Potter, 1976. (CR).

Marsy, Balthazard, 1629–1674
Gaspard, 1624–1681

7751. Hedin, Thomas. *The sculpture of Gaspard and Balthazard Marsy: art and patronage in the early reign of Louis XIV.* With a catalogue raisonné. New York, Harper and Row, 1984. (CR).

Martin, Agnes, 1912–

7752. Haskell, Barbara, ed. *Agnes Martin.* With essays by B. Haskell, Anna Chave and Rosalind Krauss. New York, Whitney Museum of American Art; distrib. by Harry N. Abrams, 1992.

7753. Martin, Agnes. *Agnes Martin: paintings and drawings, 1974–1990.* [Catalogue of an exhibition]. Paris, Musée d'Art Moderne de la Ville de Paris, 1991.

7754. ———. *Writings = Schriften.* edited by Dieter Schwarz. Winterthur, Switzerland. Kunstmuseum Winterthur; Stuttgart, Edition Cantz, 1991.

Martin, Homer Dodge, 1836–1897

7755. Martin, Elizabeth G. *Homer Martin, a reminiscence.* New York, Macbeth, 1904.

7756. Mather, Frank J., Jr. *Homer Martin, poet in landscape.* New York, [Frederick F. Sherman], 1912.

Martin, John, 1789–1854

7757. Balston, Thomas. *John Martin, 1789–1854; his life and works.* London, Duckworth, 1947.

7758. Feaver, William. *The art of John Martin.* Oxford, Clarendon Press, 1975.

7759. Johnstone, Christopher. *John Martin.* London, Academy/New York, St. Martin's, 1974.

7760. Pendered, Mary L. *John Martin, painter; his life and times.* London, Hurst & Blackett, 1923.

7761. Wees, J. Dustin. *Darkness visible: the prints of John Martin.* [By] J.D. Weess with contributions by Michael J. Campbell. Williamstown, Mass., Sterling and Francine Clark Art Institute, 1986.

Martin, Paul, 1864–1944

7762. Flukinger, Roy, et al. *Paul Martin: Victorian photographer.* Austin, University of Texas Press, 1977.

7763. Jay, Bill. *Victorian candid camera: Paul Martin, 1864–1944.* Introd. by Cecil Beaton. Newton Abbot, David & Charles, 1973.

7764. Martin, Paul. *Victorian snapshots.* With an introduction by Charles Harvard. London, Country Life/New York, Scribner, 1939. (Reprint: New York, Arno, 1973).

Martinez Montañes, Juan, 1568–1648

7765. Camon, Aznar José . . . [et al.]. *Martinez Montañes (1568–1649) y la escultura andaluza de su tiempo.* Madrid, Direccion General de Bellas Artes, Comisaria de Exposiciones, 1972.

7766. Gomez-Moreno, Maria Elena. *Juan Martinez Montanes.* Prologo de Elias Tormo. Barcelona, Ediciones Selectas, 1942. (Los grandes Maestros de la scultura, 2).

7767. Hernandez Diaz, Jose. *Juan Martinez Montañes: el Lisipo Andaluz, 1568–1649.* Sevilla, Diputacion Sevilla, 1992. 2 e. (Arte hispalense, 10).

7768. Proske, Beatrice Irene (Gilman). *Juan Martinez Montañes, Sevillian sculptor.* New York, Hispanic Society of America, 1967.

Martini, Simone, 1285–1344

7769. Bologna, Ferdinando. *Simone Martini.* Milano, Fabbri, 1966. (I maestri del colore, 119).

7770. Contini, Gianfranco [and] Gozzoli, Maria C. *L'opera completa di Simone Martini.* Milano, Rizzoli, 1970. (CR). (Classici dell'arte, 43).

7771. Gosche, Agnes. *Simone Martini, ein Beitrag zur Geschichte der sienesischen Malerei im XIV. Jahrhundert.* Leipzig, Seemann, 1899. (Beiträge zur Kunstgeschichte, Neue Folge, 26).

7772. Jannella, Cecilia. *Simone Martini.* Trans. Lisa Pelletti. New York, Riverside Books, 1989.

7773. Leone De Castris, Pierluigi. *Simone Martini: catalogo completo dei dipinti.* Firenze, Cantini, 1989. (CR).

7774. Mariani, Valerio. *Simone Martini e il suo tempo.* Napoli, Libreria Scientifica, 1968.

7775. Marle, Raimond van. *Simone Martini et les peintres de son école.* Strasbourg, Heitz, 1920.

7776. Martindale, Andrew. *Simone Martini.* Complete edition. Oxford, Phaidon; New York, New York University Press, 1988.(CR).

7777. Martini, Simone. *Simone Martini: atti del onvegno, Siena 27. 28. 29. marzo 1985.* Firenze, Centro Di, 1988.

7778. Paccagnini, Giovanni. *Simone Martini.* Milano, Martello, 1955.

7779. Rinaldis, Aldo de. *Simone Martini.* Roma, Palombi, [1936].

Martins, Nabur *see* Master of Flemalle

Masaccio, 1401–1428

7780. Baldini, Umberto. *Masaccio.* Firenze, Edizioni d'Arte Il Fiorino, 1990.

7781. Berti, Luciano. *Masaccio.* University Park, Penn., Penn. State University Press, 1967.

7782. ———. *Masaccio: catalogo completo dei dipinti.* [By] U. Berti, Rossella Foggi.Firenze, Cantini, 1989.(CR).

7783. Cole, Bruce. *Masaccio and the art of early Renaissance Florence.* Bloomington, Ind., Indiana University Press, 1980.

7784. Creutz, Max. *Masaccio; ein Versuch zur stilistischen und chronologischen Einordnung seiner Werke.* Berlin, Ebering, 1901.

7785. Hendy, Philip. *Masaccio; frescoes in Florence.* [Greenwich, Conn.], New York Graphic Society/Paris, UNESCO, 1956.

7786. Hertlein, Edgar. *Masaccios Trinität: Kunst, Geschichte und Politik der Frührenaissance in Florenz.* Firenze, Olschki, 1979. (Pocket Library of Studies in Art, 24).

7787. Joannides, Paul. *Masaccio and Masolino: a complete catalogue.* London, Phaidon; New York; distrib. in North America by H.N. Abrams, 1993. (CR).

7788. Knudtzon, Fried G. *Masaccio og den florentiniske Malerkunst.* København, Lund, 1875.

7789. Lindberg, Henrik. *To the problem of Masolino and Masaccio.* 2 v. Stockholm, Norstedt, 1931.

7790. Magherini-Graziani, Giovanni, ed. *Masaccio: ricordo delle rese in San Giovanni di Valdarno nel di XXV ottobre MCMIII in occasione del V centenario della sua nascita.* Firenze, Seeber, 1904.

7791. Masaccio. *L'Eta di Masaccio: il primo Quattrocento a Firenze.* [Catalogue of an exhibition]. A cura di Luciano Berti e Antonio Paolucci. Milano, Electa, 1990.

7792. Mesnil, Jacques. *Masaccio et les débuts de la renaissance.* La Haye, Nijhoff, 1927.

7793. Missirini, Melchior. *Masaccio, orazione.* Firenze, Piatti, 1846.

7794. Pittaluga, Mary. *Masaccio.* Firenze, LeMonnier, 1935.

7795. Procacci, Ugo. *All the paintings of Masaccio.* Trans. by Paul Colacicchi. New York, Hawthorn, 1962. (Complete Library of World Art, 6).

7796. Schmarsow, August. *Masaccio Studien.* [Issued in 3 v.] Kassel, Fisher, 1895–1899.

7797. ———. *Masolino und Masaccio.* Leipzig, [Schmarsow], 1928.

7798. Salmi, Mario. *La Cappella Brancacci a Firenze.* 2 v. [Vol. I: *Masaccio*; Vol. II: *Masaccio-Masolino-Filippino Lippi*]. Milano, Pizzi, [1948]. (Collezione Silvana, 8/10).

7799. ———. *Masaccio.* Roma, Valori Plastici, [1932].

7800. Somaré, Enrico. *Masaccio.* Milano, Bottega di Poesia, [1924].

7801. Steinbart, Kurt. *Masaccio.* Wien, Schroll, 1948.

7802. Volponi, Paolo [and] Berti, Luciano. *L'opera completa di Masaccio.* Milano, Rizzoli, 1968. (CR). (Classici dell'arte, 24).

7803. Wasserman, Gertrud. *Masaccio und Masolino; Probleme einer Zeitenwende und ihre schöpferische Gestaltung.* Strassburg, Heitz, 1935. (Zur Kunstgeschichte des Auslandes, 134).

Masereel, Frans, 1889–1972

7804. Avermaete, Roger. *Frans Masereel.* Bibliography and catalogue by Pierre Vorms and Hanns-Conon von der Gabelentz. New York, Rizzoli, 1977. (CR).

7805. Claussnitzer, Gert. *Frans Masereel.* Berlin, Henschelverlag Kunst und Gesellschaft, 1990.

7806. Durtain, Luc. *Frans Masereel.* Paris, Vorms, 1931.

7807. Hagelstange, Rudolf. *Gesang des Lebens; das Werk Frans Masereels.* Hannover, Fackelträger, 1957.

7808. Havelaar, Just. *Het werk van Frans Masereel.* Haag, De Baanbreker, 1930.

7809. Holitscher, Arthur [and] Zweig, Stefan. *Frans Masereel.* Berlin, Juncker, 1923. (Graphiker Unserer Zeit, 1).

7810. Masereel, Frans. *Frans Masereel.* Mit Beiträgen von Stefan Zweig, Pierre Vorms, Gerhard Pommeranz-Liedke; und einer Bibliographie von Hanns-Conon von der Gabelentz, 1959.

7811. ———. *Landscapes and voices.* New York, Schocken Books, 1988.

7812. ———. *Frans Masereel;* [tentoonstelling] Museum von Schone Kunsten, Gent, 26–6/ 14–9–1986. Ghent, Gemeentekrediet, 1986.

7813. ———. *Frans Masereel (1889–1972): Zur Verwirklichung des Traums von einer Freien Gesellschaft.* [Katalog einer Ausstellung, Saarlandmuseum Saarbrücken, 1989]. Saarbrücken, Saarbrücker Zeitung, 1989.

7814. ———. *Tribute Frans Masereel: an exhibition of paintings, watercolours and graphics.* September 13–October 25, 1981. Art Gallery of Windsor. Windsor, Ont., The Gallery, 1981.

7815. Pommeranz-Liedtke, Gerhard. *Der Maler Frans Masereel.* Dresden, Verlag der Kunst, 1961. 2 ed.

7816. Ritter, Paul. *Frans Masereel: eine annotierte Bibliographie.* München, K.G. Saur, 1992.

7817. Vorms, Pierre. *Gespräche mit Frans Masereel.* Dresden, Verlag der Kunst, 1967.

7818. Ziller, Gerhart. *Frans Masereel, Einführung und Auswahl.* Dresden, Sachsenverlag, 1949.

7819. Zweig, Stefan, et al. *Frans Masereel, mit Beiträgen von Stefan Zweig et al.* Dresden, Verlag der Kunst, 1961. 2 ed.

Masolino da Panicale, 1383–1440 *see also* **Masaccio**

7820. Martini, Alberto. *Masolino a Castiglione Olona.* Milano, Fabbri/Ginevra, Skira, 1965. (L'arte racconta, 3).

7821. Micheletti, Emma. *Masolino da Panicale.* Milano, Istituto Editoriale Italiano, 1959. (Arte e pensiero, 3).

7822. Toesca, Pietro. *Masolino da Panicale.* Bergamo, Istituto Italiano d'Arti Grafiche, 1908. (Collezione di monografie illustrate; pittore, scultori, architetti, 4).

Masson, André, 1896–

7823. Barrault, Jean-Louis, et al. *André Masson.* Rouen, Wolf, 1940.

7824. Clébert, Jean-Paul. *Mythologie d'André Masson.* Genève, Cailler, 1971. (Les grandes monographies, 14).

7825. Hahn, Otto. *Masson.* London, Thames & Hudson, 1965.

7826. Juin, Hubert. *André Masson.* Paris, Fall, 1963.

7827. Leiris, Michel et Limbour, Georges. *André Masson et son univers.* Genève/Paris, Editions des Trois Collines, 1947.

7828. Levaillant, Françoise. *André Masson.* Milano, Mazotta, 1988.

7829. Masson, André. *Les années surréalistes: correspondence 1916–1942.* Edition établie, présentée et annotée par Françoise Levaillant. Paris, La Manufacture, 1990.

7830. ———. *André Masson: the complete graphic work.* Catalogue, Lawrencce Saphire; preface, Stanley William Hayter. v. 1– . New York, Blue Moon Press, 1990– . (CR).

7831. ———. *André Masson, Nîmes été 85: 4.7.– 15.10.1985.* Musée des Beaux Arts. Nîmes, Association "Carré d'art", 1985.

7832. ———. *Masson.* Textes de Jean-Marie Drot . . . [et al.]. Roma, Carte segrete, 1989.

7833. ———. *Métamorphose de l'artiste.* 2 v. Genève, Cailler, 1956.

7834. ———. *Le rebelle du surréalisme; écrits.* Edition établie par Françoise Will-Levaillant. Paris, Hermann, 1976.

7835. Matthes, Axel [and] Klewan, Helmut, [eds.]. *Masson: Gesammelte Schriften.* v.1– . München, 1990– .

7836. Museum of Modern Art (New York). *André Masson.* [Text and catalogue by William Rubin and Carolyn Lancher]. New York, Museum of Modern Art, 1976.

7837. Noël, Bernard. *André Masson: la chair du regard.* Paris, Gallimard, 1993.

7838. Passeron, Roger. *André Masson et les puissances du signe.* [Paris], Denoël, 1975.

7839. ———. *André Masson: gravures, 1924– 1972.* Fribourg, Weber, 1973.

7840. Pia, Pascal. *André Masson.* Paris, Gallimard, 1930.

Massys, Quentin, 1466–1530

7841. Boon, Karel G. *Quinten Massys.* Amsterdam, Becht, [1948]. (Palet serie, 22).

7842. Bosque, Andrée de. *Quentin Metsys.* Bruxelles, Arcade, 1975. (CR).

7843. Bosschère, Jean de. *Quinten Metsys.* Bruxelles, van Oest, 1907.

7844. Brising, Harald. *Quinten Metsys und der Ursprung des Italianismus in der Kunst der Niederlande.* 2 v. Leipzig, Schumann, 1908. 2 ed.

7845. Cohen, Walter. *Studien zu Quinten Metsys.* München, Bruckmann, 1904.

7846. Friedländer, Max J. *Quentin Massys.* Comments and notes by H. Paulwels. Trans. by Heinz Norden. Leyden, Sijthoff/Brussels, La Connaissance, 1971. (Early Netherlandish Painting, 7).

7847. Génard, Pierre. *Nasporingen over de geboorteplatts en de familie van Quinten Massys.* Antwerpen, Fontaine, 1870.

7848. Roosen-Runge, Heinz. *Die Gestaltung der Farbe bei Quentin Metsys.* München, Filser, 1940. (Münchener Beiträge zur Kunstgeschichte, 6).

Master . . . [Here are grouped all monographs on those anonymous artists called *Master, Meister* or *Maestro*]

[Collective biography]

7849. Lehrs, Max. *Geschichte und kritischer Kat-*alog des deutschen, niederländischen und französischen Kupferstichs im XV. Jahrhundert. 9 v. Wien, Gesellschaft für Vervielfältigende Kunst, 1908–1934.

Master of the Amsterdam Cabinet, 15th c.

7850. Bierens de Haan, Johan Catharinus Justus. *De meester van het Amsterdamse kabinet.* Amsterdam, Balkema, 1947.

7851. Hutchison, Jane C. *The master of the housebook.* New York, Collectors Editions, 1972.

7852. Lanckorońska, Maria. *Das mittelalterliche Hausbuch der fürstlich waldburgschen Sammlung; Auftraggeber, Entstehungsgrund und Zeichner.* Darmstadt, Roether, 1975.

7853. *The Master of the Amsterdam Cabinet, or, The Housebook Master, ca. 1470–1500.* Compiled by J.P. Filedt Kok. Introductions and appendixes by K.G. Boon . . . [et al.]. Translations from the Dutch and German by Arno Pomerans, Gary Schwartz, and Patricia Wardle. Amsterdam, Rijksmuseum in association with the Rijksprentenkabinet. Princeton, N.J., Princeton University Press, 1985. (Exhibition catalogue).

7854. Naumann, Hans. *Die Holzschnitte des Meisters vom Amsterdamer Kabinett zum Spiegel Menschlicher Behaltnis.* Strassburg, Heitz, 1910. (Studien zur deutschen Kunstgeschichte, 126).

7855. Stange, Alfred. *Der Hausbuchmeister; Gesamtdarstellung und Katalog seiner Gemälde, Kupferstiche und Zeichnungen.* Strasbourg/Baden-Baden, Heitz, 1958. (Studien zur deutschen Kunstgeschichte, 316).

Master Bertram of Minden, 1345?–1415

7856. Dorner, Alexander. *Meister Bertram von Minden.* Berlin, Rembrandt, 1937. (Kunstbücher des Volkes, 17).

7857. Lichtwark, Alfred. *Meister Bertram, tätig in Hamburg, 1367–1415.* Hamburg, Lütcke & Wulff, 1905.

7858. Portmann, Paul. *Meister Bertram.* Zürich, Rabe, 1963.

Master of the Boucicaut Hours, 15th c.

7859. Champeaux, Alfred de [and] Gauchery, Paul. *Les travaux d'art exécutés pour Jean de France, duc de Berry, avec une etude biographique sur les artistes employés par ce prince.* Paris, Champion, 1894.

7860. Meiss, Millard. *French painting in the time of Jean de Berry: the Boucicaut Master.* With the assistance of Kathleen Morand and Edith W. Kirsch. London, Phaidon, 1968.

Master DS, fl. 1503–1515

7861. Bock, Elfried. *Holzschnitte des Meisters DS.*

Berlin, Deutscher Verein für Kunstwissenschaft, 1924.

Master of 1515

7862. Kristeller, Paul. *Der Meister von 1515; Nachbildungen seiner Kupferstiche.* Berlin, Cassirer, 1916. (Graphische Gesellschaft, 22).

Master of Flemalle *see also* Weyden, Roger van der

7863. Beyaert-Carlier, Louis. *Le problème van der Weyden, Flémalle, Campin.* Bruxelles, Notre Temps, 1937.

7864. Frinta, Mojmír S. *The genius of Robert Campin.* The Hague, Mouton, 1966. (Studies in Art, 1).

7865. Hasse, Carl. *Roger van Brügge, der Meister von Flémalle.* Strassburg, Heitz, 1904. (Zur Kunstgeschichte des Auslandes, 21).

7866. Maeterlinck, Louis. *Nabur Martins ou Le Maître de Flémalle.* Bruxelles/Paris, van Oest, 1913.

7867. Renders, Emile. *La solution du problème van der Weyden, Flémalle, Campin.* 2 v. Bruges, Beyaert, 1931.

7868. Winkler, Friedrich. *Der Meister von Flémalle und Rogier van der Weyden.* Strassburg, Heitz, 1913.

Master Francke, 15th c.

7869. Lichtwark, Alfred. *Meister Francke, 1424.* Hamburg, Kunsthalle zu Hamburg, 1899.

7870. Martens, Bella. *Meister Francke.* 2 v. Hamburg, Friederichsen, de Gruyter, 1929.

Master of the Gardens of Love, 15th c.

7871. Lehrs, Max. *Der Meister der Liebesgärten; ein Beitrag zur Geschichte des ältesten Kupferstichs in den Niederlanden.* Leipzig, Hiersemann, 1893.

7872. Schüler, Irmgard. *Der Meister der Liebesgärten; ein Beitrag zur frühholländischen Malerei.* Amsterdam, van Munster, 1932.

Master of Moulins, fl. 1480–1503

7873. Huillet d'Istria, Madeleine. *Le Maître de Moulins.* Paris, Presses Universitaires du France, 1961. (Le peinture française de la fin du Moyen Age, 1).

Master of Naumburg, 13th c.

7874. Beenken, Hermann. *Der Meister von Naumburg.* Berlin, Rembrandt, 1939.

7875. Hinz, Paulus. *Der Naumburger Meister.* Berlin, Evangelische-Anstalt, 1954.

Master of Petrarch

7876. Musper, Theodor. *Die Holzschnitte des Pe-*

trakameisters; ein kritisches Verzeichnis mit Einleitung. München, Verlag der Münchner Drucke, 1927.

Master of the Playing Cards, Fl. 1445

7877. Geisberg, Max. *Das Älteste Gestochene deutsche Kartenspiel vom Meister der Spielkarten.* Strassburg, Heitz, 1905. (Studien zur deutschen Kunstgeschichte, 66).

7878. Lehmann-Haupt, Hellmut. *Gutenberg and the Master of the Playing Cards.* New Haven/London, Yale University Press, 1966.

Master of San Miniato

7879. Maestro di San Miniato. *Il 'Maestro di San Miniato': Lo stato degli studi, i problemi, le riposte della filologia.* Presentazione di Federico Zeri; a cura di Gigetta Dalli Regoli, con la collaborazione di Serenella Castri, Gemma Landolfi, Paola Richetti. Pisa, Giardini, 1988.

Master of the Vyssí Brod Cycle, fl. 1350

7880. Friedl, Antonín. *Pasionál Mistrů Vyśebrodských.* Praha, Borový, 1934.

Master of the Wilton Diptych, 14th c.

7881. Bodkin, Thomas. *The Wilton diptych in the National Gallery, London.* London, Humphries, [1947]. (The Gallery books, 16).

7882. Scharf, George. *Description of the Wilton House diptych, containing a contemporary portrait of King Richard the Second.* [London], Arundel Society, 1882.

Meister des Blutenburger Apostelzyklus, 15th c.

7883. Otto, Kornelius. *Erasmus Grasser und der Meister des Blutenburger Apostelzyklus: Studien zur Münchner Plastik des späten 15, Jahrhunderts.* München, Kommissionsverlag UNI-Druck, 1988. (Neue Schriftenreihe des Stadtarchivs München, Miscellanea Bavarica Monacensia, 150).

Meister des Buxheimer Hochaltars, 17th c.

7884. Fischer, Fritz. *Der Meister des Buxheimer Hochaltars: ein Beitrag zur süddeutschen Skulptur der ersten Hälfte des 17. Jahrhunderts.* Berlin, Deutscher Verein für Kunstwissenschaft, 1988.

Meister des Marienlebens, fl. 1463–1480

7885. Schmidt, Hans M. *Der Meister des Marienlebens und sein Kreis; studien zur spätgotischen Malerei in Köln.* Düsseldorf, Schwann, 1978. (Beiträge zu den Bau- und Kunstdenkmälern im Rheinland, 22).

M

Meister des Wolfgang-Missale von Rein, 15th c.

7886. Sieveking, Hinrich. *Der Meister des Wolfgang-Missale von Rein. Zur österreichischen Buchmalerei zwischen Spätgotik und Renaissance.* München, Prestel, 1986.

Meister E. S., 15th c.

7887. Albert, Peter P. *Der Meister E. S.; sein Name, seine Heimat und sein Ende: Funde und Vermutungen.* Strassburg, Heitz, 1911. (Studien zur deutschen Kunstgeschichte, 137).

7888. Geisberg, Max. *Die Anfänge des deutschen Kupferstiches & der Meister E. S.* Leipzig, Klinkhardt & Biermann, 1910. (Meister der Graphik, 2).

7889. ———. *Die Kupferstiche der Meisters E. S.* Berlin, Cassirer, 1924.

7890. Hessig, Edith. *Die Kunst des Meisters E. S. und die Plastik der Spätgotik.* Berlin, Deutscher Verein für Kunstwissenschaft, 1935. (Forschungen zur deutschen Kunstgeschichte, 1).

Mastroianni, Umberto, 1910–

7891. Argan, Giulio C. *Umberto Mastroianni.* Venezia, Edizioni del Cavallino, 1958.

7892. De Santi, Floriano. *Umberto Mastroianni: bassorilievi, 1975–1983.* Bologna, Bora, 1984.

7893. Galleria Nazionale d'Arte Moderna (Rome). *Umberto Mastroianni.* 12 giugno–20 settembre 1974; presentazioni di Palma Bucarelli. Roma, de Luca, 1974.

7894. Mastroianni, Umberto. *Il grido e l'eco: scritti autobiografici.* Presentazione di Rafaella del Puglia. Bologna, Bora, 1986. 2 ed.

7895. Ponente, Nello. *Mastroianni.* Rome, Modern Art Editions, 1963. (Album of Contemporary Art, 2).

Mataré, Ewald, 1887–1965

7896. Flemming, Hanns F. *Ewald Mataré.* München, Prestel, 1955.

7897. Kestner-Gesellschaft Hannover. *Mataré und seine Schüler: Beuys, Haese, Heerich, Meistermann.* 2. März bis 15. April 1979. Hannover, Kestner-Gesellschaft, 1979. (Kestner-Gesellschaft Katalog 1/1979).

7898. Mataré, Ewald. *Ewald Mataré Retrospektive: das plastische Werk, 4. März bis 3. Mai 1987.* Eine Ausstellung des Erzbistums Köln und der Künstlerunion Köln in Kölnischen Kunstverein. Mit Beiträgen von Hans und Franz Josef van der Grinten . . . [et al.]. Ausstellungskonzeption und -organisation, Karl Josef Bollenbeck, Fiedhelm Hofmann und Sabine Maia Schilling. Köln, Wienand, 1987

7899. ———. *Tagebücher.* Ausgewählt und Herausgegeben von Hanna Mataré und Franz Müller. Köln, Hegner, 1973.

7900. Mataré, Sonia. *Ewald Mataré: Holzschnitte. Werkverzeichnis.* Von S. Mataré in Zusammenarbeit mit Guido de Werd. Kleve, Boss-Verlag, 1990. (CR).

7901. ———. *Ewald Mataré: Zeichnungen; Werkverzeichnis.* Von S. Mataré in Zusammenarbeit mit Guido de Werd. [Herausgeber, Städtisches Museum Haus Koekkoek Kleve und 'Freunde des Städtischen Museums Haus Koekkoek Kleve e.V.']. Kleve, Boss-Verlag, 1992.(CR).

7902. Peters, Heinz. *Ewald Mataré, das graphische Werk.* 2 v. Köln, Czwiklitzer, 1957. (CR).

7903. Schilling, Sabine Maja. *Ewald Mataré: das plastische Werk.* Werkverzeichnis. Köln, Wienand, 1987.(CR).

Matejko, Jan, 1838–1893 *see also* Grottger, Artur

7904. Bogucki, Janusz. *Matejko.* Warszawa, Wiedna Powszechna, 1955.

7905. Gintel, Jan. *Jan Matejko, biografia w wypisach.* Kraków, Literackie, 1966. 2 ed.

7906. Kunsthalle Nürnberg. *Jan Matejko, 1838–1893: Gemälde, Aquarelle, Zeichnungen.* [March 26–April 25, 1982]. Nürnburg, Kunsthalle Nürnberg, 1982.

7907. Matejko, Jan. *Ubiory w Polsce, 1200–1795.* Kraków, [n.p.], 1860. (New ed.: Kraków, Literackie, 1967).

7908. Ostrovs'kyi, Hryhorii S. *Ian Matejko; monograficheskii ocherk.* Moskva, Iskusstvo, 1965.

7909. Panstwowy Instytut Sztuki (Warsaw). *Jan Matejko; materialy z sesji naukowej póswięconej twórczości artysty.* [Nov. 23–27, 1953]. Warszawa, Arkady, 1957.

7910. Serafínska, Stanislawa, ed. *Jan Matejko: wspomnienia rodzinne.* Kraków, Literackie, 1955.

7911. Starzyński, Juliusz. *Jan Matejko.* Warszawa, Arkady, 1979. 2 ed.

7912. Tarnowski, Stanislaw. *Matejko.* Kraków, Spólki wydawnictwo, 1897.

7913. Treter, Mieczyslaw. *Matejko; osobowość artysty, twórczość, forma i styl.* Lwów/Warszawa, Książnisa-Atlas, 1939.

7914. Witkiewicz, Stanislaw. *Matejko.* Lwów, Gubrynowicza, 1912. (Nauka i sztuka, 9).

Matisse, Henri, 1869–1954

7915. Alpatov, Mikhail V. *Henri Matisse.* [Translated from the Russian]. Dresden, Verlag der Kunst, 1973.

7916. Aragon, [Louis]. *Henri Matisse, roman.* 2 v. Paris, Gallimard, 1971.

7917. Baltimore Museum of Art. *Matisse as a draughtsman.* 12 January–21 February

1971. Introduction and commentary by Victor I. Carlson. Baltimore, Md., Baltimore Museum of Art, 1971; distributed by New York Graphic Society, Greenwich, Conn.

7918. Barnes, Albert C. and de Mazia, Violette. *The art of Henri Matisse.* New York/London, Scribner, 1933.

7919. Barr, Alfred H., Jr. *Matisse, his art and his public.* New York, Museum of Modern Art, 1951. (Reprint: New York, Arno, 1966).

7920. Basler, Adolphe. *Henri Matisse.* Leipzig, Klinkhardt & Biermann, 1924. (Junge Kunst, 46).

7921. Benjamin, Roger. *Henri Matisse.* New York, Rizzoli, 1992.

7922. Bernier, Rosamond. *Matisse, Picasaso, Miro; as I knew them.* Foreword by John Russell. New York, Alfred A. Knopf; distrib. by Random House,1991.

7923. Bock, Catherine C. *Henri Matisse and neo-impressionism, 1898–1908.* Ann Arbor, Mich., University Microfilms, 1981. (Studies in the Fine Arts; the Avant-garde, 13).

7924. Bonnard, Pierre. *Bonnard—Matisse: correspondence, 1926–1946.* Préface de Jean Clair; introduction et notes d'Antoine Terrasse. Paris, Gallimard, 1991.

7925. Buchholz, Cornelia. *Henri Matisse's "papiers découpées": zur Analyse eines Mediums.* Frankfurt am Main/ New York, P. Lang, 1985. (Europäische Hochschulschriften. Reihe XXVIII. Kunstrgeschichte, 44).

7926. Courthion, Pierre. *Henri Matisse.* Paris, Rieder, 1934.

7927. Cowart, Jack. *Henri Matisse: the early years in Nice, 1916–1930.* [By] J. Cowart, Dominique Fourcade. Washington, National Gallery of Art; New York, H.N. Abrams, 1986.

7928. ———. *Le visage de Matisse.* Lausanne, Marguerat, 1942.

7929. Daftari, Fereshteh. *The influence of Persian art on Gauguin, Matisse, and Kandinsky.* New York, Garland Publishing, 1991.

7930. Delectotskaya, Lydia. *With apparent ease — Henri Matisse; paintings from 1935–1939.* Trans. from the French by Olga Tourkoff. Paris, A. Maeght, 1988.

7931. Diehl, Gaston. *Henri Matisse.* Paris, Nouvelles Editions Françaises, 1970.

7932. Durozoi, Gérard. *Matisse.* Paris, Hazan, 1989.

7933. Duthuit, Claude. *Henri Matisse: catalogue raisonné des ouvrages illustrés.* Claude Duthuit; établi ave c la collaboration de Françoise Garnaud; introduction de Jean Guichard-Meili. Paris, C. Duthuit, 1966 [c1967]. (Paris, Imprimerie Union).(CR).

7934. Duthuit-Matisse, Marguerite. *Henri Matisse: catalogue raisonné de l'oeuvre gravé.* [By] M. Duthuit-Matisse, Claude Duthuit. Etablié avec la colloboration de Françoise Garnaud. Préface de Jean Guichard-Meili. 2 v. Paris, M. Duthuit-Matisse, 1983. (Paris, Imprimerie Union).(CR).

7935. Elderfield, John. *Henri Matisse, a retrospective.* New York, Museum of Modern Art; distrib. by H.N. Abrams, 1992.

7936. Escholier, Raymond. *Matisse from the life.* Trans. by Geraldine and H. M. Colville. London, Faber, 1960.

7937. Faure, Elie, et al. *Henri Matisse.* Paris, Cahiers d'Aujourd'hui, [1920].

7938. Fels, Florent. *Henri Matisse.* Paris, Chroniques du Jour; New York, Weyhe, 1929.

7939. Flam, Jack D. *Matisse, image into sign.* [Catalogue of an exhibition at] The Saint Louis Art Musaeum, February 19–April 25, 1993. St. Louis, Mo., The Museum, 1993.

7940. ———. *Matisse on art.* [Edited by Jack D. Flam]. London, Phaidon, 1973. (Paperback ed.: New York, E.P. Dutton, 1978.

7941. ———. *Matisse: the man and his art, 1869–1918.* Ithaca, Cornell University Press, 1986.

7942. Fry, Roger. *Henri Matisse.* Paris, Chroniques du Jour, [1930].

7943. Elsen, Albert E. *The sculpture of Henri Matisse.* New York, Abrams, 1972.

7944. Girard, Xavier. *Henri Matisse, 1869–1954: Skulpturen und Druckgraphik. Kunstmuseum Bern, 1990/91 = sculptures et gravures. Musée des beaux-arts de Berne, 1990/91.* [By] X. Girard, Sandor Kuthy. Bern, Kunstmuseum, 1990.

7945. Gowing, Lawrence. *Matisse.* New York, Oxford University Press, 1979.

7946. Grand Palais (Paris). *Henri Matisse, exposition du centenaire. Avril–septembre 1970.* [Text by Pierre Schneider]. Paris, Ministère d'Etat Affaires Culturelles/Réunion des Musées Nationaux, 1970.

7947. Grünewald, Isaac. *Matisse och expressionismen.* Stockholm, Wahlström & Widstrand, 1944.

7948. Guichard-Meili, Jean. *Matisse.* Trans. by Caroline Moorehead. New York, Praeger, 1967.

7949. Guillaud, Jacqueline. *Matisse, le rhythme et la ligne.* Par Jacqueline et Maurice Guillaud. Paris/New York, Guillaud Editions, 1987.

7950. Herrera, Hayden. *Matisse: a portrait.* Harcourt Brace, 1993.

7951. Jacobus, John. *Henri Matisse.* New York, Abrams, 1973.

7952. Kostenevich, Albert Grigorievich. *Collecting Matisse.* [By] A. Kostenevich, Natalia Semyonova. Paris, Flammarion, 1993.

7953. Kunsthaus Zürich. *Henri Matisse.* 15. Oktober 1982 bis 16. Januar 1983. [Text by Felix Baumann et al.]. Zürich, Kunsthaus Zürich, 1982.

M

7954. Lassaigne, Jacques. *Matisse, biographical and critical study.* Trans. by Stuart Gilbert. Geneva, Skira, 1959. (The Taste of Our Time, 30).

7955. Lieberman, William S. *Matisse, fifty years of his graphic art.* New York, Braziller, 1956.

7956. Luzi, Mario [and] Carrà, Massimo. *L'opera di Matisse dalla rivolta fauve all'intimismo, 1904-1928.* Milano, Rizzoli, 1971. (Classici dell'arte, 49).

7957. Marchiori, Giuseppe. *Matisse.* [Milano], Pizzi, [1967].

7958. McBride, Henry. *Matisse.* New York, Knopf, 1930.

7959. Matisse, Henri. *Henri Matisse.* [Catalogue of an exhibition]. Redaktion des Kataloges, Felix Baumann; Mitarbeit, Margrit Hahnloser-Ingold, Klaus Schrenk. Zürich, Kunsthaus Zürich; Düsseldorf, Städtische Kunsthalle, Düsseldorf, 1982.

7960. ———. *Henri Matisse: drawings and sculptures.* Edited and with an introduction by Ernst-Gerhard Guse; and with contributions by Christian Arthaud . . . [et al.]; translated by John Ormond, with Iain Taylor. München, Prestel; New York, distrib. in the USA and Canada by te Neues Pub. Co., 1991.

7961. ———. *Henri Matisse: paintings and sculptures in Soviet Museums.* [Introduction by A. Izerghina. Translated by R.J. Rosengrant and V. Paperno (introduction}, Yu. Nemetsky (notes). Leningrad, Aurora Art Publishers, 1990. 4 ed.

7962. ———. *Matisse: a retrospective.* Edited by Jack Flam. New York, Hugh Lauter Levin Associates; distributed by Macmillan Pub. Co., 1988.

7963. ———. *Matisse: oeuvres de Henri Matisse.* Catalogue établi par Isabelle Monod-Fontaine, Anne Baldassari, Claude Laugier. Paris, Centre Georges Pompidou, 1989. (Collections du Musée national d'art moderne).

7964. Musée National d'Art Moderne (Paris). *Henri Matisse, dessins et sculpture.* 29 mai-7 septembre 1975. Paris, Centre National d'Art et de Culture Georges Pompidou/Musée National d'Art Moderne, 1975.

7965. ———. *Oeuvres de Henri Matisse (1869-1954).* Catalogue établi par Isabelle Monod-Fontaine. Paris, Centre Georges Pompidous, Musée National d'Art Moderne, 1979.

7966. Museum of Modern Art (New York). *Henri Matisse, retrospective exhibition.* November 3-December 6, 1931. New York, Museum of Modern Art, 1931.

7967. ———. *The last works of Henri Matisse: large cut gouaches.* October 17-December 3, 1961. [Text by Monroe Wheeler]. New York, Museum of Modern Art, 1961. Distributed by Doubleday, Garden City, N.Y.

7968. ———. *Matisse in the collection of the Museum of Modern Art, including remainder interest and promised gifts.* [Text by John Elderfield et al.]. New York, Museum of Modern Art, 1978.

7969. Orienti, Sandra. *Henri Matisse.* Firenze, Sansoni, 1971. (I maestri del novecento, 18).

7970. Philadelphia Museum of Art. *Henri Matisse, retrospective exhibition of paintings, drawings and sculpture.* Philadelphia, Philadelphia Museum of Art, 1948.

7971. Pleynet, Mercelin. *Henri Matisse: qui êtes vous?.* Lyon, La Manufacture, 1988.

7972. Reverdy, Pierre and Duthuit, Georges. *The last works of Henri Matisse, 1950-1954.* New York, Harcourt, Brace, 1958.

7973. St. Louis Art Museum. *Henri Matisse paper cut-outs.* January 29-March 12, 1978. [Catalogue by Jack Cowart et al.]. St. Louis, Mo., St. Louis Art Museum, 1977.

7974. Schacht, Roland. *Henri Matisse.* Dresden, Kaemmerer, 1922. (Künstler der Gegenwart, 4).

7975. Scheiwiller, Giovanni. *Henri Matisse.* Milano, Hoepli, 1947. 5 ed. (Arte moderna straniera, 3.—Serie A: Pittori,2).

7976. Selz, Jean. *Henri Matisse.* Trans. by A. P. H. Hamilton. New York, Crown, 1964.

7977. Sembat, Marcel. *Matisse et son oeuvre.* Paris, Gallimard, 1920. (Les peintres français nouveaux, 1).

7978. Severini, Gino. *Matisse.* Roma, Fratelli Bocca, 1944.("Anticipazioni", serie arti, 6).

7979. Swane, Leo. *Henri Matisse.* Stockholm, Nordstedt, 1944.

7980. U.C.L.A. Art Galleries (Los Angeles). *Henri Matisse.* Jan. 5-Feb. 27, 1966. [Text by Jean Leymarie et al.]. Berkeley, University of California Press, 1966.

7981. Verdet, André. *Prestiges de Matisse.* Paris, Emile-Paul, 1952.

7982. Watkins, Nicholas. *Matisse.* Oxford, Phaidon, 1984.

7983. Zervos, Christian, et al. *Henri Matisse.* Paris, Cahiers d'Art/New York, Weyhe, 1931.

7984. Zubova, Mariia V. *Grafika Matissa.* Moskva, Iskusstvo, 1977.

Matta Echaurren, Roberto Sebastián, 1911–

7985. Kestner-Gesellschaft Hannover. *Matta.* 12. Juli bis 29. September 1974. Hannover, Kestner-Gesellschaft, 1974. (Katalog 4/1974).

7986. Matta Echaurren, Roberto Sebastian. *Entretiens morphologiques: notebook no. 1. 1936-1944.* [Edited by] Germana Ferrari. London, Sistan, 1987.

7987. ———. *Matta.* Herausgegeben von Wieland Schmied. Tübingen, Wwasmuth, 1991.

7988. ———. *Matta.* [Catalogue of an exhibition

held at the] Centre Georges Pompidou, Musée national d'art moderne, 3 octobre–16 décembre 1985. [Commissaire général, Dominique Bozo]. Paris, Editions du Centre Pompidou, 1985.

7989. ———. *Matta: conversaciones.*[Edited by] Eduardo Carrasco. Santiago, Chile, CENECA: CESOC., 1987.

7990. Museum of Modern Art (New York). *Matta.* September 10–October 20, 1957. [Text by William Rubin]. New York, Museum of Modern Art, 1957.

7991. Rose Art Museum, Brandeis University (Waltham, Mass.). *Matta, the first decade.* May 9–June 20, 1982. Waltham, Mass., Rose Art Museum, 1982.

7992. Schuster, Jean. *Developpements sur l'infra-réalisme de Matta.* Paris, Losfeld, 1970.

Matteo di Giovanni, 1435–1495

7993. Hartlaub, Gustav. F. *Matteo da Siena und seine Zeit.* Strassburg, Heitz, 1910. (Zur Kunstgeschichte des Auslandes, 78).

Maufra, Maxime, 1861–1918

7994. Alexandre, Arsène. *Maxime Maufra, peintre marin et rustique (1861–1918).* Paris, Petit, 1926.

7995. Michelet, Victor-Emile. *Maufra, peintre et graveur.* Paris, Floury, 1908.

7996. Morane, Daniel. *Maxime Maufra, 1861–1918: catalogue de l'oeuvre gravé.* Pont-Aven, Musée de Pont-Aven, 1986. (CR).

7997. Ramade, Patrick. *Maxime Maufra: un ami de Gauguin en Bretagne.* Le Chasse-Marée, Editions de l'Estran, 1988.

May, Ernst, 1886–1970

7998. Buekschmitt, Justus. *Ernst May.* Stuttgart, Koch, 1963.

7999. May, Ernst. *Ernst May und das neue Frankfurt, 1925–1930.* Berlin, Ernst & Sohn, 1986.

8000. May, Ernst, et al. *Das neue Mainz.* Mainz, Margraf und Fischer, 1961.

Mayer, Constance, 1775?–1821

8001. Pilon, Edmond. *Constance Mayer.* Paris, Delpleuch, 1927.

Mazzolino, Ludovico, 1480–1528/30

8002. Zamboni, Silla. *Ludovico Mazzolino.* Milano, Silvana, 1968.

Mead, William Rutherford *see* McKim, Charles Follen

Meckenem, Israhel van, ca. 1440–1503

8003. Geisberg, Max. *Der Meister der Berliner Passion und Israhel van Meckenem; Studien*

M

zur Geschichte der westfälischen Kupferstecher im fünfzehnten Jahrhundert. Strassburg, Heitz, 1903. (Studien zur deutschen Kunstgeschichte, 42).

8004. ———. *Verzeichnis der Kupferstiche Israhels van Meckenem.* Strassburg, Heitz, 1905. (CR). (Studien zur deutschen Kunstgeschichte, 58).

8005. Schnack, Jutta. *Der Passionszyklus in der Graphik Israhel van Meckenems und Martin Schongauers.* Münster, Aschendorff, 1979. (Bocholter Quellen und Beiträge, 2).

8006. [Stadt Bocholt]. *Israhel van Meckenem, Goldschmied und Kupferstecher.* Zur 450. Wiederkehr seines Todestages. [Text by Paul Pieper et al.]. Bocholt [Germany], Stadt Bocholt, 1953.

8007. Warburg, Anni. *Israhel van Meckenem; sein Leben, sein Werk une seine Bedeutung für die Kunst des ausgehenden 15. Jahrhunderts.* Bonn, Schroeder, 1930. (Forschungen zur Kunstgeschichte Westeuropas, 7).

Meer, Jan van der *see* Vermeer, Jan

Meid, Hans, 1883–1957

8008. Brieger, Lothar. *Hans Meid.* Berlin, Verlag Neue Kunsthandlung, 1921. (Graphiker der Gegenwart, 7).

8009. Friedländer, Max J. *Der Radierer Hans Meid.* Leipzig, Thyrsos, 1923.

8010. Jentsch, Ralph. *Hans Meid, das graphische Werk.* Esslingen, Kunstgalerie Esslingen, 1978.

Meidias, 5th c. B.C.

8011. Becatti, Giovanni. *Meidia, un manierista antico.* Firenze, Sansoni, 1947.

8012. Burn, Lucilla. *The Meidias painter.* Oxford, Clarendon Press; New York, Oxford University Press, 1987.

8013. Ducati, Pericle. *I vasi dipinti nello stile del ceramista Midia; contributo alla storia della ceramica attica.* Roma, Accademia dei Lincei, 1909.

8014. Nicole, Georges. *Meidias et le style fleuri dans la céramique attique.* Genève, Kündig, 1908.

Meidner, Ludwig, 1884–1966

8015. Eliel, Carol S. *The apocalyptic landscapes of Ludwig Meidner.* C.S. Eliel, with a contribution by Eberhard Roters. Los Angeles, Los Angeles County Museum of Art; München, Prestel-Verlag, 1989.

8016. Grochowiak, Thomas. *Ludwig Meidner.* Recklinghausen, Bongers, 1966.

8017. Hodin, Joseph. *Ludwig Meidner; seine Kunst, seine Persönlichkeit, seine Zeit.* Darmstadt, von Liebig, 1975.

8018. Kunz, Ludwig, ed. *Ludwig Meidner; Dichter, Maler und Cafés.* Zürich, Arche, 1973.

8019. Leistner, Gerhard. *Idee und Wirklichkeit: Gehalt und Bedeutung des urbanen Expressionismus in Deutschland, dargestellt am Werk Ludwig Meidners.* Frankfurt am Main/New York, P. Lang, 1986. [Europäische Hochschulschriften . Reihe XXVIII. Kunstgeschichte, 66).

8020. Meidner, Ludwig. *Eine autobiographische Plauderei.* Leipzig, Klinkhardt & Biermann, 1919. (Junge Kunst, 4).

8021. ———. *Ludwig Meidner, 1884–1966.* [Catalogue of an exhibition]. Redaktion, Klaus Hoffmann. Wolfsburg, Kunstverein Wolfsburg, 1985.

8022. ———. *Ludwig Meidner: Zeichner, Maler, Literat, 1884–1966.* [Catalogue of an exhibition]. Darmstadt, Mathildenhöhe, 15. September 1991–1. Dezember 1991. [Edited by] Gerda Breuer, Ines Wagemann. 2 v. Stuttgart, G. Hatje, 1991.

8023. University of Michigan Museum of Art (Ann Arbor, Mich.). *Ludwig Meidner, an expressionist master.* October 20–November 19, 1978. Ann Arbor, Mich., University of Michigan Museum of Art, 1978.

Meissonier, Jean Louis Ernest, 1815–1891

8024. Bénédite, Léonce. *Meissonier, biographie critique.* Paris, Laurens, 1910.

8025. Galerie Georges Petit (Paris). *Exposition Meissonier.* Mars 1893. [Text by Alexandre Dumas]. Paris, Galerie Georges Petit, 1893.

8026. Gréard, Vallery C. O. *Meissonier, his life and his art.* Trans. by Mary Loyd and Florence Simmonds. New York, Armstrong, 1897.

8027. Larroumet, Gustave. *Meissonier.* Étude suivie d'une biographie par Philippe Burty. Paris, Baschet, [1893].

8028. Meissonier, Jean Louis Ernest. *Ernest Meissonier: retrospective.* [Exposition] Musée des beaux-arts de Lyon, 25 mars 27 juin 1993. [Commissaires de l'exposition, Philippe Durey, Constance Cain Hungerford]. Lyon, Musée des beaux-arts de Lyon; Paris, Réunion des musées nationaux, 1993.

8029. Mollett, John W. *Meissonier.* New York, Scribner and Welford/London, Sampson Low, 1882.

Meister . . . *see* Master . . .

Meistermann, Georg, 1911–

8030. Germanisches Nationalmuseum (Nuremberg). *Georg Meistermann.* 16. Juni bis 23. August 1981. Nürnberg, Archiv für Bildende Kunst am Germanischen Nationalmuseum, 1981. (Werke und Dokumente, Neue Folge, 3).

8031. Linfert, Carl. *Georg Meistermann.* Recklinghausen, Bongers, 1958. (Monographien zur Rheinisch-Westfälischen Kunst der Gegenwart, 6).

8032. Meistermann, Georg. *Georg Meistermann: die Kirchenfenster.* [Catalogue of an exhibition]. Freiburg, i.B., Herder, 1986.

8033. Meistermann, Georg. *Georg Meistermann: Werke und Dokumente.* [Ausstellung]. Katalog, Claus Pese; Redaktion, Claus Pese, Ludwig Veit. Nürnberg, Archiv für Bildende Kunst am Germanischen Nationalmuseum, 1981.

8034. Ruhrberg, Karl und Schäfke, Werner. *Georg Meistermann: Monographie und Werkverzeichnis.* Herausgegeben von K. Ruhrberg und W. Schäfke; mit einem Werkverzeichnis edr Gemälde von Inge Herold. Köln, Wienand, 1991. (CR)

Meit, Konrad, 1475–1550

8035. Duverger, Jozef. *Conrat Meijt (ca. 1480–1551).* Bruxelles, Académie royale de Belgique, 1934.

8036. Troescher, Georg. *Conrat Meit von Worms; ein rheinischer Bildhauer der Renaissance.* Freiburg i.Br., Urban-Verlag, 1927.

Melchior, Johann Peter, 1742–1825

8037. Hofmann, Friedrich H. *Johann Peter Melchior, 1742–1825.* München, Schmidt, 1921. (Einzeldarstellungen zur süddeutschen Kunst, 2).

Mellan, Claude, 1598–1688

8038. Brejon de Lavergnée, Barbara. *Claude Mellan, 1598–1688.* Paris, Galerie de Bayser; Boston, Mass., Ars Libri Ltd., distributor, 1987.

8039. Mellan, Claude. *Claude Mellan, gli anni romani: un incisore tra Vouet e Bernini.* Catalogo a cura di Luigi Ficacci. Roma, Multigrafico, 1989.

8040. Montaiglon, Anatole de. *Catalogue raisonné de l'oeuvre de Claude Mellan d'Abbeville, précédé d'une notice sur la vie et les ouvrages de Mellan par* [Pierre J.] *Mariette.* Abbeville, Briez, 1856. (CR).

8041. Préaud, Maxime. *L'oeil d'or Claude Mellan, 1598–1688.* [Catalogue of an exhibition]. Bibliothèque nationale, Galerie Mazarine, 26 mai–21 août 1988. Catalogue rédigé par Maxime Préaud et par Barbara Brejon de Lavergnée pour les dessins et les sculptures. Paris, Bibliothèque nationale, 1988.

8042. Sgard, Jean. *La Sainte Face de Claude Mellan; étude des bases géométriques du dessin.* Abbeville, Société d'Emulation Historique et Littéraire, 1957. (Etudes Picardes, 1).

Melozzo da Forlì, 1438–1494

8043. Buscaroli, Rezio. *Melozzo da Forlì, nei documenti nelle testimonianze dei contemporanei e nella bibliografia.* Roma, Reale Accademia d'Italia, 1938. (Reale Accademia d'Italia; architettura, pittura, scultura, 3).

8044. ———. *Melozzo e il Melozzismo.* Bologna, Athena, 1955.

8045. Clark, Nicholas. *Melozzo da Forli, pictor papalis.* London, Published for Sotheby's Publications by P. Wilson; New York, distrib. in the USA by Harper and Row, 1990.

8046. Okkonen, Onni. *Melozzo da Forli und seine Schule; eine kunsthistorische Studie.* Helsinki, Suomalaisen Teideakatemian Toimituksia, 1910.

8047. Palazzo dei Musei (Forli). *Mostra di Melozzo e del quattrocentro Romagnolo.* 2 v. Guigno–ottobre, 1938. Forlì, Città di Forlì, 1938.

8048. Ricci, Corrado. *Melozzo da Forlí.* Roma, Anderson, 1911.

8049. Schmarsow, August. *Melozzo da Forli; ein Beitrag zur kunst- und kulturgeschichte Italiens im XV. Jahrhundert.* Berlin/Stuttgart, Spemann, 1886.

Memling, Hans, 1433–1494

8050. Baldass, Ludwig von. *Hans Memling.* Wien, Schroll, 1942.

8051. Bazin, Germain. *Memling.* Paris, Tisné, 1939.

8052. Corti, Maria and Faggin, Giorgio T. *L'opera completa di Memling.* Milano, Rizzoli, 1969. (CR). (Classici dell'arte, 27).

8053. Delepierre, Joseph O. et Voisin, Auguste. *La châsse de Saint Ursule.* Bruges, Société des Beaux-Arts, 1841.

8054. Eemans, Marc. *Hans Memling.* Bruxelles, Meddens, 1970.

8055. Groeningenmuseum (Brügge). *Hans Memling.* Edited by Dirk Vos. 2 v. Brügge, Groeningenmuseum, 1994.

8056. Huisman, Georges. *Memlinc.* Paris, Alcan, 1923.

8057. Kaemmerer, Ludwig. *Memling.* Bielefeld/Leipzig, Velhagen & Klasing, 1899. (Künstler-Monographien, 39).

8058. Marlier, Georges. *Memlinc.* Bruxelles, Nouvelle Société d'Editions, 1934.

8059. McFarlane, Kenneth B. *Hans Memling.* Edited by Edgar Wind with the assistance of G. L. Harris. Oxford, Clarendon Press, 1971.

8060. Muls, Jozef. *Memling.* Naarden, In den Toren, [1939]. (New ed.: Hasselt, Heideland, 1960).

8061. Musée Communal (Bruges). *Exposition Memling.* 22 juin–1 octobre 1939. [Text by Paul Lambotte]. Bruges, Desclée, de Brouwer, 1939.

8062. Nuyens, Alvarus J. *Het mysterie van leven en werk van Hans Memlinc.* Antwerpen, Nederlandsche Boekhandel, 1944.

8063. Thiemann, Barbara M. *Hans Memling: ein Beitrag zum Verständnis seiner Gestaltungsprinzipien.* Frankfurt, Lang, 1994. (Europäische Hochschulschriften, Reihe XXVIII, Kunstgeschichte, 205).

8064. Voll, Karl. *Memling, des Meisters Gemälde.* Stuttgart/Leipzig, Deutsche Verlags-Anstalt, 1909. (Klassiker der Kunst, 14).

8065. Vos, Dirk de. *Hans Memling: the complete works.* Trans. by Ted Alkins. Ghent, Ludion Press; New York, distributed in the United States and Canada by H.N. Abrams, 1994. (CR).

8066. Wauters, Alphonse J. *Sept études pour servir à l'histoire de Hans Memling.* Bruxelles, Dietrich, 1893.

8067. Weale, W. H. James. *Hans Memlinc, a notice of his life and works.* [London], Arundel Society, 1865. (New ed.: London, Bell, 1901).

Mendelsohn, Erich, 1887–1953

8068. Beyer, Oskar, ed. *Eric Mendelsohn: letters of an architect.* Trans. by Geoffrey Strachan, with an introduction by Nikolaus Pevsner. London, Abelard-Schuman, 1967.

8069. Mendelsohn, Erich. *Amerika; Bilderbuch eines Architekten.* Berlin, Mosse, 1926. (Reprint: New York, Da Capo, 1976).

8070. ———. *Erich Mendelsohn: complete works of the architect: sketches, designs, buildings.* English translation, Antje Fritsch. New York, Princeton Architectural Press, 1992.

8071. ———. *Erich Mendelsohn, 1887–1953: Ideen, Bauten, Projekte.* Bearbeitet von Sigrid Aschenbach. Berlin, Staatliche Museen Preussischer Kulturbesitz, 1987.

8072. ———. *Erich Mendelsohn: letters of an architect.* Edited by Oskar Beyer. Translated by Geoffrey Strachan. with an introd. by Nikolaus Pevsner. London, Abelard-Schuman, 1967.

8073. ———. *Das Gesamtschaffen des Architekten: Skizzen, Entwürfe, Bauten.* Berlin, Mosse, 1930.

8074. ———. *Russland, Europa, Amerika: ein architektonischer Querschnitt.* Berlin, Mosse, 1929.

8075. ———. *Structures and sketches.* Trans. by Herman G. Scheffauer. London, Benn, 1924.

8076. ———. *Three lectures on architecture.* Berkeley, University of California Press, 1944.

8077. Morgenthaler, Hans Rudolf. *Erich Mendelsohn, 1887–1953: an annotated bibliography.* Monticello, Ill., Vance Bibliographies, 1987.

8078. Roggero, Mario F. *Il contributo di Mendel-*

sohn alla evoluzione dell'architettura moderna. Milano, Tamburini, 1952.

8079. University Art Museum, University of California (Berkeley). *The drawings of Eric Mendelsohn.* [March 1969; text by Susan King and Gerald McCue]. Berkeley, Regents of the University of California, 1969.

8080. Von Eckhardt, Wolf. *Eric Mendelsohn.* London, Mayflower/New York, Braziller, 1960.

8081. Whittick, Arnold. *Eric Mendelsohn.* London, Faber, 1940. (New ed.: London, Hill, 1956.)

8082. Zevi, Bruno. *Erich Mendelsohn: opera completa; con note biografiche di Luise Mendelsohn.* Milano, Kompass, 1970. (CR). (English edition: New York, Rizzoli, 1985).

Mengs, Anton Raphael, 1728–1779

8083. Azara, Nicolas de. *Obras de D. Antonio Rafael Mengs, primer Pintor de Camera del Rey.* Madrid, Imprenta Real, 1780. (English ed.: 2 v. London, Faulder, 1796).

8084. Biancomi, Giovanni L. *Elogio storico del Cavaliere Anton Raffaele Mengs, con un catalogo delle opere da esso fatte.* Milano, Imperial Monistero di S. Ambrogio Maggiore, 1780. (Reprint: Ann Arbor, Mich., University Microfilms, 1974).

8085. Hanisch, Dieter. *Anton Raphael Mengs und die Bildform des Frühklassizismus.* Recklinghausen, Bongers, 1965. (Münstersche Studien zur Kunstgeschichte, 1).

8086. Martinelli, Rossa C. *La ragione dell'arte; teoria e critica in Anton Raphael Mengs e Johann Joachim Winckelmann.* Napoli, Liguori, 1981.

8087. Menegazzi, Luigi. *Anton Raphael Mengs.* Milano, Fabbri, 1966. (I maestri del colore, 221).

8088. Mengs, Anton R. *Briefe an Raimondo Ghelli und Anton Maron.* Herausgegeben und kommentiert von Herbert von Einem. Göttingen, Vandenhoeck und Ruprecht, 1973.

8089. ———. *Obras de d. Antonio Rafael Mengs: primer pintor de camara del rey.* Publicadas por Joseph Nicolas de Azara. Madrid, Imprenta Real, 1797. 2 ed.

8090. Museo del Prado (Madrid). *Antonio Rafael Mengs, 1728–1779.* Junio–Julio 1980. Madrid, Ministerio de Cultura, 1980.

8091. Prange, Christian F., ed. *Anton Raphael Mengs; hinterlassene Werke.* 3 v. Halle, Hendel, 1786.

8092. Ratti, Carlo G. *Epilogo della vita del fu Cavalier Antonio Raffaello Mengs.* Genova, Casamara dalle Cinque Lampardi, 1779.

8093. Roettgen, Steffi. *Anton Raphael Mengs and his British patrons.* London, Zwemmer, 1993.

Menzel, Adolph von, 1815–1905

8094. Becker, Robert. *Adolph Menzel und seine schlesische Verwandtschaft.* Strassburg, Heitz, 1922. (Studien zur deutschen Kunstgeschichte, 222).

8095. Biberfeld, Arthur, ed. *Adolph von Menzel: Architekturen.* 4 v. Berlin, Wasmuth, 1906.

8096. Erbertshäuser, Heidi. *Adolph von Menzel, das graphische Werk.* Mit einem Vorwort von Jens Christian Jensen und einem Essay von Max Liebermann. 2 v. München, Rogner & Bernhard, 1976. (CR).

8097. Graphische Sammlung Albertina (Vienna). *Adolph von Menzel, 1815–1905: Zeichnungen, Aquarelle, Gouachen aus der Nationalgalerie, Staatliche Museen zu Berlin, Deutsche Demokratische Republik, 28. Februar bis 8. April 1985.* Katalogbearbeitung, Renate Holzschuh und Walter Koschatzky. Wien, Österreichischer Bundesverlag, 1985.

8098. Hamburger Kunsthalle. *Menzel—der Beobachter.* [22. Mai–25. Juli 1981]. München, Prestel/Hamburg, Kunsthalle, 1982.

8099. Hermand, Jost. *Adolph Menzel.* Mit Selbstzeugnissen und Bilddokumenten dargestellt von J. Hermand. Reinbek bei Hamburg, Rowohlt, 1986.

8100. Hochhuth, Rolf. *Menzel; Maler des Lichts.* Frankfurt am Main, Insel, 1991.

8101. Hütt, Wolfgang. *Adolph Menzel.* Leipzig, Seemann, 1981.

8102. Jensen, Jens C. *Adolph Menzel.* Köln, DuMont, 1982.

8103. Jordan, Max und Dohme, Robert. *Das Werk Adolph Menzels.* 2 v. München, Bruckmann, 1890.

8104. Kaiser, Konrad. *Adolph Menzel, der Maler.* Stuttgart, Schuler, 1965.

8105. ———. *Adolph Menzels Eisenwalzwerk.* Berlin, Henschel, 1953.

8106. Kirstein, Gustav. *Das Leben Adolph Menzels.* Leipzig, Seemann, 1919.

8107. Knackfuss, Hermann. *Menzel.* Bielefeld/Leipzig, Velhagen & Klasing, 1895. (Künstler-Monographien, 7).

8108. Meier-Graefe, Julius. *Der junge Menzel; ein Problem der Kunstökonomie Deutschlands.* Leipzig, Insel-Verlag, 1906.

8109. Meissner, Franz H. *Adolph von Menzel.* Berlin, Schuster & Loeffler, 1902.

8110. Menzel, Adolph. *Adolph Menzel, 1815–1905: master drawings from East Berlin.* Peter Betthausen . . . [et al.]. Alexandria, Va., Art Services International, 1990.

8111. Menzel, Adolph von. *Briefe.* Herausgegeben von Hans Wolff. Berlin, Bard, 1914.

8112. Meyerheim, Paul. *Adolf von Menzel, Erinnerungen.* Berlin, Paetel, 1906.

8113. Nationalgalerie (Berlin). *Adolph Menzel;*

Gemälde, Zeichnungen. Ausstellung 1980. [Text by Peter H. Feist et al.]. Berlin, Staatliche Museen zu Berlin, 1980.

8114. Scheffler, Karl. *Menzel; der Mensch, das Werk.* Neu herausgegeben von Carl Georg Heise. München, Bruckmann, 1955.

8115. Sondermann, Fritz. *Adolph Menzel.* Magdeburg, Rathke, 1895.

8116. Tschudi, Hugo von. *Adolph von Menzel; Abbildungen seiner Gemälde und Studien.* München, Bruckmann, 1906. (CR).

8117. Waldmann, Emil. *Der Maler Adolph Menzel.* Wien, Schroll, 1941. 3 ed.

8118. Weinhold, Renate. *Menzel Bibliographie.* Leipzig, Seemann, 1959.

8119. Wirth, Irmgard. *Mit Adolph Menzel in Berlin.* München, Prestel, 1965.

8120. ———. *Mit Menzel in Bayern und Österreich.* München, Prestel, 1974.

8121. Wolf, Georg J. *Adolf von Menzel, der Maler deutschen Wesens.* München, Bruckmann, [1915].

8122. Wolff, Hans, ed. *Zeichnungen von Adolph Menzel.* Dresden, Arnold, 1920. (Arnolds graphische Bücher, zweite Folge, 1).

8123. Zangs, Christiane. *Die künstlerische Entwicklung und das Werk Menzels im Spiegel der zeitgenössischen Kritik.* Aachen, Mainz, 1992.

Merian, Maria Sibylla, 1647–1717

8124. Kerner, Charlotte. *Seidenraupe, Dschungelblüte: die Lebensgeschichte der Maria Sibylla Merian.* Weinheim, Beltz Verlag, 1989. 3 ed.

8125. Lendorff, Gertrud. *Maria Sibylla Merian, 1647–1717; ihr Leben und ihr Werk.* Basel, Gute Schriften, 1955.

8126. Pfister-Burkhalter, Margarete. *Maria Sibylla Merian, Leben und Werk, 1647–1717.* Basel, GS-Verlag, 1980.

8127. Rücker, Elizabeth. *Maria Sibylla Merian, 1647–1717.* [Published in conjunction with an exhibition at the Germanisches Nationalmuseum, Nuremberg, April 12–June 4, 1967]. Nürnberg, Germanisches Nationalmuseum, 1967.

Merrill, John O., 1896–1975 *see* Skidmore, Louis

Meryon, Charles, 1821–1868

8128. Bouvenne, Aglaus. *Notes et souveniers sur Charles Meryon.* Paris, Charavay, 1883.

8129. Burty, Philip. *Charles Meryon; sailor, engraver, and etcher. A memoir and complete descriptive catalogue of his works.* Trans. by Marcus B. Huish. London, Fine Art Society, 1879.

8130. Collins, R. D. J. *Charles Meryon: a bibliography.* Dunedin, N.Z., University of Otago Press, 1986.

8131. Delteil, Loys. *Catalogue raisonné of the etchings of Charles Meryon, with the addition of many newly discovered states.* Edited by Harold J. L. Wright. New York, Truesdell, 1924. (CR).

8132. Ecke, Goesta. *Charles Meryon.* Leipzig, Klinkhardt & Biermann, 1923. (Meister der Graphik, 11).

8133. Geffroy, Gustave. *Charles Meryon.* Paris, Floury, 1926.

8134. Schneiderman, Richard Steven. *The catalogue raisonné of the prints of Charles Meryon.* R.S. Schneiderman with the assistance of Frank W. Raysor. London, Garton & Co. in association with Scolar Press, 1990. (CR).

8135. Städelsches Kunstinstitut und Städtische Galerie (Frankfurt). *Charles Meryon: Paris um 1850; Zeichnungen, Radierungen, Photographien.* [Oct. 23, 1975–Jan. 4, 1976]. Frankfurt a.M., Städelsches Kunstinstitut und Städtische Galerie, 1975.

8136. Wedmore, Frederick. *Meryon and Meryon's Paris, with a descriptive catalogue of the artist's work.* London, Thibaudeau, 1879.

Messel, Alfred, 1853–1909

8137. Rapsilber, Maximilian. *Das Werk Alfred Messels.* Berlin, Wasmuth, [1905]. (Sonderheft der Berliner Architekturwelt, 5).

8138. Stahl, Fritz. *Alfred Messels.* Berlin, Wasmuth, [1910]. (Sonderheft der Berliner Architekturwelt, 9).

Messina, Francesco, 1900–

8139. Bernasconi, Ugo. *Francesco Messina.* Milano, Hoepli, 1937. (Arte moderna italiana, 28).

8140. Cavallo, Luigi, ed. *Messina.* Firenze, Galleria Michaud, [1971].

8141. Cocteau, Jean. *Francesco Messina.* [Text in French, English, and German]. Milano, Pizzi, 1959.

8142. Messina, Francesco. *Francesco Messina: mostra celebrativa per i 90 anni.* Torino, U. Allemandi, 1991.

8143. ———. *Messina.* Milano, A. Mondadori; Roma, De Luca, 1987.

8144. Salmon, André. *Francesco Messina.* Paris, Chroniques du Jour, 1936.

Meštrović, Ivan, 1883–1962

8145. Ćurcin, Milan, et al. *Ivan Meštrović, a monograph.* London, Williams and Norgate, 1919.

8146. Grum, Žiljko. *Ivan Meštrović.* [Text in English]. Zagreb, Matica, 1962. (New ed., in Croatian: 1969).

8147. Kečkemet, Dusko. *Ivan Meštrović: the only way to be an artist is to work.* Zagreb, Spektar, 1970.

8148. Meštrović, Ivan. *Dennoch will ich hoffen . . . : ein Weihnachtsgespräch.* [Aus dem noch unveröffentlichen Manuskript vom Kroatischen ins Deutsche übertragen durch Dr. A. Licht]. Zürich, Rascher, 1945.

8149. ———. *Ivan Meštrovic: Skulpturen.* Ausstellung]. Katalogredaktion, Martina Jura. Berlin, Nationalgalerie, Staatliche Museen Preussischer Kulturbesitz, 1987.

8150. ———. *Uspomene na političke ljude i dogadiaje.* Zagreb, Matica, 1969.

8151. Porter, Dean A. *Ivan Meštrović, 1883–1962. A centennial exhibition: a survey of drawings and prints primarily from the Mestrovic family collection.* D.A. Porter, James Flanigan. South Bend, Ind., Snite Museum of Art, University of Notre Dame, 1983.

8152. Rice, Norman L. *The sculpture of Ivan Meštrović.* Syracuse, Syracuse University Press, 1948.

8153. Schmeckebier, Lawrence. *Ivan Meštrović, sculptor and patriot.* Syracuse, Syracuse University Press, 1959.

8154. Strajnić, Kosta. *Ivan Meštrović.* Beograd, Ćelap i Popovac, 1919.

8155. Vidović, Žarko. *Meštrović i savremeni sukob skulptora s arhitektom.* Sarajevo, Veselin Masleša, 1961.

8156. Yusuf Ali, Abd Allah. *Meštrović and Serbian sculpture.* London, Mathews 1916. (Vigo Cabinet Series, second century, 38).

Metsu, Gabriel, 1629–1667

8157. Robinson, Franklin W. *Gabriel Metsu (1629–1667); a study of his place in Dutch genre painting of the Golden Age.* New York, Schram, 1974.

Metsys, Quentin *see* **Massys, Quentin**

Metzinger, Jean, 1883–1956 *see also* **Gleizes, Albert**

8158. Metzinger, Fritz. *Ein vergessener Maler im Rijksmuseum Kröller-Müller = A forgotten painter in the Rijksmuseum Kröller-Müller.* Frankfurt am Main, R.G. Fischer, 1991.

8159. Moser, Joann. *Jean Metzinger in retrospect.* J. Moser; with an essay by Daniel Robbins. Iowa City, University of Iowa Museum of Art; Seattle, distrib. by the University of Washington Press, 1985.

Meunier, Constantin Emile, 1831–1905

8160. Bazalgette, Léon, et al. *Constantin Meunier et son oeuvre.* Paris, La Plume, 1905.

8161. Behets, Armand. *Constantin Meunier; l'homme, l'artiste et l'oeuvre.* Avec d'abon-dants extraits des lettres du maître et une lettre-préface de Mme. Jacques-Meunier, sa fille. Bruxelles, Lebègue, 1942.

8162. Demolder, Eugène. *Constantin Meunier, étude.* Bruxelles, Deman, 1901.

8163. Fontaine, André. *Constantin Meunier.* Paris, Alcan, 1923.

8164. Gensel, Walter. *Constantin Meunier.* Bielefeld/Leipzig, Velhagen und Klasing, 1905. (Künstler-Monographien, 79).

8165. Lemonnier, Camille. *Constantin Meunier, sculpteur et peintre.* Paris, Floury 1904.

8166. Nikitiuk, Olga D. *Konstantin Men'e, 1831–1905.* Moskva, Iskusstvo, 1974.

8167. Scheffler, Karl. *Constantin Meunier.* Berlin, Bard, 1908. 2 ed.

8168. Theiry, A. [and] Dievoet, E. van. *Catalogue complet des oeuvres dessinées, peintes et sculptées de Constantin Meunier.* Louvain, Nova & Vetera, [1909].

8169. Treu, Georg. *Constantin Meunier.* Dresden, Richter, 1898.

Mi Fei, 1051–1107

8170. Vandier-Nicolas, Nicole. *Art et sagesse en chine: Mi Fou (1051–1107), peintre et connaisseur d'art dans la perspective de l'esthétique des lettres.* Paris, Presses Universitaires de France, 1963.

8171. ———. *Le houa-che di Mi Fou (1051–1107), ou le carnet d'un connaisseur a l'époque des Song du Nord.* Paris, Imprimerie Nationale, 1964.

Michel, Georges, 1763–1843

8172. Larguier, Léo. *Georges Michel.* Paris, Delpeuch, 1927.

8173. Sensier, Alfred. *Etude sur Georges Michel.* Paris, Lemerre, 1873.

Michelangelo Buonarroti, 1475–1564

8174. Ackerman, James S. *The architecture of Michelangelo. With a catalogue of Michelangelo's works* by J.S. Ackerman and John Newman. Harmondsworth, Middlesex, England/ New York, Penguin Books, 1986. 2 edition. (CR).

8175. Agosti, Giovanni. *Michelangelo e l'arte classica.* [Mostra] Firenze. Casa Buonarroti, 15 aprile–15 ottobre 1987. A cura di Giovanni Agosti e Vincenzo Farinella. Firenze, Cantini edizioni d'arte, 1987.

8176. Alker, Hermann R. *Michelangelo und seine Kuppel von St. Peter in Rom.* Karlsruhe, Braun, 1968.

8177. Ancona, Paolo d', et al. *Michelangelo: architettura, pittura, scultura.* Milano, Bramante, 1964.

8178. Arbour, Renée. *Michel-Ange.* Paris, Somogy, 1962.

8179. Argan, Giulio Carlo. *Michelangelo architetto*. G.C. Argan, Bruno Contardi. Milano, Electa, 1990.

8180. ———. *Michelangelo architect*. G.C. Argan and Bruno Contardi. Trans. from the Italian by Marion L. Grayson. New York, Harry N. Abrams, 1993. (French ed.: *Michel-Ange architecte*. Trans. by Denis-Armand Canal. Paris, Gallimard/Electa, 1991.

8181. Baldini, Umberto. *Michelangelo scultore*. Fotografie di Liberto Perugi. Firenze, Sansoni, 1981.

8182. ———. *Michelangiolo: tutta la scultura*. [Testi di Umberto Baldini . . . et al.]. Firenze, Naridini, 1989. (CR).

8183. Bardeschi Ciulich, Lucilla e Barocchi, Paola, eds. *I ricordi di Michelangelo*. Firenze, Sansoni, 1970.

8184. Barocchi, Paola. *Giorgio Vasari: la vita di Michelangelo nelle redazioni del 1550 e del 1568*. Curata e commentata de Paola Barocchi. 5 v. Milano/Napoli, Ricciardi, 1962.

8185. ———. *Michelangelo e la sua scuola*. 2 v. Firenze, Olschki, 1962. (Accademia toscana di scienze e lettere, 8).

8186. Beck, James. *Michelangelo: a lesson in anatomy*. New York, Viking, 1975.

8187. Bérence, Fred. *La vie de Michel-Ange*. Paris, Editions du Sud, 1965. 2 ed.

8188. Blanc, Charles, et al. *L'oeuvre et la vie de Michel-Ange, dessinateur-sculpteur-peintre-architecte et poète*. Paris, Gazette des Beaux-Arts, 1876.

8189. Borinski, Karl. *Die Rätsel Michelangelos; Michelangelo und Dante*. München, Muller, 1908.

8190. Brandes, Georg. *Michelangelo Buonarroti*. 2 v. København, Gyldendal, 1921. (English ed., trans. by Heinz Norden: New York, Ungar, 1963).

8191. Brion, Marcel. *Michelangelo*. Trans. by James Whitall. New York, Crown, 1940.

8192. Buscaroli, Rezio. *Michelangelo; la vita, la teorica sull'arte, le opere*. Bologna, Tamari, 1959.

8193. Calí, Maria. *Da Michelangelo all'Escorial: momenti del dibattito religioso nell'arte del Cinquecento*. Torino, Einaudi, 1980.

8194. Carli, Enzo. *Michelangelo*. Bergamo, Istituto Italiano d'Arti Grafiche, 1942.

8195. Clements, Robert J. *Michelangelo's theory of art*. New York, New York University Press, 1961.

8196. ———, ed. *Michelangelo, a self-portrait*. Edited with commentaries and new translations by Robert John Clements. Englewood Cliffs, N.J., Prentice-Hall, 1963.

8197. Colombier, Pierre du, et al. *Michel-Ange*. Paris, Hachette, 1961. (Collection génies et réalitiés).

8198. Condivi, Ascanio. *Vita di Michelagnolo Buonarroti*. Roma, Blado, 1553. (English ed., trans. by Alice S. Wohl; ed. by Hellmut Wohl: Baton Rouge, La., Louisiana State University Press, 1976).

8199. Dal Poggetto, Paolo. *I disegni murali di Michelangelo e della sua scuola nella Sagrestia Nuova di San Lorenzo*. Firenze, Centro Di, 1978.

8200. Davray, Jean. *Michel-Ange, essai*. Paris, Michel, 1937.

8201. Delacre, Maurice. *Le dessin de Michel-Ange*. Bruxelles, Palais des Académies, 1938.

8202. Dening-Brylow, B. *Michel-Ange et la psychologie du Barocco*. Lausanne, Frankfurter, 1913.

8203. De Tolnay, Charles. *Michelangelo e i Medici*. [Mostra]. Firenze. Casa Buonarroti, 15 marzo–15 maggio 1980. Testo di Charles de Tolnay; schede di Charles de Tolnay e Paola Squellati Brizio. Firenze, Centro Di, 1980.

8204. De Vecchi, Pierluigi. *Michelangelo*. Translated by Alexandra Campbell. London, Barrie & Jenkins, 1992.

8205. Duppa, Richard. *The life of Michel Angelo Buonarroti, with his poetry and letters*. London, Murray, 1806.

8206. Dussler, Luitpold. *Michelangelo-Bibliographie, 1927–1970*. Weisbaden, Harrassowitz, 1974.

8207. ———. *Die Zeichnungen des Michelangelo; kritischer Katalog*. Berlin, Mann, 1959. (CR).

8208. Einem, Herbert von. *Michelangelo*. Trans. by Ronald Taylor. London, Methuen, 1973.

8209. Fagan, Louis. *The art of Michel-Angelo Buonarroti as illustrated by the various collections in the British Museum*. London, Dulau, 1883.

8210. Frey, Dagobert. *Michelangelo-Studien*. Wien, Schroll, 1920.

8211. Frey, Karl. *Die Handzeichnungen Michelagniolos Buonarroti*. [3 v., with supplement by Fritz Knapp]. Berlin, Bard, 1909–11. (CR).

8212. ———. *Michelagniolos Jugendjahre*. Berlin, Curtius, 1907.

8213. Frommel, Christoph L. *Michelangelo und Tomasso dei Cavalieri*. Amsterdam, Peregrini, 1979. 2 ed.

8214. Geymüller, Heinrich F. von. *Michelagnolo Buonarroti als Architekt*. München, Bruckmann, 1904.

8215. Giunti, Jacopo. *Esequie del divino Michelagnolo Buonarroti, celebrate in Firenze dall'Accademia de Pittori, Scultori, & Architettori nella chiesa di S. Lorenzo il di 14 Luglio, MDLXIIII*. Firenze, Giunti, 1564. (New ed., introduced, translated, and annotated by Rudolf & Margot Wittkower: London, Phaidon, 1964).

8216. Goldscheider, Ludwig. *Michelangelo: paint-*

ings, sculptures, architecture. London, Phaidon, 1962. 4 ed.

8217. ———. *A survey of Michelangelo's models in wax and clay.* London, Phaidon, 1962.

8218. Gotti, Aurelio. *Vita di Michelangelo Buonarotti.* 2 v. Firenze, Gazzetta d'Italia, 1875.

8219. Granchi, Giovanni, et al. *Atti del Convegno di Studi Michelangelo, Firenze-Roma 1964.* Roma, Ateneo, 1966.

8220. Grimm, Hermann. *Life of Michelangelo.* Trans. by Fanny E. Bunnett. 2 v. London, Smith, Elder, 1865. (New ed.: Boston, Little, Brown, 1896).

8221. Harford, John S. *The life of Michael Angelo Buonarroti, with translations of many of his poems and letters.* 2 v. London, Longman, 1857.

8222. Hartt, Frederick. *Michelangelo.* New York, Abrams, 1965.

8223. ———. *Michelangelo drawings.* New York, Abrams, 1970. (CR).

8224. ———. *Michelangelo; the complete sculpture.* New York, Abrams, 1968.

8225. ———. *Michelangelo's three pietàs: a photographic study by David Finn.* Text by Frederick Hartt. New York, Abrams, 1976.

8226. Hauchecorne, l'Abbé. *Vie de Michel-Ange Buonarotti, peintre, sculpteur et architecte de Florence.* Paris, Cellot, 1783.

8227. Heusinger, Lutz. *Michelangelo.* Antella (Florence), SCALA; New York, Riverside, 1989. (The library of great masters).

8228. Heusinger, Lutz. *Michelangelo: life and works in chronological order.* Trans. by Lisa Clark. London, Constable, 1978.

8229. Hibbard, Howard. *Michelangelo.* New York, Harper & Row, 1974. (2 ed. 1985).

8230. Hirst, Michael. *Michelangelo and his drawings.* New Haven, Yale University Press, 1988.

8231. Holroyd, Charles. *Michael Angelo Buonarroti.* London, Duckworth, 1911. 2 ed.

8232. Ipser, Karl. *Michelangelo, der Künstler-Prophet der Kirche.* Augsburg, Kraft, 1963.

8233. Jahn, Johannes. *Michelangelo.* Leipzig, Seemann, 1963.

8234. Justi, Carl. *Michelangelo; Beiträge zur Erklärung der Werke und des Menschen.* Berlin, Grote, 1922. 2 ed.

8235. Knackfuss, Hermann. *Michelangelo.* Bielefeld/Leipzig, Velhagen & Klasing, 1895; new ed.: 1914. (Künstler-Monographien, 4).

8236. Knapp, Fritz. *Michelangelo.* Stuttgart, Deutsche Verlags-Anstalt, 1906. (Klassiker der Kunst, 7).

8237. Kriegbaum, Friedrich. *Michelangelo Buonarroti, die Bildwerke.* Berlin, Rembrandt, 1940.

8238. Leites, Nathan Constantin. *Art and life: aspects of Michelangelo.* New York, New York University Press, 1986. (Psychoanalytic crosscurrents).

8239. Liebert, Robert S. *Michelangelo: a psychoanalytic study of his life and images.* New Haven, Yale University Press, 1983.

8240. Ludwig, Emil. *Michelangelo.* Berlin, Rowohlt, 1930.

8241. Mackowsky, Hans. *Michelagniolo.* Berlin, Marquardt, 1908. (New ed.: *Michelangelo.* Stuttgart, Metzler, 1939).

8242. Magherini, Giovanni. *Michelangiolo Buonarrati.* Firenze, Barbèra, 1875.

8243. Maio, Romeo de. *Michelangelo e la Controriforma.* Roma, Laterza, 1978.

8244. Mariani, Valerio. *Michelangelo, the painter.* Milano, Ricordi, 1964.

8245. Michelangelo Buonarroti. *Il carteggio di Michelangelo.* Edizione posthuma di Giovanni Poggi, a cura di Paola Barocchi e Renzo Ristori. 4 v. Firenze, Sansoni, 1965–79.

8246. ———. *Il carteggio indiretto di Michelangelo.* A cura die Paola Barocchi, Kathleen Loach Bramanti, Renzo Ristori. v. 1– . Firenze, S.P.E.S., 1988– .

8247. ———. *The letters of Michelangelo, translated from the original Tuscan.* Edited and annotated by E. H. Ramsden. 2 v. London, Owen, 1963.

8248. ———. *Making & meaning, the young Michelangelo.* London, National Gallery Publications; [New Haven], Yale University Press, 1994.

8249. ———. *Michelangelo drawings.* Edited by Craig Hugh Smyth in collaboration with Ann Gilkerson. Washington, National Gallery of Art; Hannover, N.H., distributed by the University Press of New England, 1992. (Studies in the history of art, 33. Symposium papers, 17).

8250. Montreal Museum of Fine Arts. *The genius of the sculptor in Michelangelo's work.* [Exhibition catalogue]. Montreal, Montreal Museum of Fine Arts, 1992.

8251. Morgan, Charles H. *The life of Michelangelo.* New York, Reynal, 1960.

8252. Murray, Linda. *Michelangelo.* New York, Oxford University Press, 1980.

8253. Norton, Charles Eliot. *List of the principal books relating to the life and works of Michel Angelo.* With notes by Charles Eliot Norton. Republished from the Bulletin of the Library of Harvard University, March, June, and October, 1878 and January and March 1879. Cambridge, Mass. Press of J. Wilson and Son, 1879.

8254. Ollivier, Emile. *Michel-Ange.* Paris, Garnier, 1892.

8255. Papini, Giovanni. *Dante e Michelangiolo.* Milano, Mondadori, 1961.

8256. ———, ed. *Michelangiolo Buonarroti nel IV centenario del Giudizio Universale (1541–1941).* Firenze, Sansoni, 1942.

8257. Parronchi, Alessandro. *Opere giovanili di Michelangelo.* 3 v. Firenze, Olschki, 1968–81.

8258. Passerini, Luigi. *La bibliografia di Michelangelo Buonarroti e gli incisori delle sue opere.* Firenze, Cellini, 1875.

8259. Perrig, Alexander. *Michelangelo Studien.* 4 v. Frankfurt a.M., Peter Lang/Bern, Herbert Lang, 1976–7. (Kunstwissenschaftliche Studien, 1–4).

8260. ———. *Michelangelo's drawings: the science of attribution.* Translated by Michael Joyce. New Haven, Yale Uiversity Press, 1991.

8261. Popp, Anny E. *Die Medici-Kapelle Michelangelos.* München, Recht, 1922.

8262. Powers, Harry M. *The art of Michelangelo.* New York, Macmillan, 1935.

8263. Quasimodo, Salvatore [and] Camesasca, Ettore. *L'opera completa di Michelangelo, pittore.* Milano, Rizzoli, 1966. (CR). (Classici dell'arte, 1; English ed. with an introduction by L. D. Ettinger: New York, Abrams, 1959).

8264. Quatremère de Quincy, Antoine C. *Histoire de la vie et des ouvrages de Michel-Ange Bonarroti.* Paris, Didot, 1835.

8265. Redig de Campos, Deoclezio [and] Biagetti, Biagio. *Il Giudizio Universale di Michelangelo.* Prefazione di Bartolomeo Nogara. 2 v. Roma, Faccioli, 1944.

8266. Ricci, Corrado. *Michelangelo.* Firenze, Barbèra, 1900.

8267. Roberts, Jane. *A dictionary of Michelangelo's watermarks.* Milano, Olivetti, 1988.

8268. Romdahl, Axel. *Michelangelo.* Stockholm, Norstedt, 1943.

8269. Rossi, Giuseppe I. *La libreria Medicea-Laurenziana, architettura di Michelagnolo Buonarroti.* Firenze, Stamperia Granducale, 1739.

8270. Salmi, Mario, et al. *The complete work of Michelangelo.* New York, Reynal, 1965.

8271. Salviati, Lionardo. *Orazione di Lionardo Salviati nella morte di Michelagnolo Buonarroti.* Firenze, Stamperia Ducale, 1564.

8272. Salvini, Roberto. *The hidden Michelangelo.* Oxford, Phaidon, 1978.

8273. ———. *The Sistine Chapel.* Appendix by Ettore Camesasca. With an essay by C. L. Ragghianti. 2 v. New York, Abrams, 1971.

8274. Schiavo, Armando. *La vita e le opere architettoniche di Michelangelo.* Roma, La Libreria dello Stato, 1953. 2 ed.

8275. Schmidt, Heinrich [and] Schadewaldt, Hans. *Michelangelo und die Medizin seiner Zeit.* Stuttgart, Schattauer, 1965.

8276. Schott, Rudolf. *Michelangelo.* Translated and adapted by Constance McNab. New York, Tudor, 1963.

8277. Seymour, Charles, Jr. *Michelangelo: the Sistine Chapel ceiling.* New York, Norton, 1972.

8278. ———. *Michelangelo's David: a search for identity.* Pittsburgh, University of Pittsburgh Press, 1967.

8279. Spahn, Martin. *Michelangelo und die Sixtinische Kapelle; eine psychologisch-historische Studie über die Anfänge der abendländischen Religions- und Kulturspaltung.* Berlin, Grote, 1907.

8280. Steinmann, Ernst. *Das Geheimnis der Medicigräber Michel Angelos.* Leipzig, Hiersemann, 1907.

8281. ———. *Michelangelo im Spiegel seiner Zeit.* Leipzig, [Privatdruck], 1930. (Römische Forschungen der Bibliotheca Herziana, 8).

8282. ———. *Die sixtinische Kapelle.* 2 v. München, Bruckmann, 1901/1905.

8283. ——— und Wittkower, Rudolf. *Michelangelo Bibliographie, 1510–1926.* Leipzig, Klinkhardt & Biermann, 1927. (Römische Forschungen der Bibliotheca Herziana, 1).

8284. Summers, David. *Michelangelo and the language of art.* Princeton, N.J., Princeton University Press, 1981.

8285. Symonds, John A. *The life of Michelangelo Buonarroti, based on studies in the archives of the Buonarroti family at Florence.* 2 v. London, Nimmo, 1893.

8286. Thode, Henry. *Michelangelo; kritische Untersuchungen über seine Werke.* 3 v. Berlin, Grote, 1908–1913.

8287. ———. *Michelangelo und das Ende der Renaissance.* 3 v. Berlin, Grote, 1902–1913.

8288. Tolnay, Charles de. *The art and thought of Michelangelo.* Trans. by Nan Buranelli. New York, Pantheon, 1964.

8289. ———. *Corpus dei disegni di Michelangelo.* Presentazione di Mario Salmi. 4 v. Novara, De Agostino, 1975–80. (CR).

8290. ———. *Michelangelo.* 5 v. Princeton, N.J., Princeton University Press, 1947–1960. (Reprint: 1969–70).

8291. ———. *Michelangelo: sculptor, painter, architect.* Trans. by Gaynor Woodhouse. Princeton, N.J., Princeton University Press, 1975.

8292. Torti, Luigi. *La concezione estetica di Michelangelo.* Pavia, Marelli, 1974.

8293. Varchi, Benedetto. *Orazione funerale . . . fatta e recitata da lui pubblicamente nell'essequie di Michelagnolo Buonarroti in Firenze, nella chiesa di San Lorenzo.* Firenze, Giunti, 1564.

8294. Venturi, Adolfo. *Michelangelo.* Trans. by Joan Redfern. London/New York, Warne, 1928.

M

8295. Weinberger, Martin. *Michelangelo, the sculptor.* 2 v. London, Routledge/New York, Columbia University Press, 1967.

8296. Wilde, Johannes. *Michelangelo and his studio.* Introduction by A. E. Popham. London, Trustees of the British Museum, 1953.

8297. ———. *Michelangelo: six lectures.* Oxford, Clarendon Press, 1978.

8298. Wilson, Charles H. *The life and works of Michelangelo Buonarroti.* London, Murray, 1876.

8299. Wölfflin, Heinrich. *Die Jugendwerke des Michelangelo.* München, Ackermann, 1891.

8300. Zevi, Bruno e Portoghesi, Paolo. *Michelangelo architetto.* Saggi di Giulio C. Argan et al. Catalogo delle opere a cura di Franco Barbieri e Lionello Puppi. Torino, Einaudi, 1964. (CR).

Michelozzo di Bartolommeo, 1396–1472
see also Brunelleschi, Filippo and Donatello

8301. Caplow, Harriet M. *Michelozzo.* 2 v. New York, Garland, 1977.

8302. Morisani, Ottavio. *Michelozzo architetto.* Torino, Einaudi, 1951. (Collana storica di architettura, 1).

8303. Wolff, Fritz. *Michelozzo di Bartolommeo, ein Beitrag zur Geschichte der Architektur und Plastik im Quattrocento.* Strassburg, Heitz, 1900. (Zur Kunstgeschichte des Auslandes, 2).

Mieris, Frans van, 1635–1681

8304. Naumann, Otto. *Frans von Mieris.* 2 v. Doornspijk, Davaco, 1981. (CR).

Mies van der Rohe, Ludwig, 1886–1969

8305. Art Institute of Chicago. *Mies van der Rohe.* April 27–June 30, 1968. Text by A. James Speyer. Chicago, Art Institute, 1968.

8306. ———. *Mies reconsidered: his career, legacy, and disciples.* [Exhibition] organized by John Zukowsky; with essays by Francesco Dal Co . . . [et al.]. Chicago, Art Institute of Chicago. New York, Rizzoli International Publications, 1986.

8307. Bill, Max. *Ludwig Mies van der Rohe.* Traduzione autorizzata di Cornelia Tamborini. Milano, Il Balcone, 1955.

8308. Blake, Peter. *Mies van der Rohe, architecture and structure.* Baltimore, Penguin, 1964.

8309. Blaser, Werner. *After Mies: Mies van der Rohe—teaching and principles.* New York, Van Nostrand Reinhold, 1977.

8310. ———. *Mies van der Rohe.* Trans. by D. Q. Stephenson. New York, Praeger, 1972. 2 ed.

8311. Carter, Peter. *Mies van der Rohe at work.* New York, Praeger, 1974.

8312. Drexler, Arthur. *Ludwig Mies van der Rohe.* New York, Braziller, 1960.

8313. Glaeser, Ludwig. *Ludwig Mies van der Rohe: furniture and furniture designs from the Design Collection and the Mies van der Rohe Archive* [of the Museum of Modern Art]. New York, Museum of Modern Art, 1977.

8314. Hilberseimer, Ludwig. *Mies van der Rohe.* Chicago, Theobald, 1956.

8315. Hochman, Elaine S. *Architects of Fortune: Mies van der Rohe and the Third Reich.* New York, Weidenfeld & Nilcolson, 1989.

8316. Johnson, Philip C. *Mies van der Rohe.* New York, Museum of Modern Art, 1978; distributed by New York Graphic Society, Boston. 3 ed.

8317. Machulskii, Gennadii K. *Mis van der Roe.* Moskva, Izd-vo litry po stroitel'stvu, 1969.

8318. Mies van der Rohe. Ludwig. *The Mies van der Rohe archive.* Edited by Arthur Drexler; with introductory notes by A. Drexler and Franz Schulze. v. 1–20. New York, Garland Publishing, 1986–1995.

8319. Neumeyer, Fritz. *The artless word: Mies van der Rohe on the Building Art.* Translated by Mark Jarzombek. Cambridge, Mass., MIT Press, 1991.

8320. Pawley, Martin. *Mies van der Rohe.* With photographs by Yukio Futagawa. New York, Simon & Schuster, 1970.

8321. Schulze, Franz. *Mies van der Rohe: a critical biography.* [By] F. Schulze in association with the Mies van der Rohe Archive of the Museum of Modern Art. Chicago/London, University of Chicago Press, 1985.

8322. Spaeth, David A. *Ludwig Mies van der Rohe; an annotated bibliography and chronology.* With a foreword by George E. Danforth. New York/London, Garland, 1979. (Papers of the American Association of Architectural Bibliographers, 13).

8323. ———. *Mies van der Rohe.* Preface by Kenneth Frampton. New York, Rizzoli, 1985.

Milano, Giovanni da see Giovanni da Milano

Millais, John Everett, 1829–1896

8324. Baldry, Alfred L. *Sir John Everett Millais, his art and influence.* London, Bell, 1899.

8325. Bolton Museum and Art Gallery (London). *The drawings of John Everett Millais.* July 7–August 4, 1979. London, Arts Council of Great Britain, 1979.

8326. Fish, Arthur. *John Everett Millais, 1829–1896.* London, Cassell, 1923.

8327. Hall, John N. *Trollope and his illustrators.* London, Macmillan, 1980.

8328. Lutyens, Mary. *Millais and the Ruskins.* London, Murray, 1967.

8329. Lutyens, Mary and Warner, Malcolm, eds. *Rainy days at Brig O'Turk: the highland sketchbooks of John Everett Millais, 1853.*

Westerham, England, Dalrymple Press, 1983.

8330. Millais, Geoffroy. *Sir John Everett Millais*. London, Academy, 1979.

8331. Millais, John G. *The life and letters of Sir John Everett Millais*. 2 v. London, Methuen, 1899.

8332. Pythian, John E. *Millais*. London, Allen, 1911.

8333. Ruskin, John. *Notes on some of the principal pictures of Sir John Everett Millais, exhibited at the Grosvenor Gallery, 1886, with a preface and original selected criticisms*. London, Reeves, 1886.

8334. Spielmann, Marion H. *Millais and his works, with a chapter Thoughts on our art of to-day by Sir J. E. Millais*. Edinburgh/London, Blackwood, 1898.

8335. Watson, J.N.P. *Millais. Three generations in nature, art and sport*. London, Sportsman's Press, 1988.

Miller, Kenneth Hayes, 1876–1952

8336. Burroughs, Alan. *Kenneth Hayes Miller*. New York, Whitney Museum of American Art, 1931.

8337. Goodrich, Lloyd. *Kenneth Hayes Miller*. New York, The Arts, 1930.

8338. Rothschild, Lincoln. *To keep art alive: the effort of Kenneth Hayes Miller, American painter (1876–1952)*. Philadelphia, Art Alliance Press, 1974.

Milles, Carl, 1875–1955

8339. Ångström, Astrid S. *Carl Milles*. Stockholm, Forum, 1956.

8340. Arvidsson, Karl A. *Carl Milles and Millesgården*. With photographs by Anna Riwkin-Brick. Trans. by Eric Dancy and P. E. Burke. Stockholm, Rabén & Sjögren, 1960.

8341. Cornell, Henrik. *Carl Milles and the Milles Gardens*. Photographers: Sune Sundahl and others. Stockholm, Bonniers, 1957.

8342. Köper, Conrad. *Carl Milles*. Stockholm, Norstedt, 1913.

8343. Lidén, Elisabeth. *Between water and heaven: Carl Milles, search for American commissions*. Stockholm, Almqvist & Wiksell International; Montclair, N.J., A. Schram, 1986.

8344. Rogers, Meyric R. *Carl Milles; an interpretation of his work*. New Haven, Yale University Press, 1940.

8345. Verneuil, Maurice P. *Carl Milles, sculpteur suédois; suivi de deux études*. 2 v. Paris, van Oest, 1929.

8346. Westholm, Alfred. *Milles, en bok om Carl Milles konst*. Stockholm, Norstedt, 1949.

Millet, Jean François, 1814–1875

8347. Ady, Julia Mary Cartwright. *Jean François Millet: His life and letters, by Julia Cartwright (Mrs. Henry Ady) . . . with nine photogravures by the Swan electric engraving Co., and Messrs. Braun Clement & cie,m of Paris*. London, S.Sonnenschein & Co., Ltd.; New York, The Macmillan Company, 1896.

8348. [Anonymous]. *Le livre d'or de J.-F. Millet par un ancien ami, illustré de dix-sept eauxfortes originales par Frédéric Jacques*. Paris, Ferroud, [1891].

8349. Bacou, Roseline. *Millet dessins*. Paris, Bibliothèque des Arts, 1975.

8350. Bénédite, Léonce. *The drawings of Jean-François Millet*. Philadelphia, Lippincott, 1906.

8351. Cartwright, Julia. *Jean François Millet, his life and letters*. London, Sonnenschein/New York, Macmillan, 1896.

8352. Dali, Salvador. *Le mythe tragique de l'Angelus de Millet*. Paris, Pauvert, 1963. (New ed.: 1978).

8353. Fermigier, André. *Jean-François Millet*. New York, Rizzoli, 1977.

8354. Gensel, Walther. *Millet and Rousseau*. Bielefeld/Leipzig, Velhagen & Klasing, 1902. (Künstler-Monographien, 57).

8355. Hayward Gallery (London). *Jean-François Millet. 22 January–7 March 1976*. [Text by Robert L. Herbert et al.]. London, Arts Council of Great Britain, 1976.

8356. Laughton, Bruce. *The drawings of Daumier and Millet*. New Haven, Yale University Press, 1991.

8357. Lepoittevin, Lucien. *Jean-François Millet*. 2 v. [Vol. I: *Portraitiste, essai et catalogue*; préf. par René Jullian. Vol. II: *L'ambiguité de l'image, essai*; préf. par Frédéric Mégret]. Paris, Laget, 1971/1973.

8358. ———. *Jean-François Millet, bibliographie générale*. Préf. par Pierre Leberruyer. [Cherbourg], La Fenêtre Ouverte, 1980.

8359. Marcel, Henry. *J.-F. Millet, biographie critique*. Paris, Laurens, [1904].

8360. Meixner, Laura L. *An international episode: Millet, Monet and their North American counterparts: [exhibition] the Dixon Gallery and Gardens, Memphis, November 21, 1982–December 23, 1982; Terra Museum of American Art, Evanston, Illinois, January 8–February 13, 1983; Worcester Art Museum, Worcester, Massachusetts, March 3–April 30, 1983*. Memphis, Dixon Gallery and Gardens, 1982.

8361. Moreau-Nélaton, Etienne. *Millet raconté par lui-même*. 3 v. Paris, Laurens, 1921.

8362. Murphy, Alexandra R. *Jean François Millet*. Boston, Museum of Fine Arts, 1984; distributed by Little Brown.

8363. Muther, Richard. *J. F. Millet*. Berlin, Bard, [1904]. (Die Kunst, 17).

8364. Naegely, Henry. *J. F. Millet and rustic art*. London, Stock, 1898.

8365. Sensier, Alfred. *Jean-François Millet, peasant and painter.* Trans. by Helena de Kay. Boston, Osgood, 1881.

8366. Soullié, Louis. *Peintures, aquarelles, pastels, dessins de Jean-François Millet relevés dans les catalogues de ventes de 1849 à 1900, précédé d'une notice biographique par Paul Mantz.* Paris, Souillé, 1900. (Les grands peintres aux ventes publiques, 2).

8367. Tilborgh, Louis van, Heugten, Sjraar van, and Conisbee, Philip, eds. *Van Gogh and Millet.* Zwolle, The Netherlands, Waanders; Amsterdam, Rijksmuseum Vincent van Gogh, 1989.

8368. Tomson, Arthur. *Jean-François Millet and the Barbizon school.* London, Bell, 1903.

8369. Weisberg, Gabriel P. *Millet and his Barbizon contemporaries.* Tokyo, Art Life, 1985.

8370. Yriarte, Charles. *J. F. Millet.* Paris, Rouam, 1885.

Mills, Robert, 1781–1855

8371. Bryan, John M. *Robert Mills, architect, 1781–1855.* [Published in conjunction with an exhibition at the Columbia Museum of Art, Columbia, S.C., October 1–31, 1976, and other places]. Columbia, S.C., Columbia Museum of Art, 1976.

8372. Gallagher, Helen M. *Robert Mills, architect of the Washington Monument, 1781–1855.* New York, Columbia University Press, 1935.

8373. Marsh, Blanche. *Robert Mills, architect in South Carolina.* Columbia, S.C., Bryan, 1970.

8374. Mills, Robert. *The Scholarly Resources microfilm edition of the papers of Robert Mills, 1781–1855.* Ed. by Pamela Scott. Wilmington, Delaware, Scholarly Resources, Inc., 1990.

Minne, Georg, 1866–1941

8375. Museum voor Schone Kunsten (Ghent). *George Minne en de kunst rond 1900.* 18 september 1982 tot 5 december 1982. Gent, Gemeentekrediet, 1982.

8376. Puyvelde, Leo van. *George Minne.* Bruxelles, Cahiers de Belgique, 1930.

8377. Ridder, André de. *George Minne.* Anvers, De Sikkel, 1947. (Monographies de l'art belge, 3).

Mino da Fiesole, 1429–1484

8378. Angeli, Diego. *Mino da Fiesole.* Florence, Alinari, 1905.

8379. Cionini Visani, Maria. *Mino da Fiesole.* Milano, Fabbri, 1966. (I maestri della scultura, 62).

8380. Lange, Hildegard. *Mino da Fiesole; ein Beitrag zur Geschichte der florentinischen und römischen Plastik des Quattrocentos.* Greifswald, Abel, 1928.

8381. Sciolla, Gianni C. *La scultura di Mino da Fiesole.* Torino, Giappichelli, 1970.

Miró, Joan, 1893–1983

8382. Bonnefoy, Yves. *Miró.* New York, Viking, 1967.

8383. Catalá Roca, Francesc. *Miró, ninety years.* Text by Lluís Permanyer. London, Macdonald, 1986.

8384. Cirici Pellicer, Alejandro. *Miró y la imaginación.* Barcelona, Omega, 1949.

8385. Cirlot, Juan E. *Joan Miró.* Barcelona, Cobalto, 1949.

8386. Corredor-Matheos, José. *Los carteles de Miró.* Catálogo de los carteles por Gloria Picazo. Barcelona, Polígrafa, 1980. (CR).

8387. Dupin, Jacques. *Joan Miró, life and work.* Trans. by Norbert Guterman. New York, Abrams, 1962. (CR).

8388. ———. *Miró engraver.* New York, Rizzoli, 1989.

8389. Erben, Walter. *Joan Miró.* München, Prestel, 1959.

8390. Fondation Maeght. *Joan Miró; peintures, sculptures, dessins, céramiques, 1956–1979.* 7 juillet–30 septembre 1979. Saint-Paul, Fondation Maeght, 1979.

8391. Fondation Maeght (Saint Paul). *Joan Miró: rétrospective de l'oeuvre peint.* 4 juillet–7 octobre 1990. Saint-Paul, La Fondation, 1990.

8392. Fundació Joan Miró-Centre d'Estudis d'Art Contemporani. *The Joan Miró Foundation and its collections.* [2nd ed.]. Barcelona, Fundació Joan Miró, 1993.

8393. Gallerie civiche d'arte moderna, Palazzo dei Diamanti. *Joan Miró.* 16 marzo–15 giugno 1985. [Comune di Ferrara, Assessorato istituzioni cultuali in collaborazione con la Fondazione Joan Miró di Barcelona]. [Ferrara], Cassa di risparmio di Ferrara, [1985].

8394. Gimferrer, Pere. *Miró: colpir sense nafrar.* Barcelona, Polígrafa, 1978.

8395. Gimferrer, Pere. *The roots of Miró.* Barcelona, Parets de Vallès; Ediciones Polígrafa; New York, distributed in the USA and Canada by Rizzoli, 1993.

8396. Grand Palais (Paris). *Joan Miró.* 17 mai–13 octobre 1974. Paris, Editions des Musées Nationaux, 1974.

8397. Greenberg, Clement. *Joan Miró.* New York, Quadrangle, 1948.

8398. Hirmer (München). *Joan Miró, Skulpturen.* Organisation, Peter A. Ade; Übersetzung, Ulrike Schleiffer. München, Hirmer, 1990.

8399. Hunter, Sam. *Joan Miró, his graphic work.* New York, Abrams, 1958.

8400. Jouffroy, Alain. *Miró.* Trans. by Charles Lynn Clark. New York, Universe Books; distributed to the trade by St. Martin's Press, 1987.

8401. Lassaigne, Jacques. *Miró, biographical and critical study*. Trans. by Stuart Gilbert. Lausanne, Skira, 1963. (The Taste of Our Time, 39).

8402. Leiris, Michel. *Joan Miró, lithographe*. Catalogue et notices [by] Fernand Mourlot. 4 v. Paris, Mazo, 1972–81. (CR). (English ed., vol. I only: trans. by P. Niemark, New York, Tudor, 1972).

8403. Melià, Josep. *Joan Miró, vida y testimonio*. Barcelona, Dopesa, 1975.

8404. Miró, Joan. *Joan Miró, 1893–1993*. Barcelona, Fundació Joan Miró; Milán, Leonardo Arte, 1993.

8405. Miró, Joan. *Joan Miró: Arbeiten auf Papier 1901–1977*. Mit Texten von Georges Bataille . . . [et al.]. Herausgegeben von Carl Haenlein. (Kestner Gesellschaft, Hannover, Katalog 5/6, 1989).

8406. Miró, Joan. *Joan Miró: la ceramica*. A cura di Gian Carlo Bojani e Trinidad Sanchez-Pacheco. (Strumenti di studio per la ceramica del XIX e XX secolo, 13). Centro Di cat. 252. Firenze, Centro Di, 1991.

8407. Miró, Joan. *Miró sculptures from the Fondation Maeght*. [Edinburgh], Trustees of the National Galleries of Scotland, 1992.

8408. Miró, Joan. *Joan Miró: selected writings and interviews*. Ed. by Margit Rowell. Translations from the French by Paul Aster; translations from the Spanish and Catalan by Patricia Mathews. Boston, G.K. Hall, 1986.

8409. Museo Español de Arte Contemporáneo (Madrid). *Joan Miró, pintura*. 4 mayo–23 julio 1978. [Text by Julián Gállego et al.]. Barcelona, Polígrafa, 1978.

8410. Museum of Fine Arts (Montreal). *Miró in Montreal*. Montreal, Museum of Fine Arts, 1986.

8411. Museum Ludwig (Cologne). *Miró der Bildhauer*. 10. April bis 8. Juni 1987. [Katalog von Gloria Moure]. Köln, Das Museum, 1987.

8412. Penrose, Roland. *Miró*. New York, Abrams, 1969.

8413. ———. *Miró*. New York, Thames and Hudson, 1985.

8414. Perucho, Juan. *Joan Miró y Cataluña*. [Text in Spanish, English, French, and German]. Barcelona, Polígrafa, [1968].

8415. *Picasso, Miró, Dalí und der Beginn der spanischen Moderne, 1900–1936*. In Zusammenarbeit mit dem Museo Nacional Centro de Arte Reina Sofía, Madrid. [Katalog, Gesamtredaktion, Sabine Schulze; Redaktion der Übersetzungen, Karsten Garscha]. Frankfurt am Main, Schirn Kunsthalle Frankfurt, 1991.

8416. Picon, Gaëtan, ed. *Joan Miró, carnets catalans: dessins et texte inédits*. 2 v. Genève, Skira, 1976.

8417. Pierre Matisse Gallery (New York). *Miró, the last bronze sculptures, 1981–1983*. 26 May–20 June 1987. [Introduction by Margit Rowell]. New York, The Gallery, 1987.

8418. Rose, Barbara. *Miró in America*. With essays by Judith McCandless and Duncan Hamilton. Houston, Museum of Fine Arts, 1982.

8419. Rowell, Margit. *The captured imagination: drawings by Joan Miró from the Fundació Joan Miró, Barcelona*. New York, American Federation of Arts; Philadelphia, Clothbound edition distributed by the University of Pennsylvania Press, 1987.

8420. Rowell, Margit. *Miró*. New York, Abrams, 1970.

8421. Rubin, William. *Miro in the collection of the Museum of Modern Art*. New York, Museum of Modern Art, 1973; distributed by New York Graphic Society, Greenwich, Conn.

8422. Salas de la Dirección General del Patrimonio Artístico, Archivos y Museos (Madrid). *Joan Miró, obra gráfica*. 4 mayo–23 julio 1978. [Text by Joan Teixidor]. Barcelona, Polígrafa, 1978.

8423. Serra, Pere A. *Miró and Mallorca*. With a foreword by Camilo José Cela. New York: Rizzoli, 1986.

8424. Soby, James T. *Joan Miró*. New York, Museum of Modern Art, 1959; distributed by Doubleday, Garden City, N.Y.

8425. Solomon R. Guggenheim Museum (New York). *Joan Miró, a retrospective*. New Haven, Yale University Press, 1987.

8426. South Bank Centre (London). *Joan Miró: sculpture*. [Exhibition organised by Alexandra Noble; assisted by Richard Halstead]. London, South Bank Centre, 1989.

8427. Stich, Sidra. *Joan Miró: the development of a sign language*. [Published in conjunction with an exhibition at the Washington University Gallery of Art, St. Louis, Mo., March 19–April 27, 1980]. St. Louis, Washington University, 1980.

8428. Sweeney, James J. *Joan Miró*. [Published in conjunction with an exhibition at the Museum of Modern Art, New York, 1941]. New York, Museum of Modern Art, 1941.

8429. Taillandier, Ivon. *Mirógrafías: dibujos, grabados sobre cobre, litografías, grabados sobre madera, libros, carteles*. Barcelona, Gili, 1972.

8430. Weelen, Guy. *Miró*. Trans. by Robert Erich Wolf. New York, Abrams, 1989.

Modena, Tomaso da *see* **Tomaso da Modena**

Modersohn-Becker, Paula, 1876–1907

8431. Busch, Günter. *Paula Modersohn-Becker:*

Malerin, Zeichnerin. Frankfurt a.M., Fischer, 1981. (CR).

8432. Clemens-Sels-Museum (Neuss). *Paula Modersohn-Becker, Worpswede, Paris.* 13. Oktober bis 15. Dezember 1985. [Neuss], Das Museum 1985.

8433. Harke, Peter J. *Stilleben von Paula Modersohn-Becker.* [Lilienthal], Worpsweder Verlag, 1985.

8434. Hetsch, Rolf, ed. *Paula Modersohn-Becker, ein Buch der Freundschaft.* Berlin, Rembrandt, 1932.

8435. Krininger, Doris. *Modell, Malerin, Akt: über Suzanne Valadon und Paula Modersohn-Becker.* (Sammlung Luchterhand 588). Darmstadt, Luchterhand, 1986.

8436. Kunsthalle Bremen. *Paula Modersohn-Becker zum hundertsten Geburtstag.* 8. Februar bis 4. April 1976. Bremen, Kunsthalle Bremen, 1976.

8437. Kunstverein in Hamburg. *Paula Modersohn-Becker: Zeichnungen, Pastelle, Bildentwürfe.* 25. September bis 21. November 1976. Hamburg, Kunstverein in Hamburg, 1976.

8438. Modersohn-Becker, Paula. *The letters and journals of Paula Modersohn-Becker.* Translated and annotated by J. Diane Radycki. Metuchen, N.J./London, Scarecrow Press, 1980.

8439. ———. *Paula Modersohn-Becker.* With an essay by Jane Kallir. New York, Galerie St. Etienne, 1983.

8440. ———. *Paula Modersohn-Becker in Briefen und Tagebüchern.* Herausgegeben von Günter Busch und Liselotte von Reinken. Frankfurt a.M., Fischer, 1979.

8441. ———. *Paula Modersohn-Becker, das Frühwerk.* [Lilienthal-Worphausen], Worpswede, 1985. (Zweite Veröffentlichung der Paula Modersohn-Becker-Stiftung.)

8442. Murken-Altrogge, Christa. *Paula Modersohn-Becker: Leben und Werk.* Köln, DuMont, 1980.

8443. Pauli, Gustav. *Paula Modersohn-Becker.* München, Wolff, 1919. (Das neue Bild, 1).

8444. Perry, Gillian. *Paula Modersohn-Becker, her life and work.* New York, Harper & Row, 1979.

8445. Stelzer, Otto. *Paula Modersohn-Becker.* Berlin, Rembrandt, 1958. (Die Kunst unserer Zeit, 12).

8446. Uphoff, Carl E. *Paula Modersohn.* Leipzig, Klinkhardt & Biermann, 1919. (Junge Kunst, 2).

Modigliani, Amedeo, 1884–1920

8447. Carli, Enzo. *Amedeo Modigliani, con una testimonianza di Jean Cassou.* Roma, de Luca, 1952.

8448. Ceroni, Ambrogio. *Amedeo Modigliani, dessins et sculptures.* Milano, Edizioni del Milione, 1965. (Monographes des artistes italiens modernes, 8).

8449. ———. *Amedeo Modigliani, peintre.* Milano, Edizioni del Milione, 1958. (Monographie des artistes italiens modernes, 6).

8450. Fifield, William. *Modigliani.* New York, Morrow, 1976.

8451. Gindertael, Roger V. *Modigliani e Montparnasse.* Milano, Fabbri, 1969.

8452. Hall, Douglas. *Modigliani.* Oxford, Phaidon, 1984. (Rev. and enlarged ed.).

8453. Jedlicka, Gotthard. *Modigliani, 1884–1920.* Erlenbach/Zürich, Rentsch, 1953.

8454. Lanthemann, Jacques. *Modigliani, 1884–1920; catalogue raisonné; sa vie, son oeuvre complet, son art.* Barcelona, Gráficas Condal, 1970. (CR).

8455. Mann, Carol. *Modigliani.* New York/Toronto, Oxford University Press, 1980.

8456. Modigliani, Jeanne. *Modigliani: man and myth.* Trans. by Esther R. Clifford. New York, Orion, 1958; distributed by Crown, New York.

8457. Modigliani, Jeanne. *Modigiani, une biographie.* Paris, Adam Biro, 1990.

8458. Musée d'Art Moderne de la Ville de Paris. *Amedeo Modigliani: 1884–1920.* 26 mars–28 juin 1981. [XXe anniversaire]. Paris, Musée d'Art Moderne de la Ville de Paris, 1981.

8459. Parisot, Christian. *Modigliani.* [Exposition]. Paris, P.Terrail, 1991.

8460. ———. *Modigliani: catalogue raisonné.* Ed. by Giorgio et Guido Guastella. Textes par Christian Parisot, Jeanne Modigliani, Fulvio Venturi. Livorno, Graphis Arte, 1990–1991. (CR).

8461. Patani, Osvaldo. *Amedeo Modigliani.* [catalogo]. Milano, Leonardo, 1991.

8462. Pfannstiel, Arthur. *Dessins de Modigliani.* Lausanne, Mermod, 1958.

8463. ———. *Modigiliani.* Préface de Louis Latourrettes. Paris, Seheur, 1929.

8464. ———. *Modigliani et son oeuvre; étude critique et catalogue raisonné.* Paris, Bibliothèque des Arts, 1956. (CR).

8465. Piccioni, Leone [and] Ceroni, Ambrogio. *I dipinti di Modigliani.* Milano, Rizzoli, 1970. (Classici dell'arte, 40).

8466. Rose, June. *Modigliani, the pure bohemian.* London, Constable, 1990.

8467. Roy, Claude. *Modigliani.* New York, Rizzoli; Geneva, Skira, 1985.

8468. Russoli, Franco. *Modigliani, drawings and sketches.* Trans. by John Shepley. New York, Abrams, 1969. (CR).

8469. Salmon, André. *Modigliani, a memoir.* Trans. by Dorothy and Randolph Weaver. New York, Putnam, 1961.

8470. ———. *Modigliani, sa vie et son oeuvre.* Paris, Editions des Quatre Chemins, 1926.

8471. Santini, Aldo. *Modigliani*. Milano, Rizzoli, 1987.
8472. Scheiwiller, Giovanni. *Modigliani*. Milano, Hoepli, 1927.
8473. [————, ed.]. *Omaggio a Modigliani, 1884–1920*. Milano, Società Anonima Tipografica Editoriale, 1930.
8474. Schmalenbach, Werner. *Amedeo Modigliani: Malerei, Skulpturen, Zeichungen*. München, Prestel, 1990.
8475. ————. *Amedeo Modigliani: paintings, sculptures, drawings*. Translations from the German by David Britt and Peter Underwood, from the French by Caroline Beamish, and from the Italian by Brian Binding. Munich, Prestel; New York, Distributed in the USA and Canada by te Neues Pub. Co., 1990.
8476. Sichel, Pierre. *Modigliani; a biography*. New York, Dutton, 1967.
8477. Soby, James T. *Modigliani; paintings, drawings, sculpture*. New York, Museum of Modern Art, 1951.
8478. Werner, Alfred. *Amedeo Modigliani*. New York, Abrams, 1966.

Moholy-Nagy, László, 1895–1946

8479. Caton, Joseph Harris. *The utopian vision of Moholy-Nagy*. Ann Arbor, UMI Research Press, 1984.
8480. Centre de Création Industrielle, Centre Georges Pompidou (Paris). *Laszlo Moholy-Nagy*. [18 novembre 1976 au 31 janvier 1977]. Paris, Centre National d'Art et de Culture Georges Pompidou, 1976.
8481. Haus, Andreas. *Moholy-Nagy; Fotos und Fotogramme*. München, Schirmer/Mosel, 1978.
8482. Hight, Eleanor M. *Picturing modernism: Moholy-Nagy and photography in Weimar Germany*. Cambridge, Mass., MIT Press, 1995.
8483. Kostelanetz, Richard, ed. *Moholy-Nagy*. New York/Washington, D.C., Praeger, 1970.
8484. Lusk, Irene-Charlotte. *Montagen ins Blaue: Laszlo Moholy-Nagy; Fotomontagen und -collagen, 1922–1943*. Berlin, Anabas, 1980.
8485. Moholy, Lucia. *Moholy-Nagy, marginal notes*. Krefeld, Scherpe, 1972.
8486. Moholy-Nagy, László. *Frühe Photographien*. Berlin, Nishen, 1989.
8487. ————. *Malerei, photographie, film*. München, Langen, 1925. (English ed., trans. by Janet Seligman: Cambridge, Mass., MIT Press, 1969).
8488. ————. *Moholy-Nagy, a new vision for Chicago: Illinois State Museum, Springfield and Chicago*. [Curator, Terry Suhre]. Springfield, University of Illinois Press and the Illinois State Museum, 1990.
8489. ————. *The new vision, from material to architecture*. Trans. by Daphne M. Hoffmann. New York, Brewer, Warren, 1932.
8490. ————. *60 Fotos*. Herausgegeben von Franz Roh. Berlin, Klinkhardt & Biermann, 1930.
8491. ————. *Vision in motion*. Chicago, Theobald, 1947.
8492. Moholy-Nagy, Sibyl. *Moholy-Nagy, experiment in totality*. With an introduction by Walter Gropius. New York, Harper, 1950. (New ed.: Cambridge, Mass., MIT Press, 1969).
8493. Passuth, Krisztina. *Moholy-Nagy*. New York, Thames and Hudson, 1985.
8494. Rondolino, Gianni. *Laszlo Moholy-Nagy; pittura, fotografia, film*. Con prefazione di Giulio C. Argan. Torino, Martano, 1975.

Moll, Oskar, 1875–1947

8495. Krickau, Heinz B. *Oskar Moll*. Leipzig, Klinkhardt & Biermann, 1921. (Junge Kunst, 19).
8496. Salzmann, Siegfried und Salzmann, Dorothea. *Oskar Moll, Leben und Werk*. München, Bruckmann, 1975. (CR).
8497. Scheyer, Ernst. *Die Kunstakademie Breslau und Oskar Moll*. Würzburg, Holzner, 1961.

Möller, Anton, 1563–1611

8498. Gyssling, Walter. *Anton Möller und seine Schule; ein Beitrag zur Geschichte der Niederdeutschen Renaissance-Malerei*. Strassburg, Heitz, 1917. (Studien zur deutschen Kunstgeschichte, 197).
8499. Möller, Antonius. *Der Danziger Frauen und Jungfrauen gebreuchliche Zierheit und Tracht*. Danzig, Rhodo, 1601. (Reprint: Danzig, Bertling, 1886).

Moller, Georg, 1784–1852

8500. Frölich, Marie [and] Sperlich, Hans-Günther. *Georg Moller, Baumeister der Romantik*. Darmstadt, Roether, 1959.
8501. Magistrat der Stadt Darmstadt. *Darmstadt in der Zeit des Klassizismus und der Romantik*. 19. November 1978 bis 14. Januar 1979. [Konzeption und Katalogbear-beitung zur Georg Moller: Eva Huber]. Darmstadt, Magistrat der Stadt Darmstadt, 1978.
8502. Moller, Georg. *Beiträge zu der Lehre von den Constructionen*. 7 v. Darmstadt, Leske, 1833–44.
8503. ————. *Denkmäler der deutschen Baukunst*. 3 v. [Vol. 3 ed. by Ernst Gladbach]. Leipzig/Darmstadt, Leske, [1844]. 2 ed.

Mondriaan, Pieter Cornelis, 1872–1944

8504. Art Gallery of Toronto. *Piet Mondrian, 1872–1944*. February 12–March 10, 1966. Catalogue by Robert P. Welsh. Toronto, Art Gallery of Toronto, 1966.

8505. Blok, Cor. *Piet Mondriaan, een catalogus van zijn werk in Nederlands openbaarbezit.* Amsterdam, Meulenhoff, 1974.

8506. Blotkamp, Carel. *Mondrian: the art of destruction.* New York, H.N. Abrams, 1995.

8507. Champa, Kermit Swiler. *Mondrian studies.* Chicago, University of Chicago Press, 1985.

8508. Elgar, Frank. *Mondrian.* Trans. by Thomas Walton. New York, Praeger, 1968.

8509. Jaffé, Hans Ludwig. *Mondrian und De Stijl.* Köln, Schauberg, 1967.

8510. ———. *Piet Mondrian.* New York, Abrams, 1970.

8511. ———. *Piet Mondrian.* Paris, Editions Cercle d'art, 1991.

8512. Joosten, Joop M. and Welsh, Robert. *Piet Mondrian: catalogue raisonné.* Naarden, V + K Publications, 1995. (CR).

8513. Lemoine, Serge. *Mondrian and De Stijl.* Trans. by Charles Lynn Clark. England, Art Data, 1987.

8514. Menna, Filiberto. *Mondrian, cultura e poesia.* Prefazione di Giulio C. Argan. Roma, Ateneo, 1962. (Nuovi saggi, 36).

8515. Milner, John. *Mondrian.* New York, Abbeville Press, 1992.

8516. Mondrian, Piet. *Mondrian: from figuration to abstraction.* General composition by Herbert Henkels. Trans. by Ruth Koenig. Tokyo, Tokyo Shimbun, 1987. [Catalog of an exhibition of works from the Haags Gemeentemuseum in the Netherlands and the Sidney Janis Gallery in New York held July 25–Aug. 31, 1987 at the Seibu Museum of Art, Tokyo; Sept. 5–Oct. 4, 1987 at the Miyagi Museum of Art; Oct. 10–Nov. 8, 1987 at the Museum of Modern Art, Shiga].

8517. ———. *Piet Mondrian de la figuration: a l'abstraction: oeuvres du Haags Gemeentemuseum de La Haye.* [Exposition et catalogue realisés par Jean-Louis Prat]. Saint-Paul, Fondation Maeght, 1985. [Catalog of an exhibition Mar. 23–May 16, 1985, Fondation Maeght, Saint-Paul, France].

8518. ———. *Piet Mondrian, the wall works, 1943–44.* New York, Carpenter & Hochman, 1984. [Catalog of an exhibition held Oct.–Nov. 1984, Carpenter & Hochman Gallery, New York, and Dec. 1984–Jan. 1985, Carpenter & Hochman Gallery, Dallas].

8519. ———. *Gedurende een wandeling van buiten naar de stad.* Hague, Haags Gemeentemuseum/Gravura, 1986.

8520. ———. *Le néo-plasticisme.* Paris, Editions de l'Effort Moderne, 1920. New edition: Amersfoort, Stichting Mondriaanhuis, 1994.

8521. ———. *The new art—the new life: the collected writings of Piet Mondrian.* Ed. and Trans. by Harry Holtzman and Martin S. James. Boston, G.K. Hall, 1986.

8522. ———. *Piet Mondriaan in het Haags Gemeentemuseum = Piet Mondrian in the Haags Gemeentemuseum.* Hague, Haags Gemeentemuseum, 1985.

8523. ———. *Plastic art and pure plastic art, 1937, and other essays, 1941–1943.* New York, Wittenborn, 1945.

8524. Morisani, Ottavio. *L'astrattismo di Piet Mondrian.* Venezia, Pozza, 1956. (Collezione di varia critica, 13).

8525. Ottolenghi, Maria G. *L'opera completa di Mondrian.* Milano, Rizzoli, 1974. (CR). (Classici dell'arte, 77).

8526. Ragghianti, Carlo L. *Mondrian e l'arte de XX secolo.* Milano, Edizioni di Comunità, 1962.

8527. Seuphor, Michel [pseud., Ferdinand L. Berckelaers]. *Piet Mondrian, life and work.* New York, Abrams, 1956. .

8528. Solomon R. Guggenheim Museum. *Piet Mondrian, 1872–1944; centennial exhibition.* [Oct. 8–Dec. 12, 1971]. New York, Guggenheim Foundation, 1971.

8529. Threlfall, Tim. *Piet Mondrian, his life's work and evolution, 1872 to 1944.* New York, Garland Pub., 1988.

8530. Welsh, Robert, Bakker, Boudewijn, Bax, Marty. *Piet Mondriaan: the Amsterdam years, 1892–1912.* With contributions by Peter-Paul de Baar . . . [et al.]. Ed. by Margriet de Roever. Amsterdam, Gemeentearchief; Bussum, Thoth, 1994.

8531. Wijsenbeek, Louis J. F. *Piet Mondrian.* Trans. by Irene R. Gibbons. Greenwich, Conn., New York Graphic Society, 1969.

8532. Wismer, Beat. *Mondrians: ästhetische Utopie.* Baden, LIT, 1985.

Monet, Claude, 1840–1926

8533. Alexandre, Arsène. *Claude Monet.* Paris, Bernheim, 1921.

8534. Clemenceau, Georges. *Claude Monet: the Water Lilies.* Trans. by George Boas. Garden City, N.Y., Doubleday, 1930.

8535. ———. *Georges Clemenceau á son ami Claude Monet: correspondance.* Paris, Editions de la Réunion des musées nationaux, 1993.

8536. Cogniat, Raymond. *Monet and his world.* Trans. by Wayne Dynes. New York, Viking, 1966.

8537. Crespelle, Jean Paul. *Monet.* New York, Universe Books, 1986.

8538. Decker, Michel de. *Claude Monet: une vie.* Paris, Perrin, 1992.

8539. Elder, Marc [pseud., Marcel Tendron]. *Giverny chez Claude Monet.* Paris, Blenheim, 1924.

8540. Fels, Marthe de. *La vie de Claude Monet.* Paris, Gallimard, 1929. (Vies des hommes illustres, 33).

8541. Fourny-Dargère, Sophie. *Monet*. [Paris], Chêne, 1992.

8542. Geffroy, Gustave. *Claude Monet, sa vie, son oeuvre*. Paris, Crès, 1922.

8543. Gordon, Robert and Forge, Andrew. *Monet*. New York, Abrams, 1983.

8544. Grand Palais (Paris). *Hommage à Claude Monet (1840–1926)*. 8 février–5 mai 1980. Paris, Editions de la Réunion des Musée Nationaux/Ministère de la Culture et de la Communication, 1980.

8545. Grappe, Georges. *Claude Monet*. Paris, Librairie Artistique Internationale, [1911].

8546. Gwynn, Stephen. *Claude Monet and his garden; the story of an artist's paradise*. New York, Macmillan, 1934.

8547. Hoschedé, Jean-Pierre. *Claude Monet, ce mal connu; intimité familiale d'un demi-siècle à Giverny de 1883 à 1926*. 2 v. Genève, Cailler, 1960.

8548. House, John. *Monet*. Oxford, Phaidon, 1981. (2 ed., rev. and enl.).

8549. Howard, Michael. *Monet*. London, Brompton, 1989.

8550. Isaacson, Joel. *Claude Monet: observation and reflection*. Oxford, Phaidon, 1978.

8551. ———. *Monet: Le Déjeuner sur l'Herbe*. New York, Viking, 1972.

8552. Joyes, Claire. *Monet at Giverny*. Photographic and editorial research by Robert Gordon and Jean-Marie Toulgouat. With a commentary on the paintings at Giverny by Andrew Forge. London, Mathews Miller Dunbar, 1975.

8553. Keller, Horst. *Ein Garten wird Malerei: Monets Jahre in Giverny*. Köln, DuMont, 1982.

8554. Lathom, Xenia. *Claude Monet*. London, Allan, 1931.

8555. Levine, Steven Z. *Monet and his critics*. New York, Garland, 1976.

8556. Leymarie, Jean. *Monet*. 2 v. Paris, Hazan, 1964. (Petite encyclopédie de l'art, 59–60).

8557. Martini, Alberto. *Monet*. Milano, Fabbri, 1964. (I maestri del colore, 30).

8558. Mauclair, Camille. *Claude Monet*. Trans. by J. Louis May. New York, Dodd, 1924.

8559. Metropolitan Museum of Art (New York). *Monet's years at Giverny: beyond Impressionism*. [April 22–July 9, 1978; text by Daniel Wildenstein et al.]. New York, Metropolitan Museum, 1978; distributed by Abrams, New York.

8560. Mirbeau, Octave. *Correspondance avec Claude Monet*. [Edition établie, présentée et annotée par Pierre Michel et Jean François Nivet]. Tusson, Charente, Du Lèrot, 1990.

8561. *Monet in Holland*. Zwolle, Waanders; Amsterdam, Rijksmuseum Vincent van Gogh in samenwerking met het Gemeentearchief Amsterdam, 1986.

8562. Monet, Claude. *Claude Monet: paintings in Soviet museums*. Introduction by Nina Kalitina. Notes on the plates by Anna Barskaya and Eugenia Georgievskaya. Trans. by Hugh Aplin and Ruslan Smirnov. Leningrad, Aurora Art Publishers, 1990.

8563. ———. *Monet, a retrospective*. Ed. by Charles F. Stuckey. New York, Hugh Lauter Levin Associates; distributed by the Scribner Book Companies, 1985.

8564. ———. *Monet by himself: paintings, drawings pastels, letters*. Ed. by Richard Kendall. Trans. by Bridget Strevens Romer. London, Macdonald Orbis, 1989.

8565. Morisani, Ottavio. *Il linguaggio di Monet e la crisi dell'impressionismo*. Napoli, Libreria Scientifica Editrice, 1971.

8566. Mount, Charles M. *Monet, a biography*. New York, Simon & Schuster, 1966.

8567. Murray, Elizabeth. *Monet's passion: ideas, inspiration and insights from the painter's gardens*. Illustrated by Heather O'Connor. Petaluma, Calif., Pomegranate Artbooks, 1989.

8568. Musée de l'Orangerie (Paris). *Claude Monet, exposition rétrospective*. [Text by Paul Jamot]. Paris, Les Musées Nationaux, 1931.

8569. Petrie, Brian. *Claude Monet, the first of the Impressionists*. Oxford, Phaidon/New York, Dutton, 1979.

8570. Proietti, Maria L. *Lettere di Claude Monet*. Assisi/Roma, Carucci, 1974.

8571. Reuterswärd, Oscar. *Monet, en konstnärshistorik*. Stockholm, Bonniers, 1948.

8572. Reymond, Nathalie. *Claude Monet*. Paris, Lattés, 1992.

8573. Rossi Bortolato, Luigina. *L'opera completa di Claude Monet, 1870–1889*. Milano, Rizzoli, 1972. (Classici dell'arte, 63).

8574. Rouart, Denis. *Claude Monet*. Introduction and conclusion by Léon Degand. Trans. by James Emmons. [New York], Skira, 1958. (The Taste of Our Time, 25).

8575. ———, et Rey, Jean-Dominique. *Monet: Nymphéas, ou les miroirs du temps*. Suivi d'un catalogue raisonné par Robert Maillard. Paris, Hazan, 1972. (CR).

8576. Seitz, William. *Claude Monet*. New York, Abrams, 1960. (New ed.: 1971).

8577. Spate, Virginia. *The colour of time: Claude Monet*. London, Thames and Hudson, 1992.

8578. Stuckey, Charles F. *Claude Monet, 1840–1926*. Chicago, Art Institute, 1995.

8579. Taillandier, Yvon. *Monet*. Paris, Flammarion, [1963].

8580. Tucker, Paul H. *Monet at Argenteuil*. New Haven, Yale University Press, 1982.

8581. Weekes, C. P. *Camille, a study of Claude Monet*. London, Sidgwick and Jackson, 1962. 2 ed.

8582. Wildenstein, Daniel. *Claude Monet, bio-*

graphie et catalogue raisonné [1840–1898].
3 v. Lausanne/Paris, La Bibliothèque des
Arts, 1974–1979. (CR).

Montagna, Bartolomeo, ca. 1450–1523

8583. Foratti, Aldo. *Bartolomeo Montagna*. Padova, Drucker, 1908.
8584. Puppi, Lionello. *Bartolomeo Montagna*. Venezia, Pozza, 1962.

Monticelli, Adolphe, 1824–1886

8585. Alauzen, André M. et Ripert, Pierre. *Monticelli, sa vie et son oeuvre*. Paris, Bibliothèque des Arts, 1969. (CR).
8586. Arnaud d'Agnel, G. et Isnard, Emile. *Monticelli, sa vie et son oeuvre (1824–1886)*. Paris, Occitania, 1926.
8587. Centre de la Vieille Charité (Marseille). *Adolphe Monticelli, 1824–1886*. 12 octobre 1986–4 janvier 1987. Marseille, Direction des Musées de Marseille, Editions J. Laffitte, [1986].
8588. Coquiot, Gustave. *Monticelli*. Paris, Michel, 1925.
8589. Galerie Jacques Dubourg (Paris). *Exposition Monticelli, 1824–1886*. Novembre–décembre 1942. Paris, Galerie Jacques Dubourg, [1942].
8590. Garibaldi, Charles et Garibaldi, Mario. *Monticelli*. Genève, Skira, 1991.
8591. Guinand, Louis. *La vie et les oeuvres de Monticelli*. Marseilles, Aubertin, 1894.
8592. Isnard, Guy. *Monticelli sans sa légende*. Genève, Cailler, 1967.
8593. Museum of Art, Carnegie Institute (Pittsburgh). *Monticelli; his contemporaries, his influence*. October 27, 1978 to January 7, 1979. Text by Aaron Sheon. Pittsburgh, Museum of Art, Carnegie Institute, 1978.
8594. Négis, André. *Adolphe Monticelli, chatelain des nues*. Paris, Grasset, 1929. (La vie de Bohème, 7).
8595. Sheon, Aaron. *Monticelli, his contemporaries, his influence*. [Catalogue of an exhibition at the Museum of Art, Carnegie Institute, Pittsburgh, and others, Oct. 27, 1978–Jan. 7 1979]. Pittsburgh, Museum of Art, Carnegie Institute, 1978.
8596. Stammegna, Sauveur. *Catalogue des oeuvres de Monticelli*. 2 v. Vence, Imprimerie des Ramparts, 1981–1986. (CR).
8597. ———. *Les faux Monticelli*. [Vence, Imprimérie des Ramparts], 1987.

Moore, Henry Spencer, 1898–

8598. Argan, Giulio C. *Henry Moore*. Trans. by Daniel Dichter. New York, Abrams, 1973.
8599. Berthoud, Roger. *The life of Henry Moore*. London/Boston, Faber and Faber, 1987.
8600. Clark, Kenneth. *Henry Moore, drawings*. London, Thames and Hudson, 1974.

8601. Compton, Susan P. *Henry Moore*. With contributions by Richard Cork and Peter Fuller. London, Royal Academy of Arts, in association with Weidenfeld and Nicolson, 1988.
8602. Cramer, Gérard, et al. *Henry Moore: catalogue of graphic works*. 2 v. [Vol. I: 1931–1972; Vol. II: 1973–1975]. Genève, Cramer, 1972-[1976]. (CR).
8603. Davis, Alexander, ed. and comp. *Henry Moore bibliography*. Hertfordshire, England, Henry Moore Foundation, 1992.
8604. Finn, David. *Henry Moore: sculpture and environment*. Foreword by Kenneth Clark. Commentaries by Henry Moore. New York, Abrams, 1977.
8605. Forte di Belvedere (Florence). *Mostra di Henry Moore*. 20 maggio–30 settembre 1972. A cura di Giovanni Carandente. Firenze, Il Bisonte, 1972.
8606. Garrould, Ann. *Henry Moore drawings*. New York, Rizzoli, 1988.
8607. Grigson, Geoffrey. *Henry Moore*. Harmondsworth [Eng.], Penguin, 1943.
8608. Grohmann, Will. *Henry Moore*. New York, Abrams, 1960.
8609. Hall, Donald. *Henry Moore, the life and work of a great sculptor*. New York, Harper, 1966.
8610. Hedgecoe, John [and] Moore, Henry. *Henry Moore*. Photographed and edited by John Hedgecoe; words by Henry Moore. New York, Simon & Schuster, 1968.
8611. Jianou, Ionel. *Henry Moore*. Trans. by Geoffrey Skelding. Paris, Arted, 1968.
8612. Levine, Gemma. *With Henry Moore: the artist at work*. Photographed by Gemma Levine. Preface by David Mitchinson. London, Sidgwick & Jackson, 1978.
8613. Marlborough Fine Art (London). *A tribute to Henry Moore, 1898 1986*. May–June 1987. London, Marlborough Fine Art, [1987].
8614. Melville, Robert. *Henry Moore: sculpture and drawings, 1921–1969*. New York, Abrams, 1970.
8615. Mitchinson, David. *Henry Moore, unpublished drawings*. New York, Abrams, 1972.
8616. Moore, Henry. *Henry Moore, catalogue of graphic work*. Ed. by Gerald Cramer, Alistair Grant, and David Mitchinson. Geneva, G. Cramer, 1973–1986. (CR).
8617. ———. *Henry Moore, complete sculpture*. Ed. by David Sylvester. With an introduction by Herbert Read. London, Lund Humphries, 1988. (5 ed.). (CR).
8618. ———. *Henry Moore on sculpture*. Edited with an introduction by Philip James. New York, Viking, 1971. 2 ed.
8619. ———. *Henry Moore, a Shelter sketchbook*. With a commentary by Frances Carey. Munich, Prestel; New York, distribution for the

USA and Canada only by te Neues Publishing, 1988.

8620. ———. *Henry Moore, wood sculpture.* Commentary by Henry Moore. Photographs by Gemma Levine. New York, Universe Books, 1983.

8621. ———. *Shelter sketch book.* London, Poetry London, 1940.

8622. Neumann, Erich. *The archetypal world of Henry Moore.* Trans. by R. F. C. Hull. New York, Pantheon, 1959.

8623. Read, Herbert. *Henry Moore, a study of his life and work.* New York, Praeger, 1966.

8624. ——— [and] Bowness, Alan. *Henry Moore, sculpture and drawings.* 5 v. London, Lund Humphries/Zwemmer, 1944–1983. (CR).

8625. Russell, John. *Henry Moore.* Baltimore, Penguin, 1973. 2 ed.

8626. Seldis, Henry J. *Henry Moore in America.* New York, Praeger, in association with the Los Angeles County Museum of Art, 1973.

8627. Spender, Stephen. *Henry Moore, sculptures in landscape.* Photographs and foreword by Geoffrey Shakerley. Introduction by Henry Moore. New York, Clarkson Potter, [1980]; distributed by Crown, New York.

8628. ———. *In Irina's garden with Henry Moore's sculpture.* Photographs by David Finn. London/New York, Thames and Hudson, 1986.

8629. Sweeney, James J. *Henry Moore.* New York, Museum of Modern Art, 1946.

8630. Tate Gallery (London). *Henry Moore.* 17 July to 22 September 1968. [Text by David Sylvester]. London, Arts Council of Great Britain, 1968.

8631. Teague, Edward H. *Henry Moore, bibliography and reproductions index.* Jefferson, N.C., McFarland, 1981.

8632. Wilkinson, Alan G. *Henry Moore remembered: the collection at the Art Gallery of Ontario in Toronto.* Toronto, The Gallery, Key Porter Books, 1987.

8633. ———. *The Moore collection in the Art Gallery of Ontario.* [Toronto], Art Gallery of Ontario, 1979.

Mor, Anthonis *see* Moro, Antonio

Morales, Luis de, 1509?–1580

8634. Baecksbacka, Ingjal. *Luis de Morales.* [Text in English]. Helsinki, Paava Heinon Kirjapaino, 1962. (Societas Scientiarum Fennica, Commentationes Humanorum Litterarum, 31).

8635. Berjano Escobar, Daniel. *El pintor Luis de Morales (El Divino).* Madrid, Matev, [1918?].

8636. Gaya Nuno, Juna Antonio. *Luis de Morales.* Madrid, Instituto Diego Velazquez, 1961.

8637. Tormo, Elías. *El Divino Morales.* Barcelona, Thomas, 1917.

8638. Trapier, Elizabeth du Gué. *Luis de Morales and Leonardesque influences in Spain.* New York, Trustees of the Hispanic Society of America, 1953.

Morandi, Giorgio, 1890–1964

8639. Arcangeli, Francesco. *Giorgio Morandi.* Milano, Edizioni del Milione, 1964. (Vite, lettere, testimonianze di artisti italiani, 4).

8640. Basile, Franco. *Morandi incisore.* Italy, La loggia edizioni d'arte, [1985].

8641. Beccaria, Arnaldo. *Giorgio Morandi.* Milano, Hoepli, 1939.

8642. Brandi, Cesare. *Morandi.* Firenze, Le Monnier, 1952.

8643. ———. *Morandi.* Introduzione di Vittorio Rubiu. Con il carteggio Brandi-Morandi, 1938–1963. A cura di Marilena Pasquali. Roma, Editori Riuniti, 1990.

8644. Burger, Angelika. *Die Stilleben des Giorgio Morandi: eine koloritgeschichtliche Untersuchung.* Hildesheim/New York, Olms, 1984. (Studien zur Kunstgeschichte, 35).

8645. Des Moines Art Center (Des Moines, Ia.). *Giorgio Morandi.* February 1–March 14, 1982. [Exhibition opened at the San Francisco Museum of Modern Art, September 24–November 1, 1981]. Des Moines, Des Moines Art Center, 1981.

8646. Folon, Jean Michel. *Flowers by Giorgio Morandi.* Text and photographs by Jean-Michel Folon. Trans. by R. Scott Walker. New York, Rizzoli, 1985.

8647. Galleria d'Arte Moderna (Bologna). *Giorgio Morandi.* 1 maggio–2 giugno 1975; a cura di Lamberto Vitali. Bologna, Grafis, 1975.

8648. Morandi, Giorgio. *Giorgio Morandi.* Milan, Electa, 1989.

8649. ———. *Giorgio Morandi: etchings.* Millbank, London, Tate Gallery, 1991.

8650. ———. *Morandi: acquarelli: catalogo generale.* A cura di Marilena Pasquali. Milano, Electa, 1991. (CR).

8651. ———. *Morandi alla Galleria comunale d'arte moderna di Bologna.* A cura di Franco Solmi. Collaborazione scientifica di Marilena Pasquali. Bologna, Grafis, [1985].

8652. ———. *Morandi: l'opera grafica rispondenze e variazioni.* A cura di Michele Cordaro. Milano, Electa, 1990.

8653. ———. *Omaggio a Giorgio Morandi, nel ventennale della morte: oli, acquarelli, disegni, grafiche.* Testimonianze, Francesco Arcangeli . . . [et al.]. Sasso Marconi, La Casa dell'arte di Sasso Marconi, 1984.

8654. Pasini, Roberto. *Morandi.* Bologna, CLUEB, 1989. (Arte contemporanea, 1).

8655. Pasquali, Marilena. *Morandi: riflessioni*

sull'opera. Piacenza, Galleria Braga, 1991.

8656. Pozza, Neri. *Morandi, dessins/drawings.* [Text in French and English]. Milano/Paris, Idea e, 1976.

8657. Valsecchi, Marco [and] Ruggeri, Giorgio. *Morandi disegni.* A cura di Efrem Tavoni. [Work in progress]. Bologna, Marconi, 1981– . (CR).

8658. Vitali, Lamberto. *Giorgio Morandi, pittore.* Milano, Edizioni del Milione, 1964.

8659. ———. *Morandi, catalogo generale.* 2 v. Milano, Electa, 1977. (CR).

8660. ———. *L'opera grafica di Giorgio Morandi.* 2 v. Torino, Einaudi, 1964/1968.

Morazzone, Pier Francesco, 1573–1626

8661. Musei Civici e Centro di Studi Preistorici e Archeologici Varese, Villa Mirabello (Varese). *Il Morazzone.* 14. luglio–14 ottobre 1962. Catalogo della mostra a cura di Mina Gregori. Milano, Bramante, 1962.

8662. Nicodemi, Giorgio. *Pier Francesco Mazzucchelli, detto Il Morazzone.* Varese, Cronica Prealpina, 1927.

Moreau, Gustave, 1826–1898

8663. Alexandrian, Sarane. *L'univers de Gustave Moreau.* Paris, Scrépel, 1975.

8664. Flat, Paul. *Le Musée Gustave Moreau; l'artiste, son oeuvre, son influence.* Paris, Société d'Edition Artistique, [1899].

8665. Geffroy, Gustave. *L'oeuvre de Gustave Moreau.* Paris, L'Oeuvre d'Art, [1900].

8666. Hahlbrock, Peter. *Gustave Moreau oder das Unbehagen in der Natur.* Berlin, Rembrandt, 1976.

8667. Hofstätter, Hans H. *Gustave Moreau, Leben und Werk.* Köln, DuMont, 1978.

8668. Holten, Ragnar von. *L'art fantastique de Gustave Moreau.* Paris, Pauvert 1961.

8669. Kunsthaus Zürich. *Gustave Moreau, symboliste.* 14. März bis 25. Mai 1986. [Ausstellung und Katalog, Toni Stooss; Mitarbeit, Pierre-Louis Mathieu]. Zürich, Das Kunsthaus, 1986.

8670. Lacambre, Geneviève. *Maison d'artiste, maison-musée: l'exemple de Gustave Moreau.* [Catalogue établi et rédigé par Geneviève Lacambre]. Paris, Ministère de la culture et de la communication, Editions de la Réunion des musées nationaux, 1987. (Les Dossiers du Musée d'Orsay, 12).

8671. Leprieur, Paul. *Gustave Moreau et son oeuvre.* Paris, L'Artiste, 1889.

8672. Los Angeles County Museum of Art. *Gustave Moreau.* July 23–September 1, 1974. [Text by Julius Kaplan]. Los Angeles, Los Angeles County Museum of Art, 1974; distributed by New York Graphic Society, [Greenwich, Conn.].

8673. Mathieu, Pierre-Louis. *Gustave Moreau.* With a catalogue of the finished paintings, watercolors, and drawings. Trans. by James Emmons. Boston, New York Graphic Society, 1976. (CR).

8674. ———. *Gustave Moreau, the watercolors.* New York, Hudson Hills Press, distributed in the U.S. by Viking Penguin, 1985. 1st American ed.

8675. ———. *Le Musée Gustave Moreau.* Paris, Editions de la Réunion des musées nationaux, 1986.

8676. ———. *Tout l'oeuvre peint de Gustave Moreau.* Introduction et catalogue par Pierre-Louis Mathieu. Paris, Flammarion, 1991.

8677. Moreau, Gustave. *Gustave Moreau.* Redaktie, Anke van der Laan. Heerlen, Stadsgalerij Heerlen; Gent, Imschoot, [1991].

8678. ———. *Gustave Moreau: l'elogio del poeta.* A cura di Bruno Mantura e Geneviève Lacambre. Rome, Leonardo-De Luca, 1992.

8679. Paladilhe, Jean and Pierre, José. *Gustave Moreau.* Trans. by Bettina Wadia. New York, Praeger, 1972.

8680. Renan, Ary. *Gustave Moreau (1826–1898).* Paris, Gazette des Beaux-Arts, 1900.

8681. Segalen, Victor. *Gustave Moreau, maître imagier de l'orphisme.* Introduction par P.-L. Mathieu. Texte établi et annoté par Eliane Formentelli. Fontfroide, Bibliothèque artistique & littéraire, 1984.

8682. Selz, Jean. *Gustave Moreau.* Trans. by Alice Sachs. New York, Crown, 1979.

8683. Thévenin, Léon. *L'esthétique de Gustave Moreau.* Paris, Vanier, 1897.

Moreau, Jean Michel, 1741–1815
Louis Gabriel, 1740–1805

8684. Boucher, Emmanuel. *Jean-Michel Moreau le jeune.* Paris, Morgand et Fatout, 1882. (CR). (Catalogue raisonné des estampes, vignettes, eaux-fortes, pièces en couleur au bistre et au lavis de 1700 à 1800, 6).

8685. Draibel, Henri [pseud., Henri Beraldi]. *L'oeuvre de Moreau le jeune, notice & catalogue.* Paris, Rouquette, 1874.

8686. Mahérault, Marie J. F. *L'oeuvre de Moreau le jeune; catalogue raisonné et descriptif avec notes iconographiques et bibliographiques, et précédé d'une notice biographique par Emile de Najac.* Paris, Labitte, 1880. (CR).

8687. Marcel, Pierre. *Carnet de croquis par Moreau le jeune; fac-similé de l'album du Musée du Louvre.* Introduction et description par Pierre Marcel. Paris, Terquem, 1914.

8688. Moreau, Adrien. *Les Moreau.* Paris, Pierson, [1893].

8689. Schéfer, Gaston. *Moreau le jeune, 1741–1814.* Paris, Goupil, 1915.

8690. Wildenstein, Georges. *Un peintre de paysage au XVIII siècle: Louis Moreau.* Paris, Beaux-Arts, 1923.

Moreelse, Paulus, 1571–1638

8691. Jonge, Caroline H. de. *Paulus Moreelse, portret en genreschilder te Utrecht, 1571–1638.* Assen, van Gorcum, 1938.

Moretto, Il, 1498–1554

8692. Boselli, Camillo. *Il Moretto, 1498–1554.* Brescia, Ateneo di Brescia, 1954.

8693. Cassa Salvi, Elvira. *Moretto.* Milano, Fabbri, 1966. (I maestri del colore, 145).

8694. Gombosi, György. *Moretto da Brescia.* Basel, Holbein, 1943.

8695. Molmenti, Pompeo. *Il Moretto da Brescia.* Firenze, Bemporad, 1898.

8696. Ponte, Pietro da. *L'opera del Moretto.* Brescia, Canosi, 1898.

Morisot, Berthe, 1841–1895

8697. Adler, Kathleen and Garb, Tamar. *Berthe Morisot.* Ithaca, Cornell University Press, 1987.

8698. Angoulvent, Monique. *Berthe Morisot.* Preface de Robert Rey. Paris, Morancé, [1933].

8699. Bataille, Maria-Louis et Wildenstein, Georges. *Berthe Morisot; catalogue des peintures, pastels et aquarelles.* Paris, Les Beaux-Arts, 1961. (CR).

8700. Charles E. Slatkin Galleries (New York). *Berthe Morisot: drawings, pastels, watercolors, paintings.* November 12 to December 10, 1960. [Text by Elizabeth Mongan et al.]. New York, Shorewood, 1960; in collaboration with Charles E. Slatkin Galleries, New York.

8701. Edelstein, T.J., ed. and intro. *Perspectives on Morisot.* Essays by Kathleen Adler . . . [et al.]. New York, Hudson Hills Press, distributed by Rizzoli International Publications, 1990.

8702. Fourreau, Armand. *Berthe Morisot.* Trans. by H. Wellington. New York, Dodd, Mead, 1925.

8703. Galerie Durand-Ruel (Paris). *Berthe Morisot (Madame Eugène Manet). 5 au 24 Mars 1896.* Préface de Stéphane Mallarmé. Paris, Galerie Durand-Ruel, 1896.

8704. Higonnet, Anne. *Berthe Morisot.* New York, Harper & Row, 1990.

8705. ———. *Berthe Morisot's images of women.* Cambridge, Mass., Harvard University Press, 1992.

8706. Morisot, Berthe. *Berthe Morisot, the correspondence with her family and her friends: Manet, Puvis de Chavannes, Degas, Monet, Renoir, and Mallarmé.* Compiled and ed. by Denis Rouart. Trans. by Betty W. Hubbard. With a new introduction and notes by Kathleen Adler and Tamar Garb. Mt. Kisco, N.Y., Moyer Bell, 1987.

8707. Rey, Jean D. *Berthe Morisot.* Trans. by Shirley Jennings. Naefels, Switzerland, Bonfini, 1982.

8708. Rouart, Denis, ed. *The correspondence of Berthe Morisot with her family and friends.* Trans. by Betty W. Hubbard. New York, Wittenborn, 1957.

8709. Rouart, Louis. *Berthe Morisot.* Paris, Plon, 1941.

8710. Stuckey, Charles F. and Scott, William P. *Berthe Morisot, Impressionist.* With the assistance of Suzanne G. Lindsay. New York, Hudson Hills Press, distributed in the U.S. by Rizzoli International Publications, 1987.

Morland, George, 1763–1804

8711. Baily, J. T. Herbert. *George Morland, a biographical essay.* London, Otto, 1906.

8712. Collins, William. *Memoirs of a picture . . . including a genuine biographical sketch of the late Mr. George Morland, to which is added a copious appendix, etc.* London, Symonds, 1805. 3 v.

8713. Dawe, George. *The life of George Morland, with remarks on his works.* London, Vernor, Hood, 1807. (New ed.: London, Laurie, 1904).

8714. Gilbey, Walter and Cuming, Edward D. *George Morland, his life and works.* London, Black, 1907.

8715. Hassell, John. *Memoirs of the life of the late G. Morland.* London, Cundee, 1806.

8716. Henderson, Bernard L. *Morland and Ibbetson.* London, Allan, 1923.

8717. Nettleship, John T. *George Morland and the evolution from him of some later painters.* London, Seeley, 1898. (The Portfolio, 39).

8718. Richardson, Ralph. *George Morland, painter, London (1763–1804).* London, Stock, 1895.

8719. Williamson, George C. *George Morland, his life and works.* London, Bell, 1907.

8720. Wilson, David H. *George Morland.* London, Scott/New York, Scribner, 1907.

Moro, Antonio, 1519–1576

8721. Hymans, Henri S. *Antonio Moro, son oeuvre et son temps.* Bruxelles, van Oest, 1910.

8722. Frerichs, L. C. *Antonio Moro.* Amsterdam, Becht, [1947]. (Palet serie, 23).

8723. Friedländer, Max J. *Anthonis Mor and his contemporaries.* Comments and notes by H. Pauwels and G. Lemmens; assisted by M. Gierts. Trans. by Heinz Norden. Leyden, Sijthoff/Brussels, La Connaissance, 1975. (Early Netherlandish Painting, 13).

8724. Marlier, Georges. *Anthonis Mor van Dashorst (Antonio Moro).* Bruxelles, Nouvelle Société d'Editions, 1934.

Morone, Domenico, 1442–1518

8725. Brenzoni, Raffaello. *Domenico Morone, 1458–9 c.–1517 c.; vita ed opere.* Firenze, Olschki, 1956.

8726. Dal-Gal, Niccolò. *Un pittore veronese del quattrocento: Domenico Morone e i suoi affreschi nel chiostro francescano di San Bernardino in Verona.* Roma, Tipografia Editrice Industriale, 1909.

Moroni, Giovanni Battista, 1520–1578

8727. Cugini, Davide. *Moroni, pittore.* Bergamo, Orobiche, 1939.

8728. Lendorff, Gertrud. *Giovanni Battista Moroni, der Porträtmaler von Bergamo.* Winterthur, Schönenberger & Gall, 1933.

8729. Palazzo dell Ragione (Bergamo). *Giovan Battista Moroni (1520–1578).* [Direttore della mostra: Francesco Rossi; coordinamento scientifica: Mina Gregori]. Bergamo, Azienda Autonoma di Turismo, 1979.

8730. Spina, Emma. *Giovan Battista Moroni.* Milano, Fabbri, 1966. (I maestri del colore, 139).

Morris, Robert, 1931–

8731. Contemporary Arts Museum (Houston). *Robert Morris; selected works, 1970–1980.* December 12, 1981–February 14, 1982. [Essay by Marti Mayo]. Houston, Tex., Contemporary Arts Museum, 1981.

8732. Corcoran Gallery of Art (Washington, D.C.). *Robert Morris.* November 24–December 28, 1969. [Essay by Annette Michelson]. Washington, D.C., Corcoran Gallery of Art, 1969.

8733. Tate Galley (London). *Robert Morris.* 28 April–6 June 1971. [Text by Michael Compton and David Sylvester]. London, Tate Gallery, 1971.

8734. Whitney Museum of American Art (New York). *Robert Morris.* April 9–May 31, 1970. [Text by Marcia Tucker]. New York, Whitney Museum of American Art, 1970.

Morris, William, 1834–1896

8735. Aho, Gary L. *William Morris, a reference guide.* Boston, G.K. Hall, 1985.

8736. Boris, Eileen. *Art and labor: Ruskin, Morris, and the craftsman ideal in America.* Philadelphia, Temple University Press, 1986.

8737. Bradley, Ian. *William Morris and his world.* London, Thames and Hudson, 1978.

8738. Cary, Elisabeth L. *William Morris, poet, craftsman, socialist.* New York, Putnam, 1902.

8739. Clark, Fiona. *William Morris, wallpaper and chintzes.* With a biographical note by Andrew Malvin. New York, St. Martin's, 1973.

8740. Clutton-Brock, Arthur. *William Morris: his work and influence.* London, Williams and Norgate, 1914.

8741. Crow, Gerald H. *William Morris, designer.* London, The Studio, 1934.

8742. Eshleman, Lloyd W. *A Victorian rebel; the life of William Morris.* New York, Scribner, 1940.

8743. Fairclough, Oliver and Leary, Emmeline. *Textiles by William Morris and Morris & Co., 1861–1940.* Introduction by Barbara Morris. London, Thames and Hudson, 1981.

8744. Faulkner, Peter. *Against the age: an introduction to William Morris.* London, Allen & Unwin, 1980.

8745. Forman, Harry B. *The books of William Morris described, with some account of his doings in literature and the allied crafts.* London, Hollings, 1897.

8746. Henderson, Philip. *William Morris: his life, work and friends.* London, Thames and Hudson, 1967.

8747. Jackson, Holbrook. *William Morris.* London, Cape, 1926. 2 ed.

8748. Latham, David and Latham, Sheila. *An annotated critical bibliography of William Morris.* London, Harvester Wheatsheaf; New York, St. Martin's Press, 1991.

8749. Lindsay, Jack. *William Morris, his life and work.* London, Constable, 1975.

8750. Mackail, John W. *The life of William Morris.* 2 v. New York, Longmans, Green & co., 1899.

8751. ———. *The life of William Morris.* [New impression. Two volumes in one.] London/New York, Longmans, Green & Co., 1922.

8752. ———. *The life of William Morris.* 2 v. New York, Blom, 1968.

8753. Meynell, Esther H. *Portrait of William Morris.* London, Chapman & Hall, 1947.

8754. Morris, May. *William Morris; artist, writer, socialist.* Oxford, Blackwell, 1936. 2 v.

8755. Morris, William. *Architecture, industry & wealth: collected papers.* London, Longmans, 1902.

8756. ———. *Glass: artifact and art.* Seattle, WA, distributed by University of Washington Press, 1989.

8757. ———. *Gothic architecture: a lecture for the Arts and Crafts Exhibition Society.* London, Kelmscott Press, 1893.

8758. ———. *Hopes and fears for art.* Boston, Roberts, 1882.

8759. ———. *The letters of William Morris to his family and friends.* Edited by Philip Henderson. New York, Longmans, 1950.

8760. ———. *A note by William Morris on his aims in founding the Kelmscott Press.* Together with a short description of the press by S. J. Cockerell, & an annotated list of the books printed thereat. London, Kelmscott Press, 1898.

8761. ———. *On art and socialism; essays and*

lectures. Selected with an introduction by Holbrook Jackson. London, Lehmann, 1947.

8762. ———. *William Morris by himself: designs and writings*. Ed. by Gillian Naylor Boston, Little, Brown, 1988. 1st U.S. ed.

8763. ———. *William Morris's socialist diary*. Ed. and annotated by Florence Boos. London/ West Nyack, NY, Journeyman, 1985.

8764. Parry, Linda. *William Morris textiles*. New York, Viking, 1983.

8765. Pye, John William. *A bibliography of the American editions of William Morris published by Robert Brothers Boston, 1867–1898*. Brockton, Mass. William Pye Rare Books, 1993.

8766. Schleinitz, Otto. *William Morris, sein Leben und Wirken*. 4 v. Bielefeld/Leipzig, Velhagen & Klasing, 1907–8.

8767. Schmidt-Künsemüller, Friedrich A. *William Morris und die neuere Buchkunst*. Wiesbaden, Harrassowitz, 1955.

8768. Scott, Temple. *A bibliography of the works of William Morris*. London, Bell, 1897.

8769. Sewter, A. Charles. *The stained glass of William Morris and his circle*. 2 v. New Haven/ London, Yale University Press, 1974. (CR).

8770. Skoblow, Jeffrey. *Paradise dislocated: Morris, politics, art*. Charlottesville, University Press of Virginia, 1993.

8771. Sparling Henry H. *The Kelmscott Press and William Morris, master-craftsman*. London, Macmillan, 1924.

8772. Stoppani, Leonard, et al. *William Morris & Kelmscott*. London, Design Council, 1981.

8773. Thompson, E.P. *William Morris: romantic to revolutionary*. Stanford, Stanford University Press, 1988.

8774. Thompson, Paul R. *The work of William Morris*. London, Heinemann, 1967.

8775. ———. *The work of William Morris*. Oxford, Clarendon Press; New York, Oxford University Press, 1991. 3 ed.

8776. Vallance, Aymer. *William Morris; his art, his writings and his public life*. London, Bell, 1897.

8777. Vidalenc, Georges. *William Morris*. Paris, Alcan, 1920.

8778. Walsdorf, John J. *William Morris in private press and limited editions: a descriptive bibliography of books by and about William Morris, 1891–1981*. Foreword by Sir Basil Blackwell. Phoenix, Ariz., Oryx Press, 1983.

8779. Watkinson, Ray. *William Morris as designer*. New York, Reinhold, 1967.

Morris, Wright, 1910–

8780. Bird, Roy K. *Wright Morris: memory and imagination*. New York, P. Lang, 1985. (American University Studies, Series IV, English language and literature, vol. 20).

8781. Morris, Wright. *Photographs and·words*. Edited with an introduction by James Alinder. Carmel, Calif., Friends of Photography, 1982. (Untitled: Quarterly of the Friends of Photography, 29).

8782. Phillips, Sandra S. and Szarkowski, John. *Wright Morris: origin of a species: San Francisco Museum of Modern Art*. San Francisco, The Museum, 1992.

8783. Sheldon Memorial Art Gallery, University of Nebraska (Lincoln, Nebr.). *Wright Morris: structures and artifacts; photographs 1933–1954*. October 21–November 16, 1975. Lincoln, Nebr., Sheldon Memorial Art Gallery, 1975.

Morse, Samuel Finley Breese, 1791–1872

8784. Kloss, William. *Samuel F.B. Morse*. New York, H.N. Abrams in association with the National Museum of American Art, Smithsonian Institution, 1988.

8785. Larkin, Oliver W. *Samuel F. B. Morse and American democratic art*. Boston, Little, Brown, 1954.

8786. Mabee, Carleton. *The American Leonardo; a life of Samuel F. B. Morse*. With an introduction by Allan Nevins. New York, Knopf, 1943. (Reprint: New York, Octagon, 1967).

8787. ———. *Samuel F.B. Morse: eine Biographie*. Herausgegeben von Christian Brauner. Basel, Birkhäuser, 1990.

8788. Morse, Samuel F. B. *Lectures on the affinity of painting with the other fine arts*. Edited with an introduction by Nicolai Cikovsky, Jr. Columbia, Mo./London, University of Missouri Press, 1983.

8789. ———. *Samuel F. B. Morse, his letters and journals*. Edited and supplemented by his son. 2 v. Boston/New York, Houghton Mifflin, 1914. (Reprint: New York, Da Capo, 1973).

8790. Prime, Samuel F. *The life of Samuel F. B. Morse, the inventor of the electro-magnetic telegraph*. New York, Appleton, 1875.

8791. Staiti, Paul J. *Samuel F.B. Morse*. Cambridge/ New York, Cambridge University Press, 1989.

8792. Wehle, Harry B. *Samuel F. B. Morse, American painter*. A study occasioned by an exhibition of his paintings [at the Metropolitan Museum of Art, New York] February 16 through March 27, 1932. New York, Metropolitan Museum of Art, 1932.

Moser, Lukas, ca. 1400–ca. 1450

8793. May, Helmut. *Lucas Moser*. Stuttgart, Fink, 1961.

8794. Piccard, Gerhard. *Der Magdalenenaltar des Lukas Moser in Tiefenbronn; ein Beitrag zur europäischen Kunstgeschichte*. Wiesbaden, Harrassowitz, 1969.

M

Moses, Grandma *see* **Robertson, Anna Mary**

Mostaert, Jan, ca. 1475–1556

8795. Pierron, Sander. *Les Mostaert: Jean Mostaert, dit le maître d'Oultremont; Gilles et François Mostaert; Michel Mostaert.* Bruxelles/Paris, van Oest, 1912.

Motherwell, Robert, 1915–

8796. Arnason, H. Harvard. *Robert Motherwell.* Introduction by Dore Ashton. New York, Abrams, 1982. 2 ed.

8797. Flam, Jack D. *Motherwell.* New York, Rizzoli, 1991.

8798. Mattison, Robert Saltonstall. *The art of Robert Motherwell during the 1940's.* 1985.

8799. ———. *Robert Motherwell, the formative years.* Ann Arbor, UMI Research Press, 1987. (Studies in the fine arts. The Avantgarde, 56).

8800. Motherwell, Robert. *The collected writings of Robert Motherwell.* Ed. by Stephanie Terenzio. New York, Oxford University Press, 1992.

8801. ———. *Robert Motherwell: the Dedalus sketchbooks.* Ed. and selected by Constance and Jack Glenn. Introduction by Constance Glenn. New York, H.N. Abrams, 1988.

8802. ———. *Robert Motherwell: forty-five years of printmaking.* [Exhibition]. Nov. 29–Dec. 31, 1988. New York, Associated American Artists, [1988].

8803. Museum of Modern Art (New York). *Robert Motherwell.* Sept. 30–Nov. 28, 1965. New York, Museum of Modern Art, 1965; distributed by Doubleday, Garden City, N.Y.

8804. Städtische Kunsthalle Düsseldorf. *Robert Motherwell.* [Text by Robert C. Hobbs et al., in English and German]. Düsseldorf, Städtische Kunsthalle, 1976.

8805. Terenzio, Stephanie. *The painter and the printer: Robert Motherwell's graphics, 1943–1980.* Catalogue raisonné by Dorothy C. Belknap. New York, American Federation of Arts, 1980. (CR).

8806. ———. *The prints of Robert Motherwell.* [Catalogue raisonné, 1943–1990 by Dorothy C. Belknap]. New York, Hudson Hills Press in association with the American Federation of Arts, distributed in the U.S. by Rizzoli, 1991. (CR).

Mount, William Sidney, 1807–1868

8807. Armstrong, Janice Gray. *Catching the tune: music and William Sidney Mount.* Stony Brook, NY, Museums at Stony Brook, 1984.

8808. Cassedy, David and Shrott, Gail. *William Sidney Mount: works in the collection of the Museums at Stony Brook.* Ed. by Janice Gray Armstrong. Stony Brook, N.Y., Museums at Stony Brook, 1983.

8809. Cowdrey, Bartlett and Williams, Hermann W., Jr. *William Sidney Mount, 1807–1868; an American painter.* With a foreword by Harry B. Wehle. New York, published for the Metropolitan Museum of Art by Columbia University Press, 1944.

8810. Frankenstein, Alfred. *William Sidney Mount.* New York, Abrams, 1975.

8811. Museums at Stony Brook (Stony Brook, NY). *William Sidney Mount, annotated bibliography and listings of archival holdings of the Museums at Stony Brook.* Compiled and written by David Cassedy and Gail Shrott. Ed. by Janice Gray Armstrong. Stony Brook, N.Y., The Museums, 1983.

Mucha, Alphonse Marie, 1860–1939

8812. Arwas, Victor. *Alphonse Mucha: master of art nouveau.* London, Academy Editions; New York, St. Martin's Press, 1985.

8813. Bridges, Ann, ed. *Alphonse Mucha, the complete graphic work.* Foreword by Jiři Mucha. Contributions by Marina Henderson and Anna Dvořak. New York, Harmony, 1980. (CR).

8814. Mathildenhöhe Darmstadt. *Alfons Mucha, 1860–1939.* 8. Juni bis 3. August 1980. Darmstadt, Mathildenhöhe Darmstadt/ München, Prestel, 1980. (CR).

8815. Mucha, Alphonse. *Lectures on art.* New York, St. Martin's/London, Academy, 1975.

8816. ———. *Alfons Mucha: Meditation und Botschaft.* Organisation, Documenta und Museum Fridericianum Veranstaltungs GmbH, Galerie der Hauptstadt Prag. Herausgeber des Kataloges, Veit Loers. Kassel, Museum Fridericianum, Weber & Weidemeyer, 1989.

8817. Mucha, Jiři. *Alphonse Mucha; his life and art, by his son.* London, Heinemann, 1966. (New ed.: Praha, Miadá Fronta, 1982).

8818. ———. *Alphonse Maria Mucha: his life and art.* London, Academy Editions, 1989.

8819. ———, et al. *Alphonse Mucha, revised, enlarged edition.* New York, St. Martin's/ London, Academy, 1974.

8820. Ovenden, Graham. *Alphonse Mucha, photographs.* New York, St. Martin's/London, Academy, 1974.

Muche, Georg, 1895–

8821. Busch, Ludger. *Muche: Georg Muche, Dokumentation zum malerischen Werk der Jahre 1915 bis 1920: ein Diskussionsbeitrag zum Expressionismus.* Tübingen, E. Wasmuth, 1984.

8822. Muche, Georg. *Blickpunkt: Sturm, Dada, Bauhaus, Gegenwart.* München, Langen/ Müller, 1961.

8823. ———. *Der alte Maler: Briefe von Georg Muche, 1945–1984.* [Herausgegeben vom

Bauhaus-Archiv in Berlin]. Bearbeitung und Redaktion, Ute Ackermann. Tübingen, E. Wasmuth, 1992.

8824. ———. *Georg Muche: das künstlerische Werk, 1912–1927: kritisches Verzeichnis der Gemälde, Zeichnungen, Fotos und architektonishen Arbeiten.* Bearbeitet von Magdalena Droste. Unter Mitwirkung von Christian Wolsdorff und Bauxi Mang. Mit Textbeiträgen von Georg Muche . . . [et al]. Herausgegeben vom Bauhaus-Archiv, Berlin. Berlin, Mann, 1980.

8825. Richter, Horst. *George Muche.* Recklinghausen, Bongers, 1960. (Monographien zur Rheinisch-Westfälischen Kunst der Gegenwart, 18).

8826. Schiller, Peter H. *George Muche: das druckgraphische Werk. Kritisches Verzeichnis.* Darmstadt/Berlin, Bauhaus-Archiv, 1970. (CR).

8827. Städtische Galerie Schwarzes Kloster, Freiburg im Breisgau. *Muche, Zeichnungen und Druckgraphik aus den Jahren 1912–73.* 27. Oktober bis 25. November 1973. Freiburg i.Br., Städtische Galerie Schwarzes Kloster, 1973.

Muelich, Hans, 1516–1573
8828. Röttger, Bernhard H. *Der Maler Hans Muelich.* München, Schmidt, 1925.

Müller, Friedrich, 1749–1825
8829. Bernardini, Ingrid Sattel and Schlegel, Wolfgang. *Friedrich Müller, 1749–1825: der Maler.* Landau/Pfalz, Edition PVA, 1986.

8830. Unverricht, Konrad. *Die Radierungen des Maler Müller ein Beitrag zur Geschichte der deutschen Kunst im späten achtzehnten Jahrhundert.* Speyer am Rhein, Jaeger, 1930.

Mueller, Otto, 1874–1930
8831. Buchheim, Lothar-Günther. *Otto Mueller, Leben und Werk.* Mit einem Werkverzeichnis der Graphik Otto Muellers von Florian Karsch. Feldafing, Buchheim, 1963. (CR).

8832. Galerie Nierendorf (Berlin). *Otto Mueller zum hundertsten Geburtstag: das graphische Gesamtwerk.* [November 25, 1974–March 18, 1975]. Berlin, Galerie Nierendorf, 1974. (CR).

8833. Lüttichau, Mario-Andreas von. *Otto Mueller, ein Romantiker unter den Expressionisten.* Köln, DuMont, 1993.

Münter, Gabriele, 1877–1962 *see also* Kandinsky, Wassily
8834. Galerie Neher (Essen). *Gabriele Münter und ihre Zeit: Malerei der klassischen Moderne in Deutschland.* 10. November bis 18. Dez-

ember 1990. [Texte, Marion Agathe]. Essen, Galerie Neher, 1990.

8835. Lahnstein, Peter. *Münter.* Ettal, Buch-Kunstverlag Ettal, 1971.

8836. Kleine, Gisela. *Gabriele Münter und Wassily Kandinsky: Biographie eines Paares.* Frankfurt am Main, Insel Verlag, 1990.

8837. Mochan, Anne. *Gabriele Münter: between Munich and Murnau.* [Published in conjunction with an exhibition at the Busch-Reisenger Museum, Cambridge, Mass., Sept. 25–Nov. 8, 1980]. Cambridge, Mass., President and Fellows of Harvard College, 1980.

8838. Münter, Gabriele. *Gabriele Münter, 1877–1962: Retrospektive.* Herausgegeben von Annegret Hoberg und Helmut Friedel. Mit Beiträgen von Shulamith Behr . . . [et al.]. München, Prestel, 1992.

8839. Pfeiffer-Belli, Erich. *Gabriele Münter, Zeichnungen und Aquarelle.* Mit einem Katalog von Sabine Helms. Berlin, Mann, 1979.

8840. Städtische Galerie im Lenbachhaus (Munich). *Gabriele Münter, 1877–1962; Gemälde, Zeichnungen, Hinterglasbilder und Volkskunst aus ihrem Besitz.* 22. April–3. Juli 1977. München, Städtische Galerie im Lenbachhaus, 1977.

8841. Windecker, Sabine. *Gabriele Münter: eine Künstlerin aus dem Kreis des "Blauen Reiter."* Berlin, Reimer, 1991.

Mulready, William, 1786–1863
8842. Dafforne, James. *Pictures of William Mulready, R. A., with descriptions and a biographical sketch of the painter.* London, Virtue, [1872].

8843. Heleniak, Kathryn M. *William Mulready.* New Haven/London, published for the Paul Mellon Centre for Studies in British Art by Yale University Press, 1980.

8844. Pointon, Marcia R. *Mulready: a book with catalogue,* published to accompany the exhibition *William Mulready, 1786–1863;* organised to celebrate the bicentenary of the artist's birth, at the the Victoria and Albert Museum, London, 1 July–12 October 1986, continuing at the National Gallery of Ireland, Dublin, and at the Ulster Museum, Belfast, Autumn/Winter 1986/7. London, Victoria and Albert Museum, 1986.

8845. Stephens, Frederick. *Memorials of William Mulready, R. A.* London, Sampson Low, 1890. 2 ed.

Multscher, Hans, 1400–1467
8846. Beck, Herbert und Bückling, Maraike. *Hans Multscher: das Frankfurter Trinitätsrelief: ein Zeugnis spekulativer Künstlerindividualität.* Frankfurt am Main, Fischer Taschenbuch Verlag, 1988.

8847. Dietrich, Irmtraud. *Hans Multscher, plastische Malerei—malerische Plastik: zum Einfluss der Plastik auf die Malerei der Multscher-Retabel.* Bochum, N. Brockmeyer, 1992.

8848. Gerstenberg, Kurt. *Hans Multscher.* Leipzig, Insel Verlag, 1928.

8849. Rasmo, Nicoló. *L'altare di Hans Multscher a Vipiteno.* Bolzano, Ferrari-Auer, 1963.

8850. Stadler, Fran J. *Hans Multscher und seine Werkstatt; ihre Stellung in der Geschichte der schwäbischen Kunst.* Strassburg, Heitz, 1907. (Studien zur deutschen Kunstgeschichte, 82).

8851. Tripps, Manfred. *Hans Multscher, seine Ulmer Schaffenszeit, 1427–1467.* Weissenhorn, Konrad, 1969.

Munch, Edvard, 1863–1944

8852. Amann, Per. *Edvard Munch.* Trans. by Jennifer Barnes. Thornbury, Bristol, Avon, Artline Editions, 1987.

8853. Arnold, Matthias. *Edvard Munch: mit Selbstzeugnissen und Bilddokumenten.* Reinbek bei Hamburg, Rowohlt, 1986. (Rowohlts Monographien, 351).

8854. Bë, Alf. *Edvard Munch.* Trans. by Robert Ferguson. New York, Rizzoli, 1989.

8855. Benesch, Otto. *Edvard Munch.* Trans. by Joan Spencer. Phaidon, 1943.

8856. Bjørnstad, Ketil. *Historien om Edvard Munch.* Oslo, Gyldendal, 1993.

8857. Bock, Henning und Busch, Günter, eds. *Edvard Munch: Probleme, Forschungen, Thesen.* München, Prestel, 1973. (Studien zur Kunst des neunzehnten Jahrhunderts, 21).

8858. Deknatel, Frederick B. *Edvard Munch.* With an introduction by Johan H. Langaard. Boston, Institute of Contemporary Art/New York, Chanticleer Press, 1950.

8859. Eggum, Arne. *Munch and photography.* Trans. Birgit Holm. New Haven, Yale University Press, 1989.

8860. *Ensor, Hodler, Kruyder, Munch: Wegbereiter der Moderne.* Bern, Benteli, [1988].

8861. Gauguin, Pola. *Edvard Munch.* Oslo, Aschehoug, 1946.

8862. ———. *Grafikeren Edvard Munch.* 2 v. Trondheim, Bruns, 1946.

8863. Gerlach, Hans E. *Edvard Munch, sein Leben und sein Werk.* Hamburg, Wagner, 1955.

8864. Gierloff, Christian. *Edvard Munch selv.* Oslo, Gyldendal, 1953.

8865. Glaser, Curt. *Edvard Munch.* Berlin, Cassirer, 1917.

8866. Greve, Eli. *Edvard Munch, liv og werk i lys av tresnittene.* Oslo, Cappelens, 1963.

8867. Heller, Reinhold. *Edvard Munch: The Scream.* New York, Viking, 1973.

8868. ———. *Munch: his life and work.* Chicago, University of Chicago Press, 1984.

8869. ———. *Munch, his life and work.* London, J. Murray, 1984.

8870. Hodin, Josef P. *Edvard Munch, der Genius des Nordens.* Stockholm, Neuer Verlag, 1948.

8871. Hougen, Pål, ed. *Edvard Munch, Handzeichnungen.* New York, Rathenau/Berlin, Euphorion, 1976. (CR).

8872. Hüttinger, Eduard. *Edvard Munch.* Milano, Fratelli Fabbri, 1966. (I Maestri del colore, 179).

8873. Krieger, Peter. *Edvard Munch: der Lebensfries für Max Reinhardts Kammerspiele.* Berlin, Mann, 1978.

8874. Lande, Marit.—*for aldrig meer at skilles—: fra Edvard Munchs barndom og ungdom i Christiania.* Oslo, Universitetsforlaget, 1992.

8875. Langaard, Ingrid. *Edvard Munch, modningsår; en studie i tidlig ekspresjonisme og symbolisme.* Oslo, Gyldendal, 1960.

8876. Langaard, Johan H. [and] Revold, Reidar. *Edvard Munch, masterpieces from the artist's collections in the Munch Museum in Oslo.* Trans. by Michael Bullock. New York/Toronto, McGraw-Hill, 1964.

8877. Linde, Max. *Edvard Munch.* Neue Ausgabe. Berlin-Charlottenburg, Gottheiner, 1905.

8878. Moen, Arve. *Edvard Munch.* 3 v. Oslo, Forlaget Norsk Kunstreproduksjon, 1956–58.

8879. Munch, Edvard. *Edvard Munchs brev familien: et utvalg ved Inger Munch.* Oslo, Tanum, 1949.

8880. ———. *Briefwechsel.* Von Gustav Schiefler. Bearbeitet von Arne Eggum, in Verbindung mit Sibylle Baumbach, Sissel Biornstad und Signe Bohn. 2 v. Hamburg, Verlag Verein für Hamburgische Geschichte, 1987–1990. (Veröffentlichungen des Vereins für Hamburgische Geschichte, 30, 36).

8881. ———. *Edvard Munch i Nasjonalgalleriet.* Oslo, Nasjonalgalleriet, 1989.

8882. ———. *Edvard Munch og hans modeller, 1912–1943.* Utstilling og katalog, Arne Eggum. Oslo, Munch-museet, 1988. (Katalog/Oslo kommunes kunstsamlinger, A35).

8883. Musée d'Orsay (Paris). *Munch et la France.* 24 septembre 1991–5 janvier 1992. [Oslo, Musée Munch, 27 janvier–21 avril 1992]. [Traduction, Denise Bernard-Folliot, Marie-Claire Schjoth-Iversen]. Paris, Editions de la Réunion des musées nationaux, 1991.

8884. National Gallery of Art (Washington, D.C.). *Edvard Munch: symbols & images.* Nov. 11, 1978–Feb. 19, 1979. Introd. by Robert Rosenblum; essays by Arne Eggum et al. Washington, D.C., National Gallery of Art, 1978.

8885. Prelinger, Elizabeth. *Edvard Munch, master printmaker: an examination of the artist's works and techniques based on the Philip and Lynn Straus Collection.* New York, Norton, in association with the Busch-Reisinger Museum, Harvard University, Cambridge, Mass., 1983.

8886. Przybyszewski, Stanislaw, et al. *Das Werk des Edvard Munch.* Berlin, Fischer, 1896.

8887. Sarvig, Ole. *The graphic work of Edvard Munch.* Trans. by Helen Sarvig in collaboration with Alberta Feynman and the author. Ed. by Elizabeth Pollet. Lyngby, Hamlet, 1980.

8888. Schiefler, Gustav. *Edvard Munch, das graphische Werk, 1906–1926.* Berlin, Euphorion, 1928.

8889. ———. *Verzeichnis des graphischen Werks Edvard Munchs bis 1906.* Berlin, Cassirer, 1907. (CR).

8890. Selz, Jean. *E. Munch.* Trans. by Eileen B. Hennessy. New York, Crown, 1974.

8891. Stang, Ragna T. *Edvard Munch: the man and his art.* Trans. by Geoffrey Culverwell. New York, Abbeville Press, 1979.

8892. Stenersen, Rolf. *Edvard Munch, close-up of a genius.* Trans. and edited by Reidar Dittman. Oslo, Gyldendal, 1969.

8893. Stenerud, Karl, et al. *Edvard Munch, mennesket og kunstneren.* Oslo, Gyldendal, 1946. (Kunst og kulturs serie).

8894. Svenaeus, Gösta. *Edvard Munch im männlichen Gehirn.* 2 v. Lund, Vetenskaps-Societeten i Lund, 1973. (Publications of the New Society of Letters at Lund, 66–67).

8895. ———. *Edvard Munch: das Universum der Melancholie.* Lund, Vetenskaps-Societen i Lund, 1968. (Publications of the New Society of Letters at Lund, 58).

8896. Thiis, Jens. *Edvard Munch.* Berlin, Rembrandt, 1934.

8897. Timm, Werner. *The graphic art of Edvard Munch.* Trans. by Ruth Michaelis-Jena with the collaboration of Patrick Murray. Greenwich, Conn., New York Graphic Society, 1973.

8898. Weisner, Ulrich, ed. *Edvard Munch: Liebe, Angst, Tod. Themen und Variationen; Zeichnungen und Graphiken aus dem Munch-Museum, Oslo.* Bielefeld, Kunsthalle Bielefeld, 1980.

8899. Wittlich, Petr. *Edvard Munch.* Praha, Odeon, 1988. Vyd. 2. (Malá galerie, sv. 34).

Munkacsy, Mihaly von, 1844–1900

8900. Aleshina, Liliia S. *Mikhai Munkachi, 1844–1900.* Moskva, Iskusstvo, 1960.

8901. Ilges, Franz W. *M. von Munkacsy.* Bielefeld/Leipzig, Velhagen & Klasing, 1899. (Künstler-Monographien, 40).

8902. Malonyay, Dezsö. *Munkácsy Mihály.* 2 v. Budapest, Lampel, 1907. 2 ed.

8903. Sedelmeyer, Charles. *M. von Monkácsy, sein Leben und seine künstlerische Entwicklung.* Paris, Sedelmeyer, 1914.

8904. Végvári, Lajos. *Katalog der Gemälde und Zeichnungen Mihály Munkacsys.* Budapest, Akadémiai Kiado, 1958. (CR).

8905. ———. *Munkácsy Mihály élete és müvei.* Budapest, Akadémiai Kiado, 1958.

Munthe, Gerhard Peter, 1849–1929

8906. Bakken, Hilmar. *Gerhard Munthes dekorative Kunst.* Oslo, Gyldendal, 1946.

8907. ———. *Gerhard Munthe, en biografisk studie.* With a summary in English. Oslo, Gyldendal, 1952.

Murillo, Bartolome Esteban, 1617–1682

8908. Alfonso, Luis. *Murillo; el hombre, el artista, las obras.* Barcelona, Maucci, 1883.

8909. Angulo Iñiguez, Diego. *Murillo.* 3 v. Madrid, Espasa-Calpe, 1981. (CR).

8910. Brown, Jonathan. *Murillo and his drawings.* (Published in conjunction with an exhibition of drawings by Murillo held at the Art Museum, Princeton University, Princeton, N.J., Dec. 12, 1976–Jan. 30, 1977). Princeton, N.J., Art Museum, Princeton University, 1976; distributed by Princeton University Press, Princeton, N.J. (CR).

8911. Calvert, Albert F. *Murillo, a biography and appreciation.* New York, Lane, 1907.

8912. Causa, Raffaello. *Murillo.* Milano, Fabbri, 1964. (I maestri del colore, 51).

8913. Curtis, Charles B. *Velázquez and Murillo; a descriptive and historical catalogue of the works.* London, Sampson Low/New York, Bouton, 1883. (Reprint: Ann Arbor, Mich., University Microfilms, 1973).

8914. Davies, Edward. *The life of Bartolomé E. Murillo, compiled from the writings of various authors.* London, Bensley, 1819.

8915. Elizalde, Ignacio. *En torno a las inmaculadas de Murillo.* Prologo del Marques de Lozoya. Madrid, Sapientia, 1955.

8916. Gaya Nuño, Juan A. *L'opera completa di Murillo.* (CR). Milano, Rizzoli, 1978. (Classici dell'arte, 93).

8917. Justi, Carl. *Murillo.* Leipzig, Seemann, 1892.

8918. Lafond, Paul. *Murillo; biographie critique.* Paris, Laurens, 1908.

8919. Lefort, Paul. *Murillo et ses élèves.* Paris, Rouam, 1892.

8920. Knackfuss, Hermann. *Murillo.* Bielefeld/Leipzig, Velhagen & Klasing, 1896. (Künstler-Monographien, 10).

8921. Mayer, August L. *Murillo.* Stuttgart, Deutsche Verlags-Anstalt, 1923. (Klassiker der Kunst, 22).

8922. Minor, Ellen E. *Murillo.* London, Sampson Low, 1881.
8923. Montoto de Sedas, Santiago. *Murillo.* Barcelona, Hymsa, 1932.
8924. Muñoz, Antonio. *Murillo.* Novara, Ist. Geog. de Agostini, 1942.
8925. Royal Academy of Arts (London). *Bartolomé Esteban Murillo, 1617–1682.* London, Royal Academy of Arts, in association with Weidenfeld and Nicolson, 1983.
8926. Sanchez de Palacios, Mariano. *Murillo.* Madrid, Offo, 1965.
8927. Taggard, Mindy Nancarrow. *Murillo's allegories of salvation and triumph: the Parable of the prodigal son and the Life of Jacob.* Columbia, University of Missouri Press, 1992.
8928. Tubino, Francisco M. *Murillo; su epoca, su vida, sus cuadros.* Sevilla, La Andalucia, 1864.

Muybridge, Eadweard, 1830–1904

8929. Haas, Robert B. *Muybridge, man in motion.* Berkeley/Los Angeles, University of California Press, 1976.
8930. Harris, David. *Eadweard Muybridge and the photographic panorama of San Francisco, 1850–1880.* With Eric Sandweiss. Montréal, Canadian Centre for Architecture, 1993.
8931. Hendricks, Gordon. *Eadweard Muybridge, the father of the motion picture.* New York, Grossman, 1975.
8932. MacDonnell, Kevin. *Eadweard Muybridge: the man who invented the moving picture.* Boston, Little, Brown, 1972.
8933. Muybridge, Eadweard. *Animal locomotion, an electrophoto-graphic investigation of consecutive phases of animal movements.* Philadelphia, University of Pennsylvania, 1881. 11 v. (Reprint: New York, Dover, 1979).
8934. Sheldon, James and Reynolds, Jock. *Motion and document, sequence and time: Eadweard Muybridge and contemporary American photography.* Andover, Mass., Addison Gallery of American Art, 1991.
8935. Württembergischer Kunstverein Stuttgart. *Eadweard Muybridge.* [Oct. 21–Nov. 28, 1976]. Stuttgart, Württembergischer Kunstverein, 1976.

Myron, 5th c. B.C.

8936. Klöter, Hermann. *Myron im Licht neuerer Forschungen.* Würzburg, Triltsch, 1933.
8937. Mirone, Salvatore. *Mirone d'eleutere.* Catania, Tropea, 1921.
8938. Schröder, Bruno. *Zum Diskobol des Myron, eine Untersuchung.* Strassburg, Heitz, 1913. (Zur Kunstgeschichte des Auslandes, 105).

N

Nadar *see* **Tournachon, Felix**

Nadelman, Elie, 1882–1946
8939. Kirstein, Lincoln. *Elie Nadelman.* New York, Eakins Press, [1973]. (CR).
8940. Museum of Modern Art (New York). *The sculpture of Elie Nadelman.* [Text by Lincoln Kirstein]. New York, Museum of Modern Art, 1948.
8941. Whitney Museum of American Art (New York). *The sculpture and drawings of Elie Nadelman.* September 23–November 30, 1975. [Text by John I. H. Baur]. New York, Whitney Museum of American Art, 1975.

Nagel, Otto, 1894–1967
8942. Huett, Wolfgang. *Otto Nagel.* Berlin, Henschelverlag 1964.
8943. Lüdecke, Heinz. *Otto Nagel.* Dresden, Verlag der Kunst, 1959. (Künstler der Gegenwart,1).
8944. Nagel, Otto. *Otto Nagel, Leben und Werk, 1894–1967: Gemälde, Pastelle, Zeichnungen.* Städtische Galerie Schloss Oberhausen, Ludwig-Institut für Kunst der DDR. [In Zusammenarbeit mit den Staatlichen Museen zu Berlin, Nationalgalerie, DDR und der Otto-Pankok-Gesellschaft, Haus Esselt, Drevenack. Herausgegeben vom Ludwig-Institut für Kunst der DDR, Oberhausen]. Katalogredaktion, Bernhard Mensch, Inge Ludescher. Oberhausen, Ludwig-Institut für Kunst der DDR, [1987?].
8945. Nagel, Valli. *Ríadom s Otto Nagelem: vospominaniía.* Avtorizovanny í perevod s nemetskogo V.I. Sovvy. Moskva, "Sov. Rossiía," 1984.
8946. Nagel, Wali. *Das darfst du nicht!: Erinnerungen.* Halle Leipzig: Mitteldeutscher Verlag, 1981.
8947. Pommeranz-Liedke, Gerhard. *Otto Nagel und Berlin.* Dresden, Verlag der Kunst, 1964.

8948. Schallenberg-Nagel, Sibylle. *Otto Nagel: die Gemälde und Pastelle.* Bearb. von S. Schallenberg-Nagel und Götz Schallenberg. Berlin, Herschelverlag Kunst und Gesellschaft, 1974.
8949. Städische Galerie Schloss Oberhausen. *Gemälde, Pastelle, Zeichnungen.* 10. April bis 8. Juni 1987. Städische Galerie Schloss Oberhausen, in Zusammenarbeit mit den Staatlichen Museen zu Berlin, Nationalgalerie, DDR und der Otto-Pankok-Gesellschaft, Haus Esselt, Drevenack.

Nagy, László Moholy *see* **Moholy Nagy, László**

Nanni di Banco, 1373–1421 *see also* **Donatello**
8950. Bellosi, Luciano. *Nanni di Banco.* Milano, Fabbri, 1966. (I maestri della scultura, 64).
8951. Planiscig, Leo. *Nanni di Banco.* Firenze, Arnaud, 1946.
8952. Vaccarino, Paolo. *Nanni.* Firenze, Sansoni, 1950.

Nanteuil, Celestin, 1813–1873
8953. Burty, Philippe. *Célestin Nanteuil, graveur et peintre.* 2 v. Paris, Monnier, 1887. (L'âge du romantisme, 1–2).
8954. Marie, Aristide. *Un imagier romantique: Célestin Nanteuil, peintre, aquafortiste et lithographe.* Paris, Carteret, 1910.

Nanteuil, Robert, 1623–1678
8955. Bouvy, Eugène. *Nanteuil.* Paris, Le Goupy, 1924.
8956. Loriquet, Charles. *Robert Nanteuil, sa vie & son oeuvre.* Reims, Michaud, 1886.
8957. Petitjean, Charles. *Catalogue de l'oeuvre gravé de Robert Nanteuil.* Notice biographique de François Courbon. Paris, Delteil et Le Garrec, 1925.

Nash, John, 1752–1835

8958. Davis, Terence. *The architecture of John Nash*. Introduced with a critical essay by Sir John Summerson. London, Studio, 1960.

8959. ———. *John Nash, the Prince Regent's architect*. Newton Abbot (England), David & Charles, 1973. 2 ed.

8960. Freer, Allan. *John Nash: "The Delighted Eye"*. Brookfield, VT, Scolar Press, 1993.

8961. Mansbridge, Michael. *John Nash: a complete catalogue*. Photographs and text by Michael Mansbridge. Introduction by John Summerson. New York, Rizzoli, 1991.

8962. Summerson, John. *The life and work of John Nash, architect*. Cambridge, Mass., MIT Press, 1980.

8963. Temple, Nigel. *John Nash & the village picturesque*. Gloucester (England), Sutton, 1979.

Nash, Paul, 1889–1946

8964. Bertram, Anthony. *Paul Nash, the portrait of an artist*. London, Faber, 1955.

8965. Cardinal, Roger. *The landscape vision of Paul Nash*. London, Reaktion Books, 1989.

8966. Causey, Andrew. *Paul Nash*. Oxford, Clarendon Press, 1980. (CR).

8967. ———. *Paul Nash's photographs: document and image*. London, Tate Gallery, 1973.

8968. Colvin, Clare. *Paul Nash book designs: a Minories touring exhibition*. Colchester, England, The Minories, 1982.

8969. Eates, Margot. *Paul Nash, the master of the image, 1889–1946*. London, Murray, 1973.

8970. ———, ed. *Paul Nash: paintings, drawings and illustrations*. [Memorial volume; text by Herbert Read, John Rothenstein, et al.]. London, Humphries, 1948.

8971. King, James. *Interior landscapes: a life of Paul Nash*. London, Weidenfeld and Nicolson, 1987.

8972. Nash, Paul. *Dear Mercia: Paul Nash letters to Mercia Oakley, 1909–18*. Ed. by Janet Boulton. Netherton, England, Fleece Press, 1991.

8973. ———. *Outline; an autobiography, and other writings*. With a preface by Herbert Read. London, Faber, 1949.

8974. ——— and Bottomley, Gordon. *Poet and painter; being the correspondence between Gordon Bottomley and Paul Nash, 1910–1946*. Edited by C. C. Abbott and A. Bertram. London, Oxford University Press, 1955.

8975. Postan, Alexander. *The complete graphic work of Paul Nash*. London, Secker & Warburg, 1973. (CR).

8976. Read, Herbert. *Paul Nash*. Harmondsworth (England), Penguin, 1944.

8977. Tate Gallery. *Paul Nash, paintings and watercolours. 12 November–28 December 1975*. London, Tate Gallery, 1975.

8978. Towner Art Gallery and Local History Museum, Eastbourne. *Paul Nash, places. 30 September–5 Novermber 1989*. [City Art Gallery, York, 11 November–17 December 1989. Royal Albert Memorial Museum, Exeter, 6 January–11 February 1990. The Minories, Colchester, 17 February–31 March 1990]. [Essays by Clare Colvin]. London, South Bank Centre, 1989.

Natoire, Charles Joseph, 1700–1777 *see also* Boucher, Francois

8979. Boyer, Ferdinand. *Catalogue raisonné de l'oeuvre de Charles Natoire*. Paris, Colin, 1949. (CR). (Archives de l'art français, nouvelle période, 21).

8980. Duclaux, Lise. *Charles Natoire, 1700–1777*. Paris, Galerie de Bayser; Boston, Distribution exclusive, Ars Libri, [1991]. (Cahiers du dessin français, 8).

8981. Musée des Beaux-Arts, Troyes, et al. *Charles-Joseph Natoire (Nîmes, 1700–Castel Gandolfo, 1777): peintures, dessins, estampes et tapisseries des collections publiques françaises. Mars–juin 1977*. [Nantes, Chiffoleau], 1977.

8982. Musée National du Château de Compiègne. *Don Quichotte vu par un peintre du XVIIIe siècle: Natoire. 14 mai–10 juillet 1977*. Paris, Editions des Musées Nationaux, 1977.

Nattier, Jean-Marc, 1685–1766

8983. Nolhac, Pierre de. *Nattier, peintre de la cour de Louis XV*. Paris, Floury, 1925. 3 ed.

Nay, Ernst Wilhelm, 1902–1968

8984. Germanisches Nationalmuseum Nürnberg. *E. W. Nay, 1902–1968; Bilder und Dokumente. 29 März bis 1. Juni 1980*. München, Prestel, 1980. (Werke und Dokumente, neue Folge, 1).

8985. Haftmann, Werner. *E. W. Nay*. Köln, DuMont Schauberg, 1960.

8986. ———. *E. W. Nay*. Köln, DuMont, 1991. (Erw. Neuausg.).

8987. Heise, Carl G. [and] Gabler, Karlheinz. *Ernst Wilhelm Nay, die Druckgraphik 1923–1968*. Vorwort von Carl Georg Heise . . . Werkkatalog von Karlheinz Gabler. Zürich/ Stuttgart, Belser, 1975. (CR).

8988. Nay, Elly. *Ein strahlendes Weiss*. Berlin, [s.n.], 1984.

8989. Nay, Ernst Wilhelm. *E. W. Nay, 1902–68: Bilder kommen aus Bildern: Gemälde und unveröf-fentliche Schriften aus vier Jahrzehnten*. Krefeld, Krefelder Kunstmuseen, 1985.

8990. ———. *Ernst Wilhelm Nay: Wekverzeichnis*

der Ölgemälde. Werkverzeichnis, Aurel Scheibler. Einführung, Siegfried Gohr. Herausgegeben vom Museum Ludwig Köln. Köln, DuMont Buchverlag, 1990.(CR).

8991. Usinger, Fritz. *Ernst Wilhelm Nay*. Recklinghausen, Bongers, 1961. (Monographien zur rheinisch-westfälischen Kunst der Gegenwart, 21).

Nègre, Charles, 1820–1880

8992. Borcoman, James. *Charles Nègre, 1820–1880*. [Text in English and French]. Ottawa, National Gallery of Canada, 1976.

8993. Heilbrun, Françoise. *Charles Nègre, 1820–1880: das photographische Werk*. München, Schirmer/Mosel, 1988.

8994. Jammes, André. *Charles Nègre, photographe, 1820–1880*. Préface de Jean Adhémar. Paris, Jammes, 1963.

8995. Musée Réattu (Arles). *Charles Nègre, photographe, 1820–1880*. 5 juillet–17 août 1980. [Catalogue rédigé par François Heilbrun et Philippe Neagu]. Paris, Editions des Musées Nationaux, 1980.

8996. Nègre, Charles. *De la gravure héliographique, son utilité, son origine, son application à l'étude de l'histoire des arts et des sciences naturelles*. Nice, Gauther, 1866.

Neithardt, Mathis *see* Gruenewald, Matthias

Neizvestnyĭ, Ernst, 1926–

8997. Berger, John. *Art and revolution: Ernest Neizvestny and the role of the artist in the U.S.S.R.* London, Weidenfeld and Nicolson, 1969.

8998. Egeland, Erik. *Ernst Neizvestny, life and work*. Trans. by John Poole. Oakille, Ont./ New York, Mosaic Press, 1984.

8999. Neizvestnyĭ, Ernst. *On synthesis in art (= O sinteze v iskusstve)*. Trans. by Alice Nichols. Ann Arbor, Hermitage, 1982.

9000. Städtisches Museum Leverkusen. *Ernst Neizvestny; Plastiken, Grafiken, Zeichnungen*. [Oct. 28–Dec. 18, 1977]. Leverkusen, Städtisches Museum Leverkusen, 1977.

Neri di Bicci, 1419–1491

9001. Neri di Bicci. *Le ricordanze (10 marzo 1453–24 aprile 1475)*. A cura di Bruno Santi. Pisa, Marlin, 1976. (Testimonia, 4).

9002. Santi, Bruno. *Dalle Ricordanze di Neri di Bicci*. Pisa, Scuola Vamale Superiore, 1973. (Annali, Classe di lettere e filosofia, sec.III, v.III, 1).

Neri, Manuel, 1930–

9003. Neri, Manuel. *Manuel Neri*. Introduction by Thomas Albright. San Francisco, Anne Kohs & Associates, 1988.

9004. ———. *Manuel Neri, plasters: an exhibition*. [Organized by Graham W.J. Beal. Text by Caroline A. Jones]. San Francisco, San Francisco Museum of Modern Art, 1989.

9005. ———. *Sculpture & drawings*. San Francisco, John Berggruen Gallery in co-operation with the Seattle Art Museum, 1981.

Neroccio de'Landi, 1447–1500

9006. Coor, Gertrude. *Neroccio de'Landi, 1447–1500*. Princeton, N.J., Princeton University Press, 1961.

Nervi, Pier Luigi, 1893–1979

9007. Argan, Giulio C. *Pier Luigi Nervi*. Milano, Il Balcone, 1955. (Architetti del movimento moderne, 11).

9008. Desideri, Paolo [and] Nervi, Pier Luigi, Jr. *Pier Luigi Nervi*. Bologna, Zanchelli, 1979. (Serie di architettura, 5).

9009. Huxtable, Ada L. *Pier Luigi Nervi*. New York, Braziller, 1960.

9010. Nervi, Pier L. *Aesthetics and technology in building*. Trans. by Robert Einaudi. Cambridge, Mass., Harvard University Press, 1965.

9011. ———. *Architekten—Pier Luigi Nervi*. Redaktionelle Bearbeitung, Ulla Barnbeck. Stuttgart, Informationszentrum Raum und Bau der Fraunhofer-Gesellschaft, 1987. (IRB-Literaturauslese, 1359).

9012. ———. *Architettura d'oggi*. Firenze, Vallecchi, 1955.

9013. ———. *New structures*. London, Architectural Press, 1963.

9014. ———. *Scienza o arte del construire?* Caratteristiche e possibilità del cemento armato. Roma, Bussola, 1945. (Panorama di cultura contemporanea, 3).

9015. ———. *Structures*. Trans. by Giuseppina and Mario Salvadori. New York, McGraw-Hill, 1956.

9016. Rogers, Ernesto N. *The works of Pier Luigi Nervi*. Introduction by Ernesto N. Rogers. Explanatory notes to the illustrations by Jürgen Joedicke, trans. by Ernst Priefert. London, Architectural Press, 1957.

Nesch, Rolf, 1893–1975

9017. Detroit Institute of Arts. *The graphic art of Rolf Nesch*. March 18–April 27, 1969. Detroit, Detroit Institute of Arts, 1969.

9018. Hentzen, Alfred. *Rolf Nesch; Graphik, Materialbilder, Plastik*. Stuttgart, Belser, 1960. (English ed.: New York, Atlantis, 1964).

9019. ——— und Stubbe, Wolf. *Rolf Nesch, Drucke*. Frankfurt a.M., Propyläen, 1973.

9020. Nesch, Rolf. *Rolf Nesch: grafikk fra fem årtier.* [Katalogredaksjon, Eivind Otto Hjelle]. Oslo, Riksgalleriet, [1981?].

Neuhuijs, Albert, 1844–1914

9021. Martin, Wilhelm. *Albert Neuhuys, zijn leven en zijn kunst.* Amsterdam, van Kampen & Zoon, [1915].

9022. Neuhuys, Albert. *Albert Neuhuys (1844–1914): schilderijen, aquarellen en tekeningen.* Laren NH, Singer Museum, 1987.

9023. ———. *Rijkdom der eenvoud: Albert Neuhuy, 1844–1914: schilderijen, aquarellen, tekeningen uit priveverazamelingen verworven door Jacques van Rijn, Oude Kunst, Maastricht.* Tekst, Jacques van Rijn, Foto's, Paul Mellaart. Venlo, Nederland, Van Spijk, 1987.

Neumann, Balthasar, 1687–1754

9024. Eckert, Georg. *Balthasar Neumann und die Würzburger Residenzpläne; ein Beitrag zur Entwicklungsgeschichte des Würzburger Residenzbaues.* Strassburg, Heitz, 1917. (Studien zur deutschen Kunstgeschichte, 203).

9025. Eckstein, Hans. *Vierzehnheiligen.* Berlin, Rembrandt, 1939.

9026. Freeden, Max H. von. *Balthasar Neumann als Stadt-baumeister.* Berlin, Deutscher Kunstverlag, 1937. (Kunstwissenschaftliche Studien, 20; reprint: Würzburg, Freunde Mainfränkischer Kunst und Geschichte, 1978).

9027. ———. *Balthasar Neumann, Leben und Werk.* Aufnahmen von Walter Hege. [München], Deutscher Kunstverlag, [1953].

9028. Hansmann, Wilfried. *Balthasar Neumann: Leben und Werk.* Köln, DuMont, 1986.

9029. Hirsch, Fritz. *Das sogenannte Skizzenbuch Balthasar Neumanns: ein Beitrag zur Charakteristik des Meisters und zur Philosophie der Baukunst.* Heidelberg, Winter, 1912. (Zeitschrift für Geschichte der Architektur, 8; reprint: Nendeln [Liechtenstein], Kraus, 1978).

9030. Hotz, Joachim. *Das Skizzenbuch Balthasar Neumanns; Studien zur Arbeitsweise des Würzburger Meisters und zur Dekorationskunst im 18. Jahrhundert.* 2 v. Wiesbaden, Reichert, 1981.

9031. Hubala, Erich. *Balthasar Neumann, 1687–1753, der Barockbaumeister aus Eger.* Stuttgart, Edition Cantz, 1987.

9032. Keller, Joseph. *Balthasar Neumann, Artillerie- und Ingenieur-Obrist, fürstlich Bambergischer und Würzburger Oberarchitekt und Baudirektor; eine Studie zur Kunstgeschichte des 18. Jahrhunderts.* Würzburg, Bauer, 1896.

9033. Knapp, Fritz. *Balthasar Neumann, der grosse Architekt seiner Zeit.* Bielefeld/Leipzig, Velhagen & Klasing, 1937. (Künstler-Monographien, 120).

9034. Lohmeyer, Karl, ed. *Die Briefe Balthasar Neumanns an Friedrich Karl von Schönborn, Fürstbischof von Würzburg und Bamberg, und Dokumente aus den ersten Baujahren der Würzburger Residenz.* Saarbrücken, Hofer, 1921. (Das rheinisch-fränkische Barock, 1).

9035. Neumann, Balthasar. *Balthasar Neumann: kunstgeschichtliche Beiträge zum Jubiläumsjahr 1987.* Herausgegeben von Thomas Korth und Joachim Poeschke. München, Hirmer, 1987.

9036. Neumann, Günther. *Neresheim.* Herausgegeben von Hans Jantzen. München, Filser, 1947. (Münchener Beiträge zur Kunstgeschichte, 9).

9037. Otto, Christian F. *Space into light; the churches of Balthasar Neumann.* New York, Architectural History Foundation/Cambridge, Mass. and London, MIT Press, 1979.

9038. Reuther, Hans. *Balthasar Neumann, der mainfränkische Barockbaumeister.* München, Süddeutscher Verlag, 1983.

9039. ———. *Die Kirchenbauten Balthasar Neumanns.* Berlin, Hessling, 1960.

9040. ———. *Die Zeichnungen aus dem Nachlass Balthasar Neumanns: der Bestand in der Kunstbibliothek Berlin.* Berlin, Mann, 1979. (Veröffentlichung der Kunstbibliothek Berlin, 82).

9041. Schmorl, Theodor A. *Balthasar Neumann; Räume und Symbole des Spätbarock.* Hamburg, Claassen & Goverts, 1946.

9042. Schneider, Erich. *Balthasar Neumann, 1687–1753: Vollender der mainfränkischen Barockarchitektur.* München, Haus der Bayerischen Geschichte, 1987. (Hefte zur Bayerischen Geschichte und Kultur, 4).

9043. Schütz, Bernhard. *Balthasar Neumann.* Freiburg, Herder, 1986.

9044. Sedlmaier, Richard und Pfister, Rudolf. *Die fürstbischöfliche Residenz zu Würzburg.* 2 v. München, Müller, 1923.

9045. Staatsgalerie Stuttgart. *Balthasar Neumann in Baden-Württemberg: Bruchsal-Karlsruhe-Stuttgart-Neresheim.* 28. September bis 30. November 1975. Stuttgart, Staatsgalerie Stuttgart, 1975.

9046. Teufel, Richard. *Balthasar Neumann, sein Werk in Oberfranken.* Lichtenfels, Schulze, 1953.

9047. ———. *Vierzehnheiligen.* Lichtenfels, Schulze, 1957. 2 ed.

Neutra, Richard Joseph, 1892–1970

9048. Boesiger, Willy. *Richard Neutra, buildings and projects.* 3 v. [Text in English, French, and German]. Zürich, Girsberger [Vols. 1–2]/New York, Praeger [Vol. 3], 1966.

9049. Harmon, Robert B. *Richard J. Neutra and the blending of house and nature in American architecture: a selected bibliography.* Monticello, Ill., Vance Bibliographies, 1980.

9050. Hines, Thomas S. *Richard Neutra and the search for modern architecture, a biography and history.* New York, Oxford University Press, 1982.

9051. McCoy, Esther. *Richard Neutra.* New York, Braziller, 1960.

9052. Museum of Modern Art (New York). *The architecture of Richard Neutra: from international style to California modern.* [Text by Arthur Drexler and Thomas S. Hines]. New York, Museum of Modern Art, 1982.

9053. Neutra, Richard J. *Amerika; die Stilbildung des neuen Bauens in den Vereinigten Staaten.* Wien, Schroll, 1930. (Neues Bauen in der Welt, 2).

9054. ———. *Building with nature.* New York, Universe, 1971.

9055. ———. *Life and human habitat.* [Text in English and German]. Stuttgart, Koch, 1956.

9056. ———. *Life and shape.* New York, Appleton, 1962.

9057. ———. *Nature near: late essays of Richard Neutra.* Ed. by William Marlin. Foreword by Norman Cousins. Santa Barbara, Calif., Capra Press, 1989.

9058. ———. *Richard Neutra, promise and fulfillment, 1919–1932: selections from the letters and diaries of Richard and Dione Neutra.* Comp. and trans. by Dione Neutra. Carbondale, Southern Illinois University Press, 1986.

9059. ———. *Survival through design.* New York, Oxford University Press, 1954.

9060. ———. *Wie baut Amerika?* Stuttgart, Hoffman, 1927.

9061. ———. *World and dwelling.* London, Tiranti, 1962.

9062. Sack, Manfred. *Richard Neutra: mit einem Essay von Dion Neutra, Erinnerungen an meine Zeit mit Richard Neutra.* Zürich, Verlag für Architektur, 1992.

9063. Schiattarella, Aedeo. *Richard Neutra, 1892–1970.* Roma Officina, 1993. (Dizionario monografico degli architetti moderni e contemporanei, 6).

9064. Spade, Rupert. *Richard Neutra.* Photographs by Yukio Futagawa. London, Thames and Hudson, 1971.

9065. Zevi, Bruno. *Richard Neutra.* Milano, Il Balcone, 1954.

Nevelson, Louise (Berliawski), 1900–1988

9066. Bober, Natalie. *Breaking tradition: the story of Louise Nevelson.* New York, Atheneum, 1984.

9067. Cain, Michael. *Louise Nevelson.* New York, Chelsea House, 1989.

9068. Glimcher, Arnold B. *Louise Nevelson.* New York, Dutton, 1976. 2 ed.

9069. Gordon, John. *Louise Nevelson.* [Published in conjunction with an exhibition at the Whitney Museum of American Art, New York, March 8–April 30, 1967]. New York, Whitney Museum of American Art, 1967.

9070. Lisle, Laurie. *Louise Nevelson: a passionate life.* New York, Summit Books, 1990.

9071. Nevelson, Louise. *Dawns and dusks: taped conversations with Diana MacKown.* New York, Scribner, 1976.

9072. Pace Gallery (New York). *Louise Nevelson remembered: sculpture and collages. March 31–29 April, 1989. New York, The Gallery,* [1989].

9073. Roberts, Colette. *Nevelson.* Paris, Fall, 1964.

9074. Schwartz, Constance. *Nevelson and O'Keeffe: independents of the twentieth century.* January 30, 1983–April 10, 1983, Nassau County Museum of Fine Art, Roslyn Harbor, New York. Roslyn Harbor, N.Y., The Museum, [1983].

9075. Whitney Museum of American Art (New York). *Louise Nevelson, atmospheres and environments.* May 27–September 14, 1980. [Introduction by Edward Albee]. New York, Potter, in association with the Whitney Museum of American Art, 1980; distributed by Crown, New York.

Newman, Barnett, 1905–1970

9076. Baltimore Museum of Art. *Barnett Newman: the complete drawings, 1944–1969.* April 29–June 17, 1979. [Text and catalogue by Brenda Richardson]. Baltimore, Museum of Art, 1979. (CR).

9077. Museum Ludwig (Cologne). *Barnett Newman: das zeichnerische Werk.* 20. Februar bis 29. März 1981. [Ausstellung und Katalog, Christoph Brockhaus in Zusam-menarbeit mit Bernd Vogelsang]. Köln, Das Museum, 1981.

9078. Pace Gallery (New York). *Barnett Newman, paintings.* April 8–May 7, 1988. [Text, Yve-Alain Bois]. New York, Pace Gallery, 1988.

9079. Hess, Thomas B. *Barnett Newman.* [Published in conjunction with an exhibition at the Museum of Modern Art, New York, Oct. 21, 1971–Jan. 10, 1972]. New York, Museum of Modern Art, 1971; distributed by New York Graphic Society, Greenwich, Conn.

9080. Heynen, Julian. *Barnett Newmans Texte zur Kunst.* New York/Hildesheim, Olms, 1979. (Studien zur Kunstgeschichte, 10).

9081. Rosenberg, Harold. *Barnett Newman.* New York, Abrams, 1978.

Niccolò da Foligno, 1430–1502

9082. Ergas, Rudolf. *Niccolò da Liberatore, gennant Alunno; eine kunsthistorische Studie.* München, Wolf, 1912.

9083. Frenfanelli Cibo, Serafino. *Niccolò Alunno e la scuola Umbra.* Roma, Barbèra, 1872. (Reprint: Bologna, Forni, 1975).

9084. Passavant, Johann D. *Niccolò Alunno da Foligno, saggio critico.* Roma, Barbèra, 1872.

Niccolò dell'Abbate See Abbate, Niccolò dell'

Niccolò dell'Arca, d. 1494

9085. Gnudi, Cesare. *Niccolò dell'Arca.* Torino, Einaudi, 1942. (Biblioteca d'arte, 2).

9086. ———. *Nuove ricerche su Niccolò dell'Arca.* Roma, de Luca, [1973]. (Quaderni di commentari, 3).

9087. Novelli, Mariangela. *Niccolò dell'Arca.* Milano, Fabbri, 1966. (I maestri della scultura, 15).

9088. Silvestri Baffi, Rosetta. *Lo scultore dell'Arca, Nicolò di Puglia.* Galantina (Italy), Congedo, 1971.

Niccolò di Giovanni Fiorentino, d. 1505

9089. Schulz, Anne M. *Niccolò di Giovanni Fiorentino and Venetian sculpture of the early Renaissance.* New York, New York University Press for the College Art Association of America, 1978. (Monographs on Archeology and Fine Arts, 33).

Niccolò di Liberatore *see* Niccolò da Foligno

Niccolò di Piero Lamberti *see* Lamberti, Niccolò

Nicholson, Ben, 1894–1982
William, 1872–1949

9090. Albright-Knox Art Gallery (Buffalo, N.Y.). *Ben Nicholson, fifty years of his art.* October 21–November 26, 1978. [Text by Steven A. Nash]. Buffalo, N.Y., Buffalo Fine Arts Academy, 1978.

9091. Baxandall, David. *Ben Nicholson: art in progress.* London, Methuen, 1962.

9092. Browse, Lillian. *William Nicholson.* London, Hart-Davis, 1956. (CR).

9093. Fondation di Pierre Gianadda (Martigny). *Ben Nicholson.* [Exhibition] 14 novembre 1992–24 janvier 1993. Martigny, Suisse, La Fondation, 1992.

9094. Hodin, Joseph P. *Ben Nicholson: the meaning of his art.* London, Tiranti, 1957.

9095. Lewison, Jeremy. *Ben Nicholson.* New York, Rizzoli International, 1991.

9096. Nicholson, Ben. *Appliance House.* Chicago, Chicago Institute for Architecture and Urbanism; Cambridge, MA, Distributed by MIT Press, 1990.

9097. Read, Herbert. *Ben Nicholson.* 2 v. [Vol. 1: *Paintings, reliefs, drawings;* Vol. 2: *Work since 1947*]. London, Humphries, 1948/1956.

9098. Russell, John. *Ben Nicholson: drawings, paintings and reliefs, 1911–1968.* London, Thames and Hudson, 1969.

9099. Steen, Marguerite. *William Nicholson.* London, Collins, 1943.

9100. Tate Gallery (London). *Ben Nicholson.* 19 June–27 July 1969. London, Tate Gallery, 1969; distributed by Arno Press, New York.

Niemeyer, Oscar, 1907–

9101. Khait, Vladimir L. [and] Ianitskii, O. *Oskar Nimeir.* Moskva, Gosstroiizdat, 1963.

9102. Luigi, Gilbert. *Oscar Niemeyer: une esthetique de la fluidite.* Marseille, Parentheses, 1987.

9103. Niemeyer, Oscar. *Catalogo oficial da exposicao Oscar Niemeyer: Congresso "Cidades do futuro,"* Anhembi, Sao Paulo, SP, agosto, 1985. [Exhibition]. Rio de Janeiro, Revista Modulo, [1985]. 2 ed.

9104. ———. *Niemeyer.* Paris, Alphabet, 1977.

9105. ———. *Oscar Niemeyer.* Sao Paolo, Almed, 1985.

9106. ———. *Oscar Niemeyer: Selbstdarstellung, Kritiken, Oeuvre.* Hrsg., Alexander Fils. West Germany, Frolich & Kaufmann, [1982?].

9107. ———. *Quase memórias viagens: tempos de entusiasmo e revolta, 1961–1966.* Rio de Janeiro, Civilizaçao Brasileira, 1968.

9108. Papadaki, Stamo. *Oscar Niemeyer.* New York, Braziller, 1960.

9109. ———. *Oscar Niemeyer: works in progress.* New York, Reinhold, 1956.

9110. ———. *The work of Oscar Niemeyer.* With a foreword by Lucio Costa. New York, Reinhold, 1954. 2 ed.

9111. Puppi, Lionello. *Guida a Niemeyer.* Milano, A. Mondadori, 1987.

9112. Sodré, Nelson W. *Oscar Niemeyer.* Rio de Janeiro, Graal, 1978.

9113. Spade, Rupert. *Oscar Niemeyer.* Photographs by Yukio Futagawa. New York, Simon & Schuster, 1971.

9114. Underwood, David Kendrick. *Oscar Niemeyer and Brazilian free-form modernism.* New York, George Braziller, 1994.

Niépce, Joseph Nicéphore, 1765–1833

9115. Art Institute of Chicago. *Niépce to Atget: the first century of photography from the collec-*

tion of *André Jammes*. November 16, 1977–January 15, 1978. Essay and catalogue by Marie-Thérèse and André Jammes, and an introduction by David Travis. Chicago, Art Institute of Chicago, 1977.

9116. Fouque, Victor. *The truth concerning the invention of photography: Nicéphore Niépce; his life, letters and works*. Trans. by Edward Epstean. New York, Tennant and Ward, 1935. (Reprint: New York, Arno, 1973).

9117. Jay, Paul. *Niépce, genèse d'une invention*. Chalon-sur-Saone, Société des amis du Musée Nicéphore Niépce, 1988.

9118. Joyeux, Odette. *Le troisième oeil, la vie de Nicéphore Niépce: la rèfèrence des dates, celle des événements, et la liberté de l'imaginaire*. Paris, Ramsay, 1990.

9119. Niépce, Joseph N. *Correspondances, 1825–1829*. Avec une nomenclature des sources manuscrites par Pierre G. Harmant. Rouen, Pavillon de la Photographie, 1974. (Histoire de la photographie, 2).

9120. ———. *Lettres, 1816–1817*. Correspondance conservée à Châlon-sur-Saône. Rouen, Pavillon de la Photographie, 1973. (Histoire de la photographie, 1).

9121. Société Française de Photographie et de Cinématographie. *Commémoration du centenaire de la mort de Joseph Nicéphore Niépce, inventeur de la photographie*. Manifestations organisées à Châlon-sur-Saone en Juin 1933. Paris, Société Française de Photographie et de Cinématographie, 1933.

Nittis, Giuseppe de, 1846–1884

9122. Lamacchia, Giovanni. *Giuseppe De Nittis, capolista degli impressionisti*. Firenze, Atheneum, [1990]. (Collezione Basilea. Biografie; 4).

9123. Nittis, Giuseppe de. *Notes et souvenirs*. Paris, May et Motteroz, 1895. (Italian ed.: *Taccuino, 1870/1884*. Prefazione di Emilio Cecchi. Bari, Leonardo da Vinci, 1964).

9124. Pica, Vittorio. *Giuseppe de Nittis, l'uomo e l'artista*. Milano, Alfieri & Lacroix, 1914.

9125. Piceni, Enrico. *De Nittis, l'uomo e l'opera*. Milano, Bramante, 1979.

9126. Pittaluga, Mary [and] Piceni, Enrico. *De Nittis*. Milano, Bramante, 1963. (CR).

Noakowski, Stanislaw, 1867–1928

9127. Bieganskiego, Piotra. *O Stanislawie Noakowskim*. Warszawa, Pánstwowe Wydawnictwo Naukowe, 1959.

9128. Noakowski, Stanislaw. *Pisma*. Materialy zestawil i wstepem opatrzyl Mieczyslaw Wallis. Warszawa, Wydawnictwo Budownictwo i Architektura, 1957.

9129. Wallis, Mieczyslaw. *Kraj lat dziecinnych Stanislawa Noakowskiego*. Warszawa, Czytelnik, 1960.

9130. ———. *Lata nauki i mistrzostwa Stanislawa Noakowskiego*. Warszawa, Czytelnik, 1971.

9131. ———. *Noakowski*. Warszawie/Auriga, Oficyna Wydawnicza, 1965.

9132. Zachwatowicz, Jan. *Stanislaw Noakowski, rysunki katalog*. Warszawa, Pánstwowe Wydawnictwo Naukowe, 1966. (CR).

Noguchi, Isamu, 1904–1988

9133. Altshuler, Bruce. *Noguchi*. New York, Abbeville Press, 1994. (Modern masters, 16).

9134. Gordon, John. *Isamu Noguchi*. [Published in conjunction with an exhibition at the Whitney Museum of American Art, New York, April 17–June 16, 1969]. New York, Whitney Museum of American Art, 1968.

9135. Grove, Nancy and Botnick, Diane. *The sculpture of Isamu Noguchi, 1924–1979; a catalogue*. Foreword by Isamu Noguchi. New York/London, Garland, 1980. (CR). (Garland Reference Library of the Humanities, 207).

9136. Hunter, Sam. *Isamu Noguchi*. New York, Abbeville Press, 1978.

9137. Noguchi, Isamu. *Isamu Noguchi: essays and conversatiohs*. Edited by Diane Apostolos Cappadona and Bruce Altshuler. New York, H.N. Abrams in association with the Isamu Noguchi Foundation, 1994.

9138. ———. *A sculptor's world*. Foreword by R. Buckminster Fuller. New York, Harper & Row, 1968.

9139. Tobias, Tobi. *Isamu Noguchi, the life of a sculptor*. New York, Crowell, 1974.

9140. Whitney Museum of American Art (New York). *Isamu Noguchi: the sculpture of space*. February 5–April 6, 1980. New York, Whitney Museum of American Art, 1980.

Nolan, Sidney Robert, 1917–1992

9141. Adams, Brian. *Sidney Nolan: such is life: a biography*. London, Hutchinson, 1987.

9142. Clar, Jane. *Sidney Nolan: landscapes & legends*. With an essay by Patrick McCaughey. Cambridge/New York, Cambridge University Press, 1987.

9143. Lynn, Elwyn. *Sidney Nolan: myth and imagery*. London/Melbourne, Macmillan, 1967.

9144. MacInnes, Colin and Robertson, Bryan. *Sidney Nolan*. Introduction by Kenneth Clark. London, Thames and Hudson, 1961.

Noland, Kenneth, 1924–

9145. Moffett, Kenworth. *Kenneth Noland*. New York, Abrams, 1977.

9146. Noland, Kenneth. *Kenneth Noland: an important exhibition of paintings from 1958 through 1989*. [Exhibition]. Essay by Terry

Fenton. Reprinted writings by Ken Carpenter . . . [et al.]. New York, Salander-O'Reilly Galleries, 1989.

9147. Waldman, Diane. *Kenneth Noland, a retrospective.* [Published in conjunction with an exhibition at the Solomon R. Guggenheim Museum, New York]. New York, Guggenheim Foundation in collaboration with Abrams, 1977.

9148. Wilkin, Karen. *Kenneth Noland.* New York, Rizzoli, 1990.

Nolde, Emil, 1867–1956

9149. Ackley Clifford S. *Nolde: the painter's prints.* By Clifford S. Ackley, Timothy O. Benson, and Victor Carlson. [Catalogue of an exhibition]. Museum of Fine Arts, Boston in association with the Los Angeles County Museum of Art. Boston, Museum of Fine Arts, 1995.

9150. Bradley, William S. *Emil Nolde and German expressionism: a prophet in his own land.* Ann Arbor, UMI Research Press, 1986. (Studies in the fine arts. The Avant-garde, 52).

9151. Fehr, Hans. *Emil Nolde, ein Buch der Freundschaft.* Köln, DuMont Schauberg, 1957.

9152. Haftmann, Werner. *Emil Nolde.* Trans. by Norbert Guterman. New York, Abrams, 1959.

9153. Kunstmuseum Hannover und Sammlung Sprengel (Hannover). *Emil Nolde: Gemälde, Aquarelle und Druckgraphik, Verzeichnis der Bestände.* Hannover, Kunstmuseum Hannover und Sammlung Sprengel, 1980. (CR).

9154. Nolde, Emil. *Emil Nolde: Aquarelle und figürliche Radierungen: 27.Oktober 1991– 5. Januar 1992: Westfälisches Landesmuseum für Kunst und Kulturgeschichte Münster, Landschaftsverband Westfalen-Lippe.* [Ausstellung]. [Konzeption und Be-arbeitung, Erich Franz, Annegret Rittmann]. Münster, Das Landesmuseum, 1991.

9155. ———. *Briefe aus den Jahren 1894–1926.* Herausgegeben und mit einem Vorwort versehen von Max Sauerlandt. Berlin, Furche-Kunstverlag, [1927].

9156. ———. *Das eigene Leben; die Zeit der Jugend, 1867–1902.* Herausgegeben von der Stiftung Seebüll Ada und Emil Nolde. Köln, DuMont Schauberg, 1967. 3 ed.

9157. ———. *Emil Nolde, unpainted pictures.* Seebüll, Stiftung Seebüll Ada und Emil Nolde, 1987.

9158. ———. *Emil und Ada Nolde, Karl Ernst und Gertrud Osthaus: Briefwechsel.* Herausgegeben von Herta Hesse-Frielinghaus. Bonn, Bouvier, 1985. (Abhandlungen zur Kunst-, Musik und Literaturwissenschaft, 360).

9159. ———. *Jahre der Kämpfe, 1902–1914.* Herausgegeben von der Stiftung Seebüll Ada und Emil Nolde. Flensburg, Wolff, [1957]. 2 ed.

9160. ———. *Reisen, Ächtung, Befreiung: 1919–1946.* Herausgegeben von der Stiftung Seebüll Ada und Emil Nolde. Köln, DuMont Schauberg, 1967.

9161. ———. *Welt und Heimat; die Südseereise, 1913–1918 (geschrieben 1936).* Herausgegeben von der Stiftung Seebüll Ada und Emile Nolde. Köln, DuMont Schauberg, 1965.

9162. Palmer Museum of Art (University Park, PA). *Emil Nolde: works from American collections.* April 14–June 19, 1988. University Park, Penn State, 1988.

9163. Pois, Robert. *Emil Nolde.* Washington, D.C., University Press of America, 1982.

9164. Reuther, Manfred. *Das Frühwerk Emil Noldes: vom Kunstgewerbler zum Künstler.* Köln, DuMont, 1985.

9165. Sauerlandt, Max. *Emil Nolde.* München, Wolff, 1921.

9166. Schiefler, Gustav. *Emil Nolde: das graphische Werk.* Neubearbeitet, ergänzt und mit Abbildungen versehen von Christel Mosel. 2 v. Köln, DuMont Schauberg, 1966–1967. (CR).

9167. Schleswig-Holsteinischer Kunstverein (Kiel). *Emil Nolde: Graphik aus der Sammlung der Stiftung Seebüll Ada und Emil Nolde.* [October 19–November 30, 1975; text by Martin Urban et al.]. Neukirchen über Niebüll, Stiftung Seebüll Ada und Emil Nolde, 1975.

9168. Schmidt, Paul F. *Emil Nolde.* Leipzig/Berlin, Klinkhardt & Biermann, 1929. (Junge Kunst, 53).

9169. Selz, Peter H. *Emil Nolde.* [Published in conjunction with an exhibition at the Museum of Modern Art, New York, March 4–April 30, 1963]. New York, Museum of Modern Art, 1963; distributed by Doubleday, Garden City, N.Y.

9170. Sprengel Museum (Hannover). *Emil Nolde: Reise in die Südsee, 1913–1914.* 14. 10.1992–3.1.1993. [Ausstellung und Katalog, Karin Orchard]. Hannover, Das Museum, 1992.

9171. Urban, Martin. *Emil Nolde, catalogue raisonné of the oil-paintings.* 2 v. London, Sotheby's Publications; New York, Harper & Row, 1987. (CR).

9172. ———. *Emil Nolde: landscapes; watercolors and drawings.* Trans. by Paul Stevenson. New York, Praeger, 1970.

9173. ———. *Emil Nolde: Werkverzeichnis der Gemälde.* 2 v. München, C.H. Beck, 1987–1990. (CR).

Nollekens, Joseph, 1737–1823

9174. Smith, John T. *Nollekens and his times, com-*

prehending a life of that celebrated sculptor; and the memoirs of several contemporary artists from the time of Roubiliac, Hogarth, and Reynolds to that of Fuseli, Flaxman, and Blake. 2 v. London, Colburn, 1829. (New ed., minus the parts on other contemporary artists: London, Turnstile Press, 1949).

Notke, Bernt, 1440–1509

9175. Eimer, Gerhard. *Bernt Notke: das Wirken eines niederdeutschen Künstlers im Ostseeraum.* Bonn, Kulturstiftung der deutschen Vertriebenen, 1985.

9176. Hasse, Max. *Das Triumphkreuz des Bernt Notke im Lübecker Dom.* Hamburg, Ellermann, 1952.

9177. Heise, Carl G. *Die Gregorsmesse des Bernt Notke.* Hamburg, Ellermann, 1941.

9178. Paatz, Walter. *Bernt Notke und sein Kreis.* 2 v. Berlin, Deutscher Verein für Kunstwissenschaft, 1939.

9179. Stoll, Karlheinz, et al. *Triumphkreuz im Dom zu Lübeck: ein Meisterwerk Bernt Notkes.* Wiesbaden, Reichert, 1977.

Novelli, Pietro, 1603–1647

9180. Di Stefano, Guido. *Pietro Novelli, il Monrealese.* Prefazione di Giulio Carlo Argan. Catologo delle opere e repertori a cura di Angela Mazze. Palermo, Flaccovio, 1989. (CR).

9181. Mantovani, Giuseppe. *Pietro Novelli, il monrealese e la sua famiglia.* Palermo, Edizioni librarie Siciliane, [1987?].

9182. Novelli, Pietro. *Pietro Novelli e il suo ambiente*: Palermo, Albergo dei Poveri, 10 giugno–30 ottobre 1990. Palermo, Flaccovio, 1990.

Nuzi, Allegretto, 1346–1373

9183. Romagnoli, Fernanda. *Allegretto Nuzi, pittore fabrianese.* Fabriano, Tipografia Gentile, 1927.

N

O

Oelze, Richard, 1900-

9184. Akademie der Künste (Berlin). *Richard Oelze, 1900–1980: Gemälde und Zeichnungen.* 25. Januar-4. März 1987. Herausgegeben von Wieland Schmied. [Konzeption und Planung, Wieland Schmied. Redaktion und Gestaltung, Barbara Volkmann. Mitarbeit, Renate Damsch-Wiehager, Rose-France Raddatz, Ursula Reich]. Berlin, Akademie der Künste und Autoren, Vertrieb Nicolaische Verlagsbuchh, 1987.

9185. Damsch-Wiehager, Renate. *Richard Oelze: ein alter Meister der Moderne.* München, Bucher, 1989.

9186. Schmied, Wieland. *Richard Oelze.* Göttingen, Musterschmidt, 1965. (Niedersächsische Künstler der Gegenwart, 7).

9187. Württembergischer Kunstverein Stuttgart. *Richard Oelze: Oeuvre-Katalog, 1925–1964.* 15. Januar bis 15. Februar 1965. Hannover, Kestner-Gesellschaft Hannover 1964.

Oeser, Adam Friedrich, 1717–1799

9188. Benyovszky, Karl. *Adam Friedrich Oeser, der Zeichenlehrer Goethes.* Leipzig, Thomas, 1930.

9189. Dürr, Alphons. *Adam Friedrich Oeser, ein Beitrag zur Kunstgeschichte des 18. Jahrhunderts.* Leipzig, Dürr, 1879.

9190. Schulze, Friedrich. *Adam Friedrich Oeser, der Vorläufer des Klassizismus.* Leipzig, Koehler & Amelung, [1944].

O'Keeffe, Georgia, 1887–date

9191. Goodrich, Lloyd and Bry, Doris. *Georgia O'Keeffe.* New York, published for the Whitney Museum of American Art by Praeger, 1970.

9192. Lisle, Laurie. *Portrait of an artist: a biography of Georgia O'Keeffe.* New York, Seaview Books, 1980.

9193. O'Keeffe, Georgia. *Georgia O'Keeffe.* New York, Viking, 1976.

9194. Rich, Daniel C. *Georgia O'Keeffe.* Chicago, Art Institute, 1943.

Okyo, Maruyama, 1733–1795

9195. Saint Louis Art Museum. *Okyo and the Maruyama-Shijo school of Japanese painting.* [Winter, 1980]. St. Louis, St. Louis Art Museum, 1980.

Olbrich, Josef Maria, 1867–1908

9196. Creutz, Max. *Joseph Maria Olbrich, das Warenhaus Tietz in Düsseldorf.* Berlin, Wasmuth, 1909.

9197. Hessischen Landesmuseum in Darmstadt. *Joseph M. Olbrich, 1867–1908; das Werk des Architekten.* Ausstellung anlässlich der 100. Wiederkehr des Geburtstages. Darmstadt, Hessisches Landesmuseum, 1967.

9198. Latham, Ian. *Olbrich.* London, Academy, 1980.

9199. Lux, Joseph A. *Joseph Maria Olbrich, eine Monographie.* Berlin, Wasmuth, 1919.

9200. Mathildenhöhe Darmstadt. *Joseph M. Olbrich, 1867–1908.* [Sept. 18–Nov. 27, 1983]. Darmstadt, Mathildenhöhe Darmtadt, 1983.

9201. Olbrich, Joseph M. *Architektur von Olbrich.* Berlin, Wasmuth, 1904.

9202. Schreyl, Karl Heinz [and] Neumeister, Dorothea. *Joseph Maria Olbrich: die Zeichnungen in der Kunstbibliothek Berlin; kritisher Katalog.* Berlin, Mann, 1972. (CR).

9203. Veronesi, Giulia. *Joseph Maria Olbrich.* Milano, Il Balcone, 1948. (Architetti del movimento moderno, 7).

Oldenburg, Claes, 1929–

9204. Baro, Gene. *Claes Oldenburg: drawings and prints.* London/New York, Chelsea House, 1969. (CR).

9205. Celant, Germano. *A bottle of notes and some voyages: Claes Oldenburg, Coosje van Bruggen*. Sunderland, Northern Center for Contemporary Art; Leeds, Henry Moore Centre for the Study of Sculpture, Leeds City Art Galleries; New York, distributed by Rizzoli International Publications, 1988.

9206. ———, ed. *Il Corso del coltello: Claes Oldenburg, Coosje van Bruggen, Frank O. Gehry*. New York, Rizzoli, 1987.

9207. Johnson, Ellen H. *Claes Oldenburg*. Harmondsworth (Eng.), Penguin, 1971.

9208. Kunsthalle Tübingen. *Zeichnungen von Claes Oldenburg*. Mit Textbeiträgen von Götz Adriani, Dieter Koepplin, Barbara Rose. [March 1–April 20, 1975]. Tübingen, Kunsthalle Tübingen, 1975.

9209. Oldenburg, Claes. *Claes Oldenburg: May 1974–August 1976*. Stuttgart/London/Reykjavik, H. Mayer, 1976.

9210. ———. *Claes Oldenburg, die frühen Zeichnungen*. Texte von Dieter Koepplin und Claes Oldenburg. [Herausgegeben vom Kupferstichkabinett der Öffentlichen Kunstsammlung Basel . . . anlässlich der Ausstellung vom 5. Juli bis 7. September 1992]. Basel, Wiese, [1992].

9211. ———. *Claes Oldenburg: multiples in retrospect, 1964–1990*. New York, Rizzoli International, 1991.

9212. ———. *Proposals for monuments and buildings, 1965–1969*. Chicago, Big Table Publishing Co., 1969.

9213. ———. *Raw notes; documents and scripts of the performances: Stars, Moveyhouse, Massage, The Typewriter*. With annotations by the author. Halifax (Nova Scotia), The Press of the Nova Scotia College of Art and Design, 1973.

9214. ——— and Van Bruggen, Coosje. *Claes Oldenburg: large-scale projects, 1977–1980; a chronicle*. New York, Rizzoli, 1980.

9215. ——— and Williams, Emmett. *Store days: documents from The Store (1961) and Ray Gun Theater (1962)*. Photographs by Robert R. McElroy. New York, Something Else Press, 1967.

9216. Rose, Barbara. *Claes Oldenburg*. [Published in conjunction with an exhibition at the Museum of Modern Art, New York, Sept. 25–Nov. 23, 1969]. New York, Museum of Modern Art, 1969; distributed by New York Graphic Society, Greenwich, Conn.

9217. Tate Gallery (London). *Claes Oldenburg*. 24 June–16 August 1970. London, Arts Council of Great Britain, 1970.

Olitski, Jules, 1922

9218. Fenton, Terry. *Jules Olitski and the tradition of oil painting*. [Published in conjunction with an exhibition at the Edmonton Art Gallery, Edmonton, Alberta, Sept. 12–Oct. 28, 1979]. Edmonton, Edmonton Art Gallery, 1979.

9219. Moffett, Kenworth. *Jules Olitski*. New York, Abrams, 1981.

9220. Museum of Fine Arts (Boston). *Jules Olitski*. April 6–May 13, 1973. Boston, Museum of Fine Arts, 1973.

9221. Olitski, Jules. *Jules Olitski*. [By Henry Geldzahler, Tim Hilton, Dominique Fourcade]. New York, Salander-O'Reilly Galleries, 1990.

9222. Wilkin, Karen and Long, Stephen. *The prints of Jules Olitski: a catalogue raisonné, 1954–1989*. New York, Associated American Artists, 1989. (CR).

Oliver, Isaac, 1556–1617 *see* Hilliard, Nicholas

Omodeo, Giovanni Antonio *see* Amadeo, Giovanni Antonio

Onatas, 5th c. B.C.

9223. Dörig, José. *Onatas of Aegina*. Leiden, Brill, 1977. (Monumenta graeca et romana, 1).

Opie, John, 1761–1807? *see also* Barry(ie?), James

9224. Earland, Ada. *John Opie and his circle*. London, Hutchinson, 1911.

9225. Opie, John. *Lectures on painting delivered at the Royal Academy of Arts, to which are prefixed a memoir by Mrs. Opie and other accounts of Mr. Opie's talents and character*. London, Longman, 1809.

9226. Rogers, John J. *Opie and his works; being a catalogue of 760 pictures by John Opie, R. A., preceded by a biographical sketch*. London, Colnaghi, 1878. (CR).

Oppenheimer, Max, 1907–1957 *see* Ophüls, Max

Orcagna, Andrea di Cione, 1308–1368

9227. Gronau, Hans D. *Andrea Orcagna und Nardo di Cione, eine stilgeschichtliche Untersuchung*. Berlin, Deutscher Kunstverlag, 1937. (Kunstwissenschaftliche Studien, 23).

9228. Niccolini, Giovanni B. *Elogio d'Andrea Orcagna*. Firenze, Carli, 1816.

9229. Steinweg, Klara. *Andrea Orcagna; quellengeschichtliche und stilkritische Untersuchung*. Strassburg, Heitz, 1929.

Ordonez, Bartolome, ca. 1480–1520 *see also* Berruguete, Alonso Gonzalez

9230. Gómez-Moreno, María E. *Bartolomé Ordonez*. Madrid, Instituto Diego Velázquez, 1956.

Orley, Bernaert van, 1485–1542

9231. Musée de l'Ain (Bourg-en-Bresse, France). *Van Orley et les artistes de la cour de Marguerite d'Autriche.* 19 juin–13 septembre 1981. Bourge-en-Bresse, Musée de l'Ain, 1981.

9232. Terlinden, Charles, et al. *Bernard van Orley, 1488–1541.* [Papers edited by the Société Royale d'Archéologie de Belgique], Bruxelles, Dessart, 1943.

9233. Wauters, Alphonse J. *Bernard van Orley.* Paris, Librairie de l'Art, [1893].

Orlik, Emil, 1870–1932

9234. Orlik, Emil. *Malergrüsse an Max Lehrs, 1898–1930.* Herausgegeben vom Adalbert Stifter Verein. München, Prestel, 1981.

9235. Osborn, Max. *Emil Orlik.* Berlin, Verlag Neue Kunsthandlung, 1920. (Graphiker der Gegenwart, 2).

9236. Pauli, Friedrich W. *Emil Orlik; Wege eines Zeichners und Graphikers.* Mit einem Beitrag von Walter R. Habicht. Darmstadt, Bläschke, 1972.

9237. Singer, Hans W. *Zeichnungen von Emil Orlik.* Leipzig, Schumann, 1912. (Meister der Zeichnung, 7).

Orloff, Chana, 1888–1968

9238. Courières, Edouard des. *Chana Orloff: trente reproductions de sculptures et dessins précédées d'une étude critique.* Paris, Nouvelle Revue Française, 1927. (Les sculpteurs français nouveaux, 6).

9239. Marcilhac, Félix. *Chana Orloff.* Paris, Editions de l'Amateur, 1991.

9240. Musée Rodin (Paris). *Chana Orloff, sculptures et dessins.* Paris, Musée Rodin, 1971.

9241. Werth, Leon. *Chana Orloff.* Paris, Crès, 1927.

Orlovskii, Aleksandr Osipovich, 1777–1832

9242. Atsarkina, Esfir N. *Aleksandr Osipovich Orlovskii, 1777–1832.* Moskva, Iskusstvo, 1971.

9243. Cekalska-Zborowska, Halina. *Aleksander Orlowski.* Warszawa, Wiedza Powszechna, 1962.

9244. Muzeum Narodowe (Warsaw). *Aleksander Orlowski, 1777–1832.* [December 1957–February 1958]. Warszawa, Arkady, 1957.

9245. Tatarkiewicz, Wladyslaw. *Aleksander Orlowski.* Warszawa, Gebethnera i Wolffa, 1926. (Monografje artystyczne, 7).

Orme, Philibert de L' See Delorme, Philibert

Orozco, José Clemente, 1883–1949

9246. Cardoza y Aragón, Luis. *Orozco.* [Mexico City], Universidad Nacional Autónoma de México, 1959.

9247. Fernández, Justino. *José Clemente Orozco, forma e idea.* [Mexico City], Porrua, 1956. 2 ed.

9248. Guerico, Antonio del. *José Clemente Orozco.* Milano, Fabbri, 1966 (I maestri del colore, 200).

9249. Helm, MacKinley. *Man of fire, J. C. Orozco; an interpretive memoir.* Boston, Institute of Contemporary Art/New York, Harcourt Brace, 1953. (Reprint: Westport, Conn., Greenwood, 1971).

9250. Hopkins, Jon H. *Orozco: a catalogue of his graphic work.* Flagstaff, Ariz., Northern Arizona University Publications, 1967. (CR).

9251. Hurlburt, Laurance P. *The Mexican muralists in the United States.* Foreword by David W. Scott. Albuquerque, University of New Mexico Press, 1989.

9252. Merida, Carlos. *Orozco's frescos in Guadalajara.* Photographs by Juan Arauz Lomeli. Edited by Frances Toor. [Mexico City], Toor Studios, 1940.

9253. Museum of Modern Art (Oxford, Eng.). *Orozco!: 1883–1949.* 9 November 1980–4 January 1981. Oxford, Eng., Museum of Modern Art, 1980.

9254. Orangerie Schloss Charlottenburg (Berlin). *José Clemente Orozco, 1883–1949.* Herausgegeben von Egbert Baqué und Heinz Spreitz. 24. Januar bis 1. März 1981. Berlin, Leibniz-Gesellschaft für kulturellen Austausch, 1981.

9255. Orozco, José C. *The artist in New York: letters to Jean Charlot and unpublished writings, 1925–1929.* Foreword and notes by Jean Charlot. Letters and writings trans. by Ruth L. C. Sims. Austin, Tex., University of Texas Press, 1974.

9256. ———. *An autobiography.* Trans. by Robert C. Stephenson. Introduction by John Palmer Leeper. Austin, Tex., University of Texas Press, 1962.

9257. ———. *Orozco, iconografía personal.* México, D.F., Fondo de Cultura Económica, 1983.

9258. ———. *Orozco: pintura mural; los murales de Orozco, Jorge Alberto Manrique . . . [et al.].* México, D.F., Fondo Editorial de la Plástica Mexicana, 1989.

9259. Orozco, V. Clemente. *Catálogo completo de la gráfica de Orozco.* Edición, introducción, notas, Luigi Marrozzini. Río Piedras, Instituto de Cultura Puertorriqueña, Universidad de Puerto Rico, [1970]. (CR).

9260. Reed, Alma. *Orozco.* New York, Oxford University Press, 1956.

9261. Zuno, José G. *Orozco y la ironía plástica.* [Mexico City], Cuadernos Americanos, 1953.

Orpen, William, 1878–1931

9262. Arnold, Bruce. *Orpen, mirror to an age.* London, Cape, 1981.

9263. Konody, Paul G. and Dark, Sidney. *Sir William Orpen, artist and man.* London, Seeley, 1932.

9264. National Gallery of Ireland (Dublin). *William Orpen, 1878–1931; a centenary exhibition.* 1 Nov.–15 Dec. 1978. Dublin, National Gallery of Ireland, 1978.

9265. Pickle, R. *Sir William Orpen.* London, Benn, 1923.

Ostade, Adriaen van, 1610–1685
Isaac van, 1621–1649 (?)

9266. Gaedertz, Theodor. *Adrian van Ostade, sein Leben und seine Kunst.* Lübeck, Rohden, 1869.

9267. Godefroy, Louis. *L'oeuvre gravé de Adriaen van Ostade.* Paris, L'Auteur, 1930. (CR).

9268. ———. *The complete etchings of Adriaen van Ostade.* San Francisco, Alan Wofsy Fine Arts, 1990. (CR). (Translation of selected chapters and catalogue raisonné from L'oeuvre gravé de Adriaen van Ostade. Includes a reprint of the original French edition).

9269. Rosenberg, Adolf. *Adriaen und Isack van Ostade.* Bielefeld/Leipzig, Velhagen & Klasing, 1900. (KünstlerMonographien, 44).

9270. Rovinski, Dmitri, et Tchétchouline, Nicolas. *L'oeuvre gravé d'Adrien van Ostade.* [Text in Russian and French]. Leipzig, Hiersemann/Saint-Pétersbourg, Kotov, 1912. (CR).

9271. Schnackenburg, Bernhard. *Adriaen von Ostade, Isack von Ostade: Zeichnungen und Aquarelle.* 2 v. Hamburg, Hauswedell, 1981. (CR).

9272. Wessely, Joseph E. *Adriaen van Ostade.* Hamburg, Haendcke & Lehmkuhl, 1888. (Kritische Verzeichnisse von Werken hervorragender Kupferstecher, 5).

9273. Wiele, Marguerite van de. *Les frères van Ostade.* Paris, Librairie de l'Art, 1893.

O'Sullivan, Timothy H., 1839–1882

9274. Horan, James D. *Timothy O'Sullivan, America's forgotten photographer.* Garden City, N.Y., Doubleday, 1966.

9275. Newhall, Beaumont, and Newhall, Nancy. *T. H. O'Sullivan, photographer.* With an appreciation by Ansel Adams. Rochester, N.Y., George Eastman House/Fort Worth, Tex., Amon Carter Museum of Western Art, 1966.

9276. Snyder, Joel. *American frontiers: the photographs of Timothy H. O'Sullivan, 1867–1874.* Millerton, N.Y., Aperture, 1981.

Oud, Jacobus Johannes Pieter, 1890–1963

9277. Florida State University Art Gallery (Tallahassee, Fla.). *The architecture of J. J. P. Oud, 1906–1963: an exhibition of drawings, plans, and photographs from the archives of Mrs. J. M. A. Oud-Dianux, Wassenaar, Holland.* May 4–28, 1978. Tallahassee, Fla., University Presses of Florida, 1978.

9278. Oud, Jacobus J. P. *Holländische Architektur.* Eschwege, Poeschel & Schulz-Schamburgk, 1926. (Neue Bauhausbücher, 10; reprint: Mainz/Berlin, Kupferberg, 1976).

9279. ———. *Mein weg in De Stijl.* 's Gravenhage, Nijgh en van Ditmar, 1961.

9280. Veronesi, Giulia. *J. J. Pieter Oud.* Milano, Il Balcone, 1953.

Oudry, Jean Baptiste, 1686–1755

9281. Cordey, Jean. *Esquisses de portraits peints par J.-B. Oudrey avec une étude sur Oudry portraitiste.* Paris, Société des Bibliophiles Français, 1929.

9282. Grand Palais (Paris). *J. B. Oudry, 1686–1755.* 1 octobre 1982–3 janvier 1983. [Catalogue by Hal Opperman]. Paris, Editions de la Réunion des Musées Nationaux, 1982.

9283. Hennique, Nicolette. *Jean-Baptiste Oudry, 1686–1755.* Paris, Nilsson, 1926.

9284. Locquin, Jean. *Catalogue raisonné de l'oeuvre de J. B. Oudry, peintre du roi, 1686–1755.* Paris, Schemit, 1912. (CR).

9285. Opperman, Hal. *J. B. Oudry, 1686–1755.* [Published in conjunction with an exhibition at the Kimball Art Museum, Fort Worth, Tex., February 26–June 5, 1983]. Fort Worth, Tex., Kimball Art Museum, 1983.

9286. ———. *Jean-Baptiste Oudry.* 2 v. New York/London, Garland, 1977.

Outerbridge, Paul, 1896–1958

9287. Dines, Elaine, and Howe, Graham. *Paul Outerbridge, a singular aesthetic: photographs and drawings, 1921–1941. A catalogue raisonné.* Introductory essay by Bernard Barryte. [Published in conjunction with an exhibition at the Laguna Beach Museum of Art, Laguna Beach, Calif., Nov. 21, 1981–Jan. 10, 1982]. Santa Barbara, Calif., Arabesque Books, 1981. (CR).

9288. Howe, Graham and Hawkins, G. Ray, eds. *Paul Outerbridge, Jr.: photographs.* [Additional material by Jacqueline Markham]. New York, Rizzoli, 1980.

9289. Outerbridge, Paul. *Photographing in color.* New York, Random House, 1940.

Ovens, Jürgen, 1623–1678

9290. Schlüter-Göttsche, Gertrud. *Jürgen Ovens, ein schleswig-holsteinischer Barockmaler.* Heine in Holstein, Boyens, 1978.

9291. Schmidt, Harry. *Das Nachlass-Inventar des Malers Jürgen Ovens.* Briefwechsel zwischen dem Grafen Hermann Baudissin und Geheimrat Samwer; ein Beitrag zur

Geschichte von Schleswig-Holstein in den Jahren 1863 und 1864 von Dr. Kupke. Leipzig, [n.p.], 1913. (Quellensammlung der Gesellschaft für schleswig-holsteinische Geschichte, 7).

9292. Schmidt, Harry. *Jürgen Ovens, sein Leben und seine Werke; ein Beitrag zur Geschichte der niederländischen Malerei im XVII. Jahrhundert.* Kiel, Schmidt, [1922].

Ovens, Juriaen, *see* **Ovens, Jürgen.**

Overbeck, Johann Friedrich, 1789–1869

9293. Atkinson, J. Beavington. *Overbeck.* New York, Scribner and Welford/London, Sampson Low, 1882.

9294. Heise, Karl G. *Overbeck und sein Kreis.* München, Wolff, 1928.

9295. Howitt, Margaret. *Friedrich Overbeck, sein Leben und Schaffen.* 2 v. Freiburg im Breisgau, Herder, 1886.

9296. Jensen, Jens C. *Friedrich Overbeck, die Werke im Behnhaus.* Lübeck, [Museum für Kunst und Kulturgeschichte, 1963]. (Lübecker Museumshefte, 4).

9297. ———. *Die Zeichnungen Overbecks in der Lübecker Graphiksammlung.* Lübeck, [Museum für Kunst und Kulturgeschichte, n.d.]. (Lübecker Museumshefte, 8).

9298. Laderchi, Camillo. *Sulla vita e sulle opere di Federico Overbeck.* Roma, Menicanti, 1848.

9299. Museum für Kunst und Kulturgeschichte der Hansestadt Lübeck, Behnhaus. *Johann Friedrich Overbeck, 1789–1869: zur zweihundertsten Wiederkehr seines Geburtstages.* 25. Juni bis 3. September 1989. [Herausgegeben von Andreas Blühm und Gerhard Gerkens. Mit Beiträgen von Frank Büttner . . . et al.]. Lübeck, Das Museum, [1989].

Owings, Nathaniel A., 1903– *see* **Skidmore, Louis**

O

P

Pacher, Michael, 1435–1498
Friedrich, ca. 1435–1510

9300. Allesch, Johannes von. *Michael Pacher.* Leipzig, Insel-Verlag, 1931.

9301. Doering, Oscar. *Michael Pacher und die Seinen; eine Tiroler Künstlergruppe am Ende des Mittelalters.* München Gladbach, Kühlen, 1913.

9302. Hempel, Eberhard. *Michael Pacher.* Wien, Schroll, 1931.

9303. Mannowsky, Walter. *Die Gemälde des Michael Pacher.* München, Müller, 1910.

9304. Rasmo, Nicolò. *Michele Pacher.* Milano, Electa, 1969.

9305. Schürer, Oskar. *Michael Pacher.* Bielefeld/Leipzig, Velhagen & Klasing, 1940. (Künstler-Monographien, 121).

9306. Schwabik, Aurel. *Michael Pacher.* Milano, Fabbri, 1966. (I maestri del colore, 191).

9307. ———. *Michael Pachers Grieser Altar.* München, Bruckmann, 1933.

9308. Semper, Hans. *Michael und Friedrich Pacher; ihr Kreis und ihre Nachfolger.* Esslingen, Neff, 1911.

9309. Thurmann, Peter. *Symbolsprache und Bildstruktur: Michael Pacher, der Trinitätsgedanke und die Schriften des Nikolaus von Kues.* Frankfurt am Main/New York, P. Lang, 1987. (Bochumer Schriften zur Kunstgeschichte, 9).

Palladio, Andrea, 1508–1580

9310. Ackerman, James. *Palladio.* Harmondsworth, Eng./New York, Penguin, 1977. 2 ed.

9311. ———. *Palladio's villas.* Locust Valley, N.Y., Augustin, 1967.

9312. Azzi Visentini, Margherita. *Il Palladianesimo in America e l'architettura della villa.* Milano, Polifilo, 1976.

9313. Barbieri, Franco. *The Basilica of Andrea Palladio.* University Park, Penn./London, Pennsylvania State University Press, 1970. (Corpus Palladianum, 2).

9314. Barichella, Vittorio. *Andrea Palladio e la sua scuola.* Lonigo (Italy), Gaspari, 1880.

9315. Basilica Palladiana (Vicenza). *Mostra del Palladio.* Direttore della mostra: Renato Cevese. Milano, Electa, [1974]. 2 ed.

9316. Bassi, Elena. *The Convento della Carità.* Trans. by C. W. Westfall. University Park, Penn./London, Pennsylvania State University Press, 1973. (Corpus Palladianum, 6).

9317. Battilotti, Donata. *The villas of Palladio.* Milano, Electa, 1990.

9318. Bertotti Scamozzi, Ottavio. *Le fabbriche e i disegni di Andrea Palladio, raccolti ed illustrati.* 4 v. Vicenza, Rossi, 1786. (Reprinted, with an introduction by Quentin Hughes: New York, Architectural Book Publishing Co., 1968).

9319. Bordignon Favero, Giampaolo. *The Villa Emo at Fanzolo.* Trans. by Douglas Lewis. University Park, Penn./London, Pennsylvania State University Press, 1972. (Corpus Palladianum, 5).

9320. Boucher, Bruce. *Andrea Palladio, the architect in his time.* New York, Abbeville Press, 1994.

9321. Burger, Fritz. *Die Villen des Andrea Palladio; ein Beitrag zur Entwicklungsgeschichte der Renaissance-Architektur.* Leipzig, Klinkhardt & Biermann, [1909].

9322. Burlington, Richard. *Fabbriche antiche disegnate da Andrea Palladio, vicentino.* Londra, [Burlington], 1730. (Reprint: Farnborough, Eng., Gregg, 1969).

9323. Burns, Howard, et al. *Andrea Palladio, 1508–1580; the portico and the farmyard.* Catalogue by Howard Burns in collaboration with Lynda Fairburn and Bruce Boucher. [Catalogue of an exhibition]. London, Arts Council of Great Britain, 1975.

9324. Cevese, Renato. *Invito a Palladio*. Milano, Rusconi Immagini, 1980.

9325. Constant, Caroline. *The Palladio guide*. New York, Princeton Architectural Press, 1993. 2 ed.

9326. Fancelli, Paolo. *Palladio e Praeneste: archeologia, modelli, progettazione*. Roma, Bulzoni, 1974. (Studi di storia dell'arte, 2).

9327. Ferrari, Luigi. *Palladio e Venezia*. Venezia, Cordella, 1880.

9328. Fletcher, Banister F. *Andrea Palladio, his life and works*. London, Bell, 1902.

9329. Forssman, Erik. *The Palazzo da Porta Festa in Vicenza*. Trans. by Catherine Enggass. University Park, Penn./London, Pennsylvania State University Press, 1973. (Corpus Palladianum, 8).

9330. ———. *Palladios Lehrgebäude: Studien über den Zusammenhang von Architektur und Architektur-Theorie bei Andrea Palladio*. Stockholm, Almquist & Wiksell, 1965. (Acta Universitatis Stockholmiensis, 9).

9331. ———, et al. *Palladio: la sua eredità nel mondo*. Milano, Electa, 1980.

9332. Guinness, Desmond and Sadler, Julius T., Jr. *Palladio: a western progress*. New York, Viking, 1976.

9333. Gurlitt, Cornelius. *Andrea Palladio*. Berlin, Der Zirkel, 1914. (Bibliothek alter Meister der Baukunst, 1).

9334. Harris, John. *The Palladians*. New York, Rizzoli, 1982.

9335. Hofer, Paul. *Palladios Erstling: die Villa Godi Valmarana in Lonedo bei Vicenza; Palladio-Studien, 1*. Basel und Stuttgart, Birkhäuser, 1969. (Geschichte und Theorie der Architektur, 5).

9336. Ivanoff, Nicola. *Palladio*. Milano, Edizioni per il Club del Libro, 1967. (Collana d'arte del Club del Libro, 14).

9337. Köster, Baldur. *Palladio in Amerika: die Kontinuität klassizistichen Bauens in den USA*. München, Prestel, 1990.

9338. Lewis, Douglas. *The drawings of Andrea Palladio*. [Catalogue of a traveling exhibition commencing at the National Gallery of Art, Washington, D.C.]. Washington, D.C., International Exhibitions Foundation, 1981.

9339. Magrini, Antonio. *Memorie intorno la vita e le opere di Andrea Palladio*. Padova, Tipi del Seminario, 1845.

9340. Mazzotti, Giuseppe. *Palladian and other Venetian villas*. Roma, Bestetti, 1966.

9341. Montenari, Giovanni. *Del Teatro Olimpico di Andrea Palladio in Vicenza*. Padova, Conzatti, 1733.

9342. Oosting, J. Thomas. *Andrea Palladio's Teatro Olimpico*. Ann Arbor, Mich., UMI Research Press, 1981. (Theatre and Dramatic Studies, 8).

9343. Palazzo della Gran Guardia (Verona). *Palladio e Verona*. 3 agosto al 5 novembre 1980. Catalogo della mostra a cura di Paola Martini. Verona, Pozza, 1980.

9344. Palladio, Andrea. *I quattro libri dell'architettura*. Venezia, Franceschi, 1570. (English ed.: London, Ware, 1738; reprinted, with an introduction by Adolf K. Placzek: New York, Dover, 1965).

9345. [——— and Jones, Inigo]. *Inigo Jones on Palladio; being the notes by Inigo Jones in the copy of I Quattro Libri dell'Architettura di Andrea Palladio, 1601, in the Library of Worcester College, Oxford*. 2 v. Newcastle-upon-Tyne, Oriel Press, 1970.

9346. Pane, Roberto. *Andrea Palladio*. Torino, Einaudi, 1961. (Collana storica di architettura, 5).

9347. Pée, Herbert. *Die Palastbauten des Andrea Palladio*. Würzburg-Aumühle, Triltsch, 1941. 2 ed.

9348. Pozza, Antonio M. dalla. *Palladio*. Vicenza, Edizioni del Pellicano, 1943.

9349. Puppi, Lionello. *Andrea Palladio*. Boston, New York Graphic Society, 1975.

9350. ———. *Andrea Palladio: the complete works*. London, Faber and Faber, 1989. (CR).

9351. ———. *Palladio drawings*. Trans. by Jeremy Scott. New York, Rizzoli, 1989.

9352. ———. *The Villa Badoer at Fratta Polesine*. Trans. by Catherine Enggass. University Park, Penn./London, Pennsylvania State University Press, 1975. (Corpus Palladianum, 7).

9353. ———, ed. *Palladio e Venezia*. Firenze, Sansoni, 1982.

9354. Reed, Henry H. *Palladio's architecture and its influence: a photographic guide*. Photographs by Joseph C. Farber. New York, Dover, 1980.

9355. Reynolds, James. *Andrea Palladio and the winged device*. New York, Creative Age, 1948.

9356. Rigon, Fernando. *Palladio*. Bologna, Capitol, 1980.

9357. Roop, Guy. *Villas & palaces of Andrea Palladio, 1508–1580*. Color photographs by Franca Parisi Baslini and Anna Pressi. [Text in English, French, Italian, Dutch and Spanish]. Milano, Ghezzi, 1968.

9358. Sale del Palazzo Leoni-Montanari (Vicenza). *Andrea Palladio; il testo, l'immagine, la città*. 30 agosto al 9 novembre 1980. Catalogo della mostra a cura di Lionello Puppi. Milano, Electa, 1980.

9359. Semenzato, Camillo. *The Rotunda of Andrea Palladio*. Trans. by Ann Percy. University Park, Penn./London, Pennsylvania State University Press, 1968. (Corpus Palladianum, 1).

9360. Spielmann, Heinz. *Andrea Palladio und die*

Antike; Untersuchung und Katalog der Zeichnungen aus seinem Nachlass. München, Deutscher Kunstverlag, 1966. (Kunstwissenschaftliche Studien, 37).

9361. Streitz, Robert. *Palladio: la Rotonde et sa géométrie*. Lausanne/Paris, Bibliothèque des Arts, 1973.

9362. Tavernor, Robert. *Palladio and Palladianism*. London, Thames and Hudson, 1991.

9363. Temanza, Tommaso. *Vita di Andrea Palladio, Vicentino*. Venezia, Pasquali, 1762.

9364. Timofiewitsch, Wladimir. *The Chiesa del Redentore*. University Park, Penn./London, Pennsylvania State University Press, 1971. (Corpus Palladianum, 3).

9365. ———. *Die sakrale Architektur Palladios*. München, Fink, 1968.

9366. Trager, Philip. *The villas of Palladio*. Photographs by Philip Trager. Text by Vincent Scully. Foreword by Renato Cevese. Intro. by Michael Graves. Boston, Little, Brown, 1986.

9367. Venditti, Arnaldo. *The Loggia del Capitaniato*. With a note on the pictorial decoration by Franco Barbieri. University Park, Penn./London, Pennsylvania State University Press, 1971. (Corpus Palladianum, 4).

9368. Whitehill, Walter M. *Palladio in America: the work of Andrea Palladio as represented in an exhibition sent to the United States in 1976 by the Centro Internazionale di Studi di Architettura Andrea Palladio of Vicenza*. With an essay on Palladio's influence on American architecture by Frederick Doveton Nichols. Milano, Electa, 1976; distributed by Rizzoli, New York.

9369. Wittkower, Rudolf. *Palladio and Palladianism*. New York, Braziller, 1974.

9370. Zorzi, Giangiorgio. *Le chiese e i ponti di Andrea Palladio*. Venezia, Pozza, 1967.

9371. ———. *I disegni delle antichità di Andrea Palladio*. Pref. di Giuseppe Fiocco. Venezia, Pozza, 1959.

9372. ———. *Le opere pubbliche e i palazzi privati di Andrea Palladio*. Venezia, Pozza, 1965.

9373. ———. *Le ville e i teatri di Andrea Palladio*. Venezia, Pozza, 1968.

Palma, Giacomo *see* Palma Vecchio Palma, il Giovane, 1544–1628 Palma, il Vecchio, *see* Palma, Vecchio

Palma Vecchio, 1480–1528

9374. Ballarin, Alessandro. *Palma il Vecchio*. Milano, Fabbri, 1965. (I maestri del colore, 64).

9375. Gombosi, György. *Palma Vecchio, des Meisters Gemälde und Zeichnungen*. Stuttgart/Berlin, Deutsche Verlags-Anstalt, 1937. (Klassiker der Kunst, 38).

9376. Locatelli, Pasino. *Notizie intorno a Giacomo*

Palma il Vecchio ed alle sue pitture. Bergamo, Cattaneo, 1890.

9377. Mariacher, Giovanni. *Palma il Vecchio*. Milano, Bramante, 1968.

9378. Rylands, Philip. *Palma Il Vecchio, l'opera completa*. Traduzione, Alessandro Giorgetta. Milano, A. Mondadori, 1988.

9379. ———. *Palma Vecchio*. Cambridge/New York, Cambridge University Press, 1992.

9380. Spahn, Annemarie. *Palma Vecchio*. Leipzig, Hiersemann, 1932. (Kunstgeschichtliche Monographien, 20).

Palmer, Erastus Dow, 1817–1904

9381. Webster, James Carson. *Erastus D. Palmer: Sculpture—Ideas*. Newark, University of Delaware Press, 1983.

Palmer, Samuel, 1801–1888, *see also* Burne-Jones, Edward

9382. Alexander, Russell G. *A catalogue of the etchings of Samuel Palmer*. London, Print Collector's Club, 1937. (Print Collector's Club Publications, 16).

9383. Brown, David Blayney. *Samuel Palmer, 1805–1881: catalogue raisonné of the paintings and drawings and a selection of the prints in the Ashmolean Museum*. Oxford, Ashmolean Museum, 1983. (CR).

9384. Butlin, Martin. *Samuel Palmer's sketchbook, 1824 [with] an introduction and commentary*. Preface by Geoffrey Keynes. 2 v. Paris, Trianon Press, 1962; distributed by Quaritch, London.

9385. Grigson, Geoffrey. *Samuel Palmer, the visionary years*. London, Kegan Paul, 1947.

9386. Lister, Raymond. *A catalogue raisonné of the works of Samuel Palmer*. Cambridge/New York, Cambridge University Press, 1988. (CR).

9387. ———. *Samuel Palmer, a biography*. London, Faber, 1974.

9388. ———. *Samuel Palmer and his etchings*. London, Faber, 1969.

9389. Malins, Edward. *Samuel Palmer's Italian honeymoon*. London, Oxford University Press, 1968.

9390. Palmer, Alfred H. *The life and letters of Samuel Palmer, painter and etcher*. London, Seeley, 1892.

9391. Palmer, Samuel. *The letters of Samuel Palmer*. Edited by Raymond Lister. 2 v. Oxford, Clarendon Press, 1974.

9392. Peacock, Carlos. *Samuel Palmer: Shoreham and after*. Greenwich, Conn., New York Graphic Society, 1968.

9393. Sellars, James. *Samuel Palmer*. London, Academy, 1974.

Palmezzano, Marco, 1460–1539

9394. Grigioni, Carlo. *Marco Palmezzano, pittore*

forlivese; nella vita, nelle opere, nell'arte. Faenza, Lega, 1956.

Pan Painter, 5th c. B.C.

9395. Beazley, John D. *The Pan painter.* Mainz, von Zabern, 1974. 4 ed. (Bilder griechischer Vasen, 4).

9396. Follmann, Anna-Barbara. *Der Pan-Maler.* Bonn, Bouvier, 1968. (Abhandlungen zur Kunst-, Musik- und Literaturwissenschaft, 52).

Pankok, Otto, 1893–1966

9397. Greither, Aloys. *Der junge Otto Pankok: das Frühwerk des Malers.* Düsseldorf, Droste, 1977.

9398. Pankok, Otto. *Werkverzeichnis.* Bearbeitet und eingeleitet von Rainer Zimmerman. Mitarbeit, Rolf Jäger. Herausgegeben von Hulda und Eva Pankok und der Otto-Pankok-Gesellschaft. Düsseldorf, Droste, 1985. (CR).

9399. Schifner, Kurt. *Otto Pankok.* Dresden, Verlag der Kunst, 1963.

9400. Zimmermann, Rainer. *Otto Pankok: das Werk des Malers, Holzschneiders und Bildhauers.* Berlin, Rembrandt, 1964.

Pannini, Giovanni Paolo, 1691–1765

9401. Arisi, Ferdinando. *Gian Paolo Panini.* Piacenza, Cassa di Risparmio, 1961.

9402. ———. *Gian Paolo Panini.* Soncino (Via Tinelli 11/A-26029), Edizioni dei Soncino, 1991.

9403. ———. *Giovanni Paolo Panini, 1691–1765.* A cura di Ferdinando Arisi. Milano, Electa, 1993.

9404. Kiene, Michael. *Pannini.* Paris, Réunion des musées nationaux, 1992. (Les Dossiers du Musées du Louvre. Exposition-dossier du Département des peintures, 41).

9405. Ozzòla, Leandro. *Gian Paolo Pannini, pittore.* Torino, Celanza, 1921.

Paolo, Giovanni di see Giovanni di Paolo

Paris, Matthew, 1200–1259

9406. James, Montague R. *Illustrations to the life of St. Alban in Trinity College, Dublin Manuscript E.i.40* [purported to be by Matthew Paris]. With a description of the illustrations. Oxford, Clarendon Press, 1924.

9407. Lewis, Suzanne. *The art of Matthew Paris in the Chronica majora.* Berkeley, University of California Press in collaboration with Corpus Christi College, Cambridge, 1987. (California studies in the history of art, 21).

Parler, Peter, 1330–1399

9408. Kletzl, Otto. *Peter Parler, der Dombaumeister von Prag.* Leipzig, Seemann, 1940.

9409. Neuwirth, Josef. *Peter Parler von Gmünd und seine Familie.* Prag, Calve, 1891.

9410. Reinhold, Hans. *Der Chor des Münsters zu Freiburg i. Br. und die Baukunst der Parlerfamilie.* Strassburg, Heitz, 1929. (Studien zur deutschen Kunstgeschichte, 263).

9411. Schnütgen-Museum, Kunsthalle Köln. *Die Parler und der Schöne Stil, 1350–1400; europäische Kunst unter den Luxemburgern.* 6 v. Herausgegeben von Anton Legner. Köln, Museen der Stadt Köln, 1978–80.

9412. Swoboda, Karl M. *Peter Parler, der Baukünstler und Bildhauer.* Wien, Schroll, 1940.

Parma, Benedetto di see Antelami, Benedetto

Parmigianino, Il, 1503–1540

9413. Affo, Ireneo. *Vita del graziosissimo pittore Francesco Mazzola detto Il Parmigianino.* Parma, Carmignani, 1784.

9414. Copertini, Giovanni. *Il Parmigianino.* 2 v. Parma, Fresching, 1932.

9415. Faelli, Emilio. *Bibliografia Mazzoliana.* Parma, Battei, 1884.

9416. Fagiolo dell'Arco, Maurizio. *Il Parmigianino; un saggio sull'ermetismo nel cinquecento.* Roma, Bulzoni, 1970.

9417. Freedberg, Sydney J. *Parmigianino; his works in painting.* Cambridge, Mass., Harvard University Press, 1950. (CR).

9418. Fröhlich-Bum, Lili. *Parmigianino und der Manierismus.* Wien, Schroll, 1921.

9419. Gould, Cecil Hilton Monk. *Parmigianino.* New York, Abbeville Press, 1995.

9420. Mortara, Antonio E. *Della vita e dei lavori di Francesco Mazzola detto Il Parmigianino.* Casalmaggiore, Bizzarri, 1846.

9421. Popham, Arthur E. *Catalogue of the drawings of Parmigianino.* 3 v. New Haven/London, Yale University Press, 1971. (CR).

9422. Quintavalle, Armando O. *Il Parmigianino.* Milano, Istituto Editoriale Italiano, [1948].

9423. Quintavalle, Augusta G. *Gli affreschi giovanili del Parmigianino.* Milano, Silvana, 1968.

9424. ———. *Gli ultimo affreschi del Parmigianino.* Milano, Silvana, 1971.

9425. Rossi, Paola. *L'opera completa del Parmigianino.* Milano, Rizzoli, 1980. (CR). (Classici dell'arte, 101).

Pascin, Jules, 1885–1930

9426. Brodzky, Horace. *Pascin.* With a preface by James Laver. London, Nicholson & Watson, 1946.

9427. Fels, Florent. *Dessins de Pascin: choix de dessins, maquette et mise en pages d'Arielli.* Paris, Editions du Colombier, 1966.

9428. Freudenheim, Tom L. *Pascin.* [Published in conjunction wih an exhibition at the University Art Museum, University of California, Berkeley, Nov. 15–Dec. 18, 1966]. Berkeley, Regents of the University of California, 1966.

9429. Hemin, Yves . . . et al.]. *Pascin, catalogue raisonné.* 4 v.+ 1 booklet. Paris, A. Rambert; Diffusion, La Bibliothéque des arts, 1984–1991. (CR).

9430. Leeper, John P. *Jules Pascin's Caribbean sketchbook.* Austin, Tex., University of Texas Press, 1964.

9431. Roger-Marx, Claude. *Pascin: carnet de dessins, Berlin-Tunis 1908.* 2 v. Paris, Berggruen, 1968.

9432. Warnod, André. *Pascin.* Préface de Pierre Mac Orlan. Monte Carlo, Sauret, 1954.

9433. Werner, Alfred. *Pascin.* New York, Abrams, [1959].

Pasiteles, 1st c.

9434. Borda, Maurizio. *La scuola di Pasiteles.* Bari, Adriatica Editrice, 1953.

Pasmore, Victor, 1908–

9435. Bell, Clive. *Victor Pasmore.* Harmondsworth, Eng., Penguin, 1945.

9436. Bowness, Alan and Lambertini, Luigi. *Victor Pasmore, a catalogue raisonné of the paintings, constructions and graphics, 1926–1979.* New York, Rizzoli, 1980. (CR).

9437. Lynton, Norbert. *Victor Pasmore: paintings and graphics, 1980–92.* London, Lund Humphries, 1992.

9438. Pasmore, Victor. *Victor Pasmore.* With essays by Lawrence Gowing and Leif Sjöberg and catalogue by Malcolm Cormack. New Haven, Yale Center for British Art, 1988.

Pater, Jean-Baptiste-Joseph, 1695–1736

9439. Ingersoll-Smouse, Florence. *Pater; biographie et catalogue critiques, l'oeuvre complète de l'artiste.* Paris, Beaux-Arts, 1928. (CR).

Peale, Charles Willson, 1741–1827
James, 1749–1831
Raphaelle, 1774–1825
Rembrandt, 1778–1860

9440. Briggs, Berta N. *Charles Willson Peale, artist & patriot.* New York, McGraw-Hill, 1952.

9441. Cikovsky, Nicolai. *Raphaelle Peale still lifes.* With contributions by Linda Bantel, John Wilmerding. Washington, National Gallery of Art; Philadelphia, Pennsylvania Academy of the Fine Arts; New York, Distributed by H.N. Abrams, 1988.

9442. Detroit Institute of Arts. *The Peale family: three generations of American artists.* [Catalogue of an exhibition]. Detroit, Detroit Institute of Arts, 1967.

9443. Maryland Historical Society (Baltimore). *Four generations of commissions: the Peale Collection of the Maryland Historical Society.* March 3–June 29, 1975. Baltimore, Maryland Historical Society, 1975.

9444. Miller, Lillian B. *In pursuit of fame: Rembrandt Peale, 1778–1860.* With an essay on the paintings of Rembrandt Peale, character and conventions by Carol Eaton Hevner. Washington, D.C., National Portrait Gallery; Seattle, University of Washington Press, 1992.

9445. Miller, Lillian B. and Ward, David C., eds. *New perspectives on Charles Willson Peale: a 250th anniversary celebration.* Pittsburgh, Published for the Smithsonian Institution by the University of Pittsburgh Press, 1991.

9446. Peale, Charles Willson. *The selected papers of Charles Willson Peale and his family.* Ed. by Lillian B. Miller. Assistant ed., Sidney Hart. Research historian, Toby B. Appel. New Haven, Published for the National Portrait Gallery Smithsonian Institution by Yale University Press, 1983.

9447. Pennsylvania Academy of Fine Arts (Philadelphia). *Catalogue of an exhibition of portraits by Charles Willson Peale and James Peale and Rembrandt Peale.* [April 11–May 9, 1923]. Philadelphia, Pennsylvania Academy of Fine Arts, 1923.

9448. Richardson, Edgar P., et al. *Charles Willson Peale and his world.* [Published in conjunction with an exhibition at the National Portrait Gallery, Washington, D.C.]. New York, Abrams, 1983.

9449. Sellers, Charles C. *Charles Willson Peale.* 2 v. Philadelphia, American Philosophical Society, 1947. (Memoires of the American Philosophical Society, vol. 23, parts 1–2; new ed.: New York, Scribner, 1969).

9450. ———. *Portraits and miniatures by Charles Willson Peale.* Philadelphia, American Philosophical Society, 1952. (CR). (Transactions of the American Philosophical Society, vol. 42, part 1).

Pechstein, Max, 1881–1955

9451. Biermann, Georg. *Max Pechstein.* Leipzig, Klinkhardt & Biermann, 1920. 2 ed. (Junge Kunst, 1).

9452. Heymann, Walther. *Max Pechstein.* München, Piper, 1916.

9453. Krüger, Günter. *Das druckgraphische Werk Max Pechsteins.* Herausgeber, Max Pechstein-Archiv, Hamburg. Tökendorf, R.C. Pechstein-Verlag, 1988. (CR).

9454. Kunstverein Braunschweig. *Max Pechstein.* 18. April–27. Juni 1982. Braunschweig, Kunstverein Braunschweig, 1982.

9455. Osborn, Max. *Max Pechstein.* Berlin, Propyläen, 1922.

9456. Pechstein, Max. *Erinnerungen.* Herausgegeben von L. Reidemeister. Wiesbaden, Limes, 1960.

Peiffer-Watenphul, Max, 1896–1976

9457. Pasqualucci, Grace Watenphul and Pasqualucci, Alessandra. *Max Peiffer Watenphul, Werk-verzeichnis*. Geleitwort, Bernhard Degen-hart. Köln, DuMont Buchverlag, 1989–1993. (CR).

Pellegrini, Pellegrino *see* Tibaldi, Pellegrino

Penn, Irving, 1917–

9458. Foresta, Merry A., Stepp, William F. *Irving Penn master images: the collections of the National Museum of American Art and the National Portrait Gallery*. Washington D.C., Smithsonian Institution Press, 1994.

9459. Penn, Irving. *Passage: a work record*. Irving Penn with the collaboration of Alexandra Arrowsmith and Nicola Majocchi. Intro. by Alexandra Liberman. Produced by Nicholas Callaway. New York, Knopf [in association with Callaway], 1991.

9460. Szarkowski, John. *Irving Penn*. New York, Museum of Modern Art, 1984.

Pennell, Joseph, 1860–1926

9461. Pennell, Elizabeth R. *The life and letters of Joseph Pennell*. 2 v. Boston, Little, Brown, 1929.

9462. Pennell, Joseph. *The adventures of an illustrator*. Boston, Little, Brown, 1925.

9463. ———. *Joseph Pennell's Liberty Loan poster; a text book for artists and amateurs*. Philadelphia/London, Lippincott, 1918.

9464. ———. *Joseph Pennell's pictures in the land of temples*. Philadelphia, Lippincott/London, Heinemann, 1915.

9465. ———. *Joseph Pennell's pictures of war work in America*. Philadelphia, Lippincott, 1918.

9466. ———. *Joseph Pennell's pictures of war work in England*. Philadelphia, Lippincott/London, Heinemann, 1917.

9467. ———. *Joseph Pennell's pictures of the wonder of work*. Philadelphia, Lippincott, 1916.

9468. Wuerth, Louis A. *Catalogue of the etchings of Joseph Pennell*. With an introduction by Elizabeth Robins Pennell. Boston, Little, Brown, 1928. (CR).

Permeke, Constant, 1886–1952

9469. Avermaete, Roger. *Permeke, 1886–1952*. Bruxelles, Elsevier, 1958.

9470. Bussche, Willy van den. *Permeke*. Antwerpen, Mercatorfonds, 1986.

9471. Fierens, Paul. *Permeke*. Paris, Crès, 1930.

9472. Kunstverein Hannover. *Constant Permeke,*

1886–1952. [Ausstellung]. 25. April bis 8. Juni 1987. Hannover, Der Kunstverein, [1987?].

9473. Langui, Emile. *Constant Permeke*. Anvers, De Sikkel, 1952.

9474. Ridder, André de. *Constant Permeke, 1887[sic]–1952*. Brussel, Paleis der Academiën, 1953.

Permoser, Balthasar, 1651–1732

9475. Asche, Sigfried. *Balthasar Permoser, Leben und Werk*. Berlin, Deutscher Verlag für Kunstwissenschaft, 1978.

9476. ———. *Balthasar Permoser und die Barockskulpture des Dresdener Zwingers*. Frankfurt a.M., Weidlich, 1966.

9477. Beschorner, Hans. *Permoser-Studien*. Dresden, Baensch Stiftung, 1913.

9478. Michalski, Ernst. *Balthasar Permoser*. Frankfurt a.M., Iris, 1927.

Perov, Vasilii Grigor'evich, 1833–1882

9479. Liaskovskaia, Olga A. *V. G. Perov*. Moskva, Iskusstvo, 1979.

9480. Perov, Vasilií Grigorévich. *Vasily Perov: paintings, graphic works*. Compiled and introduced by Marina Shumova. Trans. by Graham Whittaker. Leningrad, Aurora Art Publishers, 1989.

9481. Sobko, N. P. *Vasilií Grigor'evich Perov; ego zhizn' i proizvedeniia*. S. Peterburg, Stasiulevicha, 1892.

Perrault, Claude, 1613–1688

9482. Hallays, André. *Les Perrault*. Paris, Perrin, 1926.

9483. Herrmann, Wolfgang. *The theory of Claude Perrault*. London, Zwemmer, 1973. (Studies in Architecture, 12).

9484. Kambartel, Walter. *Symmetrie und Schönheit; über mögliche Voraussetzungen des neueren Kunstbewusstseins in der Architekturtheorie Claude Perraults*. München, Fink, 1972. (Theorie und Geschichte der Literatur und der Schönen Künste, 20).

9485. Perrault, Claude. *Ordonnance des cinq espèces de collones, selon la méthode des anciens*. Paris, Coignard, 1683. (English ed., trans. by John James: London, Motte/Sturt, 1708).

9486. Picon, Antoine. *Claude Perrault, 1613–1688, ou, La curiosité d'un classique*. Paris, Picard, [1988]; Editeur, Caisse nationale des monuments historiques et des sites, Déégation á l'action artistique de la ville de Paris, 1988.

Perreal, Jean, ca. 1455–1530

9487. Bancel, E. M. *Jehan Perréal dit Jehan de Paris, peintre et valet de chambre des rois*

Charles VIII, Louis XII et François I. Paris, Launette, 1885. (Reprint: Genève, Slatkine, 1970).

9488. Charvet, Léon. *Jehan Perréal, Clément Trie, et Edouard Grand.* Lyon, Glairon Mondet, 1874.

9489. Dufay, Charles J. *Essai biographique sur Jehan Perréal dit Jehan de Paris, peintre et architecte Lyonnais.* Lyon, Brun, 1864.

9490. Maulde de Clavière, René. *Jean Perréal dit Jean de Paris.* Paris, Leroux, 1896.

9491. Renouvier, Jules. *Iehan de Paris, varlet de chambre et peintre ordinaire des rois Charles VIII et Louis XII, précédé d'une notice biographique sur la vie et les ouvrages par Georges Duplessis.* Paris, Aubry, 1861.

Perugino, 1446–1524

9492. Alazard, Jean. *Pérugin, biographie critique.* Paris, Laurens, 1927.

9493. Bombe, Walter. *Perugino, des Meisters Gemälde.* Stuttgart/Berlin, Deutsche Verlags-Anstalt, 1914. (Klassiker der Kunst, 25).

9494. Broussole, Abbé. *La jeunesse du Pérugin et les origins de l'école ombrienne.* Paris, Oudin, 1901.

9495. Camesasca, Ettore. *Tutta la pittura del Perugino.* Milano, Rizzoli, 1959. (Biblioteca d'arte Rizzoli, 36/37).

9496. Canuti, Fiorenzo. *Il Perugino.* 2 v. Siena, La Diana, 1931.

9497. Castellaneta, Carlo [and] Camesasca, Ettore. *L'opera completa del Perugino.* Milano, Rizzoli, 1969. (CR). (Classici dell'arte, 30).

9498. Gnoli, Umberto. *Pietro Perugino.* Spoleto, Argentieri, 1923.

9499. Hutton, Edward. *Perugino.* London, Duckworth/New York, Dutton, [1907].

9500. Knapp, Fritz. *Perugino.* Bielefeld/Leipzig, Velhagen & Klasing, 1926. 2 ed. (Künstler-Monographien, 87).

9501. Mezzanotte, Antonio. *Della vita e delle opere di Pietro Vanucci da Castello della Pieve cognominato Il Perugino; commentario istorico.* Perugia, Baduel/Bartelli, 1836.

9502. Negri Arnoldi, Francesco. *Perugino.* Milano, Fabbri, 1965. (I maestri del colore, 68).

9503. [Orsini, Baldassare]. *Vita elogio e memorie dell'egregio pittore Pietro Perugino e degli scolari di esso.* Perugia, Stamperia Badueliana, 1804.

9504. Scarpellini, Pietro. *Perugino.* Milano, Electa, 1991. (First publ. 1984).

9505. Schmarsow, August. *Peruginos erste Schaffensperiode.* Leipzig, B.G. Teubner, 1915. (Abhandlungen der Philologisch-Historischen Klasse der Königl. Sächsischen Gesellschaft der Wissenschaften, Bd. 31, Nr. 2).

9506. Venturi, Lionello. *Il Perugino* [di] Lionello Venturi [e] *Gli affreschi del Collegio del cambio,* a cura di Giovanni Caradente. Torino, Edizioni Radio italiana, [1955].

9507. Williamson, George C. *Pietro Vannucci, called Perugino.* London, Bell, 1903.

Peruzzi, Baldassare, 1481–1536

9508. Archivio Italiano dell'Arte dei Giardini (San Quirico d'Orcia, Italy). *Baldassare Peruzzi e le ville senesi del Cinquecento.* San Quirico, Archivo Italiano dell'Arte dei Giardini, 1977.

9509. Cataldo, Noella de. *Baldassare Peruzzi, pittore.* Roma, Palombi, [1930].

9510. Comune di Sovicille, Assessorato alla Cultura (Sovicille, Italy). *Baldassare Peruzzi, architetto: V centenario della nascità di Baldassare Peruzzi.* [July 20–August 20, 1981]. Sovicille, Comune di Sovicille, 1981.

9511. Frommel, Christoph L. *Baldassare Peruzzi als Maler und Zeichner.* Wien/München, Schroll, 1967. (Beiheft zum Römischen Jahrbuch für Kunstgeschichte, 11).

9512. ———. *Die Farnesina und Peruzzis architektonisches Frühwerk.* Berlin, de Gruyter, 1961. (Neue Münchner Beiträge zur Kunstgeschichte, 1).

9513. Kent, William W. *The life and works of Baldassare Peruzzi.* New York, Architectural Book Publishing Co., 1925.

9514. Pareto, Vilfredo. *Lettere ai Peruzzi, 1872–1900.* A cura di Tommaso Giancalone-Monaco. In appendice, Lettere di Raffaele Pareto a Emilia Peruzzi. Genève, Librairie Droz, 1984, c.1968. (Travaux de droit, d'économie, de sciences politiques, de sociologie et d'anthropologie, 140. Oeuvres complètes, t. 27).

9515. Peruzzi, Baldassarre. *Baldassarre Peruzzi, Architekturzeichnungen.* Tübingen, Wasmuth, 1984. (CR).

9516. ———. *Baldassarre Peruzzi: pittura scena e architettura nel cinquecento.* A cura di Marcello Faiolo e Maria Luisa Madonna. Roma, Istituto della Enciclopedia Italiana, 1987. (Biblioteca internazionale di cultura, 20).

Pesellino, 1422–1457

9517. Weisbach, Werner. *Francesco Pesellino und die Romantik der Renaissance.* Berlin, Cassirer, 1901.

Pesne, Antoine, 1683–1757

9518. Börsch-Supan, Helmut. *Die Gemälde Antoine Pesnes in den Berliner Schlössern.* Berlin, Verwaltung der Staatlichen Schlösser und Gärten, 1982. (Aus Berliner Schlössern. Kleine Schriften, 7).

9519. ———. *Der Maler Antoine Pesne: Franzose und Preusse.* Friedberg, Podzun-Pallas, 1986.

9520. Galerie Goldschmidt-Wallerstein (Berlin).

Antoine Pesne, 1683–1757. 21. November–19. Dezember [1926]. [Text by Charles F. Foerster]. Berlin, Galerie Goldschmidt-Wallerstein, 1926.

9521. Pesne, Antoine. *Antoine Pesne, 1683–1757: Ausstellung zum 300. Geburtstag.* Bearbeitet von Gerd Bartoschek. Potsdam-Sanssouci: Generaldirektion der Staatlichen Schlösser und Gärten, 1983.

9522. Poensgen, Georg, et al. *Antoine Pesne.* Berlin, Deutscher Verein für Kunstwissenschaft, 1958. (CR).

Petrarca-Meister *see* **Weiditz, Hans**

Petrus Christus *see* **Cristus, Petrus**

Pevsner, Antoine, 1886–1962 *see also* **Gabo, Naum**

9523. Peissi, Pierre [and] Giedion-Welcker, Carola. *Antoine Pevsner.* Trans. by Haakon Chevalier. Neuchâtel (Switzerland), Editions du Griffon, 1961.

Peyron, Pierre, 1744–1814

9524. Rosenberg, Pierre, Sandt, Udolpho van de. *Pierre Peyron, 1744–1814.* Neuilly-sur-Seine, Arthena, 1983.

Pfeil, Hartmuth, 1893–1962

9525. Keil, Heinrich. *Hartmuth Pfeil: Werke aus fünf Jahrzehnten.* Darmstadt, Eduard Roether Verlag, 1987.

Phidias, ca. 500–430 B.C.

9526. Buschor, Ernst. *Phidias der Mensch.* München, Bruckmann, 1948.

9527. Caro-Delvaille, Henry. *Phidias, ou le génie grec.* Paris, Alcan, 1922.

9528. Collignon, Maxime. *Phidias.* Paris, Rouam, [1886].

9529. Diehl, August. *Die Reiter Schöpfungen der phidiasischen Kunst.* Berlin, de Gruyter, 1921.

9530. Johansen, Peter. *Phidias and the Parthenon sculptures.* Trans. by Ingeborg Andersen. Kjøbenhavn, Gyldendal, 1925.

9531. Langlotz, Ernst. *Phidiasprobleme.* Frankfurt a.M., Klostermann, 1947.

9532. Lechat, Henri. *Phidias et la sculpture grecque au Vᵉ siècle.* Paris, Librairie de l'Art Ancien et Moderne, 1906.

9533. Liegle, Josef. *Der Zeus des Phidias.* Berlin, Weidmann, 1952.

9534. Mallwitz, Alfred und Schiering, Wolfgang. *Die Werkstatt des Pheidias in Olympia.* Berlin, De Gruyter, 1964. (Olympische Forschungen, 5).

9535. Mueller, Karl O. *De Phidiae vita et operibus.* Gottingae, Dieterich, 1827.

9536. Petersen, Eugen. *Die Kunst des Pheidias am Parthenon und zu Olympia.* Berlin, Weidmann, 1873.

9537. Ronchaud, Louis de. *Phidias, sa vie et ses ouvrages.* Paris, Gide, 1861.

9538. Semler, Christian. *Die Tempelsculpturen aus der Schule des Phidias im Britischen Museum.* Hamburg, Meissner, 1858.

9539. Settis, Salvatore. *Saggio sull'Afrodite Urania di Fidia.* Pisa, Nistri-Lischi, 1966. (Studi di lettere, storia e filosofia, 30).

9540. Ubell, Hermann. *Phidias.* Berlin, Bard, Marquardt, [1904]. (Die Kunst, 31).

9541. Waldstein, Charles. *Essays on the art of Pheidias.* Cambridge, Cambridge University Press, 1885.

Piazzetta, Giovanni Battista, 1682–1754

9542. Knox, George. *Giambattista Piazzetta, 1682–1754.* Oxford, Clarendon Press; New York, Oxford University Press, 1992.

9543. ———. *Piazzetta: a tercentenary exhibition of drawings, prints, and books.* Washington, National Gallery of Art, 1983.

9544. Pallucchini, Rodolfo. *L'arte di Giovanni Battista Piazzetta.* Bologna, Maylender, 1934.

9545. Piazzetta, Giovanni Battista. *G.B. Piazzetta, disegni, incisioni, libri, manoscritti: San Giorgio maggiore, Venezia.* Introduzione di George Knox. Scritti di Alessandro Bettagno . . . [et al.]. Presentazione di Bruno Visentini. Vicenza, N. Pozza, 1983. (Grafica veneta, 4).

9546. ———. *Giambattista Piazzetta, il suo tempo, la sua scuola.* Venezia, Marsilio, 1983.

9547. [and] Mariuz, Adriano. *L'opera completa del Piazzetta.* Milano, Rizzoli, 1982. (CR). (Classici dell'arte).

9548. Ravà, Aldo. *G. B. Piazzetta.* Firenze, Alinari, 1921.

9549. Ruggeri, Ugo. *Disegni piazzetteschi; disegni inediti di raccolte bergamasche.* Bergamo, Istituto Italiano d'Arte Grafiche, 1967. (Monumenta Bergomensia, 17).

9550. White, D. Maxwell e Sewter, A. C. *I disegni di G. B. Piazzetta nella Biblioteca Reale di Torino.* Testo italiano in collaborazione con Maria Pia Nazzari di Calabiana. Roma, Istituto Poligrafico dello Stato, 1969. (CR).

Picabia, Francis, 1878–1953

9551. André, Edouard. *Picabia, le peintre & l'aqua-fortiste.* Paris, Rey, 1908.

9552. Camfield, William A. *Francis Picabia: his life, art and times.* Princeton, N.J., Princeton University Press, 1979.

9553. Fagiolo Dell'Arco, Maurizio. *Francis Picabia.* Milano, Fabbri, 1976.

9554. Galerie Haussmann (Paris). *Picabia.* 10

février au 25 février 1905. [Text by L. Roger-Milès]. Paris, Galerie Haussmann, 1905.

9555. Grand Palais (Paris). *Francis Picabia.* 23 janvier–29 mars 1976. Paris, Centre National d'Art et de Culture Georges Pompidou, 1976.

9556. La Hire, Marie de. *Francis Picabia.* Paris, Galerie La Cible, 1920.

9557. Le Bot, Marc. *Francis Picabia et la crise des valeurs figuratives, 1900–1925.* Paris, Klincksieck, 1968.

9558. Picabia, Francis. *Ecrits.* Textes réunis et présentés par Olivier Revault d'Allones. 2 v. Paris, Belfond, 1975/1978.

9559. ———. *Francis Picabia.* Herausgegeben von der Städtischen Kunsthalle Düsseldorf und dem Kunsthaus Zürich. Mit einem einführenden Text von Schuldt. Redaktion des Kataloges Marianne Heinz. Köln, DuMont Buchverlag, 1984. 2. überarbeitete Aufl.

9560. ———. *Picabia: opere, 1898–1951.* Milano, Electa, 1986.

9561. ———. *Picabia, 1879–1953.* Stuttgart, Edition Cantz; Frankfurt/Main, Galerie Neuendorf, 1988.

9562. Sanouillet, Michel. *Picabia.* Paris, L'Oeil du Temps, 1964.

Picasso, Pablo, 1881–1973

9563. Alberti, Rafael. *Picasso, el rayo que no cesa.* Barcelona, Poligrafa, 1975.

9564. Arnheim, Rudolf. *Picasso's Guernica: the genesis of a painting.* Berkeley/Los Angeles, University of California Press, 1962.

9565. Ashton, Dore, ed. *Picasso on art: a selection of views.* New York, Viking, 1972.

9566. Badisches Landesmuseum (Karlsruhe). *Picasso und die Antike.* Zusammengestellt und bearbeitet von Jürgen Thimme. [September 6–November 17, 1974]. Karlsruhe, Badisches Landesmuseum, 1974.

9567. Barr, Alfred H., Jr. *Picasso: fifty years of his art.* New York, Museum of Modern Art, 1946; distributed by Simon & Schuster, New York.

9568. Berger, John. *The success and failure of Picasso.* Harmondsworth, Eng., Penguin, 1965.

9569. Bloch, Georges. *Pablo Picasso.* 4 v. [Text in French, English, and German]. Berne, Kornfeld et Klipstein, 1968–1979. (CR).

9570. Blunt, Anthony and Pool, Phoebe. *Picasso, the formative years; a study of his sources.* Greenwich, Conn., New York Graphic Society, 1962.

9571. Boeck, Wilhelm and Sabartes, Jaime. *Picasso.* New York, Abrams, 1955.

9572. Boggs, Jean Sutherland. *Picasso & things.* With essays by Marie-Laure Bernadac & Brigitte Léal. Cleveland, Cleveland Museum of Art; New York, distributed by Rizzoli International Publications, 1992.

9573. Bollinger, Hans. *Picasso for Vollard.* Trans. by Norbert Guterman. New York, Abrams, 1956.

9574. Bonet Correa, Antonio, et al. *Picasso, 1881–1981.* Madrid, Taurus, 1981.

9575. Boudaille, Georges. *The drawings of Picasso.* London, Hamlyn, 1988.

9576. Brassaï. *Picasso and company.* Trans. by Francis Price. Preface by Henry Miller. Introd. by Roland Penrose. Garden City, N.Y., Doubleday, 1966.

9577. Cabanne, Pierre. *Pablo Picasso, his life and times.* Trans. by Harold J. Salemson. New York, Morrow, 1977.

9578. Camón Aznar, José. *Picasso y el cubismo.* Madrid, Espasa-Calpe, 1956.

9579. Cassou, Jean. *Picasso.* Trans. by Mary Chamot. New York, Hyperion Press, 1940.

9580. Champris, Pierre de. *Picasso, ombre et soleil.* Paris, Gallimard, 1960.

9581. Cirici-Pellicer, Alejandro. *Picasso avant Picasso.* Traduit de l'espagnol par Marguerite de Flores et Ventura Gasol. Genève, Cailler, 1950. 2 ed. (Peintres et sculpteurs d'hier et d'aujourd'hui, 6).

9582. Cirlot, Juan-Edouardo. *Picasso, birth of a genius.* Trans. by Paul Elek. New York, Praeger, 1972.

9583. Cocteau, Jean. *Picasso.* Paris, Stock, 1923.

9584. Cooper, Douglas. *Picasso theatre.* New York, Abrams, 1968.

9585. Czwiklitzer, Christopher. *Picasso's posters.* New York, Random House, 1971. (CR).

9586. Daix, Pierre. *La vie de peintre de Pablo Picasso.* Paris, Editions du Seuil, 1977.

9587. Daix, Pierre and Daux, Pierre. *Picasso 1900–1906: catalogue raisonné de loeuvre peint.* 1900, 1901, 1906, Pierre Daux. 1902 á 1905, Georges Boudaille. Catalogue établi avec la collaboration de Joan Rosselet. Neuchâtel, Editions Ides et Calendes, 1988. (CR).

9588. Daix, Pierre and Boudaille, Georges. *Picasso: the blue and rose periods; a catalogue raisonné of the paintings, 1900–1906.* Trans. by P. Pool. Greenwich, Conn., New York Graphic Society, 1967. (CR).

9589. Daix, Pierre and Rosselet, Joan. *Picasso, the cubist years, 1907–1916; a catalogue raisonné of the paintings and related works.* Trans. by Dorothy S. Blair. Boston, New York Graphic Society, 1979. (CR).

9590. Descargues, Pierre. *Picasso.* Trans. by Roland Balay. Introd. by John Russell. Photographs by Edward Quinn. New York, Felicie, 1974.

9591. Dufour, Pierre. *Picasso, 1950–1968; biographical and critical study.* Trans. by Robert Allen. Geneva, Skira, 1969. Distributed by World, Cleveland. (The Taste of Our Time, 49).

9592. Duncan, David D. *Goodbye, Picasso.* New York, Grosset & Dunlap, 1974.

9593. ———. *Picasso's Picassos.* New York, Harper, 1961.

9594. Elgar, Frank. *Picasso, a study of his work.* [With] a biographical study by Robert Maillard. Trans. by Francis Scarfe. New York, Praeger, 1956.

9595. Eluard, Paul. *Pablo Picasso.* Trans. by Joseph T. Shipley. New York, Philosophical Library, 1947.

9596. Fogg Art Museum (Cambridge, Mass.). *Master drawings by Picasso.* [Catalogue by Gary Tinterow]. Cambridge, Mass., President and Fellows of Harvard College, 1981.

9597. Gallwitz, Klaus. *Picasso at 90: the late work.* New York, Putnam, 1971.

9598. ———. *Picasso, the heroic years.* New York, Abbeville Press, 1985.

9599. Gayo Nuno, Juan A. *Bibliografia critica y antologica de Picasso.* San Juan, Puerto Rico, Ediciones de la Torre, Universidad de Puerto Rico, 1966.

9600. Gedo, Mary M. *Picasso: art as autobiography.* Chicago/London, University of Chicago Press, 1980.

9601. Geiser, Bernhard. *Picasso, peintre-graveur.* 2 v. Berne, Geiser, 1933/1968. (CR).

9602. ———. *Picasso, peintre-graveur.* Corrections, refonte et supplément par Brigitte Baer. Berne, Editions Kornfeld, 1986. Ed. rév. (CR).

9603. ——— and Bollinger, Hans. *Picasso, fifty-five years of his graphic work.* Trans. by Lisbeth Gombrich. New York, Abrams, 1955. (CR).

9604. Gieure, Maurice. *Initiation à l'oeuvre de Picasso.* Paris, Editions des Deux Mondes, 1951.

9605. Giraudy, Danièle, et al. *L'oeuvre de Picasso à Antibes.* 2 v. [Exhibition and catalogue organized by Danièle Giraudy, assisted by Michèle Pinguet and Gilbert Gianangelli]. Antibes, Musée Picasso/Château Grimaldi, 1981.

9606. Goeppert, Sebastian, Goeppert-Frank, Herma, and Cramer, Patrick. *Pablo Picasso, catalogue raisonné des livres illustrés.* Genève, Cramer, 1983. (CR).

9607. Hayward Gallery (London). *Picasso's Picassos.* An exhibition from the Musée Picasso, Paris. 17 July–11 October 1981. London, Arts Council of Great Britain, 1981.

9608. Hilton, Timothy. *Picasso.* London, Thames and Hudson, 1975.

9609. Horodisch, Abraham. *Picasso as a book artist.* Trans. by I. Grafe. Cleveland/New York, World, 1962.

9610. Huelin y Ruiz-Blasco, Ricardo. *Pablo Ruiz Picasso; su infancia, su adolescencia, y primeros anos de juventud, todo ello precedido de datos historicos, anecdotas, curiosidades y recuerdos de la familia Ruiz-Blasco.* Prólogo de Enrique Lafuente Ferrari. Madrid, Revista de Occidente, 1975.

9611. Jaffé, Hans L. C. *Pablo Picasso.* Trans. by Norbert Guterman. New York, Abrams, 1964.

9612. Jardot, Maurice. *Pablo Picasso: drawings.* New York, Abrams, 1959.

9613. Jouffroy, Jean P. et Ruiz, Edouard. *Picasso de l'image à la lettre.* Paris, Temps Actuels, 1981.

9614. Kahnweiler, Daniel H. *Les sculptures de Picasso.* Paris, du Chêne, 1948.

9615. ———, et al. *Picasso, 1881–1973.* London, Elek, 1973.

9616. Kibbey, Ray A. *Picasso: a comprehensive bibliography.* New York/London, Garland, 1977.

9617. Larrea, Juan. *Guernica, Pablo Picasso.* Trans. by Alexander H. Krappe. Edited by Walter Pach. Introd. by Alfred H. Barr, Jr. New York, Valentin, 1947. (Reprint: New York, Arno, 1969).

9618. Leighten, Patricia Dee. *Re-ordering the universe: Picasso and anarchism, 1897–1914.* Princeton, Princeton University Press, 1989.

9619. Leonhard, Kurt [and] Bollinger, Hans. *Picasso: recent etchings, lithographs, and linoleum cuts.* Trans. by Norbert Guterman. New York, Abrams, 1967. (CR).

9620. Level, André. *Picasso.* Paris, Crès, 1928.

9621. Leymarie, Jean. *Picasso drawings.* Trans. by Stuart Gilbert. Geneva, Skira, 1957; distributed by World, Cleveland. (The Taste of Our Time).

9622. ———. *Picasso: the artist of the century.* Trans. by James Emmons. New York, Viking, 1972.

9623. Lipton, Eunice. *Picasso criticism, 1901–1939; the making of an artist hero.* New York/London, Garland, 1976. (Outstanding Dissertations in the Fine Arts).

9624. Marrero, Vincente. *Picasso and the bull.* Trans. by Anthony Kerrigan. Chicago, Regnery, 1956.

9625. ———. *Picasso y el monstruo: una introducción.* Madrid, Editorial de la Universidad Complutense, 1986.

9626. McCully, Marilyn, ed. *A Picasso anthology: documents, criticism, reminiscences.* Princeton, N.J., Princeton University Press, 1982.

9627. Merli, Joan. *Picasso, el artista y la obra de nuestro tiempo.* Buenos Aires, El Ateneo, 1942.

9628. Ministerio de Cultura, Direccion General de Bellas Artes, Archivos y Bibliotecas (Madrid). *Una sociedad a fines del siglo XIX:*

Malaga/Estudios Picassianos/Picasso y Malaga. 3 v. [Issued in commemoration of the 100th anniversary of Picasso's birth]. Madrid, Ministerio de Cultura, 1981.

9629. Moravia, Alberto [and] Lecaldano, Paolo. *L'opera completa di Picasso, blu e rosa*. Milano, Rizzoli, 1968. (CR). (Classici dell'arte, 22).

9630. Mourlot, Fernand. *Picasso lithographe*. Préface de Jaime Sabartés. 4 v. Monte Carlo, Sauret, 1949–1964. (CR). (English ed., in a reduced format and with additional entries, trans. by Jean Didry: Boston, Boston Book and Art Co., 1970).

9631. Mujica Gallo, Manuel. *La minitauromaquia de Picasso*. Madrid, Prensa Espanola, 1971.

9632. Museum of Modern Art (New York). *Pablo Picasso, a retrospective*. Edited by William Rubin; chronology by Jane Fluegel. [May 22–September 16, 1980]. New York, Museum of Modern Art, 1980; distributed by New York Graphic Society, Boston.

9633. ———. *The sculpture of Picasso*. [Essay by Roland Penrose; chronology by Alicia Legg]. New York, Museum of Modern Art, 1967.

9634. O'Brian, Patrick. *Pablo Ruiz Picasso*. New York, Putnam, 1976.

9635. Olivier, Fernande. *Picasso et ses amis*. Préface de Paul Léautaud. Paris, Stock, 1933. (English ed., trans. by Jane Miller: New York, Appleton-Century, 1965).

9636. Oriol Anguera, A. *Guernica al desnudo*. Barcelona, Polígrafa, 1979.

9637. Ors y Rovira, Eugenio d'. *Pablo Picasso*. Trans. by Warren B. Wells. New York, Weyhe, 1930.

9638. Palau i Fabre, Josep. *Picasso en Cataluna*. [Text in English, French, Spanish, and German]. Barcelona, Polígrafa, 1966.

9639. ———. *Picasso i els seus amics catalans*. Barcelona, Aedos, 1971.

9640. ———. *Picasso: the early years, 1881–1907*. Trans. by Kenneth Lyons. New York, Rizzoli, 1981.

9641. ———. *El secret de les Menines de Picasso*. Barcelona, Polígrafa, 1981.

9642. ———. *Picasso Cubism (1907–1917)*. Translated from the Catalan by Susan Branyas, Richard-Lewis Rees, and Patrick Zabalbeascoa. New York, Rizzoli, 1990.

9643. Parmelin, Hélène. *Intimate secrets of a studio—Picasso: women, Cannes and Mougins; Picasso, the artist and his model; Picasso at Notre Dame de Vie*. 3 v. New York, Abrams, 1965–1967.

9644. ———. *Picasso plain: an intimate portrait*. Trans. by Humphrey Hare. New York, St. Martin's, 1963.

9645. Penrose, Roland. *Picasso, his life and work*. Berkeley/Los Angeles, University of California Press, 1981. 3 ed.

9646. Picasso, Pablo. *Carnet Catalan*. [Preface and notes by Douglas Cooper]. Paris, Berggruen, 1958.

9647. ———. *Carnet Picasso: La Coruna, 1894–1895*. 2 v. [Introduction by Juan Ainaud de Lasarte]. Barcelona, Gili, 1971.

9648. ———. *Carnet Picasso: Paris, 1900*. 2 v. [Introduction by Rosa Maria Subirana]. Barcelona, Gili. 1972.

9649. ———. *Je suis le cahier: the sketchbooks of Picasso*. Ed. by Arnold Glimcher and Marc Glimcher. Boston, Atlantic Monthly Press; New York, Pace Gallery, 1986. (CR).

9650. ———. *Late Picasso: paintings, sculpture, drawings, prints 1953–1972*. London, Tate Gallery, 1988.

9651. ———. *Le dernier Picasso, 1953–1973: 17 février–16 mai 1988, exposition*. [Organisée par le Musée national d'art moderne, Paris, le Musée Picasso, Paris, la Tate Gallery, Londres.] Paris, Centre Georges Pompidou, 1988.

9652. ———. *Pablo Picasso: die Lithographien*. Einleitung von Ernst-Gerhard Güse. Werkverzeichnis von Bernd Rau. Stuttgart, G. Hatje, 1988. (CR).

9653. ———. *Picasso: the Ludwig Collection: paintings, drawings, sculptures, ceramics, prints*. Ed. by Evelyn Weiss and Maria Teresa Ocaña. With contributions by Pierre Daix . . . [et al.]. Munich, Prestel-Verlag; [New York, Distributed in the USA and Canada by te Neues Publishing], 1992.

9654. ———. *Picassos Klassizismus, Werke von 1914–1934*. Herausgegeben von Ulrich Weisner. Bielefeld, Kunsthalle Bielefeld, 1988.

9655. ———. *Picassos Surrealismus: Werke 1925–1937*. Herausgegeben von Ulrich Weisner. Bielefeld, Kunsthalle Bielefeld, 1991.

9656. Quintanilla, Felix M. *Proceso a Picasso*. Barcelona, Acervo, 1972.

9657. Ramié, Alain. *Picasso: catalogue of the edited ceramic works, 1947–1971*. Vallauris, France, Madoura, 1988. (CR).

9658. Ramié, Georges. *Picasso's ceramics*. Trans. by Kenneth Lyons. New York, Viking, 1976. (CR).

9659. ———. *Ceramics of Picasso*. Trans. by Kenneth Lyons. Barcelona, Ediciones Polígrafa, 1985.

9660. Raynal, Maurice. *Picasso, biographical and critical study*. Trans. by James Emmons. Geneva, Skira, 1953. (The Taste of Our Time, 4).

9661. Richardson, John. *A life of Picasso*. With the collaboration of Marilyn McCully. New York, Random House, 1991.

9662. Rodriguez-Aguilera, Cesareo. *Picassos de Barcelona*. Barcelona, Polígrafa, 1974. (CR).

9663. Russell, Frank D. *Picasso's Guernica: the*

labyrinth of narrative and vision. London, Thames and Hudson, 1980.

9664. Russoli, Franco [and] Minervino, Fiorella. *L'opera completa di Picasso, cubista*. Milano, Rizzoli, 1972. (CR). (Classici dell'arte, 64).

9665. Sabartés, Jaime. *Picasso: an intimate portrait*. Trans. by Angel Flores. New York, Prentice-Hall, 1948.

9666. ———. *Picasso: documents iconographiques*. Avec une préface et des notes. Traduction de Félia Leal et Alfred Rosset. Genève, Cailler, 1954.

9667. ———. *Picasso: toreros*. With four original lithographs. Trans. by Patrick Gregory. New York, Braziller/Monte-Carlo, Sauret, 1961.

9668. Salas de Exposiciones de la Subdirección General de Artes Plásticas, Ministerio de Cultura (Madrid). *Picasso; obra gráfica original, 1904–1971*. 2 v. Mayo–Julio, 1981. Madrid, Ministerio de Cultura, 1981.

9669. Salinero Portero, José. *Libros sobre Picasso en el Museo de Malaga*. Madrid, Ministerio de Cultura, 1981.

9670. Schiff, Gert. *Picasso, the last years, 1963–1973*. New York, G. Braziller, in association with the Grey Art Gallery & Study Center, New York University, 1983.

9671. ———, ed. *Picasso in perspective*. Englewood Cliffs, N.J., Prentice-Hall, 1976.

9672. Schürer, Oskar. *Pablo Picasso*. Berlin/Leipzig, Klinkhardt & Biermann, 1927. (Junge Kunst, 49/50).

9673. Sopena Ibanez, Federico. *Picasso y la musica*. Madrid, Ministerio de Cultura, 1982.

9674. Spies, Werner. *Picasso, Pastelle, Zeichnungen, Aquarelle*. Stuttgart, Hatje, 1986.

9675. ———. *Sculpture by Picasso, with a catalogue of the works*. Trans. by Maxwell Brownjohn. New York, Abrams, 1971. (CR).

9676. Stein, Gertrude. *On Picasso*. Edited by Edward Burns. Afterword by Leon Katz and Edward Burns. New York, Liveright, 1970.

9677. Uhde, Wilhelm. *Picasso and the French tradition*. Trans. by F. M. Loving. New York, Weyhe, 1929.

9678. Vallentin, Antonina. *Pablo Picasso*. Paris, Michel, 1957. (English ed.: Garden City, N.Y., Doubleday, 1963).

9679. Zervos, Christian. *Pablo Picasso*. 33 v. Paris, Cahiers d'Art, 1932–1978. (CR).

Piero della Francesca *see* Francesca, Piero della

Piero Di Niccolò Lamberti *see* Lamberti, Piero

Piero di Cosimo, 1462–1521

9680. Bacci, Mina. *L'opera completa di Piero di Cosimo*. Milano, Rizzoli, 1976. (CR). (Classici dell'arte, 88).

9681. ———. *Piero di Cosimo*. Milano, Bramante, 1966. (Antichi pittori italiani, 4).

9682. Douglas, Robert L. *Piero di Cosimo*. Chicago, University of Chicago Press, 1946.

9683. Knapp, Fritz. *Piero di Cosimo: ein Übergangsmeister vom florentiner Quattrocento zum Cinquecento*. Halle, Knapp, 1899.

Pietro da Cortona, 1596–1669

9684. Abbate, Francesco. *Pietro da Cortona*. Milano, Fabbri, 1965. (I maestri del colore, 109).

9685. Briganti, Giuliano. *Pietro da Cortona, o della pittura barocca*. Firenze, Sansoni, 1962. (CR).

9686. Campbell, Malcolm. *Pietro da Cortona at the Pitti Palace; a study of the Planetary Rooms and related projects*. Princeton, N.J., Princeton University Press, 1977. (Princeton Monographs in art and archeology, 41).

9687. Merz, Jörg Martin. *Pietro da Cortona: der Aufstieg zum führenden Maler im barocken Rom*. Tübingen, E. Wasmuth, 1991. (Tübinger Studien zur Archäologie und Kunstgeschichte, 8).

9688. Noehles, Karl. *La chiesa dei SS. Luca e Martina nell' opera di Pietro da Cortona*. Con contributi di Giovanni Incisa della Rocchetta e Carlo Pietrangeli. Presentazione di Mino Maccari. Roma, Bozzi, 1970. (Saggi e studi di storia dell'arte, 3).

Pietro, Sano di *See* Sano di Pietro

Pigalle, Jean-Baptiste, 1714–1785

9689. Musée du Louvre. *Jean-Baptiste Pigalle, 1714–1785: sculptures du Musée du Louvre*. Par Jean-René Gaborit. Paris, Ministère de la culture, Editions de la Réunion des musées nationaux, 1985.

9690. Réau, Louis. *J.-B. Pigalle*. Paris, Tisné, 1950.

9691. Rocheblave, Samuel. *Jean-Baptiste Pigalle*. Paris, Lévy, 1919.

9692. Tarbé, Prosper. *La vie et les oeuvres de Jean-Baptiste Pigalle*. Paris, Renouard, 1859.

Pikov, Mikhail Ivanovich, 1903–

9693. Miamlin, Igor G. *Mikhail Ivanovich Pikov*. Leningrad, Khudozhnik RSFSR, 1968.

Pilo, Carl Gustaf, 1711–1793

9694. Byesen, Lars Rostrup. *Carl Gustaf Pilo i Danmark: utställning i Nationalmuseum 1985*. Katalogtext, Lars Rostrup Byesen. Oversåttning och katalogredaktion, Ulf G. Johnsson. Stockholm, Nationalmuseum, [1985]. (Nationalmusei utställningskatalog, 488).

9695. Jungmarker, Gunnar. *Carl Gustaf Pilo, son*

tecknare. Stockholm, Allmänna, 1973.

9696. Sirén, Osvald. *Carl Gustav Pilo och hans förhållande till den samtida porträttkonsten i Sverige och Danmark.* Stockholm, Tullberg, 1902. (Sveriges Allmänna Konstförenings Publikation, 11).

Pilon, Germain, 1536–1590

9697. Babelon, Jean. *Germain Pilon; biographie et catalogue critiques, l'oeuvre complète de l'artiste.* Paris, Beaux-Arts, 1927. (CR).

9698. Terrasse, Charles. *Germain Pilon, biographie critique.* Paris, Laurens, 1930.

Pimenov, Stepan Stepanovich, 1784–1833

9699. Petrova, E. N. *Stepan Stepanovich Pimenov.* Moskva, Izogiz, 1961.

Pineau, Dominique, 1718–1786
François Nicolas, 1746–1823
Jean Baptiste, 1652–1715
Nicolas, 1684–1754
Pierre Dominique, 1842–1886

9700. Blais, Emile. *Les Pineau, sculpteurs, dessinateurs des bâtiments du roy, graveurs, architects (1652–1886).* Paris, Société des Bibliophiles Français, 1892.

9701. Deshairs, Léon. *Dessins originaux des maîtres décorateurs; les dessins du Musée et de la Bibliothèque des arts décoratifs: Nicolas et Dominique Pineau.* Paris, Longuet, 1914.

Pinelli, Bartolomeo, 1781–1835

9702. Mariani, Valerio. *Bartolomeo Pinelli.* Roma, Olympus, 1948.

9703. Pacini, Renato. *Bartolomeo Pinelli e la Roma del tempo suo.* Milano, Treves, 1935.

9704. Palazzo Braschi (Rome). *Bartolomeo Pinelli.* A cura di Giovanni Incisa della Rocchetta. Prefazione di Valerio Mariani. Maggio-luglio, 1956. Roma, Amici dei Musei di Roma, 1956.

9705. Raggi, Oreste. *Cenni intorno alla vita ed alle opere principale di Bartolomeo Pinelli.* Roma, Salviucci, 1835.

Pinturicchio, 1454–1513

9706. Carli, Enzo. *Il Pintoricchio.* Milano, Electa, 1960.

9707. Ehrle, Francesco e Stevenson, Enrico. *Gli affreschi del Pinturicchio nell'appartamento Borgia del Palazzo Apostolica Vaticano.* Roma, Danesi, 1897.

9708. Goffin, Arnold. *Pinturicchio, biographie critique.* Paris, Laurens, 1908.

9709. Phillips, Evelyn M. *Pintoricchio.* London, Bell, 1901.

9710. Ricci, Corrado. *Pintoricchio (Bernardino di Betto of Perugia): his life, work and time.*

Trans. by Florence Simmonds. Philadelphia, Lippincott, 1902.

9711. Schmarsow, August. *Pinturicchio in Rom, eine kritische Studie.* Stuttgart, Spemann, 1882.

9712. Steinmann, Ernst. *Pinturicchio.* Bielefeld/ Leipzig, Velhagen & Klasing, 1898. (Künstler-Monographien, 37).

9713. Vermiglioli, Giovanni B. *Di Bernardino Pinturicchio, pittore Perugino de' secoli XV. XVI; memorie raccolte e pubblicate.* Perugia, Baduel, 1837.

Pinwell, George John, 1842–1875

9714. Williamson, George C. *George J. Pinwell and his works.* London, Bell, 1900.

Piombo, Sebastiano Luciani, 1485–1547

9715. Archiardi, Pietro d'. *Sebastiano del Piombo, monografia storico-artistica.* Roma, Casa Editrice de l'Arte, 1908.

9716. Bernardini, Giorgio. *Sebastiano del Piombo.* Bergamo, Istituto Italiano d'Arti Grafiche, 1908.

9717. Biagi, Pietro. *Memorie storico-critiche intorno alla vita ed alle opere di F. Sebastiano Luciani soprannominato del Piombo.* Venezia, Picotti, 1826.

9718. Dussler, Luitpold. *Sebastiano del Piombo.* Basel, Holbein, 1942.

9719. Hirst, Michael. *Sebastiano del Piombo.* Oxford, Clarendon Press, 1981. (Oxford Studies in the History of Art and Architecture).

9720. Pallucchini, Rodolfo. *Sebastian Viniziano (Fra Sebastiano del Piombo).* Milano, Mondadori, 1944.

9721. Volpe, Carlo [and] Lucco, Mauro. *L'opera completa di Sebastiano del Piombo.* Milano, Rizzoli, 1980. (CR). (Classici dell'arte).

Piper, John, 1903–1992

9722. Betjeman, John. *John Piper.* Harmondsworth, Eng., Penguin, 1944. (Penguin Modern Painters).

9723. Piper, John. *John Piper, paintings and watercolors.* [Exhibition] December 7–29, 1984, Marlborough Gallery, Inc., New York. New York, the Gallery, 1984.

9724. West, Anthony. *John Piper.* London, Secker & Warburg, 1979.

9725. Woods, Sydney J. *John Piper: paintings, drawings & theatre designs, 1932–1954.* Arranged and with an introduction by S. John Woods. London, Faber, 1955.

Pippin, Horace, 1888–1946

9726. Rodman, Selden. *Horace Pippin: a Negro painter in America.* New York, Quadrangle, 1947.

9727. and Cleaver, Carole. *Horace Pippin: the art-*

ist as a Black American. Garden City, N.Y., Doubleday, 1972.

Piranesi, Francesco, 1750–1810
Giovanni Battista, 1720–1778

9728. Bacou, Roseline. *Piranesi, etchings and drawings*. Selected and with an introduction by Roseline Bacou. Boston, New York Graphic Society, 1975.

9729. Bettagno, Alessandro, ed. *Piranesi; incisioni, rami, legature, architetture*. Presentazione di Bruno Visentini. Venezia, Pozza, 1978. (Grafica veneta, 2).

9730. Castel Sant'angelo (Rome) et al. *Piranesi nei luoghi di Piranesi*. [Catalogue of an exhibition]. Roma, Multigrafica Editrice/Palombi, 1979.

9731. Focillon, Henri. *G. B. Piranesi/Giovanni Battista Piranesi, essai de catalogue raisonné de son oeuvre*. 2 v. [issued separately]. Paris, Laurens, 1918. (CR). (New ed., ed. by Maurizio Calvesi and Augusta Monferini. Trans. by Giuseppe Guglielmi. Bologna, Alfa, 1967).

9732. Giesecke, Albert. *Giovanni Battista Piranesi*. Leipzig, Klinkhardt & Biermann, [1911]. (Meister der Graphik, 6).

9733. Hermanin, Federico. *Giambattista Piranesi*. Roma, Sansaini, 1922. 2 ed.

9734. Hind, Arthur M. *Giovanni Battista Piranesi; a critical study, with a list of his published works and detailed catalogues of the prisons and views of Rome*. London, Cotswold Gallery, 1922.

9735. Keller, Luzius. *Piranèse et les romantiques français*. Paris, Corti, 1966.

9736. Marini, Maurizio. *Le vedute di Roma di Giovanni Battista Piranesi: il mondo antico e quello moderno riscoprono la loro comune anima . . .* Roma, Newton Compton, 1989.

9737. Mayor, A. Hyatt. *Giovanni Battista Piranesi*. New York, Bittner, 1952.

9738. Miller, Norbert. *Archäologie des Traums; Versuch über Giovanni Battista Piranesi*. München/Wien, Hanser, 1978.

9739. Morazzoni, Giuseppe. *G. B. Piranesi, notizie biografiche*. Milano, Alfieri & Lacroix, [1921].

9740. Murray, Peter. *Piranesi and the grandeur of ancient Rome*. London, Thames and Hudson, 1971.

9741. Pane, Roberto. *Paestum nelle acqueforti di Piranesi*. Milano, Edizioni di Comunità, 1980.

9742. Piranesi, Giovanni B. *Le carceri: the prisons. The complete first and second states*. With a new introduction by Philip Hofer. New York, Dover, 1973.

9743. ———. *Opere [Views of Rome]*. 27 v. Paris, Firmin-Didot, 1835–1839.

9744. [Placzek, Adolf K., et al.] *The Arthur M. Sackler Collection: Piranesi; drawings and etchings at the Avery Architectural Library, Columbia University, New York*. New York, Arthur M. Sackler Foundation, 1975. (CR).

9745. Reudenbach, Bruno. *G. B. Piranesi, Architektur als Bild; der Wandel in der Architekturauffassung des achtzehnten Jahrhunderts*. München, Prestel, 1979.

9746. Ruler, Dick van. *Verbeeldingen van werkelijkheid: speurtochten vaniut de kerkers van Piranesi*. 3 v. Rotterdam, Uitgeverij 010, 1992.

9747. Samuel, Arthur. *Piranesi*. London, Batsford, 1910.

9748. Scott, Jonathan. *Piranesi*. London, Academy/ New York, St. Martin's, 1975.

9749. Stampfle, Felice. *Giovanni Battista Piranesi: drawings in the Pierpont Morgan Library*. With a foreword by Charles Ryskamp. New York, Dover, in association with the Pierpont Morgan Library, 1978.

9750. Thomas, Hylton. *The drawings of Giovanni Battista Piranesi*. London, Faber, 1954.

9751. Villa Medici (Rome), et al. *Piranèse et les français, 1740–1790*. [Catalogue of a traveling exhibition, May–November 1976]. Roma, Edizioni dell'Elefante, 1976.

9752. Volkmann, Hans. *Giovanni Battista Piranesi, Architekt und Graphiker*. Berlin, Hessling, 1965.

9753. Wilton-Ely, John. *The mind and art of Giovanni Battista Piranesi*. London, Thames and Hudson, 1978. (2 ed. 1988).

Pisanello, 1393–1455

9754. Acqua, Gian A. dell' [and] Chiarelli, Renzo. *L'opera completa del Pisanello*. Milano, Rizzoli, 1972. (CR). (Classici dell'arte, 56).

9755. Bernasconi, Cesare. *Il Pisano, grand' artefice Veronese della prima metà del secolo decimoquinto, considerato primieramento come pittore e di poi come scultore in bronzo*. Verona, Civelli, 1862.

9756. Brenzoni, Raffaello. *Pisanello, pittore*. Firenze, Olschki, 1952.

9757. Calabi, Augusto [and] Cornaggia, G. *Pisanello; l'opera medaglistica paragonata a quella pittorica. Studio critico italiano e inglese, e catalogo ragionato*. Milano, Modiano, 1927. (CR).

9758. Cavallaro, Anna and Parlato, Enrico, eds. *Da Pisanello alla nascita dei Musei capitolini: l'antico a roma alla vigilia del Rinascimento*. [Catalogo a cura di Anna Cavallaro, Enrico Parlato]. Milano, A. Mondadori; Roma, DeLuca, 1988.

9759. Degenhart, Bernhard. *Antonio Pisanello*. Wien, Schroll, 1940.

9760. Fossi Todorow, Maria. *I disegni del Pisanello e della sua cerchia*. Firenze, Olschki, 1966. (CR).

9761. Foville, Jean de. *Pisanello et les médailleurs italiens, étude critique*. Paris, Laurens, 1908.

9762. Hill, George F. *Dessins de Pisanello, choisis et reproduits avec introduction et notices*. Paris/Bruxelles, van Oest, 1929.

9763. ———. *Pisanello*. London, Duckworth/New York, Scribner, 1905.

9764. Nocq, Henry. *Les médailles d'Antonio Pisano, dit le Pisanello*. Série complète moulée et décrite. Paris, Marotte, 1912.

9765. Paccagnini, Giovanni. *Pisanello*. Trans. by Jane Carroll. London, Phaidon, 1973.

9766. ———. *Pisanello e il ciclo cavalleresco di Mantova*. Milano, Electa, 1972. (Reprint 1981).

9767. Sindona, Enio. *Pisanello*. Trans. by John Ross. New York, Abrams, 1963.

9768. Société de Reproductions des Dessins de Maîtres. *Les dessins de Pisanello & de son école conservés au Musée du Louvre*. 4 v. [Text by Jean Guiffrey]. Paris, [Société de Reproductions], 1911–1920.

9769. Venturi, Adolfo. *Pisanello*. Roma, Palombi, 1939.

9770. Zanoli, Anna. *Pisanello*. Milano, Fabbri, 1964. (I maestri del colore, 47).

Pisano, Andrea, 1270–1348/9
Nino, fl. 1358–1368
Tommaso, d. 1371?

9771. Burresi, Mariagiulia. ed. *Andrea, Nino e Tommaso scultori pisani*. A cura di M. Burresi; con un profilo storico sull' arte pisana del Trecento di Antonio Caleca; fotografie di Aurelio Amendola. Milano, Electa, 1983.

9772. Castelnuovo, Enrico. *Andrea Pisano*. Milano, Fabbri, 1966. (I maestri della scultura, 48).

9773. Falk, Ilse. *Studien zu Andrea Pisano*. Hamburg, Niemann & Moschinski, 1940.

9774. Kreytenberg, gert. *Andrea Pisano und die toskanische Skulptur des 14. Jahrhunderts*. München, Bruckmann, 1984.

9775. Moskowitz Anita Fiderer. *The sculpture of Andrea and Nino Pisano*. Cambridge/ New York, Cambridge University Press, 1986.

9776. Toesca, Ilaria. *Andrea e Nino Pisano*. Firenze, Sansoni, 1950.

Pisano, Giovanni, 1240–1320
Nicola, 1206–1280

9777. Ayrton, Michael. *Giovanni Pisano, sculptor*. Introduction by Henry Moore. Photographs by Ilario Bessi. New York, Weybright and Talley, 1969. (CR).

9778. Bacci, Pèleo. *La ricostruzione del pergamo di Giovanni Pisano nel Duomo di Pisa*. Milano/ Roma, Bestetti e Tumminelli, [1926].

9779. Bottari, Stefano. *Saggi su Nicola Pisano*. Bologna, Pàtron, 1969.

9780. Brach, Albert. *Nicola und Giovanni Pisano und die Plastik des XIV. Jahrhunderts in Siena*. Strassburg, Heitz, 1904. (Zur Kunstgeschichte des Auslandes, 16).

9781. Carli, Enzo. *Giovanni Pisano*. Pisa, Pacini, 1977.

9782. Crichton, George H. and Crichton, E. R. *Nicola Pisano and the revival of sculpture in Italy*. Cambridge, Cambridge University Press, 1938.

9783. Fassola, Giusta N. *Nicola Pisano, orientamenti sulla formazione del gusto italiano*. Roma, Palombi, 1941.

9784. Graber, Hans. *Beiträge zu Nicola Pisano*. Strassburg, Heitz, 1911. (Zur Kunstgeschichte des Auslandes, 90).

9785. Keller, Harald. *Giovanni Pisano*. Wien, Schroll, 1942.

9786. Mellini, Gian L. *Il pulpito di Giovanni Pisano a Pistoia*. Fotografia di Aurelio Amendola. Milano, Electa, 1970.

9787. Swarzenski, Georg. *Nicolo Pisano*. Frankfurt am Main, Iris, 1926.

9788. Venturi, Adolfo. *Giovanni Pisano, his life and work*. Paris, Pegasus, 1928.

9789. Wallace, Robert D. *L'influence de la France gothique sur deux des précurseurs de la Renaissance italienne: Nicola et Giovanni Pisano*. Genève, Droz, 1953.

Pisis, Filippo de, 1896–1956

9790. Ballo, Guido. *De Pisis*. Torino, Industria Libraria Tipografica Editrice, 1968.

9791. Malabotta, Manlio. *L'opera grafica di Filippo de Pisis*. Milano, Edizioni di Communità, 1969. (CR). (Studi e documenti di storia dell'arte, 9).

9792. Naldini, Nico. *De Pisis: vita solitaria di un poeta pittore*. Torino, Giulio Einaudi, 1991.

9793. Pisis, Filippo de. *De Pisis a Milano*. A cura di Claudia Gian Ferrari. Milano, Mazzotta, 1991.

9794. ———. *De Pisis: gli anni di Parigi, 1925–1939*. A cura di Giuliano Briganti. Milano, Mazzotta, 1987.

9795. ———. *Le memorie del marchesino pittore*. A cura di Bona de Pisis e Sandro Zanotto. Torino, Einausdi, 1989.

9796. ———. *De Pisis: opere su carta, 1913–1953*. [Redazione, Giorgio Bombi]. Milano, Electa, 1985.

9797. ———. *Prose e articoli*. Milano, Il Balcone, 1947. (Testi e documenti d'arte moderna, 6).

9798. Raimondi, Guiseppe. *Filippo de Pisis*. Firenze, Vallecchi, 1952.

9799. Solmi, Sergio. *Filippo de Pisis*. Milano, Hoepli, 1931. (Arte moderna italiana, 19).

P

Pissarro, Camille Jacob, 1830–1903
Lucien, 1863–1944

9800. Adler, Kathleen. *Camille Pissarro, a biography.* New York, St. Martin's, 1977.

9801. Brettell, Richard and Lloyd, Christopher. *A catalogue of the drawings by Camille Pissarro in the Ashmolean Museum, Oxford.* Oxford, Clarendon Press, 1980. (CR).

9802. ———. *Pissaro and Pontoise; the painter in a landscape.* [By] R.R. Bretell with assistance from Joachim Pissaro. New Haven/London, Yale University Press, 1990.

9803. Hayward Gallery (London). *Camille Pissarro, 1830–1903.* 30 October 1980–11 January 1981. London, Arts Council of Great Britain, 1980.

9804. Holl, J.-C. *Camille Pissarro et son oeuvre.* Paris, Daragon, 1904.

9805. Lecomte, Georges. *Camille Pissarro.* Paris, Bernheim-Jeune, 1922.

9806. Lloyd, Christopher. *Pissarro.* Geneva, Skira/ New York, Rizzoli, 1981.

9807. ———, ed. *Studies on Camille Pissarro.* London, Routledge & Kegan Paul, 1986.

9808. Malvano, Laura. *Camille Pissarro.* Milano, Fabbri, 1965. (I maestri del colore, 70).

9809. Meadmore, William S. *Lucien Pissarro, un coeur simple.* London, Constable, 1962.

9810. Pissarro, Camille. *Correspondance, 1865– 1885.* [Edited by Janine Bailly-Herzberg]. Preface de Bernard Dorival. 5v. Paris, Presses Universitaires de France, 1980– [1991].

9811. ———. *Letters to his son, Lucien.* Edited with the assistance of Lucien Pissarro by John Rewald. Trans. by Lionel Abel. New York, Pantheon, 1943. 2 ed.

9812. Pissarro, Joachim. *Camille Pissaro.* New York, Abrams, 1993.

9813. Pissarro, Lucien. *The letters of Lucien to Camille Pissaro, 1883–1930.* Edited by Anne Thorold. Cambridge, Cambridge University Press, 1993.

9814. ———. *Lucien Pissaro: his watercolours.* [Exhibition]. Spink & Son Ltd., Wednesday 3rd to Friday 20th October 1990. London, Spink & Son, 1990.

9815. Pissarro, Ludovic R. et Venturi, Lionello. *Camille Pissarro; son art, son oeuvre.* 2 v. Paris, Rosenberg, 1939. (CR).

9816. Rewald, John. *Camille Pissarro.* London, Thames and Hudson, 1963.

9817. Shikes, Ralph and Harper, Paula. *Pissarro, his life and work.* New York, Horizon, 1980.

9818. Tabarant, Adolphe. *Pissarro.* Paris, Rieder, 1924.

9819. Thorold, Anne. *Camille Pissaro and his family: the Pissaro collection in the Ashmolean Museum.* [By] Anne Thorold and Kristen Erickson. Oxford, Ashmolean Museum, 1993.

9820. ———. *A catalogue of the oil paintings of Lucien Pissarro.* Compiled by A. Thorold; with a preface by Christopher Lloyd and an introduction by John Bensusan-Butt. London, Athelney, 1983. (CR).

9821. ———. *Lucien Pissaro: his influence on English art, 1890–1914.* Canterbury, n.p., 1986.

9822. Urbanelli, Lora S. *The wood engravings of Lucien Pissarro.* Cambridge, Silent Books, 1994.

Pittoni, Giovanni Battista, 1687–1767

9823. Binion, Alice. *I disegni di Giovanni Pittoni.* Firenze, Nuova Italia, 1983. (Corpus graphicum, 4).

9824. Coggiola Pittoni, Laura. *G. B. Pittoni.* Firenze, Alinari, 1921. (Piccola collezione d'arte, 26).

9825. Pallucchini, Rodolfo. *I disegni di Giam battista Pittoni.* Padova, Le Tre Venezie, 1945. (Collana d'arte, II series, 5).

9826. Zava Boccazzi, Franca. *Pittoni.* Venezia, Alfieri, 1979. (CR).

Plimer, Andrew, 1763–1837
Nathaniel, 1757–1822

9827. Williamson, George C. *Andrew & Nathaniel Plimer, miniature painters; their lives and works.* London, Bell, 1903.

Poelzig, Hans, 1869–1936

9828. Biraghi, Marco. *Hans Poelzig; architectura, ars magna, 1869–1936.* Venezia, Arsenale, 1992.

9829. Heuss, Theodor. *Hans Poelzig, Bauten und Entwürfe; das Lebensbild eines deutschen Baumeisters.* Berlin, Wasmuth, 1939. (Reprint: Milano, Electa, 1991. (Documenti di architettura).

9830. Poelzig Hans. *Der dramatische Raum: Hans Poelzig, Malerei, Theater, Film.* [Catalogue of an exhibition] Krefeld, Museum Haus Lange, Museum Haus Esters. [Krefeld, Die Museen], 1986.

9831. ———. *Gesammelte Schriften und Werke.* Herausgegeben von Julius Posener. Berlin, Mann, 1970. (Schriftenreihe der Akademie der Kunst, 6).

9832. ———. *Hans Poelzig: ein grosses Theater und ein kleines Haus.* Mit Texten von Poelzig, Posener, Pehnt. Berlin, Aedes, 1986.

9833. Posener, Julius. *Hans Poelzig; reflections on his life and work.* [By] Julius Posener; edited by Kristin Feireiss; translated by Christine Charlesworth. New York, Architectural History Foundation; Cambridge, Mass., MIT Press, 1992.

Poeppelmann, Matthes Daniel, 1662– 1736

9834. Döring, Bruno A. *Matthes Daniel Pöppel-*

mann, der Meister des Dresdener Zwingers. Ergänzt und herausgegeben von Hubert Georg Ermisch mit einem Vorwort von Cornelius Gurlitt. Dresden, Limpert, 1930.

9835. Heckmann, Hermann. *M. D. Pöppelmann als Zeichner.* Dresden, Verlag der Kunst, 1954.

9836. ———. *Matthäus Daniel Pöppelmann und die Barockbaukunst in Dresden.* Stuttgart, Deutsche Verlagsanstalt, 1986.

9837. ——— und Pape, Johannes. *Matthes Daniel Pöppelmann.* Herford/Bonn, Maximilian, 1962.

9838. Pöppelmann, Matthäus Daniel. *Matthäus Daniel Pöppelmann: der Architekt des Dresdner Zwingers.* [Catalogue of an exhibition] Hrsg. von Harald Marx, mit Beiträgen von Harald Marx . . . [et al.] Leipzig, VEB E.A. Seemann, 1989.

Polenov, Vasilii Dmitrievich, 1844–1927

9839. Gosudarstvennyi Muzei—usad'ba V. D. Polenova (Polenova, USSR). *Gosudarstvennyi muzei—usad'ba V. D. Polenova: zhivopis i grafika.* Leningrad, RSFSR, 1979.

9840. Gramolina, Natalia Nikolaevna. *Polenovo.* Tula, Prioskskoe knizhnoe izdvo, 1987.

9841. Iurova, Tamara V. *Vasilii Dmitrievich Polenov.* Moskva, Iskusstvo, 1961.

9842. Sakharova, Ekaterina V. *Vasilii Dmitrievich Polenova i Elena Dmitrievna Polenova; khronika sem'i khudozhnikov.* Moskva, Iskusstvo, 1964.

Poliakoff, Serge, 1900–1969

9843. Brütsch, Françoise. *Serge Poliakoff 1900–1969.* Neuchâtel, Ides et Calendes, 1993.

9844. Galerie Melki (Paris). *Poliakoff.* 29 mai–15 juillet 1975. Paris, Galerie Melki, 1975.

9845. Poliakoff, Alexis. *Serge Poliakoff: les estampes.* Paris, Editions Arts et Métiers Graphiques/Yves Rivière, 1974.

9846. Ragon, Michel. *Poliakoff.* Paris, Fall, 1956. (Le musée de poche).

9847. Vallier, Dora. *Serge Poliakoff.* Paris, Cahiers d'Art, 1959.

Polidoro da Caravaggio, ca. 1495–ca. 1543

9848. Marabottini, Alerssandro. *Polidoro da Caravaggio.* 2 v. Roma, Edizioni dell'Elefante, 1969.

9849. Polidoro da Caravaggio. *Polidoro da Caravaggio: fra Napoli e Messina.* A cura di Pierluigi Leone de Castris. Milano, A. Mondadori; Roma, De Luca Edizioni d'Arte, 1988.

Polke, Sigmar, 1941–

9850. Milwaukee Art Museum. *Warhol/Beuys/ Polke.* [Catalogue of an exhibition]. Milwaukee, Milwaukee Art Museum, 1987.

9851. Polke, Sigmar. *Sigmar Polke.* [Catalogue of an exhibition]. San Francisco Museum of Modern Art. San Francisco, The Museum, 1990.

9852. Polke, Sigmar. *Sigmar Polke.* [Tentoonstelling]. Museum Boymans-van Beuningen, Rotterdam 1983; Städtisches Kunstmuseum, Bonn 1984. Redactie catalogus, Elbrig de Groot. Rotterdam, Museum Boymans-van Beuningen, 1983.

9853. ———. *Sigmar Polke: Fotografien.* [Catalogue of an exhibition]. Staatliche Kunsthalle Baden-Baden, 11. Februar bis 25. März 1990. Herausgegebn von Jochen Poetter. Stuttgart, Edition Cantz, 1990.

9854. ———. *Sigmar Polke: Zeichnungen 1963– 1969.* Herausgegeben von Johannes Gachnang. Bern, Gachnang & Springer, 1987.

9855. ———. *Sigmar Polke: Zeichnungern, Aquarelle, Skizzenbücher 1962–1988.* [Katalog der Ausstellung] 15. Juni–28. August 1988. Kunstmuseum Bonn. Ausstellung: Katharina Schmidt und Sigmar Polke. Bonn, Kunstmuseum Bonn, 1988.

Pollaiuolo, Antonio del, 1432?–1498
Piero del, 1441–1496

9856. Bovi, Arturo. *Pollaiolo.* Milano, Fabbri, 1965. (I maestri del colore, 85).

9857. Busignani, Alberto. *Pollaiolo.* Firenzi, Edizioni d'Arte il Fiorino, 1970.

9858. Colacicchi, Giovanni. *Antonio del Pollaiuolo.* Florence, Chessa, 1945. (Collection Astarte, 1).

9859. Cruttwell, Maud. *Antonio Pollaiuolo.* London, Duckworth/New York, Scribner, 1907.

9860. Ettlinger, Leopold D. *Antonio and Piero Pollaiuolo, complete edition with a critical catalogue.* London, Phaidon, 1978. (CR).

9861. Ortolani, Sergio. *Il Pollaiuolo.* Milano, Hoepli, 1948.

9862. Sabatini, Attilio. *Antonio e Piero del Pollaiolo.* Firenze, Sansoni, 1944.

9863. Schwabacher, Sascha. *Die Stickerein nach Entwürfen des Antonio Pallaiuolo in der opera di S. Maria del Fiore zu Florenz.* Strassburg, Heitz, 1911. (Zur Kunstgeschichte des Auslandes, 83).

Pollard, James, 1792–1867

9864. Selway, Neville C. *The Regency Road: the coaching prints of James Pollard.* Introd. by James Laver. London, Faber, 1957.

Pollock, Jackson, 1912–1956

9865. Cernuschi, Claude. *Jackson Pollock: meaning and significance.* New York, ICON Editions, 1992.

9866. ———. *Jackson Pollock, "psychoanalytic" drawings.* Foreword by Michael P. Mezzatesta. Durham, NC, Duke University Press in association with the Duke University Museum of Art, 1992.

9867. Doss, Erika Lee. *Benton, Pollock, and the politics of modernism: from regionalism to abstract expressionism.* Chicago, University of Chicago Press, 1991.

9868. Frank, Elizabeth. *Jackson Pollock.* New York, Abbeville Press, 1983.

9869. Friedman, Bernard H. *Jackson Pollock: energy made visible.* New York, McGraw-Hill, 1972.

9870. Landau, Ellen G. *Jackson Pollock.* New York, Abrams, 1989.

9871. Museum of Modern Art (New York). *Jackson Pollock.* [Chronology by Francis V. O'Connor]. New York, Museum of Modern Art, 1967.

9872. Naifeh, Steven W. and Smith, Gregory White. *Jackson Pollock: an American saga.* By S. Naifeh and Gregory W. Smith. New York, C.N. Potter; distrib. by Crown Publishers, 1989.

9873. O'Connor, Francis V. and Thaw, Eugene V. *Jackson Pollock; a catalogue raisonné of paintings, drawings, and other works.* 4 v. New Haven/London, Yale University Press, 1978. (CR).

9874. O'Hara, Frank. *Jackson Pollock.* New York, Braziller, 1959.

9875. Pollock, Jackson. *Jackson Pollock.* [Exposition] 21 janvier–19 avril 1982, Centre Georges Pompidou, Musée national d'art moderne. Réalisation du catalogue, Daniel Abadie et Claire Stoullig. Paris, Centre Georges Pompidou, Musée national de l'art moderne, 1982.

9876. ———. *To a violent grave: an oral biography of Jackson Pollock.* [Compiled by] Jeffrey Potter. New York, G.P. Putnam, 1985.

9877. Putz, Ekkehard. *Jackson Pollock: Theorie und Bild.* Hildesheim/New York, Olms, 1975. (Studien zur Kunstgeschichte, 4).

9878. Robertson, Bryan. *Jackson Pollock.* New York, Abrams, 1960.

9879. Rohn, Matthew. *Visual dynamics in Jackson Pollock's abstractions.* Ann Arbor, UMI Research Press, 1987.

9880. Rose, Bernice. *Jackson Pollock: works on paper.* New York, Museum of Modern Art in association with the Drawing Society, Inc., 1969; distributed by New York Graphic Society, Greenwich, Conn.

9881. Solomon, Deborah. *Jackson Pollock, a biography.* New York, Simon and Schuster, 1987.

9882. Wysuph, C. L. *Jackson Pollock: psychoanalytic drawings.* New York, Horizon, 1970.

Polyclitus, 5th c. B.C.

9883. Arias, Paolo E. *Policleto.* Milano, Edizioni per Il Club del Libro, 1964. (Collana d'arte del Club del Libro, 7).

9884. Kreikenbom, Detlev. *Bildwerke nach Polyklet: Kopienkritische Untersuchungen zu den männlichen statuarischen Typen nach polykletischen Vorbildern: <Diskophoros<, Hermes, Doryphoros, Herakles, Diadumenos.* Berlin, Gebr. Mann, 1990.

9885. Lorenz, Thuri. *Polyklet.* Wiesbaden, Steiner, 1972.

9886. Mahler, Arthur. *Polyklet und seine Schule; ein Beitrag zur Geschichte der griechischen Plastik.* Athen/Leipzig, Barth, 1902.

9887. Paris, Pierre. *Polyclète.* Paris, Librairie de l'Art, [1895].

9888. Polyclitus. *Polyklet: der Bildhauer griechischen Klassik.* [Katalog der] Ausstellung im Liebighaus, Museum alter Plastik, Frankfurt am Main. Herausgeber des Kataloges, H. Beck, P.C. Bol, M. Bückling; im Auftrag des Dezernats Kultur und Freizeit der Stadt Frankfurt am Main. Redaktion des Kataloges, D. Kreikenbom. Mainz am Rhein, P. von Zabern, 1990.

Polygnotus, 5th c. B.C.

9889. Feihl, Eugen. *Die ficoronische Cista und Polygnot.* Tübingen, Laupp, 1913.

9890. Löwy, Emanuel. *Polygnot, ein Buch von griechischer Malerei.* 2 v. Wien, Schroll, 1929.

9891. Schreiber, Theodor. *Die Wandbilder des Polygnotos in der Halle der Knidier zu Delphi.* Leipzig, Hirzel, 1897. (Abhandlungen der philologisch-historischen Classe der königl. sächsischen Gesellschaft der Wissenschaft, Bd. 17, Heft 6).

9892. Weizsäcker, Paul. *Polygnots Gemälde in der Lesche der Knidier in Delphi.* Stuttgart, Neff, 1895.

Pontormo, Jacopo Carucci, 1494–1557

9893. Becherucci, Luisa. *Disegni del Pontormo.* Bergamo, Istituto Italiano d'Arti Grafiche, 1943.

9894. Berti, Luciano. *L'opera completa di Pontormo.* Milano, Rizzoli, 1973. (Classici dell'arte, 66).

9895. ———. *Pontormo.* Firenze, Edizioni d'Arte Il Fiorino, 1966. (I più eccellenti, collana di monografie de artisti, 1).

9896. Clapp, Frederick M. *Les dessins de Pontormo; catalogue raisonné.* Paris, Champion, 1914. (CR).

9897. ———. *Jacopo Carucci da Pontormo, his life and work.* New Haven, Yale University Press, 1916.

9898. Forster, Kurt W. *Pontormo; Monographie mit kritischem Katalog.* München, Bruckmann, 1966. (CR).

9899. Lebensztejn, Jean-Claude . . . [et al.]. *Dossier Pontormo.* Paris, Macula, 1984.

9900. Nigro, Salvatore S. *Pontormo drawings.* Edited and with an introduction by S.S. Nigro. New York, H.N., Abrams, 1992.

9901. ———. *Pontormo paintings and frescoes.* New York, H.N. Abrams, 1994.

9902. Palazzo Strozzi (Florence). *Mostra del Pontormo e del primo manierismo fiorentino.* 24 marzo–15 luglio 1956. Firenze, Palazzo Strozzi, 1956.

9903. Pontormo, Jacopo Carucci. *Diario; fatto nel tempo che dipingeva il coro di San Lorenzo, 1554–1556.* A cura di Emilio Cecchi. Firenze, Le Monnier, 1956.

9904. ———. *Il libro mio.* Edizione critica a cura di Salvatore S. Nigro; presentazione di Enrico Baj; illustrazioni di Enrico Baj; disegni di Pontormo. Genova, Edizioni Costa & Nolan, 1984.

9905. ———. *Le journal de Jacopo da Pontormo;* avec un commentaire et des annexes. Traduit par Jean-Claude Lebensztejn, avec la colloboration d'Alessandro Parronchi. Paris, Aldines, 1992.

9906. Rearick, Janet C. *The drawings of Pontormo.* 2 v. Cambridge, Mass., Harvard University Press, 1964. (CR). (Reprint: New York, Hacker, 1981).

9907. Toesca, Elena. *Il Pontormo.* Roma, Tumminelli, 1943.

Popova, Liubov, 1889–1929

9908. Dabrowski, Magdalena. *Liubov Popova.* [Catalogue of an exhibition held at the Museum of Modern Art]. New York, Museum of Modern Art, 1991.

9909. Popova, Liubov. *Gouaches & drawings by Liubov Popova & Kazimir Malevich.* [Catalogue of an exhibition] April 18–May 30, 1986. New York, Leonard Hutton [Gallery], 1968.

9910. Sarab'ianov, Dmitri Vladimirovich and Adaskina, Natalia L. *Popova.* Translated from the Russian by Marian Schwartz. New York, Harry N. Abrams, 1989.

Pordenone, Giovanni Antonio, 1484–1539

9911. Cohen, Charles. *The drawings of Giovanni Antonio da Pordenone.* Firenze, Nuova Italia, 1980. (CR).

9912. Fiocco, Giuseppe. *Giovanni Antonio Pordenone.* 2 v. Pordenone, Cosarini, 1969. 3 ed.

9913. Furlan, Caterina. *Il Pordenone.* Milano, Electa, 1988.

9914. ———, ed. *Il Pordenone: atti del convegno internatzionale di studio.* Pordenone, Sala Convegni della Camera di Commercio 23–25 agosto, 1984. A cura di C. Furlan. Pordenone, Biblioteca dell'immagine, 1984.

Porter, Eliot, 1901–

9915. Porter, Eliot. *Eliot Porter.* Photographs and text by Eliot Porter; foreword by Martha A. Sandweiss. Boston, New York Graphic Society Books, Little Brown; in association with the Amon Carter Museum, 1987.

Porter, Fairfield, 1907–1975

9916. Agee, William C. *Fairfield Porter: an American painter.* [By] William C. Agee with Malama Maron-Bersin, Michele White, and Peter Blank. Southhampton, N.Y., Parrish Art Museum, 1993.

9917. Ludman, Joan. *Fairfield Porter, a catalogue raisonné of his prints, including illustrations bookjackets, and exhibition posters.* [By] J. Ludman . . . [et al.]. Westbury, N.Y., Highland House Pub., 1981.(CR).

9918. Porter, Fairfield. *Fairfield Porter (1907–1975): realist painter in the age of abstraction.* Essays by John Ashbery and Kenworth offet; contributions by John Bernard Myers . . . [et al.]. Boston, Museum of Fine Arts; distrib. by the New York Graphic Society, 1982.

9919. Spike, John T. *Fairfield Porter: an American classic.* Checklist of paintings of Fairfield Porter by Joan Ludman. New York, Abrams, 1992.

Posch, Alexander, 1890–1950

9920. Kunsthalle Darmstadt. *Alexander Posch: ein Darmstädter Maler 1890–1950.* [Catalogue of an exhibition]. Darmstadt, Kunsthalle, 21.1.–4.3. 1990. Darmstadt, Kunsthalle, 1990.

Post, Frans Janszoon, 1612?–1680

9921. Larsen, Erik. *Frans Post, interprète du Brésil.* Avec une préface par Jacques Lavalleye. Amsterdam/Rio de Janeiro, Colibris, 1962.

9922. Museu Nacional de Bellas Artes (Rio de Janeiro). *Exposiçao, Frans Post.* Rio de Janeiro, Ministério da Educaçao e Saúde, 1942.

9923. Post, Frans. *Frans Post, 1612–1680.* [Catalogue of an exhibition]. Herausgegeben von Thomas Kellein und Urs-Beat Frei. Basel, Kunsthalle Basel; Tübingen, Kunsthalle Tübingen, 1990.

9924. Sousa-Leao, Joaquim de. *Frans Post, 1612–1680.* [Text in English]. Amsterdam, van Gendt, 1973. (CR). (Painters of the Past).

Post, Pieter, 1608–1669

9925. Blok, Gerard A.C. *Pieter Post, 1608–1669: der Baumeister der Prinzen von Oranien und* des Fürsten Johann Moritz von Nassau-Siegen. Siegen, Vorlander, 1937.

9926. Loonstra, Marten. *La Sala d'Orange: un architettura di gusto italiano per una principessa olandese del '600*. Casalecchio di Reno, Grafis, 1984

9927. Terwen, J. J. *Pieter Post (1608–1669)*. By J.J. Terwen; K.A. Ottenheym. Zutphen: Walburg Pers , 1993.

Potter, Paulus, 1625-1654

9928. Michel, Emile. *Paul Potter: biographie critique*. Paris, Laurens, 1907.

9929. Walsh, Amy. *Paulus Potter: paintings, drawings and etchings*. [By] A. Walsh; Edwin Buijsen, Ben Broos. Zwolle, Waanders, 1994.

9930. Westrheene, Tobias van. *Paulus Potter, sa vie et ses oeuvres*. La Haye, M. Nijhoff, 1867.

Pougny, Jean, 1892-1956

9931. Berninger, Herman [and] Cartier, Jean-Albert. *Jean Pougny (Iwan Puni), 1892–1956; catalogue de l'oeuvre*. [par] Herman Berninger [et] Jean-Albert Cartier. 2 v. *Tome 1: Les années d'avant-garde, Russie-Berlin, 1910–1923.—t.2: Paris-Cote d'Azur 1924–1956, peintures*. Tübingen, Wasmuth, 1972–1992. (CR).

9932. Gindertael, Roger V. *Pougny*. Genève, Cailler, 1957.

9933. Haus am Waldsee (Berlin). *Iwan Puni (Jean Pougny), 1892–1956; Gemälde, Zeichnungen, Reliefs*. 15. Mai bis 22. Juni 1975. Berlin, Haus am Waldsee, 1975.

9934. Pougny, Jean. *Iwan Puni: synthetischer Musiker*. [Catalogue of an exhibition]. Mit Beiträgen von Eberhard Roters, Hubertus Gassner und Schriften zur Kunst (1915–1923) von Iwan Puni. Redaktion, Helmut Geisert, Elizabeth Moortgat, Martina Jura. Berlin, Berlinische Galerie, 1992.

9935. ———. *Jean Pougny*. [Catalogue of an exhibition]. Paris, Musée d'art moderne de la ville de Paris, 1993.

Poussin, Nicolas, 1594-1665

9936. Advielle, Victor. *Recherches sur Nicolas Poussin et sur sa famille*. Paris, Rapilly, 1902.

9937. Andresen, Andreas. *Nicolas Poussin: Verzeichniss der nach seinen Gemälden, Gefertigten . . . Kupferstiche*. Leipzig, Weigel, 1863.

9938. Badt, Kurt. *Die Kunst des Nicolas Poussin*. 2 v. Köln, DuMont Schauberg, 1969.

9939. Bätschmann, Oskar. *Nicolas Poussin, dialectics of painting*. London, Reaktion Books, 1990.

9940. Bellori, Giovanni P. *Vie de Nicolas Poussin*. [Trans. by Georges Rémond and extracted from his *Vies des peintres*, 1672]. Vésanez-Genève, Cailler, 1947. (Collection écrits de peintres).

9941. Blunt, Anthony. *The drawings of Poussin*. New Haven/London, Yale University Press, 1979.

9942. ———. *Nicolas Poussin*. 2 v. Washington, D.C., National Gallery of Art, 1967; distributed by Pantheon, New York. (Bollingen Series, 35; Mellon Lectures in the Fine Arts, 7).

9943. ———. *The paintings of Nicolas Poussin; a critical catalogue*. London, Phaidon, 1966. (CR).

9944. Bouchitté, Hervé. *Le Poussin, sa vie et son oeuvre*. Paris, Didier, 1858.

9945. Cambry, Jacques. *Essai sur la vie et sur les tableaux du Poussin*. Rome/Paris, Le Jay, 1783.

9946. Carrier, David. *Poussin's paintings: a study in art-historical methodology*. University Park, Pa., Pennsylvania State University Press, 1992.

9947. Chastel, André, ed. *Nicolas Poussin* [Symposium held Sept. 19–21, 1958]. 2 v. Paris, Editions du Centre National de la Recherche Scientifique, 1960.

9948. Courthion, Pierre. *Nicolas Poussin*. Paris, Plon, 1929.

9949. Delacroix, Eugène. *Essai sur Poussin*. Préface et notes de Pierre Jaquillard. Genève, Cailler, 1965.

9950. Denio, Elizabeth H. *Nicolas Poussin, his life and work*. London, Sampson Low/New York, Scribner, 1899.

9951. Desjardins, Paul. *Poussin, biographie critique*. Paris, Laurens, [1906].

9952. Félibien, André. *Entretiens sur la vie et les ouvrages de Nicolas Poussin*. [Extracted from his *Entretiens sur les vies et sur les ouvrages de plus excellents peintres*, 1705, and his *Conférences de l'Académie Royale*, 1705]. Vésanez-Genève, Caille, 1947. (Collection écrits et documents de peintres).

9953. Fischer, Gert. *Figuren- und Farbkomposition in ausgewählten Werken des Nicolas Poussin: zwei Studien*. Frankfurt am Main/ New York, P. Lang, 1992. (Ars faciendi, 1).

9954. Friedlaender, Walter. *The drawings of Nicolas Poussin; catalogue raisonné*. 5 v. [Vol. 5 prepared with the assistance of Anthony Blunt]. London, Warburg Institute/ University of London, 1939–1974. (CR). (Studies of the Warburg Institute, 5).

9955. ———. *Nicolas Poussin; a new approach*. New York, Abrams, 1965.

9956. ———. *Nicolas Poussin; die Entwicklung seiner Kunst*. München, Piper, 1914.

9957. Gandar, Eugène. *Les Andelys et Nicolas Poussin*. Paris, Renouard, 1860.

9958. Gault de Saint-Germain, Pierre M. *Vie de Nicolas Poussin*. Paris, Didot/Renouard, 1806.

9959. Graham, Maria. *Memoirs of the life of Nicholas Poussin*. London, Longman, 1820.

9960. Grautoff, Otto. *Nicolas Poussin, sein Werk und sein Leben*. 2 v. München, Müller, 1914.

9961. Grepmair-Müller, Angelika. *Landschaftskompositionen von Nicolaus Poussin, eine Studie*. Frankfurt am Main/ New York, P. Lang, 1992.

9962. Guibal, Nicolas. *Eloge de Nicolas Poussin, peintre ordinaire du roi*. Paris, Imprimerie Royale, 1783.

9963. Hourticq, Louis. *La jeunesse de Poussin*. Paris, Hachette, 1937.

9964. Jamot, Paul. *Connaissance de Poussin*. Paris, Floury, 1948.

9965. Kauffmann, Georg. *Poussin-Studien*. Berlin, de Gruyter, 1960.

9966. Lagerlöf, Margaretha Rossholm. *Ideal landscape: Annibale Carraci, Nicolas Poussin, and Claude Lorrain*. New Haven, Yale University Press, 1990.

9967. Lévêque, Jean Jacques. *La vie et l'oeuvre de Nicolas Poussin*. Courbevoie, Paris, ACR, 1988.

9968. Licht, Fred S. *Die Entwicklung der Landschaft in den Werken von Nicolas Poussin*. Basel/Stuttgart, Birkhäuser, 1954. (Basler Studien zur Kunstgeschichte, 11).

9969. Magne, Emile. *Nicolas Poussin, premier peintre du roi, 1594–1665*. Bruxelles/Paris, van Oest, 1914.

9970. Mahon, Denis. *Poussiniana: afterthoughts arising from the exhibition* [i.e., at the Musée du Louvre, 1960]. Paris/New York, Gazette des Beaux Arts, 1962.

9971. Mérot, Alain. *Nicolas Poussin*. London, Thames and Hudson; New York, Abbeville, 1990.

9972. Musée du Louvre (Paris). *Exposition Nicolas Poussin*. Mai–juillet 1960. Paris, Edition des Musées Nationaux, 1960.

9973. Oberhuber, Konrad. *Poussin, the early years in Rome: the origins of French classicism*. Foreword by Edmund P. Pillsbury. New York, Hudson Hills Press, in association with Kimbell Art Museum, Fort Worth, 1988.

9974. Poillon, Louis. *Nicolas Poussin, étude biographique*. Lille/Paris, Lefort, 1868.

9975. Poussin, Nicolas. *Correspondance*. Publiée d'après les originaux par Charles Jouanny. Paris, Champion, 1911.

9976. ———. *Nicolas Poussin [Nikola Pussen. English.]: paintings and drawings in Soviet museums*. Introductory articles by Yuri Zolotov and Natalia Serebriannaya; selection and commentaries by Irina Kuznetsova . . . et al.; translated from the Russian by Thomas Crane and Margarita Latsinova. Leningrad, Aurora Publishers, 1990.

9977. ———. *Oeuvres complètes*. 2 v. [Engravings after the paintings]. Paris, Didot, 1845.

9978. Rosenberg, Pierre, ed. *Nicolas Poussin 1594–1665*. Par Pierre Rosenberg pour les peintures; Louis-Antoine Prat et Pierre Rosenberg pour les dessins. 2v. Paris, Réunion des Musées nationaux, 1994.

9979. ———, and Prat, Louis-Antoine. *Nicolas Poussin, 1594–1665: catalogue raisonné des dessins*. 2v. Milano, Leonardo, 1994. (CR).

9980. Rouchès, Gabriel. *Nicolas Poussin; quatorze dessins*. Paris, Musées Nationaux, 1938.

9981. Santucci, Paola. *Poussin: tradizione ermetica e classicismo gesuita*. Salerno, 10/17, 1985. (Arte d'Occidente, 2).

9982. Thuillier, Jacques. *L'opera completa di Poussin*. Milano, Rizzoli, 1974. (CR). (Classici dell'arte, 72).

9983. ———. *Nicolas Poussin*. Paris, Fayard, 1988.

9984. Verdi, Richard. *Cézanne and Poussin: the classical vision of landscape*. Edinburgh, National Galleries of Scotland in association with Lund Humphries, London, 1990.

9985. ———. *Nicolas Poussin, 1594–1665*. [By] Richard Verdi; with an essay by Pierre Rosenberg. London, Royal Academy of Arts, 1995.

9986. Villa Medici (Rome). *Nicolas Poussin, 1594–1665*. Novembre 1977–gennaio 1978. [Organisée par l'Académie de France à Rome]. Roma, Edizioni dell'Elefante, 1977.

9987. Wild, Doris. *Nicolas Poussin*. 2 v. Zürich, Füssli, 1980. (CR).

9988. Wright, Christopher. *Poussin paintings: a catalogue raisonné*. New York, Hippocrene Books, distributed by Harlequin Books, 1985. (CR).

Powers, Hiram, 1805–1873

9989. Crane, Sylvia E. *White silence: Greenough, Powers, and Crawford; American sculptors in nineteenth-century Italy*. Coral Gables, Fla., University of Miami Press, 1972

9990. Reynolds, Donald M. *Hiram Powers and his ideal sculptures*. New York, Garland Publishing, 1977.

9991. Wunder, Richard P. *Hiram Powers: Vermont sculptor, 1805–1873*. 2 v. Newark, University of Delaware Press; London, Associated University Presses, 1991.

Pozzo, Andrea, 1642–1709

9992. Carboneri, Nino. *Andrea Pozzo, architetto (1642–1709)*. Prefazione di Giuseppe Fiocco. Trenti, Collana Artisti Trentini, 1961.

9993. De Feo, Vittorio. *Andrea Pozzo, architettura e illusione*. [By] Vittorio De Feo [e] Maurizio Gargano. Roma, Officina, 1988.

9994. Kerber, Bernhard. *Andrea Pozzo*. Berlin/New York, de Gruyter, 1971. (Beiträge zur Kunstgeschichte, 6).

9995. Marini, Remigio. *Andrea Pozzo, pittore*

(1642–1709). Trento, Collana di Artisti Trentini, 1959.

9996. Pozzo, Andrea. *Rules and examples of perspective proper for painters and architects, in English and Latin*. Trans. by John James. London, Senex, [1707].

Prandtauer, Jakob, 1660–1726

9997. Hantsch, Hugo. *Jakob Prandtauer, der Klosterarchitekt des österreichischen Barock*. Wien, Krystall, 1926.

9998. Stift Melk (Austria). *Jakob Prandtauer und sein Kunstkreis*. Ausstellung zum 300. Geburtstag des grossen österreichischen Baumeisters. 14. Mai bis 31. Oktober 1960. Wien, Österreichische Staatsdruckerei, 1960.

Praxiteles, 4th c. B.C.

9999. Collignon, Maxime. *Scopas et Praxitèle; la sculpture grecque au IV siècle jusqu'au temps d'Alexandre*. Paris, Plon, 1907.

10000. Corso, Antonio. *Prassitele: fonti epigrafiche e letterarie: vita e opere*. 2 v. Roma, De Luca, 1988–1990.

10001. Ducati, Pericle. *Prassitele*. Firenze, Le Monnier, 1927.

10002. Friedrichs, Karl. *Praxiteles und die Niobegruppe, nebst Erklärung einiger Vasenbilder*. Leipzig, Teubner, 1855.

10003. Gebhart, Emile. *Praxitèle; essai sur l'histoire de l'art et du génie grecs*. Paris, Tandou, 1864.

10004. Klein, Wilhelm. *Praxiteles*. Leipzig, Veit, 1898.

10005. Perrot, Georges. *Praxitèle, étude critique*. Paris, Laurens, [1904].

10006. Rizzo, Giulio E. *Prassitele*. Milano/Roma, Treves, 1932.

Preetorius, Emil, 1883–1973

10007. Adolf, Rudolf. *Emil Preetorius*. Aschaffenburg, Pattloch, 1960.

10008. Hölscher, Eberhard. *Emil Preetorius, das Gesamtwerk*. Berlin, Heintze & Blanckertz, 1943. (Monographien künstlerischer Schrift, 10).

10009. Preetorius, Emil. *Geheimnis des Sichtbaren: gesammelte Aufsätze zur Kunst*. München, Piper, 1963.

10010. Stuck-Villa (Munich). *Emil Preetorius; Illustrationen, Graphik, Plakate*. 21. September bis 2. Dezember 1973. München, Rossipaul, 1973.

Pregelj, Marij, 1913–1967

10011. Bihalji-Merin, Oto. *Marij Pregelj*. [Text in Slovak, German, and French]. Maribor (Yugoslavia), Zalozba Obsorja, 1971. (Likovna obzorja, 11).

10012. Moderna Galerija (Ljubljani, Yugoslavia).

Marij Pregelj; retrospektivna razstava, 1937–1967. 4. februar–9. marec 1969. [Text in Slovak and French]. Ljubljani, Moderna Galerija, 1969.

Preisler, Jan, 1872–1918

10013. Kotalík, Jirí. *Jan Preisler*. Praha, Odeon, 1968.

10014. Matejcek, Antonín. *Jan Preisler*. Praza, Melantrich, 1950.

10015. Wittlich, Petr. *Jan Preisler, kresby*. Praha, Odeon, 1988.

10016. Záhavec, Frantisek. *Jan Preisler*. Praha, Stenc, 1921.

Prendergast, Maurice Brazil, 1859–1924
Charles, 1863–1948

10017. Breuning, Margaret. *Maurice Prendergast*. New York, Macmillan, 1931.

10018. Langdale, Cecily. *Monotypes by Maurice Prendergast in the Terra Museum of American Art*. Chicago, The Museum, 1984.

10019. Mathews, Nancy Mowll. *Maurice Prendergast*. Munich, Prestel; Williamstown, Mass. Williams College Museum of Art, 1990.

10020. Prendergast, Maurice Brazil. *Maurice Brazil Prendergast, Charles Prendergast: a catalogue raisonné*. [By] Carol Clark, Nancy Mowll Mathews, Gwendolyn Owens. Williamstown, Mass. Williams College Museum of Art; Munich, Germany, Prestel, 1989. (CR).

10021. ———. *The large Boston Public Garden Sketchbook*. With introduction by George Szabo. New York, Braziller, 1987.

10022. Rhys, Hedley H. *Maurice Prendergast, 1859–1924*. [Published in conjunction with an exhibition at the Museum of Fine Arts, Boston, October 26–December 4, 1960]. Cambridge, Mass., Harvard University Press, 1960.

10023. University of Maryland Art Gallery (College Park, Md.). *Maurice Prendergast: art of impulse and color*. 1 September–6 October 1976. College Park, Md., University of Maryland, 1976.

10024. Whitney Museum of American Art (New York). *Maurice B. Prendergast, a concentration of works from the permanent collection*. January 9–March 2, 1980. New York, Whitney Museum of American Art, 1979.

Preti, Mattia, 1613–1699

10025. Cannata, Francesco. *Il cavaliere calabrese Mattia Preti*. Catanzaro, Carello Editore, 1978.

10026. Chimirri, Bruno [and] Frangipane, Alfonso. *Mattia Preti, detto il Cavalier Calabrese*. Milano, Alfieri & Lacroix, 1914.

10027. Frangipane, Alfonso. *Mattia Preti, il Cava-*

lier Calabrese. Milano, Alpes, 1929.

10028. Mariani, Valerio. *Mattia Preti a Malta*. Roma, Biblioteca d'Arte, 1929.

10029. Pelaggi, Antonio. *Mattia Preti ed il seicento italiano, col catalogo delle opere*. Catanzaro, Italy, Amministrazione Provinciale di Catanzaro, Museo Provinciale, 1972.

10030. Preti, Mattia. *Mattia Preti*. Texts by M. Marini, F. Piccirillo, J. Spike, C. Strinati, S. Vitelli. Edited by Erminia Corace. Trans. by Isabel Butters-Caleffi. Roma, Fratelli Palombi, 1989.

10031. Pujia, Carmello. *Fra Mattia Preti nel terzo suo centenario*. Napoli, Artigianelli, 1913.

10032. Refice Taschetta, Claudia. *Mattia Preti: contributi alla conoscenza del Cavalier Calabrese*. Brindisi, Italy, Abicca, [1959].

10033. Sergi, Antonino. *Mattia Preti, detto il Cavalier Calabrese: la vita, l'opera; catalogo delle opere*. Acireale, Italy, Tipografia XX Secolo, 1927.

10034. Strinati, Claudio M., ed. *Mattia Preti: disegno e colore*. [By] Claudio Strinati, Maurizio Marini, Carolina Ippoliti. Catanzaro, Abramo, 1991.

10035. Tassoni, Luigi. *La giovinezza di Mattia Preti e l'eros secentesco*. Catanzaro, La Biblioteka, 1989.

10036. ———. *Mattia Preti e il senso del disegno: sessantotto disgni del Cavaliere Calabrese*. Bergamo, Moretti & Vitali, 1990. (Le forme dell' immaginario,1).

Prikker, Johan Thorn *see* **Thorn Prikker, Johan**

Primaticcio, Francesco, 1504–1570

10037. Dimier, Louis. *Le Primatice, peintre, sculpteur et architecte des rois de France*. Essays sur la vie et les ouvrages de cet artiste suivi d'un catalogue raisonné de ses dessins et de ses compositions gravées. Paris, Leroux, 1900. (CR).

10038. ———. *Le Primatice*. Paris, A. Michel, 1928. (Les Maîtres du moyen âge et de la Renaissance . . . , 4).

Procaccini, Camillo, 1555–1629

10039. Artioli, Nerio. *Gli affreschi di Camillo Procaccini e Bernardino Camnpi in San Prospero di Reggio Emilia*. [By] Nerio Artioli [and] Elio Monducci. Reggio Emilia, Cassa di risparmio di Reggio Emilia, 1986.

10040. Neilson, Nancy W. *Camillo Procaccini: paintings and drawings*. New York, Garland, 1979. (CR). (Garland Reference Library of the Humanities, 163).

Prud'hon, Pierre Paul, 1758–1823

10041. Bricon, Etienne. *Prud'hon, biographie cri-*

tique. Paris, Laurens, [1907].

10042. Clément, Charles. *Prud'hon; sa vie, ses oeuvres et sa correspondance*. Paris, Didier, 1872.

10043. Forest, Alfred. *Pierre Paul Prud'hon, peintre français (1758–1823)*. Paris, Leroux, 1913.

10044. Gauthiez, Pierre. *Prud'hon*. Paris, Rouam, 1886.

10045. Goncourt, Edmond de. *Catalogue raisonné de l'oeuvre peinte, dessiné et gravé de P. P. Prud'hon*. Paris, Rapilly, 1876. (CR).

10046. Grappe, Georges. *P.-P. Prud'hon*. Paris, Michel, 1958.

10047. Guiffrey, Jean. *L'oeuvre de P. P. Prud'hon*. Paris, Colin, 1924. (CR).

10048. Régamey, Raymond. *Prud'hon*. Paris, Rieder, 1928.

10049. Voïart, Elise. *Notice historique sur la vie et les oeuvres de P. P. Prud'hon, peintre*. Paris, Didot, 1824.

Puget, Pierre, 1620–1694
François, 1651–1707

10050. Alibert, François P. *Pierre Puget*. Paris, Rieder, 1930.

10051. Arts et Livres de Provence. *Pierre Puget: pour le trois-cent cinquantième anniversaire de sa naissance à Marseille, le 16 octobre 1620*. Marseille, Arts et Livres de Provence, 1917. (Arts et livres de Provence, 78).

10052. Auquier, Philippe. *Pierre Puget, biographie critique*. Paris, Laurens, [1903].

10053. Baumann, Emile. *Pierre Puget, sculpteur*. Paris, Editions de l'Ecole, 1949.

10054. Brion, Marcel. *Pierre Puget*. Paris, Plon, 1930.

10055. Gloton, Marie-Christine. *Pierre et François Puget, peintres baroques*. Préface de Jacques Thuillier. Aix-en-Provence, Edisud, 1985.

10056. Herding, Klaus. *Pierre Puget, das bildnerische Werk*. Berlin, Mann, 1970. (CR).

10057. Lagrange, Léon. *Pierre Puget; peintre, sculpteur, architecte, décorateur de vaisseaux*. Paris, Didier, 1868.

10058. Pons, Zenon. *Essai sur la vie et les ouvrages de Pierre Puget*. Paris, Delaunai, 1812.

10059. Provence Historique. *Puget et son temps: actes du colloque tenu à l'Université de Provence les 15, 16 et 17 octobre 1971*. Provence, Provence Historique, 1972.

10060. Vitzthum, Walter. *Pierre Puget*. Milano, Fabbri, 1966. (I maestri della scultura, 80).

Pugin, Augustus Charles, 1768–1832
Augustus Welby Northmore, 1812–1852

10061. Atterbury, Paul and Wainwright, Clive. eds. *Pugin: a gothic passion*. Edited by P. Atterbury and Clive Wainwright. New Haven, Yale University Press, 1994

P

10062. Belcher, Margaret. *A.W.N. Pugin: an annotated critical bibliography*. London/New York, Mansell, 1988.

10063. Ferrey, Benjamin. *Recollections of A. N. Welby Pugin and his father, Augustus Pugin*. With an appendix by E. Sheridan Purcell. London, Stanford, 1861. (Reprint: New York, Blom, 1972).

10064. ———. *Recollections of A.W.N. Pugin and his father Augustus Pugin*. [By] Benjamin Ferre with an appendix by E. Sheridan Pur-cell and an introduction and index by Clive and Jane Wainwright. London, Scolar Preess, 1978.

10065. Gwynn, Denis R. *Lord Shrewsbury, Pugin, and the Catholic revival*. London, Hollis & Carter, 1946.

10066. Harries, John G. *Pugin: an illustrated life of Augustus Welby Northmore Pugin, 1812–1852*. Aylesbury (England), Shire, 1973. (Lifelines, 17). (Reprint: Princes Risborough, Shire, 1994).

10067. Pugin, Augustus W. *An apology for the revival of Christian architecture in England*. London, Weale, 1843.

10068. ———. *Contrasts, or a parallel between the noble edifices of the Middle Ages and corresponding buildings of the present day, shewing the present decay of taste*. London, Dolmon, 1841. 2 ed. (Reprint, with an introduction by Henry Russell Hitchcock: Leicester, Leicester University Press, 1969).

10069. ———. *Examples of Gothic architecture; selected from various ancient edifices in England*. 3 v. London, [Pugin], 1831.

10070. ———. *The true principles of pointed or Christian architecture*. London, Weale, 1841. (Reprint: New York, St. Martin's, 1973).

10071. ———. *Pugin: a Gothic passion*. Edited by Paul Atterbury and Clive Wainwright. New Haven, Yale University Press; London, Yale University Press in association with the Victoria & Albert Museum, 1994.

10072. Rope, Edward G. *Pugin*. Ditchling (England), Pepler & Sewell, 1935.

10073. Stanton, Phoebe. *Pugin*. Preface by Nikolaus Pevsner. London, Thames and Hudson, 1971.

10074. Trappes-Lomax, Michael. *Pugin: a medieval Victorian*. London, Sheed & Ward, 1932.

10075. Wedgwood, Alexandra. *A.W.N. Pugin and the Pugin family*. Lndon, Victoria and Albert Museum, 1985.

10076. Williams, Guy R. *Augustus Pugin versus Decimus Burton: a Victorian architectural duel*. London, Cassell, 1990.

Puni, Iwan *see* **Pougni, Jean**

Purrmann, Hans, 1880–1966
10077. Göpel, Barbara und Göpel, Erhard. *Leben und Meinungen des Malers Hans Purrmann; an Hand seiner Erzählungen, Schriften und Briefe*. Wiesbaden, Limes, 1961.

10078. Hausen, Edmund. *Der Maler Hans Purrmann*. Berlin, Lemmer, 1950.

10079. Pfalzgalerie Kaiserslautern. *Hans Purrmann zum 100. Geburtstag. 8. Juni bis 6. Juli 1980*. Mainz, Mittelrheinisches Landesmuseum, 1980.

10080. Purrmann, Hans. *Hans Purrmann: Aquarelle*: Katalog zur Ausstellung anlässlich des 20. Todestages. Kunstverein Speyer am Rhein, 2. März–31. März 1986; Museum Langenargen am Bodensee 13. April–28. Mai 1986. [Herausgeber, Kunstverein Speyer; Redaktion Friedrich Seel; wissenschaftliche Bearbeitung, Angela Heilmann]. Heidelberg, Edition Braus, 1986.

10081. ———. *Hans Purrmann, 1880–1966: Malerei, Graphik, Zeichnungen, Plastik*. [Katalogbearbeitung, Horst-Jörg Ludwig]. Berlin, Akademie der Künste der Deutschen Demokratischen Republik, 1982.

10082. ———. *Hans Purrmann: Stilleben, Akte, Interieurs*: Katalog zur Ausstellung im Kunstverein Speyer anlässlich der 2000-Jahrfeier der Heimatstadt Hans Purrmanns vom 13. Mai bis zum 24. Juni 1990 und im Städtischen Museum Lindau, vom 5. Juli bis zum 26. August 1990. [Herausgeber: Kunstverein Speyer in Verbindung mit dem Landemuseum Mainz; Redaktion, Friedrich Seel.] Heidelberg, Edition Braus, 1990.

10083. ———. *Der Maler Hans Purrmann, Speyer, 1880–1966 Basel*. Ausstellung und Katalog, Berthold Roland]. Bundeskanzleramt Bonn, 11. November 1987 bis 10. Januar 1988; Landesmuseum Mainz, 31. Januar bis 6. März 1988; Cercle municipal, Luxembourg, 15. bis 25. März 1988. Mainz, Landesmuseum, 1987.

10084. Steigelmann, Wilhelm. *Hans Purrmann und die Pfalz; erlebte Kunstgeschichte in Briefen*. Edenkoben (Germany), Edenkobener Rundschau, 1976.

10085. Villa Stuck (Munich). *Hans Purrmann, 1880–1966; Gemälde, Aquarelle, Zeichnungen, Druckgraphik. 21. Oktober 1976–16. Januar 1977*. München, Stuck-Jugendstil-Verein, 1976.

Putz, Leo, 1869–1940
10086. Kurhaus Meran. *Leo Putz, 1869–1940*. Gedächtnisausstellung zum 40. Todestag. 9. August–20.September 1980. Katalogbearbeitung, Ruth Stein; Redaktion, Siegfried Unterberger. Bozen [Bolzano], Athesia, 1980.

10087. Michel, Wilhelm. *Leo Putz, ein deutscher Künstler der Gegenwart*. Leipzig, Klinkhart & Biermann, [1909].

10088. Stein, Ruth. *Leo Putz.* Mit einem Verzeichnis der Gemälde und bildartigen Entwürfe. Wien, Tusch, 1974.

10089. Villa Stuck (Munich). *Leo Putz: Zeichnungen und Bilder aus dem Spätwerk.* [Catalogue of an exhibition], 8. Oktober bis 22. November 1981. München, Museum Villa Stuck, 1981.

Puvis de Chavannes, Pierre, 1824–1898

10090. Aynard, Edouard. *Les peintures décoratives de Puvis de Chavannes au Palais des Arts.* Lyon, Mougin-Rusand, 1884.

10091. Brown Price, Aimée. *Pierre Puvis de Chavanne.* [Catalogue of an exhibition held in the Vincent van Gogh Museum, Amsterdam from February 25 until May 29, 1994]. Zwolle, Waanders, 1994.

10092. Declairieux, A. *Puvis de Chavannes et ses oeuvres: trois conférences.* Lyon, Rey, 1928.

10093. Jean, René. *Puvis de Chavannes.* Paris, Alcan, 1914.

10094. Mauclair, Camille. *Puvis de Chavannes.* Paris, Plon, 1928.

10095. Michel, André. *Puvis de Chavannes, a biographical and critical study.* Notes by Jean Laran. Philadelphia, Lippincott/London, Heinemann, 1912.

10096. National Gallery of Canada (Ottawa). *Puvis de Chavannes, 1824–1898.* 25 March–8 May 1977. Ottawa, National Museums of Canada, 1977.

10097. Puvis de Chavannes, Pierre. *Puvis de Chavannes et le Musée des beaux-arts de Marseille.* [Catalogue of an exhibition], Marseille, Musée des beaux-arts, décembre 1984–janvier 1985. Marseilles, Le Musée, 1984.

10098. Scheid, Gustave. *L'oeuvre de Puvis de Chavannes à Amiens.* [Paris], Office d'Edition des Musées et des Arts, 1907.

10099. Vachon, Marius. *Puvis de Chavannes.* Paris, Braun, 1895.

10100. Werth, Léon. *Puvis de Chavannes.* Paris, Crès, 1926.

Pyle, Howard, 1853–1911

10101. Abbott, Charles D. *Howard Pyle: a chronicle.* With an introduction by N. C. Wyeth. New York/London, Harper, 1925.

10102. Agosta, Lucien L. *Howard Pyle.* Boston, Twayne Publishers,1987.

10103. Delaware Art Museum (Wilmington, Del.). *Howard Pyle: diversity in depth.* March 5–April 15, 1973. Wilmington, Wilmington Society of the Fine Arts, 1973.

10104. Hyland, Douglas. *Howard Pyle and the Wyeths: four generations of American imagination.* [Catalogue of an exhibition] [by] Douglas K.S. Hyland; essay by Howard P. Brokaw. Memphis, Tenn, Memphis Brooks Museum of Art, 1983.

10105. Morse, Willard S. and Brincklé, Gertrude. *Howard Pyle, a record of his illustrations and writings.* Wilmington, Del., Wilmington Society of the Fine Arts, 1921. (Reprint: Detroit, Singing Tree Press, 1969).

10106. Pitz, Henry C. *The Brandywine tradition.* Boston, Houghton Mifflin, 1969.

10107. ———. *Howard Pyle: writer, illustrator, founder of the Brandywine school.* New York, Clarkson Potter, 1975; distributed by Crown, New York.

10108. Pyle, Howard. *Howard Pyle, the artist, the legacy.* [Catalogue of an exhibition]. Wilmington, Del., Delaware Art Museum, 1987.

Pynacker, Adam, c.1620–1673

10109. Harwood, Laurie B. *Adam Pynacker (c.1620–1673).* Doornspijk, Davaco, 1988. (CR). (Aetas aurea, 7).

Q

Quarenghi, Giacomo, 1744–1817

10110. Colombo, Giuseppe. *Giacomo Quarenghi bergamasco, architetto alla corte imperiale di Petroburgo.* Torino, Artigianelli, 1879.

10111. Korshunova, Militsa F. *Dzhakomo Kvarengi.* Leningrad, Lenizdat, 1977.

10112. Palazzo della Ragione (Bergamo). *Disegni di Giacomo Quarenghi.* 30 aprile–30 giugno, 1967. Venezia, Pozza, 1967.

10113. Piljavskij, Vladimir. *Giacomo Quarenghi.* A cura di Sandro Angelini; testo di Vladimir Piljavskij; catalogo di Vanni Zanella. [Milano], Silvana, 1984.

10114. Quarenghi, Giacomo. *Fabbriche e disegni di Giacomo Quarenghi, illustrate dal cav. Giulio suo figlio.* Milano, Tosi, 1821.

10115. ———. *Giacomo Quarenghi, architetto a Pietroburgo: lettere e altri scritti.* A cura di Vanni Zanella. Venezia, Albrizzi, 1988.

10116. Severin, Dante. *Giacomo Quarenghi, architetto in Russia.* Bergamo, Orobiche, 1953.

Quercia, Jacopo della, 1372–1438

10117. Bacci, Pèleo. *Jacopo della Quercia; nuovi documenti e commenti.* Siena, Libreria Editrice Senese, 1929.

10118. Beck, James. *Jacopo della Quercia.* 2 v. New York, Columbia University Press, 1991. (CR).

10119. Biagi, Luigi. *Jacopo della Quercia.* Firenze, Arnaud, 1946.

10120. Chelazzi Dini, Giulietta, ed. *Jacopo della Quercia fra gotico e Rinascimento: atti del convegno di studi.* [Università di] Siena, Facoltà di Lettere e Filosofia, 2–5 ottobre 1975. Firenze, Centro Di, 1977.

10121. Cornelius, Carl. *Jacopo della Quercia, eine kunsthistorische Studie.* Halle, Knapp, 1896.

10122. Gielly, Louis J. *Jacopo della Quercia.* Paris, Michel, 1930.

10123. *Jacopo della Quercia fra gotico e Rinascimento: atti del Comnvegno di studi: Siena, Facolta di lettere filosofia, 2–5 ottobre 1975.* A cura di Giulietta Chelazzi Dini. Firenze, Centro Di, 1977.

10124. Mansi, Gerardo. *Ilaria del Carretto o Maria Caterina Antelminelli?: dissertazioni e varie ipotesi sul sepolcro di Jacopo della Quercia nella Cattedrale di Lucca.* Lucca, Maria Pacini Fazzi, 1991.

10125. Nicco, Giusta. *Jacopo della Quercia.* Firenze, Bemporad, 1934.

10126. Palazzo Pubblico (Siena). *Jacopo della Quercia nell'arte del suo tempo; mostra didattica.* 24 maggio–12 ottobre 1975. Firenze, Centro Di, 1975.

10127. Seymour, Charles. *Jacopo della Quercia, sculptor.* New Haven, Yale University Press, 1973. (Yale Publications in the History of Art, 23).

R

Rackham, Arthur, 1867–1939

10128. Coykendall, Frederick. *Arthur Rackham; a list of books illustrated by him,* compiled by Frederick Coykendall, with an introductory note by Martin Birnbaum. Mount Vernon, N.Y. Priv. print., 1922.

10129. Gettings, Fred. *Arthur Rackham.* New York, Macmillan, 1976.

10130. Hamilton, James. *Arthur Rackham: a life with illustration.* London, Pavilion, 1990.

10131. Hudson, Derek. *Arthur Rackham, his life and work.* London, Heinemann, 1960.

10132. Latimore, Sarah B. and Haskell, Grace C. *Arthur Rackham, a bibliography.* Los Angeles, Suttonhouse, 1936.

Raeburn, Henry, 1756–1823

10133. Andrew, William R. *Life of Sir Henry Raeburn, by his great grandson.* London, Allen, 1894.

10134. Armstrong, Walter. *Sir Henry Raeburn.* With an introduction by R. A. M. Stevenson and a biographical and descriptive catalogue by J. L. Caw. London, Heinemann/New York, Dodd, Mead, 1901.

10135. Dibdin, Edward R. *Raeburn.* London, Allen, 1925.

10136. Greig, James. *Sir Henry Raeburn, R. A.; his life and work.* London, Connoisseur, 1911.

Raffaelli, Jean François, 1850–1924

10137. Alexandre, Arsène. *Jean-Françoise Raffaelli; peintre, graveur et sculpteur.* Paris, Floury, 1909.

10138. Lecomte, Georges. *Raffaëlli.* Paris, Rieder, 1927.

10139. Raffaëlli, Jean F. *Mes promenades au Musée du Louvre.* Préface de Maurice Barres. Paris, Editions d'Art et de Littérature, 1913. 2 ed.

Raffet, Denis Auguste Marie, 1804–1860

10140. Béraldi, Henri. *Raffet, peintre national.* Paris, La Librairie Illustrée, [1892].

10141. Bry, Auguste. *Raffet, sa vie et ses oeuvres.* Paris, Bauer, 1874. 2 ed.

10142. Giacomelli, Hector. *Raffet: son oeuvre lithographique et ses eaux-fortes, suivi de la bibliographie complète.* Paris, Gazette des Beaux-Arts, 1862.

10143. Ladoué, Pierre. *Un peintre de l'Epopée française: Raffet.* Paris, Michel, 1946.

10144. L'homme, François. *Raffet.* Paris, Librairie de L'Art, [1892].

10145. Raffet, Denis. *Notes et croquis de Raffet.* Mis en ordre et publiés par August Raffet. Paris, Goupil etc., 1878.

Raibolini, Francesco *see* Francia

Raimondi, Marc Antonio, ca. 1480–1530

10146. Bartsch, Adam. *The works of Marcantonio Raimondi and of his school.* Ed. by Konrad Oberhuber. 2 v. New York, Abaris, 1978. (*The illustrated Bartsch,* 26/27; from his *Le peintre-graveur,* Wien, Degen, 1803–1821).

10147. Delaborde, Henri. *Marc-Antoine Raimondi, étude historique et critique suivie d'un catalogue raisonné des oeuvres du maître.* Paris, Librairie de l'Art, 1888. (CR).

10148. Delessert, Benjamin. *Notice sur la vie de Marc-Antoine Raimondi, graveur bolonais.* Paris, Goupil/Londres, Colnaghi, 1853.

10149. Spencer Museum of Art, University of Kansas (Lawrence, Kans.). *The engravings of Marcantonio Raimondi.* February 10–March 28, 1982. Lawrence, Kan., Spencer Museum of Art, University of Kansas, 1982.

10150. Straaten, Roelof van. *Marcantonio Raimondi and his school: an iconographic index to A. Bartsch, Le Peintre-graveur, vols. 14, 15, and 16.* Doornspijk, Davaco, 1988 (Iconclass indexes: Italian prints; v.2).

10151. Witt, Antony de. *Marcantonio Raimondi, incisioni.* Scelte e annotate di Antony de Witt. Firenze, La Nuova Italia, 1968.

Rainaldi, Carlo, 1611–1691

10152. Fasolo, Furio. *L'opera di Hieronimo e Carlo Rainaldi*. Roma, Edizioni Ricerche, 1961.

10153. Hempel, Eberhard. *Carlo Rainaldi; ein Beitrag zur Geschichte des römischen Barocks*. München, Wolf, 1919.

Rainer, Arnulf, 1929–

10154. Catoir, Barbara. *Arnulf Rainer: übermalte Bücher*. München, Prestel Verlag, 1989.

10155. Fuchs, Rudolf H. *Arnulf Rainer*. Wien, Historisches Museum der Stadt Wien. ARGE Wimmer & Sailer, 1989.

10156. Guse, Ernst-Gerhard. *Arnulf Rainer. Malerei von 1980–1990*. [Catalogue of an exhibition held at the Saarland Museum, Saarbrücken by Ernst-Gerhard Guse]. Stuttgart, Hatje, 1990.

10157. Rainer, Arnulf. *Arnulf Rainer*. [Catalogue of an exhibition curated by R.H. Fuchs]. Munich, Prestel-Verlag in association with the Solomon R. Guggenheim Museum, New York, 1989.

10158. ———. *A. Rainer: mort et sacrifice*. [Catalogue of an exhibition held at the Musée national d'art moderne, Centre Georges Pompidou, . . . 1er février–26 mars 1984]. Paris, Centre Georges Pompidou, 1984.

10159. ———. *Arnulf Rainer:* Nationalgalerie Berlin. Staatliche Museen Preussischer Kulturbesitz, 20.11. 1980–1.2. 1981. [Ausstellung und Katalog von Dieter Honisch; wissenschaftliche Mitarbeit, Adriaan Bracht . . . et al.] Berlin, Nationalgalerie, 1980.

10160. ———. *Hirndrang: Selbstkommentare und andere Texte zu Werk und Person mit 118 Bildbeigaben*. Hrsg. von Otto Breicha. Salzburg, Galerie Welz, 1980.

10161. ———. *Überdeckungen. Mit einem Werkkatalog sämtlicher Radierungren, Lithographien und Siebdrucke, 1950–1971*. Herausgegeben von Otto Breicha. Wien, Edition Tusch, 1972. (CR). (Österreichische Graphiker der Gegenwart, 7).

10162. Rychlik, Otmar. *Raineriana: Aufsätze zum Werk von Arnulf Rainer*. Wien, Böhlau, 1989.

10163. Schwaiger, Brigitte. *Malstunde*. Wien, P. Zsolnay, 1980. [An Interview with Arnulf Rainer].

Ramage, John, c. 1748–1802

10164. Morgan, John H. *A sketch of the life of John Ramage, miniature painter*. New York, New York Historical Society, 1930.

10165. Sherman, Frederic F. *John Ramage, a biographical sketch and a list of his portrait miniatures*. New York, [Sherman], 1929.

Ramsay, Allan, 1713–1784
Allan, 1685–1758

10166. Brown, Iain Gordon. *Poet and painter: Allan Ramsay, father and son, 1684–1784*. Edinburgh, National Library of Scotland, 1984.

10167. MacLaine, Allan H. *Allan Ramsay*. Boston, Twayne Publishers, 1985.

10168. National Gallery of Scotland (Edinburgh). *Allan Ramsay (1713–1784); his masters and rivals*. 9 August–15 September 1963. Edinburgh, National Galleries of Scotland, 1963.

10169. Smart, Alastair. *Allan Ramsay: painter, essayist and man of the Enlightenment*. New Haven, Published for the Paul Mellon Center for Studies in British Art by Yale University Press, 1992.

10170. ———. *The life and art of Allan Ramsay*. London, Routledge & Kegan Paul, 1952.

Raphael, 1483–1520

10171. Ames-Lewis, Francis. *The draftsman Raphael*. New Haven, Yale University Press, 1986.

10172. Astolfi, Carlo. *Raffaello Sanzio, scultore*. Roma, Palombi, 1935.

10173. Becherucci, Luisa, et al. *Raffaello; l'opera, le fonti, la fortuna*. 2 v. Novara, Istituto Geografico de Agostini, 1968.

10174. Beck, James H. *Raphael*. New York, Abrams, 1976.

10175. ———, ed. *Raphael before Rome*. Edited by James Beck. Washington, D.C., National Gallery of Art; Hanover, N.H., Distributed by the University Press of New England, 1986. (Studies in the history of art, 17; Symposium series, 5).

10176. Bellori, Giovanni P. *Descrizioni delle imagini dipinte da Raffaelle d'Urbino nelle camere del palazzo apostolico Vaticano*. Roma, Komarek, 1695.

10177. Bérence, Fred. *Raphaël ou la puissance de l'esprit*. Paris, La Colombe, 1954.

10178. Berti, Luciano. *Raffaello*. Bergamo, Istituto Italiano d'Arti Grafiche, 1961.

10179. Bockemühl, Michael. *Die Wirklichkeit des Bildes; Bildrezeption als Bildproduktion: Rothko, Newman, Rembrandt, Raphael*. Stuttgart, Urachhaus, 1985.

10180. Bolsena, Pietro. *La iconologia bisessuale segreta di Raffaello e del Rinascimento: (Il rifiuto di Javeth e il Credo dell' Ermafrodito; studi e tesi di iconologia umana su una civilta umana*. Vienna, [s.n.], 1980–1881. (Grotte di castro, Tipo-Litografia C. Ceccarelli).

10181. Bricarelli, Carlo. *Il pensiero cristiano del Cinquecento nell'arte di Raffaello*. Torino, Celanza, 1921.

10182. Brown, David A. *Raphael and America.*

[Published in conjunction with an exhibition at the National Gallery of Art, Washington, D.C., Jan. 9–May 8, 1983]. Washington, D.C., National Gallery of Art, 1983.

10183. Comolli, Angelo. *Vita inedita di Raffaello da Urbino, illustrata con note.* Roma, Salvioni, 1790.

10184. Cordellier, Dominique and Py, Bernadette. *Raphael, son atelier, ses copistes.* Paris, Réunion des Musees nationaux, 1992.

10185. Crowe, Joseph A. and Cavalcaselle, Giovanni B. *Raphael, his life and works.* 2 v. London, Murray, 1882.

10186. Dacos, Nicole. *Le logge di Raffaello; maestro e bottega di fronte all'antico.* Roma, Istituto Poligrafico dello Stato, 1977.

10187. Dussler, Luitpold. *Raphael: a critical catalogue of his pictures, wall-paintings and tapestries.* Trans. by Sebastian Cruft. London/New York, Phaidon, 1971. (CR).

10188. Ettlinger, Leopold D. and Ettlinger, Helen S. *Raphael.* Oxford, Phaidon, 1987.

10189. Euboeus, Tauriscus [pseud., W. Lepel]. *Catalogue des estampes gravées d'après Raphael.* Francfort sur le Mein, Hermann, 1819.

10190. Farabulini, David. *Saggio di nuovi studi su Raffaello d'Urbino.* Roma, Agonale, 1875.

10191. Ferino Pagden, Sylvia. *Rafaello: catalogo completo dei dipinti.* S. Ferino Pagden [con] Maria Antonietta Zancan. Firenze, Cantini, 1989. (CR).

10192. Fischel, Oskar. *Raphael.* Trans. by Bernard Rackham. 2 v. London, Kegan Paul, 1948.

10193. ———, ed. *Raphael Sanzio: Zeichnungen.* 9 v. [Vol. 9 ed. by Konrad Oberhuber]. Berlin, Grote, 1913–1941/Berlin, Mann, 1972 [Vol. 9]. (CR).

10194. Fraprie, Frank R. *The Raphael book: an account of the life of Raphael Santi of Urbino and his place in the development of art.* Boston, Page, 1912.

10195. Fusero, Clemente. *Raffaello.* [Milano], dall'Oglio, 1963. (Reprint: 1983).

10196. Frommel, Christoph Luitpold. *Raffaello architetto.*[Catalogue of an exhibition by C.L. Frommel, S. Ray, M. Tafuri]. La sezione "Rafaello e l'antico" è stata curata da H. Burns e A. Nesselrath. Roma, Electa Editrice, 1984.

10197. Geymuller, Enrico de. *Raffaello Sanzio studiato come architetto con l'aiuto di nuovi documenti.* Milano, Hoepli, 1884.

10198. Gherardi, Pompeo. *Della vita e delle opere di Raffaello Sanzio da Urbino.* Urbino, Rocchetti, 1874.

10199. Golzio, Vincenzo. *Raffaello nei documenti nelle testimonianze dei contemporanei e nella letteratura del suo secolo.* Città del Vaticano, 1936.

10200. Grand Palais (Paris). *Raphael et l'art français.* [November 15, 1983–February 13, 1984]. Paris, Galeries Nationales du Grand Palais, 1983.

10201. Grimm, Herman. *The life of Raphael.* Trans. by Sarah H. Adams. Boston, Cupples and Hurd, 1888.

10202. Gruyer, François A. *Essai sur les fresques de Raphaël au Vatican: chambres.* Paris, Gide, 1858.

10203. ———. *Essai sur les fresques de Raphaël au Vatican: loges.* Paris, Renouard, 1859.

10204. ———. *Raphaël et l'antiquité.* 2 v. Paris, Renouard, 1864.

10205. ———. *Raphaël, peintre de portraits; fragments d'histoire et d'iconographie.* 2 v. Paris, Renouard, 1881.

10206. ———. *Les vierges de Raphaël et l'iconographie de la vierge.* 3 v. Paris, Renouard, 1869.

10207. Gualazzi, Enzo. *Vita di Raffaello da Urbino.* Milano, Rusconi, 1984.

10208. Guillaud, Jacqueline et Maurice. *Raphael, la grace d'un ange la force du génie.* Par J. et M. Guillaud; avec la collabroration de Fabrizio Mancinelli. Paris/New York, Guillaud Editions, 1989.

10209. Hofmann, Theobald. *Raffael in seiner Bedeutung als Architekt.* 4 v. Zittau, Menzel, 1900–1911.

10210. Holmes, Charles. *Raphael and the modern use of the classical tradition.* New York, Dutton, 1933.

10211. Joannides, Paul. *The drawings of Raphael, with a complete catalogue.* Oxford, Phaidon, 1983. (CR).

10212. Jones, Roger and Penny, Nicholas. *Raphael.* New Haven/London, Yale University Press, 1983.

10213. Kelber, Wilhelm. *Raphael von Urbino, Leben und Werk.* Stuttgart, Urachhaus, 1979.

10214. Knab, Eckhart/Mitsch, Erwin, [and] Oberhuber, Konrad. *Raphael; die Zeichnungen.* Stuttgart, Urachhaus, 1983.

10215. Knackfuss, Hermann. *Raphael.* Trans. by Campbell Dodgson. Bielefeld/Leipzig, Velhagen & Klasing, 1898. (Monographs on Artists, 1).

10216. Lohuizen-Mulder, Mab van. *Raphael's images of justice, humanity, friendship: a mirror of princes for Scipione Borghese.* Trans. by Patricia Wardle. Wassenaar (Holland), Mirananda, 1977.

10217. McCurdy, Edward. *Raphael Santi.* London/New York, Hodder and Stoughton, 1917.

10218. Mason, Rainer Michael. *Raphael et la seconde main: 1984,* [exhibition catalogue]. Cabinet des estampes & Musée d'art et d'histoire, Genève. Genève, Le Musée, 1984.

10219. Middeldorf, Ulrich A. *Raphael's drawings.* New York, Bittner, 1945.

10220. Mulazzani, Germano. *Raffaello.* Milano, Rusconi, 1983.

R

10221. Muntz, Eugène. *Les historiens et critiques de Raphael; essai bibliographique.* Paris, Rouam, 1883.

10222. ———. *Raphael; his life, works, and times.* Edited by Walter Armstrong. London, Chapman and Hall/New York, Armstrong, 1882. (Reprint: Dover, N.H., Longwood, 1977).

10223. ———. *Les tapisseries de Raphael au Vatican et dans les principaux musées ou collections de l'Europe: étude historique et critique.* Paris, Rothschild, 1897.

10224. Nagler, Georg K. *Rafael als Mensch und Künstler.* München, Fleischmann, 1836.

10225. Oberhuber, Konrad. *Raffaello.* Milano, Mondadori, 1982.

10226. Oppé, Adolf A. *Raphael.* Edited with an introduction by Charles Mitchell. New York, Praeger, 1970. Revised ed.

10227. Palazzo Pitti (Florence). *Raffaello e l'architettura a Firenze nella prima metà del Cinquecento.* 11 gennaio–29 aprile 1984. Firenze, Palazzo Pitti, 1984.

10228. Passavant, Johann. *Rafael von Urbino und sein Vater Giovanni Santi.* 3 v. Leipzig, Brockhaus, 1839–1858. (English ed.: London/New York, Macmillan, 1872).

10229. Pedretti, Carlo. *Raffaello.* Bologna, Capitol, 1982.

10230. ———. *Raphael, his life & work in the splendors of the Italian Renaissance.* With new documents and an unpublished essay by Vincenzo Golzio. Florence, Giunti, 1989.

10231. Poggiali, Pietro. *Raphael in Rome; a study of art and life in the XVI century.* Rome, Centenari, 1889.

10232. Ponente, Nello. *Who was Raphael?* Trans. by James Emmons. Geneva, Skira, 1967; distributed by World, Cleveland.

10233. Pope-Hennessy, John. *Raphael.* New York, New York University Press, 1970.

10234. Prisco, Michele [and] Vecchi, Pier L. de. *L'opera completa di Raffaello.* Milano, Rizzoli, 1966. (Classici dell'arte, 4).

10235. Putscher, Marielene. *Raphaels sixtinische Madonna, das Werk und seine Wirkung.* Tübingen, Hopfer, 1955.

10236. Quatremère de Quincy, Antoine C. *Histoire de la vie et des ouvrages de Raphael.* Paris, Le Clere, 1833. 2 ed. (English ed., trans. by William Hazlitt: London, Bogue, 1896; Reprint: New York/London, Garland, 1979).

10237. Ray, Stefano. *Raffaello architetto: linguaggio artistico e ideologia nel Rinascimento romano.* Prefazione di Bruno Zevi. Roma, Laterza, 1974.

10238. Redig de Campos, Deoclecio. *Raffaello nelle stanze.* Milano, Martello, 1965.

10239. Rosenberg, Adolf. *Raffael, des Meisters Gemälde.* Berlin/Leipzig, Deutsche Verlags-Anstalt, 1923. 5 ed. (Klassiker der Kunst, 1).

10240. Rumohr, Carl F. *Über Raphael und sein Verhältniss zu den Zeitgenossen.* Berlin/Stettin, Nicolai, 1831.

10241. Salmi, Mario, et al. *The complete work of Raphael.* New York, Reynal & Co., 1969.

10242. Serra, Luigi. *Raffaello.* Torino, Unione Tipografica/Editrice Torinese, 1945.

10243. Shearman, John. *Raphael's cartoons in the collection of Her Majesty the Queen and the tapestries for the Sistine Chapel.* London, Phaidon, 1972.

10244. ———, ed. *The Princeton Raphael Symposium: science in the service of art history.* Edited by John Shearman and Marcia B. Hall. Princeton, N.J., Princeton University Press, 1990. (Princeton monographs in art and archaeology, 47).

10245. *Studi su Raffaello:* atti del congresso internazionale di studi. Urbino-Firenze, 6–14 aprile 1984. A cura di Micaela Sambucco Hamoud e Maria Letizia Stocchi. Contributi di Cristiaa Acidini . . . [et al.]. 2 v. Urbino, QuattroVenti; Distribuzione P.D.E., 1987.

10246. Stein, Wilhelm. *Raphael.* Berlin, Bondi, 1923.

10247. Suida, Wilhelm. *Raphael.* London, Phaidon, 1948. 2 ed.

10248. Thompson, David. *Raphael, the life and the legacy.* London, British Broadcasting Corporation, 1983.

10249. Ullmann, Ernst. *Raffael.* Leipzig, Prisma, 1983.

10250. [Valentini, Agostino]. *I freschi delle loggie vaticane dipinti da Raffaele Sanzio.* Illustrati per cura d'Agostino Valentini. 2 v. Roma, Valentini, 1851.

10251. Vecchi, Pier L. de. *Raffaello, la pittura.* Prefazione di Anna M. Brizio. Firenze, Martello, 1981.

10252. Venturi, Adolfo. *Raffaello.* Testo aggiornato da Lionello Venturi. Milano, Mondadori, 1952. (Biblioteca moderna Mondadori, 310).

10253. Wagner, Hugo. *Raffael im Bildnis.* Bern, Benteli, 1969. (Berner Schriften zur Kunst, 11).

10254. Wanscher, Vilhelm. *Raffaello Santi da Urbino, his life and works.* London, Benn, 1926.

10255. Wolzogen, Alfred. *Raphael Santi, his life and his works.* Trans. by Fanny Bunnett. London, Smith, Elder, 1866.

Rastrelli, Bartolomeo Carlo, 1675–1744
Bartolomeo Francesco, 1700–1771

10256. Arkhipov, Nikolai I. [and] Raskin, A. G. *Bartolomeo Karlo Rastrelli, 1675–1744.* Leningrad, Iskusstvo, 1964.

10257. Koz'mian, Galina K. *F. B. Rastrelli.* Leningrad, Lenizdat, 1976.

Rauch, Christian Daniel, 1777–1857

10258. Börsch-Supan, Helmut. *Die Werke Christian Daniel Rauchs im Schlossbezirk von Charlottenburg.* Berlin, Verwaltung der Staatlichen Schlösser und Gärten, 1977. (Aus Berliner Schlössern: Kleine Schriften, 3).

10259. Cheney, Ednah D. *Life of Christian Daniel Rauch of Berlin, Germany.* Boston, Lee and Shepard, 1893.

10260. Eggers, Friedrich und Eggers, Karl. *Christian Daniel Rauch.* 5 v. Berlin, Duncker, 1873–1886 [Vols. 1–4]; Berlin, Fontane, 1891 [Vol. 5].

10261. Rauch, Christian Daniel. *Christian Daniel Rauch: Familienbriefe 1796–1857.* Hrsg. Monika Peschken-Eilsberger, München, Deutscher Kunstverlag, 1989.

10262. Rauch, Christian D. [and] Rietschel, Ernst. *Briefwechsel zwischen Rauch und Rietschel.* 2 v. Herausgegeben von Karl Eggers. Berlin, Fontane, 1890/1891.

10263. Weber, Helmut und Jedicke, Günter, eds. *Jubiläumsschrift zum 200. Geburtstag des Bildhauers Christian Daniel Rauch.* Arolsen, Stadt Arolsen, 1977.

Rauschenberg, Robert, 1925–

10264. Adriani, Götz. *Robert Rauschenberg: Zeichnungen, Gouachen, Collagen, 1949 bis 1979.* München/Zürich, Piper, 1979.

10265. Feinstein, Roni. *Robert Rauschenberg: the silkscreen paintings, 1962–64.* R. Feinstein with a contribution by Calvin Tomkins. New York, Whitney Museum of American Art in association with Bulfinch Press, Little, Brown, Boston, 1990.

10266. Forge, Andrew. *Rauschenberg.* New York, Abrams, 1969.

10267. Kotz, Mary Lynn. *Rauschenberg, art and life.* New York, Abrams, 1990.

10268. Hopps, Walter. *Robert Rauschenberg: the early 1950s.* Houston, The Menil Collection, Houston Fine Art Press, 1991.

10269. National Collection of Fine Arts (Washington, D.C.). *Robert Rauschenberg.* October 30, 1976–January 2, 1977. Washington, D.C., National Collection of Fine Arts, Smithsonian Institution, 1976.

10270. Rauschenberg, Robert. *Rauschenberg.* New York, Vintage Books, 1987.

10271. ———. *Rauschenberg photographe.* [Catalogue of an exhibition]. Paris, Centre Georges Pompidou, 1981; New York, Pantheon Books, 1981.

10272. Rose, Barbara. *Robert Rauschenberg im Gespräch mit Barbara Rose.* Aus dem Amerikanischen von Lothar Gorris. Köln, Kiepenheuer & Witsch, 1989.

10273. Solomon, Alan R. *Robert Rauschenberg.* [Published in conjunction with an exhibition at the Jewish Museum, New York, March 31–May 12, 1963]. New York, Jewish Theological Seminary, 1963.

10274. Staatliche Kunsthalle, Berlin. *Robert Rauschenberg: Werke, 1950–1980.* 23. März bis 4. Mai 1980. Berlin, Staatliche Kunsthalle, 1980.

10275. Tomkins, Calvin. *Off the wall: Robert Rauschenberg and the art world of our time.* Garden City, N.Y., Doubleday, 1980.

Ray, Man, 1890–1976

10276. Baldwin, Neil. *Man Ray, American artist.* New York, C.N. Potter; distributed by Crown, 1988.

10277. Bramly, Serge. *Man Ray.* Paris, Belfond, 1980.

10278. Esten, John. *Man Ray, Bazaar years.* Introduction, Willis Hartshorn. New York, Rizzoli, 1988.

10279. Foresta, Merry. *Perpetual motif: the art of Man Ray.* By M. Foresta . . . [et al.]. Washington, D.C., National Museum of American Art, Smithsonian Institution; New York, Abbeville Press, 1988.

10280. Frankfurter Kunstverein (Frankfurt am Main). *Man Ray, Inventionen und Interpretationen.* [October 14–December 23, 1979]. Frankfurt a.M., Frankfurter Kunstverein, 1979.

10281. Janus [pseud.]. *Man Ray.* Milano, Fabbri, 1973.

10282. Palazzo delle Esposizioni (Rome). *Man Ray: l'occhio e il suo doppio; dipinti, collages, disegni, invenzioni, fotografiche, oggetti d'affezione, libri, cinema.* Luglio–settembre 1975. Roma, Assessorato Antichità Belle Arti e Problemi della Cultura, 1975.

10283. Penrose, Roland. *Man Ray.* London, Thames and Hudson, 1975.

10284. Perl, Jed. *Man Ray.* Millerton, N.Y., Aperture, 1979. (Aperture History of Photography, 15).

10285. Ray, Man. *Man Ray.* With an essay by Jed Perl. New York, Aperture Foundation, 1988. (Aperture masters of photography, 6).

10286. ———. *Man Ray in fashion.* Introduction by Willis Hartshorn, Merry Foresta; special consultant John Esten. New York, International Center for Photography, 1990.

10287. ———. *Opera grafica.* Torino, Anselmino, 1973. (CR).

10288. ———. *Photographs.* Introduction by Jean-Herbert Martin. Trans. by Carolyn Breakspear. London, Thames and Hudson, 1982. (CR).

10289. ———. *Photographs, 1920–1934.* Edited by James Thrall Soby. Paris, Cahiers d'Art/New York, Random House, 1934. (New ed., with an introduction by A. D. Coleman: New

York, East River Press, 1975).

10290. ———. *Self portrait*. With an afterword by Juliet Man Ray; foreword by Merry A. Foresta. Boston, Little, Brown, 1988. (First published, 1963).

10291. Ribemont-Dessaignes, Georges. *Man Ray*. Paris, Gallimard, 1924.

10292. Schwartz, Arturo. *Man Ray; the rigour of imagination*. New York, Rizzoli, 1977.

Rayski, Ferdinand von, 1806–1890

10293. Goeritz, Mathias. *Ferdinand von Rayski und die Kunst des neunzehnten Jahrhunderts*. Berlin, Hugo, 1942.

10294. Grautoff, Otto. *Ferdinand von Rayski*. Berlin, Grote, 1923. (Grote'sche Sammlung von Monographien zur Kunstgeschichte, 4).

10295. Rayski, Ferdinand von. *Ferdind von Rayski, 1806–1890*. Ausstellung zum 100. Todestag. Albertinum, Dresden, 1990; Städtische Galerie im Lenbachhaus, München, 1991. [Katalogredaktion, Hans Joachim Neidhardt]. Dresden, Staatliche Kunstsammlungen Dresden, Gemäldegalerie Neue Meister, Kupferstich-Kabinett, 1990.

10296. Walter, Maräuschlein. *Ferdinand von Rayski, sein Leben und sein Werk*. Bielefeld/Leipzig, Velhagen & Klasing, 1943. (CR).

Reattu, Jacques, 1760–1833

10297. Benoit, Fernand. *Les années romaines du peintre Réattu*. Aix-en-Provence, F.-N. Nicollet, 1926.

10298. Simons, Katrin. *Jacques Réattu 1766–1833; peintre de la Révolution française*. Neuilly-sur Seine, ARTHENA, 1985.

Rebeyrolle, Paul, 1926–

10299. Descargues, Pierre. *Rebeyrolle*. Paris, Maeght, 1970.

Redgrave, Richard, 1804–1888

10300. Redgrave, Richard. *Richard Redgrave, C.B., R.A.; a memoir, compiled from his diary*. London, Cassel & Co., 1891.

10301. ———. *Richard Redgrave, 1804–1888*. Edited by Susan P. Casteras and Ronald Parkinson; with essays by Elizabeth Bonython . . . [et al.]. New Haven and London, Yale University Press, in acssociation with the Victoria and Albert Museum and the Yale Center for Bitish Art, 1988.

Redon, Odilon, 1840–1916

10302. Bacou, Roseline. *Odilon Redon*. 2 v. Genève, Cailler, 1956.

10303. ———. *Odilon Redon: pastels*. Introduction and commentaries by Roseline Bacou; trans. by Beatrice Rehl. New York, G. Braziller, 1987.

10304. Berger, Klaus. *Odilon Redon; fantasy and colour*. Trans. by Michael Bullock. New York, McGraw-Hill, 1965.

10305. Coustet, Robert. *L'univers d'Odilon Redon*. Paris, H. Screpel, 1984.

10306. Destrée, Jules. *L'oeuvre lithographique de Odilon Redon, catalogue descriptif*. Bruxelles, Deman, 1891.

10307. Eisenman, Stephen F. *The temptation of Saint Redon.: Biography, ideology, and style in the 'Noirs' of Odilon Redon*. Chicago, University of Chicago Press, 1992.

10308. Fegdal, Charles. *Odilon Redon*. Paris, Rieder, 1929.

10309. Gamboni, Dario. *La plume et le pinceau: Odilon Redon et la littérature*. Paris, Editions de Minuit, 1989.

10310. Harrison, Sharon R. *The etchings of Odilon Redon: a catalogue raisonné*. With a foreword by Peter Morse. New York, Da Capo, 1986.

10311. Hobbs, Richard. *Odilon Redon*. Boston, New York Graphic Society, 1977.

10312. Klockenbring, Gérard. *Odilon Redon: Wege zum Tor der Sonne*. Stuttgart, Urachhaus, 1986.

10313. Mellerio, André. *Odilon Redon*. Paris, Société pour l'Étude de la Gravure Française, 1913. (Reprint: New York, Da Capo. 1968).

10314. ———. *Odilon Redon: Peintre, dessinateur et graveur*. Paris, Floury, 1923. (CR).

10315. Redon, Ari, ed. *Lettres à Odilon Redon*. Textes et notes par Roseline Bacou. Paris, Corti, 1960.

10316. Redon, Odilon. *Lettres d'Odilon Redon, 1878–1916*. Publiées par sa famille, avec une préface de Marius-Ary Leblond. Paris/Bruxelles, van Oest, 1923.

10317. ———. *Odilon Redon, 1840–1916*. [Exposition] Galerie des Beaux-Arts, Bordeaux: 10 mai–1er septembre 1985. [Texte: Roseline Bacou]. Bordeaux, La Galerie, 1985.

10318. ———. *Odilon Redon*. [Edited by the National Museum of Modern Art, Tokyo, Kunio Motoe, Koji Takahashi]. Tokyo, Tokyo Shimbun, 1989.

10319. ———. *Odilon Redon*. [Catalogue of an exhibition]. Hrsg. von Rudolf Rudolf Koelle. Fribourg, Office du Livre, 1983.

10320. ———. *Odilon Redon: the Ian Woodner Family Collection*. Organized by John E. Buchanan, Jr., Nanette V. Maciejunes; with a foreword by Daniel and Alec Wildenstein. Memphis, Tenn., Dixon Gallery and Gardens, 1990.

10321. ———. *To myself: Notes on life art and artists by Odilon Redon*; translated from the French by Mira Jacob and L. Wasserman. New York, Braziller, 1986.

10322. Sandström, Sven. *Le monde imaginaire*

d'Odilon Redon; étude iconologique. Lund (Sweden), Gleerup; New York, Wittenborn, 1955.

10323. Schatz, Matthias. *Der Betrachter im Werk von Odilon Redon; eine rezeptionsästhetische Studie*. Hamburg, R. Krämer, 1988.

10324. Selz, Jean. *Odilon Redon*. Trans. by Eileen B. Hennessy. New York, Crown, 1971.

10325. Vialla, Jean. *Odilon Redon*. Paris, ACR, 1988.

10326. Werner, Alfred. *The graphic works of Odilon Redon*. New York, Dover, 1969. (CR).

10327. Wildenstein, Alec. *Odilon Redon, vol. 1: Portraits et figures*. Paris, Bibliothèque des Arts, 1992.CR). (Collections 'catalogues raisonnés').

10328. Wilson, Michael. *Nature and imagination: the work of Odilon Redon*. Oxford, Phaidon, 1978.

Redouté, Pierre-Joseph, 1758–1840

10329. Hardouin-Fugier, Elisabeth. *The pupils of Redouté*. Leigh-On-Sea, F. Lewis, 1981.

10330. Hunt Botanical Library (Pittsburgh). *A catalogue of Redoutéana exhibited at the Hunt Botanical Library, 21 april to 1 august 1963*. Pittsburgh, Hunt Botanical Library, Carnegie Institute of Technology, 1963.

10331. Lawalree, André. *Fragment d'une biographie de Redouté*. San Miniato, Auderghem, Lawalree, 1969.

10332. Leger, Charles. *Redouté et son Temps*. [Paris?], Galerie Charpentier, 1945.

10333. Mathew, Brian. *Redouté: lilies and related flowers*. Woodstock, Overlook, 1982.

10334. Musée National d'Histoire Naturelle (Paris). *Redouté et les vélins du Musée national d'histoire naturelle*. Introd., Yves Laissus, préface de Jean Dorst. Paris, Henri Scrépel, 1980.

Regnault, Henri, 1843–1871

10335. Baillière, Henri. *Henri Regnault, 1843–1871*. Paris, Didier, 1872.

10336. Brey Marino, Maria. *Viaje a Espana del pintor Henri Regnault (1868–1870); Espana en la vida y en la obra de un artista francés*. Madrid, Castalia, 1964. 2 ed.

10337. Cazalis, Henri. *Henri Regnault; sa vie et son oeuvre*. Paris, Lemerre, 1872.

10338. Marx, Roger. *Henri Regnault, 1843–1871*. Paris, Rouam, [1886].

10339. Regnault, Henri. *Correspondance*. Annotée et recueillie par Arthur du Parc, suivi du catalogue complet de l'oeuvre de H. Regnault. Paris, Charpentier, 1872.

10340. ———. *Henri Regnault (1843–1871)*.[Catalogue of an exhibition]: Musée municipal de Saint-Cloud, 16 octobre 1991–5 janvier 1992. [Commissaire de l'exposition, Sophie de Juvigny; commissaire-adjoint, Odile

Caule. Saint-Cloud. Le Musée, 1991.

Reinhardt, Ad (Adolph Frederick), 1913–1967

10341. Heere, Heribert. *Ad Reinhardt und die Tradition der Moderne*. Frankfurt am Main, R.G. Fischer, 1986.

10342. Inboden, Gudrun. *Ad Reinhardt*. [Catalogue of an exibition]: Staatsgalerie Stuttgart 13.4.–2.6. 1985. [Katalogbearbeitung] Gudrun Inboden und Thomas Kellein. Stuttgart, Staatsgalerie, 1985.

10343. Lippard, Lucy R. *Ad Reinhardt*. New York, Abrams, 1981.

10344. Reinhardt, Ad. *Ad Reinhardt*. [Catalogue of an exhibition organized jointly by] the Museum of Contemporary Art, Los Angeles and the Museum of Modern Art. New York, Rizzoli International Publications, 1991.

10345. Reinhardt, Adolph F. *Art as art: the selected writings of Ad Reinhardt*. Edited and with an introduction by Barbara Rose. New York, Viking, 1975.(Reprint: Berkeley, Univ. of Calif. Press, 1991, pbck.).

10346. Rowell, Margit. *Ad Reinhardt and color*. [Published in conjunction with an exhibition at the Solomon R. Guggenheim Museum, New York]. New York, Guggenheim Foundation, 1980.

Reinhart, Johann Christian, 1761–1847

10347. Feuchtmayr, Inge. *Johann Christian Reinhart 1761–1847. Monographie und Werkverzeichnis*. München, Prestel, 1975. (CR).

Rejlander, Oscar Gustav, 1813–1875

10348. Bunnell, Peter C., ed. *The photography of O. G. Rejlander: two selections*. [On photographic composition, by O. G. Rejlander; Rejlander's photographic studies, by A. H. Wall]. New York, Arno, 1979.

10349. Jones, Edgar Y. *Father of art photography: O. G. Rejlander, 1813–1875*. Newton Abbot (England), David & Charles, 1973.

10350. Spencer, Stephanie. *O.G. Rejlander, photography as art*. Ann Arbor, UMI Research Press, 1985.

Rembrandt Hermanszoon van Rijn, 1606–1669

10351. Alpers, Svetlana. *Rembrandt's enterprises: the studio and the market*. Chicago, University of Chicago Press, 1988.

10352. Avermaete, Roger. *Rembrandt et son temps*. Paris, Payot, 1952.

10353. Bailey, Anthony. *Rembrandt's house*. Boston, Houghton Mifflin, 1978.

10354. Bal, Mieke. *Reading "Rembrandt": beyond the word-image opposition*. Cambridge; New York, Cambridge University Press,

1991. (The Northrup Frye lectures in literary theory).

10355. Bartsch, Adam. *Catalogue raisonné de toute les estampes qui forment l'oeuvre de Rembrandt et ceux de ses principaux imitateurs.* 2 v. Vienne, Blumauer, 1797. (CR).

10356. Bauch, Kurt. *Der frühe Rembrandt und seine Zeit; Studien zur geschichtlichen Bedeutung seines Frühstils.* Berlin, Mann, 1960.

10357. ———. *Die Kunst des jungen Rembrandt.* Heidelberg, Winter, 1933. (Heidelberger kunstgeschichtliche Abhandlungen, 14).

10358. Benesch, Otto. *The drawings of Rembrandt; complete edition in six volumes.* Enlarged and edited by Eva Benesch. 6 v. London, Phaidon, 1973. 2 ed. (CR).

10359. ———. *Rembrandt.* Edited by Eva Benesch. London, Phaidon, 1970. (His Collected Writings, 1).

10360. ———. *Rembrandt, biographical and critical study.* Trans. by James Emmons. Geneva, Skira, 1957; distributed by Crown, New York. (The Taste of Our Time, 22).

10361. Bernhard, Marianne. *Rembrandt: Druckgraphik, Handzeichnungen.* 2 v. München, Südwest Verlag, 1976.

10362. Bevers, Holm. *Rembrandt, the master and his workshop: drawings & etchings.* [By] H. Bevers, Peter Schatborn & Barbara Welzel. Exhibition organizer, Uwe Wieczorek; translators, Elizabeth Clegg . . . [et al.]. New Haven, Yale University Press in association with National Gallery Publications, London 1991.

10363. Biörklund, George. *Rembrandt's etchings: true and false; a summary catalogue.* [Assisted by Osbert H. Barnard]. Stockholm, Biörklund, 1968. 2 ed.

10364. Blanc, Charles. *L'oeuvre complet de Rembrandt, décrit et commenté.* Catalogue raisonné. 2 v. Paris, Guerin, [1859/1861]. (CR).

10365. Bockemühl, Michael. *Rembrandt: Zum Wandel des Bildes und seiner Anschauung im Spätwerk.* München, Mäander, 1981.

10366. ———. *Die Wirklichkeit des Bildes: Bildrezeption als Bildproduktion: Rothko, Newman, Rembrandt, Raphael.* Stuttgart, Urachhaus, 1985.

10367. Bode, Wilhelm. *The complete work of Rembrandt: history, description, and heliographic reproduction of all the master's pictures, with a study of his life and his art.* Assisted by Cornelis Hofstede de Groot. Trans. by Florence Simmonds. 8 v. Paris, Sedelmeyer, 1897–1906. (CR).

10368. Bolton, Jaap and Bolten-Rempt, H. *The hidden Rembrandt.* Trans. by Danielle Adkinson. Chicago, Rand McNally, 1977.

10369. Bomford, David. *Art in the making: Rembrandt.* [By] D. Bomford, Christopher Brown, Ashok Roy; with contributions from Jo Kirby and Raymond White. London, National Gallery Publications, 1988.

10370. Bonafoux, Pascal. *Rembrandt, master of the portrait.* New York, Abrams, 1992.

10371. Borenius, Tancred. *Rembrandt; selected paintings.* London, Phaidon, 1942.

10372. Bredius, Abraham. *Rembrandt, the complete edition of the paintings.* Revised by Horst Gerson. London, Phaidon, 1969. 3 ed. (CR).

10373. Brion, Marcel. *Rembrandt.* Paris, Michel, 1946.

10374. British Museum (London). *Drawings by Rembrandt and his circle in the British Museum.* [Edited by] Martin Royalton-Kisch. London, Published for the Trustees of the British Museum by British Museum Press, 1992.

10375. Brown, Christopher. *Rembrandt, the master & his workshop: paintings.* [By] Christopher Brown, Jan Kelch & Pieter van Thiel; [exhibition organiser, Uwe Wieczorek; translators, Elizabeth Clegg, Michael Hoyle, Paul Vincent. New Haven, Yale University Pess in association with National Gallery Publications, London, 1991.

10376. Brown, G. Baldwin. *Rembrandt, a study of his life and work.* London, Duckworth/New York, Scribner, 1907.

10377. Bruijn, I. de en Bruijn-van der Leeuw, J. G. de. *Catalogus van de verzameling etsen van Rembrandt in het bezit van I. de Bruijn en J. G. de Bruijn-van der Leeuw.* 'S-Gravenhage, Nijhoff, 1932.

10378. Bruyn, Joshua . . . [et al]. *A corpus of Rembrandt paintings.* Trans. by D. Cook-Radmore. v.1– , Dordrecht, M. Nijhoff, 1982– . [Work in progress, 5 vols. projected]; distributed by Kluwer, Boston.

10379. Burnet, John. *Rembrandt and his works, comprising a short account of his life; with a critical examination into his principles and practice of design, light, shade, and colour.* London, Bogue, 1849.

10380. Carstensen, Hans Thomas. *Empirie als Bildsprache. Überlegungen zum jüdischen Einfluss auf Rembrandts Kunst.* Ammersbek bei Hamburg, Verlag an der Lottbek, 1993. (Wissenschaftliche Beiträge aus deutschen Hochschulen, Reihe 09, Kulturgeschichte, 5).

10381. Chapman, H. Perry. *Rembrandt's self-portraits: a study in seventeenth-century identity.* Princeton, N.J., Princeton University Press, 1990.

10382. Clark, Kenneth M. *Rembrandt and the Italian renaissance.* London, Murray, 1966.

10383. Coppier, André-Charles. *Les eaux-fortes authentiques de Rembrandt.* 2 v. Paris, Didot, 1929. 2 ed.

10384. ———. *Rembrandt.* Paris, Alcan, 1920.

10385. Coquerel, Anthony. *Rembrandt et l'individualisme dans l'art*. Paris, Cherbuliez, 1869.

10386. Daulby, Daniel. *A descriptive catalogue of the works of Rembrandt and of his scholars, Bol, Livens, and van Vliet*. Compiled from the original etchings and from the catalogues of de Burgy, Gersaint, Helle and Glomy, Marcus, and Yver. Liverpool, M'Creery, 1796.

10387. Descargues, Pierre. *Rembrandt*. [Paris], J.C. Lattes, 1990

10388. Emmens, Jan A. *Rembrandt en de regels van de kunst* [with an English summary]. Utrecht, Dekker & Gumbert, 1968. (Orbis artium: Utrechtse kunsthistorische studien, 10).

10389. Focillon, Henri and Goldscheider, Ludwig. *Rembrandt; paintings, drawings, and etchings*. New York, Phaidon, 1960.

10390. Gantner, Joseph. *Rembrandt und die Verwandlung klassischer Formen*. Bern/München, Francke, 1964.

10391. Gersaint, Edme F. *Catalogue raisonné de toutes les pièces qui forment l'oeuvre de Rembrandt*. Paris, Hochereau, 1751. (CR). (Supplément [par] Pieter Yver: Amsterdam, Yver, 1756; nouvelle édition, corrigée et considérablement augmentée par M. Claussin: Paris, Didot, 1824; supplément, 1828).

10392. Gerson, Horst. *Rembrandt paintings*. Trans. by Heinz Norden. New York, Reynal, 1968. (CR).

10393. Grimm, Claus. *Rembrandt selbst: Eine Neubewertung seiner Porträtkunst*. Stuttgart, Belser, 1991.

10394. Guillaud, Jacqueline and Guillaud, Maurice. *Rembrandt: the human form and spirit*. New York, C.N. Potter; distributed by Crown Publishers [for] Guillaud Editions, Paris], 1986.

10395. Haak, Bob. *Rembrandt: his life, his work, his time*. Trans. by Elizabeth Willems-Treeman. New York, Abrams, 1969.

10396. Halewood, William H. *Six subjects of Reformation art: a preface to Rembrandt*. Toronto/Buffalo, University of Toronto Press, 1982.

10397. Hamann, Richard. *Rembrandt*. Neu herausgegeben von Richard Hamann-MacLean. Anmerkungen von Werner Sumowski. Berlin, Safari, 1969. 2 ed.

10398. ———. *Rembrandts Radierungen*. Berlin, Cassirer, 1913. 2 ed.

10399. Hanfstaengl, Eberhard. *Rembrandt Harmensz van Rijn*. München, Bruckmann, 1958. 3 ed.

10400. Hausenstein, Wilhelm. *Rembrandt*. Stuttgart, Deutsche Verlags-Anstalt, 1926.

10401. Heckscher, William S. *Rembrandt's Anatomy of Dr. Nicolaas Tulp; an iconographical study*. New York, New York University Press, 1958.

10402. Heiland, Susanne und Lüdecke, Heinz, eds. *Rembrandt und Die Nachwelt*. Leipzig, Seemann, 1960.

10403. Held, Julius S. *Rembrandt's Aristotle and other Rembrandt studies*. Princeton, N.J., Princeton University Press, 1969.

10404. ———. *Rembrandt studies*. Princeton, N.J. Princeton University Press, 1991 [Rev. and expanded ed.).

10405. Hetzer, Theodor. *Rubens und Rembrandt*. Mittenwald, Maander; Stuttgart, Urachhaus, 1984.

10406. Hijmans, Willem, et al. *Rembrandt's Nightwatch: the history of a painting*. Trans. by Patricia Wardle. Alphen aan den Rijn, Sijthoff, 1978.

10407. Hind, Arthur M. *A catalogue of Rembrandt's etchings, chronologically arranged and completely illustrated*. 2 v. London, Methuen, 1923. 2 ed. (CR). (Reprint: New York, Da Capo, 1967).

10408. ———. *Rembrandt; being the substance of the Charles Eliot Norton lectures delivered before Harvard University, 1930–31*. Cambridge, Mass., Harvard University Press, 1932.

10409. Hofstede de Groot, Cornelis. *Die Urkunden über Rembrandt (1575–1721)*. Haag, Nijhoff, 1906. (Quellenstudien zur holländischen Kunstgeschichte, 3).

10410. Holmes, Charles J. *Notes on the art of Rembrandt*. London, Chatto & Windus, 1911.

10411. Jahn, Johannes. *Rembrandt*. Leipzig, Seemann, 1956.

10412. Knackfuss, Hermann. *Rembrandt*. Bielefeld/Leipzig, Velhagen & Klasing, 1895. 2 ed. (Künstler-Monographien, 3).

10413. Knuttel, Gerhardus. *Rembrandt, de meester en zijn werk*. Amsterdam, Ploegsma, 1956.

10414. Kolloff, Eduard. *Rembrandt's Leben und Werke, nach neuen Actenstücken und Gesichtspunkten geschildert*. Mit einer Einführung und einem Register neu hrsg. von Christian Tümpel. Hamburg, F. Wittig, 1971. (Deutsches Bibel-Archiv. Abhandlungen und Vorträge, 4).

10415. Landsberger, Franz. *Rembrandt, the Jews, and the Bible*. Trans. by Felix N. Gerson. Philadelphia, Jewish Publication Society of America, 1961. 2 ed.

10416. [Langbehn, Julius]. *Rembrandt als Erzieher, von einem Deutschen* [Julius Langbehn]. Leipzig, Hirschfeld, 1890. (New ed.: Stuttgart, Kohlhammer, 1936).

10417. Laurie, Arthur P. *The brush-work of Rembrandt and his school*. London, Oxford University Press, 1932.

10418. Lippmann, Friedrich, Hofstede de Groot, Cornelis, et al. *Original drawings by Rembrandt Harmensz van Rijn, reproduced in phototype*. 4 pts. (Four series containing 10 portfolios in German and English editions). Published variously in London/Berlin/The Hague and Leipzig, by Asher and Co., K.W. Hiersemann, and Martinus Nijhoff, 1888–1911. (A second edition of the first series originally published 1888–92 was printed at the Hague by Martinus Nijhoff, 1940–42).

10419. Lugt, Frits. *Met Rembrandt in en om Amsterdam.* Amsterdam, van Kampen & Zoon, 1915.

10420. Michel, Emile. *Rembrandt, his life, his work and his time.* Trans. Florence Simmonds. 2 v. London, Heinemann, 1894.

10421. Middleton, Charles H. *A descriptive catalogue of the etched work of Rembrandt van Rijn.* London, Murray, 1878.

10422. Muller, Joseph-Emile. *Rembrandt.* Paris, Somogy, 1968.

10423. Muller, M. *De etsen van Rembrandt.* Baarn, Hollandia, 1946.

10424. ———. *Zo leefde Rembrandt in de gouden eeuw.* Mit een voorwoord van A. van Schendel. Baarn, Hollandia, 1968.

10425. Münz, Ludwig. *The etchings of Rembrandt.* 2 v. London, Phaidon, 1952.

10426. ———. *Rembrandt.* Additional commentaries by Bob Haak. New York, Abrams, 1967. 2 ed.

10427. ———, ed. *Rembrandt, etchings.* 2 v. New York, Phaidon, 1952. (CR).

10428. Museum Boymans-Van Beuningen. *The drawings by Rembrandt and his school in the Museum Boymans-Van Buningen.* Ed. by Jeroen Giltaij. Trans. by Patricia Wardle. Rotterdam, The Museum, 1988.

10429. Neumann, Carl. *Aus der Werkstatt Rembrandts.* Heidelberg, Winter, 1918. (Heidelberger kunstgeschichtliche Abhandlungen, 3).

10430. ———. *Rembrandt.* 2 v. München, Bruckmann, 1924. 4 ed.

10431. Ornstein-Van Slooten, Eva, Holtrop, Marijke, and Schatborn, Peter. *The Rembrandt House: the prints, drawings and paintings.* Trans. by Harry Lake. Zwolle, Waanders; Amsterdam, Museum het Rembrandthuis, 1991.

10432. Rentsch, Eugen. *Der Humor bei Rembrandt.* Strassburg, Heitz, 1909. (Studien zur deutschen Kunstgeschichte, 110).

10433. Rijckevorsel, J. van. *Rembrandt en de traditie.* Rotterdam, Brusse, 1932.

10434. Rijksmuseum (Netherlands). Rijksprentenkabinet. *Drawings by Rembrandt, his anonymous pupils and followers.* Ed. by Peter Schatborn. 's-Gravenhage, Staatsuitgeverij, 1985. (Catalogue of the Dutch and Flemish drawings in the Rijksprentenkabinet, Rijksmuseum, Amsterdam, 4).

10435. Roger-Marx, Claude. *Rembrandt.* [Paris], Tisné, 1960.

10436. Rosenberg, Adolf. *Rembrandt, des Meisters Gemälde.* Stuttgart/Berlin, Deutsche Verlags-Anstalt, [1908]. 3 ed.

10437. Rosenberg, Jakob. *Rembrandt, life and work.* New York, Phaidon, 1964. 2 ed.

10438. Rotermund, Hans-Martin. *Rembrandt's drawings and etchings for the Bible.* Trans. by Shierry M. Weber. Philadelphia/Boston, Pilgrim Press, 1969.

10439. Rovinski, Dmitri. *L'oeuvre gravé de Rembrandt, avec un catalogue raisonné.* 4 v. Saint-Pétersbourg, Imprimerie de l'Académie Impériale des Sciences, 1890. (CR). (Supplement, with text in French and Russian, by N. Tchétchouline: St.-Pétersbourg, Kotoff, 1914).

10440. Schmidt-Degener, Frederik. *Rembrandt.* Amsterdam, Meulenhoff, 1950.

10441. Schneider, Cynthia P. *Rembrandt's landscapes.* New Haven, Yale University Press, 1990.

10442. ———. *Rembrandt's landscapes: drawings and prints.* With contributions by Boudewijn Bakker, Nancy Ash, and Shelley Fletcher. Ed. by Mary Yakush. Washington, National Gallery of Art; Boston, distributed by Bulfinch Press, 1990.

10443. Schwartz, Gary. *Rembrandt: his life, his paintings: a new biography with all accessible paintings illustrated in colour.* New York, Viking, 1985.

10444. Seidlitz, Woldemar von. *Die Radierungen Rembrandts, mit einem kritischen Verzeichnis.* Leipzig, Seemann, 1922. (CR).

10445. Simmel, Georg. *Rembrandt, ein kunstphilosophischer Versuch.* München, Wolff, 1925. 2 ed.

10446. Singer, Hans W. *Rembrandt, des Meisters Radierungen.* Stuttgart/Leipzig, Deutsche Verlags-Anstalt, 1906. (Klassiker der Kunst, 8).

10447. Slatkes, Leonard J. *Rembrandt: catalogo completo dei dipinti.* Firenze, Cantini, 1992. (CR).

10448. Slive, Seymour. *Drawings of Rembrandt; with a selection of drawings by his pupils and followers.* With an introduction, commentary, and supplementary material by S. Slive. Based on the facsimile series edited by F. Lippmann, C. Hofstede de Groot, and others. 2 v. New York, Dover, 1965.

10449. ———. *Rembrandt and his critics, 1630–1730.* The Hague, Nijhoff, 1953. (Reprint: New York, Hacker Art Books, 1988).

10450. Strauss, Walter L. and Meulen, Marjon van der. *The Rembrandt documents.* [Prepared] with the assistance of S. A. C. Dudok van Heel and P. J. M. de Baar. New York, Abaris, 1979.

10451. Sumowski, Werner. *Drawings of the Rembrandt School.* 10v. New York, Abaris,

1991. (Translation of: Gemälde der Rembrandtschüler in vier Bänden. 5 v. [sic!]. Landau, Edition PVA, 1983).

10452. Tümpel, Christian and Tümpel, Astrid. *Rembrandt. All the paintings in colour.* Antwerpen, Mercatorfonds, 1993.

10453. Tümpel, Christian. *Rembrandt: Mythos und Methode.* Mit Beiträgen von Astrid Tümpel. Königstein im Taunus, Langewiesche, 1986. (Dutch ed.: Amsterdam, H.J.W. Becht, 1986).

10454. Valentiner, Wilhelm R. *Rembrandt and Spinoza; a study of the spiritual conflicts in seventeenth-century Holland.* London, Phaidon, 1957.

10455. ———. *Rembrandt: des Meisters Handzeichnungen.* 2 v. Stuttgart/Berlin, Deutsche Verlags-Anstalt, 1925. (Klassiker der Kunst, 31/32).

10456. ———. *Rembrandt und seine Umgebung.* Strassburg, Heitz, 1905. (Zur Kunstgeschichte des Auslandes, 29).

10457. Van Dyke, John C. *Rembrandt and his school: a critical study of the master and his pupils with a new assignment of their pictures.* New York, Scribner, 1923.

10458. Vels Heijn, Annemarie. *Rembrandt.* Trans. by Alastair Weir. London, Scala Books, published in association with the Rijksmuseum Foundation, Amsterdam; New York, distributed in the USA by Harper & Row, 1989.

10459. Verhaeren, Emile. *Rembrandt, biographie critique.* Paris, Laurens, [1907].

10460. Visser't Hooft, Willem A. *Rembrandt et la Bible.* Neuchâtel/Paris, Delachaux et Niestlé, 1947.

10461. Vogel-Köhn, Doris. *Rembrandts Kinderzeichnungen.* Köln, DuMont, 1981. (DuMont Taschenbücher, 102).

10462. Vosmaer, Carel. *Rembrandt, sa vie et ses oeuvres.* Seconde édition, entièrement refondue et augmentée. La Haye, Nijhoff, 1877.

10463. Vries, Ary B. de, et al. *Rembrandt in the Mauritshuis; an interdisciplinary study.* Trans. by James Brockway. Alphen aan de Rijn, Sijthoff & Nordhoff, 1978.

10464. Waal, Henri van de. *Steps towards Rembrandt; collected articles, 1937–1972.* Trans. by Patricia Wardle and Alan Griffiths. Ed. by R. H. Fuchs. Amsterdam/London, North-Holland Publishing Co., 1974.

10465. Weisbach, Werner. *Rembrandt.* Berlin/Leipzig, de Gruyter, 1926.

10466. Wencelius, Léon. *Calvin et Rembrandt.* Paris, Les Belles Lettres, 1973.

10467. White, Christopher. *Rembrandt and his world.* New York, Viking, 1964.

10468. ———. *Rembrandt as an etcher; a study of the artist at work.* 2 v. London, Zwemmer, 1969.

10469. Wright, Christopher. *Rembrandt: self-portraits.* New York, Viking, 1982.

Remington, Frederic, 1861–1909

10470. Balinger, James K. *Frederic Remington.* New York, Abrams in association with the National Museum of American Art, Smithsonian Institution, 1989.

10471. ———. *Frederic Remington's Southwest.* Phoenix, Phoenix Art Museum, 1992.

10472. Hassrick, Peter H. *Frederic Remington: paintings, drawings and sculpture in the Amon Carter Museum and the Sid W. Richardson Foundation collections.* Foreword by Ruth Carter Johnson. New York, Abrams/ in association with the Amon Carter Museum of Western Art, Fort Worth, Texas, 1973.

10473. Manley, Atwood. *Frederic Remington and the north country.* New York, Dutton, 1988.

10474. McCracken, Harold. *Frederic Remington, artist of the Old West.* Philadelphia, Lippincott, 1947.

10475. Remington, Frederic. *The collected writings of Frederic Remington.* Edited by Peggy and Harold Samuels. Illustrated by Frederic Remington. Garden City, N.Y., Doubleday, 1979.

10476. ———. *Frederic Remington's own West; written and illustrated by Frederic Remington.* Edited by and with an introduction by Harold McCracken. New York, Dial, 1960.

10477. ———. *Frederic Remington, selected letters.* Ed. by Allen P. and Marilyn D. Splete. New York, Abbeville Press, 1988.

10478. Samuels, Peggy and Samuels, Harold. *Frederic Remington, a biography.* Garden City, N.Y., Doubleday, 1982.

10479. ———. *Remington: the complete prints.* New York, Crown, 1990. (CR).

10480. Shapiro, Michael Edward and Hassrick, Peter H, eds. *Frederic Remington, the masterworks.* With essays by David McCullough, Doreen Bolger Burke, John Seelye. New York, Abrams, 1988.

10481. Stewart, Rick. *Frederic Remington: masterpieces from the Amon Carter Museum.* Fort Worth, Amon Carter Museum, 1992.

10482. Vorpahl, Ben M. *Frederic Remington and the West.* Austin/London, University of Texas Press, 1972.

10483. Wear, Bruce. *The bronze world of Frederic Remington.* Tulsa, Oklahoma, Gaylord, 1966.

10484. White, G. Edward. *The Eastern establish-*

R

ment and the western experience: the West of Frederic Remington, Theodore Roosevelt, and Owen Wister. Austin, University of Texas Press, 1989.

Renger-Patzsch, Albert, 1897–1966

10485. Heise, Carl G. *Albert Renger-Patzsch: der Photograph.* Berlin, Riemerschmidt, 1942.

10486. Pfingsten, Claus. *Aspekte zum fotografischen Werk Albert Renger-Patzschs.* Witterschlick, M. Wehle, 1992. (Beiträge zur Kunstgeschichte, 9).

10487. Renger-Patzsch, Albert. *Albert Renger-Patzsch: 100 photographs, 1928.* Paris, Crèatis; Köln, Schürmann und Kicken; Boston, distributio S & K Books, 1979.

10488. ———. *Die Halligen.* Geleitwort von Johann Johannsen; unter Mitwirkung von Karl Häberlein. Berlin, Albertus, 1927.

10489. ———. *Albert Renger-Patzsch: joy before the object.* Essay by Donald Kuspit. New York, Aperture Foundation, 1993. (Aperture, 131).

10490. Rheinisches Landesmuseum, Bonn. *Industrielandschaft, Industriearchitektur, Industrieprodukt: Fotographien 1925–1960 von Albert Renger-Patzsch.* [Jan. 14–Feb. 13, 1977]. Köln, Rheinland-Verlag/Bonn, Habelt, 1977.

Reni, Guido, 1575–1642

10491. Albertina (Vienna). *Guido Reni: Zeichnungen.* 14. Mai–5. Juli 1981. Katalog und Ausstellung: Veronika Birke. Wien, Albertina, 1981.

10492. Bartsch, Adam. *Catalogue raisonné des estampes gravées à l'eau-forte par Guido Reni et de celles de ses disciples.* Vienne, Blumauer, 1795. (CR).

10493. Boehn, Max von. *Guido Reni.* Bielefeld/Leipzig, Velhagen & Klasing, 1910. (Künstler-Monographien, 100).

10494. Emiliani, Andrea. *Guido Reni.* Milano, Fabbri, 1964. (I maestri del colore, 35).

10495. Garboli, Cesare [and] Baccheschi, Edi. *L'opera completa di Guido Reni.* Milano, Rizzoli, 1971. (CR). (Classici dell'arte, 48).

10496. Malaguzzi Valeri, Francesco. *Guido Reni.* Firenze, Le Monnier, 1929.

10497. Malvasia, Carlo C. *The life of Guido Reni.* Trans. and with an introduction by Catherine Enggass and Robert Enggass. University Park, Penn./London, Pennsylvania State University Press, 1980.

10498. ———. *Vita di Guido Reni.* Roma, Scipioni, 1988. (Alchimia dell'immaginario, 4).

10499. Negro, Emilio and Pirondini, Massimo. *La Scuola di Guido Reni.* Modena, Artioli, 1992.

10500. Palazzo dell'Archiginnasio (Bologna). *Mo-stra di Guido Reni.* Catalogo critico a cura di Gian Carlo Cavalli; saggio introduttivo di Cesare Gnudi. 1 settembre–31 ottobre, 1954. Bologna, Alfa, 1954.

10501. Pepper, D. Stephen. *Guido Reni: a complete catalogue of his works with an introductory text.* Oxford, Phaidon, 1984. (CR).

10502. Reni, Guido. *Guido Reni, 1575–1642.* Bologna, Nuova Alfa Editoriale, 1988.

10503. ———. *Guido Reni, 1575–1642.* Los Angeles, Los Angeles County Museum of Art; Bologna, Nuova Alfa Editoriale, 1988.

10504. ———. *Guido Reni und der Reproduktionsstich.* [Katalog und Ausstellung, Veronika Birke; redaktionelle Mitarbeit, Barbara Dossi]. Wien, Albertina; Stuttgart, In Kommission Urachhaus J.M. Mayer, 1988.

10505. ———. *Guido Reni und Europa: Ruhm und Nachruhm.* [Katalog herausgegeben von Sybille Ebert-Schifferer, Andrea Emiliani, Erich Schleier]. Frankfurt, Schirn Kunsthalle; Bologna, Nuova Alfa, 1988.

10506. Sweetser, Moses F. *Guido Reni.* Boston, Houghton, Osgood, 1878.

Renoir, Pierre Auguste, 1841–1919

10507. André, Albert [and] Elder, Marc. *L'atelier de Renoir.* 2 v. Paris, Bernheim-Jeune, 1931. (CR).

10508. Barnes, Albert C. and de Mazia, Violette. *The art of Renoir.* With a foreword by John Dewey. New York, Minton, Balch, 1935.

10509. Baudot, Jeanne. *Renoir: ses amis, ses modèles.* Paris, Editions Littéraires de France, 1949.

10510. Bünemann, Hermann. *Renoir.* Ettal, Buch-Kunstverlag, [1959].

10511. Callen, Anthea. *Renoir.* London, Oresko, 1978.

10512. Coquiot, Gustave. *Renoir.* Paris, Michel, 1925.

10513. Daulte, François. *Auguste Renoir, catalogue raisonné de l'oeuvre peint.* Avant-propos de Jean Renoir. Préface de Charles Durand-Ruel. I: *Figures, 1860–1890.* [No further volumes published]. Lausanne, Durand-Ruel, 1971. (CR).

10514. Drucker, Michel. *Renoir.* Paris, Tisné, 1944.

10515. Duret, Théodore. *Renoir.* Trans. by Madeleine Boyd. New York, Crown, 1937.

10516. Fezzi, Elda. *L'opera completa di Renoir nel periodo impressionista, 1869–1883.* Milano, Rizzoli, 1972. (CR). (Classici dell'arte, 59).

10517. Forthuny, Pascal, ed. *Renoir.* Préface d'Octave Mirbeau. Paris, Bernheim-Jeune, 1913.

10518. Fosca, François. *Renoir, l'homme et son oeuvre.* Paris, Somogy, 1961.

10519. Fouchet, Max-Pol. *Les nus de Renoir.* Lausanne, Guilde du Livre et Clairfontaine, 1974.

10520. Graber, Hans. *Auguste Renoir nach eigenen und fremden Zeugnissen.* Basel, Schwabe, 1943.

10521. Hanson, Lawrence. *Renoir: the man, the painter, and his world.* New York, Dodd, Mead, 1968.

10522. Keller, Horst. *Auguste Renoir.* München, Bruckmann, 1987.

10523. Meier-Graefe, Julius. *Renoir.* Leipzig, Klinkhardt & Biermann, 1929.

10524. Monneret, Sophie. *Renoir.* [Paris], Chène, 1989.

10525. Pach, Walter. *Pierre Auguste Renoir.* New York, Abrams, 1950.

10526. Perruchot, Henri. *La vie de Renoir.* Paris, Hachette, 1964.

10527. Renoir, Auguste. *Renoir.* [Pubished in conjunction with an exhibition at the Hayward Art Gallery, London, 30 January–21 April 1985; Galleries nationales du Grand Palais, Paris, 14 May–2 September 1985; Museum of Fine Arts, Boston, 9 October 1985–5 January 1986]. [London], Arts Council of Great Britain, 1985.

10528. ———. *Renoir.* [Exhibition organized by Susan Ferleger Brades; assisted by Jocelyn Poulton]. New York, Abrams; [London], in association with the Arts Council of Great Britain, 1985.

10529. ———. *Renoir, a retrospective.* Ed. by Nichola Wadley. New York, Hugh Lauter Levin Associates; distributed by Macmillan Pub. Co., 1987.

10530. ———. *Renoir by Renoir.* Ed. by Rachel Barnes. Exeter, Devon, Webb & Bower; Harmondsworth, Middlesex, distributed by the Penguin Group, 1990.

10531. Renoir, Jean. *Renoir, my father.* Trans. by Randolph and Dorothy Weaver. Boston, Little, Brown, 1958.

10532. Rivière, Georges. *Renoir et ses amis.* Paris, Floury, 1921.

10533. Robida, Michel, et al. *Renoir.* Paris, Librairie Hachette, 1970. (Collection génies et réalités).

10534. Roger-Marx, Claude. *Renoir.* Paris, Floury, 1937.

10535. Rouart, Denis. *Renoir.* Trans. by James Emmons. Geneva, Skira, 1954. (The Taste of Our Time, 7).

10536. Stella, Joseph G. *The graphic work of Renoir, catalogue raisonné.* London, Humphries, [1975]. (CR).

10537. Vollard, Ambroise. *Renoir, an intimate record.* Trans. by Harold L. Van Doren and Randolph T. Weaver. New York, Knopf, 1925.

10538. ———. *Tableaux, pastels & dessins de Pierre-Auguste Renoir.* 2 v. Paris, Vollard, 1918. (CR). (Reprint: Paris, Mazo, 1954).

Repin, Il'ia Efimovich, 1844–1930

10539. Brodskii, Iosif A. *Repin, pedagog.* Moskva, Akademiia Khudozhestv SSSR, 1960.

10540. Chukovskii, Kornei I. *Il'ia Repin.* Moskva, Iskusstvo, 1969.

10541. Colliander, Tito. *Ilja Repin, en konstnär fran Ukraina.* Helsingfors, Söderström, 1942. 2 ed.

10542. Ernst, Sergei R. *Il'ia Efimovich Repin.* Leningrad, Gosudarstvennyi Akademiia, 1927.

10543. Grabar, Igor E. *Repin, monografiia.* 2 v. Moskva, Izd-vo Akademiia Nauk, 1963–64. 2 ed.

10544. Liaskovskaia, Olga A. *Il'ia Efimovich Repin.* Moskva, Iskusstvo, 1962. 2 ed.

10545. Morgunova-Kudnitskaia, Natalia D. *Il'ia Repin, zhizn' i tvorchestvo.* Moskva, Iskusstvo, 1965.

10546. Parker, Fan and Parker, Stephen J. *Russia on canvas: Ilya Repin.* University Park, Penn./ London, Pennsylvania State University Press, 1980.

10547. Prorokova, Sofia A. *Repin.* Moskva, Molodaia Gvardiia, 1960. 2 ed.

10548. Repin, Il'ia. *Dalekoe blizkoe.* [Ed. by Kornei Chukovskii]. Moskva, Iskusstvo, 1944. 2 ed.

10549. ———. *Ilya Repin: painting, graphic arts.* Introduction by Grigory Sternin. Catalogue and biographical outline by Maria Karpenko . . . [et al.]. Leningrad, Aurora Art Publishers, 1985. (CR).

10550. ———. *Izbrannye pis'ma, 1867–1930.* [Ed. by I. A. Brodskii]. 2 v. Moskva, Iskusstvo, 1969.

10551. Valkenier, Elizabeth Kridl. *Ilya Repin and the world of Russian art.* New York, Columbia University Press, 1990.

Repton, Humphry, 1752–1818 *see also* Brown, Lancelot

10552. Repton, Humphry. *Landscape gardening and landscape architecture.* A new edition with an introduction and biographical notice by J. C. Loudon. London, Longman, 1840.

10553. Stroud, Dorothy. *Humphry Repton.* London, Country Life, 1962.

10554. Uhlitz, Manfred. *Humphry Reptons Einfluss auf die gartenkünstlerischen Ideen des Fürsten Pückler-Muskau.* Vorgelegt von Manfred Uhlitz. Berlin, [s.n.], 1988.

Rerikh, Nikolaiĭ Konstantinovich *see* Roerich, Nikolai Konstantinovich

Rethel, Alfred, 1816–1859

10555. Groll, Karin. *Alfred Rethel: "auch ein Totentanz aus dem Jahre 1848".* Messkirch, A. Gmeiner, 1989.

10556. Ponten, Josef. *Alfred Rethel.* Stuttgart/Leipzig, Deutsche Verlags-Anstalt, 1911. (Klassiker der Kunst, 17).

10557. Rethel, Alfred. *Briefe.* Herausgegeben von Josef Ponten. Berlin, Cassirer, 1912.

10558. Schmid, Max. *Rethel.* Bielefeld/Leipzig, Velhagen & Klasing, 1898. (Künstler-Monographien, 32).

10559. Schmidt, Heinrich. *Alfred Rethel, 1816–1859.* Neuss, Gesellschaft für Buchdruckerei, 1958. (Rheinischer Verein für Denkmalpflege und Heimatschutz, Jahrgang 1958).

Revere, Paul, 1735–1818

10560. Brigham, Clarence S. *Paul Revere's engravings.* Worcester, Mass., American Antiquarian Society, 1954. (New ed.: New York, Atheneum, 1969).

10561. Fischer, David Hackett. *Paul Revere's ride.* New York, Oxford University Press, 1994.

10562. Forbes, Esther. *Paul Revere and the world he lived in.* Boston, Houghton Mifflin, 1969.

10563. Museum of Fine Arts (Boston). *Paul Revere's Boston: 1735–1818.* April 18–October 12, 1975. Boston, Museum of Fine Arts, 1975; distributed by New York Graphic Society, Boston.

10564. Revere, Paul. *Paul Revere: artisan, businessman, and patriot—the man behind the myth.* Boston, Paul Revere Memorial Association; Lanham, Md., distributed by the AASLH Library in assocation with University Pub. Associates, 1988.

Reynolds, Joshua, 1723–1792

10565. Armstrong, Walter. *Sir Joshua Reynolds.* London, Heinemann, 1900.

10566. Boulton, William B. *Sir Joshua Reynolds.* New York, Dutton, 1905.

10567. Graves, Algernon and Cronin, William V. *A history of the works of Sir Joshua Reynolds.* 4 v. London, Graves, 1899–1901. (CR).

10568. Hamilton, Edward. *A catalogue raisonné of the engraved works of Sir Joshua Reynolds, P. R. A. from 1755 to 1822.* London, Colnaghi, 1884. 2 ed. (CR). (Reprinted, with the addition of plates and an index: Amsterdam, Hissink, 1973).

10569. Hilles, Frederick W. *The literary career of Sir Joshua Reynolds.* Cambridge, Cambridge University Press, 1936.

10570. Hudson, Derek. *Sir Joshua Reynolds, a personal study.* With Reynolds' *Journey from London to Brentford,* now first published. London, Bles, 1958.

10571. Leslie, Charles R. *Life and times of Sir Joshua Reynolds, with notices of some of his contemporaries.* Continued and concluded by Tom Taylor. 2 v. London, Murray, 1865.

10572. Molloy, Fitzgerald. *Sir Joshua and his circle.* 2 v. London, Hutchinson, 1906.

10573. Northcote, James. *Memoirs of Sir Joshua Reynolds.* London, Colburn, 1813. (New ed., revised and augmented: 2 v., 1819).

10574. Phillips, Claude. *Sir Joshua Reynolds.* New York, Scribner, 1894.

10575. Prochno, Renate. *Joshua Reynolds.* Weinheim, VCH, Acta Humaniora, 1990.

10576. Reynolds, Joshua, Sir. *Discourses.* Ed. with an introduction and notes by Pat Rogers. London/New York, Penguin, 1992.

10577. ———. *Letters.* Ed. by Frederick W. Hilles. Cambridge, Cambridge University Press, 1929.

10578. ———. *Reynolds.* Ed. by Nicholas Penny. With contributions by Diana Donald . . . [et al.]. London, Royal Academy of Arts; published in association with Weidenfeld and Nicholson, 1986.

10579. ———. *Works.* [With] an account of the life and writings of the author by Edmond Malone. 2 v. London, Cadell and Davies, 1797.

10580. Waterhouse, Ellis K. *Reynolds.* New York, Phaidon, 1973; distributed by Praeger, New York. 2 ed.

Ribera, Jusepe, 1588?–1652

10581. Art Museum, Princeton University. *Jusepe de Ribera: prints and drawings.* October–November 1973. Princeton, N.J., Princeton University Press, 1973.

10582. Conte, Edouard. *Ribera.* Paris, Nilsson, 1924.

10583. Felton, Craig M. *Jusepe de Ribera: a catalogue raisonné.* Ann Arbor, Mich., University Microfilms, 1971. (CR).

10584. Kimball Art Museum (Fort Worth, Tex.). *Jusepe de Ribera, lo Spagnoletto, 1591–1652.* December 4, 1982–February 6, 1983. Edited by Craig Felton and William B. Jordan. Fort Worth, Tex., Kimball Art Museum, 1982; distributed by Washington University Press, Seattle and London.

10585. Lafond, Paul. *Ribera et Zurbaran, biographies critiques.* Paris, Laurens, [1909].

10586. Mayer, August L. *Jusepe de Ribera (lo Spagnoletto).* Leipzig, Hiersemann, 1908. (Kunstgeschichtliche Monographien, 10).

10587. Pérez Sánchez, Alfonso E. [and] Spinosa, Nicola. *L'opera completa del Ribera.* Milano, Rizzoli, 1978. (CR). (Classici dell'-arte, 97).

10588. Pillement, Georges. *Ribera.* Paris, Rieder, 1929.

10589. Ribera, José de. *Jusepe de Ribera, 1591–1652.* Comp. by Alfonso E. Pérez Sánchez and Nicola Spinosa. New York, Metropolitan Museum of Art, 1992; distributed by Harry N. Abrams.

10590. ———. *Jusepe de Ribera, 1591–1652.* Direzione scientifica, Alfonso E. Pérez Sánchez, Nicola Spinosa. Napoli, Electa, 1992.

10591. ———. *Ribera, 1591–1652.* Dirección científica, Alfonso E. Pérez Sánchez, Nicola

Spinosa. [Madrid], Musco del Prado, 1992.

10592. Trapier, Elizabeth du Gué. *Ribera*. New York, Hispanic Society of America, 1952.

Ricci, Marco, 1676–1730
Sebastiano, 1659/60–1734

10593. Daniels, Jeffrey. *L'opera completa di Sebastiano Ricci*. Milano, Rizzoli, 1976. (CR). (Classici dell'arte, 89).

10594. ———. *Sebastiano Ricci*. Hove, Eng., Wayland, 1976.

10595. Derschau, Joachim von. *Sebastiano Ricci, ein Beitrag zu den Anfängen der venezianischen Rokokomalerei*. Heidelberg, Winter, 1922.

10596. Palazzo Sturm (Bassano del Gruppa, Italy). *Marco Ricci: catalogo della mostra con un saggio di Rodolfo Palluchini*. Venezia, Alfieri, 1964.

10597. Pilo, Guiseppe M. *Sebastiano Ricci e la pittura veneziana del settecento*. Pordenone, Grafiche Editoriali Artistiche Pordenonesi, 1976.

10598. Ricci, Marco. *Marco Ricci e il paesaggio veneto del Settecento*. A cura di Dario Succi e Annalia Delneri. Con testi di Bernard Aikema, Bram de Klerck, Isabella Reale. Milano, Electa, 1993.

10599. Scarpa Sonino, Annalisa. *Marco Ricci*. Milano, Berenice, 1991. (CR).

10600. Wessel, Thomas. *Sebastiano Ricci und die Rokokomalerei*. Freiburg, Gaggstatter, 1984.

Riccio, Andrea, 1470–1532

10601. Planiscig, Leo. *Andrea Riccio*. Wien, Schroll, 1927.

Richardson, Henry Hobson, 1838–1886

10602. Eaton, Leonard K. *American architecture comes of age: European reaction to H. H. Richardson and Louis Sullivan*. Cambridge, Mass., MIT Press, 1972.

10603. Hitchcock, Henry R. *The architecture of H. H. Richardson and his times*. New York, Museum of Modern Art, 1936. (New ed.: Hamden, Conn., Archon, 1961).

10604. Ochsner, Jeffrey K. *H. H. Richardson, complete architectural works*. Cambridge, Mass./ London, MIT Press, 1982. (CR).

10605. O'Gorman, James F. *H. H. Richardson and his office; selected drawings*. [Published in conjunction with an exhibition at the Fogg Art Museum, Harvard University, Cambridge, Mass., October 23–December 8, 1974]. Boston, Godine, 1974.

10606. ———. *H. H. Richardson: architectural forms for an American society*. Chicago, University of Chicago Press, 1987.

10607. ———. *Three American architects: Richardson, Sullivan, and Wright, 1865–1915*. Chicago, University of Chicago Press, 1991.

10608. Richardson, Henry Hobson. *The Spirit of H.*

H. Richardson on the midland prairies: regional transformations of an architectural style. Ed. by Paul Clifford Larson with Susan M. Brown. Minneapolis, University Art Museum, University of Minnesota; Ames, Iowa State University Press, 1988.

10609. Van Rensselaer, Mariana. *Henry Hobson Richardson and his works*. Boston/New York, Houghton Mifflin, 1888. (Reprint: New York, Dover, 1969).

Richter, Adrian Ludwig, 1803–1884

10610. Bauer, Franz. *Ludwig Richter, ein deutscher Malerpoet*. Stuttgart, Schuler, 1960.

10611. Franke, Willibald. *Ludwig Richters Zeichnungen*. Leipzig/Berlin, Grethlein, [1916]. 2 ed.

10612. Friedrich, Karl J. *Die Gemälde Ludwig Richters*. Berlin, Deutscher Verein für Kunstwissenschaft, 1937. (CR).

10613. ———. *Ludwig Richter und sein Schülerkreis*. Leipzig, Koehler & Amelang, 1956.

10614. Froning, Hubertus. *Ludwig Richter, 1803–1884, Zeichnungen und Graphik: eine Ausstellung aus dem Bestand des Graphischen Kabinetts, Museum Folkwang, 26. August bis 14. Oktober 1984. [Katalogbearbeitung, Hubertus Froning]. Essen, Museum Folkwang, [1984].

10615. Hoff, Johann F. *Adrian Ludwig Richter, Maler und Radierer*. Dresden, Richter, 1877.

10616. Kalkschmidt, Eugen. *Ludwig Richter, sein Leben und Schaffen*. Berlin, Grote, 1940.

10617. Kempe, Lothar. *Ludwig Richter, ein Maler des deutschen Volkes*. Dresden, Sachsenverlag, 1953.

10618. Koch, David. *Ludwig Richter, ein Künstler für das deutsche Volk*. Stuttgart, Steinkopf, 1903.

10619. Mohn, Victor P. *Ludwig Richter*. Bielefeld/ Leipzig, Velhagen & Klasing, 1896. (Künstler-Monographien, 14).

10620. Müller-Bohn, Jost. *Ludwig Richter: das geistliche Leben eines deutschen Malers*. Lahr-Dinglingen, Verlag der St.-Johannis-Druckerei C. Schweickhardt, 1983. (Telos-Präsente, 72142).

10621. Neidhardt, Hans Joachim. *Ludwig Richter*. Leipzig, E.A. Seemann, 1991.

10622. Richter, Ludwig. *Dein treuer Vater; Briefe Ludwig Richters aus vier Jahrzehnten an seinen Sohn Heinrich*. Herausgegeben von Karl J. Friedrich. Leipzig, Koehler & Amelang, 1953.

10623. ———. *Lebenserinnerungen eines deutschen Malers; Selbstbiographie*. Herausgegeben von Heinrich Richter. Frankfurt a.M., Ult, 1885.

10624. ———. *Ludwig Richter und sein Kreis: Ausstellung zum 100. Todestag im Albertinum zu Dresden, März bis Juni 1984.*

[Staatliche Kunstsammlungen Dresden, Gemäldegalerie Neue Meister, Kupferstich-Kabinett]. Königstein im Taunus, K.R. Langewiesche Nachfolger H. Köster, 1984.

10625. ———. *Richter-Album; eine Auswahl Holzschnitten nach Zeichnungen.* Leipzig, Wigand, 1848. (New ed., with notes by Otto Jahn: 2 v., 1861).

10626. Schmidt, Karl W. *Ludwig Richter, Leben und Werk.* Berlin, Deutsche Buchvertriebs- und Verlags-Gesellschaft, 1946.

10627. Stubbe, Wolf. *Das Ludwig Richter Hausbuch.* Auswahl: Aiga Matthes. München, Rogner & Bernhard, 1976.

10628. Weidner, Karl-Heinz. *Richter und Dürer: Studien zur Rezeption des altdeutschen Stils im 19. Jahrhundert.* Frankfurt am Main/New York, P. Lang, 1983. (Europäische Hochschulschriften. Reihe XXVIII, Kunstgeschichte, 26).

Richter, David (the elder), 1662–1735
David (the younger), 1664–1741

10629. Holmquist, Bengt M. *Das Problem David Richter: Studien in der Kunstgeschichte des Spätbarocks.* Stockholm, Almqvist & Wiksell, [1968]. (Acta Universitatis Stockholmiensis, 15).

Richter, Gerhard, 1932–

10630. Museum Boymans-Van Beuningen (Rotterdam). *Gerhard Richter, 1988/89.* 15/10–3/12/89. [Organisatie tentoonstelling en redactie catalogus, Gerhard Richter, Karel Schampers]. Rotterdam, Museum Boymans-Van Beuningen, [1990].

10631. Museum Overholland Amsterdam. *Gerhard Richter: werken op papier 1983–1986: notities 1982–1986.* 20.2.87–20.4.87. [Organisatie tentoonstelling, Christian Braun, Gerhard Richter]. Amsterdam, Het Museum, 1987.

10632. Richter, Gerhard. *Gerhard Richter.* Ed. by Sean Rainbird and Judith Severne. London, Tate Gallery, 1991.

10633. ———. *Gerhard Richter, Bilder 1962–1985.* [Herausgegeben von Jürgen Harten anlässlich der Ausstellung in Düsseldorf, Berlin, Bern und Wien 1986]. Mit einem von Dietmar Elger bearbeiteten Catalogue Raisonné. Köln, DuMont, 1986. (CR).

10634. ———. *Gerhard Richter: werken op papier 1983–1986: notities 1982–1986.* Amsterdam, Museum Overholland, 1987.

10635. ———. *Text: Schriften und Interviews.* Herausgegeben von Hans-Ulrich Obrist. Frankfurt am Main, Insel, 1993.

10636. Thomas-Netik, Anja. *Gerhard Richter: mögliche Aspekte eines postmodernen Bewusstseins.* Essen, Die Blaue Eule, 1986. (Kunst, Geschichte und Theorie, 7).

Richter, Hans, 1888–1976

10637. Akademie Der Künste (Berlin). *Hans Richter, 1888–1976; Dadaist, Filmpionier, Maler, Theoretiker.* 31. Januar–7. März 1982. Berlin, Akademie der Künste, 1982.

10638. Richter, Hans. *Begegnungen von Dada bis heute: Briefe, Dokumente, Erinnerungen.* Köln, DuMont Schauberg, 1973.

10639. ———. *Dada: art and anti-art.* New York, McGraw-Hill, 1965. (The Modern Artist and His World, 1).

10640. ———. *Hans Richter.* Introd. by Sir Herbert Read. Autobiographical text by the artist. Neuchâtel, Editions du Griffon, 1965.

10641. ———. *Hans Richter by Hans Richter.* Ed. by Cleve Gray. London, Thames and Hudson, 1971.

Richter, Hans Theo, 1902–1969

10642. Richter, Hans Theo. *Hans Theo Richter, 1902–1969: Zeichnungen, Aquarelle, Lithographien, Radierungen: Städtische Galerie Albstadt, 10. Mai bis 28. Juni 1981.* [Katalogredaktion und Ausstellung, Alfred Hagenlocher. Katalog der ausgestellten Werke, Brigitte Hagenlocher-Wagner]. Albstadt (Ebingen), Die Galerie, [1981]. (Veröffentlichungen der Städtischen Galerie Albstadt, 22/1981).

Ridinger, Johann Elias, 1698–1767

10643. Schwarz, Ignaz. *Katalog einer Ridinger-Sammlung.* 2 v. Wien, Verlag des Verfassers, 1918. (CR).

10644. Stubbe, Wolf. *Johann Elias Ridinger.* Hamburg/Berlin, Parey, 1966. (Die Jagd in der Kunst).

10645. Thienemann, Georg A. W. *Leben und Wirken des unvergleichlichen Thiermalers und Kupferstechers Johann Elias Ridinger.* Leipzig, Weigel, 1856.

Riemenschneider, Tilman, 1460?–1531

10646. Becker, Carl. *Leben und Werke des Bildhauers Tilmann Riemenschneider.* Leipzig, Weigel, 1849.

10647. Bier, Justus. *Tilmann Riemenschneider, die frühen Werke.* Würzburg, Verlagsdruckerei Würzburg, 1925.

10648. ———. *Tilmann Riemenschneider, die reifen Werke.* Augsburg, Filser, 1930.

10649. ———. *Tilmann Riemenschneider, die späten Werke in Holz.* Wien, Schroll, 1978.

10650. ———. *Tilmann Riemenschneider, die späten Werke in Stein.* Wien, Schroll, 1973.

10651. ———. *Tilmann Riemenschneider, his life and work.* Lexington, Ky., University Press of Kentucky, 1982.

10652. Flesche, Herman. *Tilman Riemenschneider.* Bilder von Günther Beyer und Klaus Beyer. Hanau, Dausien, 1957.

10653. Freeden, Max H. von. *Tilman Riemenschneider, Leben und Werk.* Aufnamen von Walter Hege. [München], Deutscher Kunstverlag, 1965. 3 ed.

10654. Gerstenberg, Kurt. *Tilman Riemenschneider.* München, Bruckmann, 1955. 5 ed.

10655. Hotz, Joachim. *Tilman Riemenschneider.* München, Schuler, 1977.

10656. Kirsch, Hans-Christian. *Tilman Riemenschneider, ein deutsches Schicksal.* München, Bertelsmann, 1981.

10657. Knapp, Fritz. *Riemenschneider.* Bielefeld/Leipzig, Velhagen & Klasing, 1935. (Künstler-Monographien, 119).

10658. Mainfränkisches Museum (Würzburg). *Tilman Riemenschneider frühe Werke.* 5. September bis 1. November 1981. Regensburg, Pustet, 1981.

10659. Muth, Hanswernfried [and] Schneiders, Toni. *Tilman Riemenschneider und seine Werke.* Würzburg, Popp, 1980. 2 ed.

10660. Schrade, Hubert. *Tilman Riemenschneider.* 2 v. Heidelberg, Hain, 1927.

10661. Stein, Karl H. *Tilman Riemenschneider im deutschen Bauernkrieg; Geschichte einer geistigen Haltung.* Frankfurt a.M., Gutenberg, 1944.

10662. Streit, Carl. *Tylmann Riemenschneider, 1460–1531; Leben und Kunstwerke des fränkischen Bildschnitzers.* 2 v. Berlin, Wasmuth, 1888.

10663. Tönnies, Eduard. *Leben und Werke des Würzburger Bildschnitzers Tilmann Riemenschneider, 1468–1531.* Strassburg, Heitz, 1900. (Studien zur deutschen Kunstgeschichte, 22).

10664. Weber, Georg A. *Til Riemenschneider, sein Leben und Wirken.* Regensburg, Habbel, 1911.

Rietveld, Gerrit Thomas, 1888–1964

10665. Bless, Frits. *Rietveld, 1888–1964: een biografie.* Amsterdam, Bakker/Baarn/Rap, 1982.

10666. Brown, Theodore M. *The world of G. Rietveld, architect.* Utrecht, Bruna & Zoon, 1958.

10667. Buffinga, A. *Gerrit Thomas Rietveld.* Amsterdam, Meulenhoff, 1971.

10668. Küper, Marijke and van Zijl, Ida. *Gerrit Th. Rietveld, 1888–1964: the complete works.* Trans. by Richard Denooy, Adrienne van Dorpen. Utrecht, Centraal Museum, 1992. (CR).

10669. Mulder, Bertus. *Gerrit Thomas Rietveld: leven, werken, denken.* Nijmegen, SUN, 1995.

10670. Rietveld, Gerrit Thomas. *Gerrit Rietveld, a centenary exhibition: craftsman and visionary:* Barry Friedman Ltd., New York, October 3 1988 to November 12, 1988, Struve Gallery, Chicago, December 9, 1988 to January 16, 1988, Dayton Art Institute, February 3, 1989 to March 6, 1989. New York, Barry Friedman Ltd., 1988.

10671. ———. *Gerrit Th. Rietveld: the complete works, 1888–1964.* Ed. by Marijke Küper and Ida van Zijl. Utrecht, Centraal Museum, 1992.

10672. Rodijk, G. H. *De huizen van Rietveld.* Zwolle, Wanders Uitgevers, 1991.

Rigaud, Hyacinthe, 1659–1743

10673. Ahrens, Kirsten. *Hyacinthe Rigauds Staatsporträt Ludwigs XIV: typologische und ikonologische Untersuchung zur politischen Aussage des Bildnisses von 1701.* Worms, Wernersche Verlagsgesellschaft, 1990. (Manuskripte zur Kunstwissenschaft in der Wernerschen Verlagsgesellschaft, 29).

10674. Eudel, Paul. *Les livres de comptes de Hyacinthe Rigaud.* Paris, Le Soudier, 1910.

10675. Roman, Joseph. *Le livre de raison du peintre Hyacinthe Rigaud.* Paris, Laurens, 1919.

Riis, Jacob August, 1849–1914

10676. Alland, Alexander, Sr. *Jacob A. Riis, photographer & citizen.* With a preface by Ansel Adams. Millerton, N.Y., Aperture, 1974.

10677. Fried, Lewis and Fierst, John. *Jacob A. Riis: a reference guide.* Boston, G. K. Hall, 1977.

10678. Hales, Peter B. *Silver cities: the photography of American urbanization, 1839–1915.* Philadelphia, Temple University Press, 1984.

10679. Hassner, Rune. *Jacob A. Riis, reporter med kamera i New Yorks slum.* Stockholm, Norstedt, 1970.

10680. Riis, Jacob A. *The complete photographic work of Jacob A. Riis.* Ed. by Robert J. Doherty. Introduction by Ulrich Keller. New York, Macmillan; London, Collier Macmillan, 1981. (International archives of photography, 1).

10681. ———. *How the other half lives: studies among the tenements of New York.* New York, Scribner, 1890. (Reprint, with a preface by Charles A. Madison: New York, Dover, 1971).

10682. ———. *Jacob A. Riis, socialreporter med kamera.* Text by Rune Hassner. [Helsingborg], Lucida, 1987. (Scandinavian photographers classic and contemporary, 1).

10683. Ware, Louise. *Jacob A. Riis: police reporter, reformer, useful citizen.* Introduction by Allan Nevins. New York, Appleton-Century, 1938. (Reprint: Millwood, N.Y., Kraus, 1975).

Rimmer, William, 1816–1879

10684. Bartlett, Truman H. *The art life of William Rimmer, sculptor, painter, and physician.* Boston/New York, Houghton Mifflin, 1882.

(Reprinted from the 1890 ed., with a new preface by Leonard Baskin: New York, Da Capo/Kennedy Graphics, 1970).

10685. Rimmer, William. *William Rimmer, a Yankee Michelangelo*. Essays by Jeffrey Weidman, Neil Harris, and Philip Cash. With a foreword by Theodore E. Stebbins, Jr. Hanover, NH, distributed for the Brockton Art Museum/Fuller Memorial by University Press of New England, 1985.

10686. Weidman, Jeffrey. *William Rimmer: critical catalogue raisonné*. 7 v. in 5. Ann Arbor, Mich., University Microfilms International, 1983. (CR).

10687. Whitney Museum of American Art (New York). *William Rimmer, 1816–1879*. November 5–27, 1946. [Text by Lincoln Kirstein]. [New York, Whitney Museum of American Art, 1946].

Rimša, Petras, 1881–1961

10688. Budrys, Stanislovas. *Piatras Rimsha*. Moskva, Sovetskii Khudozhnik, 1961.

10689. Rimantaš, J. *Petras Rimsa pasakoja*. Vilnius, USSR, Valstybine grožines literaturos leidykla, 1964.

Rippl-Rónai, Józef, 1861–1927

10690. Bernáth, Mária. *Rippl-Rónai József*. Budapest, Gondolat Könyvkiadó, 1976.

10691. Genthon, István. *Rippl-Rónai, le Nabi hongrois*. [Translatd from the Hungarian by Imre Kelemen]. Budapest, Corvina, 1958.

10692. Laczkó, András. *Ecset és toll: Rippl-Rónai József és az irodalom*. Budapest, Akadémiai Kiadó, 1983. (Irodalomtörténeti fúzetek, 109).

10693. Palazzo dei Conservatori in Campidoglio (Roma). *Rippl-Rónai 1861–1927: pittore, grafico, decoratore*. 9 novembre/18 dicembre 1983. [mostra; Pinacoteca capitolina]. Roma, Multigrafica, 1983.

10694. Petrovics, Elek. *Rippl-Rónai*. Budapest, Athenaeum, [n.d.].

10695. Pewny, Denise. *Rippl-Rónai József (1861–1927)*. Budapest, Sárkány, 1940.

10696. Rippl-Rónai, József. *Rippl-Rónai, emlézezései*. Budapest, Nyugat, 1911.

Ritz, Johann, 1666–1729

10697. Steinmann, Othmar. *Der Bildhauer Johann Ritz (1666–1729) von Selkingen und seine Werkstatt*. Disentis, Switzerland, Benediktinerabtei Disentis, 1952.

Ritz, Raphael, 1829–1894

10698. Ruppen, Walter. *Raphael Ritz, 1829–1894; Leben und Werk*. Bonn/Duisburg, Allitera, 1971.

Rivera, Diego, 1886–1957

10699. [Anonymous]. *Das Werk des Malers Diego Rivera*. Berlin, Neuer Deutscher Verlag, 1928.

10700. Arquin, Florence. *Diego Rivera: the shaping of an artist, 1889–1921*. Norman, Okla., University of Oklahoma Press, 1971.

10701. Evans, Ernestine. *The frescos of Diego Rivera*. New York, Harcourt, Brace, 1929.

10702. Favela, Ramón. *Diego Rivera, the cubist years*. [Guest curator, Ramón Favela. Organized by James K. Ballinger]. [Phoenix, Ariz.], Phoenix Art Museum, 1984.

10703. Fondo Editorial de la Plástica Mexicana (Mexico City). *Diego Rivera: I. Pintura de caballete y dibujos*. [Work in progress]. [Mexico City], Fondo Editorial de la Plástica Mexicana, 1979– .

10704. López Rangel, Rafael. *Diego Rivera y la arquitectura mexicana*. Rafael López Rangel. Comentario crítico de Enrique Yáñez. Asesoría en integración plástica de Alfonso Villanueva. México, D.F., SEP Dirección General de Publicaciones y Medios, 1986.

10705. Mittler, Max, ed. *Diego Rivera, Wort und Bekenntnis*. Zürich, Verlag der Arche, 1965.

10706. Museo Nacional de Artes Plásticas (Mexico City). *Diego Rivera: 50 años de su labor artistica; exposicion de homenaje nacional*. [Mexico City], Departamento de Artes Plásticas, Instituto Nacional de Bellas Artes, 1951.

10707. Museum of Modern Art (New York). *Diego Rivera*. December 23, 1931–January 27, 1932. New York, Museum of Modern Art, 1931.

10708. ———. *Frescos of Diego Rivera* [a portfolio]. New York, Museum of Modern Art, 1933.

10709. Ospovat, Lev S. *Diego Rivera*. Moskva, Molodaia Gvardiia, 1969.

10710. Pina García, Juan Pablo de. *Diego Rivera en los años radicales*. Chapingo, Mexico, DF, Universidad Autónoma Chapingo, 1990. 1. ed. en español.

10711. Ramos, Samuel. *Diego Rivera*. [Mexico City], Universidad Nacional Autónoma de México, Dirección General de Publicaciones, 1958. (Coleccion de arte, 4).

10712. Rivera, Diego. *Diego Rivera, mural painting*. Text by Antonio Rodríguez. Photography by Enrique Franco Torrijos and Bob Schalkwijk. Design by Bernardo Recamier. Editorial coordinator, Víctor Manuel Espíndola. Mexico City, Fondo Editorial de la Plástica Mexicana, Trusteeship in the Banco Nacional de Comercio Exterior, 1989.

10713. ———. *Diego Rivera, a retrospective*. New York, Founders Society, Detroit Institute of Arts/Norton, 1986.

10714. ———. *My art, my life: an autobiography.* With Gladys March. New York, Citadel, 1960. (Reprint. New York, Dover Publications, 1991).

10715. ———. *Portrait of America.* With an explanatory text by Bertram D. Wolfe. New York, Covici, Friede, 1934.

10716. Rochfort, Desmond. *The murals of Diego Rivera.* With a political chronology by Julia Engelhardt. London, South Bank Board in collaboration with Journeyman, 1987.

10717. Rodriguez, Antonio. *Diego Rivera.* [Mexico City], Ediciones de Arte, 1950.

10718. Romero, Héctor Manuel. *El México de Diego Rivera: crónicas capitalinas.* México, D.F., Panorama Editorial, 1992.

10719. Secker, Hans F. *Diego Rivera.* Dresden, Verlag der Kunst, 1957.

10720. Tibol, Raquel. *Diego Rivera ilustrador.* Texto de Raquel Tibol. Comentarios de Alberto Beltrán. [Mexico City], SEP, Dirección General de Publicaciones y Medios, 1986.

10721. Wolfe, Bertram D. *Diego Rivera; his life and times.* London, Hale, 1939.

10722. ———. *The fabulous world of Diego Rivera.* New York, Stein & Day, 1963.

Rivers, Larry, 1923–

10723. Harrison, Helen A. *Larry Rivers.* New York, Harper & Row, 1984.

10724. Hirshhorn Museum and Sculpture Garden (Washington D.C.). *Larry Rivers: the Hirshhorn Museum and Sculpture Garden collection, Smithsonian Institution.* Ed. by Phyllis Rosenzweig. Washington D.C., Smithsonian Institution Press, for sale by the Supt. of Docs., U.S. G.P.O., 1981.

10725. Hunter, Sam. *Larry Rivers.* With a memoir by Frank O'Hara. New York, Abrams, 1970.

10726. ———. *Larry Rivers.* New York, Rizzoli, 1989.

10727. Kestner-Gesellschaft, Hannover. *Larry Rivers Retrospektive: Bilder und Skulpturen.* Herausgegeben von Carl Haenlein. 19. Dezember 1980 bis 15. Februar 1981. Hannover, Kestner-Gesellschaft, 1980. (Katalog 6/1980).

10728. ———. *Larry Rivers Retrospektive: Zeichnungen.* Herausgegeben von Carl Haenlein. 20. Dezember 1980 bis 25. Januar 1981. Hannover, Kestner-Gesellschaft, 1980. (Katalog 1/1981).

10729. Marlborough Gallery (New York City). *Larry Rivers: art and the artist.* March 3–27, 1993. New York, The Gallery, 1993.

10730. Rivers, Larry. *Drawings and digressions.* By Larry Rivers with Carol Brightman. New York, Potter, 1979; distributed by Crown, New York.

10731. ———. *What did I do?: the unauthorized autobiography.* With Arnold Weinstein. New York, Aaron Asher Books, 1992.

10732. Rose Art Museum, Brandeis University (Waltham, Mass.). *Larry Rivers.* Introduction by Sam Hunter, with a memoir by Frank O'Hara and a statement by the artist. April 10–May 9, 1965. Waltham, Mass., Brandeis University, 1965.

Rizzo, Antonio, 1440–1500

10733. Schulz, Anne M. *Antonio Rizzo, sculptor and architect.* Princeton, N.J., Princeton University Press, 1982.

Robbia, Andrea Della, 1435–1525
Giovanni Della, 1469–1529
Luca Della, 1400–1482

10734. Barbet de Jouy, Henry. *Les Della Robbia, sculpteurs en terre émaillée; étude sur leurs travaux, suivie d'un catalogue de leur oeuvre fait en Italie en 1853.* Paris, Renouard, 1855.

10735. Bargellini, Piero. *I Della Robbia.* Milano, Arti Grafiche Ricordi, 1965.

10736. Burlamacchi, L. *Luca della Robbia.* London, Bell, 1900.

10737. Cavallucci, Camillo J. [and] Molinier, Emile. *Les Della Robbia, leur vie et leur oeuvre.* Paris, Rouam, 1884.

10738. Contrucci, Pietro. *Monumento Robbiano nella loggia dello Spedale di Pistoja.* Prato, Giachetti, 1835.

10739. Cruttwell, Maud. *Luca & Andrea Della Robbia and their successors.* London, Dent/ New York, Dutton, 1902.

10740. Foville, Jean de. *Les Della Robbia, biographies critiques.* Paris, Laurens, 1910.

10741. Gentilini, Giancarlo. *I Della Robbia: la scultura invetriata nel Rinascimento.* 2 v. Firenze, Cantini, [1992].

10742. Marquand, Allan. *Andrea Della Robbia and his atelier.* 2 v. Princeton, N.J., Princeton University Press, 1922. (CR). (Princeton Monographs in Art and Archeology, 11).

10743. ———. *The brothers of Giovanni Della Robbia: Fra Mattia, Luca, Girolamo, Ambrogio.* With an appendix and corrections for all the Della Robbia catalogues. Edited and extended by Frank J. Mather, Jr., and Charles R. Morey. Princeton, N.J., Princeton University Press, 1928.

10744. ———. *Della Robbias in America.* Princeton, N.J., Princeton University Press, 1912. (Princeton Monographs in Art and Archeology, 1).

10745. ———. *Giovanni Della Robbia.* Princeton, N.J., Princeton University Press, 1920. (CR). (Princeton Monographs on Art and Archeology, 8).

10746. ———. *Luca Della Robbia.* Princeton, N.J.,

Princeton University Press, 1914. (CR).
(Princeton Monographs in Art and Archeology, 3).

10747. ———. *Robbia heraldry.* Princeton, N.J., Princeton University Press, 1919. (Princeton Monographs in Art and Archeology). [Note: all of Marquand's Della Robbia volumes were reprinted by Hacker, New York, 1972].

10748. Planiscig, Leo. *Luca della Robbia.* Wien, Schroll, 1940.

10749. Pope-Hennessy, John. *Luca della Robbia.* Oxford, Phaidon, 1980. (CR).

10750. Reymond, Marcel. *Les Della Robbia.* Florence, Alinari, 1897.

10751. Schubring, Paul. *Luca della Robbia und seine Familie.* Bielefeld/Leipzig, Velhagen & Klasing, 1905. (Künstler-Monographien, 74).

Robert, Charles, 1912–1948

10752. Comment, Jean-François, et al. *Charles Robert, dessins et peintures.* Moutier, Switzerland, Robert, 1956.

10753. Junod, Roger-Louis, et al. *Le peintre Charles Robert.* Préface de Claude Roger-Marx. Neuchâtel, Editions de la Baconnière, 1961.

10754. Roger-Marx, Claude. *[Charles Robert:] Espagne/Paris.* 2 v. Neuchâtel, Switzerland, Editions de l'Orée, 1962.

Robert, Hubert, 1733–1808 *see also* Fragonard, Jean Honore

10755. Beau, Marguerite. *La collection des dessins d'Hubert Robert au Musée de Valence.* Lyon, Audin, 1968.

10756. Burda, Hubert. *Die Ruine in den Bildern Hubert Roberts.* München, Fink, 1967.

10757. Carlson, Victor. *Hubert Robert, drawings & watercolors.* [Published in conjunction with an exhibition at the National Gallery of Art, Washington, D.C., November 19, 1978–January 21, 1979]. Washington, D.C., National Gallery of Art, 1978.

10758. Gabillot, Claude. *Hubert Robert et son temps.* Paris, Librairie de L'Art, [1895].

10759. Leclère, Tristan. *Hubert Robert et les paysagistes français de XVIII siècle.* Paris, Laurens, 1913.

10760. Lévêque, Jean-Jacques. *L'univers d'Hubert Robert.* Paris, Screpel, 1979.

10761. Musée du Louvre (Paris). *Le Louvre d'Hubert Robert.* Catalogue rédigé par Marie-Catherine Sahut. 16 juin–29 octobre 1979. Paris, Editions de la Réunion des Musées Nationaux, 1979.

10762. Nolhac, Pierre de. *Hubert Robert, 1733–1808.* Paris, Goupil, 1910.

Robert, Louis Leopold, 1794–1835

10763. Clément, Charles. *Léopold Robert d'après sa correspondance inédite.* Paris, Didier, 1875.

10764. Feuillet de Conches, Félix. *Léopold Robert; sa vie, ses oeuvres et sa correspondance.* Paris, Lévy, 1854.

Robinson, Theodore, 1852–1896

10765. Baltimore Museum of Art. *Theodore Robinson, 1852–1896.* 1 May–10 June 1973. Baltimore, Baltimore Museum of Art, 1973.

10766. Baur, John I. H. *Theodore Robinson, 1852–1896.* [Published in conjunction with an exhibition at the Brooklyn Museum, New York, November 12, 1946–January 5, 1947]. New York, Brooklyn Museum, 1946.

Robinson, William Heath, 1872–1944

10767. Day, Langston. *The life and art of W. Heath Robinson.* London, Joseph, 1947.

10768. Lewis, John. *Heath Robinson, artist and comic genius.* Introd. by Nicolas Bentley. London, Constable, 1973.

10769. Robinson, Heath. *My line of life.* London/Glasgow, Blackie, 1938. (Reprint: East Ardsley, Eng., EP Publishing, 1974).

Robusti, Jacopo *see* Tintoretto, Il

Rockwell, Norman, 1894–1978

10770. Buechner, Thomas S. *Norman Rockwell, artist and illustrator.* New York, Abrams, 1970.

10771. Finch, Christopher. *Norman Rockwell's America.* New York, Abrams, 1975.

10772. Guptill, Arthur L. *Norman Rockwell, illustrator.* Preface by Dorothy Canfield Fisher; biographical introduction by Jack Alexander. New York, Watson-Guptill, 1946.

10773. Moffatt, Laurie Norton. *Norman Rockwell, a definitive catalogue.* Text and catalogue by Laurie Norton Moffat. Introduction by David H. Wood. Stockbridge, Mass., Norman Rockwell Museum at Stockbridge; Hanover, N.H., distributed by the University Press of New England, 1986.

10774. Rockwell, Norman. *My adventures as an illustrator.* As told to Thomas Rockwell. Garden City, N.Y., Doubleday, 1960.

10775. ———. *The Norman Rockwell album.* Garden City, N.Y., Doubleday, 1961.

10776. ———. *Norman Rockwell.* A cura di Davide Faccioli e Manuela Teatini. [Mostra a cura di Judy Goffman]. Milano, Electa, 1990.

10777. Walton, Donald. *A Rockwell portrait: an intimate biography.* Kansas City, Kan., Sheed, Andrews & McMeel, 1978.

Rodchenko, Aleksandr Mikhailovich, 1891–1956

10778. Elliott, David, ed. *Rodchenko and the arts of revolutionary Russia.* New York, Pantheon, 1979.

10779. Gassner, Hubertus. *Rodcenko Fotographien.*

Mit einem Vorwort von Aleksander Lavrentjev. München, Schirmer/Mosel, 1982. (English ed., without Gassner's text, trans. by John W. Gabriel: New York, Rizzoli, 1982).

10780. Khan-Magomedov, Selim Omarovich. *Rodchenko: the complete work.* Introduced and edited by Vieri Quilici. Cambridge, Mass., MIT Press, 1987.

10781. Karginov, German. *Rodchenko.* Trans. by Elisabeth Hoch. London, Thames and Hudson, 1979.

10782. Rodchenko, Aleksandr Mikhaílovich. *Alexander Rodchenko.* Introduction by Serge Lemoine. New York, Pantheon Books; Paris, Centre national de la photographie, 1987. [1st American ed].

10783. ———. *Alexander Rodchenko: works on paper, 1914–1920.* Ed. by David Elliott and Alexander Lavrentiev. Trans. by Neil Pattenden. London, Sotheby's, 1991.

10784. ———. *Rodchenko Fotograf, 1891–1956: Bilder aus dem Moskauer Familienbesitz.* [Catalogue of an exhibition held at the Kunstsammlung der Universität Göttingen, 29.10.–3.12. 1989. Göttingen, Arkana-Verlag, 1989.

10785. Volkov-Lannit, Leonid F. *Aleksandr Rodchenko risuet, fotografiruet, sporit.* Moskva, Iskusstvo, 1968.

10786. Weiss, Evelyn, ed. *Alexander Rodtschenko; Fotographien, 1920–1938.* Köln, Wienand, 1978.

Rodin, Auguste, 1840-1917

10787. Bénédite, Léonce. *Rodin.* Paris, Rieder, 1926.

10788. Bourdelle, Antoine. *Rodin's later drawings.* Interpretations by Antoine Bourdelle. Text and translations by Elisabeth C. Geissbuhler.

10789. ———. *La sculpture et Rodin.* Précédé de *Quatre pages de journal* par Claude Aveline. Paris, Emile-Paul, 1937.

10790. Busco, Marie. *Rodin and his contemporaries: the Iris & B. Gerald Cantor Collection.* Photographs by David Finn. New York, Cross River Press, 1991.

10791. Butler, Ruth, ed. *Rodin in perspective.* Englewood Cliffs, N.J., Prentice-Hall, 1980.

10792. ———. *Rodin: the shape of genius.* New Haven, Yale University Press, 1993.

10793. Champigneulle, Bernard. *Rodin.* Trans. and adapted by J. Maxwell Brownjohn. New York, Abrams, 1967.

10794. Cladel, Judith. *Rodin; the man and his art.* Trans. by S. K. Star. New York, Century, 1917.

10795. Coquiot, Gustave. *Rodin à l'Hôtel de Biron et à Meudon.* Paris, Ollendorff, 1917.

10796. ———. *Le vrai Rodin.* Paris, Tallandier, 1913.

10797. Daix, Pierre. *Rodin.* Paris, Calmann-Lévy, 1988.

10798. De Caso, Jacques and Sanders, Patricia B. *Rodin's sculpture: a critical study of the Spreckels Collection, California Palace of the Legion of Honor.* San Francisco, Fine Arts Museums of San Francisco/Rutland, Vt. and Tokyo, Tuttle, 1977. (CR).

10799. Descharnes, Robert and Chabrun, Jean F. *August Rodin.* Trans. by Haakon Chevalier. New York, Viking, 1967.

10800. Elsen, Albert E. *In Rodin's studio; a photographic record of sculpture in the making.* Ithaca, N.Y., Cornell, 1980.

10801. ———. *Rodin.* New York, Museum of Modern Art, 1963; distributed by Doubleday, Garden City, N.Y.

10802. ———. *Rodin's Gates of Hell.* Minneapolis, University of Minnesota Press, 1960.

10803. ———, ed. *Auguste Rodin: readings on his life and work.* Englewood Cliffs, N.J., Prentice-Hall, 1965.

10804. ——— and Varnedoe, J. Kirk T. *The drawings of Rodin.* With additional contributions by Victoria Thorson and Eisabeth C. Geissbuhler. New York, Praeger, 1971.

10805. Fayard, Jeanne. *La vie passionée de Rodin.* [Paris], Librairie Séguier, 1989.

10806. Grappe, Georges. *Le Musée Rodin.* Paris, Taupin, 1944.

10807. Grautoff, Otto. *Auguste Rodin.* Bielefeld/Leipzig, Velhagen & Klasing, 1908. (Künstler-Monographien, 93).

10808. Grunfeld, Frederic V. *Rodin, a biography.* New York, Holt, 1987.

10809. Jianou, Ionel and Goldscheider, Cécile. *Rodin.* Paris, Arted, 1967.

10810. Laurent, Monique. *Rodin.* Trans. by Emily Read. London, Barrie and Jenkins, 1990.

10811. Ludovici, Anthony M. *Personal reminiscences of August Rodin.* Philadelphia, Lippincott, 1926.

10812. Maillard, Léon. *Etudes sur quelques artistes originaux: Auguste Rodin, statuaire.* Paris, Floury, 1899.

10813. Mauclair, Camille. *Auguste Rodin: the man, his ideas, his works.* Trans. by Clementina Black. London, Duckworth, 1909.

10814. Mirbeau, Octave. *Correspondance avec Auguste Rodin.* Edicion établie, présentée et annotée par Pierre Michel et Jean-Francois Nivet. Tusson, Charente, Du Lérot, 1988.

10815. Musée Rodin (Paris). *Inventaire des dessins.* Ed. by Claudie Judrin. [Paris], Musée Rodin, 1984–1992.

10816. Musée Rodin (Paris). *Marbres de Rodin: collection du musée: catalogue.* Etabli par Nicole Barbier. Paris, Editions du Musée Rodin, 1987.

10817. Musée Rodin (Paris). *Rodin et les écrivains de son temps: sculptures, dessins, lettres et livres du fonds Rodin.* 23 juin–18 octobre 1976. Paris, Musée Rodin, 1976.

10818. National Gallery of Art (Washington, D.C.). *Rodin rediscovered.* June 28, 1981–May 2, 1982. [Text edited by Albert Elsen]. Washington, D.C., National Gallery of Art, 1981.

10819. Nostitz, Helene von. *Dialogues with Rodin.* Trans. by H. L. Ripperger. New York, Duffield & Green, 1931.

10820. Pinet, Hélène. *Rodin, the hands of genius.* New York, Abrams, 1992.

10821. ———. *Rodin sculpteur et les photographes de son temps.* Paris, Philippe Sers, 1985.

10822. Rilke, Rainer M. *Auguste Rodin.* Trans. by Jessie Lemont and Hans Trausil. New York, Sunwise Turn, 1919.

10823. ———. *Rodin and other prose pieces.* Trans. by G. Craig Houston. With an introduction by William Tucker. London, Quartet, 1986.

10824. Rodin, Auguste. *Art.* Trans. from the French of Paul Gsell by Romilly Fedden. Boston, Small, Maynard, 1912.

10825. ———. *Auguste Rodin, drawings and watercolors.* Ed. by Ernst-Gerhard Güse. Trans. by John Gabriel and Michael Taylor. Text by Claudie Judrin. New York, Rizzoli, 1985.

10826. ———. *Briefe an zwei deutsche Frauen.* Herausgegeben von Helene von Nostitz. Mit einer Einführung von Rudolf Alexander Schröder. Berlin, Holle, [n.d.].

10827. ———. *Correspondance de Rodin.* Textes classés et annotés par Alain Beausire et Hélène Pinet. Paris, Musée Rodin, 1985.

10828. ———. *Les cathédrales de France.* Paris, Colin, 1914. (English ed.: Trans. by Elisabeth C. Geissbuhler. With a preface by Herbert Read. Boston, Beacon Press, 1965).

10829. Schmoll gen. Eisenwerth, J. Adolf. *Rodin-Studien: Persönlichkeit, Werke, Wirkung, Bibliographie.* München, Prestel-Verlag, 1983. (Studien zur Kunst des neunzehnten Jahrhunderts, 31).

10830. Story, Sommerville. *Rodin.* New York, Phaidon, 1964. 3 ed.

10831. Sutton, Denys. *Triumphant satyr; the world of Auguste Rodin.* New York, Hawthorn, 1966.

10832. Tancock, John L. *The sculpture of Auguste Rodin.* Special photography by Murray Weiss. [Boston], Godine/Philadelphia, Philadelphia Museum of Art, 1976. (CR).

10833. Thorson, Victoria. *Rodin graphics: a catalogue raisonné of drypoints and book illustrations.* [Published in conjunction with an exhibition at the California Palace of the Legion of Honor, San Francisco, 14 June–10 August 1975]. San Francisco, Fine Arts Museums of San Francisco, 1975. (CR).

10834. Tirel, Marcelle. *The last years of Rodin.* Trans. by R. Francis. Preface by Judith Cladel. London, Philpot, [1925].

10835. Waldmann, Emil. *Auguste Rodin.* Wien, Schroll, 1945.

Roebling, John Augustus, 1806–1869 Washington Augustus, 1837–1926

10836. McCullough, David. *The Great Bridge.* New York, Simon & Schuster, 1972.

10837. Schuyler, Hamilton. *The Roeblings; a century of engineers, bridge-builders and industrialists.* Princeton, N.J., Princeton University Press, 1931.

10838. Steinman, David B. *The builders of the bridge: the story of John Roebling and his son.* New York, Harcourt Brace, 1945.

10839. Stewart, Elizabeth C., ed. *Guide to the Roebling collections at Rensselaer Polytechnic Institute and Rutgers University.* With an introduction by Robert M. Vogel. Troy, NY, Friends of the Folsom Library, Rensselaer Polytechnic Institute, 1983. (Occasional papers of the Friends of the Folsom Library, Rensselaer Polytechnic Institute, 1).

10840. Trachtenberg, Alan. *Brooklyn Bridge: fact and symbol.* New York, Oxford University Press, 1965.

Roerich, Nikolai Konstantinovich, 1874–1947

10841. Decter, Jacqueline. *Nicholas Roerich, the life and art of a Russian master.* With the Nicholas Roerich Museum. Rochester, Vt., Park Street Press; [New York], distributed to the book trade in the U.S. by Harper & Row, 1989.

10842. Ivanov, Vsevolod Nikanorovich. *Ogni v tumane; Rerikh—khudozhnik myslitel.* [Sostavitel: Í Urií Viktorovich Konoplián-nikov]. Moskva, Sovetskii pisatel, 1991.

10843. Klizovskii, Aleksandr. *Osnovy miroponimaniiá novoí épokhi.* 3 v. Riga, "Vieda", 1990–1991. Izd. 2., ispr.

10844. Kniazeva, Valentina P. *Nikolai Konstantinovich Rerikh, 1874–1947.* Moskva, Iskusstvo, 1963.

10845. Poliakova, Elena I. *Nikolai Rerikh.* Moskva, Iskusstvo, 1973.

10846. Roerich, Nikolai I. *Adamant.* New York, Corona Mundi, 1922.

10847. Selivanova, Nina. *The world of Roerich.* New York, Corona Mundi, 1922.

Rogers, John, 1829–1904

10848. Smith, Mr. and Mrs. Chetwood. *Rogers Groups: thought & wrought by John Rogers.* Introd. by Clarence S. Brigham. Boston, Goodspeed, 1934.

10849. Wallace, David H. *John Rogers, the people's sculptor.* Middletown, Conn., Wesleyan University Press, 1967. (CR).

Rogier van der Weyden *see* **Weyden, Roger van der**

Rohe, Ludwig Mies van der *see* **Mies van der Rohe, Ludwig**

Rohlfs, Christian, 1849–1938

10850. Galerie Nierendorf (Berlin). *Christian Rohlfs: zum einhundertvierzigsten Geburtstag: Gemälde, Aquarelle, Deckfarben, Zeichnungen, Holzschnitte, Linolschnitte.* 4.12. 1989–3.4.1990. Berlin, Galerie Nierendorf, 1989.

10851. Landesmuseum Münster. *Christian Rohlfs, 1849–1938; Aquarelle und Zeichnungen.* 15. Dezember 1974–26. Januar 1975. Münster, Landesmuseum Münster, 1975.

10852. Rohlfs, Christian. *Christian Rohlfs: Aquarelle, Temperablätter, Zeichnungen, Graphik aus den Sammlungen Museum Folkwang, Essen; Karl Ernst Osthaus-Museum, Hagen; Westfälisches Landesmuseum für Kunst und Kulturgeschichte, Münster, u. a.* Herausgegeben von Reinhold Happel. [Katalogredaktion, Sabine Baumann-Wilke, Friedrich Gross, Reinhold Happel]. Braunschweig, Kunstverein Braunschweig, [1992].

10853. ———. *Christian Rohlfs, Gemälde.* Herausgegeben von Klaus Bussmann. [Katalogredaktion, Reinhold Happel, Birgit Schulte, Gerhard Graulich]. Stuttgart, Edition Cantz, [1989].

10854. Scheidig, Walther. *Christian Rohlfs.* Dresden, Verlag der Kunst, 1965.

10855. Uphoff, Carl E. *Christian Rohlfs.* Leipzig, Klinkhardt & Biermann, 1923. (Junge Kunst, 34).

10856. Vogt, Paul. *Christian Rohlfs, 1849–1938, Aquarelle, Wassertemperablätter, Zeichnungen.* Recklinghausen, Bongers, 1988. 2 Aufl.

10857. Vogt, Paul. *Christian Rohlfs.* Köln, DuMont Schauberg, 1967.

10858. ———. *Christian Rohlfs: Aquarelle und Zeichnungen.* Recklinghausen, Bongers, 1958.

10859. ———. *Christian Rohlfs: das graphische Werk.* Recklinghausen, Bongers, 1960. (CR).

10860. ———. *Christian Rohlfs: Oeuvre-Katalog der Gemälde.* Recklinghausen, Bongers, 1978. (CR).

Romako, Anton, 1832–1889

10861. Novotny, Fritz. *Der Maler Anton Romako, 1832–1889.* Wien, Schroll, 1954.

10862. Oberes Belvedere Wien. *Der Aussenseiter Anton Romako 1832–1889: ein Maler der Wiener Ringstrassenzeit.* [Redaktion und Konzept, Gerbert Frodl. Katalog der ausgestellten Werke, Sabine Grabner]. Wien, Österreichische Galerie, 1992. (Wechselaus-

stellung der Österreichischen Galerie, 163).

Romanino, Girolamo, 1485–1566

10863. Cassa Salvi, Elvira. *Romanino.* Milano, Fabbri, 1965. (I maestri del colore, 95).

10864. Comune di Brescia. *Mostra di Girolamo Romanino.* Catalogo a cura di Gaetano Panazza. Prefazione di G. A. dell'Acqua. Brescia, Comitato della Mostra, 1965.

10865. Ferrari, Maria L. *Il Romanino.* Milano, Bramante, 1961.

10866. Nicodemi, Giorgio. *Gerolamo Romanino.* [Brescia, La Poligrafica, 1925].

10867. Passamani, Bruno. *Romanino in S. Maria della Neve a Pisogne.* Contributi di Gian Paolo Treccani . . . [et al.]. Brescia, Grafo, 1991. 2a ed.

10868. Romanino, Girolamo. *Romanino in Sant'-Antonio a Breno.* Saggi di Oliviero Franzoni . . . [et al.]. Appendice di Ottorino Nonfarmale. Fotografie di Gio Lodovico Baglioni. Breno, Camuna, 1991.

Romano, Giulio *see* **Giulio Romano**

Romney, George, 1734–1802

10869. Chamberlain, Arthur B. *George Romney.* New York, Scribner, 1910.

10870. Davies, Randall. *Romney.* London, Black, 1913.

10871. Gamlin, Hilda. *George Romney and his art.* London, Sonnenschein, 1894.

10872. Gower, Ronald S. *George Romney.* London, Duckworth, 1904.

10873. Hayley, William. *The life of George Romney, Esq.* London, Payne, 1809.

10874. Jaffé, Patricia. *Drawings by George Romney* [in the Fitzwilliam Museum, Cambridge]. Cambridge, Cambridge University Press for the Fitzwilliam Museum, 1977.

10875. Maxwell, Herbert E. *George Romney.* New York, Scribner, 1902.

10876. Romney, John. *Memoirs of the life and works of George Romney.* London, Baldwin and Cradock, 1830.

10877. Rump, Gerhard C. *George Romney (1734–1802); zur Bildform der bürgerlichen Mitte in der englischen Neoklassik.* 2 v. Hildesheim/New York, Olms, 1974.

10878. Ward, Thomas H., and Roberts, William. *Romney; a biographical and critical essay, with a catalogue raisonné of his work.* 2 v. New York, Scribner, 1904. (CR).

10879. Watson, Jennifer C. *George Romney in Canada.* Waterloo, Ont., Canada, published for the Kitchener-Waterloo Art Gallery by W. Laurier University Press, 1985.

Root, John Wellborn, 1850–1891

10880. Hoffmann, Donald. *The architecture of John*

Wellborn Root. Baltimore/London, Johns Hopkins University Press, 1973. (Johns Hopkins Studies in Nineteenth-Century Architecture).

10881. Monroe, Harriet. *John Wellborn Root, a study of his life and work.* Boston, Houghton Mifflin, 1896. (Reprint: Park Forest, Ill., Prairie School Press, 1966).

10882. Root, John W. *The meaning of architecture: buildings and writings by John Wellborn Root.* Ed. by Donald Hoffmann. New York, Horizon, 1967.

Rops, Felicien, 1833–1898

10883. Bory, Jean-François. *Félicien Rops: l'oeuvre graphique complète.* Paris, Hubschmid, 1977. (CR).

10884. Boyer d'Agen, Jean et Roig, Jean de. *Ropsiana.* Paris, Pellet, 1924.

10885. Brison, Charles. *Pornocrates: an introduction to the life and work of Félicien Rops, 1833–1898.* London, Skilton, 1969.

10886. Delevoy, Robert L., ed. *Félicien Rops.* Bruxelles, Lebeer Hossmann, 1985.

10887. Dubray, Jean. *Félicien Rops.* Préface de Pierre MacOrlan. [Paris], Seheur, 1928.

10888. Exsteens, Maurice. *L'oeuvre gravé et lithographié de Félicien Rops.* 4 v. Paris, Pellet, 1928. (CR).

10889. Fontainas, André. *Rops.* Paris, Alcan, 1925.

10890. Huysmans, J.-K. *L'au-dela du mal, ou, L'oeuvre érotique de Félicien Rops.* Paris, J. Damase, 1992.

10891. Lemonnier, Camille. *Félicien Rops, l'homme et l'artiste.* Paris, Floury, 1908.

10892. Mascha, Ottokar. *Félicien Rops und sein Werk.* München, Langen, 1910.

10893. Ramiro, Erastène. *Félicien Rops.* Paris, Pellet/Floury, 1905.

10894. ———. *L'oeuvre gravé de Félicien Rops, précédé d'une notice biographique et critique.* Paris, Conquet, 1887. Supplement: Paris, Floury, 1895. (CR).

10895. ———. *L'oeuvre lithographié de Félicien Rops.* Paris, Conquet, 1891. (CR).

10896. Rouir, Eugène. *Félicien Rops: catalogue raisonné de l'oeuvre gravé et lithographié.* Bruxelles, C. Van Loock, 1987. (CR).

10897. ———. *Félicien Rops: les techniques de gravure.* Bruxelles, Bibliothéque royale Albert Ier, 1991.

Rosa, Salvator, 1615–1673

10898. Cattaneo, Irene. *Salvatore Rose.* Milano, Alpes, 1929.

10899. Limentani, Uberto. *Bibliografia della vita e delle opere di Salvator Rosa.* Firenzi, Sansoni, 1955.

10900. Mahoney, Michael. *The drawings of Salvator Rosa.* 2 v. New York/London, Garland, 1977. (CR).

10901. Morgan, Sydney. *The life and times of Salvator Rosa.* 2 v. London, Colburn, 1824.

10902. Ozzola, Leandro. *Vita e opere di Salvator Rosa, pittore, poeta, incisore.* Strassburg, Heitz, 1908. (Zur Kunstgeschichte des Auslandes, 60).

10903. Rotili, Mario. *Salvator Rosa.* Napoli, Società Editrice Napoletana, 1974. (CR).

10904. Roworth, Wendy W. *Pictor Succensor: a study of Salvator Rosa as satirist, cynic, and painter.* New York/London, Garland, 1978.

10905. Salerno, Luigi. *L'opera completa di Salvator Rosa.* Milano, Rizzoli, 1975. (CR). (Classici dell'arte, 82).

10906. ———. *Salvator Rosa.* Firenze, Barbèra, 1963. (Collana d'arte, 5).

10907. Wallace, Richard W. *The etchings of Salvator Rosa.* Princeton, N.J., Princeton University Press, 1979. (CR).

Rossellino, Antonio, 1427–1479
Bernardo, 1409–1464

10908. Gottschalk, Heinz. *Antonio Rossellino.* Liegnitz, Burmeister, 1930.

10909. Planiscig, Leo. *Bernardo und Antonio Rossellino.* Wien, Schroll, 1942.

10910. Schulz, Anne M. *The sculpture of Bernardo Rossellino and his workshop.* Princeton, N.J., Princeton University Press, 1977.

10911. Tyszkiewiczowa, Maryla. *Bernardo Rossellino.* Florencja, 1928.

Rossetti, Biagio, 1447–1516

10912. Marcianó, Ada Francesca. *L'eta di Biagio Rossetti: rinascimenti di casa d'Este.* Ferrara, G. Corbo, 1991.

10913. Zevi, Bruno. *Saper vedere l'urbanistica: Ferrara di Biagio Rossetti, la prima città moderna europea.* Torino, Einaudi, 1971.

Rossetti, Dante Gabriel, 1828–1882

10914. Beerbohm, Max, Sir. *Rossetti and his circle.* A new ed. with an introduction by N. John Hall. New Haven, Yale University Press, 1987.

10915. Caine, Hall, Sir. *Recollections of Rossetti.* With an introduction by Jan Marsh. London, Century, 1990.

10916. Cary, Elisabeth L. *The Rossettis: Dante Gabriel and Christina.* New York, Putnam, 1900.

10917. Dobbs, Brian and Dobbs, Judy. *Dante Gabriel Rossetti: an alien Victorian.* London, Macdonald and Jane, 1977.

10918. Doughty, Oswald. *A Victorian romantic: Dante Gabriel Rossetti.* London, Muller, 1949.

10919. Dunn, Henry Treffry. *Recollections of Dante Gabriel Rossetti & his circle, or, Cheyne Walk life.* Ed. by Rosalie Mander. Westerham, Dalrymple Press, 1984.

10920. Faxon, Alicia Craig. *Dante Gabriel Rossetti.* New York, Abbeville Press, 1989.

10921. Fleming, Gordon H. *Rossetti and the Pre-Raphaelite Brotherhood.* London, Hart-Davis, 1967.

10922. Grieve, Alastair I. *The art of Dante Gabriel Rossetti.* 3 v. Hingham/Norwich, Real World, 1973.

10923. Henderson, Marina. *D. G. Rossetti.* Introd. by Susan Miller. London, Academy/New York, St. Martin's, 1973.

10924. Hueffer, Ford M. *Rossetti, a critical essay on his art.* London, Duckworth, 1902.

10925. Knight, Joseph. *The life of Dante Gabriel Rossetti.* Bibliography and catalogue of pictures by John P. Anderson. London, Scott, 1887.

10926. Langlade, Jacques de. *Dante Gabriel Rossetti.* Paris, Mazarine, 1985.

10927. Marillier, Henry C. *Dante Gabriel Rossetti.* London, Bell, 1899.

10928. Mourey, Gabriel. *D. G. Rossetti et les Préraphaélites anglais, biographies critiques.* Paris, Renouard, [1909].

10929. Nicoll, John. *Dante Gabriel Rossetti.* London, Studio Vista, 1975.

10930. Riede, David G. *Dante Gabriel Rossetti revisited.* New York, Twayne Publishers, 1992.

10931. Rossetti, Dante G. *Letters.* Ed. by Oswald Doughty and John R. Wall. 4 v. Oxford, Clarendon Press, 1965.

10932. Rossetti, William M. *Dante Gabriel Rossetti as designer and writer.* London, Cassell, 1889.

10933. Schulte, Edvige. *Dante Gabriel Rossetti: vita, arte, poesia.* Napoli, Liguori Editore, 1986.

10934. Sharp, William. *Dante Gabriel Rossetti, a record and a study.* London, Macmillan, 1882.

10935. Surtees, Virginia. *The paintings and drawings of Dante Gabriel Rossetti (1828–1882); a catalogue raisonné.* 2 v. Oxford, Clarendon Press, 1971. (CR).

10936. ———. *Rossetti's portraits of Elizabeth Siddal: a catalogue of the drawings and watercolours.* Aldershot, Scolar Press, in association with Ashmolean Museum, Oxford, 1991.

10937. Waugh, Evelyn. *Rossetti, his life and works.* London, Duckworth, 1928.

10938. Wood, Esther. *Dante Rossetti and the Pre-Raphaelite movement.* New York, Scribner, 1894.

Rossi, Domenico Egidio, fl. 1697–1707

10939. Passavant, Günther. *Studien über Domenico Egidio Rossi und seine baukünstlerische Tätigkeit innerhalb des süddeutschen und österreichischen Barock.* Karlsruhe, Braun, 1967.

Rossi, Giovanni Antonio, 1616–1695

10940. Spagnesi, Gianfranco. *Giovanni Antonio de Rossi, architetto romano.* Roma, Officina Edizioni, 1964.

Rossi, Karl Ivanovich, 1775–1849

10941. Piliavskii, V. I. *Zodchii Rossi.* Moskva, Gosudarstvennyi izd-vo Arkhitekturii i Gradostroitel'stva, 1951.

10942. Taranovskaia, Marianna Z. *Karl Rossi.* Leningrad, Lenizdat, 1978.

10943. ———. *Karl Rossi—arkhitektor, gradostroitel, khudozhnik.* Leningrad, Stroiizdat, Leningradskoe otd-nie, 1980.

10944. Veinert, N. *Rossi.* Moskva, Iskusstvo, 1939.

Rosso Fiorentino, 1494–1540

10945. Barocchi, Paola. *Il Rosso Fiorentino.* Roma, Gismondi, [1950].

10946. Borea, Evelina. *Rosso Fiorentino.* Milano, Fabbri, 1965. (I maestri del colore, 106).

10947. Carroll, Eugene A. *The drawings of Rosso Fiorentino.* 2 v. New York/London, Garland, 1976. (CR).

10948. ———. *Rosso Fiorentino: drawings, prints, and decorative arts.* Washington, National Gallery of Art, 1987.

10949. Ciardi, Roberto Paolo. *Rosso Fiorentino: catalogo completo del dipinti.* Firenze, Cantini, 1991.

10950. Franklin, David. *Rosso in Italy: the Italian career of Rosso Fiorentino.* New Haven, Yale University Press, 1994.

10951. Kusenberg, Kurt. *Le Rosso.* Paris, Michel, 1931.

10952. Rosso Fiorentino. *Il Rosso e volterra.* Firenze, Giunta regionale toscana; Venezia, Marsillo, 1994.

Rosso, Giovanni Battista *see* **Rosso Fiorentino**

Rosso, Medardo, 1858–1928

10953. Barr, Margaret S. *Medardo Rosso.* New York, Museum of Modern Art, 1963; distributed by Doubleday, Garden City, N.Y.

10954. Borghi, Mino. *Medardo Rosso.* Milano, Edizioni del Milione, 1950. (Monografie di artisti italiani contemporanei, 4).

10955. Fagioli, Marco. *Medardo Rosso, disegni e sculture.* [Catalogue of an exhibition]. San Miniato al Tedesco, Palazzo Migliorati, Piazza XX Settembre, 6–27 novembre, 1933. Firenze, Opus Libri, 1993.

10956. Fles, Etha. *Medardo Rosso, der Mensch und der Künstler.* Freiburg i.Br., Heinrich, 1922.

10957. Rosso, Medardo. *Medardo Rosso, impressions in wax and bronze, 1882–1906.* Essay by Luciano Caramel. New York, Kent Fine Art, 1988.

10958. Soffici, Ardengo. *Medardo Rosso (1858– 1928)*. Firenze, Vallecchi, 1929.

Rot, Diter, 1930–

10959. Roth, Dieter. *Dieter Roth, Zeichnungen*: Hamburger Kunsthalle, 5.12.1987 bis 17.1.1988; Graphische Sammlung Staats- galerie Stuttgart, 6.2. bis 20.3.1988; Kunst- museum Solothurn, 9.4. bis 29.5.1988. [Texte, Werner Hofmann . . . [et al.]. Kata- log, Hanna Hohl, André Kamber]. [Ham- burg?, Hamburger Kunsthalle?, 1987].

10960. Rot, Diter. *Frühe Schriften und typische Scheisse*. Ausgewählt und mit einem Haufen Teilverdautes von O. Wiener. Darmstadt, Luchterhand, 1973. (Sammlung Luchter- hand, 125).

10961. Rot, Diter. *Gesammelte Werke*. [Work in progress]. Köln, Hansjörg, 1969– ; distrib- uted by Wittenborn, New York. (CR). [Later imprints vary].

Roth, Dieter *see* Rot, Diter

Rothenstein, Michael, 1908–

10962. Sidey, Tessa. *The prints of Michael Roth- enstein*. Aldershot, Hants., England, Scolar Press; Brookfield, Vt., Ashgate Pub. Co., 1993.

Rothko, Mark, 1903–1970

10963. Ashton, Dore. *About Rothko*. New York, Oxford University Press, 1983.

10964. Barnes, Susan J. *The Rothko Chapel: an act of faith*. Houston, Rothko Chapel; Austin, distributed by University of Texas Press, 1989.

10965. Breslin, James E. B. *Mark Rothko: a biogra- phy*. Chicago, University of Chicago Press, 1993.

10966. Museum Boymans-van Beuningen (Rot- terdam). *Mark Rothko*. 20 november 1971– 2 januari 1972. [Rotterdam, Museum Boy- mans-van Beuningen, 1971].

10967. Rothko, Mark. *Mark Rothko's Harvard murals*. Ed. by Marjorie B. Cohn. Cam- bridge, Mass., Center for Conservation and Technical Studies, Harvard University Art Museums, 1988.

10968. Seldes, Lee. *The legacy of Mark Rothko*. New York, Holt, Rinehart and Winston, 1978.

10969. Waldman, Diane. *Mark Rothko, 1903– 1970; a retrospective*. [Published in conjunc- tion with an exhibition at the Solomon R. Guggenheim Museum, New York]. New York, Abrams, 1978.

Rottluff, Karl Schmidt *see* Schmidt- Rottluff, Karl

Rouault, Georges, 1871–1958

10970. Bellini, Paolo. *Georges Rouault, uomo e artista*. Milano, Salamon e Agustoni, 1972.

10971. Chapon, François. *Rouault: oeuvre gravé*. Catalogue établi par Isabelle Rouault avec la collaboration d'Olivier Nouaille Rouault. 2 v. Monte Carlo, Sauret, 1978/1979. (CR).

10972. Charensol, Georges. *Georges Rouault, l'homme et l'oeuvre*. Paris, Editions des Quatre Chemins, 1926.

10973. Courthion, Pierre. *Georges Rouault*. Includ- ing a catalogue of works prepared with the collaboration of Isabelle Rouault. New York, Abrams, 1962. (CR).

10974. Dorival, Bernard. *Roualt, l'oeúvre peint*. Catalogue établi par Isabelle Rouault. Monte- Carlo, Editions André Sauret, 1988. (CR).

10975. Getlein, Frank and Getlein, Dorothy. *Georges Rouault's Misèrere*. Milwaukee, Bruce, 1964.

10976. Josef-Haubrich-Kunsthalle (Cologne). *Geor- ges Rouault*. 11. März bis 8. Mai 1983. Köln, Josef-Haubrich-Kunsthalle, 1983.

10977. Koja, Stephan. *Georges Rouault: Malerei und Graphik*. München, Prestel, 1993.

10978. Musée National d'Art Moderne (Paris). *Georges Rouault; exposition du centenaire*. 27 mai–27 septembre 1971. Paris, Ministère des Affaires Culturelles, Réunion des Musées Nationaux, 1971.

10979. Rouault, Georges. *Rouault: première péri- ode, 1903–1920*. [Catalogue, sous la direc- tion de Fabrice Hergott]. Paris, Musée na- tional d'art moderne, Centre Georges Pompidou, 1992.

10980. Rouault, Georges [and] Suarès, André. *Cor- respondance*. Introd. par Marcel Arland. Paris, Gallimard, 1960.

10981. Roulet, Claude. *Rouault: souvenirs*. Neuch- âtel, Messeiller, 1961.

10982. Soby, James T. *Georges Rouault, paintings and prints*. New York, Museum of Modern Art, 1947.

10983. Venturi, Lionello. *Rouault, biographical and critical study*. Trans. by James Emmons. Paris, Skira, 1959; distributed by World, Cleveland. (The Taste of Our Time, 26).

10984. Wofsy, Alan. *Georges Rouault, the graphic work*. London, Secker & Warburg, 1976. (CR).

Roubiliac, Louis François, 1695–1762

10985. Esdaile, Katherine A. *The life and works of Louis François Roubiliac*. London, Oxford University Press, 1928.

Roubillac, Louis Francois *see* Roubiliac, Louis Francois

Rousseau, Henri Julien Felix, 1844–1910

10986. Alley, Ronald. *Portrait of a primitive: the art*

of Henri Rousseau. Oxford, Phaidon, 1978.

10987. Artieri, Giovanni [and] Vallier, Dora. *L'opera completa di Rousseau il doganiere.* Milano, Rizzoli, 1969. (CR). (Classici dell'arte, 29).

10988. Bouret, Jean. *Henri Rousseau.* Trans. by Martin Leake. Greenwich, Conn., New York Graphic Society, 1961.

10989. Certigny, Henry. *La vérité sur le douanier Rousseau.* Paris, Plon, 1961. (Supplements: Paris, Plon, 1966; Lausanne, Bibliothèque des Arts, 1971).

10990. ————. *Le Douanier Rousseau en son temps: biographie et catalogue raisonné.* Tókyó, Bunkazai Kenkyujyo Co., 1984. (CR).

10991. Courthion, Pierre. *Henri Rousseau, le douanier.* Genève, Skira, 1944.

10992. Grey, Roch. *Henri Rousseau.* Rome, Valori Plastici, 1922. (New ed., with a preface by André Salmon: Paris, Tel, 1943).

10993. Keay, Carolyn. *Henri Rousseau, le douanier.* New York, Rizzoli, 1976.

10994. Kolle, Helmud. *Henri Rousseau.* Leipzig, Klinkhardt & Biermann, 1922. (Junge Kunst, 27).

10995. Le Pichon, Yann. *Le monde du douanier Rousseau.* Paris, Laffont, 1981.

10996. Perruchot, Henri. *Le douanier Rousseau.* Paris, Editions Universitaires, 1957. (Témoins du XXe siècle, 9).

10997. Rich, Daniel C. *Henri Rousseau.* New York, Museum of Modern Art, 1942.

10998. Rousseau, Henri. *Dichtung und Zeugnis.* Mit Photos und Erinnerungen. Herausgegeben von Peter Schifferli. Übertragung von Sonja Bütler. Zürich, Verlag der Arche, 1958.

10999. Salmon, André. *Henri Rousseau.* Paris, Somogy, 1962.

11000. ————. *Henri Rousseau dit le douanier.* Paris, Crès, 1927.

11001. Soupault, Philippe. *Henri Rousseau, le douanier.* Paris, Editions des Quatre Chemins, 1927.

11002. Uhde, Wilhelm. *Henri Rousseau.* Paris, Figuière, 1911.

11003. Vallier, Dora. *Henri Rousseau.* Paris, Flammarion, 1979. (English ed.: New York, Crown, 1979).

11004. Zervos, Christian. *Rousseau.* Paris, Cahiers d'Art, 1927.

Rousseau, Pierre Etienne Théodore, 1812–1867 *see also* Millet, Jean Francois

11005. Dorbec, Prosper. *Théodore Rousseau, biographie critique.* Paris, Laurens, 1910.

11006. Musée du Louvre, Galerie Mollien (Paris). *Théodore Rousseau, 1812–1867.* 29 novembre 1967–12 février 1968. Paris, Ministère d'Etat Affaires Culturelles, Réunion des Musées Nationaux, 1967.

11007. Sensier, Alfred. *Souvenirs sur Théodore Rousseau.* Paris, Techener/Durand-Ruel, 1872.

Roussel, Ker Xavier, 1867–1944

11008. Alain [pseud., Emile Chartier]. *Introduction à l'oeuvre gravé de K. X. Roussel.* Suivie d'un essai de catalogue par Jacques Salomon. Paris, Mercure de France, 1968. (CR).

11009. Cousturier, Lucie. *K. X. Roussel.* Paris, Bernheim-Jeune, 1927.

11010. Götte, Gisela. *Ker-Xavier Roussel, 1867–1944: Untersuchungen zu seiner Entwicklung, vor allem zum Verhältnis Frühwerk-Spätwerk.* Vorgelegt von Gisela Götte. 2 v. Bremen, [s.n.], 1982.

11011. Haus der Kunst (Munich). *Edouard Vuillard, Xavier Roussel.* 16. März–12. Mai 1968. München, Haus der Kunst, 1968.

11012. Kunsthalle Bremen. *Ker-Xavier Roussel, 1867–1944: Gemälde, Handzeichnungen, Druckgraphik.* 26. September bis 21. November 1965. Bremen, Kunsthalle Bremen, 1965.

Roussy, Anne Louis Girodet de *see* Girodet-Trioson, Anne Louis

Rowlandson, Thomas, 1756–1827

11013. Art Gallery of Ontario (Toronto). *Our old friend Rolly: watercolours, prints, and book illustrations by Thomas Rowlandson in the collection of the Art Gallery of Ontario.* Ed. by Brenda D. Rix. Organized and circulated by the Art Gallery of Ontario. Toronto, Canada, Art Gallery of Ontario, 1987.

11014. Baskett, John and Snelgrove, Dudley. *The drawings of Thomas Rowlandson in the Paul Mellon Collection.* London, Barrie & Jenkins, 1977. (CR).

11015. Falk, Bernard. *Thomas Rowlandson; his life and art.* London, Hutchinson, 1949.

11016. Grego, Joseph. *Rowlandson the caricaturist; a selection from his works, with anecdotal descriptions and a sketch of his life.* 2 v. London, Chatto and Windus, 1880.

11017. Hayes, John. *The art of Thomas Rowlandson.* Alexandria, Va., Art Services International, 1990.

11018. ————. *Rowlandson, watercolours and drawings.* London, Phaidon, 1972.

11019. Oppé, Adolf P. *Thomas Rowlandson, his drawings and watercolours.* Edited by Geoffrey Holme. London, The Studio, 1923.

11020. Paulson, Ronald. *Rowlandson, a new interpretation.* London, Studio Vista/New York, Oxford University Press, 1972.

11021. Southey, Robert. *Mr. Rowlandson's England.* Ed. by John Steel. Woodbridge, Suffolk, Antique Collectors' Club, 1985.

11022. Wark, Robert R. *Drawings by Thomas Rowlandson in the Huntington Collection.* San Marino, Calif., Huntington Library, 1975. (CR).

11023. Wolf, Edward C. *Rowlandson and his illustrations of eighteenth century English literature.* Copenhagen, Munksgaard, 1945.

Royer, Louis, 1793–1868

11024. Royer, Louis. *Louis Royer, 1793–1868: Een Vlaamse beeldhouwer in Amsterdam.* Ed. by Guus van den Hout, Eugène Langendijk. Amsterdam, Van Soeren, 1994.

Rubens, Peter Paul, 1577–1640

11025. Adler, Wolfgang. *Landscapes.* London, H. Miller/Oxford and New York, Oxford University Press, 1982. (CR). (Corpus Rubenianum Ludwig Burchard, 18/1).

11026. Albertina (Vienna). *Die Rubenszeichnungen der Albertina.* Zum 400. Geburtstag, 30. März bis 12. Juni 1977. Wien, Jugend und Volk, 1977.

11027. Alpers, Svetlana L. *The decoration of the Torre de la Parada.* London/New York, Phaidon, 1971. (CR). (Corpus Rubenianum Ludwig Burchard, 9).

11028. ———. *The making of Rubens.* New Haven, Yale University Press, 1995.

11029. Arents, Prosper. *Geschriften van en over Rubens.* Antwerpen, De Sikkel, 1940.

11030. ———. *Rubens-bibliografie: geschriften van en aan Rubens.* Brussel, De Lage Landen, 1943.

11031. Avermaete, Roger. *Rubens et son temps.* Bruxelles, Arcade, 1977.

11032. Balis, Arnout. *Rubens hunting scenes.* Trans. by P.S. Falla. London, H. Miller/Oxford; New York, Oxford University Press, 1986. (CR). (Corpus Rubenianum Ludwig Burchard, 18/2).

11033. Baudouin, Frans. *Pietro Pauolo Rubens.* Anvers, Fonds Mercator, 1977.

11034. Belkin, Kristin L. *The costume book.* Brussels, Arcade, 1980. (CR). (Corpus Rubenianum Ludwig Burchard, 24).

11035. Bell Gallery, List Art Building, Brown University (Providence, R.I.). *Rubenism.* January 30–February 23, 1975. Providence, R.I., Department of Art, Brown University, 1975.

11036. Bernhard, Marianne. *Rubens Handzeichnungen.* München, Südwest Berlag, 1977.

11037. Billeter, Felix. *Zur künstlerischen Auseinandersetzung innerhalb des Rubenskreises: eine Untersuchung am Beispiel früher Historienbilder Jakob Jordaens und Anthonis van Dycks.* Frankfurt am Main/New York, P. Lang, 1993. (Ars faciendi, 4).

11038. Bodart, Didier. *Rubens, Pietro Paolo Rubens.* Catalogo a cura di Didier Bodart. Testi di Didier Bodart . . . [et al.]. Roma, De Luca edizioni d'arte, 1990.

11039. Boussard, Joseph F. *Les leçons de P. P. Rubens; ou, fragments épistolaires sur la religion, la peinture, et la politique.* Bruxelles, Lejeune, 1838.

11040. Burchard, Ludwig and Hulst, Roger A. d'. *Rubens drawings.* 2 v. Brussels, Arcade, 1963. (CR).

11041. Burckhardt, Jakob. *Erinnerungen aus Rubens.* Basel, Lendorff, 1898. (English ed., trans. by Mary Hottinger, R. H. Boothroyd and I. Graefe: New York, Phaidon, 1950; distributed by Oxford University Press).

11042. Cammaerts, Emile. *Rubens, painter and diplomat.* London, Faber, 1932.

11043. Chapin Library, Stetson Hall, Williams College (Williamstown, Mass.). *Rubens and the book: title pages by Peter Paul Rubens.* May 2–31, 1977. Williamstown, Mass., Williams College, 1977.
Corpus Rubenianum Ludwig Burchard: see under names of the authors of the individual volumes.

11044. Dillon, Edward. *Rubens.* London, Methuen, 1909.

11045. Druwé, Robert. *Peter Pauwel Rubens of Adam van Noort: een inleiding tot het Rubensprobleem.* Tielt, Lannoo, [1951].

11046. Evers, Hans G. *Peter Paul Rubens.* München, Bruckmann, 1942.

11047. Freedberg, David. *Rubens: the Life of Christ after the Passion.* New York, Oxford University Press, 1983. (Corpus Rubenianum Ludwig Burchard, 7).

11048. Geffroy, Gustave. *Rubens, biographie critique.* Paris, Laurens, [1904].

11049. Génard, Pierre. *P. P. Rubens; aanteekeningen over den grooten meester en zijne bloedverwanten.* Antwerpen, Kockx, 1877.

11050. Gerrits, Gerrit E. *Petrus Paulus Rubens, zijn tijd en zijne tijdgenooten.* Amsterdam, Portielje, 1842.

11051. Glück, Gustave. *Rubens, Van Dyck und ihr Kreis.* Wien, Schroll, 1933.

11052. Goeler von Ravensburg, Friedrich. *Rubens und die Antike.* Jena, Costenoble, 1882.

11053. Goris, Jan A. and Held, Julius. *Rubens in America.* New York, Pantheon, 1947.

11054. Hairs, Marie-Louise. *Dans le sillage de Rubens: les peintres d'histoire anversois au XVIIᵉ siècle.* Liège, Université de Liège, 1977. (Bibliothèque de la Faculté de Philosophie et Lettres de l'Université de Liège; Publications exceptionnelles, 4).

11055. Hasselt, André van. *Histoire de P. P. Rubens, suivie du catalogue général et raisonné de ses tableaux, esquisses, dessins et vignettes.* Bruxelles, Société des Beaux-Arts, 1840. (CR).

11056. Haverkamp Begemann, Egbert. *The Achilles series.* London, Phaidon, 1975. (CR). (Corpus Rubenianum Ludwig Burchard, 10).

11057. Held, Julius. *The oil sketches of Peter Paul Rubens*. 2 v. Princeton, N.J., Princeton University Press for the National Gallery of Art, 1980.

11058. ———. *Rubens and his circle; studies*. Princeton, N.J., Princeton University Press, 1982.

11059. ———. *Rubens, selected drawings*. 2 v. London, Phaidon, 1959.

11060. Hetzer, Theodor. *Rubens and Rembrandt*. Mittenwald, Maander; Stuttgart, Urachhaus, 1984. (Schriften Theodor Hetzers, 5).

11061. Hourticq, Louis. *Rubens*. Paris, Librairie de l'Art Ancien et Moderne, 1905.

11062. Hubala, Erich, ed. *Rubens; kunstgeschichtliche Beiträge*. Konstanz, Leonhardt, 1979.

11063. Huemer, Francis. *Portraits*. Brussels, Arcade, 1977; distributed by Phaidon, New York. (CR). (Corpus Rubenianum Ludwig Burchard, 19).

11064. Hulst, Roger Adolf d' and Vandenven, M. *Rubens: the Old Testament*. Trans. by P.S. Falla. London, H. Miller; New York, Oxford University Press, 1989. (CR). (Corpus Rubenianum Ludwig Burchard, 3).

11065. Hymans, Henri S. *Histoire de la gravure dans l'école de Rubens*. Bruxelles, Olivier, 1879.

11066. Jaffe, Michael. *Rubens and Italy*. Ithaca, N.Y., Cornell University Press, 1977.

11067. ———. *Rubens: catalogo completo*. Traduzione di Germano Mulazzani. Milano, Rizzoli, 1989. (CR).

11068. Jamot, Paul. *Rubens*. Paris, Floury, 1936.

11069. Judson, Jay R. and Van de Velde, Carl. *Book illustrations and title-pages*. 2 v. London, Miller/Philadelphia, Heyden, 1978. (CR). (Corpus Rubenianum Ludwig Burchard, 21).

11070. Knackfuss, Hermann. *Rubens*. Trans. by Louise M. Richter. Bielefeld/Leipzig, Velhagen & Klasing/New York, Lemcke & Buechner, 1904. (Monographs on Artists, 9).

11071. Kunsthalle Köln. *Peter Paul Rubens, 1577–1640*. 2 v. 15. Oktober bis 15. Dezember 1977. Köln, Museen der Stadt Köln, 1977.

11072. Kunstsammlung der Universität Göttingen. *Rubens in der Grafik*. 13. Mai–19. Juni 1977. Göttingen, Kunstgeschichtliches Seminar Göttingen, 1977.

11073. Larsen, Erik. *P. P. Rubens*. With a complete catalogue of his works in America. Antwerp, De Sikkel, 1952.

11074. Lehmann, Friedrich R. *Rubens und seine Welt, ein Zeitgemälde des Barock*. Stuttgart, Günther, 1954.

11075. Lescourret, Marie-Anne. *Rubens: a double life*. Chicago, I.R. Dee, 1993.

11076. Liess, Reinhard. *Die Kunst des Rubens*. Braunschweig, Waisenhaus, 1977.

11077. Logan, Anne-Marie S. *Flemish drawings in the age of Rubens: selected works from American collections*. Wellesley, Mass., Davis Museum and Cultural Center; Seattle, distributed by University of Washington Press, 1993.

11078. Martin, John R. *The ceiling paintings for the Jesuit church in Antwerp*. London/New York, Phaidon, 1968. (CR). (Corpus Rubenianum Ludwig Burchard, 1).

11079. ———. *The decorations for the Pompa introitus Ferdinandi*. London/New York, Phaidon, 1972. (CR). (Corpus Rubenianum Ludwig Burchard, 16).

11080. ———, ed. *Rubens before 1620*. Princeton, N.J., Art Museum, Princeton University, 1972; distributed by Princeton University Press.

11081. Meulen, Marjon van der. *Petrus Paulus Rubens antiquarius: collector and copyist of antique gems*. Alphen aan den Rijn, Canaletto, 1975.

11082. Michel, Emile. *Rubens: his life, his work, and his time*. Trans. by Elizabeth Lee. 2 v. London, Heinemann/New York, Scribner, 1899.

11083. Michel, J. F. M. *Histoire de la vie de P. P. Rubens, chevalier, & seigneur de Steen*. Bruxelles, De Bel, 1771.

11084. Michiels, Alfred. *Rubens et l'école d'Anvers*. Paris, Delahays, 1854.

11085. Muray, Philippe. *La gloire de Rubens*. Paris, B. Grasset, 1991.

11086. Musée du Louvre (Paris). *Rubens: ses maîtres, ses élèves; dessins du Musée du Louvre*. 10 février–15 mai 1978. Paris, Ministère de la Culture et de l'Environment/Editions de la Réunion des Musées Nationaux, 1978.

11087. Musées Royaux des Beaux-Arts de Belgique (Brussels). *Le siècle de Rubens*. 15 octobre–12 décembre 1965. Bruxelles, Musées Royaux des Beaux-Arts de Belgique, 1965.

11088. Oldenbourg, Rudolf. *P. P. Rubens: des Meisters Gemälde*. Stuttgart, Deutsche Verlags-Anstalt, 1921. 4 ed.

11089. Palazzo Ducale (Genoa). *Rubens e Genova*. 18 dicembre 1977–12 febbraio 1978. Genova, Palazzo Ducale, 1977.

11090. Palazzo Pitti (Florence). *Rubens e la pittura fiamminga del Seicento nelle collezioni pubbliche fiorentine*. [July 22–October 9, 1977; text in Italian and French]. Firenze, Centro Di, 1977.

11091. Pohlen, Ingeborg. *Untersuchungen zur Reproduktionsgraphik der Rubenswerkstatt*. München, R.A. Klein, 1985. (Beiträge zur Kunstwissenschaft, 6).

11092. Poorter, Nora de. *The Eucharist series*. 2 v. London, Miller/Philadelphia, Heyden, 1978. (CR). (Corpus Rubenianum Ludwig Burchard, 2).

11093. Puyvelde, Leo van. *Les esquisses de Rubens*.

Bâle, Holbein, 1940.

11094. ———. *Rubens.* Bruxelles, Meddens, 1964. 2 ed. (Les peintres flamands du XVIIe siècle, 2).

11095. Rooses, Max. *L'oeuvre de P. P. Rubens, histoire et description de ses tableaux et dessins.* 5 v. Anvers, Maes, 1886–1892. (CR).

11096. ———. *Rubens.* Trans. by Harold Child. 2 v. London, Duckworth, 1904.

11097. Rosenberg, Adolf. *P. P. Rubens, des Meisters Gemälde.* Stuttgart/Leipzig, Deutsche Verlags-Anstalt, 1905. (Klassiker der Kunst, 5).

11098. Rowlands, John. *Rubens, drawings and sketches: catalogue of an exhibition at the Department of Prints and Drawings in the British Museum, 1977.* London, Trustees of the British Museum, 1977.

11099. Roy, Jean-Joseph van. *Vie de Pierre-Paul Rubens.* Bruxelles, de Mat, 1840.

11100. Royal Museum of Fine Arts (Antwerp). *P. P. Rubens; paintings, oil-sketches, drawings.* 29th June–30th September 1977. Antwerp, Royal Museum of Fine Arts, 1977.

11101. Rubens, Peter P. *Correspondance et documents épistolaires concernant sa vie et ses oeuvres.* [Vol. 1: ed. by Charles Ruelens. Anvers, de Backer, 1887; Vol. 2–3: ed. by Max Rooses and Charles Ruelens. Anvers, Maes, 1898– 1900; Vols. 4–6: ed. by Max Rooses and Charles Ruelens. Anvers, Buschmann, 1904–1909]. (Codex Diplomaticus Rubenianus, 1–6; reprint: Soest (Holland), Davaco, 1973).

11102. ———. *Lettere italiane.* A cura di Irene Cotta. Con il "Profilo di un intellettuale europeo" di Claudio Mutini. Roma, Istituto della Enciclopedia italiana, [1987].

11103. ———. *Letters.* Trans. and ed. by Ruth Saunders Magurn.. Cambridge, Mass., Harvard University Press, 1955. 2 ed. 1971. (Reprint: Evanston, Ill. Northwestern University Press, 1991).

11104. Sainsbury, William N., ed. *Original unpublished papers illustrative of the life of Sir Peter Paul Rubens as an artist and a diplomat.* London, Bradbury & Evans, 1859.

11105. Sauerländer, Willibald, et al. *Peter Paul Rubens: Werk und Nachruhm.* Herausgegeben vom Zentralinstitut für Kunstgeschichte und von den Bayerischen Staatsgemäldesammlungen. [München], Fink, 1981.

11106. Scribner, Charles. *Peter Paul Rubens.* New York, Abrams, 1989.

11107. Stechow, Wolfgang. *Rubens and the classical tradition.* Cambridge, Mass., Harvard University Press for Oberlin College, 1968. (Martin Classical Lectures, 22).

11108. Verachter, Frédéric. *Généalogie de Pierre Paul Rubens et de sa famille.* Anvers, Lacroix, 1840.

11109. Vergara, Lisa. *Rubens and the poetics of landscape.* New Haven/London, Yale University Press, 1982.

11110. Vlieghe, Hans. *Saints.* Trans. by P. S. Falla. London/New York, Phaidon, 1973. (CR). (Corpus Rubenianum Ludwig Burchard, 8).

11111. Waagen, Gustav F. *Peter Paul Rubens, his life and genius.* Trans. by Robert R. Noel. London, Saunders and Otley, 1840.

11112. White, Christopher. *Peter Paul Rubens, man and artist.* New Haven, Yale University Press, 1987.

11113. White, Christopher. *Rubens and his world.* New York, Viking, 1968.

Rublev, Andrei, 1360/70–1427/30

11114. Alpatov, Mikhail V. *Andrei Rublev i ego epokha; sbornik statei.* Moskva, Iskusstvo, 1971.

11115. ———. *Andrei Rublev, okolo 1370–1430.* Moskva, Izobrazitel'noe Iskusstvo, 1972.

11116. Demina, Natal'ia A. *Andrei Rublev i khudozhniki ego kruga.* Moskva, Nauka, 1972.

11117. Lazarev, Viktor N. *Andrej Rublev.* [Trans. from the Russian by Ettore Lo Gatto]. Milano, Club del Libro, 1966. (Collana d'arte del Club del Libro, 13).

11118. Lebedewa, Julia A. *Andrei Rubljow und seine Zeitgenossen.* [Trans. from the Russian by Gerhard Hallmann]. Dresden, Verlag der Kunst, 1962.

11119. Mainka, Rudolf M. *Andrej Rublev's Dreifaltigkeitsikone: Geschichte, Kunst, und Sinngehalt des Bildes.* Ettal, Buch-Kunstverlag Ettal, 1964.

11120. Plugin, Vladimir. *Andrei Rublev.* Compiled and introduced by V. Pugin. Trans. from the Russian by Thomas Crane and Margarita Latsinova. Leningrad, Aurora Art Publishers, 1987.

11121. Pribytkov, Vladimir S. *Andrei Rublev.* Moskva, Molodaia Gvardiia, 1960.

11122. Sergeev, Valerii Nilolaevich. *Rublev.* Moskva, Molodaia Gvardiia, 1990.

Rude, François, 1784–1855

11123. Bertrand, Alexis. *François Rude.* Paris, Librairie de l'Art, [1888].

11124. Calmette, Joseph. *François Rude.* Paris, Floury, 1920.

11125. Fourcaud, Louis de. *François Rude, sculpteur; ses oeuvres et son temps, 1784–1855.* Paris, Librairie de l'Art Ancien et Moderne, 1904.

Ruisdael, Jacob Isaacszoon van, 1628–1682

11126. Levey, Michael. *Ruisdael: Jacob van Ruisdael and other painters of his family.* London, National Gallery, 1977. (Themes and Painters in the National Gallery, Series 2, No. 7).

11127. Michel, Emile. *Jacob van Ruysdael et les paysagistes de l'école de Harlem*. Paris, Librairie de l'Art, 1890.

11128. Riat, Georges. *Ruysdael, biographie critique*. Paris, Laurens, [1905].

11129. Rosenberg, Jakob. *Jacob van Ruisdael*. Berlin, Cassirer, 1928.

11130. Schmidt, Winfried. *Studien zur Landschaftskunst Jacob van Ruisdaels: Frühwerke und Wanderjahre*. Hildesheim/New York, Olms, 1981. (Studien zur Kunstgeschichte, 15).

11131. Slive, Seymour and Hoetink, H. R. *Jacob van Ruisdael*. [Published in conjunction with an exhibition at the Fogg Art Museum, Harvard University, Cambridge, Mass., 18 January–11 April 1982]. New York, Abbeville Press, 1981.

11132. Walford, E. John. *Jacob van Ruisdael and the perception of landscape*. New Haven, Yale University Press, 1991.

Ruisdael, Salomon van *see* Ruysdael, Salomon van

Runge, Philipp Otto, 1777–1810

11133. Aubert, Andreas. *Runge und die Romantik*. Berlin, Cassirer, 1909.

11134. Berefelt, Gunnar. *Philipp Otto Runge: zwischen Aufbruch und Opposition, 1777–1802*. Stockholm, Almqvist & Wiksell, 1961. (Stockholm Studies in History of Art, 7).

11135. Betthausen, Peter. *Philipp Otto Runge*. Leipzig, Seemann, 1980.

11136. Bisanz, Rudolf M. *German romanticism and Philipp Otto Runge; a study in nineteenth century art theory and iconography*. DeKalb, Ill., Northern Illinois University Press, 1970.

11137. Bohner, Theodor P. *Philipp Otto Runge, ein Malerleben der Romantik*. Berlin, Frundsberg, 1937.

11138. Böttcher, Otto. *Philipp Otto Runge: sein Leben, Wirken und Schaffen*. Hamburg, Friederichsen, de Gruyter, 1937.

11139. Grundy, John B. *Tieck and Runge; a study in the relationship of literature and art in the Romantic period, with especial reference to "Franz Sternbald."* Strassburg, Heitz, 1930. (Studien zur deutschen Kunstgeschichte, 270).

11140. Hamburger Kunsthalle. *Runge in seiner Zeit*. 21. Oktober 1977 bis 8. January 1978. München, Prestel/Hamburg, Hamburger Kunsthalle, 1977.

11141. Isermeyer, Christian A. *Philipp Otto Runge*. Berlin, Rembrandt, 1940. (Die Kunstbücher des Volkes, 32).

11142. Jensen, Jens C. *Philipp Otto Runge, Leben und Werk*. Köln, DuMont, 1977.

11143. Leinkauf, Thomas. *Kunst und Reflexion: Untersuchungen zum Verhältnis Philip Otto Runges zur philosophischen Tradition*. München, Fink, 1987.

11144. Matile, Heinz. *Die Farbenlehre Philipp Otto Runges; ein Beitrag zur Geschichte der Künstlerfarbenlehre*. München/Mittenwald, Mäander, 1979. 2 ed. (Kunstwissenschaftliche Studientexte, 5).

11145. Richter, Cornelia. *Philipp Otto Runge: Ich weiss eine schöne Blume; Werkverzeichnis der Scherenschnitte*. München, Schirmer/Mosel, 1981. (CR).

11146. Roch, Wolfgang. *Philipp Otto Runges Kunstanschauung und ihr Verhältnis zur Frühromantik*. Strassburg, Heitz, 1909. (Studien zur deutschen Kunstgeschichte, 111).

11147. Rosenblum, Robert. *The romantic child: from Runge to Sendak*. New York, Thames and Hudson, 1989.

11148. Runge, Philipp O. *Briefe und Schriften*. Herausgegeben und kommentiert von Peter Betthausen. München, Beck, 1982.

11149. ———. *Hinterlassene Schriften*. Herausgegeben von dessen ältestem Bruder. 2 v. Hamburg, Perthes, 1840–1841.

11150. Schmidt, Paul F. *Philipp Otto Runge, sein Leben und sein Werk*. Leipzig, Insel-Verlag, 1923.

11151. Traeger, Jörg. *Die Hülsenbeckschen Kinder: von der Reflexion des Naiven im Kunstwerk der Romantik*. Frankfurt am Main, Fischer Taschenbuch, 1987.

11152. ———. *Philipp Otto Runge, oder die Geburt einer neuen Kunst*. München, Prestel, 1977.

11153. ———. *Philipp Otto Runge und sein Werk; Monographie und kritischer Katalog*. München, Prestel, 1975. (CR).

Ruscha, Edward, 1937–

11154. Auckland City Art Gallery (Auckland, New Zealand). *Graphic works of Edward Ruscha*. August to October 1978. Auckland, Auckland City Art Gallery, 1978.

11155. Bois, Ive Alain. *Edward Ruscha, romance with liquids: paintings 1966–1969*. [Catalogue of an exhibition at the Gagosian Gallery; and a conversation between Walter Hopps and Edward Ruscha]. New York, Rizzoli 1993.

11156. Lannan Museum (Lake Worth, Fla.). *Edward Ruscha*. [Catalogue of an exhibition]. Lake Worth, Fla., Lannan Museum; New York, distributed by H.N. Abrams, 1988.

11157. ———. *Guacamole Airlines and other drawings*. New York, Abrams, 1980.

11158. Ruscha, Edward. *Edward Ruscha: paintings*. Catalogue of an exhibition held at the Museum Boymans-van Beunigen, Rotterdam; Serpentine Gallery, London; the Museum of Contemporary Art, Los Angeles. Catalogue edited by Elbrig de Groot. Rotterdam, Museum Boymans-Van Beunigen; Los Angeles,

Museum of Contemporary Art, 1990.

11159. ———. *Edward Ruscha: stains.* New York, Robert Miller, 1992.

11160. San Francisco Museum of Modern Art. *The works of Edward Ruscha.* March 25–May 23, 1982. Essays by Dave Hickey and Peter Plagens; introduction by Anne Livet. With a foreword by Henry T. Hopkins. New York, published by Hudson Hills Press in association with the San Francisco Museum of Modern Art; distributed by Viking, New York, 1982.

Rush, William, 1756–1833

11161. Marceau, Henri. *William Rush, 1756–1833, the first native American sculptor.* Philadelphia, Pennsylvania Museum of Art, 1937.

11162. Pennsylvania Academy of the Fine Arts (Philadelphia). *William Rush, American sculptor.* June 20–November 21, 1982. Philadelphia, Pennsylvania Academy of the Fine Arts, 1982.

Ruskin, John, 1819–1900

11163. Walton, Paul H. *The drawings of John Ruskin.* Oxford, Clarendon Press, 1972.

Russell, Charles Marion, 1864–1926

11164. Amon Carter Museum of Western Art (Fort Worth, Texas). *Inaugural exhibition: selected works of Frederic Remington and Charles Marion Russell.* Forth Worth, The Museum, 1961.

11165. Dippie, Brian W. *Remington & Russell: The Sid Richardson Collection.* Austin. University of Texas Press, 1982.

11166. ———. *Looking at Russell.* Fort Worth, Tex., Amon Carter Museum, 1987.

11167. Hassrick, Peter H. *Charles M. Russell.* New York, Harry N. Abrams in association with the National Museum of American Art, Smithsonian Institution, 1989.

11168. McCracken, Harold. *The Charles M. Russell book; the life and work of the Cowboy artist.* Garden City, Doubleday, 1957.

11169. Russell, Charles M. *Charles M. Russell: the Frederic G. Renner Collection.* [Catalogue of an exhibition] Phoenix Art Museum, Phoenix, Arizona, April 11 to June 7, 1981, C.M. Russell Museum, Great Falls, Montana, June 15 to September 10, 1981, Denver Art Museum, Denver, Colorado, October 3 to December 6, 1981. Phoenix, Phoenix Art Museum, 1981.

Russell, John, 1745–1806

11170. Williamson, George Charles. *John Russell, R.A.* With an introduction by Lord Ronald Gower. London, George Bell, 1894.

Russell, Morgan, 1886–1953

11171. Kushner, Marilyn S. *Morgan Russell.* Introduction by William C. Agee. [Catalogue of an exhibition]. New York, Hudson Hills Press in association with the Montclair Art Museum; distributed in the U.S., its territories and possessions . . . by Rizzoli International Publications, 1990.

Russolo, Luigi, 1885–1947

11172. Ca' Corner della Regina (Venice). *Russolo/ L'arte dei rumori, 1913–1931.* 15 ottobre–20 novembre 1977. Venezia, Tipografia Emiliana, 1977. (La Biennale di Venezia, Archivio storico delle arti contemporanee, 3).

11173. Maffina, G. Franco. *Luigi Russolo e l'arte dei rumori; con tutti gli scritti musicali.* Prefazione di Fred K.Prieberg. Torino, Martano, 1978.

11174. Russolo, Luigi. *L'arte dei rumori: manifesto futurista.* Milano, Poesia, 1916.

Ruysch, Rachel, 1664–1750

11175. Grant, Maurice H. *Rachel Ruysch, 1664–1750.* Leigh-on-Sea, Lewis, 1956.

Ruysdael, Salomon van, 1600–1670

11176. Stechow, Wolfgang. *Salomon van Ruysdael: eine Einführung in seine Kunst, mit kritischem Katalog der Gemälde.* Berlin, Mann, 1975. 2 ed. (CR).

Ryder, Albert Pinkham, 1847–1917

11177. Broun, Elizabeth. *Albert Pinkham Ryder.* With catalogue by Eleanor L. Jones . . . [et al.]. [Catalogue of an exhibition held at the National Museum of American Art, Washington, D.C.]. Washington, D.C., Smithsonian Institution Press, 1989.

11178. Evans, Dorinda. *Albert Pinkham Ryder's use of visual sources.* Chicago, published for the Winterthur Museum by the University of Chicago Press, 1986.

11179. Goodrich, Lloyd. *Albert P. Ryder.* New York, Braziller, 1959.

11180. Homer, William Innes and Goodrich, Lloyd. *Albert Pinkham Ryder: painter of dreams.* New York, Harry N. Abrams, 1989.

11181. Price, Frederic N. *Ryder (1847–1917); a study of appreciation.* New York, Rudge, 1932.

11182. Sherman, Frederic F. *Albert Pinkham Ryder.* New York, Sherman, 1920.

11183. Whitney Museum of American Art (New York). *Albert P. Ryder, centenary exhibition.* October 18 to November 30, 1947. [Text by Lloyd Goodrich]. New York, Whitney Museum of American Art, 1947.

S

Saarinen, Eero, 1910–1961
Eliel, 1873–1950

11184. Christ-Janer, Albert. *Eliel Saarinen: Finnish-American architect and educator.* Foreword by Alvar Aalto. Chicago, University of Chicago Press, 1979. 2 ed.

11185. Gerard John. *A quiet grandeur: the architectural drawings of Eliel Saarinen for Kingswood School Cranbrook.* Bloomfield Hills, Mich., Cranbrook Academy of Art Museum, 1984.

11186. Hausen, Marika . . . [et al.]. *Eliel Saarinen: projects, 1896–1923.* Trans. by Desmond O'Rourke, Michael Wynne-Ellis, and the English Centre. Cambridge, Mass., MIT Press, 1990.

11187. Saarinen, Aline B., ed. *Eero Saarinen on his work; a selection of buildings dating from 1947 to 1964, with statements by the architect.* New Haven, Yale University Press, 1968. 2 ed.

11188. Saarinen, Eliel. *The city: its growth, its decay, its future.* New York, Reinhold, 1943.

11189. ———. *Search for form, a fundamental approach to art.* New York, Reinhold, 1948.

11190. Spade, Rupert. *Eero Saarinen.* Photographs by Yukio Futagawa. New York, Simon & Schuster, 1971.

11191. Temko, Allan. *Eero Saarinen.* New York, Braziller, 1962.

Sabatini, Andrea, *see* Andrea da Salerno

Sacchi, Andrea, 1599–1661

11192. D'Avossa. Antonio. *Andrea Sacchi.* Roma, Kappa, 1985.

11193. Harris Ann Sutherland. *Andrea Sacchi: complete edition of the paintings with a critical catalogue.* Oxford, Phaidon, 1977.(CR).

11194. Posse, Hans. *Der römische Maler Andrea Sacchi; ein Beitrag zur Geschichte der klassizistischen Bewegung im Barock.* Leipzig, Seemann, 1924. (Italienische Forschungen, Neue Folge, 1).

Sacchi, Giovanni Antonio de *see* Pordenone

Saenredam, Pieter Janszoon, 1579–1665

11195. Heckmanns, Friedrich Wilhelm. *Pieter Janszoon Saenredam; das Problem seiner Raumform.* Recklinghausen, Bongers, 1965. (Münstersche Studien zur Kunstgeschichte, 3).

11196. Museum Boymans-Van Beuningen (Rotterdam). *Catalogus, schilderijen en tekeningen: Pieter Jansz Saenredam, 1697–1665.* [Tentoonstelling] 24 dec. 1937–1 Febr. 1938. Rotterdam, The Museum, 1938

11197. ———. *Perspectives: Saenredam and the architectural painters of the 17th century.* [Exhibition] organised by Jeroen Giltaij and Guido Jansen; trans. Yvette Rosenberg. Rotterdam: Museum Boymans-Van Beuningen; Seattle; distributed by University of Washington Press, 1991.

11198. Ruurs, Rob. *Saenredam, the art of perspective.* Amsterdam,; Philadelphia: Benjamins/Forsten, 1987.

11199. Saenredam, Pieter Jansz. *Saenredam. 1597–1665; peintre des églises.* Exposition, Institut Néerlandais, Paris, 31 janvier–15 mars, 1970. Paris, l'Institut, 1970.

11200. Schwartz, Gary. *Pieter Saenredam: the painter and his time.* G. Schwartz and Marten Jan Bok. Maarssen, G. Schwartz/SDU, 1990.

11201. Swillens, P.T.A. *Pieter Janszoon Saenredam; schilder van Haarlem, 1597–1665.* Met een inleiding van W. Vogelsang. Amsterdam, N. v. Uitgeversbdrijf "De Spieghel," 1935.

Saftleven, Cornelis, 1607–1681
Herman, 1609–1685

11202. Schultz, Wolfgang. *Cornelis Saftleven, 1607–1681; Leben und Werke.* Mit einem kritischen Katalog der Gemälde und Zeichnungen. Berlin/New York, de Gruyter, 1978. (CR). (Beiträge zur Kunstgeschichte, 14).

11203. ———. *Herman Saftleven, 1609–1685: Leben und Werke.* Mit einem kritischen Katalog der Gemälde und Zeichnungen. Berlin/New York, de Gruyter, 1982. (CR). (Beiträge zur Kunstgeschichte, 18).

Saint-Aubin, Auguste de, 1736–1807
Gabriel Jacques de, 1724–1780

11204. Bocher, Emmanuel. *Augustin de Saint-Aubin.* Paris, Morgand et Fatout, 1879. (CR). (Les gravures françaises du XVIIIᵉ siècle, 5).

11205. Dacier, Emile. *Gabriel de Saint-Aubin, peintre, dessinateur et graveur (1724–1780); l'homme et l'oeuvre; catalogue raisonné.* 2 v. Paris/Bruxelles, van Oest, 1929–1931. (CR).

11206. Davidson Art Center, Wesleyan University (Middletown, Conn.). *Prints and drawings by Gabriel de Saint-Aubin, 1724–1780.* March 7–April 13, 1975. Middletown, Conn., Davidson Art Center, Wesleyan University, 1975.

11207. Moreau, Adrien. *Les Saint-Aubin.* Paris, Librairie de l'art.[1894].

Saint-Gaudens, Augustus, 1848–1907

11208. Cortissoz, Royal. *Augustus Saint-Gaudens.* Boston, Houghton Mifflin, 1907.

11209. Dryfhout, John H. *The work of Augustus Saint-Gaudens.* Hanover,N.H./London, University Presses of New England, 1982. (CR).

11210. Hind, Charles L. *Augustus Saint-Gaudens.* London, Lane, 1908.

11211. Saint-Gaudens, Augustus. *Reminiscences.* Edited and amplified by Homer Saint-Gaudens. 2 v. New York, Century, 1913. (Reprint: New York, Garland, 1976).

11212. Tharp, Louise H. *Saint-Gaudens and the Gilded Era.* Boston, Little, Brown, 1969.

Saint-Phalle, Niki de, 1930–

11213. Bourdon, David. *Niki at Nassau: fantastic vision: works by Niki de Saint Phalle, 27 September 1987–3 January 1988.* Nassau County Museum of Fine Arts, Roslyn, New York. Writings by David Bourdon, John Cage, Harry Mathews. Roslyn, N.Y., Nassau County Museum of Fine Art , 1987.

11214. Hulten, Karl Gunnar Pontus. *Niki de Saint Phalle.* [Catalogue of an exhibition] Kunst und Ausstellungshalle der Bundesrepublik Deutschland. [Bonn]. Stuttgart, Verlag Gerd Hatje, 1992.

11215. Mock, Jean Yves. *Niki de Saint-Phalle; exposition rétrospective,* 2 juillet–1er septembre 1980. Centre Georges Pompidou, Musée Nationale d'art moderne, Paris. Paris, Musée national d'art moderne, 1980.

11216. Saint-Phalle, Niki. *Niki de Saint-Phalle: das graphische Werk, 1968–1980: Figuren.* [Ausstellung] 18. Mai bis 6. Juli 1980, Ulmer Museum. Katalogbearbeitung, Dominique Chenivesse, Brigitte Kühn. Ulm, Das Museum, 1980.

11217. ———. *Niki de Saint Phalle: Retrospektive 1954–80.* [Exhibition catalogue]. Wilhelm-Lehmbruck-Museum der Stadt Duisburg, 1980. Duisburg, Das Museum, 1980.

Sakonides, 6th c. B.C.

11218. Rumpf, Andreas. *Sakonides.* Leipzig, Keller, 1937. (Bilder griechischer Vasen, 11).

Salimbeni, Jacopo, d. ca. 1427
Lorenzo, 1374–ca. 1419

11219. Rossi, Alberto. *I Salimbeni.* Milano, Electa, 1976.

11220. Salimei, Franco. *I Salimbeni di Siena.* Roma, Editalia, 1986.

11221. Zampetti, Pietro. *Gli affreschi di Lorenzo e Jacopo Salimbeni nell'Oratorio di San Giovanni di Urbino.* Urbino, Istituto Statale d'Arte di Urbino, 1956. (Collana di studi archeologici ed artistici marchigiani, 6).

Salomon, Erich, 1866–1944

11222. Hunter-Salomon, Peter. *Erich Salomon.* Millerton, N.Y., Aperture, 1978. (Aperture History of Photography, 10).

11223. Salomon, Erich. *Berühmte Zeitgenossen in unbewachten Augenblicken.* Stuttgart, Engelhorns, 1931. (New ed.: München, Schirmer/Mosel, 1978).

11224. ———. *Erich Salomon, 1866–1944: de la vie d'un photogrqaphe* (150 photographies originales, ducuments et objects): catalogue de l'exposition. Bruxelles, Bibliothèque royale Albert Ier, 1984.

11225. ———. *Portrait of an age.* Selected by Hans de Vries and Peter Hunter-Salomon. Biography and notes by Peter Hunter-Salomon. Trans. by Sheila Tobias. New York, Macmillan, 1967.

Sánchez-Coello, Alonso, d. 1588

11226. Breuer, Stephanie. *Alonso Sanchez Coello.* [Dissertation] vorgelegt von Stephanie Breuer. München, Uni Druck, 1984.

11227. Hispanic Society of America. *Sánchez Coello.* New York, Trustees of the Hispanic Society, 1927.

11228. San Román y Fernandez, Francisco de. *Alonso Sánchez Coello, ilustraciones a su biografia.* Lisboa, Amigos do Museu Nacional de Arte Antiga, 1938.

Sandberg, Ragnar Gösta Leopold, 1902–1972

11229. Linde, Ulf. *Ragnar Sandberg.* [Stockholm],

Sveriges Allmänna Konstförening, 1979. (Sveriges allmänna konstförening, 88).

11230. Mörner, Stellan. *Ragnar Sandberg.* Stockholm, Forum, 1950. (Forums små konstböcker).

11231. Sandberg, Ragnar. *Anteckningar.* Göteborg, Palettens Skriftserie, 1953. (Palettens skriftserie, 4).

Sandberg, Willem Jabob Henri Berend, 1897–

11232. *Sandberg: typograf als museumman;* [catalogus, tekst, Jan Bons . . . et al.]. Amersfoort: Amersfoortse Culturele Rad, 1982.

Sandby, Paul, 1725–1809
Thomas, 1721–1798

11233. Faigen, Julian. *Paul Sandby drawings.* [Published in conjunction with an exhibition at the City of Hamilton Art Gallery, Hamilton, Australia, October 3–October 25, 1981, and other places]. Sydney, Australian Gallery Directors' Council, 1981.

11234. Oppé, Adolf P. *The drawings of Paul and Thomas Sandby in the collection of His Majesty the King at Windsor Castle.* Oxford/London, Phaidon, 1947.

11235. Sandby, William. *Thomas and Paul Sandby, Royal Academians; some account of their lives and works.* London, Seeley, 1892.

Sander, August, 1876–1964

11236. Newhall, Beaumont and Kramer, Robert. *August Sander: photographs of an epoch, 1904–1959.* [Published in conjunction with an exhibition at the Philadelphia Museum of Art, March 1–April 27, 1980, and other places]. Millerton, N.Y., Aperture, 1980.

11237. Sander, August. *Antlitz der Zeit: sechzig Aufnahmen deutscher Menschen des 20. Jahrhunderts.* Mit einer Einleitung von Alfred Döblin. München, Transmare Verlag, 1929.

11238. ———. *Rheinlandschaften: Photographien 1929–1946.* Mit einem Text von Wolfgang Kemp. München, Schirmer/Mosel, 1975.

11239. Von Hartz, John. *August Sander.* Millerton, N.Y., Aperture, 1977. (Aperture History of Photography, 7).

Sanders van Hemessen, Jan, 16th c.

11240. Graefe, Felix. *Jan Sanders von Hemessen und seine Identification mit dem Braunschweiger Monogrammisten.* Leipzig, Hiersemann, 1909. (Kunstgeschichtliche Monographien, 13).

Sandrart, Joachim von, 1606–1688

11241. Kutter, Paul. *Joachim von Sandrart als Künstler, nebst Versuch eines Katalogs seiner noch vorhandenen Arbeiten.* Strassburg, Heitz, 1907. (Studien zur deutschen Kunstgeschichte, 83).

11242. Sandrart, Joachim von. *L'Academia todesca dell' architectura, scultura et pictura: oder Teutsche Academie der edlen Bau-, Bild-, und Mahlerey-Künste.* Nürnberg, Sandrart/Frankfurt, Merian, 1675.

11243. ———. *Der Teutschen Academie zweyter und letzter Haupt-Teil, von der edlen Bau-, Bild- und Mahlerey-Künste.* Nürnberg, Endtern/Frankfurt, Sandrart, 1679.

Sangallo, Antonio da, the elder, 1455–1535
Antonio da, the younger, 1483–1546
Giuliano da, 1445–1516

11244. Clausse, Gustave. *Les San Gallo, architectes, peintres, sculpteurs, médailleurs, XV et XVI siècles.* 3 v. Paris, Leroux, 1900–1902.

11245. Fabriczy, Cornelius von. *Die Handzeichnungen Giulianos da San Gallo; kritisches Verzeichnis.* Stuttgart, Gerschel, 1902. (CR).

11246. Falb, Rodolfo. *Il taccuino senese di Giuliano da San Gallo.* Siena, Marzocchi, 1899.

11247. Giovannoni, Gustavo. *Antonio da Sangallo il giovane.* 2 v. Roma, Tipografia Regionale, 1959.

11248. Huelsen, Cristiano. *Il libro di Giuliano da Sangallo, con introduzione e note.* 2 v. Lipsia, Harrassowitz, 1910. (Codices e Vaticanis selecti, 11).

11249. Loukomski, Georgii K. *Les Sangallo.* Paris, Vincent, Fréal, 1934.

11250. Marchini, Giuseppe. *Giuliano da Sangallo.* Firenze, Sansoni, 1942. (Monographie e studi a cura dell' Istituto di Storia dell'Arte, Reale Università di Firenze, 3).

11251. Severini, Giancarlo. *Architetture militari di Giuliano da Sangallo.* Pisa, Istituto di Architettura e Urbanistica dell'Università di Pisa, 1970.

Sanmicheli, Michele, 1484–1559

11252. Fiocco, Giuseppe, et al. *Michele Sanmicheli: studi raccolti dall'Accademia di Agricoltura, Scienze e Lettere di Verona per la celebrazione del IV centenario della morte.* Verona, Valdonega, 1960.

11253. Langenskiöld, Eric. *Michel Sanmicheli, the architect of Verona; his life and works.* Uppsala (Sweden), Almqvist & Wiksell, 1938. (CR). (Uppsala studier i arkeologi och konsthistoria, 1).

11254. Palazzo Canossa (Verona). *Michel Sanmicheli.* Maggio–ottobre 1960. Catalogo a cura di Piero Gazzola. Venezia, Pozza, 1960.

11255. Pompei, Alessandro. *Li cinque ordini dell'architettura civile di Michel Sanmicheli rilevati dalle sue fabriche, e descritti e publicati con quelli di Vitruvio, Alberti, Palladio, Sca-*

mozzi, Serlio, e Vignola. Verona, Vallarsi, 1735.

11256. Puppi, Lionello. *Michele Sanmicheli, architetto di Verona.* Padova, Marsilio, 1971.

11257. Ronzani, Francesco e Luciolli, Gerolamo. *Le fabbriche civile, ecclesiastiche e militari di Michele Sanmicheli.* Verona, Moroni, 1823. (New ed., with textual notes by Francesco Zanotto: Torino, Basadonna, 1862).

Sano di Pietro, 1406–1481

11258. Gaillard, Emile. *Un peintre siennois aux XV siècle, Sano di Pietro, 1406–1481.* Chambéry, Dardel, 1923.

11259. Trübner, Jörg. *Die stilistische Entwicklung der Tafelbilder des Sano di Pietro, 1405–1481.* Strassburg, Heitz, 1925. (Etudes sur l'art de tous les pays et de toutes les époques, 6).

Sansovino, Andrea, 1460–1529

11260. Huntley, George H. *Andrea Sansovino, sculptor and architect of the Italian Renaissance.* Cambridge, Mass., Harvard University Press, 1935.

11261. Schönfeld, Paul. *Andrea Sansovino und seine Schule.* Stuttgart, Metzler, 1881.

Sansovino, Jacopo Tatti, 1486–1570

11262. Howard, Deborah. *Jacopo Sansovino: architecture and patronage in Renaissance Venice.* New Haven, Yale University Press, 1975.

11263. Lorenzetti, Giulia. *Itinerario Sansoviniano a Venezia.* Venezia, Comitato per le Onoranze Sansoviniane, 1929.

11264. Mariacher, Giovanni. *Il Sansovino.* Milano, Mondadori, 1962. (Biblioteca moderna Mondadori, 717).

11265. Pittoni, Laura. *Jacopo Sansovino, scultore.* Venezia, Istituto Veneto di Arti Grafiche, 1909.

11266. Sapori, Francesco. *Jacopo Tatti, detto il Sansovino.* Roma, Libreria dello Stato, 1928.

11267. Tafuri, Manfredo. *Jacopo Sansovino e l'architettura del '500 a Venezia.* Fotografie di Diego Birelli. Padova, Marsilio, 1972. 2 ed.

11268. Weihrauch, Hans R. *Studien zum bildernischen Werke des Jacopo Sansovino.* Strassburg, Heitz, 1935. (Zur Kunstgeschichte des Auslandes, 135).

Santini Aichl, Jan Blažej, 1677–1723

11269. Muzeum Knihy (Saar). *Pruvodce expozici Jan Santini.* Ve žd'áru nad Sázavou, Okr. památková správa, 1977.

Sanzio, Giovanni, 1435–1494 *see also* Raphael

11270. Schmarsow, August. *Giovanni Santi, der Vater Raphaels.* Berlin, Haack, 1887.

Sargent, John Singer, 1856–1925

11271. Charteris, Evan E. *John Sargent.* New York, Scribner, 1927.

11272. Coe Kerr Gallery (New York). *John Singer Sargent, his own work.* May 28–June 27, 1980. New York, Coe Kerr Gallery/Wittenborn, 1980.

11273. Corcoran Gallery of Art (Washington, D.C.). *John Singer Sargent: drawings from the Corcoran Gallery of Art.* [Text by Edward J. Nygren]. Washington, D.C., Smithsonian Institution and Corcoran Gallery of Art, 1983.

11274. Downes, William H. *John S. Sargent, his life and work.* Boston, Little Brown, 1925.

11275. Lomax, James and Ormond, Richard. *John Singer Sargent and the Edwardian age.* [Published in conjunction with an exhibition at the Leeds Art Galleries at Lotherton Hall, Leeds, 5 April to 10 June 1979, and other places]. Leeds, Leeds Art Galleries/London, National Portrait Gallery, 1979.

11276. McKibbin, David. *Sargent's Boston, with an essay & biographical summary & a complete checklist of Sargent's portraits.* [Published in conjunction with a centennial exhibition at the Museum of Fine Arts, Boston]. Boston, Museum of Fine Arts, 1956.

11277. Metropolitan Museum of Art (New York). *Memorial exhibition of the work of John Singer Sargent.* January 4–February 14, 1926. New York, Metropolitan Museum of Art, 1926.

11278. Meynell, Alice C. *The work of John S. Sargent, R. A.* London, Heinemann, 1903.

11279. Mount, Charles M. *John Singer Sargent, a biography.* New York, Norton, 1955.

11280. Ormond, Richard. *John Singer Sargent: paintings, drawings, watercolors.* New York, Harper & Row, 1970.

11281. Ratcliff, Carter. *John Singer Sargent.* New York, Abbeville Press, 1982.

Sarto, Andrea del, 1486–1531

11282. Biadi, Luigi. *Notizie inedite della vita d'Andrea del Sarto raccolte da manoscritti e documenti autentici.* Firenze, Bonducciana, 1829.

11283. Comandé, Giovanni B. *Introduzione allo studio dell'arte di Andrea del Sarto.* Palermo, Palumbo, 1952.

11284. Fraenckel, Ingeborg. *Andrea del Sarto; Gemälde und Zeichnungen.* Strassburg, Heitz, 1935. (Zur Kunstgeschichte des Auslandes, 136).

11285. Freedberg, Sydney J. *Andrea del Sarto.* 2 v. Cambridge, Mass., Harvard University Press, 1963. (CR).

11286. Guinness, H. *Andrea del Sarto.* London, Bell, 1899.

11287. Knapp, Fritz. *Andrea del Sarto.* Bielefeld/

Leipzig, Velhagen & Klasing, 1907. (Künstler-Monographien, 90).

11288. Monti, Raffaele. *Andrea del Sarto.* Milano, Edizioni di Comunità, 1965. (Studi e documenti di storia dell'arte, 8).

11289. Reumont, Alfred. *Andrea del Sarto.* Leipzig, Brockhaus, 1835.

11290. Shearman, John. *Andrea del Sarto.* 2 v. New York, Oxford University Press, 1965.

11291. Sricchia Santoro, Fiorella. *Andrea del Sarto.* Milano, Fabbri, 1964. (I maestri del colore, 53).

Sassetta, 1392–1450

11292. Berenson, Bernard. *A Sienese painter of the Franciscan legend.* London, Dent, 1910.

11293. Carli, Enzo. *Sassetta e il Maestro dell'Osservanza.* Milano, Martello, 1957.

11294. Pope-Hennessy, John. *Sassetta.* London, Chatto & Windus, 1939.

Savoldo, Giovanni Girolamo, 1480–1548

11295. Boschetto, Antonio. *Giovanni Girolamo Savoldo.* Milano, Bramante, 1963.

11296. Gilbert, Creighton. *The works of Girolamo Savoldo.* 2 v. Ann Arbor, Mich., University Microfilms, 1962. (CR).

Scamozzi, Vincenzo, 1552–1616

11297. Barbieri, Franco. *Vincenzo Scamozzi.* Vicenza, Cassa di Risparmio di Verona e Vicenza, 1952.

11298. Donin, Richard K. *Vincenzo Scamozzi und der Einfluss Venedigs auf die Salzburger Architektur.* Innsbruck, Rohrer, 1948.

11299. Scamozzi, Vincenzo. *Discorsi sopra l'antichità di Roma.* Venezia, Ziletti, 1582.

11300. ———. *L'idea della architettura universale.* Venezia, Valentino, 1615. (Reprint: Ridgewood, N.J., Gregg, 1964).

11301. ———. *Taccuino di viaggio da Parigi a Venezia, 14 marzo–11 maggio 1600.* Edizioni e commento a cura di Franco Barbieri. Venezia, Istituto per la Collaborazione Culturale, 1959.

Schadow, Johann Gottfried, 1764–1850

11302. Kaiser, Konrad. *Gottfried Schadow als Karikaturist.* Dresden, Verlag der Kunst, 1955.

11303. Mackowsky, Hans. *Johann Gottfried Schadow, Jugend und Aufstieg, 1764 bis 1797.* Berlin, Grote, 1927.

11304. ———. *Schadows Graphik.* Berlin, Deutscher Verein für Kunstwissenschaft, 1936. (Forschungen zur deutschen Kunstgeschichte, 19).

11305. Nemitz, Fritz. *Gottfried Schadow der Zeichner.* Berlin, Mann, 1937.

11306. Schadow, Johann G. *Aufsätze und Briefe.* Nebst einem Verzeichnis seiner Werke zur hundertjährigen Feier seiner Geburt, 20. Mai

1764. Herausgegeben von Julius Friedlaender. Stuttgart, Ebner & Seubert, 1890. 2 ed. (See following for reprint).

11307. ———. *Kunst-Werke und Kunst-Ansichten.* Berlin, Decker, 1849. (Both reprinted in one vol.: Berlin, Seitz, 1980).

11308. Staatliche Museen zu Berlin, Nationalgalerie. *Johann Gottfried Schadow, 1764–1850: Bildwerke und Zeichnungen.* Oktober 1964 bis März 1965. Berlin, Staatliche Museen zu Berlin, Nationalgalerie, 1964.

Schaeufelein, Hans Leonard, 1490–1540
see also Kuhlbach, Hans Suess von

11309. Schreyl, Karl Heinz, Hrsg. *Hans Schäufelein: das druckgraphische Werk.* 2 v. Nördlingen, Verlag A. Uhl, 1990.(CR).

11310. Oldenbourg, Consuelo. *Die Buchholzschnitte des Hans Schäufelein, ein bibliographisches Verzeichnis ihrer Verwendungen.* 2 v. Baden-Baden/Strasbourg, Heitz, 1964. (CR). (Studien zur deutschen Kunstgeschichte, 340/341).

11311. Thieme, Ulrich. *Hans Leonhard Schaeufeleins malerische Thätigkeit.* Leipzig, Seemann, 1892. (Beiträge zur Kunstgeschichte, Neue Folge, 16).

Schaffner, Martin, 16th c.

11312. Pückler-Limpurg, Siegfried G. *Martin Schaffner.* Strassburg, Heitz, 1899. (Studien zur deutschen Kunstgeschichte, 20).

11313. Ulmer Museum. *Martin Schaffner, Maler zu Ulm.* 20. September bis 15. November, 1959. Ulm, Ulmer Museum, 1959. (Schriften des Ulmer Museums, Neue Folge, 2).

Scharoun, Hans, 1893–1972

11314. Akademie der Künste (Berlin). *Hans Scharoun.* 5. März–30. April 1967. Berlin, Akademie der Künste, 1967.

11315. Pfankuch, Peter, ed. *Hans Scharoun; Bauten, Entwürfe, Texte.* Berlin, Mann, [1974]. (Schriftenreihe der Akademie der Künste, 10).

Scheffer, Ary, 1795–1858

11316. Grote, Harriet L. *Memoir of the life of Ary Scheffer.* London, Murray, 1860.

11317. Institut Néerlandais (Paris). *Ary Scheffer, 1795–1858: dessins, aquarelles, esquisses à l'huile.* 16 octobre–30 novembre 1980. Paris, Institut Néerlandais, 1980.

11318. Kolb, Marthe. *Ary Scheffer et son temps, 1795–1858.* Paris, Boivin, 1937.

11319. Wellicz, Léopold. *Les amis romantiques: Ary Scheffer et ses amis polonais.* Paris, Trianon, 1933.

Schiele, Egon, 1890–1918

11320. Comini, Alessandra. *Egon Schiele's portraits.*

Berkeley, University of California Press, 1974.

11321. ———. *Schiele in prison.* Greenwich, Conn., New York Graphic Society, 1973.

11322. Kallir, Jane. *Egon Schiele.* With an essay by Alessandra Comini. [Book and catalogue accompanying the travelling exhibition: Washington, D.C. National Gallery of Art, 1994–5]. New York, H.N. Abrams; Alexandria, Va., Art Services International, 1994.

11323. ———. *Egon Schiele, the complete works; including a biography and a catalogue raisonné.* With an essay by Wolfgang G. Fischer. New York, H.N. Abrams in association with Leonardo Editore, Milano; Meulenhoff/Landshoff, Amsterdam; Julio Ollero, Madrid; Thames and Hudson, London, 1990. (CR).

11324. Kallir, Otto. *Egon Schiele, the graphic work.* [Text in German and English]. New York, Crown, 1970. (CR).

11325. ———. *Egon Schiele, Oeuvre-Katalog der Gemälde.* [Text in German and English]. Wien, Zsolnay, 1966. (CR).

11326. Leopold, Rudolf. *Egon Schiele: paintings, watercolors, drawings.* Trans. by Alexander Lieven. London, Phaidon, 1973. (CR).

11327. Malafarina, Gianfranco. *L'opera di Schiele.* Milano, Rizzoli, 1982. (CR). (Classici dell'-arte, 105).

11328. Mitsch, Erwin. *The art of Egon Schiele.* Trans. by W. Keith Haughan. London, Phaidon, 1975.

11329. Nebehay, Christian M. *Egon Schiele, 1890–1918: Leben, Briefe, Gedichte.* Salzburg/Wien, Residenz, 1979.

11330. ———. *Egon Schiele: sketchbooks.* London, Thames and Hudson, 1989.

11331. Roessler, Arthur. *Erinnerungen an Egon Schiele.* Wien/Leipzig, Konegen, 1922. (New ed.: Wien, Wiener Volksbuchverlag, 1948).

11332. Sabarsky, Serge. *Egon Schiele, watercolors and drawings.* New York, Abbeville Press, 1983.

11333. Schiele, Egon. *Briefe und Prosa.* Herausgegeben von Arthur Roessler. Wien, Lányi, 1921.

11334. ———. *A sketchbook.* Commentary by Otto Kallir. 2 v. New York, Johannes Press, 1967.

11335. Whitford, Frank. *Egon Schiele.* New York, Oxford University Press, 1981.

11336. Werkner, Patrick. *Egon Schiele: art, sexuality, and Viennese modernism.* Palo Alto, Calif., Society for the promotion of Science and Scholarship; distrib. by University of Washington Press, Seattle. 1994.

11337. Wilson, Simon. *Egon Schiele.* Oxford, Phaidon, 1980.

Schindler, Emil Jakob, 1842–1892

11338. Fuchs, Heinrich. *Emil Jakob Schindler:*

Zeugnisse eines ungewöhnlichen Kunstlebens; Werkkatalog. Wien, Fuchs, 1970. (CR).

Schinkel, Karl Friedrich, 1781–1841

11339. Bergdoll, Barry. *Karl Friedrich Schinkel: an architecture for Prussia.* New York, Rizzoli, 1994.

11340. Brües, Eva. *Die Rheinlande.* Berlin, Deutscher Kunstverlag, 1968. (Karl Friedrich Schinkel. Das Lebenswerk).

11341. Forssman, Erik. *Karl Friedrich Schinkel: Bauwerke und Baugedanken.* München/Zürich, Schnell & Steiner, 1981.

11342. Grisebach, August. *Carl Friedrich Schinkel.* Leipzig, Insel-Verlag, 1924. (New ed.: München, Piper, 1981).

11343. Kania, Hans. *Mark Brandenburg.* Berlin, Deutscher Kunstverlag, 1960. (Karl Friedrich Schinkel. Das Lebenswerk).

11344. ———. *Potsdam, Staats- und Bürgerbauten.* Berlin, Deutscher Kunstverlag, 1939. (Karl Friedrich Schinkel. Das Lebenswerk).

11345. Kugler, Franz. *Karl Friedrich Schinkel: eine Charakteristik seiner künstlerischen Wirksamkeit.* Berlin, Gropius, 1842.

11346. Lorck, Carl von. *Karl Friedrich Schinkel.* Berlin, Rembrandt, 1939.

11347. Ohff, Heinz. *Karl Friedrich Schinkel.* Berlin, Stapp, 1981.

11348. Orangerie des Schlosses Charlottenburg. *Karl Friedrich Schinkel: Architektur, Malerei, Kunstgewerbe. 13. März bis 13. September 1981.* Charlottenburg, Verwaltung der Staatlichen Schlösser und Gärten, 1981.

11349. Peschken, Goerd. *Das architektonische Lehrbuch.* München/Berlin, Deutscher Kunstverlag, 1979. (Karl Friedrich Schinkel. Das Lebenswerk).

11350. Posener, Julius, ed. *Festreden: Schinkel zu Ehren, 1846–1980.* Berlin, Architekten- und Ingenieur-Verein zu Berlin, [1981].

11351. Pundt, Hermann G. *Schinkel's Berlin: a study in environmental planning.* Cambridge, Mass., Harvard University Press, 1972.

11352. Rave, Paul O. *Berlin.* 3 v. Berlin, Deutscher Kunstverlag, 1941–62. (CR). (Reprint, ed. by Margarete Kühn: München/Berlin, Deutscher Kunstverlag, 1981; Karl Friedrich Schinkel. Das Lebenswerk).

11353. Schinkel, Karl F. *Aus Schinkel's Nachlass: Reisetage-bücher, Briefe und Aphorismen.* Mitgetheilt und mit einem Verzeichniss sämtlicher Werke Schinkel's Versehen. 4 v. Berlin, Decker, 1862–1864.

11354. ———. *Reisen nach Italien: Tagebücher, Briefe, Zeichnungen, Aquarelle.* Herausgegeben von Gottfried Riemann. Berlin, Rütten & Loening, 1979.

11355. ———. *Sammlung architektonische Entwürfe.* Berlin, Ernst & Korn, 1866. (Reprint: Chicago, Exedra, 1981).

11356. Schreiner, Ludwig. *Westfalen*. München/Berlin, Deutscher Kunstverlag, 1969. (Karl Friedrich Schinkel. Das Lebenswerk).

11357. Sievers, Johannes. *Die Arbeiten von Karl Friedrich Schinkel für Prinz Wilhelm, späteren König von Preussen*. Berlin, Deutscher Kunstverlag, 1955. (Karl Friedrich Schinkel. Das Lebenswerk).

11358. ———. *Bauten für die Prinzen August, Friedrich und Albrecht von Preussen; ein Beitrag zur Geschichte der Wilhelmstrasse in Berlin*. Berlin, Deutscher Kunstverlag, 1954. (Karl Friedrich Schinkel. Das Lebenswerk).

11359. ———. *Die Möbel*. Berlin, Deutscher Kunstverlag, 1950. (Karl Friedrich Schinkel. Das Lebenswerk).

11360. Snodin, Michael. *Karl Friedrich Schinkel, a universal man*. New Haven, Yale University Press, in association with the Victoria and Albert Museum, London, 1991.

11361. Springer, Peter. *Schinkels Schlossbrücke in Berlin: Zweckbau und Monument*. Wien, Propyläen, 1981.

11362. Vogel, Hans. *Pommern*. Berlin, Deutscher Kunstverlag, 1952. (Karl Friedrich Schinkel. Das Lebenswerk).

11363. Volk, Waltraud, ed. *Karl Friedrich Schinkel; sein Wirken als Architekt*. Ausgewählte Bauten in Berlin und Potsdam im 19. Jahrhundert. Berlin, Verlag für Bauwesen, 1981.

11364. Wolzogen, Alfred von. *Schinkel als Architekt, Maler und Kunstphilosoph; ein Vortrag*. Berlin, Ernst & Korn, 1864.

11365. Zadow, Mario. *Karl Friedrich Schinkel*. Berlin, Rembrandt, 1980.

11366. Ziller, Hermann. *Schinkel*. Bielefeld/Leipzig, Velhagen & Klasing, 1897. (Künstler-Monographien, 28).

Schjerfbeck, Helena Sofia, 1862–1946

11367. Ahtela, H. [pseud., Einar Reuter]. *Helena Schjerfbeck*. Stockholm, Ráben & Sjögren, 1953.

11368. Appelberg, Hanna och Appelberg, Eilif. *Helene Schjerfbeck, en biografisk konturteckning*. Helsingfors, Soderström, 1949.

Schlaun, Johann Conrad, 1695–1773

11369. Hartmann, Heinrich. *Johann Conrad Schlaun; sein Leben und seine Bautätigkeit*. Münster, Coppenrath, 1910.

11370. Kunsthalle Bielefeld. *Johann Conrad Schlaun, 1695–1773; Baukunst des Barock*. 16. März–11. Mai 1975. Bielefeld, Kunsthalle Bielefeld, 1975.

11371. Landesmuseum Münster. *Johann Conrad Schlaun, 1695–1773: Ausstellung zu seinem 200. Todestag*. 2 v. 21. Oktober–30. Dezember 1973. Münster, Landesmuseum Münster, 1973.

11372. Rensing, Theodor. *Johann Conrad Schlaun, Leben und Werk des westfälischen Barockbaumeisters*. München/Berlin, Deutscher Kunstverlag, 1954.

Schlemmer, Oskar, 1888–1943

11373. Grohmann, Will. *Oskar Schlemmer: Zeichnungen und Graphik; Oeuvrekatalog*. Stuttgart, Hatje, 1965. (CR).

11374. Herzogenrath, Wulf. *Oskar Schlemmer: die Wandegestaltung der neuen Architektur*. München, Prestel, 1973.

11375. Hildebrandt, Hans. *Oskar Schlemmer*. München, Prestel, 1952.

11376. Lehman, Arnold L. and Richardson, Brenda. *Oskar Schlemmer*. With texts by Vernon L. Lidke . . . et al. [Catalogue of an exhibition held at te Baltimore Museum of Art.] Baltimore, Md., 1986.

11377. Maur, Karin von. *Oskar Schlemmer*. 2 v. München, Prestel, 1979. (CR).

11378. Schlemmer, Oskar. *The letters and diaries of Oskar Schlemmer*. Selected and edited by Tut Schlemmer. Trans. by Krishna Winston. Middletown, Conn., Wesleyan University Press, 1972.

11379. ———. *Man: teaching notes from the Bauhaus*. Ed. by Heimo Kuchling. Trans. by Janet Seligman. Cambridge, Mass., MIT Press, 1971.

11380. Staatsgalerie Stuttgart. *Oskar Schlemmer*. 11. August bis 18. September 1977. Stuttgart, Württembergischer Kunstverein Stuttgart, 1977.

Schlüter, Andreas, 1664–1714

11381. Benkard, Ernst. *Andreas Schlüter*. Frankfurt am Main, Iris, 1925.

11382. Gurlitt, Cornelius. *Andreas Schlüter*. Berlin, Wasmuth, 1891.

11383. Ladendorf, Heinz. *Andreas Schlüter*. Berlin, Rembrandt, 1937.

Schmidt-Rottluff, Karl, 1884–1976

11384. Brix, Karl. *Karl Schmidt-Rottluff*. Wien/München, Schroll, 1972.

11385. Grohmann, Will. *Karl Schmidt-Rottluff*. Stuttgart, Kohlhammer, 1956.

11386. Kunstverein Braunschweig. *Karl Schmidt-Rottluff: Werke, 1905–1961*. 16. Dezember 1979–27. Januar 1980. Braunschweig, Kunst-verein Braunschweig, 1979.

11387. Schapire, Rosa and Rathenau, Ernest. *Karl Schmidt-Rottluffs graphisches Werk bis 1923*. 2 v. Berlin/New York, Euphorion Verlag & Ernest Rathenau, 1964.(CR).

11388. ———. *Karl Schmidt-Rottluff: das graphische Werk seit 1923*. 1 v. Berlin & New York, Euphorion Verlag & Ernest Rathenau, 1987. (CR)

11389. Thiem, Gunther. *Karl Schmidt-Rottluff, Aquarelle und Zeichnungen.* München, Bruckmann, 1963.

11390. Valentiner, Wilhelm R. *Schmidt-Rottluff.* Leipzig, Klinkhardt & Biermann, 1920. (Junge Kunst, 16).

11391. Wietek, Gerhard. *Schmidt-Rottluff Graphik.* München, Thiemig, 1971.

Schnorr von Carolsfeld, Julius, 1794–1872

11392. Nowald, Inken. *Die Nibelungenfresken von Julius Schnorr von Carolsfeld im Königsbau der Münchner Residenz, 1827–1867.* Kiel, Kunsthalle zu Kiel, 1978. (Schriften der Kunsthalle zu Kiel, 3).

11393. Schnorr von Carolsfeld, Julius. *Bible pictures.* With letter-press descriptions by John Tatlock. Boston, Carter & Karrick, 1888.

11394. ———. *Briefe aus Italien geschrieben in den Jahren 1817 bis 1827.* Gotha, Perthes, 1886.

11395. ———. *Das Nibelungen-Lied nach den Fresko-Gemälden.* Photographiert von Josef Albert. [Text by H. Holland]. München, Albert, [1868].

11396. Singer, Hans W. *Julius Schnorr von Carolsfeld.* Bielefeld/Leipzig, Velhagen & Klasing, 1911. (Künstler-Monographien, 103).

Schongauer, Martin, 1430/50–1491

11397. Baum, Julius. *Martin Schongauer.* Wien, Schroll, 1948.

11398. Bernhard, Marianne. *Martin Schongauer und sein Kreis: Druckgraphik, Handzeichnungen.* München, Südwest, 1980.

11399. Buchner, Ernst. *Martin Schongauer als Maler.* Berlin, Deutscher Verein für Kunstwissenschaft, 1941.

11400. Champion, Claude. *Schongauer.* Paris, Alcan, 1925.

11401. Flechsig, Eduard. *Martin Schongauer.* Strasbourg, Heitz, 1951.

11402. Girodie, André. *Martin Schongauer et l'art du Haut-Rhin au XVe siècle.* Paris, Plon, [1911].

11403. Rosenberg, Jakob. *Martin Schongauer, Handzeichnungen.* München, Piper, 1923.

11404. Shestack, Alan. *The complete engravings of Martin Schongauer.* New York, Dover, 1969.

11405. Wendland, Hans. *Martin Schongauer als Kupferstecher.* Berlin, Meyer, 1907.

11406. Winzinger, Franz. *Die Zeichnungen Martin Schongauers.* Berlin, Deutscher Verein für Kunstwissenschaft, 1962. (CR).

11407. Wurzbach, Alfred von. *Martin Schongauer, eine kritische Untersuchung seines Lebens und seiner Werke.* Wien, Manz, 1880.

Schultze, Bernard, 1915–

11408. Romain, Lothar and Wedewert, Rolf. *Ber-*

nard Schultze. München, Hirmer, 1991.

Schulze, Alfred Otto Wolfgang *see* Wols

Schumacher, Emil, 1912–

11409. Galerie Thomas (Munich). *Emil Schumacher: Werke aus den Jahren 1955–1990.* [Ausstellung 8. Mai–10. Juni 1992]. München, Galerie Thomas, 1992.

11410. Güse, Ernst-Gerhard. *Emil Schumacher; die Gouachen der 80er Jahre.* Mit einem Beitrag des Künstlers, München, Prestel, 1992.

11411. Schmalenbach, Werner. *Emil Schumacher.* Köln, DuMont, 1981.

11412. Schumacher, Emil. *Emil Schumacher; Gouachen 1980–1991.* [Catalogue of an exhibition]. Saarbrücken, Saarland Museum, 1992–1993.

11413. ———. *Emil Schumacher: späte Bilder.* Mitarbeit an Katalog und Ausstellung, Michaela Herrmann, Margret Kampmeyer-Käding, Ulrich Krempell. Berlin: Nationalgalerie, Staatliche Museen Preussischer Kulturbesitz; Düsseldorf, Kunstsammlung Nordrhein-Westfalen, 1988.

11414. ———. *Emil Schumacher, Werke 1936–1984.* Ausstellung: Kunsthalle Bremen, Ausstellung in Zusammenarbeit mit dem Förderkreis für Gegenwartskunst im Kunstverein in Bemen, 14.10.–25.11.1984; Badischer Kunstverein Karlsruhe, 22.1.–10.3. 1985. [Katlogredaktion, Annette Meyer zu Eissen. Bremen, Kunsthalle, 1984.

Schwanthaler, Ludwig Michael, 1802–1848
Thomas, 1634–1707

11415. Augustinerchorherrenstift (Reichersberg, Austria). *Die Bildhauerfamilie Schwanthaler, 1633–1848: vom Barock zum Klassizismus.* 3. Mai bis 13. Oktober 1974. Linz, Landesverlag Linz, 1974.

11416. Oberes Belvedere in Wien. *Thomas Schwanthaler, 1634–1707.* 21. November 1974–16. Februar 1975. Wien, Osterreichische Galerie, 1974.

11417. Otten, Frank. *Ludwig Michael Schwanthaler, 1802–1848: ein Bildhauer unter König Ludwig I von Bayern; Monographie und Werkverzeichnis.* München, Prestel, 1970. (CR). (Studien zur Kunst des neunzehnten Jahrhunderts, 12).

11418. Trautmann, Franz. *Ludwig Schwanthalers Reliquien.* München, Fleischmann, 1858.

Schwind, Moritz von, 1804–1871

11419. Elster, Hanns M. *Moritz von Schwind, sein Leben und Schaffen.* Berlin, Flemming und Wiskott, 1924.

11420. Führich, Lukas von. *Moritz von Schwind, eine Lebensskizze.* Leipzig, Dürr, 1871.

11421. Haack, Friedrich. *Moritz von Schwind.* Bielefeld/Leipzig, Velhagen & Klasing, 1898. (Künstler-Monographien, 31).

11422. Holland, Hyazinth. *Moritz von Schwind, sein Leben und seine Werke.* Stuttgart, Neff, 1873.

11423. Kalkschmidt, Eugen. *Moritz von Schwind, der Mann und das Werk.* München, Bruckmann, 1943.

11424. Müller, August W. *Moritz von Schwind, sein Leben und künstlerisches Schaffen.* Eisenbach, Baerecke, 1871.

11425. Pommeranz-Liedtke, Gerhard. *Moritz von Schwind, Maler und Poet.* Wien/München, Schroll, 1974.

11426. Schwind, Moritz von. *Briefe.* Herausgegeben von Otto Stoeffl. Leipzig, Bibliographisches Institut, [1924].

11427. Weigmann, Otto. *Schwind: des Meisters Werke.* Stuttgart/Leipzig, Deutsche Verlags-Anstalt, 1904. (Klassiker der Kunst, 9).

Schwitters, Kurt, 1887–1948

11428. Bailly, Jean Christophe. *Kurt Schwitters.* Paris, Hazen, 1993.

11429. Bazzoli, François. *Kurt Schwitters.* Marseille, Images et manoeuvres, 1991.

11430. Galerie Gmurzynska (Cologne). *Kurt Schwitters.* Oktober–Dezember 1978. Köln, Galerie Gmurzynska, 1978.

11431. Nündel, Ernst, ed. *Kurt Schwitters in Selbstzeugnissen und Bilddokumenten.* Reinbeck bei Hamburg, Rowohlt, 1981. (Rowohlts Monographien).

11432. Schmalenbach, Werner. *Kurt Schwitters.* New York, Abrams, 1970. (CR).

11433. Schwitters, Kurt. *Wir spielen bis uns der Tod abholt; Briefe aus fünf Jahrzehnten.* Gesammelt, ausgewählt und kommentiert von Ernst Nündel. Frankfurt a.M., Ullstein, 1975.

11434. Steinitz, Kate T. *Kurt Schwitters; a portrait from life.* With *Collision, a science fiction opera libretto in banalities* by Kurt Schwitters and Kate T. Steinitz, and other writings. Trans. by Robert B. Haas. Berkeley, University of California Press, 1968.

Scopas, 395–350 B.C. see also Praxiteles

11435. Arias, Paolo E. *Skopas.* Roma, L'Erma, 1952.

11436. Lehmann, Phyllis W. *Skopas in Samothrace.* Northampton, Mass., Smith College, 1975.

11437. Neugebauer, Karl A. *Studien über Skopas.* Leipzig, Seemann, 1913. (Beiträge zur Kunstgeschichte, Neue Folge, 39).

11438. Stewart, Andrew F. *Skopas of Paros.* Park Ridge, N.J., Noyes Press, 1977.

11439. Urlichs, Ludwig. *Skopas: Leben und Werke.* Greifswald, Germany, Koch, 1863.

Scorel, Jan van, 1495–1562 see also Coecke, Pieter

11440. Centraal Museum Utrecht. *Jan van Scorel in Utrecht.* 5 maart–1 mei 1977. Utrecht, Centraal Museum, 1977.

11441. Hoogewerff, Godefritus J. *Jan van Scorel, peintre de la renaissance hollandaise.* La Haye, Nijhoff, 1923.

11442. Toman, Hugo. *Studien über Jan van Scorel, den Meister vom Tode Mariä.* Leipzig, Seemann, 1889. (Beiträge zur Kunstgeschichte, Neue Folge, 8).

Scott, George Gilbert, Jr., 1811–1878

11443. Bayley, Stephen. *The Albert Memorial; the monument in its social and architectural context.* London, Scolar Press, 1981.

11444. Cole, David. *The work of Sir Gilbert Scott.* London, Architectural Press, 1980.

11445. Scott, George G. *An essay on the history of English church architecture prior to the separation of England from Roman obedience.* London, Simpkin, Marshall, 1881.

11446. ———. *Gleanings from Westminister Abbey.* Oxford/London, Parker, 1863.

11447. ———. *Lectures on the rise and development of mediaeval architecture delivered at the Royal Academy.* 2 v. London, Murray, 1879.

11448. ———. *Personal and professional recollections.* Edited by his son. London, Sampson Low, 1879. (Reprint: New York, Da Capo, 1977).

11449. ———. *Remarks on secular & domestic architecture, present and future.* London, Murray, 1857.

Scott, M. H. Baillie, 1865–1945

11450. Kornwolf, James D. *M. H. Baillie Scott and the Arts and Crafts Movement: pioneers of modern design.* Baltimore/London, Johns Hopkins Press, 1972. (Johns Hopkins Studies in Nineteenth Century Architecture, 2).

11451. Medici-Mall, Katharina. *Das Landhaus Waldbühl von M. H. Baillie Scott; ein Gesamtkunstwerk zwischen Neugotik und Jugendstil.* Bern, Gesellschaft für Schweizerische Kunstgeschichte, 1979. (Beiträge zur Kunstgeschichte der Schweiz, 4).

11452. Scott, M. H. Baillie. *Houses and gardens.* London, Newnes, 1906.

Seago, Edward, 1910–1974

11453. Marlborough Fine Art, Ltd. (London). *Edward Seago.* [Exhibition catalogue]. London, Marlborough Fine Art, 1976.

11454. Ranson, Ron. *Edward Seago, the vintage years.* Newton Abbott, Devon., David & Charles, 1992.

11455. Reid, James W. *Edward Seago: the landscape art.* Foreword by HRH the Duke of Edinburgh. London, Sotheby's Publications, 1991.

Seekatz, Johann Conrad, 1719–1768

11456. Bamberger, Ludwig. *Das Leben des Malers Johann Conrad Seekatz.* Heidelberg, Winter, 1916.

11457. Emmerling, Ernst. *Johann Conrad Seekatz, 1719–1768: ein Maler aus der Zeit des jungen Goethe: Leben und Werk,* von E. Emmerling. Überarbeitet von Brigitte Rechberg und Horst Wilhelm. Landau/Pfalz, Edition PVA, 1991.

Seewald, Richard, 1889–1976

11458. Neue Kunst Hans Goltz [Galerie] (Munich). *Richard Seewald: Das graphische Werk, 1916–1918.* Münchern, Neue Kunst Hans Goltz, 1916.

11459. ———. *Sonder-Ausstellung R. Seewald, November 1916.* München, Neue Kunst Hans Goltz, 1916.

11460. Saedler, Heinrich. *Richard Seewald.* München-Gladbach, Führer-Verlag, 1924.

11461. Seewald, Richard. *Kunst in der Kirche.* Freiburg i. Br., Christophorus-Verlag, 1988.

11462. Seewald, Richard. *Richard Seewald.* [Catalogue of an exhibition]. Aarau, das Kunsthaus, 1979.

11463. ———. *Richard Seewald 85 Jahre: Bilder, Zeichnungen. Graphik, 1912–1973.*[Catalogue of an exhibition] München, Galerie Wolfgang Ketterer, 1973.

11464. ———. *Richard Seewald: Das graphische Werk.* [Hrsg. Ralph Jentsch]. Esslingen, Verlag Kunstgalerie Esslingen, 1973. (CR).

11465. ———. *Seewald.* München, K. Thiemig, 1977.

Segal, George, 1924–

11466. Friedman, Martin and Beal, Graham W. J. *George Segal: sculptures.* With commentaries by George Segal. [Published in conjunction with an exhibition at the Walker Art Center, Minneapolis, 29 October 1978–7 January 1979]. Minneapolis, Walker Art Center, 1978.

11467. Hunter, Sam. *George Segal.*[By] S. Hunter [and] Don Hawthorne. New York, Rizzoli, 1984.

11468. Price, Maria. *George Segal: still lifes and related works.* [Catalogue of an exhibition]. Fort Worth, Tex. Modern Art Museum of Fort Worth, 1990.

11469. Robe-Grillet, Alain. *Georges Segal, invasion blanche.* Paris, Editions de la Différance: Galerie Beaubourg, 1990.

11470. Teuber, Dirk. *George Segal: Wege zur Kör-* *perüberformung.* Fankfurt am Main/New York, P. Lang, 1987.

11471. Tuchman, Phyllis. *George Segal.* New York, Abbeville Press, 1983.

11472. Van der Marck, Jan. *George Segal.* New York, Abrams, 1975.

Segall, Lasar, 1891–1957

11473. Bardi, Pietro M. *Lasar Segall.* Trans. by John Drummond. Milano, Edizioni del Milione, 1959.

11474. Fierens, Paul. *Lasar Segall.* Paris, Chroniques du Jour, 1938.

11475. George, Waldemar. *Lasar Segall.* Paris, Le Triangle, 1932.

Segantini, Giovanni, 1858–1899

11476. Abraham, Karl. *Giovanni Segantini: ein psychoanalytischer Versuch.* Leipzig, F. Deuticke, 1911. (Schriften zur angewandten Seelenkunde, 11).

11477. Arcangeli, Francesco [and] Gozzoli, Maria C. *L'opera completa di Segantini.* Milano, Rizzoli, 1973. (CR). (Classici dell'arte, 67).

11478. Belli, Gabriella. *Segantini.* [Exhibition catalogue] a cura di G. Belli. Milano, Electa, 1987.

11479. Budigna, Luciano. *Giovanni Segantini.* Milano, Bramante, 1962. (I grandi pittori italiani dell'ottocento).

11480. Lüthy, Hans A. [and] Maltese, Corrado. *Giovanni Segantini.* Zürich, Füssli, 1981.

11481. Montandon, Marcel. *Segantini.* Bielefeld/ Leipzig, Velhagen & Klasing, 1904. (Künstler-Monographien, 72).

11482. Nicodemi, Giorgio. *Giovanni Segantini.* Milano, L'Arte, 1956.

11483. Quinsac, Annie-Paule. *Segantini, catalogo generale.* 2 v. Milano, Electa, 1982. (CR).

11484. Roedel, Reto. *Giovanni Segantini.* Roma, Bulzoni, 1978. (Biblioteca di cultura, 123).

11485. Segantini, Giovanni. *Giovanni Segantini, 1858–1899: Kunsthaus Zürich, 9. November 1990–3. Februar 1991.*[Organisation der Ausstellung Felix Baumann, Guido Magnaguagno. Katalogredaktion, Daniela Tobler, Guido Magnaguagno. Übersetzungen, Marianne Karabelnik-Maqtta, Danyiela Tobler, Brigit Wettstein]. Zürich, Das Kunsthaus, 1990.

11486. ———. *Scritti e lettere.* A cura di Bianca Segantini. Torino, Bocca, 1910.

11487. Servaes, Franz. *Giovanni Segantini, sein Leben und sein Werk.* Wien, Gerlach, 1902.

11488. Sgarbi, Vittorio. *Giovanni Segantini: i capolavori.* Trento, L. Reverdito, 1989.

11489. Villari, Luigi. *Giovanni Segantini: the story of his life.* London, Unwin, 1901.

Seghers, Gerard, 1591–1651

11490. Bieneck, Dorothea. *Gerard Seghers, 1591–*

1651: Leben und Werk des Antwerpener Historienmalers. Lingen, Luca Verlag, 1992.

Seghers, Hercules Pieterszoon, ca. 1590–1645

11491. Collins, Leo C. *Hercules Seghers.* Chicago, University of Chicago Press, 1953.

11492. Fraenger, Wilhelm. *Die Radierungen des Hercules Seghers; ein physiognomischer Versuch.* [herausgegeben und mit einem Nachwort von Hilmar Frank]. Leipzig, Reclam, 1984. (First published: Erlenbach/Zürich, Rentsch, 1922).

11493. Haverkamp Begemann, Egbert. *Hercules Segers, the complete etchings.* With an introduction by K. G. Boon. 2 v. Amsterdam, Scheltema & Holkema/The Hague, Nijhoff, 1973. (CR).

11494. Pfister, Kurt. *Herkules Segers.* München, Piper, 1921.

11495. Rowlands, John. *Hercules Segers.* New York, Braziller, 1979.

11496. Springer, Jaro. *Die Radierungen des Herkules Seghers.* 3 v. Berlin, Cassirer, 1910–1912. (CR). (Graphische Gesellschaft, 13/14/16).

Segonzac, André Dunoyer de, 1884–1974

11497. Distel, Anne. *A. Dunoyer de Segonzac.* Paris, Flammarion, 1980.

11498. Fosca, François. *Segonzac Provence.* Trans. by Diana Imber. Lausanne, International Art Book, 1969. (Rhythm and Colour, Second series, 6).

11499. Hugault, Henry. *Dunoyer de Segonzac.* Paris, La Bibliothèque des Arts, 1973.

11500. Jamot, Paul. *Dunoyer de Segonzac.* Paris, Floury, 1929.

11501. Jean, René. *A. Dunoyer de Segonzac.* Paris, Nouvelle Revue Française, 1922. (Les peintres français nouveaux, 11).

11502. Kyriazi, Jean M. *André Dunoyer de Segonzac; sa vie, son oeuvre.* Lausanne, Harmonies et Couleurs, 1976.

11503. Lioré, Aimée et Cailler, Pierre. *Catalogue de l'oeuvre gravé de Dunoyer de Segonzac.* 8 v. Genève, Cailler, 1958–1970. (CR).

11504. Passeron, Roger. *Dunoyer de Segonzac, aquarelles.* Avec un texte inédit de l'artiste et une étude de son oeuvre d'aquarelliste. Neuchâtel, Ides et Calendes, 1976.

11505. ———. *Les gravures de Dunoyer de Segonzac.* Paris, La Bibliothèque des Arts, 1970.

11506. Roger-Marx, Claude. *Dunoyer de Segonzac.* Paris, Crès, 1925.

11507. ———. *Dunoyer de Segonzac.* Genève, Cailler, 1951.

11508. Segonzac, André D. de. *Dessins, 1900–1970.* Genève, Cailler, 1970.

Seitz, Gustav, 1906–1969

11509. Busch, Günter. *Gustav Seitz: Bildhauer-Zeichnungen.* Frankfurt a.M., Societäts-Verlag, 1970.

11510. Flemming, Hans T. *Der Bildhauer Gustav Seitz.* Frankfurt a.M., Societäts-Verlag, 1963.

11511. Hachmeister, H.A. *Gustav Seitz: Catcher und Idole: Handzeichnungen, Reliefs, Plastiken aus dem Spätwerk.* Münster, Hachmeister Galerie, 1990.

11512. Grohn, Ursel. *Gustav Seitz, das plastische Werk: Werkverzeichnis.* Mit einer Einführung von Alfred Hentzen. Hamburg, Hauswedell, 1980. (CR).

11513. Kunsthalle Bremen. *Gustav Seitz: Skulpturen und Handzeichnungen.* 15. August bis 10. Oktober 1976. Bremen, Kunsthalle Bremen, 1976.

11514. Schüler, Gerhard. *Wertstruktur und Leiblichkeit: eine kunstsoziologische Studie zum Werk des Bildhauers Gustav Seitz (1906–1969).* Frankfurt am Main, R.G. Fischer, 1992.

11515. Seitz, Gustav. *Gustav Seitz: Skulpturen, Handzeichnungen.* Münster, Hachmeister & Schnake, 1982.

11516. ———. *Gustav Seitz: Werke und Dokumente [im] Archiv für Bildende Kunst im Germanischen Nationalmuseum Nürnberg.* Katalog, Ursula Frenzel. München, Prestel-Verlag, 1984.

Semper, Gottfried, 1803–1879

11517. Börsch-Supan, Eva, ed. *Gottfried Semper und die Mitte des 19. Jahrhunderts: Symposion von 2. bis 6. Dezember 1974.* Basel/Stuttgart, Birkhäuser, 1976.

11518. Fröhlich, Martin. *Gottfried Semper.* Zürich, Verlag für Architektur, 1991.

11519. ———. *Gottfried Semper: zeichnerischer Nachlass an der ETH Zürich, kritischer Katalog.* Basel/Stuttgart, Birkhäuser, 1974. (CR).

11520. Herrmann, Wolfgang. *Gottfried Semper im Exil: Paris/London, 1849–1855; zur Entstehung des Stil, 1840–1877.* Basel/Stuttgart, Birkhäuser, 1978. (Geschichte und Theorie der Architektur, 19).

11521. ———. *Gottfried Semper: in search of architecture.* Cambridge, Mass., MIT Press, 1984.

11522. ———. *Gottfried Semper: theoretischer Nachlass an der ETH Zürich.* Katalog und Kommentare, Wolfgang Herrmann. Basel/Boston, Birkhäuser, 1981.

11523. Laudel, Heidrun. *Gottfried Semper: Architektur und Stil.* Dresden, Verlag der Kunst, 1991.

11524. Quitzsch, Heinz. *Gottfried Semper: prak-*

tische Ästhetik und politischer Kampf. Braunschweig, Vieweg, 1981. (Bauwelt Fundamente, 58).

11525. Semper, Gottfried. *Gottfried Semper und die Mitte des 19.Jahrhunderts.* Symposion vom 2.–6. Dezember 1974; veranstaltet durch das Institut für Geschichte und Theorie der Architektur an der Eidg. Technischen Hochschule Zürich. Beiträge von Eva Börsch-Supan . . . [et al.]. Basel Birkhäuser, 1976.

11526. ———. *Kleine Schriften.* Herausgegeben von Hans und Manfred Semper. Berlin/Stuttgart, Spemann, 1884. (Reprint: Mittenwald, Mäander Kunstverlag, 1979. Kunstwissenschaftliche Studientexte, 7).

11527. ———. *Der Stil in den technischen und tektonischen Künsten oder Praktische Aesthetik.* 2 v. München, Bruckmann, 1878/1879.

11528. ———. *Die vier Elemente der Baukunst.* Braunschweig, Vieweg, 1851. (Reprinted, in Quitzsch title above, 1981).

11529. Staatliche Kunstsammlungen Dresden, Institut für Denkmalpflege. *Gottfried Semper, 1803–1879; Baumeister zwischen Revolution und Historismus.* München, Callwey, 1979.

Sengai, 1751–1837

11530. Suzuki, Daisetz T. *Sengai, the Zen master.* Edited by Eva von Hoboken. Preface by Sir Herbert Read. London, Faber, 1971.

Sequeira, Domingos Antonio de, 1768–1837

11531. Correia, Vergílio. *Sequeira em Roma, duas épocas (1788–1795; 1826–1837).* Coimbra, Imprensa da Universidade, 1923. (Subsidios para a história da arte portuguesa, 6).

11532. Costa, Luiz X. da. *A obra litográfica de Domingos Antonio de Sequeira, com um emboço histórico dos inícios da litográfia em Portugal.* Lisboa, Tipografia do Comércio, 1925.

11533. Mourisca Beaumont, Maria A. *Domingos Antonio de Sequeira, desenhos.* Lisboa, Instituto de Alta Cultura, 1975. (CR).

Serebriakova, Zinaida Evgen'evna, 1884–1967

11534. Kniazeva, Valentina P. *Zinaida Evgen'evna Serebriakova.* Moskva, Izobrazitel'noe Iskusstvo, 1979.

Sergel, Johan Tobias, 1740–1814

11535. Antonsson, Oscar. *Sergels ungdom och romtid.* Stockholm, Norstedt publikationer, 1942. (Sveriges allmänna konstförenings, 50).

11536. Brising, Harald. *Sergels konst.* Stockholm, Norstedt, 1914.

11537. Göthe, Georg. *Johan Tobias Sergel, hans lefnad och verksamhet.* Stockholm, Wahlström & Widstrand, 1898.

11538. ———. *Johan Tobias Sergels skulpturverk.* Stockholm, Norstedt, 1921.

11539. Hamburger Kunsthalle. *Johann Tobias Sergel, 1740–1814.* 22. Mai bis 21. September 1975. München, Prestel/Hamburg, Hamburger Kunsthalle, 1975.

11540. Josephson, Ragnar. *Bellmann, Kellgren, Sergel.* Stockholm, Natur och kultur, 1955.

11541. ———. *Sergels fantasi.* 2 v. Stockholm, Natur och Kultur, 1956.

11542. Lange, Julius. *Sergel og Thorvaldsen; studier i den nordiske Klassicismes.* Kjøbenhavn, Høst, 1886.

11543. Looström, Ludwig. *Johan Tobias Sergel, en gustaviansk tidsbild.* Stockholm, Cederquist, 1914.

11544. Sergel Johan Tobias. *Sergel.* [Exhibition]. Katalogredaktion, Nils-Göran Hökby, Ulf Cedarlöf, Magnus Olausson. Stockholm, Nationalmusuem, 1990.

11545. Thorvaldsens Museum (Copenhagen). *Johan Tobias Sergel, 1740–1814.* 29. januar–1. april 1976. [Text in Danish and English]. København, Thorvaldsens Museum, 1976.

Serlio, Sebastiano, 1475–c. 1554

11546. Bolognini Amorini, Antonio. *Elogio di Sebastiano Serlio, architetto bolognese.* Bologna, Nobili, 1823.

11547. Charvet, Léon. *Sebastien Serlio, 1475–1554.* Lyon, Mondet, 1869.

11548. Rosci, Marco. *Il trattato di architettura di Sebastiano Serlio.* 2 v. Milano, ITEC, 1966.

11549. Rosenfeld, Myra N. *Sebastiano Serlio on domestic architecture: different dwellings from the meanest hovel to the most ornate palace.* Foreword by Adolf K. Placzek; introduction by James S. Ackerman. Cambridge, Mass., MIT Press, 1978.

11550. Serlio, Sebastiano. *Sebastiano Serlio: sesto Seminario internazionale di storia dell'architettura, Vicenza, 31 agosto–4 settembre 1987; a cura di Christof Thoenes.* Milano, Electa, 1989.

11551. Serlio, Sebastiano. *Tutte l'opere d'architettura et prospetiva.* Venezia, Franceschi, 1584. (Reprint of 1619 ed.: Ridgewood, N.J., Gregg, 1964. English ed.: *The first book of architecture.* London, Peake, 1611; reprinted: New York, Blom, 1970).

Serodine, Giovanni, 1584–1631

11552. Papi, Gianni. *Ampliamenti per Giovanni Serodine.* [By] G. Papi [and] Roberto Contini. Bellinzona, Humilibus Consentienties, 1989. (Strumenti e Documenti per lo studio del passato della svizzera italiana, 6).

11553. Schoenenberger, Walter. *Giovanni serodine*

pittore di Ascona. Basel, Birkhäuser, 1957.

11554. Serodine, Giovanni. *Giovanni Serodine (1594/1600–1630) e i precedenti romani.* [Catalogue of an exhibition]. A cura di Roberto Contini e Gianni Papi. Lugano, Fidia edizioni d'arte, 1993.

11555. ———. *Serodine: l'opera completa.* Milano, Electa, 1987. (CR).

11556. ———. *Serodine: la pittura oltre Caravaggio.* Milano , Electa, 1987.

Serov, Valentin Aleksandrovich, 1865–1911

11557. Efimova, Nina I. *Vospominaniia o Valentine Aleksandroviche Serove.* Leningrad, Khudozhnik RSFSR, 1964.

11558. Ernst, Sergei R. *V. A. Serov.* Peterburg, Rossiiskoi Akademeii Istorii Material'noi Kul'tury, 1921.

11559. Grabar, Igor E. *Valentin Aleksandrovich Serov; zhizn'i tvorchestvo, 1865–1911.* Moskva, Iskusstvo, 1980. 2 ed.

11560. Ivanova, Veneta K. *V. A. Serov, 1865–1911.* Sofiia, Nauka, 1960.

11561. Kopshitser, Mark I. *Valentin Serov.* Moskva, Iskusstvo, 1967.

11562. Leniashin, Vladimir A. *Portretnaia zhivopis V. A. Serova, 1900–kh godov: osnovnye problemy.* Leningrad, Khudozhnik RSFSR, 1980.

11563. Sarabyanov, Dmitry and Arbuzov, Grigory, eds. *Valentin Serov: paintings, graphic works, stage designs.* New York, Abrams/ Leningrad, Aurora, 1982. (CR).

11564. Serov, Valentin A. *Perepiska, 1884–1911.* [Ed. by Natalii Sokolovoi]. Leningrad, Iskusstvo, 1937.

11565. ———. *Valentin Serov, paintings, graphic works, stage designs.* Selection by Dmitry Sarabyanov; catalogue and biographical outline by Grigory Arbuzov. New York, Abrams; Leningrad, Aurora, 1982.

11566. Smirnova-Rakitina, Vera I. *Valentin Serov.* Moskva, Molodaia Gvardiia, 1961.

Serpotta, Giacomo, 1656–1732

11567. Basile, Ernesto. *Le scolture e gli stucchi di Giacomo Serpotta.* Torino, Crudo, 1911.

11568. Carandente, Giovanni. *Giacomo Serpotta.* Torino, Edizioni Radiotelevisione Italiana, 1967.

11569. Fazio, Peppe. *Serpotta.* Palermo, Priulla, 1956.

11570. Garstang, Donald. *Giacomo Serpotta and the stuccatori of Palermo, 1560–1790.* Photographs by G. Ffoulke d'Urso. London, A. Zwemmer, 1984. (Italian ed.: Palermo, Sellario, 1990).

11571. Meli, Filippo. *Giacomo Serpotta: vita ed opere.* Palermo, s.n., 1934.

11572. Società Siciliana per la Storia Patria (Palermo). *Secondo centenario della morte di Giacomo Serpotta (1732–1932).* 2 v. [Vol. 2: Meli, Filippo. Giacomo Serpotta, vita ed opere]. Palermo, Società Siciliana, 1934.

Serra, Richard, 1939–

11573. Centre Georges Pompidou (Paris). *Richard Serra.* Paris, Le centre, 1983.

11574. Güse, Ernst-Gerhard., ed. *Richard Serra.* Edited by E. -G. Güse; with contributions by Yve-Alain Bois . . . [et al.];[translations, Michael Robinson (texts by E.-G. Güse and Amin Zweite), John Shepley (text by by Yve-Alain Bois]. New York, Rizzoli, 1988.

11575. Kraus, Rosalind E . . . [et. al.]. *Richard Serra: sculpture.* [Published on the occasion of of an exhibition at the Museum of Modern Art, New York, February 27–May 13, 1986. Edited and with an introduction by Laura Rosenstock; essay by Douglas Crimp. New York, The Museum of Modern Art, 1986.

11576. Pacquement, Alfred. *Richard Serra.* Paris, Centre Georges Pompidou, 1993. (Jalons: collections du Musée national d'art moderne et du Centre de création industrielle).

11577. Serra, Richard. *Richard Serra, deadweights 1991–1992.* [Exhibition] March 21–April 18, 1992. New York, Pace Gallery, 1992.

11578. ———. *Richard Serra, drawings 1969–1990: catalogue raisonné, edited by Hans Janssen = Richard Serra, Zeichnungen 1969–1990, Werkverzeichnis, herausgegbn von Hans Janssen.* Bern, Benteli, 1990[?] (CR).

11579. ———. *Richard Serra: das druckgraphische Werk, 1972–1988 = prints, a catalogue raisonné , 1972–1988.* Neuer Berliner Kunstverein, e.V., 1. Juli–6. August 1988 . . . Text, Richard Hoppe-Sailer. Bochum, Galerie für Film, Video, Neue Konkrete Kunst und Video, 1988.(CR).

11580. ———. *Richard Serra: weight and measure 1992.* [Catalogue of an exhibition held at the Tate Gallery, London], Seattle, University of Washington Press, 1992.

Serre, Michel, 1658–1733

11581. Homet, Marie-Claude. *Michel Serre et la peinture baroque en Provence (1658–1733).* Préface de Jean-Jacques Gloton. Aix-en-Provence, Edisud, 1987.(CR).

Sert, José Luis, 1902–1983

11582. Borràs, Maria L. *Sert: mediterranean architecture.* Boston, New York Graphic Society, 1975.

11583. Freixa, Jaume. *Josep L. Sert.* Barcelona, Gili, 1979. (Spanish/English ed.: 1989).

11584. Harvard University. Graduate School of Design. *The Josep Lluis Sert Collection: a de-*

scriptive inventory of the archival holdings in the Frances Loeb Library, Harvard University, GSD. Cambridge, Mass., The Library, 1900.

11585. Sert, Jose L. *Architecture, city planning, urban design*. Ed. by Knud Bastlund. New York, Praeger, 1966.

11586. ———. *Can our cities survive?* Cambridge, Mass., Harvard University Press/London, Oxford University Press, 1942.

11587. ———. *Josep Lluis Sert: his work and ways*. Editor in charge, Katsuhiko Ichinowatari. Tokyo, Process Architecture; New York, distrib. Van Nostrand Reinhold, 1982.

Sert y Badia, José María, 1876–1945

11588. Castillo, Alberto del. *José María Sert, su vida y su obra*. Barcelona/Buenos Aires, Argos, 1949. 2 ed.

Sérusier, Paul, 1864–1927

11589. Boyle-Turner, Caroline. *Paul Sérusier*. Ann Arbor, Mich., University Microfilms, 1983.

11590. Sérusier, Paul. *ABC de la peinture*. Suivie d'une correspondance inédite recueillie par Madame P. Sérusier. Paris, Floury, 1950.

11591. ———. *ABC de la peinture*. Suivie d'une étude sur la vie et l'oeuvre de Paul Sérusier par Maurice Denis. Paris, Floury, 1942. [2 ed. 1950].

11592. ———. *Hommage à Sérusier et aux peintres du groupe de Pont-Aven*. Catalogue [exhibition] 6 juillet–30 septembre 1958, Musée de Quimper. Quimper, France, 1958.

Servaes, Albert, 1883–1966

11593. Huys, Paul. *Albert Servaes, een kunstnaarsloopbaan. Op documenten van Georges Chabot*. (Kultureel jaarboek voor de provincie Oostvlanderen, 15. jaar, 1 bd., 1961, pp. 65–198.)

11594. Servaes, Albert. *Albert Servaes: de zwitserse periode 1945–1966*. [Catalogue of an exhibition] Koninklijk Museum Antwerpen, 18 Oktober 1970–10 januarie 1971. Catalogus: A. Servaes, L.M.A. Schoonbaerten, Th. Voragen. Antwerpen, Koninklijk Museum voor Schone Kunsten, 1970.

11595. Stubbe, Achilles. *Albert Servaes en de eerste en tweede Latemse kunstenaarsgroep*. Leuwen, Davidsfonds, 1956.

Sesshu, 1420–1506

11596. Covell, Jon E.H. Carter. *Under the seal of Sesshu*. New York, De Pamphilis Press, 1941.

Settignano, Desiderio da *see* Desiderio da Settignano

Seurat, Georges Pierre, 1859–1891

11597. Alexandrian, Sarane. *Seurat*. Trans. by Alice

Sachs. New York, Crown, 1980.

11598. Art Institute of Chicago. *Seurat, paintings and drawings*. January 16–March 7, 1958. Chicago, Art Institute of Chicago, 1958.

11599. Blunt, Anthony. *Seurat*. With an essay by Roger Fry. London, Phaidon, 1965; distributed by New York Graphic Society, Greenwich, Conn.

11600. Broude, Norma, ed. *Seurat in perspective*. Englewood Cliffs, N.J., Prentice-Hall, 1978.

11601. Chastel, André [and] Minervino, Fiorella. *L'opera completa di Seurat*. Milano, Rizzoli, 1972. (CR). (Classici dell'arte, 55).

11602. Coquoit, Gustave. *Georges Seurat*. Paris, Michel, 1924.

11603. Courthion, Pierre. *Georges Seurat*. Trans. by Norbert Guterman. New York, Abrams, 1968.

11604. Coustierier, Lucie. *Seurat*. Paris, Crès, 1926.

11605. Dorra, Henri et Rewald, John. *Seurat: l'oeuvre peint; biographie et catalogue critique*. Paris, Les Beaux-Arts, 1959. (CR).

11606. Grenier, Catherine. *Seurat, catalogo completo dei dipinti*. Firenze, Cantini, 1990. (CR).

11607. Hauke, César M. de. *Seurat et son oeuvre*. 2 v. Paris, Grund, 1961. (CR).

11608. Herbert, Robert L . . . [et al.] *Georges Seurat, 1859–1891*. Robert L. Herbert, with Françoise Cachin, Anne Distel and Gary Tinterow. [Published in conjunction with the exhibition at the Metropolitan Museum of Art]. New York, Metropolitan Museum of Art, 1991.

11609. ———. *Seurat's drawings*. New York, Shorewood, 1962.

11610. Homer, William I. *Seurat and the science of painting*. Cambridge, Mass., MIT Press, 1964.

11611. Kahn, Gustave. *Les dessins de Georges Seurat, 1859–1891*. 2 v. Paris, Bernheim-Jeune, 1928.

11612. Madeleine-Perdrillat, Alain. *Seurat*. New York, Skira/Rizzoli, 1990.

11613. Perruchot, Henri. *La vie de Seurat*. Paris, Hachette, 1966.

11614. Rewald, John. *Georges Seurat*. Trans. by Lionel Abel. New York, Wittenborn, 1943.

11615. ———. *Georges Seurat, a biography*. New York, H.N. Abrams, 1990.

11616. Rich, Daniel C. *Seurat and the evolution of La Grande Jatte*. Chicago, University of Chicago Press, 1935.

11617. Russell, John. *Seurat*. New York, Praeger, 1965.

11618. Seligman, Germain. *The drawings of Georges Seurat*. New York, Valentin, 1947.

11619. Seurat, Georges. *Seurat correspondence, témoinages, notes inédites, critiques*. Préface d'Eric Darragon; choix de textes d'Hélène Seyrès. Paris, Acropole, 1991.

11620. Terrasse, Antoine. *L'univers de Seurat*. Paris,

Scrépel, 1976. (Les carnets de dessins).

11621. Thomson, Richard. *Seurat*. Oxford, Phaidon, 1986.

11622. Wotte, Herbert. *Georges Seurat: Wesen, Werk, Wirkung*. Dresden, VEB Verlag der Kunst, 1988.

11623. Zimmermann, Michael. *Seurat and the art theory of his time*. Antwerp, Fonds Mercator, 1991. (German ed.: Seurat, sein Werk und die kunsttheoretische Debatte seiner Zeit. Weinheim, Verlag Acta Humaniora, 1991).

Severini, Gino, 1883–1966

11624. Fonti, Daniela. *Gino Severini, catalogo ragionato*. Consulenza di Maurizio Fagiolo dell'Arco, Gina Severini Franchina; biografia di Maurizio Fagiolo dell'Arco; Testi critici di Maurizio Fagiolo dell'Arco . . . [et al.]. Milano, A. Mondadori: Edizioni P. Daverio, 1988.

11625. Quinti, Aldo e Quinti, Jolanda. *Severini e Cortona*. Roma, Officina Edizioni, 1976.

11626. Ruggeri, Giorgio. *Il tempo di Gino Severini*. [Catalogue of an exhibition] saggio critico introduttivo di Maurizio Fagiolo dell'Arco. Bologna, Galeria Marescalchi, 1981.

11627. Severini, Gino. *Dal cubismo al classicismo e altri saggi sulla divina proporzione e sul numero d'oro*. A cura di Piero Pacini. Firenze, Marchi & Bertolli, 1972.

11628. ———. *Écrits sur l'art*. Préface de Serge Fauchereau. Paris, Editions cercle d'art, 1987.

11629. ———. *Gino Severini: affreschi, mosaici, decorazioni monumentali, 1921–1941*.[Exhibition catalogue] a cura di Fabio Benzi. Roma, Leonardo-De Luca, 1992.

11630. ———. *Severini*. [Exhibition catalogue] a cura di Gillo Dorfles e Pier Luigi Siena. Milano, Mazzotta, 1987.

11631. ———. *Témoignages: 50 ans de réflexion*. Avec un préface de Georges Borgeaud. Rome, Editions Art Moderne, 1963. (Témoignages, 1).

11632. ———. *La vita di un pittore*. Milano, Edizioni di Comunità, 1965.

11633. Venturi, Lionello. *Gino Severini*. Roma, de Luca, 1961.

Seyssaud, René, 1867–1952

11634. Humbourg, Pierre et Humbourg, Denise. *Seyssaud, avec une biographie, une bibliographie et une documentation complète sur le peintre et son oeuvre*. Genève, Cailler, 1967. (CR).

11635. Roger-Marx, Claude. *René Seyssaud, 1867–1952*. Paris, Braun, 1958.

11636. Seyssaud, René. *Retrospective Seyssaud, 1867–1952*. [Catalogue of an exhibition held at] Hôtel des Ventes d'Aix-en-Provence . . . du 15 au 31 juillet 1957.

11637. Silvestre, Yvonne. *Seyssaud, documents et souvenirs*. Paris, Braun, 1959.

Shahn, Ben, 1898–1969

11638. Bentivoglio, Mirella. *Ben Shahn*. Roma, de Luca, [1963].

11639. McNulty, Kneeland. *The collected prints of Ben Shahn*. Essay and commentary by the artist. [Published in conjunction with an exhibition at the Philadelphia Museum of Art, November 15–December 31, 1967]. Philadelphia, Philadelphia Museum of Art, 1967.

11640. Pohl, Frances Kathryn. *Ben Shahn*. By Frances K. Pohl; with Ben Shahn's writings. San Francisco, Pomegranate Art Books, 1993.

11641. ———. *Ben Shahn, New Deal artist in a cold war climate., 1847–1954*. Austin, University of Texas Press, 1989.

11642. Morse, John D. *Ben Shahn*. New York, Praeger, 1972.

11643. Pratt, Davis, ed. *The photographic eye of Ben Shahn*. Cambridge, Mass., Harvard University Press, 1975.

11644. Prescott, Kenneth W. *The complete graphic works of Ben Shahn*. New York, Quadrangle, 1973. (CR).

11645. Rodman, Selden. *Portrait of the artist as an American: Ben Shahn*. New York, Harper, 1951.

11646. Shahn, Ben. *The shape of content*. Cambridge, Mass., Harvard University Press, 1957.

11647. Shahn, Bernarda B. *Ben Shahn*. New York, Abrams, 1972.

11648. Soby, James T. *Ben Shahn, his graphic art*. New York, Braziller, 1957.

11649. ———. *Ben Shahn, paintings*. New York, Braziller, 1963.

11650. Weiss, Margaret R., ed. *Ben Shahn, photographer: an album from the thirties*. New York, Da Capo, 1973.

Sharaku, Toshusai, fl. 1794

11651. Henderson, Harold G. and Ledoux, Louis V. *The surviving works of Sharaku*. New York, Weyhe, 1939. (CR).

11652. Huguette Berès (Paris). *Sharaku; portraits d'acteurs, 1794–1795*. [Catalogue of an exhibition]. Paris, Huguette Berès, 1980.

11653. Kondo, Ichitaro. *Toshusai Sharaku*. English adaptation by Paul C. Blum. Rutland, Vt., Tuttle, 1955. (Kodansha Library of Japanese Art, 2).

11654. Kurth, Julius. *Sharaku*. München, Piper, 1922. 2 ed.

11655. Rumpf, Fritz. *Sharaku*. Berlin-Lankwitz, Würfel, 1932. 2 ed.

11656. Sharaku, Toshusai. *Sharaku: portraits d'act-eurs 1794–1795.* [Exposition} Huguette Be-rès. Paris, Huguette Berès, 1980.

11657. Suzuki, Juzo. *Sharaku.* Trans. by John Bester. Tokyo/Palo Alto, Calif., Kodansha, 1968. (Masterworks of Ukiyo-e, 2).

Shaw, Richard Norman, 1831–1912

11658. Blomfield, Reginald. *Richard Norman Shaw, R. A., architect 1831–1912.* London, Bats-ford, 1940.

11659. Saint, Andrew. *Richard Norman Shaw.* New Haven/London, Yale University Press, 1976.

Shchusev, Aleksei Viktorovich, 1873–1949

11660. Afanas'ev, Kirill N. *A. V. Shchusev.* Moskva, Stroiizdat, 1978.

11661. Sokolov, N. B. *A. V. Shchusev.* Moskva, God. Izd'vo Lit'ry po Stroitelstvu i Arkhitekture, 1952.

Sheeler, Charles, 1883–1965

11662. Friedman, Martin. *Charles Sheeler.* New York, Watson-Guptill, 1975.

11663. Lucic, Karen. *Charles Sheeler and the cult of the machine.* Cambridge, Mass., Harvard University Press, 1991.

11664. Museum of Modern Art (New York). *Charles Sheeler: paintings, drawings, photo-graphs.* With an introduction by William Carlos Williams. New York, Museum of Modern Art, 1939.

11665. National Collection of Fine Arts, Smithson-ian Institution (Washington, D.C.). *Charles Sheeler.* 10 October–24 November 1968. Washington, D.C., Smithsonian Institution Press, 1968.

11666. Rourke, Constance M. *Charles Sheeler, art-ist in the American tradition.* New York, Harcourt, 1938.

11667. Stebbins, Theodore E. *Charles Sheeler, the photographs.* [By] Theodore E. Stebbins, Jr. and Norman Keyes. Boston, Little Brown, 1987.

11668. Troyen, Carol. *Charles Sheeler, paintings and drawings.* By Carol Troyen and Erica E. Hirshler. Boston, Little Brown, 1987.

Shen Chou, 1427–1509

11669. Edwards, Richard. *The field of stones: a study of the art of Shen Chou (1427–1509).* Washington, D.C., Smithsonian Institution Press, 1962.

11670. Kotzenberg, Heike. *Bild und Aufschrift in der Malerei Chinas, unter besonderer Brück-sichtigung der Literartenmaler der Ming-Zeit (1368–1644): Tang Yin, Wen Cheng-ming und Shen Chou.* Wiesbaden, Steiner, 1981.

11671. Shen Chou. *Shen Chou shan sui = Landscape paintings of Shen Chou.* Tai-pei shih: I shu tu shu kung ssu, min kuo 74 [1985].

Sheridan, Clare, 1885–1959

11672. Leslie, Anita. *Cousin Clare, the tempestuous career of Clare Sheridan.* London, Hutch-inson, 1976.

Sherman, Cindy, 1954–

11673. Krauss, Rosalind E. *Cindy Sherman, 1975–1993.* With an essay by Norman Bryson. New York, Rizzoli, 1993.

11674. Sherman, Cindy. *Cindy Sherman.* Amster-dam, Stedelijk Museum, 1982.

11675. ———. *Cindy Sherman.* [Catalogue edited and designed by Thomas Kellein; translation, Sebastian Wormell]. Stuttgart, Edition Cantz, 1991.

11676. ———. *Cindy Sherman.* [Catalogue of an exhibition]. Essays by Peter Schjeldahl and Lisa Phillipos. New York, Whitney Museum of American Art, 1987.

11677. ———. *Cindy Sherman.* Mit Texten von Els Barents und Schjeldahl. Munich, Schirmer/Mosel, 1987.

11678. ———. *Cindy Sherman.* With an introduc-tion by Peter Schjeldahl and an afterword by I. Michael Danoff. New York, Pantheon Books, 1984. 3 ed.

Shih-Tao *see* Tao Chi

Shishkin, Ivan Ivanovich, 1832–1898

11679. Savinov, Alexei and Fiodorov-Davydov, Alexei. *Shishkin.* Selection and biographical outline by Irina Shuvalova. Leningrad, Au-rora, 1981.

11680. Shishkin, Ivan Ivanovich. *Ivan Ivanovich Shishkin.* [Avtor i sostavitel, Nikolaii Niko-laevich Novouspenskii]. Leningrad," Khud-ozhnik SFSR", 1990.

11681. Shuvalova, Irina. *Ivan Ivanovich Shishkin: perepiska, dnevnik, sovremenniki o khud-oznike.* Leningrad, Iskusstvo Leningradskoe Otd-nie, 1978.

11682. ———. *Shishkin.* [Text in English, French, German, and Russian]. Leningrad, Aurora, 1971.

Shubin, Fedot Ivanovich, 1740–1805

11683. Iakovleva. Nonna Aleksandrovna. *Fedot Ivanovich Shubin, 1740–1805.* Leningrad, "Khudozhnik RSFSR", 1984.

11684. Lazareva, Ol'ga P. *Russkii skul'ptor Fedot Shubin.* Moskva, Iskusstvo, 1965.

Shubun, early 15th c.

11685. Nakamura, Nihei. *Die Tuschmalerei des Shubun und das Problem der unbemalten weissen Flächen.* Mit einem Vorwort von Joseph Gantner. Konstanz, Leonhardt, 1981.

Shunshō, Katsukawa, 1726–1792

11686. Boller, Willy. *Japanische Farbholzschnitte von Katsukawa Shunsho.* Bern, Hallwag, 1953.

11687. Succo, Friedrich. *Katsukawa Shunsho.* Plauen im Vogtland, Schulz, 1922.

Sickert, Walter, 1860–1942

11688. Baron, Wendy. *Sickert.* London, Phaidon, 1973. (CR).

11689. Browse, Lillian. *Sickert.* London, Hart-Davis, 1960.

11690. Connett, Maureen. *Walter Sickert and the Camden Town Group.* Newton Abbott, Devon., David & Charles, 1992.

11691. Emmons, Robert. *The life and opinions of Walter Richard Sickert.* London, Faber, 1941.

11692. Lilly, Marjorie. *Sickert: the painter and his circle.* London, Elek, 1971.

11693. Shone, Richard. *Walter Sickert.* Oxford, Phaidon, 1988.

11694. Sickert, Walter R. *A free house!, or the artist as craftsman; being the writings of Walter Richard Sickert.* Edited by Osbert Sitwell. London, Macmillan, 1947.

11695. ———. *Sickert: paintings.* [Catalogue of an exhibition] edited by Wendy Baron and Richard Shone; with contributions from Wendy Baron . . . [et al.]. London, Royal Academy of Arts; New Haven, Yale University Press, 1992.

11696. Sutton, Denys. *Walter Sickert, a biography.* London, Joseph, 1976.

11697. Troyen, Aimée. *Walter Sickert as printmaker.* [Published in conjunction with an exhibition at the Yale Center for British Art, New Haven, February 21–April 15, 1979]. New Haven, Yale Center for British Art, 1979.

Signac, Paul, 1863–1935

11698. Besson, George. *Signac, dessins.* Paris, Braun, 1950.

11699. Cachin, Françoise. *Paul Signac.* Paris, Bibliothèque des Arts, 1971.

11700. Coustorier, Lucie. *Signac.* Paris, Crès, 1922.

11701. Kornfeld, E. W., and Wick, P. A. *Catalogue raisonné de l'oeuvre gravé et lithographié de Paul Signac.* Berne, Kornfeld et Klipstein, 1974. (CR).

11702. Mura, Anna M. *Signac.* Milano. Fabbri, 1967. (I maestri del colore, 180).

11703. Musée du Louvre (Paris). *Signac.* Déc. 1963–fév. 1964. Paris, Ministère d'Etat Affaires Culturelles, [1963].

11704. Ratliff, Floyd. *Paul Signac and color in neo-impressionism; including the first English edition of From Eugène Delacroix to neo-impressionism by Paul Signac; translated* from the third French edition (H. Floury, Paris, 1921) by Willa Sivermnan.. New York, Rockefeller University Press, 1992.

11705. Signac, Paul. *D'Eugène Delacroix au neo-impressionisme.* Introd. et notes par Françoise Cachin. Paris, Hermann, 1978. (First ed.: Paris, Floury, 1899).

Signorelli, Luca, 1441–1523

11706. Baldini, Umberto. *Luca Signorelli.* Milano, Fabbri, 1966. (I maestri del colore, 176).

11707. Cruttwell, Maud. *Luca Signorelli.* London, Bell, 1899.

11708. Dussler, Luitpold. *Signorelli, des Meisters Gemälde.* Stuttgart, Deutsche Verlags-Anstalt, 1927. (Klassiker der Kunst, 34).

11709. Gizzi, Corrado. *Signorelli e Dante.* [Catalogue of an exhibition]. A cura di C. Gizzi. Milano, Electa, 1991.

11710. Kury, Gloria. *The early work of Luca Signorelli: 1465–1490.* New York/London, Garland, 1978.

11711. Mancini, Girolamo. *Vita di Luca Signorelli.* Firenze, Carnesecchi, 1903.

11712. Moriondo, Margherita. *Mostra di Luca Signorelli, catalogo: Cortona, maggio–agosto; Firenze, settembre–ottobre, 1953.* Firenze, L'Arte della Stampa, 1953.

11713. Paolucci, Antonio. *Luca Signorelli.* Antella (Florence), Scala; New York, Riverside, 1990. (The Library of great masters).

11714. Salmi, Mario. *Luca Signorelli.* Novara, Istituto Geografico de Agostini, 1953.

11715. Scarpellini, Pietro. *Luca Signorelli.* Milano, Club del Libro, 1964. (Collana d'arte del Club del Libro, 10).

11716. Venturi, Adolfo. *Luca Signorelli.* Firenze, Alinari, 1922.

11717. Vischer, Robert. *Luca Signorelli und die italienische Renaissance; eine kunsthistorische Monographie.* Leipzig, Viet, 1879.

Signorini, Telemaco, 1835–1901

11718. Dini, Piero. *Telemaco Signorini.* [Catalogue of an exhibition]. A cura di Piero Dini; collaborazione di Aide Maltagliati. Montecatini Terme, il Comune, assessorato alla cultura, 1987.

11719. Masini, Lara Vinca. *Telemaco Signorini.* Firenze, Edizioni d'arte il Fiorino, 1983. (Collana "La Specola". I Macchiaioli, 2).

11720. Monti, Raffaele. *Signorini e il naturalismo europeo.* Roma, De Luca, 1984.

Siloe, Diego de, ca. 1495–1563 *see also* Berruguete, Alonso Gonzalez

11721. Gomez-Moreno, Manuel. *Diego Siloe: homenaje en el IV centenario de su muerte.* Granada, Universidad de Granada, 1963.

Silva, Maria Elena Vieira da *see* **Vieira da Silva, Maria Elena**

Silva y Velazquez, Diego Rodriguez de *see* **Velazquez, Diego Rodriguez de Silva y**

Sima, Josef, 1891–1971.
11722. Smejkal, Frantisek. *Josef Sima*. Praha, Odeon, 1988.
11723. Sima, Josef. *Sima: oeuvres récentes*. [Catalogue of an exhibition], 30 novemmbre 1971–fin janvier 1972. Galérie le Point cardinal, Paris. Préface par Jean Starobinski; poèmes de Claude Esteban, Octavio Paz et Jacques Dupin, Paris, Galérie le apoint cardinal, 1971.
11724. ———. *Sima: 3 avril–21 juin 1992*. [Catalogue of an exhibition], Musée d'art moderne de la Ville de Paris. Paris, le Musée, 1992.

Sinan, Koca, mimar, 1489 or 90–1588
11725. Egli, Ernst. *Sinan, der Baumeister osmanischer Glanzzeit*. Erlenbach-Zürich/Stuttgart, Rentsch, 1976. 2 ed.
11726. Gennaro, Paola. *Istanbul: l'opera di Sinan*. Milano, Cittàstudi, 1992.
11727. Stratton, Arthur. *Sinan*. New York, Scribner, 1971.

Sintenis, Renée, 1888–1965
11728. Buhlmann, Britta. *Renée Sintenis: Plastiken, Zeichnungen, Druckgraphik*. Berlin, Frölich und Kaufmann, 1983.
11729. ———. *Renée Sintenis: Werkmonographie der Skulpturen*. Darmstadt, Wissenschaftliche Buchgemeinschaft, 1987. (CR).
11730. Crevel, René und Biermann, Georg. *Renée Sintenis*. Berlin, Klinkhardt & Biermann, 1930. (Junge Kunst, 57).
11731. Hagelstange, Rudolf, et al. *Renée Sintenis*. Berlin, Aufbau, 1947.
11732. Kiel, Hanna. *Renée Sintenis*. Berlin, Rembrandt, 1956. (Die Kunst unserer Zeit, 10).

Siqueiros, David Alfaro, 1896–1974
11733. Azpeitia, Rafael C., ed. *Siqueiros*. México, D.F., Secretaría de Educación Pública, 1974.
11734. Folgarait, Leonard. *So far from Heaven: David Alfaro Siqueiros' The march of humanity and Mexican revolutionary politics*. Cambridge/New York, Cambridge University Press, 1987.
11735. Orsanmichele/Palazzo Vecchio (Florence). *Siqueiros: David Alfaro Siqueiros e il muralismo messicano*. 10 novembre 1976–15 febbraio 1977. Firenze, Calenzano, 1976.
11736. Rochfort, Desmond. Mexican muralists: Orozco, Rivera, *Siqueiros*. London, L. King, 1993.

11737. Rodriguez, Antonio. *David Alfaro Siqueiros*. Mexico, D.F., Consejo Nacional de Recursos para la Atencion de la juventud: Terra Nova, 1985.
11738. Siqueiros, David A. *Como se pinta un mural*. México, D.F., Ediciones Mexicanas, 1951.
11739. ———. *Me llamaban el Coronelazo: memorias*. México, D.F., Grijalbo, 1977.
11740. Tibol, Raquel. *Siqueiros, introductor de realidades*. México, D.F., Universidad Nacional Autonoma de México, 1961.

Sirani, Elisabetta, 1638–1665
11741. Bianchini, Andrea. *Prove legali sull'avvelenamento della celebre pittrice bolognese Elisabetta Sirani*. Bologna, Guidi all'Ancora, 1854.
11742. Manaresi, Antonio. *Elisabetta Sirani; la vita, l'arte, la morte*. Bologna, Zanichelli, 1898.
11743. Mazzoni Toselli, Ottavio. *Di Elisabetta Sirani, pittrice bolognese ed il supposto veneficio onde credesi morta nell'anno XXVII di sua età; racconto storico*. Bologna, Tipografia del Genio, 1833.
11744. Moretti, Valeria. *Il pennello lacrimato: sulle trace di Elisabetta Sirani*. Ancona, Il Lavoro, 1990.

Sironi, Mario, 1885–1961
11745. Bellonzi, Fortunato. *Sironi*. [By] F. Bellonzi. Apparati biografici e bibliografici di Claudia Gian Ferrari. Milano, Electa, 1985.
11746. Benzi, Babio. *Sironi illustratore: catalogo ragionato*. [By] F. Benzi, Andrea Sironi. Roma, De Luca Edizioni d'Arte, 1988.(CR).
11747. Bonfand, Alain. *L'ombre de la nuit: essai sur la mélancolie et l'angoisse dans les oeuvres de Mario Sironi et de Paul Klee entre 1933 et 1940*. Paris, La Différence, 1993.
11748. Bossaglia, Rossana. *Sironi: il tessuti e le arti applicate*. Nuoro, Ilisaso, 1992.
11749. Gallo, Francesco. *Sironi: paesaggi*. [By] F. Gallo; catalogo, Francesca Dogana. Milano, Fabbri, 1991.
11750. Penelope, Mario. *Sironi: opere 1902–1960*. [Catalogue of an exhibition] a cura di Mario Penelope. Milano, A. Mondadori; Roma, De Luca, 1985.
11751. Pica, Agnoldomenico. *Mario Sironi, metodo e tecnica*. Catalogo a cura di Francesco Melonio; testi di Agnoldomenico Pica e di Paolo Baldacci. Milano, Edizioni Philippe Daverio: Arnoldo Mondadori editore, 1984.
11752. Sironi, Mario. *Mario Sironi (1885–1961)*. [Catalogue of an exhibition] hrsg. von Jürgen Harten und Jochen Poetter mit Textbeiträgen von Paolo Baldacci, Guido Ballo, Emily Braun und Vittorio Magnano Lampugnani; Gastkurator, Guido Ballo. Köln, DuMont Buchverlag, 1988.

Siskind, Aaron, 1903–

11753. Chiarenza, Carl. *Aaron Siskind: pleasures and terrors.* Foreword by James L. Enyeart. Boston, Little, Brown, 1982.

11754. Lyons, Nathan, ed. *Aaron Siskind, photographer.* Rochester, N.Y., George Eastman House, 1965. (George Eastman House Monograph, 5).

11755. Siskind, Aaron. *Harlem photographs 1932–1940.* Aaron Siskind; foreword, Gordon Parks; Harlem, a document, Marcia Battle; text from Federal Writers' project edited by Ann Banks. Washington, National Museum of American Art, 1990. Smithsonian Institution Press, 1990.

11756. Siskind, Aaron. *Photographs.* Introduction by Harold Rosenberg. New York, Horizon Press, 1959.

11757. ———. *Road trip: photographs, 1980–1988.* Introduction by Charles Traub. San Francisco, Friends of Photography, 1989.

11758. ———. *The Siskind variations: a quartet of photographs & contemplations,* by Aaron Siskind; orchestrated & edited by Michael Torosian. Toronto, Lumière Press, 1990.

Sisley, Alfred, 1839–1899

11759. Couldrey, Vivienne. *Alfred Sisley, the English Impressionist.* London, Newton Abbot, David & Charles, 1992.

11760. Cogniat, Raymond. *Sisley.* Paris, Flammarion, 1978. 2 ed. 1992.

11761. Daulte, François. *Alfred Sisley; catalogue raisonné de l'oeuvre peint.* Lausanne, Durand-Ruel, 1959. (CR).

11762. ———. *Sisley: les saisons.* Paris, Bibliothèque des arts, 1992.

11763. Geffroy, Gustave. *Sisley.* Paris, Crès, 1923. (Les cahiers d'aujourd'hui).

11764. Shone, Richard. *Sisley.* London, Phaidon, 1992.

11765. Stevens, Mary Anne, ed. *Alfred Sisley, 1839–1899.* Ed. by M.A. Stevens with contributions by Isabelle Cahn . . . [et al.] New Haven, Yale University Press; London, Royal Academy of Arts, 1992.

Skidmore, Owings and Merrill, I.E.: Skidmore, Louis, 1897–1962 Merrill, John O., 1896–1975 Owings, Nathaniel A., 1903–1984

11766. Danz, Ernst. *The architecture of Skidmore, Owings & Merrill, 1950–1962.* Introduction by Henry R. Hitchcock. Trans. by Ernst van Haagen. New York, Praeger, 1963.

11767. Drexler, Arthur and Mengs, Axel. *The architecture of Skidmore, Owings & Merrill, 1963–1973.* New York, Architectural Book Publishing Co., 1974.

11768. Owings, Nathaniel A. *The spaces in between: an architect's journey.* Boston, Houghton Mifflin, 1973.

11769. Skidmore, Owings & Merrill. *Representative projects of SOM: Skidmore, Owings & Merrill Architects-Engineers.* Chicago, SOM, 1977.

11770. Woodward, Christopher. *Skidmore, Owings & Merrill.* New York, Simon & Schuster, 1970.

Slevogt, Max, 1868–1932

11771. Alten, Wilken von. *Max Slevogt.* Bielefeld/Leipzig, Velhagen & Klasing, 1926. (Künstler-Monographien, 116).

11772. Guthmann, Johannes. *Scherz und Laune: Max Slevogt und seine Gelegenheitsarbeiten.* Berlin, Cassirer, 1920.

11773. Imiela, Hans-Jürgen. *Max Slevogt, eine Monografie.* Karlsruhe, Braun, 1968.

11774. ———. *Slevogt und Mozart: Werke von Max Slevogt zu den Opern "Don Giovanni" und "Die Zauberflöte".* [Catalogue of an exhibition [by] H.-J. Imiela, Berthold Roland, mit Texten von Bruno Eisner . . . [et al.]. Mainz, P. von Zabern, 1991.

11775. Kunsthalle Bremen. *Max Slevogt und seine Zeit: Gemälde, Handzeichnungen, Aquarelle, Druckgraphik.* 13. September bis 27. Oktober 1968. Bremen, Kunsthalle Bremen, 1968.

11776. Roland, Berthold, Hrsg. *Max Slevogt: Äyptenreise 1914.* [Katalog-Handbuch]. Mainz, Philipp von Zabern, 1989.

11777. Roland, Berthold. *Max Slevogt: pfälzische Landschaften.* [By] Bertold Roland; mit Texten von Wilken von Alten . . . [et al.]; und einem Beitrag von Hans-Jürgen Imiela. München, Hirmer, 1991.

11778. ———. *Max Slevogt: Illustrationen zu James Fenimore Cooper "Lederstrumpf-Erzählungen".* [Ausstellungskonzept und Katalogbearbeitung, Berthold Roland]. Edenkoben, Max-Slevogt-Galerie, Schloss "Villa Ludwigshöhe", 1984.

11779. Scheffler, Karl. *Max Slevogt.* Berlin, Rembrandt, 1940. (Die Kunstbibliothek des Volkes, 43).

11780. Sievers, Johannes [and] Waldmann, Emil. *Max Slevogt: das druckgraphische Werk, 1890–1914.* Herausgegeben von Hans-Jürgen Imiela. Heidelberg/Berlin, Impuls-Verlag, 1962.(CR). 2 ed.with English translations: San Francisco, A. Wofsy, 1991.

11781. Slevogt, Max. *Max Slevogt: Gemälde, Aquarelle, Zeichnungen.* Hrsg. von Ernst-Gerhard Güse, Hans-Jürgen Imiela, Berthold Roland; mit Beiträgen von Lorenz Dittmann . . . [et al.]. Stuttgart, G. Hatje, 1992.

11782. Waldmann, Emil. *Max Slevogt.* Berlin, Cassirer, 1923.

Sloan, John, 1871–1951

11783. Brooks, Van Wyck. *John Sloan; a painter's life.* New York, Dutton, 1955.

11784. DuBois, Guy P. *John Sloan.* New York, Whitney Museum of Art, 1931.

11785. Goodrich, Lloyd. *John Sloan.* New York, Macmillan, 1952.

11786. Hawkes, Elizabeth H. *John Sloan's illustrations in magazines and books.* Wilmington, Delaware Art Museum, 1993. (Delaware Art Museum occasional paper, 4).

11787. Morse, Peter. *John Sloan's prints: a catalogue raisonné of the etchings, lithographs, and posters.* With a foreword by Jacob Kainen. New Haven/London, Yale University Press, 1969. (CR).

11788. National Gallery of Art (Washington, D.C.). *John Sloan, 1871–1951: his life and paintings, his graphics.* September 18, 1971–October 31, 1971. [Text by David W. Scott and E. John Bullard]. Washington, D.C., National Gallery of Art, 1971.

11789. Scott, David. *John Sloan.* New York, Watson-Guptill, 1975.

11790. Sloan, John. *Gist of art: principles and practise expounded in the classroom and studio.* Recorded with the assistance of Helen Farr. New York, American Artists Group, 1939.

11791. ———. *John Sloan's New York scene, from the diaries, notes, and correspondence, 1906–1913.* Edited by Bruce St. John; with an introduction by Helen Farr Sloan. New York, Harper & Row, 1965.

11771. ———. *John Sloan's oil paintings: a catalogue raisonné.* Comp. by Rowland Elzea. Newark, University of Delaware Press; London, Associated University Presses, 1991. (CR).

11792. St. John, Bruce. *John Sloan.* New York, Praeger, 1971.

Sluter, Claus, ca. 1355–ca. 1406

11793. Arnoldi, Francesco N. *Sluter e la scultura borgognona.* Milano, Fabbri, 1966. (I maestri della scultura, 79).

11794. David, Henri. *Claus Sluter.* Paris, Tisné, 1951.

11795. Kleinclausz, Arthur J. *Claus Sluter et la sculpture bourguignonne au XV siècle.* Paris, Librairie de l'Art Ancien et Moderne, 1905.

11796. Liebreich, Aenne. *Claus Sluter.* Bruxelles, Dietrich, 1936.

11797. Morand, Kathleen. *Claus Sluter: artist at the court of Burgundy.* Photographs by David Finn. Austin, University of Texas Press; London, Harvey Miller, 1991.

11798. Schreckenberg, Hella. *Claus Sluter.* Bochum, Brockmeyer, 1987. (Bochumer historische Studien. Mittelalterliche Geschichte, 6).

11799. Sluter, Claus. *Actes des journées internationales Claus Sluter: Septembre 1990.* Dijon, Association Claus Sluter, 1992.

11800. Troescher, Georg. *Claus Sluter und die burgundische Plastik um die Wende des XIV. Jahrhunderts.* Freiburg i.Br., Urban-Verlag, [1932].

Smibert, John, 1688–1751

11801. Foote, Henry W. *John Smibert, painter.* Cambridge, Mass., Harvard University Press, 1950.

11802. Smibert, John. *The notebook of John Smibert.* With essays by Sir David Evans, John Kerslake and Andrew Oliver. Boston, Massachusetts Historical Society, 1969.

Smith, David, 1906–1965

11803. Carmean, E. A., Jr. *David Smith.* [Published in conjunction with an exhibition at the National Gallery of Art, Washington, D.C., November 7, 1982–April 24, 1983]. Washington, D.C., National Gallery of Art, 1982.

11804. Clark, Trinkett. *The drawings of David Smith.* Organized and circulated by the International Exhibitions Foundation. Washington, D.C., The Foundation, 1985.

11805. Cummings, Paul. *David Smith, the drawings.* [Published in conjunction with an exhibition at the Whitney Museum of American Art, New York]. New York, Whitney Museum, 1979.

11806. Fogg Art Museum, Harvard University (Cambridge, Mass.). *David Smith, 1906–1965; a retrospective exhibition.* September 28–November 15, 1966. Cambridge, Mass., President and Fellows of Harvard College, 1966.

11807. Fry, Edward F. *David Smith.* [Published in conjunction with an exhibition at the Solomon R. Guggenheim Museum, New York]. New York, Guggenheim Foundation, 1969.

11808. Krauss, Rosalind E. *The sculpture of David Smith, a catalogue raisonné.* New York/London, Garland, 1977. (CR). (Garland Reference Library of the Humanities, 73).

11809. ———. *Terminal iron works: the sculpture of David Smith.* Cambridge, Mass., MIT Press, 1971.

11810. Marcus, Stanley E. *David Smith: the sculptor and his work.* Ithaca, N.Y., Cornell University Press, 1984.

11811. Schwartz, Alexandra. *David Smith: the prints.* Introductory essay by Paul Cummings. New York, Pace Prints, 1987. (CR).

11812. Smith, David. *David Smith.* Edited by Garnett McCoy. New York, Praeger, 1973.

11813. ———. *David Smith by David Smith.* Text and photographs by the author. Edited by Cleve Gray. New York, Holt, Rinehart and Winston, 1968.

11814. ———. *David Smith, nudes: drawings and*

paintings from 1927–1964: March 29 to April 26, 1990. New York, Knoedler & Co., 1990.

11815. ———. David Smith, sculpture and drawings. Ed. by Jorn Merkert. With contributions by Hannelore Kersting, Rachel Kirby and Jorn Merkert, and selected writings by David Smith. Munich, Prestel, 1986.

11816. ———. David Smith—sculptures and writings. Ed. by Cleve Gray. New York, Thames and Hudson, 1988.

Smith, William Eugene, 1918–1978

11817. Hansen, Henning. Myth and vision: on the Walk to Paradise Garden and the photography of W. Eugene Smith. [Lund] Sweden, University of Lund, Institute of Art History, 1987. (Aris, nova ser., 3).

11818. Hughes, Jim. W. Eugene Smith: shadow & substance: the life and work of an American photographer. New York, McGraw-Hill, 1989.

11819. Johnson, William S. W. Eugene Smith, master of the photographic essay. Foreword by James L. Enyeart. Millerton, N.Y., Aperture, 1981.

11820. Maddow, Ben. Let truth be the prejudice: W. Eugene Smith, his life and photographs. Illustrated biography by Ben Maddow. Afterword by John G. Morris. New York, Aperture; distributed in the U.S. by Viking Penguin, 1985.

11821. Smith, W. Eugene. W. Eugene Smith. Intro. by William Johnson. New York, Pantheon Books; Paris, Centre national de la photographie, 1986.

11822. ———. Eugene Smith: his photographs and notes. Afterword by Lincoln Kirstein. New York, Aperture, 1969.

11823. Willumson, Glenn Gardner. W. Eugene Smith and the photographic essay. Cambridge/New York, Cambridge University Press, 1992.

Smithson, Robert, 1938–1973

11824. Hobbs, Robert C., et al. Robert Smithson, sculpture. Ithaca, N.Y., Cornell University Press, 1981.

11825. Smithson, Robert. Robert Smithson: drawings from the estate. Westfälisches Landesmuseum für Kunst und Kulturgeschichte Münster, 25. Juni 1989–27. August 1989, Vestsjllands Kunstmuseum Sor, 16. September 1989–15. Oktober 1989, Kunstraum München e.V., 28. November 1989–3. Februar 1990. [Übersetzungen, Brigitte Kalthoff. Ausstellung und Katalog, Friedrich Meschede. Katalogredaktion, Friedrich Meschede, Brigitte Kalthoff]. Münster, Landschaftsverband Westfalen-Lippe, [1989?].

11826. ———. Robert Smithson: el paisage en-tropico: una retrospectiva, 1960–1973. Valencia, IVAM Centre Julio Gonzalez, Generalitat Valenciana, Conselleria de Cultura, Educacio i Ciencia, 1993.

11827. ———. The writings of Robert Smithson; essays with illustrations. Edited by Nancy Holt. New York, New York University Press, 1979.

11828. Sobieszek, Robert A. Robert Smithson: photo works. Los Angeles, Los Angeles County Museum of Art; Albuquerque, University of New Mexico Press, 1993.

11829. Tsai, Eugenie. Robert Smithson unearthed: drawings, collages, writings. New York, Columbia University Press, 1991. (Columba studies on art, 4).

Smythson, Robert, 1534/5–1614

11830. Girouard, Mark. Robert Smythson & the Elizabethan country house. New Haven, Yale University Press, 1983. 2 ed.

Snyders, Frans, 1579–1657

11831. Robels, Hella. Frans Snyders, Stilleben- und Tiermaler, 1579–1657. München, Deutscher Kunstverlag, [1989].

Soane, John, 1753–1837

11832. Bolton, Arthur T. The portrait of John Soane (1753–1837) set forth in letters from his friends (1775–1837). London, Butler, 1927.

11833. Du Prey, Pierre de la Ruffinière. John Soane, the making of an architect. Chicago, University of Chicago Press, 1982.

11834. ———. Sir John Soane. London, Victoria and Albert Museum, 1985.

11835. Millenson, Susan Feinberg. Sir John Soane's Museum. Ann Arbor, UMI Research Press, 1987. (Architecture and urban design, 18).

11836. Schumann-Bacia, Eva. John Soane und die Bank of England 1788 bis 1833. Hildesheim/New York, G. Olms, 1990. (Studien zur Kunstgeschichte, 58).

11837. ———. John Soane and the Bank of England. New York, Princeton Architectural Prss, 1991.

11838. Stroud, Dorothy. The architecture of Sir John Soane. With an introduction by Henry Russell Hitchcock. London, Studio, 1961.

11839. Summerson, John N. Sir John Soane, 1753–1837. London, Art and Technics, 1952.

11840. Thornton, Peter and Dorey, Helen. Sir John Soane: the architect as collector, 1753–1837. Photographs by Ole Woldbye. New York, Harry N. Abrams, Inc., 1992.

Sodoma, Il, 1477–1549

11841. Cust, Robert H. Giovanni Antonio Bazzi, hitherto usually styled Sodoma: the man and the painter, 1477–1549; a study. New York, Dutton, 1909.

11842. Faccio, Cesare. *Giovan Antonio Bazzi (Il Sodoma), pittore vercellese del secolo XVI.* Vercelli, Gallardi & Ugo, 1902.

11843. Gielly, Louis. *Le Sodoma.* Paris, Plon, [1911].

11844. Hauvette, Henri. *Le Sodoma, biographie critique.* Paris, Laurens, 1911.

11845. Hayum, Andrée. *Giovanni Antonio Bazzi— Il Sodoma.* New York/London, Garland, 1976.

11846. Jacobsen, Emil. *Sodoma und das Cinquecento in Siena.* Strassburg, Heitz, 1910. (Zur Kunstgeschichte des Auslandes, 74).

11847. Jansen, Albert. *Leben und Werke des Malers Giovannantonio Bazzi von Vercelli, genannt Il Sodoma.* Stuttgart, Ebner & Seubert, 1870.

11848. Marciano-Agostinelli Tozzi, M. T. *Il Sodoma.* Messina, d'Amico, 1951.

11849. Priuli-Bon, Lilian. *Sodoma.* London, Bell, 1900.

11850. Segard, Achille. *Giov.-Antonio Bazzi detto Sodoma et la fin de l'école de Sienne aux XVI siècle.* Paris, Floury, 1910.

11851. Terrasse, Charles. *Sodoma.* Paris, Alcan, 1925.

Soest, Conrad von, fl. 1402–1404

11852. Hölker, Carl. *Meister Conrad von Soest und seine Bedeutung für die norddeutsche Malerei in der ersten Hälfte des 15. Jahrhunderts.* Münster in Westfalen, Coppenrath, 1921. (Beiträge zur westfälischen Kunstgeschichte, 7).

11853. Meier, Paul J. *Werk und Wirkung des Meisters Konrad von Soest.* Münster in Westfalen, Coppenrath, 1921. (Westfalen, 1).

11854. Steinbart, Kurt. *Konrad von Soest.* Wien, Schroll, 1946.

Solario, Andrea, 1460–1524

11855. Badt, Kurt. *Andrea Solario, sein Leben und seine Werke; ein Beitrag zur Kunstgeschichte der Lombardei.* Leipzig, Klinkhardt & Biermann, 1914.

11856. Béguin, Sylvie. *Andrea Solario en France.* Catalogue établi et rédigé par Sylvie Béguin. Paris, Ministère de la culture, Editions de la Réunion des musées nationaux, 1985. (Les Dossiers du Département des peintures, 31).

11857. Brown, David Alan. *Andrea Solario.* Milano, Electa, 1987. (CR).

11858. Cogliati Arano, Luisa. *Andrea Solario.* Milano, Edizioni Tecnografico Italiano, 1965.

Sole, Giovan Gioseffo, Dal, 1654–1719

11859. Thiem, Christel. *Giovan Gioseffo Dal Sole, dipinti, affreschi, disegni.* Bologna, Nuova Alfa, 1990.

Somaini, Francesco, 1926–

11860. Barilli, Renato. *Somaini realizzazione, progetti, utopie.* Como, Comune di Como; Bologna, Edizioni Bora, 1984.

11861. Bossaglia, Rossana and Farina, Franco. *Francesco Somaini, l'opera recente.* [Catalog of an exhibition held in Ferrara at the Galleria civica d'arte moderna, Palazzo dei Diamanti, April–May 1986]. Bologna, Bora, [1986].

11862. Somaini, Francesco. *Somaini per Sorrento: sculture 1967–1988.* A cura di Ciro Ruji. Napoli, Electa Napoli, 1989.

Sommer, Frederick, 1905–

11863. Sommer, Frederick. *All children are ambassadors.* Munich, Nazraeli Press, 1992.

11864. ———. *Frederick Sommer: the constellations that surround us: the conjunction of general aesthetics and poetic logic in an artist's life.* Surveyed and ed. by Michael Torosian. Toronto, Lumière Press, 1992. (Homage, 6).

11865. ———. *The mistress of this world has no name.* Essay by Stephen Aldrich. Denver, Denver Art Museum, 1987.

Sonne, Jorgen Valentin, 1801–1890

11866. Damsgaard, Nina . . . [et al.]. *Jørgen Sonne, 1801–1890.* [Catalog of an exhibition held at the Thorvaldsens Museum, Copenhagen, Nov. 17, 1988–Jan. 8, 1989 and at the Aarhus Kunstmuseum, Feb. 4–Mar. 27, 1989]. København, Thorvaldsens Museum, Aarhus Kunstmusem, 1988.

Sorolla y Bastida, Joaquín, 1863–1923

11867. Anderson, Ruth M. *Costumes painted by Sorolla in his provinces of Spain.* New York, Hispanic Society of America, 1957.

11868. Beruete, Aureliano de, et al. *Eight essays on Joaquín Sorolla y Bastida.* 2 v. New York, Hispanic Society of America, 1909.

11869. Doménech, Rafael. *Sorolla, su vida y su arte.* Barcelona, Bayés, 1907.

11870. Manaut Viglietti, José. *Cronica del pintor Joaquín Sorolla.* Madrid, Editora Nacional, 1964.

11871. Pantorba, Bernardino de [pseud., Lopez Jiménez, José]. *La vida y la obra de Joaquín Sorolla, estudio biografico y critico.* Madrid, Gráficas Monteverde, 1970. 2 ed. (CR).

11872. Sorolla, Joaquín. *The painter Joaquín Sorolla y Bastida.* Ed. by Edmund Peel. With essays by Francisco Pons Sorolla, Carmen Gracia, Priscilla Muller. London, Sotheby's Publications; San Diego, Cal., San Diego Museum of Art; New York, distributed by in the United States by Sotheby's Publications, Harper and Row, 1989.

11873. Vehils, Rafael, et al. *Sorolla, 1863–1923.*

Buenos Aires, Institución Cultural Española, 1942.

Sotatsu, Tawaraya, 1576–1643 *see also* Koetsu And Korin

11874. Croissant, Doris. *Sotatsu und der Sotatsu-Stil: Untersuchungen zu Repertoire, Ikonographie und Ästhetik der Malerei des Tawaraya Sotatsu (um 1600–1640)*. Wiesbaden, F. Steiner, 1978. (Münchener ostasiatische Studien: Sonderreihe, 3).

11875. Grilli, Elise. *Tawaraya Sotatsu*. Edited by Ichimatsu Tanaka. Tokyo/Rutland, Vt., Tuttle, 1956. (Kodansha Library of Japanese Art, 6).

11876. Watson, William. *Sotatsu*. Based on the Japanese text of Yamane Yuzo. London, Faber, 1959.

Soufflot, Jacques-Gabriel, 1713–1780

11877. Caisse Nationale des Monuments Historiques et des Sites (Paris). *Soufflot et son temps, 1780–1980*. 9 octobre 1980–25 janvier 1981. Paris, Caisse Nationale des Monuments Historiques et des Sites, 1980.

11878. Centre National de la Recherche Scientifique (Paris). *Soufflot et l'architecture des lumières*. [Published after a colloquium organized by l'Institut d'Histoire de l'Art de l'Université de Lyon II, 18–22 juin, 1980]. Paris, Centre National de la Recherche Scientifique, 1980.

11879. Mondain-Monval, Jean. *Soufflot: sa vie, son oeuvre, son esthétique (1713–1780)*. Paris, Lemerre, 1918.

11880. ———, ed. *Correspondance de Soufflot avec les directeurs des batiments concernant la manufacture des Gobelins (1756–1780)*. Paris, Lemerre, 1918.

11881. Petzet, Michael. *Soufflots Sainte-Geneviève und der französische Kirchenbau des 18. Jahrhunderts*. Berlin, de Gruyter, 1961. (Neue Münchner Beiträge zur Kunstgeschichte, 2).

11882. Université de Lyon II, Institut d'Histoire de l'Art. *L'oeuvre de Soufflot à Lyon: ètudes et documents*. Lyon, Presses Universitaires de Lyon, 1982.

Soulages, Pierre, 1919–

11883. Ceysson, Bernard. *Soulages*. Trans. by Shirley Jennings. New York, Crown, 1980.

11884. Daix, Pierre and Sweeney, James Johnson. *Pierre Soulages*. Neuchâtel, Ides et Calendes, 1991.

11885. Duby, Georges, et al. *Soulages: eaux-fortes, lithographies, 1952–1973*. Paris, Arts et Métiers Graphiques, 1974.

11886. Juin, Hubert. *Soulages*. Paris, Fall, 1958.

11887. Museum Moderner Kunst, Stiftung Ludwig (Vienna). *Soulages, peintures recentes*. Oktober–1. Dezember 1991. [Mit einem Beitrag von Loránd Hegyi und Alfred Pacuement. Übersetzung, Theresia Leitner]. Pacquement Wien, Das Museum, 1991.

11888. Soulages, Pierre. *Soulages: Pierre Soulages, l'oeuvres*. Lyon, Musée Saint-Pierre art contem-porain, 1987.

11889. ———. *Soulages, 40 Jahre Malerei*. Mit einem Beitrag von Bernard Ceysson. Herausgegeben von Veit Loers. Stuttgart, Edition Cantz, 1989.

11890. Sweeney, James J. *Soulages*. London, Phaidon, 1972.

Southworth, Albert Sands, 1811–1894 Hawes, Josiah Johnson, 1808–1901

11891. Homer, Rachel J. *The legacy of Josiah Johnson Hawes: 19th century photographs of Boston*. Barre, Mass., Barre Publishers, 1972.

11892. Sobieszak, Robert A. and Appel, Odette M. *The spirit of fact: the daguerreotypes of Southworth & Hawes, 1843–1862*. Boston, Godine, 1976.

Soutine, Chaim, 1894–1943

11893. Castaing, Marcellin and Leymarie, Jean. *Soutine*. Trans. by John Ross. New York, Abrams, 1964.

11894. Courthion, Pierre. *Soutine, peintre du déchirant*. Lausanne, Edita/Denoël, 1972. (CR).

11895. Soutine, Chaim. *Soutine*. [Catalogue of an exhibition held at the Musée de Chartres, June 29–Oct. 30, 1989]. Chartres, Musée de Chartres, 1989.

11896. Szittya, Emil. *Soutine et son temps*. Paris, Bibliothèque des Arts, 1955.

11897. Tuchman, Maurice, Dunow, Esti, and Perls, Klaus. *Chaim Soutine (1893–1943): a catalogue raisonné*. 2 v. Köln, Benedikt Taschen, 1993. (CR).

11898. Werner, Alfred. *Chaim Soutine*. New York, Abrams, 1977.

11899. Westfälisches Landesmuseum für Kunst und Kulturgeschichte Münster. *C. Soutine, 1893–1943*. Edited by Ernst-Gerhard Güse; English version edited by Michael Raeborn. December 13, 1981–February 28, 1982. London, Arts Council of Great Britain, 1982.

11900. Wheeler, Monroe. *Soutine*. [Published in conjunction with an exhibition at the Museum of Modern Art, New York]. New York, Museum of Modern Art, 1950.

Spagna, 1450–1528

11901. Gualdi Sabatini, Fausta. *Giovanni di Peitro*

detto lo Spagna. Spoleto, Accademia spoletina, 1984. (CR).

Spagnoletto, Lo *see* **Ribera, Jusepe**

Spalletti, Ettore, 1940–

11902. Spalletti, Ettore. *Ettore Spalletti: [Ausstellung] Museum Folkwang, Essen, Museum van hedendaagse kunst, Gent. [Redaktion des Kataloges, Zdenek Felix].* Essen, Das Museum, 1982.

11903. ———. *Gli anni del Caffé Michelangelo (1848–1861).* Roma, De Luca, 1985.

Spencer, Stanley, 1891–1959

11904. Bell, Keith. *Stanley Spencer: a complete catalogue of the paintings.* London, Phaidon Press; New York, distributed in North America by H.N. Abrams, 1992. (CR).

11905. Carline, Richard. *Stanley Spencer at war.* London, Faber, 1978.

11906. Collis, Louise. *A private view of Stanley Spencer.* London, Heinemann, 1972.

11907. Collis, Maurice. *Stanley Spencer, a biography.* London, Harvill Press, 1962.

11908. Pople, Kenneth. *Stanley Spencer: a biography.* London, Collins, 1991.

11909. Robinson, Duncan. *Stanley Spencer.* Oxford, Phaidon; New York, Phaidon Universe, 1990.

11910. ———. *Stanley Spencer: visions from a Berkshire village.* Oxford, Phaidon, 1979.

11911. Rothenstein, Elizabeth. *Stanley Spencer.* Oxford & London, Phaidon/New York, Oxford University Press, 1945.

11912. Rothenstein, John, ed. *Stanley Spencer, the man: correspondence and reminiscences.* London, Elek, 1979.

11913. Spencer, Gilbert. *Stanley Spencer.* London, Gollancz, 1961.

Spinelli, Spinello di Luca See Spinello Aretino

Spinello Aretino, 1346–1410

11914. Gombosi, Georg. *Spinello Aretino, eine stilgeschichtliche Studie über die florentinische Malerei des ausgehenden XIV. Jahrhunderts.* Budapest, [Gombosi], 1926.

11915. Masetti, Anna R. *Spinello Aretino giovane.* Firenze, Centro Di, 1973. (Raccolta pisana di saggi e studi, 35).

Spitzweg, Carl, 1808–1888

11916. Albrecht, Manuel. *Carl Spitzwegs Malerparadies.* Stuttgart, Schuler, 1968.

11917. Boehn, Max von. *Carl Spitzweg.* Bielefeld/Leipzig, Velhagen & Klasing, 1924. (Künstler-Monographien, 110).

11918. Elsen, Alois. *Carl Spitzweg.* Wien, Schroll, 1948.

11919. Jensen, Jens C. *Carl Spitzweg.* Köln, DuMont, 1980.

11920. Kalkschmidt, Eugen. *Carl Spitzweg und seine Welt.* München, Bruckmann, 1945.

11921. Roennefahrt, Günther. *Carl Spitzweg: beschreibendes Verzeichnis seiner Gemälde, Ölstu-dien und Aquarelle.* München, Brucmann, 1960. (CR).

11922. Spitzweg, Carl. *Carl Spitzweg, der Münchner Maler-Poet.* Gesammelt und mit einem Nachwort herausgegeben von Michael Dirrigl. München, Langen-Müller, 1969.

11923. Spitzweg, Wilhelm, ed. *Der unbekannte Spitzweg; ein Bild aus der Welt des Biedermeier: Dokumente, Briefe, Aufzeichnungen.* München, Braun & Schneider, 1958.

11924. Städtische Galerie im Prinz-Max-Palais (Karlsruhe). *Spitzweg, Schwind, Schleich.* 14. April bis 24. Juni 1984. [Redaktion, Erika Rodiger-Diruf, Helga Walter-Dressler unter Mitarbeit von Sylvia Bieber]. Karlsruhe, Die Galerie, 1984.

11925. Uhde-Bernays, Hermann. *Carl Spitzweg, des Meisters Werk und seine Bedeutung in der Geschichte der Münchner Kunst.* München, Delphin, 1913.

11926. Wichmann, Siegfried. *Carl Spitzweg.* München, Bruckmann, 1990.

11927. ———. *Carl Spitzweg: Kunst, Kosten und Konflikte.* Frankfurt am Main, Propylaen, 1991.

11928. ———. *Carl Spitzweg und die französischen Zeichner Daumier, Grandville, Gavarni, Dore: Haus der Kunst München.* [Catalog of an exhibition, Nov. 23, 1985–Feb. 2, 1986]. Herrsching, Schuler Verlagsgesellschaft, 1985.

11929. ———. *Spitzweg: Begegnungen mit Moritz von Schwind und Arnold Böcklin und die kleine Landschaft.* [Catalogue of an exhibition]. Munchen, Lipp, 1985.

11930. ———. *Spitzweg, Zeichnungen und Skizzen.* Munchen, Bruckmann, 1985.

Springer, Cornelis, 1817–1891

11931. Laanstra, Willem. *Cornelis Springer (1817–1891).* Door W. Laanstra, H.C. de Bruijn, J.H.A. Ringeling. Utrecht, Tableau, 1984. [New ed. Amsterdam, Rokin Art, 1994].

Staccioli, Mauro, 1937–

11932. University Gallery (University of Massachusetts at Amherst). *Mauro Staccioli.* Sept. 15–Dec. 16, 1984. [Comp. by Hugh M. Davies, Giuseppe Panza and Helaine Posner. Critical texts by V. Accame . . . et al.]. Milan, Puntoelinea, 1984.

Staël, Nicolas de, 1915–1955

11933. Chastel, André. *Nicolas de Staël.* Lettres

annotées par Germain Viatte; catalogue raisonné des peintures établi par Jacques Dubourg et Françoise de Staël. Paris, Le Temps, 1968. (CR).

11934. Cooper, Douglas. *Nicolas de Staël.* New York, Norton, 1962.

11935. Dumur, Guy. *Staël.* Paris, Flammarion, 1975.

11936. Galeries Nationales du Grand Palais (Paris). *Nicolas de Staël.* 22 mai–24 août 1981. Paris, Musée National d'Art Moderne, Centre Georges Pompidou, 1981.

11937. Jouffroy, Jean P. *La mesure de Nicolas de Staël.* Neuchâtel, Editions Ides et Calendes, 1981.

11938. Mansar, Arno. *Nicolas de Stael.* Paris, La Manufacture, 1990.

11939. Rathbone, Eliza E. *Nicolas de Stael in America.* Essays by Nicholas Fox Weber, John Richardson. [Prepared in conjunction with the exhibition organized by the Phillips Collection and shown there June 9–Sept. 9, 1990, and at the Cincinnati Art Museum Oct. 16–Dec. 31, 1990]. Washingon, D.C., Phillips Collection, 1990.

11940. Sutton, Denys, ed. *Nicolas de Staël: notes on painting.* Trans. by Rita Barisse. New York, Grove, 1960.

11941. Tudal, Antoine. *Nicolas de Staël.* Paris, Fall, 1958.

Stauffer-Bern, Karl, 1857–1891

11942. Arx, Bernhard von. *Der Fall Karl Stauffer, Chronik eines Skand.* Bern/Stuttgart, Hallwag, 1969. [2 ed.: *Karl Stauffer und Lydia Welti-Escher: Chronik eines Skandals.* Bern, Zytglogge,1992].

11943. Brahm, Otto. *Karl Stauffer-Bern; sein Leben, seine Briefe, seine Gedichte.* Stuttgart, Göschen, 1892.

11944. Stauffer-Bern, Karl. *Familienbriefe und Gedichte.* Herausgegeben von U. W. Züricher. Leipzig, Insel-Verlag/München, Verlag der Süddeutschen Monatshefte, 1914.

Steen, Jan, 1626–1679

11945. Bredius, Abraham. *Jan Steen.* Amsterdam, Scheltema & Holkema, [1927].

11946. Groot, Cornelis W. de. *Jan Steen, beeld en woord.* Utrecht, Dekker & van de Vegt, 1952.

11947. Gudlaugsson, Sturla. *The comedians in the work of Jan Steen and his contemporaries.* Trans. by James Brockway. Soest, Netherlands, Davaco, 1974.

11948. Kirschenbaum, Baruch D. *The religious and historical paintings of Jan Steen.* New York/Montclair, N.J., Allanheld & Schram, 1977.

11949. Martin, Wilhelm. *Jan Steen.* Amsterdam, Meulenhoff, 1954.

11950. Rosenberg Adolf. *Terborch und Jan Steen.* Bielefeld/Leipzig, Velhagen & Klasing, 1897.

(Künstler-Monographien, 19).

11951. Schmidt-Degener, Frederik. *Jan Steen.* Trans. by G. J. Renier. London, Lane, 1927.

11952. Vries, Lyckle de. *Jan Steen, de schilderende Uilenspiegel.* Amsterdam, Amsterdam Boek, 1976.

11953. Westrheene, Tobias van. *Jan Steen, étude sur l'art en Hollande.* La Haye, Nijhoff, 1856.

Stefano di Giovanni *see* Sassetta

Steichen, Edward, 1879–1973

11954. Kelton, Ruth. *Edward Steichen.* Millerton, N.Y., Aperture, 1978. (Aperture History of Photography, 9).

11955. Longwell, Dennis. *Steichen; the master prints; 1895–1914: the symbolist period.* New York, Museum of Modern Art, 1978; distributed by New York Graphic Society, Boston.

11956. Phillips, Christopher. *Steichen at war.* New York, Abrams, 1981.

11957. Sandburg, Carl. *Steichen, the photographer.* New York, Harcourt, Brace, 1929.

11958. Steichen, Edward. *A life in photography.* London, Allen, 1963.

11959. ———. *The paintings of Eduard Steichen.* [Catalog of an exhibition held June 29–Aug. 18, 1985, at the Heckscher Museum, Huntington, N.Y. Includes essay by Anne Cohen DePietro]. Huntington, Heckscher Museum, 1985.

Steinberg, Saul, 1914–

11960. Barthes, Roland and Steinberg, Saul. *All except you.* Paris, Galerie Maeght, 1983. [Text in French].

11961. Butor, Michel et Rosenberg, Harold. *Steinberg: le masque.* Photographies d'Inge Morath. Paris, Maeght, 1966.

11962. Kölnischer Kunstverein. *Saul Steinberg: Zeichnungen, Aquarelle, Collagen, Gemälde, Reliefs, 1963–1974.* 14. November-31. Dezember 1974. Köln, Kölnischer Kunstverein, 1974.

11963. Pace Gallery (New York). *Still life and architecture.* [Text by Italo Calvino]. April 3–May 1, 1982. New York, Pace Gallery, 1982.

11964. Richard Gray Gallery (Chicago). *Saul Steinberg, mixed media works on paper and wood.* November 13–December 15, 1982. Chicago, The Gallery, 1982.

11965. Rosenberg, Harold. *Saul Steinberg.* [Published in conjunction with an exhibition at the Whitney Museum of American Art, April 14–July 9, 1978]. New York, Knopf, 1978.

11966. Steinberg, Saul. *All in line.* New York, Duell, Sloan & Pearce, 1945.

11967. ———. *The art of living.* New York, Harper, 1949.

11968. ———. *Dal vero.* Portraits by Saul Steinberg. Text by John Hollander. New York, Library Fellows of the Whitney Museum of American Art, 1983. [Limited to one hundred & forty copies signed by the author].

11969. ———. *The inspector.* New York, Viking, 1973.

11970. ———. *The labyrinth.* New York, Harper, 1960.

11971. ———. *The new world.* New York, Harper, 1965.

Steinhardt, Jacob, 1887–

11972. Steinhardt, Jacob. *Jakob Steinhardt, das grapische Werk.* Herausgegeben und bearbeitet von Stefan Behrens. Berlin, Kunstamt Wedding, 1987.

Steinlen, Théophile-Alexandre, 1859–1923

11973. Bargiel, Rejane et Zagrodzki, Christophe. *Steinlen affichiste: catalogue raisonné.* Lausanne, Editions du Grand-Pont, 1986. (CR).

11974. Cate, Phillip D. and Gill, Susan. *Théophile-Alexandre Steinlen.* [Published in conjunction with an exhibition at the Voorhees Art Museum, Rutgers University, New Brunswick, N.J.]. Salt Lake City, Smith, 1982.

11975. Crauzat, Ernest de. *L'oeuvre gravé et lithographié de Steinlen.* Préface de Roger Marx. Paris, Société de Propagation des Livres d'Art, 1913. (CR).

11976. Dittmar, Peter. *Steinlen: Théophile Alexandra Steinlen, ein poetischer Realist in der Epoche des Jugendstils.* Zurich, ABC, 1984.

11977. Gute, Herbert. *A. Th. Steinlens Vermächtnis.* Berlin, Henschel, 1954.

11978. Jourdain, Francis. *Un grand imagier: Alexandre Steinlen.* Paris, Cercle d'Art, 1954.

11979. Staatliche Kunsthalle Berlin. *Théophile-Alexandre Steinlen, 1859–1923.* 15. Januar–15. Februar 1978. Berlin, Staatliche Kunsthalle, 1978.

11980. Steinlen, Theophile Alexandre. *Théophile-Alexandre Steinlen: Bilder und Graphik: eine Auswahl aus dem Petit Palais Genf, Rupertinum, 5. April bis 8. Juli 1990.* Genf, Petit Palais; Salzburg, Rupertinum, 1990.

Steir, Pat, 1940–

11981. Broun, Elizabeth. *Form, illusion, myth: prints and drawings of Pat Steir.* [Exhibition and catalogue prepared by Elizabeth Broun, with the assistance of Jan Howard]. Lawrence, Kan., Spencer Museum of Art, University of Kansas, 1983.

11982. Contemporary Arts Museum (Houston). *Arbitrary order: paintings by Pat Steir.* May 27-July 17, 1983. [Prepared by Marti Mayo]. Houston, the Museum, 1983.

11983. Steir, Pat. *Pat Steir paintings.* Essay, interview by Carter Ratcliff. New York, Abrams, 1986.

11984. ———. *Pat Steir: prints: 1976–1988.* Ed. by Juliane Willi . . . [et al.]. [Catalog of an exhibition held at the Cabinet des estampes, June 30–Sept. 18, 1988 and the Tate Gallery, London, Nov. 14, 1988–Feb. 12, 1989]. Genève, Cabinet des estampes, Musée d'art et d'histoire; London, Tate Gallery, 1988.

Stella, Frank, 1936–

11985. Axsom, Richard H. *The prints of Frank Stella: a catalogue raisonné, 1967–1982.* With the assistance of Phyllis Floyd and Matthew Rohn. Foreword by Evan M. Maurer. New York, Hudson Hills Press; Ann Arbor, University of Michigan Museum of Art, 1983. [Exhibition held at the University of Michigan, Museum of Art and other institutions from Sept. 25, 1982 through Mar. 2, 1986]. (CR).

11986. Fort Worth Art Museum (Fort Worth, Tex.). *Stella since 1970.* March 19–April 30, 1978. Fort Worth, Tex., Fort Worth Art Museum, 1978.

11987. Geelhaar, Christian. *Frank Stella: working drawings, 1956–1970.* [Catalog of an exhibition held May 22–July 27, 1980 at the Kunstmuseum Basel]. Basel, Das Kunstmuseum, 1980.

11988. Kunsthalle Bielefeld. *Frank Stella: Werke 1958–1976.* 17. April bis 29. Mai 1977. Bielefeld, Kunsthalle Bielefeld, 1977.

11989. Pacquement, Alfred. *Frank Stella, la creation contemporaine.* Paris, Flammarion, 1988.

11990. Rosenblum, Robert. *Frank Stella.* Harmondsworth, Eng., Penguin, 1971. (Penguin New Art, 1).

11991. Rubin, Lawrence. *Frank Stella, paintings 1958 to 1965: a catalogue raisonné.* Intro. by Robert Rosenblum. New York, Stewart, Tabori & Chang, distributed by Workman Pub., 1986. (CR).

11992. Rubin, William S. *Frank Stella.* New York, Museum of Modern Art, 1970; distributed by New York Graphic Society, Greenwich, Conn.

11993. ———. *Frank Stella, 1970–1987.* [Published in conjunction with an exhibition shown at the Museum of Modern Art, New York, and other museums]. New York, Museum of Modern Art; Boston, distributed by New York Graphic Society Books/Little, Brown, 1987.

11994. Staatsgalerie Stuttgart. *Frank Stella: black paintings, 1958–1960: cones and pillars, 1984–1987.* 10.11.1988–12.2.1989. [Ausstellung und Katalog, Gudrun Inboden, Mitarbeit, Jens Kraubig]. Stuttgart, Die Staatsgalerie, 1988.

Stella, Joseph, 1879–1946

11995. Baur, John I. *Joseph Stella.* New York, Praeger, 1971.

11996. Gerdts, William H. *Drawings of Joseph Stella from the collection of Rabin & Krueger.* Newark, N.J., Rabin & Krueger Gallery, 1962.

11997. Haskell, Barbara. *Joseph Stella.* [Catalog of an exhibition held at the Whitney Museum of American Art, Apr. 21–Sept. 18, 1994]. New York, Whitney Museum of American Art, distributed by H.N. Abrams, 1994.

11998. Jaffe, Irma B. *Joseph Stella.* Cambridge, Mass., Harvard University Press, 1970. [Rev. ed. New York, Fordham University Press, 1988].

11999. Stella, Joseph. *Visual poetry: the drawings of Joseph Stella.* Comp. by Joann Moser. [Catalog of an exhibition held at the Amon Carter Museum, Ft. Worth, Tex., Feb. 23–Apr. 22, 1990; Museum of Fine Arts, Boston, May 19–Jul. 22, 1990; and the National Museum of American Art, Smithsonian Institution, Washington, D.C., Sept. 7–Nov. 12, 1990]. Washington, published for the National Museum of American Art by the Smithsonian Institution Press, 1990.

12000. Zilczer, Judith. *Joseph Stella, the Hirshhorn Museum and Sculpture Garden Collection.* [Catalog of an exhibition held at Hirshhorn Museum and Sculpture Garden, Washington D.C., May 12–July 17, 1983; Columbus Museum of Art, Columbus, Ohio, February 11–March 25, 1984]. Washington D.C., published for the Hirshhorn Museum and Sculpture Garden by the Smithsonian Institution Press, 1983.

Stepanova, Varvara Fedorovna, 1894–1958

12001. Jaffe, Irma B. *Joseph Stella.* New York, Fordham University Press, 1988. Rev. ed.

12002. Lavrent'ev, Aleksandr Nikolaevich. *Varvara Stepanova, the complete work.* Ed. by John E. Bowlt. Trans. by Wendy Salmond. Cambridge, Mass., MIT Press, 1988.

12003. Rodchenko, Aleksandr Mikhailovich. *A.M. Rodchenko, V.F. Stepanova.* Moskva, "Kniga", 1989.

12004. Rodchenko, Aleksandr Mikhailovich and Stepanova, Varvara F. *The future is our only goal.* Ed. by Peter Noever. Essays by Aleksandr N. Lavrent'yev and Angela Volker. [Published in conjunction with the exhibition at the Österreichisches Museum für angewandte Kunst, Vienna (2 May–31 July, 1991) and the A.S. Pushkin State Museum of Fine Arts Moscow (25 October–15 November, 1991)]. Munich, Prestel; New York, distributed in the USA and Canada by te Neues Pub. Co., 1991.

12005. ———. *Alexander Rodtschenko und Warwara Stepanowa: Werke aus sowjetischen Museen, der Sammlung der Familie Rodtschenko und aus anderen Sammlungen.* Wilhelm-Lehmbruck-Museum der Stadt Duisburg, 7. November 1982–2. Januar 1983; Staatliche Kunsthalle Baden-Baden, 16. Januar 1983–13. Marz 1983. Duisburg, Wilhelm Lehmbruck-Museum; Baden-Baden, Staatliche Kunsthalle, 1982.

Stettheimer, Florine, 1871–1944

12006. McBride, Henry. *Florine Stettheimer.* New York, Museum of Modern Art, 1946; distributed by Simon & Schuster, New York.

12007. Tyler, Parker. *Florine Stettheimer; a life in art.* New York, Farrar, Straus, 1963.

Stevens, Alfred, 1817–1875

12008. Armstrong, Walter. *Alfred Stevens; a biographical study.* Paris, Librairie de L'Art, 1881.

12009. Beattie, Susan. *Alfred Stevens, 1817–75.* [Published in conjunction with an exhibition at the Victoria & Albert Museum]. London, HMSO, 1975.

12010. Physick, John. *The Wellington Monument.* London, HMSO, 1970.

12011. Stevens, Alfred G. *Drawings of Alfred Stevens.* New York, Scribner, 1908.

12012. Towndrow, Kenneth R. *Alfred Stevens, architectural sculptor, painter, and designer: a biography.* With a preface by D. S. MacColl. London, Constable, 1939.

12013. ———. *The works of Alfred Stevens in the Tate Gallery.* With an introduction and descriptive catalogue of classified works and a foreword by John Rothenstein. London, Tate Gallery, 1950.

Stevens, Alfred Emile Leopold, 1823–1906
Joseph, 1819–1892

12014. Boucher, François. *Alfred Stevens.* Paris, Rieder, 1931.

12015. Coles, William A. *Alfred Stevens.* [Published in conjunction with an exhibition at the University of Michigan Museum of Art, Ann Arbor, Mich., September 10–October 16, 1977]. Ann Arbor, University of Michigan Museum of Art, 1977.

12016. Lemonnier, Camille. *Alfred Stevens et son oeuvre, suivi des impressions sur la peinture par Alfred Stevens.* Bruxelles, van Oest, 1906.

12017. Stevens, Alfred. *Impressions on painting.* Trans. by Charlotte Adams. New York, Coombes, 1886.

12018. Vanzype, Gustave. *Les frères Stevens.* Bruxelles, Nouvelle Société d'Editions, 1936.

Stieglitz, Alfred, 1864–1946

12019. Abrahams, Edward. *The Lyrical Left: Randolph Bourne, Alfred Stieglitz, and the origins of cultural radicalism in America.* Charlottesville, University Press of Virginia, 1986.

12020. Eisler, Benita. *O'Keeffe and Stieglitz: an American romance.* New York, Doubleday, 1991.

12021. Frank, Waldo. *America & Alfred Stieglitz: a collective portrait.* New, revised edition. Millerton, N.Y., Aperture, 1979.

12022. Green, Jonathan, ed. *Camera Work: a critical anthology.* Millerton, N.Y., Aperture, 1973.

12023. Greenough, Sarah [and] Hamilton, Juan. *Alfred Stieglitz, photographs & writings.* [Published in conjunction with an exhibition at the National Gallery of Art, Washington, D.C.]. Washington, D.C., National Gallery of Art, 1982.

12024. Homer, William I. *Alfred Stieglitz and the American avant-garde.* Boston, New York Graphic Society, 1977.

12025. ———. *Alfred Stieglitz and the Photo-Secession.* Boston, New York Graphic Society, 1983.

12026. Kiefer Geraldine W. *Alfred Stieglitz: scientist, photographer, and avatar of modernism, 1880–1913.* New York, Garland, 1991.

12027. Lowe, Sue D. *Stieglitz, a memoir/biography.* New York, Farrar, Straus & Giroux, 1983.

12028. Lynes, Barbara Buhler. *O'Keeffe, Stieglitz and the critics, 1916–1929.* Ann Arbor, UMI Research Press, 1989. (Studies in the fine arts. Criticism, 30).

12029. Norman, Dorothy. *Alfred Stieglitz.* Millerton, N.Y., Aperture, 1976. (Aperture History of Photography, 3).

12030. ———. *Alfred Stieglitz: an American seer.* New York, Random House, 1973. 2 ed.

12031. Seligmann, Herbert. *Alfred Stieglitz talking; notes on some of his conversations, 1925–1931.* New Haven, Yale University Library, 1966.

12032. Stieglitz, Alfred. *Alfred Stieglitz.* With an essay by Dorothy Norman. New York, Aperture Foundation, 1989. (Aperture masters of photography, 6).

12033. ———. *Alfred Stieglitz: photographs from the collection of Georgia O'Keeffe.* With an afterword by Peter C. Bunnell. [Published in conjunction wth an exhibition held at Pace/MacGill Gallery, Sept. 9–Oct. 23, 1993, and Gerald Peters Gallery, Dec. 10, 1993–Jan. 7, 1994]. New York, Pace/MacGill Gallery; Santa Fe, Gerald Peters Gallery, 1993.

12034. ———. *Alfred Stieglitz's camera notes.* Ed. by Christian A. Peterson. ["Alfred Stieglitz's Camera notes exhibition tour: The Minneapolis Institute of Arts, July 17–October 10, 1993 . . ."]. Minneapolis, Minn., published by the Minneapolis Institute of Art, in association with W.W. Norton, 1993.

12035. ———. *Dear Stieglitz, Dear Dove.* Ed. by Ann Lee Morgan. Newark, University of Delaware Press; London, Associated University Presses, 1988.

12036. Stieglitz, Alfred and O'Keeffe, Georgia. *Two lives, Georgia O'Keeffe & Alfred Stieglitz: a conversation in paintings and photographs.* Essays by Belinda Rathbone, Roger Shattuck, and Elizabeth Hutton Turner. Ed. by Alexandra Arrowsmith and Thomas West. [Catalog of an exhibition held at the Phillips Collection, Washington, D.C., Dec. 12, 1992–April 4, 1993 and at three other locations through Dec. 5, 1993]. New York, HarperCollins, in association with the Phillips Collection, Washington D.C., 1992.

12037. Thomas, F. Richard. *Literary admirers of Alfred Stieglitz.* Carbondale, Ill., Southern Illinois University Press, 1983.

Still, Clyfford, 1904–

12038. Still, Clyfford. *Clyfford Still 1904–1980: the Buffalo and San Francisco collections.* Ed. by Thomas Kellein. With contributions by Michael Auping . . . [et al.]. [Published on the occasion of an exhibition of works in the collections of the Albright-Knox Art Gallery, Buffalo and the San Francisco Museum of Modern Art and held at the Kunsthalle Basel, Jan. 26–Mar. 22, 1992, and elsewhere in Europe and the U.S. through June 13, 1993]. Munich, Prestel; New York, distributed in the USA and Canada by te Neues Publishing, 1992.

Stirling, James Frazer, 1926–1992

12039. Aedes Galerie für Architektur und Raum (Berlin). *James Stirling, Wissenschaftszentrum Berlin.* 27. Juni bis 27. Juli 1985. Berlin, Die Galerie, 1985.

12040. Dal Co, Francesco and Muirhead, Tom. *I musei di James Stirling, Michael Wilford, and Associates.* Milano, Electa, 1990. (Documenti di architettura, 54).

12041. Stirling, James Frazer. *Biblioteca pubblica e giardini a Latina di James Stirling.* A cura di Claudio Greco. Rome, Officina, 1989. (Architettura e città/Laboratorio di progettazione di Roma, 2).

12042. ———. *James Stirling, buildings and projects.* Intro. by Colin Rowe. Comp. and ed. by Peter Arnell and Ted Bickford. New York, Rizzoli, 1984.

12043. ———. *James Stirling, buildings and projects: James Stirling, Michael Wilford and Associates.* Intro. by Colin Rowe. Comp. and ed. by Peter Arnell and Ted Bickford. London, Architectural Press, 1984.

12044. Stirling, James and Wilford, Michael. *James Stirling and Michael Wilford*. London, Academy Editions; New York, St. Martin's Press, 1993. (Architectural monographs, 32).

12045. Stirling, James, Wilford, Michael, and Associates. *James Stirling, Michael Wilford, and Associates: buildings & projects, 1975–1992*. Intro. by Robert Maxwell. Essays by Michael Wilford and Thomas Muirhead. London, Thames & Hudson, 1994.

Stone, Edward Durell, 1902–1978

12046. Stone, Edward D. *The evolution of an architect*. New York, Horizon Press, 1962.

12047. ———. *Recent and future architecture*. New York, Horizon Press, 1967.

Stoss, Veit, 1440/50–1533

12048. Barthel, Gustav. *Die Ausstrahlungen der Kunst des Veit Stoss im Osten*. München, Bruckmann, 1944.

12049. Daun, Berthold. *Veit Stoss und seine Schule in Deutschland, Polen, Ungarn und Siebenbürgen*. Leipzig, Hiersemann, 1916. 2 ed. (Kunstgeschichtliche Monographien, 17).

12050. Dettloff, Szczesny. *Wit Stosz*. 2 v. Wrocław, Polskiej Akademii Nauk, 1961.

12051. Funk, Veit. *Veit Stoss: der Krakauer Marienaltar*. Beschrieben und gedeutet von Veit Funk. Freiburg i.Br., Herder, 1985.

12052. Jaeger, Adolf. *Veit Stoss und sein Geschlecht*. Neustadt/Aisch, Degener, 1958.

12053. Kepiński, Zdzisław. *Wit Stwosz w starciu ideologii religijnych Odrodzenia Ołtarz Salwatora*. Wrocław, Polskiej Akademii Nauk, 1969.

12054. Lossnitzer, Max. *Veit Stoss, die Herkunft seiner Kunst, seine Werke und sein Leben*. Leipzig, Zeitler, 1912.

12055. Lutze, Eberhard. *Veit Stoss*. Berlin, Deutscher Kunstverlag, 1938.

12056. Sello, Gottfried. *Veit Stoss: Aufnahmen Albert Hirmer*. München, Hirmer, 1988.

12057. Skubiszewski, Piotr. *Rzeźba nagrobna Wita Stwosza*. Warszawa, Pánstwowym Instytucie Wydawniczym, 1957.

12058. Stoss, Veit. *Veit Stoss: die Vorträge des Nürnberger Symposions*. Herausgegeben von Germanischen Nationalmuseum Nürnberg und vom Zentralinstitut für Kunstgeschichte München. Schriftleitung, Rainer Kahsnitz. München, Deutscher Kunstverlag, [1985].

12059. ———. *Veit Stoss in Nürnberg: Werke des Meisters und seiner Schule in Nürnberg und Umgebung*. Herausgegeben vom Germanischen Nationalmuseum Nürnberg. Leitung, Gerhard Bott. Konzeption und Redaktion, Rainer Kahsnitz. München, Deutscher Kunstverlag, 1983.

12060. ———. *Wit Stwosz w Krakowie: praca zbiorowa*. Pod redakcja Lecha Kalinowskiego i Franciszka Stolota. Krakow, Wydawn Literackie, 1987.

12061. Stuhr, Michael. *Der Krakauer Marienaltar von Veit Stoss*. Fotos, Zbyszko Siemaszko, Danuta Rago Nowakowska. Leipzig, E.A. Seeman, 1992.

Stowasser, Friedrich *see* Hundertwasser, Friedensreich

Strand, Paul, 1890–1976

12062. Adams, Robert . . . [et al.]. *Paul Strand: essays on his life and work*. Ed. by Maren Stange. New York, Aperture, [1990].

12063. Greenough, Sarah. *Paul Strand: an American vision*. [Catalog of an exhibition held at the National Gallery of Art, Washington, Dec. 2, 1990–Feb. 3, 1991 and at 6 other museums through Nov. 22, 1992]. New York, Aperture Foundation in association with the National Gallery of Art, Washington, 1990.

12064. Hoffman, Michael E., ed. *Paul Strand: sixty years of photographs*. Profile by Calvin Tomkins. Millerton, N.Y., Aperture, 1976.

12065. Newhall, Nancy. *Paul Strand: photographs, 1915–1945*. [Published in conjunction with an exhibition at the Museum of Modern Art, New York]. New York, Museum of Modern Art, 1945.

12066. Strand, Paul. *Paul Strand*. New York, Aperture Foundation, 1987. (Aperture masters of photography, 1).

12067. ———. *Paul Strand*. [Text, Wolfgang Wiemann. Interviews, Naomi and Walter Rosenblum . . . et al.] Zurich, Switzerland, Galerie Zur Stockeregg, 1987. (Katalog/Galerie für Kunstphotographie Zur Stockeregg, 5).

12068. ———. *Paul Strand: a retrospective monograph*. 2 v. Millerton, N.Y., Aperture, 1971.

Stretton, Lord *see* Leighton, Frederick

Strickland, William, 1788–1854

12069. Gilchrist, Agnes E. *William Strickland, architect and engineer, 1788–1854*. Philadelphia, University of Pennsylvania Press, 1950.

Strigel, Bernhard, 1460/61–1528

12070. Otto, Gertrud. *Bernhard Strigel*. München/Berlin, Deutschen Kunstverlag, 1964.

Strozzi, Bernardo, 1581–1644

12071. Fiocco, Giuseppe. *Bernardo Strozzi*. Roma, Biblioteca d'Arte Illustrata, 1921. (Biblioteca d'arte illustrata, 9).

12072. Matteucci, Anna M. *Bernardo Strozzi*. Milano, Fabbri, 1966. (I maestri del colore, 134).

12073. Mortari, Luisa. *Bernardo Strozzi*. Roma, de Luca, 1966.

Stuart, Gilbert, 1755–1828

12074. Flexner, James T. *Gilbert Stuart*. New York, Knopf, 1955.

12075. Mason, George C. *The life and works of Gilbert Stuart*. New York, Scribner, 1879.

12076. McLanathan, Richard B. K. *Gilbert Stuart*. New York, Abrams; in association with the National Museum of American Art, Smithsonian Institution, 1986.

12077. Morgan, John H. *Gilbert Stuart and his pupils*. New York, New York Historical Society, 1939.

12078. Mount, Charles M. *Gilbert Stuart, a biography*. New York, Norton, 1964.

12079. Museum of Art, Rhode Island School of Design (Providence, R.I.). *Gilbert Stuart: portraitist of the new republic, 1755–1828*. Providence, Museum of Art, Rhode Island School of Design, 1967.

12080. Park, Lawrence. *Gilbert Stuart: an illustrated descriptive list of his works*. With an account of his life by John Hill Morgan and an appreciation by Royal Cortissoz. 4 v. New York, Rudge, 1926. (CR).

12081. Whitley, William T. *Gilbert Stuart*. Cambridge, Mass., Harvard University Press, 1932.

Stubbs, George, 1724–1806

12082. Doherty, Terence. *The anatomical works of George Stubbs*. Boston, Godine, 1975.

12083. Egerton, Judy. *George Stubbs, anatomist and animal painter*. [Published in conjunction with an exhibition at the Tate Gallery, London, 25 August–3 October 1976]. London, Tate Gallery, 1976.

12084. Gilbey, Walter. *Life of George Stubbs, R. A.* London, Vinton, 1898.

12085. Lennox-Boyd, C. A, Dixon, Rob and Clayton, Tim. *George Stubbs: the complete engraved works*. Abingdon, Stipple; New York, distributed in the USA by Harper & Row, 1989. (CR).

12086. Morrison, Venetia. *The art of George Stubbs*. London, Headline, 1989.

12087. Parker, Constance-Anne. *George Stubbs: art, animals & anatomy*. London, J.A. Allan, 1984.

12088. ———. *Mr. Stubbs, the horse painter*. London, Allen, 1971.

12089. Rump, Gerhard Charles. *Pferde- und Jagdbilder in der englischen Kunst: Studien zu George Stubbs und dem Genre der "sporting Art" von 1650–1830*. Hildesheim/New York, G. Olms, 1983. (Studien zur Kunstgeschichte, 23).

12090. Sparrow, Walter S. *George Stubbs and Ben Marshall*. London, Cassell/New York, Scribner, 1929.

12091. Stubbs, George. *George Stubbs, 1724–1806*. [Exhibition held at the Tate Gallery, London, Oct. 17, 1984–Jan. 6, 1985, and at the Yale Center for British Art, New Haven, Conn., Feb. 13–Apr. 7, 1985]. London, Tate Gallery; Salem, N.H., Salem House, 1984 (1985 printing).

12092. Tattersall, Bruce. *Stubbs & Wedgewood: unique alliance between artist and potter*. With an introduction by Basil Taylor. [Published in conjunction with an exhibition at the Tate Gallery, London, 19 June–18 August 1974]. London, Tate Gallery, 1974.

12093. Taylor, Basil. *Stubbs*. London, Phaidon, 1975. 2 ed.

Stuck, Franz von, 1863–1928

12094. Bierbaum, Otto J. *Stuck*. Bielefeld/Leipzig, Velhagen & Klasing, 1899. (Künstler-Monographien, 42).

12095. Ostini, Fritz von. *Franz von Stuck: Gesamtwerk*. Muenchen, Hanfstaengl, [1909].

12096. Schmoll, J. August, ed. *Franz von Stuck*. München, Stuck-Jugendstil-Verein, 1968.

12097. ———. *Das Phänomen Franz von Stuck: Kritiken, Essays, Interviews, 1968–1972*. München, Stuck-Jugendstil-Verein, 1972.

12098. Singer, Hans W. *Zeichnungen von Franz von Stuck*. Leipzig, Schumann, 1912. (Meister der Zeichnung, 3).

12099. Voss, Heinrich. *Franz von Stuck, 1863–1928*. Werkkatalog der Gemälde mit einer Einführung in seinen Symbolismus. München, Prestel, 1973. (CR).

Stwosz, Wit *see* Stoss, Veit

Sudek, Josef, 1896–1976

12100. Bulláty, Sonja. *Sudek*. Barre, Mass., Imprint Society, 1978; distributed by Crown, New York,

12101. Kirschner, Zdenek. *Josef Sudek*. New York, Takarajima Books, distributed by D.A.P./ Distributed Art Publishers, 1993.

12102. Linharta, Lubomíra. *Josef Sudek, fotografie*. Praha, Státní Nakladatelství Krásné Literatury, 1956.

12103. Sudek, Josef. *Josef Sudek, poet of Prague: a deepening vision*. New York, Aperture, 1990. (Aperture, 118).

12104. ———. *Josef Sudek, poet of Prague: a photographer's life*. Biographical profile by Anna Farova. New York, Aperture, 1990. (Aperture, 117).

12105. Sudek, Josef. *Magic in stone*. Text by Martin S. Briggs. London, Lincolns-Prager, 1947.

12106. ———. *Praha panoramatická*. [Praha], Státní Nakladatelství Krásné Literatury, 1959.

Sugiyama, Yasushi, 1909–

12107. National Museum of Modern Art (Tokyo). *Yasushi Sugiyama exhibition. 18 August–27 September, 1987.* [Organized by the National Museum of Modern Art Tokyo, Nihon Keizai Shimbun, Inc.]. Tokyo, Nihon Keizai Shimbun, 1987.

Sullivan, Louis Henry, 1856–1924 *see also* Richardson, Henry Hobson

12108. Andrew, David S. *Louis Sullivan and the polemics of modern architecture: the present against the past.* Urbana, University of Illinois Press, 1985.

12109. Bush-Brown, Albert. *Louis Sullivan.* New York, Braziller, 1960.

12110. Connely, Willard. *Louis Sullivan as he lived: the shaping of American architecture.* New York, Horizon Press, 1960.

12111. Duncan, Hugh Dalziel. *Culture and democracy: the struggle for form in society and architecture in Chicago and the Middle West during the life and times of Louis H. Sullivan.* With a new introduction by Scott A. Greer. New Brunswick, Transaction, 1989.

12112. Frei, Hans. *Louis Henry Sullivan.* Zurich, Artemis, 1992.

12113. Menocal, Narciso G. *Architecture as nature: the transcendentalist idea of Louis Sullivan.* Madison, Wis., University of Wisconsin Press, 1981.

12114. Morrison, Hugh. *Louis Sullivan, prophet of modern architecture.* New York, Museum of Modern Art/Norton, 1935.

12115. Paul, Sherman. *Louis Sullivan, an architect in American thought.* Englewood Cliffs, N.J., Prentice-Hall, 1962.

12116. Sprague, Paul E. *The drawings of Louis Henry Sullivan: a catalogue of the Frank Lloyd Wright Collection at the Avery Architectural Library.* Foreword by Adolf K. Placzek. Princeton, N.J., Princeton University Press, 1979.

12117. Sullivan, Louis H. *The autobiography of an idea.* New York, American Institute of Architects, 1926. (New ed., with a foreword by Claude Bragdon and an introduction by Ralph Marlowe Line: New York, Dover, 1956).

12118. ———. *Kindergarten chats and other writings.* Ed. by Isabella Athey. New York, Wittenborn, 1947.

12119. ———. *Louis Sullivan, the public papers.* Ed. by Robert Twombly. Chicago, University of Chicago Press, 1988.

12120. ———. *Louis Sullivan in the Art Institute of Chicago: the illustrated catalogue of collections.* Ed. by Sarah C. Mollman. With a foreword by John Zukowsky. New York, Garland Pub. 1989.

12121. ———. *The testament of stone: themes of idealism and indignation from the writings of Louis Sullivan.* Ed. by Maurice English. Evanston, Ill., Northwestern University Press, 1963.

12122. Szarkowski, John. *The idea of Louis Sullivan.* Minneapolis, University of Minnesota Press, 1956.

12123. Twombly, Robert C. *Louis Sullivan, his life and work.* New York, Viking, 1986.

Sully, Thomas, 1783–1872

12124. Biddle, Edward and Fielding, Mantle. *The life and work of Thomas Sully, 1783–1872.* Philadelphia, [privately printed], 1921. (CR).

12125. Fabian, Monroe H. *Mr. Sully, portrait painter: the works of Thomas Sully (1783–1872).* [An exhibition at the National Portrait Gallery, June 3 to Sept. 5, 1983]. Washington, published for the National Portrait Gallery by the Smithsonian Institution, 1983.

12126. Hart, Charles H. *A register of portraits painted by Thomas Sully, 1801–1871.* Philadelphia, [Hart], 1909.

12127. Sully, Thomas. *Hints to young painters and the process of portrait painting.* Philadelphia, Stoddart, 1873. (Reprinted, with an introduction by Faber Birren: New York, Reinhold, 1965).

Survage, Léopold, 1879–1968

12128. Abadie, Daniel. *Survage: les années heroiques: [exposition] Musee d'art moderne, Troyes, Musée Matisse, Musée d'eparte-mental, Le Cateau-Cambresis, Nord.* Arcueil, Anthese, 1993.

12129. Gauthier, Maximilien. *Survage.* Paris, Les Gémeaux, 1953.

12130. Putnam, Samuel. *The glistening bridge: Léopold Survage and the spatial problem in painting.* With an autobiographical sketch, an essay, and notes by M. Survage. New York, Covici-Friede, 1929.

12131. Survage, Leopold. *Ecrits sur la peinture.* Suivi de *Survage au regard de la critique.* Textes réunis et présentés par Hélène Seyres. Paris, L'Archipel, 1992.

Sutherland, Graham, 1903–1980

12132. Alley, Ronald. *Graham Sutherland.* [Published in conjunction with an exhibition at the Tate Gallery, London, 19 May–4 July, 1982]. London, Tate Gallery, 1982.

12133. Arcangeli, Francesco. *Graham Sutherland.* Trans. by Helen Barolini and H. Joseph Marks. New York, Abrams, 1975.

12134. Berthoud, Roger. *Graham Sutherland, a biography.* London, Faber, 1982.

12135. Cooper, Douglas. *The work of Graham Sutherland.* London, Lund Humphries, 1961.

12136. Hayes, John. *The art of Graham Sutherland.*

Oxford, Phaidon, 1980.

12137. Nicholls, Paul C., Pinottini, Marzio and Zoppi, Sergio. *Bestiaires de Graham Sutherland*. [Catalog of an exhibition held at Tour Fromage, Aosta]. Milano, Fabbri, 1985.

12138. Sackville-West, Edward. *Graham Sutherland*. Harmondsworth, Eng., Penguin, 1943. (Penguin Modern Painters).

12139. Sutherland, Graham Vivian. *Graham Sutherland: early etchings*. London, Gordon Cooke; Aldershot, Hampshire, Scolar Press, 1993.

12140. Tassi, Roberto. *Graham Sutherland: complete graphic work*. New York, Rizzoli, 1978. (CR).

12141. ———. *Sutherland: disegni di guerra*. Milano, Electa, 1979.

Suttermans, Justus, 1597–1681

12142. Bautier, Pierre. *Juste Suttermans, peintre des Médicis*. Bruxelles, van Oest, 1912.

Szinyei-Merse, Pál, 1845–1920

12143. Lázár, Béla. *Paul Merse von Szinyei, ein Vorläufer der Pleinairmalerei*. Leipzig, Klinkhardt & Biermann, [1911].

12144. Pataky, Dénes. *Pál Szinyei Merse*. Trans. by Edna Lenárt. Budapest, Corvina, 1965.

12145. Rajnai, Miklós. *Szinyei-Merse Pál, 1845–1920*. Budapest, Müvészeti Könyvek, 1953.

12146. Szinyei-Merse, Pál. *Szinyei-Merse Pál*. [A bevezeto tanulmanyt irta es a kepeket valogatta, Bernath Maria]. Budapest, Corvina, 1981.

T

Taddeo di Bartolo, 1362–1422

12147. Symeonides, Sibilla. *Taddeo di Bartolo*. Siena, Accademia Senese degli Intronati, 1965. (Monografie d'arte senese, 7).

Taeuber-Arp, Sophie Henriette, 1889–1943

12148. Kuthy, Sandor. *Sophie Taeuber-Hans Jean Arp: Künstlerpaare, Künstlerfreunde = dialogues d'artistes, resonances. Mit Texten von Christian Derouet . . . [et al.]*. Kunstmuseum Bern, Stiftung Hans Arp und Sophie Taeuber-Arp, Rolandseck, Von der Heydt-Museum, Wuppertal. Bern, Das Museum, 1988.

12149. Museum of Modern Art (New York). *Sophie Taeuber-Arp*. September 16–November 29, 1981. New York, Museum of Modern Art, 1981.

12150. Schmidt, Georg. *Sophie Taeuber-Arp*. Basel, Holbein-Verlag, 1948.

12151. Taeuber-Arp, Sophie. *Sophie Taeuber-Arp, 1889–1943*. Herausgeber, Siegfried Gohr. [Catalog of an exhibition held at the Bahnhof Rolandseck, Feb. 10–Apr. 12, 1993]. Stuttgart, G. Hatje; [Rolandseck], Stiftung Hans Arp und Sophie Taeuber-Arp e.v., 1993.

12152. ———. *Sophie Taeuber: [exposition] 15 decembre 1989–18 mars 1990, Musée d'art moderne de la ville de Paris: 30 mars–13 mai 1990, Musée cantonal des beaux-arts de Lausanne*. Paris, Paris-Musées, 1989.

12153. Watts, Harriett. *Hans Arp und Sophie Taeuber-Arp: die Elemente der Bilder und Bücher*. [Catalog of an exhibition held at the Herzog August Bibliothek, Jan. 19–Mar. 12, 1989]. Wolfenbüttel, Herzog August Bibliothek, [1989]. (Malerbuchkataloge der Herzog August Bibliothek, 2).

Taft, Lorado, 1860–1936

12154. Garvey, Timothy J. *Public sculptor: Lorado Taft and the beautification of Chicago*. Urbana, University of Illinois Press, 1988.

12155. Taft, Ada B. *Lorado Taft, sculptor and citizen*. Greensboro, N.C., Smith, 1946.

12156. Taft, Lorado. *The history of American sculpture*. New edition, revised and with new matter. New York, Macmillan, 1925.

12157. ———. *Modern tendencies in sculpture*. Chicago, University of Chicago Press, 1921.

Talbot, William Henry Fox, 1800–1877

12158. Arnold, Harry J. P. *William Henry Fox Talbot, pioneer of photography and man of science*. London, Hutchinson Benham, 1977.

12159. Booth, Arthur H. *William Henry Fox Talbot, father of photography*. London, Barker, 1965.

12160. Buckland, Gail. *Fox Talbot and the invention of photography*. Boston, Godine, 1980.

12161. Jammes, André. *William H. Fox Talbot, inventor of the negative-positive process*. New York, Macmillan, 1974.

12162. Lassam, Robert. *Fox Talbot, photographer*. Tisbury, Eng., Compton Press, 1979.

12163. Schaef, Larry J. *Out of the shadows: Herschel, Talbot & the invention of photography*. New Haven, Yale University Press, 1992.

12164. Talbot, William Henry Fox. *Henry Fox Talbot: selected texts and bibliography*. Ed. by Mike Weaver. Oxford, England, Clio Press, 1992. (World photographers reference series, v. 3).

12165. ———. *The pencil of nature*. London, Longman, 1844–1846. (Reprinted with a new introduction by Beaumont Newhall: New York, Da Capo, 1969).

12166. ———. *Some account of the art of photogenic drawing*. London, Taylor, 1839.

Tamayo, Rufino, 1900–

12167. Alba, Victor. *Coloquios de Coyoacan con Rufino Tamayo*. Mexico, D.F., Costa-Amic, [1956].

12168. Centro de Arte Reina Sofia (Madrid). *Rufino

Tamayo, pintures. 29 de junio–3 de octubre, 1988. Madrid, Ministerio de Cultura, Direccion General de Bellas Artes y Archivos, Centro Nacional de Exposiciones, [1988].

12169. Cogniat, Raymond. *Rufino Tamayo*. Paris, Presses Littéraires de France, 1951.

12170. Corredor Matheos, Jose. *Tamayo*. Trans. by Kenneth Lyons. New York, Rizzoli, 1987.

12171. Genauer, Emily. *Rufino Tamayo*. New York, Abrams, 1974.

12172. Goldwater, Robert. *Rufino Tamayo*. New York, Quadrangle, 1947.

12173. Museo Tamayo (Mexico City). *Rufino Tamayo: arte y proceso de la mixografia*. México, D.F., Museo Tamayo, 1983.

12174. Palazzo Strozzi (Florence). *Rufino Tamayo*. 1 marzo–30 aprile 1975. Firenze, Centro Di, 1975.

12175. Paz, Octavio. *Tamayo en la pintura mexicana*. México, D.F., Universidad Nacional Autonoma de México, 1959.

12176. ———— [and] Lassaigne, Jacques. *Rufino Tamayo*. Trans. by Kenneth Lyons. New York, Rizzoli, 1982.

12177. Solomon R. Guggenheim Museum (New York). *Rufino Tamayo, myth and magic*. New York, Guggenheim Foundation, 1979.

12178. Tamayo, Rufino. *Nature and the artist: the work of art and the observer, Rufino Tamayo: a fiftieth-anniversary exhibition of Rufino Tamayo's fresco for Smith College*. Northampton, Mass., Smith College Museum of Art, 1993.

12179. ————. *Rufino Tamayo*. Redaktion, Dieter Ruckhaberle, Elke Coldeway. Berlin, Staatliche Kunsthalle Berlin, 1990.

12180. ————. *Tamayo 70: Rufino Tamayo, 70 años de creacion*. Ciudad de Mexico, Instituto Nacional de Bellas Artes, Secretaria de Educacion Publica, 1987.

T'ang-Tai, 1673?–1732

12181. Goepper, Roger. *T'ang-Tai, ein Hofmaler der Ch'ing Zeit*. München, Staatliches Museum für Völkerkunde, 1956.

Tanguy, Yves, 1900–1955

12182. Breton, André. *Yves Tanguy*. Trans. by Bravig Imbs. New York, Pierre Matisse Editions, 1946.

12183. Musée National d'Art Moderne, Centre Georges Pompidou (Paris). *Yves Tanguy, rétrospective, 1925–1955*. 17 juin–21 septembre 1982. Paris, Musée National d'Art Moderne, Centre Georges Pompidou, 1982.

12184. Soby, James T. *Yves Tanguy*. [Published in conjunction with an exhibition at the Museum of Modern Art, New York]. New York, Museum of Modern Art, 1955.

12185. Tanguy, Kay S., et al. *Yves Tanguy, a summary of his works*. [Text in French and En-glish]. New York, Pierre Matisse, 1963. (CR).

12186. Tanguy, Yves. *Yves Tanguy: a retrospective*. New York, Solomon R. Guggenheim Museum, 1983.

12187. ————. *Yves Tanguy: Staatliche Kunsthalle Baden-Baden*. Herausgegeben von Katharine Schmidt, mit Beiträgen von Reinhold Hohl . . . [et al.]. Baden-Baden, Die Kunsthalle; München, Prestel, [1982].

12188. Wolfgang Wittrock Kunsthandel (Düsseldorf). *Yves Tanguy, das druckgraphische Werk: Ausstellung April–Mai 1976*. [Text in German, French, and English]. Düsseldorf, Wolfgang Wittrock Kunsthandel, 1976. (CR).

T'ang Yin, 1470–1524

12189. Chu, Doris. *C. J. Tang Yin, 1470–1524 [i.e. 1523]: the man and his art*. New York, Highlight International, 1985.

12190. Clapp, Anne de Coursey. *The painting of T'ang Yin*. Chicago, University of Chicago Press, 1991.

12191. Kotzenberg, Heike. *Bild und Aufschrift in der Malerei Chinas: unter besonderer Berucksichtigung der Literatenmaler der Ming-Zeit (1368–1644) Tang Yin, Wen Chengming und Shen Chou*. Wiesbaden, Steiner, 1981.

12192. Lai, T. C. *T'ang Yin, poet/painter, 1470–1524*. Hong Kong, Kelley and Walsh, 1971.

Tanner, Henry Ossawa, 1859–1937

12193. Mathews, Marcia M. *Henry Ossawa Tanner, American artist*. Chicago/London, University of Chicago Press, 1969.

12194. Mosby, Dewey F. *Henry Ossawa Tanner*. Introductory essay and catalogue chapters by Dewey F. Mosby. Catalogue entries by Dewey F. Mosby and Darrel Sewell. Bibliographic essay by Rae Alexander-Minter. Philadelphia, Philadelphia Museum of Art; New York, Rizzoli International Publications, 1991.

12195. National Collection of Fine Arts, Smithsonian Institution, Washington, D.C. *The art of Henry O. Tanner (1859–1937)*. 23 July through 7 September 1969. Washington, D.C., Frederick Douglass Institute in collaboration with the National Collection of Fine Arts, 1969.

12196. Simon, Walter A. *Henry O. Tanner: a study of the development of an American Negro artist, 1859–1937*. Ann Arbor, Mich., University Microfilms, 1960.

Tanning, Dorothea, 1910–

12197. Tanning, Dorothea. *Birthday*. Santa Monica, Lapis Press, 1986.

12198. ————. *Dorothea Tanning: between lives:*

works on paper: 15 September–13 October 1989. Introduction by Sarah Wilson. London, Runkel-Hue-Williams Ltd., 1989.

12199. ———. *Dorothea Tanning: hail, delirium!: a catalogue raisonné of the artist's illustrated books and prints, 1942–1991.* Ed. by Roberta Waddell and Louisa Wood Ruby. With an essay by Donald Kuspit: chronology and commentaries by Dorothea Tanning. New York, Miriam and Ira D. Wallach Division of Art, Prints and Photographs, New York Public Library, 1992. (CR).

Tao Chi, 1630–1707

12200. Coleman, Earle J. *Philosophy of painting by Shih-T'ao: a translation and exposition of his Hua-P'u.* The Hague, Mouton, 1978.

12201. Fu, Marilyn and Fong, Wen. *The wilderness colors of Tao-Chi.* Introduction, commentary, and translations by Marilyn Fu and Wen Fong. New York, Metropolitan Museum of Art, 1973.

12202. Keim, Jean. *Che T'ao (1630–1707): paysages; album en huit feuilles.* 2 v. Paris, Euros, 1957.

12203. Museum of Art, University of Michigan (Ann Arbor, Mich.). *The painting of Tao-Chi, 1641–ca. 1720.* August 13–September 17, 1967. Ann Arbor, Mich., Museum of Art, University of Michigan, 1967.

Tapie, Michel, 1909–

12204. Tapié, Michel. *Observations.* Edited by Paul and Esther Jenkins. New York, Wittenborn, 1956.

12205. Vicens, Francesc, ed. *Prolégomènes à une esthétique autre de Michel Tapié.* Barcelone, Centre International de Recherches Esthétiques, 1960.

Tàpies, Antoni, 1923–

12206. Albright-Knox Art Gallery (Buffalo, N.Y.). *Antoni Tàpies: thirty-three years of his work.* With an essay by José Luis Barrio-Garay. January 22–March 6, 1977. Buffalo, Buffalo Fine Arts Academy/Albright-Knox Art Gallery, 1977.

12207. Bonet, Blai. *Tàpies: selección, montaje, interpretación.* Barcelona, Polígrafa, 1964.

12208. Cirici, Alexandre. *Tàpies: testimonio del silencio.* Barcelona, Polígrafa, 1973.

12209. Cirlot, Juan-Eduardo. *Significacion de la pintura de Tàpies.* Barcelona, Seix Barral, 1962.

12210. Combalia Dexeus, Victoria. *Tapies.* New York, Rizzoli, 1990.

12211. Fernandez-Braso, Miguel. *Conversaciones con Tàpies.* Madrid, Rayuela, 1981.

12212. Franzke, Andreas. *Tàpies.* Trans. by John William Gabriel. Munich, Prestel; New York, distributed in the USA and Canada on behalf of Prestel by te Neues Publishing Co., 1992.

12213. Gatt, Giuseppe. *Antoni Tàpies.* Prefazione di Giulio Carlo Argan. Bologna, Cappelli, 1967.

12214. Gimferrer, Pere. *Tàpies and the Catalan spirit.* Trans. by Kenneth Lyons. New York, Rizzoli, 1975. New ed., Barcelona, Ediciones Polígrafa, 1986.

12215. Kunsthalle Bremen. *Antoni Tàpies: Handzeichnungen, Aquarelle, Gouachen, Collagen, 1944–1976.* 4. September bis 23. Oktober 1977. Bremen, Kunsthalle Bremen, 1977.

12216. Messer, Thomas M. *Antoni Tàpies: eine Retrospektive: [vom 19. Juni bis 5. September 1993].* Köln, Wienand Verlag, 1993.

12217. Penrose, Roland. *Tàpies.* New York, Rizzoli, 1978.

12218. Permanyer, Lluís. *Tàpies and the new culture.* Trans. by Kenneth Lyons. New York, Rizzoli, 1986.

12219. Schmalenbach, Werner. *Antoni Tàpies: Zeichnungen.* Frankfurt a.M., Propyläen, 1974.

12220. Tapié, Michel. *Antoni Tàpies.* Barcelona, Editorial RM, 1959.

12221. Tàpies, Antoni. *Memória personal: fragment per a una autobiografia.* Barcelona, Editorial Crítica, 1977.

12222. ———. *Tàpies, the complete works.* Direction and cataloging, Anna Agusti. Foreword, Georges Raillard. Chronology, Miguel Tapies. Trans. by Richard-Lewis Rees and Asti Hustvedt. Vol. 1– . New York, Rizzoli, 1989– . (CR).

12223. Teixidor, Joan. *Antoni Tàpies.* Barcelona, Sala Gaspar, 1964.

12224. Watts, Harriett. *Antoni Tàpies: die Bildzeichen und das Buch.* Wolfenbüttel, Herzog August Bibliothek, 1988. Malerbuchkataloge der Herzog August Bibliothek, 1).

12225. Wye, Deborah. *Antoni Tàpies in print.* New York, Museum of Modern Art, distributed by H.N. Abrams, 1991.

Tassi, Agostino, 1565–1644

12226. Hess, Jacob. *Agostino Tassi, der Lehrer des Claude Lorrain; ein Beitrag zur Geschichte der Barockmalerei in Rom.* München, [Hess], 1935.

12227. Pugliatti, Teresa. *Agostino Tassi tra conformismo e libertà.* Roma, de Luca, 1977.

Tatlin, Vladimir Yevgrafovich, 1885–1953

12228. Milner, John. *Vladimir Tatlin and the Russian avant-garde.* New Haven, Yale University Press, 1983.

12229. Moderna Museet (Stockholm). *Vladimir*

Tatlin. Juli–september 1968. [Text in Swedish and English]. Stockholm, Moderna Museet, 1968.

12230. Nakov, Andrei B. *Tatlin's dream: Russian suprematist and constructivist art, 1910–1923.* [Published in conjunction with an exhibition at Fischer Fine Art, Ltd., London, November 1973–January 1974]. London, Fischer Fine Art, Ltd., 1974.

12231. Tatlin, Vladimir Y. *V. Y. Tatlin: katalog vystavki proizvedenii.* Moskva, Sovetskaia Khudozhnikov, 1977.

12232. ———. *Vladimir Tatlin: Leben, Werk, Wirkung: ein internationales Symposium.* Herausgegeben von Jürgen Harten. Köln, DuMont, 1993.

12233. Zhadova, Larissa Alekseevna, ed. *Tatlin.* New York, Rizzoli, 1988.

Tatti, Jacopo *see* Sansovino, Jacopo Tatti

Tchelitchew, Pavel, 1898–1957

12234. Soby, James T. *Tchelitchew: paintings, drawings.* [Published in conjunction with an exhibition at the Museum of Modern Art, New York]. New York, Museum of Modern Art, 1942.

12235. Tchelitchew, Pavel. *Drawings.* Edited by Lincoln Kirstein. New York, Bittner, 1947.

12236. Tyler, Parker. *The divine comedy of Pavel Tchelitchew, a biography.* New York, Fleet, 1967.

Teniers, David (the elder), 1582–1649
David (the younger), 1610–1690

12237. Bocquet, Léon. *David Teniers.* Paris, Nilsson, 1924.

12238. Davidson, Jane P. *David Teniers the younger.* Boulder, Colo., Westview Press, 1979.

12239. Díaz Padrón, Matías and Royo-Villanova, Mercedes. *David Teniers, Jan Brueghel y los gabinetes de pinturas.* Madrid, Museo del Prado, 1992.

12240. Duverger, Erik [and] Vlieghe, Hans. *David Teniers der Ältere; ein vergessener flämischer Nachfolger Adam Elsheimers.* Utrecht, Haentjens Dekker & Gumbert, 1971.

12241. Klinge, Margret. *David Teniers the younger: paintings, drawings: [exhibition] Antwerp, Koninklijk Museum voor schone Kunsten, 11 May–1 September 1991.* Ghent, Snoeck-Ducaju & Zoon, [1991].

12242. Marillier, Henry C. *Handbook to the Teniers tapestries.* London, Oxford University Press, 1932.

12243. Meerbeke, Chris. *David Teniers de Jongere: de verloren zoon.* Antwerpen, Hadewijch, 1991.

12244. Peyre, Roger R. *David Teniers, biographie critique.* Paris, Laurens, 1910.

12245. Rosenberg, Adolf. *Teniers der Jüngere.* Bielefeld/Leipzig, Velhagen & Klasing, 1895. (Künstler-Monographien, 8).

12246. Vermoelen, John. *Teniers le jeune; sa vie, ses oeuvres.* Anvers, Donné, 1865.

Tenniel, John, Sir, 1820–1914

12247. Engen, Rodney K. *Sir John Tenniel: Alice's white knight.* Aldershot, Hants., Scolar Press; Brookfield, Vt., Gower Pub., 1991.

12248. Hancher, Michael. *The Tenniel illustrations to the "Alice" books.* Columbus, Ohio State University Press, 1985.

12249. Simpson, Roger. *Sir John Tenniel: aspects of his work.* Rutherford, N.J., Fairleigh Dickinson University Press; London, Associated University Presses, 1994.

Terborch, Gerard, 1617–1681 *see also* Steen, Jan

12250. Gudlaugsson, Sturla J. *Geraert Ter Borch.* 2 v. Den Haag, Nijhoff, 1959. (CR).

12251. Hellens, Franz. *Gérard Terborch.* Bruxelles, van Oest, 1911.

12252. Landesmuseum Münster. *Gerard ter Borch: Zwolle 1617, Deventer 1681.* 12. Mai–23. Juni 1974. Münster, Landesmuseum für Kunst und Kulturgeschichte, 1974.

12253. Michel, Emile. *Gérard Terburg (Ter Borch) et sa famille.* Paris, Rouam, 1887.

12254. Plietzsch, Eduard. *Gerard ter Borch.* Wien, Schroll, 1944.

12255. Rijksmuseum (Netherlands). Rijksprentenkabinet. *Drawings from the Ter Borch studio estate.* Ed. by Alison McNeil Kettering. s'-Gravenhage, Staatsuitgeverij, 1988. (Catalogus van de Nederlandse tekeningen in het Rijksprentenkabinet, Rijksmuseum, Amsterdam, 5).

Terbrugghen, Hendrick, 1588–1629

12256. Blankert, Albert and Slatkes, Leonard J. Holländische. *Malerei in neuem Licht: Hendrick ter Brugghen und seine Zeitgenossen. Beiträge von Marten Jan Bok . . . [et al.].* Utrecht, Centraal Museum; Braunschweig, Herzog Anton Ulrich-Museum, [1986].

12257. Klessmann, Rüdiger. *Hendrick ter Brugghen und die Nachfolger Caravaggios in Holland.* Braunschweig, Herzog Anton Ulrich-Museum, [1987].

12258. Nicholson, Benedict. *Hendrick Terbrugghen.* London, Lund, Humphries, 1958. (CR).

Tessai, Tomioka, 1836–1924

12259. Odakane, Taro. *Tessai, master of the literary style.* Translation and adaptation by Money L. Hickman. Tokyo, Kodansha, 1965; distributed by Japan Publications Trading Co., Rutland, Vt.

12260. University of California Art Museum (Berkeley). *The works of Tomioka Tessai, a travelling exhibition organized by the International Exhibitions Foundation.* November 1968–November 1969. Takaruzuka (Japan), Kiyoshi Kojin Seichoji, 1968.

Tessin, Nicodemus (the elder), 1615–1681 Nicodemus (the younger), 1654–1728

12261. Josephson, Ragnar. *L'architecte de Charles XII: Nicodème Tessin à la cour de Louis XIV.* Paris/Bruxelles, van Oest, 1930.
12262. ———. *Nicodemus Tessin D. Y.: tiden, mannen, verket.* Stockholm, Norstedt, 1931. (Sveriges allmänna Konstförenings publikation, 39).
12263. Kommer, Björn R. *Nicodemus Tessin und das Stockholmer Schloss.* Heidelberg, Winter, 1974. (Heidelberger Kunstgeschichtliche Abhandlungen, Neue Folge, 11).
12264. Sirén, Osvald. *Nicodemus Tessin d.y.: studieresor i Danmark, Tyskland, Holland, Frankrike och Italien.* Stockholm, Norstedt, 1914.
12265. Weigert, R. A. et Hernmarck, Carl, eds. *L'art en France et en Suède, 1693–1718: extraits d'une correspondance entre l'architecte Nicodème Tessin le jeune et Daniel Cronström.* Stockholm, Egnellska Boktryc-keriet, 1964.

Testa, Pietro, 1611–1650

12266. Cropper, Elizabeth. *The ideal of painting: Pietro Testa's Düsseldorf notebook.* Princeton, Princeton University Press, 1984.
12267. ———. *Pietro Testa, 1612–1650: prints and drawings.* With essays by Charles Dempsey . . . [et al.]. Aldershot, Scolar, 1988.

Thayer, Abbott Handerson, 1849–1921

12268. Anderson, Ross. *Abbott Handerson Thayer.* [Published in conjunction with an exhibition at the Everson Museum, Syracuse, N.Y.]. Syracuse, Everson Museum, 1982.
12269. Thayer, Gerald H. *Concealing-coloration in the animal kingdom: an exposition of the laws of disguise through color and pattern, being a summary of Abbott Handerson Thayer's discoveries.* New York, Macmillan, 1909.
12270. While, Nelson C. *Abbott H. Thayer, painter and naturalist.* Hartford, Conn., Connecticut Printers, 1951.

Theotocopoulos, Domenicos *see* Greco, El

Theus, Jeremiah, 1716–1774

12271. Middleton, Margaret S. *Jeremiah Theus, colonial artist of Charles Town.* Columbia, S.C., University of South Carolina Press, 1953.

Thiebaud, Wayne, 1920–

12272. Thiebaud, Wayne. *Vision and revision: hand colored prints by Wayne Thiebaud.* Intro. by Wayne Thiebaud. Essays by Bill Berkson and Robert Flynn Johnson. San Francisco, Chronicle Books, 1991.
12273. ———. *Wayne Thiebaud—private drawings: the artist's sketchbook.* Selected and ed. by Constance and Jack Glenn. Intro. by Constance Glenn. New York, Abrams, 1987.
12274. ———. *Wayne Thiebaud: Works on paper from the collection of the artist.* Chicago, Arts Club of Chicago; Atlanta, Georgia State University Art Gallery, [1987].
12275. Tsujimoto, Karen. *Wayne Thiebaud.* Seattle, published for the San Francisco Museum of Modern Art by the University of Washington Press, 1985.

Thiersch, Friedrich, 1852–1921

12276. Marschall, Horst K. *Friedrich von Thiersch (1852–1921): ein Münchner Architekt des Späthistorismus.* München, Prestel, 1982.
12277. Münchner Stadtmuseum. *Friedrich von Thiersch, ein Münchner Architekt des Späthistorismus, 1852–1921.* München, Lipp, 1977.
12278. Thiersch, Hermann. *Friedrich von Thiersch der Architekt, 1852–1921; ein Lebensbild.* München, Bruckmann, 1925.

Thoma, Hans, 1839–1924

12279. Augustinermuseum Freiburg im Breisgau. *Hans Thoma, Lebensbilder: Gemäldeausstellung zum 150. Geburtstag. 2. Oktober–3. Dezember 1989.* [Katalogbearbeitung, Markus Ewel, Brigitte Rechberg, Margret Zimmermann]. Königstein im Taunus, K.R. Langewiesche, 1989.
12280. Beringer, Joseph A. *Hans Thoma.* München, Bruckmann, 1922.
12281. Böhm, Heinrich. *Hans Thoma, sein Exlibris-Werk.* Berlin, Maximilian, 1959.
12282. Busse, Hermann E. *Hans Thoma, Leben und Werk.* Berlin, Rembrandt, 1935.
12283. Helmolt, Christa von. *Hans Thoma, Spiegelbilder.* Stuttgart, Klett-Clotta, 1989.
12284. Meissner, Franz. *Hans Thoma.* Berlin/Leipzig, Schuster & Loeffler, 1899. (Das Künstlerbuch, 4).
12285. Ostini, Fritz von. *Thoma.* Bielefeld/Leipzig, Velhagen & Klasing, 1900. (Künstler-Monographien, 46).
12286. Thode, Henry. *Thoma, des Meisters Gemälde.* Stuttgart/Leipzig, Deutsche Verlags-Anstalt, 1909. (Klassiker der Kunst, 15).
12287. Thoma, Hans. *Briefe an Frauen.* Heraus-

gegeben von Joseph A. Beringer. Stuttgart, Strecker und Schröder, 1936.

12288. ———. *Gesammelte Schriften und Briefe.* Herausgegeben von Joseph A. Beringer. 2 v. Leipzig, Koehler & Amelang, 1927/1928.

12289. ———. *Hans Thoma in Frankfurt und im Taunus.* Herausgegeben von der Museumsgesellschaft Kronberg im Taunus. Frankfurt am Main, W. Kramer, 1983. (Dokumentation der Museumsgesellschaft Kronberg e.V. Schriften, 3).

12290. ———. *Im Herbst des Lebens.* München, Süddeutsche Monatshefte, 1908.

Thorn Prikker, Johan, 1868–1932

12291. Hoff, August. *Johan Thorn Prikker.* Recklinghausen, Bongers, 1958. (Monographien zur rheinisch-westfälischen Kunst der Gegenwart, 12).

12292. Wember, Paul. *Johan Thorn Prikker: Glasfenster, Wandbilder, Ornamente, 1891–1932.* Bearbeitung des Werkverzeichnisses von Johannes Cladders. [Published in conjunction with an exhibition at the Kaiser Wilhelm Museum, Krefeld]. Krefeld, Scherpe, 1966. (CR).

12293. Wex, Johanna Luise. *Johan Thorn Prikker: Abstraktion und Konkretion in freier und angewandter Kunst.* [Bochum?, s.n., 1984].

Thornycroft, Hamo, 1850–1925

12294. Manning, Elfrida. *Marble & bronze: the art and life of Hamo Thornycroft.* Introduction by Benedict Read. London, Trefoil Books, 1982.

Thorvaldsen, Bertel, 1770–1844 *see also* Sergel, Johann Tobias

12295. Barnard, Mordaunt R. *The life of Thorvaldsen.* Collated from the Danish of J. M. Thiele. London, Chapman and Hall, 1865.

12296. Bott, Gerhard, et al. *Bertel Thorvaldsen: Untersuchungen zu seinem Werk und zur Kunst seiner Zeit.* [Published in conjunction with an exhibition at Kunsthalle Köln, February 5–April 3, 1977]. Köln, Museen der Stadt Köln, 1977.

12297. Hartmann, Jørgen B. *Antike Motive bei Thorvaldsen; Studien zur Antikenrezeption des Klassizismus.* Bearbeitet und herausgegeben von Klaus Parlasca. Tübingen, Wasmuth, 1979.

12298. ———. *Thorvaldsen a Roma.* Con prefazione di Antonio Munoz. Roma, Palombi, 1959.

12299. Helsted, Dyveke, Henschen, Eva, and Jrns, Bjarne. *Thorvaldsen.* Trans. by Ann and Janus Paludan. Copenhagen, Thorvaldsen Museum, 1990.

12300. Konrádsson, Helgi. *Bertel Thorvaldsen.* Reykjavík, Gunnarsson, 1944.

12301. Moltesen, Erik. *Bertel Thorvaldsen.* København, Navers, 1929.

12302. Müller, Sigurd. *Thorvaldsen, hans liv og hans vaerker.* Kjøbenhavn, Stochholm, 1893.

12303. Oppermann, Theodor. *Thorvaldsen.* 3 v. Kjøbenhavn, Gads, 1924–1930.

12304. Plon, Eugene. *Thorvaldsen, his life and works.* Trans. by I. M. Luyster. Boston, Roberts, 1873.

12305. Rave, Paul O. *Thorvaldsen.* Berlin, Rembrandt, 1947.

12306. Rosenberg, Adolf. *Thorwaldsen.* Bielefeld/Leipzig, Velhagen & Klasing, 1896. (Künstler-Monographien, 16).

12307. Sass, Else K. *Thorvaldsens portraetbuster.* 3 v. København, Gads, 1963/1965. (CR).

12308. Thiele, Just M. *Den danske billedhugger Bertel Thorvaldsen og hans vaerker.* 4 v. København, Forfatterens Forlag i Thieles Bogtrykkeri, 1831–1850.

12309. ———. *Thorvaldsens biographi.* 4 v. Kjøbenhavn, Reitzel, 1851–1856.

12310. Thorvaldsen, Bertel. *Bertel Thorvaldsen, 1770–1844: scultore danese a Roma.* A cura di Elena di Majo, Bjarne Jrnaes, Stefano Susinno. Roma, De Luca, 1989.

12311. ———. *Künstlerleben in Rom: Bertel Thorvaldsen (1770–1844), der dänische Bildhauer und seine deutschen Freunde:* Germanisches Nationalmuseum, Nürnberg, 1. Dezember 1991 bis 1. März 1992, Schleswig-Holsteinisches Landesmuseum Schloss Gottorf, Schleswig, 22. März bis 21. Juni 1992. [Katalog bearbeitet von Ursula Peters, in Zusammenarbeit mit Andrea M. Kluxen . . . et al. Redaktion, Wolfgang Pülhorn. Autoren, Katharina Bott . . . et al.]. Nürnberg, Verlag des Germanischen Nationalmuseums, 1991.

12312. ———. *Thorvaldsen: l'ambiente, l'influsso, il mito.* A cura di Patrick Kragelund e Mogens Nykjaer. Roma, L'Erma di Bretschneider, 1991. (Analecta Romana Instituti Danici. Supplementum, 18).

12313. Wallraf-Richartz-Museum/Kunsthalle Köln. *Bertel Thorvaldsen: Skulpturen, Modelle, Bozzetti, Handzeichnungen.* 5. Februar bis 3. April 1977. Köln, Museen der Stadt Köln, 1977.

Tibaldi, Pellegrino, 1527–1596

12314. Briganti, Giuliano. *Il manierismo e Pellegrino Tibaldi.* Roma, Cosmopolita, 1945.

12315. Hiersche, Waldemar. *Pellegrino dei Pellegrini als Architekt.* Parchim, Germany, Freise, 1913.

12316. Rocco, Giovanni. *Pellegrino Pellegrini, l'architetto di S. Carlo e le sue opere nel duomo di Milano.* Milano, Hoepli, 1939.

12317. Tibaldi, Pellegrino. *L'architettura di Leon Battista Alberti nel commento di Pellegrino*

Tibaldi. Edizione critica e apparato delle varianti, Sandro Orlando. Esegesi e saggio introduttivo, Giorgio Simoncini. Roma, De Luca Edizioni d'Arte, 1988.

Tiepolo, Giovanni Battista, 1696–1770
Giovanni Domenico, 1726–1804
Lorenzo, 1736–1776

12318. Alpers, Svetlana and Baxandall, Michael. *Tiepolo and the pictorial intelligence.* New Haven, Yale University Press, 1994.

12319. Barcham, William L. *Giambattista Tiepolo.* New York, N.N. Abrams, 1992.

12320. ———. *The religious paintings of Giambattista Tiepolo: piety and tradition in eighteenth-century Venice.* Oxford, Clarendon Press, 1989.

12321. Brown, Beverly Louise. *Giambattista Tiepolo: master of the oil sketch.* With essays by Terisio Pignatti, Oreste Ferrari, Teresa Longyear. Milan, Electa; New York, Abbeville; Fort Worth, Kimball Art Museum, 1993.

12322. Büttner, Frank. *Giovanni Battista Tiepolo: die Fresken in der Residenz zu Würzburg.* Aufnahmen von Wolf-Christian von der Mülbe. Würzburg, Popp, 1980.

12323. Chennevières, Henry de. *Les Tiepolo.* Paris, Librairie de l'Art, 1898.

12324. Fogg Art Museum, Harvard University (Cambridge, Mass.). *Tiepolo: a bicentenary exhibition, 1770–1970.* March 14–May 3, 1970. Cambridge, Mass., Trustees of Harvard College, 1970.

12325. Freeden, Max H. von und Lamb, Carl. *Das Meisterwerk des Giovanni Battista Tiepolo: die Fresken der Würzburger Residenz.* München, Hirmer, 1956.

12326. Gemin, Massimo and Pedrocco, Filippo. *Giambattista Tiepolo: i dipinti, opera completa.* Venezia, Arsenale Editrice, 1993. (Monografie, 1).

12327. Hadeln, Detlev von. *The drawings of G. B. Tiepolo.* 2 v. Paris, Pegasus, 1928.

12328. Hegemann, Hans W. *Giovanni Battista Tiepolo.* Berlin, Rembrandt, 1940.

12329. Knox, George. *Catalogue of the Tiepolo drawings in the Victoria and Albert Museum.* London, HMSO, 1975. (CR).

12330. ———. *Etchings by the Tiepolos.* [Published in conjunction with an exhibition at the National Gallery of Canada, Ottawa; text in English and French]. Ottawa, National Gallery of Canada, 1976.

12331. ———. *Giambattista and Domenico Tiepolo: a study and catalogue raisonné of the chalk drawings.* 2 v. Oxford, Clarendon Press, 1980. (CR).

12332. Leitschuh, Franz F. *Giovanni Battista Tiepolo, eine Studie zur Kunstgeschichte des 18. Jahrhunderts.* Würzburg, Bauer, 1896.

12333. Levey, Michael. *Giambattista Tiepolo, his life and art.* New Haven, Yale University Press, 1986.

12334. Mariuz, Adriano. *Giandomenico Tiepolo.* Venezia, Alfieri, [1971]. (CR). (Profile e saggi di arte veneta, 9).

12335. Mazzariol, Giuseppe [and] Pignatti, Terisio. *Itinerario tiepolesco.* Venezia, Lombroso, 1951.

12336. Meissner, Franz H. *Tiepolo.* Bielefeld/Leipzig, Velhagen & Klasing, 1897. (Künstler-Monographien, 22).

12337. Molmenti, Pompeo G. *G. B. Tiepolo, la sua vita e le sue opere.* Milano, Hoepli, 1909.

12338. Morassi, Antonio. *A complete catalogue of the paintings of G. B. Tiepolo.* London, Phaidon, 1962. (CR).

12339. ———. *G. B. Tiepolo, his life and work.* London, Phaidon, 1955; distributed by Garden City Books, New York.

12340. Palazzo Ducale (Venice). *Tiepolo, tecnica e immaginazione.* Luglio–settembre 1979. Venezia, Alfieri, 1979.

12341. Pedrocco, Filippo. *Disegni di Giandomenico Tiepolo.* Milano, Berenice, 1990.

12342. Pignatti, Terisio. *Tiepolo disegni.* Scelti e annotati da Terisio Pignatti. Firenze, La Nuova Italia, 1974.

12343. Piovene, Guido [and] Pallucchini, Anna. *L'opera completa di Giambattista Tiepolo.* Milano, Rizzoli, 1968. (CR). (Classici dell'arte, 25).

12344. Porcella, Antonio. *La giovinezza di Giambattista Tiepolo.* Roma, de Luca, 1973.

12345. Precerutti Garberi, Mercedes. *Giambattista Tiepolo, gli affreschi.* Torino, ERI, 1970.

12346. Rigon, Fernando . . . [et al.], eds. *I Tiepolo e il Settecento vicentino.* Milano, Electa, 1990.

12347. Sack, Eduard. *Giambattista und Domenico Tiepolo, ihr Leben und ihre Werke.* Hamburg, Clarmann, 1910.

12348. Semenzato, Camillo. *Giambattista Tiepolo.* Milano, Fabbri, 1964. (I maestri del colore, 37).

12349. Shaw, J. Byam. *The drawings of Domenico Tiepolo.* London, Faber, 1962.

12350. Succi, Dario, ed. *I Tiepolo, virtuosismo e ironia.* Catalogo della mostra, Mirano (Venezia), Barchessa Villa XXV Aprile, 11 settembre–30 novembre, 1988. Scritti di Madeleine Barbin . . . [et al.]. Torino, Allemandi, 1988.

12351. Tiepolo, Giovanni Battista. *Giambattista Tiepolo: il segno e l'enigma.* Catalogo della mostra a cura di Dario Succi; saggio introduttivo di Terisio Pignatti; scritti di D. Succi, Federico Montecuccoli degli Erri, Filippo Pedrocco. [Ponzano?], Vianelli Libri/foligraf, 1985.

12352. Urbani de Ghelthof, Giuseppe M. *Tiepolo e*

la sua famiglia. Venezia, Kirchmayr e Scozzi, 1879.

12353. Vigni, Giorgio. *Disegni del Tiepolo.* seconda edizione, riveduta e ampliata dall'autore. Trieste, Editoriale Libraria, 1972. (CR).

12354. Villa Manin di Passariano. *Mostra del Tiepolo.* 2 v. 27 giugno–31 ottobre 1971. Milano, Electa, 1971.

Timmermans, Felix, 1886–1947

12355. Cordemans, Marcel. *Raymond de la Haye en Felix Timmermans, herinneringen.* Gent, Story-Scientia, 1967.

12356. Peeters, Denijs. *Felix Timmermans, tekenaar en schilder.* Leuven, Davidsfonds, [1956].

12357. Remoortere, Julien van. *Felix Timmermans; mens, schrijver, schilder, tekenaar.* Antwerpen, Mercatorfonds, 1972. (CR).

12358. Rutten, Th. *Felix Timmermans.* Groningen/Den Haag, Wolters, 1928.

12359. Timmermans, Felix. *Al mijn dagen: dagboeken archief Felix Timmermans.* Ed. by Ingrid van de Wijer. Wommelgem, Gulden Engel, 1986.

12360. Timmermans, Lia. *Mijn Vader.* Amsterdam, De Brouwer, 1951.

12361. Vercammen, Louis. *Felix Timmermans: de mens—het Werk.* Hasselt, Heideland-Orbis, 1972.

12362. Veremans, Renaat. *Herinneringen aan Felix Timmermans.* Antwerpen, Vink, 1950.

Timotheus, 4th c. B.C.

12363. Schlörb, Barbara. *Timotheos.* Berlin, de Gruyter, 1965. (Jahrbuch des Archäologischen Instituts des Deutschen Reichs, Ergänzungsheft, 22).

Tinguely, Jean, 1925–

12364. Bezzola, Leonardo. *Jean Tinguely, 166 Fotos.* Zeichnungen, Texte, Gedichte, Briefe etc. von Eva Aeppli et al. Zürich, Arche, 1974.

12365. Hulten, Karl Gunnar Pontus. *Jean Tinguely: a magic stronger than death.* New York, Abbeville Press, 1987.

12366. Monteil, Annemarie. *Der Tinguely-Brunnen in Basel.* Basel, Birkhäuser, 1980.

12367. Stumm, Reinhardt and Wyss, Kurt. *Jean Tinguely.* Basel, F. Reinhardt, 1985.

12368. Tinguely, Jean. *Briefe von Jean Tinguely an Maja Sacher.* Herausgegeben von Margrit Hahnloser. Bern, Benteli, 1992.

12369. ———. *Jean Tinguely: catalogue raisonné: sculptures and reliefs, 1954–1968.* Comp. by Christina Bischofberger. Küsnacht/Zürich, Edition Galerie Bruno Bischofberger; New York, distributed by Edition Galerie Bruno Bischofberger, 1982. (CR).

12370. ———. *Pandamonium, Jean Tinguely.* Text von Margrit Hahnloser-Ingold. Fotografien von Leonardo Bezzola. Bern, Benteli, 1988.

12371. Wilhelm-Lehmbruck-Museum der Stadt Duisburg. *Jean Tinguely: Meta-Maschinen.* [December 17, 1978–February 4, 1979]. Duisburg, Wilhelm-Lehmbruck-Museum, 1978.

Tino da Camaino, 1280–1337

12372. Carli, Enzo. *Tino di Camaino, scultore.* Firenze, Le Monnier, 1934.

12373. Dan, Naoki. *La tomba di Arrigo VII di Tino di Camaino e il Rinascimento.* Firenze, Pan arte, 1983.

12374. Kreytenberg, Gert. *Die Werke von Tino di Camaino.* Frankfurt am Main, Liebighaus, 1987.

12375. Morisani, Ottavio. *Tino di Camaino a Napoli.* Napoli, Libreria Scientifica Editrice, 1945.

12376. Tino, di Camaino. *Tino di Camaino.* Testo di G. Kreytenberg. Firenze, Museo nazionale del Bargello, 1986. (Lo Specchio del Bargello, 30).

12377. Valentiner, Wilhelm R. *Tino di Camaino, a Sienese sculptor of the fourteenth century.* Trans. by Josephine Walker. Paris, Pegasus, 1935.

Tintoretto, II, 1518–1594

12378. Bercken, Erich von der und Mayer, August L. *Jacopo Tintoretto.* 2 v. München, Piper, 1923.

12379. Bernari, Carlo [and] Vecchi, Pierluigi de. *L'opera completa del Tintoretto.* Milano, Rizzoli, 1970. (CR). (Classici dell'arte, 36).

12380. Bianchini, M. A. *Tintoretto.* Milano, Fabbri, 1964. (I maestri del colore, 17).

12381. Dobai, Katharina. *Studien zu Tintoretto und die florentinische Skulptur der Michelangelo-Nachfolge.* Bern/New York, P. Lang, 1991. (European university studies. Series XXVIII, History of art, vol. 120).

12382. Fosca, François [pseud., Georges de Traz]. *Tintoret.* Paris, Michel, 1929.

12383. Hadeln, Detlev von. *Zeichnungen des Giacomo Tintoretto.* Berlin, Cassirer, 1922.

12384. Holborn, John B. *Jacopo Robusti, called Tintoretto.* London, Bell, 1903.

12385. Loos, Viggo. *Tintoretto, motreformationens malare.* [Stockholm], Wahlström & Widstrand, 1940.

12386. Newton, Eric. *Tintoretto.* London, Longmans, Green, 1952.

12387. Osler, William R. *Tintoretto.* New York, Scribner and Welford/London, Sampson Low, 1879.

12388. Osmaston, Francis P. *The art and genius of Tintoret.* 2 v. London, Bell, 1915.

12389. Pallucchini, Rodolfo. *La giovinezza del Tintoretto.* Milano, Guarnati, 1950.

12390. ———. *Tintoretto a San Rocco.* Con note

storiche di Mario Brunetti. Venezia, Le Tre Venezie, 1937.

12391. —— [and] Rossi, Paola. *Tintoretto: le opere sacre e profane.* 2 v. Venezia, Alfieri/ Milano, Electa, 1982.

12392. Phillips, Evelyn M. *Tintoretto.* London, Methuen, 1911.

12393. Pittaluga, Mary. *Il Tintoretto.* Bologna, Zanichelli, 1925.

12394. Ridolfi, Carlo. *Vita di Giacopo Robusti detto il Tintoretto, celebre pittore cittadino venetiano.* Venetia, Oddoni, 1642.

12395. Rossi, Paola. *I disegni di Jacopo Tintoretto.* Firenze, La Nuova Italia, 1975. (Corpus graphicum, 1).

12396. ——. *Jacopo Tintoretto: i ritratti.* Prefazione di Rodolfo Pallucchini. Venezia, Alfieri, 1974.

12397. Soulier, Gustave. *Le Tintoret, biographie critique.* Paris, Laurens, [1911].

12398. Stearns, Frank P. *Life and genius of Jacopo Robusti, called Tintoretto.* New York, Putnam, 1894.

12399. Thode, Henry. *Tintoretto.* Bielefeld/Leipzig, Velhagen & Klasing, 1901. (Künstler-Monographien, 49).

12400. Tietze, Hans. *Tintoretto: the paintings and drawings.* London, Phaidon, 1948.

12401. Valcanover, Francesco. *Tintoretto.* Text by Francesco Valcanover and Terisio Pignatti. Trans. by Robert Erich Wolf. New York, H.N. Abrams, 1985.

12402. Villa alla Farnesina alla Lungara (Rome). *Immagini dal Tintoretto stampe dal XVI al XIX secolo nelle collezioni del Gabinetto delle Stampe.* 23 marzo–30 maggio 1982. Roma, de Luca, 1982.

12403. Waldmann, Emil. *Tintoretto.* Berlin, Cassirer, 1921.

Tischbein, Christian Wilhelm, 1751–1824
Johann Friedrich August, 1750–1812
Johann Heinrich, 1722–1789
Johann Heinrich Wilhelm, 1751–1829

12404. Bahlmann, Hermann. *Johann Heinrich Tischbein.* Strassburg, Heitz, 1911. (Studien zur deutschen Kunstgeschichte, 142).

12405. Goethe, Johann W. *Wilhelm Tischbeins Idyllen.* München, Bruckmann, 1970.

12406. Landsberger, Franz. *Wilhelm Tischbein, ein Künstlerleben des 18. Jahrhunderts.* Leipzig, Klinkhardt & Biermann, 1908. (Bücher der Kunst, 3).

12407. Lenz, Christian. *Tischbein: Goethe in der Campagna di Roma.* [Published in conjunction with an exhibition at the Städelsches Kunstinstitut und Städtische Galerie, Frankfurt a.M.]. Frankfurt a.M., Städelsches Kunstinstitut und Städtische Galerie, 1970.

12408. Michel, Edmond. *Etude biographique sur les Tischbein, peintres allemands du XVIIIᵉ siècle.* Lyon, Georg, 1881.

12409. Mildenberger, Hermann. *Johann Heinrich Wilhelm Tischbein, Goethes Maler und Freund.* Mit Beiträgen von Margret E. Burscheidt . . . [et al.]. Neumünster, Wachholtz, 1986. (Kunst in Schleswig-Holstein, 29).

12410. Nonn, Konrad. *Christian Wilhelm Tischbein: Maler und Architekt, 1751–1824.* Strassburg, Heitz, 1912. (Studien zur deutschen Kunstgeschichte, 148).

12411. Schnyder-Seidel, Barbara. *J. H. Füssli und seine schönen Zürcherinnen: Verwirrungen um Bildnisse im Umkreis von Goethe, Füssli, und Tischbein.* Zürich, W. Classen, 1986.

12412. Stoll, Adolf. *Der Maler Johann Friedrich August Tischbein und seine Familie.* Stuttgart, Strecker und Schröder, 1923.

12413. Tischbein, Johann Heinrich Wilhelm. *Johann Heinrich Wilhelm Tischbein: Zeichnungen aus Goethes Kunstsammlung.* Auswahl, Einleitung und Katalog, Margarete Oppell. Weimar, Verlag der Klassikerstätten, 1991.

12414. Tischbein, Heinrich W. *Aus meinem Leben.* Herausgegeben von Kuno Mittelstädt. Berlin, Henschel, 1956.

Tissot, James Jacques Joseph, 1836–1902

12415. Ash, Russell. *James Tissot.* London, Pavilion, 1992.

12416. Musée des Beaux-arts de Besançon (France). *James Tissot, 1836 1902.* 6 juillet–30 septembre 1985. [Conception et réalisation du catalogue, Nathalie Alourafi]. [Besançon, Le Musée, 1985]. (Collection du Musée, 7).

12417. Tissot, James Jacques Joseph. *James Tissot.* Ed. by Krystyna Matyjaszkiewicz. Oxford, Phaidon; London, Barbican Art Gallery, 1984.

12418. Wentworth, Michael. *James Tissot.* Oxford, Clarendon Press; New York, Oxford University Press, 1984.

12419. Wood, Christopher. *Tissot, the life and works of Jacques Joseph Tissot 1836–1902.* Boston, Little, Brown, 1986.

Titian, 1477–1576

12420. Archivio General di Simancas (Simancas, Spain). *Tiziano e la corte di Spagna nei documenti dell'Archivio Generale di Simancas.* Madrid, Istituto Italiano di Cultura, 1975.

12421. Babelon, Jean. *Titien.* Paris, Plon, 1950.

12422. Barfoed, Christian. *Titian Vecellio, hans samtid, liv og kunst.* København, Lind, 1889.

12423. Basch, Victor. *Titien.* Paris, Librairie Française, 1920.

12424. Beltrame, Francesco. *Cenni illustrativi sul monumento a Tiziano Vecellio*. Venezia, Naratovich, 1852.

12425. Bergmann, Werner. *Tizian: Bilder aus seinem Leben und seiner Zeit*. 2 v. Hannover, Klindworth, 1865.

12426. Beroqui, Pedro. *Tiziano en el Museo del Prado*. Madrid, [Museo del Prado], 1946.

12427. Bettini, Sergio, et al. *Tiziano nel quarto centenario della sua morte, 1576–1976*. Venezia, Ateneo Veneto, 1977.

12428. Bortolatto, Luigina and Pilo, Giuseppe M., eds. *Tiziano dopo Tiziano: induzioni e deduzioni dagli atti del Convegno internazionale di studi promesso da Magnifica comunitá di Cadore nel quinto centenario della nascita Pieve di Cadore, 17–18 agosto 1990*. Udine, Arte documento; Le Venezie, Editrice SIT, 1991. (Arte documento. Liber extra, 2).

12429. Cadorin, Giuseppe. *Dello amore ai veneziani di Tiziano Vecellio delle sue case in Cadore e in Venezia e delle vite de' suoi figli*. Venezia, Hopfner, 1833.

12430. Cagli, Corrado [and] Valcanover, Francesco. *L'opera completa di Tiziano*. Milano, Rizzoli, 1969. (CR). (Classici dell'arte, 32).

12431. Caro-Delvaille, Henry. *Titien*. Paris, Alcan, 1913.

12432. Caroli, Flavio and Zuffi, Stefano. *Tiziano*. Milano, Rusconi, 1990. 2a ed.

12433. Carpani, Giuseppe. *Le Majeriane ovvero lettere sul bello ideale, in riposta al libro Della Imitazione Pittorica del Andrea Majer*. Edizione terza, riveduta ed accresciuta dall'autore. Padova, Tipografia della Minerva, 1824.

12434. Christoffel, Ulrich. *Tizian*. Zürich/Wien, Europa, 1957. (Urban-Bücher, 25).

12435. Clausse, Gustav. *Les Farnèses peints par Titien*. Paris, Gazette des Beaux-Arts, 1905.

12436. Comitato promotore per le manifestazioni espositive Firenze e Prato. *Tiziano nelle gallerie fiorentine*. Firenze, Centro Di, 1978.

12437. Crowe, Joseph A. and Cavalcaselle, G. B. *Titian: his life and times*. 2 v. London, Murray, 1877.

12438. Fage, Gilles, ed. *Le Siècle de Titien: l'age d'or de la peinture à Venise*. Paris, Réunion des Musées nationaux, 1993. 2 ed.

12439. Feghelm-Aebersold, Dagmar. *Zeitgeschichte in Tizians religiösen Historienbildern*. Hildesheim/New York, G. Olms, 1991. (Studien zur Kunstgeschichte, 62).

12440. Fischel, Oskar. *Tizian, des Meisters Gemälde*. Stuttgart/Leipzig, Deutsche Verlags-Anstalt, 1904. (Klassiker der Kunst, 3).

12441. Fondazione Giorgio Cini (Venice). *Disegni di Tiziano e della sua cerchia*. Catalogo a cura di Konrad Oberhuber con l'assistenza di Hilliard Goldfarb. Presentazione di Rodolfo Pallucchini. Venezia, Pozza, 1976. (Cataloghi di mostre, 38).

12442. Freedman, Luba. *Titian's independent self-portraits*. Firenze, L.S. Olschki, 1990. (Pocket library of "studies" in art, 26).

12443. Galleria degli Uffizi (Florence). *Tiziano e il disegno veneziano del suo tempo*. Firenze, Olschki, 1976.

12444. Gentili, Augusto. *Da Tiziano a Tiziano: mito e allegoria nella cultura veneziana del cinquecento*. Milano, Feltrinelli, 1980. [2a ed., Roma, Bulzoni, 1988. (Biblioteca del Cinquecento, 42)].

12445. Gilbert, Josiah. *Cadore, or Titian's country*. London, Longmans, Green, 1869.

12446. Gronau, Georg. *Titian*. Trans. by Alice M. Todd. London, Duckworth/New York, Scribner, 1904.

12447. Hadeln, Detlev von. *Titian's drawings*. London, Macmillan, 1927.

12448. Hamel, Maurice. *Titien, biographie critique*. Paris, Laurens, [1904].

12449. Heath, Richard F. *Titian*. New York, Scribner and Welford, 1882.

12450. Hetzer, Theodor. *Tizian: Geschichte seiner Farbe*. Frankfurt a.M., Klostermann, 1935.

12451. ———. *Tizian: Geschichte seiner Farbe; die frühen Gemälde: Bildnisse*. Stuttgart, Urachhaus, 1992. (Schriften Theodor Hetzers, 7).

12452. Hope, Charles. *Titian*. New York, Harper & Row, 1980.

12453. Hourticq, Louis. *La jeunesse de Titien*. Paris, Hachette, 1919.

12454. Hume, Abraham. *Notice of the life and works of Titian*. London, Rodwell, 1829.

12455. Knackfuss, Hermann. *Tizian*. Bielefeld/Leipzig, Velhagen & Klasing, 1897. (Künstler-Monographien, 29).

12456. Lafenestre, Georges. *La vie et l'oeuvre de Titien*. Paris, May, 1886.

12457. Maier, Andrea. *Apologia del libro Delle Imitazione pittorica e delle eccellenza delle opere di Tiziano contro tre lettere di Giuseppe Carpani a Giuseppe Acerbi*. Ferrara, Pomatelli, 1820.

12458. ———. *Delle imitazione pittorica* [and] *della eccellenza delle opere di Tiziano e della Vita di Tiziano scritta da Stefano Ticozzi*. Venezia, Alvisopoli, 1818.

12459. Manca, Joseph, ed. *Titian 500*. Washington, National Gallery of Art; Hanover, N.H., distributed by the University Press of New England, 1993. (Studies in the history of art, 45; Symposium papers, 25).

12460. Mauroner, Fabio. *Le incisioni di Tiziano*. Venezia, Le Tre Venezie, 1941.

12461. Morassi, Antonio. *Titian*. Greenwich, Conn., New York Graphic Society, 1965.

12462. Northcote, James. *The life of Titian*. 2 v. London, Colburn and Bentley, 1830.

12463. Ost, Hans. *Tizian-Studien*. Köln, Böhlau, 1992.

12464. Palazzo Reale (Milan). *Omaggio a Tiziano: la cultura artistica milanese nell'età di Carlo V.* 27 aprile–20 luglio 1977. Milano, Electa, 1977.

12465. Pallucchini, Rodolfo. *Tiziano*. 2 v. Firenze, Sansoni, 1969.

12466. ———, ed. *Tiziano e il manierismo europeo*. Firenze, Olschki, 1978. (Civiltà veneziana, 24).

12467. Panofsky, Erwin. *Problems in Titian, mostly iconographic*. New York, New York University Press, 1969. (Wrightsman Lectures, 2).

12468. Phillips, Claude. *The earlier work of Titian*. London, Seeley, 1897. (Portfolio, 34).

12469. ———. *The later work of Titian*. London, Seeley, 1898. (Portfolio, 37).

12470. Pilla, Eugenio. *Tiziano: il pittore dell'Assunta*. Napoli, Treves, 1969.

12471. Pope, Arthur. *Titian's Rape of Europa: a study of the composition and the mode of representation in this and related paintings*. Cambridge, Mass., Harvard University Press, 1960.

12472. Ricketts, Charles. *Titian*. London, Methuen, 1910.

12473. Rosand, David. *Titian*. New York, Abrams, 1978.

12474. ——— ed. *Titian: his world and his legacy*. New York, Columbia University Press, 1982.

12475. ——— and Muraro, Michelangelo. *Titian and the Venetian woodcut*. [Published in conjunction with an exhibition at the National Gallery of Art, Washington, D.C., and other places]. Washington, D.C., National Gallery of Art, 1976.

12476. Suida, Wilhelm. *Tizian*. Zürich/Leipzig, Füssli, 1933.

12477. Sweetser, Moses F. *Titian*. Boston, Osgood, 1877.

12478. Ticozzi, Stefano. *Vite dei pittori Vecelli di Cadore*. Milano, Stella, 1817.

12479. Tietze, Hans. *Titian: paintings and drawings*. London, Phaidon, 1950. 2 ed.

12480. Titian. *Le Siécle de Titien: l'áge d'or de la peinture á Venise: [exposition] Grand Palais 9 mars–14 juin 1993.* [Commissariat général, Michel Laclotte, Giovanna Nepi Sciré. Comité scientifique, Alessandro Ballarin . . . et al.]. Paris, Réunion des musées nationaux, 1993.

12481. ———. *Titian drawings*. Ed. by M. Agnese Chiari Moretto Wiel. New York, Rizzoli, 1990. (CR).

12482. ———. *Titian, prince of painters*. Munich, Prestel; New York, distributed in the USA and Canada by te Neues Publishing, 1990.

12483. Tiziano Vecellio. *Le lettere*. Presentazioni di Giuseppe Vecellio. Introduzione di Ugo Fasolo. Prefazione di Clemente Gandini. Cadore, Magnifica Comunità di Cadore, 1977.

12484. Università degli Studi di Venezia. *Tiziano e Venezia: convegno internazionale di studi*. Vicenza, Pozza, 1980.

12485. Valcanover, Francesco. *All the paintings of Titian*. Trans. by Sylvia J. Tomalin. 4 v. New York, Hawthorn, 1960. (CR). (Complete Library of World Art, 29–32).

12486. Verdizzotti, Giovanni M. *Breve compendio della vita del famoso Tiziano Vecellio di Cadore*. Venetia, Appresso Santo Grillo, 1622.

12487. Villa alla Farnesina alla Lungara (Rome). *Immagini da Tiziano: stampe dal secolo XVI al secolo XIX dalle collezioni del Gabinetto Nationale delle Stampe*. 16 dicembre 1976–15 gennaio 1977. Roma, de Luca, 1976.

12488. Waldmann, Emil. *Tizian*. Berlin, Propyläen, 1922.

12489. Walther, Angelo. *Tizian*. Leipzig, Seemann, 1978.

12490. Wethey, Harold E. *The paintings of Titian, complete edition*. 3 v. London, Phaidon, 1969–1975. (CR).

12491. ———. *Titian and his drawings: with reference to Giorgione and some close contemporaries*. Princeton, Princeton University Press, 1987. (National Gallery of Art Kress Foundation studies in the history of European art, 8).

12492. Wiel, Taddeo. *Tiziano a Venezia*. Venezia, Kirchmayr e Scozzi, 1880.

Tiziano Vecelli *see* Titian

Tobey, Mark, 1890–1976

12493. Feininger, Lyonel. *Feininger and Tobey: years of friendship, 1944–1956: the complete correspondence*. Ed. and annotated by Stephan E. Hauser. New York, Achim Moeller Fine Art, 1991.

12494. Galerie Beyeler (Basel). *Mark Tobey, a centennial exhibition*. November 1990–Januar 1991. Basel, Galerie Beyeler, 1990.

12495. Heidenheim, Hanns H. *Mark Tobey: das graphische Werk*. Düsseldorf, Ursus, 1975. (CR).

12496. Musée des Arts Décoratifs (Paris). *Rétrospective Mark Tobey*. 18 octobre–1 décembre 1961. Paris, Musée des Arts Décoratifs, 1961.

12497. National Collection of Fine Arts, Smithsonian Institution (Washington, D.C.). *Tribute to Mark Tobey*. June 7–September 8, 1974. Washington, D.C., Smithsonian Institution Press, 1974.

12498. Rathbone, Eliza. *Mark Tobey, city paintings*. [Published in conjunction with an exhibition at the National Gallery of Art, Washington, D.C.]. Washington, D.C., National Gallery of Art, 1984.

12499. Roberts, Colette. *Tobey.* Paris, Fall, 1959.

12500. Seitz, William C. *Mark Tobey.* [Published in conjunction with an exhibition at the Museum of Modern Art, New York]. New York, Museum of Modern Art, 1962; distributed by Doubleday, Garden City, N.Y.

12501. Tobey, Mark. *Mark Tobey: späte Werke, Bilder auf Styropor, Radierungen.* Herausgeber, Matthias Bärmann. Siegburg, Stadtmuseum Siegburg, Rheinlandia Verlag, 1990.

12502. ———. *Mark Tobey, Tempera Gouaches Aquarelle Zeichnungen: [Ausstellung] 25. Oktober 1986–28. Februar 1987.* [Redaktion, Franz Larese und Jürg Janett]. St. Gallen, Erker-Galerie, [1986].

12503. Yao, Min-Chih. *The influence of Chinese and Japanese calligraphy on Mark Tobey (1890–1976).* San Francisco, Chinese Materials Center, 1983. (Asian library series, 23).

Tocqué, Louis, 1696–1772

12504. Doria, Arnauld. *Louis Tocqué.* Paris, Beaux-Arts, 1929. (CR).

Toepffer, Rodolphe, 1799–1846

12505. Blondel, Auguste [and] Mirabaud, Paul. *Rodolphe Töpffer: l'écrivain, l'artiste et l'homme.* Paris, Hachette, 1886.

12506. Chaponnière, Paul. *Notre Töpffer.* Lausanne, Payot, 1930.

12507. Courthion, Pierre. *Genève, ou le portrait de Töpffer.* Préface de Jean Cassou. Paris, Grasset, 1936.

12508. Gagnebin, Marianne. *Rodolphe Töpffer.* Neuchâtel, Editions du Griffon, 1947.

12509. Relave, Pierre M. *Rodolphe Töpffer, biographie et extraits.* Lyon, Vitte, 1899.

12510. Toepffer, Rodolphe. *Caricatures (oeuvres complètes).* 17 v. Genève, Skira, 1943–1945. (CR).

12511. Wiese, Ellen P. *Enter: the comics; Rodolphe Töpffer's Essay on Physiognomy and The True Story of Monsieur Crépin.* Trans. and edited, with an introduction, by E. Wiese. Lincoln, Nebr., University of Nebraska Press, 1965.

Togores, Josep de, 1893–1970

12512. Fàbregas i Barri, Esteve. *Josep de Togores; l'obra, l'home, l'època (1893–1970).* Barcelona, Editorial Aedos, 1970. (Biblioteca biogràfica catalana, 46).

12513. Mas i Vives, Joan. *Josep de Togores i Sanglada, comte d'Aiamans, 1767–1831: biografia d'un illustrat liberal.* Palma de Mallorca, Universitat de les Illes Balears,

Departament de Filologia; Barcelona, Publicacions de l'Abadia de Montserrat, 1994. (Biblioteca Miquel dels Sants Oliver, 1).

Tomaso da Modena, 1325/26–1379

12514. Coletti, Luigi. *Tomaso da Modena.* A cura di Clara R. Coletti; prefazione di Sergio Bettini. Venezia, Pozza, 1963. (Saggi e studi di storia dell'arte, 7).

12515. Santa Caterina, Capitolo dei Domenicani (Treviso). *Tomaso da Modena. 5 luglio–5 novembre 1979.* Treviso, Edizioni Canova, 1979.

12516. Tomaso da Modena. *Tomaso da Modena: Treviso, S. Caterina-Capitolo dei Domenicani. 5 luglio–5 novembre 1979.* Catalogo a cura di Luigi Menegazzi. Introduzione di Luigi Menegazzi. Saggi di Enrica Cozzi . . . [et al.]. Treviso, Canova, 1979.

12517. Zava Boccazzi, Franca. *Tommaso da Modena.* Milano, Fabbri, 1966. (I maestri del colore, 193).

Tommaso da Modena See Tomaso da Modena

Toorop, Jan Theodoor, 1858–1928

12518. Haags Gemeentemuseum (The Hague). *Jan Toorop: [exhibition] 18 February–9 April, 1989.* [Catalog text by Victorine Hefting. Ed. by Ellinoor Bergvelt. Trans. by Patricia Wardle]. Organized by Haags Gemeentemuseum, the Netherlands Office for Fine Arts. Hague, Haags Gemeentemuseum, 1989.

12519. Institut Néerlandais (Paris). *Jan Toorop, 1858–1928; impressioniste, symboliste, pointilliste.* 19 octobre–4 décembre 1977. Paris, Institut Néerlandais, 1977.

12520. Knipping, John B. *Jan Toorop.* Amsterdam, Becht, [1947]. (Palet serie).

12521. Rijksmuseum Kröller-Müller (Otterlo, The Netherlands). *J. Th. Toorop, de jaren 1885 tot 1910.* 9 december 1978–11 februari 1979. Otterlo, Rijksmuseum Kröller-Müller, 1978.

Torii, Kiyonaga, 1752–1815

12522. Hirano, Chie. *Kiyonaga: a study of his life and works.* Boston, Museum of Fine Arts, 1969.

12523. Narazaki, Muneshige. *Kiyonaga.* Trans. by John Bester. Tokyo/Palo Alto, Calif., Kodansha, 1969. (Masterworks of Ukiyo-e).

12524. Noguchi, Yone. *Kiyonaga.* [Text in English and Japanese]. Tokyo, Seibundo, 1932.

12525. Takahashi, Seiichiro. *Torii Kiyonaga (1752–1815).* English adaptation by Thomas Kaasa. Tokyo/Rutland, Vt., Tuttle, 1956. (Kodansha Library of Japanese Art, 8).

Torrentius, Johannes, 1589–1644

12526. Bredius, Abraham. *Johannes Torrentius, schilder, 1589–1644*. 's Gravenhage, Nijhoff, 1909.

12527. Rehorst, A. J. *Torrentius*. Rotterdam, Brusse, 1939.

Torres-García, Joaquín, 1874–1949

12528. Biblioteca Nacional, Montevideo. *Joaquín Torres-García: centenario de su nacimiento, 1874–28 de Julio–1974; bibliografía*. Montevideo, Biblioteca Nacional, 1974.

12529. Castillo, Jorge . . . [et al.]. *The antagonistic link: Joaquín Torres-García, Theo van Doesburg*. Ed. by Rolinka Kattouw. Trans. by Donald Gardner . . . [et al.]. [Published in conjunction with an exhibition held at the Institute of Contemporary Art, Amsterdam, in 1992]. Amsterdam, Institute of Contemporary Art, 1991.

12530. Gradowczyk, Mario H. *Joaquín Torres García*. Buenos Aires, Argentina, Ediciones de Arte Gaglianone, 1985. (Colección "Artistas de América," 1).

12531. Jardí, Enric. *Torres García*. Trans. by Kenneth Lyons. Barcelona, Polígrafa, 1974. (CR).

12532. Robbins, Daniel. *Joaquín Torres-García, 1874–1949*. [Published in conjunction with an exhibition at the Museum of Art, Rhode Island School of Design, Providence R.I., and other places]. Providence, Museum of Art, Rhode Island School of Design, 1970.

12533. Schaefer, Claude. *Joaquín Torres-García*. Buenos Aires, Poseidón, 1945.

12534. Torres García, Joaquín. *Escritos*. Selección, analítica y prólogo: Juan Fló. Montevideo, Arca, 1974.

12535. ———. *Estructura*. Montevideo, Alfar, [1935].

12536. ———. *Historia de mi vida*. Montevideo, Talleres Gráficos Sur, 1939.

12537. ———. *Universalismo constructivo*. Buenos Aires, Poseidón, 1944.

12538. University of Texas at Austin Art Museum. *Joaquín Torres-García, 1874–1949; chronology and catalogue of the family collection*. 13 October–24 November 1974. Austin, Tex., University of Texas at Austin, 1974.

Toshusai Sharaku *see* Sharaku, Toshusai

Toulouse-Lautrec, Henri de, 1864–1901

12539. Adhémar, Jean. *Toulouse-Lautrec: his complete lithographs and drypoints*. New York, Abrams, 1965. (CR).

12540. Adriani, Götz. *Toulouse-Lautrec: das gesamte graphische Werk*. [Published in conjunction with an exhibition at Kunsthalle Tübingen, October–November 1976]. Köln, DuMont, 1976. (CR).

12541. ———. *Toulouse-Lautrec, the complete graphic works: a catalogue raisonné: the Gerstenberg collection*. London, Thames and Hudson, 1988. (CR).

12542. ———. *Toulouse-Lautrec und das Paris um 1900*. Köln, DuMont, 1978.

12543. Astre, Achille. *H. de Toulouse-Lautrec*. Paris, Nillson, 1926.

12544. Beaute, Georges. *Il y a cent ans Henri de Toulouse-Lautrec*. Genève, Cailler, 1964.

12545. ———. *Toulouse-Lautrec vu par les photographes*. Suivi de témoignages inédits. Lausanne, Edita, 1988.

12546. Bouret, Jean. *Toulouse-Lautrec*. Paris, Somogy, 1963. (Les plus grands, 6).

12547. Caproni, Giorgio [and] Sugana, Gabriele M. *L'opera completa di Toulouse-Lautrec*. Milano, Rizzoli, 1969. (CR). (Classici d'arte, 31).

12548. Cooper, Douglas. *Toulouse-Lautrec*. New York, Abrams, 1966.

12549. Coquiot, Gustave. *H. de Toulouse-Lautrec*. Paris, Blaizot, 1913. (New ed.: *Lautrec ou quinze ans de moeurs parisiennes*. Paris, Ollendorff, 1920).

12550. Denvir, Bernard. *Toulouse-Lautrec*. London, Thames and Hudson, 1991.

12551. Dortu, M. G. *Toulouse-Lautrec et son oeuvre*. 6 v. New York, Collectors Editions, 1971. (CR).

12552. Duret, Théodore. *Lautrec*. Paris, Bernheim, 1920.

12553. Esswein, Hermann. *Henri de Toulouse-Lautrec*. München/Leipzig, Piper, [1916]. (Moderne Illustratoren, 3).

12554. Fermigier, André. *Toulouse-Lautrec*. Paris, Hazan, 1969.

12555. Fréches-Thory, Claire. *Toulouse-Lautrec: les lumiéres de la nuit*. Paris, Gallimard, Réunion des musées nationaux, 1991.

12556. Frey, Julia Bloch. *Toulouse-Lautrec: a life*. New York, Viking, 1994.

12557. Gauzi, François. *Lautrec et son temps*. Paris, Perret, 1954.

12558. Gimferrer, Pere. *Toulouse-Lautrec*. New York, Rizzoli, 1990.

12559. Hanson, Lawrence and Hanson, Elisabeth. *The tragic life of Toulouse-Lautrec*. New York, Random House, 1956.

12560. Hayward Gallery (London). *Toulouse-Lautrec*: [exhibition], 10 October 1991–19 January 1992; Galeries nationales du Grand Palais, Paris, 21 February–1 June 1992. London, South Bank Centre; Paris, Réunion des musées nationaux, 1991.

12561. Huisman, Philippe and Dortu, M. G. *Lautrec by Lautrec*. Trans. by Corinne Bellow. London, Macmillan, 1964.

12562. Jedlicka, Gotthard. *Henri de Toulouse-Lautrec*. Zürich, Rentsch, 1943. 2 ed.

12563. Jourdain, Francis [and] Adhémar, Jean. *T.-Lautrec*. Paris, Tisné, 1952.

12564. Joyant, Maurice. *Henri de Toulouse-Lautrec, 1864–1901*. 2 v. Paris, Floury, 1926–1927.

12565. Julien, Edouard. *Les affiches de Toulouse-Lautrec*. Catalogue par Fernand Mourlot. Monte-Carlo, Sauret, 1967. 2 ed. (CR).

12566. Jarrassé, Dominique. *Henri de Toulouse-Lautrec-Monfa: entre le mythe et la modernité*. Marseille, AGEP; Saint-Julian-aux-Bois France, P. Sers, [1991].

12567. Keller, Horst. *Toulouse-Lautrec: painter of Paris*. Trans. by Erika Bizzarri. New York, Abrams, 1969.

12568. Lapparent, P. de. *Toulouse-Lautrec*. Paris, Rieder, 1927.

12569. Lassaigne, Jacques. *Lautrec, biographical and critical studies*. Trans. by Stuart Gilbert. Geneva, Skira, 1953. (The Taste of Our Time, 3).

12570. Leclercq, Paul. *Autour de Toulouse-Lautrec*. Paris, Floury, 1920. (New ed.: Genève, Cailler, 1954).

12571. Le Targat, François. *Toulouse-Lautrec*. Commentaires des hors-texte, Armelle Barré . . . [et al.]. Paris, Editions Cercle d'art, 1988.

12572. Mack, Gerstle. *Toulouse-Lautrec*. New York, Knopf, 1938.

12573. MacOrlan, Pierre. *Lautrec, peintre de la lumière froide*. Paris, Floury, 1934.

12574. Mourlot, Fernand. *Les affiches de Toulouse-Lautrec*. Monte-Carlo, Editions A. Sauret/Editions M. Trinckvel, 1992.

12575. Natanson, Thadée. *Un Henri de Toulouse-Lautrec*. Genève, Cailler, 1951. (Les grands artistes racontés par eux-mêmes et par leurs amis, 11). [New ed. with préface d'Annette Vaillant published Paris, Ecole nationale superieure des beaux-arts, 1992].

12576. Novotny, Fritz. *Toulouse-Lautrec*. Trans. by Michael Glenney. London, Phaidon, 1969.

12577. Palais de la Berbie (Albi)/Petit Palais (Paris). *Centenaire de Toulouse-Lautrec*. [June–December 1964]. Paris, Ministère d'Etat Affaires Culturelles, 1964.

12578. Palais de la Berbie, Musée Toulouse-Lautrec (Albi). *Catalogue*. Albi, Palais de la Berbie, Musée Toulouse-Lautrec, 1973.

12579. Perruchot, Henri. *La vie de Toulouse-Lautrec*. Paris, Hachette, 1958.

12580. Polásek, Jan. *Toulouse-Lautrec: drawings*. New York, St. Martin's, 1976.

12581. Roger-Marx, Claude. *Toulouse-Lautrec*. Paris, Editions Universitaires, 1957. (Témoins du XXᵉ siècle, 7).

12582. Sagne, Jean. *Toulouse-Lautrec*. Paris, Fayard, 1988.

12583. Schaub-Koch, Emile. *Psychoanalyse d'un peintre moderne: Henri de Toulouse-Lautrec*. Paris, Editions Littéraire Internationale, 1935.

12584. Stevenson, Lesley. *H. de Toulouse Lautrec*. London, Weidenfeld and Nicolson, 1991.

12585. Stuckey, Charles F. *Toulouse-Lautrec: paintings*. [Publ. in conjunction with an exhibition at the Art Institute of Chicago]. Chicago, Art Institute of Chicago, 1979.

12586. Tapié de Céleyran, Mary. *Notre oncle Lautrec*. Genève, Cailler, 1953.

12587. Thomson, Richard. *Toulouse-Lautrec*. London, Oresko, 1977.

12588. Toulouse-Lautrec, Henri de. *Toulouse-Lautrec: a retrospective*. Ed. by Gayle Murray. New York, Hugh Lauter Levin Associates, distributed by Macmillan Pub. Co., 1992.

12589. ———. *Tout l'oeuvre peint de Toulouse-Lautrec*. Introduction par Bruno Foucart. Documentation par G. M. Sugana. Ed. français, mise á jour par Jean Devoisins et Christine Gonella, [Traduit de l'Italien par Simone de Vergennes]. Paris, Flammarion, 1986.

12590. ———. *Unpublished correspondence*. Edited by Lucien Goldschmidt and Herbert Schimmel, with an introduction and notes by Jean Adhémar and Theodore Reff. London, Phaidon, 1969.

12591. Wittrock, Wolfgang. *Toulouse-Lautrec, the complete prints*. Ed. and trans. by Catherine E. Kuehn. London, for Sotheby's Publications by P. Wilson Publishers; New York, distributed in the USA by Harper and Row Publishers, 1985. (CR).

Tournachon, Gaspard Felix, 1820–1910

12592. Barret, André. *Nadar: 50 photographies de ses illustres contemporains*. Paris, Trésors de la Photographie, 1975.

12593. Gosling, Nigel. *Nadar*. New York, Knopf, 1976.

12594. Greaves, Roger. *Nadar, ou le paradoxe vital*. Paris, Flammarion, 1980.

12595. Meyer, Catherine et Meyer, Bertrand. *Nadar: photographe, caricaturiste, journaliste*. Paris, Encre, 1979.

12596. Nadar [pseud. of Felix Tournachon]. *Nadar: caricatures et photographies*. Paris, Paris Musées, 1990.

12597. ———. *Quand j'étais étudiant; édition définitive*. Paris, Dentu, 1881.

12598. ———. *Quand j'étais photographe*. Préface de Léon Daudet. Paris, Flammarion, 1899.

12599. Néagu, Philippe, et Poulet-Allamagny, Jean-Jacques. *Nadar*. Préface de Jean-François Bory. 2 v. Paris, Hubschmid, 1979. 2 v. (CR).

12600. Prinet, Jean et Dilasser, Antoinette. *Nadar*.

Paris, Colin, 1966. (Italian ed., with additional text by Lamberto Vitali and photographs by Nadar: Torino, Einaudi, 1973).

Town, Ithiel, 1784–1844 *see* **Davis, Alexander Jackson**

Towne, Francis, 1740–1816
12601. Bury, Adrian. *Francis Towne, lone star of water-colour painting.* London, Skilton, 1962.

Toyokuni, Utagawa Ichiyōsai, 1769–1825
12602. Izzard, Sebastian. *Kunisada's world.* With essays by J. Thomas Rimer, John T. Carpenter. New York, Japan Society, in collaboration with Ukiyo-e Society of America, 1993.
12603. Strange, Edward F. *Japanese colour prints by Utagawa Toyokuni.* London, HMSO, 1908.
12604. Succo, Friedrich. *Utagawa Toyokuni und seine Zeit.* 2 v. München, Piper, 1913. (CR).

Traini, Francesco, 14th c.
12605. Bonaini, Francesco. *Memorie inedite intorno alla vita e ai dipinti di Francesco Traini.* Pisa, Nistri, 1846.
12606. Meiss, Millard. *Francesco Traini.* Edited and with an introduction by Hayden B. J. Maginnis. Washington, D.C., Decatur House, 1983. (Art History Series, 6).
12607. Oertel, Robert. *Francesco Traini: der Triumph des Todes im Campo Santo zu Pisa.* Berlin, Mann, 1948.

Troost, Cornelis, 1697–1750
12608. Buijsen, Edwin and Niemeijer, J.W. *Cornelis Troost en het theater: tonelen van de 18de eeuw.* Met bijdragen van Marjolein de Boer. The Hague, Mauritshuis; Zwolle, Waanders, 1993.
12609. Knoef, Jan. *Cornelis Troost.* Amsterdam, Becht, [1947]. (Palet serie).
12610. Museum Boymans-van Beuningen (Rotterdam). *Cornelis Troost en zijn tijd.* [July 27–September 15, 1946]. Rotterdam, van Waesberge, Hoogewerff & Richards, 1946.
12611. Niemeijer, J. W. *Cornelis Troost, 1696 [sic]–1750.* Assen, van Gorcum, 1973.
12612. Ver Huell, Alexander. *Cornelis Troost en zijn werken.* Arnhem, Gouda Quint, 1873.

Trova, Ernest Tino, 1927–
12613. Alloway, Lawrence. *Trova; selected works, 1953–1966.* New York, Pace Gallery, 1966.
12614. Bush, Martin H. *Ernest Trova.* [Published in conjunction with an exhibition at the Edwin A. Ulrich Museum of Art, Wichita State University, Wichita, Kan., March 21–April 8, 1979, and other places]. Wichita, Edwin A. Ulrich Museum of Art, 1977.

12615. Heitmüller, Corinna. *Ernest Trova: Study Falling Man, 1963–1987: eine Monographie.* Frankfurt am Main; New York, P. Lang, 1993. (European University Studies, History of Art, 156).
12616. Kagan, Andrew. *Trova.* With a foreword by James R. Mellow. St. Louis, Trova Foundation; New York, H.N. Abrams, distributor, 1987.
12617. Kultermann, Udo. *Trova.* New York, Abrams, 1978.

Troyon, Constant, 1810–1865 *see also* **Corot, Jean-Baptiste Camille**
12618. Dumesnil, Henri. *Troyon; souvenirs intimes.* Avec un portrait d'aprés un médaillon d'Aimé Millet, gravé par Alph. Leroy. Paris, H. Laurens etc., 1888.
12619. Hustin, Arthur. *Constant Troyon.* Paris, Librairie de l'Art, 1895.
12620. Soullié, Louis. *Peintures, pastels, aquarelles, dessins de Constant Troyon relevés dans les catalogues de ventes de 1833 à 1900.* Paris, Soullié, 1900.

Trübner, Wilhelm, 1851–1917
12621. Beringer, Joseph A. *Trübner, des Meisters Gemälde.* Stuttgart/Berlin, Deutsche Verlags-Anstalt, 1917. (Klassiker der Kunst, 26).
12622. Fuchs, Georg. *Wilhelm Trübner und sein Werk.* München/Leipzig, Müller, 1908.
12623. Rosenhagen, Hans. *Wilhelm Trübner.* Bielefeld/Leipzig, Velhagen & Klasing, 1909. (Künstler-Monographien, 98).
12624. Trübner, Wilhelm. *Personalien und Prinzipien.* Eingeleitet von Emil Waldmann. Berlin, Cassirer, [1918]. 2 ed.

Trumbull, John, 1756–1843
12625. Cooper, Helen A. *John Trumbull: the hand and spirit of a painter.* [Published in conjunction with an exhibition at the Yale University Art Gallery, New Haven, October 28, 1982–January 16, 1983]. New Haven, Yale University Art Gallery, 1982.
12626. Jaffe, Irma B. *John Trumbull, patriot-artist of the American Revolution.* Boston, New York Graphic Society, 1975.
12627. ———. *Trumbull: the Declaration of Independence.* New York, Viking, 1976.
12628. Sizer, Theodore. *The works of Colonel John Trumbull, artist of the American Revolution.* New Haven/London, Yale University Press, 1967. 2 ed. (CR).
12629. Trumbull, John. *The autobiography of Colonel John Trumbull, patriot-artist, 1756–1843.* Ed. by Theodore Sizer. New Haven, Yale University Press, 1953.
12630. Weir, John F. *John Trumbull, a brief sketch of his life to which is added a catalogue of his works.* New York, Scribner, 1901.

T

Tura, Cosimo, 1430–1495 *see also* **Cossa, Francesco del**

12631. Bentini, Jadranka. *San Giorgio e la principessa di Cosmè Tura.* A cura di J. Bentini. Dipinti restaurati per l'officina ferrarese. Bologna, Nuova Alfa, 1985. (Rapporti, 51).

12632. Cittadella, Luigi N. *Ricordi e documenti intorno alla vita di Cosimo Tura detto Cosmè, pittor ferrarese del secolo XV.* Ferrara, Taddei, 1866.

12633. Molajoli, Rosemarie. *L'opera completa di Cosmè Tura e i grandi pittori ferraresi del suo tempo: Francesco Cossa e Ercole de' Roberti.* Milano, Rizzoli, 1974. (CR). (Classici dell'arte, 73).

12634. Neppi, Alberto. *Cosmè Tura, saggio critico.* Milano, Gastaldi, 1952.

12635. Ruhmer, Eberhard. *Tura, paintings and drawings; complete edition.* London, Phaidon, 1958.

12636. Salmi, Mario. *Cosmè Tura.* Milano, Electa, 1957.

Turner, Joseph Mallord William, 1775–1851

12637. Anderson, John. *The unknown Turner: revelations concerning the life and art of J. M. W. Turner.* New York, Privately printed for the author, 1926.

12638. Armstrong, Walter. *Turner.* London, Agnew/New York, Scribner, 1902.

12639. Bock, Henning und Prinz, Ursula. *J. M. W. Turner, der Maler des Lichts.* Berlin, Mann, 1972.

12640. British Museum (London). *Turner in the British Museum: drawings and watercolours.* [Catalogue by Andrew Wilton]. London, British Museum Publications, 1975.

12641. Brooke, Stopford. *Notes on the Liber Studiorum of J. M. W. Turner.* London, The Autotype Company, 1885.

12642. Brown, David Blayney. *The art of J.M.W. Turner.* London, Headline, 1990.

12643. Burnet, John. *Turner and his works.* London, Bogue, 1852.

12644. Butlin, Martin and Joll, Evelyn. *The paintings of J. M. W. Turner.* 3 v. New Haven/London, Yale University Press, 1977. (CR).

12645. Centre Culturel du Marais (Paris). *Turner en France.* [October 7, 1981–January 10, 1982; text in French and English]. Paris, Centre Culturel du Marais, 1981.

12646. Clare, Charles. *J. M. W. Turner, his life and work.* London, Phoenix House, 1951.

12647. Cumming, Robert. *Discovering Turner.* London, Tate Gallery Publications, 1990.

12648. Dafforne, James. *The works of J. M. W. Turner.* London, Virtue, 1877.

12649. Dawson, Barbara. *Turner in the National Gallery of Ireland.* Dublin, National Gallery of Ireland, 1988.

12650. Finberg, Alexander J. *A complete inventory of the drawings of the Turner bequest* [to the National Gallery]. 2 v. London, HMSO, 1909.

12651. ———. *The history of Turner's Liber Studiorum with a new catalogue raisonné.* London, Benn, 1924. (CR).

12652. ———. *In Venice with Turner.* London, Cotswold Gallery, 1930.

12653. ———. *The life of J. M. W. Turner.* With a supplement by Hilda F. Finberg. Oxford, Clarendon Press, 1961. 2 ed.

12654. ———. *Turner's sketches and drawings.* London, Methuen, 1910. (New ed., with an introduction by Lawrence Gowing: New York, Schocken, 1968).

12655. Finley, Gerald. *Landscapes of memory: Turner as illustrator to Scott.* London, Scolar Press, 1980.

12656. Gage, John. *Color in Turner: poetry & truth.* New York, Praeger, 1969.

12657. ———. *J.M.W. Turner: a wonderful range of mind.* New Haven, Yale University Press, 1987.

12658. ———. *Turner: Rain, steam & speed.* New York, Viking, 1972.

12659. Gaunt, William. *Turner.* Oxford, Phaidon, 1981. 2 ed.

12660. Gowing, Lawrence. *Turner: imagination and reality.* New York, Museum of Modern Art, 1966; distributed by Doubleday, Garden City, N.Y.

12661. Hamburger Kunsthalle. *William Turner und die Landschaft seiner Zeit.* 19. Mai bis 18. Juli 1976. München, Prestel, 1976.

12662. Hamerton, Philip G. *The life of J. M. W. Turner, R. A.* Boston, Roberts, 1879.

12663. Herrmann, Luke. *Ruskin and Turner.* London, Faber, 1968.

12664. ———. *Turner: paintings, watercolors, prints & drawings.* Boston, New York Graphic Society, 1975.

12665. ———. *Turner prints: the engraved work of J.M.W. Turner.* Oxford, Phaidon, 1990

12666. Hill, David. *Turner on the Thames: river journeys in the year 1805.* New Haven, Yale University Press, 1993.

12667. Hind, C. Lewis. *Turner's golden visions.* London, Jack, 1910.

12668. Lee, Eric M. *Translations: Turner and printmaking.* New Haven, Yale Center for British Art, 1993.

12669. Lindsay, Jack. *J. M. W. Turner; a critical biography.* Greenwich, Conn., New York Graphic Society, 1966.

12670. Lyles, Anne and Perkins, Diane. *Colour into line: Turner and the art of engraving.* London, Tate Gallery, 1989.

12671. Mauclair, Camille. *Turner.* Trans. by E. B. Shaw. London, Heinemann, 1939.

12672. Monkhouse, W. Cosmo. *Turner.* New York,

Scribner and Welford/London, Sampson Low, 1879.

12673. Nicholson, Kathleen Dukeley. *Turner's classical landscapes: myth and healing.* Princeton, Princeton University Press, 1990.

12674. Perkins, Diane. *The third decade: Turner watercolours 1810–1820.* London, Tate Gallery, 1990.

12675. Powell, Cecilia. *Turner in the South: Rome, Naples, Florence.* New Haven, published for the Paul Mellon Centre for Studies in British Art by Yale University Press, 1987.

12676. ———. *Turner's rivers of Europe: the Rhine, Meuse and Mosel.* London, Tate Gallery, 1991.

12677. Rawlinson, William G. *The engraved work of J. M. W. Turner.* 2 v. London, Macmillan, 1908–1913. (CR).

12678. Reynolds, Graham. *Turner.* New York, Abrams, 1969.

12679. Rothenstein, John and Butlin, Martin. *Turner.* New York, Braziller, 1964.

12680. Ruskin, John. *Notes by Mr. Ruskin on his collection of drawings by the late J. M. W. Turner, R. A.* London, Fine Art Society, 1878.

12681. ———. *Ruskin on Turner.* Ed. by Dinah Birch. Boston, Bulfinch Press, 1990.

12682. Russell, John. *Turner in Switzerland.* Survey and notes with a checklist of the finished Swiss watercolours by Andrew Wilton. Zurich, De Clivo Press, 1976.

12683. Shanes, Eric. *Turner's England.* London, Cassell, 1990.

12684. ———. *Turner's human landscape.* London, Heinemann, 1990.

12685. ———. *Turner's picturesque views in England and Wales, 1825–1838.* With an introduction by Andrew Wilton. London, Chatto & Windus, 1979.

12686. ———. *Turner's rivers, harbours and coasts.* London, Chatto & Windus, 1981.

12687. Stainton, Lindsay. *Turner's Venice.* London, British Museum Publications 1985.

12688. Swinburne, Charles A. *Life and work of J. M. W. Turner.* London, Bickers, 1902.

12689. Tate Gallery (London). *The Turner collection in the Clore Gallery: an illustrated guide.* London, Tate Gallery, 1987. 2 ed.

12690. Thornbury, Walter. *The life of J. M. W. Turner, R. A., founded on letters and papers furnished by his friends and fellow academians.* 2 v. London, Hurst and Blackett, 1862.

12691. Townsend, Joyce. *Turner's painting techniques.* London, Tate Gallery, 1993.

12692. Turner, J. M. W. *Collected correspondence.* With an early diary and a memoir by George Jones. Ed. by John Gage. Oxford, Clarendon Press, 1980.

12693. University Art Museum, University of California (Berkeley). *J. M. W. Turner: works on paper from American collections.* [September 30–November 23, 1975]. Berkeley, University Art Museum, 1975.

12694. Upstone, Robert. *Turner, the final years: watercolours 1840–1851.* London, Tate Gallery, 1993.

12695. ———. *Turner, the second decade: watercolours and drawings from the Turner Bequest 1800–1810.* London, Tate Gallery, 1989.

12696. Walker, John. *Joseph Mallord William Turner.* New York, Abrams, 1976.

12697. Warrell, Ian. *Turner, the fourth decade: watercolours 1820–1830.* London, Tate Gallery, 1991.

12698. Wilkinson, Gerald. *Turner on landscape: the Liber Studiorum.* London, Barrie & Jenkins, 1982.

12699. ———. *Turner sketches, 1802–20: romantic genius.* London, Barrie & Jenkins, 1974.

12700. ———. *Turner's colour sketches, 1820–34.* London, Barrie & Jenkins, 1975.

12701. ———. *Turner's early sketchbooks: drawings in England, Wales, and Scotland from 1789 to 1802.* London, Barrie & Jenkins, 1972.

12702. Wilton, Andrew. *J. M. W. Turner.* New York, Rizzoli, 1979.

12703. ———. *Painting and poetry: Turner's Verse book and his work of 1804–1812.* With transcriptions by Rosalind Mallord Turner. London, Tate Gallery, 1990.

12704. ———. *Turner and the sublime.* [Published in conjunction with an exhibition at the Art Gallery of Ontario, Toronto, 1 November 1980–4 January 1981, and other places]. Toronto, Art Gallery of Ontario/New Haven, Yale Center for British Art, 1980.

12705. ———. *Turner watercolors in the Clore Gallery.* Selected and introduced by Andrew Wilton. London, Tate Gallery, 1987.

12706. Winthrop, Grenville L. *A catalogue of the collection of prints from the Liber Studiorum of Joseph Mallord William Turner formed by the late Francis Bullard of Boston, Massachusetts.* Boston, Merrymount Press, 1916.

12707. Wyllie, William L. *J. M. W. Turner.* London, Bell, 1905.

Twombly, Cy, 1928–

12708. Bastian, Heiner, ed. *Cy Twombly, catalogue raisonné of the paintings.* München, Schirmer/Mosel, 1992–. (CR).

12709. ———, ed. *Cy Twombly: das Graphische Werk, 1953–1984: a catalogue raisonné of the printed graphic work.* München/New York, Edition Schellmann; New York, New York University Press, 1985. (CR).

12710. Lambert, Yvon. *Cy Twombly: catalogue raisonné des oeuvres sur papier de Cy Twombly*. Milano, Multhipla, 1979–. (CR).

12711. Museum Haus Lange (Krefeld). *Cy Twombly: Skulpturen: 23 Arbeiten aus den Jahren 1955 bis 1981*. Museum Haus Lange 1981. Krefeld, Kunstmuseen der Stadt Krefeld, 1981.

12712. Städtisches Kunstmuseum (Bonn). *Cy Twombly, Serien auf Papier*. 2. Juni–9. August 1987. [Katalogredaktion und Gestaltung, Katharina Schmidt]. Bonn, Das Kunstmuseum, 1987.

12713. Szeemann, Harald, ed. *Cy Twombly: paintings, works on paper, sculpture*. With contributions by Démosthénes Davvetas, Roberta Smith and Harald Szeemann. Foreword by Nicholas Serota. Munich, Prestel, 1987.

12714. Twombly, Cy. *24 short pieces*. Herausgegeben und mit einem Text versehen von Heiner Bastian. Trans. by Melanie Flemming. München, Schirmer/Mosel, 1989.

12715. ———. *Cy Twombly*. Houston, Menil Collection, Houston Fine Art Press, 1990.

12716. ———. *Cy Twombly, Bilder, Arbeiten auf Papier, Skulpturen*. [Ausstellung und Katalog, Harald Szeemann]. Zürich, Kunsthaus Zürich, 1987.

12717. ———. *Cy Twombly photographs*. New York, Matthew Marks Gallery, 1993.

12718. ———. *Poems to the sea*. Herausgegeben und mit einem Text versehen von Heiner Bastian. München, Schirmer/Mosel, 1990. (Edition Heiner Bastian, 2).

12719. Varnedoe, Kirk. *Cy Twombly: a retrospective*. [Exhibition: New York, Museum of Modern Art, 1994]. New York, Abrams, 1994.

Tzara, Tristan, 1896–1963

12720. Schrott, Raoul. *Dada 15/25: Post Scriptum oder die himmlischen Abenteuer des Hr.n Tristan Tzara und ein Suspensarium von Gerald Nitsche zu Elde Steeg & Raoul Hausmann*. Innsbruck, Haymon, 1992.

12721. Tzara, Tristan. *Seven Dada manifestos and lampisteries*. Trans. by Barbara Wright. London, Calder, 1977.

U

Ubertini, Francesco, 1494–1557

12722. Merritt, Howard S. *Bachiacca studies: the uses of imitation.* Ann Arbor, Mich., University Microfilms, 1975.

12723. Nikolenko, Lada. *Francesco Ubertini called il Bacchiacca.* Locust Valley, N.Y., Augustin, 1966.

12724. Tinti, Mario. *Il Bachiacca.* Firenze, Alinari, 1925. (Piccola collezione d'arte, 39).

Uccello, Paolo, 1397–1475

12725. Antoine, Jean-Philippe. *La chair de l'oiseau: vie imaginaire de Paolo Uccello.* Paris, Gallimard, 1991.

12726. Boeck, Wilhelm. *Paolo Uccello, der Florentiner Meister und sein Werk.* Berlin, Grote, 1939.

12727. Carli, Enzo. *All the paintings of Paolo Uccello.* Trans. by Marion Fitzallan. New York, Hawthorn, 1963. (Complete Library of World Art, 22).

12728. Flaiano, Ennio [and] Tongiorgi Tomasi, Lucia. *L'opera completa di Paolo Uccello.* Milano, Rizzoli, 1971. (CR). (Classici dell'arte, 46).

12729. Parronchi, Alessandro. *Paolo Uccello.* Bologna, Boni, 1974.

12730. Pittaluga, Mary. *Paolo Uccello.* Roma, Tumminelli, 1946.

12731. Pope-Hennessy, John. *Paolo Uccello, complete edition.* London, Phaidon, 1969. 2 ed.

12732. Salmi, Mario. *Paolo Uccello, Andrea del Castagno, Domenico Veneziano.* Milano, Hoepli, 1938.

12733. Schefer, Jean L. *La déluge, la peste: Paolo Uccello.* Paris, Galilée, 1976.

12734. Soupault, Philippe. *Paolo Uccello.* Paris, Rieder, 1929.

Uelsmann, Jerry Norman, 1934–

12735. Enyeart, James L. *Jerry N. Uelsmann; twenty-five years: a retrospective.* Boston, New York Graphic Society, 1982.

12736. Uelsmann, Jerry. *Silver meditations.* Introd. by Peter C. Bunnell. Dobbs Ferry, N.Y., Morgan & Morgan, 1975.

12737. ———. *Uelsmann, process and perception: photographs and commentary.* Essay by John Ames. Gainsville, University Presses of Florida, 1985.

12738. Ward, John L. *The criticism of photography as art: the photographs of Jerry Uelsmann.* Gainesville, University of Florida Press, 1970. (University of Florida Humanities Monographs, 32).

Ugriumov, Grigorii Ivanovich, 1764–1823

12739. Iakovleva, N. A. *Grigoriĭ Ivanovich Ugriúmov, 1764–1823.* Leningrad, "Khudozhnik RSFSR", 1982.

12740. Zonova, Zinaida T. *Grigorii Ivanovich Ugriumov, 1764–1823.* Moskva, Iskusstvo, 1966.

Uhde, Fritz von, 1848–1911

12741. Bierbaum, Otto J. *Fritz von Uhde.* München, Albert, 1893.

12742. Ostini, Fritz von. *Uhde.* Bielefeld/Leipzig, Velhagen & Klasing, 1902. (Künstler-Monographien, 61).

12743. Rosenhagen, Hans. *Uhde, des Meisters Gemälde.* Stuttgart/Leipzig, Deutsche Verlags-Anstalt, 1908. (Klassiker der Kunst, 12).

Uhlmann, Hans, 1900–1975

12744. Akademie der Künste (Berlin). *Hans Uhlmann.* 17. März bis 15. April 1968. Berlin, Akademie der Künste, 1968.

12745. Baumgart, Fritz. *Uhlmann, Handzeichnungen.* Frankfurt a.M., Kiefer, 1960.

12746. Haftmann, Werner. *Hans Uhlmann, Leben und Werk.* Oeuvre-verzeichnis der Skulpturen von Ursula Lehmann-Brockhaus. Berlin, Mann, 1975. (CR). (Schriftenreihe der Akademie der Künste, 11).

12747. Uhlmann, Hans. *Hans Uhlmann (1900–*

1975): die Aquarelle und Zeichnungen. Mit dem Werkverzeichnis bearbeitet von Carmela Thiele. Herausgegeben von Christoph Brockhaus und Jörn Merkert. Duisburg, Wilhelm-Lehmbruck-Museum; Berlin, Berlinische Galerie, 1990.

Ukhtomskii, Dmitri Vasil'evich, 1719–1774/5
12748. Mikhailov, Aleksei I. *Arkhitektor D. V. Ukhtomskii i ego shkola.* Moskva, Gosudarstvennyi Izd-vo Lit-ry po Stroitel'stvu i Arkhitekture, 1954.

Umlauf, Charles, 1911–
12749. Goodall, Donald B. *Charles Umlauf, sculptor.* Foreword by Gibson A. Danes. Austin/London, University of Texas Press, 1967.

Umlauf, Karl, 1939–
12750. Umlauf, Karl. *Karl Umlauf: the first twenty years.* An exhibition organized by the Tyler Museum of Art, May 21 through July 3, 1983. Introduction by Frederick Haitt. Tyler, Texas, The Museum, 1983.

Unold, Max, 1885–1964
12751. Hausenstein, Wilhelm. *Max Unold.* Leipzig, Klinkhart & Biermann, 1921. (Junge Kunst, 23).
12752. Ruck, Germaid. *Max Unold (1885–1964) und die Münchner Malerei: mit einem Werkkatalog der Ölgemälde.* Memmingen, Curt Visel, 1992. (CR).
12753. Unold, Max. *Max Unold, 1885–1964: austellung in Memmingen,* 18. September bis 13. Oktober 1985. Memmingen, Stadt Memmingen, 1985.
12754. ———. *Über die Malerei.* Hamburg, Claassen & Goverts, 1948.

Upjohn, Richard, 1802–1878
12755. Upjohn, Everard M. *Richard Upjohn, architect and churchman.* New York, Columbia University Press, 1939.
12756. Upjohn, Richard. *Upjohn's rural architecture: designs, working drawings and specifications for a wooden church and other rural structures.* New York, Putnam, 1852. (Reprint: New York, Da Capo, 1975).

Urbano da Cortona, fl. 1446
12757. Schubring, Paul. *Urbano da Cortona, ein Beitrag zur Kenntnis der Schule Donatellos und der sieneser Plastik im Quattrocento.* Strassburg, Heitz, 1903. (Zur Kunstgeschichte des Auslandes, 15).

Ury, Lesser, 1861–1931
12758. Brieger, Lothar. *Lesser Ury.* Berlin, Verlag Neue Kunsthandlung, 1921.

12759. Donath, Adolph. *Lesser Ury, seine Stellung in der modernen deutschen Malerei.* Berlin, Perl, 1921.
12760. Galerie Pels-Leusden (Berlin). *Lesser Ury zum 50. Todestag.* 1. Juni 1981 bis 19. August 1981. Berlin, Galerie Pels-Leusden, 1981.
12761. Seyppel, Joachim Hans. *Lesser Ury, der Maler der alten City: Leben-Kunst-Wirkung, eine Monographie.* Berlin, Mann, 1987.

Ushakov, Simon Fedorovich, 1626–1686
12762. Anayeva, T. *Simon Ushakov.* [Text in English and Russian]. Leningrad, Aurora, 1971.
12763. Bekeneva, N. G. *Simon Ushakov: 1626–1686.* Leningrad, "Khudozhnik RSFSR", 1984.
12764. Filimonov, Georgii D. *Simon Ushakov.* Moskva, Universitetskoi Tipografii, 1873.

Utamaro Kitigawa, 1754–1806
12765. Goncourt, Edmond. *Outamaro: le peintre des maison vertes.* Paris, Charpentier, 1904.
12766. Hillier, Jack R. *Utamaro, colour prints and paintings.* London, Phaidon, 1961.
12767. Kobayashi, Tadashi. *Utamaro.* Trans. by Mark A. Harbison. Tokyo/New York, Kodansha, 1982; distributed by Harper & Row, New York.
12768. Kitagawa, Utamaro. *Utamaro (1753–1806): Nihon Ukiyoe Hakubutsukan shozo.* Henshu Nihon Ukiyoe Gakkai; shukan Sakai Ganko. [The loan exhibition from the Japan Ukiyoe Museum]. Ed. by the Japan Ukiyoe Academy. Chief ed., Gankow N. Sakai. Kariya-shi, Kariya-shi Bijutsukan, 1989.
12769. Kondo, Ichitaro. *Kitagawa Utamaro (1753–1806).* English adaptation by Charles S. Terry. Tokyo/Rutland, Vt., Tuttle, 1956. (Kodansha Library of Japanese Art, 5).
12770. Kurth, Julius. *Utamaro.* Leipzig, Brockhaus, 1907.
12771. Narazaki, Muneshige and Kikuchi, Sadao. *Utamaro.* Trans. by John Bester. Tokyo/Palo Alto, Calif., Kodansha, 1968.
12772. Noguchi, Yone. *Utamaro.* London, Mathews, 1924.
12773. Trotter, Massey. *Catalogue of the work of Kitagawa Utamaro.* Introduction by Harold G. Henderson. New York, New York Public Library, 1950.

Utrillo, Maurice, 1883–1955
12774. Basler, Adolphe. *Maurice Utrillo.* Paris, Crès, 1931.
12775. Beachboard, Robert. *La trinité maudite: Valadon, Utrillo, Utter.* Paris, Amiot-Dumont, 1952.
12776. Carco, Francis. *Utrillo.* Paris, Grasset, 1956.
12777. Champigneulle, Bernard. *Utrillo.* Paris, Editions Universitaires, 1959. (Témoins du XXe

siècle, 16).

12778. Crespello, Jean-Paul. *Utrillo: la bohème et l'ivresse à Montmartre.* Paris, Presses de la Cité, 1970.

12779. Fabris, Jean. *Maurice Utrillo.* Paris, Edition Galerie Pétridés, 1992.

12780. ———. *Utrillo: sa vie, son oeuvre.* [Paris], Birr, 1982. (CR).

12781. Gros, Gabriel J. *Maurice Utrillo.* Paris, Crès, 1927.

12782. Pétridès, Paul. *L'oeuvre complet de Maurice Utrillo.* Avant-propos d'Edmond Heuzé.

Présentation de Florence G. Poisson. *5* v. Paris, Pétridès, 1959–1974. (CR).

12783. Tabarant, Adolphe. *Utrillo.* Paris, Bernheim, 1926.

12784. Valore, Lucie. *Maurice Utrillo, mon mari.* Paris, Foret, 1956.

12785. Werner, Alfred. *Maurice Utrillo.* New York, Abrams, 1981. 3 ed.

Uytewael, Joachim Anthoniszoon *see*
Wtewael, Joachim Anthowiszoon

V

Valadier, Giuseppe, 1762–1839

12786. Debenedetti, Elisa. *Valadier: diario architettonico.* Roma, Bulzoni, 1979.

12787. ———. *Valadier: segno e architettura: catalogo.* Roman, Multigrafica Editrice, 1985.

12788. Marconi, Paolo. *Giuseppe Valadier.* [Roma], Officina Edizioni, 1964.

12789. Schulze-Battman, Elfriede. *Giuseppe Valadier: ein klassizistischer Architekt Roms, 1762–1839.* Dresden, Zetzsche, 1939.

12790. Servi, Gaspare. *Notizie intorno alla vita del cav. Giuseppe Valadier, architetto romano.* Bologna, Tipi delle Muse alla Capra, 1840.

Valadon, Suzanne, 1865–1938 *see also* Utrillo, Maurice

12791. Basler, Adolphe. *Suzanne Valadon.* Paris, Crès, 1929.

12792. Baylis, Sarah. *Utrillo's mother.* London/New York, Pandora, 1987.

12793. Bonnat, Yves. *Valadon.* Paris, Club d'Art Bordas, 1968.

12794. Bouret, Jean. *Suzanne Valadon.* Paris, Pétridès, 1947.

12795. Champion, Jeanne. *Suzanne Valadon: ou, La recherche de la verite.* Paris, Presses de la Renaissance, 1984.

12796. Jacometti, Nesto. *Suzanne Valadon.* Genève, Cailler, 1947.

12797. Krininger, Doris. *Modell, Malerin, Akt: über Suzanne Valadon und Paula Modersohn-Becker.* Darmstadt, Luchterhand, 1986. (Sammlung Luchterhand, 588).

12798. Musée National d'Art Moderne (Paris). *Suzanne Valadon.* 17 mars–30 avril 1967. Paris, Ministère des Affaires Culturelles/Réunion des Musées Nationaux, 1967.

12799. Pétridès, Paul. *L'oeuvre complet de Suzanne Valadon.* Paris, Compagnie Française des Arts Graphiques, 1971. (CR).

12800. Rey, Robert. *Suzanne Valadon.* Paris, Nouvelle Revue Française, 1922. (Les peintres français nouveaux, 14).

12801. Rosinsky, Therese Diamand. *Suzanne Valadon.* New York, Universe, 1993.

12802. Storm, John. *The Valadon drama; the life of Suzanne Valadon.* New York, Dutton, 1958.

Valckenborch, Marten van 1534–1612 Lucas van, 1535?–1597

12803. Wied, Alexander. *Lucas und Marten van Valckenborch (1535–1597 und 1534–1612): das Gesamtwerk mit kritischem oeuvrekatalog.* Freren, Luca, 1990. (CR).

Valdés Leal, Juan de, 1622–1690

12804. Beruete y Moret, Aureliano de. *Valdés Leal, estudio critico.* Madrid, Suarez, 1911.

12805. *Exposición Valdés Leal y de Art Retrospectivo (Seville). Catálogo.* Mayo, 1922. Sevilla, Tipográfica Gironés, 1923.

12806. Gestoso y Pérez, José. *Biographía del pintor sevillano Juan de Valdés Leal.* Sevilla, Tipográfica Gironés, 1916.

12807. Lafond, Paul. *Juan de Valdés Leal; essai sur sa vie et son oeuvre.* Paris, Sansot, 1914.

12808. Lopez y Martinez, Celestino. *Valdés Leal y sus discipulos.* Sevilla, Diaz, 1907.

12809. Trapier, Elizabeth du Gué. *Valdés Leal, Spanish baroque painter.* New York, Hispanic Society of America, 1960.

12810. Valdivieso, Enrique. *Valdés Leal.* Madrid, Museo del Prado, Junt de Andalucía, [1991].

Valentin, de Boulogne, 1591–1632

12811. Mojana, Marina. *Valentin de Boulogne.* Milano, Eikonos, 1989. (CR).

Vallayer-Coster, Anne, 1744–1818

12812. Roland-Michel, Marianne. *Anne Vallayer-Coster, 1744–1818.* Paris, Comptoir International du Livre, 1970. (CR).

Vallotton, Félix, 1865–1925

12813. Bianconi, Piero. *Félix Vallotton.* Milano, Fabbri, 1966. (I maestri del colore, 126).

12814. Gourmont, Remy de. *Le livre des masques dessinés par Félix Vallotton*. Paris, Mercure de France, 1896–1898. 2 v. (Reprint: 1963).

12815. Guisan, Gilbert et Jakubec, Doris. *Félix Vallotton: documents pour une biographie et pour l'histoire d'une oeuvre*. 3 v. Lausanne/Paris, Bibliothèque des Arts, 1973–1975.

12816. Hahnloser-Bühler, Hedy. *Félix Vallotton et ses amis*. Paris, Sedrowski, 1936.

12817. Johnson, Antoinette Spanos. *Félix Vallotton: prints and preparatory drawings*. Birmingham, Visual Arts Gallery, the University of Alabama at Birmingham, 1993.

12818. Jourdain, Francis. *Félix Vallotton*. Avec une étude d'Edmond Jaloux de l'Académie Française. Genève, Cailler, 1953. (Peintres et sculpteurs d'hier et d'aujourd'hui, 29).

12819. Kunsthalle Bremen. *Félix Vallotton, das druckgraphische Werk*. 3. Mai bis 14. Juni 1981. Bremen, Kunsthalle Bremen, 1981.

12820. Kunstmuseum Winterthur. *Félix Vallotton: Bilder, Zeichnungen, Graphik*. 1. Oktober bis 12. November 1978. Winterthur, Kunstmuseum Winterthur, 1978.

12821. Meier-Graefe, Julius. *Félix Vallotton, biographie*. [Text in German and French]. Berlin, Stargardt/Paris, Sagot, 1898.

12822. Monnier, Jacques. *Félix Vallotton*. Lausanne, Rencontre, 1970.

12823. Newman, Sasha M. *Félix Vallotton*. With essays by Marina Ducrey . . . [et al.]. Ed. by Lesley K. Baier. New Haven, Yale University Art Gallery; New York, Abbeville Press, 1991.

12824. Vallotton, Félix. *F. Vallotton: Félix Vallotton, Leben und Werk*. Mit Texten von Günter Busch, Bernard Dorival, Doris Jakubec. Frauenfeld, Edition Scheidegger im Verlag Huber, 1982.

12825. ———. *Félix Vallotton: gravures sur bois*. Préface de Manuel Jover. Monaco, Editions Sauret, [1993].

12826. ———. *Vallotton*. Textes de Günter Busch . . . [et al.]. Lausanne, Bibliothèque des Arts, 1985.

12827. Vallotton, Maxime [and] Goerg, Charles. *Félix Vallotton, catalogue raisonné de l'oeuvre gravé et lithographié*. [Text in French and English]. Genève, Bonvent, 1972. (CR).

12828. Von Kirschen, Ivo. *The graphic art of Vallotton & the Nabis* [catalogue of an exhibition] Kovler Gallery: Chicago, May–July 1970; Museum of Art, University of Iowa, Iowa City, August–September 1970. Chicago, Kovler Gallery, 1970.

Valtat, Louis, 1869–1952

12829. Cogniat, Raymond. *Louis Valtat*. Neuchâtel, Ides et Calendes, 1963.

12830. Valtat, Jean. *Louis Valtat: catalogue de l'oeuvre peint*. Neuchâtel, Ides et Calendes, 1977. (CR).

Vanbrugh, John, 1664–1726

12831. Barman, Christian. *Sir John Vanbrugh*. New York, Scribner, 1924.

12832. Beard, Geoffrey W. *The work of John Vanbrugh*. Ill. by Anthony Kersting. London, B.T. Batsford, 1986.

12833. Bingham, Madeleine. *Masks and façades; Sir John Vanbrugh: the man in his setting*. London, Allen & Unwin, 1974.

12834. Downes, Kerry. *Sir John Vanbrugh: a biography*. London, Sidgwick & Jackson, 1987.

12835. ———. *Vanbrugh*. London, Zwemmer, 1977.

12836. Mavor, William F. *A new description of Blenheim*. London, Cadell, 1793. (Reprint: New York, Garland, 1982).

12837. McCormick, Frank. *Sir John Vanbrugh: the playwright as architect*. University Park, Pennsylvania State University Press, 1991.

12838. Vanbrugh, John. *The complete works of Sir John Vanbrugh*. Edited by Bonamy Dobrée and Geoffrey Webb. 4 v. London, Nonesuch, 1927–1928.

12839. Whistler, Laurence. *The imagination of Vanbrugh and his fellow artists*. London, Batsford, 1954.

12840. ———. *Sir John Vanbrugh, architect and dramatist, 1664–1726*. New York, Macmillan, 1939.

Van der Rohe, Ludwig Mies *see* Mies van der Rohe, Ludwig

Van der Zee, James, 1886–1983

12841. De Cock, Liliane and McGhee, Reginald, eds. *James van der Zee*. Introduction by Regina A. Perry. Dobbs Ferry, N.Y., Morgan & Morgan, 1973.

12842. Haskins, James. *James Van Der Zee: the picture-takin' man*. Trenton, Africa World Press, 1991.

12843. McGhee, Reginald. *The world of James van der Zee: a visual record of Black Americans*. New York, Grove, 1969.

12844. Van Der Zee, James, et al. *The Harlem book of the dead*. Foreword by Toni Morrison. Dobbs Ferry, N.Y., Morgan & Morgan, 1978.

12845. Willis-Braithwaite, Deborah. *Van Der Zee, photographer, 1886–1983*. Biographical essay by Rodger C. Birt. New York, H.N. Abrams, 1993.

van Dyck, Anthony *see* Dyck, Anthony van

van Gogh, Vincent *see* Gogh, Vincent van

Vannucci, Pietro di Cristoforo *see* Perugino

Vantongerloo, Georges, 1886–1965

12846. Corcoran Gallery of Art (Washington, D.C.). *Georges Vantongerloo, a traveling retrospective exhibition.* April 22–June 17, 1980. [Brussels], Ministry of French Culture in Belgium, 1980.

12847. Vantongerloo, Georges. *Paintings, sculptures, reflections.* Trans. by Dollie P. Chareau and Ralph Manheim. New York, Wittenborn, Schultz, 1948. (Problems of Contemporary Art, 5).

12848. ———. *Vantongerloo.* Milano, Electa, 1986.

Vanvitelli, Gaspare *see* Wittel, Gaspar Adriaenszoon van

Vanvitelli, Luigi, 1700–1773

12849. Carreras, Pietro. *Studi su Luigi Vanvitelli.* Firenze, La Nuova Italia, 1977.

12850. Chierici, Gino. *La reggia di Caserta.* Prefazione di Bruno Malojoli. Roma, Libreria dello Stato, 1969.

12851. Convegno Vanvitelliano (Ancona). *L'attivà architettonica di Luigi Vanvitelli nelle Marche e i suoi epigoni.* 27–28 aprile 1974. Ancona, Presso la Deputazione di Storia Patria per le Marche, 1975.

12852. Fichera, Francesco. *Luigi Vanvitelli.* Prefazione di Gustavo Giovannoni. Roma, Reale Accademia d'Italia, 1937.

12853. Fiengo, Giuseppe. *Gioffredo e Vanvitelli nei palazzi dei Casacalenda.* Napoli, Editoriale Scientifica, 1976.

12854. Fusco, Renato de, et al. *Luigi Vanvitelli.* [Napoli], Edizioni Scientifiche Italiane, 1973.

12855. Strazzullo, Franco, ed. *Le lettere di Luigi Vanvitelli della Biblioteca Palatina di Caserta.* Introduzione di Roberto Pane. Prefazione di Guerriera Guerrieri. 3 v. Galatina, Congedo, 1976/1977. (Biblioteca napoletana di storia e arte, 1–3).

12856. Vanvitelli, Luigi [Jr.]. *Vita dell'architetto Luigi Vanvitelli.* Napoli, Trani, 1823. (New ed., edited by Mario Rotili: Napoli, Società Editrice Napoletana, 1975).

Varin, Jean, 1604–1672

12857. Courajod, Louis. *Jean Warin et ses oeuvres de sculpture.* Paris, Champion, 1881.

12858. Mazerolle, F. *Jean Varin.* Paris, Bourgey et Schemit, 1932.

12859. Pény, Frédéric. *Jean Varin de Liège, 1607 [sic]–1672.* Liège, Imprimerie de L'Académie, 1947.

Varo, Remedios, 1908–1963

12860. Kaplan, Janet A. *Unexpected journeys: the art and life of Remedios Varo.* New York, Abbeville Press, 1988.

Vasarely, Victor, 1908–

12861. Dahhan, Bernard. *Victor Vasarely, ou la connaissance d'un art moléculaire.* Paris, Denoël/Gonthier, 1979.

12862. Ferrier, Jean-Louis. *Entretiens avec Victor Vasarely.* Paris, Belfond, 1969.

12863. La Motte, Manfred de and Tolnay, Alexander. *Vasarely: Werke aus sechs jahrzehnten.* Stüttgart, Klett-Cotta, 1986.

12864. Spies, Werner. *Victor Vasarely.* Trans. by Robert E. Wolf. New York, Abrams, 1971.

12865. Vasarely, Victor. *Notes brutes.* Introduction de Claude Desailly. Paris, Denoël/Gonthier, 1972.

12866. ———. *Plasticien.* Paris, Laffont, 1979.

12867. ———. *Vasarely.* Introductions by Marcel Joray. Texts and designs by Victor Vasarely. Trans. by Haakon Chevalier. 3 v. Neuchâtel, Editions du Griffon, 1969–1974.

Vasari, Giorgio, 1511–1574

12868. Barolsky, Paul. *Why Mona Lisa smiles and other tales by Vasari.* University Park, Pennsylvania State University Press, 1991.

12869. Barocchi, Paola. *Studi vasariani.* Torino, G. Einaudi, 1984. (Saggi, 667).

12870. ———. *Vasari, pittore.* Milano, Il Club del Libro, 1964. (Collana d'arte del Club del Libro, 9).

12871. Boase, Thomas S. R. *Giorgio Vasari: the man and the book.* Princeton, N.J., Princeton University Press, 1979. (Bollingen Series XXXV, 20).

12872. Capriglione, Anna A. *Giorgio Vasari pittore e sua influenza sulla pittura napoletana.* [Napoli], Libreria Editrice Ferraro, 1970.

12873. Carden, Robert W. *The life of Giorgio Vasari, a study of the later Renaissance in Italy.* London, Warner, 1910.

12874. Churchill, Sydney J. *Bibliografia vasariana.* [Firenze], [n.p.], 1912.

12875. Conforti, Claudia. *Vasari architetto.* Milano, Electa, 1993.

12876. Hall, Marcia B. *Renovation and Counter-Reformation: Vasari and Duke Cosimo in Santa Maria Novella and Santa Croce, 1567–1577.* Oxford, Clarendon Press, 1979. (Oxford-Warburg Studies).

12877. Istituto Nazionale di Studi sul Rinascimento (Florence). *Il Vasari: storiografo e artista; atti del congresso internazionale nel IV centenario della morte, 2–8 settembre 1974.* Firenze, Istituto Nazionale di Studi sul Rinascimento, 1976.

12878. ———. *Studi vasariani: atti del convegno internazationale per il IV centenario della prima edizione delle Vite del Vasari. 16–19 settembre, 1950.* Firenze, Sansoni, 1952.

12879. Kallab, Wolfgang. *Vasaristudien.* Wien, Graeser, 1908.

12880. Le Molle, Roland. *Georges Vasari et le vocabulaire de la critique d'art dans les "Vite"*. Grenoble, Ellug, Université Stendhal—Grenoble 3, 1988.

12881. Ragghianti Collobi, Licia. *Il libro de disegni del Vasari*. 2 v. Firenze, Vallecchi, 1974.

12882. Rubin, Patricia Lee. *Giorgio Vasari: art and history*. New Haven, Yale University Press, 1994.

12883. Rud, Einar. *Vasari's life and Lives: the first art historian*. Trans. by Reginald Spink. London, Thames and Hudson, 1963.

12884. Satkowski, Leon George. *Giorgio Vasari: architect and courtier*. With photographs by Ralph Lieberman. Princeton, Princeton University Press, 1993.

12885. Sottochiesa di San Francesco (Arezzo). *Giorgio Vasari: principi, letterati e artisti nelle carte di Giorgio Vasari*. 26 settembre–29 novembre 1981. Firenze, Edam, 1981.

12886. Vasari, Giorgio. *Giorgio Vasari: principi, letterati e artisti nelle carte di Giorgio Vasari, Casa Vasari: pittura vasariana dal 1532 al 1554, Sottochiesa di S. Francesco*. [Catalogo delle mostre, Arezzo, 26 settembre–29 novembre 1981]. Firenze, Edam, 1981.

12887. ———. *Giorgio Vasari: tra decorazione ambientale e storiografia artistica: convegno di studi, Arezzo, 8–10 ottobre, 1981*. A cura di Gian Carlo Garfagnini. Firenze, L.S. Olschki, 1985. (Atti di convegni, 15).

12888. ———. *Il carteggio di Giorgio Vasari dal 1563 al 1565*. [Edited by Karl Frey; Italian edition by Alessandro del Vita]. Roma, Reale Istituto d'Archeologia e Storia dell'Arte, 1941.

12889. ———. *Il libro delle ricordanze di Giorgio Vasari*. A cura di Alessandro del Vita. Roma, Reale Istituto d'Archeologia e Storia dell'-Arte, 1938.

12890. ———. *Ragionamenti del Signore Cavaliere Giorgio Vasari, pittore et architetto aretino*. Firenze, Giunti, 1588.

12891. ———. *Vasari on technique*. Trans. by Louisa S. Maclehose. Edited with an introduction and notes by G. Baldwin Brown. London, Dent, 1907. (Reprint: New York, Dover, 1960).

12892. ———. *Le vite de' piu eccellenti pittori, scultori e architettori*. Di nuovo dal medesimo riviste et ampliate. 3 v. Fiorenza, Giunti, 1568. (English ed., edited and annotated by E. H. and E. W. Blashfield and A. A. Hopkins: New York, Scribner, 1896. 4 v.).

12893. ———. *Lo zibaldone di Giorgio Vasari*. A cura di Alessandro del Vita. Roma, Reale Istituto d'Archeologia e Storia dell'Arte, 1938.

12894. Vita, Alessandro del. *Inventorio e regesto dei manoscritti dell'Archivio Vasariano*. Roma, Reale Istituto d'Archeologia e Storia dell'-Arte, 1938.

Vauban, Sebastien le Preste de, 1633–1707

12895. Blomfield, Reginald T. *Sebastien le Preste de Vauban, 1633–1707*. London, Methuen, 1938.

12896. Decorps, Aimée-Charlotte. *Essai pour etablir un parallele entre les ecrits de Vauban et les cahiers de doléances de 1789*. Saint-Léger-Vauban, Association des amis de la Maison Vauban, 1989.

12897. Lazard, Pièrre E. *Vauban, 1633–1707*. Paris, Alcan, 1934.

12898. Michel, Georges. *Histoire de Vauban*. Paris, Plon, 1879.

12899. Parent, Michel et Verroust, Jacques. *Vauban*. Paris, Fréal, 1971.

12900. Rochas d'Aiglun, Albert de, ed. *Vauban: sa famille et ses écrits, ses oisivetés et sa correspondance*. 2 v. Paris, Berger-Levrault, 1910.

12901. Vauban, Sebastien le Preste de. *Traité de l'attaque et de la défense des places*. Nouvelle édition. La Haye, de Hondt, 1742.

Vázquez-Díaz, Daniel, 1882–1969

12902. Benito, Angel. *Vázquez-Díaz, vida y pintura*. Madrid, Direccion General de Bellas Artes/ Ministerio de Educacion y Ciencia, 1971. (CR). (Arte de Espana, 1).

12903. Martinez, Elena M. *El discurso dialogico de La era imaginaria de Rene Vázques Díaz*. Madrid, Editorial Betania, 1991.

Vecchio, Palma *see* Palma, Giacomo

Vecelli, Tiziano *see* Titian

Vedder, Elihu, 1836–1923

12904. Kennedy Galleries (New York). *Three simultaneous exhibitions*. May 1986. New York, Kennedy Galleries, 1986.

12905. National Collection of the Fine Arts, Smithsonian Institution (Washington, D.C.). *Perceptions and evocations: the art of Elihu Vedder*. October 13, 1978–February 4, 1979. Washington, D.C., Smithsonian Institution, 1979.

12906. Soria, Regina. *Elihu Vedder, American visionary artist in Rome (1836–1923)*. Rutherford, N.J., Fairleigh Dickinson University Press, 1970.

12907. Vedder, Elihu. *The digressions of V., written for his own fun and that of his friends*. Boston, Houghton Mifflin, 1910.

Veen, Gerrit Jan van der, 1902–1944

12908. Helman, Albert [pseud., Lou Lichtveld].

Gerrit Jan van der Veen, een doodgewone held. Baarn, Het Wereldvenster, 1977. 2 ed.

12909. Ommeren, Anita van and Scherphuis, Ageeth. *'Die man had moeten blijven leven': Gerrit Jan van der Veen en het verzet.* Amsterdam, Sijthoff, 1988.

Veit, Philipp, 1793–1877

12910. Jungnitz, Ingobert. *Die Nazarener-Fresken im Mainzer Dom zum 100. Todestag von Philipp Veit.* Fotos von Winfried G. Popp. [Text in German and English]. Mainz, Krach, 1976.

12911. Spahn, Martin. *Philipp Veit.* Bielefeld/ Leipzig, Velhagen & Klasing, 1901. (Künstler-Monographien, 51).

12912. Suhr, Norbert. *Philipp Veit: Porträts aus dem Mittelrheinischen Landesmuseum, Mainz und aus Privatbesitz.* Mainz, Mittelrheinisches Landesmuseum, 1978.

12913. ———. *Philipp Veit, 1793–1877: Leben und Werk eines Nazareners: Monographie und Werkverzeichnis.* Weinheim [Germany], VCH, Acta Humaniora, 1991. (CR).

Velasco, José María, 1840–1912

12914. Altamirano Piolle, María Elena. *Homenaje nacional, José María Velasco.* Introducción, Fausto Ramírez. Prólogo, Xavier Moyssén. Mexico, Amigos del Museo Nacional de Arte, 1993.

12915. Encina, Juan de la. *El paisajista José María Velasco (1840–1912).* México, D.F., Colegio de México, 1943.

12916. Moyssén, Xavier . . . [et al.]. *José María Velasco: homenaje.* México, D.F., Universidad Nacional Autónoma de México, 1989.

12917. Trabulse, Elías. *José María Velasco: un paisaje de la ciencia en México.* Toluca, Instituto Mexiquense de Cultura, 1992.

12918. Velasco, José María. *José María Velasco, pinturas, dibujos, acuarelas.* Con un prólogo y tres sonetos de Carlos Pellicer. México, Fondo Editorial de la Plástica Mexicana, 1981. 2a ed.

12919. ———. *Velasco en blanco y negro.* Prólogo, José Yurrieta Valdés. Introducción, Rodrigo Almanza Villanueva. Comentario, José A. Bernal Obregón. Toluca, Instituto Mexiquense de Cultura, 1992. Ed. especial.

Velázquez, Diego Rodriguez de Silva y, 1599–1660 *see also* Murillo, Bartolomé Esteban

12920. Alfaro, Juan de. *Memoria de las pinturas que la magestad catholica del Rey nuestro señor Don Philipe IV embia al Monasterio de San Laurencio el Real del Escurial este ano de MDCLVI, descriptas y colocadas por*

Diego de Sylva Velázquez. Roma, Grignano, 1658. (New ed., trans. into French and edited by Charles Davillier: Paris, Aubry, 1874).

12921. Allende-Salazar, Juan. *Velázquez, des Meisters Gemälde.* Einleitung von Walter Gensel. Stuttgart, Deutsche Verlags-Anstalt, 1925. 4 ed. (Klassiker der Kunst, 6).

12922. Aman-Jean, Edmond F. *Velázquez.* Paris, Alcan, 1913.

12923. Angulo Iñiguez, Diego. *Velázquez: cómo compuso sus principales cuadros.* Sevilla, Universidad de Sevilla, 1947.

12924. Armstrong, Walter. *The art of Velázquez.* London, Seeley, 1896. (Portfolio Artistic Monographs, 29).

12925. ———. *The life of Velázquez.* London, Seeley, 1896. (Portfolio Artistic Monographs, 28).

12926. Asturias, Miguel A. [and] Bardi, P. M. *L'opera completa di Velázquez.* Milano, Rizzoli, 1969. (CR). (Classici dell'arte, 26).

12927. Beruete, Aureliano de. *Velázquez.* Trans. by Hugh E. Poynter. London, Methuen, 1906.

12928. Brasil, Jaime. *Velázquez.* Lisboa, Portugália Editora, 1960.

12929. Brown, Dale. *The world of Velázquez, 1599– 1660.* New York, Time-Life, 1969.

12930. Brown, Jonathan. *Velázquez, painter and courtier.* New Haven, Yale University Press, 1986.

12931. Calvert, Albert F. and Hartley, C. Gasquoine. *Velázquez, an account of his life and works.* London, Lane, 1908.

12932. Camón Aznar, José. *Velázquez.* 2 v. Madrid, Espasa-Calpe, 1964.

12933. Campo y Francés, Angel del. *La magia de la meninas: une iconología velazqueña.* Madrid, Colegio de Ingenieros de Caminos, Canales, y Puertos, 1978.

12934. Casa de Velázquez (Madrid). *Velázquez; son temps, son influence: actes du colloque tenu à la Casa de Velázquez les 7, 9 et 10 décembre 1960.* Paris, Arts et Métiers Graphiques, 1963.

12935. Cruzada Villaamil, Gregorio. *Anales de la vida y de las obras de Diego de Silva Velázquez.* Madrid, Guijarro, 1885.

12936. Curtis, Charles Boyd. *Velázquez and Murillo: a descriptive and historical catalogue of the works of Don Diego de Silva Velázquez and Bartolomé Estéban Murillo.* London, Sampson Low, Marston, Searle, and Rivington; New York, J.W. Bouton, 1883.

12937. Díez del Corral, Luis. *Velázquez, la monarquía, e italia.* Madrid, Espasa-Calpe, 1979.

12938. Dmitrienko, Mariia F. *Velaskes.* Moskva, Molodaia Gvardiia, 1965.

12939. Domínguez Ortiz, Antonio, Pérez Sánchez,

Alfonso E., Gállego, Julián. *Velázquez*. New York, Metropolitan Museum of Art, distributed by H.N. Abrams, 1989.

12940. ———. *Velázquez: Museo del Prado 23 enero/31 marzo 1990*. Madrid, Ministerio de Cultura, 1990.

12941. Encina, Juan de la. *Sombra y enigma de Velázquez*. Buenos Aires, Espasa-Calpe, 1952.

12942. Faure, Elie. *Velázquez, biographie critique*. Paris, Laurens, [1903].

12943. Gállego, Julián. *Velázquez en Sevilla*. Sevilla, Diputación Provincial de Sevilla, 1974.

12944. Gaya Nuño, Juan A. *Bibliografia critica y antologia de Velázquez*. Madrid, Galdiano, 1963.

12945. ———. *Velázquez, biografía ilustrada*. Barcelona, Ediciones Destino, 1970.

12946. Gerstenberg, Kurt. *Diego Velázquez*. München, Deutscher Kunstverlag, 1957.

12947. Gudiol Ricart, Josep. *Velázquez, 1599–1660*. Trans. by Kenneth Lyons. New York, Viking, 1974.

12948. Harris, Enriqueta. *Velázquez*. Oxford, Phaidon, 1982.

12949. Hind, C. Lewis. *Days with Velázquez*. London, A & C Black, 1906.

12950. Instituto Diego Velázquez (Madrid). *Velázquez: homenaje en el tercer centenario de su muerte*. Madrid, Instituto Diego Velázquez, 1960.

12951. Jornadas de Arte. *Velázquez y el arte de su tiempo: V Jornadas de Arte*. Madrid, Editorial Alpuerto, 1991.

12952. Justi, Carl. *Diego Velázquez and his times*. Trans. by A. H. Keane. London, Grevel, 1889.

12953. Kahr, Madlyn M. *Velázquez: the art of painting*. New York, Harper & Row, 1976.

12954. Kapterewa, Tatjana. *Velázquez und die spanische Porträtmalerei*. [Trans. from the Russian by Ulrich Kuhirt]. Leipzig, Seemann, 1961.

12955. Kehrer, Hugo. *Die Meninas des Velázquez*. München, Bruckmann, 1966.

12956. Kemenov, Vladimir. *Velázquez in Soviet museums*. Trans. by Roger Keys. Leningrad, Aurora, 1977.

12957. Knackfuss, Hermann. *Velázquez*. Bielefeld/Leipzig, Velhagen & Klasing, 1895. (Künstler-Monographien, 6).

12958. Lafuente Ferrari, Enrique. *Velázquez, biographical and critical study*. Trans. by James Emmons. Lausanne, Skira, 1960; distributed by World, Cleveland. (The Taste of Our Time, 33).

12959. Lefort, Paul. *Velázquez*. Paris, Librairie de l'Art, 1888.

12960. López-Rey, José. *Velázquez: the artist as a maker, with a catalogue raisonné of his ex-

tant works*. Lausanne/Paris, Bibliothèque des Arts, 1979. (CR).

12961. Maravall, José A. *Velázquez y el espiritu de la modernidad*. Madrid, Guadarrama, 1960.

12962. Mayer, August L. *Diego Velázquez*. Berlin, Propyläen, 1924.

12963. ———. *Velázquez: a catalogue raisonné of the pictures and drawings*. London, Faber, 1936. (CR).

12964. McKim-Smith, Gridley, Andersen-Bergdoll, Greta, and Newman, Richard. *Examining Velázquez*. With technical photography by Andrew Davidhazy. New Haven, Yale University Press, 1988.

12965. Mesonero Romanos, Manuel. *Velázquez fuera del Museo del Prado, apuntes para un catálogo de los cuadros que se le atribuyen en las principales galerías públicas y particulares de Europa*. Madrid, Hernández, 1899.

12966. Ministerio de Educacion Nacional (Madrid). *Varia velazqueña: homenaje a Velázquez en el III centenario de su muerte, 1660–1960*. 2 v. Madrid, Ministerio de Educacion Nacional, 1960.

12967. Muñoz, Antonio. *Velázquez*. Leipzig, Goldmann, 1941.

12968. Orozco Diaz, Emilio. *El barroquismo de Velázquez*. Madrid, Rialp, 1965.

12969. Orso, Steven N. *Velázquez, Los Borrachos, and painting at the Court of Philip IV*. Cambridge/New York, Cambridge University Press, 1993.

12970. Ortega y Gasset, José. *Velasquez, Goya and the dehumanization of art*. Trans by Alexis Brown. Intro. by Philip Troutman. New York, Norton, 1972.

12971. Pantorba, Bernardino de [pseud., José López Jiménez]. *La vida y la obra de Velázquez*. Madrid, Compañia Bibliografica Española, 1955.

12972. Pérez Sánchez, Alfonso E. *Velázquez*. Bologna, Capitol, 1980.

12973. Picon, Jacinto O. *Vida y obras de Don Diego Velázquez*. Madrid, Fé, 1899.

12974. Pompey, Francisco. *Velázquez, estudio biografico y critico*. Madrid, Offo, 1961.

12975. Saint-Paulien, J. [pseud., Maurice I. Sicard]. *Velázquez et son temps*. Paris, Fayard, 1961.

12976. Sérullaz, Maurice. *Velázquez*. Trans. by I. Mark Paris. New York, Abrams, 1981.

12977. ———. *Velázquez*. Text by Maurice Sérullaz, with the collaboration of Christian Pouillon. Trans. by I. Mark Paris. New York, H.N. Abrams, 1987.

12978. Stirling, William. *Velázquez and his works*. London, Parker, 1855.

12979. Stowe, Edwin. *Velázquez*. New York, Scribner & Welford, 1881.

12980. Trapier, Elizabeth du Gué. *Velázquez*. New

York, Hispanic Society of America, 1948.

12981. Wind, Barry. *Velázquez's bodegones: a study in seventeenth-century Spanish genre painting.* Fairfax, George Mason University Press; Lanham, distributed by arrangement with University Pub. Associates, 1987.

12982. Znamerovskaia, Tat'iana P. *Velaskes.* Moskva, Izobrazitel'noe Iskusstvo, 1978.

Velde, Bram van, 1895–1981

12983. Beckett, Samuel, et al. *Bram van Velde.* Trans. by Olive Classe and Samuel Beckett. New York, Grove, 1960.

12984. Cabinet des Estampes, Musée d'Art et d'Histoire (Geneva). *Bram van Velde: les lithographies, 1923–1973.* Paris Rivière, 1973.

12985. Greshoff, Jan . . . [et al.]. *Bram van Velde, 1895–1981.* Samenstelling Bonnefantenmuseum. 's-Gravenhage, SDU Uitgeverij, 1989.

12986. Gribaudo, Ezio, ed. *Bram van Velde.* [Text in English]. Torino, Pozzo, [1970]. (CR).

12987. Juliet, Charles. *Rencontres avec Bram van Velde.* Montpellier, Fata Morgana, 1978.

12988. Putnam, Jacques et Juliet, Charles. *Bram van Velde.* Paris, Maeght, 1975.

12989. Velde, Bram van. *Bram van Velde*: [exposition] été 1985, Musée d'art et d'industrie Saint-Etienne. Saint-Etienne, Le Musée, 1985.

12990. ———. *Bram van Velde*: Musée national d'art moderne, Centre Georges Pompidou. [Documentation et iconographie Nathalie Schoeller. Traductions, J. Hannard, Yves Kobry, Martine Reyss]. Paris, Le Centre, 1989. (Collection Classiques du XXe siécle).

Velde, Henry van de, 1863–1957 *see also* Kirchner, Ernst Ludwig

12991. Canning, Susan Marie. *Henry van de Velde (1863–1957): paintings and drawings.* J.F. Buyck, hoofdredactie. Antwerpen, Koninklijk Museum voor Schone Kunsten; Otterlo, Rijksmuseum Kröller-Müller, [1987].

12992. Hammacher, Abraham M. *Die Welt Henry van de Velde.* Antwerpen, Mercator/Köln, DuMont Schauberg, 1967.

12993. Hüter, Karl-Heinz. *Henry van de Velde: sein Werk bis zum Ende seiner Tätigkeit in Deutschland.* Berlin, Akademie, 1967. (Schriften zur Kunstgeschichte, 9).

12994. Kerckhove, Fabrice van de . . . [et al.]. *Henry van de Velde dans les collections de la Bibliothéque royale Albert Ier.* Introduction, A.M. Hammacher. Bruxelles, La Bibliothèque, 1993.

12995. Palais des Beaux-Arts (Brussels). *Henry van de Velde, 1863–1957.* 13 au 29 décembre 1963. Bruxelles, Palais des Beaux-Arts, 1963.

12996. Ploegaerts, Léon and Puttemans, Pierre. *L'oeuvre architecturale de Henry van de Velde.* Bruxelles, Atelier Vokaer; Québec, Presses de l'Université Laval, 1987.

12997. Rességuier von Brixen, Clemens. *Die Schriften Henry van de Veldes.* New York, Delphic Press, 1955.

12998. Sharp, Dennis, ed. *Henri van de Velde: theatre designs 1904–1914.* [Text in English and French]. London, Architectural Association, 1974.

12999. Velde, Henry van de. *Die drei Sünden wider die Schönheit.* Deutsche berechtigte Uebersetzung mitsamt dem französischen Original. Zürich, Rascher, 1918. (Europäische Bibliothek, 5).

13000. ———. *Essays.* Leipzig, Insel-Verlag, 1910.

13001. ———. *Geschichte meines Lebens.* Herausgegeben und übertragen von Hans Curjel. München, Piper, 1962.

13002. ———. *Kunstgewerbliche Laienpredigten.* Leipzig, Seemann, 1902.

13003. ———. *Vom neuen Stil: der Laienpredigten, II Teil.* Leipzig, Insel-Verlag, 1907.

Velde, Jan van de, 1593–1641

13004. Franken, Daniel et Kellen, J. P. van der. *L'oeuvre de Jan van de Velde.* Amsterdam, Muller/Paris, Rapilly, 1883. (New ed., with additions and corrections in German by Simon Laschitzer: Amsterdam, Hissink, 1968).

13005. Gelder, Jan G. van. *Jan van de Velde, 1593–1641: teekenaar, schilder.* 's-Gravenhage, Nijhoff, 1933.

Velde, Willem van de, the elder, 1611–1693
Willem van de, the younger, 1633–1707

13006. Baard, Henricus P. *Willem van de Velde de oude; Willem van de Velde de jonge.* Amsterdam, Becht, [1942]. (Palet serie, 25).

13007. Michel, Emile. *Les van de Velde.* Paris, Allison, [1892].

13008. Museum Boymans-van Beuningen (Rotterdam). *The Willem van de Velde drawings in the Boymans-van Beuningen Museum.* 3 v. Rotterdam, Museum Boymans-van Beuningen Foundation, 1979. (CR).

13009. National Maritime Museum (Greenwich). *Van de Velde Drawings.* 2 v. Cambridge, Cambridge University Press, 1958/1974.

13010. Robinson, M. S. *Van de Velde: a catalogue of the paintings of the elder and the younger Willem van de Velde.* Greenwich, National Maritime Museum; Den Haag, distributed by Gary Schwartz/SDU, 1990. (CR).

13011. Zoege von Manteuffel, Kurt. *Die Künstlerfamilie van de Velde.* Bielefeld/Leipzig, Velhagen & Klasing, 1927. (Künstler-Monographien, 117).

Venetsianov, Aleksei Gavrilovich, 1780–1847

13012. Efros, Abram M. [and] Miuller, A. P., eds. *Venetsianov v pis'makh Khudozhnika i vospominaniiakh sovremennikov.* Moskva, Academia, 1931.

13013. Smirnov, G. *Venetsianov and his school.* [Text in English, French, German, and Russian]. Leningrad, Aurora, 1973.

13014. Venetsianov, Aleksei Gavrilovich. *Alexei Venetsianov.* [Comp. and introduced by Dmitry Sarabyanov. Trans. by Christina Staros]. Leningrad, Aurora Art Publishers, 1988.

13015. ———. *Venetsianov and his school.* [Comp. and introduced by Tatyana Alexeyeva. Trans. by Carolyn Justice and Yuri Kleiner]. Leningrad, Aurora Art Publishers, 1984.

Veneziano, Domenico, 1410–1461

13016. Bacci, Mina. *Domenico Veneziano.* Milano, Fabbri, 1965. (I maestri del colore, 60).

13017. Wohl, Hellmut. *The paintings of Domenico Veneziano, ca. 1410–1461: a study of Florentine art of the early Renaissance.* New York, New York University Press, 1980.

Verhulst, Rombout, 1624–1698

13018. Van Notten, Marinus. *Rombout Verhulst, beeldhouwer, 1624–1698.* 's-Gravenhage, Nijhoff, 1907.

Vermeer, Jan, 1632–1675 *see also* Fabritius, Carel

13019. Aillaud, Gilles, Blankert, Albert, Montias, John Michael. *Vermeer.* [Traduzione, Serena Marchi]. Milano, A. Mondadori, 1986.

13020. Badt, Kurt. *Modell und Maler von Jan Vermeer.* Köln, DuMont Schauberg, 1961.

13021. Blankert, Albert. *Vermeer of Delft, complete edition of the paintings.* With contributions by Rob Ruurs and Willem L. van de Watering. Oxford, Phaidon, 1978.

13022. Blum, André. *Vermeer et Thoré-Bürger.* Genève, Editions du Mont-Blanc, 1945.

13023. Bonafoux, Pascal. *Vermeer.* Paris, Chène, 1992.

13024. Brion, Marcel. *Vermeer.* Paris, Somogy, 1963.

13025. Chantavoine, Jean. *Ver Meer de Delft, biographie critique.* Paris, Laurens, 1926.

13026. Descargues, Pierre. *Vermeer, biographical and critical study.* Trans. by James Emmons. Geneva, Skira, 1966. (The Taste of Our Time, 45).

13027. Goldscheider, Ludwig. *Jan Vermeer: the paintings, complete edition.* London, Phaidon, 1967. 2 ed.

13028. Gowing, Lawrence. *Vermeer.* London, Faber, 1952.

13029. Grimme, Ernst G. *Jan Vermeer van Delft.* Köln, DuMont Schauberg, 1974.

13030. Hale, Philip L. *Jan Vermeer of Delft.* Boston, Small, Maynard, 1913. (New ed., completed and prepared by Frederick W. Coburn and Ralph T. Hale: Boston, Hale, 1937.

13031. Jacob, John [and] Bianconi, Piero. *The complete paintings of Vermeer.* New York, Abrams, 1970. (CR).

13032. Malraux, André, ed. *Vermeer de Delft.* Paris, Gallimard, 1952.

13033. Martini, Alberto. *Johannes Vermeer.* Milano, Fabbri, 1965. (I maestri del colore, 54).

13034. Menzel, Gerhard W. *Vermeer.* Leipzig, Seemann, 1977.

13035. Mistler, Jean. *Vermeer.* Paris, Scrépel, 1973.

13036. Montias, John Michael. *Vermeer and his milieu: a web of social history.* Princeton, Princeton University Press, 1989.

13037. Nash, J. M. *Vermeer.* London, Scala Books; New York, distributed in the United States and Canada by Rizzoli International, 1991.

13038. Plietzsch, Eduard. *Vermeer van Delft.* Leipzig, Hiersemann, 1911.

13039. Slatkes, Leonard J. *Vermeer and his contemporaries.* New York, Abbeville, 1981.

13040. Snow, Edward A. *A study of Vermeer.* Berkeley, University of California Press, 1979. [Rev. and enl. ed., Berkeley, University of California Press, 1994].

13041. Swillens, P. T. A. *Johannes Vermeer, painter of Delft, 1632–1675.* Trans. by C. M. Breuning-Williamson. Utrecht, Spectrum, 1950.

13042. Vanzype, Gustave. *Vermeer de Delft.* Bruxelles, van Oest, 1908.

13043. Vries, Ary B. de. *Jan Vermeer van Delft.* Trans. by Robert Allen. London, Batsford, 1948.

13044. Walicki, Michał. *Jan Vermeer van Delft.* [Trans. from the Polish by Peter Panomarow]. Dresden, Verlag der Kunst, [1970].

13045. Wheelock, Arthur, Jr. *Jan Vermeer.* New York, Abrams, 1981.

13046. ———. *Vermeer and the art of painting.* New Haven, Yale University Press, 1995.

Vernet, Antoine Charles Horace *see* Vernet, Carle

Vernet, Carle, 1758–1836
Horace, 1789–1863
Joseph, 1714–1789

13047. Académie de France à Rome/Ecole Nationale Supérieure des Beaux-Arts, Paris. *Horace Vernet (1789–1863).* Mars–juillet 1980. Roma, de Luca, 1980.

13048. Arlaud, Pierre. *Catalogue raisonné des estampes gravées d'après Joseph Vernet.* Avignon, Rulliere-Libeccio, 1976. (CR).

13049. Blanc, Charles. *Une famille d'artistes; les trois Vernet: Joseph, Carle, Horace.* Paris, Laurens, [1898].

13050. [Buizard, L. M.]. *Catalogue de l'oeuvre lithographique de Mr. J. E. Horace Vernet.* Paris, Gratiot, 1826.

13051. Dayot, Armand. *Carle Vernet, étude sur l'artiste.* Paris, Le Goupy, 1925. (CR).

13052. ———. *Les Vernet: Joseph, Carle, Horace.* Paris, Magnier, 1898.

13053. Durande, Amédée, ed. *Joseph, Carle et Horace Vernet: correspondance et biographies.* Paris, Hetzel, [1864].

13054. Ingersoll-Smouse, Florence. *Joseph Vernet, peintre de marine, 1714–1789.* 2 v. Paris, Bignou, 1926. (CR).

13055. Lagrange, Léon. *Joseph Vernet et la peinture au XVIIIᵉ siècle.* Paris, Didier, 1864.

13056. Mirecourt, Eugène de. *Horace Vernet.* Paris, Roret, 1855.

13057. Musée de la Marine, Palais de Chaillot (Paris). *Joseph Vernet, 1714–1789.* 15 octobre 1976–9 janvier 1977. Paris, Musée de la Marine, Palais de Chaillot, 1976.

Vernet, Claude Joseph *see* **Vernet, Joseph**

Vernet, Emile Jean Horace *see* **Vernet, Horace**

Verona, Giovanni da *see* **Giovanni da Verona**

Veronese, Paolo, 1528–1588

13058. Badt, Kurt. *Paolo Veronese.* Köln, DuMont, 1981.

13059. Ca' Giustinian (Venice). *Mostra di Paolo Veronese.* Catalogo delle opere a cura di Rodolfo Pallucchini. 25 aprile–4 novembre 1939. Venezia, Libreria Serenissima, 1939.

13060. Caliari, Pietro. *Paolo Veronese: sua vita e sue opere; studi storico-estetici.* Roma, Forzani, 1888.

13061. Fiocco, Giuseppe. *Paolo Veronese, 1528–1588.* Bologna, Apollo, 1928.

13062. Gould, Cecil. *The Family of Darius before Alexander by Paolo Veronese; a resumé, some new deductions, and some new facts.* London, National Gallery, [1978].

13063. Loukomski, Georgii K. *Les fresques de Paul Véronèse et de ses disciples.* Préface de Paul Valéry. Paris, Seheur, 1928.

13064. Meissner, Franz H. *Veronese.* Bielefeld/Leipzig, Velhagen & Klasing, 1897. (Künstler-Monographien, 26).

13065. Osmond, Percy H. *Paolo Veronese, his career and work.* London, Sheldon Press, 1927.

13066. Pallucchini, Rodolfo. *Veronese.* Bergamo, Istituto Italiano d'Arti Grafiche, 1953. 3 ed.

13067. Pignatti, Terisio. *Veronese.* 2 v. Venezia, Alfieri, 1976. (CR).

13068. Piovene, Guido [and] Marini, Remigio. *L'opera completa del Veronese.* Milano, Rizzoli, 1968. (CR). (Classici dell'arte, 20).

13069. Venturi, Adolfo. *Paolo Veronese (per il IV centenario dalla nascità).* Milano, Hoepli, 1928.

13070. Villa alla Farnesina alla Lungara (Rome). *Immagini dal Veronese: incisioni dal secolo XVI al XIX dalle collezioni del Gabinetto Nazionale delle Stampe.* 21 novembre 1978–31 gennaio 1979. Roma, de Luca, 1978.

13071. Yriarte, Charles. *Paul Véronèse.* Paris, Librairie de l'Art, [1888].

Verrocchio, Andrea del, 1435–1488

13072. Adorno, Piero. *Il Verrocchio: nuove proposte nella civiltá artistica del tempo di Lorenzo il Magnifico.* Firenze, Casa editrice EDAM, 1991.

13073. Bule, Steven; Darr, Alan Phipps; Gioffredi, Fiorella Superbi, eds. *Verrocchio and late Quattrocento Italian sculpture.* Firenze, Le Lettere, 1992.

13074. Busignani, Alberto. *Verrocchio.* Firenze, Sadea/Sansoni, 1966.

13075. Cruttwell, Maud. *Verrocchio.* London, Duckworth, 1904.

13076. Dolcini, Loretta. *La scultura del Verrocchio: itinerario fiorentino.* Firenze, Le Lettere, 1992.

13077. Mackowsky, Hans. *Verrocchio.* Bielefeld/Leipzig, Velhagen & Klasing, 1901. (Künstler-Monographien, 52).

13078. Passavant, Günther. *Verrocchio: sculptures, paintings, and drawings; complete edition.* Trans. by Katherine Watson. London, Phaidon, 1969. (CR).

13079. Planiscig, Leo. *Andrea del Verrocchio.* Wien, Schroll, 1941.

13080. Reymond, Marcel. *Verrocchio.* Paris, Librairie de l'Art, 1906.

13081. Seymour, Charles, Jr. *The sculpture of Verrocchio.* Greenwich, Conn., New York Graphic Society, 1971.

Vestier, Antoine, 1740–1824

13082. Passez, Anne-Marie. *Antoine Vestier, 1740–1824.* Paris, Publié par la Fondation Wildenstein avec le concours de Joseph Baillio et Marie-Christine Maufus, 1989.

Vieira da Silva, Maria Elena, 1908–1992

13083. Descargues, Pierre. *Vieira da Silva.* Paris, Presses Littéraires de France, 1950.

13084. França, José-Augusto. *Vieira da Silva.* Lisboa, Artis, 1958.

13085. Fundação Calouste Gulbenkian (Lisbon). *Vieira da Silva.* Junho-Julho 1970. [Text in

Portuguese and French]. Lisboa, Fundação Calouste Gulbenkian, 1970.

13086. Lassaigne, Jacques and Weelen, Guy. *Vieira da Silva*. Trans. by John Shepley. New York, Rizzoli, 1979. [New ed., Paris, Editions Cercle d'art, 1987].

13087. Philipe, Anne, ed. *L'éclat de la lumière: entretiens avec Marie-Hélène Vieira da Silva et Arpad Szenes*. Paris, Gallimard, 1978.

13088. Solier, René de. *Vieira da Silva*. Paris, Fall, 1956.

13089. Vallier, Dora. *Vieira da Silva*. Paris, Weber, 1971.

13090. Viera da Silva. *Vieira da Silva*. [Commissaire, Alberte Grynpas Nguyen]. Genève, Skira; Paris, Centre national des arts plastiques, [1988].

13091. Weelen, Guy. *Vieira da Silva: les estampes, 1929–1976*. Paris, Rivière, 1977. (CR).

Vigée-Le Brun, Elisabeth Louise, 1755–1842

13092. Baillio, Joseph. *Elisabeth Louise Vigée Le Brun, 1755–1842*. [Published in conjunction with an exhibition at the Kimball Art Museum, Fort Worth, Tex., June 5–August 8, 1982]. Fort Worth, Kimball Art Museum, 1982.

13093. Blum, André. *Madame Vigée-Lebrun; peintre des grandes dames du XVIIIᵉ siècle*. Paris, Piazza, 1919.

13094. Hautecoeur, Louis. *Madame Vigée-Le Brun; étude critique*. Paris, Laurens, 1917.

13095. Helm, William H. *Vigée-Lebrun, 1755–1842; her life, works, and friendships*. With a catalogue raisonné of the artist's pictures. Boston, Small, Maynard, 1915. (CR).

13096. Mycielski, Jerzy i Wasylewski, Stanisław. *Portrety polskie Elżbiety Vigée-Lebrun, 1755–1842*. Lwów, Wegner, 1928.

13097. Nolhac, Pierre de. *Madame Vigée-Le Brun, peintre de la reine Marie Antoinette, 1755–1842*. Paris, Goupil, 1908.

13098. Pillet, Charles. *Madame Vigée-Le Brun*. Paris, Librairie de l'Art, [1890].

13099. Vigée-LeBrun, Elisabeth L. *Memoirs*. Trans. by Gerald Shelley. New York, Doran, 1927.

13100. ———. *Elisabeth Vigée Le Brun: mémoires d'une portraitiste 1755–1842*. Préface de Jean Chalon. Paris, Scala, 1989.

13101. ———. *The memoirs of Elisabeth Vigée-Le Brun: member of the Royal Academy of Paris, Rouen, Saint-Luke of Rome, Parma, Bologna, Saint-Petersburg, Berlin, Geneva and Avignon*. Trans. by Sián Evans. London, Camden Press, 1989.

13102. ———. *Souvenirs*. 2 v. Une édition féministe de Claudine Herrmann. Paris, Des femmes, 1984.

Vigeland, Gustav, 1869–1943

13103. Brenna, Arne. *Guide to Gustav Vigeland's sculpture park in Oslo*. Oslo, Enersen, 1960. 3 ed.

13104. Hale, Nathan C. *Embrace of life: the sculpture of Gustav Vigeland*. Photographs by David Finn. New York, Abrams, 1969.

13105. Romdahl, Axel L., et al. *Gustav Vigeland*. Oslo, Gyldendal, 1949.

13106. Stang, Ragna. *Gustav Vigeland, the sculptor and his works*. Trans. by Ardis Grosjean. Oslo, Tanum, 1965.

13107. Vigeland, Gustav. *Dagbok*. Utdrag av Harald Aars' etterlatte dagboknotater. [Edited with a foreword by Carl Just]. Oslo, Mortensen, 1955.

13108. Wikborg, Tone. *Gustav Vigeland: his art and sculpture park*. Trans. by Ruth Waaler. Oslo, Aschehoug, 1990.

Vignola, Giacinto, 1540–1584
Giacomo, 1507–1573

13109. Anzivino, Ciro L. *Jacopo Barozzi, il Vignola e gli architetti italiani del Cinquecento: repertorio bibliografico*. Vignola, Lions Club di Vignola, 1974.

13110. Barozzi, P. *Vita e opere di Jacopo Barozzi*. Modena, Arti Grafiche Modenesi, 1949.

13111. Cassa di Risparmio di Vignola, ed. *La vita e le opere di Jacopo Barozzi da Vignola, 1507–1573, nel quarto centenario della morte*. Vignola, Cassa di Risparmio di Vignola, 1975.

13112. Comitato Preposto alle Onoranze a Jacopo Barozzi, ed. *Memorie e studi intorno a Jacopo Barozzi pubblicati nel IV centenario dalla nascita*. Vignola, Monti, 1908.

13113. Domiani Almeyda, Giuseppe. *Giacomo Barozzi da Vignola ed il suo libro dei Cinque Ordini di Architettura*. Palermo, Giliberti, 1878.

13114. Lotz, Wolfgang. *Vignola-studien*. Würzburg, Triltsch, 1939.

13115. Lukomskii, Georgii K. *Vignole (Jacopo Barozzi da Vignola)*. Paris, Vincent, 1927.

13116. Spinelli, Alessandro G. *Bio-bibliografia dei due Vignola*. Roma, Società Multigrafica Editrice, 1968.

13117. Vignola, Giacomo. *Regola delle cinque ordini d'architettura*. Venetia, Ziletti, 1562. (English ed., trans. by Joseph Moxon: London, Moxon, 1655).

13118. Walcher Casotti, Maria. *Il Vignola*. 2 v. Trieste, Istituto di Storia dell'Arte Antica e Moderna, 1960. (Istituto di Storia dell'Arte, 11).

13119. Ware, William R. *The American Vignola*. 2 v. Boston, American Architect and Building News Co., 1902/Scranton, International

Textbook Co., 1906. (New ed., with introductory notes by John Barrington Bayley and Henry Hope Reed: New York, Norton, 1977).

13120. Willich, Hans. *Giacomo Barozzi da Vignola.* Strassburg, Heitz, 1906. (Zur Kunstgeschichte des Auslandes, 46).

Vignon, Claude, 1593–1670

13121. Pacht Bassani, Paola. *Claude Vignon, 1593–1670.* Préface de Jacques Thuillier. Vignon et compagnie, étude d'Antoine Schnapper. Paris, Arthena, 1992. (CR).

Vilar, Manuel, 1812–1860

13122. Moreno, Salvador. *El escultor Manuel Vilar.* México, D. F., Instituto de Investigaciones Estéticas, Universidad Nacional Autónoma de México, 1969.

13123. Vilar, Manuel. *Copiador de cartas (1846–1860) y diario particular (1854–1860).* Palabras preliminares y notas de Salvador Moreno. México, D. F., Universidad Nacional Autónoma de México, 1979.

Villard de Honnecourt, 13th c.

13124. Barnes, Carl F., Jr. *Villard de Honnecourt: the artist and his drawings; a critical bibliography.* Boston, G.K. Hall, 1982.

13125. Bechmann, Roland. *Villard de Honnecourt: la pensée technique au XIIIe siècle et sa communication.* Préface de Jacques Le Goff. Paris, Picard, 1991.

13126. Bowie, Theodore R., ed. *The sketchbook of Villard de Honnecourt.* Bloomington, Indiana University Press, 1959.

13127. Erlande-Brandenburg, Alain . . . [et al.], présenté et commenté. *Carnet de Villard de Honnecourt: d'après le manuscrit conservé á la Bibliothèque nationale de Paris.* Paris, Stock, 1986.

13128. Hahnloser, Hans R. *Villard de Honnecourt.* Wien, Schroll, 1935.

Villon, Jacques, 1875–1963 *see also* Duchamp, Marcel

13129. Auberty, Jacqueline, et Perussaux, Charles. *Jacques Villon: catalogue de son oeuvre gravé.* Paris, Prouté, 1950. (CR). (Les grands peintres graveurs français, 1).

13130. Eluard, Paul [and] René-Jean. *Jacques Villon, ou l'art glorieux.* Paris, Carré, 1948.

13131. Fogg Art Museum, Harvard University (Cambridge, Mass.). *Jacques Villon.* January 17–February 29, 1976. Cambridge, Mass., President and Fellows of Harvard College, 1976; distributed by Godine, Boston.

13132. Ginestet, Colette de et Pouillon, Catherine. *Jacques Villon: les estampes et les illustrations; catalogue raisonné.* Paris, Arts et Métiers Graphiques, 1979. (CR).

13133. Lassaigne, Jacques. *Jacques Villon.* Paris, Editions de Beaune, 1950.

13134. Naumann, Francis M. *Marcel Duchamp et ses frères.* Textes par Francis M. Naumann, Bertrand Lorquin, Pierre Cabanne. Paris, Galerie Dina Vierny, 1988.

13135. Rijksprentenkabinet Amsterdam. *Jacques Villon: grafiek uit een particuliere verzameling.* 2 juni–9 september 1984. [Samenstelling catalogus, Irene M. de Groot]. Amsterdam, Rijksmuseum, 1984.

13136. Vallier, Dora. *Jacques Villon: oeuvres de 1897 à 1956.* Paris, Cahiers d'Art, [1957].

13137. Villon, Jacques. *Jacques Villon, l'oeuvre gravé: exposition autour d'une collection,* 2 juin–3 septembre 1989, Musée du dessin et de l'estampe originale, Gravelines (Nord) [et] octobre–novembre 1989, Musée de l'imprimerie & de la Banque-Lyon. [Catalogue établi par Roland Pressat]. Gravelines, Le Musée, [1989].

13138. ———. *Jacques Villon: peintures, 1940–1960.* [Texte, Dora Vallier]. Paris, Louis Carré & Cie, 1991.

Villon, Raymond Duchamp *see* Duchamp-Villon, Raymond

Vinci, Leonardo da *see* Leonardo da Vinci

Viollet-le-Duc, Eugène Emmanuel, 1814–1879

13139. Abraham, Pol. *Viollet-le-Duc et le rationalisme médiéval.* Paris, Vincent, Fréal, 1934.

13140. Auzas, Pierre-Marie. *Eugène Viollet-le-Duc, 1814–1879.* Paris, Caisse Nationale des Monuments Historique et des Sites, 1979.

13141. Bekaert, Geert, ed. *A la recherche de Viollet-le-Duc.* Bruxelles, Mardaga, [1980].

13142. Bercé, Françoise and Foucart, Bruno. *Viollet-le-Duc: architect, artist, master of historic preservation.* With contributions by Jean-Jacques Aillagon . . . [et al.]. Washington, D.C., Trust for Museum Exhibitions, 1988.

13143. Ecole Nationale Supérieure des Beaux-Arts, Chapelle des Petits-Augustins (Paris). *Le voyage d'Italie d'Eugène Viollet-le-Duc, 1836–1837.* Janvier–mars 1980. Florence, Centro Di, 1980.

13144. Galeries Nationales du Grand Palais (Paris). *Viollet-le-Duc.* 19 février–5 mai 1980. Paris, Editions de la Réunion des Musées Nationaux, Ministère de la Culture et de la Communication, 1980.

13145. Gout, Paul. *Viollet-le-duc; sa vie, son oeuvre, sa doctrine.* Paris, Champion, 1914.

13146. Musée Historique de l'Ancien-Evêché (Lausanne). *Viollet-le-Duc: centenaire de la mort à Lausanne.* 22 juin–30 septembre 1979. Lausanne, Musée Historique de l'Ancien-Evêché, 1979.

13147. Saint-Paul, Anthyme. *Viollet-le-Duc, ses travaux d'art et son système archéologique.* Paris, Bureaux de l'Année Archéologique, 1881. 2 ed.

13148. Sauvageot, Claude. *Viollet-le-Duc et son oeuvre dessiné.* Paris, Morel, 1880.

13149. Tagliaventi, Ivo. *Viollet-le-Duc e la cultura architettonica dei revivals.* Bologna, Pàtron, 1976.

13150. Viollet-le-Duc, Eugène-Emmanuel. *Actes du Colloque international Viollet-le Duc, Paris, 1980.* Paris, Nouvelles Editions Latines, 1982.

13151. ———. *The architectural theory of Viollet-le-Duc: readings and commentary.* Ed. by M.F. Hearn. Cambridge, Mass., MIT Press, 1990.

13152. ———. *Dictionnaire raisonné de l'architecture française du XIe au XVIe siècle.* 10 v. Paris, Bance/Morel, 1854–1868.

13153. ———. *Dictionnaire raisonné du mobilier français de l'époque carolingienne à la Renaissance.* 6 v. Paris, Bance/Morel, 1858–1875.

13154. ———. *E. Viollet-le-Duc et le Massif du Mont-Blanc, 1868–1879.* Ouvrage publié sous la direction de Pierre A. Frey. Lausanne, Payot, 1988.

13155. ———. *Entretiens sur l'architecture.* 2 v. Paris, Morel, 1863/1872. (English ed., trans. by Benjamin Bucknell: New York, Grove, 1959).

13156. ———. *Habitations modernes.* 2 v. Paris, Morel, 1875–1877. (Reprint: Bruxelles, Mardaga, 1976).

13157. ———. *Lettres d'Italie, 1836–1837.* Annotées par Geneviève Viollet-le-Duc. Paris, Laget, 1971.

Vischer, Peter (the elder), 1460–1529 (the younger), 1487–1528

13158. Daun, Berthold. *P. Vischer und A. Krafft.* Bielefeld/Leipzig, Velhagen & Klasing, 1905. (Künstler-Monographien, 75).

13159. Headlam, Cecil. *Peter Vischer.* London, Bell, 1901.

13160. Meller, Simon. *Peter Vischer der Ältere und seine Werkstatt.* Leipzig, Insel-Verlag, 1925.

13161. Pilz, Kurt. *Das Sebaldusgrabmal im Ostchor der St.-Sebaldus-Kirche in Nürnberg; ein Messingguss aus der Giesshütte der Vischer.* Nürnberg, Carl, 1970.

13162. Réau, Louis. *Peter Vischer et la sculpture franconienne du XIV au XVI siècle.* Paris, Plon, 1909.

13163. Reindel, Albert. *Die wichtigsten Bildwerke am Sebaldusgrabe zu Nürnberg von Peter Vischer.* 2 v. [Text in German, English, and French]. Nürnberg, Schrag, [1851/1856].

13164. Seeger, Georg. *Peter Vischer der Jüngere.* Leipzig, Seemann, 1897. (Beiträge zur Kunstgeschichte, Neue Folge, 23).

13165. Stafski, Heinz. *Der jüngere Peter Vischer.* Nürnberg, Carl, 1962.

13166. Stasiak, Ludwik. *Prawda o Piotrze Vischerze.* Kraków, [Stasiak], 1910.

Vitale da Bologna, fl. 1320–1359

13167. D'Amico, Rosalba e Medica, Massimo. *Vitale da Bologna.* Per la Pinacoteca Nazionale di Bologna. Bologna, Nuova Alfa Editoriale, 1986. (Rapporti, 57).

13168. Gnudi, Cesare. *Vitale da Bologna and Bolognese painting in the fourteenth century.* Trans. by Olga Ragusa. New York, Abrams, 1964.

13169. Quintavalle, Carlo. *Vitale da Bologna.* Milano, Fabbri, 1966. (I maestri del colore, 157).

13170. Vitale da Bologna. *Itinerari di Vitale da Bologna: affreschi a Udine e a Pomposa*: Bologna, San Giorgio in Poggiale, 29 settembre–11 novembre 1990. Scritti di Cesare Gnudi e di Paolo Casadio. Bologna, Nuova Alfa Editoriale, 1990.

Vitruvius, ca. 90–ca. 20 b.c.

13171. Mikhailov, Boris P. *Vitruvii i Ellada; osnovy antichnoi teorii arkhitektury.* Moskva, Stroiizdat, 1967.

13172. Nohl, Hermann. *Index Vitruvianus.* Stuttgart, Teubner, 1983.

13173. Philandrier, Guillaume. *De architectura, annotationes.* Cum indicibus graeco & latino locupletissimis. Romae, Dossena, 1544.

13174. Prestel, Jakob. *Des Marcus Vitruvius Pollio Basilika zu Fanum Fortunae.* Strassburg, Heitz, 1901. (Zur Kunstgeschichte des Auslandes, 4).

13175. Romano, Elisa. *La capanna e il tempio: Vitruvio o dell'architettura.* Palermo, Palumbo, 1987. (Letteratura classica, 15).

13176. Vagnetti, Luigi, ed. *2000 [i.e., due mille] anni di Vitruvio.* Firenze, Edizioni della Cattedra di Composizione Architettonica I A, 1978. (Studi e documenti di architettura, 8).

13177. Vitruvius. *De architectura.* [Roma, Herolt, 1486]. (English eds.: *Vitruvius on architecture.* Trans. by Frank Granger. 2 v. [Text in Latin and English]. Cambridge, Mass., Harvard University Press, 1931 . . . Loeb Classical Library . . . ; *Vitruvius: the ten books of architecture.* Trans. by Morris H. Morgan. Cambridge, Mass., Harvard University Press, 1914).

Vittone, Bernardo Antonio, 1702–1770

13178. Accademia delle Scienze di Torino. *Bernardo Vittone e la disputa fra classicismo e barocco nel settecento: atti del convegno internaz-*

ionale. 2 v. 21–24 settembre 1970. Torino, Accademia delle Scienze, 1972.

13179. Città di Vercelli. *Bernardo Vittone, architetto: mostra organizzata nella restaurata chiesa vittoniana di Santa Chiara.* 21 ottobre–26 novembre 1967. Vercelli, Città di Vercelli, 1967.

13180. Oechslin, Werner. *Bildungsgut und Antikenrezeption im frühen Settecento in Rom; Studien zum römischen Aufenthalt Bernardo Antonio Vittones.* Zürich, Atlantis, 1972.

13181. Olivero, Eugenio. *Le opere di Bernardo Antonio Vittone.* Torino, Collegio degli Artigianelli, 1920.

13182. Portoghesi, Paolo. *Bernardo Vittone, un architetto tra illuminismo e rococò.* Roma, Edizioni dell'Elefante, 1966.

Vivarini, Alvise, 1445–1505
Antonio, 1415–1484
Bartolommeo, 1432–1499

13183. Flores d'Arcais, Francesca. *Antonio Vivarini.* Milano, Fabbri, 1966. (I maestri del colore, 151).

13184. Moschini, Vittorio. *I Vivarini.* Milano, Pizzi, 1946.

13185. Pallucchini, Rodolfo. *I Vivarini: Antonio, Bartolommeo, Alvise.* Venezia, Pozza, 1962.

13186. Sinigaglia, Giorgio. *De' Vivarini, pittori da Murano.* Bergamo, Istituto Italiano d'Arti Grafiche, 1905.

Vlaminck, Maurice de, 1876–1958 *see also* **Derain, André**

13187. Carco, Francis. *M. de Vlaminck; trente et une reproductions précédées d'une étude critique.* Paris, Nouvelle Revue Française, 1920. (Les peintres français nouveaux, 7).

13188. Crespelle, Jean-Paul. *Vlaminck, fauve de la peinture.* Paris, Gallimard, 1958.

13189. Fels, Florent. *Vlaminck.* Paris, Seheur, 1928. (L'Art et la vie, 8).

13190. Genevoix, Maurice. *Vlaminck.* Paris, Flammarion, 1954.

13191. Henry, Daniel [pseud., Daniel-Henry Kahnweiler]. *Maurice de Vlaminck.* Leipzig, Klinkhardt & Biermann, 1920. (Junge Kunst, 11).

13192. MacOrlan, Pierre. *Vlaminck.* Trans. by J. B. Sidgwick. New York, Universe, 1958.

13193. Mantaigne, André. *Maurice Vlaminck.* Paris, Crès, 1929.

13194. Perls, Klaus G. *Vlaminck.* New York, Hyperion Press, 1941.

13195. Sauvage, Marcel. *Vlaminck, sa vie et son message.* Genève, Cailler, 1956.

13196. Selz, Jean. *Vlaminck.* Paris, Flammarion, 1962.

13197. Vlaminck, Maurice de. *Maurice de Vlaminck.* Comp. and intro. by Natalia Brod-

skaya. Trans. by Michael Molnar. Leningrad, Aurora Art Publishers, 1987.

13198. ———. *Paysages et personnages.* Paris, Flammarion, 1953.

13199. ———. *Tournant dangereux: souvenirs de ma vie.* Paris, Stock, 1929.

13200. ———. *Vlaminck, il pittore e la critica.* Milano, Fabbri, 1988.

13201. Walterskirchen, Katalin von. *Maurice de Vlaminck: Verzeichnis des graphischen Werkes.* Bern, Benteli, 1974. (CR).

Vogeler, Heinrich, 1872–1942

13202. Bonner Kunstverein (Bonn). *Heinrich Vogeler: vom Romantiker zum Revolutionär.* 23. Juni–1. August 1982. Bonn, Bonner Kunstverein, 1982.

13203. Erlay, David. *Vogeler: ein Maler und seine Zeit.* Bremen, Atelier im Bauernhaus, 1981.

13204. ———. *Worpswede-Bremen-Moskau: der Weg des Heinrich Vogeler.* Bremen, Schünemann, 1972.

13205. Hundt, Walter. *Bei Heinrich Vogeler in Worpswede, Erinnerungen.* Mit einem Nachwort von Berndt Stenzig. Worpswede, Worpsweder Verlag, 1981.

13206. Petzet, Heinrich W. *Von Worpswede nach Moskau: Heinrich Vogeler; ein Künstler zwischen den Zeiten.* Köln, DuMont Schauberg, 1972.

13207. Rief, Hans-Herman. *Heinrich Vogeler: das graphische Werk.* Bremen, Schmalfeldt, 1974. (CR).

13208. Schütze, Karl-Robert. *Heinrich Vogeler, Worpswede: Leben und architektonisches Werk.* Berlin, Frölich & Kaufmann, 1980.

13209. Staatliche Kunsthalle Berlin. *Heinrich Vogeler: Kunstwerke, Gebrauchsgegenstände, Dokumente.* 1.–6. Mai 1983. Berlin, Frölich & Kaufmann, 1983.

13210. Vogeler, Heinrich. *Erinnerungen.* Herausgegeben von Erich Weinert. Berlin, Rütten & Loening, 1952.

13211. ———. *Das neue Leben: ausgewählte Schriften zur proletarischen Revolution und Kunst.* Herausgegeben von Dietger Pforte. Darmstadt, Luchterhand, 1972.

Volterra, Daniele da, 1509–1566

13212. Barolsky, Paul. *Daniele da Volterra, a catalogue raisonné.* New York/London, Garland, 1979. (CR). (Garland Reference Library of the Humanities, 130).

13213. Levie, Simon H. *Der Maler Daniele da Volterra, 1509–1566.* Köln, [s.n.], 1962.

13214. Mez, Marie L. *Daniele da Volterra, saggio storico-artistico.* Volterra, Vanzi, 1935.

13215. Pugliatti, Teresa. *Giulio Mazzoni e la decorazione a Roma nella cerchia di Daniele da Volterra.* Roma, Istituto poligrafico e Zecca dello Stato, Libreria dello Stato, 1984.

Von Holst, Theodor, 1810–1844

13216. Browne, Max. *The romantic art of Theodor von Holst, 1810–44: an introduction to the life and work of the artist on the occasion of his sesquicentenary exhibition in London and Cheltenham, 1994.* London, Lund Humphries, 1994.

Vostell, Wolf, 1932–

13217. Daadgalerie (Berlin). *Vostell und Berlin.* 30. Januar bis 7. März 1982. [Toni Stooss, Wolf Vostell. Redaktion, Rita Dalle Carbonare, Toni Stooss]. Berlin, Berliner Künstlerprogramm des Deutschen Akademischen Austauschdienstes (DAAD), 1982.

13218. Musée d'art moderne de Strasbourg. *Wolf Vostell, environnement, vidéo, peintures, dessins, 1977–1985.* 7.12.85–9.2.86. [Conception du catalogue: Wolf Vostell et Nadine Lehni]. Strasbourg, Le Musée, 1985.

13219. Vostell, Wolf. *Vostell: [Ausstellungen] Bonn, Köln, Leverkusen, Mannheim, Mülheim an der Ruhr.* Mit Texten von Michael Euler-Schmidt . . . [et al.]. Herausgegeben von Rolf Wedewer. Heidelberg, Braus, 1992.

13220. ———. *Vostell, Fluxus Zug: das mobile Museum Vostell: 7 Environments über Liebe, Tod, Arbeit: (eine mobile Kunstakademie):* [Ausstellung] 1.5.81–29.9.81. West Germany, Frölich and Kaufmann, [1981].

13221. ———. *Wolf Vostell: Tauromaquie, Automaquie, Frauenmaquie 1987–88.* Text, Dieter Ronte. Wien, Galerie Chobot, 1989.

Vouet, Aubin, 1595–1641
Simon, 1590–1649

13222. Brejon de Lavergnée, Barbara. *Dessins de Simon Vouet, 1590–1649.* Paris, Ministère de la culture et de la communication, Editions de la Réunion des musées nationaux, 1987.

13223. Crelly, William R. *The painting of Simon Vouet.* New Haven/London, Yale University Press, 1962. (CR). (Yale Publications in the History of Art, 14).

13224. Galeries nationales du Grand Palais (Paris). *Simon Vouet: actes du colloque international.* 5–6–7 février 1991. Publiés sous la direction de Stéphane Loire. Paris, Documentation française, 1992.

13225. Picart, Yves. *La vie et l'oeuvre d'Aubin Vouet (1595–1641): un cadet bien oublié.* Paris, Quatre Chemins, 1982.

13226. ———. *La vie et l'oeuvre de Simon Vouet.* 2 v. Paris, Cahiers de Paris, 1958.

13227. Thuillier, Jacques, Brejon de Lavergnée, Barbara, Lavalle, Denis. *Vouet: Galeries nationales du Grand Palais,* Paris, 6 novembre 1990–11 février 1991. Paris, Réunion des musées nationaux, 1990.

13228. Vouet, Simon. *Simon Vouet: 100 neuentdeckte Zeichnungen: aus den Beständen der Bayerischen Staatsbibliothek.* [Textbeiträge, Richard Harprath, Laurentius Koch, Jackques Thuillier. Katalog, Richard Harprath, Barbara Brejon de Lavergnée, Helge Siefert]. München, Staatliche Graphische Sammlung München, [1991]. (Ausstellungskataloge/Bayerische Staatsbibliothek, 56).

Voysey, Charles Francis Annesley, 1857–1941

13229. Durant, Stuart. *CFA Voysey.* London, Academy; New York, St. Martin's Press, 1992. (Architectural monographs, 19).

13230. Gebhard, David. *Charles F. A. Voysey, architect.* Los Angeles, Hennessey & Ingalls, 1975.

13231. Simpson, Duncan. *C. F. A. Voysey: an architect of individuality.* London, Lund Humphries, 1979.

13232. Voysey, Charles F. A. *Individuality.* Longmead, Shaftesbury, Dorset, Element Books, Ltd., 1986.

Vries, Adriaen de, 1545?–1626

13233. Böttinger, Johan. *Bronsarbeten of Adriaen de Vries I Sverige, Särskilt å Drottningholm.* Stockholm, Central, 1884.

13234. Buchwald, Conrad. *Adriaen de Vries.* Leipzig, Seemann, 1899. (Beiträge zur Kunstgeschichte, Neue Folge, 25).

13235. Cahn, Erich B. *Adriaen de Vries und seine kirchlichen Bronzekunstwerke in Schaumburg.* Rinteln, Bösendahl, 1966.

13236. Larsson, Lars O. *Adrian de Vries: Adrianus Fries Hagiensis Batavus, 1545–1626.* Wien/München, Schroll, 1967.

Vries, Jan Vredeman de, 1527–1604

13237. Iwanoyko, Eugeniusz. *Gdański okres Hansa Vredemana de Vries; studium na temat cyklu malarskiego z ratuszu w Gdansku.* Poznań, Uniwersytet im. Adama Mickiewicza, 1963.

13238. Mielke, Hans. *Hans Vredeman de Vries; Verzeichnis der Stichwerke und Beschreibung seines Stils sowle Beiträge zum Werk Gerard Groennings.* (Inaugural-Diss. Freie Universität Berlin) Berlin, 1967.

13239. Vries, Jan V. de. *Perspective.* Leiden, Hondius, 1604. (New ed., with an introduction by Adolf K. Placzek: New York, Dover, 1968).

Vroman, Adam Clark, 1856–1916

13240. Mahood, Ruth I. *Photographer of the Southwest: Adam Clark Vroman, 1856–1916.* Introduction by Beaumont Newhall. [Los Angeles], Ward Ritchie, 1961.

13241. Webb, William and Weinstein, Robert A.

Dwellers at the source: southwestern Indian photographs of A. C. Vroman, 1895–1904. New York, Grossman, 1973.

Vroom, Cornelis, 1591/or 2–1661

13242. Keyes, George S. *Cornelis Vroom: marine and landscape artist.* 2 v. Alphen aan den Rijn, 1975. (CR). The author's published dissertation.

Vrubel', Mikhail Aleksandrovich, 1856–1910

13243. Gavrilova, Evgeniia I. *Mikhail Vrubel'.* Moskva, Izobrazitel'noe Iskusstvo, 1973.

13244. Gomberg-Verzhbinskaia, Eleonora P., et al. *Vrubel': perepiska, vospominaniia o khudozhnike.* Leningrad, Iskusstvo, 1976.

13245. Iagodovskaia, Anna T. *Mikhail Aleksandrovich Vrubel'.* Leningrad, Khudizhnik RSFSR, 1966.

13246. Kogan, Dora Z. *M. A. Vrubel'.* Moskva, Iskusstvo, 1980.

13247. Rakitin, Vasilii I. *Mikhail Vrubel'.* Moskva, Iskusstvo, 1971.

13248. Suzdalev, Petr K. *Vrubel' i Lermontov.* Moskva, Izobrazitel'noe Iskusstvo, 1980.

13249. Tarabukin, Nikolai M. *Mikhail Aleksandrovich Vrubel'.* Moskva, Iskusstvo, 1974.

13250. Vrubel', Mikhail Aleksandrovich. *Mikhail Vrubel'.* [Selection, introduction, and biographical outline by Mikhail Guerman. Catalogue compiled by Alla Gaiduk . . . et al. Trans. by John Greenfield and Valery Dereviaghin]. Leningrad, Aurora Art Publishers, 1985.

Vuillard, Edouard, 1868–1940 *see also* Roussel, Ker Xavier

13251. Chastel, André. *Vuillard, 1868–1940.* Paris, Floury, 1946.

13252. Easton, Elizabeth Wynne. *The intimate interiors of Edouard Vuillard.* Washington, D.C., [Published for] the Museum of Fine Arts, Houston by the Smithsonian Institution Press, 1989.

13253. Groom, Gloria Lynn. *Edouard Vuillard: painter-decorator: patrons and projects, 1892–1912.* New Haven, Yale University Press, 1993.

13254. Preston, Stuart. *Edouard Vuillard.* New York, Abrams, 1974.

13255. Ritchie, Andrew C. *Edouard Vuillard.* [Published in conjunction with an exhibition at the Museum of Modern Art, New York]. New York, Museum of Modern Art, 1954.

13256. Roger-Marx, Claude. *The graphic work of Edouard Vuillard.* San Francisco, Alan Wofsy Fine Arts, 1990. (CR).

13257. ———. *L'oeuvre gravé de Vuillard.* Monte-Carlo, Sauret, 1948.

13258. ———. *Vuillard, his life and work.* Trans. by E. B. d'Auvergne. London, Elek, 1946.

13259. Russell, John, ed. *Vuillard.* Greenwich, Conn., New York Graphic Society, 1971.

13260. Salomon, Jacques. *Auprès de Vuillard.* Paris, La Palme, 1953.

13261. ———. *Vuillard.* Avant-propos de John Rewald. Paris, Gallimard, 1968. 2 ed.

13262. Schweicher, Curt. *Die Bildraumgestaltung, das Dekorative und das Ornamentale im Werke von Edouard Vuillard.* Trier, Paulinus, 1949.

13263. Thomson, Belinda. *Vuillard.* New York, Abbeville Press, 1988.

13264. Vuillard, Edouard. *Vuillard.* Sous la direction de Ann Dumas et Guy Cogeval. Introduction par André Chastel. Paris, Flammarion, 1990.

V

Wagner, Otto, 1841–1918

13265. Geretsegger, Heinz and Peintner, Max. *Otto Wagner, 1841–1918: the expanding city, the beginning of modern architecture.* Introduction by Richard Neutra. Trans. by Gerald Onn. New York, Rizzoli, 1979. [Another ed., London, Pall Mall, 1970].

13266. Giusti Baculo, Adriana. *Otto Wagner: dall'architettura di stile allo stile utile.* Napoli, Edizioni Scientifiche Italiane, 1970.

13267. Graf, Otto Antonia. *Master drawings of Otto Wagner: an exhibition of the Otto Wagner-Archiv, Academy of Fine Arts, Vienna.* New York, The Drawing Center, 1987.

13268. ———. *Otto Wagner.* Wien, H. Böhlau, 1985– . (Schriften des Instituts für Kunstgeschichte, Akademie der Bildenden Künste, Wien, 2).

13269. Hessisches Landesmuseum (Darmstadt). *Otto Wagner, das Werk des Wiener Architekten, 1841–1918.* 22. November 1963–2. Februar 1964. Darmstadt, Hessisches Landesmuseum, 1964.

13270. Lux, Joseph A. *Otto Wagner; eine Monographie.* München, Delphin, 1914.

13271. Mallgrave, Harry Francis, ed. *Otto Wagner: reflections on the raiment of modernity.* Santa Monica, Cal., Getty Center for the History of Art and the Humanities, 1993.

13272. Ostwald, Hans. *Otto Wagner; ein Beitrag zum Verständnis seines baukünstlerischen Schaffens.* Baden-Baden, Verlag Buchdrucker, 1948.

13273. Tietze, Hans. *Otto Wagner.* Wien, Rikola, 1922.

13274. Trevisiol, Robert. *Otto Wagner.* Roma-Bari, Editori Laterza, 1990. 1a ed.

13275. Wagner, Otto. *Die Baukunst unserer Zeit.* Wien, Schroll, 1914. (Reprint: Wien, Löcker, 1979).

13276. ———. *Die Kunst des Otto Wagner.* Herausgegeben von Gustav Peichl. Wien, Akademie der bildenden Künste, [1984]. (Wiener Aka-demie-Reihe, 16).

13277. ———. *Einige Skizzen: Projecte und ausgeführte Bauwerke.* 4 v. Wien, Schroll, 1892.

13278. Zednicek, Walter. *Otto Wagner: vierzig Photographien.* Mit einem Essay von Harald Sterk. Wien, Edition Tusch, 1983.

Waldmüller, Ferdinand Georg, 1793–1865

13279. Altes Rathaus (Schweinfurt). *Ferdinand Georg Waldmüller: Gemälde aus der Sammlung Georg Schäfer, Schweinfurt.* 17. September bis 29. Oktober 1978. Schweinfurt, Sammlung Georg Schäfer, 1978.

13280. Eberlein, Kurt K. *Ferdinand Georg Waldmüller, das Werk des Malers.* Berlin, Juncker, 1938.

13281. Grabner, Sabine. *Ferdinand Georg Waldmüller, 1793–1865.* Salzburg, Salzburger Museum Carolino Augusteum, 1993.

13282. Grimschitz, Bruno. *Ferdinand Georg Waldmüller.* Salzburg, Galerie Welz, 1957.

13283. Roessler, Arthur und Pisko, Gustav. *Ferdinand Georg Waldmüller, sein Leben, sein Werk und seine Schriften.* 2 v. Wien, Pisko, [1908].

13284. Schröder, Klaus Albrecht. *Ferdinand Georg Waldmüller.* München, Prestel-Verlag, 1990.

13285. Waldmüller, Ferdinand G. *Andeutungen zur Belebung der vaterländischen bildenden Kunst.* Wien, Gerold, 1857.

13286. Wolf, Georg J. *Waldmüller: Bilder und Erlebnisse.* München, Delphin, [1916].

Walther, Franz Erhard, 1939–

13287. Adriani, Götz, ed. *Franz Erhard Walther: Arbeiten 1955–1963; Material zum 1. Werksatz, 1963–1969.* Köln, DuMont Schauberg, 1972.

13288. Kunstraum München. *Diagramme zum 1. Werksatz.* [January 29–March 20, 1976]. München, Kunstraum München, 1976.

13289. Kunstverein Braunschweig. *Franz Erhard*

Walther: Ich bin die Skulptur: Wandform-
ationen 1978–1985 und Zeichnungen. 17.
April bis 1. Juni 1986. [Ausstellung und
Katalog, Wilhelm Bojescul, Franz Erhard
Walther]. Braunschweig, Der Kunstverein,
[1986].

13290. Kupferstichkabinett Berlin. *Franz Erhard
Walther: Zeichnungen, Werkzeichnungen,
1957–1984.* 24.3.–2.7. 1989. [Ausstellung
und Katalog, Alexander Dückers. Mitarbeit,
Uwe Wieczorek]. Berlin, Kupferstichkabinett, Staatliche Museen Preussischer Kulturbesitz, 1989.

13291. Museum Ludwig (Cologne). *Franz Erhard
Walther, 2. Werksatz: Skulpturen, Zeich-
nungen.* 6. Mai bis 26. Juni 1977. Köln,
Museen der Stadt Köln, 1977.

13292. Walther, Franz Erhard. *Franz Erhard Walther, Antwort der Körper.* Herausgegeben von
Renate Damsch-Wiehager. Stuttgart, Cantz,
1993.

Wang Chien, 1598–1677
Hui, 1632–1717
Shih-Min, 1592–1680
Yüan-Chi, 1642–1715

13293. Chiang Fu-ts'ung. *Catalogue of Wang Hui's
paintings.* [Text in Chinese and English].
Taipei, National Palace Museum, 1970.

13294. Contag, Victoria. *Die sechs berühmten
Maler der Ch'ing Dynastie.* Leipzig, Seemann, 1940.

13295. Pang, Mae A. *Wang Yüan-Ch'i (1642–1715)
and formal construction in Chinese landscape painting.* Ann Arbor, Mich., University
Microfilms, 1976.

Wang Wei, 701–761

13296. Ch'eng Hsi. *An album of Wang Wei; pictures
in illustration of his poems with translations
by Ch'eng Hsi and Henry W. Wells.* [Text in
English and Chinese]. Hong Kong, Ling-
ch'ao-hsüan, 1974.

13297. Walmsley, Lewis C. and Walmsley, Dorothy
B. *Wang Wei, the painter-poet.* Rutland, Vt.,
Tuttle, 1968.

Wappers, Gustav, 1803–1874

13298. Koninklijk Museum van Schone Kunsten
(Antwerp). *Gustav Wappers en zijn school.*
26 juni tot 29 augustus 1976. Antwerpen,
Ministerie van Nederlandse Cultuur, 1976.

Ward, James, 1769–1859
William, 1766–1826

13299. Frankau, Julia. *William Ward, James Ward;
their lives and works.* 2 v. London, Macmillan, 1904.

13300. Fussell, George E. *James Ward, R. A., animal
painter, 1769–1859, and his England.* London, Joseph, 1974.

13301. Grundy, C. Reginald. *James Ward, R. A.: his
life and works.* London, Otto, 1909.

13302. Ward, James. *James Ward R.A. 1769–1859.*
Cambridge, Fitzwilliam Museum, [1991].

Warhol, Andy, 1928–1987

13303. Bockris, Victor. *The life and death of Andy
Warhol.* New York, Bantam Books, 1989.

13304. Bourdon, David. *Warhol.* New York, H.N.
Abrams, 1989.

13305. Colacello, Bob. *Holy terror: Andy Warhol
close up.* New York, HarperCollins, 1990.

13306. Coplans, John. *Andy Warhol.* With contributions by Jonas Mekas and Calvin Tomkins. [Published in conjunction with an exhibition at the Pasadena Art Museum,
Pasadena, Calif., May 12–June 21, 1970].
Greenwich, Conn., New York Graphic Society, 1970.

13307. Crone, Rainer. *Andy Warhol.* Trans. by John
W. Gabriel. New York, Praeger, 1970.

13308. Finkelstein, Nat. *Andy Warhol, the Factory
years, 1964–1967.* New York, St. Martin's
Press, 1989.

13309. Geldzahler, Henry and Rosenblum, Robert.
*Andy Warhol: portraits of the seventies and
eighties.* With additional text by Vincent
Fremont and Leon Paroissien. London, An-
thony d'Offay Gallery in association with
Thames and Hudson, 1993.

13310. Gidal, Peter. *Andy Warhol, films and paintings.* New York, Dutton, 1971.

13311. Kestner-Gesellschaft, Hannover. *Andy Warhol, Bilder 1961 bis 1981.* 23. Oktober bis
13. Dezember 1981. Hannover, Kestner-
Gesellschaft, 1981. (Katalog 7/1981).

13312. Koch, Stephen. *Stargazer: the life, world, and
films of Andy Warhol.* New York, M.
Boyars, distributed in the United States and
Canada by Rizzoli International Publications, 1991. Rev. and updated ed.

13313. Kunsthaus Zürich. *Andy Warhol: ein Buch
zur Ausstellung 1978.* 16. Mai–30. Juli
1978. Zürich, Kunsthaus Zürich, 1978.

13314. Obalk, Hector. *Andy Warhol n'est pas un
grand artiste.* Paris, Aubier, 1990.

13315. Ratcliff, Carter. *Andy Warhol.* New York,
Abbeville, 1983. (Abbeville Modern Masters, 4).

13316. Romain, Lothar. *Andy Warhol.* München,
Bruckmann, 1993.

13317. Smith, Patrick S. *Andy Warhol's art and films.*
Ann Arbor, UMI Research Press, 1986. (Studies in the fine arts. The Avante-garde, 54).

13318. ———. *Warhol: conversations about the artist.* Ann Arbor, UMI Research Press, 1988.
(Studies in the fine arts. The Avant-garde,
59).

13319. Ultra Violet. *Famous for 15 minutes: my
years with Andy Warhol.* San Diego, Harcourt Brace Jovanovich, 1988.

13320. Warhol, Andy. *The Andy Warhol diaries*. Ed. by Pat Hackett. New York, Warner Books, 1989.

13321. ———. *Andy Warhol: heaven and hell are just one breath away!: late paintings and related works, 1984–1986*. Essay by Charles Stuckey. Foreword by Vincent Fremont. Afterword by John Richardson. New York, Gagosian Gallery/Rizzoli, 1992.

13322. ———. *Andy Warhol: a picture show by the artist*. Ed. by Rainer Crone. New York, Rizzoli, 1987.

13323. ———. *Andy Warhol prints: a catalogue raisonné*. Ed. by Frayda Feldman and Jörg Schellmann. New York, R. Feldman Fine Arts, 1985. (CR).

13324. ———. *Andy Warhol, a retrospective*. Ed. by Kynaston McShine. With essays by Kynaston McShine . . . [et al.]. New York, Museum of Modern Art; Boston, distributed by Bulfinch Press/Little, Brown, 1989.

13325. ———. *Andy Warhol's exposures: photographs by Andy Warhol*. Text by Andy Warhol with Bob Colacello. New York, Grosset & Dunlap, 1979.

13326. ———. *The philosophy of Andy Warhol (from A to B and back again)*. New York, Harcourt, Brace, Jovanovich, 1975.

13327. ——— and Hackett, Pat. *Popism: the Warhol '60's*. New York, Harcourt, Brace, Jovanovich, 1980.

13328. Whitney Museum of American Art (New York). *Andy Warhol: portraits of the '70's*. November 20, 1979–January 27, 1980. New York, Whitney Museum of American Art, 1979.

13329. Württembergischer Kunstverein (Stuttgart). *Andy Warhol: das zeichnerische Werk, 1942–1975*. Stuttgart, Württembergischer Kunstverein, 1976.

13330. Wünsche, Hermann. *Andy Warhol, das graphische Werk, 1962–1980*. Köln, Bonner Universität Buchdruckerei, [1980]; distributed by Castelli Graphics, New York. (CR).

Wasmann, Friedrich, 1805–1886

13331. Nathan, Peter. *Friedrich Wasmann, sein Leben und sein Werk*. München, Bruckmann, 1954. (CR).

13332. Wasmann, Friedrich. *Friedrich Wasmann, ein deutsches Künstlerleben*. Herausgegeben von Bernt Grönvold. Leipzig, Insel-Verlag, 1915.

Watanabe, Kazan, 1793–1841

13333. Abiko, Bonnie F. *Watanabe Kazan, the man and his times*. 2 v. in 1. Ann Arbor, University Microfilms International, 1985. (Ph.D. diss., Princeton University, 1982.)

13334. Dombrady, G.S. *Watanabe Kazan: ein japanischer Gelehrter des 19. Jahrhunderts*. Hamburg, Gesellschaft für Natur- und Völkerkunde Ostasiens, 1968.

13335. Suganuma, Teizo. *Watanabe Kazan, hito to geijutsu*. Tokyo, Nigensha,1982. (First published 1962).

Waterhouse, John William, 1849–1917

13336. Hobson, Anthony. *The art and life of J. W. Waterhouse, R. A., 1849–1917*. New York, Rizzoli, 1980.

13337. ———. *J. W. Waterhouse*. Oxford, Phaidon-Christie's, 1989.

Watkins, Carleton E., 1829–1916

13338. Alinder, James, ed. *Carleton E. Watkins: photographs of the Columbia River and Oregon*. Essays by David Featherstone and Russ Anderson. Carmel, Calif., Friends of Photography, 1979.

13339. Johnson, J. W. *The early Pacific Coast photographs of Carleton E. Watkins*. [Berkeley], University of California Water Resources Center, 1960. (Archives Series Report, 8).

13340. Palmquist, Peter E. *Carleton E. Watkins: photographer of the American West*. Foreword by Martha A. Sandweiss. Albuquerque, published for the Amon Carter Museum by the University of New Mexico Press, 1983.

13341. Watkins, Carleton E. *Carleton E. Watkins, photographs, 1861–1874*. Essay by Peter E. Palmquist. San Francisco, Fraenkel Gallery in association with Bedford Arts, 1989.

13342. Ziebarth, Marilyn, ed. *Carleton E. Watkins*. San Francisco, California Historical Society, 1978.

Watkins, Franklin Chenault, 1894–1972

13343. Ritchie, Andrew C. *Franklin C. Watkins*. [Published in conjunction with an exhibition at the Museum of Modern Art, New York]. New York, Museum of Modern Art, 1950.

13344. Wolf, Ben. *Franklin C. Watkins: portrait of a painter*. Philadelphia, University of Pennsylvania Press, 1966.

Watteau, Jean Antoine, 1684–1721

13345. Adhémar, Hélène. *Watteau, sa vie, son oeuvre*. Paris, Tisné, 1950.

13346. Banks, Oliver T. *Watteau and the North: studies in the Dutch and Flemish baroque influences on French rococo painting*. New York, Garland, 1977.

13347. Barker, Gilbert W. *Antoine Watteau*. London, Duckworth, 1939.

13348. Brinckmann, Albert E. *J. A. Watteau*. Wien, Schroll, 1943.

13349. Cellier, L. *Watteau; son enfance, ses contemporains*. Valenciennes, Henry, 1867.

13350. Champion, Pierre. *Notes critiques sur les vies anciennes d'Antoine Watteau.* Paris, Edouard Champion, 1921.

13351. Dacier, Emile et Vuaflart, Albert. *Jean de Jullienne et les graveurs de Watteau au XVIIIᵉ siècle.* 4 v. Paris, Société pour l'Etude de la Gravure Française, 1929–31.

13352. Dargenty, G. [pseud., Arthur A. M. du Cluseau d'Echerac]. *Antoine Watteau.* Paris, Librairie de l'Art, [1891].

13353. Eaubonne, Françoise d'. *Le coeur de Watteau.* [Monaco], Editions Littéraires de Monaco, 1944.

13354. Eidelberg, Martin P. *Watteau's drawings: their use and significance.* New York/London, Garland, 1977.

13355. Ferré, Jean, ed. *Watteau, critiques.* 4 v. Madrid, Athéna, 1972. (CR).

13356. Gillet, Louis. *Watteau, un grand maître du XVIII siècle.* Paris, Plon, 1943. 4 ed.

13357. Goncourt, Edmond de. *Catalogue raisonné de l'oeuvre peint, dessiné et gravé d'Antoine Watteau.* Paris, Rapilly, 1875. (CR).

13358. Guillaume, Georges. *Antoine Watteau; sa vie, son oeuvre, et les monuments élevés à sa mémoire.* Lille, Danel, 1884.

13359. Hildebrandt, Edmund. *Antoine Watteau.* Berlin, Propyläen, 1922.

13360. Hôtel de la Monnaie (Paris). *Pèlerinage à Watteau.* 4 v. [Catalogue of an exhibition]. Paris, Hôtel de la Monnaie, 1977.

13361. Huyghe, René. *L'univers de Watteau.* Paris, Scrépel, 1968.

13362. Josz, Virgile. *Antoine Watteau.* Paris, Piazza, [1904].

13363. Kunstler, Charles. *Watteau, l'enchanteur.* Paris, Floury, 1936.

13364. Lavallée, Pierre. *Antoine Watteau, 1684–1721; quatorze dessins.* Paris, Musées Nationaux, 1939.

13365. Macchia, Giovanni [and] Montagni, E. C. *L'opera completa di Watteau.* Milano, Rizzoli, 1968. (CR). (Classici dell'arte, 21).

13366. Mathey, Jacques. *Antoine Watteau: peintures réapparues, inconnues, ou négligées par les historiens.* Paris, de Nobele, 1959.

13367. Mauclair, Camille. *Antoine Watteau.* Trans. by Madame Simon Bussy. London, Duckworth, [1905].

13368. Maurel, André. *L'enseigne de Gersaint; étude sur le tableau de Watteau: son histoire, les controverses, solution du problème.* Paris, Hachette, 1913.

13369. Mollett, John W. *Watteau.* New York, Scribner & Welford/London, Sampson Low, 1883.

13370. Nemilova, Inna S. *Vatto i ego proizvedeniia v Ermitazhe.* Leningrad, Sovetskii Khudozhnik, 1964.

13370. Nordenfalk, Carl. *Antoine Watteau och andra franska sjutton hundratalsmästare i Nationalmuseum.* Stockholm, Ehlins, 1953.

13372. Parker, Karl T. *The drawings of Antoine Watteau.* London, Batsford, 1931.

13373. ——— et Mathey, Jacques. *Antoine Watteau, catalogue complet de son oeuvre dessiné.* 2 v. Paris, de Nobele, 1957. (CR).

13374. Phillips, Claude. *Antoine Watteau.* London, Seeley, 1895. (Portfolio, 13357).

13375. Pilon, Edmond. *Watteau et son école.* Bruxelles/Paris, van Oest, 1912.

13376. Posner, Donald. *Antoine Watteau.* London, Weidenfeld and Nicolson Ithaca, Cornell University Press, 1984.

13377. ———. *Watteau.* London, Weidenfeld and Nicolson, 1983.

13378. ———. *Watteau: A Lady at her Toilet.* New York, Viking, 1973. (Art in context).

13379. Roland Michel, Marianne. *Watteau, an artist of the eighteenth century.* London, Trefoil Books, 1984.

13380. Rosenberg, Adolf. *Antoine Watteau.* Bielefeld/Leipzig, Velhagen & Klasing, 1896. (Künstler-Monographien, 15).

13381. Schneider, Pierre. *The world of Watteau, 1684–1721.* New York, Time, Inc., 1967.

13382. Séailles, Gabriel. *Watteau, biographie critique.* Paris, Laurens, 1907.

13383. Staley, Edgcumbe. *Watteau and his school.* London, Bell, 1902.

13384. Watteau, Antoine. *Antoine Watteau (1684–1721): le peintre, son temps et sa légende.* Textes recueillis par François Moreau et Margaret Morgan Grasselli. Prèface de H.A. Millon, P. Rosenberg et F. Moreau. Paris, Champion-Slatkine, 1987.

13385. ———. *Tout l'oeuvre peint de Watteau.* Introduction par Pierre Rosenberg. Documentation par Ettore Camesasca. [Traduit de l'italien par Alain Veinstein]. Paris, Flammarion, 1982. Nouv. éd. rev. et mise á jour. (CR).

13386. ———. *Watteau, 1684–1721:* [exposition] National Gallery of Art, Washington, 17 juin–23 septembre 1984; Galeries nationales du Grand Palais, Paris, 23 octobre 1984–28 janvier 1985; Château de Charlottenbourg, Berlin, 22 février–26 mai 1985. Paris, Ministère de la culture, Editions de la Réunion des musées nationaux, 1984.

13387. Zimmermann, E. Heinrich. *Watteau, des Meisters Werke.* Stuttgart/Leipzig, Deutsche Verlags-Anstalt, 1912. (Klassiker der Kunst, 21).

Watts, George Frederick, 1817–1904

13388. Barrington, Emilie I. *G. F. Watts, reminiscences.* New York, Macmillan, 1905.

13389. Blunt, Wilfrid. *England's Michelangelo: a biography of George Frederick Watts.* London, Hamilton, 1904.

13390. Chapman, Ronald. *The laurel and the thorn: a study of G. F. Watts*. London, Faber, 1945.

13391. Chesterton, Gilbert K. *G. F. Watts*. London, Duckworth, [1909].

13392. Macmillan, Hugh. *The life-work of George Frederick Watts*. London, Dent, 1903.

13393. National Portrait Gallery (London). *G. F. Watts: the Hall of Fame; portraits of his famous contemporaries*. London, HMSO, 1975.

13394. Schleinitz, Otto von. *George Frederick Watts*. Bielefeld/Leipzig, Velhagen & Klasing, 1904. (Künstler-Monographien, 73).

13395. Spielmann, Marion H. *The works of Mr. George F. Watts, R. A., with a complete catalogue of his pictures*. [London], Pall Mall Gazette, 1886. (Pall Mall Gazette Extra, 22).

13396. Watts, Mary S. *George Frederick Watts*. 3 v. London, Macmillan, 1912.

Waugh, Frederick Judd, 1861–1940

13397. Havens, George R. *Frederick J. Waugh, American marine painter*. Orono, Maine, University of Maine Press, 1969. (University of Maine Studies, 89).

Wayne, June, 1918–

13398. Baskett, Mary W. *The art of June Wayne*. New York, Abrams, 1969.

Weber, Andreas Paul, 1893–1981

13399. Dorsch, Klaus. *A. Paul Weber: Werkverzeichnis der Lithographien*. Lübeck, Kunsthaus Lübeck, 1991.

13400. Noll, Thomas. *Zwischen den Stühlen: A. Paul Weber—Britische Bilder und 'Leviathan'-Reihe: Studien zum Werk des Künstlers im Dritten Reich*. Münster, Lit., [1993]. (Göttinger Beiträge zur Kunstgeschichte, 1–2).

13401. Privates A. Paul Weber-Archiv. *Sascha Schneider, A. Paul Weber*. [Vaihingen Ensingen, s.n., 1986]. (Schriftenreihe des Privaten A. Paul Weber-Archivs Vaihingen-Ensingen, 3).

13402. Reinhardt, Georg, ed. *A. Paul Weber: das graphische Werk, 1930–1978; Handzeichnungen, Lithographien*. [Based on an exhibition held at the Rheinisches Landesmuseum, Bonn, October 26–December 10, 1978]. München, Schirmer-Mosel, 1980. (CR).

13403. Schartel, Werner, ed. *A. Paul Weber: das anti-faschistische Werk*. Berlin/Hamburg, Elefanten Press, 1977.

13404. Schumacher, Helmut. *A. Paul Weber: Werkverzeichnis der Gebrauchsgraphik*. Lübeck, Kunsthaus Lübeck, 1990. (CR).

13405. Weber, Andreas Paul. *A. Paul Weber, 1893–1980: Kritische Graphik und Britische Bilder: Retrospektive der Griffelkunst*. Herausgegeben von Erich Arp. Hamburg, Christians Verlag, 1985.

13406. Weber, Andreas Paul. *A. Paul Weber, Waldbilder: Zeichnungen aus dem Gefängnis 1937*. Herausgegeben von Hermann Krämer. Hamburg, Christians, 1985.

13407. Wolandt, Gerd. *Bild und Wort: Überlegungen zum Werk A. Paul Webers*. Hamburg, Christian, 1977. (Schriften der A. Paul Weber-Gesellschaft, 1).

Weber, Max, 1881–1961

13408. Goodrich, Lloyd. *Max Weber*. New York, Macmillan, 1949.

13409. Rubenstein, Daryl R. *Max Weber: a catalogue raisonné of his graphic work*. Foreword by Alan Fern. Chicago, University of Chicago Press, 1980. (CR).

13410. Weber, Max. *Essays on art*. New York, Rudge, 1916.

13411. ———. *Max Weber: the cubist decade, 1910–1920*. Essay by Percy North. Introduction by Susan Krane. Atlanta, High Museum of Art, 1991.

13412. Werner, Alfred. *Max Weber*. New York, Abrams, 1975.

Wedgwood, Josiah, 1730–1795 see also Stubbs, George

13413. Burton, Anthony. *Josiah Wedgwood, a biography*. New York, Stein and Day, 1976.

13414. Burton, William. *Josiah Wedgwood and his pottery*. London, Cassell, 1922.

13415. Church, Arthur H. *Josiah Wedgwood, master-potter*. London, Seeley, 1894. (Portfolio Artistic Monographs, 3).

13416. Jewitt, Llewellynn. *The Wedgwoods: being a life of Josiah Wedgwood with notices of his works and their productions*. London, Virtue, 1865.

13417. Meteyard, Eliza. *The life of Josiah Wedgwood, from his private correspondence and family papers*. With an introductory sketch of the art of pottery in England. 2 v. London, Hurst and Blackett, 1865.

13418. ———. *Wedgwood and his works: a selection of his plaques, cameos, medallions, vases, etc*. London, Bell and Daldy, 1873.

13419. National Portrait Gallery, Smithsonian Institution (Washington, D.C.). *Wedgwood portraits and the American Revolution*. Washington, D.C., Smithsonian Institution, 1976.

13420. Rathbone, Frederick. *Old Wedgwood: the decorative or artistic ceramic work in colour and relief*. London, Quaritch, 1898.

13421. Reilly, Robin and Savage, George. *Wedgwood: the portrait medallions*. London, Barrie & Jenkins, 1973. (CR).

13422. Science Museum (London). *Josiah Wedgwood: the arts and sciences united*. 21 March to 24 September 1978. Barlaston, England, Wedgwood, 1978.

13423. Smiles, Samuel. *Josiah Wedgwood, his personal history.* New York, Harper, 1895.

13424. Wedgwood, Josiah. *Selected letters.* Edited by Ann Finer and George Savage. New York, Born & Hawes, 1965.

13425. Wedgwood, Julia. *The personal life of Josiah Wedgwood, the potter.* Revised and edited by C. H. Herford. London, Macmillan, 1915.

Weiditz, Hans, 16th c. *see also* Master of Petrarch

13426. Fraenger, Wilhelm. *Hans Weiditz und Sebastian Brandt. Leipzig, Stubenrauch, 1930. (Denkmale der Volkskunst, 2).*

13427. Röttinger, Heinrich. *Hans Weiditz, der Petrarkameister.* Strassburg, Heitz, 1904. (Studien zur deutschen Kunstgeschichte, 50).

13428. Scheidig, Walther. *Die Holzschnitte des Petrarcameisters.* Berlin, Henschel, 1955.

Weinbrenner, Friedrich, 1766–1826

13429. Koebel, Max. *Friedrich Weinbrenner.* Berlin, Wasmuth, [1920].

13430. Lankheit, Klaus. *Friedrich Weinbrenner und der Denkmalskult um 1800.* Basel/Stuttgart, Birkhäuser, 1979. (Geschichte und Theorie der Architektur, 21).

13431. Staatliche Kunsthalle Karlsruhe. *Friedrich Weinbrenner, 1766–1826; eine Ausstellung des Instituts für Baugeschichte an der Universität Karlsruhe.* 29. Oktober 1977– 15. Januar 1978. Karlsruhe, Institut für Baugeschichte an der Universität Karlsruhe, 1977.

13432. Valdenaire, Arthur. *Friedrich Weinbrenner, sein Leben und seine Bauten.* Karlsruhe, Druck, 1919. (New eds.: Karlsruhe, C. F. Müller, 1976/1985).

13433. Weinbrenner, Friedrich. *Briefe und Aufsätze.* Herausgegeben von Arthur Valdenaire. Karlsruhe, Braun, 1926.

13434. ———. *Denkwürdigkeiten.* Herausgegeben und bearbeitet von Arthur von Schneider. Karlsruhe, Braun, 1958.

13435. ———. *Friedrich Weinbrenner, architect of Karlsruhe: a catalogue of the drawings in the Architectural Archives of the University of Pennsylvania.* Ed. by David B. Brownlee. Philadelphia, University of Pennsylvania Press, 1986.

Weir, Julian Alden, 1852–1919

13436. Cummings, Hildegard, Fusscas, Helen K., Larkin, Susan G. *J. Alden Weir: a place of his own.* Storrs, William Benton Museum of Art, University of Connecticut, 1991.

13437. Flint, Janet A. *J. Alden Weir, an American printmaker, 1852–1919.* [Published in con-

junction with an exhibition at the National Collection of Fine Arts, Smithsonian Institution, Washington, D.C., May 5–June 4, 1972, and other places]. Provo, Utah, Brigham Young University Press, 1972.

13438. Phillips, Duncan, et al. *Julian Alden Weir, an appreciation of his life and works.* New York, Century Club, 1921.

13439. Young, Dorothy W. *The life and letters of J. Alden Weir.* Edited with an introduction by Lawrence W. Chisholm. New Haven, Yale University Press, 1960.

13440. Zimmerman, Agnes. *An essay towards a catalogue raisonné of the etchings, dry-points, and lithographs of Julian Alden Weir.* New York, Metropolitan Museum of Art, 1923. (Metropolitan Museum of Art papers, I:2). (CR).

Welch, Lucy Elizabeth Kemp *see* Kemp-Welch, Lucy Elizabeth

Wên Chê Ng-Ming, 1470–1559

13441. Chih-yung, Chu Sui-liang, Wen, Cheng-Ming. *Chi'ien tzu wen.* Pei-ching, Pei-ching ch'u pan she, Hsin hua shu tien Pei-ching fa hsing so fa hsing, 1991.

13442. Chou, Tao-chen, pien chu. *Wen Cheng-ming shu hua chien piao.* Pei-ching, Jen min mei shu ch'u pan she, Hsin hua shu tien Pei-ching fa hsing so fa hsing, 1985.

13443. Dubosc, Jean-Pierre. *Wen Tcheng-Ming et son école.* Lausanne, Bridel, 1961.

13444. University of Michigan Museum of Art (Ann Arbor, Mich.). *The art of Wen Cheng-Ming (1470–1559).* January 25–February 29, 1976. [Text by Richard Edwards, with an essay by Anne de Coursey Clapp]. Ann Arbor, Mich., University of Michigan Museum of Art, 1976.

Wengenroth, Stow, 1906–1978

13445. McCord, David. *Stow Wengenroth's New England.* Barre, Mass., Barre Publishers, 1969.

13446. Stuckey, Ronald and Stuckey, Joan. *The lithographs of Stow Wengenroth, 1931– 1972.* Barre, Mass., Barre Publishers, 1974. (CR).

13447. ———. *Stow Wengenroth's lithographs: a supplement.* With an essay by Albert Reese. Huntington, N.Y., Black Oaks Publishers, 1982. (CR).

13448. Wengenroth, Stow. *Making a lithograph.* London, The Studio, 1936.

Werefkin, Marianne, 1860–1938

13449. Fathke, Bernd. *Marianne Werefkin, Leben und Werk, 1860–1938.* München, Prestel, 1988.

13450. Hahl-Koch, Jelena. *Marianne Werefkin und der russische Symbolismus: Studien zur Ästhetik und Kunsttheorie.* München, Sagner, 1967. (Slavistische Beiträge, 24).

13451. Museum Wiesbaden. *Marianne Werefkin: Gemälde und Skizzen.* [September 28–November 23, 1980]. Wiesbaden, Museum Wiesbaden, 1980.

13452. Werefkin, Marianne. *Briefe an einen Unbekannten, 1901–1905.* Herausgegeben von Clemens Weiler. Köln, DuMont Schauberg, 1960.

Werff, Adriaen van der, 1659–1722

13453. Gaehtgens, Barbara. *Adriaen van der Werff, 1659–1722.* München, Deutscher Kunstverlag, [1987]. (CR).

13454. Werff, Adriaen van der. *Adriaen van der Werff, Kralingen 1659–1722 Rotterdam*: [tentoonstelling] Historisch Museum, Rotterdam, 3 september–1 november, 1973. Amsterdam, The Museum, 1973.

Werner, Anton von, 1843–1915

13455. Bartmann, Dominik. *Anton von Werner: zur Kunst und Kunstpolitik im Deutschen Kaiserreich.* Berlin, Deutscher Verlag für Kunstwissenschaft, 1985.

13456. Rosenberg, Adolf. *A. von Werner.* Bielefeld/Leipzig, Velhagen & Klasing, 1895. (Künstler-Monographien, 9).

13457. Werner, Anton von. *Anton von Werner: Geschichte in Bildern.* Herausgegeben von Dominik Bartmann. Mit Beiträgen von Dominik Bartmann . . . [et al.]. München, Hirmir, 1993.

Wesselmann, Tom, 1931–

13458. Ileana Sonnabend (Gallery), (Paris). *Tom Wesselman.* Novembre 1966. [Prèface par Jean-Louis Ferrier]. Paris, Galerie I. Sonnabend, 1966.

13459. Wesselmann, Tom. *Tom Wesselmann.* Ed. by Slim Stealingworth. New York, Abbeville Press, 1980.

13460. ———. *Wesselmann.* New York, Sidney Janis Gallery, 1983.

West, Benjamin, 1738–1820
Raphael Lamar, 1769–1850

13461. Abrams, Ann Uhry. *The valiant hero: Benjamin West and grand-style history painting.* Washington, D.C., Smithsonian Institution Press, 1985.

13462. Alberts, Robert C. *Benjamin West, a biography.* Boston, Houghton Mifflin, 1978.

13463. Allentown Art Museum (Allentown, Pa.). *The world of Benjamin West.* [May 1–July 31, 1962]. Allentown, Allentown Art Museum, 1962.

13464. Dillenberger, John. *Benjamin West: the context of his life's work with particular attention to paintings with religious subject matter.* San Antonio, Tex., Trinity University Press, 1977.

13465. Erffa, Helmut von and Staley, Allen. *The paintings of Benjamin West.* New Haven, Yale University Press, 1986. (CR).

13466. Evans, Grose. *Benjamin West and the taste of his times.* Carbondale, Ill., Southern Illinois University Press, 1959.

13467. Galt, John. *The life and studies of Benjamin West.* London, Cadell and Davies, 1816. (Reprinted with an introduction by Nathalia Wright: Gainesville, Florida, Scholar's Facsimiles & Reprints, 1960).

13468. Kraemer, Ruth S. *Drawings by Benjamin West and his son Raphael Lamar West.* New York, Pierpont Morgan Library, 1975. (CR).

13469. Weintraub, Stanley and Ploog, Randy. *Benjamin West drawings from the Historical Society of Pennsylvania, May 31 through September 17, 1987.* University Park, Museum of Art, Penn State, 1987.

13470. West, Benjamin. *Benjamin West, American painter at the English Court: June 4–August 20, 1989.* Baltimore, Baltimore Museum of Art, 1989.

Westmacott, Richard, 1775–1856

13471. Busco, Marie. *Sir Richard Westmacott, sculptor.* Cambridge/New York, Cambridge University Press, 1994.

Weston, Brett, 1911–1993
Edward, 1886–1958

13472. Armitage, Merle. *Brett Weston, photographs.* New York, Weyhe, 1956.

13473. Cravens, R. H. *Brett Weston, photographs from five decades.* Millerton, N.Y., Aperture, 1980.

13474. Maddow, Ben. *Edward Weston, his life and photographs: the definitive volume of his photographic work.* Millerton, N.Y., Aperture, 1979. 2 ed.

13475. Weston, Brett. *Brett Weston, a personal selection.* Intro. by Dody W. Thompson. Carmel, Calif., Photography West Graphics, 1986.

13476. ———. *Voyage of the eye.* Afterword by Beaumont Newhall. Millerton, N.Y., Aperture, 1975. [Rev. ed., with photographs of Hawaii, 1978–1992: New York, Aperture, (1992)].

13477. Weston, Charis W. and Weston, Edward. *California and the West.* New York, Duell, Sloan, and Pearce, 1940.

13478. Weston, Edward. *The daybooks of Edward Weston.* Edited by Nancy Newhall. 2 v. Millerton, N.Y., Aperture, 1973.

13479. ———. *Edward Weston.* With an essay by R.H. Cravens. New York, Aperture, 1988. (Aperture masters of photography, 7).

13480. ———. *Edward Weston omnibus: a critical anthology.* Ed. and with intro.'s by Beaumont Newhall and Amy Conger. Salt Lake City, G.M. Smith/Peregrine Smith Books, 1984.

13481. ———. *EW:100: centennial essays in honor of Edward Weston.* Ed. by Peter C. Bunnell, David Featherstone. Contributors, Robert Adams . . . [et al.]. Carmel, Calif., Friends of Photography, 1986.

13482. ———. *The Heritage of Edward Weston: an exhibition, a tribute.* An invitational exhibition sponsored by the Friends of the Museum of Art, University of Oregon. January 12–February 7, 1965. Organized by Gerald H. Robinson . . . and Mark Clarke. Eugene, University of Oregon Press, 1965.

Weyden, Roger van der, c. 1400–1464 *see also* Master of Flemalle

13483. Beenken, Hermann. *Rogier van der Weyden.* München, Bruckmann, 1951.

13484. Burger, Willy. *Roger van der Weyden.* Leipzig, Hiersemann, 1923.

13485. Campbell, Lorne. *Van der Weyden.* New York, Harper & Row, 1980.

13486. City Museum of Brussels. *Rogier van der Weyden: official painter to the city of Brussels.* October 6–November 18, 1979. Brussels, City Museum of Brussels, 1979.

13487. Davies, Martin. *Rogier van der Weyden; an essay with a critical catalogue of paintings assigned to him and to Robert Campin.* London, Phaidon, 1972. (CR).

13488. Dijkstra Jeltje. *Origineel en kopie: een onderzoek naar de navolging van de Meester van Flémalle en Rogier van der Weyden.* [Amsterdam?, J. Dijkstra, 1990?].

13489. Gondinet-Wallstein, Eliane. *Un retable pour l'au-delà le Jugement dernier de Rogier van der Weyden, Hôtel-Dieu de Beaune.* Photographies de Jacques Michot. Paris, Mame, 1990.

13490. Drestrée, Jules. *Roger de la Pasture van der Weyden.* 2 v. Paris/Bruxelles, van Oest, 1930.

13491. Hasse, Carl. *Roger van der Weyden und Roger van Brügge.* Strassburg, Heitz, 1905. (Zur Kunstgeschichte des Auslandes, 30).

13492. Koninklijke Academie voor Wetenschappen, Letteren en Schone Kunsten van België. *Rogier van der Weyden en zijn tijd: internationael colloquium, 11–12 juni 1964.* [Text alternatingly in French or Dutch]. Brussel, Paleis der Academiën, 1974.

13493. Lafond, Paul. *Roger van der Weyden.* Bruxelles, van Oest, 1912.

13494. Sonkes, Micheline. *Dessins du XVe siècle: groupe van der Weyden; essai de catalogue des originaux du maître, des copies, et des dessins anonymes inspirés par son style.* Bruxelles, Centre National du Recherches Primitifs Flamands, 1969. (Les primitifs flamands: contributions à l'étude des primitifs flamands, 5).

Whistler, James Abbot McNeill, 1834–1903

13495. Art Institute of Chicago. *James McNeill Whistler.* January 13–February 25, 1968. Chicago, Art Institute of Chicago, 1968.

13496. Arts Council Gallery (London). *James McNeill Whistler.* September 1–24, 1960. London, Arts Council of Great Britain, 1960.

13497. Bacher, Otto H. *With Whistler in Venice.* New York, Century, 1908.

13498. Barbier, Carl P., ed. *Correspondance Mallarmé-Whistler.* Paris, Nizet, 1964.

13499. Cabanne, Pierre. *Whistler.* Trans. by Nicholas Max Jennings. New York, Crown, 1985.

13500. Cary, Elisabeth L. *The works of James McNeill Whistler.* New York, Moffat, 1907.

13501. Cheney, Liana DeGirolami and Marks, Paul G., eds. *The Whistler papers.* Lowell, Mass., Whistler House Museum, 1986.

13502. Dorment, Richard, MacDonald, Margaret F. *James McNeill Whistler.* With contributions by Nicolai Cikovsky, Jr., Ruth Fine, Geneviève Lacambre. New York, H.N. Abrams, 1995.

13503. Duret, Théodore. *Whistler.* Trans. by Frank Rutter. Philadelphia, Lippincott, 1917.

13504. Eddy, Arthur J. *Recollections and impressions of James A. McNeill Whistler.* Philadelphia/London, Lippincott, 1903.

13505. Fine, Ruth E. *James McNeill Whistler: a reexamination.* Washington, National Gallery of Art; Hanover, distributed by the University Press of New England, 1987. (Studies in the history of art, v. 19, Symposium papers, 6).

13506. Fleming, Gordon H. *James Abbott McNeil Whistler: a life.* New York, St. Martin's Press, 1991.

13507. ———. *The young Whistler.* London, Allen & Unwin, 1978.

13508. Getscher, Robert H., Marks, Paul G. *James McNeill Whistler and John Singer Sargent: two annotated bibliographies.* New York, Garland, 1986. (Garland reference library of the humanities, 467).

13509. Gregory, Horace. *The world of James McNeill Whistler.* New York, Nelson, 1959.

13510. Hartmann, Sadakichi. *The Whistler book: a monograph on the life and position in art of James McNeill Whistler.* Boston, Page, 1910.

13511. Holden, Donald. *Whistler landscapes and seascapes.* New York, Watson-Guptill, 1969.

13512. Honour, Hugh and Fleming, John. *The Venetian hours of Henry James, Whistler and Sargent.* London, Walker, 1991.

13513. Kennedy, Edward G. *The etched work of Whistler.* 4 v. New York, Grolier Club, 1910. (CR).

13514. Laver, James. *Whistler.* London, Faber, 1930.

13515. Levy, Mervyn. *Whistler lithographs: an illustrated catalogue raisonné.* With an essay on Whistler the printmaker by Allen Staley. London, Jupiter, 1975. (CR).

13516. Lochnan, Katharine Jordan. *Whistler's etchings and the sources of his etching style, 1855–1880.* New York, Garland Pub., 1988.

13517. Mansfield, Howard. *A descriptive catalogue of the etchings and dry-points of James Abbott McNeill Whistler.* Chicago, Caxton Club, 1909. (CR).

13518. McMullen, Roy. *Victorian outsider: a biography of J. A. M. Whistler.* New York, Dutton, 1973.

13519. McNamara, Carole and Siewert, John. *Whistler, prosaic views, poetic vision: works on paper from the University of Michigan Museum of Art.* New York, Thames and Hudson; Ann Arbor, University of Michigan Museum of Art, 1994.

13520. Menpes, Mortimer. *Whistler as I knew him.* London, Black, 1904.

13521. Merrill, Linda. *A pot of paint: aesthetics on trial in Whistler v. Ruskin.* Washington, Smithsonian Institution Press in collaboration with the Freer Gallery of Art, Smithsonian Institution, 1992.

13522. Montesquiou, Robert de. *La chauve-souris et le papillon: correspondence Montesquiou-Whistler.* Editée par Joy Newton. Glasgow, University of Glasgow French and German Publications, 1990.

13523. Pearson, Hesketh. *The man Whistler.* London, Methuen, 1952.

13524. Pennell, Elizabeth R. *Whistler the friend.* Philadelphia/London, Lippincott, 1930.

13525. Pennell, Elizabeth R. and Pennell, Joseph. *The life of James McNeill Whistler.* 2 v. Philadelphia, Lippincott, 1908.

13526. ———. *The Whistler journal.* Philadelphia, Lippincott, 1921.

13527. Pocock, Tom. *Chelsea Reach: the brutal friendship of Whistler and Walter Greaves.* London, Hodder and Stoughton, 1970.

13528. Prideaux, Tom. *The world of Whistler, 1834–1903.* New York, Time-Life, 1970.

13529. Rutter, Frank V. *James McNeill Whistler: an estimate & a biography.* New York, Kennerley, 1911.

13530. Salaman, Malcolm. *James McNeill Whistler.* 2 v. London, The Studio, 1927/1932. (Modern Masters of Etching, 13/32).

13531. Seitz, Don C. *Whistler stories.* New York, Harper, 1913.

13532. ———. *Writings by and about James Abbott McNeill Whistler, a bibliography.* Edinburgh, Schulze, 1910.

13533. Singer, Hans W. *James McNeill Whistler.* New York, Scribner, 1905. (Langham Series of Art Monographs, 12).

13534. Sutton, Denys. *James McNeill Whistler: paintings, etchings, pastels & watercolours.* London, Phaidon, 1966.

13535. ———. *Nocturne: the art of James McNeill Whistler.* London, Country Life, 1963.

13536. Taylor, Hilary. *James McNeill Whistler.* New York, Putnam, 1978.

13537. Walker, John. *James McNeill Whistler.* New York, H.N. Abrams; Washington, D.C., National Museum of American Art, Smithsonian Institution, 1987.

13538. Way, Thomas R. *Memories of James McNeill Whistler, the artist.* London, Lane, 1912.

13539. ———. *Mr. Whistler's lithographs: the catalogue.* London, Bell, 1896. (CR). (Rev. ed.: 1905).

13540. ——— and Dennis, G. R. *The art of James McNeill Whistler, an appreciation.* London, Bell, 1903.

13541. Wedmore, Frederick. *Whistler's etchings: a study and a catalogue.* London, Thibadeau, 1886. (Rev. ed.: London, Colnaghi, 1899).

13542. Weintraub, Stanley. *Whistler, a biography.* New York, Weybright and Talley, 1974.

13543. Whistler, James A. *Eden versus Whistler: the baronet & the butterfly.* Paris, May, 1899.

13544. ———. *The gentle art of making enemies.* Edited by Sheridan Ford. Paris, Delabrosse, 1890.

13545. ———. *James Abbott McNeill Whistler, pastels.* Intro. and commentaries by Robert H. Getscher. New York, G. Braziller, 1991.

13546. ———. *Mr. Whistler's Ten o'clock.* London, Chatto & Windus, 1888.

13547. ———. *Whistler: a retrospective.* Ed. by Robin Spencer. New York, H. Lauter Levin, distributed by Macmillan, 1989.

13548. ———. *Whistler v. Ruskin: art & art critics.* London, Chatto & Windus, 1878.

13549. Wildenstein Gallery (New York). *From Realism to Symbolism: Whistler and his world, an exhibition organized by the Department of Art History and Archaeology of Columbia University.* March 4–April 3, 1971. New York, Trustees of Columbia University, 1971.

13550. Young, Andrew M., et al. *The paintings of James McNeill Whistler.* 2 v. New Haven/London, Yale University Press, 1980. (CR).

Whistler, Rex, 1905–1944

13551. Whistler, Laurence. *The laughter and the urn: the life of Rex Whistler.* London, Weidenfeld and Nicolson, 1985.

13552. Whistler, Rex. *Rex Whistler, 1905–1944: a memorial exhibition.* London, The Arts Council, 1960.

White, Charles Wilbert, 1918–1979

13553. Horowitz, Benjamin. *Images of dignity: the drawings of Charles White.* Foreword by Harry Belafonte; introduction by James Porter. Los Angeles, Ward Ritchie, 1967.

White, Clarence H., 1871–1925

13554. Delaware Art Museum (Wilmington, Del.). *Symbolism of light: the photographs of Clarence H. White.* April 15–May 22, 1977. Wilmington, Delaware Art Museum, 1977.

13555. White, Maynard P. *Clarence H. White.* Millerton, N.Y., Aperture, 1979. (Aperture History of Photography, 11).

White, Minor, 1908–1976

13556. Bunnell, Peter C. *Minor White, the eye that shapes.* With Maria B. Pellerano and Joseph B. Rauch. Princeton, Art Museum, Princeton University; Boston, in association with Bulfinch Press, 1989.

13557. Hall, James B., ed. *Minor White: rites and passages; his photographs accompanied by excerpts from his diaries and letters.* Millerton, N.Y., Aperture, 1978.

13558. White, Minor. *Mirrors, messages, manifestations.* Millerton, N.Y., Aperture, 1969.

13559. ———. *Zone system manual.* Hastings-on-Hudson, Morgan & Morgan, 1968. (New ed., with additional material by Richard Zakia and Peter Lorenz: Dobbs Ferry, Morgan & Morgan, 1976).

White, Stanford, 1853–1906

13560. Baldwin, Charles C. *Stanford White.* New York, Dodd Mead, 1931. (Reprint: New York, Da Capo Press, 1976).

13561. Baker, Paul R. *Stanny: the gilded life of Stanford White.* New York, Free Press; London, Collier Macmillan, 1989.

13562. Lowe, David. *Stanford White's New York.* New York, Doubleday, 1992.

13563. Wodehouse, Lawrence. *White of McKim, Mead, and White.* New York, Garland, 1988.

Whittredge, Worthington, 1820–1910

13564. Janson, Anthony F. *Worthington Whittredge.* Cambridge/New York, Cambridge University Press, 1989.

Wiertz, Antoine, 1806–1865

13565. Colleye, Hubert. *Antoine Wiertz.* Bruxelles, La Renaissance du Livre, 1957.

13566. Fierens-Gevaert, Hippolyte. *Antoine Wiertz.* Turnhout, Brepols, 1920.

13567. Sikes, Wert, et al. *Catalogue of the Wiertz-Museum.* Brussels, Weissenbruch, 1899.

13568. Terlinden, Charles. *La correspondance d'Antoine Wiertz, Prix de Rome, au cours de son voyage d'Italie.* Bruxelles/Rome, Academia Belgica, 1953. (Bibliothèque de l'Institut Historique Belge de Rome, 5).

Wiligelmus, fl. 1099–1110

13569. Armandi, Marina . . . [et al.], redazione del catalogo. *Lanfranco e Wiligelmo: Il Duomo di Modena.* Modena, Panini, [1984].

13570. Castelnuovo, Enrico; Peroni, Adriano; Settis, Salvatore, comitato scientifico. *Wiligelmo e Lanfranco nell'Europa romanica.* Modena, Panini, [1989].

13571. Francovich, Géza de. *Wiligelmo da Modena e gli inizi della scultura romanica in Francia e in Spagna.* Roma, Istituto Poligrafico dello Stato Libreria, 1940.

13572. Quintavalle, Arturo Carlo. *Wiligelmo e Matilde: l'officina romanica.* Catalogo delle opere a cura di Arturo Calzona, Arturo Carlo Quintavalle. Con schede di Gloria Bianchino, Maria Pia Branchi, Giorgio Voltini. Le schede dei codici di San Benedetto Po sono di Giuseppa Z. Zanichelli. Milano, Electa, 1991.

13573. Salvini, Roberto. *Wiligelmo e le origini della scultura romanica.* Milano, Martello, 1956.

Wilkie, David, 1785–1841

13574. [Anonymous]. *The Wilkie Gallery: a selection of the best pictures of the late Sir David Wilkie, R. A., with notices biographical and critical.* London/New York, Virtue, [1848].

13575. Brown, David Blayney. *Sir David Wilkie, drawings and sketches in the Ashmolean Museum.* London, Morton Morris in association with the Ashmolean Museum, Oxford, 1985.

13576. Cunningham, Allan. *The life of Sir David Wilkie.* 3 v. London, Murray, 1843.

13577. Errington, Lindsay. *David Wilkie, 1785–1841.* Edinburgh, National Galleries of Scotland, 1988. (Scottish masters, 10).

13578. Gower, Ronald S. *Sir David Wilkie.* London, Bell, 1902.

13579. Heaton, Mrs. Charles. *The great works of Sir David Wilkie; twenty-six photographs with a descriptive account of the pictures and a memoir of the artist.* London, Bell and Daldy, 1868.

13580. Mollett, John W. *Sir David Wilkie.* New York, Scribner and Welford/London, Sampson Low, 1881.

13581. Pinnington, Edward. *Sir David Wilkie and the Scots school of painters.* Edinburgh/London, Oliphant, Anderson & Ferrier, [1900]. (Famous Scots).

Willink, Albert Carel, 1900–1983

13582. Jaffé, Hans L. *Willink*. Amsterdam, Meulenhoff/Landshoff, 1979. (CR).

13583. Willink, Carel. *Willinks kopstukken: portretten geschilderd door Carel Willink*: [tentoonstelling] Singer Museum, Laren, 8 februari 1986–6 april 1986, Museum Van Bommel-Van Dam, Venlo, 18 april 1986–8 juni 1986. Interviews, Hans Melissen en Loek Brons. Research, samenstelling en eindredactie, Loek Brons. Amsterdam, G. Kemme, 1986.

Wilson, Richard, 1714–1782

13584. Bury, Adrian. *Richard Wilson, the grand classic*. Leigh-on-Sea, Lewis, 1947.

13585. Constable, William G. *Richard Wilson*. Cambridge, Mass., Harvard University Press, 1953.

13586. Fletcher, Beaumont. *Richard Wilson, R. A.* London, Scott, 1908.

13587. Ford, Brinsley. *The drawings of Richard Wilson*. London, Faber, 1950.

13588. Solkin, David H. *Richard Wilson: the landscape of reaction*. London, Tate Gallery, 1982.

13589. Sutton, Denys, ed. *An Italian sketchbook by Richard Wilson, R. A.* With a catalogue by Ann Clements. 2 v. London, Paul Mellon Foundation for British Art, 1968.

13590. Wright, Thomas. *Some account of the life of Richard Wilson, R. A.* London, Longmans, 1824.

Winter, Fritz, 1905–1976

13591. Buchner, Joachim. *Fritz Winter*. Recklinghausen, Bongers, 1963. (Monographien zur rheinisch-westfälischen Kunst der Gegenwart, 25).

13592. Keller, Horst. *Fritz Winter*. München, Bruckmann, 1976.

13594. Kunstverein Hannover. *Fritz Winter zum 60. Geburtstag*. 16. Januar–13. Februar 1966. Hannover, Kunstverein Hannover, 1966.

13594. Lohberg, Gabriele. *Fritz Winter, Leben und Werk: mit Werkverzeichnis der Gemälde und einem Anhang der sonstigen Techniken*. München, Bruckmann, 1986. (CR).

13595. Westfälisches Landesmuseum für Kunst und Kulturgeschichte (Münster). *Fritz Winter: Triebkräfte der Erde*. 8. November 1981–10. Januar 1982. Münster, Westfälisches Landesmuseum, [1981].

13596. Winter, Fritz. *Fritz Winter*. [Herausgeber, Johann-Karl Schmidt. Ausstellung und Katalog, Johann-Karl Schmidt, Ursula Zeller]. Stuttgart, G. Hatje, 1990.

Winterhalter, Franz Xaver, 1805–1873

13597. Ormond, Richard and Blackett-Ord, Carol. *Franz Xaver Winterhalter and the courts of Europe 1830–70*. With contributions by Susan Foister . . . [et al.]. London, National Portrait Gallery, 1987.

Wittel, Gaspar Adriaenszoon van, 1653–1736

13598. Briganti, Giuliano. *Caspar van Wittel e l'origine della veduta settecentesca*. Roma, Bozzi, 1966.

13599. Lorenzetti, Constanza. *Gaspare Vanvitelli*. Milano, Treves, 1934.

13600. Vitzthum, Walter. *Drawings by Gaspar van Wittel (1652/53–1736) from Neapolitan collections*. Trans. and ed. by Catherine Johnston. [Text in English and French; published in conjunction with an exhibition at the National Gallery of Canada, Ottawa]. Ottawa, National Gallery of Canada, 1977.

13601. Wittel, Gaspar van. *Gaspare Vanvitelli (1652/53–1736): Zeichnungen und Aquarelle*: Ausstellung in der Neuen Pinakothek, 2. März bis 30. April 1983. München, Staatliche Graphische Sammlung, 1983.

Witten, Hans, fl. 1501–1512

13602. Fründt, Edith. *Der Bornaer Altar von Hans Witten*. Berlin, Union, 1975.

13603. Hentschel, Walter. *Hans Witten, der Meister H. W.* Leipzig, Seemann, 1938.

Witz, Konrad, 1400–1446

13604. Barrucand, Marianne. *Le retable du miroir du salut dans l'oeuvre de Konrad Witz*. Genève, Droz, 1972.

13605. Escherich, Mela. *Konrad Witz*. Strassburg, Heitz, 1916. (Studien zur deutschen Kunstgeschichte, 183).

13606. Feldges-Henning, Uta. *Werkstatt und Nachfolge des Konrad Witz: ein Beitrag zur Geschichte der Basler Malerei des 15. Jahrhunderts*. Basel, Werner & Bischoff, 1968.

13607. Gantner, Joseph. *Konrad Witz*. Wien, Schroll, 1942.

13608. Ganz, Paul L. *Meister Konrad Witz von Rottweil*. Bern, Urs Graf, 1947.

13609. Graber, Hans. *Konrad Witz*. Basel, Schwabe, 1922.

13610. Meng-Koehler, Mathilde. *Die Bilder des Konrad Witz und ihre Quellen*. Basel, Holbein, 1947.

13611. Miegroet, Hans J. van. *De invloed van de vroege Nederlandse schilderkunst in de eerste helft van de 15de eeue op Konrad Witz*. Brussel, AWLsK, 1986. (Verhandelingen van de Koninklijke Academie voor Wetenschappen, Letteren en Schone Kunsten van Belgie, Klasse der Schone Kunsten, jaarg. 48, nr. 42).

13612. Ueberwasser, Walter. *Konrad Witz*. Basel,

Cratander, [1938]. (Baseler Kunstbücher, 1).

13613. Wendland, Hans. *Konrad Witz: Gemäldestudien*. Basel, Schwabe, 1924.

Wols (Alfred Otto Wolfgang Schulze), 1913–1951

13614. Collin, Bernard. *Wols avec une loupe*. Paris, Fourbis, 1990.

13615. Dorfles, Gillo. *Wols*. Milano, All'Insegna del Pesce d'Oro, 1958. (Nuova serie illustrata, 1).

13616. Frankfurter Kunstverein. *Wols: Gemälde, Aquarelle, Zeichnungen, Fotos*. 20. November 1965 bis 2. Januar 1966. Frankfurt a.M., Kunstverein, 1965.

13617. Glozer, Laszlo. *Wols: Photograph*. [Published in conjunction with an exhibition at the Kestner-Gesellschaft Hannover, June 30–August 14, 1978]. Hannover, Kestner-Gesellschaft, 1978. (Katalog 3/1978).

13618. Goethe-Institut London. *Wols: drawings and water-colours*. 17 May–29 June 1985. [Exhibition organized, catalogue and text, Ewald Rathke. Trans. by Anthony Vivis and Goethe-Institut London]. London, Goethe-Institut London; Köln, Vertrieb, Buchhandlung Walther König, 1985.

13619. Haftmann, Werner. *Wols Aufzeichnungen*. Köln, DuMont Schauberg, 1963.

13620. Nationalgalerie Berlin. *Wols, 1913–1951: Gemälde, Aquarelle, Zeichnungen*. 13. September–5. November 1973. Berlin, Nationalgalerie Berlin, 1973.

13621. Wols. *Wols: Bilder, Aquarelle, Zeichnungen, Photographien, Druckgraphik*: Kunsthaus Zürich, 24. November 1989 bis 11. Februar 1990, Kunstsammlung Nordrhein-Westfalen, Düsseldorf, 31. Marz bis 27. Mai 1990. [Katalogredaktion, Marianne Karabelnik-Matta. Mitarbeit, Theres Abbt. Ubersetzungen, Theres Abbt, Marianne Karabelnik-Matta, Dieter Portmann]. Zürich, Kunsthaus Zürich, 1989.

Wolvens, Henri-Victor, 1894–1977

13622. Bussche, Willy van den. *Henri-Victor Wolvens, 1894–1977*. Bruges, Stichting Kunstboek, 1994.

Wood, Grant, 1892–1942 *see also* Benton, Thomas Hart and Curry, John Steuart

13623. Brown, Hazel E. *Grant Wood and Marvin Cone: artists of an era*. Ames, Iowa, Iowa State University Press, 1972.

13624. Cole, Sylvan, Jr. *Grant Wood: the lithographs: a catalogue raisonné*. Ed. by Susan Teller. New York, Associated American Artists, 1984. (CR).

13625. Corn, Wanda M. *Grant Wood: the regionalist vision*. [Published in conjunction with an

exhibition at the Whitney Museum for American Art, New York, June 16–September 4, 1983, and other places]. New Haven/London, Yale University Press, 1983.

13626. Dennis, James M. *Grant Wood: a study in American art and culture*. New York, Viking, 1975.

13627. Garwood, Darrell. *Artist in Iowa: a life of Grant Wood*. New York, Norton, 1944.

13628. Liffring-Zug, Joan, ed. *This is Grant Wood country*. Davenport, Iowa, Davenport Municipal Art Gallery, 1977.

Wotruba, Fritz, 1907–1975

13629. Akademie der bildenden Künste in Wien. *Wotruba: Figur als Widerstand: Bilder und Schriften zu Leben und Werk*. [October 20–December 23, 1977]. Salzburg, Galerie Welz, 1977.

13630. Breicha, Otto, ed. *Um Wotruba: Schriften zum Werk*. Wien, Europa, 1967.

13631. Canetti, Elias. *Fritz Wotruba*. Wien, Rosenbaum, 1955.

13632. Heer, Friedrich. *Fritz Wotruba*. St. Gallen, Erker, 1977. (Künstler unserer Zeit, 19).

13633. Salis, Jean R. de. *Fritz Wotruba*. Zürich, Edition Graphis, 1948.

13634. Smithsonian Institution Traveling Exhibition Service (Washington, D.C.). *The human form: sculpture, prints and drawings [by] Fritz Wotruba*. Washington, D.C., Smithsonian Institution, 1977.

13635. Wotruba, Fritz. *Fritz Wotruba*. [Redaktion, Otto Breicha, Jürg Janett]. St. Gallen, Erker, 1992.

13636. ———. *Überlegungen: Gedanken zur Kunst*. Zürich, Oprecht, 1945.

Wouters, Rik, 1882–1916

13637. Avermaete, Roger. *Rik Wouters*. Bruxelles, Editions L'Arcade, 1962.

13638. Bertrand, Olivier and Hautekeete, Stefaan. *Rik Wouters, jalons d'une vie*. Anvers, Pandora, 1994.

13639. Koninklijk Museum voor Schone Kunsten (Antwerpen). *Rik Wouters*. 7 juli–15 september 1957. [Antwerpen, 1957].

13640. Musée national d'art moderne (Paris). *Rik Wouters*. Octobre–Novembre 1957. [Avant-propos, Jean Cassou]. Paris, les Presses artistiques, 1957.

Wren, Christopher, 1632–1723

13641. Amery, Colin. *Wren's London*. Luton, Bedfordshire, [England], Lennard, 1988.

13642. Beard, Geoffrey W. *The work of Christopher Wren*. Edinburgh, Bartholomew, 1982.

13643. Bennett, J. A. *The mathematical science of Christopher Wren*. Cambridge, Cambridge University Press, 1982.

13644. Bolton, Arthur T. and Hendry, H. Duncan,

eds. *The Wren Society.* 20 v. Oxford, Wren Society, 1924–1943. (CR).

13645. Briggs, Martin S. *Wren, the incomparable.* London, Allen & Unwin, 1953.

13646. Caröe, William D., ed. *Tom tower, Christ Church, Oxford: some letters of Sir Christopher Wren to John Fell.* [With chapters by Herbert H. Turner and Arthur Cochrane]. Oxford, Clarendon Press, 1923.

13647. Downes, Kerry. *The architecture of Wren.* London, Granada, 1982. [Rev. ed., Reading, England, Redhedge, 1988].

13648. Dutton, Ralph. *The age of Wren.* London, Batsford, 1951.

13649. Elmes, James. *Memoirs of the life and works of Sir Christopher Wren.* London, Priestley and Weale, 1823.

13650. Fürst, Viktor. *The architecture of Sir Christopher Wren.* London, Lund Humphries, 1956.

13651. Gray, Ronald D. *Christopher Wren and St. Paul's Cathedral.* Cambridge, Cambridge University Press, 1979.

13652. Hutchinson, Harold F. *Sir Christopher Wren: a biography.* London, Gollancz, 1976.

13653. Little, Bryan D. *Sir Christopher Wren: a historical biography.* London, Hale, 1975.

13654. Milman, Lena. *Sir Christopher Wren.* London, Duckworth, 1908.

13655. Pevsner, Nikolaus. *Christopher Wren, 1632–1723.* New York, Universe, 1960.

13656. Phillimore, Lucy. *Sir Christopher Wren: his family and his times.* London, Kegan Paul, 1881.

13657. Royal Institute of British Architects. *Sir Christopher Wren, A.D. 1632–1723: bicentenary memorial volume.* Ed. by Rudolf Dirks. London, Hodder & Stoughton, 1923.

13658. Sekler, Eduard F. *Wren and his place in European architecture.* New York, Macmillan, 1956.

13659. Summerson, John. *Sir Christopher Wren.* New York, Macmillan, 1953.

13660. Weaver, Lawrence. *Sir Christopher Wren; scientist, scholar, and architect.* London, Country Life, 1923.

13661. Webb, Geoffrey. *Wren.* London, Duckworth, 1937.

13662. Whinney, Margaret. *Wren.* London, Thames and Hudson, 1971.

13663. Whitaker-Wilson, Cecil. *Sir Christopher Wren, his life and times.* London, Methuen, 1932.

13664. Wren, Christopher, [Jr.]. *Parentalia, or memoirs of the family of the Wrens.* London, Osborn, 1750. (New ed., edited by E. J. Enthoven: London, Arnold, 1903).

Wright, Frank Lloyd, 1869–1959

13665. Alofsin, Anthony. *Frank Lloyd Wright—the lost years, 1910–1922: a study of influence.* Chicago, University of Chicago Press, 1993.

13666. Bardeschi, Marco D. *Frank Lloyd Wright.* London, Hamlyn, 1972.

13667. Blake, Peter. *Frank Lloyd Wright, architecture and space.* Baltimore, Penguin, 1964.

13668. Brooks, Harold A. *The Prairie School: Frank Lloyd Wright and his midwest contemporaries.* Toronto, University of Toronto Press, 1972.

13669. ———, comp. *Writings on Wright: selected comments.* Cambridge, Mass./London, MIT Press, 1981.

13670. Brownell, Baker and Wright, Frank L. *Architecture and modern life.* New York, Harper, 1937.

13671. Costantino, Maria. *Frank Lloyd Wright.* New York, Crescent Books, 1991.

13672. Doremus, Thomas. *Frank Lloyd Wright and Le Corbusier: the great dialogue.* New York, Van Nostrand Reinhold, 1985.

13673. Drexler, Arthur. *The drawings of Frank Lloyd Wright.* [Published in conjunction with an exhibition at the Museum of Modern Art, New York, March 14–May 6, 1962]. New York, Horizon/Museum of Modern Art, 1962.

13674. Eaton, Leonard K. *Two Chicago architects and their clients: Frank Lloyd Wright and Howard Van Doren Shaw.* Cambridge, Mass./London, MIT Press, 1969.

13675. Etlin, Richard A. *Frank Lloyd Wright and Le Corbusier: the romantic legacy.* Manchester/New York, Manchester University Press; New York, distributed exclusively in the USA and Canada by St. Martin's Press, 1994.

13676. Farr, Finis. *Frank Lloyd Wright, a biography.* New York, Scribner, 1961.

13677. Gebhard, David. *Romanza: the California architecture of Frank Lloyd Wright.* Text by David Gebhard. Photographs by Scot Zimmerman. San Francisco, Chronicle Books, 1988.

13678. Gill, Brendan. *Many masks: a life of Frank Lloyd Wright.* New York, Putnam, 1987.

13679. Guerrero, Pedro E. *Picturing Wright: an album from Frank Lloyd Wright's photographer.* Foreword by Martin Fuller. San Francisco, Pomegranate Artbooks, 1994.

13680. Guggenheim, Harry T. and Wright, Frank L. *The Solomon R. Guggenheim Museum; architect: Frank Lloyd Wright.* New York, Horizon/Guggenheim Foundation, 1960.

13681. Hamilton, Mary Jane. *Frank Lloyd Wright and the book arts*: an exhibition in the Department of Special Collections, Memorial Library, Fall 1992. Madison, Friends of the University of Wisconsin-Madison Libraries, 1993.

13682. Hanks, David A. *The decorative designs of*

Frank Lloyd Wright. New York, Dutton, 1979.

13683. Hanna, Paul R. and Hanna, Jean S. *Frank Lloyd Wright's Hanna House, the clients' report*. Cambridge, Mass./London, MIT Press, 1981. (Architectural History Foundation Series, 5).

13684. Heinz, Thomas A. *Frank Lloyd Wright*. New York, St. Martin's, 1982.

13685. ———. *Frank Lloyd Wright: glass art*. London, Academy Editions; Berlin, Ernst & Sohn; New York, distributed in U.S. by St. Martin's Press, 1994.

13686. Hertz, David Michael. *Frank Lloyd Wright in word and form*. New York, G.K. Hall, 1995.

13687. Hitchcock, Henry-Russell. *In the nature of materials, 1887–1941. the buildings of Frank Lloyd Wright*. New York, Duell, 1942. (Reprinted, with a new foreword and bibliography by the author: New York, Da Capo, 1975).

13688. Hoffmann, Donald. *Frank Lloyd Wright, architecture and nature*. New York, Dover Publications, 1986.

13689. ———. *Frank Lloyd Wright's Fallingwater: the house and its history*. With an introduction by Edgar Kaufmann, Jr. New York, Dover, 1978.

13690. Jacobs, Herbert. *Building with Frank Lloyd Wright, an illustrated memoir*. With Katherine Jacobs. San Francisco, Chronicle Books, 1978.

13691. James, Cary. *The Imperial Hotel: Frank Lloyd Wright and the architecture of unity*. Rutland, Vt./Tokyo, Tuttle, 1968.

13692. Johnson, Donald Leslie. *Frank Lloyd Wright versus America: the 1930's*. Cambridge, Mass., MIT Press, 1990.

13693. Levine, Neil. The architecture of Frank Lloyd Wright. Princeton, NJ, Princeton University Press, 1996.

13694. Manson, Grant C. *Frank Lloyd Wright to 1910: the first golden age*. With a foreword by Henry-Russell Hitchcock. New York, Reinhold, 1958.

13695. Meehan, Patrick. *Frank Lloyd Wright: a research guide to archival sources*. With a foreword by Adolf K. Placzek. New York/London, Garland, 1983.

13696. Morton, Terry B., ed. *The Pope-Leighey house*. Washington, D.C., Presentation Press, 1983.

13697. Muschamp, Herbert. *Man about town: Frank Lloyd Wright in New York City*. Cambridge, Mass./London, MIT Press, 1983.

13698. Nute, Kevin. *Frank Lloyd Wright and Japan: the role of traditional Japanese art and architecture in the work of Frank Lloyd Wright*. New York, Van Nostrand Reinhold, 1993.

13699. O'Gorman, James F. *Three American architects: Richardson, Sullivan, and Wright, 1865–1915*. Chicago, University of Chicago Press, 1991.

13700. Patterson, Terry L. *Frank Lloyd Wright and the meaning of materials*. New York, Van Nostrand Reinhold, 1994.

13701. Pfeiffer, Bruce Brooks. *Frank Lloyd Wright drawings: masterworks from the Frank Lloyd Wright archives*. New York, Abrams, 1990.

13702. ——— and Nordland, Gerald, eds. *Frank Lloyd Wright in the realm of ideas*. Carbondale, Southern Illinois University Press, 1988.

13703. Scully, Vincent. *Frank Lloyd Wright*. New York, Braziller, 1960.

13704. Secrest, Meryle. *Frank Lloyd Wright*. New York, Alfred A. Knopf, 1992.

13705. Sergeant, John. *Frank Lloyd Wright's usonian houses: the case for organic architecture*. New York, Watson-Guptill, 1976.

13706. Smith, Norris K. *Frank Lloyd Wright: a study in architectural content*. Englewood Cliffs, N.J., Prentice-Hall, 1966. (New ed.: Watkins Glen, N.Y., American Life Foundation, 1979).

13707. Storrer, William A. *The architecture of Frank Lloyd Wright, a complete catalog*. Cambridge, Mass./London, MIT Press, [1974]/1978. (CR).

13708. ———. *The Frank Lloyd Wright companion*. Chicago, University of Chicago Press, 1993.

13709. Sweeney, Robert L. *Frank Lloyd Wright: an annotated bibliography*. Los Angeles, Hennessey & Ingalls, 1978.

13710. Tafel, Edgar. *About Wright: an album of recollections by those who knew Frank Lloyd Wright*. New York, Wiley, 1993.

13711. ———. *Apprentice to genius: years with Frank Lloyd Wright*. New York, McGraw-Hill, 1979.

13712. Twombly, Robert C. *Frank Lloyd Wright, his life and architecture*. New York, Wiley, 1979. 2 ed.

13713. Willard, Charlotte. *Frank Lloyd Wright: American architect*. New York, Macmillan, 1972.

13714. Wright, Frank Lloyd. *An American architecture*. Ed. by Edgar Kaufman. New York, Horizon, 1955.

13715. ———. *Ausgeführte Bauten und Entwürfe*. Berlin, Wasmuth, 1910. (English ed.: *Studies and executed buildings*. Palos Park, Ill., Prairie School Press, 1975).

13716. ———. *An autobiography*. California, Reprint Services Corp., 1991.

13717. ———. *An autobiography*. New York, Duell, Sloan and Pearce, 1943. (New ed.: New

York, Horizon, 1977).

13718. ———. *Drawings for a living architecture.* New York, Horizon, 1959.

13719. ———. *Frank Lloyd Wright, architect.* Ed. by Terence Riley with Peter Reed. Essays by Anthony Alofsin . . . [et al.]. New York, Museum of Modern Art, distributed by H.N. Abrams, 1994.

13720. ———. *Frank Lloyd Wright: a primer on architectural principles.* Ed. by Robert McCarter. Kenneth Frampton . . . [et al.]. New York, Princeton Architectural Press, 1991.

13721. ———. *Frank Lloyd Wright remembered.* Ed. by Patrick J. Meehan. Washington, DC, Preservation Press, National Trust for Historic Preservation, 1991.

13722. ———. *Frank Lloyd Wright selected houses.* Text by Bruce Brooks Pfeiffer. Ed. and photographed by Yukio Futagawa. Tokyo, A.D.A. EDITA, 1989– .

13723. ———. *Frank Lloyd Wright: the complete 1925 "Wendingen" series.* [With a new introduction by Donald Hoffman]. New York, Dover Publications, 1992.

13724. ———. *Frank Lloyd Wright: the masterworks.* Ed. by David Larkin and Bruce Brooks Pfeiffer. Text by Bruce Brooks Pfeiffer. New York, Rizzoli in association with the Frank Lloyd Wright Foundation, 1993.

13725. ———. *The future of architecture.* New York, Horizon, 1953.

13726. ———. *Genius and Mobocracy.* New York, Duell, Sloan and Pearce, 1949. (New ed.: New York, Horizon, 1971).

13727. ———. *In the cause of architecture: essays by Frank Lloyd Wright for Architectural Record, 1908–1952.* New York, Architectural Record, 1975.

13728. ———. *Letters to apprentices.* Selected and with commentary by Bruce B. Pfeiffer. Fresno, The Press at California State University, 1982.

13729. ———. *Letters to architects.* Selected and with commentary by Bruce B. Pfeiffer. Fresno, The Press at California State University, 1982.

13730. ———. *The life-work of the American architect Frank Lloyd Wright.* Santpoort, Holland, Mees, 1925. (New ed.: with an introduction by Mrs. Frank Lloyd Wright: New York, Horizon, 1965).

13731. ———. *The living city.* New York, Horizon, 1958.

13732. ———. *The master architect: conversations with Frank Lloyd Wright.* Ed. by Patrick J. Meehan. New York, Wiley, 1984.

13733. ———. *Monograph 1887–1901.* Ed. and photographed by Yukio Futagawa. Text by

Bruce Brooks Pfeiffer. Tokyo, A.D.A. Edita, 1986. (Complete works).

13734. ———. *Monograph, 1902–1906.* Ed. and photographed by Yukio Futagawa. Text by Bruce Brooks Pfeiffer. Tokyo, A.D.A. Edita, 1987. (Complete works).

13735. ———. *Monograph, 1914–1923.* Ed. and photographed by Yukio Futagawa. Text by Bruce Brooks Pfeiffer. Tokyo, A.D.A. Edita, 1985. (Complete works).

13736. ———. *Monograph, 1924–1936.* Ed. and photographed by Yukio Futagawa. Text by Bruce Brooks Pfeiffer. Tokyo, A.D.A. Edita, 1985. (Complete works).

13737. ———. *Monograph, 1937–1941.* Ed. and photographed by Yukio Futagawa. Text by Bruce Brooks Pfeiffer. Tokyo, A.D.A. Edita, 1986. (Complete works).

13738. ———. *Monograph, 1942–1950.* Ed. and photographed by Yukio Futagawa. Text by Bruce Brooks Pfeiffer. Tokyo, A.D.A. Edita, 1988. (Complete works).

13739. ———. *Monograph, 1951–1959.* Ed. and photographed by Yukio Futagawa. Text by Bruce Brooks Pfeiffer. Tokyo, A.D.A. Edita, 1988. (Complete works).

13740. ———. *The natural house.* New York, Horizon, 1954.

13741. ———. *On architecture: selected writings, 1894–1940.* Ed. by Frederick Gutheim. New York, Duell, Sloan and Pearce, 1941.

13742. ———. *Preliminary studies, 1889–1916.* Ed. by Yukio Futagawa. Text by Bruce Brooks Pfeiffer. Tokyo, A.D.A. Edita, 1985. (Complete works).

13743. ———. *Preliminary studies, 1917–1932.* Ed. by Yukio Futagawa. Text by Bruce Brooks Pfeiffer. Tokyo, A.D.A. Edita, 1986. (Complete works).

13744. ———. *Preliminary studies, 1933–1959.* Ed. by Yukio Futagawa. Text by Bruce Brooks Pfeiffer. Tokyo, A.D.A. Edita, 1987. (Complete works).

13745. ———. *Selected drawings proposal.* Selected and arranged by A.D.A. Edita Tokyo Co., Ltd. 3 v. New York, Horizon, 1977–1982.

13746. ———. *A testament.* New York, Horizon, 1957.

13747. ———. *Truth against the world: Frank Lloyd Wright speaks for an organic architecture.* Ed. with introductions by Patrick J. Meehan. New York, Wiley, 1987.

13748. ———. *Writings and buildings.* Selected by Edgar Kaufmann and Ben Raeburn. Cleveland/New York, World, 1960.

13749. Wright, John L. *My father who is on earth.* New York, Putnam, 1946. [New ed., including comments, responses, and documents by Frank Lloyd Wright and John Lloyd Wright. Ed. and with an introduction by Narciso G.

Menocal. Postscript by Elizabeth Wright Ingraham.] Carbondale, Southern Illinois University Press, 1994.

13750. Wright, Olgivanna L. *Frank Lloyd Wright, his life, his work, his words.* New York, Horzion, 1966.

13751. ———. *Our house.* New York, Horizon, 1959.

13752. Zevi, Bruno. *Frank Lloyd Wright.* Zürich, Artemis, 1980.

Wright, Joseph, 1734–1797

13753. Bemrose, William. *The life and works of Joseph Wright, A. R. A., commonly called Wright of Derby.* With a preface by Cosmo Monkhouse. Illustrated with two etchings by Mr. F. Seymour Haden, and other plates and woodcuts. London, Derby, Bemrose & Sons, 1885.

13754. Egerton, Judy. *Wright of Derby.* London, Tate Gallery, 1990.

13755. Nicholson, Benedict. *Joseph Wright of Derby, painter of light.* 2 v. London, Routledge and Kegan Paul, 1968. (CR).

13756. Smith, Solomon C. and Bemrose, H. Cheney. *Wright of Derby.* New York, Stokes, 1922.

Wright of Derby, Joseph *see* Wright, Joseph

Wtewael, Joachim Anthoniszoon, 1566–1638

13757. Lindeman, Catherinus M. *Joachim Anthonisz. Wtewael.* Utrecht, Oosthoek, 1929.

13758. Lowenthal, Anne W. *Joachim Wtewael and Dutch mannerism.*Doornspijk, The Netherlands, Davaco, 1986. (Aetas aurea, monographs on Dutch and Flemish painting, 6).

Wu Chên, 1280–1354

13759. Cahill, James F. *Wu Chên, a Chinese landscapist and bamboo painter of the 14th century.* Ann Arbor, Mich., University Microfilms, 1958.

Wu Li, 1632–1718

13760. Chaves, Jonathan. *Singing of the source: nature and god in the poetry of the Chinese painter Wu Li.* Honolulu, University of Hawaii Press, 1993.

Wunderlich, Paul, 1927–

13761. Bense, Max, et al. *Paul Wunderlich: Werkverzeichnis der Lithografien von 1949–1971.* Berlin, Propyläen, [1977]. (CR).

13762. Jensen, Jens C. *Paul Wunderlich: eine Werkmonographie.* Mit Beiträgen von Max Bense und Philippe Roberts-Jones. Offenbach a.M., Huber, 1980. (CR).

13763. Raddatz, Fritz J. *Paul Wunderlich: litho-*

graphies et peintures. Traduit de l'allemand par Cornélius Heim. Paris, Denoël, 1972.

13764. Wunderlich, Paul and Székessy, Karin. *Correspondenzen.* Herausgegeben von Fritz J. Raddatz. Stuttgart/Zürich, Belser, 1977.

Wyatt, James, 1746–1813
Samuel, 1737–1807

13765. Dale, Antony. *James Wyatt.* Oxford, Blackwell, 1956. 2 ed.

13766. Robinson, John M. *The Wyatts, an architectural dynasty.* With a foreword by Woodrow Wyatt. Oxford, Oxford University Press, 1979.

13767. Turnor, Reginald. *James Wyatt, 1746–1813.* London, Art and Technics, 1950.

Wyatville, Jeffry, 1766–1840 *see also* Wyatt, James

13768. Linstrum, Derek. *Sir Jeffry Wyatville, architect to the king.* Oxford, Clarendon Press, 1972.

Wyeth, Andrew, 1911–
James, 1946–
Newell Convers, 1882–1945
see also Pyle, Howard

13769. Allen, Douglas and Allen, Douglas Jr. *N. C. Wyeth: the collected paintings, illustrations, and murals.* New York, Crown, 1972.

13770. Corn, Wanda M. *The art of Andrew Wyeth.* [Published in conjunction with an exhibition at the De Young Memorial Museum, San Francisco, June 16–September 3, 1973]. Greenwich, Conn., New York Graphic Society, 1973.

13771. Duff, James H. *The western world of N. C. Wyeth.* [Published in conjunction with an exhibition at the Buffalo Bill Historical Center, Cody, Wyo., and other places]. Cody, Wyo., Buffalo Bill Historical Center, 1980.

13772. ——— . . . [et al.], essays. *An American vision: three generations of Wyeth art: N.C. Wyeth, Andrew Wyeth, James Wyeth.* Boston, Little, Brown, 1987.

13773. Fogg Art Museum, Harvard University (Cambridge, Mass.). *Andrew Wyeth: dry brush and pencil drawings; a loan exhibition.* Cambridge, Mass., President and Fellows of Harvard College, 1963.

13774. Harris, Gene E. *N.C. Wyeth's wild west.* Chadds Ford, Pa., Brandywine River Museum, 1990.

13775. Logsdon, Gene. *Wyeth people: a portrait of Andrew Wyeth as he is seen by his friends and neighbors.* Garden City, N.Y., Doubleday, 1971.

13776. ———. *Wyeth people: a portrait of Andrew Wyeth as seen by his friends and neighbors.* Dallas, Taylor Pub. Co., 1988.

13777. Meryman, Richard. *Andrew Wyeth*. Boston, Houghton Mifflin, 1968.

13778. Metropolitan Museum of Art (New York). *Two worlds of Andrew Wyeth: Kuerners and Olsons*. New York, Metropolitan Museum of Art, 1976. (Metropolitan Museum of Art Bulletin, XXXIV: 2).

13779. Museum of Fine Arts (Boston). *Andrew Wyeth*. Introduction by David McCord; selection by Frederick A. Sweet. Boston, Museum of Fine Arts, 1970; distributed by New York Graphic Society, Greenwich, Conn.

13780. Wyeth, Andrew. *Andrew Wyeth: the Helga pictures*. Text by John Wilmerding. New York, H.N. Abrams, 1987.

13781. Wyeth, Betsy J. *Christina's World: paintings and pre-studies of Andrew Wyeth*. Boston, Houghton Mifflin, 1982.

13782. ———. *Wyeth at Kuerners*. Boston, Houghton Mifflin, 1976.

13783. ———, ed. *The Wyeths: the letters of N. C. Wyeth*. Boston, Gambit, 1971.

13784. Wyeth, James. *Jamie Wyeth*. Boston, Houghton Mifflin, 1980.

13785. ———. *Jamie Wyeth, an American view*: [exhibition] Portland Museum of Art, Portland, Maine, 19 June–9 September 1984; Columbia Museum, Columbia, South Carolina, 16 September–11 November 1984; Oklahoma Art Center, Oklahoma City, Ok- lahoma, 30 November 1984–20 January 1985. Portland, Me., Portland Museum of Art, 1984.

Wyspiański, Stanisław, 1869–1907

13786. Blum, Napisała H. *Stanisław Wyspiański*. Warszawa, Auriga, 1969.

13787. Kępiński, Zdzislaw. *Stanisław Wyspiański*. Warszawa, Krajowa Agencja Wydawnicza, 1984.

13788. Makowiecki, Tadeusz. *Poeta-malarz: studjum o Stanisławie Wyspiańskim*. Warszawa, Mickiewicza, 1935.

13789. Przybyszewski, Stanisław, iuk-Skarszewski, Tadeusz. *Stanisław Wyspiański, dziełła malarskie*. [Warszawa], Bibljoteka Polska, 1925.

13790. Skierkowska, Elżbieta. *Wyspiański-artysta książki*. Wrocław, Ossolineum, 1970. 2 ed.

13791. Stokowa, Maria. *Stanisław Wyspiański: monografia bibliograficzna*. 4 v. Kraków, Wydawnicka Literackie, 1967/1968.

13792. Wojtak, Maria. *O języku i stylu "Wesela" Stanislawa Wyspiańskiego*. Lublin, Uniwersytet Marii Curie-Sklodowskiej w Lublinie, Wydzial Humanistyczny, 1988.

13793. Zbijewska, Krystyna. *Krakowskim szlakiem Stanislawa Wyspianskiego*. Warszawa/Krakow, Wydawnictwo PTTK "Kraf", 1986.

X

Xugu, *see* Hsü-Kuo, 1823–1896

Y

Yeats, Jack Butler, 1871–1957
John Butler, 1839–1922

13794. MacGreevy, Thomas. *Jack B. Yeats, an appreciation and an interpretation.* Dublin, Waddington, 1945.

13795. Murphy, William M. *Prodigal father: the life of John Butler Yeats (1839–1922).* Ithaca/London, Cornell University Press, 1978.

13796. National Gallery of Ireland (Dublin). *Jack B. Yeats, a centenary exhibition.* September–December 1971. London, Secker & Warburg, 1971.

13797. ———. *Jack B. Yeats in the National Gallery of Ireland.* Dublin, The Gallery, 1986.

13798. Pyle, Hilary. *Jack B. Yeats, a biography.* London, Routledge, 1970. [Rev. ed., London, A. Deutsch, 1989].

13799. ———. *Jack B. Yeats: a catalogue raisonné of the oil paintings.* 3 v. London, A. Deutsch, 1992. (CR).

13800. ———. *Jack B. Yeats: his watercolours, drawings and pastels.* Dublin/Portland, Or., Irish Academic Press, 1993. (CR).

13801. Rosenthal, T. G. *The art of Jack B. Yeats.* Chronology, list of exhibitions, bibliography and notes on the plates by Hilary Pyle. London, A. Deutsch, 1993.

13802. Yeats, Jack Butler. *Jack B. Yeats: the late paintings.* [Co-ordination of catalogue and organisation of exhibition by Stephen Snoddy, Felicity Lunn and Franz Kaiser]. Bristol, Arnolfini; London, Whitechapel Art Gallery; The Hague, Haags Gemeentemuseum, 1991.

13803. ———. *Sailing swiftly.* London, Putnam, 1933.

13804. Yeats, John B. *Letters to his son W. B. Yeats and others, 1869–1922.* Edited with a memoir by Joseph Hone, and a preface by Oliver Elton. London, Faber, 1944.

Yeh Shih, 1150–1223

13805. Lo, Winston W. *The life and thought of Yeh Shih.* Gainesville, Florida, University Presses of Florida; Hong Kong, Chinese University of Hong Kong, 1974.

Yoshitoshi, Taiso, 1839–1892

13806. Ing, Eric van den and Schaap, Robert. *Beauty & violence: Japanese prints by Yoshitoshi, 1839–1892.* Intro. by John Stevenson. Bergeyk, The Netherlands Society for Japanese Arts, 1992.

13807. Keyes, Roger S. *Courage and silence: a study of the life and color woodblock prints of Tsukioka Yoshitoshi: 1839–1892.* 2 v. 1982 Dec.

13808. ——— and Kuwayama, George. *The bizarre imagery of Yoshitoshi: the Herbert R. Cole Collection.* Los Angeles, Los Angeles County Museum of Art, 1980.

13809. Museum für Ostasiatische Kunst der Stadt Köln. *Taiso Yoshitoshi, 1839–1892; ein Holzschnittmeister an der Schwelle zur Neuzeit.* [Katalogbearbeitung, W. Schamoni . . . et al.]. [Köln, 1971?].

13810. Rijksmuseum (Netherlands). Rijksprentenkabinet. *The age of Yoshitoshi: Japanese prints from the Meiji and Taisho periods: Nagasaki, Yokohama and Kamigata prints: recent acquisitions.* [Catalogue by Charlotte van Rappard-Boon. Ed. by J.P. Filedt Kok and J.F. Heijbroek]. Amsterdam, Rijksprentenkabinet/Rijksmuseum; Maarsens-Gravenhage, Gary Schwartz/SDU, 1990. (Catalogue of the collection of Japanese prints, 5).

13811. Stevenson, John. *Yoshitoshi's One hundred aspects of the moon.* Redmond, Wash., San Francisco Graphic Society, [1992].

13812. ———. *Yoshitoshi's thirty-six ghosts.* With an intro. by Donald Richie. New York, Weatherhill/Blue Tiger, 1983.

13813. Taiso, Yoshitoshi. *Yoshitoshi: the splendid decadent.* Ed. by Shinichi Segi. Trans. by Alfred Birnbaum. Tokyo/New York, Kodansha International; New York, distributed in the U.S. by Kodansha International/USA, through Harper & Row Publishers, 1985.

Yün Shou-P'ing, 1633–1690

13814. Chung, Saehyang P. *Yün Shou-p'ing (1633–1690) and the orthodox tradition of Chinese bird-and-flower painting.* (Ph.D. diss., Columbia University, 1983). Ann Arbor, University Microfilms International, 1986. Photocopy.

13815. Tong, Ginger. *Yun Shou-p'in (1633–1690) and his landscape art.* (Ph.D. diss., Stanford University, 1983). Ann Arbor, University Microfilms International, 1986. Photocopy.

Z

Zadkine, Ossip, 1890–1967

13816. Buchanan, Donald. *The secret world of Zadkine*. [Text by Zadkine; in French and English]. Paris, Arted, 1966.

13817. Czwiklitzer, Christophe. *Ossip Zadkine, le sculpteur-graveur de 1919 à 1967*. Préface de Jean Adhémar. Paris, Art-Christophe Czwiklitzer, 1967.

13818. Hammacher, Abraham M. *Zadkine*. Amsterdam, De Lange, 1954.

13819. Jianou, Ionel. *Zadkine*. Paris, Arted, 1979. 2 ed. (CR).

13820. Lecombe, Sylvain. *Ossip Zadkine. L'Oeuvre sculpté*. Includes writings by Zadkine. Paris, 1994.

13821. Lichtenstern, Christa. *Ossip Zadkine (1890–1967), der Bildhauer und seine Ikonographie*. Berlin, Mann, 1980. (Frankfurter Forschungen zur Kunst, 8).

13822. Marchal, Gaston-Louis. *Ossip Zadkine: la sculpture . . . toute une vie*. Rodez, Editions du Rouergue, 1992.

13823. Prax, Valentine. *Avec Zadkine: souvenirs de notre vie*. Lausanne/Paris, Bibliothèque des Arts, 1973.

13824. Raynal, Maurice. *Ossip Zadkine*. Rome, Valori Plastici, 1921.

13825. Zadkine, Ossip. *Lettres à André de Ridder*. Introduction de Jean Cassou. Anvers, Librairie des Arts, 1963.

13826. ———. *Le maillet et le ciseau: souvenirs de ma vie*. Paris, Michel, 1968.

13827. ———. *Voyage en Grèce/Trois Lumières*. [Amsterdam, Boeschoten, 1955].

Zakhariev, Vasil, 1895–1971

13828. Svintila, Vladimir. *Vasil Zakhariev*. Sofia, Iskusstvo Bulgarski Khudozhnik, 1972.

13829. Tomov, Evtim. *Vassil Zachariev*. Sofia, Bulgarian Artist, 1954.

Zampieri, Domenico *see* Domenichino

Zandomeneghi, Federico, 1841–1917

13830. Cinotti, Mia. *Zandomeneghi*. Busto Arsizio, Bramante, 1960. (I grandi pittori italiani dell'ottocento, 3).

13831. Dini, Francesca. *Federico Zandomeneghi: la vita e le opere*. Firenze, Il Torchio, [1989].

13832. Piceni, Enrico. *Zandomeneghi*. Milano, Bramante, 1967. (CR).

13833. Zandomeneghi, Federico. *Federico Zandomeneghi: un veneziano a Parigi*. Milano, Mazzotta, 1988.

Zao Wou-Ki, 1921–

13834. Galeries Nationales du Grand Palais (Paris). *Zao Wou-Ki; peintures, encres de Chine*. 12 juin–10 août 1981. Paris, Ministère de la Culture et de la Communication, 1981.

13835. Jacometti, Nesto. *Zao Wou-Ki: catalogue raisonné de l'oeuvre gravée et lithographiée, 1949–1954*. Berne, Gutekunst et Klipstein, 1955. (CR).

13836. Laude, Jean. *Zao Wou-Ki*. Bruxelles, La Connaissance, 1974.

13837. Leymarie, Jean. *Zao Wou-Ki*. Trans. by Kenneth Lyons. New York, Rizzoli, 1979.

13838. Roy, Claude. *Zao Wou-Ki*. Paris, Fall, 1957.

13839. ———. *Zao Wou-Ki*. Paris, Cercle d'art, 1988.

13840. Zao Wou-Ki. *Les estampes, 1937–1974*. Paris, Arts et Métiers Graphiques, 1975. (CR).

13841. ———. *Zao Wou-ki, paintings 1980–1985*. New York, Pierre Matisse Gallery, 1986.

13842. ——— et Marquet, Françoise. *Autoportrait*. Paris, Fayard, 1988.

Zauffely, Johann *see* Zoffany, John

Zeiller, Johann Jakob, 1708–1783

13843. Fischer, Pius. *Der Barockmaler Johann Jakob Zeiller und sein Ettaler Werk*. Vorwort von Norbert Lieb. München, Herold, 1964.

Zelotti, Battista, 1526–1578

13844. Brugnolo Meloncelli, Katia. *Battista Zelotti.* Prefazione di Lionello Puppi. Milano, Berenice, 1992. (CR).

Zevio, Altechiero da *see* **Altechieri, Altechiero**

Zichy, Mihály, 1827–1906

13845. Aleshina, Liliia S. *Mikhai Zichi.* Moskva, Izobrazitel'noe Iskusstvo, 1975.

13846. Berkovits, Ilona. *Zichy Mihály, élete és munkássága (1827–1906).* Budapest, Akadémiai Kiado, 1964.

13847. Lázár, Béla. *Zichy Mihály, élete és müvészete.* Budapest, Atheneum, 1928.

Ziem, Felix, 1821–1911

13848. Fournier, Louis. *Un grand peintre, Félix Ziem; notes biographiques.* Beaune, Lambert, 1897.

13849. Roger-Milès, Léon. *Félix Ziem.* Paris, Librairie de l'Art Ancien et Moderne, 1903.

13850. Miquel, Pierre. *Félix Ziem, 1821–1911.* 2 v. Maurs-la-Jolie, Editions de la Martinelle, 1978. (CR).

13851. Musée de l'Annonciade (Saint-Tropez). *Ziem en marge.* 20 juin–15 septembre [1980]. Saint-Tropez, Musée de l'Annonciade, [1980].

Zille, Heinrich, 1858–1929

13852. Flügge, Gerhard. *Heinrich Zille: Ernstes und Heiteres aus seinem Leben.* Rudolstadt, Greifenverlag, 1960.

13853. Köhler-Zille, Margarete. *Mein Vater, Heinrich Zille.* Erzählt von Gerhard Flügge. Berlin, Verlag Neues Leben, 1955.

13854. Luft, Friedrich. *Mein Photo-Milljöh: 100 X Alt-Berlin aufgenommen von Heinrich Zille.* Hannover, Fackelträger, 1967.

13855. Murmann, Geerte. *"Heinrich, lieber Heinrich!": Zille und seine Zeit.* Düsseldorf, Droste, 1994.

13856. Nagel, Otto. *H. Zille.* Berlin, Henschel, 1955.

13857. Oschilewski, Walther G. *Heinrich Zille Bibliographie; Veröffentlichungen von ihm und über ihn.* Herausgegeben von Gustav Schmidt-Küster. Hannover, Heinrich-Zille-Stiftung, 1979.

13858. Paust, Otto. *Vater Zille: der Meister in seinem Milljöh.* Berlin, Franke, 1941.

13859. Ranke, Winfried. *Heinrich Zille: Photographien Berlin, 1890–1910.* München, Schirmer/Mosel, 1985.

13860. ———. *Vom Milljöh ins Milieu: Heinrich Zilles Aufstieg in der Berliner Gesellschaft.* Hannover, Fackelträger, 1979.

13861. Schumann, Werner. *Zille sein Milljöh.* Hannover, Fackelträger, 1952.

13862. Zille, Heinrich. *Das dicke Zillebuch.* Herausgegeben von Gerhard Flügge. Berlin, Eulenspiegel, 1972. 2 ed.

13863. ———. *Das grosse Zille-Album.* Einleitung von Werner Schumann. Hannover, Fackelträger, 1957.

13864. ———. *Heinrich Zille, das graphische Werk.* Herausgegeben von Detlev Rosenbach; in zusammenarbeit mit Renate Altner und Matthias Flügge. Hannover, Rosenbach, 1984.

Zimmermann, Dominikus, 1685–1766
Johann Baptist, 1680–1758

13865. Bauer, Hermann und Anna. *Johann Baptist und Dominikus Zimmermann: Entstehung und Vollendung des bayerischen Rokoko.* Fotografische Aufnahmen, Wolf-Christian von der Mülbe. Regensburg, F. Pustet, 1985.

13866. Hitchcock, Henry R. *German Rococo: the Zimmermann brothers.* London, Lane, 1968.

13867. Lamb, Carl. *Die Wies: das Meisterwerk von Dominikus Zimmermann.* Berlin, Rembrandt, 1937.

13868. Muchall-Viebrook, Thomas W. *Dominicus Zimmermann, ein Beitrag zur Geschichte der süddeutschen Kunst im 18. Jahrhundert.* Leipzig, Hiersemann, 1912.

13869. Thon, Christina. *Johann Baptist Zimmermann als Stukkator.* München/Zürich, Schnell & Steiner, 1977.

13870. Zimmermann, Dominikus. *Dominikus Zimmermann, 1685–1766: Ausstellung im Alten Rathaus in Landsberg a. Lech 29. 6. 1985 bis 24. 7. 1985.* [Herausgeber, Alois Epple]. München, Verlag Schnell & Steiner, 1985.

Zoffany, John, 1733–1810

13871. Manners, Victoria and Williamson, George C. *John Zoffany, R. A.* London, Lane, 1920.

13872. Millar, Oliver. *Zoffany and his Tribuna.* London, Paul Mellon Foundation/Routledge & Kegan Paul, 1967.

13873. National Portrait Gallery (London). *Johann Zoffany, 1733–1810.* January 14–March 27, 1977. London, National Portrait Gallery, 1976.

13874. Webster, Mary. *Johann Zoffany.* Milano, Fabbri, 1966. (I maestri del colore, 237).

Zoller, Anton, 1695–1768
Joseph Anton, 1730–1791

13875. Krall, Gertrud. *Anton und Joseph Anton Zoller: ein Beitrag zur Barockmalerei in Tirol.* Innsbruck, Universität Innsbruck, 1978. (Veröffentlichungen der Universität Innsbruck, 115; Kunstgeschichtliche Studien, 3).

Zoppo, Marco, 1433–1478

13876. Armstrong, Lilian. *The paintings and drawings of Marco Zoppo.* New York, Garland, 1976.

13877. Ruhmer, Eberhard. *Marco Zoppo. 188 illustrazioni in nero e 8 a colori . . . e 8 tavole a colori.* Venezia, Neri Pozza, [1966]. (Saggi e studi di storia dell'arte, 9).

13878. Zoppo, Marco. *Marco Zoppo, Cento 1433–1478. Venezia.* Atti del Convegno internazionale di studi sulla pittura del Quattrocento padano, Cento, 8–9 ottobre 1993. A cura di Berenice Giovannucci Vigi. Bologna, Nuova Alfa editoriale, 1993.

Zorach, Marguerite, 1887–1968
William, 1887–1966

13879. Bauer, John I. *William Zorach.* New York, Whitney Museum of American Art/Praeger, 1959.

13880. Brooklyn Museum (New York). *William Zorach; paintings, watercolors and drawings, 1911–1922.* November 26, 1968–January 19, 1969. New York, Brooklyn Museum, 1968.

13881. Hoffman, Marilyn Friedman. *Marguerite and William Zorach: the cubist years, 1915–1918.* Manchester, N.H., Currier Gallery of Art; Hanover, distributed by the University Press of New England, 1987.

13882. Wingert, Paul S. *The sculpture of William Zorach.* New York, Pitman, 1938.

13883. Zorach, Marguerite. *Marguerite Zorach: the early years, 1908–1920.* Washington, published for the National Collection of Fine Arts by the Smithsonian Institution Press, 1973.

13884. Zorach, William. *Art is my life.* Cleveland, World, 1967.

13885. ———. *Zorach explains sculpture: what it means and how it is made.* New York, American Artists Group, 1947.

Zorn, Anders Leonard, 1860–1920

13886. Asplund, Karl. *Anders Zorn, his life and work.* Edited by Geoffrey Holme. Trans. by Henry Alexander. London, The Studio, 1921.

13887. ———. *Zorn's engraved work: a descriptive catalogue.* Trans. by Edward Adams-Ray. 2 v. Stockholm, Bukowski, 1920. (CR).

13888. Boëthius, Gerda. *Zorn: människan och konstnären.* Stockholm, Konst och Kultur, 1960.

13889. ———. *Zorn: Swedish painter and world traveller.* Trans. by Albert Read. Stockholm, Raben & Sjögren, 1959.

13890. ———. *Zorn: tecknaren, malaren, etsaren, skulptören.* Stockholm, Nordisk Rotogravyr, 1949.

13891. Broun, Elizabeth. *The prints of Anders Zorn.* [Published in conjunction with an exhibition at the Spencer Museum of Art, University of Kansas, Lawrence, Kansas]. Lawrence, Kan., Spencer Museum of Art, 1979.

13892. Brummer, Hans H. *Zorn, svensk målare i världen.* Stockholm, Bonniers, 1975.

13893. Engström, Albert. *Anders Zorn.* Stockholm, Bonniers, 1928.

13894. Hedberg, Tor. *Anders Zorn, ungdomstiden.* 2 v. Stockholm, Norstedt, 1923–1924. (Sveriges allmänna konstförenings publikation, 32/33).

13895. Hjert, Svenolof [and] Hjert, Bertil. *Zorn: engravings/etsningar; a complete catalogue/ en komplett katalog.* Preface by Hans H. Brummer. [Text in English and Swedish]. Uppsala, Hjert & Hjert, 1980. (CR).

13896. Hyland, Douglas K.S., Brummer, Hans Henrik. *Zorn, paintings, graphics, and sculpture.* Catalogue by Marguerite J. Harbert. Birmingham, Ala., Birmingham Museum of Art, 1986.

13897. Servaes, Franz. *Anders Zorn.* Bielefeld/Leipzig, Velhagen & Klasing, 1910. (Künstler-Monographien, 102).

13898. Zorn, Anders. *Anders Zorn, 1860–1920: Gemälde, Aquarelle, Zeichnungen, Radierungen.* Herausgegeben von Jens Christian Jensen. München, Prestel, [1989].

Zrzavý, Jan, 1890–

13899. Lamač, Miroslav. *Jan Zrzavý.* Praha, Odeon, 1980.

13900. Plichta, Dalibor. *The modern symbolist: the painter Jan Zrzavý.* Trans. by Roberta F. Samsour. Prague, Artia, [1958].

13901. Šourek, Karel, ed. *Dílo Jana Zrzavého, 1906–1940.* Praze, Umělecka Beseda a Družstevní Práce, 1941.

Zuccari, Federigo *see* Zuccaro, Federigo

Zuccari, Taddeo *see* Zuccaro, Taddeo

Zuccaro, Federigo, 1530–1609
Taddeo, 1529–1566

13902. Cleri, Bonita. *Per Taddeo e Federico Zuccari nelle Marche.* A cura di Bonita Cleri. Introduzione di Paolo Dal Poggetto. Sant'-Angelo in Vado, Grafica Vadese, 1993.

13903. Gere, John. *Taddeo Zuccaro: his development studied in his drawings.* London, Faber, 1969.

13904. Gizzi, Corrado. *Federico Zuccari e Dante.* Milano, Electa, 1993.

13905. Körte, Werner. *Der Palazzo Zuccari in Rom; sein Freskenschmuck und seine Geschichte.* Leipzig, Keller, 1935. (Römische Forschungen der Bibliotheca Hertziana, 7).

13906. Mundy, E. James. *Renaissance into baroque: Italian master drawings by the Zuccari, 1550–1600.* With the assistance of Elizabeth Ourusoff de Fernandez-Gimenez. Milwaukee, Wis., Milwaukee Art Museum; Cambridge, Cambridge University Press, 1989.

13907. Zuccaro, Federico. *L'idea de' pittori, scultori ed architetti.* Torino, Disserolio, 1607. (Reprint included in: *Scritti d'arte di Federico Zuccaro.* A cura di Detlef Heikamp. Firenze, Olschki, 1961. Fonti per lo studio della storia dell'arte, 1).

Zuloaga, Ignacio, 1870–1945

13908. Arozamena, Jesus M. de. *Ignacio Zuloaga; el pintor, el hombre.* San Sebastián, Spain, Sociedad Guipuzcoana, 1970.

13909. Bénédite, Léonce. *Ignacio Zuloaga.* Paris, Librairie Artistique Internationale, [1912].

13910. Encina, Juan de la [pseud., Ricardo Gutierrez Abascal]. *El arte de Ignacio Zuloaga.* Madrid, Sociedad Española de Librería, [1916].

13911. Hispanic Society of America (New York). *Catalogue of paintings by Ignacio Zuloaga exhibited March 21 to April 11, 1909.* With introduction by Christian Brinton. New York, Hispanic Society of America, 1909.

13912. Inmaculada, Juan J. de la. *La incognita de Zuloaga.* Burgos, El Monte Carmelo, 1951.

13913. Lafuente Ferrari, Enrique. *La vida y el arte de Ignacio Zuloaga.* San Sebastián, Spain, Editora Internacional, 1950; distributed by Mayfe, Madrid. (New ed.: Madrid, Revista de Occidente, 1972).

13914. Milhou, Mayi. *Ignacio Zuloaga (1870–1945) et la France.* St. Loubes, Graphilux, 1981.

13915. Rodriguez del Castillo, Jesús. *Ignacio Zuloaga, el hombre.* Zarauz, Icharopena, 1970.

13916. Utrillo, Miguel, et al. *Five essays on the art of Ignacio Zuloaga.* [Text in either French or Spanish]. New York, Hispanic Society of America, 1909.

13917. Zuloaga, Ignacio. *Ignacio Zuloaga, 1870–1945: erakusketa, Bilbo, Bilboko Arte Ederretako Museoa, S.A.* Bilbo, Eusko Jaurlaritza, Kultura eta Turismo Saila; Dallas Meadows Museum, [1991].

13918. ———. *Ignacio Zuloaga in America, 1909–1925:* [exhibition] February 2–April 29, 1989. New York, Spanish Institute, [1989].

Zurbarán, Francisco de, 1598–1664 *see also* Ribera, Jusepe

13919. Baticle, Jeannine. *Zurbarán.* With essays by Yves Bottineau, Jonathan Brown, Alfons Pérez Sánchez. New York, Metropolitan Museum of Art, distributed by Abrams, 1987.

13920. Brown, Jonathan. *Francisco de Zurbarán.* New York, Abrams, 1973.

13921. Calzada, Andrés M. y Santa Marina, Luys. *Estampas de Zurbarán.* Barcelona, Canosa, 1929.

13922. Carrascal Muñoz, José. *Francisco de Zurbarán.* Madrid, Giner, 1973.

13923. Cascales y Muñoz, José. *Francisco de Zurbarán; his epoch, his life and his works.* Trans. by Nellie S. Evans. New York, [privately printed], 1918.

13924. Cason del Buen Retiro (Madrid). *Exposicion Zurbarán en el III centenario de su muerte.* Noviembre 1964–Febrero 1965. Madrid, Ministerio de Educación Nacional/Dirección General de Bellas Artes, 1964.

13925. Caturla, Maria Louisa. *Francisco de Zurbarán.* Paris, Bibliothèque des arts, 1994.

13926. Gállego, Julián [and] Gudiol, José. *Zurbarán, 1598–1664.* New York, Rizzoli, 1977. (CR).

13927. Gaya Nuño, Juan A. *Zurbarán.* Barcelona, Aedos, 1948.

13928. Gregori, Mina [and] Frati, Tiziana. *L'opera completa di Zurbarán.* Milano, Rizzoli, 1973. (CR). (Classici dell'arte, 69).

13929. Guinard, Paul. *Zurbarán et les peintres espagnols de la vie monastique.* Photographies de Roger Catherineau. Paris, Editions du Temps, 1960. (CR).

13930. Kehrer, Hugo. *Francisco de Zurbarán.* München, Schmidt, 1918.

13931. Museo del Prado (Madrid). *Zurbarán.* 3 mayo/30 julio 1988. Madrid, Ministerio de Cultura, Banco Bilbao Vizcaya, 1988.

13932. Pemán y Pemartín, César. *Zurbarán y otros estudios sobre pintura del XVII español.* Prólogo de Alfonso E. Pérez Sánchez. Introducción de Jonathan Brown. Madrid, Editorial Alpuerto, 1989.

13933. Pompey, Francisco. *Zurbarán, su vida y sus obras.* Madrid, Aguado, [1948].

13934. Sanchez de Palacios, Mariano. *Zurbarán, estudio biografico y critico.* Madrid, Offo, 1964.

13935. Soria, Martin S. *The paintings of Zurbarán, complete edition.* London, Phaidon, 1953; distributed by Garden City Books, New York.

13936. Torres Martín, Ramón. *Zurbarán, el pintor gótico del siglo XVII.* Sevilla, Gráficas del Sur, 1963.

13937. Zurbarán, Francisco. *Zurbarán, 1598–1664.* Biographie et étude critique, Julián Gállego. Catalogue des oeuvres, José Gudiol. Traduit de l'espanol par Robert Marrast. Paris, Editions cercle d'art, 1987.

Index of Authors, Editors and Compilers

Numbers refer to entry, not page numbers.

Albrecht, Manuel 11916
Albright, Thomas 9003
Albright-Knox Art Gallery (Buffalo, N.Y.) 326, 2713, 3794, 7461, 9090, 12206
Albrizzi, Isabella 1620
Alcala Flecha, Roberto 4625
Alce, Venturino 199
Aldrich, Stephen 11865
Aleshina, Liliia S. 8900, 13845
Alessi, Galeazzo 109
Alexander, Constance G. 112
Alexander, David 5928
Alexander, Jack 10772
Alexander, Russell G. 9382
Alexander-Minter, Rae 12194
Alexandre, Arsène 558, 2517, 4049, 5354, 7994, 8533, 10137
Alexandrian, Sarane 8663, 11597
Alexeyeva, Tatyana 13015
Alfaro, Juan de 12920
Alfons, Harriet 6483
Alfons, Sven 6483
Alfonso, Luis 8908
Alibert, François P. 10050
Alibert, Pierre 4433
Alinder, James 8781, 13338
Alinder, Mary Street 53
Alison, Filippo 7361
Alker, Hermann R. 8176
Alland, Alexander, Sr. 10676
Allard, Roger 6394, 6536
Allderidge, Patricia 2447
Allen, Brian 5176
Allen, Douglas 13769
Allen, Douglas, Jr. 13769
Allen, Virginia 2807
Allen Memorial Art Museum (Oberlin, Ohio) 4118
Allende-Salazar, Juan 12921
Allentown Art Museum (Allentown, Pa.) 13463
Allesch, Johannes von 9300
Alley, Ronald 394, 10986, 12132
Allgeyer, Julius 3547, 3548
Alloway, Lawrence 409, 7070, 12613
Allyn, Nancy E. 4428
Almanza Villanueva, Rodrigo 12919
Almoisna, José 4626
Alofsin, Anthony 13665, 13719
Alourafi, Nathalie 12416
Alpatov, Mikhail V. 5703, 7915, 11114, 11115
Alpers, Svetlana L. 10351, 11027, 11028, 12318
Alphen, Ernst van 395
Altamirano Piolle, María Elena 12914
Alten, Wilken von 11771, 11777
Altenberg, Peter 7230
Alterocca, Arnaldo 7168
Altes Rathaus (Schweinfurt) 13279
Altonaer Museum in Hamburg 5098
Altshuler, Bruce 9133, 9137
Alvarez Lopera, José 4808
Alves Guimaraes, Renato 7171
Alviani, Getulio 74

Aman-Jean, Edmond F. 12922
Amann, Per 8852
Amanshauser, Hildegund 5150
Amaury-Duval, Eugène E. 5639, 5640
American Association of Architectural Bibliographers 5849
Amery, Colin 13641
Ames, John 12737
Ames-Lewis, Francis 10171
Amiet, Jacob 4735
Amishai-Maisels, Ziva 4050
Amman, Jean-Christophe 328, 2426
Ammann, Edith 5899
Amon Carter Museum of Western Art (Fort Worth, Texas) 11164
Amor, Anne Clark 5614
Amoretti, Carlo 6819
Amsden, Dora 5291
Ananoff, Alexandre 1200, 1201, 3704
Anayeva, T. 12762
Ancona, Paolo d' 8177
Anderberg, Adolf 5267
Anderegg-Tille, Maria 5005
Andersen, Troels 5800, 7487, 7495
Andersen-Bergdoll, Greta 12964
Anderson, John 12637
Anderson, Laurie 5840
Anderson, Nancy K. 918
Anderson, Ross 12268
Anderson, Russ 13338
Anderson, Ruth M. 11867
Anderson, Wayne 1848, 4051
André, Albert 10507
André, Édouard 9551
Andre Emmerich Gallery (New York) 108
Andree, Rolf 1027
Andreeva, G. B. 7023
Andreotti, Giulio 2011
Andreotti, Margherita 298
Andresen, Andreas 9937
Andrew, David S. 12108
Andrew, William R. 10133
Andrew Crispi Gallery (New York) 285
Andrews, Keith 3227
Andriesse, Emmy 4458
Aners, Gonzalo 4654
Angeli, Diego 8378
Angelini, Luigi 566, 2124, 7267
Angelini, Sandro 10113
Angell, Henry C. 5625
Angoulvent, Monique 8698
Angrand, Pierre 1827, 5641
Angström, Astrid S. 8339
Angulo Iniguez, Diego 249, 846, 8909, 12923
Anonymous 8348, 10699, 13574
Anquetil, Marie-Amélie 4069
Antal, Frederick 3911, 5375
Antoine, Jean-Philippe 12725
Antoniewicz, Jan B. 4920
Antonsson, Oscar 11535
Anzelewsky, Fedja 3035, 3036

Auberty, Jacqueline 13129
Aubier, Dominique 5116
Aubrun, Marie M. 3026
Auckland City Art Gallery (Auckland, New Zealand) 11154
Auerbach, Erna 5280
Auger, Elmina 6448
Augustinerchorherrenstift (Reichersberg, Austria) 11415
Augustinermuseum Freiburg im Breisgau 12279
Auping, Michael 12038
Auquier, Philippe 10052
Aurenhammer, Hans 168, 3579, 3580, 3581
Auricoste, Emmanuel 1231
Austin, Henry *see* Dobson
Auzas, Pierre-Marie 13140
Avenarius, Ferdinand 6156
Avermaete, Roger 7804, 9469, 10352, 11031, 13637
Avery, Charles 1833, 4389
Avon Caffi, Guiseppe 1496
Avril, Françoise 3694
Axsom, Richard H. 5958, 11985
Ayers, David 7026
Aynard, Edouard 10090
Ayres, Linda 763
Ayrton, Michael 9777
Azara, Nicolas de 8083
Azcarate, José Maria de 847
Azpeitia, Rafael C. 11733
Azzi Visentini, Margherita 9312

B
Baard, Henricus P. 5066, 13006
Babelon, Jean 9697, 12421
Baboni, Andrea 3464
Baccheschi, Edi 1347, 2946, 4346, 10495
Bacci, Mina 65, 9680, 9681, 13016
Bacci, Pèleo 2448, 3908, 9778, 10117
Bachelin, Léopold 7481
Bacher, Otto H. 13497
Bachert, Hildegard 6280
Bachman, John 359
Bachmann, Dieter 7203
Bachmann, Fredo 1570
Bacou, Roseline 8349, 9728, 10302, 10303, 10315, 10317
Badischer Kunstverein, Karlsruhe 2179
Badisches Landesmuseum (Karlsruhe) 9566
Badt, Kurt 1849, 2683, 4461, 9938, 11855, 13020, 13058
Badura-Triska, Eva 5699
Baecksbacka, Ingjal 8634
Baer, Rudolf 1345
Baer, Wolfram 5483
Baetjer, Katharine 1578
Bagni, Prisco 478, 479, 480, 483, 4002
Bahlmann, Hermann 12404
Baier, Lesley K. 12823
Baigell, Matthew 774, 777, 917, 1461, 2130
Bailey, Anthony 10353

Bailey, Martin 4462, 4502
Bailly, Jean Christophe 11428
Bailly-Herzberg, Janine 2512, 9810
Baillière, Henri 10335
Baillio, Joseph 13092
Baily, J. T. Herbert 8711
Baily, Jean Christophe 11428
Bain, Ian 896
Bajou, Thierry 6494
Baker, Charles H. 2401, 6787
Baker, Geoffrey Howard 6619, 6654
Baker, Paul R. 13561
Bakken, Hilmar 8906, 8907
Bakker, Boudewijn 8530, 10442
Bal, Mieke 10354
Balanci, Bernard 6448
Baldacci, Paolo 11751, 11752
Baldanzi, Ferdinando 7150
Baldass, Ludwig von 144, 145, 1116, 2107, 3383, 4312, 7304, 8050
Baldassari, Anne 7963
Baldini, Umberto 200, 202, 1170, 7151, 7152, 7780, 8181, 8182, 11706
Baldinucci, Filippo 812, 813, 814, 1418
Baldry, Alfred L. 5237, 6773, 8324
Baldwin, Charles C. 13560
Baldwin, Neil 10276
Balet, Leo 4125
Balinger, James K. 10470, 10471
Baljeu, Joost 2833
Balken, Debra Bricker 7716
Balla, Elica 452
Ballarin, Alessandro 9374
Ballasi, Pietro 416
Ballo, Ferdinando 4905
Ballo, Guido 1015, 3633, 4762, 9790, 11752
Ballot de Sovot 6415
Balston, Thomas 7757
Baltimore Museum of Art 2131, 7917, 9076, 10765
Balzer, Wolfgang 2518
Bamberger, Ludwig 11456
Bancel, E. M. 9487
Bandera Bistoletti, Sandrina 4347
Bang, Marie L'drup 2455
Bange, E. F. 3608
Banks, Oliver T. 13346
Bantel, Linda 9441
Bantens, Robert James 1759
Banti, Anna 7268
Banzato, Davide 4325
Baqué, Egbert 9254
Baranow, Sonja von 6803
Barasch, Moshe 4348
Baratta, Mario 6822, 6823
Barbet de Jouy, Henry 10734
Barbier, Carl P. 4295, 13498
Barbieri, Franco 1623, 8300, 9313, 9367, 11297, 11301
Barbin, Madeleine 12350
Barbosa, Waldemar de Almeida 7173

Bianconi, Piero 1378, 1380, 1381, 3741, 4938, 7271, 12813, 13031
Biberfeld, Arthur 8095
Biblioteca Nacional (Montevideo) 12528
Bibliothèque Municipale (La Rochelle) 3878
Bibliothèque Nationale (Paris) 1532, 1912, 2111, 2216, 2521, 2522, 3294, 3663, 6390, 7606
Bickford, Ted 12042, 12043
Biddle, Edward 5574, 12124
Bidermanis, Izis 1913
Biederman, Charles 1853
Biedermann, Margret 6194
Biedermann, Rolf 5017
Bieganskiego, Piotra 9127
Bieneck, Dorothea 11490
Biennali d'Arte Antica, Bologna 1746, 1747
Bier, Justus 10647, 10648, 10649, 10650, 10651
Bierbaum, Otto J. 12094, 12741
Bierens de Haan, Johan Catharinus Justus 7850
Biermann, Georg 2180, 2181, 6215, 9451, 11730
Biesboer, Peter 5084, 7052
Biez, Jacques de 7537
Bigi, Quirino 2244
Bigongiari, Piero 1738
Bihalji-Merin, Oto 10011
Bijl, Martin 5084
Bill, Max 5862, 8307
Billcliffe, Roger 7364, 7365, 7366, 7376
Billeter, Erika 4601
Billeter, Felix 11037
Bindeman, Barry 5107
Binder, M. J. 5068
Binding, Rudolf G. 6245
Bindman, David 954, 955, 971, 1605, 5379
Bingham, Madeleine 12833
Binion, Alice 4983, 9823
Binyon, Laurence 956, 1174, 2290, 2402, 4412
Biörklund, George 10363
Biornstad, Sissel 8880
Biraghi, Marco 9828
Birch, Dinah 12681
Bird, Paul 6341
Bird, Roy K. 8780
Birindello, Massimo 820
Birke, Veronika 10491, 10504
Birnbaum, Martin 420, 10128
Birnholz, Alan C. 7182
Birolli, Zeno 1017
Birren, Faber 12127
Birtwistle, Graham 5803
Bisanz, Hans 6317
Bisanz, Rudolf M. 11136
Bischof, Marco 932
Bischof, René 933
Bischofberger, Christina 12369
Bischoff, Ulrich 6058
Bishop, Morchand 2500
Bissell, Raymond Ward 4147, 4148
Bissell, Willard 5165
Bisthoven, A. Jannssens de 3390
Bittner, Herbert 6255

Bizardel, Yvon 2719
Bjelajac, David 119
Blache, Gérard 6449
Black, Charles C. 6885
Black, Peter 5177
Black, Robert 3269
Blackburn, Henry 1506
Blackert, Albert 377, 1048, 1049, 12256, 13019, 13021
Blackett-Ord, Carol 13597
Blackwell, Basil, Sir 8778
Blad, E. Maurice 929
Blais, Emile 9700
Blake, Peter 1340, 6621, 8308, 13667
Blanc, Charles 4749, 5642, 8188, 10364, 13049
Blanchard, Paula 1732
Blanche, Jacques-Emile 7538
Blank, Peter 9916
Blankert, Albert 377, 1048, 1049, 12256, 13019, 13021
Blaser, Werner 8309, 8310
Blatter, Silvio 3291
Blauensteiner, Kurt 2895
Bleikasten, Aimée 300
Blesh, Rudi 2609
Bless, Frits 10665
Blimlinger, Eva 5585
Bliss, Douglas Percy 7367
Bliss, Frank E. 6751
Bloberg, Maurice 5578
Bloch, Georges 9569
Bloch, Vitale 6495
Bloemink, Barbara 6389
Blok, Cor 8505
Blok, Gerard A. C. 9925
Blomberg, Erik 5268, 5809, 5810, 5811
Blomfield, Reginald T. 11658, 12895
Blondel, Auguste 12505
Bloomfield, Lin 7119
Blotkamp, Carel 8506
Blühm, Andreas 9299
Blum, André 1149, 2075, 5380, 7619, 13022, 13093
Blum, Gerd 5552
Blum, Ilse 7620
Blum, Napisala H. 13786
Blunden, Edmund 898
Blunden, Geofrey 7124
Blunt, Anthony 957, 990, 1102, 1807, 1809, 2723, 7602, 9570, 9941, 9942, 9943, 11599
Blunt, Wilfrid 13389
Bo, Carlo 1176
Boas, George 2300
Boase, Thomas S. R. 12871
Bober, Natalie 9066
Bocher, Emmanuel 6391, 6416, 11204
Bock, Catherine C. 7923
Bock, Elfried 7861
Bock, Franz 4939
Bock, Henning 8857, 12639
Bock, Paul A. de 2731

Botkin, Izdal M. 5704
Botnick, Diane 9135
Bott, Gerhard 12296
Bott, Katharina 12311
Bottari, Stefano 251, 252, 253, 476, 491, 704, 2246, 9779
Böttcher, Otto 11138
Botteon, Vincenzo 2061
Bottineau, Yves 3940, 13919
Böttinger, Johan 13233
Bottomley, Gordon 8974
Bouche, Louis 5226
Boucher, Bruce 9320, 9323
Boucher, Emmanuel 8684
Boucher, François 12014
Bouchet, André du 4213, 4214
Bouchitté, Hervé 9944
Bouchot-Saupique, Jacqueline 1534
Boudaille, Georges 2303, 4055, 5749, 9575, 9588
Boulton, Janet 8972
Boulton, William B. 3956, 10566
Bourchard, Gustave 1450
Bourdelle, Antoine 10788, 10789
Bourdon, David 1509, 2041, 2042, 2043, 11213, 13304
Bouret, Jean 1777, 2778, 10988, 12546, 12794
Bourget, Pierre 7607
Bourgier, Annette M. 6496
Bourniquel, Camille 4468
Boussard, Joseph F. 11039
Boussel, Patrice 6830
Bouvenne, Aglaus 8128
Bouvet, François 1067
Bouvier, Jean Bernard 2070
Bouvier, Marguette 7462
Bouvy, Eugène 2523, 8955
Bouyer, Raymond 2076
Bovero, Anna 2392, 2393
Bovi, Arturo 6831, 9856
Bovy, Adrien 534
Bowdoin College Museum of Fine Arts (Brunswick, Maine) 587
Bowen, Marjorie 5381
Bowie, Theodore R. 5413, 13126
Bowlt, John E. 12002
Bown-Taevernier, Sabine 3251, 3259
Bowness, Alan 2304, 5229, 5304, 8624, 9436
Boyd, James D. 1283
Boyer, Ferdinand 8979
Boyer d'Agen, Jean 10884
Boyle-Turner, Caroline 807, 4056, 11589
Bozzoni, Corrado 1422
Brach, Albert 9780
Brackett, Oliver 1999
Brachot, Isy 7441
Bradley, Ian 8737
Bradley, John W. 2120
Bradley, William S. 9150
Brady, Darlene 6623
Brady, Elizabeth A. 4266

Bragdon, Claude 778
Braham, Allan 3626, 7603
Braham, Helen 6216
Brahm, Otto 11943
Braider, Donald 753
Bramanti, Kathleen L. 8246
Bramly, Serge 6832, 10277
Bramsen, Alfred 5094
Branchi, Maria Pia 13572
Branchick, Thomas 778
Brandani, Edoardo 2006
Brandes, Georg 8190
Brandi, Cesare 1581, 2947, 4401, 5040, 7656, 8642, 8643
Brandt, Klaus J. 3225
Brangwyn, Rodney 1285
Brasil, Jaime 6833, 12928
Brassaï 9576
Brauer, Heinrich 819
Braun, Christian 10631
Braun, Emily 778, 11752
Braun, Wilhelm 166
Brauner, Christian 8787, 10631
Brauner, Lothar 7083
Braunfels, Wolfgang 2442, 4469
Braunfels-Esche, Sigrid 6834
Braungart, Richard 786
Bray, Salomon de 6000
Brayer, Yves 2301
Bredius, Abraham 10372, 11945, 12526
Bredt, Ernst W. 2020, 6318
Breeskins, Adelyn D. 379, 382, 1355, 1783, 1784
Brehm, Margrit Franziska 1664
Breicha, Otto 6133, 6228, 6319, 10160, 10161, 13630, 13635
Brejon de Lavergnée, Barbara 8038, 8041, 13222, 13227, 13228
Bremmer, Henricus P. 4470
Brenna, Arne 13103
Brenzoni, Raffaello 4302, 7062, 8725, 9756
Breslin, James E. B. 10965
Breton, André 2977, 4601, 12182
Brett, David 7370
Brettell, Richard 4099, 9801, 9802
Breuer, Gerda 8022
Breuer, Stephanie 11226
Breuning, Margaret 10017
Breuning, Mary 1786
Brewer, Robert 7257
Brewer, Roy 4267
Brey Marino, Maria 10336
Brezianu, Barbu 1266
Bricarelli, Carlo 10181
Bricon, Etienne 10041
Bridenbaugh, Carl 5110
Bridges, Ann 8813
Brieger-Wasservogel, Lothar 6157, 7106, 8008, 12758
Brielle, Roger 7054
Briganti, Giuliano 1495, 2007, 2279, 5001, 9685, 9794, 12314, 13598

Buddensieg, Tilmann 691
Buderath, Bernhard 690, 5580
Budigna, Luciano 11479
Budrys, Stanislovas 10688
Buechner, Thomas S. 10770
Buekschmitt, Justus 7998
Buerkel, Ludwig von 1443
Buffalo Fine Arts Academy 420
Buffinga, A. 10667
Buhlmann, Britta 11728, 11729
Buijsen, Edwin 4722, 9929, 12608
Buisson, Dominique 3683
Buisson, Sylvie 3683
Buizard, L. M. 13050
Bule, Steven 13073
Bullard, E. John 1787, 11788
Bulláty, Sonja 12100
Bullock, Albert E. 4251
Bullock, Barbara 1455, 1456
Bultmann, Bernhard 6217
Bünemann, Hermann 7675, 10510
Bunge, Matthias 7084
Bunnell, Peter C. 1525, 1654, 10348, 12033,
    12736, 13481, 13556
Bunt, Cyril G. E. 1286, 1287, 2139
Buono, O. del 3744
Burchard, Ludwig 11040
Burchfield, Charles 5557
Burchfield Center at State University College,
    Buffalo, N.Y. 1464
Burckhardt, Carl J. 3282
Burckhardt, Jacqueline 882
Burckhardt, Jakob 11041
Burckhardt, Rudolf F. 2062, 4122
Burda, Hubert 10756
Burdin, Arthur 814
Burgbacher-Krupka, Ingrid 883
Burger, Angelika 8644
Bürger, Fritz 6532, 9321
Burger, Willy 13484
Burke, Doreen Bolger 10480
Burke, James 1167
Burke, Joseph 5383
Burke, Peter 3757
Burkhard, Arthur 1469, 4941
Burlamacchi, L. 10736
Burlington, Richard 9322
Burlington Fine Arts Club (London) 685, 2347,
    4413
Burn, Lucilla 8012
Burne-Jones, Georgina M. 1474
Burnet, John 10379, 12643
Burnett, David 6100
Burnett, Robert 4057
Burns, Edward 9676
Burns, Howard 9323, 10196
Burova, G. 248
Burr, Frederick M. 192
Burresi, Mariagiulia 9771
Burri, René 932, 933
Burri, Rosellina Bischof 933

Burroughs, Alan 8336
Burroughs, Polly 779
Burscheidt, Margret E. 12409
Burton, Anthony 13413
Burton, William 13414
Burty, Philippe 4589, 5598, 8027, 8129, 8953
Bury, Adrian 4260, 6511, 12601, 13584
Buscaroli, Rezio 8043
Busch, Günter 673, 7085, 7093, 8431, 8440, 8857,
    11509, 12824, 12826
Busch, Ludger 8821
Busche, Ernst A. 7071
Buschmann, Paul, Jr. 5788
Buschor, Ernst 9526
Busch-Reisinger Museum, Harvard University
    (Cambridge, Mass.) 4879
Busco, Marie 10790, 13471
Bush, Martin H. 5103, 12614
Bush Memorial Library, Hamline University (St.
    Paul, Minn.) 7611
Bush-Brown, Albert 12109
Bushart, Bruno 5437
Bushman, Richard L. 3184
Busignani, Alberto 9857, 13074
Busiri Vici, Andrea 7130
Bussche, Willy van den 9470, 13622
Busse, Hermann E. 12282
Bussmann, Georg 431
Bussmann, Klaus 10853
Bustamante Garcia, Augustin 4801
Butler, Arthur S. 7330
Butler, Ruth 10791, 10792
Butlin, Martin 959, 960, 961, 9384, 12644, 12679
Butor, Michel 2732, 11961
Büttner, Frank 12322
Byesen, Lars Rostrup 9694

C

C. G. Boerner (Düsseldorf) 5923
Ca' Corner della Regina (Venice) 11172
Ca' Giustinian (Venice) 13059
Cabanne, Pierre 2956, 2957, 2958, 3706, 4474,
    7595, 7600, 9577, 13134, 13499
Cabinet des Dessins, Musée du Louvre (Paris) 696
Cabinet des Estampes, Musée d'Art et d'Histoire
    (Geneva) 12984
Cachin, Françoise 2627, 4058, 4059, 7539, 11608,
    11699, 11705
Cadorin, Giuseppe 12429
Caemmerer, H. Paul 6811
Caflisch, Nina 7394
Cage, John 11213
Cagli, Corrado 12430
Cahen, Gustave 1216
Cahiers d'Art 3296
Cahill, James F. 13759
Cahn, Erich B. 13235
Cahn, Isabelle 11765
Caillaux, Henriette 2495
Cailler, Pierre 370, 535, 1777, 2757, 3283, 4297,
    7544, 11503

Cain, Julien 1914, 2522
Cain, Michael 9067
Caine, Hall, Sir 10915
Caisse Nationale des Monuments Historiques et des Sites (Paris) 11877
Calabi, Augusto 9757
Calabrese, Omar 3753
Calamandrei, Piero 1828
Calder, Ritchie 6837
Calderini, Marco 3654
Caldwell, Colin 5383
Calí, Maria 8193
Caliari, Pietro 13060
Callen, Anthea 10511
Calley, Kathryn L. 131
Callman, Ellen 263
Callow, Philip 4475
Calmette, Joseph 11124
Calvert, Albert F. 4633, 4767, 8911, 12931
Calvesi, Maurizio 1014, 1019, 1665, 1666, 1746, 4313, 7731, 9731
Calvi, Gerolamo 6839
Calvi, Ignazio 6840
Calvi, Jacopo A. 481, 3789
Calvino, Italo 11963
Calvo Serraller, Francisco 4768
Calvocoressi, Richard 6218, 6236
Calzá, Gianni 6630
Calzada, Andrés M. 13921
Calzona, Arturo 13572
Cambry, Jacques 9945
Camesasca, Ettore 735, 1834, 5666, 7621, 7622, 8263, 9495, 9497, 13385
Camfield, William A. 3297, 9552
Cammaerts, Emile 11042
Cammell, Charles Richard 236, 237
Camón Aznar, Jose 4634, 4769, 7765, 9578, 12932
Campana, Adelemo 6841
Campbell, Lorne 13485
Campbell, Malcolm 2280, 9686
Campbell, Michael J. 7761
Campo y Francés, Angel del 12933
Canaday, John 31
Canella, Guido 4007
Canetti, Elias 13631
Caneva, Caterina 1177
Cannata, Francesco 10025
Canning, Susan Marie 12991
Cannon-Brookes, P. 1232
Canova, Giordana 1090
Cantaro, Maria Teresa 3631
Cantelli, Giuseppe 3909
Cantinelli, Richard 808, 2574
Cantone, Gaetana 3461
Canuti, Fiorenzo 9496
Capa, Cornell 67, 1645, 5992
Cape Ann Historical Association (Gloucester, Mass.) 6429
Caplow, Harriet M. 8301
Capote, Truman 372

Cappadona, Diane A. 9137
Capriglione, Anna A. 12872
Caprile, Luciano 415
Caproni, Giorgio 12547
Capuis, Loredana 98
Caramel, Luciano 10957
Carandente, Giovanni 8605, 9506, 11568
Caravaggi, Giovanni 3625
Carbonare, Rita Dalle 13217
Carboneri, Nino 5008, 9992
Carco, Francis 12776, 13187
Cardazzo, Carlo 1573
Cardellini, Ida 2776
Carden, Robert W. 12873
Cardinal, Roger 8965
Cardon, Roger 6790
Cardoza y Aragón, Luis 9246
Carey, Frances 8619
Cario, Louis 1217
Carli, Enzo 1424, 2948, 4355, 7063, 7248, 8194, 8447, 9706, 9781, 11293, 12372, 12727
Carline, Richard 11905
Carls, Carl D. 505
Carlson, Victor 7917, 9149
Carlton House Terrace (London) 6789
Carluccio, Luigi 4212
Carmean, E. A., Jr. 3808, 11803
Carnegie Institute (Pittsburgh) 3155
Caro-Delvaille, Henry 9527, 12431
Caröe, William D. 13646
Carofano, Pierluigi 7213
Caroli, Flavio 229, 625, 6838, 7272, 12432
Carotti, Giulio 6842
Carpani, Giuseppe 12433
Carpeggiani, Paolo 4419, 4420
Carpenter, John T. 12602
Carpenter, William H. 3119
Carpi, Piera 4421
Carpiceci, Alberto C. 6843
Carr, Carolyn Kinder 6374
Carr, Gerald L. 2052
Carr-Gom, Sarah 7540
Carrà, Carlo 2758, 3655, 4356
Carrà, Massimo 1738, 1739, 3656, 7956
Carracciolo, Maria Teresa 1495
Carrascal Munoz, José 13922
Carrasco, Eduardo 7989
Carreras, Pietro 12849
Carrier, David 9946
Carrieri, Raffaele 2105
Carroll, Eugene A. 10947, 10948
Cars, Jean des 5152, 5154
Carson, Julia M. 1788
Carstensen, Hans Thomas 10380
Carter, Edward C. 6525, 6526
Carter, Edward G. 6529
Carter, Peter 8311
Cartier, Etienne 209
Cartier, Jean-Albert 9931
Cartwright, Julia 3790, 8351
Cary, Elisabeth L. 962, 2524, 8738, 10916, 13500

Casa de Velázquez (Madrid) 12934
Casa del Mantegan (Mantua) 3995
Casadio, Paolo 4988, 13170
Casanelles, Enric 4013
Cascales y Muñoz, José 13923
Casey, Robert J. 1099
Cash, Philip 10685
Cason del Buen Retiro (Madrid) 13924
Cassa di Risparmio di Vignola 13111
Cassa Salvi, Elvira 8693, 10863
Cassedy, David 8808, 8811
Cassou, Jean 1574, 1915, 2525, 2685, 2722, 2993,
    4434, 4770, 5643, 6360, 6724, 9579, 12507,
    13640
Castagnary, Jules A. 2305
Castaing, Marcellin 11893
Castel Sant'angelo (Rome) 9730
Castelfranchi-Vegas, Liana 4393
Castelfranco, Giorgio 6844
Castelfranco Veneto (Venice) 4314
Castellaneta, Carlo 5172, 9497
Castello Sforzesco (Milan) 3634
Castellanos, Jordi 4034
Castelnuovo, Enrico 3689, 9772, 13570
Casteras, Susan P. 10301
Castillo, Alberto del 11588
Castillo, Jorge 12529
Castleden, Louise D. 1812
Castleman, Riva 5750
Castri, Serenella 7879
Castro, Luis de 848
Catalá Roca, Francesc 8383
Cataldo, Noella de 9509
Cate, Phillip D. 11974
Cathelin, Jean 308
Catoir, Barbara 10154
Caton, Joseph Harris 8479
Cattaneo, Irene 10898
Cattaui, Georges 7607
Caturla, Maria Louisa 13925
Caumont, Jacques 2975, 6122
Causa, Raffaello 8912
Causey, Andrew 8966, 8967
Cavadini, Luigi 4394
Cavalcaselle, Giovanni B. 10185, 12437
Cavallaro, Anna 9758
Cavalli, Gian Carlo 10500
Cavallo, Luigi 8140
Cavallucci, Camillo J. 10737
Caversazzi, Ciro 1703
Caws, Mary Ann 2209
Cayrol, Jean 7531
Cazalis, Henri 10337
Cazort, Mimi 4003
Ceán Bermúdez 7401
Ceccarelli, Anna 6845
Cecchi, Doretta 2098
Cecci, Emilio 2852, 4357, 4358, 7249, 9123, 9903
Cecil, David 1475, 1560
Cedarlöf, Ulf 11544
Cela, Camilo José 8423

Celant, Germano 330, 884, 7640, 7641, 7644,
    7668, 7669, 7670, 9205, 9206
Cellier, L. 13349
Cendali, Lorenzo 768
Centraal Museum Utrecht 265, 11440
Centre Culturel du Marais (Paris) 12645
Centre de Création Industrielle (Paris) 8480
Centre de la Vieille Charitè (Marseille) 8587
Centre Georges Pompidou (Paris) 317, 344, 948,
    1439, 1908, 2463, 2464, 2841, 2982, 3009,
    6450, 6685, 7143, 7501, 7964, 7965, 10978,
    11573, 12183, 12798, 13640
Centre National d'Art Contemporaine (Paris) 266,
    729, 922
Centre National de la Recherche Scientifique
    (Paris) 11878
Centro d'Arte Dolomiti (Cortina d'Ampezzo) 3466
Centro de Arte Reina Sofia (Madrid) 12168
Cercle de la Librairie (Paris) 2899
Ceriani, Franco Buzzi 4007
Cermenati, Mario 6895
Cerni, Vicente Aguilera 4591, 4592
Cernuschi, Claude 9865, 9866
Cerny, Vratislav 1843
Ceroni, Ambrogio 8448, 8449, 8465
Certigny, Henry 10989, 10990
Cerutti Fusco, Annarosa 5768
Cervigni, Dino S. 1837
Cevese, Renato 9315, 9324, 9366
Ceysson, Bernard 11883, 11889
Ch'eng Hsi 13296
Chabrun, Jean-François 4635, 10799
Chaim, John 7673
Chalon, Jean 13100
Chamberlain, Arthur B. 3958, 5438, 10869
Chamberlaine, John 5439
Chambers, Charles E. S. 6714
Chamot, Mary 6464
Champa, Kermit Swiler 8507
Champeaux, Alfred de 7859
Champfleury [pseud., Jules Fleury] 2526, 6512,
    6798
Champigneulle, Bernard 10793, 12777
Champion, Claude 11400
Champion, Jeanne 12795
Champion, Pierre 13350
Champris, Pierre de 9580
Chamson, Lucie 3874
Chancellor, John 362
Chang, Wan-li 2050
Chanin, Abraham 3938
Chanlaine, Pierre 2789
Channin, Richard 283
Chantavoine, Jean 13025
Chantelou, Paul Friart de 823, 824
Chanzit, Gwen Finkel 614
Chapelle, Arnaud de la 2103
Chapin Library, Stetson Hall, Williams
    College (Williamstown, Mass.) 11043
Chaplin, Harry F. 7120
Chapman, Brian 5153

Chapman, H. Perry 10381
Chapman, Joan M. 5153
Chapman, Ronald 13390
Chapon, François 10971
Chaponnière, Paul 12506
Chappell, Miles L. 117
Chappuis, Adrien 1856, 1861, 1862
Charensol, Georges 823, 6042, 10972
Charles E. Slatkin Galleries (New York) 8700
Charlot, Jean 9255
Charpentier, Françoise-Thérèse 3981
Charteris, Evan E. 11271
Chartier, Emile *see* Alain
Charvet, Léon 9488, 11547
Chassé, Charles 4060, 4061
Chastel, André 1178, 6846, 6906, 9947, 11601,
    11933, 13251, 13264
Chastenet, Jacques 4636
Chateau de Blois (Blois, France) 2527
Château de Versailles 6596
Chaumeil, Louis 2884
Chaumelin, Marius 2618
Chave, Anna 1267, 7752
Chaves, Jonathan 13760
Chedid, Andrée 5002
Chegodaev, Andrei 5973
Cheim, John 6308
Chelazzi Dini, Giulietta 10120, 10123
Chen, Shih-Hsiang 6315
Cheney, Ednah D. 10259
Cheney, Liana DeGirolami 13501
Chenivesse, Dominique 11216
Chennevières, Henry de 12323
Cherchi, Placido 6059
Cherpin, Jean 1863
Chesson, Wilfred H. 2411
Chester, Gilbert Keith 963
Chesterton, Gilbert K. 13391
Chetham, Charles S. 4476
Chetwood, Mrs. 10848
Chevalier, Denys 7463
Chevalier, Jean 4435
Chevalley, Denis A. 2942
Chevillard, Valbert 1984
Chiang Fu-ts'ung 13293
Chiappini, Rudy 780
Chiarelli, Renzo 9754
Chiarenza, Carl 11753
Chiarini, Marco 4201, 6533
Chiasserini, Vera 3745
Chierici, Gino 12850
Chiesa del Gesù (Ancona, Italy) 7273
Chih-yung, Chu Sui-liang 13441
Chimirri, Bruno 10026
Chinard, Gilbert 5569
Chiodi, Luigi 7274
Chipp, Herschel B. 5606
Chisholm, Lawrence W. 13439
Chitty, Susan 6574
Choay, Françoise 6625
Choing, Alan 4131

Chou, Tao-chen 13442
Christ, Yvan 6698
Christ-Janer, Albert 11184
Christensen, Laura J. 3190
Christiansen, Keith 4142, 7633
Christin, Anne-Marie 3879, 3882
Christman, Margaret C. S. 6374
Christoffel, Ulrich 2077, 3549, 4132, 5440, 12434
Chu, Doris C. J. 12189
Chukovskii, Kornei I. 10540, 10548
Chung, Saehyang P. 13814
Church, Arthur H. 13415
Churchill, Karen L. 2632
Churchill, Sydney J. 12874
Chytil, Karel 7519
Cianci, Giovanni 7035
Ciardi, Roberto Paolo 7213, 10949
Cicognara, Leopoldo 1621, 1628, 1629
Ciervo, Joaquin 3675
Cikovsky, Nicolai, Jr. 5510, 5511, 5672, 5673,
    5674, 8788, 9441, 13502
Cinotti, Mia 1667, 1668, 1691, 13830
Cionini Visani, Maria 2121, 8379
Cipriani, Renata 3658, 7623
Ciranna, Alfonso 2012, 7657, 7661
Cirici, Alexandre 12208
Cirici Pellicer, Alejandro 8384, 9581
Cirlot, Juan-Eduardo 4014, 8385, 9582, 12209
Cisternino del Poccianti (Livorno) 3467
Città di Vercelli 13179
Cittadella, Luigi N. 12632
City Art Galleries (Sheffield) 128
City Art Gallery (Bristol) 2499
City Art Museum of St. Louis 2633
City Museum of Brussels 13486
Civico Istituto di Cultura Popolare (Luino) 7318
Cladders, Johannes 12292
Cladel, Judith 7464, 10794, 10834
Clair, Jean 2732, 2959, 2960, 2961, 2962, 7924
Clairet, Alain 2844
Clapp, Anne de Coursey 12190, 13444
Clapp, Frederick M. 9896, 9897
Clar, Jane 9142
Clare, Charles 12646
Clarenbach, Dietrich 6208
Clark, Anthony M. 600
Clark, Carol 10020
Clark, Fiona 8739
Clark, Kenneth 629, 1179, 3746, 6847, 6952,
    8600, 8604, 9144, 10382
Clark, Nicholas 8045
Clark, Timothy J. 2306, 7541
Clark, Trinkett 11804
Clarke, Michael 2217
Claus, Hugo 267
Clausen, G. 597
Clausse, Gustave 11244, 12435
Claussnitzer, Gert 7805
Clay, Rotha M. 5631
Clayton, Tim 12085
Clearwater, Bonnie 2963

Crowe, Joseph A. 10185, 12437
Cruttwell, Maud 7624, 9859, 10739, 11707, 13075
Cruzada Villaamil, D. G. 4637, 12935
Cugini, Davide 8727
Cuming, Edward D. 8714
Cumming, Robert 12647
Cummings, Hildegard 13436
Cummings, Paul 11805, 11811
Cunningham, Allan 13576
Cunningham, Peter 5769
Cuno, James B. 6380
Cuppers, Joachim 601
Curcin, Milan 8145
Curjel, Hans 432, 13001
Curry, David Park 5140
Curtis, Atherton 1061, 5683
Curtis, Charles B. 8913, 12936
Curtis, Penelope 5230
Curtis, William J. R. 6628
Cust, Lionel H. 3120, 3121
Cust, Robert H. 1838, 11841
Cuypers, Firmin 3246
Cuzin, Jean Pierre 3707
Czestochowski, Joseph H. 2438, 2601
Czwiklitzer, Christophe 9585, 13817
Çekalska-Zborowska, Halina 9243

D

D. Caz-Delbo Galleries (New York) 3666
Daadgalerie (Berlin) 13217
Dabrowski, Magdalena 5035, 9908
Dacier, Emile 11205, 13351
Dacos, Nicole 4397, 10186
D'adda, Gerolamo 6855
Dafforne, James 6419, 8842, 12648
Daftari, Fereshteh 7929
D'Agen, Boyer 5645
Daguerre, Isabelle Neto 4754
Dahhan, Bernard 12861
Dahlem, Franz 575
Daingerfield, Elliott 5675
Daix, Pierre 4066, 5117, 9586, 9587, 9588, 9589, 9653, 10797, 11884
Dake, Carel L. 5689
Dal Co, Francesco 8306, 12040
Dal Poggetto, Paolo 8199, 13902
Dal-Gal, Niccolò 8726
Dale, Antony 13765
Dali, Ana Maria 2465
Dali, Salvador 8352
Dalisi, Riccardo 4017
Dalli Regoli, Gigetta 7258, 7879
Damase, Jacques 2716, 3247
Damerini, Gino 4985
D'Amico, Rosalba 13167
Damon, Samuel Foster 964
Damsch-Wiehager, Renate 9184, 9185, 13292
Damsgaard, Nina 11866
Dan, Naoki 12373
Dana, Richard H. 118

Danes, Gibson A. 12749
Danforth, George E. 8322
Danforth Museum (Framingham, Mass.) 3667
Daniel, Howard 1120, 1538
Daniel, Pete 5765
Daniels, Jeffrey 10593, 10594
Danielsson, Bengt 4064, 4065
Daninos, Andrea 7216
Danly, Susan 3158
Danniell, Frederick B. 2287
Danoff, I. Michael 11678
Danto, Arthur C. 7671
Dantzig, Maurits M. van 4481, 5069
Danz, Ernst 11766
Danziger, James 645
D'Arco, Carlo 4423
Darel, Henri 535
Dargenty, G. [pseud., Arthur Auguste Mallebay Du Cluseau D'Echérac] 4895, 13352
Daria, Sophie 6629
Dark, Sidney 9263
Darr, Alan Phipps 2858, 13073
Darracott, Joseph 2144
Darragon, Eric 7545, 11619
D'Aruia, Antonio 5358
Dater, Judy 2432
Dauberville, Henry 1069
Dauberville, Jean 1069
Däubler, Theodor 271, 1921, 6117
Daudet, Alphonse 3668
Daudet, Léon 12598
Daulby, Daniel 10386
Daulte, François 620, 621, 10513, 11761, 11762
Daun, Berthold 6294, 12049, 13158
Daux, Pierre 9587
David d'Angers, Robert 2593
David, Henri 11794
Davidson, Angus 6575
Davidson, Jane P. 12238
Davidson Art Center, Wesleyan University (Middletown, Conn.) 11206
Davies, Edward 8914
Davies, Gerald S. 4202, 5070, 5442
Davies, Hugh M. 11932
Davies, Jane B. 2607
Davies, Martin 2394, 13487
Davies, Randall 4414, 10870
D'Aviler, Augustin C. 7001
Davillier, Jean C. 3676
Davis, Alexander 8603
Davis, John, Jr. 7486
Davis, Margaret D. 3749
Davis, Melinda D. 5514
Davis, Richard A. 6353
Davis, Terence 8958, 8959
D'Avossa, Antonio 11192
Davray, Jean 8200
Davvetas, Démosthénes 12713
Davy, d'Annick 6662
Davydova, Alla S. 6298
Dawe, George 8713

Diehl, Gaston 2760, 3298, 6730, 7931
Diel, Louise 6258
Dienst, Rolf-Gunter 7114
Dieran, Bernard van 3271
Dierkens-Aubry, Françoise 5562, 5563
Dierks, Hermann 5570
Dietrich, Irmtraud 8847
Dietschi, Peter 5321
Dieterle, Jean 2237
Dievoet, E. van 8168
Díez Del Corral, Luis 12937
Di Fabio, Clario 7414
Digne, Danielle 1052
Dijkstra, Jeltje 13488
Dilasser, Antoinette 12600
Dillenberger, John 13464
Dillon, Edward 11044
Dillon, Gianvittorio 7277
Dilworth, Ira 1733
Di Micheli, Mario 3468
Dimier, Louis 10037, 10038
Dines, Elaine 9287
Dini, Francesca 13831
Dini, Piero 25, 11718
Dippie, Brian W. 1818, 11165, 11166
Di Provvido, Sandra 2395
Dirks, Rudolf 13657
Dirr, Pius 5481
Dirrigl, Michael 11922
Di San Lazzaro, Gualtieri 6062, 7739
Di Stefano, Guido 9180
Distel, Anne 1499, 11497, 11608
Distl, Dieter 6805
Dittman, Lorenz 4942, 11781
Dittman, Reider 8892
Dittmar, Peter 11976
Dittrich, Christian 7307
Dixon, Rob 12085
Dixon Gallery and Gardens (Memphis, Tenn.)
    3027
Dmitrienko, Mariia F. 12938
Dobai, Johannes 6135, 6140, 6147
Dobai, Katharina 12381
Dobbs, Brian 10917
Dobbs, Judy 10917
Döblin, Alfred 11237
Dobrée, Bonamy 12838
Dobryzcka, Anna 4721
Dobson, Austin 900, 5385
Doderer, Heimito von 5021, 5022
Dodgson, Campbell 2351, 3041, 3669, 5740, 6751
D'Oench, Ellen 2808
Doering, Oscar 9301
Doezema, Marianne 755
Doherty, Robert J. 10680
Doherty, Terence 12082
Dohme, Robert 8103
Doiteau, Victor 4482
Dolcini, Loretta 13076
Dolenský, Antonin 5489
Dombrady, G. S. 13334

Doménech, Rafael 11869
Domenikos Theotokopoulos Kres 4774
Domiani Almeyda, Giuseppe 13113
Domínguez Ortiz, Antonio 12939, 12940
Domm, Anne-S 7703, 7710, 7712
Donald, Diana 10578
Donath, Adolph 12759
Donati, Pier P. 3945
Donati, Ugo 7395
Doner, Alexander 616
Donin, Richard K. 11298
Dönz-Breimaier, Maria Gertrud 5202
Dorazio, Virginia Dortch 455
Dorbec, Prosper 3880, 11005
Dordrechts Museum (Dordrecht, Netherlands) 2444
Doré Gallery (London) 2901
Doremus, Thomas 13672
Dorey, Helen 11840
Dorfles, Gillo 3492, 11630, 13615
Doria, Arnauld 12504
Dörig, José 9223
Döring, Bruno A. 9834
Dorival, Bernard 343, 1864, 1952, 1953, 1954,
    1956, 2408, 2717, 2718, 2779, 3005, 3009,
    9810, 10974, 12824
Dorment, Richard 13502
Dorn, Roland 4504
Dorner, Alexander 858, 7856
Dorra, Henri 11605
Dorsch, Klaus 13399
Dorst, Jean 10334
Dortu, M. G. 12551, 12561
Doss, Erika Lee 781, 9867
Dossi, Barbara 10504
Dostál, Eugène 5490
Doughty, Oswald 10918, 10931
Douglas, Charlotte 7489, 7490
Douglas, Robert L. 211, 9682
Douvee, D. H. 167
Dowd, David 2577
Downes, Kerry 5161, 12834, 12835, 13647
Downes, William H. 5515, 11274
Draibel, Henri [pseud., Henri Beraldi] 8685
Draper, James David 857
Dréolle De Nodon, Ernest 6516
Drestrée, Jules 13490
Drexler, Arthur 8312, 8318, 9052, 11767, 13673
Drey, Franz 2396
Dreyfous, Georges 4320
Dreyfous, Maurice 2497
Driggs, Howard R. 5710
Driscoll, John P. 2603
Dross, Friedrich 499
Drost, Willi 3229, 3230
Droste, Magdalena 8824
Drot, Jean-Marie 7731, 7832
Drucker, Malka 5840
Drucker, Michel 10514
Druick, Douglas 3448, 4056
Druwé, Robert 11045
Dryfhout, John H. 11209

Dube, Annemarie 5180, 6023
Dube, Wolf-Dieter 5180, 6023
Dube-Heynig, Annemarie 6024, 6033, 6036
DuBois, Guy P. 5548, 11784
Du Bois, Guy Pène 6570
Dubosc, Jean-Pierre 13443
Du Bouchet, André 4213, 4214
Dubray, Jean 1760, 5053, 10887
Dubuisson, A. 1062
Duby, Georges 11885
Du Carrois, Norbert R. 4215
Ducati, Pericle 8013, 10001
Duchateau, Jacques 2617
Dückers, Alexander 400, 4909, 6158, 13290
Duclaux, Lise 1221, 8980
Du Colombier, Pierre 2620, 4617
Ducret, André 6631
Ducrey, Marina 12823
Ducrot, Nicolas 5994, 5997
Dufay, Charles J. 9489
Dufet, Michel 1233, 1234
Duff, James H. 13771, 13772
Duflo, Pierre 5054
Dufour, Pierre 9591
Duhamel, George 2522
Duhem, Pierre 6856
Dülberg, Franz 5072
Duliere, Cecile 5564
Dulles, Owen J. 2082
Dumanthier, Ernest 5712
Dumas, Alexandre 8025
Dumas, Ann 13264
Dumesnil, Henri 12618
Dumont-Wilden, Louis 6003
Dumur, Guy 11935
Duncan, David D. 9592, 9593
Duncan, Hugh Dalziel 12111
Duncan, J. L. 636
Dunlop, Ian 2637
Dunn, Henry Treffry 10919
Dunow, Esti 11897
Dunoyer de Segonzac, André 2761
Du Pasquier, Jacqueline 2450
Dupin, Jacques 4216, 8387, 8388, 11723
Duplaquet, Charles-Vincent 6517
Duplessis, Georges 1153
Duppa, Richard 8205
Du Prey, Pierre de la Ruffinière 11833, 11834
Duran i Albareda, Montserrat 5822
Durand, John 3029
Durand-Greveille, E. 3394
Durand-Ruel, Charles 10513
Durande, Amédée 13053
Durant, Stuart 13229
Durbe, Dario 3469
Dürck-Kaulbach, Josefa 5935
Duret, Théodore 2312, 4483, 7546, 7547, 10515, 12552, 13503
Durozoi, Gérard 7932
Dürr, Alphons 9189
Durrell, Lawrence 1325

Durrieu, Paul 3692, 3693
Dürst, Hans 7410
Durtain, Luc 7806
Dussieux, Louis E. 7009
Dussler, Luitpold 705, 769, 8206, 8207, 9718, 10187, 11708
Duthuit, Claude 7933, 7934
Duthuit, Georges 7972
Duthuit-Matisse, Marguerite 7934
Dutton, Ralph 13648
Duve, Thierry de 2969
Duverger, Erik 12240
Duverger, Jozef 8035
Duyckinck, Evert Augustus 193
Dvořák, Anna 8813
Dvorák, Frantisek 6355
Dvorak, Max 1384, 3395

E
Earland, Ada 9224
Earp, Thomas W. 2832, 5741
Eastlake, Elizabeth R. 4258
Easton, Elizabeth Wynne 13252
Easton, Malcolm 5742
Eates, Margot 8969, 8970
Eaton, Leonard K. 10602, 13674
Eaubonne, Françoise d' 13353
Eberhardt, Hans-Joachim 7065
Eberhardt, Joachim 703
Eberlein, Kurt K. 13280
Ebers, Georg 129
Ebert, Hans 4133
Ebert-Schifferer, Sybille 488, 10505
Ecke, Goesta 8132
Ecker, Jürgen 3550
Eckert, Christian L. M. 2204
Eckert, Georg 9024
Eckstein, Hans 9025
Ecole Nationale des Beaux-Arts (Paris) 7548
Ecole Nationale Supérieure des Beaux-Arts, Chapelle des Petits-Augustins (Paris) 13143
Eddy, Arthur J. 13504
Ede, H. S. 4038, 4039
Edelstein, T. J. 8701
Edgerton, Samuel 4361
Edkins, Diane E. 5711
Edmond, Mary 5281
Edmondson, Amy 3897
Edwards, Paul 7028
Edwards, Richard 5593, 11669, 13444
Eemans, Marc 8054
Eerde, Katherine S. van 5491
Efimova, Nina I. 11557
Efros, Abram M. 1923, 13012
Eganbiuri, Eli 6465
Egeland, Erik 8998
Egerton, Judy 12083, 13754
Eggeling, Tilo 6189
Egger, Hermann 5192, 7396
Eggers, Friedrich 10260
Eggers, George W. 756

Fernow, Carl Ludwig 1765
Ferrari, Claudia Gian 9793
Ferrari, Germana 7986
Ferrari, Giulio 1586
Ferrari, Luigi 9327
Ferrari, Maria L. 10865
Ferrari, Oreste 4307, 4308, 12321
Ferrario, Luigi 6910
Ferré, Jean 13355
Ferrey, Benjamin 10063, 10064
Ferrier, Jean-Louis 853, 1875, 12862, 13458
Ferriguto, Arnaldo 4321
Fessenden, De Witt H. 2775
Feu de Carvalho, Theophilo 7175
Feuchtmayr, Inge 10347
Feuchtmeyr, Karl 1471
Feuchtmüller, Rupert 4045, 4046, 6358
Feuillet de Conches, Félix 10764
Feuillet, Maurice 3708
Feulner, Adolf 5013, 5014
Feurstein, Heinrich 4944
Fezzi, Elda 10516
Ffoulkes, Constance J. 3659
Ficacci, Luigi 8039
Fichera, Francesco 12852
Fidell-Beaufort, Madeleine 2512
Fiedler, Conrad 7704
Fiege, Gertrud 3839
Field, Richard S. 5752
Field, William B. 6577, 6715
Fielding, Mantle 12124
Fiengo, Giuseppe 12853
Fierens, Paul 1388, 2887, 3252, 4493, 6799, 9471, 11474
Fierens-Gevaert, Hippolyte 3126, 5790, 13566
Fierst, John 10677
Fifield, William 8450
Figgis, Darrell 970
Figueiredo, José de 4583
Filedt Kok, J. P. 7853, 13810
Filimonov, Georgii D. 12764
Filippi, Elena 5188
Fillon, Benjamin 2136
Fils, Alexander 9106
Finberg, Alexander J. 12650, 12651, 12652, 12653, 12654
Finch, Christopher 10771
Finamore, Daniel 1223
Fine, Ruth E. 3797, 7073, 7718, 13502, 13505
Fine Art Society, London 421
Finer, Ann 13424
Finkelstein, Louis 4240
Finkelstein, Nat 13308
Finley, Gerald 12655
Finn, David 8604
Fiocco, Giuseppe 256, 1711, 1712, 4322, 4986, 7625, 7626, 7627, 9912, 9992, 11252, 12071, 13061
Fiodorov-Davydov, Alexei 7018, 11679
Fiore, F. Paolo 3778
Firmenich, Andrea 1568

Firmenich-Richartz, Eduard 1435
Firpo, Luigi 6862
Fischel, L. 4155
Fischel, Oskar 10192, 10193, 12440
Fischer, A. M. 582, 3324
Fischer, Chris 551
Fischer, David Hackett 10561
Fischer, Friedhelm W. 675, 676
Fischer, Fritz 7884
Fischer, Gert 9953
Fischer, Guido 350
Fischer, Lothar 2816
Fischer, Otto 434
Fischer, Pius 13843
Fischer, Wolfgang 11323
Fish, Arthur 8326
Fisher, Dorothy Canfield 10772
Fisher, Jay McKean 7550
Fitch, James M. 4881, 4882
Fitzgerald, Percy 44
Fitzsimmons, James 2929
Fitzwilliam Museum (Cambridge, England) 971, 7128
Flagg, Jared 120
Flaiano, Ennio 12728
Flam, Jack D. 7939, 7940, 7941, 7962, 8797
Flat, Paul 8664
Flavell, Mary Kay 4910
Flechsig, Eduard 3046, 11401
Fleig, Karl 2
Fleming, Gordon H. 10921, 13506, 13507
Fleming, John 45, 13512
Fleming-Williams, Ian 2145, 2151
Flemming, Hanns T. 5203, 7896, 11510
Flemming, Willi 92, 508
Fles, Etha 10956
Flesche, Herman 10652
Fletcher, Banister F. 9328
Fletcher, Beaumont 13586
Fletcher, John E. 4068
Fletcher, Shelley 10442
Fletcher, Valerie J. 4217
Fleuret, Fernand 3870
Fleury, Jules see Champfleury
Flexner, James T. 2171, 2172, 5516, 12074
Flint, Janet A. 13437
Floerke, Gustav 1033
Floerke, Hanns 1033
Flora, Francesco 6863
Florence, Penny 7551
Flores, Carlos 4018, 5823
Flores d'Arcais, Francesca 13183
Florida State University Art Gallery (Tallahassee, Fla.) 9277
Florisoone, Michel 1763, 1962, 2583, 4494, 7552
Flüeler, Niklaus 934
Flügge, Gerhard 13852, 13853, 13862
Flukinger, Roy 7762
Focarino, Joseph 6417
Focillon, Henri 3750, 5416, 9731, 10389
Fogaccia, Piero 3444

Fogg Art Museum, Harvard University (Cambridge, Mass.) 1985, 5648, 9596, 11806, 12324, 13131, 13773
Foggi, Rossella 7782
Fohl, Thomas 5209
Foister, Susan 13597
Folena, Gianfranco 4000
Folgarait, Leonard 11734
Follmann, Anna-Barbara 9396
Folnesics, Hans 1427
Folon, Jean Michel 8646
Fong, Wen 12201
Fondation di Pierre Gianadda (Martigny) 9093
Fondation Maeght (Paris/Saint Paul) 1070, 1300, 1514, 4218, 5967, 7115, 8390, 8391, 9093
Fondazione Giorgio Cini (Venice) 12441
Fondo Editorial de la Plástica Mexicana (Mexico City) 10703
Fontainas, André 2541, 5073, 10889
Fontaine, André 6597, 8163
Fontana, Vincenzo 4303
Fonti, Daniela 11624
Fonvielle, Lloyd 3368
Foote, Henry W. 3512, 11801
Foratti, Aldo 1630, 1751, 8583
Forberg, Gabriele 2903
Forbes, Esther 10562
Ford, Brinsley 13587
Ford, Colin 5274
Ford, Ford Madox see Hueffer, Ford Madox
Ford, Sheridan 13544
Forest, Alfred 10043
Foresta, Merry A. 9458, 10279, 10286, 10290
Forestier, Sylvie 1925
Forge, Andrew 4240, 8543, 8552, 10266
Formaggio, Dino 3751, 4495, 4647
Forman, Harry B. 8745
Fornes, Eduard 2477, 2478
Forno, Federico dal 3463
Forrer, Matthi 5417, 5418, 5419, 6348
Forrester, Viviane 4496
Forsee, Aylesa 5706
Forssman, Erik 9329, 9330, 9331, 11341
Forster, Kurt W. 239, 9898
Förster, Otto H. 1258, 7196
Fort Worth Art Museum (Fort Worth, Tex.) 11986
Forte di Belvedere (Florence) 8605
Forthuny, Pascal 10517
Fortuna, Alberto M. 1799
Fosca, François [pseud., Georges de Traz] 2071, 2242, 2672, 2752, 2989, 3733, 7131, 10518, 11498, 12382
Foshay, Toby 7029
Foskett, Daphne 2166, 2168
Fossi, Gloria 7153
Fossi, Mazzino 190
Fossi, Piero 4323
Fossi Todorow, Maria 9760
Foster, Allen E. 5517
Foster, Hal 7226
Foster, Joshua J. 2167

Foster, Kathleen 27, 3159
Foucart, Bruno 2318, 12589, 13142
Foucault, Michel 7427
Fouchet, Max Pol 946, 10519
Fougerat, Emmanuel 5443
Fouque, Victor 9116
Fouquet, Jacques 5649
Fourcade, Dominique 7927, 9221
Fourcaud, Louis de 596, 1963, 11125
Fournier, Louis 13848
Fourny-Dargère, Sophie 8541
Fourreau, Armand 2113, 8702
Foville, Jean de 9761, 10740
Fox, Caroline 6188, 7036
Fox, Helen M. 6815
Fox, Howard N. 7226
Fox-Weber, Nicholas 11938
Fraenckel, Ingeborg 11284
Fraenger, Wilhelm 1121, 1122, 1123, 1389, 4945, 11492, 13426
Frampton, Kenneth 8323, 13720
França, José-Augusto 13084
Francastel, Pierre 3345, 4404
Francés, José 7244
Franchi, Anna 3470, 3471
Franchini Guelfi, Fausta 7411
Francini Ciaranfi, Anna M. 3472
Francis, Anne F. 4584
Francis, Mark 570
Francisci, Françoise 4229
Franciscono, Marcel 4883, 6063
Franck, Hans 509
Franclieu, Franoise 6675
François, Giuseppe 6910
Francovich, Géza de 240, 13571
Frangipane, Alfonso 10026, 10027
Frank, Elizabeth 9868
Frank, Hilmar 11492
Frank, Waldo 12021
Frankau, Julia 13299
Franke, Willibald 10611
Frankel, Stephen Robert 7014
Franken, Daniel 13004
Frankenburger, Max 5718
Frankenstein, Alfred 2173, 5109, 8810
Frankfurter Kunstkabinett Hanna Bekker vom Rath 602
Frankfurter Kunstverein 13616
Frankl, Volker 6277
Franklin, David 10950
Franz, Erich 7712, 9154
Franz, Heinrich G. 2795
Franzini, Elio 6864
Franzoni, Oliviero 10868
Franzke, Andreas 576, 2930, 2931, 12212
Fraprie, Frank R. 10194
Frary, Ihna T. 5731
Fraschetti, Stanislao 827
Fraser, John Lloyd 2146
Fratelli Treves 6865
Frati, Tiziana 13928

Frauenfelder, Rudolf 1414
Fréches-Thory, Claire 12555
Freedberg, David 11047
Freedberg, Sydney J. 9417, 11285
Freeden, Max H. von 9026, 9027, 10653, 12325
Freedman, Luba 12442
Freer, Allan 8960
Frei, Hans 12112
Freifrau von Tiesenhausen, Maria 6248
Freise, Kurt 6491
Freixa, Jaume 11586
Fremont, Vincent 13309, 13321
French, Mrs. Daniel Chester 3819
Frenfanelli Cibo, Serafino 9083
Frenzel, Ursula 7692, 11516
Frère, Henri 7467
Frerichs, L. C. 8722
Frese, Werner 7352
Freud, Anna 4538
Freud, Sigmund 6866
Freudenheim, Tom L. 9428
Freuler, Gaudenz 547
Frey, Adolf 5322
Frey, Dagobert 3583, 8210
Frey, Julia Bloch 12556
Frey, Karl 8211, 12888
Frey, Stefan 6075
Frick, George F. 1814
Fridlander, Ernest D. 7745
Frieberg, Axel 6484
Fried, Lewis 10677
Fried, Michael 2319, 3160
Friedel, Helmut 8838
Friedenthal, Richard 6867
Friedl, Antonin 7880
Friedländer, Julius 11306
Friedländer, Max J. 149, 1390, 2127, 2357, 3047,
    3397, 4126, 4451, 7087, 7309, 7846, 8009,
    8723
Friedländer, Salomon *see* Mynona
Friedländer, Walter F. 1670, 2083, 9954, 9955,
    9956
Friedman, Bernard H. 9869
Friedman, Martin 11466, 11662
Friedrich, Carl 5302
Friedrich, Karl J. 10002, 10612, 10613, 10622
Fries, Waldemar H. 363
Friesen, Astrid von 7349
Frieze, Henry Simmons 3025
Frinta, Mojmír S. 7864
Frith, William P. 3868, 6716
Fritz, Rolf 100
Fritzsche, Hellmuth A. 736
Frodel, Gerbert 7482
Frodl, Gerbert 6137
Fröhlich, Martin 11518, 11519
Fröhlich-Bum, Lili 5650, 9418
Frölich, Marie 8500
Frölicher, Elsa 5444
Frommel, Christoph L. 8213, 9511, 9512, 10196
Frommhold, Erhard 4930

Froning, Hubertus 6025, 10614
Fründt, Edith 13602
Fry, Edward F. 6738, 11807
Fry, Roger E. 707, 1867, 7942, 11599
Fu, Marilyn 12201
Fu, Shen 1957
Fuchs, Eduard 2542, 2543, 2544
Fuchs, Georg 12622
Fuchs, Heinrich 11338
Fuchs, Rudi 5246
Fuchs, Rudolf H. 10155, 10464
Fuehmann, Franz 510
Fuerst, Margot 4848, 4849, 4850, 4855, 4856
Fuess, David 1457
Führich, Lukas von 11420
Fulcher, George W. 3961
Fuller, Martin 13679
Fuller, Peter 8601
Fumagalli, Giuseppina 6868, 6869
Fumet, Stanislas 1301
Fundaçao Calouste Gulbenkian (Lisbon) 13085
Fundació Joan Miró-Centre d'Estudis d'Art
    Contemporani 8392
Funk, Veit 12051
Furhange, Maguy 1780
Furlan, Caterina 4397, 9913, 9914
Furness, S. M. 6497
Furst, Herbert E. A. 1288, 1964
Fürst, Viktor 13650
Fusco, Renato de 6634, 12854
Fusero, Clemente 10195
Fusscas, Helen K. 13436
Fussell, George E. 13300
Futagawa, Yukio 13733, 13734, 13735, 13736,
    13737, 13738, 13739, 13742, 13743, 13744

G

Gabelentz, Hans von der 552, 7804
Gabetti, Roberto 6635
Gabillot, Claude 10758
Gabler, Karlheinz 6039, 8987
Gablik, Suzi 7428
Gaborit, Jean-René 9689
Gabrielli, Margherita 4362
Gabus, Jean 3290
Gachet, Paul 1863
Gachnang, Johannes 580, 9854
Gadney, Reg 2147
Gadol, Joan 93
Gaedertz, Theodor 9266
Gaehtgens, Barbara 13453
Gaertner, Friedrich W. 5956
Gaffé, René 6396
Gafner, Raymond 3291
Gage, John 12656, 12657, 12658, 12692
Gagnebin, Marianne 12508
Gagnon, François 2932
Gagnon, François-Marc 1092, 1094, 1095
Gaiduk, Alla 13250
Gailhabaud, Jules 4618
Gaillard, Agathe 5991

Heugten, Sjraar van 8367
Heusinger, Lutz 8227, 8228
Heuss, Theodor 9829
Heuzé, Edmond 12782
Hevesi, Ludwig 139
Hevesy, André de 474, 6888
Heyck, Eduard 2360, 3554
Heydenreich, Ludwig H. 6889, 6890, 6891, 6925
Heyman, Therese T. 1344, 6434
Heymann, Walther 9452
Heyne, Hildegard 6159, 6163
Heynen, Julian 9080
Heywood, Florence 3697
Hibbard, Benjamin H. 831
Hibbard, Howard 844, 1671, 7397, 8229
Hickey, Dave 11160
Hildesheimer, Wolfgang 5720
Hieber, Hermann 5482
Hieronimus, Ekkehard 4447, 7108, 7111
Hiersche, Waldemar 12315
Higgler, Max 232
Higgott, Gordon 5771
Hight, Eleanor M. 8482
Higonnet, Anne 8704, 8705
Hijmans, Willem 10406
Hilaire, Georges 2765
Hilberseimer, Ludwig 8314
Hildebrandt, Edmund 3439, 6892, 13359
Hildebrandt, Hans 273, 11375
Hilger, Ernst 5585
Hill, Brian 1559
Hill, David 12666
Hill, Draper 4288, 4290
Hill, Frederick P. 7388
Hill, George F. 9762, 9763
Hill, John T. 3370
Hilles, Frederick W. 10569, 10577
Hillier, Jack R. 5421, 5422, 12766
Hilpert, Thilo 6645
Hilton, Timothy 9221, 9608
Hinckley, F. Lewis 5228
Hind, Arthur M. 556, 1205, 2087, 2088, 3056,
    3130, 3131, 5493, 9734, 10407, 10408
Hind, C. Lewis 12667, 12949
Hind, Charles L. 11210
Hines, Thomas S. 1480, 9050, 9052
Hinks, Roger P. 1672
Hinrichs, Walther T. 6445
Hinson, Hal 5992
Hintze, Bertel 3197
Hinz, Berthold 3847
Hinz, Paulus 7875
Hinz, Renate 6261
Hipkiss, Edwin J. 7384
Hirano, Chie 12522
Hirano, Imao 4138
Hirmer (München) 8398
Hirsch, Fritz 9029
Hirschfeld, Susan B. 5880
Hirschl and Adler Galleries (New York) 2990
Hirschmann, Otto 4571, 4572

Hirsh, Sharon L. 5324
Hirshhorn Museum and Sculpture Garden
    (Washington, D.C.) 10724
Hirshler, Erica E. 11668
Hirst, Michael 8230, 9719
Hispanic Society of America (New York) 11227,
    13911
Hitchcock, Henry-Russell 4020, 5758, 10068,
    10603, 11766, 11838, 13687, 13694, 13866
Hjelle, Eivind Otto 9020
Hjert, Bertil 13895
Hjert, Svenolof 13895
Hlaváček, Luboš 7520
Ho, Tao 5593
Hobbs, Richard 8804, 10311, 11824
Hobbs, Robert C. 385, 5104, 6305
Hoberg, Annegret 8838
Hoboken, Eva von 11530
Hobson, Anthony 13336, 13337
Hochhuth, Rolf 8100
Hochman, Elaine S. 8315
Hodin, Josef P. 5235, 6221, 6222, 6223, 7532,
    8017, 8870, 9094
Hoeber, Fritz 692
Hoecker, Rudolf 7509
Hoerth, Otto 6893
Hoetink, H. R. 11131
Hofer, Paul 9335
Hofer, Philip 6579, 6580, 6581, 9742
Hoff, August 6755, 6756, 12291
Hoff, Johann F. 10615
Hoffman, Marilyn Friedman 13881
Hoffman, Michael E. 12064
Hoffmann, Dieter 33
Hoffmann, Donald 10880, 10882, 13688, 13689,
    13723
Hoffmann, Edith 6224
Hoffmann, Josef 7241
Hoffmann, Klaus 8021
Hoffmann, Marguerite 6604
Hoffmann, Raimund 4981
Hofmaier, James 662
Hofmann, Friedhelm 7898
Hofmann, Friedrich H. 8037
Hofmann, Julius 4665
Hofmann, Theobald 10209
Hofmann, Walter J. 3057
Hofmann, Werner 700, 1024, 1305, 1306, 2322,
    3848, 4666, 6054, 6138, 6232, 6547, 10959
Hofmannsthal, Hugo von 4479
Hofrichter, Ferima Fox 1263, 7051
Hofstätter, Hans H. 3849, 6139, 8667
Hofstede de Groot, Cornelis 3427, 10367, 10409,
    10418, 10448, 11946
Hohl, Hanna 10959
Hohl, Reinhold 4217, 4232, 12187
Höhne, Erich 1363
Hökby, Nils-Göran 11544
Holborn, John B. 12384
Holcomb, Adele M. 2291
Holden, Donald 13511

Humbourg, Pierre 11634
Hume, Abraham 12454
Humfrey, Peter 1714, 2064
Hundt, Walter 13205
Huneke, Andreas 3495, 5350
Hunt, John Dixon 5982
Hunt Botanical Library (Pittsburgh) 10330
Hunter, Sam 3003, 5372, 7733, 8399, 9136,
    10725, 10726, 10732, 11467
Hunter-Salomon, Peter 11222, 11225
Huntington, David C. 2053
Huntley, George H. 11260
Hurlburt, Laurance P. 9251
Hurley, F. Jack 6711
Hürlimann, Martin 4950, 6228
Hurll, Estelle M. 6420
Huse, Norbert 715
Hussey, Christopher 1372, 5983, 7333
Hustin, Arthur 12619
Hutchinson, Harold F. 13652
Hutchinson, John 6010
Hutchison, Jane C. 3059, 7851
Hüter, Karl-Heinz 12993
Hütt, Wolfgang 3060, 4934, 8101
Hutter, Heribert 5025
Hüttinger, Eduard 8872
Hutton, Edward 9499
Huxley, Aldous L. 4669, 5171
Huxtable, Ada L. 9009
Huys, Paul 11593
Huyghe, René 1876, 2316, 2583, 2693, 4086,
    4087, 4088, 4519, 4752, 13361
Huysmans, Joris K. 4951, 4952, 10890
Hyams, Edward 1371
Hyland, Douglas 6540, 10104, 13896
Hyman, Isabelle 1428
Hyman, Linda 5530
Hyman, Susan 6581,6587
Hymans, Henri S. 3400, 8721, 11065
Hyslop, Francis E. 3375, 3378

I

Iagodovskaia, Anna T. 13245
Iakovkva, Nonna A. 11683, 12739
Ianitskii, O. 9101
Ichinowatari, Katsuhiko 11587
Igitian, Genrikh 389, 390
Ileana Sonnabend Gallery (Paris) 13458
Ilg, Albert 3584
Ilges, Franz W. 8901
Image, Selwyn 897
Imiela, Hans-Jürgen 11773, 11774, 11777, 11780,
    11781
Inboden, Gudrun 10342, 11994
Ing, Eric van den 13806
Ingersoll-Smouse, Florence 9439, 13054
Inmaculada, Juan J. de la 13912
Innes, Christopher D. 2352
Inness, George, Jr. 5677
Inskip, Peter 5677
Institut Néerlandais (Paris) 5496, 11317, 12519

Institute of Contemporary Art (Boston) 2046,
    6230, 7721
Instituto Diego Velázquez (Madrid) 12950
International Center for Photography (New York)
    5090
International Congress on M.C. Escher 3340
International Galleries (Chicago) 651
Ippoliti, Carolina 10034
Ipser, Karl 4787, 8232
Ireland, John 5391
Ireland, Le Roy 5678
Irving, Robert G. 7334
Irwin, David 3599
Isaacs, Reginald 4891
Isaacson, Joel 8550, 8551
Isermeyer, Christian A. 11141
Isnard, Émile 8586
Isnard, Guy 8592
Istituto di Studi Vinciani di Roma 6895
Istituto Italo-Latino Americano (Rome)
    3641
Istituto Nazionale di Studi sul Rinascimento
    (Florence) 12877
Istituto Statale d'Arte, Firenze 2864
Iurova, Tamara V. 9841
Ivanoff, Nicola 7404, 7405, 9336
Ivanov, Vsevolod N. 10842
Ivanova, Veneta K. 11560
Ives, Colta 1074
Ivinski, Patricia R. 131
Ivy, Judy Crosby 2149
Iwanoyko, Eugeniusz 13237
Iwasaki, Yoshikazu 7439
Izerghina, A. 7961
Izzard, Sebastian 12602

J

Jackson, Clarence S. 5707
Jackson, Holbrook 8747, 8761
Jacob, John 13031
Jacob, Mira 2733
Jacobowitz, Ellen 7311
Jacobs, Herbert 13690
Jacobs, Katherine 13690
Jacobs, Ottokar von 6145
Jacobsen, Emil 11846
Jacobsen, R. 7510
Jacobus, John 5759, 7951
Jacometti, Nesto 4298, 12796, 13835
Jaeger, Adolf 12052
Jaffe, Cynthia 1159
Jaffé, Ernst 6203
Jaffé, Hans L. C. 2835, 8509, 8510, 8511, 9611,
    13582
Jaffe, Irma B. 11998, 12001, 12626, 12627
Jaffe, Michael 3124, 11066, 11067
Jaffé, Patricia 10874
Jaguer, Edouard 2210
Jahn, Carl 6119
Jahn, Fred 580
Jahn, Johannes 2032, 2361, 3061, 8233, 10411

Jahn, Otto 10625
Jahnsen, Angeli 3761
Jakovsky, Anatole 7056
Jakstein, Werner 5099
Jakubec, Doris 12815, 12824
Jaloux, Edmond 3921, 12818
James, Cary 13691
James, John 9485
James, Philip 8618
James, Martin S. 8521
James, Montague R. 9406
James R. Osgood and Company (Boston, Mass.)
    3432
Jamieson, I. 2342
Jamis, Randa 5842
Jammes, André 610, 8994, 9115, 12161
Jammes, Isabelle 995
Jamot, Paul 2642, 2753, 6498, 6801, 7561, 7575,
    8568, 9964, 11068, 11500
Janasch, Adolf 678
Janett, Jürg 12502, 13635
Janis, Eugenia P. 2643
Janitschek, Hubert 85
Jannella, Cecilia 2949, 7772
Janowitz, Günther J. 6896
Jansen, Albert 11847
Jansen, Dieter 3401
Jansen, Elmar 502, 514, 515
Jansen, Guido 11197
Jansen, Per Hofman 5804
Janson, Anthony F. 13564
Janson, Horst W. 2865
Janssens, Jacques 3254
Jantzen, Hans 9036
Janzen, Reinhild 151
Janus [pseud.] 10281
Jaquillard, Pierre 9949
Jardí, Enric 6077, 12531
Jardot, Maurice 6663, 6734, 6740, 9612
Jarrassé, Dominique 12566
Jarrin, Charles 4619
Jarzombek, Mark 94
Jawlensky, Angelica 5725
Jawlensky, Lucia 5725
Jawlensky, Maria 5725
Jaworska, Wladyslawa 4089
Jay, Bill 2741, 7763
Jay, Paul 9117
Jean, Marcel 299, 303
Jean, René 10093, 11501
Jean-Aubry, Georges 1218, 1219
Jean-Richard, Pierette 1211, 1212
Jedicke, Günter 10263
Jedlicka, Gotthard 178, 1397, 4299, 7562, 8453,
    12562
Jelenski, Constantin 730, 731
Jencks, Charles 6646
Jenkins, David Fraser 7140
Jenkins, Esther 12204
Jenkins, Paul 12204
Jenni, Ulrike 4047, 5586

Jensen, Jens C. 243, 2824, 3621, 8096, 8102,
    9296, 9297, 11142, 11919, 13762, 13898
Jensen, Johannes V. 6474
Jentsch, Ralph 8010, 11464
Jerrold, Blanchard 2416, 2906, 2907
Jestaz Bertrand 7209
Jewitt, Llewellynn 13416
Jianou, Ionel 39, 313, 1233, 1272, 6457, 8611,
    10809
Joachim, Harold 4096
Joachimides, Christos M. 888
Joannides, Paul 7787, 10211
Joffroy, Berne 1673
Johannsen, Johann 10488
Johansen, Peter 3192, 9530
Johns, Elizabeth 3158, 3167
Johnson, Antionette Spanos 12817
Johnson, Donald Leslie 13692
Johnson, Edward M. 2289
Johnson, Ellen H. 9207
Johnson, Franklin P. 7340
Johnson, Fridolf 5977, 5978, 5981
Johnson, J. W. 13339
Johnson, Lee 2694, 2695, 2696
Johnson, Philip C. 8316
Johnson, R. Stanley 4876
Johnson, Robert Flynn 12272
Johnson, Ruth Carter 10472
Johnson, Una E. 380
Johnson, William R. 1088
Johnson, William S. 11819, 11821
Johnston, Catherine 13600
Johnston, William R. 131
Johnstone, Christopher 7759
Joliffe, John 5167
Jolinon, Joseph 5905
Joll, Evelyn 12644
Jolly, Alphonse 2115
Jombert, Charles-Antoine 6611
Jones, Anthony 7375
Jones, Caroline A. 9004
Jones, Dan B. 5979, 5981
Jones, Edgar Y. 10349
Jones, Eleanor L. 11177
Jones, Elizabeth B. 5709
Jones, Roger 10212
Jones, William C. 5709
Jonge, Caroline H. de 8691
Joosten, Joop M. 7497, 8512
Joppien, Rüdiger 7303
Joppolo, Giovanni 3640, 3642
Joray, Marcel 6643, 12867
Jordan, Jim M. 4602
Jordan, Max 6897, 8103
Jordan, Robert F. 6647
Jordan, William B. 10584
Jorge, Fernando 7176
Jorge, Ricardo 4788
Jornadas de Arte (Madrid) 12951
Josef-Haubrich-Kunsthalle (Cologne) 3484, 10976
Josefowitz, Samuel 4056

Joselit, David 7670
Josephson, Ragnar 11540, 11541, 12261, 12262
Josten, Hanns H. 4953
Josz, Virgile 3715, 13362
Joubin, André 2688, 2690, 2703
Jouffroy, Alain 734, 2385, 8400
Jouffroy, Jean P. 9613, 11937
Jouin, Henri A. 2344, 2591, 2596, 4620, 6599
Jourdain, Francis 11978, 12563, 12818
Jourdain, Margaret 5983
Jover, Manuel 12825
Joyant, Maurice 12564
Joyes, Claire 8552
Joyeux, Odette 9118
Jrnaes, Bjarne 12299, 12310
Judey-Barosin, Jacob 658
Judge, Mary A. 5531
Judrin, Claudie 10815, 10825
Judson, J. Richard 5541
Judson, Jay R. 497, 11069
Juin, Hubert 7826, 11886
Julien, Edouard 12565
Juliet, Charles 12987, 12988
Jullian, René 8357
Jullien, Adolphe 3455
Jungmarker, Gunnar 9695
Jungnitz, Ingobert 12910
Junod, Roger-Louis 10753
Jura, Martina 8149, 9934
Jussim, Estelle 2615, 3201
Justi, Carl 8234, 8917, 12952, 13107
Justi, Ludwig 2193, 4329, 6246

K

Kadatz, Hans-Joachim 693, 6190
Kaemmerer, Ludwig 2033, 3402, 6262, 8057
Kagan, Andrew 6078, 12616
Kaganovich, A. L. 7265
Kahn, Gustave 1206, 3456, 3716, 11611
Kahn, Rosy 7312
Kahn-Rossi, Manuela 3497
Kahnweiler, Daniel-Henry 2764, 4867, 4869,
    4870, 4871, 6079, 6547, 9614, 9615, 13191
Kahr, Madlyn M. 12953
Kahsnitz, Rainer 12058, 12059
Kainen, Jacob 1588, 11787
Kaiser, Konrad 1775, 8104, 8105, 11302
Kaiser-Wilhelm-Museum (Krefeld, Germany) 3196
Kalinowskiego, Lecha 12060
Kalitina, Nina N. 2549, 2766, 8562
Kalkschmidt, Eugen 10616, 11423, 11920
Kallab, Wolfgang 12879
Kallir, Jane 8439, 11322, 11323
Kallir, Otto 11324, 11325, 11334
Kalthoff, Brigitte 11825
Kambartel, Walter 9484
Kamber, André 10959
Kamensky, Aleksandr 1927
Kamphausen, Alfred 1767
Kampmeyer-Käding, Margret 11413
Kandinsky, Nina 5871

Kanelski, Paul 60
Kania, Hans 11343, 11344
Kanteckiego, Klemensa 4921
Kaplan, Daile 5288
Kaplan, Janet A. 12860
Kaplan, Julius 8672
Kapterewa, Tatjana 12954
Karabelnik-Matta, Marianne 11485, 13621
Karcher, Eva 2820, 2821, 2822
Karginov, German 10781
Karia, Bhupendra 933, 1647
Karpenko, Maria 10549
Karsch, Florian 2823, 8831
Karshan, Donald 274, 276, 1783, 7493
Kath, Ruth R. 7695
Kattouw, Rolinka 12529
Katz, Leon 9676
Katz, William 5632
Kauffmann, Georg 9965
Kauffmann, Hans 832, 2866, 3062
Kaufmann, Edgar 13689, 13714, 13748
Kaufmann, Emil 6648, 6700
Kaulbach, Isidore 5936
Kautzsch, Paul 392
Kawakita, Michiaki 6214
Kayafas, Gus 3201
Kazanjian, Dodie 7067
Kearns, Martha 6263
Keay, Carolyn 10993
Keckemet, Dusko 8147
Kehl, Anton 4954
Kehrer, Hugo 3063, 4789, 4790, 4791, 12955,
    13930
Keil, Heinrich 9525
Keim, Jean A. 3216, 12202
Kelber, Wilhelm 10213
Kelch, Jan 10375
Kelder, Diane 2611
Kelemen, Pál 4792
Kellein, Thomas 9923, 10342, 11675, 12038
Kellen, J. P. van der 13004
Keller, Harald 9785
Keller, Horst 2191, 4520, 8553, 10522, 12567,
    13592
Keller, Joseph 9032
Keller, Luzius 9735
Keller, Ulrich 3362, 10680
Keller-Dorian, Georges 2345
Kellermann, Michel 2767
Kelly, Franklin 2054, 2055
Kelterborn-Haemmerli, Anna 3867
Kelton, Ruth 11954
Kemenov, Vladimir 12956
Kemp, Martin 6849, 6898, 6915
Kemp, Wolfgang 11238
Kempe, Lothar 10617
Kempter, Lothar 1415
Kendall, M. Sue 2440
Kendall, Richard 1857, 2635, 2644, 8564
Kennedy, Edward G. 13513
Kennedy, Ruth W. 428

Kennedy Galleries (New York) 12904
Kenner, Hugh 3902, 7041
Kent, William W. 9513
Keopplin, Dieter 438
Kepiński, Zdzislaw 12053, 13787
Kerber, Bernard 7197, 9994
Kerbert, Ottmar 3403
Kerckhove, Fabrice van de 12994
Kerner, Charlotte 8124
Kerouac, Jack 3805
Kerrich, Thomas 5193
Kerslake, John 11802
Kersten, Michiel 1264
Kersten, Wolfgang 6094
Kersting, Hannelore 11815
Kertesz, Janine 5611
Kertesz, Klaus 7698
Kesel, Joseph 6044
Kesnerova, Gabriela 5492
Kesser, Herman 5331
Kessler, Charles S. 679
Kessler, Johann H. H. 4127
Kestner-Gesellschaft, Hannover 732, 925, 5151,
    5211, 5610, 5721, 5806, 7897, 7985, 10727,
    10728, 13311
Kettenmann, Andrea 5844
Ketterer, Roman N. 6031, 6036
Kettering, Alison McNeil 12255
Keuerleber, Eugen 2817
Keulen, Jan van 4518
Keyes, George S. 13242
Keyes, Norman 11667
Keyes, Roger S. 13807, 13808
Keynes, Geoffrey Langdon 950, 951, 976, 977,
    978, 9384
Khait, Vladimir L. 9101
Khan-Magomedov, Selim Omarovich 10780
Kibbey, Ray A. 9616
Kiefer, Geraldine W. 12026
Kiel, Hanna 11732
Kiene, Michael 9404
Kikuchi, Sadao 12771
Killanin, Michael M. 6185
Killian, James R., Jr. 3199, 3200, 3201
Killy, Herta Elisabeth 604, 700
Kimball, Fiske 5733, 7386
Kimball Art Museum (Fort Worth, Tex.) 10584
King, Ethel M. 2511
King, James 8971
King, Susan 8079
Kinkel, Hans 2823
Kinney, Peter 191
Kinsman, Jane 6046
Kirby, Jo 10369
Kirby, Rachel 11815
Kirker, Harold 1453
Kirker, James 1453
Kirsch, Hans-Christian 10656
Kirschenbaum, Baruch D. 11948
Kirschner, Zdenek 12101
Kirsta, Georg 1674

Kirstein, Gustav 8106
Kirstein, Lincoln 1770, 3361, 6378, 8939, 8940,
    10687, 11822, 12235
Kisling, Jean 6045
Kitaj, R.B. 3829
Kitao, Timothy K. 833
Kite, Elizabeth S. 6812
Kitson, Michael 1675, 2091
Kitson, Sydney D. 2292
Kitton, Fred G. 6718
Klaiber, Hans 6899
Klee, Felix 6080, 6083, 6090
Klein, H. Arthur 1398, 6264
Klein, Ian 1273
Klein, Mina C. 6264
Klein, Rudolf 2189, 5332, 7089
Klein, Wilhelm 3356, 10004
Kleinclausz, Arthur J. 11795
Kleine, Gisela 5885, 8836
Kleiner, Leopold 5362
Klessmann, Rüdiger 12257
Kletzl, Otto 9408
Klewan, Helmut 7835
Klinge, Margret 12241
Klipstein, August 6265
Klipstein and Kornfeld (Bern) 314, 3796
Klizovskii, Aleksandr 10843
Klockenbring, Gérard 10312
Kloek, Wouter 57
Kloss, William 8784
Klossowski, Erich 2550
Klossowski de Rola, Stanislaus 466
Klöter, Hermann 8936
Klotz, Heinrich 1429
Klumpke, Anna 1054
Klüser, Bernd 876
Kluxen, Andrea M. 12311
Knab, Eckhart 4747, 10214
Knackfuss, Hermann 3132, 3133, 5078, 5457,
    8107, 8235, 8920, 10215, 10412, 11070,
    12455, 12957
Knapp, Fritz 553, 4521, 6900, 7629, 8211, 8236,
    9033, 9500, 9683, 10657, 11287
Knapp, Oswald G. 6566
Knapp, Peter 4247
Knappe, Karl Adolf 3064
Kniazeva, Valentina P. 10844, 11534
Knight, Carleton, III 5761
Knight, Joseph 10925
Knipping, John B. 4452, 12520
Knobling, Harald 516
Knoedler & Company, New York 3134
Knoef, Jan 12609
Knorr, Georg W. 3065
Knowles, John 3922
Knowlton, Helen M. 5626, 5627
Knox, George 9542, 9543, 9545, 12329, 12330,
    12331
Knudtzon, Fried G. 7788
Knust, Herbert 4911
Knuttel, Gerhardus 1364, 3404, 10413

Kunsthalle Baden-Baden 4872
Kunsthalle Basel 4447, 7045
Kunsthalle Bern 179, 180, 351, 3004, 5969, 6123
Kunsthalle Bielefeld 4041, 6166, 11370, 11988
Kunsthalle Bremen 352, 517, 581, 8436, 11012, 11513, 11775, 12215, 12819
Kunsthalle Darmstadt 9920
Kunsthalle Düsseldorf 2845
Kunsthalle Hamburg [also Hamburger Kunsthalle] 973, 2322, 3598, 3801, 3846, 3920, 4662, 8098, 11140, 11539, 12661
Kunsthalle Köln 2191, 6736, 11071
Kunsthalle Nürnberg 7906
Kunsthalle Tübingen 9208
Kunsthalle zu Kiel 2824
Kunsthandel P. de Boer Amsterdam 1399
Kunsthaus Zürich 181, 926, 3923, 6649, 7953, 8669, 13313
Kunsthistorisches Museum (Wien) 2363
Kunstler, Charles 4090, 13363
Künstler, Gustav 7239
Kunstmuseum Basel 438, 1036, 5459
Kunstmuseum Bern 234, 2697, 7651
Kunstmuseum Düsseldorf 4121, 4977
Kunstmuseum Hannover 3307, 9153
Kunstmuseum Winterthur (Switzerland) 4441, 12820
Kunstraum München 13288
Kunstreich, Jan S. 1493
Kunstsammlung der Universität Göttingen 6327, 11072
Kunstverein Braunschweig 943, 1705, 9454, 11386, 13289
Kunstverein Hamburg 3485, 8437
Kunstverein Hannover 6458, 9472, 13594
Kunstverein München 2625
Kunstverein und Kunsthaus Hamburg 7432
Kunz, Ludwig 8018
Kunzl, Martin 4578
Kuo, Chi-seng 5593
Kuoni, Carin 875
Küper, Marijke 10668, 10671
Kupferstichkabinett (Berlin) 13290
Kupper, Daniel 3555
Küppers, Paul E. 4204
Kurhaus Meran 10086
Kurochkina, Tatiana I. 6302
Kurth, Julius 5129, 11654, 12770
Kurth, Willi 498, 3068
Kurtz, Donna C. 798
Kury, Gloria 11710
Kusenberg, Kurt 10951
Kush, Thomas 7032
Kuspit, Donald B. 268, 289, 2883, 4581, 5917, 10489, 12199
Küster, Bernd 1490, 7090
Kuthy, Sandor 233, 6548, 7944, 12148
Kutter, Erich 7707
Kutter, Paul 11241
Kuwayama, George 13808

Kuznetsova, Irina A. 2579, 9976
Kyriazi, Jean M. 11502

L
Laan, Anke van der 8677
Laanstra, Willem 11931
Labaree, Benjamin W. 7385
LaBelle, Jenijoy 3595
Laboureur, Sylvain 6372
Lacambre, Geneviève 8670, 13502
Lackner, Stephan 680
Laclotte, Michel 12480
LaCombe, Joseph F. de 1981
La Cour, Tage 6475, 6476, 6477
Laczkó, András 10692
Ladendorf, Heinz 11383
Ladengalerie (West Berlin) 4935
Lader, Melvin P. 4603, 4604
Laderchi, Camillo 9298
Ladis, Andrew 3946
Ladoué, Pierre 10143
Lafaille, Maurice 3001, 3005, 3006
Lafenestre, Georges 3698, 12456
Lafond, Paul 1128, 1129, 2645, 4670, 4763, 4793, 8918, 10585, 12807, 13493
Lafouge, Jean-pierre 3886
Lafourcade, Bernard 7039
Lafuente Ferrari, Enrique 4671, 4705, 4794, 9610, 12958, 13913
Lagaisse, Marcelle 4729
Lagan, Guido 7377
Lagerlöf, Margaretha Rossholm 9966
Lagrange, Andrée 3887
Lagrange, Léon 10057, 13055
La Greca, Bianci Tavassi 5008
La Hire, Marie de 9556
Lahnstein, Peter 8835
Lahuerta, Juan José 4021, 4034
Lai, T. C. 12192
Lainez Alcala, Rafael 851
Laissus, Yves 10334
Lake, Carlton 2481
Lake, Johannes auf der 3308
Lalanne, Ludovic 824, 2336
Lalique, Marie-Claud 6402
Lamac, Miroslav 7522, 13899
Lamacchia, Giovanni 9122
Lamb, Carl 12325, 13867
Lambert, Jean-Clarence 264
Lambert, Yvon 12710
Lamberti, Maria Mimita 3752
Lambertin, Pierre 1781
Lambertini, Luigi 9436
Lambeth, William A. 5734
Lambotte, Paul 3379, 8061
La Meridiana di Palazzo Pitti (Florence) 3476
La Motte, Manfred de 12863
Lampert, Catherine 3825
Lampsonius, Dominicus 7206
Lancaster, Jan 2921
Lanchner, Carolyn 6087, 7836

Marchal, Gaston-Louis 13822
Marchesseau, Daniel 1517, 4230, 6542
Marchini, Giuseppe 4192, 7155, 11250
Marchiori, Giuseppe 315, 5047, 7957
Marcianó, Ada Francesca 10912
Marciano-Agostinelli Tozzi, M. T. 11848
Marcilhac, Félix 6405, 9239
Marck, Jan van der 290, 3643
Marcolongo, Roberto 6933
Marconi, Paolo 12788
Marcos, Fouad 3888
Marcucci, Luigi 461
Marcus, Aage 6477, 6479, 6934
Marcus, Penelope 1478
Marcus, Stanley E. 11810
Marechal, Dominique 1291
Maret, Jacques 2580
Mariacher, Giovanni 719, 9377, 11264
Marian Goodman Gallery (New York) 6014
Mariani, Valerio 294, 295, 837, 4369, 4370, 7774,
    8244, 9702, 9704, 10028
Mariani Canova, Giordana 7285
Marianno Filho, José 7178
Marias, Fernando 4801, 4812
Marie, Alfred 7604, 7605
Marie, Aristide 1227, 8954
Marie, Jeanne 7604, 7605
Marignane, M. 3875
Marijnissen, Roger H. 1135, 1136, 1403
Marilaun, Karl 7238
Marillier, Henry C. 632, 10927, 12242
Marinelli, Sergio 741
Marinetti, F. 1021
Marini, Maurizio 1679, 9736, 10030, 10034
Marini, Paola 591
Marini, Remigio 9995, 13068
Marinoni, Augusto 6881, 6935, 6936
Marion Kogler McNay Art Museum (San Antonio)
    6467
Mariuz, Adriano 9547, 12334
Mark, Hans 6205
Marks, Alfred 6328
Marks, Paul G. 13501, 13508
Marks, Robert W. 3903
Marlborough Fine Art, Ltd. (London) 3257, 8613,
    11453
Marlborough Gallery (New York) 30, 399, 10729
Marlborough-Gerson Gallery (New York) 404
Marle, Raimond van 4372, 7775
Marlier, Georges 770, 1404, 2128, 8058, 8724
Marlin, William 9057
Marling, Karal Ann 784
Marlowe, Ralph 12117
Marmottan, Paul 1047
Marnau, Alfred 6227
Maron-Bersin, Malama 9916
Marotte, Léon 2094
Marquand, Allan 10742, 10743, 10744, 10745,
    10746, 10747
Marquardt, Hans 4852
Marquet, Françoise 2892, 13842

Marrozzini, Luigi 9259
Marrero, Vincente 9624, 9625
Marrey, Bernard 3217, 3218
Marriott, Charles 4281
Marrow, Bradford 7039
Marsan, Anna 6493
Marschall, Horst K. 12276
Marsh, Blanche 8373
Marsh, Jan 10915
Marshall, Hans 4134
Marshall, Richard 7674
Martano, Giuliano 6124
Marteau, Robert 1941
Marteneau, Robert 1943
Martens, Bella 3803, 7870
Martens, Friedrich A. 859
Martens, Maximiliaan P. 2387
Marter, Joan 1518, 1519
Martin, Elizabeth G. 7755
Martin, Gregory 1593
Martin, Henry 286
Martin, Jean 2465, 4839
Martin, Jean-Herbert 10288
Martin, John R. 11078, 11079, 11080
Martin, Kurt 439
Martin, Leslie 3933
Martin, Wilhelm 2918, 2919, 2920, 5080, 9021,
    11949
Martín Gonzales, Juan José 5829
Martindale, Andrew 7632, 7776
Martineau, Emmanuel 7500
Martineau, Jane 7633
Martinell, Cèsar 4022
Martinell i Brunet, Cèsar 4023
Martinelli, Rossa C. 8086
Martinelli, Valentino 838, 839
Martinez, Elena 12903
Martinez, Romeo 340, 1646
Martinez Chumillas, Manuel 1618
Martini, Alberto 4239, 7820, 8557, 13033
Martini, Paoli 9343
Martini, Pietro 2258, 4802
Marx, Harald 9838
Marx, Roger 10338, 11975
Maryland Historical Society (Baltimore) 9443
März, Roland 7684
Marzorati, Gerald 4582
Mascha, Ottokar 10892
Mascherpa, Giorgio 7281, 7282
Masetti, Anna R. 11915
Mashek, Joseph 2980
Masini, Lara Vinca 11719
Mas i Vives, Joan 12513
Maslyn, David 3210
Mason, Eudo C. 3924
Mason, George C. 12075
Mason, James 7321
Mason, Lauris 759
Mason, Rainer Michael 3486, 10218
Masravell, Nicholas P. 5918
Massar, Phyllis D. 695

Medica, Massimo 13167
Medici-Mall, Katharina 11451
Meehan, Patrick 13695, 13721, 13732, 13747
Meek, Harold 5009
Meerbeke, Chris 12243
Mégret, Frédéric 8357
Mehl, Sonia 6806
Mehta, Jaimini 5851
Meier, Cordula 6016
Meier, Michael 4962
Meier, Paul J. 11853
Meier-Graefe, Julius 1037, 1883, 1884, 2141,
    2227, 2228, 2328, 2329, 2656, 2657, 4532,
    4533, 5397, 7573, 7713, 7714, 8108, 10523,
    12821
Meiss, Millard 7634, 7860, 12606
Meissner, Carl 3243
Meissner, Franz H. 6168, 6169, 8109, 12284,
    12336, 13064
Meissner, Günter 7095
Meixner, Laura L. 8360
Mekas, Jonas 13306
Mele, Giuseppe L. 1575
Melet-Sanson, J. 3699
Meli, Filippo 2073, 11571
Melià, Josep 8403
Melia, Paul 5315
Melion, Walter S. 7513
Mellen, Peter 2117
Meller, Simon 13160
Mellerio, André 10313, 10314
Mellini, Gian Lorenzo 163, 9786
Mellow, James R. 12616
Melonio, Francesco 11751
Meltzer, Milton 6442
Melville, Ralph 5495
Melville, Robert 8614
Memes, John Smythe 1633
Mende, Matthias 440, 3074
Mendelsohn, Henriette 2915, 7156
Mendes, Murillo 1523, 7422
Menegazzi, Luigi 2065, 8087, 12516
Menekes, Friedhelm 5589
Meng-Koehler, Mathilde 13610
Mengin, Urbain 4730, 7157
Mengs, Axel 11767
Menna, Filiberto 8514
Menocal, Narciso G. 12113, 13749
Menpes, Mortimer 13520
Mensch, Bernhard 8944
Mentienne, Adrien 2454
Mentze, Ernst 6480
Menzel, Gerhard W. 13034
Méras, Mathieu 2782
Mercereau, Alexandre 7060
Meredith, Roy 1247, 1248
Merediz, José A. 4806
Merida, Carlos 9252
Merkel, Ursula 3575
Merkert, Jörn 3935, 11815, 12747
Merli, Joan 9627

Mérot, Alain 7011, 9971
Merriam, Dana 7316
Merrill, Linda 13521
Merriman, Mira Pajes 2381, 2382
Merritt, Howard S. 2131, 12722
Merson, Olivier 5656
Meryman, Richard 13777
Merz, Jörg Martin 9687
Meschede, Friedrich 11825
Mesnil, Jacques 1187, 7792
Mesonero Romanos, Manuel 12965
Messer, Thomas M. 892, 941, 12216
Messerer, Richard 2804
Messina, Bruno Salvatore 6681
Messum, David 5971
Meteyard, Eliza 13417, 13418
Metken, Günter 61, 2903
Metropolitan Museum of Art (New York) 132,
    316, 405, 760, 1681, 2056, 2602, 3170,
    4534, 5224, 5532, 5963, 6387, 8559, 11277,
    13778
Metzinger, Fritz 8158
Metzinger, Jean 4436, 4437
Meulen, Marjon van der 10450, 11081
Meuris, Jacques 7442
Meyenburg, Ernst von 7251
Meyer, Agnes E. 7061
Meyer, Alfred G. 1634, 2868
Meyer, Bertrand 12595
Meyer, Catherine 12595
Meyer, Ferdinand 2035
Meyer, Franz 179, 1933, 1934, 4241
Meyer, Julius 2260, 2261
Meyer, Rudolph 1594
Meyer zu Eissen, Annette 581, 11414
Meyerheim, Paul 8112
Meyers, Jeffrey 7040
Meynell, Alice C. 5615, 11278
Meynell, Esther H. 8753
Meynell, Everard 2229
Mez, Marie L. 13214
Mezzanotte, Antonio 9501
Mezzatesta, Michael P. 9866
Mezzetti, Amalia 1730, 2916
Miamlin, Igor G. 9693
Michael, Erika 5464
Michaëlis, Sophus 5094
Michaels, Barbara 5911
Michaelsen, Katherine Janszky 279
Michalski, Ernst 9478
Michalski, Martin 6170
Michel, André 10095
Michel, Edmond 12408
Michel, Emile 1405, 2230, 5308, 9928, 10420,
    11082, 11127, 12253, 13007
Michel, Georges 12898
Michel, J. F. M. 11083
Michel, Pierre 8560, 10814
Michel, Sally 381
Michel, Walter 7036, 7041
Michel, Wilhelm 10087

Montandon, Marcel 11481
Montclair Art Museum (Montclair, New Jersey) 3032
Montecuccoli degli Erri, Federico 4996, 12351
Monteil, Annemarie 12366
Montenari, Giovanni 9341
Montesquiou-Fezensac, Robert 5215, 13522
Monti, Raffaele 11288, 11720
Montias, John Michael 13036
Montoto de Sedas, Santiago 8923
Montreal Museum of Fine Arts 2483, 8250
Montrond, Maxime de 5660
Mooney, Michael M. 1816
Mooradian, Karlen 4606
Moore, Charles H. 1481, 7390
Moore, Henry 9777
Moore, Robert E. 5398
Moore, Thomas S. 2262
Moorhead, Desirée 5177
Moorhouse, Paul 1706
Moortgat, Elizabeth 9934
Moos, Stanislaus von 3565, 6682, 6683, 6684
Mora, Gilles 3364, 3370
Moran, Lord237
Morand, Kathleen 7860, 11797
Morand, Paul 1357, 3685
Morane, Daniel 7996
Morante, Elsa 200
Morassi, Antonio 4332, 4990, 4991, 4992, 12338, 12339, 12461
Moravia, Alberto [pseud.] 1158, 5048, 9629
Morazzoni, Giuseppe 9739
Moreau, Adolphe 2621
Moreau, Adrien 8688, 11207
Moreau, François 13384
Moreau, Marc 291
Moreau-Nélaton, Etienne 1087, 2118, 2119, 2220, 2236, 2238, 2239, 2515, 2699, 7574, 8361
Moreau-Vauthier, Charles 4184
Moreno, Paolo 7344, 7345
Moreno, Salvador 13122, 13123
Moretti, Valeria 11744
Morey, Charles R. 10743
Morgan, Ann Lee 12035
Morgan, Charles H. 759, 761, 762, 8251
Morgan, John H. 2174, 10164, 12077, 12080
Morgan, Sydney 10901
Morgenthaler, Hans Rudolf 8077
Morgtenthaler, Jean Georges 7058
Morgunova-Kudnitskaia, Natalia D. 10545
Morice, Charles 1762, 4097
Moriondo, Margherita 11712
Morisani, Ottavio 83, 2870, 8302, 8524, 8565, 12375
Mornard, Pierre 805
Mörner, Stellan 11230
Morosini, Duilio 5049
Morphet, Richard 5092, 6051
Morris, John G. 11820
Morris, May 8754
Morrison, Hugh 12114

Morrison, Toni 12844
Morrison, Venetia 12086
Morschel, Jürgen 6310
Morse, Albert Reynolds 2484, 2485
Morse, John D. 11642
Morse, Peter 10310, 11787
Morse, Willard S. 10105
Mortara, Antonio E. 9420
Mortari, Luisa 12073
Morton, Terry B. 13696
Mosby, Dewey F. 2622, 12194
Moschini, Vittorio 716, 717, 1595, 4993, 7217, 13184
Moser, Joann 8159, 11999
Moskowitz, Anita Fiderer 9775
Moss, Armand 2700
Mösser, Andeheinz 6099
Mosso, Leon 14
Mostra Biennale d'Arte Antica (VII), Bologna 494
Motoe, Kunio 10318
Mottini, Guido E. 2263
Mottram, Ralph H. 2405
Moulin, Raoul-Jean 4242
Mount, Charles M. 8566, 11279, 12078
Moure, Gloria 8411
Moureau, Adrien 1596
Mourey, Gabriel 865, 3973, 10928
Mourgue, Géraqrd 6941
Mourisca Beaumont, Maria A. 11533
Mourlot, Fernand 1315, 1445, 1914, 8402, 9630, 12565, 12574
Moxey, Keith P. F. 58
Moyssén, Xavier 12914, 12916
Mras, George P. 2701
Muccigrosso, Robert 2354
Mucha, Jiri 8813, 8817, 8818, 8819
Muchall-Viebrook, Thomas W. 13868
Mueller, Karl O. 9535
Muenier, Pierre-Alexis 5220
Mühlestein, Hans 5335, 5336
Muirhead, Tom 12040, 12045
Mujica Gallo, Manuel 9631
Mulazzani, Germano 1253, 10220
Mulder, Bertus 10669
Müller, August W. 11424
Müller, Christin 5465
Müller, Franz L. 3075, 7899
Müller, Hans 5938
Müller, Heinrich 2192
Müller, Josef 182
Muller, Joseph-Emile 3347, 10422
Müller, Jürgen 7515
Muller, M. 10423, 10424
Muller, Priscilla 11872
Müller, Sigurd 12302
Müller, Werner Y. 5318
Müller, Wolfgang J. 3604
Müller-Bohn, Jost 10620
Müller-Thalheim, Wolfgang K. 6330
Müller-Walde, Paul 6942
Muls, Jozef 8060

Museum für Kunst und Kulturgeschichte der
Hansestadt Lübeck, Behnhaus 9299
Museum für Ostasiatische Kunst der Stadt Köln
(Köln) 13809
Museum Haus Lange (Krefeld) 12711
Museum Ludwig (Cologne) 582, 2983, 8411,
9077, 13291
Museum Moderner Kunst Stiftung Ludwig (Wien)
11887
Museum of Art, Carnegie Institute (Pittsburgh) 8593
Museum of Art, Rhode Island School of
Design (Providence, R.I.) 12079
Museum of Art, University of Connecticut (Storrs,
Conn.) 4574
Museum of Art, University of Michigan (Ann
Arbor, Mich.) 12203
Museum of Fine Arts (Boston) 3076, 5628, 5779,
6040, 9220, 10563, 13779
Museum of Fine Arts (Montreal) 8410
Museum of Fine Arts (Springfield, Mass.) 3673
Museum of Modern Art (New York) 12, 76, 1075,
1339, 1886, 2283, 3312, 3371, 3504, 3938,
4098, 4243, 4536, 4537, 4596, 4873, 4892,
5373, 5557, 5998, 6311, 6378, 6443, 7049,
7144, 7444, 7727, 7836, 7966, 7967, 7968,
7990, 8803, 8940, 9052, 9632, 9633, 9871,
10707, 10708, 11664, 12149
Museum of Modern Art (Oxford, Eng.) 9253
Museum Overholland Amsterdam 10631
Museum voor Schone Kunsten (Ghent) 866, 3259,
8375
Museum Wiesbaden 13451
Museumsgesellschaft Kronberg im Taunus 12289
Museums of Stony Brook (Stony Brook, NY) 8811
Musgrave, Clifford 48
Musper, Theodor 3077, 3078, 3079, 3080, 7876
Musso y Valiente 7401
Muth, Hanswernfried 10659
Muther, Richard 4683, 4742, 8363
Muzeum Knihy (Saar) 11269
Muzeum Narodowe (Warsaw) 9244
Muzzi, Andrea 2251
Mycielski, Jerzy 13096
Myers, Jane 763
Myers, John Bernard 9918
Mynona [pseud., Salomon Friedländer] 4916

N

Nadeau, Maurice 2736
Naef, Hans 5659, 5663
Naef, Weston J. 5999
Naegely, Henry 8364
Nagassé, Takeshiro 5428
Nagel, Otto 6278, 6279, 13856
Nagel, Valli 8945
Nagel, Wali 8946
Nagera, Humberto 4538
Nagler, Georg K. 10224
Naifeh, Steven W. 9872
Nakamura, Nihei 11685
Nakov, Andrei B. 6466, 12230

Naldini, Nico 9792
Naquet, Félix 3723
Narazaki, Muneshige 5295, 5429, 5430, 12523,
12771
Nardini, Bruno 6921
Nash, George 2353
Nash, J. M. 13037
Nash, Steven 3935, 4168, 9090
Nasjonal galleriet (Oslo) 2456, 2457, 2458
Nasse, Hermann 1541, 6765
Natanson, Thadée 1076, 12575
Nathan, Peter 6453, 13331
National Collection of Fine Arts, Smithsonian
Institution (Washington, D.C.) 2057, 2613,
10269, 11665, 12195, 12497, 12905
National Gallery of Art (Washington, D.C.) 1542,
2175, 2266, 3081, 3171, 4099, 5533, 6757,
7576, 8884, 10818, 11788
National Gallery of Canada (Ottawa) 3143, 5795,
6100, 10096
National Gallery of Ireland (Dublin) 9264, 13796,
13797
National Gallery of Scotland (Edinburgh) 10168
National Gallery of Victoria (Melbourne) 6172
National Maritime Museum (Greenwich) 13009
National Museum for Modern Art (Tokyo) 3854,
12107
National Museum of Western Art (Tokyo) 3724
National Portrait Gallery, Smithsonian
Institution (Washington, D.C.) 767, 13419
National Portrait Gallery (London) 2168, 13393,
13873
Nationalgalerie (Berlin) 583, 608, 701, 998, 2193,
7096, 8113, 13620
Naubert-Riser, Constance 6101
Naumann, Francis M. 2976, 13134
Naumann, Hans H. 4961, 7854
Naumann, Otto 8304
Naumann, Uwe 4908
Nava Cellini, Antonia 7400
Navarro de Adriaensens, José M. 4901
Nay, Elly 8988
Naylor, Gillian 8762
Néagu, Philippe 8995, 12599
Nebbia, Ugo 909
Nebehay, Christian M. 6143, 6144, 6145, 6146,
11329, 11330
Nebelthau, Eberhard 6397
Négis, André 8594
Negri, Emmina de 111
Negri, Mario 4244
Negri Arnoldi, Francesco 9502
Negro, Emilio 10499
Neidhardt, Hans Joachim 10295, 10621
Neilson, Katherine B. 7158
Neilson, Nancy W. 10040
Nelson, Junek 854
Nemilova, Inna S. 13370
Nemitz, Fritz 3855, 6210, 11305
Neppi, Alberto 12634
Nerdinger, Winfried 3952, 4879

O

Obalk, Hector 13314
Ober, William B. 5060
Oberdorfer, Aldo 6944
Oberes Belvedere in Wien 10862, 11416
Oberhuber, Konrad 9973, 10146, 10193, 10214, 10225, 12441
Oberhuber, Oswald 5360
O'Brian, John 2659
O'Brian, Patrick 9634
Obrist, Hans-Ulrich 10635
Ocaña, Maria Teresa 9653
Ochsner, Jeffrey K. 10604
O'Connor, Francis V. 9873
Odakane, Taro 12259
Oechelhaeuser, Adolf von 3556
Oechslin, Werner 13180
Oehlers, Helmut 3314, 7447
Oertel, Richard 4685
Oertel, Robert 7159, 12607
Oesterreichische Kulturvereinigung (Vienna) 742
Oettingen, Wolfgang von 2028, 2036, 3566
Oettinger, Karl 152, 5097
Öffentliche Kunstsammlung Basel 318
O'Gorman, James F. 10605, 10606, 10607, 13699
O'Hara, Frank 4601, 9874, 10725, 10732
O'Hara, J. Philip 3315
Ohff, Heinz 11347
Ohly, Friedrich 2367
Ohnesorge, Karl 2800
Ohrn, Karin B. 6444
Oka, Isaburo 5298, 5299
Okkonen, Onni 20, 3993, 8046
Olausson, Magnus 11544
Oldenbourg, Maria Consuelo 441, 11310
Oldenbourg, Rudolf 3545, 11088
Oliva, Achille Bonito 1806, 7426
Oliver, Andrew 11802
Olivero, Eugenio 13181
Olivier, Fernande 9635
Ollinger-Zinque, Gisèlde 3260, 6002
Ollivier, Émile 8254
Olmedo, Lola 5846
Olmo, Carlo 6635
Olney, Clarke 5168
Olsen, Harald 531
Olson, Ruth 3938
Ommeren, Anita van 12909
Oncken, Alste 4293
O'Neal, Hank 31
O'Neal, William B. 4024, 5738
O'Neil, Doris C. 3221
O'Neill, Daniel 7337
Onieva, Antonio J. 4686
Oostens-Wittamer, Yolande 5566, 5567
Oosting, J. Thomas 9342
Opel, Adolf 7234
Oppé, Adolf P. 2349, 5401, 10226, 11019, 11234
Oppell, Margarete 12413

Opperman, Hal 9282, 9285, 9286
Oppermann, Theodor 12303
Oprescu, Georges 4176
Orangerie des Tuileries (Paris) 1890, 1956, 2722, 4540
Orangerie Schloss Charlottenburg (Berlin) 9254, 11348
Orchard, Karin 9170
Orchier, Poppy Gandler 5635
O'Reilly, Patrick 4065, 4100
Oresko, Robert 41
Organ, Violet 5223
Orgel, Stephen 5775
Orienti, Sandra 1870, 7565, 7592, 7969
Oriol Anguera, A. 9636
Orlando, Fernando 6141
Orlando, Sandro 12317
Orlando, Stefano 215
Ormond, Leonée 6778
Ormond, Richard 6424, 6425, 6778, 11275, 11280, 13597
Ornstein-van Slooten, Eva 7104, 10431
Orozco, V. Clemente 9259
Orozco Diaz, Emilio 12968
Ors y Rovira, Eugenio d' 9637
Orsanmichele (Florence) 11735
Orsini, Baldassare 9503
Orso, Steven N. 12969
Ortega y Gasset, José 4687, 12970
Ortolani, Sergio 2284, 9861
Orton, Fred 4546
Orueta, Ricardo de 852
Osborn, Max 1244, 9235, 9455
Oschilewski, Walther G. 13857
Osler, William R. 12387
Osmaston, Francis P. 12388
Osmond, Marion W. 5687
Osmond, Percy H. 13065
Ospovat, Lev S. 10709
Ost, Hans 6945, 12463
Osten, Gert von der 442, 2194
Osterman, Gunhold 790
Osterwold, Tilman 6102
Ostini, Fritz von 1038, 5939, 5940, 12095, 12285, 12742
Ostrovs'kyi, Hryhorii S. 7908
Ostwald, Hans 13272
Otmezguine, Jane 291
Ottani Cavina, Anna 476, 6501
Otten, Frank 11417
Ottenheym, K. A. 9927
Ottino della Chiesa, Angela 1686, 6909, 6946
Otto, Christian F. 9037
Otto, Gertrud 12070
Otto, Kornelius 4761, 7883
Ottolenghi, Maria G. 8525
Ovenden, Graham 1560, 8820
Overy, Paul 5890
Owens, Gwendolyn 10020
Ozzòla, Leandro 9405, 10902

Peters, Ursula 12311
Peters-Schildgen, Susanne 7160
Petersen, Eugen 9536
Peterson, Christian A. 12034
Peterson, Elmer 2967
Peterson, Roger Tory 355
Petit Palais (Paris) 4899
Petit, Jean 418, 6690
Petitjean, Charles 8957
Petraccone, Enzo 4310
Pétridès, Paul 12782, 12799
Petrie, Brian 8569
Petrini, Enzo 3024
Petrova, E. N. 9699
Petrova, Evgeniya 7503
Petrovics, Elek 3531, 10694
Petrowa, Jewgenija 3569
Petrucci, Alfredo 1689
Pettenella, Plinia 164
Petzet, Heinrich W. 13206
Petzet, Michael 6768, 11881
Pevsner, Alexei 3939
Pevsner, Nikolaus 4962, 7239, 7381, 8068, 8072,
    10073, 13655
Pewny, Denise 10695
Peyre, Roger R. 12244
Peyre, Yves 3348, 3490
Pfäfflin, Friedrich 4855
Pfalzgalerie Kaiserslautern 10079
Pfankuch, Peter 11315
Pfannstiel, Arthur 8462, 8463, 8464
Pfefferkorn, Rudolph 6118
Pfeiffer, Bruce Brooks 13701, 13702, 13722,
    13724, 13728, 13729, 13733, 13734, 13735,
    13736, 13737, 13738, 13739, 13742, 13743,
    13744
Pfeiffer, H. G. 6161, 6174
Pfeiffer-Belli, Erich 6104, 8839
Pfingsten, Claus 10486
Pfister, Kurt 1137, 3410, 4453, 4543, 11494
Pfister, Rudolf 9044
Pfister-Burkhalter, Margarete 8126
Pforte, Dietger 13211
Philadelphia Museum of Art 984, 2235, 2332,
    5131, 6425, 7579, 7728, 7970
Philandrier, Guillaume 13173
Philip, Lotte Brand 3411
Philipe, Anne 13087
Philippe, Joseph 3412
Philipson, Morris 6957
Phillimore, Lucy 13656
Phillipos, Lisa 11676
Phillips, Christopher 11956
Phillips, Claude 10574, 12468, 12469, 13374
Phillips, Duncan 4336, 13438
Phillips, Evelyn M. 9709, 12392
Phillips, Laughlin 2921
Phillips, Sandra S. 5999, 8782
Phillips Collection (Washington, D.C.) 1892
Phillips Memorial Art Gallery (Washington, D. C.)
    2604

Phipps, Alan 13073
Photography Gallery (Philadelphia) 1655
Physick, John F. 4278, 4279, 12010
Phythian, J. Ernest 5695
Pia, Pascal 7840
Piantanida, Sandro 6958
Piantoni, Gianna 1473
Piatkowski, Henryk 197
Pica, Agnoldomenico 3648, 11751
Pica, Vittorio 9124
Picart, Yves 13225, 13226
Piccard, Gerhard 8794
Piccioni, Leone 8465
Piccirillo, F. 10030
Piceni, Enrico 9125, 9126, 13832
Pichi, Giovanni F. 3766
Pickle, R. 9265
Pickvance, Ronald 4102, 4544
Pican, Antoine 9486
Picon, Gaëtan 472, 2938, 5665, 8416
Picon, Jacinto O. 12973
Pieper, Paul 8006
Pierantoni, Amalia C. 6959
Piérard, Louis 4545, 7580
Pierre, José 6056, 8679
Pierre Matisse Gallery (New York) 468, 469, 4245,
    8417
Pierron, Sander 8795
Piers, Harry 3562
Piersanti, Gilda 5058
Pietro, Filippo di 532
Pietsch, Ludwig 5242
Pieyre de Mandiargues, André 282, 733
Pigler, Andor 2896
Pignatti, Terisio 720, 1599, 1600, 1601, 1602,
    1603, 4337, 4997, 7216, 7218, 7219, 7220,
    7221, 7627, 12321, 12335, 12342, 12351,
    12401, 13067
Piliavskii, V. I. 10941
Piljavskij, Vladimir 10113
Pilla, Eugenio 12470
Pillement, Georges 10588
Pillep, Rudolf 668
Pillet, Charles 13098
Pillsbury, Edmund P. 9973
Pilo, Giuseppe Maria 1731, 10597, 12428
Pilon, Edmond 4843, 8001, 13375
Pilz, Kurt 13161
Pina García, Juan Pablo de 10710
Pincus, Robert L. 6020
Pincus-Witten, Robert 7079
Pinder, Wilhelm 5467, 6249
Pinet, Hélène 10820, 10821, 10827
Pinnington, Edward 13581
Pino, Domenico 6960
Pinottini, Marzio 12137
Pionault, Madeleine 5579
Piovene, Guido 12343, 13068
Pirchan, Emil 6148, 7484
Pires, Heliodoro 7179
Pirondini, Massimo 10499

Pirovano, Carlo 7730, 7737
Pisis, Bona de 9795
Pisko, Gustav 13283
Pissaro, Joachim 9812
Pissarro, Ludovic R. 9815
Pita Andrade, José Manuel 4808
Pittaluga, Mary 1497, 7161, 7794, 9126, 12393, 12730
Pittoni, Laura 11265
Pitz, Henry C. 10106, 10107
Piva, Paolo 2268
Pivar, Stuart 561
Place, Charles A. 1454
Placzek, Adolf K. 2799, 9344, 9744, 11549, 12116, 13695
Plagens, Peter 11160
Plan, Pierre Paul 1543
Planet, Louis de 2703
Planiscig, Leo 2777, 2872, 4195, 8951, 10601, 10748, 10909, 13079, 13239
Planque, Jean 2928
Plant, Margaret 6105
Plate, Robert 1821
Pleasants, J. Hall 5767
Plettinck, Leopold 7517
Pleynet, Mercelin 7971
Plichta, Dalibor 13900
Plietzsch, Eduard 12254, 13038
Ploegaerts, Léon 12996
Plon, Eugène 1840, 12304
Ploog, Randy 13469
Plugin, Vladimir S. 11120
Pocock, Tom 13527
Podobedova, O. I. 6447
Poensgen, Georg 3622, 9522
Poeschel, Erwin 4246
Poeschke, Joachim 2873, 2874, 9035
Poetter, Jochen 11752
Poggetto, Paolo Dal 7273, 8199, 13902
Poggi, Giovanni 8245
Poggiali, Pietro 10231
Poggianella, Sergio 458
Pogliarani, Elio 7639
Pogorilovschi, Ion 1275
Pohl, Frances Kathryn 11640, 11641
Pohlen, Ingeborg 11091
Pohlmann, Ulrich 4448
Poillon, Louis 9974
Point, Daniël 3425
Point Cardinal, Le (Paris) 3309
Pointer, Andy 66
Pointon, Marcia R. 3118, 8844
Pois, Robert 9163
Poland, William C. 3513
Polano, Sergio 2838
Polásek, Jan 12580
Polazzo, Marco 450, 451
Poley, Stefanie 319
Polfeldt, Ingegerd 5271
Poliakoff, Alexis 9845
Poliakova, Elena I. 10845

Polifolo [pseud. Luca Beltrami] 6961
Pollak, Oskar 814
Pollet, Elizabeth 8887
Pollock, Griselda 2644, 4546
Poma, Anna Maria 1425
Pomilio, Mario 6962
Pommer, Richard 5834
Pommeranz-Liedtke, Gerhard 2370, 2812, 7810, 7815, 8947, 11425
Pompei, Alessandro 11255
Pompey, Francisco 3679, 4690, 12974, 13933
Ponente, Nello 1893, 6106, 7895, 10232
Ponert, Dietmar J. 609
Ponge, Francis 1314, 1315
Pons, Nicoletta 1188
Pons, Zenon 10058
Ponsonailhe, Charles 1238
Ponte, Pietro da 8696
Ponten, Josef 10556, 10557
Pool, Phoebe 7565, 9570
Poore, Charles 4691
Poorter, Nora de 5792, 11092
Pope, Arthur 12471
Pope, Willard Bissell 5165
Pope-Hennessy, John 216, 217, 1829, 2847, 2875, 3767, 4402, 5282, 10233, 10749, 11294, 12731
Popelier, F. 2729
Popham, Arthur E. 2269, 6963, 8296, 9421
Popitz, Klaus 1335
Pople, Kenneth 11908
Popp, Anny E. 8261
Popper, Frank 62
Porcella, Antonio 12344
Porta, Marco 4006
Portalis, Roger 3726, 6368
Porter, Dean A. 5249, 8151
Porter, Fairfield 3174
Porter, James A. 5780, 13553
Porteus, Hugh G. 7043
Portmann, Paul 7858
Portmas, Paul Ferdinand 860
Portoghesi, Paolo 84, 1110, 1111, 1112, 5011, 5560, 5561, 8300, 13182
Posener, Julius 7240, 9831, 9833, 11350
Posner, Donald 1754, 13376, 13377, 13378
Posner, Helaine 11932
Pospisil, Maria 7416
Posse, Hans 2368, 11194
Postan, Alexander 8975
Potocki, Antoni 4922
Potter, Jeffrey 9876
Potterton, Homan 1604
Pottier, Edmond 3114
Pougetoux, Alain 340
Pouillon, Catherine 13132
Pouillon, Christian 12977
Pouillon, Nadine 1294
Poulain, Gaston 622, 623
Poulet, Anne L. 2108
Poulet-Allamagny, Jean-Jacques 12599

Rizzi, Aldo 1701, 1702
Rizzo, Giulio E. 10006
Robaut, Alfred 2236, 2237, 2238, 2239, 2704
Robbins, Daniel 8159, 12532
Robe-Grillet, Alain 11469
Robels, Hella 11831
Robert, Guy 1097, 1098
Roberts, Colette 9073, 12499
Roberts, Jane 8267
Roberts, William 5559, 10878
Roberts-Jones, Philippe 2535, 2729, 7450, 13762
Robertson, Bruce 5535
Robertson, Bryan 6306, 9144, 9878
Robertson, David A. 3189
Robertson, Donald W. 3905
Robertson, Giles 722, 1813
Robida, Michel 10533
Robin, Michel 4547
Robinson, Basil W. 6349, 6350
Robinson, Duncan 11909, 11910
Robinson, Franklin W. 8157
Robinson, John M. 13766
Robinson, M. S. 13010
Robinson, Susan Barnes 462
Robiquet, Jacques 4623
Rocco, Giovanni 12316
Roch, Wolfgang 11146
Rochas d'Aiglun, Albert de 12900
Roche, Denis 424, 7025
Roché, H. P. 2977
Rocheblave, Samuel 9691
Rochfort, Desmond 10716, 11736
Rodiger-Diruf, Erika 11924
Rodijk, G. H. 10672
Roditi, Eduard 5989
Rodman, Selden 9726, 11645
Rodrigues dos Santos, Cecilia 6693
Rodriguez, Antonio 10712, 10717, 11737
Rodriguez-Aguilera, Cesareo 9662
Rodriguez del Castillo, Jesús 13915
Roe, F. Gordon 3353
Roeck, Bernd 5483, 5484
Roedel, Reto 11484
Roehm, Marjorie Catlin 1817
Roennefahrt, Günther 11921
Roessler, Arthur 1416, 11331, 11333, 13283
Roethel, Hans K. 5892
Roethlisberger, Marcel 1002, 1326, 7136
Roettgen, Steffi 8093
Roffler, Thomas 5338
Roger-Ballu 562
Roger-Marx, Claude 2522, 2557, 2561, 2787,
    2788, 5786, 9431, 10435, 10534, 10754,
    11506, 11507, 11635, 12581, 13256, 13257,
    13258
Roger-Milès, Léon 1056, 6969, 9554, 13849
Rogers, Ernesto N. 9016
Rogers, John J. 9226
Rogers, Meyric R. 8344
Rogers, Pat 10576
Rogge, Henning 691

Roggero, Mario F. 8078
Rogosz, Josef 4924
Roh, Franz 8490
Rohn, Matthew 9879
Roi, Pia 2273
Roig, Jean de 10884
Roland, Berthold 5495, 10083, 11774, 11776,
    11777, 11778, 11781
Roland-Michel, Marianne 1971, 12812, 13379
Rolfs, Wilhelm 4965, 6535
Roli, Renato 476, 491
Romagnoli, Fernanda 9183
Romain, Lothar 889, 5207, 11408, 13316
Romains, Jules 6722
Roman, Joseph 10675
Romanelli, Giandomenico 1626
Romanini, Angiola Maria 296
Romano, Elisa 13175
Romano, Giovanni 3535
Romanus, Peter 3495
Romdahl, Axel L. 8268, 13105
Romero, Héctor Manuel 10718
Romero, Luis 2488
Romney, John 10876
Römpler, Karl 6766
Ronchaud, Louis de 9537
Rondolino, Gianni 8494
Ronner, Heinz 5857
Ronte, Dieter 13221
Ronzani, Francesco 11257
Roop, Guy 9357
Roosen-Runge, Heinz 7848
Rooses, Max 5797, 11095, 11096, 11101
Roosevelt, Blanche [pseud.] 2911
Root, Elihu, Jr. 1812
Rope, Edward G. 10072
Rosand, David 4714, 12473, 12474, 12475
Rosci, Marco 569, 4151, 6970, 11548
Roscoe, S. 903
Rose, Barbara 283, 3812, 5962, 6309, 6377, 7069,
    8418, 9208, 9216, 10272, 10345
Rose, Bernice 891, 9880
Rose, June 8466
Rose, Millicent 2912
Rose, W. K. 7034
Rose Art Museum, Brandeis University (Waltham,
    Mass.) 3813, 3906, 7991, 10732
Rosenauer, Artur 2876
Rosenauer, Monika 3407
Rosenbach, A. S. W. 2420
Rosenbach, Detlev 1336, 13864
Rosenberg, Adolf 688, 2626, 4123, 5941, 6808,
    6971, 9269, 10239, 10436, 11097, 11950,
    12245, 12306, 13380, 13384, 13385, 13456
Rosenberg, Harold 2679, 4608, 9081, 11756,
    11961, 11965
Rosenberg, Jakob 2357, 10437, 11129, 11403
Rosenberg, Marc 5719
Rosenberg, Pierre 1972, 1973, 2343, 3729, 6494,
    6504, 6505, 6513, 9524, 9978, 9979, 9985
Rosenberg, Yvette 4503

Schmalenbach, Werner 944, 945, 8474, 8475, 11411, 11432, 12219
Schmarsow, August 3418, 7796, 7797, 8049, 9505, 9711, 11270
Schmeckebier, Laurence E. 2434, 2441, 8153
Schmid, Heinrich Alfred 1041, 1042, 5471
Schmid, Max 6175, 10558
Schmidt, Dieter 2815, 5209
Schimdt, Adriana 5986
Schmidt, Georg 5336, 12150
Schmidt, Hans M. 7885
Schmidt, Hans-Werner 6021
Schmidt, Harry 9291, 9292
Schmidt, Heinrich A. 4968, 8275, 10559
Schmidt, Johann Karl 2829, 13596
Schmidt, Justus 3589
Schmidt, Karl W. 10626
Schmidt, Katharina 1994, 9855, 12187, 12712
Schmidt, Paul F. 6334, 9168, 11150
Schmidt, Werner 6275
Schmidt, Winfried 11130
Schmidt-Degener, Frederik 1365, 10440, 11951
Schmidt-Dengler, Maria 3408, 3409
Schmidt-Künsemüller, Friedrich A. 8767
Schmidt-Küster, Gustav 13857
Schmied, Wieland 1483, 3860, 5212, 5808, 6335, 7987, 9184, 9186
Schmit, Robert 1218, 1222
Schmitz, Hermann 443
Schmoll, J. August 12096, 12097
Schmollgen. Eisenwerth, Josef Adolf 702, 10829
Schmorl, Theodor A. 9041
Schmücking, Rolf 5124
Schnack, Jutta 8005
Schnackenburg, Bernhard 9271
Schnapper, Antoine 2585, 5820, 13121
Schneditz, Wolfgang 6336
Schneeberger, Pierre-Francis 4109
Schneede, Marina 5814
Schneede, Uwe M. 3320, 4919, 5814, 6281, 7452
Schneider, Angela 608, 4220
Schneider, Arthur von 1694, 3623, 13434
Schneider, Cynthia P. 10441, 10442
Schneider, Edouard 221
Schneider, Erich 9042
Schneider, Hans 7105
Schneider, Hans-Karl 4901
Schneider, Laurie 4382
Schneider, Max F. 1043
Schneider, Pierre 7946, 13381
Schneider, Reinhold 6211
Schneiderman, Richard S. 8134
Schneiders, Toni 10659
Schnell, Werner 5990
Schnütgen-Museum, Kunsthalle Köln 9411
Schnyder-Seidel, Barbara 3929, 12411
Schöber, David G. 3089
Schoeller, André 2237, 2238, 2239
Schoeller, Nathalie 12990
Schoenberger, Arno 5016
Schoenberger, Guido 4969

Schoenenberger, Walter 11553
Schönberg, Arnold 5884
Schöne, Wolfgang 1241
Schönfeld, Paul 11261
Schoonbaerten, L. M. A. 11594
Schopenhauer, Johanna 3419
Schott, Rudolf 8276
Schottmüller, Frida 222, 2878
Schouvaloff, Alexander 425
Schrade, Hubert 7199, 10660
Schram, Wilhelm 5932
Schreckenberg, Hella 11798
Schreiber, Theodor 9891
Schreiner, Ludwig 11356
Schrenk, Klaus 2565, 7959
Schreyl, Karl Heinz 9202, 11309
Schröder, Bruno 8938
Schröder, Klaus Albrecht 6234, 13284
Schröder, Rudolf A. 10826
Schroeder, Thomas 1545
Schrott, Raoul 12720
Schubert, Dietrich 2830, 6759
Schubring, Paul 165, 2879, 10751, 12757
Schuchardt, Christian 2371
Schuder, Rosemarie 1140
Schudt, Ludwig 1695
Schüler, Gerhard 11514
Schüler, Irmgard 7872
Schult, Friedrich 518, 519, 520
Schulte, Birgit 10853
Schulte, Edvige 10933
Schultz, Wolfgang 11202, 11203
Schultze, Ingrid 4970
Schultze, Jürgen 5728
Schulz, Anne M. 1458, 9089, 10733, 10910
Schulz, Katharina 6236
Schulz-Hoffmann, Carla 1309, 3645, 7740
Schulze, Franz 8318, 8321
Schulze, Friedrich 9190
Schulze, Hanns 1352
Schulze, Sabine 8415
Schulze-Battman, Elfriede 12789
Schumacher, Helmut 13404
Schumacher, Joachim 6976
Schumann, Werner 13861, 13863
Schumann-Bacia, Eva 11836, 11837
Schurek, Paul 521, 522
Schürer, Oskar 9305, 9672
Schurian, Walter 5581
Schurmeyer, Walter 1141
Schuster, Jean 7992
Schuster, Peter-Klaus 1000, 6054, 6208, 7680, 7688
Schuster, Thomas E. 4824
Schütz, Bernhard 9043
Schütze, Karl-Robert 13208
Schuurman, K. E. 3428
Schuyler, Hamilton 10837
Schvey, Henry I. 6235
Schwabacher, Ethel 4609

Schwabacher, Sascha 9863
Schwabik, Aurel 9306, 9307
Schwaiger, Brigitte 10163
Schwartz, Alexandra 11811
Schwartz, Arturo 10292
Schwartz, Constance 9074
Schwartz, Gary 10443, 11200
Schwartzman, Myron 626
Schwarz, Arturo 2966, 2985, 2986
Schwarz, Dieter 7754
Schwarz, Heinrich 5276
Schwarz, Herbert 2372
Schwarz, Ignaz 10643
Schwarz, Karl 2197, 5303
Schwarz, Michael 2898
Schweicher, Curt 13262
Schweizerisches Institut für Kunstwissenschaft
    (Zurich) 5339
Schwemmer, Wilhelm 6120, 6295
Schwenger, Marlis 4286
Sciascio, Leonardo 250
Science Museum (London) 13422
Sciolla, Gianni C. 8381
Sciré, Giovanna Nepi 12480
Scott, David W. 2737, 9251, 11788, 11789
Scott, Gayl R. 5125
Scott, Jonathan 9748
Scott, Leader [pseud.] 549
Scott, McDougall 6426
Scott, Pamela 8374
Scott, Temple 8768
Scott, William P. 8710
Scottish Arts Council (Edinburgh) 1771
Scottish Arts Council Gallery (Edinburgh) 5277
Scribner, Charles 842, 11106
Scricchia Santoro, Fiorella 255, 257, 656, 11291
Scully, Vincent, Jr. 5853, 5858, 6814, 9366, 13703
Scutenaire, Louis 7453
Séailles, Gabriel 1764, 6977, 13382
Secker, Hans F. 10719
Secrest, Meryle 1358, 2491, 13704
Secrétain, Roger 4044
Sedelmeyer, Charles 8903
Sedlmaier, Richard 9044
Sedlmayr, Hans 1113, 3590
Seeger, Georg 13164
Seel, Friedrich 10080, 10082
Seelye, John 10480
Segalen, Victor 8681
Segantini, Bianca 11486
Segard, Achille 1795, 4615, 11850
Segi, Shinichi 13813
Seidlitz, Woldemar von 6978, 10444
Seipel, Wilfried 6337
Seitz, Don C. 13531
Seitz, William C. 4610, 5373, 8576, 12500
Sekler, Eduard F. 5364, 13658
Sekler, Mary P. 6694
Seldes, Lee 10968
Seldis, Henry J. 8626
Selevoy, Robert L. 861

Seligman, Germain 6398, 11618
Seligman, Herbert J. 7725, 12031
Seligman, Janet 2508, 8487
Selivanova, Nina 10847
Sellars, James 9393
Sellers, Charles C. 9449, 9450
Sello, Gottfried 3233, 4753, 12056
Selway, Neville C. 9864
Selz, Jean 2240, 7976, 8682, 8890, 10324, 13196
Selz, Peter H. 671, 682, 2939, 3799, 5340, 9169
Sembat, Marcel 7977
Semenzato, Camillo 7215, 9359, 12348
Semler, Christian 9538
Semper, Hans 2880, 2881, 9308, 11526
Semper, Manfred 11526
Senghor, Léopold 1938, 3286
Sensier, Alfred 1757, 8173, 8365, 11007
Sentenac, Paul 7477
Serafinska, Stanislawa 7910
Serebriannaya, Natalia 9976
Serenyi, Peter 6695
Sergeant, John 13705
Sergeev, Valerii Nilolaevich 11122
Sergi, Antonino 10033
Serota, Nicholas 570, 5036, 12713
Serov, Valentin A. 11564, 11565
Serra, Luigi 2848, 10242
Serra, Pere A. 8423
Serret, Georges 5031
Sert, Josep Lluís 4033
Sérullaz, Maurice 2241, 2584, 2687, 2707, 2708,
    12976, 12977
Servaes, Franz 6176, 11487, 13897
Servi, Gaspare 12790
Servolini, Luigi 475, 1154
Servot, Martine 2231, 2232
Settis, Salvatore 9539, 13570
Seuphor, Michel [pseud., Berckelaers, Ferdinand
    Louis] 246, 320, 322, 6459, 8527
Severin, Dante 10116
Severini, Giancarlo 11251
Severini, Gino 7978
Severne, Judith 10632
Sewell, Darrel 3177, 12194
Sewter, A. Charles 8769, 9550
Seymour, Charles, Jr. 8277, 8278, 10127, 13081
Seyppel, Joachim Hans 12761
Seyres, Helene 12131
Sgarbi, Vittorio 1163, 5003, 11488
Sgard, Jean 8042
Shadbolt, Doris 1735
Shahn, Bernarda B. 11647
Shakerley, Geoffrey 8627
Shanes, Eric 1276, 12683, 12684, 12685, 12686
Shannon, Martha A. S. 5629
Shapiro, David 2809, 5755
Shapiro, Michael Edward 10480
Sharp, Dennis 12998
Sharp, William 10934
Shattuck, Roger 12036
Shaw, J. Byam 4998. 12349

Stoll, Karlheinz 9179
Stoloff, Bernard 6709
Stolota, Franciszka 12060
Stone, David M. 495
Stone, Irving 4551
Stooss, Toni 8669, 13217
Stoppani, Leonard 8772
Stoppenbach, Robert 2496
Storm, John 12802
Storr, Robert 2110, 5038
Storrer, William A. 13707, 13708
Story, Alfred T. 7129
Story, Sommerville 10830
Stoullig, Claire 9875
Stowe, Edwin 12979
Straaten, Roelof van 10150
Strachey, Constance 6592, 6593
Strajnić, Kosta 8154
Strange, Alfred 5462
Strange, Edward F. 5300, 5434, 12603
Strangos, Niklos 5316
Stratton, Arthur 11727
Strauss, Eva 7108
Strauss, Gerhard 6284
Strauss, Walter L. 3092, 3093, 3094, 3095, 4577,
    10450
Strazzullo, Franco 12855
Streicher, Elizabeth 6181
Streichhan, Annelise 6191
Streit, Carl 10662
Streitz, Robert 9361
Stridbeck, Carl Gustaf 1409
Strieder, Peter 3096, 3097
Strinati, Claudio M. 10030, 10034
Strobl, Alice 6151
Strömberg, Martin 5826
Strong, Roy 5274, 5284, 5473, 5775
Stroud, Dorothy 1372, 10553, 11838
Strub, Marcel 4129
Strutt, Edward C. 7165
Stuart, Jan 1957
Stubbe, Achilles 11595
Stubbe, Wolf 524, 525, 9019, 10627, 10644
Stubblebine, James H. 2950, 5026
Stuchbury, Howard E. 1564
Stuck-Villa (Munich) 10010
Stuckey, Charles F. 4071, 8563, 8578, 8710,
    12585, 13321
Stuckey, Joan 13446, 13447
Stuckey, Ronald 13446, 13447
Studentenstudio für Moderne Kunst (Tübingen)
    4857
Studi su Raffaello atti del congresso internatzionale
    de studi 10245
Studniczka, Franz 1505
Stuhr, Michael 12061
Stumm, Lucie 7653
Stumm, Reinhardt 12367
Stupples, Peter 6366
Stuttmann, Ferdinand 7101
Stutzer, Beat 4226, 4249

Suarès, André 10980
Subirana, Rosa Maria 9648
Succi, Dario 10598, 12350, 12351
Succo, Friedrich 11687, 12604
Sugana, Gabriele M. 4110, 12547
Suganuma, Teizo 13335
Sugranes, Jose M. a Guix 4032
Suhr, Norbert 5495, 12912, 12913
Suida, William Emil 1260, 1551, 3098, 6984,
    10247, 12476
Suida Manning, Bertina 1549, 1551
Sullivan, Edward J. 1166
Summers, David 8284
Summerson, John 5778, 8958, 8961, 8962, 11839,
    13659
Sumner, Heyward 2376
Sumowski, Werner 3863, 10397, 10451
Supino, Igino B. 1841, 4385, 7166, 7167
Surtees, Virginia 1367, 10935, 10936
Survage, M. 12130
Susinno, Stefano 12310
Suter, Margrit 328
Sutton, Denys 1078, 2773, 7598, 10831, 11696,
    11940, 13534, 13535, 13589
Sutton, Peter C. 1223, 5544
Sutton, Thomas 2502
Suzdalev, Petr K. 13248
Suzuki, Daisetz T. 11530
Suzuki, Juzo 11657
Svenaeus, Gösta 8894, 8895
Svietlov, V. 424
Svintila, Vladimir 13828
Swane, Leo 7979
Swanson, Vern G. 131, 136, 137
Swarbrick, John 51
Swarzenski, Georg 9787
Sweeney, James J. 1522, 1945, 2614, 4033, 8428,
    8629, 11884, 11890
Sweeney, Robert L. 13709
Sweet, Frederick A. 1796, 13779
Sweetman, David 4552
Sweetser, Moses F. 124, 2100, 3149, 6428, 6985,
    10506, 12477
Swillens, P. T. A. 1565, 11201, 13041
Swinburne, Algernon Charles 987
Swinburne, Charles A. 12688
Swoboda, Karl M. 9412
Syamken, Georg G. 7417
Sydow, Eckart von 184
Sýkorová, Libuše 4111
Sylvester, David 410, 7438, 7454, 7455, 8617,
    8630, 8733
Symeonides, Sibilla 12147
Symmons, Sarah 3601, 4709
Symonds, Emily Morse see Paston, George
Symonds, John A. 8285
Symons, Arthur 988
Syre, Cornelia 3646
Szabo, George 10021
Szarkowski, John 342, 1528, 3371, 5998, 8782,
    9460, 12122

Szeeman, Harald 12713, 12716
Székessy, Karin 13764
Szittya, Emilio 3574, 11896
Szwykowski, Ignaz von 3150

T

Tabarant, Adolphe 7589, 7590, 9818, 12783
Táborský, Frantisek 4925, 5916
Tadashi, Kobayashi 5424
Tadgell, Christopher 3943
Taevernier, Aug 3263, 3264
Tafel, Edgar 13710, 13711
Taft, Ada B. 12155
Tafuri, Manfredo 10196, 11267
Taggard, Mindy Nancarrow 8927
Tagliaventi, Ivo 13149
Taigny, Edmond 5688
Taillandier, Yvon 107, 8429, 8579
Takahashi, Koji 10318
Takahashi, Seiichiro 5133, 5301, 5946, 12525
Takeda, Tsuneo 5898
Talbot, Charles W. 3081
Tanaka, Ichimatsu 11875
Tanaka, Jo 3686
Tancock, John L. 10832
Tanguy, Kay S. 12185
Tannenbaum, Libby 3265
Tapié, Michel 1653, 2484, 3295, 3650, 12220
Tapié de Céleyran, Mary 12586
Tarabukin, Nikolai M. 13249
Taranovskaia, Marianna Z. 10942, 10943
Tarbé, Prosper 9692
Tarnowski, Stanislaw 7912
Tassi, Roberto 3864, 12140, 12141
Tassoni, Luigi 10035, 10036
Tatarinoff-Eggenschwiler, Adele 185
Tatarkiewicz, Wladyslaw 9245
Tate Gallery (London) 64, 412, 471, 990, 2161,
     2296, 3013, 3329, 3865, 3930, 3975, 4112,
     5305, 6237, 6746, 8630, 8733, 8977, 9100,
     9217, 12689
Tatham, David 5536
Tattersall, Bruce 12092
Tauber, Henry 6179
Tavel, Hans C. von 5701, 7654
Tavernor, Robert 9362
Tavoni, Efrem 8657
Taylor, Basil 2162, 12092, 12093
Taylor, Hilary 13536
Taylor, Ina 4826
Taylor, John L. 4238
Taylor, Joshua Charles 1022
Taylor, Paul S. 6440, 6441
Taylor, Tom 5171, 10571
Tchétchouline, Nicolas 9270, 10439
Teague, Edward H. 8631
Teatini, Manuela 10776
Technau, Werner 3382
Teixidor, Joan 12223
Teller, Susan Pirpiris 938, 13624
Telluccini, Augusto 5836

Temanza, Tommaso 9363
Temkin, Ann 891
Temko, Allan 11191
Temple, Nigel 8963
Templeman, William D. 4296
Tendron, Marcel *see* Elder, Marc
Terenzio, Stephanie 388, 8800, 8805, 8806
Terez, Gabriel (Gabor) von 446, 447
Tériade, E. 6747
Terlinden, Charles 9232, 13568
Ternois, Daniel 1546, 1547, 5662, 5669
Terrasse, Antoine 1067, 1072, 1079, 1080, 2739,
     7924, 11620
Terrasse, Charles 4553, 4710, 9698, 11851
Terrier, A. 424
Terwen, J. J. 9927
Testori, Giovanni 3541, 7225
Teuber, Dirk 11470
Teuber, M. L. 3340
Teufel, Richard 9046, 9047
Tharp, Louise H. 11212
Thater-Schulz, Cornelia 5309
Thausing, Moritz 3099
Thaw, Eugene V. 9873
Theiry, A. 8168
Thelen, Heinrich 1114
Theuriet, André 597
Thévenin, Léon 8683
Thévoz, Michel 4443
Thibaudeau, A. 6752
Thiel, Pieter van 10375
Thiele, Carmela 12747
Thiele, Just M. 12308, 12309
Thiele, Vladimir 1650
Thiem, Christel 11859
Thiem, Günther 5436, 6035, 11389
Thiemann, Barbara M. 8063
Thieme, Ulrich 11311
Thienemann, Georg A. W. 10645
Thienen, Frithjof Willem Sophi van 5545
Thiersch, Hermann 12278
Thiis, Jens 6986, 8896
Thimme, Jürgen 9566
Thirion, Henri 2109
Thode, Henry 1044, 2274, 4386, 7636, 8286,
     8287, 12286, 12399
Thoenes, Christof 11550
Thoma, Hans 6785
Thomas, Denis 5260
Thomas, Duncan 284
Thomas, F. Richard 12037
Thomas, Hylton 9750
Thomas-Netik, Anja 10636
Thome, Antoine 2586
Thompson, David 10248
Thompson, Dody W. 13475
Thompson, E. P. 8773
Thompson, Henry Y. 3702
Thompson, Jerry L. 3365
Thompson, Paul R. 8774, 8775
Thomson, Belinda 4113, 13263

Visser't Hooft, Willem A. 10460
Vita, Alessandro del 3773, 12889, 12893, 12894
Vitali, Christoph 1947
Vitali, Lamberto 8647, 8658, 8659, 8660, 12600
Vitelli, S. 10030
Vitelli Buscaroli, Syra 2059
Vitet, Ludovic 7013
Vitra, Paul 2138
Vitrac, Roger 7148
Vitry, Paul 2345, 4622, 7615
Vittorini, Elio 5051
Vitzthum, Walter 10060, 13600
Vitzthum Von Eckstädt, Georg 2449
Vladych, Leonid V. 5913
Vlieghe, Hans 1045, 2379, 11110, 12240
Vöge, Wilhelm 5065
Vogel, Hans 11362
Vogel, Julius 4744, 6182, 6183
Vogel, Robert M. 10839
Vogel-Köhn, Doris 10461
Vogelsang, Bernd 9077
Vogelsang, W. 4128, 11201
Vogt, Adolf M. 4972
Vogt, Paul 5187, 10856, 10857, 10858, 10859, 10860
Vogt, Wilhelm 5485
Voïart, Elise 10049
Voisin, Auguste 8053
Volavková, Hana 7530
Volbehr, Theodor 7314
Volhard, Hans 4723
Volk, Peter 5018
Volk, Waltraud 11363
Volker, Angela 12004
Volkmann, Barbara 7243, 9184
Volkmann, Hans 9752
Volkov-Lannit, Leonid F. 10785
Voll, Karl 8064
Vollard, Ambroise 804, 1905, 2674, 10537, 10538
Volpe, Carlo 7255, 9721
Volponi, Paolo 7802
Voltini, Giorgio 13572
Von Bothmer, Dietrich 173, 174
Von Eckhardt, Wolf 8080
Von Hartz, John 11239
Von Kirschen, Ivo 12858
Von Wagner, Johann Martin 3952
Voragen, Th. 11594
Vorarlberger Landesmuseum (Bregenz) 5934
Vorms, Pierre 7804, 7810, 7817
Vorpahl, Ben M. 10482
Vos, Dirk de 8055, 8065
Vos, Rik 7315
Vosmaer, Carel 10462
Voss, Heinrich 12099
Voss, Hermann G. A. 155
Vries, Ary B. de 10463, 13043
Vries, Lyckle de 5247, 11952
Vries, Simonetta de 1996
Vriesen, Gustav 7358

Vuaflart, Albert 13351
Vuilliaud, Paul 6996

W

Waagen, Gustav Friedrich 3420, 11111
Waal, Henri Van de 4724, 10464
Wächter, Bernhard 3524, 4931
Waddell, Roberta 12199
Wadley, Nicholas 4563, 10529
Wadsworth Atheneum (Hartford, Conn.) 2135, 4845
Waern, Cecilia 6388
Waetzoldt, Wilhelm 3101, 5474
Wagemann, Ines 8022
Wagenseil, Christian Jakob 5486
Wagner, A. 6285
Wagner, Anne Middleton 1729
Wagner, Geoffrey 7044
Wagner, Helga 5248
Wagner, Hugo 354, 2697, 10253
Wagner, Robert 4047
Wainwright, Clive 10061, 10064, 10071
Wainwright, Jane 10064
Wakefield, David 3734
Walcher Casotti, Maria 13118
Wälchli, Gottfried 1440, 1442
Waldberg, Michel 3800
Waldberg, Patrick 3331, 3332, 6554, 7459, 7739
Waldemar-George [pseud.] 39, 2018
Walden, Russell 6697
Waldkirch, Bernhard von 5328
Waldman, Diane 572, 1708, 2428, 4611, 5966, 7081, 7082, 9147, 10969
Waldmann, Emil 156, 3102, 3103, 3104, 3560, 4116, 6769, 6770, 7593, 8117, 9541, 10835, 11780, 11782, 12403, 12488, 12624
Waldstein, Charles 9541
Walford, E. John 11132
Walicki, Michal 13044
Walker, Barry 5921
Walker, John 2164, 12696, 13537
Walker, R. A. 635
Walker Art Center (Minneapolis) 2681
Walker Art Gallery (Liverpool) 1370, 5623
Wall, John R. 10931
Wallace, David H. 10849
Wallace, Richard W. 10907
Wallace, Robert D. 9789
Waller, Mark 6401
Wallis, Brian 7226
Wallis, Mieczyslaw 749, 9129, 9130, 9131
Wallraf-Richartz-Museum (Cologne) 1436, 6771, 12313
Walmsley, Dorothy B. 13297
Walmsley, Lewis C. 13297
Walsdorf, John J. 8778
Walsh, Amy 9929
Walter, Ingo F. 2822
Walter, Maräuschlein 10296
Walter-Dressler, Helga 11924
Walters, William T. 564

Wyatt, Woodrow 13766
Wye, Deborah 12225
Wyeth, Betsy J. 13781, 13782, 13783
Wyeth, N. C. 10101
Wyl, Wilhelm [pseud., Wilhelm Ritter von
　　Wymetal] 6810
Wyler, Eva 5340
Wyllie, William L. 12707
Wymetal, Wilhelm Ritter von *see* Wyl, Wilhelm
Wynn Jones, Michael 2424
Wyss, Kurt 12367
Wysuph, C. L. 9882

Y

Yakush, Mary 10442
Yale University Art Gallery (New Haven) 27, 80
Yao, Min-Chih 12503
Yard, Sally 2048
Yarnall, James L. 6389
Yarrow, William 5226
Yarwood, Doreen 52
Yashiro, Yukio 1197
Yglesias, Helen 939
Yorke, Malcolm 4282
Young, Andrew M. 7382, 13550
Young, Dorothy 13439
Young, Eric 800
Young, Mahonri S. 766
Yriarte, Charles E. 2074, 3680, 4718, 7638, 8370,
　　13071
Yurrieta Valdés, José 12919
Yusuf Ali, Abd Allah 8156
Yxart y Morgas, José 3681

Z

Zacharias, Thomas 3591
Zachwatowicz, Jan 9132
Zadow, Mario 11365
Zagrodzki, Christophe 11973
Zahar, Marcel 2334
Záhavec, Frantisek 10016
Zahle, Eric 3194
Zahn, Albert von 3113
Zahn, Leopold 1548, 1674, 6116
Zakia, Richard 13559
Zaknic, Ivan 6658
Zamboni, Silla 8002
Zamora, Martha 5848
Zampetti, Pietro 589, 593, 1719, 1723, 2397,
　　2399, 2400, 4344, 5000, 7273, 7280, 7284,
　　7287, 7288, 7289, 7407, 11221
Zancan, Maria Antonietta 10191
Zandomeneghi, Luigi 7211
Zanella, Vanni 10115
Zangs, Christiane 8123
Zanoli, Anna 1804, 9770
Zanotti, Giovanni Pietro Cavazzoni 24
Zanotto, Francesco 11257
Zanotto, Sandro 9795

Zarnecki, George 4418
Zava Boccazzi, Franca 7212, 9826, 12517
Zbijewska, Krystyna 13793
Zdunić, Drago 4137
Zednicek, Walter 13278
Zehder, Hugo 5897
Zemel, Carol M. 4568
Zendralli, A. M. 4250
Zennström, Per-Olav 5817
Zerbst, Rainer 4035
Zeri, Federico 2251, 3464, 7879
Zermani, Paolo 4009
Zerner, Catherine Wilkinson 5243
Zervos, Christian 1279, 3015, 4822, 7983, 9679,
　　11004
Zhadova, Larisa 7506, 12233
Ziebarth, Marilyn 13342
Zieseniss, Charles Otto 565
Zigrosser, Carl 5145, 5976, 6286, 7728
Zijl, Ida van 10668, 10671
Zilcken, Philippe 5694
Zilczer, Judith 12000
Ziller, Gerhart 7818
Ziller, Hermann 11366
Ziloty, Alexandre 3423
Zimmer, Jürgen 5208
Zimmerman, Agnes 13440
Zimmermann, E. Heinrich 13387
Zimmermann, Margret 12279
Zimmermann, Michael 11623
Zimmermann, Rainer 9398, 9400
Zimmermanns, Klaus 5943
Zimmern, Helen 138
Zinsli, Paul 7655
Znamerovskaia, Tat'iana P. 12982
Zocchi, Juan 3651
Zoege von Manteuffel, Kurt 5478, 5479, 13011
Zola, Emile 7548, 7594
Zolotov, Iurii K. 1978, 6509, 9976
Zonova, Zinaida T. 12740
Zoppi, Sergio 12137
Zorn, Amy Mizrahi 5754
Zorzi, Giangiorgio 9370, 9371, 9372, 9373
Zottmann, Ludwig 594
Zschelletzschky, Herbert 104, 689
Zubov, Vasilii P. 6999
Zubova, Mariia V.7984
Zuffi, Stefano 724, 12432
Zukowsky, John 12120
Zuk-Skarszewski, Tadeusz 13789
Zülch, Walter K. 4974
Zuno, José G. 9261
Zuntz, Dora 3618
Zurcher, Bernard 1320, 4569
Zwanziger, Walter C. 2917
Zweig, Stefan 7112, 7809, 7810, 7819
Zweigbergk, Eva von 6490
Zweite, Armin 3362, 5805, 5881, 6012, 11574